Creating
Mobile Apps
with Xamarin.Forms

Cross-platform C# programming

for iOS, Android, and Windows Phone

Charles Petzold

PUBLISHED BY
Microsoft Press
A Division of Microsoft Corporation
One Microsoft Way
Redmond, Washington 98052-6399

ISBN: 978-1-5093-0298-7

Printed and bound in the United States of America.

2   16

Microsoft Press books are available through booksellers and distributors worldwide. If you need support related to this book, email Microsoft Press Support at mspinput@microsoft.com. Please tell us what you think of this book at http://aka.ms/tellpress.

This book is provided "as-is" and expresses the author's views and opinions. The views, opinions and information expressed in this book, including URL and other Internet website references, may change without notice.

Some examples depicted herein are provided for illustration only and are fictitious. No real association or connection is intended or should be inferred.

Microsoft and the trademarks listed at http://www.microsoft.com on the "Trademarks" webpage are trademarks of the Microsoft group of companies. All other marks are property of their respective owners.

Acquisitions and Project Editor: Devon Musgrave
Editorial production: John Pierce, Flying Squirrel Press
Cover illustration: Serena Zhang

Contents

Foreword

The idea for producing a book on Xamarin.Forms is one we've had for almost as long as we've been working on the product. Of course, we didn't know it would be written by such a talented and highly regarded author. We couldn't have asked for a better-qualified person, nor someone who would require so little of us to get inside our minds! Charles offers insights in such beautiful and simple ways, as you'll soon discover.

This book distills more than three years of effort to create a modern, cross-platform toolkit as an easy to understand, organized progression of ideas. The examples contained within this book are simple enough to be understood without the need for a fancy IDE or compiler, yet they retain the complexity required to be applicable to problems faced by real applications. Better, the following chapters don't focus on a single platform but take a holistic approach to understanding mobile development for all platforms, not just iOS or Android or Windows.

We wanted to avoid the pitfalls commonly associated with cross-platform toolkits: either they have an alien-feeling user experience, or they are limited to the lowest common denominator across all the target platforms. The pattern we fell in love with was to use native APIs, as is the traditional Xamarin way. Xamarin.Forms offers the user the smallest usable subset of APIs that are required to write the majority of an app in a unified codebase, and then gives access to the underlying toolkit for fit and finish. The end result is that the user has the ability to express the majority of their app in unified code, without losing the flexibility of per-platform implementation.

It works, too, by removing the need to provide every feature inside the abstraction. Instead, we allow simple access down to the toolkit so that application developers are able to bring out those platform-specific features that make their app shine. Ninety percent of what makes your app work is the same as for every other app out there, but working across platforms shouldn't force you to give up the 10 percent that makes your app unique.

Because of this, Xamarin.Forms is in many ways the "untoolkit," a toolkit that isn't so much a toolkit as it is a way to look at mobile development and use it as a pattern to create mobile apps. If the authors of Xamarin.Forms can offer you anything to retain as you read this book, it is that toolkits, platforms, and technologies change very rapidly, but patterns, especially good patterns, rarely die.

When I read the preview editions of this book, I was blown away. Charles understood what we were trying to do better than anyone else ever had. This book is written knowing that Xamarin.Forms is about the pattern of creating mobile apps. I believe that by the time you finish reading, you too will understand what it is we set out to create.

Xamarin.Forms cocreator,
Jason Smith

Introduction

This is the third version of a book about writing applications with Xamarin.Forms, the exciting mobile development platform for iOS, Android, and Windows unveiled by Xamarin in May 2014. (The first two versions of this book were Preview Editions.) Xamarin.Forms lets you write shared user-interface code in C# and XAML (the Extensible Application Markup Language) that maps to native controls on these platforms.

The Windows support of Xamarin.Forms includes the Windows Runtime (WinRT) for targeting Windows 8.1 and Windows Phone 8.1 devices, and the Universal Windows Platform (UWP), which is a form of the Windows Runtime that targets Windows 10 and Windows 10 Mobile devices with a single program.

The two previous versions of this book were called Preview Editions because they were not complete. At 1200 pages, this is the first edition that can claim to be complete, even though several topics are not included and Xamarin.Forms continues to be progressively enhanced with no sign of slowing down.

All information about this book can be found on the book's home page at:

https://developer.xamarin.com/r/xamarin-forms/book/

Who should read this book

This book is for C# programmers who want to write applications using a single code base that targets the three most popular mobile platforms: iOS, Android, and Windows, encompassing the Universal Windows Platform and Windows Phone.

Xamarin.Forms also has applicability for those programmers who eventually want to use C# and the Xamarin.iOS and Xamarin.Android libraries to target the native application programming interfaces (APIs) of these platforms. Xamarin.Forms can be a big help in getting programmers started with these platforms or in constructing a prototype or proof-of-concept application.

This book assumes that you know C# and are familiar with the use of the .NET Framework. However, when I discuss some C# and .NET features that might be somewhat exotic or unfamiliar to recent C# programmers, I adopt a somewhat slower pace.

Conventions and features in this book

This book has just a few typographical conventions:

- All programming elements referenced in the text—including classes, methods, properties, variable names, etc.—are shown in a monospaced font, such as the `StackLayout` class.

- Items that appear in the user interface of Visual Studio or Xamarin Studio, or the applications discussed in these chapters, appear in boldface, such as the **Add New Project** dialog.

- Application solutions and projects also appear in boldface, such as **MonkeyTap**.

The various editions of this book

This book is intended as a tutorial to learn Xamarin.Forms programming. It is not a replacement for the online API documentation, which can be found at the Xamarin.Forms Framework link on this page:

https://developer.xamarin.com/api/

The first Preview Edition of this book was published in October 2014 to coincide with the Xamarin Evolve 2014 conference. It contained six chapters but no coverage of XAML.

This second Preview Edition was reconceived to contain shorter and more focused chapters. The sixteen chapters of the second Preview Edition were published in April 2015 to coincide with the Microsoft Build 2015 conference. Over the next six months, eight more chapters were published online, bringing the total to 24.

This edition has 27 chapters and is being published to coincide with the Xamarin Evolve 2016 conference taking place April 24–28, 2016. But the deadline for this book is about a month earlier than Evolve, and several topics did not make it into this edition. These include maps, `ControlTemplate`, `DataTemplateSelector`, the `Margin` property, and `CarouselView`. Of the classes that derive from `GestureRecognizer`, only `TapGestureRecognizer` is covered, and not `PanGestureRecognizer` or `PinchGestureRecognizer`. Although `RelativeLayout` dates from the very first release of Xamarin.Forms, somehow it never made it into this book.

Between the second Preview Edition and this edition, a big change occurred for the Windows platforms: The sample programs no longer support the Silverlight API of Windows Phone 8.0. Instead, all the sample programs support the Universal Windows Platform for targeting Windows 10 and Windows 10 Mobile, and the Windows Runtime for targeting Windows 8.1 and Windows Phone 8.1.

However, there was insufficient time to update this book's sample programs and screenshots to reflect Android AppCompat and Material Design, which is expected to be supported in a forthcoming Visual Studio and Xamarin Studio project template for Xamarin.Forms.

For updates and additions to this edition, check the Xamarin webpage devoted to this book.

System requirements

This book assumes that you'll be using Xamarin.Forms to write applications that simultaneously target all the supported mobile platforms—iOS, Android, the Universal Windows Platform, and perhaps Windows Phone 8.1 as well. However, it's possible that some readers will be targeting only one or two platforms in their Xamarin.Forms solutions. The platforms you target govern your hardware and software requirements. For targeting iOS devices, you'll need a Mac installed with Apple Xcode and the Xamarin Platform, which includes Xamarin Studio. For targeting any of the Windows platforms, you'll need Visual Studio 2015 on a PC, and you'll need to have installed the Xamarin Platform.

However, you can also use Visual Studio on the PC to target iOS devices through a Wi-Fi-accessible Mac installed with Xcode and the Xamarin Platform. You can target Android devices from Visual Studio on the PC or from Xamarin Studio on the Mac.

Chapter 1, "How does Xamarin.Forms fit in?" has more details on the various configurations you can use and resources for additional information and support. My setup for creating this book consisted of a Microsoft Surface Pro 2 (with external monitor, keyboard, and mouse) installed with Visual Studio 2015 and the Xamarin Platform, connected by Wi-Fi with a MacBook Pro installed with Xcode and the Xamarin Platform.

Most of the screenshots in this book show an iPhone, an Android phone, and a Windows 10 Mobile device in that order. The three devices shown in these screenshots reflect my setup and hardware:

- The iPhone 6 simulator on the MacBook Pro running iOS 8.2

- An LG Nexus 5 running Android 6.0.1

- A Nokia Lumia 925 running Windows 10 Mobile

Additional screenshots use an iPad Air 2 simulator, a Microsoft Surface Pro 3 running Windows 10 in tablet mode, a Windows 10 Mobile phone running a program targeting Windows Phone 8.1, and the Windows 10 desktop running a program targeting Windows 8.1.

Some of the early triple screenshots in this book used devices with somewhat earlier versions of the operating systems, for example Android 5.0 or 5.1. Although I tried to use real devices for all the Android and Windows screenshots, in the interests of expediency some Windows Phone and Windows 10 Mobile screenshots were taken with a Windows 10 Mobile emulator.

Downloads: Code samples

The sample programs shown in the pages of this book were compiled in late March 2016 with Xamarin.Forms version 2.1.0. The source code of these samples is hosted on a repository on GitHub:

http://aka.ms/xamarinbook/codesamples

You can clone the directory structure to a local drive on your machine or download a big ZIP folder. I'll try to keep the code updated with the latest release of Xamarin.Forms and to fix (and comment) any errors that might have sneaked through.

You can report problems, bugs, or other kinds of feedback about the book or source code by clicking the **Issues** button on this GitHub page. You can search through existing issues or file a new one. To file a new issue, you'll need to join GitHub (if you haven't already).

Use this GitHub page only for issues involving the book. For questions or discussions about Xamarin.Forms itself, use the Xamarin.Forms forum:

http://forums.xamarin.com/categories/xamarin-forms

Updating the code samples

The libraries that make up Xamarin.Forms are distributed via the NuGet package manager. The Xamarin.Forms package consists of a collection of dynamic-link libraries, the most significant of which are:

- Xamarin.Forms.Core.dll

- Xamarin.Forms.Xaml.dll

- Xamarin.Forms.Platform.dll

- Xamarin.Forms.Platform.iOS.dll

- Xamarin.Forms.Platform.Android.dll

- Xamarin.Forms.Platform.WinRT.dll

- Xamarin.Forms.Platform.WinRT.Phone.dll

- Xamarin.Forms.Platform.WinRT.Tablet.dll

- Xamarin.Forms.Platform.UAP.dll

The Xamarin.Forms package also requires five Android support libraries, currently identified with the version number 23.0.1.3. These should be automatically included.

When you create a new Xamarin.Forms solution using Visual Studio or Xamarin Studio, a version of the Xamarin.Forms package becomes part of that solution. However, that might not be the latest Xamarin.Forms version available from NuGet. You'll probably want to update that package to the most recent version.

Also, the source code for this book that is stored on GitHub does not include the actual NuGet packages. Xamarin Studio will automatically download them when you load the solution, but by default Visual Studio will not.

In Visual Studio, you can handle both these jobs by right-clicking the solution name in the **Solution Explorer** and selecting **Manage NuGet Packages for Solution**. The **Manage Packages for Solution** dialog lets you download and restore the NuGet packages and to update them.

In Xamarin Studio, the process is somewhat more automatic, but you can also use the **Update NuGet Packages** and **Restore NuGet Packages** options on the **Project** menu.

Some of the projects contain references to libraries in the **Libraries** folder of the sample code. You'll want to load those library solutions into Visual Studio or Xamarin Studio separately and restore (or update) the NuGet packages. Then load projects referencing these libraries.

Acknowledgments

It's always seemed peculiar to me that authors of programming books are sometimes better known to programmers than the people who actually created the product that is the subject of the book! The real brains behind Xamarin.Forms are Jason Smith, Eric Maupin, Stephane Delcroix, Seth Rosetter, Rui Marinho, Chris King, E.Z. Hart, Samantha Houts, Paul DiPietro, and interim product manager Bryan Hunter. Congratulations, guys! We've been enjoying the fruits of your labor!

Over the months that these various editions of the book were in progress, I have benefited from valuable feedback, corrections, and edits from several people. This book wouldn't exist without the collaboration of Bryan Costanich at Xamarin and Devon Musgrave at Microsoft Press. Both Bryan and Craig Dunn at Xamarin read some of my drafts of early chapters and managed to persuade me to take a somewhat different approach to the material. Later on, Craig kept me on track and reviewed the chapters while John Meade did the copyediting. For the first Preview Edition, Stephane Delcroix at Xamarin and Andy Wigley with Microsoft offered essential technical reads and persistently prodded me to make the book better. Rui Marinho was often willing to explore technical questions that I had. Reader Albert Mata found a number of typos. Microsoft's copyeditor for the second Preview Edition and this edition was John Pierce.

Almost nothing I do these days would be possible without the daily companionship and support of my wife, Deirdre Sinnott.

Charles Petzold
March 21, 2016

Free ebooks from Microsoft Press

From technical overviews to in-depth information, the free ebooks from Microsoft Press cover a wide range of topics. These ebooks are available in PDF, EPUB, and Mobi for Kindle formats, ready for you to download at http://aka.ms/mspressfree.

We want to hear from you

At Microsoft Press, your satisfaction is our top priority and your feedback our most valuable asset. Please tell us what you think of this book at http://aka.ms/tellpress. Your feedback goes directly to the editors at Microsoft Press. (No personal information will be requested.) Thanks in advance for your input!

Chapter 1
How does Xamarin.Forms fit in?

There is much joy in programming. There is joy in analyzing a problem, breaking it down into pieces, formulating a solution, mapping out a strategy, approaching it from different directions, and crafting the code. There is very much joy in seeing the program run for the first time, and then more joy in eagerly diving back into the code to make it better and faster.

There is also often joy in hunting down bugs, in ensuring that the program runs smoothly and predictably. Few occasions are quite as joyful as finally identifying a particularly recalcitrant bug and definitively stamping it out.

There is even joy in realizing that the original approach you took is not quite the best. Many developers discover that they've learned a lot while writing a program, including that there's a better way to structure the code. Sometimes, a partial or even a total rewrite can result in a much better application, or simply one that is structurally more coherent and easier to maintain. The process is like standing on one's own shoulders, and there is much joy in attaining that perspective and knowledge.

However, not all aspects of programming are quite so joyful. One of the nastier programming jobs is taking a working program and rewriting it in an entirely different programming language or porting it to another operating system with an entirely different application programming interface (API).

A job like that can be a real grind. Yet, such a rewrite may very well be necessary: an application that's been so popular on the iPhone might be even more popular on Android devices, and there's only one way to find out.

But here's the problem: As you're going through the original source code and moving it to the new platform, do you maintain the same program structure so that the two versions exist in parallel? Or do you try to make improvements and enhancements?

The temptation, of course, is to entirely rethink the application and make the new version better. But the further the two versions drift apart, the harder they will be to maintain in the future.

For this reason, a sense of dread pervades the forking of one application into two. With each line of code that you write, you realize that all the future maintenance work, all the future revisions and enhancements, have become two jobs rather than one.

This is not a new problem. For over half a century, developers have craved the ability to write a single program that runs on multiple machines. This is one of the reasons that high-level languages were invented in the first place, and this is why the concept of "cross-platform development" continues to exert such a powerful allure for programmers.

Cross-platform mobile development

The personal computer industry has experienced a massive shift in recent years. Desktop computers still exist, of course, and they remain vital for tasks that require keyboards and large screens: programming, writing, spread-sheeting, data tracking. But much of personal computing now occurs on smaller devices, particularly for quick information, media consumption, and social networking. Tablets and smartphones have a fundamentally different user-interaction paradigm based primarily on touch, with a keyboard that pops up only when necessary.

The mobile landscape

Although the mobile market has the potential for rapid change, currently two major phone and tablet platforms dominate:

- The Apple family of iPhones and iPads, all of which run the iOS operating system.

- The Android operating system, developed by Google based on the Linux kernel, which runs on a variety of phones and tablets.

How the world is divided between these two giants depends on how they are measured: there are more Android devices currently in use, but iPhone and iPad users are more devoted and spend more time with their devices.

There is also a third mobile development platform, which is not as popular as iOS and Android but involves a company with a strong history in the personal computer industry:

- Microsoft's Windows Phone and Windows 10 Mobile.

In recent years, these platforms have become a more compelling alternative as Microsoft has been merging the APIs of its mobile, tablet, and desktop platforms. Both Windows 8.1 and Windows Phone 8.1 are based on a single API called the Windows Runtime (or WinRT), which is based on Microsoft .NET. This single API means that applications targeted for desktop machines, laptops, tablets, and phones can share very much of their code.

Even more compelling is the Universal Windows Platform (UWP), a version of the Windows Runtime that forms the basis for Windows 10 and Windows 10 Mobile. A single UWP application can target every form factor from the desktop to the phone.

For software developers, the optimum strategy is to target more than just one of these platforms. But that's not easy. There are four big obstacles:

Problem 1: Different user-interface paradigms

All three platforms incorporate similar ways of presenting the graphical user interface (GUI) and interaction with the device through multitouch, but there are many differences in detail. Each platform has different ways to navigate around applications and pages, different conventions for the presentation of data, different ways to invoke and display menus, and even different approaches to touch.

Users become accustomed to interacting with applications on a particular platform and expect to leverage that knowledge with future applications as well. Each platform acquires its own associated culture, and these cultural conventions then influence developers.

Problem 2: Different development environments

Programmers today are accustomed to working in a sophisticated integrated development environment (IDE). Such IDEs exist for all three platforms, but of course they are different:

- For iOS development, Xcode on the Mac.

- For Android development, Android Studio on a variety of platforms.

- For Windows development, Visual Studio on the PC.

Problem 3: Different programming interfaces

All three of these platforms are based on different operating systems with different APIs. In many cases, the three platforms all implement similar types of user-interface objects but with different names.

For example, all three platforms have something that lets the user toggle a Boolean value:

- On the iPhone or iPad, it's a "view" called `UISwitch`.

- On Android devices, it's a "widget" called `Switch`.

- In the Windows Runtime API, it's a "control" called `ToggleSwitch`.

Of course, the differences go far beyond the names into the programming interfaces themselves.

Problem 4: Different programming languages

Developers have some flexibility in choosing a programming language for each of these three platforms, but, in general, each platform is very closely associated with a particular programming language:

- Objective-C for the iPhone and iPad

- Java for Android devices

- C# for Windows

Objective-C, Java, and C# are cousins of sorts because they are all object-oriented descendants of C, but they have become rather distant cousins.

For these reasons, a company that wants to target multiple platforms might very well employ three different programmer teams, each team skilled and specialized in a particular language and API.

This language problem is particularly nasty, but it's the problem that is the most tempting to solve: If you could use the same programming language for these three platforms, you could at least share some code between the platforms. This shared code likely wouldn't be involved with the user interface because each platform has different APIs, but there might well be application code that doesn't touch the user interface at all.

A single language for these three platforms would certainly be convenient. But what language would that be?

The C# and .NET solution

A roomful of programmers would come up with a variety of answers to the question just posed, but a good argument can be made in favor of C#. Unveiled by Microsoft in the year 2000, C# is a fairly new programming language, at least when compared with Objective-C and Java. At first, C# seemed to be a rather straightforward, strongly typed, imperative object-oriented language, certainly influenced by C++ (and Java as well), but with a much cleaner syntax than C++ and none of the historical baggage. In addition, the first version of C# had language-level support for properties and events, which turn out to be member types that are particularly suited for programming graphical user interfaces.

But C# has continued to grow and get better over the years. The support of generics, lambda functions, LINQ, and asynchronous operations has successfully transformed C# so that it is now properly classified as a multiparadigm programming language. C# code can be traditionally imperative, or the code can be flavored with declarative or functional programming paradigms.

Since its inception, C# has been closely associated with the Microsoft .NET Framework. At the lowest level, .NET provides an infrastructure for the C# basic data types (`int`, `double`, `string`, and so forth). But the extensive .NET Framework class library provides support for many common chores encountered in many different types of programming. These include:

- Math
- Debugging
- Reflection
- Collections
- Globalization
- File I/O
- Networking

- Security

- Threading

- Web services

- Data handling

- XML and JSON reading and writing

Here's another big reason for C# and .NET to be regarded as a compelling cross-platform solution:

It's not just hypothetical. It's a reality.

Soon after Microsoft's announcement of .NET way back in June 2000, the company Ximian (founded by Miguel de Icaza and Nat Friedman) initiated an open-source project called Mono to create an alternative implementation of the C# compiler and the .NET Framework that could run on Linux.

A decade later, in 2011, the founders of Ximian (which had been acquired by Novell) founded Xamarin, which still contributes to the open-source version of Mono but which has also adapted Mono to form the basis of cross-platform mobile solutions.

The year 2014 saw some developments in C# and .NET that bode well for its future. An open-source version of the C# compiler, called the .NET Compiler Platform (formerly known by its code name "Roslyn") has been published. And the .NET Foundation was announced to serve as a steward for open-source .NET technologies, in which Xamarin plays a major part.

In March 2016, Microsoft acquired Xamarin with the goal of bringing cross-platform mobile development to the wider Microsoft developer community. Xamarin.Forms is now freely available to all users of Visual Studio.

A single language for all platforms

For the first three years of its existence, Xamarin focused mainly on compiler technologies and three basic sets of .NET libraries:

- Xamarin.Mac, which has evolved from the MonoMac project.

- Xamarin.iOS, which evolved from MonoTouch.

- Xamarin.Android, which evolved from Mono for Android or (more informally) MonoDroid.

Collectively, these libraries are known as the Xamarin platform. The libraries consist of .NET versions of the native Mac, IOS, and Android APIs. Programmers using these libraries can write applications in C# to target the native APIs of these three platforms, but also (as a bonus) with access to the .NET Framework class library.

Developers can use Visual Studio to build Xamarin applications, targeting iOS and Android as well as all the various Windows platforms. However, iPhone and iPad development also requires a Mac connected to the PC through a local network. This Mac must have Xcode installed as well as Xamarin Studio, an OS X–based integrated development environment that lets you develop iPhone, iPad, Mac OS X, and Android applications on the Mac. Xamarin Studio does not allow you to target Windows platforms.

Sharing code

The advantage of targeting multiple platforms with a single programming language comes from the ability to share code among the applications.

Before code can be shared, an application must be structured for that purpose. Particularly since the widespread use of graphical user interfaces, programmers have understood the importance of separating application code into functional layers. Perhaps the most useful division is between user-interface code and the underlying data models and algorithms. The popular MVC (Model-View-Controller) application architecture formalizes this code separation into a Model (the underlying data), the View (the visual representation of the data), and the Controller (which handles input from the user).

MVC originated in the 1980s. More recently, the MVVM (Model-View-ViewModel) architecture has effectively modernized MVC based on modern GUIs. MVVM separates code into the Model (the underlying data), the View (the user interface, including visuals and input), and the ViewModel (which manages data passing between the Model and the View).

When a programmer develops an application that targets multiple mobile platforms, the MVVM architecture helps guide the developer into separating code into the platform-specific View—the code that requires interacting with the platform APIs—and the platform-independent Model and View-Model.

Often this platform-independent code needs to access files or the network or use collections or threading. Normally these jobs would be considered part of an operating system API, but they are also jobs that can make use of the .NET Framework class library, and if .NET is available on each platform, then this code is effectively platform independent.

The part of the application that is platform independent can then be isolated and—in the context of Visual Studio or Xamarin Studio—put into a separate project. This can be either a Shared Asset Project (SAP)—which simply consists of code and other asset files accessible from other projects—or a Portable Class Library (PCL), which encloses all the common code in a dynamic-link library (DLL) that can then be referenced from other projects.

Whichever method you use, this common code has access to the .NET Framework class library, so it can perform file I/O, handle globalization, access web services, decompose XML, and so forth.

This means that you can create a single Visual Studio solution that contains four C# projects to target the three major mobile platforms (all with access to a common PCL or SAP), or you can use Xamarin Studio to target iPhone and Android devices.

The following diagram illustrates the interrelationships between the Visual Studio or Xamarin Studio projects, the Xamarin libraries, and the platform APIs. The third column refers to any .NET-based Windows Platform regardless of the device:

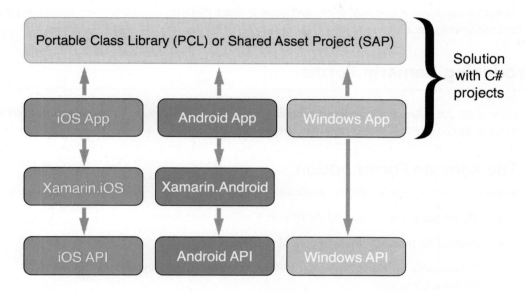

The boxes in the second row are the actual platform-specific applications. These apps make calls into the common project and also (with the iPhone and Android) the Xamarin libraries that implement the native platform APIs.

But the diagram is not quite complete: it doesn't show the SAP or PCL making calls to the .NET Framework class library. Exactly what version of .NET this is depends on the common code: A PCL has access to its own version of .NET, while an SAP uses the version of .NET incorporated into each particular platform.

In this diagram, the Xamarin.iOS and Xamarin.Android libraries seem to be substantial, and while they are certainly important, they're mostly just language bindings and do not significantly add any overhead to API calls.

When the iOS app is built, the Xamarin C# compiler generates C# Intermediate Language (IL) as usual, but it then makes use of the Apple compiler on the Mac to generate native iOS machine code just like the Objective-C compiler. The calls from the app to the iOS APIs are the same as though the application were written in Objective-C.

For the Android app, the Xamarin C# compiler generates IL, which runs on a version of Mono on the device alongside the Java engine, but the API calls from the app are pretty much the same as though the app were written in Java.

For mobile applications that have very platform-specific needs, but also a potentially shareable chunk of platform-independent code, Xamarin.iOS and Xamarin.Android provide excellent solutions. You have access to the entire platform API, with all the power (and responsibility) that implies.

But for applications that might not need quite so much platform specificity, there is an alternative that will simplify your life even more.

Introducing Xamarin.Forms

On May 28, 2014, Xamarin introduced Xamarin.Forms, which allows you to write user-interface code that can be compiled for the iOS, Android, and Windows devices.

The Xamarin.Forms option

Xamarin.Forms supports five distinct application platforms:

- iOS for programs that run on the iPhone, iPad, and iPod Touch.

- Android for programs that run on Android phones and tablets.

- The Universal Windows Platform (UWP) for applications that runs under Windows 10 or Windows 10 Mobile.

- The Windows Runtime API of Windows 8.1.

- The Windows Runtime API of Windows Phone 8.1.

In this book, "Windows" or "Windows Phone" will generally be used as a generic term to describe all three of the Microsoft platforms.

In the general case, a Xamarin.Forms application in Visual Studio consists of five separate projects for each of these five platforms, with a sixth project containing common code. But the five platform projects in a Xamarin.Forms application are typically quite small—often consisting of just stubs with a little boilerplate startup code. The PCL or SAP contains the bulk of the application, including the user-interface code. The following diagram shows just the iOS, Android, and Universal Windows Platform. The other two Windows platforms are similar to UWP:

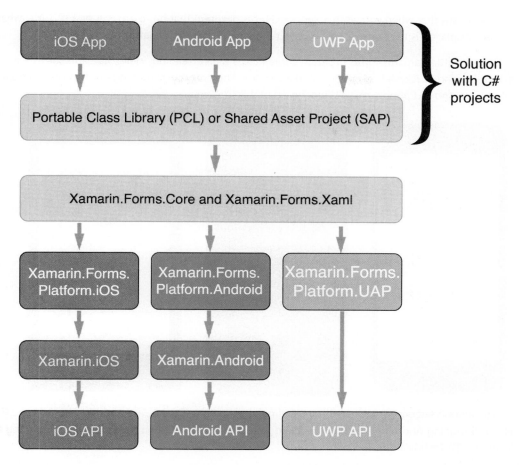

The **Xamarin.Forms.Core** and **Xamarin.Forms.Xaml** libraries implement the Xamarin.Forms API. Depending on the platform, **Xamarin.Forms.Core** then makes use of one of the **Xamarin.Forms.Platform** libraries. These libraries are mostly a collection of classes called *renderers* that transform the Xamarin.Forms user-interface objects into the platform-specific user interface.

The remainder of the diagram is the same as the one shown earlier.

For example, suppose you need the user-interface object discussed earlier that allows the user to toggle a Boolean value. When programming for Xamarin.Forms, this is called a `Switch`, and a class named `Switch` is implemented in the **Xamarin.Forms.Core** library. In the individual renderers for the three platforms, this `Switch` is mapped to a `UISwitch` on the iPhone, a `Switch` on Android, and a `ToggleSwitch` on Windows Phone.

Xamarin.Forms.Core also contains a class named `Slider` for displaying a horizontal bar that the user manipulates to choose a numeric value. In the renderers in the platform-specific libraries, this is mapped to a `UISlider` on the iPhone, a `SeekBar` on Android, and a `Slider` on Windows Phone.

This means that when you write a Xamarin.Forms program that has a `Switch` or a `Slider`, what's actually displayed is the corresponding object implemented in each platform.

Here's a little Xamarin.Forms program containing a `Label` reading "Hello, Xamarin.Forms!", a `Button` saying "Click Me!", a `Switch`, and a `Slider`. The program is running on (from left to right) the iPhone, an Android phone, and a Windows 10 Mobile device:

The iPhone screenshot is of an iPhone 6 simulator running iOS 9.2. The Android phone is an LG Nexus 5 running Android version 6. The Windows 10 Mobile device is a Nokia Lumia 935 running a Windows 10 Technical Preview.

You'll encounter triple screenshots like this one throughout this book. They're always in the same order—iPhone, Android, and Windows 10 Mobile—and they're always running the same program.

As you can see, the `Button`, `Switch`, and `Slider` all have different appearances on the three phones because they are all rendered with the object specific to each platform.

What's even more interesting is the inclusion in this program of six `ToolBarItem` objects, three identified as primary items with icons, and three as secondary items without icons. On the iPhone these are rendered with `UIBarButtonItem` objects as the three icons and three buttons at the top of the page. On the Android, the first three are rendered as items on an `ActionBar`, also at the top of the page. On Windows 10 Mobile, they're realized as items on the `CommandBar` at the page's bottom.

The Android `ActionBar` has a vertical ellipsis and the Universal Windows Platform `CommandBar` has a horizontal ellipsis. Tapping this ellipsis causes the secondary items to be displayed in a manner appropriate to these two platforms:

Xamarin.Forms was originally conceived as a platform-independent API for mobile devices. However, Xamarin.Forms is not limited to phones. Here's the same program running on an iPad Air 2 simulator:

Most of the programs in this book are fairly simple, and hence designed to look their best on a phone screen in portrait mode. But they will also run in landscape mode and on tablets.

Here's the UWP project on a Microsoft Surface Pro 3 running Windows 10:

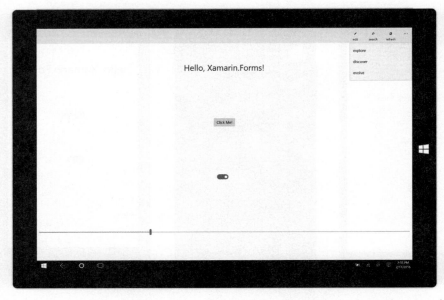

Notice the toolbar at the top of the screen. The ellipsis has already been pressed to reveal the three secondary items.

The other two platforms supported by Xamarin.Forms are Windows 8.1 and Windows Phone 8.1. Here's the Windows 8.1 program running in a window on the Windows 10 desktop, and the Windows 8.1 program running on the Windows 10 Mobile device:

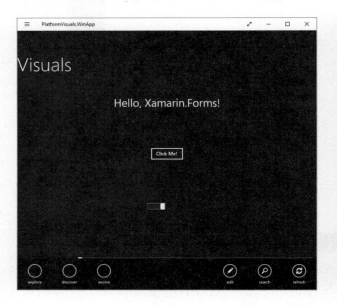

The Windows 8.1 screen has been left-clicked with the mouse to reveal the toolbar items at the bottom. On this screen, the secondary items are at the left, but the program neglectfully forgot to assign them icons. On the Windows Phone 8.1 screen, the ellipsis at the bottom has been pressed.

The various implementations of the toolbar reveals that, in one sense, Xamarin.Forms is an API that virtualizes not only the user-interface elements on each platform, but also the user-interface paradigms.

XAML support

Xamarin.Forms also supports XAML (pronounced "zammel" to rhyme with "camel"), the XML-based Extensible Application Markup Language developed at Microsoft as a general-purpose markup language for instantiating and initializing objects. XAML isn't limited to defining initial layouts of user interfaces, but historically that's how it's been used the most, and that's what it's used for in Xamarin-.Forms.

Here's the XAML file for the program whose screenshots you've just seen:

```xml
<ContentPage xmlns="http://xamarin.com/schemas/2014/forms"
             xmlns:x="http://schemas.microsoft.com/winfx/2009/xaml"
             x:Class="PlatformVisuals.PlatformVisualsPage"
             Title="Visuals">

    <StackLayout Padding="10,0">
        <Label Text="Hello, Xamarin.Forms!"
               FontSize="Large"
               VerticalOptions="CenterAndExpand"
               HorizontalOptions="Center" />

        <Button Text = "Click Me!"
                VerticalOptions="CenterAndExpand"
                HorizontalOptions="Center" />

        <Switch VerticalOptions="CenterAndExpand"
                HorizontalOptions="Center" />

        <Slider VerticalOptions="CenterAndExpand" />
    </StackLayout>

    <ContentPage.ToolbarItems>
        <ToolbarItem Text="edit" Order="Primary">
            <ToolbarItem.Icon>
                <OnPlatform x:TypeArguments="FileImageSource"
                            iOS="edit.png"
                            Android="ic_action_edit.png"
                            WinPhone="Images/edit.png" />
            </ToolbarItem.Icon>
        </ToolbarItem>

        <ToolbarItem Text="search" Order="Primary">
            <ToolbarItem.Icon>
```

```
                    <OnPlatform x:TypeArguments="FileImageSource"
                                iOS="search.png"
                                Android="ic_action_search.png"
                                WinPhone="Images/feature.search.png" />
                </ToolbarItem.Icon>
            </ToolbarItem>

            <ToolbarItem Text="refresh" Order="Primary">
                <ToolbarItem.Icon>
                    <OnPlatform x:TypeArguments="FileImageSource"
                                iOS="reload.png"
                                Android="ic_action_refresh.png"
                                WinPhone="Images/refresh.png" />
                </ToolbarItem.Icon>
            </ToolbarItem>

            <ToolbarItem Text="explore" Order="Secondary" />
            <ToolbarItem Text="discover" Order="Secondary" />
            <ToolbarItem Text="evolve" Order="Secondary" />
        </ContentPage.ToolbarItems>
    </ContentPage>
```

Unless you have experience with XAML, some syntax details might be a little obscure. (Don't worry; you'll learn all about them later on in this book.) But even so, you can see the `Label`, `Button`, `Switch`, and `Slider` tags. In a real program, the `Button`, `Switch`, and `Slider` would probably have event handlers attached that would be implemented in a C# code file. Here they do not. The `VerticalOptions` and `HorizontalOptions` attributes assist in layout; they are discussed in the next chapter.

Platform specificity

In the section of that XAML file involving the `ToolbarItem`, you can also see a tag named `OnPlatform`. This is one of several techniques in Xamarin.Forms that allow introducing some platform specificity in otherwise platform-independent code or markup. It's used here because each of the separate platforms has somewhat different image format and size requirements associated with these icons.

A similar facility exists in code with the `Device` class. It's possible to determine what platform the code is running on and to choose values or objects based on the platform. For example, you can specify different font sizes for each platform or run different blocks of code based on the platform. You might want to let the user manipulate a `Slider` to select a value in one platform but pick a number from a set of explicit values in another platform.

In some applications, deeper platform specificities might be desired. For example, suppose your application requires the GPS coordinates of the user's phone. This is not something that Xamarin.Forms provides, so you'd need to write your own code specific to each platform to obtain this information.

The `DependencyService` class provides a way to do this in a structured manner. You define an interface with the methods you need (for example, `IGetCurrentLocation`) and then implement that interface with a class in each of the platform projects. You can then call the methods in that interface from the Xamarin.Forms project almost as easily as if it were part of the API.

Each of the standard Xamarin.Forms visual objects—such as `Label`, `Button`, `Switch`, and `Slider`—are supported by a renderer class in the various **Xamarin.Forms.Platform** libraries. Each renderer class implements the platform-specific object that maps to the Xamarin.Forms object.

You can create your own custom visual objects with your own custom renderers. The custom visual object goes in the common code project, and the custom renderers go in the individual platform projects. To make it a bit easier, generally you'll want to derive from an existing class. Within the individual Xamarin.Forms platform libraries, all the corresponding renderers are public classes, and you can derive from them as well.

Xamarin.Forms allows you to be as platform independent or as platform specific as you need to be. Xamarin.Forms doesn't replace Xamarin.iOS and Xamarin.Android; rather, it integrates with them.

A cross-platform panacea?

For the most part, Xamarin.Forms defines its abstractions with a focus on areas of the mobile user interface that are common to the iOS, Android, and Windows Runtime APIs. These Xamarin.Forms visual objects are mapped to platform-specific objects, but Xamarin.Forms has tended to avoid implementing anything that is unique to a particular platform.

For this reason, despite the enormous help that Xamarin.Forms can offer in creating platform-independent applications, it is not a complete replacement for native API programming. If your application relies heavily on native API features such as particular types of controls or widgets, then you might want to stick with Xamarin.iOS, Xamarin.Android, and the native Windows Phone API.

You'll probably also want to stick with the native APIs for applications that require vector graphics or complex touch interaction. The current version of Xamarin.Forms is not quite ready for these scenarios.

On the other hand, Xamarin.Forms is great for prototyping or making a quick proof-of-concept application. And after you've done that, you might just find that you can continue using Xamarin.Forms features to build the entire application. Xamarin.Forms is ideal for line-of-business applications.

Even if you begin building an application with Xamarin.Forms and then implement major parts of it with platform APIs, you're doing so within a framework that allows you to share code and that offers structured ways to make platform-specific visuals.

Your development environment

How you set up your hardware and software depends on what mobile platforms you're targeting and what computing environments are most comfortable for you.

The requirements for Xamarin.Forms are no different from the requirements for using Xamarin.iOS or Xamarin.Android or for programming for Windows Runtime platforms.

This means that nothing in this section (and the remainder of this chapter) is specific to Xamarin.Forms. There exists much documentation on the Xamarin website on setting up machines and software for Xamarin.iOS and Xamarin.Android programming, and on the Microsoft website about Windows Phone.

Machines and IDEs

If you want to target the iPhone, you're going to need a Mac. Apple requires that a Mac be used for building iPhone and other iOS applications. You'll need to install Xcode on this machine and, of course, the Xamarin platform that includes the necessary libraries and Xamarin Studio. You can then use Xamarin Studio and Xamarin.Forms on the Mac for your iPhone development.

Once you have a Mac with Xcode and the Xamarin platform installed, you can also install the Xamarin platform on a PC and program for the iPhone by using Visual Studio. The PC and Mac must be connected via a network (such as Wi-Fi). Visual Studio communicates with the Mac through a Secure Shell (SSH) interface, and uses the Mac to build the application and run the program on a device or simulator.

You can also do Android programming in Xamarin Studio on the Mac or in Visual Studio on the PC.

If you want to target the Windows platforms, you'll need Visual Studio 2015. You can target all the platforms in a single IDE by running Visual Studio 2015 on a PC connected to the Mac via a network. (That's how the sample programs in this book were created.) Another option is to run Visual Studio in a virtual machine on the Mac.

Devices and emulators

You can test your programs on real phones connected to the machines via a USB cable, or you can test your programs with onscreen emulators.

There are advantages and disadvantages to each approach. A real phone is essential for testing complex touch interaction or when getting a feel for startup or response time. However, emulators allow you to see how your application adapts to a variety of sizes and form factors.

The iPhone and iPad emulators run on the Mac. However, because Mac desktop machines don't have touchscreens, you'll need to use the mouse or trackpad to simulate touch. The touch gestures on the Mac touchpad do not translate to the emulator. You can also connect a real iPhone to the Mac, but you'll need to provision it as a developer device.

Historically, Android emulators supplied by Google have tended to be slow and cranky, although they are often extremely versatile in emulating a vast array of actual Android devices. Fortunately, Visual Studio now has its own Android emulator that works rather better. It's also very easy to connect a real Android phone to either a Mac or PC for testing. All you really need do is enable USB Debugging on the device.

The Windows Phone emulators are capable of several different screen resolutions and also tend to run fairly smoothly, albeit consuming lots of memory. If you run the Windows Phone emulator on a touchscreen, you can use touch on the emulator screen. Connecting a real Windows Phone to the PC is fairly easy but requires enabling the phone in the **Settings** section for developing. If you want to un-lock more than one phone, you'll need a developer account.

Installation

Before writing applications for Xamarin.Forms, you'll need to install the Xamarin platform on your Mac, PC, or both (if you're using that setup). See the articles on the Xamarin website at:

   https://developer.xamarin.com/guides/cross-platform/getting_started/installation/

You're probably eager to create your first Xamarin.Forms application, but before you do, you'll want to try creating normal Xamarin projects for the iPhone and Android and normal Windows, Windows Phone, and Windows 10 Mobile projects.

This is important: if you're experiencing a problem using Xamarin.iOS, Xamarin.Android, or Windows, that's not a problem with Xamarin.Forms, and you'll need to solve that problem before using Xamarin.Forms.

Creating an iOS app

If you're interested in using Xamarin.Forms to target the iPhone, first become familiar with the appro-priate Getting Started documents on the Xamarin website:

   https://developer.xamarin.com/guides/ios/getting_started/

This will give you guidance on using the Xamarin.iOS library to develop an iPhone application in C#. All you really need to do is get to the point where you can build and deploy a simple iPhone application on either a real iPhone or the iPhone simulator.

If you're using Visual Studio, and if everything is installed correctly, you should be able to select **File > New > Project** from the menu, and in the **New Project** dialog, from the left, select **Visual C#** and **iOS** and then **Universal** (which refers to targeting both iPhone and iPad), and from the template list in the center, select **Blank App (iOS)**.

If you're using Xamarin Studio, you should be able to select **File > New > Solution** from the menu, and in the **New Project** dialog, from the left, select **iOS** and then **App**, and from the template list in the center, select **Single View App**.

In either case, select a location and name for the solution. Build and deploy the skeleton application created in the project. If you're having a problem with this, it's not a Xamarin.Forms issue. You might want to check the Xamarin.iOS forums to see if anybody else has a similar problem:

http://forums.xamarin.com/categories/ios/

Creating an Android app

If you're interested in using Xamarin.Forms to target Android devices, first become familiar with the Getting Started documents on the Xamarin website:

https://developer.xamarin.com/guides/android/getting_started/

If you're using Visual Studio, and if everything is installed correctly, you should be able to select **File > New > Project** from the menu, and in the **New Project** dialog, from the left, select **Visual C#** and then **Android**, and from the template list in the center, select **Blank App (Android)**.

If you're using Xamarin Studio, you should be able to select **File > New > Solution** from the menu, and in the **New Project** dialog, from the left, select **Android** and **App**, and in the template list in the center, select **Android App**.

Give it a location and a name; build and deploy. If you can't get this process to work, it's not a Xamarin.Forms issue, and you might want to check the Xamarin.Android forums for a similar problem:

http://forums.xamarin.com/categories/android/

Creating a Windows app

If you're interested in using Xamarin.Forms to target Windows, Windows Phone, or Windows 10 Mobile, you'll need to become familiar with at least the rudiments of using Visual Studio to develop Windows applications:

http://dev.windows.com/

In Visual Studio 2015, if everything is installed correctly, you should be able select **File > New > Project** from the menu, and in the **New Project** dialog, at the left, select **Visual C#** and **Windows**. You'll see a hierarchy under the **Windows** heading something like this:

The first **Universal** heading under **Windows** is for creating a Universal Windows Platform application that can target either Windows 10 or Windows 10 Mobile. Select that, and from the center area select **Blank App (Universal Windows)** to create a UWP app.

The other two project types supported by Xamarin.Forms are under the Windows 8 header. The **Universal** item actually creates two projects—a Windows desktop application and a Windows Phone application with some shared code. For creating just a Windows application, choose **Windows** and then from the center section **Blank App (Windows 8.1)**. For a Windows Phone application, choose **Windows Phone** and **Blank App** This creates a project that targets Windows Phone 8.1.

These are the three project types supported by Xamarin.Forms.

You should be able to build and deploy the skeleton application to the desktop or to a real phone or an emulator. If not, search the Microsoft website or online forums such as Stack Overflow.

All ready?

If you can build Xamarin.iOS, Xamarin.Android, and Windows applications (or some subset of those), then you're ready to create your first Xamarin.Forms application. It's time to say "Hello, Xamarin.Forms" to a new era in cross-platform mobile development.

Chapter 2
Anatomy of an app

The modern user interface is constructed from visual objects of various sorts. Depending on the operating system, these visual objects might go by different names—controls, elements, views, widgets—but they are all devoted to the jobs of presentation or interaction or both.

In Xamarin.Forms, the objects that appear on the screen are collectively called *visual elements*. They come in three main categories:

- page
- layout
- view

These are not abstract concepts! The Xamarin.Forms application programming interface (API) defines classes named `VisualElement`, `Page`, `Layout`, and `View`. These classes and their descendants form the backbone of the Xamarin.Forms user interface. `VisualElement` is an exceptionally important class in Xamarin.Forms. A `VisualElement` object is anything that occupies space on the screen.

A Xamarin.Forms application consists of one or more pages. A page usually occupies all (or at least a large area) of the screen. Some applications consist of only a single page, while others allow navigating between multiple pages. In many of the early chapters in this book, you'll see just one type of page, called a `ContentPage`.

On each page, the visual elements are organized in a parent-child hierarchy. The child of a `ContentPage` is generally a layout of some sort to organize the visuals. Some layouts have a single child, but many layouts have multiple children that the layout arranges within itself. These children can be other layouts or views. Different types of layouts arrange children in a stack, in a two-dimensional grid, or in a more freeform manner. In this chapter, however, our pages will contain just a single child.

The term *view* in Xamarin.Forms denotes familiar types of presentation and interactive objects: text, bitmaps, buttons, text-entry fields, sliders, switches, progress bars, date and time pickers, and others of your own devising. These are often called controls or widgets in other programming environments. This book refers to them as views or elements. In this chapter, you'll encounter the `Label` view for displaying text.

Say hello

Using either Microsoft Visual Studio or Xamarin Studio, let's create a new Xamarin.Forms application by using a standard template. This process creates a solution that contains up to six projects: five platform projects—for iOS, Android, the Universal Windows Platform (UWP), Windows 8.1, and Windows Phone 8.1—and a common project for the greater part of your application code.

In Visual Studio, select the menu option **File > New > Project**. At the left of the **New Project** dialog, select **Visual C#** and then **Cross-Platform**. In the center part of the dialog you'll see several available solution templates, including three for Xamarin.Forms:

- **Blank App (Xamarin.Forms Portable)**

- **Blank App (Xamarin.Forms Shared)**

- **Class Library (Xamarin.Forms)**

Now what? We definitely want to create a **Blank App** solution, but what kind?

Xamarin Studio presents a similar dilemma but in a different way. To create a new Xamarin.Forms solution in Xamarin Studio, select **File > New > Solution** from the menu, and at the left of the **New Project** dialog, under **Multiplatform** select **App**, pick **Forms App**, and press the **Next** button. Toward the bottom of the next screen are a pair of radio buttons labeled **Shared Code**. These buttons allow you to choose one of the following options:

- **Use Portable Class Library**

- **Use Shared Library**

The term "Portable" in this context refers to a Portable Class Library (PCL). All the common application code becomes a dynamic-link library (DLL) that is referenced by all the individual platform projects.

The term "Shared" in this context means a Shared Asset Project (SAP) containing loose code files (and perhaps other files) that are shared among the platform projects, essentially becoming part of each platform project.

For now, pick the first one: **Blank App (Xamarin.Forms Portable)** in Visual Studio or **Use Portable Class Library** in Xamarin Studio. Give the project a name—for example, **Hello**—and select a disk location for it in that dialog (in Visual Studio) or in the dialog that appears after pressing the **Next** button again in Xamarin Studio.

If you're running Visual Studio, six projects are created: one common project (the PCL project) and five application projects. For a solution named **Hello**, these are:

- A Portable Class Library project named **Hello** that is referenced by all five application projects;

- An application project for Android, named **Hello.Droid**;

- An application project for iOS, named **Hello.iOS**;

- An application project for the Universal Windows Platform of Windows 10 and Windows Mobile 10, named **Hello.UWP**;

- An application project for Windows 8.1, named **Hello.Windows**; and

- An application project for Windows Phone 8.1, named **Hello.WinPhone**.

If you're running Xamarin Studio on the Mac, the Windows and Windows Phone projects are not created.

When you create a new Xamarin.Forms solution, the Xamarin.Forms libraries (and various support libraries) are automatically downloaded from the NuGet package manager. Visual Studio and Xamarin Studio store these libraries in a directory named **packages** in the solution directory. However, the particular version of the Xamarin.Forms library that is downloaded is specified within the solution template, and a newer version might be available.

In Visual Studio, in the **Solution Explorer** at the far right of the screen, right-click the solution name and select **Manage NuGet Packages for Solution**. The dialog that appears contains selectable items at the upper left that let you see what NuGet packages are installed in the solution and let you install others. You can also select the **Update** item to update the Xamarin.Forms library.

In Xamarin.Studio, you can select the tool icon to the right of the solution name in the **Solution** list and select **Update NuGet Packages**.

Before continuing, check to be sure that the project configurations are okay. In Visual Studio, select the **Build > Configuration Manager** menu item. In the **Configuration Manager** dialog, you'll see the PCL project and the five application projects. Make sure the **Build** box is checked for all the projects and the **Deploy** box is checked for all the application projects (unless the box is grayed out). Take note of the **Platform** column: If the **Hello** project is listed, it should be flagged as **Any CPU**. The **Hello.Droid** project should also be flagged as **Any CPU**. (For those two project types, **Any CPU** is the only option.) For the **Hello.iOS** project, choose either **iPhone** or **iPhoneSimulator** depending on how you'll be testing the program.

For the **Hello.UWP** project, the project configuration must be **x86** for deploying to the Windows desktop or an on-screen emulator, and **ARM** for deploying to a phone.

For the **Hello.WinPhone** project, you can select **x86** if you'll be using an on-screen emulator, **ARM** if you'll be deploying to a real phone, or **Any CPU** for deploying to either. Regardless of your choice, Visual Studio generates the same code.

If a project doesn't seem to be compiling or deploying in Visual Studio, recheck the settings in the **Configuration Manager** dialog. Sometimes a different configuration becomes active and might not include the PCL project.

In Xamarin Studio on the Mac, you can switch between deploying to the iPhone and iPhone simulator through the **Project > Active Configuration** menu item.

In Visual Studio, you'll probably want to display the iOS and Android toolbars. These toolbars let you choose among emulators and devices and allow you to manage the emulators. From the main menu, make sure the **View > Toolbars > iOS** and **View > Toolbars > Android** items are checked.

Because the solution contains anywhere from two to six projects, you must designate which program starts up when you elect to run or debug an application.

In the **Solution Explorer** of Visual Studio, right-click any of the five application projects and select the **Set As StartUp Project** item from the menu. You can then select to deploy to either an emulator or a real device. To build and run the program, select the menu item **Debug > Start Debugging**.

In the **Solution** list in Xamarin Studio, click the little tool icon that appears to the right of a selected project and select **Set As Startup Project** from the menu. You can then pick **Run > Start Debugging** from the main menu.

If all goes well, the skeleton application created by the template will run and you'll see a short message:

As you can see, these platforms have different color schemes. The iOS and Windows 10 Mobile screens display dark text on a light background, while the Android device displays light text on a black background. By default, the Windows 8.1 and Windows Phone 8.1 platforms are like Android in displaying light text on a black background.

By default, all the platforms are enabled for orientation changes. Turn the phone sideways, and you'll see the text adjust to the new center.

The app is not only run on the device or emulator but deployed. It appears with the other apps on the phone or emulator and can be run from there. If you don't like the application icon or how the app name displays, you can change that in the individual platform projects.

Inside the files

Clearly, the program created by the Xamarin.Forms template is very simple, so this is an excellent opportunity to examine the generated code files and figure out their interrelationships and how they work.

Let's begin with the code that's responsible for drawing the text that you see on the screen. This is the App class in the **Hello** project. In a project created by Visual Studio, the App class is defined in the App.cs file, but in Xamarin Studio, the file is Hello.cs. If the project template hasn't changed too much since this chapter was written, it probably looks something like this:

```csharp
using System;
using System.Collections.Generic;
using System.Linq;
using System.Text;

using Xamarin.Forms;

namespace Hello
{
    public class App : Application
    {
        public App()
        {
            // The root page of your application
            MainPage = new ContentPage
            {
                Content = new StackLayout
                {
                    VerticalOptions = LayoutOptions.Center,
                    Children = {
                        new Label {
                            HorizontalTextAlignment = TextAlignment.Center,
                            Text = "Welcome to Xamarin Forms!"
                        }
                    }
                }
            };
        }

        protected override void OnStart()
        {
            // Handle when your app starts
        }

        protected override void OnSleep()
        {
            // Handle when your app sleeps
        }

        protected override void OnResume()
```

```
        {
            // Handle when your app resumes
        }
    }
}
```

Notice that the namespace is the same as the project name. This `App` class is defined as public and derives from the Xamarin.Forms `Application` class. The constructor really has just one responsibility: to set the `MainPage` property of the `Application` class to an object of type `Page`.

The code that the Xamarin.Forms template has generated here shows one very simple approach to defining this constructor: The `ContentPage` class derives from `Page` and is very common in single-page Xamarin.Forms applications. (You'll see a lot of `ContentPage` throughout this book.) It occupies most of the phone's screen with the exception of the status bar at the top of the Android screen, the buttons on the bottom of the Android screen, and the status bar at the top of the Windows Phone screen. (As you'll discover, the iOS status bar is actually part of the `ContentPage` in single-page applications.)

The `ContentPage` class defines a property named `Content` that you set to the content of the page. Generally this content is a layout that in turn contains a bunch of views, and in this case it's set to a `StackLayout`, which arranges its children in a stack.

This `StackLayout` has only one child, which is a `Label`. The `Label` class derives from `View` and is used in Xamarin.Forms applications to display up to a paragraph of text. The `VerticalOptions` and `HorizontalTextAlignment` properties are discussed in more detail later in this chapter.

For your own single-page Xamarin.Forms applications, you'll generally be defining your own class that derives from `ContentPage`. The constructor of the `App` class then sets an instance of the class that you define to its `MainPage` property. You'll see how this works shortly.

In the **Hello** solution, you'll also see an AssemblyInfo.cs file for creating the PCL and a pack-ages.config file that contains the NuGet packages required by the program. In the **References** section under **Hello** in the solution list, you'll see at least the four libraries this PCL requires:

- .NET (displayed as .NET Portable Subset in Xamarin Studio)

- **Xamarin.Forms.Core**

- **Xamarin.Forms.Xaml**

- **Xamarin.Forms.Platform**

It is this PCL project that will receive the bulk of your attention as you're writing a Xamarin.Forms application. In some circumstances the code in this project might require some tailoring for the various platforms, and you'll see shortly how to do that. You can also include platform-specific code in the five application projects.

The five application projects have their own assets in the form of icons and metadata, and you must pay particular attention to these assets if you intend to bring the application to market. But during the time that you're learning how to develop applications using Xamarin.Forms, these assets can generally be ignored. You'll probably want to keep these application projects collapsed in the solution list because you don't need to bother much with their contents.

But you really should know what's in these application projects, so let's take a closer look.

In the **References** section of each application project, you'll see references to the common PCL project (**Hello** in this case), as well as various .NET assemblies, the Xamarin.Forms assembles listed above, and additional Xamarin.Forms assemblies applicable to each platform:

- **Xamarin.Forms.Platform.Android**

- **Xamarin.Forms.Platform.iOS**

- **Xamarin.Forms.Platform.UAP** (not explicitly displayed in the UWP project)

- **Xamarin.Forms.Platform.WinRT**

- **Xamarin.Forms.Platform.WinRT.Tablet**

- **Xamarin.Forms.Platform.WinRT.Phone**

Each of these libraries defines a static `Forms.Init` method in the `Xamarin.Forms` namespace that initializes the Xamarin.Forms system for that particular platform. The startup code in each platform must make a call to this method.

You've also just seen that the PCL project derives a public class named `App` that derives from `Application`. The startup code in each platform must also instantiate this `App` class.

If you're familiar with iOS, Android, or Windows Phone development, you might be curious to see how the platform startup code handles these jobs.

The iOS project

An iOS project typically contains a class that derives from `UIApplicationDelegate`. However, the Xamarin.Forms.Platform.iOS library defines an alternative base class named `FormsApplicationDelegate`. In the **Hello.iOS** project, you'll see this AppDelegate.cs file, here stripped of all extraneous `using` directives and comments:

```
using Foundation;
using UIKit;

namespace Hello.iOS
{
    [Register("AppDelegate")]
    public partial class AppDelegate :
                    global::Xamarin.Forms.Platform.iOS.FormsApplicationDelegate
```

```
    {
        public override bool FinishedLaunching(UIApplication app, NSDictionary options)
        {
            global::Xamarin.Forms.Forms.Init();
            LoadApplication(new App());

            return base.FinishedLaunching(app, options);
        }
    }
}
```

The `FinishedLaunching` override begins by calling the `Forms.Init` method defined in the **Xamarin.Forms.Platform.iOS** assembly. It then calls a `LoadApplication` method (defined by the `FormsApplicationDelegate`), passing to it a new instance of the `App` class defined in the `Hello` namespace in the shared PCL. The page object set to the `MainPage` property of this `App` object can then be used to create an object of type `UIViewController`, which is responsible for rendering the page's contents.

The Android project

In the Android application, the typical `MainActivity` class must be derived from a Xamarin.Forms class named `FormsApplicationActivity`, defined in the **Xamarin.Forms.Platform.Android** assembly, and the `Forms.Init` call requires some additional information:

```
using Android.App;
using Android.Content.PM;
using Android.OS;

namespace Hello.Droid
{
    [Activity(Label = "Hello", Icon = "@drawable/icon", MainLauncher = true,
        ConfigurationChanges = ConfigChanges.ScreenSize | ConfigChanges.Orientation)]
    public class MainActivity : global::Xamarin.Forms.Platform.Android.FormsApplicationActivity
    {
        protected override void OnCreate(Bundle bundle)
        {
            base.OnCreate(bundle);

            global::Xamarin.Forms.Forms.Init(this, bundle);
            LoadApplication(new App());
        }
    }
}
```

The new instance of the `App` class in the `Hello` namespace is then passed to a `LoadApplication` method defined by `FormsApplicationActivity`. The attribute set on the `MainActivity` class indicates that the activity is *not* re-created when the phone changes orientation (from portrait to landscape or back) or the screen changes size.

The Universal Windows Platform project

In the UWP project (or either of the two Windows projects), look first in the App.xaml.cs file tucked underneath the App.xaml file in the project file list. In the `OnLaunched` method you will see the call to `Forms.Init` using the event arguments:

```
Xamarin.Forms.Forms.Init(e);
```

Now look at the MainPage.xaml.cs file tucked underneath the MainPage.xaml file in the project file list. This file defines the customary `MainPage` class, but it actually derives from a Xamarin.Forms class specified as the root element in the MainPage.xaml file. A newly instantiated `App` class is passed to the `LoadApplication` method defined by this base class:

```
namespace Hello.UWP
{
    public sealed partial class MainPage
    {
        public MainPage()
        {
            this.InitializeComponent();

            LoadApplication(new Hello.App());
        }
    }
}
```

Nothing special!

If you've created a Xamarin.Forms solution under Visual Studio and don't want to target one or more platforms, simply delete those projects.

If you later change your mind about those projects—or you originally created the solution in Xamarin Studio and want to move it to Visual Studio to target one of the Windows platforms—you can add new platform projects to the Xamarin.Forms solution. In the **Add New Project** dialog, you can create a Unified API (not Classic API) Xamarin.iOS project by selecting the iOS project **Universal** type and **Blank App** template. Create a Xamarin.Android project with the Android **Blank App** template, or a Windows project by selecting **Universal** under the **Windows** heading (for a UWP project), or **Windows** or **Windows Phone** under the **Windows 8** heading, and then **Blank App**.

For these new projects, you can get the correct references and boilerplate code by consulting the projects generated by the standard Xamarin.Forms template.

To summarize: there's really nothing all that special in a Xamarin.Forms app compared with normal Xamarin or Windows Phone projects—except the Xamarin.Forms libraries.

PCL or SAP?

When you first created the **Hello** solution in Visual Studio, you had a choice of two application templates:

- **Blank App (Xamarin.Forms Portable)**

- **Blank App (Xamarin.Forms Shared)**

In Xamarin Studio, the choice is embodied in a pair of radio buttons:

- **Use Portable Class Library**

- **Use Shared Library**

The first option creates a Portable Class Library (PCL), whereas the second creates a Shared Asset Project (SAP) consisting only of shared code files. The original **Hello** solution used the PCL template. Now let's create a second solution named **HelloSap** with the SAP template.

As you'll see, everything looks pretty much the same, except that the **HelloSap** project itself contains only one item: the App.cs file.

With both the PCL and SAP approaches, code is shared among the five applications, but in decidedly different ways: With the PCL approach, all the common code is bundled into a dynamic-link library that each application project references and binds to at run time. With the SAP approach, the common code files are effectively included with each of the five application projects at build time. By default, the SAP has only a single file named App.cs, but effectively it's as if this **HelloSap** project did not exist and instead there were five different copies of this file in the five application projects.

Some subtle (and not-so-subtle) problems can manifest themselves with the shared library approach:

The iOS and Android projects have access to pretty much the same version of .NET, but it is not the same version of .NET that the Windows projects use. This means that any .NET classes accessed by the shared code might be somewhat different depending on the platform. As you'll discover later in this book, this is the case for some file I/O classes in the `System.IO` namespace.

You can compensate for these differences by using C# preprocessor directives, particularly `#if` and `#elif`. In the projects generated by the Xamarin.Forms template, the various application projects define symbols that you can use with these directives.

What are these symbols?

In Visual Studio, right-click the project name in the **Solution Explorer** and select **Properties**. At the left of the properties screen, select **Build**, and look for the **Conditional compilation symbols** field.

In Xamarin Studio, select an application project in the **Solution** list, invoke the drop-down tools menu, and select **Options**. In the left of the **Project Options** dialog, select **Build > Compiler**, and look for the **Define Symbols** field.

Here are the symbols that you can use:

- iOS project: You'll see the symbol `__IOS__` (that's two underscores before and after)

- Android project: You won't see any symbols defined for indicating the platform, but the identifier `__ANDROID__` is defined anyway, as well as multiple `__ANDROID_nn__` identifiers, where `nn` is each Android API level supported.

- UWP project: The symbol `WINDOWS_UWP`

- Windows project: The symbol `WINDOWS_APP`

- Windows Phone project: The symbol `WINDOWS_PHONE_APP`

Your shared code file can include blocks like this:

```
#if __IOS__
          // iOS specific code
#elif __ANDROID__
          // Android specific code
#elif WINDOWS_UWP
          // Universal Windows Platform specific code
#elif WINDOWS_APP
          // Windows 8.1 specific code
#elif WINDOWS__PHONE_APP
          // Windows Phone 8.1 specific code
#endif
```

This allows your shared code files to run platform-specific code or access platform-specific classes, including classes in the individual platform projects. You can also define your own conditional compilation symbols if you'd like.

These preprocessor directives make no sense in a Portable Class Library project. The PCL is entirely independent of the five platforms, and these identifiers in the platform projects are not present when the PCL is compiled.

The concept of the PCL originally arose because every platform that uses .NET actually uses a somewhat different subset of .NET. If you want to create a library that can be used among multiple .NET platforms, you need to use only the common parts of those .NET subsets.

The PCL is intended to help by containing code that is usable on multiple (but specific) .NET platforms. Consequently, any particular PCL contains some embedded flags that indicate what platforms it supports. A PCL used in a Xamarin.Forms application must support the following platforms:

- .NET Framework 4.5

- Windows 8

- Windows Phone 8.1

- Xamarin.Android

- Xamarin.iOS

- Xamarin.iOS (Classic)

This is known as PCL Profile 111.

If you need platform-specific behavior in the PCL, you can't use the C# preprocessor directives because those work only at build time. You need something that works at run time, such as the Xamarin-.Forms `Device` class. You'll see an example shortly.

The Xamarin.Forms PCL can access other PCLs supporting the same platforms, but it cannot directly access classes defined in the individual application projects. However, if that's something you need to do—and you'll see an example in Chapter 9, "Platform-specific API calls"—Xamarin.Forms provides a class named `DependencyService` that allows you to access platform-specific code from the PCL in a methodical manner.

Most of the programs in this book use the PCL approach. This is the recommended approach for Xamarin.Forms and is preferred by many programmers who have been working with Xamarin.Forms for a while. However, the SAP approach is also supported and definitely has its advocates as well. Programs within these pages that demonstrate the SAP approach always contain the letters **Sap** at the end of their names, such as the **HelloSap** program.

But why choose? You can have both in the same solution. If you've created a Xamarin.Forms solution with a Shared Asset Project, you can add a new PCL project to the solution by selecting the **Class Library (Xamarin.Forms Portable)** template. The application projects can access both the SAP and PCL, and the SAP can access the PCL as well.

Labels for text

Let's create a new Xamarin.Forms PCL solution, named **Greetings**, using the same process described above for creating the **Hello** solution. This new solution will be structured more like a typical Xamarin.Forms program, which means that it will define a new class that derives from `ContentPage`. Most of the time in this book, every class and structure defined by a program will get its own file. This means that a new file must be added to the **Greetings** project:

In Visual Studio, you can right-click the **Greetings** project in the **Solution Explorer** and select **Add > New Item** from the menu. At the left of the **Add New Item** dialog, select **Visual C#** and **Cross-Platform**, and in the center area, select **Forms ContentPage**. (Watch out: There's also a **Forms ContentView** option. Don't pick that one!)

In Xamarin Studio, from the tool icon on the **Greetings** project, select **Add > New File** from the menu. In the left of the **New File** dialog, select **Forms**, and in the central area, select **Forms ContentPage**. (Watch out: There are also **Forms ContentView** and **Forms ContentPage Xaml** options. Don't pick those!)

In either case, give the new file a name of GreetingsPage.cs.

The GreetingsPage.cs file will be initialized with some skeleton code for a class named `Greet-ingsPage` that derives from `ContentPage`. Because `ContentPage` is in the `Xamarin.Forms` namespace, a `using` directive includes that namespace. The class is defined as public, but it need not be because it won't be directly accessed from outside the **Greetings** project.

Let's delete all the code in the `GreetingsPage` constructor and most of the `using` directives, so the file looks something like this:

```
using System;
using Xamarin.Forms;

namespace Greetings
{
    public class GreetingsPage : ContentPage
    {
        public GreetingsPage()
        {

        }
    }
}
```

In the constructor of the `GreetingsPage` class, instantiate a `Label` view, set its `Text` property, and set that `Label` instance to the `Content` property that `GreetingsPage` inherits from `ContentPage`:

```
using System;
using Xamarin.Forms;

namespace Greetings
{
    public class GreetingsPage : ContentPage
    {
        public GreetingsPage()
        {
            Label label = new Label();
            label.Text = "Greetings, Xamarin.Forms!";
            this.Content = label;
        }
    }
}
```

Now change the `App` class in App.cs to set the `MainPage` property to an instance of this `Greet-ingsPage` class:

```
using System;
using Xamarin.Forms;
```

```
namespace Greetings
{
    public class App : Application
    {
        public App()
        {
            MainPage = new GreetingsPage();
        }

        protected override void OnStart()
        {
            // Handle when your app starts
        }

        protected override void OnSleep()
        {
            // Handle when your app sleeps
        }

        protected override void OnResume()
        {
            // Handle when your app resumes
        }
    }
}
```

It's easy to forget this step, and you'll be puzzled that your program seems to completely ignore your page class and still says "Welcome to Xamarin Forms!"

It is in the `GreetingsPage` class (and others like it) where you'll be spending most of your time in early Xamarin.Forms programming. For some single-page, UI-intensive programs, this class might contain the only application code that you'll need to write. Of course, you can add additional classes to the project if you need them.

In many of the single-page sample programs in this book, the class that derives from `ContentPage` will have a name that is the same as the application but with `Page` appended. That naming convention should help you identify the code listings in this book from just the class or constructor name without seeing the entire file. In most cases, the code snippets in the pages of this book won't include the `using` directives or the `namespace` definition.

Many Xamarin.Forms programmers prefer to use the C# 3.0 style of object creation and property initialization in their page constructors. You can do this for the `Label` object. Following the `Label` constructor, a pair of curly braces enclose one or more property settings separated by commas. Here's an alternative (but functionally equivalent) `GreetingsPage` definition:

```
public class GreetingsPage : ContentPage
{
    public GreetingsPage()
    {
        Label label = new Label
```

```
        {
            Text = "Greetings, Xamarin.Forms!"
        };
        this.Content = label;
    }
}
```

This style of property initialization allows the `Label` instance to be set to the `Content` property directly, so that the `Label` doesn't require a name, like so:

```
public class GreetingsPage : ContentPage
{
    public GreetingsPage()
    {
        Content = new Label
        {
            Text = "Greetings, Xamarin.Forms!"
        };
    }
}
```

For more complex page layouts, this style of instantiation and initialization provides a better visual analogue of the organization of layouts and views on the page. However, it's not always as simple as this example might indicate if you need to call methods on these objects or set event handlers.

Whichever way you do it, if you can successfully compile and run the program on the iOS, Android, and Windows 10 Mobile platforms on either an emulator or a device, here's what you'll see:

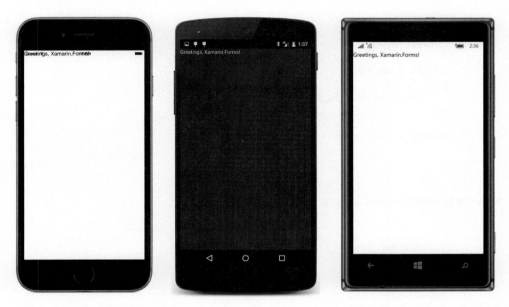

The most disappointing version of this **Greetings** program is definitely the iPhone: Beginning in iOS 7, a single-page application shares the screen with the status bar at the top. Anything the application displays at the top of its page will occupy the same space as the status bar unless the application compensates for it.

This problem disappears in multipage-navigation applications discussed later in this book, but until that time, here are four ways (or five ways if you're using an SAP) to solve this problem right away.

Solution 1. Include padding on the page

The Page class defines a property named Padding that marks an area around the interior perimeter of the page into which content cannot intrude. The Padding property is of type Thickness, a structure that defines four properties named Left, Top, Right, Bottom. (You might want to memorize that order because that's the order you'll define the properties in the Thickness constructor as well as in XAML.) The Thickness structure also defines constructors for setting the same amount of padding on all four sides or for setting the same amount on the left and right and on the top and bottom.

A little research in your favorite search engine will reveal that the iOS status bar has a height of 20. (Twenty what? you might ask. Twenty pixels? Actually, no. For now, just think of them as 20 "units." For much of your Xamarin.Forms programming, you shouldn't need to bother with numeric sizes, but Chapter 5, "Dealing with sizes," will provide some guidance when you need to get down to the pixel level.)

You can accommodate the status bar like so:

```
namespace Greetings
{
    public class GreetingsPage : ContentPage
    {
        public GreetingsPage ()
        {
            Content = new Label
            {
                Text = "Greetings, Xamarin.Forms!"
            };

            Padding = new Thickness(0, 20, 0, 0);
        }
    }
}
```

Now the greeting appears 20 units from the top of the page:

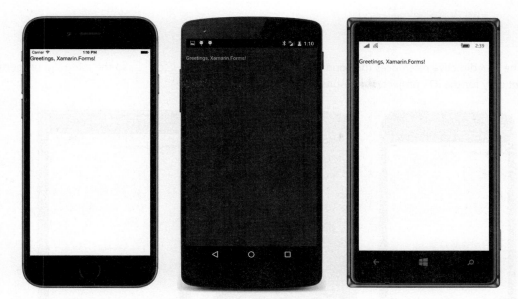

Setting the `Padding` property on the `ContentPage` solves the problem of the text overwriting the iOS status bar, but it also sets the same padding on the Android and Windows Phone, where it's not required. Is there a way to set this padding only on the iPhone?

Solution 2. Include padding just for iOS (SAP only)

One of the advantages of the Shared Asset Project (SAP) approach is that the classes in the project are extensions of the application projects, so you can use conditional compilation directives.

Let's try this out. We'll need a new solution named **GreetingsSap** based on the SAP template, and a new page class in the **GreetingsSap** project named `GreetingsSapPage`. To set the `Padding` in iOS only, that class looks like this:

```
namespace GreetingsSap
{
    public class GreetingsSapPage : ContentPage
    {
        public GreetingsSapPage ()
        {
            Content = new Label
            {
                Text = "Greetings, Xamarin.Forms!"
            };

#if __IOS__

            Padding = new Thickness(0, 20, 0, 0);

#endif
```

```
            }
        }
    }
}
```

The `#if` directive references the conditional compilation symbol `__IOS__`, so the `Padding` property is set only for the iOS project. The results look like this:

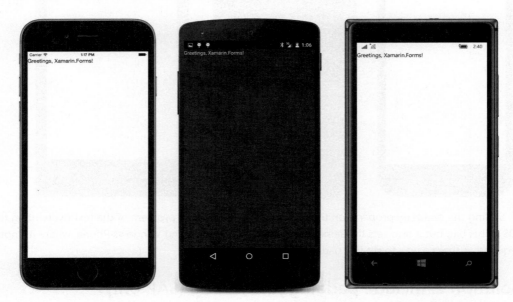

However, these conditional compilation symbols affect only the compilation of the program, so they have no effect in a PCL. Is there a way for a PCL project to include different `Padding` for different platforms?

Solution 3. Include padding just for iOS (PCL or SAP)

Yes! The static `Device` class includes several properties and methods that allow your code to deal with device differences at run time in a very simple and straightforward manner:

- The `Device.OS` property returns a member of the `TargetPlatform` enumeration: `iOS`, `Android`, `WinPhone`, or `Other`. The `WinPhone` member refers to all the Windows and Windows Phone platforms.

- The `Device.Idiom` property returns a member of the `TargetIdiom` enumeration: `Phone`, `Tablet`, `Desktop`, or `Unsupported`.

You can use these two properties in `if` and `else` statements, or a `switch` and `case` block, to execute code specific to a particular platform.

Two methods named `OnPlatform` provide even more elegant solutions:

- The static generic method `OnPlatform<T>` takes three arguments of type `T`—the first for iOS, the second for Android, and the third for Windows Phone (encompassing all the Windows platforms)—and returns the argument for the running platform.

- The static method `OnPlatform` has four arguments of type `Action` (the .NET function delegate that has no arguments and returns void), also in the order iOS, Android, and Windows Phone, with a fourth for a default, and executes the argument for the running platform.

Rather than setting the same `Padding` property on all three platforms, you can restrict the `Padding` to just the iPhone by using the `Device.OnPlatform` generic method:

```
Padding = Device.OnPlatform<Thickness>(new Thickness(0, 20, 0, 0),
                                       new Thickness(0),
                                       new Thickness(0));
```

The first `Thickness` argument is for iOS, the second is for Android, and the third is for Windows Phone. Explicitly specifying the type of the `Device.OnPlatform` arguments within the angle brackets isn't required if the compiler can figure it out from the arguments, so this works as well:

```
Padding = Device.OnPlatform(new Thickness(0, 20, 0, 0),
                            new Thickness(0),
                            new Thickness(0));
```

Or, you can have just one `Thickness` constructor and use `Device.OnPlatform` for the second argument:

```
Padding = new Thickness(0, Device.OnPlatform(20, 0, 0), 0, 0);
```

This is how the `Padding` will usually be set in the programs that follow when it's required. Of course, you can substitute some other numbers for the zeroes if you want some additional padding on the page. Sometimes a little padding on the sides makes for a more attractive display.

However, if you just need to set `Padding` for iOS, you can use the version of `Device.OnPlatform` with `Action` arguments. These arguments are `null` by default, so you can just set the first for an action to be performed on iOS:

```
public class GreetingsPage : ContentPage
{
    public GreetingsPage()
    {
        Content = new Label
        {
            Text = "Greetings, Xamarin.Forms!"
        };

        Device.OnPlatform(() =>
            {
                Padding = new Thickness(0, 20, 0, 0);
            });
    }
}
```

Now the statement to set the padding is executed only when the program is running on iOS. Of course, with just that one argument to `Device.OnPlatform`, it could be a little obscure to people who need to read your code, so you might want to include the parameter name preceding the argument to make it explicit that this statement executes just for iOS:

```
Device.OnPlatform(iOS: () =>
    {
        Padding = new Thickness(0, 20, 0, 0);
    });
```

Naming the argument like that is a feature introduced in C# 4.0.

The `Device.OnPlatform` method is very handy and has the advantage of working in both PCL and SAP projects. However, it can't access APIs within the individual platforms. For that you'll need `DependencyService`, which is discussed in Chapter 9.

Solution 4. Center the label within the page

The problem with the text overlapping the iOS status bar occurs only because the default display of the text is at the upper-left corner. Is it possible to center the text on the page?

Xamarin.Forms supports a number of facilities to ease layout without requiring the program to perform calculations involving sizes and coordinates. The `View` class defines two properties, named `HorizontalOptions` and `VerticalOptions`, that specify how a view is to be positioned relative to its parent (in this case the `ContentPage`). These two properties are of type `LayoutOptions`, an exceptionally important structure in Xamarin.Forms.

Generally you'll use the `LayoutOptions` structure by specifying one of the eight public static read-only fields that it defines that return `LayoutOptions` values:

- `Start`

- `Center`

- `End`

- `Fill`

- `StartAndExpand`

- `CenterAndExpand`

- `EndAndExpand`

- `FillAndExpand`

However, you can also create a `LayoutOptions` value yourself. The `LayoutOptions` structure also defines two instance properties that let you create a value with these same combinations:

- An `Alignment` property of type `LayoutAlignment`, an enumeration with four members:

`Start`, `Center`, `End`, and `Fill`.

- An `Expands` property of type `bool`.

A fuller explanation of all these options awaits you in Chapter 4, "Scrolling the stack," but for now you can set the `HorizontalOptions` and `VerticalOptions` properties of the `Label` to one of the static fields defined by `LayoutOptions` values. For `HorizontalOptions`, the word `Start` means left and `End` means right; for `VerticalOptions`, `Start` means top and `End` means bottom.

Mastering the use of the `HorizontalOptions` and `VerticalOptions` properties is a major part of acquiring skill in the Xamarin.Forms layout system, but here's a simple example that positions the `Label` in the center of the page:

```csharp
public class GreetingsPage : ContentPage
{
    public GreetingsPage()
    {
        Content = new Label
        {
            Text = "Greetings, Xamarin.Forms!",
            HorizontalOptions = LayoutOptions.Center,
            VerticalOptions = LayoutOptions.Center
        };
    }
}
```

Here's how it looks:

For this paragraph of text, setting `HorizontalOptions` to `Start`, `Center`, or `End` on iOS or Windows Phone will shift the entire paragraph horizontally slightly to the left, center, or right. (Android works a little differently for multiple lines of text.) The shifting is only slight because the width of the paragraph is the width of the longest line of text. Since word wrapping is governed by the page width (minus the padding), the paragraph likely occupies just slightly less width than the width available for it on the page.

But setting the `HorizontalTextAlignment` property of the `Label` has a much more profound effect: Setting this property affects the alignment of the individual lines. A setting of `TextAlignment.Center` will center all the lines of the paragraph, and `TextAlignment.Right` aligns them all at the right. You can use `HorizontalOptions` in addition to `HorizontalTextAlignment` to shift the entire paragraph slightly to the center or the right.

However, after you've set `VerticalOptions` to `Start`, `Center`, or `End`, any setting of `VerticalTextAlignment` has no effect.

`Label` defines a `LineBreakMode` property that you can set to a member of the `LineBreakMode` enumeration if you don't want the text to wrap or to select truncation options.

There is no property to specify a first-line indent for the paragraph, but you can add one of your own with space characters of various types, such as the em space (Unicode \u2003).

This is the version of the **Greetings** program that is included in the sample code for this chapter. You can use various combinations of `HorizontalOptions` and `VerticalOptions` to position the text in any of nine places relative to the page.

Solution 5. Center the text within the label

The `Label` is intended to display text up to a paragraph in length. It is often desirable to control how the lines of text are horizontally aligned: left justified, right justified, or centered.

The `Label` view defines a `HorizontalTextAlignment` property for that purpose and also a `VerticalTextAlignment` property for positioning text vertically. Both properties are set to a member of the `TextAlignment` enumeration, which has members named `Start`, `Center`, and `End` to be versatile enough for text that runs from right to left or from top to bottom. For English and other European languages, `Start` means left or top and `End` means right or bottom.

For this final solution to the iOS status bar problem, set `HorizontalTextAlignment` and `VerticalTextAlignment` to `TextAlignment.Center`:

```
public class GreetingsPage : ContentPage
{
    public GreetingsPage()
    {
        Content = new Label
        {
            Text = "Greetings, Xamarin.Forms!",
            HorizontalTextAlignment = TextAlignment.Center,
            VerticalTextAlignment = TextAlignment.Center
        };
    }
}
```

Visually, the result with this single line of text is the same as setting `HorizontalO` `VerticalOptions` to `Center`, and you can also use various combinations of these tion the text in one of nine different locations around the page.

However, these two techniques to center the text are actually quite different, a next chapter.

Chapter 3   Deeper into text

Notice the use of embedded Unicode codes for opened and closed "smart quotes" (\u201C and \u201D) and the em dash (\u2014). `Padding` has been set for 5 units around the page to avoid the text butting up against the edges of the screen, but the `VerticalOptions` property has been used as well to vertically center the entire paragraph on the page:

Chapter 3
Deeper into text

Despite how sophisticated graphical user interfaces have become, text remains the backbone of most applications. Yet text is potentially one of the most complex visual objects because it carries baggage of hundreds of years of typography. The primary consideration is that text must be readable. This requires that text not be too small, yet text mustn't be so large that it hogs a lot of space on the screen.

For these reasons, the subject of text is continued in several subsequent chapters, most notably Chapter 5, "Dealing with sizes." Very often, Xamarin.Forms programmers define font characteristics in styles, which are the subject of Chapter 12.

Wrapping paragraphs

Displaying a paragraph of text is as easy as displaying a single line of text. Just make the text long enough to wrap into multiple lines:

```
public class BaskervillesPage : ContentPage
{
    public BaskervillesPage()
    {
        Content = new Label
        {
            VerticalOptions = LayoutOptions.Center,
            Text =
                "Mr. Sherlock Holmes, who was usually very late in " +
                "the mornings, save upon those not infrequent " +
                "occasions when he was up all night, was seated at " +
                "the breakfast table. I stood upon the hearth-rug " +
                "and picked up the stick which our visitor had left " +
                "behind him the night before. It was a fine, thick " +
                "piece of wood, bulbous-headed, of the sort which " +
                "is known as a \u201CPenang lawyer.\u201D Just " +
                "under the head was a broad silver band, nearly an " +
                "inch across, \u201CTo James Mortimer, M.R.C.S., " +
                "from his friends of the C.C.H.,\u201D was engraved " +
                "upon it, with the date \u201C1884.\u201D It was " +
                "just such a stick as the old-fashioned family " +
                "practitioner used to carry\u2014dignified, solid, " +
                "and reassuring."
        };

        Padding = new Thickness(5, Device.OnPlatform(20, 5, 5), 5, 5);
    }
}
```

Notice the use of embedded Unicode codes for opened and closed "smart quotes" (\u201C and \u201D) and the em dash (\u2014). `Padding` has been set for 5 units around the page to avoid the text butting up against the edges of the screen, but the `VerticalOptions` property has been used as well to vertically center the entire paragraph on the page:

For this paragraph of text, setting `HorizontalOptions` to `Start`, `Center`, or `End` on iOS or Windows Phone will shift the entire paragraph horizontally slightly to the left, center, or right. (Android works a little differently for multiple lines of text.) The shifting is only slight because the width of the paragraph is the width of the longest line of text. Since word wrapping is governed by the page width (minus the padding), the paragraph likely occupies just slightly less width than the width available for it on the page.

But setting the `HorizontalTextAlignment` property of the `Label` has a much more profound effect: Setting this property affects the alignment of the individual lines. A setting of `TextAlignment.Center` will center all the lines of the paragraph, and `TextAlignment.Right` aligns them all at the right. You can use `HorizontalOptions` in addition to `HorizontalTextAlignment` to shift the entire paragraph slightly to the center or the right.

However, after you've set `VerticalOptions` to `Start`, `Center`, or `End`, any setting of `VerticalTextAlignment` has no effect.

`Label` defines a `LineBreakMode` property that you can set to a member of the `LineBreakMode` enumeration if you don't want the text to wrap or to select truncation options.

There is no property to specify a first-line indent for the paragraph, but you can add one of your own with space characters of various types, such as the em space (Unicode \u2003).

`Start`, `Center`, `End`, and `Fill`.

- An `Expands` property of type `bool`.

A fuller explanation of all these options awaits you in Chapter 4, "Scrolling the stack," but for now you can set the `HorizontalOptions` and `VerticalOptions` properties of the `Label` to one of the static fields defined by `LayoutOptions` values. For `HorizontalOptions`, the word `Start` means left and `End` means right; for `VerticalOptions`, `Start` means top and `End` means bottom.

Mastering the use of the `HorizontalOptions` and `VerticalOptions` properties is a major part of acquiring skill in the Xamarin.Forms layout system, but here's a simple example that positions the `Label` in the center of the page:

```
public class GreetingsPage : ContentPage
{
    public GreetingsPage()
    {
        Content = new Label
        {
            Text = "Greetings, Xamarin.Forms!",
            HorizontalOptions = LayoutOptions.Center,
            VerticalOptions = LayoutOptions.Center
        };
    }
}
```

Here's how it looks:

This is the version of the **Greetings** program that is included in the sample code for this chapter. You can use various combinations of `HorizontalOptions` and `VerticalOptions` to position the text in any of nine places relative to the page.

Solution 5. Center the text within the label

The `Label` is intended to display text up to a paragraph in length. It is often desirable to control how the lines of text are horizontally aligned: left justified, right justified, or centered.

The `Label` view defines a `HorizontalTextAlignment` property for that purpose and also a `VerticalTextAlignment` property for positioning text vertically. Both properties are set to a member of the `TextAlignment` enumeration, which has members named `Start`, `Center`, and `End` to be versatile enough for text that runs from right to left or from top to bottom. For English and other European languages, `Start` means left or top and `End` means right or bottom.

For this final solution to the iOS status bar problem, set `HorizontalTextAlignment` and `VerticalTextAlignment` to `TextAlignment.Center`:

```
public class GreetingsPage : ContentPage
{
    public GreetingsPage()
    {
        Content = new Label
        {
            Text = "Greetings, Xamarin.Forms!",
            HorizontalTextAlignment = TextAlignment.Center,
            VerticalTextAlignment = TextAlignment.Center
        };
    }
}
```

Visually, the result with this single line of text is the same as setting `HorizontalOptions` and `VerticalOptions` to `Center`, and you can also use various combinations of these properties to position the text in one of nine different locations around the page.

However, these two techniques to center the text are actually quite different, as you'll see in the next chapter.

You can display multiple paragraphs with a single `Label` view by ending each paragraph with one or more line feed characters (\n). However, a better approach is to use the string returned from the `Environment.NewLine` static property. This property returns "\n" on iOS and Android devices and "\r\n" on all Windows and Windows Phone devices. But rather than embedding line feed characters to create paragraphs, it makes more sense to use a separate `Label` view for each paragraph, as will be demonstrated in Chapter 4, "Scrolling the stack."

The `Label` class has lots of formatting flexibility. As you'll see shortly, properties defined by `Label` allow you to specify a font size or bold or italic text, and you can also specify different text formatting within a single paragraph.

`Label` also allows specifying color, and a little experimentation with color will demonstrate the profound difference between the `HorizontalOptions` and `VerticalOptions` properties and the `HorizontalTextAlignment` and `VerticalTextAlignment` properties.

Text and background colors

As you've seen, the `Label` view displays text in a color appropriate for the device. You can override that behavior by setting two properties, named `TextColor` and `BackgroundColor`. `Label` itself defines `TextColor`, but it inherits `BackgroundColor` from `VisualElement`, which means that `Page` and `Layout` also have a `BackgroundColor` property.

You set `TextColor` and `BackgroundColor` to a value of type `Color`, which is a structure that defines 17 static fields for obtaining common colors. You can experiment with these properties with the **Greetings** program from the previous chapter. Here are two of these colors used in conjunction with `HorizontalTextAlignment` and `VerticalTextAlignment` to center the text:

```
public class GreetingsPage : ContentPage
{
    public GreetingsPage()
    {
        Content = new Label
        {
            Text = "Greetings, Xamarin.Forms!",
            HorizontalTextAlignment = TextAlignment.Center,
            VerticalTextAlignment = TextAlignment.Center,
            BackgroundColor = Color.Yellow,
            TextColor = Color.Blue
        };
    }
}
```

The result might surprise you. As these screenshots illustrate, the `Label` actually occupies the entire area of the page (including underneath the iOS status bar), and the `HorizontalTextAlignment` and `VerticalTextAlignment` properties position the text within that area:

In contrast, here's some code that colors the text the same but instead centers the text using the `HorizontalOptions` and `VerticalOptions` properties:

```
public class GreetingsPage : ContentPage
{
    public GreetingsPage()
    {
        Content = new Label
        {
            Text = "Greetings, Xamarin.Forms!",
            HorizontalOptions = LayoutOptions.Center,
            VerticalOptions = LayoutOptions.Center,
            BackgroundColor = Color.Yellow,
            TextColor = Color.Blue
        };
    }
}
```

Now the `Label` occupies only as much space as required for the text, and that's what's positioned in the center of the page:

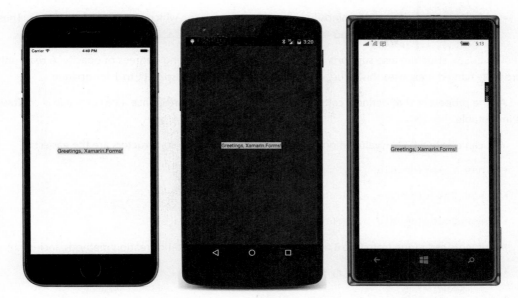

The default value of `HorizontalOptions` and `VerticalOptions` is not `LayoutOptions.Start`, as the default appearance of the text might suggest. The default value is instead `LayoutOptions.Fill`. This is the setting that causes the `Label` to fill the page. The default `Horizontal-TextAlignment` and `VerticalTextAlignment` value of `TextAlignment.Start` is what caused the text to be positioned at the upper-left in the first version of the **Greetings** program in the previous chapter.

You can combine various settings of `HorizontalOptions`, `VerticalOptions`, `HorizontalText-Alignment`, and `VerticalTextAlignment` for different effects.

You might wonder: What are the default values of the `TextColor` and `BackgroundColor` properties, because the default values result in different colors for the different platforms?

The default value of `TextColor` and `BackgroundColor` is actually a special color value named `Color.Default,` which does not represent a real color but instead is used to reference the text and background colors appropriate for the particular platform.

Let's explore color in more detail.

The Color structure

Internally, the `Color` structure stores colors in two different ways:

- As red, green, and blue (RGB) values of type `double` that range from 0 to 1. Read-only properties named `R`, `G`, and `B` expose these values.

- As hue, saturation, and luminosity values of type `double`, which also range from 0 to 1. These values are exposed with read-only properties named `Hue`, `Saturation`, and `Luminosity`.

The `Color` structure also supports an alpha channel for indicating degrees of opacity. A read-only property named `A` exposes this value, which ranges from 0 for transparent to 1 for opaque.

All the properties that define a color are read-only. In other words, once a `Color` value is created, it is immutable.

You can create a `Color` value in one of several ways. The three constructors are the easiest:

- `new Color(double grayShade)`

- `new Color(double r, double g, double b)`

- `new Color(double r, double g, double b, double a)`

Arguments can range from 0 to 1. `Color` also defines several static creation methods, including:

- `Color.FromRgb(double r, double g, double b)`

- `Color.FromRgb(int r, int g, int b)`

- `Color.FromRgba(double r, double g, double b, double a)`

- `Color.FromRgba(int r, int g, int b, int a)`

- `Color.FromHsla(double h, double s, double l, double a)`

The two static methods with integer arguments assume that the values range from 0 to 255, which is the customary representation of RGB colors. Internally, the constructor simply divides the integer values by 255.0 to convert to `double`.

Watch out! You might think that you're creating a red color with this call:

```
Color.FromRgb(1, 0, 0)
```

However, the C# compiler will assume that these arguments are integers. The integer `FromRgb` method will be invoked, and the first argument will be divided by 255.0, with a result that is nearly zero. If you want to invoke the method that has `double` arguments, be explicit:

```
Color.FromRgb(1.0, 0, 0)
```

`Color` also defines static creation methods for a packed `uint` format and a hexadecimal format in a string, but these are used less frequently.

The `Color` structure also defines 17 public static read-only fields of type `Color`. In the table below, the integer RGB values that the `Color` structure uses internally to define these fields are shown together with the corresponding `Hue`, `Saturation`, and `Luminosity` values, somewhat rounded for purposes of clarity:

Color Fields	Color	Red	Green	Blue	Hue	Saturation	Luminosity
White		255	255	255	0	0	1.00
Silver		192	192	192	0	0	0.75
Gray		128	128	128	0	0	0.50
Black		0	0	0	0	0	0
Red		255	0	0	1.00	1	0.50
Maroon		128	0	0	1.00	1	0.25
Yellow		255	255	0	0.17	1	0.50
Olive		128	128	0	0.17	1	0.25
Lime		0	255	0	0.33	1	0.50
Green		0	128	0	0.33	1	0.25
Aqua		0	255	255	0.50	1	0.50
Teal		0	128	128	0.50	1	0.25
Blue		0	0	255	0.67	1	0.50
Navy		0	0	128	0.67	1	0.25
Pink		255	102	255	0.83	1	0.70
Fuchsia		255	0	255	0.83	1	0.50
Purple		128	0	128	0.83	1	0.25

With the exception of `Pink`, you might recognize these as the color names supported in HTML. An 18th public static read-only field is named `Transparent`, which has R, G, B, and A properties all set to zero.

When people are given an opportunity to interactively formulate a color, the HSL color model is often more intuitive than RGB. The `Hue` cycles through the colors of the visible spectrum (and the rainbow) beginning with red at 0, green at 0.33, blue at 0.67, and back to red at 1.

The `Saturation` indicates the degree of the hue in the color, ranging from 0, which is no hue at all and results in a gray shade, to 1 for full saturation.

The `Luminosity` is a measure of lightness, ranging from 0 for black to 1 for white.

Color-selection programs in Chapter 15, "The interactive interface," let you explore the RGB and HSL models more interactively.

The `Color` structure includes several interesting instance methods that allow creating new colors that are modifications of existing colors:

- `AddLuminosity(double delta)`

- `MultiplyAlpha(double alpha)`

- `WithHue(double newHue)`

- `WithLuminosity(double newLuminosity)`

- `WithSaturation(double newSaturation)`

Finally, `Color` defines two special static read-only properties of type `Color`:

- `Color.Default`

- `Color.Accent`

The `Color.Default` property is used extensively within Xamarin.Forms to define the default color of views. The `VisualElement` class initializes its `BackgroundColor` property to `Color.Default`, and the `Label` class initializes its `TextColor` property as `Color.Default`.

However, `Color.Default` is a `Color` value with its `R`, `G`, `B`, and `A` properties all set to –1, which means that it's a special "mock" value that means nothing in itself but indicates that the actual value is platform specific.

For `Label` and `ContentPage` (and most classes that derive from `VisualElement`), the `BackgroundColor` setting of `Color.Default` means transparent. The background color you see on the screen is the background color of the page. The `BackgroundColor` property of the page has a default setting of `Color.Default`, but that value means something different on the various platforms. The meaning of `Color.Default` for the `TextColor` property of `Label` is also device dependent.

Here are the default color schemes implied by the `BackgroundColor` of the page and the `TextColor` of the `Label`:

Platform	Color Scheme
iOS	Dark text on a light background
Android	Light text on a dark background
UWP	Dark text on a light background
Windows 8.1	Light text on a dark background
Windows Phone 8.1	Light text on a dark background

On Android, Windows, and Windows Phone devices, you can change this color scheme for your application. See the next section.

You have a couple of possible strategies for working with color: You can choose to do your Xamarin.Forms programming in a very platform-independent manner and avoid making any assumptions about the default color scheme of any phone. Or, you can use your knowledge about the color schemes of the various platforms and use `Device.OnPlatform` to specify platform-specific colors.

But don't try to just ignore all the platform defaults and explicitly set all the colors in your application to your own color scheme. This probably won't work as well as you hope because many views use other colors that relate to the color theme of the operating system but that are not exposed through Xamarin.Forms properties.

One straightforward option is to use the `Color.Accent` property for an alternative text color. On the iPhone and Android platforms, this is a color that is visible against the default background but is not the default text color. On the Windows platforms, it's a color selected by the user as part of the color theme.

You can make text semitransparent by setting `TextColor` to a `Color` value with an `A` property less than 1. However, if you want a semitransparent version of the default text color, use the `Opacity` property of the `Label` instead. This property is defined by the `VisualElement` class and has a default value of 1. Set it to values less than 1 for various degrees of transparency.

Changing the application color scheme

When targeting your application for Android, Windows, and Windows Phone, it is possible to change the color scheme for the application. In this case, the settings of `Color.Default` for the `Back-groundColor` of the `ContentPage` and the `TextColor` property of the `Label` will have different meanings.

There are several ways to set color schemes in Android, but the simplest requires only a single attribute setting in the AndroidManifest.xml file in the **Properties** folder of the Android project. That file normally looks like this:

```
<manifest xmlns:android="http://schemas.android.com/apk/res/android">
    <uses-sdk android:minSdkVersion="15" />
    <application>
    </application>
</manifest>
```

Add the following attribute to the `application` tag:

```
<manifest xmlns:android="http://schemas.android.com/apk/res/android">
    <uses-sdk android:minSdkVersion="15" />
    <application android:theme="@style/android:Theme.Holo.Light">
    </application>
</manifest>
```

Now your Android application will display dark text on a light background.

For the three Windows and Windows Phone projects, you'll need to change the App.xaml file located in the particular project.

In the **UWP** project, the default App.xaml file looks like this:

```
<Application
    x:Class="Baskervilles.UWP.App"
    xmlns="http://schemas.microsoft.com/winfx/2006/xaml/presentation"
    xmlns:x="http://schemas.microsoft.com/winfx/2006/xaml"
    xmlns:local="using:Baskervilles.UWP"
    RequestedTheme="Light">

</Application>
```

That `RequestedTheme` attribute is what gives the UWP application a color scheme of dark text on a light background. Change it to `Dark` for light text on a dark background. Remove the `Requested-Theme` attribute entirely to allow the user's setting to determine the color scheme.

The App.xaml file for the Windows Phone 8.1 and Windows 8.1 projects is similar, but the `Request-edTheme` attribute is not included by default. Here's the App.xaml file in the **WinPhone** project:

```
<Application
    x:Class="Baskervilles.WinPhone.App"
```

```
xmlns="http://schemas.microsoft.com/winfx/2006/xaml/presentation"
xmlns:x="http://schemas.microsoft.com/winfx/2006/xaml"
xmlns:local="using:Baskervilles.WinPhone">

</Application>
```

By default, the color scheme is determined by the user's setting. You can include a `RequestedTheme` attribute and set it to `Light` or `Dark` to override the user's preference and take control of the color scheme.

By setting `RequestedTheme` on your Windows Phone and Windows projects, your application should have complete knowledge of the underlying color schemes on all the platforms.

Font sizes and attributes

By default, the `Label` uses a system font defined by each platform, but `Label` also defines several properties that you can use to change this font. `Label` is one of only two classes with these font-related properties; `Button` is the other.

The properties that let you change this font are:

- `FontFamily` of type `string`

- `FontSize` of type `double`

- `FontAttributes` of type `FontAttributes`, an enumeration with three members: `None`, `Bold`, and `Italic`.

There is also a `Font` property and corresponding `Font` structure, but this is deprecated and should not be used.

The hardest of these to use is `FontFamily`. In theory you can set it to a font family name such as "Times Roman," but it will work only if that particular font family is supported on the particular platform. For this reason, you'll probably use `FontFamily` in connection with `Device.OnPlatform`, and you'll need to know each platform's supported font family names.

The `FontSize` property is a little awkward as well. You need a number that roughly indicates the height of the font, but what numbers should you use? This is a thorny issue, and for that reason, it's relegated to Chapter 5, "Dealing with sizes," when the tools to pick a good font size will become available.

Until then, however, the `Device` class helps out with a static method called `GetNamedSize`. This method requires a member of the `NamedSize` enumeration:

- `Default`

- `Micro`

- Small

- Medium

- Large

GetNamedSize also requires the type of the class that you're sizing with this font size, and that argument will be either typeof(Label) or typeof(Button). You can also use an instance of Label or Button itself rather than the Type, but this option is often less convenient.

As you'll see later in this chapter, the NamedSize.Medium member does not necessarily return the same size as NamedSize.Default.

FontAttributes is the least complicated of the three font-related properties to use. You can specify Bold or Italic or both, as this little snippet of code (adapted from the **Greetings** program from the previous chapter) demonstrates:

```
class GreetingsPage : ContentPage
{
    public GreetingsPage()
    {
        Content = new Label
        {
            Text = "Greetings, Xamarin.Forms!",
            HorizontalOptions = LayoutOptions.Center,
            VerticalOptions = LayoutOptions.Center,
            FontSize = Device.GetNamedSize(NamedSize.Large, typeof(Label)),
            FontAttributes = FontAttributes.Bold | FontAttributes.Italic
        };
    }
}
```

Here it is on the three platforms:

The Windows 10 Mobile screen is not quite wide enough to display the text in a single line.

Formatted text

As you've seen, `Label` has a `Text` property that you can set to a string. But `Label` also has an alternative `FormattedText` property that constructs a paragraph with nonuniform formatting.

The `FormattedText` property is of type `FormattedString`, which has a `Spans` property of type `IList<Span>`, a collection of `Span` objects. Each `Span` object is a uniformly formatted chunk of text that is governed by six properties:

- `Text`

- `FontFamily`

- `FontSize`

- `FontAttributes`

- `ForegroundColor`

- `BackgroundColor`

Here's one way to instantiate a `FormattedString` object and then add `Span` instances to its `Spans` collection property:

```
public class VariableFormattedTextPage : ContentPage
{
```

```
    public VariableFormattedTextPage()
    {
        FormattedString formattedString = new FormattedString();

        formattedString.Spans.Add(new Span
        {
            Text = "I "
        });

        formattedString.Spans.Add(new Span
        {
            Text = "love",
            FontSize = Device.GetNamedSize(NamedSize.Large, typeof(Label)),
            FontAttributes = FontAttributes.Bold
        });

        formattedString.Spans.Add(new Span
        {
            Text = " Xamarin.Forms!"
        });

        Content = new Label
        {
            FormattedText = formattedString,
            HorizontalOptions = LayoutOptions.Center,
            VerticalOptions = LayoutOptions.Center,
            FontSize = Device.GetNamedSize(NamedSize.Large, typeof(Label))
        };
    }
}
```

As each Span is created, it is directly passed to the Add method of the Spans collection. Notice that the Label is given a FontSize of NamedSize.Large, and the Span with the Bold setting is also explicitly given that same size. When a Span is given a FontAttributes setting, it does not inherit the FontSize setting of the Label.

Alternatively, it's possible to initialize the contents of the Spans collection by following it with a pair of curly braces. Within these curly braces, the Span objects are instantiated. Because no method calls are required, the entire FormattedString initialization can occur within the Label initialization:

```
public class VariableFormattedTextPage : ContentPage
{
    public VariableFormattedTextPage()
    {
        Content = new Label
        {
            FormattedText = new FormattedString
            {
                Spans =
                {
                    new Span
                    {
                        Text = "I "
```

```
                },
                new Span
                {
                    Text = "love",
                    FontSize = Device.GetNamedSize(NamedSize.Large, typeof(Label)),
                    FontAttributes = FontAttributes.Bold
                },
                new Span
                {
                    Text = " Xamarin.Forms!"
                }
            }
        },

        HorizontalOptions = LayoutOptions.Center,
        VerticalOptions = LayoutOptions.Center,
        FontSize = Device.GetNamedSize(NamedSize.Large, typeof(Label))
    };
    }
}
```

This is the version of the program that you'll see in the collection of sample code for this chapter. Regardless of which approach you use, here's what it looks like:

You can also use the `FormattedText` property to embed italic or bold words within an entire paragraph, as the **VariableFormattedParagraph** program demonstrates:

```
public class VariableFormattedParagraphPage : ContentPage
{
    public VariableFormattedParagraphPage()
    {
```

```
Content = new Label
{
    FormattedText = new FormattedString
    {
        Spans =
        {
            new Span
            {
                Text = "\u2003There was nothing so "
            },
            new Span
            {
                Text = "very",
                FontAttributes = FontAttributes.Italic
            },
            new Span
            {
                Text = " remarkable in that; nor did Alice " +
                    "think it so "
            },
            new Span
            {
                Text = "very",
                FontAttributes = FontAttributes.Italic
            },
            new Span
            {
                Text = " much out of the way to hear the " +
                    "Rabbit say to itself \u2018Oh " +
                    "dear! Oh dear! I shall be too late!" +
                    "\u2019 (when she thought it over " +
                    "afterwards, it occurred to her that " +
                    "she ought to have wondered at this, " +
                    "but at the time it all seemed quite " +
                    "natural); but, when the Rabbit actually "
            },
            new Span
            {
                Text = "took a watch out of its waistcoat-pocket",
                FontAttributes = FontAttributes.Italic
            },
            new Span
            {
                Text = ", and looked at it, and then hurried on, " +
                    "Alice started to her feet, for it flashed " +
                    "across her mind that she had never before " +
                    "seen a rabbit with either a waistcoat-" +
                    "pocket, or a watch to take out of it, " +
                    "and, burning with curiosity, she ran " +
                    "across the field after it, and was just " +
                    "in time to see it pop down a large " +
                    "rabbit-hold under the hedge."
            }
        }
```

```
            },

            HorizontalOptions = LayoutOptions.Center,
            VerticalOptions = LayoutOptions.Center
        };
    }
}
```

The paragraph begins with an em space (Unicode \u2003) and contains so-called smart quotes (\u201C and \u201D), and several words are italicized:

You can persuade a single `Label` to display multiple lines or paragraphs with the insertion of end-of-line characters. This is demonstrated in the **NamedFontSizes** program. Multiple `Span` objects are added to a `FormattedString` object in a `foreach` loop. Each `Span` object uses a different `NamedFont` value and also displays the actual size returned from `Device.GetNamedSize`:

```
public class NamedFontSizesPage : ContentPage
{
    public NamedFontSizesPage()
    {
        FormattedString formattedString = new FormattedString();
        NamedSize[] namedSizes =
        {
            NamedSize.Default, NamedSize.Micro, NamedSize.Small,
            NamedSize.Medium, NamedSize.Large
        };

        foreach (NamedSize namedSize in namedSizes)
        {
            double fontSize = Device.GetNamedSize(namedSize, typeof(Label));
```

```
formattedString.Spans.Add(new Span
    {
        Text = String.Format("Named Size = {0} ({1:F2})",
                                namedSize, fontSize),
        FontSize = fontSize
    });

if (namedSize != namedSizes.Last())
{
    formattedString.Spans.Add(new Span
        {
            Text = Environment.NewLine + Environment.NewLine
        });
}
    }

    Content = new Label
    {
        FormattedText = formattedString,
        HorizontalOptions = LayoutOptions.Center,
        VerticalOptions = LayoutOptions.Center
    };
    }
}
```

Notice that a separate `Span` contains the two platform-specific end-of-line strings to space the individual lines. This ensures that the line spacing is based on the default font size rather than the font size just displayed:

These are not pixel sizes! As with the height of the iOS status bar, it's best to refer to these sizes only vaguely as some kind of "units." Some additional clarity is coming in Chapter 5.

The `Default` size is generally chosen by the operating system, but the other sizes were chosen by the Xamarin.Forms developers. On iOS, `Default` is the same as `Medium`, but on Android `Default` is the same as `Small`, and on Windows 10 Mobile, `Default` is smaller than `Micro`.

The sizes on the iPad and Windows 10 are the same as the iPhone and Windows 10 Mobile, respectively. However, the sizes on the Windows 8.1 and Windows Phone 8.1 platforms show more of discrepancy:

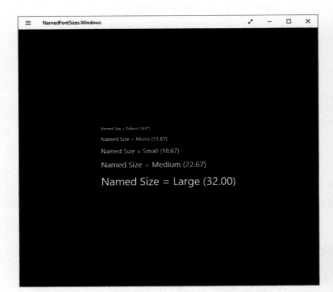

Of course, the use of multiple `Span` objects in a single `Label` is not a good way to render multiple paragraphs of text. Moreover, text often has so many paragraphs that it must be scrolled. This is the job for the next chapter and its exploration of `StackLayout` and `ScrollView`.

Chapter 4
Scrolling the stack

If you're like most programmers, as soon as you saw that list of static `Color` properties in the previous chapter, you wanted to write a program to display them all, perhaps using the `Text` property of `Label` to identify the color, and the `TextColor` property to show the actual color.

Although you could do this with a single `Label` using a `FormattedString` object, it's much easier with multiple `Label` objects. Because multiple `Label` objects are involved, this job also requires some way to display all the `Label` objects on the screen.

The `ContentPage` class defines a `Content` property of type `View` that you can set to an object—but only one object. Displaying multiple views requires setting `Content` to an instance of a class that can have multiple children of type `View`. Such a class is `Layout<T>`, which defines a `Children` property of type `IList<T>`.

The `Layout<T>` class is abstract, but four classes derive from `Layout<View>`, a class that can have multiple children of type `View`. In alphabetical order, these four classes are:

- `AbsoluteLayout`

- `Grid`

- `RelativeLayout`

- `StackLayout`

Each of them arranges its children in a characteristic manner. This chapter focuses on `StackLayout`.

Stacks of views

The `StackLayout` class arranges its children in a stack. It defines only two properties on its own:

- `Orientation` of type `StackOrientation`, an enumeration with two members: `Vertical` (the default) and `Horizontal`.

- `Spacing` of type `double`, initialized to 6.0.

`StackLayout` seems ideal for the job of listing colors. You can use the `Add` method defined by `IList<T>` to add children to the `Children` collection of a `StackLayout` instance. Here's some code that creates multiple `Label` objects from two arrays and then adds each `Label` to the `Children` collection of a `StackLayout`:

```
Color[] colors =
```

```
{
    Color.White, Color.Silver, Color.Gray, Color.Black, Color.Red,
    Color.Maroon, Color.Yellow, Color.Olive, Color.Lime, Color.Green,
    Color.Aqua, Color.Teal, Color.Blue, Color.Navy, Color.Pink,
    Color.Fuchsia, Color.Purple
};

string[] colorNames =
{
    "White", "Silver", "Gray", "Black", "Red",
    "Maroon", "Yellow", "Olive", "Lime", "Green",
    "Aqua", "Teal", "Blue", "Navy", "Pink",
    "Fuchsia", "Purple"
};

StackLayout stackLayout = new StackLayout();

for (int i = 0; i < colors.Length; i++)
{
    Label label = new Label
    {
        Text = colorNames[i],
        TextColor = colors[i],
        FontSize = Device.GetNamedSize(NamedSize.Large, typeof(Label))
    };
    stackLayout.Children.Add(label);
}
```

The `StackLayout` object can then be set to the `Content` property of the page.

But the technique of using parallel arrays is rather perilous. What if they're out of sync or have a different number of elements? A better approach is to keep the color and name together, perhaps in a tiny structure with `Color` and `Name` fields, or as an array of `Tuple<Color, string>` values, or as an anonymous type, as demonstrated in the **ColorLoop** program:

```
class ColorLoopPage : ContentPage
{
    public ColorLoopPage()
    {
        var colors = new[]
        {
            new { value = Color.White, name = "White" },
            new { value = Color.Silver, name = "Silver" },
            new { value = Color.Gray, name = "Gray" },
            new { value = Color.Black, name = "Black" },
            new { value = Color.Red, name = "Red" },
            new { value = Color.Maroon, name = "Maroon" },
            new { value = Color.Yellow, name = "Yellow" },
            new { value = Color.Olive, name = "Olive" },
            new { value = Color.Lime, name = "Lime" },
            new { value = Color.Green, name = "Green" },
            new { value = Color.Aqua, name = "Aqua" },
            new { value = Color.Teal, name = "Teal" },
```

```
            new { value = Color.Blue, name = "Blue" },
            new { value = Color.Navy, name = "Navy" },
            new { value = Color.Pink, name = "Pink" },
            new { value = Color.Fuchsia, name = "Fuchsia" },
            new { value = Color.Purple, name = "Purple" }
        };

        StackLayout stackLayout = new StackLayout();

        foreach (var color in colors)
        {
            stackLayout.Children.Add(
                new Label
                {
                    Text = color.name,
                    TextColor = color.value,
                    FontSize = Device.GetNamedSize(NamedSize.Large, typeof(Label))
                });
        }

        Padding = new Thickness(5, Device.OnPlatform(20, 5, 5), 5, 5);
        Content = stackLayout;
    }
}
```

Or you can initialize the `Children` property of `StackLayout` with an explicit collection of views (similar to the way the `Spans` collection of a `FormattedString` object was initialized in the previous chapter). The **ColorList** program sets the `Content` property of the page to a `StackLayout` object, which then has its `Children` property initialized with 17 `Label` views:

```
class ColorListPage : ContentPage
{
    public ColorListPage()
    {
        Padding = new Thickness (5, Device.OnPlatform (20, 5, 5), 5, 5);
        double fontSize = Device.GetNamedSize(NamedSize.Large, typeof(Label));
        Content = new StackLayout
        {
            Children =
            {
                new Label
                {
                    Text = "White",
                    TextColor = Color.White,
                    FontSize = fontSize
                },
                new Label
                {
                    Text = "Silver",
                    TextColor = Color.Silver,
                    FontSize = fontSize
                },
```

```
            ...
            new Label
            {
                Text = "Fuchsia",
                TextColor = Color.Fuchsia,
                FontSize = fontSize
            },
            new Label
            {
                Text = "Purple",
                TextColor = Color.Purple,
                FontSize = fontSize
            }
        }
    };
}
}
```

You don't need to see the code for all 17 children to get the idea! Regardless of how you fill the `Children` collection, here's the result:

Obviously, this isn't optimum. Some colors aren't visible at all, and some of them are too faint to read well. Moreover, the list overflows the page on two platforms, and there's no way to scroll it up.

One solution is to reduce the text size. Instead of using `NamedSize.Large`, try one of the smaller values.

Another partial solution can be found in `StackLayout` itself: `StackLayout` defines a `Spacing` property of type `double` that indicates how much space to leave between the children. By default, it's

6.0, but you can set it to something smaller (for example, zero) to help ensure that all the items will fit:

```
Content = new StackLayout
{
    Spacing = 0,
    Children =
    {
        new Label
        {
            Text = "White",
            TextColor = Color.White,
            FontSize = fontSize
        },
        …
```

Now all the `Label` views occupy only as much vertical space as required for the text. You can even set `Spacing` to negative values to make the items overlap!

But the best solution is scrolling. Scrolling is not automatically supported by `StackLayout` and must be added with another element called `ScrollView`, as you'll see in the next section.

But there's another issue with the color programs shown so far: they need to either explicitly create an array of colors and names, or explicitly create `Label` views for each color. To programmers, this is somewhat tedious, and hence somewhat distasteful. Might it be automated?

Scrolling content

Keep in mind that a Xamarin.Forms program has access to the .NET base class libraries and can use .NET reflection to obtain information about all the classes and structures defined in an assembly, such as **Xamarin.Forms.Core**. This suggests that obtaining the static fields and properties of the `Color` structure can be automated.

Most .NET reflection begins with a `Type` object. You can obtain a `Type` object for any class or structure by using the C# `typeof` operator. For example, the expression `typeof(Color)` returns a `Type` object for the `Color` structure.

In the version of .NET available in the PCL, an extension method for the `Type` class, named `GetTypeInfo`, returns a `TypeInfo` object from which additional information can be obtained. Although that's not required in the program shown below; it needs other extension methods defined for the `Type` class, named `GetRuntimeFields` and `GetRuntimeProperties`. These return the fields and properties of the type in the form of collections of `FieldInfo` and `PropertyInfo` objects. From these, the names as well as the values of the properties can be obtained.

This is demonstrated by the **ReflectedColors** program. The ReflectedColorsPage.cs file requires a `using` directive for `System.Reflection`.

In two separate `foreach` statements, the `ReflectedColorsPage` class loops through all the fields and properties of the `Color` structure. For all the public static members that return `Color` values, the two loops call `CreateColorLabel` to create a `Label` with the `Color` value and name, and then add that `Label` to the `StackLayout`.

By including all the public static fields and properties, the program lists `Color.Transparent`, `Color.Default`, and `Color.Accent` along with the 17 static fields displayed in the earlier program. A separate `CreateColorLabel` method creates a `Label` view for each item. Here's the complete listing of the `ReflectedColorsPage` class:

```
public class ReflectedColorsPage : ContentPage
{
    public ReflectedColorsPage()
    {
        StackLayout stackLayout = new StackLayout();

        // Loop through the Color structure fields.
        foreach (FieldInfo info in typeof(Color).GetRuntimeFields())
        {
            // Skip the obsolete (i.e. misspelled) colors.
            if (info.GetCustomAttribute<ObsoleteAttribute>() != null)
                continue;

            if (info.IsPublic &&
                info.IsStatic &&
                info.FieldType == typeof(Color))
            {
                stackLayout.Children.Add(
                    CreateColorLabel((Color)info.GetValue(null), info.Name));
            }
        }

        // Loop through the Color structure properties.
        foreach (PropertyInfo info in typeof(Color).GetRuntimeProperties())
        {
            MethodInfo methodInfo = info.GetMethod;

            if (methodInfo.IsPublic &&
                methodInfo.IsStatic &&
                methodInfo.ReturnType == typeof(Color))
            {
                stackLayout.Children.Add(
                    CreateColorLabel((Color)info.GetValue(null), info.Name));
            }
        }

        Padding = new Thickness(5, Device.OnPlatform(20, 5, 5), 5, 5);

        // Put the StackLayout in a ScrollView.
        Content = new ScrollView
        {
            Content = stackLayout
        };
    }
```

```
Label CreateColorLabel(Color color, string name)
{
    Color backgroundColor = Color.Default;

    if (color != Color.Default)
    {
        // Standard luminance calculation.
        double luminance = 0.30 * color.R +
                           0.59 * color.G +
                           0.11 * color.B;

        backgroundColor = luminance > 0.5 ? Color.Black : Color.White;
    }

    // Create the Label.
    return new Label
    {
        Text = name,
        TextColor = color,
        FontSize = Device.GetNamedSize(NamedSize.Large, typeof(Label)),
        BackgroundColor = backgroundColor
    };
}
}
```

Toward the end of the constructor, the `StackLayout` is set to the `Content` property of a `ScrollView`, which is then set to the `Content` property of the page.

The `CreateColorLabel` method in the class attempts to make each color visible by setting a contrasting background. The method calculates a luminance value based on a standard weighted average of the red, green, and blue components and then selects a background of either white or black.

This technique won't work for `Transparent`, so that item can't be displayed at all, and the method treats `Color.Default` as a special case and displays that color (whatever it may be) against a `Color.Default` background.

Here are the results, which are still quite short of being aesthetically satisfying:

But you can scroll the display because the StackLayout is the child of a ScrollView.

StackLayout and ScrollView are related in the class hierarchy. StackLayout derives from Lay-out<View>, and you'll recall that the Layout<T> class defines the Children property that Stack-Layout inherits. The generic Layout<T> class derives from the nongeneric Layout class, and ScrollView also derives from this nongeneric Layout. Theoretically, ScrollView is a type of layout object—even though it has only one child.

As you can see from the screenshot, the background color of the Label extends to the full width of the StackLayout, which means that each Label is as wide as the StackLayout.

Let's experiment a bit to get a better understanding of Xamarin.Forms layout. For these experiments, you might want to temporarily give the StackLayout and the ScrollView distinct background colors:

```
public ReflectedColorsPage()
{
    StackLayout stackLayout = new StackLayout
    {
        BackgroundColor = Color.Blue
    };
    …
    Content = new ScrollView
    {
        BackgroundColor = Color.Red,
        Content = stackLayout
    };
}
```

Layout objects usually have transparent backgrounds by default. Although they occupy an area on the screen, they are not directly visible. Giving layout objects temporary colors is a great way to see exactly where they are on the screen. It's a good debugging technique for complex layouts.

You will discover that the blue `StackLayout` peeks out in the space between the individual `Label` views. This is a result of the default `Spacing` property of `StackLayout`. The `StackLayout` is also visible through the `Label` for `Color.Default`, which has a transparent background.

Try setting the `HorizontalOptions` property of all the `Label` views to `LayoutOptions.Start`:

```
return new Label
{
    Text = name,
    TextColor = color,
    FontSize = Device.GetNamedSize(NamedSize.Large, typeof(Label)),
    BackgroundColor = backgroundColor,
    HorizontalOptions = LayoutOptions.Start
};
```

Now the blue background of the `StackLayout` is even more prominent because all the `Label` views occupy only as much horizontal space as the text requires, and they are all pushed over to the left side. Because each `Label` view is a different width, this display looks even uglier than the first version!

Now remove the `HorizontalOptions` setting from the `Label`, and instead set a `HorizontalOptions` on the `StackLayout`:

```
StackLayout stackLayout = new StackLayout
{
    BackgroundColor = Color.Blue,
    HorizontalOptions = LayoutOptions.Start
};
```

Now the `StackLayout` becomes only as wide as the widest `Label` (at least on iOS and Android) with the red background of the `ScrollView` now clearly in view.

As you begin constructing a tree of visual objects, these objects acquire a parent-child relationship. A parent object is sometimes referred to as the *container* of its child or children because the child's location and size is contained within its parent.

By default, `HorizontalOptions` and `VerticalOptions` are set to `LayoutOptions.Fill`, which means that each child view attempts to fill the parent container. (At least with the containers encountered so far. As you'll see, other layout classes have somewhat different behavior.) Even a `Label` fills its parent container by default, although without a background color, the `Label` appears to occupy only as much space as it requires.

Setting a view's `HorizontalOptions` or `VerticalOptions` property to `LayoutOptions.Start`, `Center`, or `End` effectively forces the view to shrink down—either horizontally, vertically, or both—to only the size the view requires.

A `StackLayout` has this same effect on its child's vertical size: every child in a `StackLayout` occupies only as much height as it requires. Setting the `VerticalOptions` property on a child of a `StackLayout` to `Start`, `Center`, or `End` has no effect! However, the child views still expand to fill the width of the `StackLayout`, except when the children are given a `HorizontalOptions` property other than `LayoutOptions.Fill`.

If a `StackLayout` is set to the `Content` property of a `ContentPage`, you can set `HorizontalOptions` or `VerticalOptions` on the `StackLayout`. These properties have two effects: first, they shrink the `StackLayout` width or height (or both) to the size of its children; and second, they govern where the `StackLayout` is positioned relative to the page.

If a `StackLayout` is in a `ScrollView`, the `ScrollView` causes the `StackLayout` to be only as tall as the sum of the heights of its children. This is how the `ScrollView` can determine how to vertically scroll the `StackLayout`. You can continue to set the `HorizontalOptions` property on the `StackLayout` to control the width and horizontal placement.

However, you should avoid setting `VerticalOptions` on the `ScrollView` to `LayoutOptions.Start`, `Center`, or `End`. The `ScrollView` must be able to scroll its child content, and the only way `ScrollView` can do that is by forcing its child (usually a `StackLayout`) to assume a height that reflects only what the child needs and then to use the height of this child and its own height to calculate how much to scroll that content. If you set `VerticalOptions` on the `ScrollView` to `LayoutOptions.Start`, `Center`, or `End`, you are effectively telling the `ScrollView` to be only as tall as it needs to be. But what is that height? Because `ScrollView` can scroll its contents, it doesn't need to be any particular height, so in theory it will shrink down to nothing. Xamarin.Forms protects against this eventuality, but it's best for you to avoid code that suggests something you don't want to happen.

Although putting a `StackLayout` in a `ScrollView` is normal, putting a `ScrollView` in a `StackLayout` doesn't seem quite right. In theory, the `StackLayout` will force the `ScrollView` to have a height of only what it requires, and that required height is basically zero. Again, Xamarin.Forms protects against this eventuality, but you should avoid such code.

There is a proper way to put a `ScrollView` in a `StackLayout` that is in complete accordance with Xamarin.Forms layout principles, and that will be demonstrated shortly.

The preceding discussion applies to vertically oriented `StackLayout` and `ScrollView` elements. `StackLayout` has a property named `Orientation` that you can set to a member of the `StackOrientation` enumeration—`Vertical` (the default) or `Horizontal`. Similarly, `ScrollView` also has an `Orientation` property that you set to a member of the `ScrollOrientation` enumeration. Try this:

```
public ReflectedColorsPage()
{
    StackLayout stackLayout = new StackLayout
    {
        Orientation = StackOrientation.Horizontal
    };
    ...
    Content = new ScrollView
```

```
    {
        Orientation = ScrollOrientation.Horizontal,
        Content = stackLayout
    };
}
```

Now the `Label` views are stacked horizontally, and the `ScrollView` fills the page vertically but allows horizontal scrolling of the `StackLayout`, which vertically fills the `ScrollView`:

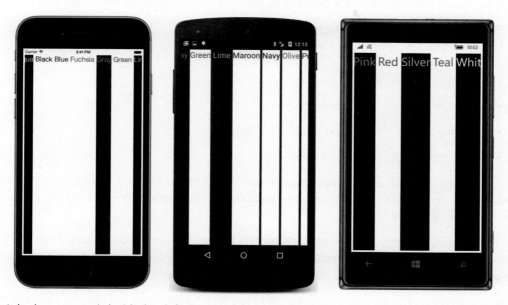

It looks pretty weird with the default vertical layout options, but those could be fixed to make it look a little better.

The Expands option

You probably noticed that the `HorizontalOptions` and `VerticalOptions` properties are plurals, as if there's more than one option. These properties are generally set to a static field of the `LayoutOptions` structure—another plural.

The discussions so far have focused on the following static read-only `LayoutOptions` fields that returned predefined values of `LayoutOptions`:

- `LayoutOptions.Start`

- `LayoutOptions.Center`

- `LayoutOptions.End`

- `LayoutOptions.Fill`

The default—established by the `View` class—is `LayoutOptions.Fill`, which means that the view fills its container.

As you've seen, a `VerticalOptions` setting on a `Label` doesn't make a difference when the `Label` is a child of a vertical `StackLayout`. The `StackLayout` itself constrains the height of its children to only the height they require, so the child has no freedom to move vertically within that slot.

Be prepared for this rule to be slightly amended!

The `LayoutOptions` structure has four additional static read-only fields not discussed yet:

- `LayoutOptions.StartAndExpand`

- `LayoutOptions.CenterAndExpand`

- `LayoutOptions.EndAndExpand`

- `LayoutOptions.FillAndExpand`

`LayoutOptions` also defines two instance properties, named `Alignment` and `Expands`. The four instances of `LayoutOptions` returned by the static fields ending with `AndExpand` all have the `Expands` property set to `true`.

This `Expands` property is recognized only by `StackLayout`. It can be very useful for managing the layout of the page, but it can be confusing on first encounter. Here are the requirements for `Expands` to play a role in a vertical `StackLayout`:

- The contents of the `StackLayout` must have a total height that is less than the height of the `StackLayout` itself. In other words, some extra unused vertical space must exist in the `Stack-Layout`.

- That first requirement implies that the vertical `StackLayout` cannot have its own `Vertical-Options` property set to `Start`, `Center`, or `End` because that would cause the `StackLayout` to have a height equal to the aggregate height of its children, and it would have no extra space.

- At least one child of the `StackLayout` must have a `VerticalOptions` setting with the `Expands` property set to `true`.

If these conditions are satisfied, the `StackLayout` allocates the extra vertical space equally among all the children that have a `VerticalOptions` setting with `Expands` equal to `true`. Each of these children gets a larger slot in the `StackLayout` than normal. How the child occupies that slot depends on the `Alignment` setting of the `LayoutOptions` value: `Start`, `Center`, `End`, or `Fill`.

Here's a program, named **VerticalOptionsDemo,** that uses reflection to create `Label` objects with all the possible `VerticalOptions` settings in a vertical `StackLayout`. The background and foreground colors are alternated so that you can see exactly how much space each `Label` occupies. The program uses Language Integrated Query (LINQ) to sort the fields of the `LayoutOptions` structure in a visually more illuminating manner:

```
public class VerticalOptionsDemoPage : ContentPage
{
    public VerticalOptionsDemoPage()
    {
        Color[] colors = { Color.Yellow, Color.Blue };
        int flipFlopper = 0;

        // Create Labels sorted by LayoutAlignment property.
        IEnumerable<Label> labels =
            from field in typeof(LayoutOptions).GetRuntimeFields()
            where field.IsPublic && field.IsStatic
            orderby ((LayoutOptions)field.GetValue(null)).Alignment
            select new Label
            {
                Text = "VerticalOptions = " + field.Name,
                VerticalOptions = (LayoutOptions)field.GetValue(null),
                HorizontalTextAlignment = TextAlignment.Center,
                FontSize = Device.GetNamedSize(NamedSize.Medium, typeof(Label)),
                TextColor = colors[flipFlopper],
                BackgroundColor = colors[flipFlopper = 1 - flipFlopper]
            };

        // Transfer to StackLayout.
        StackLayout stackLayout = new StackLayout();

        foreach (Label label in labels)
        {
            stackLayout.Children.Add(label);
        }

        Padding = new Thickness(0, Device.OnPlatform(20, 0, 0), 0, 0);
        Content = stackLayout;
    }
}
```

You might want to study the results a little:

The `Label` views with yellow text on blue backgrounds are those with `VerticalOptions` properties set to `LayoutOptions` values *without* the `Expands` flag set. If the `Expands` flag is not set on the `LayoutOptions` value of an item in a vertical `StackLayout`, the `VerticalOptions` setting is ignored. As you can see, the `Label` occupies only as much vertical space as it needs in the vertical `StackLayout`.

The total height of the children in this `StackLayout` is less than the height of the `StackLayout`, so the `StackLayout` has extra space. It contains four children with their `VerticalOptions` properties set to `LayoutOptions` values with the `Expands` flag set, so this extra space is allocated equally among those four children.

In these four cases—the `Label` views with blue text on yellow backgrounds—the `Alignment` property of the `LayoutOptions` value indicates how the child is aligned within the area that includes the extra space. The first one—with the `VerticalOptions` property set to `LayoutOptions.StartAnd-Expand`—is above this extra space. The second (`CenterAndExpand`) is in the middle of the extra space. The third (`EndAndExpand`) is below the extra space. However, in all these three cases, the `Label` is getting only as much vertical space as it needs, as indicated by the background color. The rest of the space belongs to the `StackLayout`, which shows the background color of the page.

The last `Label` has its `VerticalOptions` property set to `LayoutOptions.FillAndExpand`. In this case, the `Label` occupies the entire slot including the extra space, as the large area of yellow background indicates. The text is at the top of this area; that's because the default setting of `Vertical-TextAlignment` is `TextAlignment.Start`. Set it to something else to position the text vertically within the area.

The `Expands` property of `LayoutOptions` plays a role only when the view is a child of a `Stack-Layout`. In other contexts, it's ignored.

Frame and BoxView

Two simple rectangular views are often useful for presentation purposes:

The `BoxView` is a filled rectangle. It derives from `View` and defines a `Color` property with a default setting of `Color.Default` that's transparent by default.

The `Frame` displays a rectangular border surrounding some content. `Frame` derives from `Layout` by way of `ContentView`, from which it inherits a `Content` property. The content of a `Frame` can be a single view or a layout containing a bunch of views. From `VisualElement`, `Frame` inherits a `Back-groundColor` property that's white on the iPhone but transparent on Android and Windows Phone. From `Layout`, `Frame` inherits a `Padding` property that it initializes to 20 units on all sides to give the content a little breathing room. `Frame` itself defines a `HasShadow` property that is `true` by default (but the shadow shows up only on iOS devices) and an `OutlineColor` property that is transparent by default but doesn't affect the iOS shadow, which is always black and always visible when `HasShadow` is set to `true`.

Both the `Frame` outline and the `BoxView` are transparent by default, so you might be a little uncertain how to color them without resorting to different colors for different platforms. One good choice is `Color.Accent`, which is guaranteed to show up regardless. Or, you can take control over coloring the background as well as the `Frame` outline and `BoxView`.

If the `BoxView` or `Frame` is not constrained in size in any way—that is, if it's not in a `StackLayout` and has its `HorizontalOptions` and `VerticalOptions` set to default values of `LayoutOptions-.Fill`—these views expand to fill their containers.

For example, here's a program that has a centered `Label` set to the `Content` property of a `Frame`:

```
public class FramedTextPage : ContentPage
{
    public FramedTextPage()
    {
        Padding = new Thickness(20);
        Content = new Frame
        {
            OutlineColor = Color.Accent,
            Content = new Label
            {
                Text = "I've been framed!",
                FontSize = Device.GetNamedSize(NamedSize.Large, typeof(Label)),
                HorizontalOptions = LayoutOptions.Center,
                VerticalOptions = LayoutOptions.Center
            }
        };
```

```
        }
}
```

The `Label` is centered in the `Frame`, but the `Frame` fills the whole page, and you might not even be able to see the `Frame` clearly if the page had not been given a `Padding` of 20 on all sides:

To display centered framed text, you want to set the `HorizontalOptions` and `VerticalOptions` properties on the `Frame` (rather than the `Label`) to `LayoutOptions.Center`:

```csharp
public class FramedTextPage : ContentPage
{
    public FramedTextPage()
    {
        Padding = new Thickness(20);
        Content = new Frame
        {
            OutlineColor = Color.Accent,
            HorizontalOptions = LayoutOptions.Center,
            VerticalOptions = LayoutOptions.Center,
            Content = new Label
            {
                Text = "I've been framed!",
                FontSize = Device.GetNamedSize(NamedSize.Large, typeof(Label))
            }
        };
    }
}
```

Now the `Frame` hugs the text (but with the frame's 20-unit default padding) in the center of the page:

The version of **FramedText** included with the sample code for this chapter exercises the freedom to give everything a custom color:

```
public class FramedTextPage : ContentPage
{
    public FramedTextPage()
    {
        BackgroundColor = Color.Aqua;

        Content = new Frame
        {
            OutlineColor = Color.Black,
            BackgroundColor = Color.Yellow,
            HorizontalOptions = LayoutOptions.Center,
            VerticalOptions = LayoutOptions.Center,

            Content = new Label
            {
                Text = "I've been framed!",
                FontSize = Device.GetNamedSize(NamedSize.Large, typeof(Label)),
                FontAttributes = FontAttributes.Italic,
                TextColor = Color.Blue
            }
        };
    }
}
```

The result looks roughly the same on all three platforms:

Try setting a `BoxView` to the `Content` property of a `ContentPage`, like so:

```
public class SizedBoxViewPage : ContentPage
{
    public SizedBoxViewPage()
    {
        Content = new BoxView
        {
            Color = Color.Accent
        };
    }
}
```

Be sure to set the `Color` property so you can see it. The `BoxView` fills the whole area of its container, just as `Label` does with its default `HorizontalOptions` or `VerticalOptions` settings:

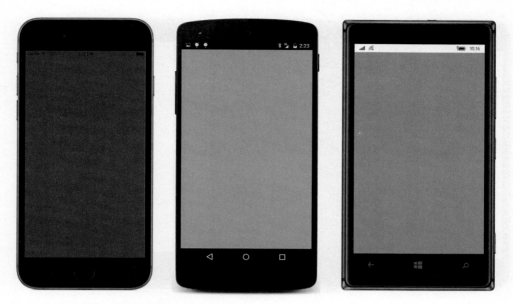

It's even underlying the iOS status bar!

Now try setting the `HorizontalOptions` and `VerticalOptions` properties of the `BoxView` to something other than `Fill`, as in this code sample:

```
public class SizedBoxViewPage : ContentPage
{
    public SizedBoxViewPage()
    {
        Content = new BoxView
        {
            Color = Color.Accent,
            HorizontalOptions = LayoutOptions.Center,
            VerticalOptions = LayoutOptions.Center
        };
    }
}
```

In this case, the `BoxView` will assume its default dimensions of 40 units square:

The `BoxView` is now 40 units square because the `BoxView` initializes its `WidthRequest` and `HeightRequest` properties to 40. These two properties require a little explanation:

`VisualElement` defines `Width` and `Height` properties, but these properties are read-only. `VisualElement` also defines `WidthRequest` and `HeightRequest` properties that are both settable and gettable. Normally, all these properties are initialized to –1 (which effectively means they are un-defined), but some `View` derivatives, such as `BoxView`, set the `WidthRequest` and `HeightRequest` properties to specific values.

After a page has organized the layout of its children and rendered all the visuals, the `Width` and `Height` properties indicate actual dimensions of each view—the area that the view occupies on the screen. Because `Width` and `Height` are read-only, they are for informational purposes only. (Chapter 5, "Dealing with sizes," describes how to work with these values.)

If you want a view to be a specific size, you can set the `WidthRequest` and `HeightRequest` prop-erties. But these properties indicate (as their names suggest) a *requested* size or a *preferred* size. If the view is allowed to fill its container, these properties will be ignored.

`BoxView` sets its default size to values of 40 by overriding the `OnSizeRequest` method. You can think of these settings as a size that `BoxView` would like to be if nobody else has any opinions in the matter. You've already seen that `WidthRequest` and `HeightRequest` are ignored when the `BoxView` is allowed to fill the page. The `WidthRequest` kicks in if the `HorizontalOptions` is set to `LayoutOp-tions.Left`, `Center`, or `Right`, or if the `BoxView` is a child of a horizontal `StackLayout`. The `HeightRequest` behaves similarly.

Here's the version of the **SizedBoxView** program included with the code for this chapter:

```
public class SizedBoxViewPage : ContentPage
{
    public SizedBoxViewPage()
    {
        BackgroundColor = Color.Pink;

        Content = new BoxView
        {
            Color = Color.Navy,
            HorizontalOptions = LayoutOptions.Center,
            VerticalOptions = LayoutOptions.Center,
            WidthRequest = 200,
            HeightRequest = 100
        };
    }
}
```

Now we get a `BoxView` with that specific size and the colors explicitly set:

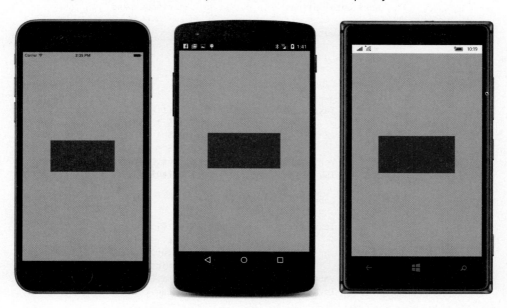

Let's use both `Frame` and `BoxView` in an enhanced color list. The **ColorBlocks** program has a page constructor that is virtually identical to the one in **ReflectedColors**, except that it calls a method named `CreateColorView` rather than `CreateColorLabel`. Here's that method:

```
class ColorBlocksPage : ContentPage
{
    ...

    View CreateColorView(Color color, string name)
    {
```

```
        return new Frame
        {
            OutlineColor = Color.Accent,
            Padding = new Thickness(5),
            Content = new StackLayout
            {
                Orientation = StackOrientation.Horizontal,
                Spacing = 15,
                Children =
                {
                    new BoxView
                    {
                        Color = color
                    },
                    new Label
                    {
                        Text = name,
                        FontSize = Device.GetNamedSize(NamedSize.Large, typeof(Label)),
                        FontAttributes = FontAttributes.Bold,
                        VerticalOptions = LayoutOptions.Center,
                        HorizontalOptions = LayoutOptions.StartAndExpand
                    },
                    new StackLayout
                    {
                        Children =
                        {
                            new Label
                            {
                                Text = String.Format("{0:X2}-{1:X2}-{2:X2}",
                                                (int)(255 * color.R),
                                                (int)(255 * color.G),
                                                (int)(255 * color.B)),
                                VerticalOptions = LayoutOptions.CenterAndExpand,
                                IsVisible = color != Color.Default
                            },
                            new Label
                            {
                                Text = String.Format("{0:F2}, {1:F2}, {2:F2}",
                                                color.Hue,
                                                color.Saturation,
                                                color.Luminosity),
                                VerticalOptions = LayoutOptions.CenterAndExpand,
                                IsVisible = color != Color.Default
                            }
                        },
                        HorizontalOptions = LayoutOptions.End
                    }
                }
            }
        };
    }
}
```

The `CreateColorView` method returns a `Frame` containing a horizontal `StackLayout` with a `Box-View` indicating the color, a `Label` for the name of the color, and another `StackLayout` with two more `Label` views for the RGB composition and the `Hue`, `Saturation`, and `Luminosity` values. The RGB and HSL displays are meaningless for the `Color.Default` value, so that inner `StackLayout` has its `IsVisible` property set to `false` in that case. The `StackLayout` still exists, but it's ignored when the page is rendered.

The program doesn't know which element will determine the height of each color item—the `Box-View`, the `Label` with the color name, or the two `Label` views with the RGB and HSL values—so it centers all the `Label` views. As you can see, the `BoxView` expands in height to accommodate the height of the text:

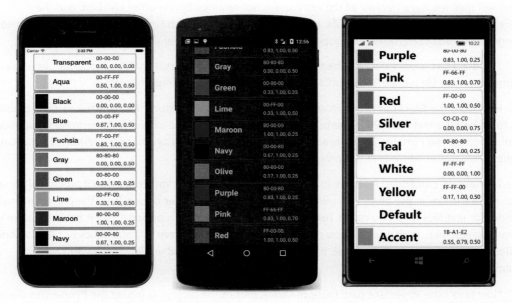

Now this is a scrollable color list that's beginning to be something we can take a little pride in.

A ScrollView in a StackLayout?

It's common to put a `StackLayout` in a `ScrollView`, but can you put a `ScrollView` in a `StackLayout`? And why would you even want to?

It's a general rule in layout systems like the one in Xamarin.Forms that you can't put a scroll in a stack. A `ScrollView` needs to have a specific height to compute the difference between the height of its content and its own height. That difference is the amount that the `ScrollView` can scroll its contents. If the `ScrollView` is in a `StackLayout`, it doesn't get that specific height. The `StackLayout` wants the `ScrollView` to be as short as possible, and that's either the height of the `ScrollView` contents or zero, and neither solution works.

So why would you want a `ScrollView` in a `StackLayout` anyway?

Sometimes it's precisely what you need. Consider a primitive e-book reader that implements scrolling. You might want a `Label` at the top of the page always displaying the book's title, followed by a `ScrollView` containing a `StackLayout` with the content of the book itself. It would be convenient for that `Label` and the `ScrollView` to be children of a `StackLayout` that fills the page.

With Xamarin.Forms, such a thing is possible. If you give the `ScrollView` a `VerticalOptions` setting of `LayoutOptions.FillAndExpand`, it can indeed be a child of a `StackLayout`. The `StackLayout` will give the `ScrollView` all the extra space not required by the other children, and the `ScrollView` will then have a specific height. Interestingly, Xamarin.Forms protects against other settings of that `VerticalOptions` property, so it works with whatever you set it to.

The **BlackCat** project displays the text of Edgar Allan Poe's short story "The Black Cat," which is stored in a text file named TheBlackCat.txt in a one-line-per-paragraph format.

How does the **BlackCat** program access the file with this short story? Perhaps the easiest approach is to embed the text file right in the program executable or—in the case of a Xamarin.Forms application—right in the Portable Class Library DLL. These files are known as *embedded resources*, and that's what TheBlackCat.txt file is in this program.

To make an embedded resource in either Visual Studio or Xamarin Studio, you'll probably first want to create a folder in the project by selecting the **Add > New Folder** option from the project menu. A folder for text files might be called **Texts**, for example. The folder is optional, but it helps organize program assets. Then, in that folder, you can select **Add > Existing Item** in Visual Studio or **Add > Add Files** in Xamarin Studio. Navigate to the file, select it, and click **Add** in Visual Studio or **Open** in Xamarin Studio.

Now here's the important part: Once the file is part of the project, bring up the **Properties** dialog from the menu associated with the file. Specify that the **Build Action** for the file is **EmbeddedResource**. This is an easy step to forget, but it is essential.

This was done for the **BlackCat** project, and consequently the TheBlackCat.txt file becomes embedded in the BlackCat.dll file.

In code, the file can be retrieved by calling the `GetManifestResourceStream` method defined by the `Assembly` class in the `System.Reflection` namespace. To get the assembly of the PCL, all you need to do is get the `Type` of any class defined in the assembly. You can use `typeof` with the page type you've derived from `ContentPage` or `GetType` on the instance of that class. Then call `GetTypeInfo` on this `Type` object. `Assembly` is a property of the resultant `TypeInfo` object:

```
Assembly assembly = GetType().GetTypeInfo().Assembly;
```

In the `GetManifestResourceStream` method of `Assembly`, you'll need to specify the name of the resource. For embedded resources, that name is not the filename of the resource but the *resource ID*. It's easy to confuse these because that ID might look vaguely like a fully qualified filename.

The resource ID begins with the default namespace of the assembly. This is not the .NET namespace! To get the default namespace of the assembly in Visual Studio, select **Properties** from the project menu, and in the properties dialog, select **Library** at the left and look for the **Default namespace** field. In Xamarin Studio, select **Options** from the project menu, and in the **Project Options** dialog, select **Main Settings** at the left, and look for a field labeled **Default Namespace**.

For the **BlackCat** project, that default namespace is the same as the assembly: "BlackCat". However, you can actually set that default namespace to whatever you want.

The resource ID begins with that default namespace, followed by a period, followed by the folder name you might have used, followed by another period and the filename. For this example, the resource ID is "BlackCat.Texts.TheBlackCat.txt"—and that's what you'll pass to the `GetManifestResourceStream` method in the code. The method returns a .NET `Stream` object, and from that a `StreamReader` can be created to read the lines of text.

It's a good idea to use `using` statements with the `Stream` object returned from `GetManifestResourceStream` and the `StreamReader` object because that will properly dispose of the objects when they're no longer needed or if they raise exceptions.

For layout purposes, the `BlackCatPage` constructor creates two `StackLayout` objects: `mainStack` and `textStack`. The first line from the file (containing the story's title and author) becomes a bolded and centered `Label` in `mainStack`; all the subsequent lines go in `textStack`. The `mainStack` instance also contains a `ScrollView` with `textStack`.

```
class BlackCatPage : ContentPage
{
    public BlackCatPage()
    {
        StackLayout mainStack = new StackLayout();
        StackLayout textStack = new StackLayout
        {
            Padding = new Thickness(5),
            Spacing = 10
        };

        // Get access to the text resource.
        Assembly assembly = GetType().GetTypeInfo().Assembly;
        string resource = "BlackCat.Texts.TheBlackCat.txt";

        using (Stream stream = assembly.GetManifestResourceStream (resource))
        {
            using (StreamReader reader = new StreamReader (stream))
            {
                bool gotTitle = false;
                string line;

                // Read in a line (which is actually a paragraph).
```

```
                    while (null != (line = reader.ReadLine()))
                    {
                        Label label = new Label
                        {
                            Text = line,

                            // Black text for ebooks!
                            TextColor = Color.Black
                        };

                        if (!gotTitle)
                        {
                            // Add first label (the title) to mainStack.
                            label.HorizontalOptions = LayoutOptions.Center;
                            label.FontSize = Device.GetNamedSize(NamedSize.Medium, label);
                            label.FontAttributes = FontAttributes.Bold;
                            mainStack.Children.Add(label);
                            gotTitle = true;
                        }
                        else
                        {
                            // Add subsequent labels to textStack.
                            textStack.Children.Add(label);
                        }
                    }
                }
            }

            // Put the textStack in a ScrollView with FillAndExpand.
            ScrollView scrollView = new ScrollView
            {
                Content = textStack,
                VerticalOptions = LayoutOptions.FillAndExpand,
                Padding = new Thickness(5, 0),
            };

            // Add the ScrollView as a second child of mainStack.
            mainStack.Children.Add(scrollView);

            // Set page content to mainStack.
            Content = mainStack;

            // White background for ebooks!
            BackgroundColor = Color.White;

            // Add some iOS padding for the page.
            Padding = new Thickness (0, Device.OnPlatform (20, 0, 0), 0, 0);
        }
    }
```

Because this is basically an e-book reader, and humans have been reading black text on white paper for hundreds of years, the `BackgroundColor` of the page is set to white and the `TextColor` of each `Label` is set to black:

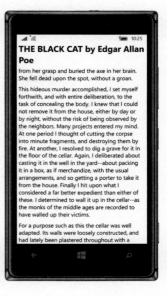

BlackCat is a PCL application. It is also possible to write this program using a Shared Asset Project rather than a PCL. To prove it, a **BlackCatSap** project is included with the code for this chapter. However, because the resource actually becomes part of the application project, you'll need the default namespace for the application, and that's different for each platform. The code to set the resource variable looks like this:

```
#if __IOS__
            string resource = "BlackCatSap.iOS.Texts.TheBlackCat.txt";
#elif __ANDROID__
            string resource = "BlackCatSap.Droid.Texts.TheBlackCat.txt";
#elif WINDOWS_UWP
            string resource = "BlackCatSap.UWP.Texts.TheBlackCat.txt";
#elif WINDOWS_APP
            string resource = "BlackCatSap.Windows.Texts.TheBlackCat.txt";
#elif WINDOWS_PHONE_APP
            string resource = "BlackCatSap.WinPhone.Texts.TheBlackCat.txt";
#endif
```

If you're having problems referencing an embedded resource, you might be using an incorrect name. Try calling `GetManifestResourceNames` on the `Assembly` object to get a list of the resource IDs of all embedded resources.

Chapter 5
Dealing with sizes

Already you've seen some references to sizes in connection with various visual elements:

- The iOS status bar has a height of 20, which you can adjust for with a `Padding` setting on the page.

- The `BoxView` sets its default width and height to 40.

- The default `Padding` within a `Frame` is 20.

- The default `Spacing` property on the `StackLayout` is 6.

And then there's `Device.GetNamedSize`, which for various members of the `NamedSize` enumeration returns a platform-dependent number appropriate for `FontSize` values for a `Label` or `Button`.

What are these numbers? What are their units? And how do we intelligently set properties requiring sizes to other values?

Good questions. As you've seen, the various platforms have different screen sizes and different text sizes, and all display a different quantity of text on the screen. Is that quantity of text something that a Xamarin.Forms application can anticipate or control? And even if it's possible, is it a proper programming practice? Should an application adjust font sizes to achieve a desired text density on the screen?

In general, when programming a Xamarin.Forms application, it's best not to get too close to the actual numeric dimensions of visual objects. It's preferable to trust Xamarin.Forms and the individual platforms to make the best default choices.

However, there are times when a programmer needs to know something about the size of particular visual objects and the size of the screen on which they appear.

Pixels, points, dps, DIPs, and DIUs

Video displays consist of a rectangular array of pixels. Any object displayed on the screen also has a pixel size. In the early days of personal computers, programmers sized and positioned visual objects in units of pixels. But as a greater variety of screen sizes and pixel densities became available, working with pixels became undesirable for programmers attempting to write applications that look roughly the same on many devices. Another solution was required.

These solutions began with operating systems for desktop computers and were then adapted for mobile devices. For this reason, it's illuminating to begin this exploration with the desktop.

Desktop video displays have a wide range of pixel dimensions, from the nearly obsolete 640 × 480 on up into the thousands. The aspect ratio of 4:3 was once standard for computer displays—and for movies and television as well—but the high-definition aspect ratio of 16:9 (or the similar 16:10) is now more common.

Desktop video displays also have a physical dimension usually measured along the diagonal of the screen in inches or centimeters. The pixel dimension combined with the physical dimension allows you to calculate the video display's resolution or pixel density in dots per inch (DPI), sometimes also referred to as pixels per inch (PPI). The display resolution can also be measured as a dot pitch, which is the distance between adjacent pixel centers, usually measured in millimeters.

For example, you can use the Pythagorean theorem to calculate that an ancient 800 × 600 display has a diagonal length of 1,000, the square root of 800 squared plus 600 squared. If this monitor has a 13-inch diagonal, that's a pixel density of 77 DPI, or a dot pitch of 0.33 millimeters. However, a 13-inch screen on a modern laptop might have pixel dimensions of 2560 × 1600, which is a pixel density of about 230 DPI, or a dot pitch of about 0.11 millimeters. A 100-pixel square object on this screen is one-third the size of the same object on the older screen.

Programmers should have a fighting chance when attempting to size visual elements correctly. For this reason, both Apple and Microsoft devised systems for desktop computing that allow programmers to work with the video display in some form of device-independent units instead of pixels. Most of the dimensions that a programmer encounters and specifies are in these device-independent units. It is the responsibility of the operating system to convert back and forth between these units and pixels.

In the Apple world, desktop video displays were traditionally assumed to have a resolution of 72 units to the inch. This number comes from typography, where many measurements are in units of *points*. In classical typography, there are approximately 72 points to the inch, but in digital typography the point has been standardized to be exactly one seventy-second of an inch. By working with points rather than pixels, a programmer has an intuitive sense of the relationship between numeric sizes and the area that visual objects occupy on the screen.

In the Windows world, a similar technique was developed, called *device-independent pixels* (DIPs) or *device-independent units* (DIUs). To a Windows programmer, desktop video displays are assumed to have a resolution of 96 DIUs, which is exactly one-third higher than 72 DPI, although it can be adjusted by the user.

Mobile devices, however, have somewhat different rules: The pixel densities achieved on modern phones are typically much higher than on desktop displays. This higher pixel density allows text and other visual objects to shrink much more in size before becoming illegible.

Phones are also typically held much closer to the user's face than is a desktop or laptop screen. This difference also implies that visual objects on the phone can be smaller than comparable objects on desktop or laptop screens. Because the physical dimensions of the phone are much smaller than desktop displays, shrinking down visual objects is very desirable because it allows much more to fit on the screen.

Apple continues to refer to the device-independent units on the iPhone as *points*. Until recently, all of Apple's high-density displays—which Apple refers to by the brand name Retina—have a conversion of two pixels to the point. This was true for the MacBook Pro, iPad, and iPhone. The recent exception is the iPhone 6 Plus, which has three pixels to the point.

For example, the 640 × 960 pixel dimension of the 3.5-inch screen of the iPhone 4 has an actual pixel density of about 320 DPI. There are two pixels to the point, so to an application program running on the iPhone 4, the screen appears to have a dimension of 320 × 480 points. The iPhone 3 actually did have a pixel dimension of 320 × 480, and points equaled pixels, so to a program running on these two devices, the displays of the iPhone 3 and iPhone 4 appear to be the same size. Despite the same perceived sizes, graphical objects and text are displayed in greater resolution on the iPhone 4 than the iPhone 3.

For the iPhone 3 and iPhone 4, the relationship between the screen size and point dimensions implies a conversion factor of 160 points to the inch rather than the desktop standard of 72.

The iPhone 5 has a 4-inch screen, but the pixel dimension is 640 × 1136. The pixel density is about the same as the iPhone 4. To a program, this screen has a size of 320 × 768 points.

The iPhone 6 has a 4.7-inch screen and a pixel dimension of 750 × 1334. The pixel density is also about 320 DPI. There are two pixels to the point, so to a program, the screen appears to have a point size of 375 × 667.

However, the iPhone 6 Plus has a 5.5-inch screen and a pixel dimension of 1080 × 1920, which is a pixel density of 400 DPI. This higher pixel density implies more pixels to the point, and for the iPhone 6 Plus, Apple has set the point equal to three pixels. That would normally imply a perceived screen size of 360 × 640 points, but to a program, the iPhone 6 Plus screen has a point size of 414 × 736, so the perceived resolution is about 150 points to the inch.

This information is summarized in the following table:

Model	iPhone 2, 3	iPhone 4	iPhone 5	iPhone 6	iPhone 6 Plus*
Pixel size	320 × 480	640 × 960	640 × 1136	750 × 1334	1080 × 1920
Screen diagonal	3.5 in.	3.5 in.	4 in.	4.7 in.	5.5 in.
Pixel density	165 DPI	330 DPI	326 DPI	326 DPI	401 DPI
Pixels per point	1	2	2	2	3
Point size	320 × 480	320 × 480	320 × 568	375 × 667	414 × 736
Points per inch	165	165	163	163	154

* Includes 115 percent downsampling.

Android does something quite similar: Android devices have a wide variety of sizes and pixel dimensions, but an Android programmer generally works in units of density-independent pixels (dps). The relationship between pixels and dps is set assuming 160 dps to the inch, which means that Apple and Android device-independent units are very similar.

Microsoft took a different approach with Windows Phone 7. The original Windows Phone 7 devices had a screen dimension of 480 × 800 pixels, which is often referred to as WVGA (Wide Video Graphics

Array). Applications worked with this display in units of pixels. If you assume an average screen size of 4 inches for a 480 × 800 Windows Phone 7 device, this means that Windows Phone 7 implicitly assumed a pixel density of about 240 DPI. That's 1.5 times the assumed pixel density of iPhone and Android devices. Eventually, several larger screen sizes were allowed: 768 × 1280 (WXGA or Wide Extended Graphics Array), 720 × 1280 (referred to using high-definition television lingo as 720p), and 1080 × 1920 (called 1080p). For these additional display sizes, programmers worked in device-independent units. An internal scaling factor translated between pixels and device-independent units so that the width of the screen in portrait mode always appeared to be 480 pixels.

With the Windows Runtime API in Windows Phone 8.1, different scaling factors were introduced based on both the screen's pixel size and the physical size of the screen. The following table was put together based on the Windows Phone 8.1 emulators using a program named **WhatSize,** which you'll see shortly:

Screen type	WVGA 4″	WXGA 4.5″	720p 4.7″	1080p 5.5″	1080p 6″
Pixel size	480 × 800	768 × 1280	720 × 1280	1080 × 1920	1080 × 1920
Size in DIUs	400 × 640	384 × 614.5	400 × 684	450 × 772	491 × 847
Scaling factor	1.2	2	1.8	2.4	2.2
DPI	194	161	169	167	167

The scaling factors were calculated from the width because the height in DIUs displayed by the **What-Size** program excludes the Windows Phone status bar. The final DPI figures were calculated based on the full pixel size, the diagonal size of the screen in inches, and the scaling factor.

Aside from the WVGA outlier, the calculated DPI is close enough to the 160 DPI criterion associated with iOS and Android devices.

Windows 10 Mobile uses somewhat higher scaling factors, and in multiples of 0.25 rather than 0.2. The following table was put together based on the Windows 10 Mobile emulators:

Screen type	WVGA 4″	QHD 5.2″	WXGA 4.5″	720p 5″	1080p 6″
Pixel size	480 × 800	540 × 960	768 × 1280	720 × 1280	1080 × 1920
Size in DIUs	320 × 512	360 × 616	341 × 546	360 × 616	432 × 744
Scaling factor	1.5	1.5	2.25	2	2.5
DPI	155	141	147	147	141

You might conclude from this that a good average DPI for Windows 10 Mobile is 144 (rounded to the nearest multiple of 16) rather than 160. Or you might say that it's close enough to 160 to assume that it's consistent with iOS and Windows Phone.

Xamarin.Forms has a philosophy of using the conventions of the underlying platforms as much as possible. In accordance with this philosophy, a Xamarin.Forms programmer works with sizes defined by each particular platform. All sizes that the programmer encounters through the Xamarin.Forms API are in these platform-specific, device-independent units.

Xamarin.Forms programmers can generally treat the phone display in a device-independent manner, with the following resolution:

- 160 units to the inch

- 64 units to the centimeter

The `VisualElement` class defines two properties, named `Width` and `Height`, that provide the rendered dimensions of views, layouts, and pages in these device-independent units. However, the initial settings of `Width` and `Height` are "mock" values of –1. The values of these properties become valid only when the layout system has positioned and sized everything on the page. Also, keep in mind that the default `Fill` setting for `HorizontalOptions` or `VerticalOptions` often causes a view to occupy more space than it would otherwise. The `Width` and `Height` values reflect this extra space. The `Width` and `Height` values also include any `Padding` that may be set on the element and are consistent with the area colored by the view's `BackgroundColor` property.

`VisualElement` defines an event named `SizeChanged` that is fired whenever the `Width` or `Height` property of the visual element changes. This event is part of several notifications that occur when a page is laid out, a process that involves the various elements of the page being sized and positioned. This layout process occurs following the first definition of a page (generally in the page constructor), and a new layout pass takes place in response to any change that might affect layout—for example, when views are added to a `ContentPage` or a `StackLayout`, removed from these objects, or when properties are set on visual elements that might result in their sizes changing.

A new layout is also triggered when the screen size changes. This happens mostly when the phone is swiveled between portrait and landscape modes.

A full familiarity with the Xamarin.Forms layout system often accompanies the job of writing your own `Layout<View>` derivatives. This task awaits us in Chapter 26, "Custom layouts." Until then, simply knowing when `Width` and `Height` properties change is helpful for working with sizes of visual objects. You can attach a `SizeChanged` handler to any visual object on the page, including the page itself. The **WhatSize** program demonstrates how to obtain the page's size and display it:

```
public class WhatSizePage : ContentPage
{
    Label label;

    public WhatSizePage()
    {
        label = new Label
        {
            FontSize = Device.GetNamedSize(NamedSize.Large, typeof(Label)),
            HorizontalOptions = LayoutOptions.Center,
            VerticalOptions = LayoutOptions.Center
        };

        Content = label;

        SizeChanged += OnPageSizeChanged;
    }

    void OnPageSizeChanged(object sender, EventArgs args)
```

```
    {
        label.Text = String.Format("{0} \u00D7 {1}", Width, Height);
    }
}
```

This is the first example of event handling in this book, and you can see that events are handled in the normal C# and .NET manner. The code at the end of the constructor attaches the `OnPageSize-Changed` event handler to the `SizeChanged` event of the page. The first argument to the event handler (customarily named `sender`) is the object firing the event, in this case the instance of `WhatSize-Page`, but the event handler doesn't use that. Nor does the event handler use the second argument—the so-called *event arguments*—which sometimes provides more information about the event.

Instead, the event handler accesses the `Label` element (conveniently saved as a field) to display the `Width` and `Height` properties of the page. The Unicode character in the `String.Format` call is a times (×) symbol.

The `SizeChanged` event is not the only opportunity to obtain an element's size. `VisualElement` also defines a protected virtual method named `OnSizeAllocated` that indicates when the visual element is assigned a size. You can override this method in your `ContentPage` derivative rather than handling the `SizeChanged` event, but `OnSizeAllocated` is sometimes called when the size isn't actually changing.

Here's the program running on the three standard platforms:

For the record, these are the sources of the screens in these three images:

- The iPhone 6 simulator, with pixel dimensions of 750 × 1334.

- An LG Nexus 5 with a screen size of 1080 × 1920 pixels.

- A Nokia Lumia 925 with a screen size of 768 × 1280 pixels.

Notice that the vertical size perceived by the program on the Android does not include the area occupied by the status bar or bottom buttons; the vertical size on the Windows 10 Mobile device does not include the area occupied by the status bar.

By default, all three platforms respond to device orientation changes. If you turn the phones (or emulators) 90 degrees counterclockwise, the phones display the following sizes:

The screenshots for this book are designed only for portrait mode, so you'll need to turn this book sideways to see what the program looks like in landscape. The 598-pixel width on the Android excludes the area for the buttons; the 335-pixel height excludes the status bar, which always appears above the page. On the Windows 10 Mobile device, the 728-pixel width excludes the area for the status bar, which appears in the same place but with rotated icons to reflect the new orientation.

Here's the program running on the iPad Air 2 simulator with a pixel dimension of 2048 × 1536.

Obviously, the scaling factor is 2. The screen is 9.7 inches in diagonal for a resolution of 132 DPI.

The Surface Pro 3 has a pixel dimension of 2160 × 1440. The scaling factor is selectable by the user to make everything on the screen larger or smaller, but the recommended scaling factor is 1.5:

The height displayed by **WhatSize** excludes the taskbar at the bottom of the screen. The screen is 12" in diagonal for a resolution of 144 DPI.

A few notes on the **WhatSize** program itself:

WhatSize creates a single `Label` in its constructor and sets the `Text` property in the event handler. That's not the only way to write such a program. The program could use the `SizeChanged` handler to create a whole new `Label` with the new text and set that new `Label` as the content of the page, in which case the previous `Label` would become unreferenced and hence eligible for garbage collection. But creating new visual elements is unnecessary and wasteful in this program. It's best for the program to create only one `Label` view and just set the `Text` property to indicate the page's new size.

Monitoring size changes is the only way a Xamarin.Forms application can detect orientation changes without obtaining platform-specific information. Is the width greater than the height? That's landscape. Otherwise, it's portrait.

By default, the Visual Studio and Xamarin Studio templates for Xamarin.Forms solutions enable device orientation changes for all three platforms. If you want to disable orientation changes—for example, if you have an application that just doesn't work well in portrait or landscape mode—you can do so.

For iOS, first display the contents of Info.plist in Visual Studio or Xamarin Studio. In the **iPhone Deployment Info** section, use the **Supported Device Orientations** area to specify which orientations are allowed.

For Android, in the `Activity` attribute on the `MainActivity` class in the MainActivity.cs file, add:

```
ScreenOrientation = ScreenOrientation.Landscape
```

or

```
ScreenOrientation = ScreenOrientation.Portrait
```

The `Activity` attribute generated by the solution template contains a `ConfigurationChanges` argument that also refers to screen orientation, but the purpose of `ConfigurationChanges` is to inhibit a restart of the activity when the phone's orientation or screen size changes.

For the two Windows Phone projects, the class and enumeration to use is in the `Windows-.Graphics.Display` namespace. In the `MainPage` constructor in the MainPage.xaml.cs file, set the static `DisplayInformation.AutoRotationPreferences` property to one or more members of the `DisplayOrientations` enumeration combined with the C# bitwise OR operation. To restrict the program to landscape or portrait, use:

```
DisplayInformation.AutoRotationPreferences = DisplayOrientations.Landscape
```

or:

```
DisplayInformation.AutoRotationPreferences = DisplayOrientations.Portrait;
```

Metrical sizes

Now that you know how sizes in a Xamarin.Forms application approximately correspond to metrical dimensions of inches and centimeters, you can size elements so that they are approximately the same size on various devices. Here's a program called **MetricalBoxView** that displays a `BoxView` with a width of approximately one centimeter and a height of approximately one inch:

```
public class MetricalBoxViewPage : ContentPage
{
    public MetricalBoxViewPage()
    {
        Content = new BoxView
        {
            Color = Color.Accent,
            WidthRequest = 64,
            HeightRequest = 160,
            HorizontalOptions = LayoutOptions.Center,
            VerticalOptions = LayoutOptions.Center
        };
    }
}
```

If you actually take a ruler to the object on your phone's screen, you'll find that it's not exactly the desired size but certainly close to it, as these screenshots also confirm:

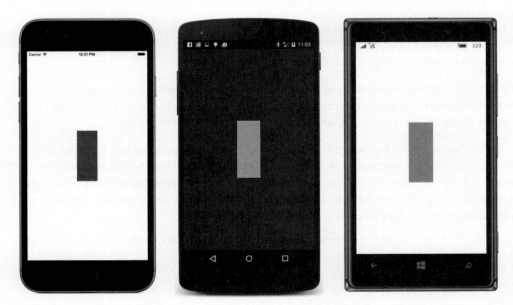

This program is intended to run on phones. If you want to run it on tablets as well, you might use the `Device.Idiom` property to set a somewhat smaller factor for the iPad and Windows tablets.

Estimated font sizes

The `FontSize` property on `Label` and `Button` specifies the approximate height of font characters from the bottom of descenders to the top of ascenders, often (depending on the font) including diacritical marks as well. In most cases you'll want to set this property to a value returned by the `Device.GetNamedSize` method. This allows you to specify a member of the `NamedSize` enumeration: `Default`, `Micro`, `Small`, `Medium`, or `Large`.

Alternatively, you can set the `FontSize` property to actual numeric font sizes, but there's a little problem involved (to be discussed in detail shortly). For the most part, you specify font sizes in the same device-independent units used throughout Xamarin.Forms, which means that you can calculate device-independent font sizes based on the platform resolution.

For example, suppose you want to use a 12-point font in your program. The first thing you should know is that while a 12-point font might be a comfortable size for printed material or a desktop screen, on a phone it's quite large. But let's continue.

There are 72 points to the inch, so a 12-point font is one-sixth of an inch. Multiply by the DPI resolution of 160 and that's about 27 device-independent units.

Let's write a little program called **FontSizes**, which begins with a display similar to the **NamedFontSizes** program in Chapter 3 but then displays some text with numeric point sizes, converted to device-independent units using the device resolution:

```
public class FontSizesPage : ContentPage
{
    public FontSizesPage()
    {
        BackgroundColor = Color.White;
        StackLayout stackLayout = new StackLayout
        {
            HorizontalOptions = LayoutOptions.Center,
            VerticalOptions = LayoutOptions.Center
        };

        // Do the NamedSize values.
        NamedSize[] namedSizes =
        {
            NamedSize.Default, NamedSize.Micro, NamedSize.Small,
            NamedSize.Medium, NamedSize.Large
        };

        foreach (NamedSize namedSize in namedSizes)
        {
            double fontSize = Device.GetNamedSize(namedSize, typeof(Label));

            stackLayout.Children.Add(new Label
                {
                    Text = String.Format("Named Size = {0} ({1:F2})",
```

```
                                    namedSize, fontSize),
                FontSize = fontSize,
                TextColor = Color.Black
            });
    }

    // Resolution in device-independent units per inch.
    double resolution = 160;

    // Draw horizontal separator line.
    stackLayout.Children.Add(
        new BoxView
        {
            Color = Color.Accent,
            HeightRequest = resolution / 80
        });

    // Do some numeric point sizes.
    int[] ptSizes = { 4, 6, 8, 10, 12 };

    foreach (double ptSize in ptSizes)
    {
        double fontSize = resolution * ptSize / 72;

        stackLayout.Children.Add(new Label
            {
                Text = String.Format("Point Size = {0} ({1:F2})",
                                     ptSize, fontSize),
                FontSize = fontSize,
                TextColor = Color.Black
            });
    }

    Content = stackLayout;
    }
}
```

To facilitate comparisons among the three screens, the backgrounds have been uniformly set to white and the labels to black. Notice the `BoxView` inserted into the `StackLayout` between the two `foreach` blocks: the `HeightRequest` setting gives it a device-independent height of approximately one-eightieth of an inch, and it resembles a horizontal rule.

Interestingly, the resultant visual sizes based on the calculation are more consistent among the platforms than the named sizes. The numbers in parentheses are the numeric `FontSize` values in device-independent units:

Fitting text to available size

You might need to fit a block of text to a particular rectangular area. It's possible to calculate a value for the `FontSize` property of `Label` based on the number of text characters, the size of the rectangular area, and just two numbers.

The first number is line spacing. This is the vertical height of a `Label` view per line of text. For the default fonts associated with the three platforms, it is roughly related to the `FontSize` property as follows:

- iOS: `lineSpacing` = 1.2 * `label.FontSize`

- Android: `lineSpacing` = 1.2 * `label.FontSize`

- Windows Phone: `lineSpacing` = 1.3 * `label.FontSize`

The second helpful number is average character width. For a normal mix of uppercase and lower-case letters for the default fonts, this average character width is about half of the font size, regardless of the platform:

- `averageCharacterWidth` = 0.5 * `label.FontSize`

For example, suppose you want to fit a text string containing 80 characters in a width of 320 units, and you'd like the font size to be as large as possible. Divide the width (320) by half the number of characters (40), and you get a font size of 8, which you can set to the `FontSize` property of `Label`. For text that's somewhat indeterminate and can't be tested beforehand, you might want to make this calculation a little more conservative to avoid surprises.

The following program uses both line spacing and average character width to fit a paragraph of text on the page, minus the area at the top of the iPhone occupied by the status bar. To make the exclusion of the iOS status bar a bit easier in this program, the program uses a `ContentView`.

`ContentView` derives from `Layout` but only adds a `Content` property to what it inherits from `Layout`. `ContentView` is also the base class to `Frame`. Although `ContentView` has no functionality other than occupying a rectangular area of space, it is useful for two purposes: Most often, `ContentView` can be a parent to other views to define a new custom view. But `ContentView` can also simulate a margin.

As you might have noticed, Xamarin.Forms has no concept of a margin, which traditionally is similar to padding except that padding is inside a view and a part of the view, while a margin is outside the view and actually part of the parent's view. A `ContentView` lets us simulate this. If you find a need to set a margin on a view, put the view in a `ContentView` and set the `Padding` property on the `ContentView`. `ContentView` inherits a `Padding` property from `Layout`.

The **EstimatedFontSize** program uses `ContentView` in a slightly different manner: It sets the customary padding on the page to avoid the iOS status bar, but then it sets a `ContentView` as the content of that page. Hence, this `ContentView` is the same size as the page, but excluding the iOS status bar. It is on this `ContentView` that the `SizeChanged` event is attached, and it is the size of this `ContentView` that is used to calculate the text font size.

The `SizeChanged` handler uses the first argument to obtain the object firing the event (in this case the `ContentView`), which is the object in which the `Label` must fit. The calculation is described in comments:

```
public class EstimatedFontSizePage : ContentPage
{
    Label label;

    public EstimatedFontSizePage()
    {
        label = new Label();
        Padding = new Thickness(0, Device.OnPlatform(20, 0, 0), 0, 0);
        ContentView contentView = new ContentView
        {
            Content = label
        };
        contentView.SizeChanged += OnContentViewSizeChanged;
        Content = contentView;
    }

    void OnContentViewSizeChanged(object sender, EventArgs args)
    {
        string text =
            "A default system font with a font size of S " +
```

```
            "has a line height of about ({0:F1} * S) and an " +
            "average character width of about ({1:F1} * S). " +
            "On this page, which has a width of {2:F0} and a " +
            "height of {3:F0}, a font size of ?1 should " +
            "comfortably render the ??2 characters in this " +
            "paragraph with ?3 lines and about ?4 characters " +
            "per line. Does it work?";

        // Get View whose size is changing.
        View view = (View)sender;

        // Define two values as multiples of font size.
        double lineHeight = Device.OnPlatform(1.2, 1.2, 1.3);
        double charWidth = 0.5;

        // Format the text and get its character length.
        text = String.Format(text, lineHeight, charWidth, view.Width, view.Height);
        int charCount = text.Length;

        // Because:
        //    lineCount = view.Height / (lineHeight * fontSize)
        //    charsPerLine = view.Width / (charWidth * fontSize)
        //    charCount = lineCount * charsPerLine
        // Hence, solving for fontSize:
        int fontSize = (int)Math.Sqrt(view.Width * view.Height /
                        (charCount * lineHeight * charWidth));

        // Now these values can be calculated.
        int lineCount = (int)(view.Height / (lineHeight * fontSize));
        int charsPerLine = (int)(view.Width / (charWidth * fontSize));

        // Replace the placeholders with the values.
        text = text.Replace("?1", fontSize.ToString());
        text = text.Replace("??2", charCount.ToString());
        text = text.Replace("?3", lineCount.ToString());
        text = text.Replace("?4", charsPerLine.ToString());

        // Set the Label properties.
        label.Text = text;
        label.FontSize = fontSize;
    }
}
```

The text placeholders named "?1", "??2", "?3", and "?4" were chosen to be unique but also to be the same number of characters as the numbers that replace them.

If the goal is to make the text as large as possible without the text spilling off the page, the results validate the approach:

A default system font with a font size of S has a line height of about (1.2 * S) and an average character width of about (0.5 * S). On this page, which has a width of 375 and a height of 647, a font size of 34 should comfortably render the 334 characters in this paragraph with 15 lines and about 22 characters per line. Does it work?

A default system font with a font size of S has a line height of about (1.2 * S) and an average character width of about (0.5 * S). On this page, which has a width of 360 and a height of 567, a font size of 31 should comfortably render the 334 characters in this paragraph with 15 lines and about 23 characters per line. Does it work?

A default system font with a font size of S has a line height of about (1.3 * S) and an average character width of about (0.5 * S). On this page, which has a width of 341 and a height of 546, a font size of 29 should comfortably render the 334 characters in this paragraph with 14 lines and about 23 characters per line. Does it work?

Not bad. Not bad at all. The text actually displays in one less line that indicated on all three platforms, but the technique seems sound. It's not always the case that the same `FontSize` is calculated for landscape mode, but it happens sometimes:

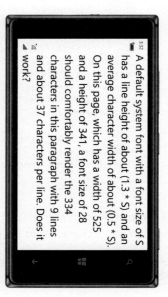

A default system font with a font size of S has a line height of about (1.2 * S) and an average character width of about (0.5 * S). On this page, which has a width of 667 and a height of 355, a font size of 34 should comfortably render the 334 characters in this paragraph with 8 lines and about 39 characters per line. Does it work?

A default system font with a font size of S has a line height of about (1.2 * S) and an average character width of about (0.5 * S). On this page, which has a width of 598 and a height of 335, a font size of 31 should comfortably render the 334 characters in this paragraph with 9 lines and about 38 characters per line. Does it work?

A default system font with a font size of S has a line height of about (1.3 * S) and an average character width of about (0.5 * S). On this page, which has a width of 525 and a height of 341, a font size of 28 should comfortably render the 334 characters in this paragraph with 9 lines and about 37 characters per line. Does it work?

A fit-to-size clock

The `Device` class includes a static `StartTimer` method that lets you set a timer that fires a periodic event. The availability of a timer event means that a clock application is possible, even if it displays the time only in text.

The first argument to `Device.StartTimer` is an interval expressed as a `TimeSpan` value. The timer fires an event periodically based on that interval. (You can go down as low as 15 or 16 milliseconds, which is about the period of the frame rate of 60 frames per second common on video displays.) The event handler has no arguments but must return `true` to keep the timer going.

The **FitToSizeClock** program creates a `Label` for displaying the time and then sets two events: the `SizeChanged` event on the page for changing the font size, and the `Device.StartTimer` event for one-second intervals to change the `Text` property.

Many C# programmers these days like to define small event handlers as anonymous lambda functions. This allows the event-handling code to be very close to the instantiation and initialization of the object firing the event instead of somewhere else in the file. It also allows referencing objects within the event handler without storing those objects as fields.

In this program, both event handlers simply change a property of the `Label`, and they are both expressed as lambda functions so that they can access the `Label` without it being stored as a field:

```
public class FitToSizeClockPage : ContentPage
{
    public FitToSizeClockPage()
    {
        Label clockLabel = new Label
        {
            HorizontalOptions = LayoutOptions.Center,
            VerticalOptions = LayoutOptions.Center
        };

        Content = clockLabel;

        // Handle the SizeChanged event for the page.
        SizeChanged += (object sender, EventArgs args) =>
            {
                // Scale the font size to the page width
                //      (based on 11 characters in the displayed string).
                if (this.Width > 0)
                    clockLabel.FontSize = this.Width / 6;
            };

        // Start the timer going.
        Device.StartTimer(TimeSpan.FromSeconds(1), () =>
            {
                // Set the Text property of the Label.
                clockLabel.Text = DateTime.Now.ToString("h:mm:ss tt");
```

```
            return true;
        });
    }
}
```

The `StartTimer` handler specifies a custom formatting string for `DateTime` that results in 10 or 11 characters, but two of those are capital letters, and those are wider than average characters. The `SizeChanged` handler implicitly assumes that 12 characters are displayed by setting the font size to one-sixth of the page width:

Of course, the text is much larger in landscape mode:

This one-second timer doesn't tick exactly at the beginning of every second, so the displayed time might not precisely agree with other time displays on the same device. You can make it more accurate by setting a more frequent timer tick. Performance won't be impacted much because the display still changes only once per second and won't require a new layout cycle until then.

Accessibility issues

The **EstimatedFontSize** program and the **FitToSizeClock** program both have a subtle flaw, but the problem might not be so subtle if you're one of the many people who can't comfortably read text on a mobile device and uses the device's accessibility features to make the text larger.

On iOS, run the **Settings** app, and choose **General**, and **Accessibility**, and **Larger Text**. You can then use a slider to make text on the screen larger or smaller. The page indicates that text will only be adjusted in iOS applications that support the **Dynamic Type** feature.

On Android, run the **Settings** app, and choose **Display** and then **Font size**. You are presented with four radio buttons for selecting **Small**, **Normal** (the default), **Large**, or **Huge**.

On a Windows 10 Mobile device, run the **Settings** app, and choose **Ease of Access** and then **More options**. You can then move a slider labeled **Text scaling** from 100% to 200%.

Here's what you will discover:

The iOS setting has no effect on Xamarin.Forms applications.

The Android setting affects the values returned from `Device.GetNamedSize`. If you select something other than **Normal** and run the **FontSizes** program again, you'll see that for the `NamedSize.Default` argument, `Device.GetNamedSize` returns 14 when the setting is **Normal** (as the earlier screenshot shows), but returns 12 for a setting of **Small**, 16 for **Large**, and 18 1/3 for **Huge.**

Also, *all* the text displayed on the Android screen is a different size—either smaller or larger depending on what setting you selected—even for constant `FontSize` values.

On Windows 10 Mobile, the values returned from `Device.GetNamedSize` do not depend on the accessibility setting, but all the text is displayed larger.

This means that the **EstimatedFontSize** or **FitToSizeClock** programs do not run correctly on Android or Windows 10 Mobile with the accessibility setting for larger text. Part of the text is truncated.

Let's explore this a little more. The **AccessibilityTest** program displays two `Label` elements on its page. The first has a constant `FontSize` of 20, and the second merely displays the size of the first `Label` when its size changes:

```
public class AccessibilityTestPage : ContentPage
{
    public AccessibilityTestPage()
    {
        Label testLabel = new Label
        {
            Text = "FontSize of 20" + Environment.NewLine + "20 characters across",
            FontSize = 20,
            HorizontalTextAlignment = TextAlignment.Center,
            HorizontalOptions = LayoutOptions.Center,
            VerticalOptions = LayoutOptions.CenterAndExpand
        };

        Label displayLabel = new Label
        {
            HorizontalOptions = LayoutOptions.Center,
            VerticalOptions = LayoutOptions.CenterAndExpand
        };

        testLabel.SizeChanged += (sender, args) =>
        {
            displayLabel.Text = String.Format("{0:F0} \u00D7 {1:F0}", testLabel.Width,
                                                                       testLabel.Height);
        };

        Content = new StackLayout
        {
            Children =
            {
                testLabel,
                displayLabel
            }
        };
    }
}
```

```
}
```

Normally, the second `Label` displays a size that is roughly consistent with the assumptions described earlier:

But now go into the accessibility settings and crank them all the way up. Both Android and Windows 10 Mobile display larger text:

The character size assumptions described earlier are no longer valid, and that's why the programs fail to fit the text.

But there is an alternative approach to sizing text to a rectangular area.

Empirically fitting text

Another approach to fitting text within a rectangle of a particular size involves empirically determining the size of the rendered text based on a particular font size and then adjusting that font size up or down. This approach has the advantage of working on all devices regardless of the accessibility settings.

But the process can be tricky: The first problem is that there is not a clean linear relationship between the font size and the height of the rendered text. As text gets larger relative to the width of its container, more line breaks result, with more wasted space. A calculation to find the optimum font size often involves a loop that narrows in on the value.

A second problem involves the actual mechanism of obtaining the size of a `Label` rendered with a particular font size. You can set a `SizeChanged` handler on the `Label`, but within that handler you don't want to make any changes (such as setting a new `FontSize` property) that will cause recursive calls to that handler.

A better approach is calling the `GetSizeRequest` method defined by `VisualElement` and inherited by `Label` and all other views. `GetSizeRequest` requires two arguments—a width constraint and a height constraint. These values indicate the size of the rectangle in which you want to fit the element, and one or the other can be infinity. When using `GetSizeRequest` with a `Label`, generally you set the width constraint argument to the width of the container and the height constraint to `Double.PositiveInfinity`.

The `GetSizeRequest` method returns a value of type `SizeRequest`, a structure with two properties, named `Request` and `Minimum`, both of type `Size`. The `Request` property indicates the size of the rendered text. (More information on this and related methods can be found in Chapter 26.)

The **EmpiricalFontSize** project demonstrates this technique. For convenience, it defines a small structure named `FontCalc` whose constructor makes the call to `GetSizeRequest` for a particular `Label` (already initialized with text), a trial font size, and a text width:

```
struct FontCalc
{
    public FontCalc(Label label, double fontSize, double containerWidth)
        : this()
    {
        // Save the font size.
        FontSize = fontSize;

        // Recalculate the Label height.
```

```
            label.FontSize = fontSize;
            SizeRequest sizeRequest =
                label.GetSizeRequest(containerWidth, Double.PositiveInfinity);

            // Save that height.
            TextHeight = sizeRequest.Request.Height;
        }

        public double FontSize { private set; get; }

        public double TextHeight { private set; get; }
    }
```

The resultant height of the rendered `Label` is saved in the `TextHeight` property.

When you make a call to `GetSizeRequest` on a page or a layout, the page or layout needs to obtain the sizes of all its children down through the visual tree. This has a performance penalty, of course, so you should avoid making calls like that unless necessary. But a `Label` has no children, so calling `GetSizeRequest` on a `Label` is not nearly as bad. However, you should still try to optimize the calls. Avoid looping through a sequential series of font size values to determine the maximum value that doesn't result in text exceeding the container height. A process that algorithmically narrows in on an optimum value is better.

`GetSizeRequest` requires that the element be part of a visual tree and that the layout process has at least partially begun. Don't call `GetSizeRequest` in the constructor of your page class. You won't get information from it. The first reasonable opportunity is in an override of the page's `OnAppearing` method. Of course, you might not have sufficient information at this time to pass arguments to the `GetSizeRequest` method.

However, calling `GetSizeRequest` doesn't have any side effects. It doesn't cause a new size to be set on the element, which means that it doesn't cause a `SizeChanged` event to be fired, which means that it's safe to call in a `SizeChanged` handler.

The `EmpiricalFontSizePage` class instantiates `FontCalc` values in the `SizeChanged` handler of the `ContentView` that hosts the `Label`. The constructor of each `FontCalc` value makes `GetSize-Request` calls on the `Label` and saves the resultant `TextHeight`. The `SizeChanged` handler begins with trial font sizes of 10 and 100 under the assumption that the optimum value is somewhere between these two and that these represent lower and upper bounds. Hence the variable names `lower-FontCalc` and `upperFontCalc`:

```
public class EmpiricalFontSizePage : ContentPage
{
    Label label;

    public EmpiricalFontSizePage()
    {
        label = new Label();

        Padding = new Thickness(0, Device.OnPlatform(20, 0, 0), 0, 0);
```

```
            ContentView contentView = new ContentView
            {
                Content = label
            };
            contentView.SizeChanged += OnContentViewSizeChanged;
            Content = contentView;
    }

    void OnContentViewSizeChanged(object sender, EventArgs args)
    {
        // Get View whose size is changing.
        View view = (View)sender;

        if (view.Width <= 0 || view.Height <= 0)
            return;

        label.Text =
            "This is a paragraph of text displayed with " +
            "a FontSize value of ?? that is empirically " +
            "calculated in a loop within the SizeChanged " +
            "handler of the Label's container. This technique " +
            "can be tricky: You don't want to get into " +
            "an infinite loop by triggering a layout pass " +
            "with every calculation. Does it work?";

        // Calculate the height of the rendered text.
        FontCalc lowerFontCalc = new FontCalc(label, 10, view.Width);
        FontCalc upperFontCalc = new FontCalc(label, 100, view.Width);

        while (upperFontCalc.FontSize - lowerFontCalc.FontSize > 1)
        {
            // Get the average font size of the upper and lower bounds.
            double fontSize = (lowerFontCalc.FontSize + upperFontCalc.FontSize) / 2;

            // Check the new text height against the container height.
            FontCalc newFontCalc = new FontCalc(label, fontSize, view.Width);

            if (newFontCalc.TextHeight > view.Height)
            {
                upperFontCalc = newFontCalc;
            }
            else
            {
                lowerFontCalc = newFontCalc;
            }
        }

        // Set the final font size and the text with the embedded value.
        label.FontSize = lowerFontCalc.FontSize;
        label.Text = label.Text.Replace("??", label.FontSize.ToString("F0"));
    }
}
```

In each iteration of the `while` loop, the `FontSize` properties of those two `FontCalc` values are averaged and a new `FontCalc` is obtained. This becomes the new `lowerFontCalc` or `upperFontCalc` value depending on the height of the rendered text. The loop ends when the calculated font size is within one unit of the optimum value.

About seven iterations of the loop are sufficient to get a value that is clearly better than the estimated value calculated in the earlier program:

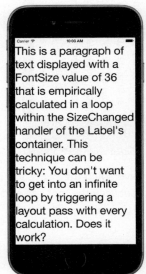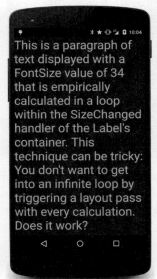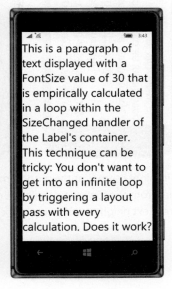

Turning the phone sideways triggers another recalculation that results in a similar (though not necessarily the same) font size:

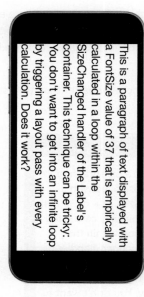

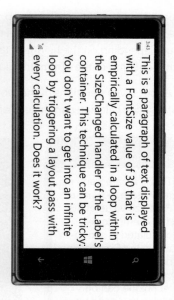

It might seem that the algorithm could be improved beyond simply averaging the `FontSize` properties from the lower and upper `FontCalc` values. But the relationship between the font size and rendered text height is rather complex, and sometimes the easiest approach is just as good.

Chapter 6
Button clicks

The components of a graphical user interface can be divided roughly into views that are used for presentation, which display information *to* the user, and interaction, which obtain input *from* the user. While the `Label` is the most basic presentation view, the `Button` is probably the archetypal interactive view. The `Button` signals a command. It's the user's way of telling the program to initiate some action—to do something.

A Xamarin.Forms button displays text, with or without an accompanying image. (Only text buttons are described in this chapter; adding an image to a button is covered in Chapter 13, "Bitmaps.") When the user's finger presses on a button, the button changes its appearance somewhat to provide feedback to the user. When the finger is released, the button fires a `Clicked` event. The two arguments of the `Clicked` handler are typical of Xamarin.Forms event handlers:

- The first argument is the object firing the event. For the `Clicked` handler, this is the particular `Button` object that's been tapped.

- The second argument sometimes provides more information about the event. For the `Clicked` event, the second argument is simply an `EventArgs` object that provides no additional information.

Once an application begins implementing user interaction, some special needs arise: The application should make an effort to save the results of that interaction if the program happens to be terminated before the user has finished working with it. For that reason, this chapter also discusses how an application can save transient data, particularly in the context of application lifecycle events. These are described in the section "Saving transient data."

Processing the click

Here's a program named **ButtonLogger** with a `Button` that shares a `StackLayout` with a `Scroll-View` containing another `StackLayout`. Every time the `Button` is clicked, the program adds a new `Label` to the scrollable `StackLayout`, in effect logging all the button clicks:

```
public class ButtonLoggerPage : ContentPage
{
    StackLayout loggerLayout = new StackLayout();

    public ButtonLoggerPage()
    {
        // Create the Button and attach Clicked handler.
        Button button = new Button
```

```
        {
            Text = "Log the Click Time"
        };
        button.Clicked += OnButtonClicked;

        this.Padding = new Thickness(5, Device.OnPlatform(20, 0, 0), 5, 0);

        // Assemble the page.
        this.Content = new StackLayout
        {
            Children =
            {
                button,
                new ScrollView
                {
                    VerticalOptions = LayoutOptions.FillAndExpand,
                    Content = loggerLayout
                }
            }
        };
    }

    void OnButtonClicked(object sender, EventArgs args)
    {
        // Add Label to scrollable StackLayout.
        loggerLayout.Children.Add(new Label
        {
            Text = "Button clicked at " + DateTime.Now.ToString("T")
        });
    }
}
```

In the programs in this book, event handlers are given names beginning with the word On, followed by some kind of identification of the view firing the event (sometimes just the view type), followed by the event name. The resultant name in this case is OnButtonClicked.

The constructor attaches the Clicked handler to the Button right after the Button is created. The page is then assembled with a StackLayout containing the Button and a ScrollView with another StackLayout, named loggerLayout. Notice that the ScrollView has its VerticalOptions set to FillAndExpand so that it can share the StackLayout with the Button and still be visible and scrollable.

Here's the display after several Button clicks:

As you can see, the `Button` looks a little different on the three screens. That's because the button is rendered natively on the individual platforms: on the iPhone it's a `UIButton`, on Android it's an Android `Button`, and on Windows 10 Mobile it's a Windows Runtime `Button`. By default the button always fills the area available for it and centers the text inside.

`Button` defines several properties that let you customize its appearance:

- `FontFamily` of type `string`

- `FontSize` of type `double`

- `FontAttributes` of type `FontAttributes`

- `TextColor` of type `Color` (default is `Color.Default`)

- `BorderColor` of type `Color` (default is `Color.Default`)

- `BorderWidth` of type `double` (default is 0)

- `BorderRadius` of type `double` (default is 5)

- `Image` (to be discussed in Chapter 13)

`Button` also inherits the `BackgroundColor` property (and a bunch of other properties) from `VisualElement` and inherits `HorizontalOptions` and `VerticalOptions` from `View`.

Some `Button` properties might work a little differently on the various platforms. As you can see, none of the buttons in the screenshots has a border. (However, the Windows Phone 8.1 button has a visible white border by default.) If you set the `BorderWidth` property to a nonzero value, the border becomes visible only on the iPhone, and it's black. If you set the `BorderColor` property to something other than `Color.Default`, the border is visible only on the Windows 10 Mobile device. If you want a visible border on both iOS and Windows 10 mobile devices, set both `BorderWidth` and `BorderColor`. But the border still won't show up on Android devices unless you also set the `BackgroundColor` property. Customizing a button border is a good opportunity for using `Device.OnPlatform` (as you'll see in Chapter 10, "XAML markup extensions").

The `BorderRadius` property is intended to round off the sharp corners of the border, and it works on iOS and Android if the border is displayed, but it doesn't work on Windows 10 and Windows 10 Mobile. The `BorderRadius` works on Windows 8.1 and Windows Phone 8.1, but if you use it with `BackgroundColor`, the background is not enclosed within the border.

Suppose you wrote a program similar to **ButtonLogger** but did not save the `loggerLayout` object as a field. Could you get access to that `StackLayout` object in the `Clicked` event handler?

Yes! It's possible to obtain parent and child visual elements by a technique called *walking the visual tree*. The `sender` argument to the `OnButtonClicked` handler is the object firing the event, in this case the `Button`, so you can begin the `Clicked` handler by casting that argument:

```
Button button = (Button)sender;
```

You know that the `Button` is a child of a `StackLayout`, so that object is accessible from the `Parent` property. Again, some casting is required:

```
StackLayout outerLayout = (StackLayout)button.Parent;
```

The second child of this `StackLayout` is the `ScrollView`, so the `Children` property can be indexed to obtain that:

```
ScrollView scrollView = (ScrollView)outerLayout.Children[1];
```

The `Content` property of this `ScrollView` is exactly the `StackLayout` you were looking for:

```
StackLayout loggerLayout = (StackLayout)scrollView.Content;
```

Of course, the danger in doing something like this is that you might change the layout someday and forget to change your tree-walking code similarly. But the technique comes in handy if the code that assembles your page is separate from the code handling events from views on that page.

Sharing button clicks

If a program contains multiple `Button` views, each `Button` can have its own `Clicked` handler. But in some cases it might be more convenient for multiple `Button` views to share a common `Clicked` handler.

Consider a calculator program. Each of the buttons labeled 0 through 9 basically does the same thing, and having 10 separate `Clicked` handlers for these 10 buttons—even if they share some common code—simply wouldn't make much sense.

You've seen how the first argument to the `Clicked` handler can be cast to an object of type `Button`. But how do you know which `Button` it is?

One approach is to store all the `Button` objects as fields and then compare the `Button` object firing the event with these fields.

The **TwoButtons** program demonstrates this technique. This program is similar to the previous program but with two buttons—one to add `Label` objects to the `StackLayout`, and the other to remove them. The two `Button` objects are stored as fields so that the `Clicked` handler can determine which one fired the event:

```
public class TwoButtonsPage : ContentPage
{
    Button addButton, removeButton;
    StackLayout loggerLayout = new StackLayout();

    public TwoButtonsPage()
    {
        // Create the Button views and attach Clicked handlers.
        addButton = new Button
        {
            Text = "Add",
            HorizontalOptions = LayoutOptions.CenterAndExpand
        };
        addButton.Clicked += OnButtonClicked;

        removeButton = new Button
        {
            Text = "Remove",
            HorizontalOptions = LayoutOptions.CenterAndExpand,
            IsEnabled = false
        };
        removeButton.Clicked += OnButtonClicked;

        this.Padding = new Thickness(5, Device.OnPlatform(20, 0, 0), 5, 0);

        // Assemble the page.
        this.Content = new StackLayout
        {
            Children =
            {
                new StackLayout
                {
                    Orientation = StackOrientation.Horizontal,
                    Children =
                    {
                        addButton,
                        removeButton
                    }
```

```
                    },

                    new ScrollView
                    {
                        VerticalOptions = LayoutOptions.FillAndExpand,
                        Content = loggerLayout
                    }
                }
            };
        }

        void OnButtonClicked(object sender, EventArgs args)
        {
            Button button = (Button)sender;

            if (button == addButton)
            {
                // Add Label to scrollable StackLayout.
                loggerLayout.Children.Add(new Label
                {
                    Text = "Button clicked at " + DateTime.Now.ToString("T")
                });
            }
            else
            {
                // Remove topmost Label from StackLayout.
                loggerLayout.Children.RemoveAt(0);
            }

            // Enable "Remove" button only if children are present.
            removeButton.IsEnabled = loggerLayout.Children.Count > 0;
        }
    }
```

Both buttons are given a `HorizontalOptions` value of `CenterAndExpand` so that they can be displayed side by side at the top of the screen by using a horizontal `StackLayout`:

Notice that when the `Clicked` handler detects `removeButton`, it simply calls the `RemoveAt` method on the `Children` property:

```
loggerLayout.Children.RemoveAt(0);
```

But what happens if there are no children? Won't `RemoveAt` raise an exception?

It can't happen! When the **TwoButtons** program begins, the `IsEnabled` property of the `remove-Button` is initialized to `false`. When a button is disabled in this way, a dim appearance signals to the user that it's nonfunctional. It does not provide feedback to the user and it does not fire `Clicked` events. Toward the end of the `Clicked` handler, the `IsEnabled` property on `removeButton` is set to `true` only if the `loggerLayout` has at least one child.

This illustrates a good general rule: if your code needs to determine whether a button `Clicked` event is valid, it's probably better to prevent invalid button clicks by disabling the button.

Anonymous event handlers

As with any event handler, you can define a `Clicked` handler as an anonymous lambda function. Here's a program named **ButtonLambdas** that has a `Label` displaying a number and two buttons. One button doubles the number, and the other halves the number. Normally, the number and `Label` variables would be saved as fields. But because the anonymous event handlers are defined right in the constructor after these variables are defined, the event handlers have access to these local variables:

```
public class ButtonLambdasPage : ContentPage
{
```

```
public ButtonLambdasPage()
{
    // Number to manipulate.
    double number = 1;

    // Create the Label for display.
    Label label = new Label
    {
        Text = number.ToString(),
        FontSize = Device.GetNamedSize(NamedSize.Large, typeof(Label)),
        HorizontalOptions = LayoutOptions.Center,
        VerticalOptions = LayoutOptions.CenterAndExpand
    };

    // Create the first Button and attach Clicked handler.
    Button timesButton = new Button
    {
        Text = "Double",
        FontSize = Device.GetNamedSize(NamedSize.Large, typeof(Button)),
        HorizontalOptions = LayoutOptions.CenterAndExpand
    };
    timesButton.Clicked += (sender, args) =>
    {
        number *= 2;
        label.Text = number.ToString();
    };

    // Create the second Button and attach Clicked handler.
    Button divideButton = new Button
    {
        Text = "Half",
        FontSize = Device.GetNamedSize(NamedSize.Large, typeof(Button)),
        HorizontalOptions = LayoutOptions.CenterAndExpand
    };
    divideButton.Clicked += (sender, args) =>
    {
        number /= 2;
        label.Text = number.ToString();
    };

    // Assemble the page.
    this.Content = new StackLayout
    {
        Children =
        {
            label,
            new StackLayout
            {
                Orientation = StackOrientation.Horizontal,
                VerticalOptions = LayoutOptions.CenterAndExpand,
                Children =
                {
                    timesButton,
                    divideButton
```

```
                                    }
                               }
                          }
                    };
             }
      }
```

Notice the use of `Device.GetNamedSize` to get large text for both the `Label` and the `Button`. When used with `Label`, the second argument of `GetNamedSize` should indicate a `Label`, and when used with the `Button` it should indicate a `Button`. The sizes for the two elements might be different.

Like the previous program, the two buttons share a horizontal `StackLayout`:

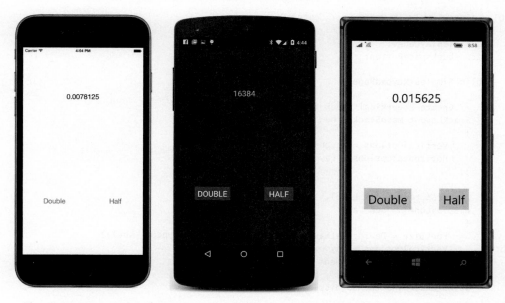

The disadvantage of defining event handlers as anonymous lambda functions is that they can't be shared among multiple views. (Actually they can, but some messy reflection code is involved.)

Distinguishing views with IDs

In the **TwoButtons** program, you saw a technique for sharing an event handler that distinguishes views by comparing objects. This works fine when there aren't very many views to distinguish, but it would be a terrible approach for a calculator program.

The `Element` class defines a `StyleId` property of type `string` specifically for the purpose of identifying views. It's not used for anything internal to Xamarin.Forms, so you can set it to whatever is convenient for the application. You can test the values by using `if` and `else` statements or in a `switch` and `case` block, or you can use a `Parse` method to convert the strings into numbers or enumeration members.

The following program isn't a calculator, but it is a numeric keypad, which is certainly part of a calculator. The program is called **SimplestKeypad** and uses a `StackLayout` for organizing the rows and columns of keys. (One of the intents of this program is to demonstrate that `StackLayout` is not quite the right tool for this job!)

The program creates a total of five `StackLayout` instances. The `mainStack` is vertically oriented, and four horizontal `StackLayout` objects arrange the 10 digit buttons. To keep things simple, the keypad is arranged with telephone ordering rather than calculator ordering:

```
public class SimplestKeypadPage : ContentPage
{
    Label displayLabel;
    Button backspaceButton;

    public SimplestKeypadPage()
    {
        // Create a vertical stack for the entire keypad.
        StackLayout mainStack = new StackLayout
        {
            VerticalOptions = LayoutOptions.Center,
            HorizontalOptions = LayoutOptions.Center
        };

        // First row is the Label.
        displayLabel = new Label
        {
            FontSize = Device.GetNamedSize(NamedSize.Large, typeof(Label)),
            VerticalOptions = LayoutOptions.Center,
            HorizontalTextAlignment = TextAlignment.End
        };
        mainStack.Children.Add(displayLabel);

        // Second row is the backspace Button.
        backspaceButton = new Button
        {
            Text = "\u21E6",
            FontSize = Device.GetNamedSize(NamedSize.Large, typeof(Button)),
            IsEnabled = false
        };
        backspaceButton.Clicked += OnBackspaceButtonClicked;
        mainStack.Children.Add(backspaceButton);

        // Now do the 10 number keys.
        StackLayout rowStack = null;

        for (int num = 1; num <= 10; num++)
        {
            if ((num - 1) % 3 == 0)
            {
```

```
                rowStack = new StackLayout
                {
                    Orientation = StackOrientation.Horizontal
                };
                mainStack.Children.Add(rowStack);
            }

            Button digitButton = new Button
            {
                Text = (num % 10).ToString(),
                FontSize = Device.GetNamedSize(NamedSize.Large, typeof(Button)),
                StyleId = (num % 10).ToString()
            };
            digitButton.Clicked += OnDigitButtonClicked;

            // For the zero button, expand to fill horizontally.
            if (num == 10)
            {
                digitButton.HorizontalOptions = LayoutOptions.FillAndExpand;
            }
            rowStack.Children.Add(digitButton);
        }

        this.Content = mainStack;
    }

    void OnDigitButtonClicked(object sender, EventArgs args)
    {
        Button button = (Button)sender;
        displayLabel.Text += (string)button.StyleId;
        backspaceButton.IsEnabled = true;
    }

    void OnBackspaceButtonClicked(object sender, EventArgs args)
    {
        string text = displayLabel.Text;
        displayLabel.Text = text.Substring(0, text.Length - 1);
        backspaceButton.IsEnabled = displayLabel.Text.Length > 0;
    }
}
```

The 10 number keys share a single `Clicked` handler. The `StyleId` property indicates the number associated with the key, so the program can simply append that number to the string displayed by the `Label`. The `StyleId` happens to be identical to the `Text` property of the `Button`, and the `Text` property could be used instead, but in the general case, things aren't always quite that convenient.

The backspace `Button` is sufficiently different in function to warrant its own `Clicked` handler, although it would surely be possible to combine the two methods into one to take advantage of any code they might have in common.

To give the keypad a slightly larger size, all the text is given a `FontSize` using `NamedSize.Large`. Here are the three renderings of the **SimplestKeypad** program:

Of course, you'll want to press the keys repeatedly until you see how the program responds to a really large string of digits, and you'll discover that it doesn't adequately anticipate such a thing. When the Label gets too wide, it begins to govern the overall width of the vertical StackLayout, and the buttons start shifting as well.

Moreover, if the buttons contain letters or symbols rather than numbers, the buttons will be misaligned because each button width is based on its content.

Can you fix this problem with the Expands flag on the HorizontalOptions property? No. The Expands flag causes extra space to be distributed equally among the views in the StackLayout. Each view will increase additively by the same amount, but the buttons start out with different widths, and they will always have different widths. For example, take a look at the two buttons in the **TwoButtons** or **ButtonLambdas** program. Those buttons have their HorizontalOptions properties set to Fill-AndExpand, but they are different widths because the width of the button content is different.

A better solution for these programs is the layout known as the Grid, coming up in Chapter 17.

Saving transient data

Suppose you're entering an important number in the **SimplestKeypad** program and you're interrupted—perhaps with a phone call. Later on, you shut off the phone, effectively terminating the program.

What should happen the next time you run **SimplestKeypad**? Should the long string of numbers you entered earlier be discarded? Or should it seem as though the program resumed from the state you last left it? Of course, it doesn't matter for a simple demo program like **SimplestKeypad**, but in the general case, users expect mobile applications to remember exactly what they were doing the last time they interacted with the program.

For this reason, the `Application` class supports two facilities that help the program save and restore data:

- The `Properties` property of `Application` is a dictionary with `string` keys and `object` items. The contents of this dictionary are automatically saved prior to the application being terminated, and the saved contents become available the next time the application runs.

- The `Application` class defines three protected virtual methods, named `OnStart`, `OnSleep`, and `OnResume`, and the `App` class generated by the Xamarin.Forms template overrides these methods. These methods help an application deal with what are known as *application lifecycle* events.

To use these facilities, you need to identify what information your application needs to save so that it can restore its state after being terminated and restarted. In general, this is a combination of *application settings*—such as colors and font sizes that the user might be given an opportunity to set—and *transient data*, such as half-entered entry fields. Application settings usually apply to the entire application, while transient data is unique to each page in the application. If each item of this data is an entry in the `Properties` dictionary, each item needs a dictionary key. However, if a program needs to save a large file such as a word-processing document, it shouldn't use the `Properties` dictionary, but instead should access the platform's file system directly. (That's a job for Chapter 20, "Async and file I/O.")

Also, you should restrict the data types used with `Properties` to the basic data types supported by .NET and C#, such as `string`, `int`, and `double`.

The **SimplestKeypad** program needs to save only a single item of transient data, and the dictionary key "displayLabelText" seems reasonable.

Sometimes a program can use the `Properties` dictionary to save and retrieve data without getting involved with application lifecycle events. For example, the **SimplestKeypad** program knows exactly when the `Text` property of `displayLabel` changes. It happens only in the two `Clicked` event handlers for the number keys and the delete key. Those two event handlers could simply store the new value in the `Properties` dictionary.

But wait: `Properties` is a property of the `Application` class. Do we need to save the instance of the `App` class so that code in the `SimplestKeypadPage` can get access to the dictionary? No, it's not necessary. `Application` defines a static property named `Current` that returns the current application's instance of the `Application` class.

To store the `Text` property of the `Label` in the dictionary, simply add the following line at the bottom of the two `Clicked` event handlers in **SimplestKeypad**:

```
Application.Current.Properties["displayLabelText"] = displayLabel.Text;
```

Don't worry if the `displayLabelText` key does not yet exist in the dictionary: The `Properties` dictionary implements the generic `IDictionary` interface, which explicitly defines the indexer to replace the previous item if the key already exists or to add a new item to the dictionary if the key does not exist. That behavior is exactly what you want here.

The `SimplestKeypadPage` constructor can then conclude by initializing the `Text` property of the `Label` with the following code, which retrieves the item from the dictionary:

```
IDictionary<string, object> properties = Application.Current.Properties;

if (properties.ContainsKey("displayLabelText"))
{
    displayLabel.Text = properties["displayLabelText"] as string;
    backspaceButton.IsEnabled = displayLabel.Text.Length > 0;
}
```

This is all your application needs to do: just save information in the `Properties` dictionary and retrieve it. Xamarin.Forms itself is responsible for the job of saving and loading the contents of the dictionary in platform-specific application storage.

In general, however, it's better for an application to interact with the `Properties` dictionary in a more structured manner, and here's where the application lifecycle events come into play. These are the three methods that appear in the `App` class generated by the Xamarin.Forms template:

```
public class App : Application
{
    public App()
    {
        …
    }

    protected override void OnStart()
    {
        // Handle when your app starts
    }

    protected override void OnSleep()
    {
        // Handle when your app sleeps
    }

    protected override void OnResume()
    {
        // Handle when your app resumes
    }
}
```

The most important is the `OnSleep` call. In general, an application goes into sleep mode when it no longer commands the screen and has become inactive (apart from some background jobs it might have initiated). From this sleep mode, an application can be resumed (signaled by an `OnResume` call) or terminated. But this is important: After the `OnSleep` call, there is no further notification that an application is being terminated. The `OnSleep` call is as close as you get to a termination notification, and it always precedes a termination. For example, if your application is running and the user turns off the phone, the application gets an `OnSleep` call as the phone is shutting down.

Actually, there are some exceptions to the rule that a call to `OnSleep` always precedes program termination: a program that crashes does not get an `OnSleep` call first, but you probably expect that. But here's a case that you might not anticipate: When you are debugging a Xamarin.Forms application, and use Visual Studio or Xamarin Studio to stop debugging, the program is terminated without a preceding `OnSleep` call. This means that when you are debugging code that uses these application lifecycle events, you should get into the habit of using the phone itself to put your program to sleep, to resume the program, and to terminate it.

When your Xamarin.Forms application is running, the easiest way to trigger an `OnSleep` call on a phone or simulator is by pressing the phone's **Home** button. You can then bring the program back to the foreground and trigger an `OnResume` call by selecting the application from the home menu (on iOS devices or Android devices) or by pressing the **Back** button (on Android and Windows Phone devices).

If your Xamarin.Forms program is running and you invoke the phone's application switcher—by pressing the **Home** button twice on iOS devices, by pressing the **Multitask** button on Android devices (or by holding down the **Home** button on older Android devices), or by holding down the **Back** button on a Windows Phone—the application gets an `OnSleep` call. If you then select that program, the application gets an `OnResume` call as it resumes execution. If you instead terminate the application—by swiping the application's image upward on iOS devices or by tapping the X on the upper-right corner of the application's image on Android and Windows Phone devices—the program stops executing with no further notification.

So here's the basic rule: Whenever your application gets a call to `OnSleep`, you should ensure that the `Properties` dictionary contains all the information about the application you want to save.

If you're using lifecycle events solely for saving and restoring program data, you don't need to handle the `OnResume` method. When your program gets an `OnResume` call, the operating system has already automatically restored the program contents and state. If you want to, you can use `OnResume` as an opportunity to clear out the `Properties` dictionary because you are assured of getting another `OnSleep` call before your program terminates. However, if your program has established a connection with a web service—or is in the process of establishing such a connection—you might want to use `OnResume` to restore that connection. Perhaps the connection has timed out in the interval that the program was inactive. Or perhaps some fresh data is available.

You have some flexibility when you restore the data from the `Properties` dictionary to your application as your program starts running. When a Xamarin.Forms program starts up, the first opportunity you have to execute some code in the Portable Class Library is the constructor of the `App` class. At that time, the `Properties` dictionary has already been filled with the saved data from platform-specific storage. The next code that executes is generally the constructor of the first page in your application instantiated from the `App` constructor. The `OnStart` call in `Application` (and `App`) follows that, and then an overridable method called `OnAppearing` is called in the page class. You can retrieve the data at any time during this startup process.

The data that an application needs to save is usually in a page class, but the `OnSleep` override is in the `App` class. So somehow the page class and the `App` class must communicate. One approach is to define an `OnSleep` method in the page class that saves the data to the `Properties` dictionary and then call the page's `OnSleep` method from the `OnSleep` method in `App`. This approach works fine for a single-page application—indeed, the `Application` class has a static property named `MainPage` that is set in the `App` constructor and which the `OnSleep` method can use to get access to that page—but it doesn't work nearly as well for multipage applications.

Here's a somewhat different approach: You first define all the data you need to save as public properties in the `App` class, for example:

```
public class App : Application
{
    public App()
    {
        ...
    }

    public string DisplayLabelText { set; get; }
    ...

}
```

The page class (or classes) can then set and retrieve those properties when convenient. The `App` class can restore any such properties from the `Properties` dictionary in its constructor prior to instantiating the page and can store the properties in the `Properties` dictionary in its `OnSleep` override.

That's the approach taken by the **PersistentKeypad** project. This program is identical to **SimplestKeypad** except that it includes code to save and restore the contents of the keypad. Here's the `App` class that maintains a public `DisplayLabelText` property that is saved in the `OnSleep` override and loaded in the `App` constructor:

```
namespace PersistentKeypad
{
    public class App : Application
    {
        const string displayLabelText = "displayLabelText";

        public App()
        {
            if (Properties.ContainsKey(displayLabelText))
            {
                DisplayLabelText = (string)Properties[displayLabelText];
            }
```

```
        MainPage = new PersistentKeypadPage();
    }

    public string DisplayLabelText { set; get; }

    protected override void OnStart()
    {
        // Handle when your app starts
    }

    protected override void OnSleep()
    {
        // Handle when your app sleeps
        Properties[displayLabelText] = DisplayLabelText;
    }

    protected override void OnResume()
    {
        // Handle when your app resumes
    }
}
}
```

To avoid spelling errors, the App class defines the string dictionary key as a constant. It's the same as the property name except that it begins with a lowercase letter. Notice that the DisplayLabelText property is set prior to instantiating PersistentKeypadPage so that it's available in the PersistentKeypadPage constructor.

An application with many more items might want to consolidate them in a class named AppSettings (for example), serialize that class to an XML or a JSON string, and then save the string in the dictionary.

The PersistentKeypadPage class accesses that DisplayLabelText property in its constructor and sets the property in its two event handlers:

```
public class PersistentKeypadPage : ContentPage
{
    Label displayLabel;
    Button backspaceButton;

    public PersistentKeypadPage()
    {

        ...

        // New code for loading previous keypad text.
        App app = Application.Current as App;
        displayLabel.Text = app.DisplayLabelText;
        backspaceButton.IsEnabled = displayLabel.Text != null &&
                                    displayLabel.Text.Length > 0;

    }
```

```
void OnDigitButtonClicked(object sender, EventArgs args)
{
    Button button = (Button)sender;
    displayLabel.Text += (string)button.StyleId;
    backspaceButton.IsEnabled = true;

    // Save keypad text.
    App app = Application.Current as App;
    app.DisplayLabelText = displayLabel.Text;
}

void OnBackspaceButtonClicked(object sender, EventArgs args)
{
    string text = displayLabel.Text;
    displayLabel.Text = text.Substring(0, text.Length - 1);
    backspaceButton.IsEnabled = displayLabel.Text.Length > 0;

    // Save keypad text.
    App app = Application.Current as App;
    app.DisplayLabelText = displayLabel.Text;
}
}
```

When testing programs that use the `Properties` dictionary and application lifecycle events, you'll want to occasionally uninstall the program from the phone or simulator. Uninstalling a program from a device also deletes any stored data, so the next time the program is deployed from Visual Studio or Xamarin Studio, the program encounters an empty dictionary, as though it were being run for the very first time.

Chapter 7
XAML vs. code

C# is undoubtedly one of the greatest programming languages the world has ever seen. You can write entire Xamarin.Forms applications in C#, and it's conceivable that you've found C# to be so ideally suited for Xamarin.Forms that you haven't even considered using anything else.

But keep an open mind. Xamarin.Forms provides an alternative to C# that has some distinct advantages for certain aspects of program development. This alternative is XAML (pronounced "zammel"), which stands for the Extensible Application Markup Language. Like C#, XAML was developed at Microsoft Corporation, and it is only a few years younger than C#.

As its name suggests, XAML adheres to the syntax of XML, the Extensible Markup Language. This book assumes that you have familiarity with the basic concepts and syntax of XML.

In the most general sense, XAML is a declarative markup language used for instantiating and initializing objects. That definition might seem excessively general, and XAML is indeed quite flexible. But most real-world XAML has been used for defining tree-structured visual user interfaces characteristic of graphical programming environments. The history of XAML-based user interfaces begins with the Windows Presentation Foundation (WPF) and continues with Silverlight, Windows Phone 7 and 8, and Windows 8 and 10. Each of these XAML implementations supports a somewhat different set of visual elements defined by the particular platform. Likewise, the XAML implementation in Xamarin.Forms supports the visual elements defined by Xamarin.Forms, such as `Label`, `BoxView`, `Frame`, `Button`, `StackLayout`, and `ContentPage`.

As you've seen, a Xamarin.Forms application written entirely in code generally defines the initial appearance of its user interface in the constructor of a class that derives from `ContentPage`. If you choose to use XAML, the markup generally replaces this constructor code. You will find that XAML provides a more succinct and elegant definition of the user interface and has a visual structure that better mimics the tree organization of the visual elements on the page.

XAML is also generally easier to maintain and modify than equivalent code. Because XAML is XML, it is also potentially toolable: XAML can more easily be parsed and edited by software tools than the equivalent C# code. Indeed, an early impetus behind XAML was to facilitate a collaboration between programmers and designers: Designers can use design tools that generate XAML, while programmers focus on the code that interacts with the markup. While this vision has perhaps only rarely been fulfilled to perfection, it certainly suggests how applications can be structured to accommodate XAML. You use XAML for the visuals and code for the underlying logic.

Yet, XAML goes beyond that simple division of labor. As you'll see in a future chapter, it's possible to define bindings right in the XAML that link user-interface objects with underlying data.

When creating XAML for Microsoft platforms, some developers use interactive design tools such as Microsoft Blend, but many others prefer to handwrite XAML. No design tools are available for Xamarin.Forms, so handwriting is the only option. Obviously, all the XAML examples in this book are handwritten. But even when design tools are available, the ability to handwrite XAML is an important skill.

The prospect of handwriting XAML might cause some consternation among developers for another reason: XML is notoriously verbose. Yet, you'll see almost immediately that XAML is often more concise than the equivalent C# code. The real power of XAML becomes evident only incrementally, however, and won't be fully apparent until Chapter 19, "Collection views," when you use XAML for constructing templates for multiple items displayed in a `ListView`.

It is natural for programmers who prefer strongly typed languages such as C# to be skeptical of a markup language where everything is a text string. But you'll see shortly how XAML is a very strict analog of programming code. Much of what's allowed in your XAML files is defined by the classes and properties that make up the Xamarin.Forms application programming interface. For this reason, you might even begin to think of XAML as a "strongly typed" markup language. The XAML parser does its job in a very mechanical manner based on the underlying API infrastructure. One of the objectives of this chapter and the next is to demystify XAML and illuminate what happens when the XAML is parsed.

Yet, code and markup are very different: Code defines a process while markup defines a state. XAML has several deficiencies that are intrinsic to markup languages: XAML has no loops, no flow control, no algebraic calculation syntax, and no event handlers. However, XAML defines several features that help compensate for some of these deficiencies. You'll see many of these features in future chapters.

If you do not want to use XAML, you don't need to. Anything that can be done in XAML can be done in C#. But watch out: Sometimes developers get a little taste of XAML and get carried away and try to do everything in XAML! As usual, the best rule is "moderation in all things." Many of the best techniques involve combining code and XAML in interactive ways.

Let's begin this exploration with a few snippets of code and the equivalent XAML, and then see how XAML and code fit together in a Xamarin.Forms application.

Properties and attributes

Here is a Xamarin.Forms `Label` instantiated and initialized in code, much as it might appear in the constructor of a page class:

```
new Label
{
    Text = "Hello from Code!",
    IsVisible = true,
    Opacity = 0.75,
    HorizontalTextAlignment = TextAlignment.Center,
    VerticalOptions = LayoutOptions.CenterAndExpand,
    TextColor = Color.Blue,
```

```
    BackgroundColor = Color.FromRgb(255, 128, 128),
    FontSize = Device.GetNamedSize(NamedSize.Large, typeof(Label)),
    FontAttributes = FontAttributes.Bold | FontAttributes.Italic
};
```

Here is a very similar `Label` instantiated and initialized in XAML, which you can see immediately is more concise than the equivalent code:

```
<Label Text="Hello from XAML!"
       IsVisible="True"
       Opacity="0.75"
       HorizontalTextAlignment="Center"
       VerticalOptions="CenterAndExpand"
       TextColor="Blue"
       BackgroundColor="#FF8080"
       FontSize="Large"
       FontAttributes="Bold,Italic" />
```

Xamarin.Forms classes such as `Label` become XML elements in XAML. Properties such as `Text`, `IsVisible`, and the rest become XML attributes in XAML.

To be instantiated in XAML, a class such as `Label` must have a public parameterless constructor. (In the next chapter, you'll see that there is a technique to pass arguments to a constructor in XAML, but it's generally used for special purposes.) The properties set in XAML must have public `set` accessors. By convention, spaces surround an equal sign in code but not in XML (or XAML), but you can use as much white space as you want.

The concision of the XAML results mostly from the brevity of the attribute values—for example, the use of the word "Large" rather than a call to the `Device.GetNamedSize` method. These abbreviations are not built into the XAML parser. The XAML parser is instead assisted by various converter classes defined specifically for this purpose.

When the XAML parser encounters the `Label` element, it can use reflection to determine whether Xamarin.Forms has a class named `Label`, and if so, it can instantiate that class. Now it is ready to initialize that object. The `Text` property is of type `string`, and the attribute value is simply assigned to that property.

Because XAML is XML, you can include Unicode characters in the text by using the standard XML syntax. Precede the decimal Unicode value with `&#` (or the hexadecimal Unicode value with `&#x`) and follow it with a semicolon:

```
Text="Cost &#x2014; &#x20AC;123.45"
```

Those are the Unicode values for the em dash and euro symbol. To force a line break, use the line-feed character `&#x000A,` or (because leading zeros aren't required) `&#xA,` or, in decimal, `&#10.`

Angle brackets, ampersands, and quotation marks have a special meaning in XML, so to include those characters in a text string, use one of the standard predefined entities:

- `&lt;` for <

- `&gt;` for >

- `&amp;` for &

- `&apos;` for '

- `&quot;` for "

The HTML predefined entities such as ` ` are not supported. For a nonbreaking space use ` ` instead.

In addition, in Chapter 10, "XAML markup extensions," you'll discover that curly braces ({ and }) have a special meaning in XAML. If you need to begin an attribute value with a left curly brace, begin it with a pair of curly braces ({}) and then the left curly brace.

Back to the example: The `IsVisible` and `Opacity` properties of `Label` are of type `bool` and `double`, respectively, and these are as simple as you might expect. The XAML parser uses the `Boolean.Parse` and `Double.Parse` methods to convert the attribute values. The `Boolean.Parse` method is case insensitive, but generally Boolean values are capitalized as "True" and "False" in XAML. The `Double.Parse` method is passed a `CultureInfo.InvariantCulture` argument, so the conversion doesn't depend on the local culture of the programmer or user.

The `HorizontalTextAlignment` property of `Label` is of type `TextAlignment`, which is an enumeration. For any property that is an enumeration type, the XAML parser uses the `Enum.Parse` method to convert from the string to the value.

The `VerticalOptions` property is of type `LayoutOptions`, a structure. When the XAML parser references the `LayoutOptions` structure using reflection, it discovers that the structure has a C# attribute defined:

```
[TypeConverter (typeof(LayoutOptionsConverter))]
public struct LayoutOptions
{
    …
}
```

(Watch out! This discussion involves two types of attributes: XML attributes such as `HorizontalTextAlignment` and C# attributes such as this `TypeConverter`.)

The `TypeConverter` attribute is supported by a class named `TypeConverterAttribute`. This particular `TypeConverter` attribute on `LayoutOptions` references a class named `LayoutOptionsConverter`, which derives from a public abstract class named `TypeConverter` that defines methods named `CanConvertFrom` and `ConvertFrom`. When the XAML parser encounters this `TypeConverter` attribute, it instantiates the `LayoutOptionsConverter`. The `VerticalOptions` attribute in the XAML is assigned the string "Center", so the XAML parser passes that "Center" string to the `ConvertFrom` method of `LayoutOptionsConverter`, and out pops a `LayoutOptions` value. This is assigned to the `VerticalOptions` property of the `Label` object.

Similarly, when the XAML parser encounters the `TextColor` and `BackgroundColor` properties, it uses reflection to determine that those properties are of type `Color`. The `Color` structure is also adorned with a `TypeConverter` attribute:

```
[TypeConverter (typeof(ColorTypeConverter))]
public struct Color
{
    …
}
```

You can create an instance of `ColorTypeConverter` and experiment with it in code if you'd like. It accepts color definitions in several formats: It can convert a string like "Blue" to the `Color.Blue` value, and the "Default" and "Accent" strings to the `Color.Default` and `Color.Accent` values. `Color-TypeConverter` can also parse strings that encode red-green-blue values, such as "#FF8080", which is a red value of 0xFF, a green value of 0x80, and a blue value also of 0x80.

All numeric RGB values begin with a number-sign prefix, but that prefix can be followed with eight, six, four, or three hexadecimal digits for specifying color values with or without an alpha channel. Here's the most extensive syntax:

```
BackgroundColor="#aarrggbb"
```

Each of the letters represents a hexadecimal digit, in the order alpha (opacity), red, green, and blue. For the alpha channel, keep in mind that 0xFF is fully opaque and 0x00 is fully transparent. Here's the syntax without an alpha channel:

```
BackgroundColor="#rrggbb"
```

In this case the alpha value is set to 0xFF for full opacity.

Two other formats allow you to specify only a single hexadecimal digit for each channel:

```
BackgroundColor="#argb"
BackgroundColor="#rgb"
```

In these cases, the digit is repeated to form the value. For example, #CF3 is the RGB color 0xCC-0xFF-0x33. These short formats are rarely used.

The `FontSize` property of `Label` is of type `double`. This is a little different from properties of type `LayoutOptions` and `Color`. The `LayoutOptions` and `Color` structures are part of Xamarin.Forms, so they can be flagged with the C# `TypeConverter` attribute, but it's not possible to flag the .NET `Double` structure with a `TypeConverter` attribute just for font sizes!

Instead, the `FontSize` property within the `Label` class has the `TypeConverter` attribute:

```
public class Label : View, IFontElement
{
    …
    [TypeConverter (typeof (FontSizeConverter))]
    public double FontSize
    {
```

```
        ...
    }
        ...
}
```

The `FontSizeConverter` class determines whether the string passed to it is one of the members of the `NamedSize` enumeration. If not, `FontSizeConverter` assumes the value is a `double`.

The last attribute set in the example is `FontAttributes`. The `FontAttributes` property is an enumeration named `FontAttributes`, and you already know that the XAML parser handles enumeration types automatically. However, the `FontAttributes` enumeration has a C# `Flags` attribute set like so:

```
[Flags]
public enum FontAttributes
{
    None = 0,
    Bold = 1,
    Italic = 2
}
```

The XAML parser therefore allows multiple members separated by commas:

```
FontAttributes="Bold,Italic"
```

This demonstration of the mechanical nature of the XAML parser should be very good news. It means that you can include custom classes in XAML, and these classes can have properties of custom types, or the properties can be of standard types but allow additional values. All you need is to flag these types or properties with a C# `TypeConverter` attribute and provide a class that derives from `TypeConverter`.

Property-element syntax

Here is some C# that is similar to the **FramedText** code in Chapter 4. In one statement it instantiates a `Frame` and a `Label` and sets the `Label` to the `Content` property of the `Frame`:

```
new Frame
{
    OutlineColor = Color.Accent,
    HorizontalOptions = LayoutOptions.Center,
    VerticalOptions = LayoutOptions.Center,
    Content = new Label
    {
        Text = "Greetings, Xamarin.Forms!"
    }
};
```

But when you start to duplicate this in XAML, you might become a little stymied at the point where you set the `Content` attribute:

```
<Frame OutlineColor="Accent"
```

```
             HorizontalOptions="Center"
             VerticalOptions="Center"
             Content=" what goes here? " />
```

How can that `Content` attribute be set to an entire `Label` object?

The solution to this problem is the most fundamental feature of XAML syntax. The first step is to separate the `Frame` tag into start and end tags:

```
<Frame OutlineColor="Accent"
       HorizontalOptions="Center"
       VerticalOptions="Center">

</Frame>
```

Within those tags, add two more tags that consist of the element (`Frame`) and the property you want to set (`Content`) connected with a period:

```
<Frame OutlineColor="Accent"
       HorizontalOptions="Center"
       VerticalOptions="Center">
    <Frame.Content>

    </Frame.Content>
</Frame>
```

Now put the `Label` within those tags:

```
<Frame OutlineColor="Accent"
       HorizontalOptions="Center"
       VerticalOptions="Center">
    <Frame.Content>
        <Label Text="Greetings, Xamarin.Forms!" />
    </Frame.Content>
</Frame>
```

That syntax is how you set a `Label` to the `Content` property of the `Frame`.

You might wonder if this XAML feature violates XML syntax rules. It does not. The period has no special meaning in XML, so `Frame.Content` is a perfectly valid XML tag. However, XAML imposes its own rules about these tags: The `Frame.Content` tags must appear within `Frame` tags, and no attributes can be set in the `Frame.Content` tag. The object set to the `Content` property appears as the XML content of those tags.

Once this syntax is introduced, some terminology becomes necessary. In the final XAML snippet shown above:

- `Frame` and `Label` are C# objects expressed as XML elements. They are called *object elements*.

- `OutlineColor`, `HorizontalOptions`, `VerticalOptions`, and `Text` are C# properties expressed as XML attributes. They are called *property attributes*.

- `Frame.Content` is a C# property expressed as an XML element, and it is therefore called a *property element*.

Property elements are very common in real-life XAML. You'll see numerous examples in this chapter and future chapters, and you'll soon find property elements becoming second nature to your use of XAML. But watch out: Sometimes developers must remember so much that we forget the basics. Even after you've been using XAML for a while, you'll probably encounter a situation where it doesn't seem possible to set a particular object to a particular property. The solution is very often a property element.

You can also use property-element syntax for simpler properties, for example:

```
<Frame HorizontalOptions="Center">
    <Frame.VerticalOptions>
        Center
    </Frame.VerticalOptions>
    <Frame.OutlineColor>
        Accent
    </Frame.OutlineColor>
    <Frame.Content>
        <Label>
            <Label.Text>
                Greetings, Xamarin.Forms!
            </Label.Text>
        </Label>
    </Frame.Content>
</Frame>
```

Now the `VerticalOptions` and `OutlineColor` properties of `Frame` and the `Text` property of `Label` have all become property elements. The value of these attributes is always the content of the property element without quotation marks.

Of course, it doesn't make much sense to define these properties as property elements. It's unnecessarily verbose. But it works as it should.

Let's go a little further: Instead of setting `HorizontalOptions` to "Center" (corresponding to the static property `LayoutOptions.Center`), you can express `HorizontalOptions` as a property element and set it to a `LayoutOptions` value with its individual properties set:

```
<Frame>
    <Frame.HorizontalOptions>
        <LayoutOptions Alignment="Center"
                       Expands="False" />
    </Frame.HorizontalOptions>
    <Frame.VerticalOptions>
        Center
    </Frame.VerticalOptions>
    <Frame.OutlineColor>
        Accent
    </Frame.OutlineColor>
    <Frame.Content>
```

```
            <Label>
                <Label.Text>
                    Greetings, Xamarin.Forms!
                </Label.Text>
            </Label>
        </Frame.Content>
</Frame>
```

And you can also express these properties of `LayoutOptions` as property elements:

```
<Frame>
    <Frame.HorizontalOptions>
        <LayoutOptions>
            <LayoutOptions.Alignment>
                Center
            </LayoutOptions.Alignment>
            <LayoutOptions.Expands>
                False
            </LayoutOptions.Expands>
        </LayoutOptions>
    </Frame.HorizontalOptions>
    ...
</Frame>
```

You can't set the same property as a property attribute and a property element. That's setting the property twice, and it's not allowed. And remember that nothing else can appear in the property-element tags. The value being set to the property is always the XML content of those tags.

Now you should know how to use a `StackLayout` in XAML. First express the `Children` property as the property element `StackLayout.Children`, and then include the children of the `StackLayout` as XML content of the property-element tags. Here's an example where each child of the first `StackLayout` is another `StackLayout` with a horizontal orientation:

```
<StackLayout>
    <StackLayout.Children>
        <StackLayout Orientation="Horizontal">
            <StackLayout.Children>
                <BoxView Color="Red" />
                <Label Text="Red"
                       VerticalOptions="Center" />
            </StackLayout.Children>
        </StackLayout>

        <StackLayout Orientation="Horizontal">
            <StackLayout.Children>
                <BoxView Color="Green" />
                <Label Text="Green"
                       VerticalOptions="Center" />
            </StackLayout.Children>
        </StackLayout>

        <StackLayout Orientation="Horizontal">
            <StackLayout.Children>
```

```
                    <BoxView Color="Blue" />
                    <Label Text="Blue"
                           VerticalOptions="Center" />
                </StackLayout.Children>
            </StackLayout>
        </StackLayout.Children>
    </StackLayout>
```

Each horizontal `StackLayout` has a `BoxView` with a color and a `Label` with that color name.

Of course, the repetitive markup here looks rather scary! What if you wanted to display 16 colors? Or 140? You might succeed at first with a lot of copying and pasting, but if you then needed to refine the visuals a bit, you'd be in bad shape. In code you'd do this in a loop, but XAML has no such feature.

When markup threatens to be overly repetitious, you can always use code. Defining some of a user interface in XAML and the rest in code is perfectly reasonable. But there are other solutions, as you'll see in later chapters.

Adding a XAML page to your project

Now that you've seen some snippets of XAML, let's look at a whole XAML page in the context of a complete program. First, create a Xamarin.Forms solution named **CodePlusXaml** using the Portable Class Library solution template.

Now add a XAML `ContentPage` to the PCL. Here's how: In Visual Studio, right-click the **CodePlusXaml** project in the **Solution Explorer**. Select **Add > New Item** from the menu. In the **Add New Item** dialog, select **Visual C#** and **Cross-Platform** at the left, and **Forms Xaml Page** from the central list. Name it CodePlusXamlPage.cs.

In Xamarin Studio, invoke the drop-down menu on the **CodePlusXaml** project in the **Solution** list, and select **Add > New File**. In the **New File** dialog, select **Forms** at the left and **Forms ContentPage Xaml** in the central list. (Watch out: There's also a **Forms ContentView Xaml** in the list. You want a content *page*.) Name it CodePlusXamlPage.

In either case, two files are created:

- CodePlusXamlPage.xaml, the XAML file; and

- CodePlusXamlPage.xaml.cs, a C# file (despite the odd double extension on the filename).

In the file list, the second file is indented underneath the first, indicating their close relationship. The C# file is often referred to as the *code-behind* of the XAML file. It contains code that supports the markup. These two files both contribute to a class named `CodePlusXamlPage` that derives from `ContentPage`.

Let's examine the code file first. Excluding the `using` directives, it looks like this:

```
namespace CodePlusXaml
{
    public partial class CodePlusXamlPage : ContentPage
    {
        public CodePlusXamlPage()
        {
            InitializeComponent();
        }
    }
}
```

It is indeed a class named `CodePlusXamlPage` that derives from `ContentPage`, just as anticipated. However, the class definition includes a `partial` keyword, which usually indicates that this is only part of the `CodePlusXamlPage` class definition. Somewhere else there should be another partial class definition for `CodePlusXamlPage`. So if it exists, where is it? It's a mystery! (For now.)

Another mystery is the `InitializeComponent` method that the constructor calls. Judging solely from the syntax, it seems as though this method should be defined or inherited by `ContentPage`. Yet you won't find `InitializeComponent` in the API documentation.

Let's set those two mysteries aside temporarily and look at the XAML file. The Visual Studio and Xamarin Studio templates generate two somewhat different XAML files. If you're using Visual Studio, delete the markup for the `Label` and replace it with `ContentPage.Content` property-element tags so that it looks like the version in Xamarin Studio:

```
<ContentPage xmlns="http://xamarin.com/schemas/2014/forms"
             xmlns:x="http://schemas.microsoft.com/winfx/2009/xaml"
             x:Class="CodePlusXaml.CodePlusXamlPage">
    <ContentPage.Content>
    </ContentPage.Content>
</ContentPage>
```

The root element is `ContentPage`, which is the class that `CodePlusXamlPage` derives from. That tag begins with two XML namespace declarations, both of which are URIs. But don't bother checking the web addresses! There's nothing there. These URIs simply indicate who owns the namespace and what function it serves.

The default namespace belongs to Xamarin. This is the XML namespace for elements in the file with no prefix, such as the `ContentPage` tag. The URI includes the year that this namespace came into being and the word `forms` as an abbreviation for Xamarin.Forms.

The second namespace is associated with a prefix of `x` by convention, and it belongs to Microsoft. This namespace refers to elements and attributes that are intrinsic to XAML and are found in every XAML implementation. The word `winfx` refers to a name once used for the .NET Framework 3.0, which introduced WPF and XAML. The year 2009 refers to a particular XAML specification, which also implies a particular collection of elements and attributes that build upon the original XAML specification, which is dated 2006. However, Xamarin.Forms implements only a subset of the elements and attributes in the 2009 specification.

The next line is one of the attributes that is intrinsic to XAML, called `Class`. Because the `x` prefix is almost universally used for this namespace, this attribute is commonly referred to as `x:Class` and pronounced "x class."

The `x:Class` attribute can appear only on the root element of a XAML file. It specifies the .NET namespace and name of a derived class. The base class of this derived class is the root element. In other words, this `x:Class` specification indicates that the `CodePlusXamlPage` class in the `CodePlusXaml` namespace derives from `ContentPage`. That's exactly the same information as the `CodePlusXamlPage` class definition in the CodePlusXamlPage.xaml.cs file.

Let's add some content to this `ContentPage` in the XAML file. This requires setting something to the `Content` property, which in the XAML file means putting something between `ContentPage.Content` property-element tags. Begin the content with a `StackLayout`, and then add a `Label` to the `Children` property:

```xml
<ContentPage xmlns="http://xamarin.com/schemas/2014/forms"
             xmlns:x="http://schemas.microsoft.com/winfx/2009/xaml"
             x:Class="CodePlusXaml.CodePlusXamlPage">
    <ContentPage.Content>
        <StackLayout>
            <StackLayout.Children>
                <Label Text="Hello from XAML!"
                       IsVisible="True"
                       Opacity="0.75"
                       HorizontalTextAlignment="Center"
                       VerticalOptions="CenterAndExpand"
                       TextColor="Blue"
                       BackgroundColor="#FF8080"
                       FontSize="Large"
                       FontAttributes="Bold,Italic" />
            </StackLayout.Children>
        </StackLayout>
    </ContentPage.Content>
</ContentPage>
```

That's the XAML `Label` you saw at the beginning of this chapter.

You'll now need to change the `App` class to instantiate this page just like you do with a code-only derivative of `ContentPage`:

```csharp
namespace CodePlusXaml
{
    public class App : Application
    {
        public App()
        {
            MainPage = new CodePlusXamlPage();
        }
        ...
    }
}
```

You can now build and deploy this program. After you do so, it's possible to clear up a couple of mysteries encountered earlier in this section:

In Visual Studio, in the **Solution Explorer**, select the **CodePlusXaml** project, find the icon at the top with the tooltip **Show All Files**, and toggle that on.

In Xamarin Studio, in the **Solution** file list, invoke the drop-down menu for the whole solution, and select **Display Options > Show All Files**.

In the **CodePlusXaml** Portable Class Library project, find the **obj** folder and within that, the **Debug** folder. You'll see a file named CodePlusXamlPage.xaml.g.cs. Notice the *g* in the filename. That stands for *generated*. Here it is, complete with the comment that tells you that this file is generated by a tool:

```
//------------------------------------------------------------------------------
// <auto-generated>
//     This code was generated by a tool.
//     Runtime Version:4.0.30319.42000
//
//     Changes to this file may cause incorrect behavior and will be lost if
//     the code is regenerated.
// </auto-generated>
//------------------------------------------------------------------------------

namespace CodePlusXaml {
    using System;
    using Xamarin.Forms;
    using Xamarin.Forms.Xaml;

    public partial class CodePlusXamlPage : global::Xamarin.Forms.ContentPage {

        [System.CodeDom.Compiler.GeneratedCodeAttribute("Xamarin.Forms.Build.Tasks.XamlG",
                                                         "0.0.0.0")]
        private void InitializeComponent() {
            this.LoadFromXaml(typeof(CodePlusXamlPage));
        }
    }
}
```

During the build process, the XAML file is parsed, and this code file is generated. Notice that it's a partial class definition of `CodePlusXamlPage`, which derives from `ContentPage`, and the class contains a method named `InitializeComponent`.

In other words, it's a perfect fit for the CodePlusXamlPage.xaml.cs code-behind file. After the CodePlusXamlPage.xaml.g.cs file is generated, the two files can be compiled together as if they were just normal C# partial class definitions.

At run time, the `App` class instantiates the `CodePlusXamlPage` class. The `CodePlusXamlPage` constructor (defined in the code-behind file) calls `InitializeComponent` (defined in the generated file), and `InitializeComponent` calls `LoadFromXaml`. This is an extension method for `View` defined in the `Extensions` class in the **Xamarin.Forms.Xaml** assembly. What `LoadFromXaml` does depends on whether you've chosen to compile the XAML or not (as discussed in the next section). But when the `InitializeComponent` method returns, the whole page is in place, just as though everything had been instantiated and initialized in code in the `CodePlusXamlPage` constructor.

It's possible to continue adding content to the page in the constructor of the code-behind file, but only after the `InitializeComponent` call returns. Let's take this opportunity to create another `Label` by using some code from earlier in this chapter:

```
namespace CodePlusXaml
{
    public partial class CodePlusXamlPage : ContentPage
    {
        public CodePlusXamlPage()
        {
            InitializeComponent();

            Label label = new Label
            {
                Text = "Hello from Code!",
                IsVisible = true,
                Opacity = 0.75,
                HorizontalTextAlignment = TextAlignment.Center,
                VerticalOptions = LayoutOptions.CenterAndExpand,
                TextColor = Color.Blue,
                BackgroundColor = Color.FromRgb(255, 128, 128),
                FontSize = Device.GetNamedSize(NamedSize.Large, typeof(Label)),
                FontAttributes = FontAttributes.Bold | FontAttributes.Italic
            };

            (Content as StackLayout).Children.Insert(0, label);
        }
    }
}
```

The constructor concludes by accessing the `StackLayout` that we know is set to the `Content` property of the page and inserting the `Label` at the top. (In the next chapter, you'll see a much better way to reference objects in the XAML file by using the `x:Name` attribute.) You can create the `Label` prior to the `InitializeComponent` call, but you can't add it to the `StackLayout` at that time because `InitializeComponent` is what causes the `StackLayout` (and all the other XAML elements) to be instantiated. Here's the result:

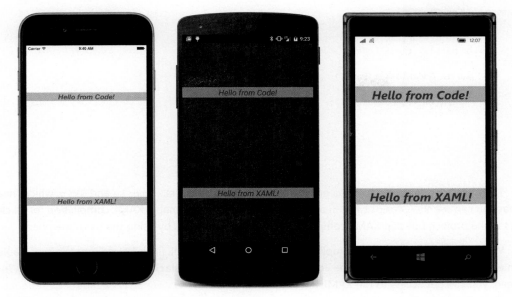

Aside from the text, the two buttons are identical.

You don't have to spend much time examining the generated code file that the XAML parser cre-ates, but it's helpful to understand how the XAML file plays a role both in the build process and during run time. Also, sometimes an error in the XAML file raises a run-time exception at the `LoadFromXaml` call, so you will probably see the generated code file pop up frequently, and you should know what it is.

The XAML compiler

You have an option whether to compile the XAML during the build process. Compiling the XAML per-forms validity checks during the build process, reduces the size of the executable, and improves load-ing time, but it's somewhat newer than the noncompilation approach, so there might be issues sometimes.

To indicate that you want to compile all the XAML files in your application, you can insert the fol-lowing assembly attribute somewhere in a code file. The most convenient place is the Assembly.cs file in the **Properties** folder of the PCL project:

```
[assembly: XamlCompilation(XamlCompilationOptions.Compile)]
```

You can put it in another C# file, but because it's an assembly attribute, it needs to be outside any `namespace` block. You'll also need a `using` directive for `Xamarin.Forms.Xaml`.

You can alternatively specify that the XAML file for a particular class is compiled:

```
namespace CodePlusXaml
{
    [XamlCompilation(XamlCompilationOptions.Compile)]
    public partial class CodePlusXamlPage : ContentPage
    {
        public CodePlusXamlPage()
        {
            InitializeComponent();

            …
        }
    }
}
```

The `XamlCompilationOptions` enumeration has two members, `Compile` and `Skip`, which means that you can use `XamlCompilation` as an assembly attribute to enable XAML compilation for all classes in the project, but skip XAML compilation for individual classes by using the `Skip` member.

When you do *not* choose to compile the XAML, the entire XAML file is bound into the executable as an embedded resource, just like the Edgar Allan Poe story in the **BlackCat** program in Chapter 4. Indeed, you can get access to the XAML file at run time by using the `GetManifestResourceStream` method. That's similar to what the `LoadFromXaml` call in `InitializeComponent` does. It loads the XAML file and parses it for a second time, instantiating and initializing all the elements in the XAML file except for the root element, which already exists.

When you choose to compile the XAML, this process is streamlined somewhat, but the `LoadFromXaml` method still needs to instantiate all the elements and build a visual tree.

Platform specificity in the XAML file

Here is the XAML file for a program named **ScaryColorList** that's similar to a snippet of XAML that you saw earlier. But now the repetition is even scarier because each color item is surrounded by a `Frame`:

```xml
<ContentPage xmlns="http://xamarin.com/schemas/2014/forms"
             xmlns:x="http://schemas.microsoft.com/winfx/2009/xaml"
             x:Class="ScaryColorList.ScaryColorListPage">
    <ContentPage.Content>
        <StackLayout>
            <StackLayout.Children>
                <Frame OutlineColor="Accent">
                    <Frame.Content>
                        <StackLayout Orientation="Horizontal">
                            <StackLayout.Children>
                                <BoxView Color="Red" />
                                <Label Text="Red"
                                       VerticalOptions="Center" />
                            </StackLayout.Children>
                        </StackLayout>
                    </Frame.Content>
```

```
            </Frame>

            <Frame OutlineColor="Accent">
                <Frame.Content>
                    <StackLayout Orientation="Horizontal">
                        <StackLayout.Children>
                            <BoxView Color="Green" />
                                <Label Text="Green"
                                       VerticalOptions="Center" />
                        </StackLayout.Children>
                    </StackLayout>
                </Frame.Content>
            </Frame>

            <Frame OutlineColor="Accent">
                <Frame.Content>
                    <StackLayout Orientation="Horizontal">
                        <StackLayout.Children>
                            <BoxView Color="Blue" />
                            <Label Text="Blue"
                                   VerticalOptions="Center" />
                        </StackLayout.Children>
                    </StackLayout>
                </Frame.Content>
            </Frame>
        </StackLayout.Children>
    </StackLayout>
  </ContentPage.Content>
</ContentPage>
```

The code-behind file contains only the standard call to InitializeComponent.

Aside from the repetitious markup, this program has a more practical problem: When it runs on iOS, the top item overlaps the status bar. This problem can be fixed with a call to Device.OnPlatform in the page's constructor (just as you saw in Chapter 2). Because Device.OnPlatform sets the Padding property on the page and doesn't require anything in the XAML file, it could go either before or after the InitializeComponent call. Here's one way to do it:

```
public partial class ScaryColorListPage : ContentPage
{
    public ScaryColorListPage()
    {
        Padding = Device.OnPlatform(new Thickness(0, 20, 0, 0),
                                    new Thickness(0),
                                    new Thickness(0));

        InitializeComponent();
    }
}
```

Or, you could set a uniform Padding value for all three platforms right in the root element of the XAML file:

```
<ContentPage xmlns="http://xamarin.com/schemas/2014/forms"
             xmlns:x="http://schemas.microsoft.com/winfx/2009/xaml"
             x:Class="ScaryColorList.ScaryColorListPage"
             Padding="0, 20, 0, 0">
    <ContentPage.Content>
       ...
    </ContentPage.Content>
</ContentPage>
```

That sets the `Padding` property for the page. The `ThicknessTypeConverter` class requires the values to be separated by commas, but you have the same flexibility as with the `Thickness` constructor. You can specify four values in the order left, top, right, and bottom; two values (the first for left and right, and the second for top and bottom); or one value.

However, you can also specify platform-specific values right in the XAML file by using the `OnPlatform` class, whose name suggests that it is similar in function to the `Device.OnPlatform` static method.

`OnPlatform` is a very interesting class, and it's worthwhile to gain a sense of how it works. The class is generic, and it has three properties of type `T`, as well as an implicit conversion of itself to `T` that makes use of the `Device.OS` value:

```
public class OnPlatform<T>
{
    public T iOS { get; set; }

    public T Android { get; set; }

    public T WinPhone { get; set; }

    public static implicit operator T(OnPlatform<T> onPlatform)
    {
        // returns one of the three properties based on Device.OS
    }
}
```

In theory, you might use the `OnPlatform<T>` class in code, perhaps like this in the constructor of a `ContentPage` derivative:

```
Padding = new OnPlatform<Thickness>
{
    iOS = new Thickness(0, 20, 0, 0),
    Android = new Thickness(0),
    WinPhone = new Thickness(0)
};
```

You can set an instance of this `OnPlatform` class directly to the `Padding` property because the `OnPlatform` class defines an implicit conversion of itself to the generic argument (in this case `Thickness`).

However, you shouldn't use `OnPlatform` in code. Use `Device.OnPlatform` instead. `OnPlatform` is designed for XAML, and the only really tricky part is figuring out how to specify the generic type argument.

Fortunately, the XAML 2009 specification includes an attribute designed specifically for generic classes, called `TypeArguments`. Because it's part of XAML itself, it's used with an `x` prefix, so it appears as `x:TypeArguments`. Here's how `OnPlatform` is used in XAML to select among three `Thickness` values:

```
<OnPlatform x:TypeArguments="Thickness"
            iOS="0, 20, 0, 0"
            Android="0"
            WinPhone="0" />
```

In this example (and in the previous code example), the `Android` and `WinPhone` settings aren't required because they are the defaults. Notice that the `Thickness` strings can be set directly to the properties because those properties are of type `Thickness`, and hence the XAML parser will use the `ThicknessTypeConverter` for converting those strings.

Now that we have the `OnPlatform` markup, how do we set it to the `Padding` property of the `Page`? By expressing `Padding` using property-element syntax, of course!

```
<ContentPage xmlns="http://xamarin.com/schemas/2014/forms"
             xmlns:x="http://schemas.microsoft.com/winfx/2009/xaml"
             x:Class="ScaryColorList.ScaryColorListPage">

    <ContentPage.Padding>
        <OnPlatform x:TypeArguments="Thickness"
                    iOS="0, 20, 0, 0" />
    </ContentPage.Padding>

    <ContentPage.Content>
        ...
    </ContentPage.Content>
</ContentPage>
```

This is how the **ScaryColorList** program appears in the collection of samples from this book and here's how it looks:

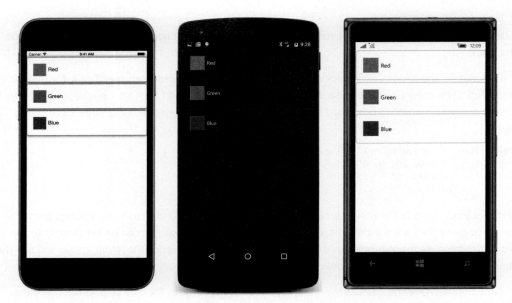

Similar to `OnDevice`, `OnIdiom` distinguishes between `Phone` and `Tablet`. For reasons that will become apparent in the next chapter, you should try to restrict the use of `OnDevice` and `OnIdiom` to small chunks of markup rather than large blocks. Their use shouldn't become a structural element in your XAML files.

The content property attribute

The XAML file in the **ScaryColorList** program is actually somewhat longer than it needs to be. You can delete the `ContentPage.Content` tags, all the `StackLayout.Children` tags, and all the `Frame.Content` tags, and the program will work the same:

```
<ContentPage xmlns="http://xamarin.com/schemas/2014/forms"
             xmlns:x="http://schemas.microsoft.com/winfx/2009/xaml"
             x:Class="ScaryColorList.ScaryColorListPage">

    <ContentPage.Padding>
        <OnPlatform x:TypeArguments="Thickness"
                    iOS="0, 20, 0, 0" />
    </ContentPage.Padding>

    <StackLayout>
        <Frame OutlineColor="Accent">
            <StackLayout Orientation="Horizontal">
                <BoxView Color="Red" />
                <Label Text="Red"
                       VerticalOptions="Center" />
            </StackLayout>
```

```
                </Frame>

            <Frame OutlineColor="Accent">
                <StackLayout Orientation="Horizontal">
                    <BoxView Color="Green" />
                    <Label Text="Green"
                           VerticalOptions="Center" />
                </StackLayout>
            </Frame>

            <Frame OutlineColor="Accent">
                <StackLayout Orientation="Horizontal">
                    <BoxView Color="Blue" />
                    <Label Text="Blue"
                           VerticalOptions="Center" />
                </StackLayout>
            </Frame>
        </StackLayout>
</ContentPage>
```

It looks a lot cleaner now. The only property element left is for the `Padding` property of `ContentPage`.

As with almost everything about XAML syntax, this elimination of some property elements is supported by the underlying classes. Every class used in XAML is allowed to define one property as a *content property* (sometimes also called the class's *default property*). For this content property, the property-element tags are not required, and any XML content within the start and end tags is automatically assigned to this property. Very conveniently, the content property of `ContentPage` is `Content`, the content property of `StackLayout` is `Children`, and the content property of `Frame` is `Content`.

These content properties are documented, but you need to know where to look. A class specifies its content property by using the `ContentPropertyAttribute`. If this attribute is attached to a class, it appears in the online Xamarin.Forms API documentation along with the class declaration. Here's how it appears in the documentation for `ContentPage`:

```
[Xamarin.Forms.ContentProperty("Content")]
public class ContentPage : TemplatedPage
```

If you say it aloud, it sounds a bit redundant: The `Content` property is the content property of `ContentPage`.

The declaration for the `Frame` class is similar:

```
[Xamarin.Forms.ContentProperty("Content")]
public class Frame : ContentView
```

`StackLayout` doesn't have a `ContentProperty` attribute applied, but `StackLayout` derives from `Layout<View>`, and `Layout<T>` has a `ContentProperty` attribute:

```
[Xamarin.Forms.ContentProperty("Children")]
public abstract class Layout<T> : Layout, IViewContainer<T>
where T : View
```

The ContentProperty attribute is inherited by the classes that derive from Layout<T>, so Children is the content property of StackLayout.

Certainly, there's no problem if you include the property elements when they're not required, but in most cases they will no longer appear in the sample programs in this book.

Formatted text

Text displayed by a XAML file might involve just a word or two, but sometimes an entire paragraph is required, perhaps with some embedded character formatting. Specifying character formatting is not always as obvious, or as easy, in XAML as might be suggested by our familiarity with HTML.

The **TextVariations** solution has a XAML file that contains seven Label views in a scrollable StackLayout:

```
<ContentPage xmlns="http://xamarin.com/schemas/2014/forms"
             xmlns:x="http://schemas.microsoft.com/winfx/2009/xaml"
             x:Class="TextVariations.TextVariationsPage">

    <ContentPage.Padding>
        <OnPlatform x:TypeArguments="Thickness"
                    iOS="0, 20, 0, 0" />
    </ContentPage.Padding>

    <ScrollView>
        <StackLayout>
            ...
        </StackLayout>
    </ScrollView>
</ContentPage>
```

Each of the seven Label views shows a somewhat different way of defining the displayed text. For reference purposes, here's the program running on all three platforms:

The simplest approach involves just setting a few words to the `Text` attribute of the `Label` element:

```
<Label VerticalOptions="CenterAndExpand"
       Text="Single lines of text are easy." />
```

You can also set the `Text` property by breaking it out as a property element:

```
<Label VerticalOptions="CenterAndExpand">
    <Label.Text>
        Text can also be content of the Text property.
    </Label.Text>
</Label>
```

`Text` is the content property of `Label`, so you don't need the `Label.Text` tags:

```
<Label VerticalOptions="CenterAndExpand">
    Text is the content property of Label.
</Label>
```

When you set text as the content of the `Label` (whether you use the `Label.Text` tags or not), the text is trimmed: all white space, including carriage returns, is removed from the beginning and end of the text. However, all embedded white space is retained, including end-of-line characters.

When you set the `Text` property as a property attribute, all white space within the quotation marks is retained, but if the text occupies more than one line in the XAML file, each end-of-line character (or character sequence) is converted to a single space.

As a result, displaying a whole paragraph of uniformly formatted text is somewhat problematic. The most foolproof approach is setting `Text` as a property attribute. You can put the whole paragraph as a single line in the XAML file, but if you prefer to use multiple lines, you should left justify the whole paragraph in the XAML file surrounded by quotation marks, like so:

```
<Label VerticalOptions="CenterAndExpand"
        Text=
"Perhaps the best way to define a paragraph of
uniformly formatted text is by setting the Text
property as an attribute and left justifying
the block of text in the XAML file. End-of-line
characters are converted to a space character." />
```

The end-of-line characters are converted to space characters so the individual lines are properly concatenated. But watch out: Don't leave any stray characters at the end or beginning of the individual lines. Those will show up as extraneous characters within the paragraph.

When multiple lines of text are specified as content of the Label, only white space at the beginning and end of the text is trimmed. All embedded white space is retained, including end-of-line characters:

```
<Label VerticalOptions="CenterAndExpand">
Text as content has the curse
Of breaks at each line's close.
That's a format great for verse
But not the best for prose.
    </Label>
```

This text is rendered as four separate lines. If you're displaying lists or poetry in your Xamarin.Forms application, that's exactly what you want. Otherwise, probably not.

If your line or paragraph of text requires some nonuniform paragraph formatting, you'll want to use the FormattedText property of Label. As you might recall, you set this to a FormattedString object and then set multiple Span objects to the Spans collection of the FormattedString. In XAML, you need property-element tags for Label.FormattedString, but Spans is the content property of FormattedString:

```
<Label VerticalOptions="CenterAndExpand">
    <Label.FormattedText>
        <FormattedString>
            <Span Text="A single line with " />
            <Span Text="bold" FontAttributes="Bold" />
            <Span Text=" and " />
            <Span Text="italic" FontAttributes="Italic" />
            <Span Text=" and " />
            <Span Text="large" FontSize="Large" />
            <Span Text=" text." />
        </FormattedString>
    </Label.FormattedText>
</Label>
```

Notice that the Text properties of the nonformatted items have spaces at the end or beginning of the text string, or both, so that the items don't run into each other.

In the general case, however, you might be working with an entire paragraph. You can set the `Text` attribute of `Span` to a long line, or you can wrap it on multiple lines. As with `Label`, keep the entire block left justified in the XAML file:

```
<Label VerticalOptions="CenterAndExpand">
    <Label.FormattedText>
        <FormattedString>
            <Span Text=
"A paragraph of formatted text requires left justifying
it within the XAML file. But the text can include multiple
kinds of character formatting, including " />
            <Span Text="bold" FontAttributes="Bold" />
            <Span Text=" and " />
            <Span Text="italic" FontAttributes="Italic" />
            <Span Text=" and " />
            <Span Text="large" FontSize="Large" />
            <Span Text=
" and whatever combinations you might desire to adorn
your glorious prose." />
        </FormattedString>
    </Label.FormattedText>
</Label>
```

You'll notice in the screenshot that the text with the large font size is aligned with the regular text on the baseline, which is the typographically proper approach, and the line spacing is adjusted to accommodate the larger text.

In most Xamarin.Forms programs, neither XAML nor code exist in isolation but work together. Elements in XAML can trigger events handled in code, and code can modify elements in XAML. In the next chapter you'll see how this works.

Chapter 8

Code and XAML in harmony

A code file and a XAML file always exist as a pair. The two files complement each other. Despite being referred to as the "code-behind" file to the XAML, very often the code is prominent in taking on the more active and interactive parts of the application. This implies that the code-behind file must be able to refer to elements defined in XAML with as much ease as objects instantiated in code. Likewise, elements in XAML must be able to fire events that are handled in code-based event handlers. That's what this chapter is all about.

But first, let's explore a couple of unusual techniques for instantiating objects in a XAML file.

Passing arguments

When you run an application containing a XAML file, each element in the XAML file is instantiated with a call to the parameterless constructor of the corresponding class or structure. The load process continues with initialization of the resultant object by setting properties from attribute values. This seems reasonable. However, developers using XAML sometimes have a need to instantiate objects with constructors that require arguments or by calling a static creation method. These needs usually don't involve the API itself, but instead involve external data classes referenced by the XAML file that interact with the API.

The 2009 XAML specification introduced an `x:Arguments` element and an `x:FactoryMethod` attribute for these cases, and Xamarin.Forms supports them. These techniques are not often used in ordinary circumstances, but you should see how they work in case the need arises.

Constructors with arguments

To pass arguments to a constructor of an element in XAML, the element must be separated into start and end tags. Follow the start tag of the element with `x:Arguments` start and end tags. Within those `x:Arguments` tags, include one or more constructor arguments.

But how do you specify multiple arguments of common types, such as `double` or `int`? Do you separate the arguments with commas?

No. Each argument must be delimited with start and end tags. Fortunately, the XAML 2009 specification defines XML elements for common basic types. You can use these tags to clarify the types of elements, to specify generic types in `OnPlatform`, or to delimit constructor arguments. Here's the complete set supported by Xamarin.Forms. Notice that they duplicate the .NET type names rather than the C# type names:

- `x:Object`

- `x:Boolean`

- `x:Byte`

- `x:Int16`

- `x:Int32`

- `x:Int64`

- `x:Single`

- `x:Double`

- `x:Decimal`

- `x:Char`

- `x:String`

- `x:TimeSpan`

- `x:Array`

- `x:DateTime` (supported by Xamarin.Forms but not the XAML 2009 specification)

You'll be hard-pressed to find a use for all of these, but you'll certainly discover uses for some of them.

The **ParameteredConstructorDemo** sample demonstrates the use of `x:Arguments` with arguments delimited by `x:Double` tags using three different constructors of the `Color` structure. The constructor with three parameters requires red, green, and blue values ranging from 0 to 1. The constructor with four parameters adds an alpha channel as the fourth parameter (which is set here to 0.5), and the constructor with a single parameter indicates a gray shade from 0 (black) to 1 (white):

```
<ContentPage xmlns="http://xamarin.com/schemas/2014/forms"
             xmlns:x="http://schemas.microsoft.com/winfx/2009/xaml"
             x:Class="ParameteredConstructorDemo.ParameteredConstructorDemoPage">

    <StackLayout>
        <BoxView WidthRequest="100"
                 HeightRequest="100"
                 HorizontalOptions="Center"
                 VerticalOptions="CenterAndExpand">
            <BoxView.Color>
                <Color>
                    <x:Arguments>
                        <x:Double>1</x:Double>
                        <x:Double>0</x:Double>
                        <x:Double>0</x:Double>
                    </x:Arguments>
                </Color>
            </BoxView.Color>
```

```
            </BoxView.Color>
        </BoxView>

        <BoxView WidthRequest="100"
                 HeightRequest="100"
                 HorizontalOptions="Center"
                 VerticalOptions="CenterAndExpand">
            <BoxView.Color>
                <Color>
                    <x:Arguments>
                        <x:Double>0</x:Double>
                        <x:Double>0</x:Double>
                        <x:Double>1</x:Double>
                        <x:Double>0.5</x:Double>
                    </x:Arguments>
                </Color>
            </BoxView.Color>
        </BoxView>

        <BoxView WidthRequest="100"
                 HeightRequest="100"
                 HorizontalOptions="Center"
                 VerticalOptions="CenterAndExpand">
            <BoxView.Color>
                <Color>
                    <x:Arguments>
                        <x:Double>0.5</x:Double>
                    </x:Arguments>
                </Color>
            </BoxView.Color>
        </BoxView>
    </StackLayout>
</ContentPage>
```

The number of elements within the x:Arguments tags, and the types of these elements, must match one of the constructors of the class or structure. Here's the result:

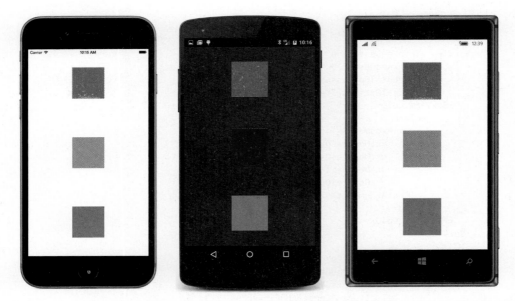

The blue `BoxView` is light against the light background and dark against the dark background because it's 50 percent transparent and lets the background show through.

Can I call methods from XAML?

At one time, the answer to this question was "Don't be ridiculous," but now it's a qualified "Yes." Don't get too excited, though. The only methods you can call in XAML are those that return objects (or values) of the same type as the class (or structure) that defines the method. These methods must be public and static. They are sometimes called *creation methods* or *factory methods*. You can instantiate an element in XAML through a call to one of these methods by specifying the method's name using the `x:FactoryMethod` attribute and its arguments using the `x:Arguments` element.

The `Color` structure defines seven static methods that return `Color` values, so these qualify. This XAML file makes use of three of them:

```
<ContentPage xmlns="http://xamarin.com/schemas/2014/forms"
             xmlns:x="http://schemas.microsoft.com/winfx/2009/xaml"
             x:Class="FactoryMethodDemo.FactoryMethodDemoPage">

    <StackLayout>
        <BoxView WidthRequest="100"
                 HeightRequest="100"
                 HorizontalOptions="Center"
                 VerticalOptions="CenterAndExpand">
            <BoxView.Color>
                <Color x:FactoryMethod="FromRgb">
                    <x:Arguments>
                        <x:Int32>255</x:Int32>
                        <x:Int32>0</x:Int32>
```

```
                        <x:Int32>0</x:Int32>
                    </x:Arguments>
                </Color>
            </BoxView.Color>
        </BoxView>

        <BoxView WidthRequest="100"
                 HeightRequest="100"
                 HorizontalOptions="Center"
                 VerticalOptions="CenterAndExpand">
            <BoxView.Color>
                <Color x:FactoryMethod="FromRgb">
                    <x:Arguments>
                        <x:Double>0</x:Double>
                        <x:Double>1.0</x:Double>
                        <x:Double>0</x:Double>
                    </x:Arguments>
                </Color>
            </BoxView.Color>
        </BoxView>

        <BoxView WidthRequest="100"
                 HeightRequest="100"
                 HorizontalOptions="Center"
                 VerticalOptions="CenterAndExpand">
            <BoxView.Color>
                <Color x:FactoryMethod="FromHsla">
                    <x:Arguments>
                        <x:Double>0.67</x:Double>
                        <x:Double>1.0</x:Double>
                        <x:Double>0.5</x:Double>
                        <x:Double>1.0</x:Double>
                    </x:Arguments>
                </Color>
            </BoxView.Color>
        </BoxView>
    </StackLayout>
</ContentPage>
```

The first two static methods invoked here are both named `Color.FromRgb`, but the types of elements within the `x:Arguments` tags distinguish between `int` arguments that range from 0 to 255 and `double` arguments that range from 0 to 1. The third one is the `Color.FromHsla` method, which creates a `Color` value from hue, saturation, luminosity, and alpha components. Interestingly, this is the only way to define a `Color` value from HSL values in a XAML file by using the Xamarin.Forms API. Here's the result:

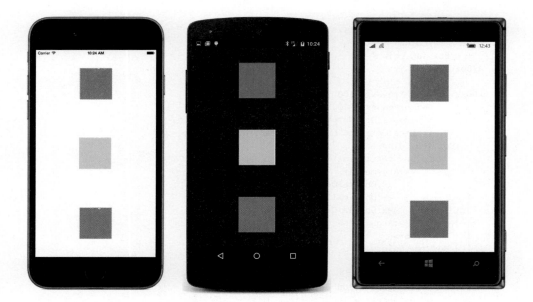

The x:Name attribute

In most real applications, the code-behind file needs to reference elements defined in the XAML file. You saw one way to do this in the **CodePlusXaml** program in the previous chapter: If the code-behind file has knowledge of the layout of the visual tree defined in the XAML file, it can start from the root element (the page itself) and locate specific elements within the tree. This process is called "walking the tree" and can be useful for locating particular elements on a page.

Generally, a better approach is to give elements in the XAML file a name similar to a variable name. To do this you use an attribute that is intrinsic to XAML, called `Name`. Because the prefix `x` is almost universally used for attributes intrinsic to XAML, this `Name` attribute is commonly referred to as `x:Name`.

The **XamlClock** project demonstrates the use of `x:Name`. Here is the XamlClockPage.xaml file containing two `Label` controls, named `timeLabel` and `dateLabel`:

```
<ContentPage xmlns="http://xamarin.com/schemas/2014/forms"
             xmlns:x="http://schemas.microsoft.com/winfx/2009/xaml"
             x:Class="XamlClock.XamlClockPage">
    <StackLayout>
        <Label x:Name="timeLabel"
               FontSize="Large"
               HorizontalOptions="Center"
               VerticalOptions="EndAndExpand" />

        <Label x:Name="dateLabel"
               HorizontalOptions="Center"
               VerticalOptions="StartAndExpand" />
```

```
    </StackLayout>
</ContentPage>
```

The rules for x:Name are the same as for C# variable names. (You'll see why shortly.) The name must begin with a letter or an underscore and can contain only letters, underscores, and numbers.

Like the clock program in Chapter 5, **XamlClock** uses Device.StartTimer to fire a periodic event for updating the time and date. Here's the XamlClockPage code-behind file:

```
namespace XamlClock
{
    public partial class XamlClockPage
    {
        public XamlClockPage()
        {
            InitializeComponent();

            Device.StartTimer(TimeSpan.FromSeconds(1), OnTimerTick);
        }

        bool OnTimerTick()
        {
            DateTime dt = DateTime.Now;
            timeLabel.Text = dt.ToString("T");
            dateLabel.Text = dt.ToString("D");
            return true;
        }
    }
}
```

This timer callback method is called once per second. The method must return true to continue the timer. If it returns false, the timer stops and must be restarted with another call to Device.Start-Timer.

The callback method references timeLabel and dateLabel as though they were normal variables and sets the Text properties of each:

This is not a visually impressive clock, but it's definitely functional.

How is it that the code-behind file can reference the elements identified with x:Name? Is it magic? Of course not. The mechanism is very evident when you examine the XamlClockPage.xaml.g.cs file that the XAML parser generates from the XAML file as the project is being built:

```
//------------------------------------------------------------------------------
// <auto-generated>
//     This code was generated by a tool.
//     Runtime Version:4.0.30319.42000
//
//     Changes to this file may cause incorrect behavior and will be lost if
//     the code is regenerated.
// </auto-generated>
//------------------------------------------------------------------------------

namespace XamlClock {
    using System;
    using Xamarin.Forms;
    using Xamarin.Forms.Xaml;

    public partial class XamlClockPage : global::Xamarin.Forms.ContentPage {

        [System.CodeDom.Compiler.GeneratedCodeAttribute("Xamarin.Forms.Build.Tasks.XamlG",
                                                         "0.0.0.0")]
        private global::Xamarin.Forms.Label timeLabel;

        [System.CodeDom.Compiler.GeneratedCodeAttribute("Xamarin.Forms.Build.Tasks.XamlG",
                                                         "0.0.0.0")]
        private global::Xamarin.Forms.Label dateLabel;
```

```
[System.CodeDom.Compiler.GeneratedCodeAttribute("Xamarin.Forms.Build.Tasks.XamlG",
                                "0.0.0.0")]
    private void InitializeComponent() {
        this.LoadFromXaml(typeof(XamlClockPage));
        timeLabel = this.FindByName<global::Xamarin.Forms.Label>("timeLabel");
        dateLabel = this.FindByName<global::Xamarin.Forms.Label>("dateLabel");
    }
  }
}
```

It might be a little hard to see because of the attributes and fully qualified types, but as the build-time
XAML parser chews through the XAML file, every x:Name attribute becomes a private field in this generated code file. This allows code in the code-behind file to reference these names as though they were
normal fields—which they definitely are. However, the fields are initially null. Only when InitializeComponent is called at run time are the two fields set via the FindByName method, which is defined in the NameScopeExtensions class. If the constructor of your code-behind file tries to reference
these two fields prior to the InitializeComponent call, they will have null values.

This generated code file also implies another rule for x:Name values that is now very obvious but
rarely stated explicitly: the names cannot duplicate names of fields or properties defined in the code-
behind file.

Because these are private fields, they can be accessed only from the code-behind file and not from
other classes. If a ContentPage derivative needs to expose public fields or properties to other classes,
you must define those yourself.

Obviously, x:Name values must be unique within a XAML page. This can sometimes be a problem if
you're using OnPlatform for platform-specific elements in the XAML file. For example, here's a XAML
file that expresses the iOS, Android, and WinPhone properties of OnPlatform as property elements
to select one of three Label views:

```
<ContentPage xmlns="http://xamarin.com/schemas/2014/forms"
            xmlns:x="http://schemas.microsoft.com/winfx/2009/xaml"
            x:Class="PlatformSpecificLabels.PlatformSpecificLabelsPage">

    <OnPlatform x:TypeArguments="View">
        <OnPlatform.iOS>
            <Label Text="This is an iOS device"
                    HorizontalOptions="Center"
                    VerticalOptions="Center" />
        </OnPlatform.iOS>

        <OnPlatform.Android>
            <Label Text="This is an Android device"
                    HorizontalOptions="Center"
                    VerticalOptions="Center" />
        </OnPlatform.Android>

        <OnPlatform.WinPhone>
            <Label Text="This is an Windows device"
```

```
                            HorizontalOptions="Center"
                            VerticalOptions="Center" />
            </OnPlatform.WinPhone>
        </OnPlatform>
</ContentPage>
```

The x:TypeArguments attribute of OnPlatform must match the type of the target property exactly. This OnPlatform element is implicitly being set to the Content property of ContentPage, and this Content property is of type View, so the x:TypeArguments attribute of OnPlatform must specify View. However, the properties of OnPlatform can be set to any class that derives from that type. The objects set to the iOS, Android, and WinPhone properties can in fact be different types just as long as they all derive from View.

Although that XAML file works, it's not exactly optimum. All three Label views are instantiated and initialized, but only one is set to the Content property of the ContentPage. The problem with this approach arises if you need to refer to the Label from the code-behind file and you give each of them the same name, like so:

The following XAML file does not work!

```
<ContentPage xmlns="http://xamarin.com/schemas/2014/forms"
             xmlns:x="http://schemas.microsoft.com/winfx/2009/xaml"
             x:Class="PlatformSpecificLabels.PlatformSpecificLabelsPage">

    <OnPlatform x:TypeArguments="View">
        <OnPlatform.iOS>
            <Label x:Name="deviceLabel"
                   Text="This is an iOS device"
                   HorizontalOptions="Center"
                   VerticalOptions="Center" />
        </OnPlatform.iOS>

        <OnPlatform.Android>
            <Label x:Name="deviceLabel"
                   Text="This is an Android device"
                   HorizontalOptions="Center"
                   VerticalOptions="Center" />
        </OnPlatform.Android>

        <OnPlatform.WinPhone>
            <Label x:Name="deviceLabel"
                   Text="This is a Windows device"
                   HorizontalOptions="Center"
                   VerticalOptions="Center" />
        </OnPlatform.WinPhone>
    </OnPlatform>
</ContentPage>
```

This will not work because multiple elements cannot have the same name.

You could give them different names and handle the three names in the code-behind file by using

`Device.OnPlatform`, but a better solution is to keep the platform-specific markup as small as possible. In this example, all the `Label` properties are the same except for `Text`, so only the `Text` property needs to be platform specific. Here's the version of the **PlatformSpecificLabels** program that is included with the sample code for this chapter. It has a single `Label`, and everything is platform independent except for the `Text` property:

```
<ContentPage xmlns="http://xamarin.com/schemas/2014/forms"
             xmlns:x="http://schemas.microsoft.com/winfx/2009/xaml"
             x:Class="PlatformSpecificLabels.PlatformSpecificLabelsPage">

    <Label x:Name="deviceLabel"
           HorizontalOptions="Center"
           VerticalOptions="Center">
        <Label.Text>
            <OnPlatform x:TypeArguments="x:String"
                        iOS="This is an iOS device"
                        Android="This is an Android device"
                        WinPhone="This is a Windows device" />
        </Label.Text>
    </Label>
</ContentPage>
```

Here's what it looks like:

The `Text` property is the content property for `Label`, so you don't need the `Label.Text` tags in the previous example. This works as well:

```
<ContentPage xmlns="http://xamarin.com/schemas/2014/forms"
             xmlns:x="http://schemas.microsoft.com/winfx/2009/xaml"
             x:Class="PlatformSpecificLabels.PlatformSpecificLabelsPage">
```

```
<Label x:Name="deviceLabel"
       HorizontalOptions="Center"
       VerticalOptions="Center">
    <OnPlatform x:TypeArguments="x:String"
                iOS="This is an iOS device"
                Android="This is an Android device"
                WinPhone="This is a Windows device" />
</Label>
</ContentPage>
```

Custom XAML-based views

The **ScaryColorList** program in the previous chapter listed a few colors in a `StackLayout` using `Frame`, `BoxView`, and `Label`. Even with just three colors, the repetitive markup was starting to look very ominous. Unfortunately there is no XAML markup that duplicates the C# `for` and `while` loops, so your choice is to use code for generating multiple similar items, or to find a better way to do it in markup.

In this book, you'll see several ways to list colors in XAML, and eventually, a very clean and elegant way to do this job will become clear. But that requires a few more steps into learning Xamarin.Forms. Until then, we'll be looking at some other approaches that you might find useful in similar circumstances.

One strategy is to create a custom view that has the sole purpose of displaying a color with a name and a colored box. And while we're at it, let's display the hexadecimal RGB values of the colors as well. You can then use that custom view in a XAML page file for the individual colors.

What might a reference to such a custom view look like in XAML?

Or the better question is: How would you *like* it to look?

If the markup looked something like this, the repetition is not bad at all, and not so much worse than explicitly defining an array of `Color` values in code:

```
<StackLayout>
    <MyColorView Color="Red" />
    <MyColorView Color="Green" />
    <MyColorView Color="Blue" />
    ...
</StackLayout>
```

Well, actually, it won't look exactly like that. `MyColorView` is obviously a custom class and not part of the Xamarin.Forms API. Therefore, it cannot appear in the XAML file without a namespace prefix that is defined in an XML namespace declaration.

With this XML prefix applied, there won't be any confusion about this custom view being part of the Xamarin.Forms API, so let's give it a more dignified name of `ColorView` rather than `MyColorView`.

This hypothetical `ColorView` class is an example of a fairly easy custom view because it consists solely of existing views—specifically `Label`, `Frame`, and `BoxView`—arranged in a particular way using `StackLayout`. Xamarin.Forms defines a view designed specifically for the purpose of parenting such an arrangement of views, and it's called `ContentView`. Like `ContentPage`, `ContentView` has a `Content` property that you can set to a visual tree of other views. You can define the contents of the `ContentView` in code, but it's more fun to do it in XAML.

Let's put together a solution named **ColorViewList**. This solution will have two sets of XAML and code-behind files, the first for a class named `ColorViewListPage`, which derives from `ContentPage` (as usual), and the second for a class named `ColorView`, which derives from `ContentView`.

To create the `ColorView` class in Visual Studio, use the same procedure as when adding a new XAML page to the **ColorViewList** project: Right-click the project name in the **Solution Explorer**, and select **Add > New Item** from the context menu. In the **Add New Item** dialog, select **Visual C# > Cross-Platform** at the left and then **Forms Xaml Page**. Enter the name ColorView.cs. But right away, before you forget, go into the ColorView.xaml file and change the `ContentPage` start and end tags to `ContentView`. In the ColorView.xaml.cs file, change the base class to `ContentView`.

The process is a little easier in Xamarin Studio. From the tool menu for the **ColorViewList** project, select **Add > New File**. In the **New File** dialog, select **Forms** at the left and **Forms ContentView Xaml** (not **Forms ContentPage Xaml**). Give it a name of ColorView.

You'll also need to create a XAML file and code-behind file for the `ColorViewListPage` class, as usual.

The ColorView.xaml file describes the layout of the individual color items but without any actual color values. Instead, the `BoxView` and two `Label` views are given names:

```xml
<ContentView xmlns="http://xamarin.com/schemas/2014/forms"
             xmlns:x="http://schemas.microsoft.com/winfx/2009/xaml"
             x:Class="ColorViewList.ColorView">

    <Frame OutlineColor="Accent">
        <StackLayout Orientation="Horizontal">
            <BoxView x:Name="boxView"
                     WidthRequest="70"
                     HeightRequest="70" />

            <StackLayout>
                <Label x:Name="colorNameLabel"
                    FontSize="Large"
                    VerticalOptions="CenterAndExpand" />

                <Label x:Name="colorValueLabel"
                    VerticalOptions="CenterAndExpand" />
            </StackLayout>
        </StackLayout>
    </Frame>
</ContentView>
```

In a real-life program, you'll have plenty of time later to fine-tune the visuals. Initially, you'll just want to get all the named views in there.

Besides the visuals, this `ColorView` class will need a new property to set the color. This property must be defined in the code-behind file. At first, it seems reasonable to give `ColorView` a property named `Color` of type `Color` (as the earlier XAML snippet with `MyColorView` seems to suggest). But the `ColorView` class needs to display the color *name*, and it can't get the color name from a `Color` value.

Instead, it makes more sense to define a property named `ColorName` of type `string`. The code-behind file can then use reflection to obtain the static field of the `Color` class corresponding to that name.

But wait: Xamarin.Forms includes a public `ColorTypeConverter` class that the XAML parser uses to convert a text color name like "Red" or "Blue" into a `Color` value. Why not take advantage of that?

Here's the code-behind file for `ColorView`. It defines a `ColorName` property with a `set` accessor that sets the `Text` property of the `colorNameLabel` to the color name, and then uses `ColorType-Converter` to convert the name to a `Color` value. This `Color` value is then used to set the `Color` property of `boxView` and the `Text` property of the `colorValueLabel` to the RGB values:

```
public partial class ColorView : ContentView
{
    string colorName;
    ColorTypeConverter colorTypeConv = new ColorTypeConverter();

    public ColorView()
    {
        InitializeComponent();
    }

    public string ColorName
    {
        set
        {
            // Set the name.
            colorName = value;
            colorNameLabel.Text = value;

            // Get the actual Color and set the other views.
            Color color = (Color)colorTypeConv.ConvertFrom(colorName);
            boxView.Color = color;
            colorValueLabel.Text = String.Format("{0:X2}-{1:X2}-{2:X2}",
                                        (int)(255 * color.R),
                                        (int)(255 * color.G),
                                        (int)(255 * color.B));
        }
        get
        {
            return colorName;
        }
```

```
    }
}
```

The `ColorView` class is finished. Now let's look at `ColorViewListPage`. The ColorViewList-Page.xaml file must list multiple `ColorView` instances, so it needs a new XML namespace declaration with a new namespace prefix to reference the `ColorView` element.

The `ColorView` class is part of the same project as `ColorViewListPage`. Generally, programmers use an XML namespace prefix of `local` for such cases. The new namespace declaration appears in the root element of the XAML file (like the other two) with the following format:

```
xmlns:local="clr-namespace:ColorViewList;assembly=ColorViewList"
```

In the general case, a custom XML namespace declaration for XAML must specify a common language runtime (CLR) namespace—also known as the .NET namespace—and an assembly. The keywords to specify these are `clr-namespace` and `assembly`. Often the CLR namespace is the same as the assembly, as they are in this case, but they don't need to be. The two parts are connected by a semicolon.

Notice that a colon follows `clr-namespace`, but an equal sign follows `assembly`. This apparent inconsistency is deliberate: the format of the namespace declaration is intended to mimic a URI found in conventional namespace declarations, in which a colon follows the URI scheme name.

You use the same syntax for referencing objects in external portable class libraries. The only difference in those cases is that the project also needs a reference to that external PCL. (You'll see an example in Chapter 10, "XAML markup extensions.").

The `local` prefix is common for code in the same assembly, and in that case the `assembly` part is not required:

```
xmlns:local="clr-namespace:ColorViewList"
```

For a XAML file in a PCL, you can include the `assembly` part to reference something in the same assembly if you want but it's not necessary. For a XAML file in an SAP, however, you must *not* include the `assembly` part to reference a local class because there is no assembly associated with an SAP. The code in the SAP is actually part of the individual platform assemblies, and those all have different names.

Here's the XAML for the `ColorViewListPage` class. The code-behind file contains nothing beyond the `InitializeComponent` call:

```
<ContentPage xmlns="http://xamarin.com/schemas/2014/forms"
             xmlns:x="http://schemas.microsoft.com/winfx/2009/xaml"
             xmlns:local="clr-namespace:ColorViewList"
             x:Class="ColorViewList.ColorViewListPage">

    <ContentPage.Padding>
        <OnPlatform x:TypeArguments="Thickness"
                    iOS="0, 20, 0, 0" />
    </ContentPage.Padding>
```

```
<ScrollView>
    <StackLayout Padding="6, 0">
        <local:ColorView ColorName="Aqua" />
        <local:ColorView ColorName="Black" />
        <local:ColorView ColorName="Blue" />
        <local:ColorView ColorName="Fuchsia" />
        <local:ColorView ColorName="Gray" />
        <local:ColorView ColorName="Green" />
        <local:ColorView ColorName="Lime" />
        <local:ColorView ColorName="Maroon" />
        <local:ColorView ColorName="Navy" />
        <local:ColorView ColorName="Olive" />
        <local:ColorView ColorName="Purple" />
        <local:ColorView ColorName="Pink" />
        <local:ColorView ColorName="Red" />
        <local:ColorView ColorName="Silver" />
        <local:ColorView ColorName="Teal" />
        <local:ColorView ColorName="White" />
        <local:ColorView ColorName="Yellow" />
    </StackLayout>
</ScrollView>
</ContentPage>
```

This is not quite as odious as the earlier example seemed to suggest, and it demonstrates how you can encapsulate visuals in their own XAML-based classes. Notice that the `StackLayout` is the child of a `ScrollView`, so the list can be scrolled:

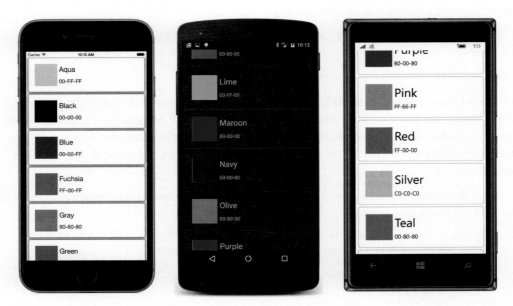

However, there is one aspect of the **ColorViewList** project that does not qualify as a "best practice." It is the definition of the `ColorName` property in `ColorView`. This should really be implemented as a

`BindableProperty` object. Delving into bindable objects and bindable properties is a high priority and will be explored in Chapter 11, "The bindable infrastructure."

Events and handlers

When you tap a Xamarin.Forms `Button`, it fires a `Clicked` event. You can instantiate a `Button` in XAML, but the `Clicked` event handler itself must reside in the code-behind file. The `Button` is only one of a bunch of views that exist primarily to generate events, so the process of handling events is crucial to coordinating XAML and code files.

Attaching an event handler to an event in XAML is as simple as setting a property; it is, in fact, visually indistinguishable from a property setting. The **XamlKeypad** project is a XAML version of the **PersistentKeypad** project from Chapter 6. It illustrates setting event handlers in XAML and handling these events in the code-behind file. It also includes logic to save keypad entries when the program is terminated.

If you take a look back at the constructor code of the `SimplestKeypadPage` or `PersistentKeypadPage` classes, you'll see a couple of loops to create the buttons that make up the numeric part of the keypad. Of course, this is precisely the type of thing you can't do in XAML, but look at how much cleaner the markup in `XamlKeypadPage` is when compared with that code:

```
<ContentPage xmlns="http://xamarin.com/schemas/2014/forms"
             xmlns:x="http://schemas.microsoft.com/winfx/2009/xaml"
             x:Class="XamlKeypad.XamlKeypadPage">

    <StackLayout VerticalOptions="Center"
                 HorizontalOptions="Center">

        <Label x:Name="displayLabel"
               Font="Large"
               VerticalOptions="Center"
               HorizontalTextAlignment="End" />

        <Button x:Name="backspaceButton"
                Text="&#x21E6;"
                Font="Large"
                IsEnabled="False"
                Clicked="OnBackspaceButtonClicked" />

        <StackLayout Orientation="Horizontal">
            <Button Text="7" StyleId="7" Font="Large"
                    Clicked="OnDigitButtonClicked" />
            <Button Text="8" StyleId="8" Font="Large"
                    Clicked="OnDigitButtonClicked" />
            <Button Text="9" StyleId="9" Font="Large"
                    Clicked="OnDigitButtonClicked" />
        </StackLayout>
```

```xml
        <StackLayout Orientation="Horizontal">
            <Button Text="4" StyleId="4" Font="Large"
                    Clicked="OnDigitButtonClicked" />
            <Button Text="5" StyleId="5" Font="Large"
                    Clicked="OnDigitButtonClicked" />
            <Button Text="6" StyleId="6" Font="Large"
                    Clicked="OnDigitButtonClicked" />
        </StackLayout>

        <StackLayout Orientation="Horizontal">
            <Button Text="1" StyleId="1" Font="Large"
                    Clicked="OnDigitButtonClicked" />
            <Button Text="2" StyleId="2" Font="Large"
                    Clicked="OnDigitButtonClicked" />
            <Button Text="3" StyleId="3" Font="Large"
                    Clicked="OnDigitButtonClicked" />
        </StackLayout>

        <Button Text="0" StyleId="0" Font="Large"
                Clicked="OnDigitButtonClicked" />

    </StackLayout>
</ContentPage>
```

The file is a lot shorter than it would have been had the three properties on each numeric `Button` been formatted into three lines, but packing these all together makes the uniformity of the markup very obvious and provides clarity rather than obscurity.

The big question is this: Which would you rather maintain and modify? The code in the `Simplest-KeypadPage` or `PersistentKeypadPage` constructors or the markup in the `XamlKeypadPage` XAML file?

Here's the screenshot. You'll see that these keys are now arranged in calculator order rather than telephone order:

The backspace button has its `Clicked` event set to the `OnBackspaceButtonClicked` handler, while the digit buttons share the `OnDigitButtonClicked` handler. As you'll recall, the `StyleId` property is often used to distinguish views sharing the same event handler, which means that the two event handlers can be implemented in the code-behind file exactly the same as in the code-only program:

```csharp
public partial class XamlKeypadPage
{
    App app = Application.Current as App;

    public XamlKeypadPage()
    {
        InitializeComponent();

        displayLabel.Text = app.DisplayLabelText;
        backspaceButton.IsEnabled = displayLabel.Text != null &&
                                    displayLabel.Text.Length > 0;
    }

    void OnDigitButtonClicked(object sender, EventArgs args)
    {
        Button button = (Button)sender;
        displayLabel.Text += (string)button.StyleId;
        backspaceButton.IsEnabled = true;

        app.DisplayLabelText = displayLabel.Text;
    }

    void OnBackspaceButtonClicked(object sender, EventArgs args)
    {
        string text = displayLabel.Text;
        displayLabel.Text = text.Substring(0, text.Length - 1);
```

```
            backspaceButton.IsEnabled = displayLabel.Text.Length > 0;

            app.DisplayLabelText = displayLabel.Text;
        }
}
```

Part of the job of the `LoadFromXaml` method called by `InitializeComponent` involves attaching these event handlers to the objects instantiated from the XAML file.

The **XamlKeypad** project also includes the code that was added to the page and `App` classes in **PersistentKeypad** to save the keypad text when the program is terminated. The `App` class in **XamlKeypad** is basically the same as the one in **PersistentKeypad**.

Tap gestures

The Xamarin.Forms `Button` responds to finger taps, but you can actually get finger taps from any class that derives from `View`, including `Label`, `BoxView`, and `Frame`. These tap events are not built into the `View` class, but the `View` class defines a property named `GestureRecognizers`. Taps are enabled by adding an object to this `GestureRecognizers` collection. An instance of any class that derives from `GestureRecognizer` can be added to this collection, but undoubtedly the most useful is `TapGestureRecognizer`.

Here's how to add a `TapGestureRecognizer` to a `BoxView` in code:

```
BoxView boxView = new BoxView
{
    Color = Color.Blue
};
TapGestureRecognizer tapGesture = new TapGestureRecognizer();
tapGesture.Tapped += OnBoxViewTapped;
boxView.GestureRecognizers.Add(tapGesture);
```

`TapGestureRecognizer` also defines a `NumberOfTapsRequired` property with a default value of 1. Set it to 2 to implement double taps.

To generate `Tapped` events, the `View` object must have its `IsEnabled` property set to `true`, its `IsVisible` property set to `true` (or it won't be visible at all), and its `InputTransparent` property set to `false`. These are all default conditions.

The `Tapped` handler looks just like a `Clicked` handler for the `Button`:

```
void OnBoxViewTapped(object sender, EventArgs args)
{
    ...
}
```

As you know, the `sender` argument of an event handler is normally the object that fires the event, which in this case would be the `TapGestureRecognizer` object. That would not be of much use. Instead, the `sender` argument to the `Tapped` handler is the view being tapped, in this case the `BoxView`. That's *much* more useful!

Like `Button`, `TapGestureRecognizer` also defines `Command` and `CommandParameter` properties; these are used when implementing the MVVM design pattern, and they are discussed in a later chapter.

`TapGestureRecognizer` also defines properties named `TappedCallback` and `TappedCallback-Parameter` and a constructor that includes a `TappedCallback` argument. These are all deprecated and should not be used.

In XAML, you can attach a `TapGestureRecognizer` to a view by expressing the `GestureRecognizers` collection as a property element:

```
<BoxView Color="Blue">
    <BoxView.GestureRecognizers>
        <TapGestureRecognizer Tapped="OnBoxViewTapped" />
    </BoxView.GestureRecognizers>
</BoxView>
```

As usual, the XAML is a little shorter than the equivalent code.

Let's make a program that's inspired by one of the first standalone computer games.

The Xamarin.Forms version of this game is called **MonkeyTap** because it's an imitation game. It contains four `BoxView` elements, colored red, blue, yellow, and green. When the game begins, one of the `BoxView` elements flashes, and you must then tap that `BoxView`. That `BoxView` flashes again followed by another one, and now you must tap both in sequence. Then those two flashes are followed by a third and so forth. (The original had sound as well, but **MonkeyTap** does not.) It's a rather cruel game because there is no way to win. The game just keeps on getting harder and harder until you lose.

The MonkeyTapPage.xaml file instantiates the four `BoxView` elements and a `Button` in the center labeled "Begin".

```
<ContentPage xmlns="http://xamarin.com/schemas/2014/forms"
             xmlns:x="http://schemas.microsoft.com/winfx/2009/xaml"
             x:Class="MonkeyTap.MonkeyTapPage">

    <ContentPage.Padding>
        <OnPlatform x:TypeArguments="Thickness"
                    iOS="0, 20, 0, 0" />
    </ContentPage.Padding>

    <StackLayout>
        <BoxView x:Name="boxview0"
                 VerticalOptions="FillAndExpand">
            <BoxView.GestureRecognizers>
                <TapGestureRecognizer Tapped="OnBoxViewTapped" />
            </BoxView.GestureRecognizers>
```

```
            </BoxView>

            <BoxView x:Name="boxview1"
                     VerticalOptions="FillAndExpand">
                <BoxView.GestureRecognizers>
                    <TapGestureRecognizer Tapped="OnBoxViewTapped" />
                </BoxView.GestureRecognizers>
            </BoxView>

            <Button x:Name="startGameButton"
                    Text="Begin"
                    Font="Large"
                    HorizontalOptions="Center"
                    Clicked="OnStartGameButtonClicked" />

            <BoxView x:Name="boxview2"
                     VerticalOptions="FillAndExpand">
                <BoxView.GestureRecognizers>
                    <TapGestureRecognizer Tapped="OnBoxViewTapped" />
                </BoxView.GestureRecognizers>
            </BoxView>

            <BoxView x:Name="boxview3"
                     VerticalOptions="FillAndExpand">
                <BoxView.GestureRecognizers>
                    <TapGestureRecognizer Tapped="OnBoxViewTapped" />
                </BoxView.GestureRecognizers>
            </BoxView>
        </StackLayout>
</ContentPage>
```

All four `BoxView` elements here have a `TapGestureRecognizer` attached, but they aren't yet assigned colors. That's handled in the code-behind file because the colors won't stay constant. The colors need to be changed for the flashing effect.

The code-behind file begins with some constants and variable fields. (You'll notice that one of them is flagged as protected; in the next chapter, a class will derive from this one and require access to this field. Some methods are defined as protected as well.)

```
public partial class MonkeyTapPage
{
    const int sequenceTime = 750;        // in msec
    protected const int flashDuration = 250;

    const double offLuminosity = 0.4;    // somewhat dimmer
    const double onLuminosity = 0.75;    // much brighter

    BoxView[] boxViews;
    Color[] colors = { Color.Red, Color.Blue, Color.Yellow, Color.Green };
    List<int> sequence = new List<int>();
    int sequenceIndex;
    bool awaitingTaps;
    bool gameEnded;
```

```
Random random = new Random();

public MonkeyTapPage()
{
    InitializeComponent();
    boxViews = new BoxView[] { boxview0, boxview1, boxview2, boxview3 };
    InitializeBoxViewColors();
}

void InitializeBoxViewColors()
{
    for (int index = 0; index < 4; index++)
        boxViews[index].Color = colors[index].WithLuminosity(offLuminosity);
}
...
}
```

The constructor puts all four `BoxView` elements in an array; this allows them to be referenced by a simple index that has values of 0, 1, 2, and 3. The `InitializeBoxViewColors` method sets all the `BoxView` elements to their slightly dimmed nonflashed state.

The program is now waiting for the user to press the **Begin** button to start the first game. The same `Button` handles replays, so it includes a redundant initialization of the `BoxView` colors. The `Button` handler also prepares for building the sequence of flashed `BoxView` elements by clearing the `sequence` list and calling `StartSequence`:

```
public partial class MonkeyTapPage
{
    ...
    protected void OnStartGameButtonClicked(object sender, EventArgs args)
    {
        gameEnded = false;
        startGameButton.IsVisible = false;
        InitializeBoxViewColors();
        sequence.Clear();
        StartSequence();
    }

    void StartSequence()
    {
        sequence.Add(random.Next(4));
        sequenceIndex = 0;
        Device.StartTimer(TimeSpan.FromMilliseconds(sequenceTime), OnTimerTick);
    }
    ...
}
```

`StartSequence` adds a new random integer to the `sequence` list, initializes `sequenceIndex` to 0, and starts the timer.

In the normal case, the timer tick handler is called for each index in the `sequence` list and causes the corresponding `BoxView` to flash with a call to `FlashBoxView`. The timer handler returns `false` when the sequence is at an end, also indicating by setting `awaitingTaps` that it's time for the user to imitate the sequence:

```
public partial class MonkeyTapPage
{
    …
    bool OnTimerTick()
    {
        if (gameEnded)
            return false;

        FlashBoxView(sequence[sequenceIndex]);
        sequenceIndex++;
        awaitingTaps = sequenceIndex == sequence.Count;
        sequenceIndex = awaitingTaps ? 0 : sequenceIndex;
        return !awaitingTaps;
    }

    protected virtual void FlashBoxView(int index)
    {
        boxViews[index].Color = colors[index].WithLuminosity(onLuminosity);
        Device.StartTimer(TimeSpan.FromMilliseconds(flashDuration), () =>
            {
                if (gameEnded)
                    return false;

                boxViews[index].Color = colors[index].WithLuminosity(offLuminosity);
                return false;
            });
    }
    …
}
```

The flash is just a quarter second in duration. The `FlashBoxView` method first sets the luminosity for a bright color and creates a "one-shot" timer, so called because the timer callback method (here expressed as a lambda function) returns `false` and shuts off the timer after restoring the color's luminosity.

The `Tapped` handler for the `BoxView` elements ignores the tap if the game is already over (which only happens with a mistake by the user), and ends the game if the user taps prematurely without waiting for the program to go through the sequence. Otherwise, it just compares the tapped `BoxView` with the next one in the sequence, flashes that `BoxView` if correct, or ends the game if not:

```
public partial class MonkeyTapPage
{
    …
    protected void OnBoxViewTapped(object sender, EventArgs args)
    {
        if (gameEnded)
            return;

        if (!awaitingTaps)
```

```
        {
            EndGame();
            return;
        }

        BoxView tappedBoxView = (BoxView)sender;
        int index = Array.IndexOf(boxViews, tappedBoxView);

        if (index != sequence[sequenceIndex])
        {
            EndGame();
            return;
        }

        FlashBoxView(index);

        sequenceIndex++;
        awaitingTaps = sequenceIndex < sequence.Count;

        if (!awaitingTaps)
            StartSequence();
    }

    protected virtual void EndGame()
    {
        gameEnded = true;

        for (int index = 0; index < 4; index++)
            boxViews[index].Color = Color.Gray;

        startGameButton.Text = "Try again?";
        startGameButton.IsVisible = true;
    }
}
```

If the user manages to "ape" the sequence all the way through, another call to StartSequence adds a new index to the sequence list and starts playing that new one. Eventually, though, there will be a call to EndGame, which colors all the boxes gray to emphasize the end, and reenables the Button for a chance to try it again.

Here's the program after the Button has been clicked and hidden:

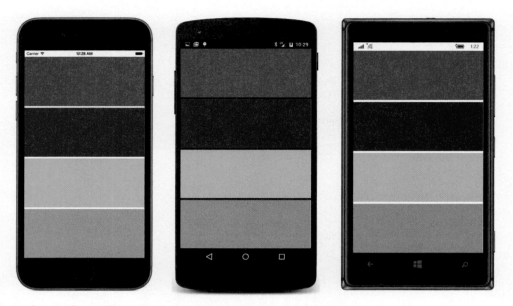

I know, I know. The game is a real drag without sound.

Let's take the opportunity in the next chapter to fix that.

Chapter 9
Platform-specific API calls

An emergency has arisen. Anyone playing with the **MonkeyTap** game from the previous chapter will quickly come to the conclusion that it desperately needs a very basic enhancement, and it simply cannot be allowed to exist without it.

> **MonkeyTap** needs sound.

It doesn't need very sophisticated sound—just little beeps to accompany the flashes of the four `BoxView` elements. But the Xamarin.Forms API doesn't support sound, so sound is not something we can add to **MonkeyTap** with just a couple of API calls. Supporting sound requires going somewhat beyond Xamarin.Forms to make use of platform-specific sound-generation facilities. Figuring out how to make sounds in iOS, Android, and Windows Phone is hard enough. But how does a Xamarin.Forms program then make calls into the individual platforms?

Before tackling the complexities of sound, let's examine the different approaches to making platform-specific API calls with a much simpler example. The first three short programs shown in this chapter are all functionally identical: They all display two tiny items of information supplied by the underlying platform's operating system that reveal the model of the device running the program and the operating system version.

Preprocessing in the Shared Asset Project

As you learned in Chapter 2, "Anatomy of an app," you can use either a Shared Asset Project (SAP) or a Portable Class Library (PCL) for the code that is common to all three platforms. An SAP contains code files that are shared among the platform projects, while a PCL encloses the common code in a library that is accessible only through public types.

Accessing platform APIs from a Shared Asset Project is a little more straightforward than from a Portable Class Library because it involves more traditional programming tools, so let's try that approach first. You can create a Xamarin.Forms solution with an SAP using the process described in Chapter 2. You can then add a XAML-based `ContentPage` class to the SAP the same way you add one to a PCL.

Here's the XAML file for a project that displays platform information, named **PlatInfoSap1**:

```
<ContentPage xmlns="http://xamarin.com/schemas/2014/forms"
             xmlns:x="http://schemas.microsoft.com/winfx/2009/xaml"
             x:Class="PlatInfoSap1.PlatInfoSap1Page">

    <StackLayout Padding="20">
```

```
            <StackLayout VerticalOptions="CenterAndExpand">
                <Label Text="Device Model:" />

                <ContentView Padding="50, 0, 0, 0">
                    <Label x:Name="modelLabel"
                           FontSize="Large"
                           FontAttributes="Bold" />
                </ContentView>
            </StackLayout>

            <StackLayout VerticalOptions="CenterAndExpand">
                <Label Text="Operating System Version:" />

                <ContentView Padding="50, 0, 0, 0">
                    <Label x:Name="versionLabel"
                           FontSize="Large"
                           FontAttributes="Bold" />
                </ContentView>
            </StackLayout>
        </StackLayout>
</ContentPage>
```

The code-behind file must set the `Text` properties for `modelLabel` and `versionLabel`.

Code files in a Shared Asset Project are extensions of the code in the individual platforms. This means that code in the SAP can make use of the C# preprocessor directives `#if`, `#elif`, `#else`, and `#endif` with conditional-compilation symbols defined for the three platforms, as demonstrated in Chapters 2 and 4. These symbols are:

- `__IOS__` for iOS

- `__ANDROID__` for Android

- `WINDOWS_UWP` for the Universal Windows Platform

- `WINDOWS_APP` for Windows 8.1

- `WINDOWS_PHONE_APP` for Windows Phone 8.1

The APIs involved in obtaining the model and version information are, of course, different for the three platforms:

- For iOS, use the `UIDevice` class in the `UIKit` namespace.

- For Android, use various properties of the `Build` class in the `Android.OS` namespace.

- For the Windows platforms, use the `EasClientDeviceInformation` class in the `Windows.Security.ExchangeActiveSyncProvisioning` namespace.

Here's the PlatInfoSap1.xaml.cs code-behind file showing how `modelLabel` and `versionLabel` are set based on the conditional-compilation symbols:

```
using System;
```

```csharp
using Xamarin.Forms;

#if __IOS__
using UIKit;

#elif __ANDROID__
using Android.OS;

#elif WINDOWS_APP || WINDOWS_PHONE_APP || WINDOWS_UWP
using Windows.Security.ExchangeActiveSyncProvisioning;

#endif

namespace PlatInfoSap1
{
    public partial class PlatInfoSap1Page : ContentPage
    {
        public PlatInfoSap1Page ()
        {
            InitializeComponent ();

#if __IOS__

            UIDevice device = new UIDevice();
            modelLabel.Text = device.Model.ToString();
            versionLabel.Text = String.Format("{0} {1}", device.SystemName,
                                                    device.SystemVersion);

#elif __ANDROID__

            modelLabel.Text = String.Format("{0} {1}", Build.Manufacturer,
                                                    Build.Model);
            versionLabel.Text = Build.VERSION.Release.ToString();

#elif WINDOWS_APP || WINDOWS_PHONE_APP || WINDOWS_UWP

            EasClientDeviceInformation devInfo = new EasClientDeviceInformation();
            modelLabel.Text = String.Format("{0} {1}", devInfo.SystemManufacturer,
                                                    devInfo.SystemProductName);
            versionLabel.Text = devInfo.OperatingSystem;

#endif

        }
    }
}
```

Notice that these preprocessor directives are used to select different `using` directives as well as to make calls to platform-specific APIs. In a program as simple as this, you could simply include the namespaces with the class names, but for longer blocks of code, you'll probably want those `using` directives.

And of course it works:

The advantage of this approach is that you have all the code for the three platforms in one place. But the preprocessor directives in the code listing are—let's face it—rather ugly, and they harken back to a much earlier era in programming. Using preprocessor directives might not seem so bad for short and less frequent calls such as this example, but in a larger program you'll need to juggle blocks of platform-specific code and shared code, and the multitude of preprocessor directives can easily become confusing. Preprocessor directives should be used for little fixes and generally not as structural elements in the application.

Let's try another approach.

Parallel classes and the Shared Asset Project

Although the Shared Asset Project is an extension of the platform projects, the relationship goes both ways: just as a platform project can make calls into code in a Shared Asset Project, the SAP can make calls into the individual platform projects.

This means that we can restrict the platform-specific API calls to classes in the individual platform projects. If the names and namespaces of these classes in the platform projects are the same, then code in the SAP can access these classes in a transparent, platform-independent manner.

In the **PlatInfoSap2** solution, each of the five platform projects has a class named `PlatformInfo` that contains two methods that return `string` objects, named `GetModel` and `GetVersion`. Here's the version of this class in the iOS project:

```
using System;
```

```
using UIKit;

namespace PlatInfoSap2
{
    public class PlatformInfo
    {
        UIDevice device = new UIDevice();

        public string GetModel()
        {
            return device.Model.ToString();
        }

        public string GetVersion()
        {
            return String.Format("{0} {1}", device.SystemName,
                                            device.SystemVersion);
        }
    }
}
```

Notice the namespace name. Although the other classes in this iOS project use the `PlatInfo-Sap2.iOS` namespace, the namespace for this class is just `PlatInfoSap2`. This allows the SAP to access this class directly without any platform specifics.

Here's the parallel class in the Android project. Same namespace, same class name, and same method names, but different implementations of these methods using Android API calls:

```
using System;
using Android.OS;

namespace PlatInfoSap2
{
    public class PlatformInfo
    {
        public string GetModel()
        {
            return String.Format("{0} {1}", Build.Manufacturer,
                                            Build.Model);
        }

        public string GetVersion()
        {
            return Build.VERSION.Release.ToString();
        }
    }
}
```

And here's the class that exists in three identical copies in the three Windows and Windows Phone projects:

```
using System;
using Windows.Security.ExchangeActiveSyncProvisioning;
```

```
namespace PlatInfoSap2
{
    public class PlatformInfo
    {
        EasClientDeviceInformation devInfo = new EasClientDeviceInformation();

        public string GetModel()
        {
            return String.Format("{0} {1}", devInfo.SystemManufacturer,
                                            devInfo.SystemProductName);
        }

        public string GetVersion()
        {
            return devInfo.OperatingSystem;
        }
    }
}
```

The XAML file in the **PlatInfoSap2** project is basically the same as the one in **PlatInfoSap1** project. The code-behind file is considerably simpler:

```
using System;
using Xamarin.Forms;

namespace PlatInfoSap2
{
    public partial class PlatInfoSap2Page : ContentPage
    {
        public PlatInfoSap2Page ()
        {
            InitializeComponent ();

            PlatformInfo platformInfo = new PlatformInfo();
            modelLabel.Text = platformInfo.GetModel();
            versionLabel.Text = platformInfo.GetVersion();
        }
    }
}
```

The particular version of `PlatformInfo` that is referenced by the class is the one in the compiled project. It's almost as if we've defined a little extension to Xamarin.Forms that resides in the individual platform projects.

DependencyService and the Portable Class Library

Can the technique illustrated in the **PlatInfoSap2** program be implemented in a solution with a Portable Class Library? At first, it doesn't seem possible. Although application projects make calls to libraries all the time, libraries generally can't make calls to applications except in the context of events or callback functions. The PCL is bundled with a device-independent version of .NET and closed up tight—capable only of executing code within itself or other PCLs it might reference.

But wait: When a Xamarin.Forms application is running, it can use .NET reflection to get access to its own assembly and any other assemblies in the program. This means that code in the PCL can use reflection to access classes that exist in the platform assembly from which the PCL is referenced. Those classes must be defined as public, of course, but that's just about the only requirement.

Before you start writing code that exploits this technique, you should know that this solution already exists in the form of a Xamarin.Forms class named `DependencyService`. This class uses .NET reflection to search through all the other assemblies in the application—including the particular platform assembly itself—and provide access to platform-specific code.

The use of `DependencyService` is illustrated in the **DisplayPlatformInfo** solution, which uses a Portable Class Library for the shared code. You begin the process of using `DependencyService` by defining an interface type in the PCL project that declares the signatures of the methods you want to implement in the platform projects. Here's `IPlatformInfo`:

```
namespace DisplayPlatformInfo
{
    public interface IPlatformInfo
    {
        string GetModel();

        string GetVersion();
    }
}
```

You've seen those two methods before. They're the same two methods implemented in the `PlatformInfo` classes in the platform projects in **PlatInfoSap2**.

In a manner very similar to **PlatInfoSap2**, all three platform projects in **DisplayPlatformInfo** must now have a class that implements the `IPlatformInfo` interface. Here's the class in the iOS project, named `PlatformInfo`:

```
using System;
using UIKit;
using Xamarin.Forms;

[assembly: Dependency(typeof(DisplayPlatformInfo.iOS.PlatformInfo))]

namespace DisplayPlatformInfo.iOS
{
    public class PlatformInfo : IPlatformInfo
    {
        UIDevice device = new UIDevice();

        public string GetModel()
        {
            return device.Model.ToString();
```

```
        }

        public string GetVersion()
        {
            return String.Format("{0} {1}", device.SystemName,
                                            device.SystemVersion);
        }
    }
}
```

This class is not referenced directly from the PCL, so the namespace name can be anything you want. Here it's set to the same namespace as the other code in the iOS project. The class name can also be anything you want. Whatever you name it, however, the class must explicitly implement the `IPlat-formInfo` interface defined in the PCL:

```
public class PlatformInfo : IPlatformInfo
```

Furthermore, this class must be referenced in a special attribute outside the namespace block. You'll see it near the top of the file following the `using` directives:

```
[assembly: Dependency(typeof(DisplayPlatformInfo.iOS.PlatformInfo))]
```

The `DependencyAttribute` class that defines this `Dependency` attribute is part of Xamarin.Forms and used specifically in connection with `DependencyService`. The argument is a `Type` object of a class in the platform project that is available for access by the PCL. In this case, it's this `PlatformInfo` class. This attribute is attached to the platform assembly itself, so code executing in the PCL doesn't have to search all over the library to find it.

Here's the Android version of `PlatformInfo`:

```
using System;
using Android.OS;
using Xamarin.Forms;

[assembly: Dependency(typeof(DisplayPlatformInfo.Droid.PlatformInfo))]

namespace DisplayPlatformInfo.Droid
{
    public class PlatformInfo : IPlatformInfo
    {
        public string GetModel()
        {
            return String.Format("{0} {1}", Build.Manufacturer,
                                            Build.Model);
        }

        public string GetVersion()
        {
            return Build.VERSION.Release.ToString();
        }
    }
}
```

And here's the one for the UWP project:

```
using System;
using Windows.Security.ExchangeActiveSyncProvisioning;
using Xamarin.Forms;

[assembly: Dependency(typeof(DisplayPlatformInfo.UWP.PlatformInfo))]

namespace DisplayPlatformInfo.UWP
{
    public class PlatformInfo : IPlatformInfo
    {
        EasClientDeviceInformation devInfo = new EasClientDeviceInformation();

        public string GetModel()
        {
            return String.Format("{0} {1}", devInfo.SystemManufacturer,
                                            devInfo.SystemProductName);
        }

        public string GetVersion()
        {
            return devInfo.OperatingSystem;
        }
    }
}
```

The Windows 8.1 and Windows Phone 8.1 projects have similar files that differ only by the namespace.

Code in the PCL can then get access to the particular platform's implementation of IPlatform-Info by using the DependencyService class. This is a static class with three public methods, the most important of which is named Get. Get is a generic method whose argument is the interface you've defined, in this case IPlatformInfo.

```
IPlatformInfo platformInfo = DependencyService.Get<IPlatformInfo>();
```

The Get method returns an instance of the platform-specific class that implements the IPlatform-Info interface. You can then use this object to make platform-specific calls. This is demonstrated in the code-behind file for the **DisplayPlatformInfo** project:

```
namespace DisplayPlatformInfo
{
    public partial class DisplayPlatformInfoPage : ContentPage
    {
        public DisplayPlatformInfoPage()
        {
            InitializeComponent();

            IPlatformInfo platformInfo = DependencyService.Get<IPlatformInfo>();
            modelLabel.Text = platformInfo.GetModel();
            versionLabel.Text = platformInfo.GetVersion();
        }
    }
```

```
}
```

`DependencyService` caches the instances of the objects that it obtains through the `Get` method. This speeds up subsequent uses of `Get` and also allows the platform implementations of the interface to maintain state: any fields and properties in the platform implementations will be preserved across multiple `Get` calls. These classes can also include events or implement callback methods.

`DependencyService` requires just a little more overhead than the approach shown in the **PlatInfoSap2** project and is somewhat more structured because the individual platform classes implement an interface defined in shared code.

`DependencyService` is not the only way to implement platform-specific calls in a PCL. Adventurous developers might want to use dependency-injection techniques to configure the PCL to make calls into the platform projects. But `DependencyService` is very easy to use, and it eliminates most reasons to use a Shared Asset Project in a Xamarin.Forms application.

Platform-specific sound generation

Now for the real objective of this chapter: to give sound to **MonkeyTap**. All three platforms support APIs that allow a program to dynamically generate and play audio waveforms. This is the approach taken by the **MonkeyTapWithSound** program.

Commercial music files are often compressed in formats such as MP3. But when a program is algorithmically generating waveforms, an uncompressed format is much more convenient. The most basic technique—which is supported by all three platforms—is called pulse code modulation or PCM. Despite the fancy name, it's quite simple, and it's the technique used for storing sound on music CDs.

A PCM waveform is described by a series of samples at a constant rate, known as the sampling rate. Music CDs use a standard rate of 44,100 samples per second. Audio files generated by computer programs often use a sampling rate of half that (22,050) or one-quarter (11,025) if high audio quality is not required. The highest frequency that can be recorded and reproduced is one-half the sampling rate.

Each sample is a fixed size that defines the amplitude of the waveform at that point in time. The samples on a music CD are signed 16-bit values. Samples of 8 bits are common when sound quality doesn't matter as much. Some environments support floating-point values. Multiple samples can accommodate stereo or any number of channels. For simple sound effects on mobile devices, monaural sound is often fine.

The sound generation algorithm in **MonkeyTapWithSound** is hard-coded for 16-bit monaural samples, but the sampling rate is specified by a constant and can easily be changed.

Now that you know how `DependencyService` works, let's examine the code added to **Monkey-**

Tap to turn it into **MonkeyTapWithSound**, and let's look at it from the top down. To avoid reproducing a lot of code, the new project contains links to the MonkeyTap.xaml and MonkeyTap.xaml.cs files in the **MonkeyTap** project.

In Visual Studio, you can add items to projects as links to existing files by selecting **Add > Existing Item** from the project menu. Then use the **Add Existing Item** dialog to navigate to the file. Choose **Add as Link** from the drop-down on the **Add** button.

In Xamarin Studio, select **Add > Add Files** from the project's tool menu. After opening the file or files, an **Add File to Folder** alert box pops up. Choose **Add a link to the file**.

However, after taking these steps in Visual Studio, it was also necessary to manually edit the MonkeyTapWithSound.csproj file to change the MonkeyTapPage.xaml file to an **EmbeddedResource** and the **Generator** to **MSBuild:UpdateDesignTimeXaml**. Also, a **DependentUpon** tag was added to the MonkeyTapPage.xaml.cs file to reference the MonkeyTapPage.xaml file. This causes the code-behind file to be indented under the XAML file in the file list.

The `MonkeyTapWithSoundPage` class then derives from the `MonkeyTapPage` class. Although the `MonkeyTapPage` class is defined by a XAML file and a code-behind file, `MonkeyTapWithSoundPage` is code only. When a class is derived in this way, event handlers in the original code-behind file for events in the XAML file must be defined as `protected`, and this is the case.

The `MonkeyTap` class also defined a `flashDuration` constant as `protected`, and two methods were defined as `protected` and `virtual`. The `MonkeyTapWithSoundPage` overrides these two methods to call a static method named `SoundPlayer.PlaySound`:

```
namespace MonkeyTapWithSound
{
    class MonkeyTapWithSoundPage : MonkeyTap.MonkeyTapPage
    {
        const int errorDuration = 500;

        // Diminished 7th in 1st inversion: C, Eb, F#, A
        double[] frequencies = { 523.25, 622.25, 739.99, 880 };

        protected override void BlinkBoxView(int index)
        {
            SoundPlayer.PlaySound(frequencies[index], flashDuration);
            base.BlinkBoxView(index);
        }

        protected override void EndGame()
        {
            SoundPlayer.PlaySound(65.4, errorDuration);
            base.EndGame();
        }
    }
}
```

The `SoundPlayer.PlaySound` method accepts a frequency and a duration in milliseconds. Everything else—the volume, the harmonic makeup of the sound, and how the sound is generated—is the responsibility of the `PlaySound` method. However, this code makes an implicit assumption that `SoundPlayer.PlaySound` returns immediately and does not wait for the sound to complete playing. Fortunately, all three platforms support sound-generation APIs that behave in this way.

The `SoundPlayer` class with the `PlaySound` static method is part of the **MonkeyTapWithSound** PCL project. The responsibility of this method is to define an array of the PCM data for the sound. The size of this array is based on the sampling rate and the duration. The `for` loop calculates samples that define a triangle wave of the requested frequency:

```
namespace MonkeyTapWithSound
{
    class SoundPlayer
    {
        const int samplingRate = 22050;

        // Hard-coded for monaural, 16-bit-per-sample PCM
        public static void PlaySound(double frequency = 440, int duration = 250)
        {
            short[] shortBuffer = new short[samplingRate * duration / 1000];
            double angleIncrement = frequency / samplingRate;
            double angle = 0;    // normalized 0 to 1

            for (int i = 0; i < shortBuffer.Length; i++)
            {
                // Define triangle wave
                double sample;

                // 0 to 1
                if (angle < 0.25)
                    sample = 4 * angle;

                // 1 to -1
                else if (angle < 0.75)
                    sample = 4 * (0.5 - angle);

                // -1 to 0
                else
                    sample = 4 * (angle - 1);

                shortBuffer[i] = (short)(32767 * sample);
                angle += angleIncrement;

                while (angle > 1)
                    angle -= 1;
            }

            byte[] byteBuffer = new byte[2 * shortBuffer.Length];
            Buffer.BlockCopy(shortBuffer, 0, byteBuffer, 0, byteBuffer.Length);

            DependencyService.Get<IPlatformSoundPlayer>().PlaySound(samplingRate, byteBuffer);
```

```
        }
    }
}
```

Although the samples are 16-bit integers, two of the platforms want the data in the form of an array of bytes, so a conversion occurs near the end with `Buffer.BlockCopy`. The last line of the method uses `DependencyService` to pass this byte array with the sampling rate to the individual platforms.

The `DependencyService.Get` method references the `IPlatformSoundPlayer` interface that defines the signature of the `PlaySound` method:

```
namespace MonkeyTapWithSound
{
    public interface IPlatformSoundPlayer
    {
        void PlaySound(int samplingRate, byte[] pcmData);
    }
}
```

Now comes the hard part: writing this `PlaySound` method for the three platforms!

The iOS version uses `AVAudioPlayer`, which requires data that includes the header used in Waveform Audio File Format (.wav) files. The code here assembles that data in a `MemoryBuffer` and then converts that to an `NSData` object:

```
using System;
using System.IO;
using System.Text;
using Xamarin.Forms;
using AVFoundation;
using Foundation;

[assembly: Dependency(typeof(MonkeyTapWithSound.iOS.PlatformSoundPlayer))]

namespace MonkeyTapWithSound.iOS
{
    public class PlatformSoundPlayer : IPlatformSoundPlayer
    {
        const int numChannels = 1;
        const int bitsPerSample = 16;

        public void PlaySound(int samplingRate, byte[] pcmData)
        {
            int numSamples = pcmData.Length / (bitsPerSample / 8);

            MemoryStream memoryStream = new MemoryStream();
            BinaryWriter writer = new BinaryWriter(memoryStream, Encoding.ASCII);

            // Construct WAVE header.
            writer.Write(new char[] { 'R', 'I', 'F', 'F' });
            writer.Write(36 + sizeof(short) * numSamples);
            writer.Write(new char[] { 'W', 'A', 'V', 'E' });
            writer.Write(new char[] { 'f', 'm', 't', ' ' });          // format chunk
```

```
        writer.Write(16);                                              // PCM chunk size
        writer.Write((short)1);                                        // PCM format flag
        writer.Write((short)numChannels);
        writer.Write(samplingRate);
        writer.Write(samplingRate * numChannels * bitsPerSample / 8);  // byte rate
        writer.Write((short)(numChannels * bitsPerSample / 8));        // block align
        writer.Write((short)bitsPerSample);
        writer.Write(new char[] { 'd', 'a', 't', 'a' });               // data chunk
        writer.Write(numSamples * numChannels * bitsPerSample / 8);

        // Write data as well.
        writer.Write(pcmData, 0, pcmData.Length);

        memoryStream.Seek(0, SeekOrigin.Begin);
        NSData data = NSData.FromStream(memoryStream);
        AVAudioPlayer audioPlayer = AVAudioPlayer.FromData(data);
        audioPlayer.Play();
    }
  }
}
```

Notice the two essentials: `PlatformSoundPlayer` implements the `IPlatformSoundPlayer` interface, and the class is flagged with the `Dependency` attribute.

The Android version uses the `AudioTrack` class, and that turns out to be a little easier. However, `AudioTrack` objects can't overlap, so it's necessary to save the previous object and stop it playing before starting the next one:

```
using System;
using Android.Media;
using Xamarin.Forms;

[assembly: Dependency(typeof(MonkeyTapWithSound.Droid.PlatformSoundPlayer))]

namespace MonkeyTapWithSound.Droid
{
    public class PlatformSoundPlayer : IPlatformSoundPlayer
    {
        AudioTrack previousAudioTrack;

        public void PlaySound(int samplingRate, byte[] pcmData)
        {
            if (previousAudioTrack != null)
            {
                previousAudioTrack.Stop();
                previousAudioTrack.Release();
            }

            AudioTrack audioTrack = new AudioTrack(Stream.Music,
                                                   samplingRate,
                                                   ChannelOut.Mono,
                                                   Android.Media.Encoding.Pcm16bit,
                                                   pcmData.Length * sizeof(short),
```

```
                                                             AudioTrackMode.Static);

            audioTrack.Write(pcmData, 0, pcmData.Length);
            audioTrack.Play();

            previousAudioTrack = audioTrack;
        }
    }
}
```

The three Windows and Windows Phone platforms can use `MediaStreamSource`. To avoid a lot of repetitive code, the **MonkeyTapWithSound** solution contains an additional SAP project named **WinRuntimeShared** consisting solely of a class that all three platforms can use:

```csharp
using System;
using System.Runtime.InteropServices.WindowsRuntime;
using Windows.Media.Core;
using Windows.Media.MediaProperties;
using Windows.Storage.Streams;
using Windows.UI.Xaml.Controls;

namespace MonkeyTapWithSound.WinRuntimeShared
{
    public class SharedSoundPlayer
    {
        MediaElement mediaElement = new MediaElement();
        TimeSpan duration;

        public void PlaySound(int samplingRate, byte[] pcmData)
        {
            AudioEncodingProperties audioProps =
                AudioEncodingProperties.CreatePcm((uint)samplingRate, 1, 16);
            AudioStreamDescriptor audioDesc = new AudioStreamDescriptor(audioProps);
            MediaStreamSource mss = new MediaStreamSource(audioDesc);

            bool samplePlayed = false;
            mss.SampleRequested += (sender, args) =>
            {
                if (samplePlayed)
                    return;

                IBuffer ibuffer = pcmData.AsBuffer();
                MediaStreamSample sample =
                    MediaStreamSample.CreateFromBuffer(ibuffer, TimeSpan.Zero);
                sample.Duration = TimeSpan.FromSeconds(pcmData.Length / 2.0 / samplingRate);
                args.Request.Sample = sample;
                samplePlayed = true;
            };

            mediaElement.SetMediaStreamSource(mss);
        }
    }
}
```

This SAP project is referenced by the three Windows and Windows Phone projects, each of which contains an identical (except for the namespace) PlatformSoundPlayer class:

```
using System;
using Xamarin.Forms;

[assembly: Dependency(typeof(MonkeyTapWithSound.UWP.PlatformSoundPlayer))]

namespace MonkeyTapWithSound.UWP
{
    public class PlatformSoundPlayer : IPlatformSoundPlayer
    {
        WinRuntimeShared.SharedSoundPlayer sharedSoundPlayer;

        public void PlaySound(int samplingRate, byte[] pcmData)
        {
            if (sharedSoundPlayer == null)
            {
                sharedSoundPlayer = new WinRuntimeShared.SharedSoundPlayer();
            }

            sharedSoundPlayer.PlaySound(samplingRate, pcmData);
        }
    }
}
```

The use of DependencyService to perform platform-specific chores is very powerful, but this approach falls short when it comes to user-interface elements. If you need to expand the arsenal of views that adorn the pages of your Xamarin.Forms applications, that job involves creating platform-specific renderers, a process discussed in the final chapter of this book.

Chapter 10
XAML markup extensions

In code, you can set a property in a variety of different ways from a variety of different sources:

```
triangle.Angle1 = 45;
triangle.Angle1 = 180 * radians / Math.PI;
triangle.Angle1 = angles[i];
triangle.Angle1 = animator.GetCurrentAngle();
```

If this `Angle1` property is a `double`, all that's required is that the source be a `double` or otherwise provide a numeric value that is convertible to a `double`.

In markup, however, a property of type `double` usually can be set only from a string that qualifies as a valid argument to `Double.Parse`. The only exception you've seen so far is when the target property is flagged with a `TypeConverter` attribute, such as the `FontSize` property.

It might be desirable if XAML were more flexible—if you could set a property from sources other than explicit text strings. For example, suppose you want to define another way to set a property of type `Color`, perhaps using the `Hue`, `Saturation`, and `Luminosity` values but without the hassle of the `x:FactoryMethod` element. Just offhand, it doesn't seem possible. The XAML parser expects that any value set to an attribute of type `Color` is a string acceptable to the `ColorTypeConverter` class.

The purpose of XAML *markup extensions* is to get around this apparent restriction. Rest assured that XAML markup extensions are *not* extensions to XML. XAML is always legal XML. XAML markup extensions are extensions only in the sense that they extend the possibilities of attribute settings in markup. A markup extension essentially *provides* a value of a particular type without necessarily being a text representation *of* a value.

The code infrastructure

Strictly speaking, a XAML markup extension is a class that implements `IMarkupExtension`, which is a public interface defined in the regular **Xamarin.Forms.Core** assembly but with the namespace `Xamarin.Forms.Xaml`:

```
public interface IMarkupExtension
{
    object ProvideValue(IServiceProvider serviceProvider);
}
```

As the name suggests, `ProvideValue` is the method that provides a value to a XAML attribute. `IServiceProvider` is part of the base class libraries of .NET and defined in the `System` namespace:

```
public interface IServiceProvider
{
    object GetService(Type type);
}
```

Obviously, this information doesn't provide much of a hint on writing custom markup extensions, and in truth, they can be tricky. (You'll see an example shortly and other examples later in this book.) Fortunately, Xamarin.Forms provides several valuable markup extensions for you. These fall into three categories:

- Markup extensions that are part of the XAML 2009 specification. These appear in XAML files with the customary `x` prefix and are:

  - `x:Static`

  - `x:Reference`

  - `x:Type`

  - `x:Null`

  - `x:Array`

  These are implemented in classes that consist of the name of the markup extension with the word `Extension` appended—for example, the `StaticExtension` and `ReferenceExtension` classes. These classes are defined in the **Xamarin.Forms.Xaml** assembly.

- The following markup extensions originated in the Windows Presentation Foundation (WPF) and, with the exception of `DynamicResource`, are supported by Microsoft's other implementations of XAML, including Silverlight, Windows Phone 7 and 8, and Windows 8 and 10:

  - `StaticResource`

  - `DynamicResource`

  - `Binding`

  These are implemented in the public `StaticResourceExtension`, `DynamicResourceExtension`, and `BindingExtension` classes.

- There is only one markup extension that is unique to Xamarin.Forms: the `ConstraintExpression` class used in connection with `RelativeLayout`.

Although it's possible to play around with public markup-extension classes in code, they really only make sense in XAML.

Accessing static members

One of the simplest and most useful implementations of `IMarkupExtension` is encapsulated in the `StaticExtension` class. This is part of the original XAML specification, so it customarily appears in XAML with an `x` prefix. `StaticExtension` defines a single property named `Member` of type `string` that you set to a class and member name of a public constant, static property, static field, or enumeration member.

Let's see how this works. Here's a `Label` with six properties set as they would normally appear in XAML.

```
<Label Text="Just some text"
       BackgroundColor="Accent"
       TextColor="Black"
       FontAttributes="Italic"
       VerticalOptions="Center"
       HorizontalTextAlignment="Center" />
```

Five of these attributes are set to text strings that eventually reference various static properties, fields, and enumeration members, but the conversion of those text strings occurs through type converters and the standard XAML parsing of enumeration types.

If you want to be more explicit in setting these attributes to those various static properties, fields, and enumeration members, you can use `x:StaticExtension` within property element tags:

```
<Label Text="Just some text">
    <Label.BackgroundColor>
        <x:StaticExtension Member="Color.Accent" />
    </Label.BackgroundColor>

    <Label.TextColor>
        <x:StaticExtension Member="Color.Black" />
    </Label.TextColor>

    <Label.FontAttributes>
        <x:StaticExtension Member="FontAttributes.Italic" />
    </Label.FontAttributes>

    <Label.VerticalOptions>
        <x:StaticExtension Member="LayoutOptions.Center" />
    </Label.VerticalOptions>

    <Label.HorizontalTextAlignment>
        <x:StaticExtension Member="TextAlignment.Center" />
    </Label.HorizontalTextAlignment>
</Label>
```

`Color.Accent` is a static property. `Color.Black` and `LayoutOptions.Center` are static fields. `FontAttributes.Italic` and `TextAlignment.Center` are enumeration members.

Considering the ease with which these attributes are set with text strings, the approach using Stat-icExtension initially seems ridiculous, but notice that it's a general-purpose mechanism. You can use *any* static property, field, or enumeration member in the StaticExtension tag if its type matches the type of the target property.

By convention, classes that implement IMarkupExtension incorporate the word Extension in their names, but you can leave that out in XAML, which is why this markup extension is usually called x:Static rather than x:StaticExtension. The following markup is marginally shorter than the previous block:

```
<Label Text="Just some text">
    <Label.BackgroundColor>
        <x:Static Member="Color.Accent" />
    </Label.BackgroundColor>

    <Label.TextColor>
        <x:Static Member="Color.Black" />
    </Label.TextColor>

    <Label.FontAttributes>
        <x:Static Member="FontAttributes.Italic" />
    </Label.FontAttributes>

    <Label.VerticalOptions>
        <x:Static Member="LayoutOptions.Center" />
    </Label.VerticalOptions>

    <Label.HorizontalTextAlignment>
        <x:Static Member="TextAlignment.Center" />
    </Label.HorizontalTextAlignment>
</Label>
```

And now for the really major markup reduction—a change in syntax that causes the property-element tags to disappear and the footprint to shrink considerably. XAML markup extensions almost always appear with the markup extension name and the arguments within a pair of curly braces:

```
<Label Text="Just some text"
       BackgroundColor="{x:Static Member=Color.Accent}"
       TextColor="{x:Static Member=Color.Black}"
       FontAttributes="{x:Static Member=FontAttributes.Italic}"
       VerticalOptions="{x:Static Member=LayoutOptions.Center}"
       HorizontalTextAlignment="{x:Static Member=TextAlignment.Center}" />
```

This syntax with the curly braces is so ubiquitously used in connection with XAML markup extensions that many developers consider markup extensions to be synonymous with the curly-brace syntax. And that's nearly true: while curly braces always signal the presence of a XAML markup extension, in many cases a markup extension can appear in XAML without the curly braces (as demonstrated earlier) and it's sometimes convenient to use them in that way.

Notice there are no quotation marks within the curly braces. Within those braces, very different syntax rules apply. The `Member` property of the `StaticExtension` class is no longer an XML attribute. In terms of XML, the entire expression delimited by the curly braces is the value of the attribute, and the arguments within the curly braces appear without quotation marks.

Just like elements, markup extensions can have a `ContentProperty` attribute. Markup extensions that have only one property—such as the `StaticExtension` class with its single `Member` property—invariably mark that sole property as the content property. For markup extensions using the curly-brace syntax, this means that the `Member` property name and the equal sign can be removed:

```
<Label Text="Just some text"
       BackgroundColor="{x:Static Color.Accent}"
       TextColor="{x:Static Color.Black}"
       FontAttributes="{x:Static FontAttributes.Italic}"
       VerticalOptions="{x:Static LayoutOptions.Center}"
       HorizontalTextAlignment="{x:Static TextAlignment.Center}" />
```

This is the common form of the `x:Static` markup extension.

Obviously, the use of `x:Static` for these particular properties is unnecessary, but you can define your own static members for implementing application-wide constants, and you can reference these in your XAML files. This is demonstrated in the **SharedStatics** project.

The **SharedStatics** project contains a class named `AppConstants` that defines some constants and static fields that might be of use for formatting text:

```
namespace SharedStatics
{
    static class AppConstants
    {
        public static Color LightBackground = Color.Yellow;
        public static Color DarkForeground = Color.Blue;

        public static double NormalFontSize = 18;
        public static double TitleFontSize = 1.4 * NormalFontSize;
        public static double ParagraphSpacing = 10;

        public const FontAttributes Emphasis = FontAttributes.Italic;
        public const FontAttributes TitleAttribute = FontAttributes.Bold;

        public const TextAlignment TitleAlignment = TextAlignment.Center;
    }
}
```

You could use `Device.OnPlatform` in these definitions if you need something different for each platform.

The XAML file then uses 18 `x:Static` markup extensions to reference these items. Notice the XML namespace declaration that associates the `local` prefix with the namespace of the project:

```
<ContentPage xmlns="http://xamarin.com/schemas/2014/forms"
```

```
                    xmlns:x="http://schemas.microsoft.com/winfx/2009/xaml"
                    xmlns:local="clr-namespace:SharedStatics"
                    x:Class="SharedStatics.SharedStaticsPage"
                    BackgroundColor="{x:Static local:AppConstants.LightBackground}">

        <ContentPage.Padding>
            <OnPlatform x:TypeArguments="Thickness"
                        iOS="0, 20, 0, 0" />
        </ContentPage.Padding>

        <StackLayout Padding="10, 0"
                     Spacing="{x:Static local:AppConstants.ParagraphSpacing}">

            <Label Text="The SharedStatics Program"
                   TextColor="{x:Static local:AppConstants.DarkForeground}"
                   FontSize="{x:Static local:AppConstants.TitleFontSize}"
                   FontAttributes="{x:Static local:AppConstants.TitleAttribute}"
                   HorizontalTextAlignment="{x:Static local:AppConstants.TitleAlignment}" />

            <Label TextColor="{x:Static local:AppConstants.DarkForeground}"
                   FontSize="{x:Static local:AppConstants.NormalFontSize}">
                <Label.FormattedText>
                    <FormattedString>
                        <Span Text="Through use of the " />
                        <Span Text="x:Static"
                              FontSize="{x:Static local:AppConstants.NormalFontSize}"
                              FontAttributes="{x:Static local:AppConstants.Emphasis}" />
                        <Span Text=
" XAML markup extension, an application can maintain a collection of
common property settings defined as constants, static properties or fields,
or enumeration members in a separate code file. These can then be
referenced within the XAML file." />
                    </FormattedString>
                </Label.FormattedText>
            </Label>

            <Label TextColor="{x:Static local:AppConstants.DarkForeground}"
                   FontSize="{x:Static local:AppConstants.NormalFontSize}">
                <Label.FormattedText>
                    <FormattedString>
                        <Span Text=
"However, this is not the only technique to share property settings.
You'll soon discover that you can store objects in a " />
                        <Span Text="ResourceDictionary"
                              FontSize="{x:Static local:AppConstants.NormalFontSize}"
                              FontAttributes="{x:Static local:AppConstants.Emphasis}" />
                        <Span Text=" and access them through the " />
                        <Span Text="StaticResource"
                              FontSize="{x:Static local:AppConstants.NormalFontSize}"
                              FontAttributes="{x:Static local:AppConstants.Emphasis}" />
                        <Span Text=
" markup extension, and even encapsultate multiple property settings in a " />
                        <Span Text="Style"
                              FontSize="{x:Static local:AppConstants.NormalFontSize}"
```

```
                        FontAttributes="{x:Static local:AppConstants.Emphasis}" />
                <Span Text=" object." />
            </FormattedString>
        </Label.FormattedText>
    </Label>
  </StackLayout>
</ContentPage>
```

Each of the `Span` objects with a `FontAttributes` setting repeats the `FontSize` setting that is set on the `Label` itself because `Span` objects do not inherit font-related settings from the `Label` when another font-related setting is applied.

And here it is:

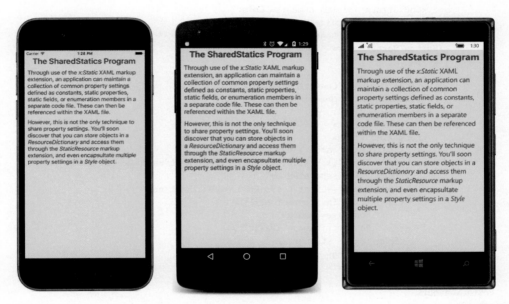

This technique allows you to use these common property settings on multiple pages, and if you ever need to change the values, you need only change the `AppSettings` file.

It is also possible to use `x:Static` with static properties and fields defined in classes in external libraries. The following example, named **SystemStatics,** is rather contrived—it sets the `BorderWidth` of a `Button` equal to the `PI` static field defined in the `Math` class and uses the static `Environment.New-Line` property for line breaks in text. But it demonstrates the technique.

The `Math` and `Environment` classes are both defined in the .NET `System` namespace, so a new XML namespace declaration is required to define a prefix named (for example) `sys` for `System`. Notice that this namespace declaration specifies the CLR namespace as `System` but the assembly as `mscorlib`, which originally stood for Microsoft Common Object Runtime Library but now stands for Multilanguage Standard Common Object Runtime Library:

```xml
<ContentPage xmlns="http://xamarin.com/schemas/2014/forms"
             xmlns:x="http://schemas.microsoft.com/winfx/2009/xaml"
             xmlns:sys="clr-namespace:System;assembly=mscorlib"
             x:Class="SystemStatics.SystemStaticsPage">
    <StackLayout>
        <Button Text=" Button with &#x03C0; border width "
                BorderWidth="{x:Static sys:Math.PI}"
                HorizontalOptions="Center"
                VerticalOptions="CenterAndExpand">
            <Button.BackgroundColor>
                <OnPlatform x:TypeArguments="Color"
                            Android="#404040" />
            </Button.BackgroundColor>
            <Button.BorderColor>
                <OnPlatform x:TypeArguments="Color"
                            Android="White"
                            WinPhone="Black" />
            </Button.BorderColor>
        </Button>

        <Label VerticalOptions="CenterAndExpand"
               HorizontalTextAlignment="Center"
               FontSize="Medium">
            <Label.FormattedText>
                <FormattedString>
                    <Span Text="Three lines of text" />
                    <Span Text="{x:Static sys:Environment.NewLine}" />
                    <Span Text="separated by" />
                    <Span Text="{x:Static sys:Environment.NewLine}" />
                    <Span Text="Environment.NewLine"
                          FontSize="Medium"
                          FontAttributes="Italic" />
                    <Span Text=" strings" />
                </FormattedString>
            </Label.FormattedText>
        </Label>
    </StackLayout>
</ContentPage>
```

The button border doesn't show up in Android unless the background color is set, and on both Android and Windows Phone the border needs a nondefault color, so some additional markup takes care of those problems. On iOS platforms, a button border tends to crowd the button text, so the text is defined with spaces at the beginning and end.

Judging solely from the visuals, we really have to take it on trust that the button border width is about 3.14 units wide, but the line breaks definitely work:

The use of curly braces for markup extensions implies that you can't display text surrounded by curly braces. The curly braces in this text will be mistaken for a markup extension:

```
<Label Text="{Text in curly braces}" />
```

That won't work. You can have curly braces elsewhere in the text string, but you can't begin with a left curly brace.

If you really need to, however, you can ensure that text is not mistaken for a XAML markup extension by beginning the text with an escape sequence that consists of a pair of left and right curly braces:

```
<Label Text="{}{Text in curly braces}" />
```

That will display the text you want.

Resource dictionaries

Xamarin.Forms also supports a second approach to sharing objects and values, and while this approach has a little more overhead than the `x:Static` markup extension, it is somewhat more versatile because everything—the shared objects and the visual elements that use them—can be expressed in XAML.

`VisualElement` defines a property named `Resources` that is of type `ResourceDictionary`—a dictionary with `string` keys and values of type `object`. Items can be added to this dictionary right in XAML, and they can be accessed in XAML with the `StaticResource` and `DynamicResource` markup extensions.

Although `x:Static` and `StaticResource` have somewhat similar names, they are quite different: `x:Static` references a constant, a static field, a static property, or an enumeration member, while `StaticResource` retrieves an object from a `ResourceDictionary`.

While the `x:Static` markup extension is intrinsic to XAML (and hence appears in XAML with an `x` prefix), the `StaticResource` and `DynamicResource` markup extensions are not. They were part of the original XAML implementation in the Windows Presentation Foundation, and `StaticResource` is also supported in Silverlight, Windows Phone 7 and 8, and Windows 8 and 10.

You'll use `StaticResource` for most purposes and reserve `DynamicResource` for some special applications, so let's begin with `StaticResource`.

StaticResource for most purposes

Suppose you've defined three buttons in a `StackLayout`:

```xml
<StackLayout>
    <Button Text=" Carpe diem "
            HorizontalOptions="Center"
            VerticalOptions="CenterAndExpand"
            BorderWidth="3"
            TextColor="Red"
            FontSize="Large">
        <Button.BackgroundColor>
            <OnPlatform x:TypeArguments="Color"
                        Android="#404040" />
        </Button.BackgroundColor>
        <Button.BorderColor>
            <OnPlatform x:TypeArguments="Color"
                        Android="White"
                        WinPhone="Black" />
        </Button.BorderColor>
    </Button>

    <Button Text=" Sapere aude "
            HorizontalOptions="Center"
            VerticalOptions="CenterAndExpand"
            BorderWidth="3"
            TextColor="Red"
                FontSize="Large">
        <Button.BackgroundColor>
            <OnPlatform x:TypeArguments="Color"
                        Android="#404040" />
        </Button.BackgroundColor>
        <Button.BorderColor>
            <OnPlatform x:TypeArguments="Color"
                        Android="White"
                        WinPhone="Black" />
        </Button.BorderColor>
    </Button>

    <Button Text=" Discere faciendo "
```

```
                HorizontalOptions="Center"
                VerticalOptions="CenterAndExpand"
                BorderWidth="3"
                TextColor="Red"
                FontSize="Large">
        <Button.BackgroundColor>
            <OnPlatform x:TypeArguments="Color"
                        Android="#404040" />
        </Button.BackgroundColor>
        <Button.BorderColor>
            <OnPlatform x:TypeArguments="Color"
                        Android="White"
                        WinPhone="Black" />
        </Button.BorderColor>
    </Button>
</StackLayout>
```

Of course, this is somewhat unrealistic. There are no `Clicked` events set for these buttons, and generally button text is not in Latin. But here's what they look like:

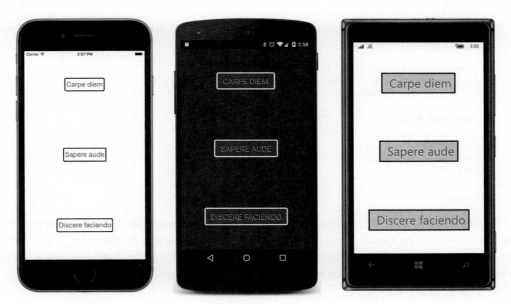

Aside from the text, all three buttons have the same properties set to the same values. Repetitious markup such as this tends to rub programmers the wrong way. It's an affront to the eye and difficult to maintain and change.

Eventually you'll see how to use styles to really cut down on the repetitious markup. For now, however, the goal is not to make the markup shorter but to consolidate the values in one place so that if you ever want to change the `TextColor` property from `Red` to `Blue`, you can do so with one edit rather than three.

Obviously, you can use `x:Static` for this job by defining the values in code. But let's do the whole thing in XAML by storing the values in a *resource dictionary*. Every class that derives from `VisualElement` has a `Resources` property of type `ResourceDictionary`. Resources that are used throughout a page are customarily stored in the `Resources` collection of the `ContentPage`.

The first step is to express the `Resources` property of `ContentPage` as a property element:

```
<ContentPage xmlns="http://xamarin.com/schemas/2014/forms"
             xmlns:x="http://schemas.microsoft.com/winfx/2009/xaml"
             x:Class="ResourceSharing.ResourceSharingPage">

    <ContentPage.Resources>

    </ContentPage.Resources>
    ...
</ContentPage>
```

If you're also defining a `Padding` property on the page by using property-element tags, the order doesn't matter.

For performance purposes, the `Resources` property is `null` by default, so you need to explicitly instantiate the `ResourceDictionary`:

```
<ContentPage xmlns="http://xamarin.com/schemas/2014/forms"
             xmlns:x="http://schemas.microsoft.com/winfx/2009/xaml"
             x:Class="ResourceSharing.ResourceSharingPage">

    <ContentPage.Resources>
        <ResourceDictionary>

        </ResourceDictionary>
    </ContentPage.Resources>
    ...
</ContentPage>
```

Between the `ResourceDictionary` tags, you define one or more objects or values. Each item in the dictionary must be identified with a dictionary key that you specify with the XAML `x:Key` attribute. For example, here's the syntax for including a `LayoutOptions` value in the dictionary with a descriptive key that indicates that this value is defined for setting horizontal options:

```
<LayoutOptions x:Key="horzOptions">Center</LayoutOptions>
```

Because this is a `LayoutOptions` value, the XAML parser accesses the `LayoutOptionsConverter` class to convert the content of the tags, which is the text "Center".

A second way to store a `LayoutOptions` value in the dictionary is to let the XAML parser instantiate the structure and set `LayoutOptions` properties from attributes you specify:

```
<LayoutOptions x:Key="vertOptions"
               Alignment="Center"
               Expands="True" />
```

The `BorderWidth` property is of type `double`, so the `x:Double` datatype element defined in the XAML 2009 specification is ideal:

```
<x:Double x:Key="borderWidth">3</x:Double>
```

You can store a `Color` value in the resource dictionary with a text representation of the color as content. The XAML parser uses the normal `ColorTypeConverter` for the text conversion:

```
<Color x:Key="textColor">Red</Color>
```

You can also specify hexadecimal ARGB values following a hash sign.

You can't initialize a `Color` value by setting its `R`, `G`, and `B` properties because those are get-only. But you can invoke a `Color` constructor using `x:Arguments` or one of the `Color` factory methods using `x:FactoryMethod` and `x:Arguments`.

```
<Color x:Key="textColor"
       x:FactoryMethod="FromHsla">
    <x:Arguments>
        <x:Double>0</x:Double>
        <x:Double>1</x:Double>
        <x:Double>0.5</x:Double>
        <x:Double>1</x:Double>
    </x:Arguments>
</Color>
```

Notice both the `x:Key` and `x:FactoryMethod` attributes.

The `BackgroundColor` and `BorderColor` properties of the three buttons shown above are set to values from the `OnPlatform` class. Fortunately you can put `OnPlatform` objects right in the dictionary:

```
<OnPlatform x:Key="backgroundColor"
            x:TypeArguments="Color"
            Android="#404040" />

<OnPlatform x:Key="borderColor"
            x:TypeArguments="Color"
            Android="White"
            WinPhone="Black" />
```

Notice both the `x:Key` and `x:TypeArguments` attributes.

A dictionary item for the `FontSize` property is somewhat problematic. The `FontSize` property is of type `double`, so if you're storing an actual numeric value in the dictionary, that's no problem. But you can't store the word "Large" in the dictionary as if it were a `double`. Only when a "Large" string is set to a `FontSize` attribute does the XAML parser use the `FontSizeConverter`. For that reason, you'll need to store the `FontSize` item as a string:

```
<x:String x:Key="fontSize">Large</x:String>
```

Here's the complete dictionary at this point:

```
<ContentPage xmlns="http://xamarin.com/schemas/2014/forms"
             xmlns:x="http://schemas.microsoft.com/winfx/2009/xaml"
             x:Class="ResourceSharing.ResourceSharingPage">

    <ContentPage.Resources>
        <ResourceDictionary>
            <LayoutOptions x:Key="horzOptions">Center</LayoutOptions>

            <LayoutOptions x:Key="vertOptions"
                           Alignment="Center"
                           Expands="True" />

            <x:Double x:Key="borderWidth">3</x:Double>

            <Color x:Key="textColor">Red</Color>

            <OnPlatform x:Key="backgroundColor"
                        x:TypeArguments="Color"
                        Android="#404040" />

            <OnPlatform x:Key="borderColor"
                        x:TypeArguments="Color"
                        Android="White"
                        WinPhone="Black" />

            <x:String x:Key="fontSize">Large</x:String>
        </ResourceDictionary>
    </ContentPage.Resources>
    ...
</ContentPage>
```

This is sometimes referred to as a *resources section* for the page. In real-life programming, very many XAML files begin with a resources section.

You can reference items in the dictionary by using the `StaticResource` markup extension, which is supported by `StaticResourceExtension`. The class defines a property named `Key` that you set to the dictionary key. You can use a `StaticResourceExtension` as an element within property-element tags, or you can use `StaticResourceExtension` or `StaticResource` in curly braces. If you're using the curly-brace syntax, you can leave out the `Key` and equal sign because `Key` is the content property of `StaticResourceExtension`.

The following complete XAML file in the **ResourceSharing** project illustrates three of these options:

```
<ContentPage xmlns="http://xamarin.com/schemas/2014/forms"
             xmlns:x="http://schemas.microsoft.com/winfx/2009/xaml"
             x:Class="ResourceSharing.ResourceSharingPage">

    <ContentPage.Resources>
        <ResourceDictionary>
            <LayoutOptions x:Key="horzOptions">Center</LayoutOptions>

            <LayoutOptions x:Key="vertOptions"
                           Alignment="Center"
```

```
                                    Expands="True" />

            <x:Double x:Key="borderWidth">3</x:Double>

            <Color x:Key="textColor">Red</Color>

            <OnPlatform x:Key="backgroundColor"
                        x:TypeArguments="Color"
                        Android="#404040" />

            <OnPlatform x:Key="borderColor"
                        x:TypeArguments="Color"
                        Android="White"
                        WinPhone="Black" />

            <x:String x:Key="fontSize">Large</x:String>
        </ResourceDictionary>
    </ContentPage.Resources>

    <StackLayout>
        <Button Text=" Carpe diem ">
            <Button.HorizontalOptions>
                <StaticResourceExtension Key="horzOptions" />
            </Button.HorizontalOptions>

            <Button.VerticalOptions>
                <StaticResourceExtension Key="vertOptions" />
            </Button.VerticalOptions>

            <Button.BorderWidth>
                <StaticResourceExtension Key="borderWidth" />
            </Button.BorderWidth>

            <Button.TextColor>
                <StaticResourceExtension Key="textColor" />
            </Button.TextColor>

            <Button.BackgroundColor>
                <StaticResourceExtension Key="backgroundColor" />
            </Button.BackgroundColor>

            <Button.BorderColor>
                <StaticResourceExtension Key="borderColor" />
            </Button.BorderColor>

            <Button.FontSize>
                <StaticResourceExtension Key="fontSize" />
            </Button.FontSize>
        </Button>

        <Button Text=" Sapere aude "
                HorizontalOptions="{StaticResource Key=horzOptions}"
                VerticalOptions="{StaticResource Key=vertOptions}"
                BorderWidth="{StaticResource Key=borderWidth}"
```

```
                    TextColor="{StaticResource Key=textColor}"
                    BackgroundColor="{StaticResource Key=backgroundColor}"
                    BorderColor="{StaticResource Key=borderColor}"
                    FontSize="{StaticResource Key=fontSize}" />

        <Button Text=" Discere faciendo "
                HorizontalOptions="{StaticResource horzOptions}"
                VerticalOptions="{StaticResource vertOptions}"
                BorderWidth="{StaticResource borderWidth}"
                TextColor="{StaticResource textColor}"
                BackgroundColor="{StaticResource backgroundColor}"
                BorderColor="{StaticResource borderColor}"
                FontSize="{StaticResource fontSize}" />
    </StackLayout>
</ContentPage>
```

The simplest syntax in the third button is the most common, and indeed, that syntax is so ubiquitous that many longtime XAML developers might be entirely unfamiliar with the other variations. But if you use a version of `StaticResource` with the `Key` property, do not put an x prefix on it. The `x:Key` attribute is only for defining dictionary keys for items in the `ResourceDictionary`.

Objects and values in the dictionary are shared among all the `StaticResource` references. That's not so clear in the preceding example, but it's something to keep in mind. For example, suppose you store a `Button` object in the resource dictionary:

```
<ContentPage.Resources>
    <ResourceDictionary>
        <Button x:Key="button"
                Text="Shared Button?"
                HorizontalOptions="Center"
                VerticalOptions="CenterAndExpand"
                FontSize="Large" />
    </ResourceDictionary>
</ContentPage.Resources>
```

You can certainly use that `Button` object on your page by adding it to the `Children` collection of a `StackLayout` with the `StaticResourceExtension` element syntax:

```
<StackLayout>
    <StaticResourceExtension Key="button" />
</StackLayout>
```

However, you can't use that same dictionary item in hopes of putting another copy in the `StackLayout`:

```
<StackLayout>
    <StaticResourceExtension Key="button" />
    <StaticResourceExtension Key="button" />
</StackLayout>
```

That won't work. Both these elements reference the same `Button` object, and a particular visual element can be in only one particular location on the screen. It can't be in multiple locations.

For this reason, visual elements are not normally stored in a resource dictionary. If you need multiple elements on your page that have mostly the same properties, you'll want to use a `Style`, which is explored in Chapter 12.

A tree of dictionaries

The `ResourceDictionary` class imposes the same rules as other dictionaries: all the items in the dictionary must have keys, but duplicate keys are not allowed.

However, because every instance of `VisualElement` potentially has its own resource dictionary, your page can contain multiple dictionaries, and you can use the same keys in different dictionaries just as long as all the keys within each dictionary are unique. Conceivably, every visual element in the visual tree can have its own dictionary, but it really only makes sense for a resource dictionary to apply to multiple elements, so resource dictionaries are only commonly found defined on `Layout` or `Page` objects.

Using this technique you can construct a tree of dictionaries with dictionary keys that effectively override the keys on other dictionaries. This is demonstrated in the **ResourceTrees** project. The XAML file for the `ResourceTreesPage` class shows a `Resources` dictionary for the `ContentPage` that defines resources with keys of `horzOptions`, `vertOptions`, and `textColor`.

A second `Resources` dictionary is attached to an inner `StackLayout` for resources named `textColor` and `FontSize`:

```
<ContentPage xmlns="http://xamarin.com/schemas/2014/forms"
             xmlns:x="http://schemas.microsoft.com/winfx/2009/xaml"
             x:Class="ResourceTrees.ResourceTreesPage">

    <ContentPage.Resources>
        <ResourceDictionary>
            <LayoutOptions x:Key="horzOptions">Center</LayoutOptions>

            <LayoutOptions x:Key="vertOptions"
                           Alignment="Center"
                           Expands="True" />

            <OnPlatform x:Key="textColor"
                        x:TypeArguments="Color"
                        iOS="Red"
                        Android="Pink"
                        WinPhone="Blue" />
        </ResourceDictionary>
    </ContentPage.Resources>

    <StackLayout>
        <Button Text=" Carpe diem "
                HorizontalOptions="{StaticResource horzOptions}"
                VerticalOptions="{StaticResource vertOptions}"
                BorderWidth="{StaticResource borderWidth}"
                TextColor="{StaticResource textColor}"
```

```
                        BackgroundColor="{StaticResource backgroundColor}"
                        BorderColor="{StaticResource borderColor}"
                        FontSize="{StaticResource fontSize}" />

        <StackLayout>
            <StackLayout.Resources>
                <ResourceDictionary>
                    <Color x:Key="textColor">Default</Color>
                    <x:String x:Key="fontSize">Default</x:String>
                </ResourceDictionary>
            </StackLayout.Resources>

            <Label Text="The first of two labels"
                    HorizontalOptions="{StaticResource horzOptions}"
                    TextColor="{StaticResource textColor}"
                    FontSize="{StaticResource fontSize}" />

            <Button Text=" Sapere aude "
                    HorizontalOptions="{StaticResource horzOptions}"
                    BorderWidth="{StaticResource borderWidth}"
                    TextColor="{StaticResource textColor}"
                    BackgroundColor="{StaticResource backgroundColor}"
                    BorderColor="{StaticResource borderColor}"
                    FontSize="{StaticResource fontSize}" />

            <Label Text="The second of two labels"
                    HorizontalOptions="{StaticResource horzOptions}"
                    TextColor="{StaticResource textColor}"
                    FontSize="{StaticResource fontSize}" />
        </StackLayout>

        <Button Text=" Discere faciendo "
                HorizontalOptions="{StaticResource horzOptions}"
                VerticalOptions="{StaticResource vertOptions}"
                BorderWidth="{StaticResource borderWidth}"
                TextColor="{StaticResource textColor}"
                BackgroundColor="{StaticResource backgroundColor}"
                BorderColor="{StaticResource borderColor}"
                FontSize="{StaticResource fontSize}" />
    </StackLayout>
</ContentPage>
```

The `Resources` dictionary on the inner `StackLayout` applies only to items within that `StackLay-out`, which are the items in the middle of this screenshot:

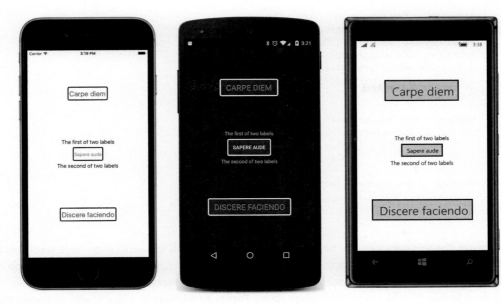

Here's how it works:

When the XAML parser encounters a `StaticResource` on an attribute of a visual element, it begins a search for that dictionary key. It first looks in the `ResourceDictionary` for that visual element, and if the key is not found, it looks for the key in the visual element's parent's `ResourceDictionary`, and up and up through the visual tree until it reaches the `ResourceDictionary` on the page.

But something's missing here! Where are the entries in the page's `ResourceDictionary` for `borderWidth`, `backgroundColor`, `borderColor`, and `fontSize`? They aren't in the ResourceTreesPage.xaml file!

Those items are elsewhere. The `Application` class—from which every application's `App` class derives—also defines a `Resources` property of type `ResourceDictionary`. This is handy for defining resources that apply to the entire application and not just to a particular page or layout. When the XAML parser searches up the visual tree for a matching resource key, and that key is not found in the `ResourceDictionary` for the page, it finally checks the `ResourceDictionary` defined by the `Application` class. Only if it's not found there is a `XamlParseException` raised for the `StaticResource` key-not-found error.

You can add items to your `App` class's `ResourceDictionary` object in two ways:

One approach is to add the items in code in the `App` constructor. Make sure you do this before instantiating the main `ContentPage` class:

```
public class App : Application
{
    public App()
    {
```

```
        Resources = new ResourceDictionary();
        Resources.Add("borderWidth", 3.0);
        Resources.Add("fontSize", "Large");
        Resources.Add("backgroundColor",
            Device.OnPlatform(Color.Default,
                              Color.FromRgb(0x40, 0x40, 0x40),
                              Color.Default));

        Resources.Add("borderColor",
            Device.OnPlatform(Color.Default,
                              Color.White,
                              Color.Black));

        MainPage = new ResourceTreesPage();
    }
    …
}
```

However, the `App` class can also have a XAML file of its own, and the application-wide resources can be defined in the `Resources` collection in that XAML file. To do this, you'll want to delete the App.cs file created by the Xamarin.Forms solution template. There's no template item for an `App` class, so you'll need to fake it. Add a new XAML page class—**Forms Xaml Page** in Visual Studio or **Forms ContentPage Xaml** in Xamarin Studio—to the project. Name it `App`. And immediately—before you forget—go into the App.xaml file and change the root tags to `Application`, and go into the App.xaml.cs file and change the base class to `Application`.

Now you have an `App` class that derives from `Application` and has its own XAML file. In the App.xaml file you can then instantiate a `ResourceDictionary` within `Application.Resources` property-element tags and add items to it:

```
<Application xmlns="http://xamarin.com/schemas/2014/forms"
             xmlns:x="http://schemas.microsoft.com/winfx/2009/xaml"
             x:Class="ResourceTrees.App">
    <Application.Resources>
        <ResourceDictionary>
            <x:Double x:Key="borderWidth">3</x:Double>
            <x:String x:Key="fontSize">Large</x:String>

            <OnPlatform x:Key="backgroundColor"
                        x:TypeArguments="Color"
                        Android="#404040" />

            <OnPlatform x:Key="borderColor"
                        x:TypeArguments="Color"
                        Android="White"
                        WinPhone="Black" />
        </ResourceDictionary>
    </Application.Resources>
</Application>
```

The constructor in the code-behind file needs to call `InitializeComponent` to parse the App.xaml file at run time and add the items to the dictionary. This should be done prior to the normal job of instantiating the `ResourceTreesPage` class and setting it to the `MainPage` property:

```
public partial class App : Application
{
    public App()
    {
        InitializeComponent();

        MainPage = new ResourceTreesPage();
    }

    protected override void OnStart()
    {
        // Handle when your app starts
    }

    protected override void OnSleep()
    {
        // Handle when your app sleeps
    }

    protected override void OnResume()
    {
        // Handle when your app resumes
    }
}
```

Adding the lifecycle events is optional.

Be sure to call `InitializeComponent` before instantiating the page class. The constructor of the page class calls its own `InitializeComponent` to parse the XAML file for the page, and the `StaticResource` markup extensions need access to the `Resources` collection in the `App` class.

Every `Resources` dictionary has a particular scope: For the `Resources` dictionary on the `App` class, that scope is the entire application. A `Resources` dictionary on the `ContentPage` class applies to the whole page. A `Resources` dictionary on a `StackLayout` applies to all the children in the `StackLayout`. You should define and store your resources based on how you use them. Use the `Resources` dictionary in the `App` class for application-wide resources; use the `Resources` dictionary on the `ContentPage` for page-wide resources; but define additional `Resources` dictionaries deeper in the visual tree for resources required only in one part of the page.

As you'll see in Chapter 12, the most important items in a `Resources` dictionary are usually objects of type `Style`. In the general case, you'll have application-wide `Style` objects, `Style` objects for the page, and `Style` objects associated with smaller parts of the visual tree.

DynamicResource for special purposes

An alternative to `StaticResource` for referencing items from the `Resources` dictionary is `DynamicResource`, and if you just substitute `DynamicResource` for `StaticResource` in the example shown above, the program will seemingly run the same. However, the two markup extensions are very different. `StaticResource` accesses the item in the dictionary only once while the XAML is being parsed and the page is being built. But `DynamicResource` maintains a link between the dictionary key and the property set from that dictionary item. If the item in the resource dictionary referenced by the key changes, `DynamicResource` will detect that change and set the new value to the property.

Skeptical? Let's try it out. The **DynamicVsStatic** project has a XAML file that defines a resource item of type `string` with a key of `currentDateTime`, even though the item in the dictionary is the string "Not actually a DateTime"!

This dictionary item is referenced four times in the XAML file, but one of the references is commented out. In the first two examples, the `Text` property of a `Label` is set using `StaticResource` and `DynamicResource`. In the second two examples, the `Text` property of a `Span` object is set similarly, but the use of `DynamicResource` on the `Span` object appears in comments:

```
<ContentPage xmlns="http://xamarin.com/schemas/2014/forms"
             xmlns:x="http://schemas.microsoft.com/winfx/2009/xaml"
             x:Class="DynamicVsStatic.DynamicVsStaticPage"
             Padding="5, 0">

    <ContentPage.Resources>
        <ResourceDictionary>
            <x:String x:Key="currentDateTime">Not actually a DateTime</x:String>
        </ResourceDictionary>
    </ContentPage.Resources>

    <StackLayout>
        <Label Text="StaticResource on Label.Text:"
               VerticalOptions="EndAndExpand"
               FontSize="Medium" />

        <Label Text="{StaticResource currentDateTime}"
               VerticalOptions="StartAndExpand"
               HorizontalTextAlignment="Center"
               FontSize="Medium" />

        <Label Text="DynamicResource on Label.Text:"
               VerticalOptions="EndAndExpand"
               FontSize="Medium" />

        <Label Text="{DynamicResource currentDateTime}"
               VerticalOptions="StartAndExpand"
               HorizontalTextAlignment="Center"
               FontSize="Medium" />

        <Label Text="StaticResource on Span.Text:"
               VerticalOptions="EndAndExpand"
               FontSize="Medium" />

        <Label VerticalOptions="StartAndExpand"
               HorizontalTextAlignment="Center"
```

```
                    FontSize="Medium">
            <Label.FormattedText>
                <FormattedString>
                    <Span Text="{StaticResource currentDateTime}" />
                </FormattedString>
            </Label.FormattedText>
        </Label>

        <!-- This raises a run-time exception! -->

        <!--<Label Text="DynamicResource on Span.Text:"
                VerticalOptions="EndAndExpand"
                FontSize="Medium" />

        <Label VerticalOptions="StartAndExpand"
                HorizontalTextAlignment="Center"
                FontSize="Medium">
            <Label.FormattedText>
                <FormattedString>
                    <Span Text="{DynamicResource currentDateTime}" />
                </FormattedString>
            </Label.FormattedText>
        </Label>-->
    </StackLayout>
</ContentPage>
```

You'll probably expect all three of the references to the `currentDateTime` dictionary item to result in the display of the text "Not actually a DateTime". However, the code-behind file starts a timer going. Every second, the timer callback replaces that dictionary item with a new string representing an actual `DateTime` value:

```
public partial class DynamicVsStaticPage : ContentPage
{
    public DynamicVsStaticPage()
    {
        InitializeComponent();

        Device.StartTimer(TimeSpan.FromSeconds(1),
            () =>
            {
                Resources["currentDateTime"] = DateTime.Now.ToString();
                return true;
            });
    }
}
```

The result is that the `Text` properties set with `StaticResource` stay the same, while the one with `DynamicResource` changes every second to reflect the new item in the dictionary:

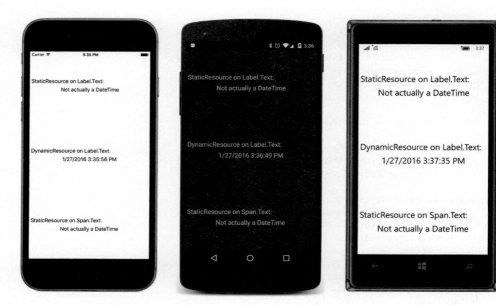

Here's another difference: if there is no item in the dictionary with the specified key name, Static-Resource will raise a run-time exception, but DynamicResource will not.

You can try uncommenting the block of markup at the end of the **DynamicVsStatic** project, and you will indeed encounter a run-time exception to the effect that the Text property could not be found. Just offhand, that exception doesn't sound quite right, but it's referring to a very real difference.

The problem is that the Text properties in Label and Span are defined in significantly different ways, and that difference matters a lot for DynamicResource. This difference will be explored in the next chapter, "The bindable infrastructure."

Lesser-used markup extensions

Three markup extensions are not used as much as the others. These are:

- x:Null

- x:Type

- x:Array

You use the x:Null extension to set a property to null. The syntax looks like this:

```
<SomeElement SomeProperty="{x:Null}" />
```

This doesn't make much sense unless SomeProperty has a default value that is not null when it's desirable to set the property to null. But as you'll see in Chapter 12, sometimes a property can acquire a non-`null` value from a style, and `x:Null` is pretty much the only way to override that.

The `x:Type` markup extension is used to set a property of type `Type`, the .NET class describing the type of a class or structure. Here's the syntax:

```
<AnotherElement TypeProperty="{x:Type Color}" />
```

You'll also use `x:Type` in connection with `x:Array`. The `x:Array` markup extension is always used with regular element syntax rather than curly-brace syntax. It has a required argument named `Type` that you set with the `x:Type` markup extension. This indicates the type of the elements in the array. Here's how an array might be defined in a resource dictionary:

```
<x:Array x:Key="array"
         Type="{x:Type x:String}">
    <x:String>One String</x:String>
    <x:String>Two String</x:String>
    <x:String>Red String</x:String>
    <x:String>Blue String</x:String>
</x:Array>
```

A custom markup extension

Let's create our own markup extension named `HslColorExtension`. This will allow us to set any property of type `Color` by specifying values of hue, saturation, and luminosity, but in a manner much simpler than the use of the `x:FactoryMethod` tag demonstrated in Chapter 8, "Code and XAML in harmony."

Moreover, let's put this class in a separate Portable Class Library so that you can use it from multiple applications. Such a library can be found with the other source code for this book. It's in a directory named **Libraries** that is parallel to the separate chapter directories. The name of this PCL (and the namespace of the classes within it) is **Xamarin.FormsBook.Toolkit**.

You can use this library yourself in your own applications by adding a reference to it. You can then add a new XML namespace declaration in your XAML files like so to specify this library:

```
xmlns:toolkit="clr-namespace:Xamarin.FormsBook.Toolkit;assembly=Xamarin.FormsBook.Toolkit"
```

With this `toolkit` prefix you can then reference the `HslColorExtension` class in the same way you use other XAML markup extensions:

```
<BoxView Color="{toolkit:HslColor H=0.67, S=1, L=0.5}" />
```

Unlike other XAML markup extensions shown so far, this one has multiple properties, and if you're setting them as arguments with the curly-brace syntax, they must be separated with commas.

Would something like that be useful? Let's first see how to create such a library for classes that you'd like to share among applications:

In Visual Studio, from the **File** menu, select **New** and **Project**. In the **New Project** dialog, select **Visual C#** and **Cross-Platform** at the left, and **Class Library (Xamarin.Forms)** from the list. Find a location for the project and give it a name. For the PCL created for this example, the name is **Xamarin.FormsBook.Toolkit**. Click **OK**. Along with all the overhead for the project, the template creates a code file named Xamarin.FormsBook.Toolkit.cs containing a class named `Xamarin.Forms-Book.Toolkit`. That's not a valid class name, so just delete that file.

In Xamarin Studio, from the **File** menu, select **New** and **Solution**. In the **New Project** dialog, select **Multiplatform** and **Library** at the left, and **Forms** and **Class Library** from the list. Find a location for it and give it a name (**Xamarin.FormsBook.Toolkit** for this example). Click **OK**. The solution template creates several files, including a file named MyPage.cs. Delete that file.

You can now add classes to this project in the normal way:

In Visual Studio, right-click the project name, select **Add** and **New Item**. In the **Add New Item** dialog, if you're just creating a code-only class, select **Visual C#** and **Code** at the left, and select **Class** from the list. Give it a name (HslColorExtension.cs for this example). Click the **Add** button.

In Xamarin Studio, in the tool menu for the project, select **Add** and **New File**. In the **New File** dialog, if you're just creating a code-only class, select **General** at the left and **Empty Class** in the list. Give it a name (HslColorExtension.cs for this example). Click the **New** button.

The **Xamarin.FormsBook.Toolkit** library will be built up and accumulate useful classes during the course of this book. But the first class in this library is `HslColorExtension`. The HslColorExtension.cs file (including the required `using` directives) looks like this:

```
using System;
using Xamarin.Forms;
using Xamarin.Forms.Xaml;

namespace Xamarin.FormsBook.Toolkit
{
    public class HslColorExtension : IMarkupExtension
    {
        public HslColorExtension()
        {
            A = 1;
        }

        public double H { set; get; }

        public double S { set; get; }

        public double L { set; get; }

        public double A { set; get; }

        public object ProvideValue(IServiceProvider serviceProvider)
        {
            return Color.FromHsla(H, S, L, A);
```

```
        }
    }
}
```

Notice that the class is public, so it's visible from outside the library, and that it implements the `IMarkupExtension` interface, which means that it must include a `ProvideValue` method. However, the method doesn't make use of the `IServiceProvider` argument at all, mainly because it doesn't need to know about anything else external to itself. All it needs are the four properties to create a `Color` value, and if the `A` value isn't set, a default value of 1 (fully opaque) is used.

This **Xamarin.FormsBook.Toolkit** solution contains only a PCL project. The project can be built to generate a PCL assembly, but it cannot be run without an application that uses this assembly.

There are two ways to access this library from an application solution:

- From the PCL project of your application solution, add a reference to the library PCL assembly, which is the dynamic-link library (DLL) generated from the library project.

- Include a link to the library project from your application solution, and add a reference to that library project from the applicationt's PCL project.

The first option is necessary if you have only the DLL and not the project with source code. Perhaps you're licensing the library and don't have access to the source. But if you have access to the project, it's usually best to include a link to the library project in your solution so that you can easily make changes to the library code and rebuild the library project.

The final project in this chapter is **CustomExtensionDemo,** which makes use of the `HslColorEx-tension` class in the new library. The **CustomExtensionDemo** solution contains a link to the **Xamarin.FormsBook.Toolkit** PCL project, and the **References** section in the **CustomExtensionDemo** project lists the **Xamarin.FormsBook.Toolkit** assembly.

Now the application project is seemingly ready to access the library project to use the `HslColor-orExtension` class within the application's XAML file.

But first there's another step. Unless you've enabled XAML compilation, a reference to an external library from XAML is insufficient to ensure that the library is included with the application. The library needs to be accessed from actual code. For this reason, **Xamarin.FormsBook.Toolkit** also contains a class and method that might seem from the name to be performing important initialization for the library:

```
namespace Xamarin.FormsBook.Toolkit
{
    public static class Toolkit
    {
        public static void Init()
        {
        }
    }
}
```

Whenever you use anything from this library, try to get into the habit of calling this `Init` method first thing in the `App` file:

```
namespace CustomExtensionDemo
{
    public class App : Application
    {
        public App()
        {
            Xamarin.FormsBook.Toolkit.Toolkit.Init();

            MainPage = new CustomExtensionDemoPage();
        }
        …
    }
}
```

The following XAML file shows the XML namespace declaration for the **Xamarin.Forms-Book.Toolkit** library and three ways to access the custom XAML markup extension—by using an `HslColorExtension` element set with property-element syntax on the `Color` property and by using both `HslColorExtension` and `HslColor` with the more common curly-brace syntax. Again, notice the use of commas to separate the arguments within the curly braces:

```
<ContentPage xmlns="http://xamarin.com/schemas/2014/forms"
             xmlns:x="http://schemas.microsoft.com/winfx/2009/xaml"
             xmlns:toolkit=
                 "clr-namespace:Xamarin.FormsBook.Toolkit;assembly=Xamarin.FormsBook.Toolkit"
             x:Class="CustomExtensionDemo.CustomExtensionDemoPage">

    <StackLayout>
        <!-- Red -->
        <BoxView HorizontalOptions="Center"
                 VerticalOptions="CenterAndExpand">
            <BoxView.Color>
                <toolkit:HslColorExtension H="0" S="1" L="0.5" />
            </BoxView.Color>
        </BoxView>

        <!-- Green -->
        <BoxView HorizontalOptions="Center"
                 VerticalOptions="CenterAndExpand">
            <BoxView.Color>
                <toolkit:HslColorExtension H="0.33" S="1" L="0.5" />
            </BoxView.Color>
        </BoxView>

        <!-- Blue -->
        <BoxView Color="{toolkit:HslColor H=0.67, S=1, L=0.5}"
                 HorizontalOptions="Center"
                 VerticalOptions="CenterAndExpand" />

        <!-- Gray -->
        <BoxView Color="{toolkit:HslColor H=0, S=0, L=0.5}"
```

```
                        HorizontalOptions="Center"
                        VerticalOptions="CenterAndExpand" />

        <!-- Semitransparent white -->
        <BoxView Color="{toolkit:HslColor H=0, S=0, L=1, A=0.5}"
                        HorizontalOptions="Center"
                        VerticalOptions="CenterAndExpand" />

        <!-- Semitransparent black -->
        <BoxView Color="{toolkit:HslColor H=0, S=0, L=0, A=0.5}"
                        HorizontalOptions="Center"
                        VerticalOptions="CenterAndExpand" />
    </StackLayout>
</ContentPage>
```

The last two examples set the A property for 50 percent transparency, so the boxes show up as a shade of gray (or not at all) depending on the background:

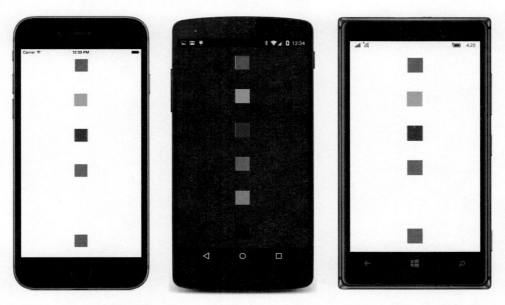

Two major uses of XAML markup extensions are yet to come. In Chapter 12, you'll see the Style class, which is without a doubt the most popular item for including in resource dictionaries, and in Chapter 16, you'll see the powerful markup extension named Binding.

Chapter 11
The bindable infrastructure

One of the most basic language constructs of C# is the class member known as the *property*. All of us very early on in our first encounters with C# learned the general routine of defining a property. The property is often backed by a private field and includes `set` and `get` accessors that reference the private field and do something with a new value:

```
public class MyClass
{
    …
    double quality;

    public double Quality
    {
        set
        {
            quality = value;
            // Do something with the new value
        }
        get
        {
            return quality;
        }
    }
    …
}
```

Properties are sometimes referred to as *smart fields*. Syntactically, code that accesses a property resembles code that accesses a field. Yet the property can execute some of its own code when the property is accessed.

Properties are also like methods. Indeed, C# code is compiled into intermediate language that implements a property such as `Quality` with a pair of methods named `set_Quality` and `get_Quality`. Yet despite the close functional resemblance between properties and a pair of *set* and *get* methods, the property syntax reveals itself to be much more suitable when moving from code to markup. It's hard to imagine XAML built on an underlying API that is missing properties.

So you may be surprised to learn that Xamarin.Forms implements an enhanced property definition that builds upon C# properties. Or maybe you won't be surprised. If you already have experience with Microsoft's XAML-based platforms, you'll encounter some familiar concepts in this chapter.

The property definition shown above is known as a *CLR property* because it's supported by the .NET common language runtime. The enhanced property definition in Xamarin.Forms builds upon the CLR property and is called a *bindable property*, encapsulated by the `BindableProperty` class and supported by the `BindableObject` class.

The Xamarin.Forms class hierarchy

Before exploring the details of the important `BindableObject` class, let's first discover how `BindableObject` fits into the overall Xamarin.Forms architecture by constructing a class hierarchy.

In an object-oriented programming framework such as Xamarin.Forms, a class hierarchy can often reveal important inner structures of the environment. The class hierarchy shows how various classes relate to one another and the properties, methods, and events that they share, including how bindable properties are supported.

You can construct such a class hierarchy by laboriously going through the online documentation and taking note of what classes derive from what other classes. Or you can write a Xamarin.Forms program to do the work for you and display the class hierarchy on the phone. Such a program makes use of .NET reflection to obtain all the public classes, structures, and enumerations in the **Xamarin.Forms.Core** and **Xamarin.Forms.Xaml** assemblies and arrange them in a tree. The **ClassHierarchy** application demonstrates this technique.

As usual, the **ClassHierarchy** project contains a class that derives from `ContentPage`, named `ClassHierarchyPage`, but it also contains two additional classes, named `TypeInformation` and `ClassAndSubclasses`.

The program creates one `TypeInformation` instance for every public class (and structure and enumeration) in the **Xamarin.Forms.Core** and **Xamarin.Forms.Xaml** assemblies, plus any .NET class that serves as a base class for any Xamarin.Forms class, with the exception of `Object`. (These .NET classes are `Attribute`, `Delegate`, `Enum`, `EventArgs`, `Exception`, `MulticastDelegate`, and `ValueType`.) The `TypeInformation` constructor requires a `Type` object identifying a type but also obtains some other information:

```
class TypeInformation
{
    bool isBaseGenericType;
    Type baseGenericTypeDef;

    public TypeInformation(Type type, bool isXamarinForms)
    {
        Type = type;
        IsXamarinForms = isXamarinForms;
        TypeInfo typeInfo = type.GetTypeInfo();
        BaseType = typeInfo.BaseType;

        if (BaseType != null)
        {
            TypeInfo baseTypeInfo = BaseType.GetTypeInfo();
            isBaseGenericType = baseTypeInfo.IsGenericType;

            if (isBaseGenericType)
            {
                baseGenericTypeDef = baseTypeInfo.GetGenericTypeDefinition();
```

```
                }
            }
        }

    public Type Type { private set; get; }
    public Type BaseType { private set; get; }
    public bool IsXamarinForms { private set; get; }

    public bool IsDerivedDirectlyFrom(Type parentType)
    {
        if (BaseType != null && isBaseGenericType)
        {
            if (baseGenericTypeDef == parentType)
            {
                return true;
            }
        }
        else if (BaseType == parentType)
        {
            return true;
        }
        return false;
    }
}
```

A very important part of this class is the `IsDerivedDirectlyFrom` method, which will return `true` if passed an argument that is this type's base type. This determination is complicated if generic classes are involved, and that issue largely accounts for the complexity of the class.

The `ClassAndSubclasses` class is considerably shorter:

```
class ClassAndSubclasses
{
    public ClassAndSubclasses(Type parent, bool isXamarinForms)
    {
        Type = parent;
        IsXamarinForms = isXamarinForms;
        Subclasses = new List<ClassAndSubclasses>();
    }

    public Type Type { private set; get; }
    public bool IsXamarinForms { private set; get; }
    public List<ClassAndSubclasses> Subclasses { private set; get; }
}
```

The program creates one instance of this class for every `Type` displayed in the class hierarchy, including `Object`, so the program creates one more `ClassAndSubclasses` instance than the number of `TypeInformation` instances. The `ClassAndSubclasses` instance associated with `Object` contains a collection of all the classes that derive directly from `Object`, and each of those `ClassAndSubclasses` instances contains a collection of all the classes that derive from that one, and so forth for the remainder of the hierarchy tree.

The `ClassHierarchyPage` class consists of a XAML file and a code-behind file, but the XAML file contains little more than a scrollable `StackLayout` ready for some `Label` elements:

```xml
<ContentPage xmlns="http://xamarin.com/schemas/2014/forms"
             xmlns:x="http://schemas.microsoft.com/winfx/2009/xaml"
             x:Class="ClassHierarchy.ClassHierarchyPage">

    <ContentPage.Padding>
        <OnPlatform x:TypeArguments="Thickness"
                    iOS="5, 20, 0, 0"
                    Android="5, 0, 0, 0"
                    WinPhone="5, 0, 0, 0" />
    </ContentPage.Padding>

    <ScrollView>
        <StackLayout x:Name="stackLayout"
                     Spacing="0" />
    </ScrollView>
</ContentPage>
```

The code-behind file obtains references to the two Xamarin.Forms `Assembly` objects and then accumulates all the public classes, structures, and enumerations in the `classList` collection. It then checks for the necessity of including any base classes from the .NET assemblies, sorts the result, and then calls two recursive methods, `AddChildrenToParent` and `AddItemToStackLayout`:

```csharp
public partial class ClassHierarchyPage : ContentPage
{
    public ClassHierarchyPage()
    {
        InitializeComponent();

        List<TypeInformation> classList = new List<TypeInformation>();

        // Get types in Xamarin.Forms.Core assembly.
        GetPublicTypes(typeof(View).GetTypeInfo().Assembly, classList);

        // Get types in Xamarin.Forms.Xaml assembly.
        GetPublicTypes(typeof(Extensions).GetTypeInfo().Assembly, classList);

        // Ensure that all classes have a base type in the list.
        //   (i.e., add Attribute, ValueType, Enum, EventArgs, etc.)
        int index = 0;

        // Watch out! Loops through expanding classList!
        do
        {
            // Get a child type from the list.
            TypeInformation childType = classList[index];

            if (childType.Type != typeof(Object))
            {
                bool hasBaseType = false;
```

```
            // Loop through the list looking for a base type.
            foreach (TypeInformation parentType in classList)
            {
                if (childType.IsDerivedDirectlyFrom(parentType.Type))
                {
                    hasBaseType = true;
                }
            }

            // If there's no base type, add it.
            if (!hasBaseType && childType.BaseType != typeof(Object))
            {
                classList.Add(new TypeInformation(childType.BaseType, false));
            }
        }
        index++;
    }
    while (index < classList.Count);

    // Now sort the list.
    classList.Sort((t1, t2) =>
    {
        return String.Compare(t1.Type.Name, t2.Type.Name);
    });

    // Start the display with System.Object.
    ClassAndSubclasses rootClass = new ClassAndSubclasses(typeof(Object), false);

    // Recursive method to build the hierarchy tree.
    AddChildrenToParent(rootClass, classList);

    // Recursive method for adding items to StackLayout.
    AddItemToStackLayout(rootClass, 0);
}

void GetPublicTypes(Assembly assembly,
                    List<TypeInformation> classList)
{
    // Loop through all the types.
    foreach (Type type in assembly.ExportedTypes)
    {
        TypeInfo typeInfo = type.GetTypeInfo();

        // Public types only but exclude interfaces.
        if (typeInfo.IsPublic && !typeInfo.IsInterface)
        {
            // Add type to list.
            classList.Add(new TypeInformation(type, true));
        }
    }
}

void AddChildrenToParent(ClassAndSubclasses parentClass,
                         List<TypeInformation> classList)
```

```
    {
        foreach (TypeInformation typeInformation in classList)
        {
            if (typeInformation.IsDerivedDirectlyFrom(parentClass.Type))
            {
                ClassAndSubclasses subClass =
                    new ClassAndSubclasses(typeInformation.Type,
                                           typeInformation.IsXamarinForms);
                parentClass.Subclasses.Add(subClass);
                AddChildrenToParent(subClass, classList);
            }
        }
    }
}

void AddItemToStackLayout(ClassAndSubclasses parentClass, int level)
{
    // If assembly is not Xamarin.Forms, display full name.
    string name = parentClass.IsXamarinForms ? parentClass.Type.Name :
                                               parentClass.Type.FullName;

    TypeInfo typeInfo = parentClass.Type.GetTypeInfo();

    // If generic, display angle brackets and parameters.
    if (typeInfo.IsGenericType)
    {
        Type[] parameters = typeInfo.GenericTypeParameters;
        name = name.Substring(0, name.Length - 2);
        name += "<";

        for (int i = 0; i < parameters.Length; i++)
        {
            name += parameters[i].Name;
            if (i < parameters.Length - 1)
            {
                name += ", ";
            }
        }
        name += ">";
    }

    // Create Label and add to StackLayout.
    Label label = new Label
    {
        Text = String.Format("{0}{1}", new string(' ', 4 * level), name),
        TextColor = parentClass.Type.GetTypeInfo().IsAbstract ?
                        Color.Accent : Color.Default
    };

    stackLayout.Children.Add(label);

    // Now display nested types.
    foreach (ClassAndSubclasses subclass in parentClass.Subclasses)
    {
        AddItemToStackLayout(subclass, level + 1);
```

```
        }
    }
}
```

The recursive `AddChildrenToParent` method assembles the linked list of `ClassAndSubclasses` instances from the flat `classList` collection. The `AddItemToStackLayout` method is also recursive because it is responsible for adding the `ClassesAndSubclasses` linked list to the `StackLayout` object by creating a `Label` view for each class, with a little blank space at the beginning for the proper indentation. The method displays the Xamarin.Forms types with just the class names, but the .NET types include the fully qualified name to distinguish them. The method uses the platform accent color for classes that are not instantiable because they are abstract or static:

Overall, you'll see that the Xamarin.Forms visual elements have the following general hierarchy:

```
System.Object
    BindableObject
        Element
            VisualElement
                View
                    ...
                    Layout
                        ...
                        Layout<T>
                            ...
                Page
                    ...
```

Aside from `Object`, all the classes in this abbreviated class hierarchy are implemented in the Xamarin.Forms.Core.dll assembly and associated with a namespace of `Xamarin.Forms`.

Let's examine some of these major classes in detail.

As the name of the `BindableObject` class implies, the primary function of this class is to support data binding—the linking of two properties of two objects so that they maintain the same value. But `BindableObject` also supports styles and the `DynamicResource` markup extension as well. It does this in two ways: through `BindableObject` property definitions in the form of `BindableProperty` objects and also by implementing the .NET `INotifyPropertyChanged` interface. All of this will be discussed in much more detail in this chapter and future chapters.

Let's continue down the hierarchy: as you've seen, user-interface objects in Xamarin.Forms are often arranged on the page in a parent-child hierarchy, and the `Element` class includes support for parent and child relationships.

`VisualElement` is an exceptionally important class in Xamarin.Forms. A visual element is anything in Xamarin.Forms that occupies an area on the screen. The `VisualElement` class defines 28 public properties related to size, location, background color, and other visual and functional characteristics, such as `IsEnabled` and `IsVisible`.

In Xamarin.Forms the word *view* is often used to refer to individual visual objects such as buttons, sliders, and text-entry boxes, but you can see that the `View` class is the parent to the layout classes as well. Interestingly, `View` adds only three public members to what it inherits from `VisualElement`. These are `HorizontalOptions` and `VerticalOptions`—which make sense because these properties don't apply to pages—and `GestureRecognizers` to support touch input.

The descendants of `Layout` are capable of having children views. A child view appears on the screen visually within the boundaries of its parent. Classes that derive from `Layout` can have only one child of type `View`, but the generic `Layout<T>` class defines a `Children` property, which is a collection of multiple child views, including other layouts. You've already seen the `StackLayout`, which arranges its children in a horizontal or vertical stack. Although the `Layout` class derives from `View`, layouts are so important in Xamarin.Forms that they are often considered a category in themselves.

ClassHierarchy lists all the public classes, structures, and enumerations defined in the **Xamarin.Forms.Core** and **Xamarin.Forms.Xaml** assemblies, but it does not list interfaces. Those are important as well, but you'll just have to explore them on your own. (Or enhance the program to list them.)

Nor does **ClassHierarchy** list the many public classes that help implement Xamarin.Forms on the various platforms. In the final chapter of this book, you'll see a version that does.

A peek into BindableObject and BindableProperty

The existence of classes named `BindableObject` and `BindableProperty` is likely to be a little confusing at first. Keep in mind that `BindableObject` is much like `Object` in that it serves as a base class to a large chunk of the Xamarin.Forms API, and particularly to `Element` and hence `VisualElement`.

`BindableObject` provides support for objects of type `BindableProperty`. A `BindableProperty` object extends a CLR property. The best insights into bindable properties come when you create a few of your own—as you'll be doing before the end of this chapter—but you can also glean some understanding by exploring the existing bindable properties.

Toward the beginning of Chapter 7, "XAML vs. code," two buttons were created with many of the same property settings, except that the properties of one button were set in code using the C# 3.0 object initialization syntax and the other button was instantiated and initialized in XAML.

Here's a similar (but code-only) program named **PropertySettings** that also creates and initializes two buttons in two different ways. The properties of the first `Label` are set the old-fashioned way, while the properties of the second `Label` are set with a more verbose technique:

```
public class PropertySettingsPage : ContentPage
{
    public PropertySettingsPage()
    {
        Label label1 = new Label();
        label1.Text = "Text with CLR properties";
        label1.IsVisible = true;
        label1.Opacity = 0.75;
        label1.HorizontalTextAlignment = TextAlignment.Center;
        label1.VerticalOptions = LayoutOptions.CenterAndExpand;
        label1.TextColor = Color.Blue;
        label1.BackgroundColor = Color.FromRgb(255, 128, 128);
        label1.FontSize = Device.GetNamedSize(NamedSize.Medium, new Label());
        label1.FontAttributes = FontAttributes.Bold | FontAttributes.Italic;

        Label label2 = new Label();
        label2.SetValue(Label.TextProperty, "Text with bindable properties");
        label2.SetValue(Label.IsVisibleProperty, true);
        label2.SetValue(Label.OpacityProperty, 0.75);
        label2.SetValue(Label.HorizontalTextAlignmentProperty, TextAlignment.Center);
        label2.SetValue(Label.VerticalOptionsProperty, LayoutOptions.CenterAndExpand);
        label2.SetValue(Label.TextColorProperty, Color.Blue);
        label2.SetValue(Label.BackgroundColorProperty, Color.FromRgb(255, 128, 128));
        label2.SetValue(Label.FontSizeProperty,
                    Device.GetNamedSize(NamedSize.Medium, new Label()));
        label2.SetValue(Label.FontAttributesProperty,
                    FontAttributes.Bold | FontAttributes.Italic);

        Content = new StackLayout
        {
```

```
            Children =
            {
                label1,
                label2
            }
        };
    }
}
```

These two ways to set properties are entirely consistent:

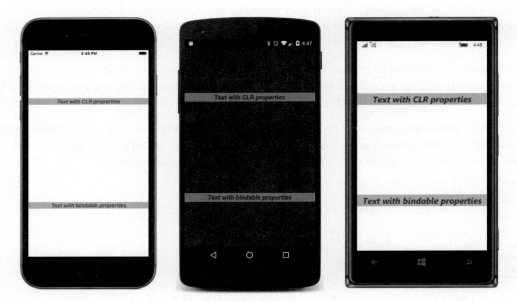

Yet the alternative syntax seems very odd. For example:

```
label2.SetValue(Label.TextProperty, "Text with bindable properties");
```

What is that `SetValue` method? `SetValue` is defined by `BindableObject`, from which every visual object derives. `BindableObject` also defines a `GetValue` method.

That first argument to `SetValue` has the name `Label.TextProperty`, which indicates that `TextProperty` is static, but despite its name, it's not a property at all. It's a static *field* of the `Label` class. `TextProperty` is also read-only, and it's defined in the `Label` class something like this:

```
public static readonly BindableProperty TextProperty;
```

That's an object of type `BindableProperty`. Of course, it may seem a little disturbing that a field is named `TextProperty`, but there it is. Because it's static, however, it exists independently of any `Label` objects that might or might not exist.

If you look in the documentation of the `Label` class, you'll see that it defines 10 properties, including `Text`, `TextColor`, `FontSize`, `FontAttributes`, and others. You'll also see 10 corresponding public static read-only fields of type `BindableProperty` with the names `TextProperty`, `TextColorProperty`, `FontSizeProperty`, `FontAttributesProperty`, and so forth.

These properties and fields are closely related. Indeed, internal to the `Label` class, the `Text` CLR property is defined like this to reference the corresponding `TextProperty` object:

```
public string Text
{
    set { SetValue(Label.TextProperty, value); }
    get { return (string)GetValue(Label.TextProperty); }
}
```

So you see why it is that your application calling `SetValue` with a `Label.TextProperty` argument is exactly equivalent to setting the `Text` property directly, and perhaps just a tinier bit faster!

The internal definition of the `Text` property in `Label` isn't secret information. This is standard code. Although any class can define a `BindableProperty` object, only a class that derives from `BindableObject` can call the `SetValue` and `GetValue` methods that actually implement the property in the class. Casting is required for the `GetValue` method because it's defined as returning `object`.

All the real work involved with maintaining the `Text` property is going on in those `SetValue` and `GetValue` calls. The `BindableObject` and `BindableProperty` objects effectively extend the functionality of standard CLR properties to provide systematic ways to:

- Define properties

- Give properties default values

- Store their current values

- Provide mechanisms for validating property values

- Maintain consistency among related properties in a single class

- Respond to property changes

- Trigger notifications when a property is about to change and has changed

- Support data binding

- Support styles

- Support dynamic resources

The close relationship of a property named `Text` with a `BindableProperty` named `TextProperty` is reflected in the way that programmers speak about these properties: Sometimes a programmer says that the `Text` property is "backed by" a `BindableProperty` named `TextProperty` because `TextProperty` provides infrastructure support for `Text`. But a common shortcut is to say that `Text` is itself a "bindable property," and generally no one will be confused.

Not every Xamarin.Forms property is a bindable property. Neither the `Content` property of `ContentPage` nor the `Children` property of `Layout<T>` is a bindable property. Of the 28 properties defined by `VisualElement`, 26 are backed by bindable properties, but the `Bounds` property and the `Resources` properties are not.

The `Span` class used in connection with `FormattedString` does not derive from `BindableObject`. Therefore, `Span` does not inherit `SetValue` and `GetValue` methods, and it cannot implement `BindableProperty` objects.

This means that the `Text` property of `Label` is backed by a bindable property, but the `Text` property of `Span` is not. Does it make a difference?

Of course it makes a difference! If you recall the **DynamicVsStatic** program in the previous chapter, you discovered that `DynamicResource` worked on the `Text` property of `Label` but not the `Text` property of `Span`. Can it be that `DynamicResource` works only with bindable properties?

This supposition is pretty much confirmed by the definition of the following public method defined by `Element`:

```
public void SetDynamicResource(BindableProperty property, string key);
```

This is how a dictionary key is associated with a particular property of an element when that property is the target of a `DynamicResource` markup extension.

This `SetDynamicResource` method also allows you to set a dynamic resource link on a property in code. Here's the page class from a code-only version of **DynamicVsStatic** called **DynamicVsStatic-Code**. It's somewhat simplified to exclude the use of a `FormattedString` and `Span` object, but otherwise it pretty accurately mimics how the previous XAML file is parsed and, in particular, how the `Text` properties of the `Label` elements are set by the XAML parser:

```
public class DynamicVsStaticCodePage : ContentPage
{
    public DynamicVsStaticCodePage()
    {
        Padding = new Thickness(5, 0);

        // Create resource dictionary and add item.
        Resources = new ResourceDictionary
        {
            { "currentDateTime", "Not actually a DateTime" }
        };

        Content = new StackLayout
        {
            Children =
            {
                new Label
                {
                    Text = "StaticResource on Label.Text:",
                    VerticalOptions = LayoutOptions.EndAndExpand,
```

```
                FontSize = Device.GetNamedSize(NamedSize.Medium, typeof(Label))
            },

            new Label
            {
                Text = (string)Resources["currentDateTime"],
                VerticalOptions = LayoutOptions.StartAndExpand,
                HorizontalTextAlignment = TextAlignment.Center,
                FontSize = Device.GetNamedSize(NamedSize.Medium, typeof(Label))
            },

            new Label
            {
                Text = "DynamicResource on Label.Text:",
                VerticalOptions = LayoutOptions.EndAndExpand,
                FontSize = Device.GetNamedSize(NamedSize.Medium, typeof(Label))
            }
        }
    };

    // Create the final label with the dynamic resource.
    Label label = new Label
    {
        VerticalOptions = LayoutOptions.StartAndExpand,
        HorizontalTextAlignment = TextAlignment.Center,
        FontSize = Device.GetNamedSize(NamedSize.Medium, typeof(Label))
    };

    label.SetDynamicResource(Label.TextProperty, "currentDateTime");

    ((StackLayout)Content).Children.Add(label);

    // Start the timer going.
    Device.StartTimer(TimeSpan.FromSeconds(1),
        () =>
        {
            Resources["currentDateTime"] = DateTime.Now.ToString();
            return true;
        });
    }
}
```

The Text property of the second Label is set directly from the dictionary entry and makes the use of the dictionary seem a little pointless in this context. But the Text property of the last Label is bound to the dictionary key through a call to SetDynamicResource, which allows the property to be updated when the dictionary contents change:

Consider this: What would the signature of this `SetDynamicResource` method be if it could not refer to a property using the `BindableProperty` object? It's easy to reference a property *value* in method calls, but not the property itself. There are a couple of ways, such as the `PropertyInfo` class in the `System.Reflection` namespace or the LINQ `Expression` object. But the `BindableProperty` object is designed specifically for this purpose, as well as the essential job of handling the underlying link between the property and the dictionary key.

Similarly, when we explore styles in the next chapter, you'll encounter a `Setter` class used in connection with styles. `Setter` defines a property named `Property` of type `BindableProperty`, which mandates that any property targeted by a style must be backed by a bindable property. This allows a style to be defined prior to the elements targeted by the style.

Likewise for data bindings. The `BindableObject` class defines a `SetBinding` method that is very similar to the `SetDynamicResource` method defined on `Element`:

```
public void SetBinding(BindableProperty targetProperty, BindingBase binding);
```

Again, notice the type of the first argument. Any property targeted by a data binding must be backed by a bindable property.

For these reasons, whenever you create a custom view and need to define public properties, your default inclination should be to define them as bindable properties. Only if after careful consideration you conclude that it is not necessary or appropriate for the property to be targeted by a style or a data binding should you retreat and define an ordinary CLR property instead.

So whenever you create a class that derives from `BindableObject`, one of the first pieces of code you should be typing in that class begins "public static readonly BindableProperty"—perhaps the most characteristic sequence of four words in all of Xamarin.Forms programming.

Defining bindable properties

Suppose you'd like an enhanced `Label` class that lets you specify font sizes in units of points. Let's call this class `AltLabel` for "alternative `Label`." It derives from `Label` and includes a new property named `PointSize`.

Should `PointSize` be backed by a bindable property? Of course! (Although the real advantages of doing so won't be demonstrated until upcoming chapters.)

The code-only `AltLabel` class is included in the **Xamarin.FormsBook.Toolkit** library, so it's accessible to multiple applications. The new `PointSize` property is implemented with a `BindableProperty` object named `PointSizeProperty` and a CLR property named `PointSize` that references `PointSizeProperty`:

```
public class AltLabel : Label
{
    public static readonly BindableProperty PointSizeProperty … ;
    …
    public double PointSize
    {
        set { SetValue(PointSizeProperty, value); }
        get { return (double)GetValue(PointSizeProperty); }
    }
    …
}
```

Both the field and the property definition must be public.

Because `PointSizeProperty` is defined as `static` and `readonly`, it must be assigned either in a static constructor or right in the field definition, after which it cannot be changed. Generally, a `BindableProperty` object is assigned in the field definition by using the static `BindableProperty.Create` method. Four arguments are required (shown here with the argument names):

- `propertyName`   The text name of the property (in this case "PointSize")

- `returnType`   The type of the property (a `double` in this example)

- `declaringType`   The type of the class defining the property (`AltLabel`)

- `defaultValue`   A default value (let's say 8 points)

The second and third arguments are generally defined with `typeof` expressions. Here's the assignment statement with these four arguments passed to `BindableProperty.Create`:

```
public class AltLabel : Label
{
    public static readonly BindableProperty PointSizeProperty =
        BindableProperty.Create("PointSize",        // propertyName
                                typeof(double),      // returnType
                                typeof(AltLabel),    // declaringType
                                8.0,                 // defaultValue
                                ...);
    ...
}
```

Notice that the default value is specified as 8.0 rather than just 8. Because `BindableProperty.Create` is designed to handle properties of any type, the `defaultValue` parameter is defined as `object`. When the C# compiler encounters just an 8 as that argument, it will assume that the 8 is an `int` and pass an `int` to the method. The problem won't be revealed until run time, however, when the `BindableProperty.Create` method will be expecting the default value to be of type `double` and respond by raising a `TypeInitializationException`.

You must be explicit about the type of the value you're specifying as the default. Not doing so is a very common error in defining bindable properties. A *very* common error.

`BindableProperty.Create` also has six optional arguments. Here they are with the argument names and their purpose:

- `defaultBindingMode`   Used in connection with data binding

- `validateValue`   A callback to check for a valid value

- `propertyChanged`   A callback to indicate when the property has changed

- `propertyChanging`   A callback to indicate when the property is about to change

- `coerceValue`   A callback to coerce a set value to another value (for example, to restrict the values to a range)

- `defaultValueCreator`   A callback to create a default value. This is generally used to instantiate a default object that can't be shared among all instances of the class; for example, a collection object such as `List` or `Dictionary`.

Do not perform any validation, coercion, or property-changed handling in the CLR property. The CLR property should be restricted to `SetValue` and `GetValue` calls. Everything else should be done in the callbacks provided by the bindable property infrastructure.

It is very rare that a particular call to `BindableProperty.Create` would need all of these optional arguments. For that reason, these optional arguments are commonly indicated with the named argument feature introduced in C# 4.0. To specify a particular optional argument, use the argument name followed by a colon. For example:

```
public class AltLabel : Label
{
    public static readonly BindableProperty PointSizeProperty =
        BindableProperty.Create("PointSize",          // propertyName
                                typeof(double),        // returnType
                                typeof(AltLabel),      // declaringType
                                8.0,                   // defaultValue
                                propertyChanged: OnPointSizeChanged);
    ...
}
```

Without a doubt, `propertyChanged` is the most important of the optional arguments because the class uses this callback to be notified when the property changes, either directly from a call to `Set-Value` or through the CLR property.

In this example, the property-changed handler is called `OnPointSizeChanged`. It will be called only when the property truly changes and not when it's simply set to the same value. However, because `On-PointSizeChanged` is referenced from a static field, the method itself must also be static. Here's what it looks like:

```
public class AltLabel : Label
{
    ...
    static void OnPointSizeChanged(BindableObject bindable, object oldValue, object newValue)
    {
        ...
    }
    ...
}
```

This seems a little odd. We might have multiple `AltLabel` instances in a program, yet whenever the `PointSize` property changes in any one of these instances, this same static method is called. How does the method know exactly which `AltLabel` instance has changed?

The method can tell which instance's property has changed because that instance is always the first argument to the property-changed handler. Although that first argument is defined as a `BindableObject`, in this case it's actually of type `AltLabel` and indicates which `AltLabel` instance's property has changed. This means that you can safely cast the first argument to an `AltLabel` instance:

```
static void OnPointSizeChanged(BindableObject bindable, object oldValue, object newValue)
{
    AltLabel altLabel = (AltLabel)bindable;
    ...
}
```

You can then reference anything in the particular instance of `AltLabel` whose property has changed. The second and third arguments are actually of type `double` for this example and indicate the previous value and the new value.

Often it's convenient for this static method to call an instance method with the arguments converted to their actual types:

```
public class AltLabel : Label
{
    …

    static void OnPointSizeChanged(BindableObject bindable, object oldValue, object newValue)
    {
        ((AltLabel)bindable).OnPointSizeChanged((double)oldValue, (double)newValue);
    }

    void OnPointSizeChanged(double oldValue, double newValue)
    {
        …
    }
}
```

The instance method can then make use of any instance properties or methods of the underlying base class as it would normally.

For this class, this `OnPointSizeChanged` method needs to set the `FontSize` property based on the new point size and a conversion factor. In addition, the constructor needs to initialize the `Font-Size` property based on the default `PointSize` value. This is done through a simple `SetLabelFont-Size` method. Here's the final complete class:

```
public class AltLabel : Label
{
    public static readonly BindableProperty PointSizeProperty =
        BindableProperty.Create("PointSize",            // propertyName
                                typeof(double),         // returnType
                                typeof(AltLabel),       // declaringType
                                8.0,                    // defaultValue
                                propertyChanged: OnPointSizeChanged);

    public AltLabel()
    {
        SetLabelFontSize((double)PointSizeProperty.DefaultValue);
    }

    public double PointSize
    {
        set { SetValue(PointSizeProperty, value); }
        get { return (double)GetValue(PointSizeProperty); }
    }

    static void OnPointSizeChanged(BindableObject bindable, object oldValue, object newValue)
    {
        ((AltLabel)bindable).OnPointSizeChanged((double)oldValue, (double)newValue);
    }

    void OnPointSizeChanged(double oldValue, double newValue)
    {
        SetLabelFontSize(newValue);
    }

    void SetLabelFontSize(double pointSize)
```

```
    {
        FontSize = 160 * pointSize / 72;
    }
}
```

It is also possible for the instance `OnPointSizeChanged` property to access the `PointSize` property directly rather than use `newValue`. By the time the property-changed handler is called, the underlying property value has already been changed. However, you don't have direct access to that underlying value, as you do when a private field backs a CLR property. That underlying value is private to `BindableObject` and accessible only through the `GetValue` call.

Of course, nothing prevents code that's using `AltLabel` from setting the `FontSize` property and overriding the `PointSize` setting, but let's hope such code is aware of that. Here's some code that is—a program called **PointSizedText**, which uses `AltLabel` to display point sizes from 4 through 12:

```xml
<ContentPage xmlns="http://xamarin.com/schemas/2014/forms"
             xmlns:x="http://schemas.microsoft.com/winfx/2009/xaml"
             xmlns:toolkit=
                 "clr-namespace:Xamarin.FormsBook.Toolkit;assembly=Xamarin.FormsBook.Toolkit"
             x:Class="PointSizedText.PointSizedTextPage">
    <ContentPage.Padding>
        <OnPlatform x:TypeArguments="Thickness"
                    iOS="5, 20, 0, 0"
                    Android="5, 0, 0, 0"
                    WinPhone="5, 0, 0, 0" />
    </ContentPage.Padding>

    <StackLayout x:Name="stackLayout">
        <toolkit:AltLabel Text="Text of 4 points" PointSize="4" />
        <toolkit:AltLabel Text="Text of 5 points" PointSize="5" />
        <toolkit:AltLabel Text="Text of 6 points" PointSize="6" />
        <toolkit:AltLabel Text="Text of 7 points" PointSize="7" />
        <toolkit:AltLabel Text="Text of 8 points" PointSize="8" />
        <toolkit:AltLabel Text="Text of 9 points" PointSize="9" />
        <toolkit:AltLabel Text="Text of 10 points" PointSize="10" />
        <toolkit:AltLabel Text="Text of 11 points" PointSize="11" />
        <toolkit:AltLabel Text="Text of 12 points" PointSize="12" />
    </StackLayout>
</ContentPage>
```

And here are the screenshots:

The read-only bindable property

Suppose you're working with an application in which it's convenient to know the number of words in the text that is displayed by a `Label` element. Perhaps you'd like to build that facility right into a class that derives from `Label`. Let's call this new class `CountedLabel`.

By now, your first thought should be to define a `BindableProperty` object named `WordCount-Property` and a corresponding CLR property named `WordCount`.

But wait: It only makes sense for this `WordCount` property to be set from within the `CountedLabel` class. That means the `WordCount` CLR property should not have a public `set` accessor. It should be defined this way:

```
public int WordCount
{
    private set { SetValue(WordCountProperty, value); }
    get { return (double)GetValue(WordCountProperty); }
}
```

The `get` accessor is still public, but the `set` accessor is private. Is that sufficient?

Not exactly. Despite the private `set` accessor in the CLR property, code external to `CountedLabel` can still call `SetValue` with the `CountedLabel.WordCountProperty` bindable property object. That type of property setting should be prohibited as well. But how can that work if the `WordCountProp-erty` object is public?

The solution is to make a *read-only* bindable property by using the `BindableProperty.Create-ReadOnly` method. The

Xamarin.Forms API itself defines several read-only bindable properties—for example, the `Width` and `Height` properties defined by `VisualElement`.

Here's how you can make one of your own:

The first step is to call `BindableProperty.CreateReadOnly` with the same arguments as for `BindableProperty.Create`. However, the `CreateReadOnly` method returns an object of `BindablePropertyKey` rather than `BindableProperty`. Define this object as `static` and `readonly`, as with the `BindableProperty`, but make it be private to the class:

```
public class CountedLabel : Label
{
    static readonly BindablePropertyKey WordCountKey =
        BindableProperty.CreateReadOnly("WordCount",          // propertyName
                                        typeof(int),           // returnType
                                        typeof(CountedLabel),  // declaringType
                                        0);                    // defaultValue
    ...
}
```

Don't think of this `BindablePropertyKey` object as an encryption key or anything like that. It's much simpler—really just an object that is private to the class.

The second step is to make a public `BindableProperty` object by using the `BindableProperty` property of the `BindablePropertyKey`:

```
public class CountedLabel : Label
{
    ...
    public static readonly BindableProperty WordCountProperty = WordCountKey.BindableProperty;
    ...
}
```

This `BindableProperty` object is public, but it's a special kind of `BindableProperty`: It cannot be used in a `SetValue` call. Attempting to do so will raise an `InvalidOperationException`.

However, there is an overload of the `SetValue` method that accepts a `BindablePropertyKey` object. The CLR `set` accessor can call `SetValue` using this object, but this `set` accessor must be private to prevent the property from being set outside the class:

```
public class CountedLabel : Label
{
    ...
    public int WordCount
    {
        private set { SetValue(WordCountKey, value); }
        get { return (int)GetValue(WordCountProperty); }
    }
    ...
}
```

The `WordCount` property can now be set from within the `CountedLabel` class. But when should the class set it? This `CountedLabel` class derives from `Label`, but it needs to detect when the `Text` property has changed so that it can count up the words.

Does `Label` have a `TextChanged` event? No it does not. However, `BindableObject` implements the `INotifyPropertyChanged` interface. This is a very important .NET interface, particularly for applications that implement the Model-View-ViewModel (MVVM) architecture. In Chapter 18 you'll see how to use it in your own data classes.

The `INotifyPropertyChanged` interface is defined in the `System.ComponentModel` namespace like so:

```
public interface INotifyPropertyChanged
{
    event PropertyChangedEventHandler PropertyChanged;
}
```

Every class that derives from `BindableObject` automatically fires this `PropertyChanged` event whenever any property backed by a `BindableProperty` changes. The `PropertyChangedEventArgs` object that accompanies this event includes a property named `PropertyName` of type `string` that identifies the property that has changed.

So all that's necessary is for `CountedLabel` to attach a handler for the `PropertyChanged` event and check for a property name of "Text". From there it can use whatever technique it wants for calculating a word count. The complete `CountedLabel` class uses a lambda function on the `Property-Changed` event. The handler calls `Split` to break the string into words and see how many pieces result. The `Split` method splits the text based on spaces, dashes, and em dashes (Unicode \u2014):

```
public class CountedLabel : Label
{
    static readonly BindablePropertyKey WordCountKey =
        BindableProperty.CreateReadOnly("WordCount",           // propertyName
                                        typeof(int),           // returnType
                                        typeof(CountedLabel),  // declaringType
                                        0);                    // defaultValue

    public static readonly BindableProperty WordCountProperty = WordCountKey.BindableProperty;

    public CountedLabel()
    {
        // Set the WordCount property when the Text property changes.
        PropertyChanged += (object sender, PropertyChangedEventArgs args) =>
            {
                if (args.PropertyName == "Text")
                {
                    if (String.IsNullOrEmpty(Text))
                    {
                        WordCount = 0;
                    }
                    else
                    {
                        WordCount = Text.Split(' ', '-', '\u2014').Length;
```

```
                        }
                    }
                };
        }

        public int WordCount
        {
            private set { SetValue(WordCountKey, value); }
            get { return (int)GetValue(WordCountProperty); }
        }
}
```

The class includes a `using` directive for the `System.ComponentModel` namespace for the `Property-ChangedEventArgs` argument to the handler. Watch out: Xamarin.Forms defines a class named `PropertyChangingEventArgs` (present tense). That's not what you want for the `PropertyChanged` handler. You want `PropertyChangedEventArgs` (past tense).

Because this call of the `Split` method splits the text at blank characters, dashes, and em dashes, you might assume that `CountedLabel` will be demonstrated with text that contains some dashes and em dashes. This is true. The **BaskervillesCount** program is a variation of the **Baskervilles** program from Chapter 3, but here the paragraph of text is displayed with a `CountedLabel`, and a regular `Label` is included to display the word count:

```
<ContentPage xmlns="http://xamarin.com/schemas/2014/forms"
             xmlns:x="http://schemas.microsoft.com/winfx/2009/xaml"
             xmlns:toolkit=
                 "clr-namespace:Xamarin.FormsBook.Toolkit;assembly=Xamarin.FormsBook.Toolkit"
             x:Class="BaskervillesCount.BaskervillesCountPage"
             Padding="5, 0">

    <StackLayout>
        <toolkit:CountedLabel x:Name="countedLabel"
                              VerticalOptions="CenterAndExpand"
                              Text=
"Mr. Sherlock Holmes, who was usually very late in
the mornings, save upon those not infrequent
occasions when he was up all night, was seated at
the breakfast table. I stood upon the hearth-rug
and picked up the stick which our visitor had left
behind him the night before. It was a fine, thick
piece of wood, bulbous-headed, of the sort which
is known as a &#x201C;Penang lawyer.&#x201D; Just
under the head was a broad silver band, nearly an
inch across, &#x201C;To James Mortimer, M.R.C.S.,
from his friends of the C.C.H.,&#x201D; was engraved
upon it, with the date &#x201C;1884.&#x201D; It was
just such a stick as the old-fashioned family
practitioner used to carry&#x2014;dignified, solid,
and reassuring." />

        <Label x:Name="wordCountLabel"
               Text="???"
```

```
            FontSize="Large"
            VerticalOptions="CenterAndExpand"
            HorizontalOptions="Center" />

    </StackLayout>
</ContentPage>
```

That regular `Label` is set in the code-behind file:

```
public partial class BaskervillesCountPage : ContentPage
{
    public BaskervillesCountPage()
    {
        InitializeComponent();

        int wordCount = countedLabel.WordCount;
        wordCountLabel.Text = wordCount + " words";
    }
}
```

The word count that it calculates is based on the assumption that all hyphens in the text separate two words and that "hearth-rug" and "bulbous-headed" should be counted as two words each. That's not always true, of course, but word counts are not quite as algorithmically simple as this code might imply:

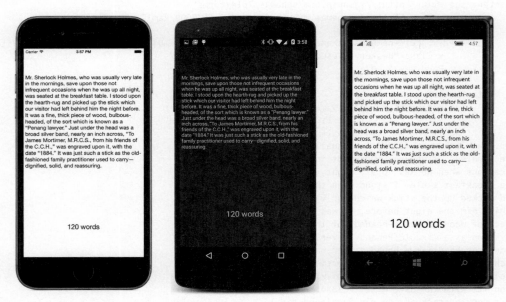

How would the program be structured if the text changed dynamically while the program was running? In that case, it would be necessary to update the word count whenever the `WordCount` property of the `CountedLabel` object changed. You could attach a `PropertyChanged` handler on the `CountedLabel` object and check for the property named "WordCount".

However, exercise caution if you try to set such an event handler from XAML—for example, like so:

```
<toolkit:CountedLabel x:Name="countedLabel"
                      VerticalOptions="CenterAndExpand"
                      PropertyChanged="OnCountedLabelPropertyChanged"
                      Text=" … " />
```

You'll probably want to code the event handler in the code-behind file like this:

```
void OnCountedLabelPropertyChanged(object sender,
                                   PropertyChangedEventArgs args)
{
    wordCountLabel.Text = countedLabel.WordCount + " words";
}
```

That handler will fire when the `Text` property is set by the XAML parser, but the event handler is trying to set the `Text` property of the second `Label`, which hasn't been instantiated yet, which means that the `wordCountLabel` field is still set to `null`. This is an issue that will come up again in Chapter 15 when working with interactive controls, but it will be pretty much solved when we work with data binding in Chapter 16.

There is another variation of a bindable property coming up in Chapter 14 on the `AbsoluteLay-out`: this is the *attached bindable property,* and it is very useful in implementing certain types of layouts, as you'll also discover in Chapter 26, "Custom layouts."

Meanwhile, let's look at one of the most important applications of bindable properties: styles.

Chapter 12

Styles

Xamarin.Forms applications often contain multiple elements with identical property settings. For example, you might have several buttons with the same colors, font sizes, and layout options. In code, you can assign identical properties to multiple buttons in a loop, but loops aren't available in XAML. If you want to avoid a lot of repetitive markup, another solution is required.

The solution is the `Style` class, which is a collection of property settings consolidated in one convenient object. You can set a `Style` object to the `Style` property of any class that derives from `VisualElement`. Generally, you'll apply the same `Style` object to multiple elements, and the style is shared among these elements.

The `Style` is the primary tool for giving visual elements a consistent appearance in your Xamarin.Forms applications. Styles help reduce repetitive markup in XAML files and allow applications to be more easily changed and maintained.

Styles were designed primarily with XAML in mind, and they probably wouldn't have been invented in a code-only environment. However, you'll see in this chapter how to define and use styles in code and how to combine code and markup to change program styling dynamically at run time.

The basic Style

In Chapter 10, "XAML markup extensions," you saw a trio of buttons that contained a lot of identical markup. Here they are again:

```
<StackLayout>
    <Button Text=" Carpe diem "
            HorizontalOptions="Center"
            VerticalOptions="CenterAndExpand"
            BorderWidth="3"
            TextColor="Red"
            FontSize="Large">
        <Button.BackgroundColor>
            <OnPlatform x:TypeArguments="Color"
                        Android="#404040" />
        </Button.BackgroundColor>
        <Button.BorderColor>
            <OnPlatform x:TypeArguments="Color"
                        Android="White"
                        WinPhone="Black" />
        </Button.BorderColor>
    </Button>
```

```
    <Button Text=" Sapere aude "
            HorizontalOptions="Center"
            VerticalOptions="CenterAndExpand"
            BorderWidth="3"
            TextColor="Red"
                FontSize="Large">
        <Button.BackgroundColor>
            <OnPlatform x:TypeArguments="Color"
                        Android="#404040" />
        </Button.BackgroundColor>
        <Button.BorderColor>
            <OnPlatform x:TypeArguments="Color"
                        Android="White"
                        WinPhone="Black" />
        </Button.BorderColor>
    </Button>

    <Button Text=" Discere faciendo "
            HorizontalOptions="Center"
            VerticalOptions="CenterAndExpand"
            BorderWidth="3"
            TextColor="Red"
            FontSize="Large">
        <Button.BackgroundColor>
            <OnPlatform x:TypeArguments="Color"
                        Android="#404040" />
        </Button.BackgroundColor>
        <Button.BorderColor>
            <OnPlatform x:TypeArguments="Color"
                        Android="White"
                        WinPhone="Black" />
        </Button.BorderColor>
    </Button>
</StackLayout>
```

With the exception of the `Text` property, all three buttons have the same property settings.

One partial solution to this repetitious markup involves defining property values in a resource dictionary and referencing them with the `StaticResource` markup extension. As you saw in the **ResourceSharing** project in Chapter 10, this technique doesn't reduce the markup bulk, but it does consolidate the values in one place.

To reduce the markup bulk, you'll need a `Style`. A `Style` object is almost always defined in a `ResourceDictionary`. Generally, you'll begin with a `Resources` section at the top of the page:

```
<ContentPage xmlns="http://xamarin.com/schemas/2014/forms"
             xmlns:x="http://schemas.microsoft.com/winfx/2009/xaml"
             x:Class="BasicStyle.BasicStylePage">

    <ContentPage.Resources>
        <ResourceDictionary>
            …
        </ResourceDictionary>
```

```
        </ContentPage.Resources>
        ...
    </ContentPage>
```

Instantiate a `Style` with separate start and end tags:

```
<ContentPage xmlns="http://xamarin.com/schemas/2014/forms"
             xmlns:x="http://schemas.microsoft.com/winfx/2009/xaml"
             x:Class="BasicStyle.BasicStylePage">

    <ContentPage.Resources>
        <ResourceDictionary>
            <Style x:Key="buttonStyle" TargetType="Button">
                ...
            </Style>
        </ResourceDictionary>
    </ContentPage.Resources>
    ...
</ContentPage>
```

Because the `Style` is an object in a `ResourceDictionary`, you'll need an `x:Key` attribute to give it a descriptive dictionary key. You must also set the `TargetType` property. This is the type of the visual element that the style is designed for, which in this case is `Button`.

As you'll see in the next section of this chapter, you can also define a `Style` in code, in which case the `Style` constructor requires an object of type `Type` for the `TargetType` property. The `TargetType` property does not have a public `set` accessor; hence the `TargetType` property cannot be changed after the `Style` is created.

`Style` also defines another important get-only property named `Setters` of type `IList<Setter>`, which is a collection of `Setter` objects. Each `Setter` is responsible for defining a property setting in the style. The `Setter` class defines just two properties:

- `Property` of type `BindableProperty`
- `Value` of type `Object`

Properties set in the `Style` must be backed by bindable properties! But when you set the `Property` property in XAML, don't use the entire fully qualified bindable property name. Just specify the text name, which is the same as the name of the related CLR property. Here's an example:

```
<Setter Property="HorizontalOptions" Value="Center" />
```

The XAML parser uses the familiar `TypeConverter` classes when parsing the `Value` settings of these `Setter` instances, so you can use the same property settings that you use normally.

`Setters` is the content property of `Style`, so you don't need the `Style.Setters` tags to add `Setter` objects to the `Style`:

```
<ContentPage xmlns="http://xamarin.com/schemas/2014/forms"
             xmlns:x="http://schemas.microsoft.com/winfx/2009/xaml"
```

```
            x:Class="BasicStyle.BasicStylePage">

    <ContentPage.Resources>
        <ResourceDictionary>
            <Style x:Key="buttonStyle" TargetType="Button">
                <Setter Property="HorizontalOptions" Value="Center" />
                <Setter Property="VerticalOptions" Value="CenterAndExpand" />
                <Setter Property="BorderWidth" Value="3" />
                <Setter Property="TextColor" Value="Red" />
                <Setter Property="FontSize" Value="Large" />
                ...
            </Style>
        </ResourceDictionary>
    </ContentPage.Resources>
    ...
</ContentPage>
```

Two more `Setter` objects are required for `BackgroundColor` and `BorderColor`. These involve `OnPlatform` and might at first seem to be impossible to express in markup. However, it's possible to express the `Value` property of `Setter` as a property element, with the `OnPlatform` markup between the property element tags:

```
            <Setter Property="BackgroundColor">
                <Setter.Value>
                    <OnPlatform x:TypeArguments="Color"
                                Android="#404040" />
                </Setter.Value>
            </Setter>
            <Setter Property="BorderColor">
                <Setter.Value>
                    <OnPlatform x:TypeArguments="Color"
                                Android="White"
                                WinPhone="Black" />
                </Setter.Value>
            </Setter>
```

The final step is to set this `Style` object to the `Style` property of each `Button`. Use the familiar `StaticResource` markup extension to reference the dictionary key. Here is the complete XAML file in the **BasicStyle** project:

```
<ContentPage xmlns="http://xamarin.com/schemas/2014/forms"
             xmlns:x="http://schemas.microsoft.com/winfx/2009/xaml"
             x:Class="BasicStyle.BasicStylePage">

    <ContentPage.Resources>
        <ResourceDictionary>
            <Style x:Key="buttonStyle" TargetType="Button">
                <Setter Property="HorizontalOptions" Value="Center" />
                <Setter Property="VerticalOptions" Value="CenterAndExpand" />
                <Setter Property="BorderWidth" Value="3" />
                <Setter Property="TextColor" Value="Red" />
                <Setter Property="FontSize" Value="Large" />
                <Setter Property="BackgroundColor">
```

```
                            <Setter.Value>
                                <OnPlatform x:TypeArguments="Color"
                                            Android="#404040" />
                            </Setter.Value>
                        </Setter>
                        <Setter Property="BorderColor">
                            <Setter.Value>
                                <OnPlatform x:TypeArguments="Color"
                                            Android="White"
                                            WinPhone="Black" />
                            </Setter.Value>
                        </Setter>
                    </Style>
                </ResourceDictionary>
            </ContentPage.Resources>

            <StackLayout>
                <Button Text=" Carpe diem "
                        Style="{StaticResource buttonStyle}" />

                <Button Text=" Sapere aude "
                        Style="{StaticResource buttonStyle}" />

                <Button Text=" Discere faciendo "
                        Style="{StaticResource buttonStyle}" />
            </StackLayout>
        </ContentPage>
```

Now all these property settings are in one `Style` object that is shared among multiple `Button` elements:

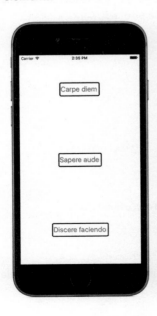  

The visuals are the same as those in the **ResourceSharing** program in Chapter 10, but the markup is a lot more concise.

Even after working with Style objects in markup, it's easy to be flummoxed with an unwieldy Value property. Suppose you'd like to define a Setter for the TextColor using the Color.FromHsla static method. You can define such a color by using the x:FactoryMethod attribute, but how can you possibly set such an unwieldy chunk of markup to the Value property of the Setter object? As you saw earlier, the solution is almost always property-element syntax:

```
<ResourceDictionary>
    <Style x:Key="buttonStyle" TargetType="Button">
        ...
        <Setter Property="TextColor">
            <Setter.Value>
                <Color x:FactoryMethod="FromHsla">
                    <x:Arguments>
                        <x:Double>0.83</x:Double>
                        <x:Double>1</x:Double>
                        <x:Double>0.75</x:Double>
                        <x:Double>1</x:Double>
                    </x:Arguments>
                </Color>
            </Setter.Value>
        </Setter>
        ...
    </Style>
</ResourceDictionary>
```

Here's another way to do it: Define the Color value as a separate item in the resource dictionary, and then use StaticResource to set it to the Value property of the Setter:

```
<ResourceDictionary>
    <Color x:Key="btnTextColor"
           x:FactoryMethod="FromHsla">
        <x:Arguments>
            <x:Double>0.83</x:Double>
            <x:Double>1</x:Double>
            <x:Double>0.75</x:Double>
            <x:Double>1</x:Double>
        </x:Arguments>
    </Color>

    <Style x:Key="buttonStyle" TargetType="Button">
        ...
        <Setter Property="TextColor" Value="{StaticResource btnTextColor}" />
        ...
    </Style>
</ResourceDictionary>
```

This is a good technique if you're sharing the same Color value among multiple styles or multiple setters.

You can override a property setting from a `Style` by setting a property directly in the visual element. Notice that the second `Button` has its `TextColor` property set to `Maroon`:

```
<StackLayout>
    <Button Text=" Carpe diem "
            Style="{StaticResource buttonStyle}" />

    <Button Text=" Sapere aude "
            TextColor="Maroon"
            Style="{StaticResource buttonStyle}" />

    <Button Text=" Discere faciendo "
            Style="{StaticResource buttonStyle}" />
</StackLayout>
```

The center `Button` will have maroon text while the other two buttons get their `TextColor` settings from the `Style`. A property directly set on the visual element is sometimes called a *local setting* or a *manual setting*, and it always overrides the property setting from the `Style`.

The `Style` object in the **BasicStyle** program is shared among the three buttons. The sharing of styles has an important implication for the `Setter` objects. Any object set to the `Value` property of a `Setter` must be shareable. Don't try to do something like this:

```
<!-- Invalid XAML! -->
<Style x:Key="frameStyle" TargetType="Frame">
    <Setter Property="OutlineColor" Value="Accent" />
    <Setter Property="Content">
        <Setter.Value>
            <Label Text="Text in a Frame" />
        </Setter.Value>
    </Setter>
</Style>
```

This XAML doesn't work for two reasons: `Content` is not backed by a `BindableProperty` and therefore cannot be used in a `Setter`. But the obvious intent here is for every `Frame`—or at least every `Frame` on which this style is applied—to get that same `Label` object as content. A single `Label` object can't appear in multiple places on the page. A much better way to do something like this is to derive a class from `Frame` and set a `Label` as the `Content` property, or to derive a class from `ContentView` that includes a `Frame` and `Label`.

You might want to use a style to set an event handler for an event such as `Clicked`. That would be useful and convenient, but it is not supported. Event handlers must be set on the elements themselves. (However, the `Style` class does support objects called *triggers*, which can respond to events or property changes. Triggers are discussed in Chapter 23, "Triggers and behaviors.")

You cannot set the `GestureRecognizers` property in a style. That would be useful as well, but `GestureRecognizers` is not backed by a bindable property.

If a bindable property is a reference type, and if the default value is `null`, you can use a style to set the property to a non-`null` object. But you might also want to override that style setting with a local setting that sets the property back to `null`. You can set a property to `null` in XAML with the {x:Null} markup extension.

Styles in code

Although styles are mostly defined and used in XAML, you should know what they look like when defined and used in code. Here's the page class for the code-only **BasicStyleCode** project. The constructor of the `BasicStyleCodePage` class uses object-initialization syntax to mimic the XAML syntax in defining the `Style` object and applying it to three buttons:

```
public class BasicStyleCodePage : ContentPage
{
    public BasicStyleCodePage()
    {
        Resources = new ResourceDictionary
        {
            { "buttonStyle", new Style(typeof(Button))
                {
                    Setters =
                    {
                        new Setter
                        {
                            Property = View.HorizontalOptionsProperty,
                            Value = LayoutOptions.Center
                        },
                        new Setter
                        {
                            Property = View.VerticalOptionsProperty,
                            Value = LayoutOptions.CenterAndExpand
                        },
                        new Setter
                        {
                            Property = Button.BorderWidthProperty,
                            Value = 3
                        },
                        new Setter
                        {
                            Property = Button.TextColorProperty,
                            Value = Color.Red
                        },
                        new Setter
                        {
                            Property = Button.FontSizeProperty,
                            Value = Device.GetNamedSize(NamedSize.Large, typeof(Button))
                        },
                        new Setter
                        {
                            Property = VisualElement.BackgroundColorProperty,
                            Value = Device.OnPlatform(Color.Default,
                                                Color.FromRgb(0x40, 0x40, 0x40),
```

```
                                                        Color.Default)
                },
                new Setter
                {
                    Property = Button.BorderColorProperty,
                    Value = Device.OnPlatform(Color.Default,
                                              Color.White,
                                              Color.Black)
                }
            }
        }
    }
};

Content = new StackLayout
{
    Children =
    {
        new Button
        {
            Text = " Carpe diem ",
            Style = (Style)Resources["buttonStyle"]
        },
        new Button
        {
            Text = " Sapere aude ",
            Style = (Style)Resources["buttonStyle"]
        },
        new Button
        {
            Text = " Discere faciendo ",
            Style = (Style)Resources["buttonStyle"]
        }
    }
};
    }
}
```

It's much more obvious in code than in XAML that the `Property` property of the `Setter` is of type `BindableProperty`.

The first two `Setter` objects in this example are initialized with the `BindableProperties` objects named `View.HorizontalOptionsProperty` and `View.VerticalOptionsProperty`. You could use `Button.HorizontalOptionsProperty` and `Button.VerticalOptionsProperty` instead because `Button` inherits these properties from `View`. Or you can change the class name to any other class that derives from `View`.

As usual, the use of a `ResourceDictionary` in code seems pointless. You could eliminate the dictionary and just assign the `Style` objects directly to the `Style` properties of the buttons. However, even in code, the `Style` is a convenient way to bundle all the property settings together into one compact package.

Style inheritance

The `TargetType` of the `Style` serves two different functions: One of these functions is described in the next section on implicit styles. The other function is for the benefit of the XAML parser. The XAML parser must be able to resolve the property names in the `Setter` objects, and for that it needs a class name provided by the `TargetType`.

All the properties in the style must be defined by or inherited by the class specified in the `Target-Type` property. The type of the visual element on which the `Style` is set must be the same as the `TargetType` or a derived class of the `TargetType`.

If you need a `Style` only for properties defined by `View`, you can set the `TargetType` to `View` and still use the style on buttons or any other `View` derivative, as in this modified version of the **BasicStyle** program:

```
<ContentPage xmlns="http://xamarin.com/schemas/2014/forms"
             xmlns:x="http://schemas.microsoft.com/winfx/2009/xaml"
             x:Class="BasicStyle.BasicStylePage">

    <ContentPage.Resources>
        <ResourceDictionary>
            <Style x:Key="viewStyle" TargetType="View">
                <Setter Property="HorizontalOptions" Value="Center" />
                <Setter Property="VerticalOptions" Value="CenterAndExpand" />
                <Setter Property="BackgroundColor" Value="Pink" />
            </Style>
        </ResourceDictionary>
    </ContentPage.Resources>

    <StackLayout>
        <Button Text=" Carpe diem "
                Style="{StaticResource viewStyle}" />

        <Label Text ="A bit of text"
               Style="{StaticResource viewStyle}" />

        <Button Text=" Sapere aude "
                Style="{StaticResource viewStyle}" />

        <Label Text ="Another bit of text"
               Style="{StaticResource viewStyle}" />

        <Button Text=" Discere faciendo "
                Style="{StaticResource viewStyle}" />
    </StackLayout>
</ContentPage>
```

As you can see, the same style is applied to all the `Button` and `Label` children of the `StackLayout`:

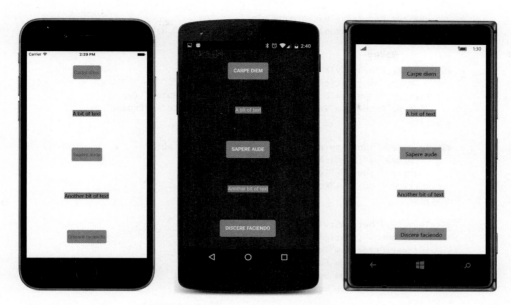

But suppose you now want to expand on this style, but differently for `Button` and `Label`. Is that possible?

Yes, it is. Styles can derive from other styles. The `Style` class includes a property named `BasedOn` of type `Style`. In code, you can set this `BasedOn` property directly to another `Style` object. In XAML you set the `BasedOn` attribute to a `StaticResource` markup extension that references a previously created `Style`. The new `Style` can include `Setter` objects for new properties or use them to override properties in the earlier `Style`. The `BasedOn` style must target the same class or an ancestor class of the new style's `TargetType`.

Here's the XAML file for a project named **StyleInheritance**. The application has a reference to the **Xamarin.FormsBook.Toolkit** assembly for two purposes: It uses the `HslColor` markup extension to demonstrate that markup extensions are legitimate value settings in `Setter` objects and to demonstrate that a style can be defined for a custom class, in this case `AltLabel`.

The `ResourceDictionary` contains four styles: The first has a dictionary key of "visualStyle". The `Style` with the dictionary key of "baseStyle" derives from "visualStyle". The styles with keys of "labelStyle" and "buttonStyle" derive from "baseStyle":

```
<ContentPage xmlns="http://xamarin.com/schemas/2014/forms"
             xmlns:x="http://schemas.microsoft.com/winfx/2009/xaml"
             xmlns:toolkit=
                 "clr-namespace:Xamarin.FormsBook.Toolkit;assembly=Xamarin.FormsBook.Toolkit"
             x:Class="StyleInheritance.StyleInheritancePage">

    <ContentPage.Resources>
        <ResourceDictionary>
            <Style x:Key="visualStyle" TargetType="VisualElement">
```

```
                    <Setter Property="BackgroundColor"
                            Value="{toolkit:HslColor H=0, S=1, L=0.8}" />
            </Style>

            <Style x:Key="baseStyle" TargetType="View"
                    BasedOn="{StaticResource visualStyle}">
                <Setter Property="HorizontalOptions" Value="Center" />
                <Setter Property="VerticalOptions" Value="CenterAndExpand" />
            </Style>

            <Style x:Key="labelStyle" TargetType="toolkit:AltLabel"
                    BasedOn="{StaticResource baseStyle}">
                <Setter Property="TextColor" Value="Black" />
                <Setter Property="PointSize" Value="12" />
            </Style>

            <Style x:Key="buttonStyle" TargetType="Button"
                    BasedOn="{StaticResource baseStyle}">
                <Setter Property="TextColor" Value="Blue" />
                <Setter Property="FontSize" Value="Large" />
                <Setter Property="BorderColor" Value="Blue" />
                <Setter Property="BorderWidth" Value="2" />
            </Style>
        </ResourceDictionary>
    </ContentPage.Resources>

    <ContentPage.Style>
        <StaticResourceExtension Key="visualStyle" />
    </ContentPage.Style>

    <StackLayout>
        <Button Text=" Carpe diem "
                Style="{StaticResource buttonStyle}" />

        <toolkit:AltLabel Text ="A bit of text"
                        Style="{StaticResource labelStyle}" />

        <Button Text=" Sapere aude "
                Style="{StaticResource buttonStyle}" />

        <toolkit:AltLabel Text ="Another bit of text"
                        Style="{StaticResource labelStyle}" />

        <Button Text=" Discere faciendo "
                Style="{StaticResource buttonStyle}" />
    </StackLayout>
</ContentPage>
```

Immediately after the `Resources` section is some markup that sets the `Style` property of the page itself to the "visualStyle" `Style`:

```
<ContentPage.Style>
    <StaticResourceExtension Key="visualStyle" />
</ContentPage.Style>
```

Because `Page` derives from `VisualElement` but not `View`, this is the only style in the resource dictionary that can be applied to the page. However, the style can't be applied to the page until after the `Resources` section, so using the element form of `StaticResource` is a good solution here. The entire background of the page is colored based on this style, and the style is also inherited by all the other styles:

If the `Style` for the `AltLabel` only included `Setter` objects for properties defined by `Label`, the `TargetType` could be `Label` instead of `AltLabel`. But the `Style` has a `Setter` for the `PointSize` property. That property is defined by `AltLabel`, so the `TargetType` must be `toolkit:AltLabel`.

A `Setter` can be defined for the `PointSize` property because `PointSize` is backed by a bindable property. If you change the accessibility of the `BindableProperty` object in `AltLabel` from `public` to `private`, the property will still work for many routine uses of `AltLabel`, but now `PointSize` cannot be set in a style `Setter`. The XAML parser will complain that it cannot find `PointSizeProperty`, which is the bindable property that backs the `PointSize` property.

You discovered in Chapter 10 how `StaticResource` works: When the XAML parser encounters a `StaticResource` markup extension, it searches up the visual tree for a matching dictionary key. This process has implications for styles. You can define a style in one `Resources` section and then override it with another style with the same dictionary key in a different `Resources` section lower in the visual tree. When you set the `BasedOn` property to a `StaticResource` markup extension, the style you're deriving from must be defined in the same `Resources` section (as demonstrated in the **StyleInheritance** program) or a `Resources` section higher in the visual tree.

This means that you can structure your styles in XAML in two hierarchical ways: You can use `BasedOn` to derive styles from other styles, and you can define styles at different levels in the visual tree that derive from styles higher in the visual tree or replace them entirely.

For larger applications with multiple pages and lots of markup, the recommendation for defining styles is very simple—define your styles as close as possible to the elements that use those styles.

Adhering to this recommendation aids in maintaining the program and becomes particularly important when working with *implicit styles*.

Implicit styles

Every entry in a `ResourceDictionary` requires a dictionary key. This is an indisputable fact. If you try to pass a `null` key to the `Add` method of a `ResourceDictionary` object, you'll raise an `Argument-NullException`.

However, there is one special case where a programmer is not required to supply this dictionary key. A dictionary key is instead generated automatically.

This special case is for a `Style` object added to a `ResourceDictionary` without an `x:Key` setting. The `ResourceDictionary` generates a key based on the `TargetType`, which is always required. (A little exploration will reveal that this special dictionary key is the fully qualified name associated with the `TargetType` of the `Style`. For a `TargetType` of `Button`, for example, the dictionary key is "Xamarin.Forms.Button". But you don't need to know that.)

You can also add a `Style` to a `ResourceDictionary` without a dictionary key in code: an overload of the `Add` method accepts an argument of type `Style` but doesn't require anything else.

A `Style` object in a `ResourceDictionary` that has one of these generated keys is known as an *implicit style*, and the generated dictionary key is very special. You can't refer to this key directly using `StaticResource`. However, if an element within the scope of the `ResourceDictionary` has the same type as the dictionary key, and if that element does not have its `Style` property explicitly set to another `Style` object, then this implicit style is automatically applied.

The following XAML from the **ImplicitStyle** project demonstrates this. It is the same as the **BasicStyle** XAML file except that the `Style` has no `x:Key` setting and the `Style` properties on the buttons aren't set using `StaticResource`:

```
<ContentPage xmlns="http://xamarin.com/schemas/2014/forms"
             xmlns:x="http://schemas.microsoft.com/winfx/2009/xaml"
             x:Class="ImplicitStyle.ImplicitStylePage">

    <ContentPage.Resources>
        <ResourceDictionary>
            <Style TargetType="Button">
                <Setter Property="HorizontalOptions" Value="Center" />
                <Setter Property="VerticalOptions" Value="CenterAndExpand" />
                <Setter Property="BorderWidth" Value="3" />
                <Setter Property="TextColor" Value="Red" />
```

```
                    <Setter Property="FontSize" Value="Large" />
                    <Setter Property="BackgroundColor">
                        <Setter.Value>
                            <OnPlatform x:TypeArguments="Color"
                                        Android="#404040" />
                        </Setter.Value>
                    </Setter>

                    <Setter Property="BorderColor">
                        <Setter.Value>
                            <OnPlatform x:TypeArguments="Color"
                                        Android="White"
                                        WinPhone="Black" />
                        </Setter.Value>
                    </Setter>
                </Style>
            </ResourceDictionary>
        </ContentPage.Resources>

    <StackLayout>
        <Button Text=" Carpe diem " />

        <Button Text=" Sapere aude " />

        <Button Text=" Discere faciendo " />
    </StackLayout>
</ContentPage>
```

Despite the absence of any explicit connection between the buttons and the style, the style is definitely applied:

An implicit style is applied only when the class of the element matches the `TargetType` of the `Style` exactly. If you include an element that derives from `Button` in the `StackLayout`, it would not have the `Style` applied.

You can use local property settings to override properties set through the implicit style, just as you can override property settings in a style set with `StaticResource`.

You will find implicit styles to be very powerful and extremely useful. Whenever you have several views of the same type and you determine that you want them all to have an identical property setting or two, it's very easy to quickly define an implicit style. You don't have to touch the elements themselves.

However, with great power comes at least *some* programmer responsibility. Because no style is referenced in the elements themselves, it can be confusing when simply examining the XAML to determine whether some elements are styled or not. Sometimes the appearance of a page indicates that an implicit style is applied to some elements, but it's not quite obvious where the implicit style is defined. If you then want to change that implicit style, you have to manually search for it up the visual tree.

For this reason, you should define implicit styles *as close as possible* to the elements they are applied to. If the views getting the implicit style are in a particular `StackLayout`, then define the implicit style in the `Resources` section on that `StackLayout`. A comment or two might help avoid confusion as well.

Interestingly, implicit styles have a built-in restriction that might persuade you to keep them close to the elements they are applied to. Here's the restriction: You can derive an implicit style from a `Style` with an explicit dictionary key, but you can't go the other way around. You can't use `BasedOn` to reference an implicit style.

If you define a chain of styles that use `BasedOn` to derive from one another, the implicit style (if any) is always at the end of the chain. No further derivations are possible.

This implies that you can structure your styles with three types of hierarchies:

- From styles defined on the `Application` and `Page` down to styles defined on layouts lower in the visual tree.

- From styles defined for base classes such as `VisualElement` and `View` to styles defined for specific classes.

- From styles with explicit dictionary keys to implicit styles.

This is demonstrated in the **StyleHierarchy** project, which uses a similar (but somewhat simplified) set of styles as you saw earlier in the **StyleInheritance** project. However, these styles are now spread out over three `Resources` sections.

Using a technique you saw in the **ResourceTrees** program in Chapter 10, the **StyleHierarchy** project was given a XAML-based `App` class. The App.xaml class has a `ResourceDictionary` containing a style with just one property setter:

```
<Application xmlns="http://xamarin.com/schemas/2014/forms"
             xmlns:x="http://schemas.microsoft.com/winfx/2009/xaml"
             x:Class="StyleHierarchy.App">

    <Application.Resources>
        <ResourceDictionary>
            <Style x:Key="visualStyle" TargetType="VisualElement">
                <Setter Property="BackgroundColor" Value="Pink" />
            </Style>
        </ResourceDictionary>
    </Application.Resources>
</Application>
```

In a multipage application, this style would be used throughout the application.

The code-behind file for the `App` class calls `InitializeComponent` to process the XAML file and sets the `MainPage` property:

```
public partial class App : Application
{
    public App()
    {
        InitializeComponent();
        MainPage = new StyleHierarchyPage();
    }
    ...
}
```

The XAML file for the page class defines one `Style` for the whole page that derives from the style in the `App` class and also two implicit styles that derive from the `Style` for the page. Notice that the `Style` property of the page is set to the `Style` defined in the `App` class:

```
<ContentPage xmlns="http://xamarin.com/schemas/2014/forms"
             xmlns:x="http://schemas.microsoft.com/winfx/2009/xaml"
             x:Class="StyleHierarchy.StyleHierarchyPage"
             Style="{StaticResource visualStyle}">

    <ContentPage.Resources>
        <ResourceDictionary>
            <Style x:Key="baseStyle" TargetType="View"
                   BasedOn="{StaticResource visualStyle}">
                <Setter Property="HorizontalOptions" Value="Center" />
                <Setter Property="VerticalOptions" Value="CenterAndExpand" />
            </Style>
        </ResourceDictionary>
    </ContentPage.Resources>

    <StackLayout>
        <StackLayout.Resources>
```

```
            <ResourceDictionary>
                <Style TargetType="Label"
                        BasedOn="{StaticResource baseStyle}">
                    <Setter Property="TextColor" Value="Black" />
                    <Setter Property="FontSize" Value="Large" />
                </Style>

                <Style TargetType="Button"
                        BasedOn="{StaticResource baseStyle}">
                    <Setter Property="TextColor" Value="Blue" />
                    <Setter Property="FontSize" Value="Large" />
                    <Setter Property="BorderColor" Value="Blue" />
                    <Setter Property="BorderWidth" Value="2" />
                </Style>
            </ResourceDictionary>
        </StackLayout.Resources>

        <Button Text=" Carpe diem " />

        <Label Text ="A bit of text" />

        <Button Text=" Sapere aude " />

        <Label Text ="Another bit of text" />

        <Button Text=" Discere faciendo " />
    </StackLayout>
</ContentPage>
```

The implicit styles are defined as close to the target elements as possible.

Here's the result:

The incentive to separate `Style` objects into separate dictionaries doesn't make a lot of sense for very tiny programs like this one, but for larger programs, it becomes just as important to have a structured hierarchy of style definitions as it is to have a structured hierarchy of class definitions.

Sometimes you'll have a `Style` with an explicit dictionary key (for example "myButtonStyle"), but you'll want that same style to be implicit as well. Simply define a style based on that key with no key or setters of its own:

```
<Style TargetType="Button"
       BasedOn="{StaticResource myButtonStyle}" />
```

That's an implicit style that is identical to `myButtonStyle`.

Dynamic styles

A `Style` is generally a static object that is created and initialized in XAML or code and then remains unchanged for the duration of the application. The `Style` class does not derive from `BindableObject` and does not internally respond to changes in its properties. For example, if you assign a `Style` object to an element and then modify one of the `Setter` objects by giving it a new value, the new value won't show up in the element. Similarly, the target element won't change if you add a `Setter` or remove a `Setter` from the `Setters` collection. For these new property setters to take effect, you need to use code to detach the style from the element by setting the `Style` property to `null` and then re-attach the style to the element.

However, your application can respond to style changes dynamically at run time through the use of `DynamicResource`. You'll recall that `DynamicResource` is similar to `StaticResource` in that it uses a dictionary key to fetch an object or a value from a resource dictionary. The difference is that `Static-Resource` is a one-time dictionary lookup while `DynamicResource` maintains a link to the actual dictionary key. If the dictionary entry associated with that key is replaced with a new object, that change is propagated to the element.

This facility allows an application to implement a feature sometimes called *dynamic styles*. For example, you might include a facility in your program for stylistic themes (involving fonts and colors, perhaps), and you might make these themes selectable by the user. The application can switch between these themes because they are implemented with styles.

There's nothing in a style itself that indicates a dynamic style. A style becomes dynamic solely by being referenced using `DynamicResource` rather than `StaticResource`.

The **DynamicStyles** project demonstrates the mechanics of this process. Here is the XAML file for the `DynamicStylesPage` class:

```
<ContentPage xmlns="http://xamarin.com/schemas/2014/forms"
             xmlns:x="http://schemas.microsoft.com/winfx/2009/xaml"
             x:Class="DynamicStyles.DynamicStylesPage">

    <ContentPage.Padding>
        <OnPlatform x:TypeArguments="Thickness"
                    iOS="0, 20, 0, 0"
                    Android="0"
                    WinPhone="0" />
    </ContentPage.Padding>

    <ContentPage.Resources>
        <ResourceDictionary>
            <Style x:Key="baseButtonStyle" TargetType="Button">
                <Setter Property="FontSize" Value="Large" />
            </Style>

            <Style x:Key="buttonStyle1" TargetType="Button"
                   BasedOn="{StaticResource baseButtonStyle}">
                <Setter Property="HorizontalOptions" Value="Center" />
                <Setter Property="VerticalOptions" Value="CenterAndExpand" />
                <Setter Property="TextColor" Value="Red" />
            </Style>

            <Style x:Key="buttonStyle2" TargetType="Button"
                   BasedOn="{StaticResource baseButtonStyle}">
                <Setter Property="HorizontalOptions" Value="Start" />
                <Setter Property="VerticalOptions" Value="EndAndExpand" />
                <Setter Property="TextColor" Value="Green" />
                <Setter Property="FontAttributes" Value="Italic" />
            </Style>

            <Style x:Key="buttonStyle3" TargetType="Button"
```

```
                    BasedOn="{StaticResource baseButtonStyle}">
                <Setter Property="HorizontalOptions" Value="End" />
                <Setter Property="VerticalOptions" Value="StartAndExpand" />
                <Setter Property="TextColor" Value="Blue" />
                <Setter Property="FontAttributes" Value="Bold" />
            </Style>
        </ResourceDictionary>
    </ContentPage.Resources>

    <StackLayout>
        <Button Text=" Switch to Style #1 "
                Style="{DynamicResource buttonStyle}"
                Clicked="OnButton1Clicked" />

        <Button Text=" Switch to Style #2 "
                Style="{DynamicResource buttonStyle}"
                Clicked="OnButton2Clicked" />

        <Button Text=" Switch to Style #3 "
                Style="{DynamicResource buttonStyle}"
                Clicked="OnButton3Clicked" />

        <Button Text=" Reset "
                Style="{DynamicResource buttonStyle}"
                Clicked="OnResetButtonClicked" />
    </StackLayout>
</ContentPage>
```

The `Resources` section defines four styles: a simple style with the key "baseButtonStyle", and then three styles that derive from that style with the keys "buttonStyle1", "buttonStyle2", and "buttonStyle3".

However, the four `Button` elements toward the bottom of the XAML file all use `DynamicResource` to reference a style with the simpler key "buttonStyle". Where is the `Style` with that key? It does not exist. However, because the four button `Style` properties are set with `DynamicResource`, the missing dictionary key is not a problem. No exception is raised. But no `Style` is applied, which means that the buttons have a default appearance:

Each of the four `Button` elements has a `Clicked` handler attached, and in the code-behind file, the first three handlers set a dictionary entry with the key "buttonStyle" to one of the three numbered styles already defined in the dictionary:

```
public partial class DynamicStylesPage : ContentPage
{
    public DynamicStylesPage()
    {
        InitializeComponent();
    }

    void OnButton1Clicked(object sender, EventArgs args)
    {
        Resources["buttonStyle"] = Resources["buttonStyle1"];
    }

    void OnButton2Clicked(object sender, EventArgs args)
    {
        Resources["buttonStyle"] = Resources["buttonStyle2"];
    }

    void OnButton3Clicked(object sender, EventArgs args)
    {
        Resources["buttonStyle"] = Resources["buttonStyle3"];
    }

    void OnResetButtonClicked(object sender, EventArgs args)
    {
        Resources["buttonStyle"] = null;
    }
}
```

When you press one of the first three buttons, all four buttons get the selected style. Here's the program running on all three platforms showing the results (from left to right) when buttons 1, 2, and 3 are pressed:

Pressing the fourth button returns everything to the initial conditions by setting the value associated with the "buttonStyle" key to `null`. (You might also consider calling `Remove` or `Clear` on the `ResourceDictionary` object to remove the key entirely, but that doesn't work in the version of Xamarin.Forms used for this chapter.)

Suppose you want to derive another `Style` from the `Style` with the key "buttonStyle". How do you do this in XAML, considering that the "buttonStyle" dictionary entry doesn't exist until one of the first three buttons is pressed?

You can't do it like this:

```
<!-- This won't work! -->
<Style x:Key="newButtonStyle" TargetType="Button"
       BasedOn="{StaticResource buttonStyle}">
    ...
</Style>
```

`StaticResource` will raise an exception if the "buttonStyle" key does not exist, and even if the key does exist, the use of `StaticResource` won't allow changes in the dictionary entry to be reflected in this new style.

However, changing `StaticResource` to `DynamicResource` won't work either:

```
<!-- This won't work either! -->
<Style x:Key="newButtonStyle" TargetType="Button"
```

```
      BasedOn="{DynamicResource buttonStyle}">
    ...
</Style>
```

`DynamicResource` works only with properties backed by bindable properties, and that is not the case here. `Style` doesn't derive from `BindableObject`, so it can't support bindable properties.

Instead, `Style` defines a property specifically for the purpose of inheriting dynamic styles. The property is `BaseResourceKey`, which is intended to be set directly to a dictionary key that might not yet exist or whose value might change dynamically, which is the case with the "buttonStyle" key:

```
<!-- This works!! -->
<Style x:Key="newButtonStyle" TargetType="Button"
      BaseResourceKey="buttonStyle">
    ...
</Style>
```

The use of `BaseResourceKey` is demonstrated by the **DynamicStylesInheritance** project, which is very similar to the **DynamicStyles** project. Indeed, the code-behind processing is identical. Toward the bottom of the `Resources` section, a new `Style` is defined with a key of "newButtonStyle" that uses `BaseResourceKey` to reference the "buttonStyle" entry and add a couple of properties, including one that uses `OnPlatform`:

```
<ContentPage xmlns="http://xamarin.com/schemas/2014/forms"
             xmlns:x="http://schemas.microsoft.com/winfx/2009/xaml"
             x:Class="DynamicStylesInheritance.DynamicStylesInheritancePage">
    <ContentPage.Padding>
        <OnPlatform x:TypeArguments="Thickness"
                    iOS="0, 20, 0, 0"
                    Android="0"
                    WinPhone="0" />
    </ContentPage.Padding>

    <ContentPage.Resources>
        <ResourceDictionary>
            <Style x:Key="baseButtonStyle" TargetType="Button">
                <Setter Property="FontSize" Value="Large" />
            </Style>

            <Style x:Key="buttonStyle1" TargetType="Button"
                   BasedOn="{StaticResource baseButtonStyle}">
                <Setter Property="HorizontalOptions" Value="Center" />
                <Setter Property="VerticalOptions" Value="CenterAndExpand" />
                <Setter Property="TextColor" Value="Red" />
            </Style>

            <Style x:Key="buttonStyle2" TargetType="Button"
                   BasedOn="{StaticResource baseButtonStyle}">
                <Setter Property="HorizontalOptions" Value="Start" />
                <Setter Property="VerticalOptions" Value="EndAndExpand" />
                <Setter Property="TextColor" Value="Green" />
                <Setter Property="FontAttributes" Value="Italic" />
```

```
        </Style>

        <Style x:Key="buttonStyle3" TargetType="Button"
               BasedOn="{StaticResource baseButtonStyle}">
            <Setter Property="HorizontalOptions" Value="End" />
            <Setter Property="VerticalOptions" Value="StartAndExpand" />
            <Setter Property="TextColor" Value="Blue" />
            <Setter Property="FontAttributes" Value="Bold" />
        </Style>

        <!-- New style definition. -->
        <Style x:Key="newButtonStyle" TargetType="Button"
               BaseResourceKey="buttonStyle">
            <Setter Property="BackgroundColor">
                <Setter.Value>
                    <OnPlatform x:TypeArguments="Color"
                                iOS="#C0C0C0"
                                Android="#404040"
                                WinPhone="Gray" />
                </Setter.Value>
            </Setter>
            <Setter Property="BorderColor" Value="Red" />
            <Setter Property="BorderWidth" Value="3" />
        </Style>
    </ResourceDictionary>
</ContentPage.Resources>

<StackLayout>
    <Button Text=" Switch to Style #1 "
            Style="{StaticResource newButtonStyle}"
            Clicked="OnButton1Clicked" />

    <Button Text=" Switch to Style #2 "
            Style="{StaticResource newButtonStyle}"
            Clicked="OnButton2Clicked" />

    <Button Text=" Switch to Style #3 "
            Style="{StaticResource newButtonStyle}"
            Clicked="OnButton3Clicked" />

    <Button Text=" Reset "
            Style="{DynamicResource buttonStyle}"
            Clicked="OnResetButtonClicked" />
</StackLayout>
</ContentPage>
```

Notice that the first three `Button` elements reference the "newButtonStyle" dictionary entry with `StaticResource`. `DynamicResource` is not needed here because the `Style` object associated with the "newButtonStyle" will not itself change except for the `Style` that it derives from. The `Style` with the key "newButtonStyle" maintains a link with "buttonStyle" and internally alters itself when that underlying style changes. When the program begins to run, only the properties defined in the "newButtonStyle" are applied to those three buttons:

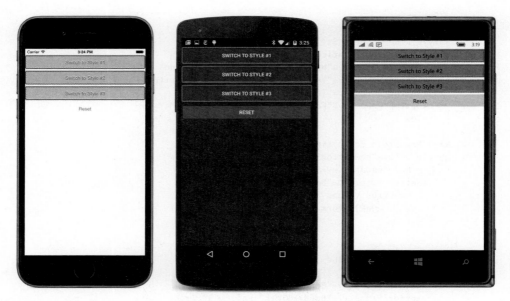

The **Reset** button continues to reference the "buttonStyle" entry.

As in the **DynamicStyles** program, the code-behind file sets that dictionary entry when you click one of the first three buttons, so all the buttons pick up the "buttonStyle" properties as well. Here are the results for (from left to right) clicks of buttons 3, 2, and 1:

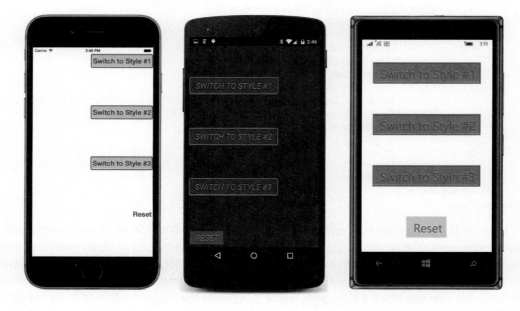

Device styles

Xamarin.Forms includes six built-in dynamic styles. These are known as *device styles*, and they are members of a nested class of `Device` named `Styles`. This `Styles` class defines 12 `static` and `readonly` fields that help reference these six styles in code:

- `BodyStyle` of type `Style`.

- `BodyStyleKey` of type `string` and equal to "BodyStyle."

- `TitleStyle` of type `Style`.

- `TitleStyleKey` of type `string` and equal to "TitleStyle."

- `SubtitleStyle` of type `Style`.

- `SubtitleStyleKey` of type `string` and equal to "SubtitleStyle."

- `CaptionStyle` of type `Style`.

- `CaptionStyleKey` of type `string` and equal to "CaptionStyle."

- `ListItemTextStyle` of type `Style`.

- `ListItemTextStyleKey` of type `string` and equal to "ListItemTextStyle."

- `ListItemDetailTextStyle` of type `Style`.

- `ListItemDetailTextStyleKey` of type `string` and equal to "ListItemDetailTextStyle."

All six styles have a `TargetType` of `Label` and are stored in a dictionary—but not a dictionary that application programs can access directly.

In code, you use the fields in this list for accessing the device styles. For example, you can set the `Device.Styles.BodyStyle` object directly to the `Style` property of a `Label` for text that might be appropriate for the body of a paragraph. If you're defining a style in code that derives from one of these device styles, set the `BaseResourceKey` to `Device.Styles.BodyStyleKey` or simply "BodyStyle" if you're not afraid of misspelling it.

In XAML, you'll simply use the text key "BodyStyle" with `DynamicResource` for setting this style to the `Style` property of a `Label` or to set `BaseResourceKey` when deriving a style from `Device.Styles.BodyStyle`.

The **DeviceStylesList** program demonstrates how to access these styles—and to define a new style that inherits from `SubtitleStyle`—both in XAML and in code. Here's the XAML file:

```
<ContentPage xmlns="http://xamarin.com/schemas/2014/forms"
             xmlns:x="http://schemas.microsoft.com/winfx/2009/xaml"
             x:Class="DeviceStylesList.DeviceStylesListPage">
```

```
<ContentPage.Padding>
    <OnPlatform x:TypeArguments="Thickness"
                iOS="10, 20, 10, 0"
                Android="10, 0"
                WinPhone="10, 0" />
</ContentPage.Padding>

<ContentPage.Resources>
    <ResourceDictionary>
        <Style x:Key="newSubtitleStyle" TargetType="Label"
            BaseResourceKey="SubtitleStyle">
            <Setter Property="TextColor" Value="Accent" />
            <Setter Property="FontAttributes" Value="Italic" />
        </Style>
    </ResourceDictionary>
</ContentPage.Resources>

<ScrollView>
    <StackLayout Spacing="20">

        <!-- Device styles set with DynamicResource -->
        <StackLayout>
            <StackLayout HorizontalOptions="Start">
                <Label Text="Device styles set with DynamicResource" />
                <BoxView Color="Accent" HeightRequest="3" />
            </StackLayout>

            <Label Text="No Style whatsoever" />

            <Label Text="Body Style"
                Style="{DynamicResource BodyStyle}" />

            <Label Text="Title Style"
                Style="{DynamicResource TitleStyle}" />

            <Label Text="Subtitle Style"
                Style="{DynamicResource SubtitleStyle}" />

            <!-- Uses style derived from device style. -->
            <Label Text="New Subtitle Style"
                Style="{StaticResource newSubtitleStyle}" />

            <Label Text="Caption Style"
                Style="{DynamicResource CaptionStyle}" />

            <Label Text="List Item Text Style"
                Style="{DynamicResource ListItemTextStyle}" />

            <Label Text="List Item Detail Text Style"
                Style="{DynamicResource ListItemDetailTextStyle}" />
        </StackLayout>

        <!-- Device styles set in code -->
        <StackLayout x:Name="codeLabelStack">
```

```
                    <StackLayout HorizontalOptions="Start">
                        <Label Text="Device styles set in code:" />
                        <BoxView Color="Accent" HeightRequest="3" />
                    </StackLayout>
                </StackLayout>
            </StackLayout>
        </ScrollView>
</ContentPage>
```

The StackLayout contains two Label and BoxView combinations (one at the top and one at the bottom) to display underlined headers. Following the first of these headers, Label elements reference the device styles with DynamicResource. The new subtitle style is defined in the Resources dictionary for the page.

The code-behind file accesses the device styles by using the properties in the Device.Styles class and creates a new style by deriving from SubtitleStyle:

```
public partial class DeviceStylesListPage : ContentPage
{
    public DeviceStylesListPage()
    {
        InitializeComponent();

        var styleItems = new[]
        {
            new { style = (Style)null, name = "No style whatsoever" },
            new { style = Device.Styles.BodyStyle, name = "Body Style" },
            new { style = Device.Styles.TitleStyle, name = "Title Style" },
            new { style = Device.Styles.SubtitleStyle, name = "Subtitle Style" },

            // Derived style
            new { style = new Style(typeof(Label))
            {
                BaseResourceKey = Device.Styles.SubtitleStyleKey,
                Setters =
                {
                    new Setter
                    {
                        Property = Label.TextColorProperty,
                        Value = Color.Accent
                    },
                    new Setter
                    {
                        Property = Label.FontAttributesProperty,
                        Value = FontAttributes.Italic
                    }
                }
            }, name = "New Subtitle Style" },

            new { style = Device.Styles.CaptionStyle, name = "Caption Style" },
            new { style = Device.Styles.ListItemTextStyle, name = "List Item Text Style" },
            new { style = Device.Styles.ListItemDetailTextStyle,
                  name = "List Item Detail Text Style" },
```

```
    };

    foreach (var styleItem in styleItems)
    {
        codeLabelStack.Children.Add(new Label
            {
                Text = styleItem.name,
                Style = styleItem.style
            });
    }
  }
}
```

The code and XAML result in identical styles, of course, but each platform implements these device styles in a different way:

The dynamic nature of these styles is easily demonstrated on iOS: While the **DeviceStyles** program is running, tap the **Home** button and run **Settings**. Pick the **General** item, then **Accessibility**, and **Larger Text**. A slider is available to make text smaller or larger. Change that slider, double tap the **Home** button to show the current applications, and select **DeviceStyles** again. You'll see the text set from device styles (or the styles that derive from device styles) change size, but none of the unstyled text in the application changes size. New objects have replaced the device styles in the dictionary.

The dynamic nature of device styles is not quite as obvious on Android because changes to the **Font size** item of the **Display** section in **Settings** affect all font sizes in a Xamarin.Forms program.

On a Windows 10 Mobile device, the **Text scaling** item in the **Ease of Access** and **More Options** section of **Settings** also affects all text.

The next chapter includes a program that demonstrates how to make a little e-book reader that lets you read a chapter of *Alice in Wonderland*. This program uses device styles for controlling the formatting of all the text, including the book and chapter titles.

But what this little e-book reader also includes are illustrations, and that requires an exploration into the subject of bitmaps.

Chapter 13
Bitmaps

The visual elements of a graphical user interface can be roughly divided between elements used for presentation (such as text) and those capable of interaction with the user, such as buttons, sliders, and list boxes.

Text is essential for presentation, but pictures are often just as important as a way to supplement text and convey crucial information. The web, for example, would be inconceivable without pictures. These pictures are often in the form of rectangular arrays of picture elements (or pixels) known as *bitmaps*.

Just as a view named `Label` displays text, a view named `Image` displays bitmaps. The bitmap formats supported by iOS, Android, and the Windows Runtime are a little different, but if you stick to JPEG, PNG, GIF, and BMP in your Xamarin.Forms applications, you'll probably not experience any problems.

`Image` defines a `Source` property that you set to an object of type `ImageSource`, which references the bitmap displayed by `Image`. Bitmaps can come from a variety of sources, so the `ImageSource` class defines four static creation methods that return an `ImageSource` object:

- `ImageSource.FromUri` for accessing a bitmap over the web.

- `ImageSource.FromResource` for a bitmap stored as an embedded resource in the application PCL.

- `ImageSource.FromFile` for a bitmap stored as content in an individual platform project.

- `ImageSource.FromStream` for loading a bitmap by using a .NET `Stream` object.

`ImageSource` also has three descendant classes, named `UriImageSource`, `FileImageSource`, and `StreamImageSource`, that you can use instead of the first, third, and fourth static creation methods. Generally, the static methods are easier to use in code, but the descendant classes are sometimes required in XAML.

In general, you'll use the `ImageSource.FromUri` and `ImageSource.FromResource` methods to obtain platform-independent bitmaps for presentation purposes and `ImageSource.FromFile` to load platform-specific bitmaps for user-interface objects. Small bitmaps play a crucial role in `MenuItem` and `ToolbarItem` objects, and you can also add a bitmap to a `Button`.

This chapter begins with the use of platform-independent bitmaps obtained from the `Image-Source.FromUri` and `ImageSource.FromResource` methods. It then explores some uses of the `Im-ageSource.FromStream` method. The chapter concludes with the use of `ImageSource.FromFile` to obtain platform-specific bitmaps for toolbars and buttons.

Platform-independent bitmaps

Here's a code-only program named **WebBitmapCode** with a page class that uses `Image-Source.FromUri` to access a bitmap from the Xamarin website:

```
public class WebBitmapCodePage : ContentPage
{
    public WebBitmapCodePage()
    {
        string uri = "https://developer.xamarin.com/demo/IMG_1415.JPG";

        Content = new Image
        {
            Source = ImageSource.FromUri(new Uri(uri))
        };
    }
}
```

If the URI passed to `ImageSource.FromUri` does not point to a valid bitmap, no exception is raised.

Even this tiny program can be simplified. `ImageSource` defines an implicit conversion from `string` or `Uri` to an `ImageSource` object, so you can set the string with the URI directly to the `Source` property of `Image`:

```
public class WebBitmapCodePage : ContentPage
{
    public WebBitmapCodePage()
    {
        Content = new Image
        {
            Source = "https://developer.xamarin.com/demo/IMG_1415.JPG"
        };
    }
}
```

Or, to make it more verbose, you can set the `Source` property of `Image` to a `UriImageSource` object with its `Uri` property set to a `Uri` object:

```
public class WebBitmapCodePage : ContentPage
{
    public WebBitmapCodePage()
    {
        Content = new Image
        {
            Source = new UriImageSource
            {
                Uri = new Uri("https://developer.xamarin.com/demo/IMG_1415.JPG")
            }
        };
    }
}
```

The `UriImageSource` class might be preferred if you want to control the caching of web-based images. The class implements its own caching that uses the application's private storage area available on each platform. `UriImageSource` defines a `CachingEnabled` property that has a default value of `true` and a `CachingValidity` property of type `TimeSpan` that has a default value of one day. This means that if the image is reaccessed within a day, the cached image is used. You can disable caching entirely by setting `CachingEnabled` to `false`, or you can change the caching expiry time by setting the `CachingValidity` property to another `TimeSpan` value.

Regardless which way you do it, by default the bitmap displayed by the `Image` view is stretched to the size of its container—the `ContentPage` in this case—while respecting the bitmap's aspect ratio:

This bitmap is square, so blank areas appear above and below the image. As you turn your phone or emulator between portrait and landscape mode, a rendered bitmap can change size, and you'll see some blank space at the top and bottom or the left and right, where the bitmap doesn't reach. You can color that area by using the `BackgroundColor` property that `Image` inherits from `VisualElement`.

The bitmap referenced in the **WebBitmapCode** program is 4,096 pixels square, but a utility is installed on the Xamarin website that lets you download a much smaller bitmap file by specifying the URI like so:

```
Content = new Image
{
    Source = "https://developer.xamarin.com/demo/IMG_1415.JPG?width=25"
};
```

Now the downloaded bitmap is 25 pixels square, but it is again stretched to the size of its container. Each platform implements an interpolation algorithm in an attempt to smooth the pixels as the image is expanded to fit the page:

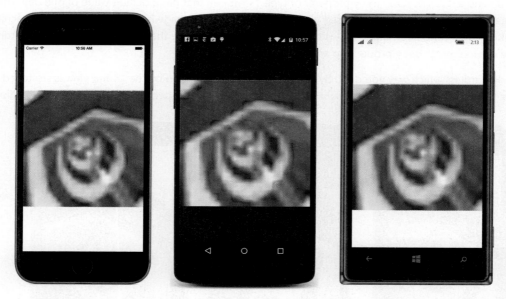

However, if you now set `HorizontalOptions` and `VerticalOptions` on the `Image` to `Center`— or put the `Image` element in a `StackLayout`—this 25-pixel bitmap collapses into a very tiny image. This phenomenon is discussed in more detail later in this chapter.

You can also instantiate an `Image` element in XAML and load a bitmap from a URL by setting the `Source` property directly to a web address. Here's the XAML file from the **WebBitmapXaml** program:

```
<ContentPage xmlns="http://xamarin.com/schemas/2014/forms"
             xmlns:x="http://schemas.microsoft.com/winfx/2009/xaml"
             x:Class="WebBitmapXaml.WebBitmapXamlPage">

    <Image Source="https://developer.xamarin.com/demo/IMG_3256.JPG" />

</ContentPage>
```

A more verbose approach involves explicitly instantiating a `UriImageSource` object and setting the `Uri` property:

```
<Image>
    <Image.Source>
        <UriImageSource Uri="https://developer.xamarin.com/demo/IMG_3256.JPG" />
    </Image.Source>
</Image>
```

Regardless, here's how it looks on the screen:

Fit and fill

If you set the `BackgroundColor` property of `Image` on any of the previous code and XAML examples, you'll see that `Image` actually occupies the entire rectangular area of the page. `Image` defines an `Aspect` property that controls how the bitmap is rendered within this rectangle. You set this property to a member of the `Aspect` enumeration:

- `AspectFit` — the default

- `Fill` — stretches without preserving the aspect ratio

- `AspectFill` — preserves the aspect ratio but crops the image

The default setting is the enumeration member `Aspect.AspectFit`, meaning that the bitmap fits into its container's boundaries while preserving the bitmap's aspect ratio. As you've already seen, the relationship between the bitmap's dimensions and the container's dimensions can result in background areas at the top and bottom or at the right and left.

Try this in the **WebBitmapXaml** project:

```
<Image Source="https://developer.xamarin.com/demo/IMG_3256.JPG"
       Aspect="Fill" />
```

Now the bitmap is expanded to the dimensions of the page. This results in the picture being stretched vertically, so the car appears rather short and stocky:

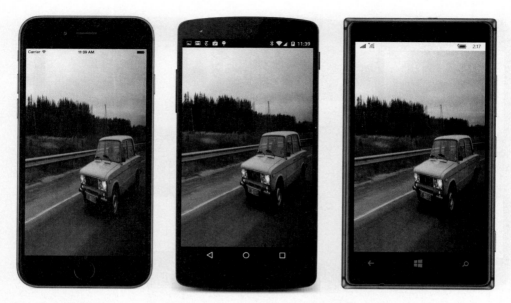

If you turn the phone sideways, the image is stretched horizontally, but the result isn't quite as extreme because the picture's aspect ratio is somewhat landscape to begin with.

The third option is `AspectFill`:

```
<Image Source="https://developer.xamarin.com/demo/IMG_3256.JPG"
       Aspect="AspectFill" />
```

With this option the bitmap completely fills the container, but the bitmap's aspect ratio is maintained at the same time. The only way this is possible is by cropping part of the image, and you'll see that the image is indeed cropped, but in a different way on the three platforms. On iOS and Android, the image is cropped on either the top and bottom or the left and right, leaving only the central part of the bitmap visible. On the Windows Runtime platforms, the image is cropped on the right or bottom, leaving the upper-left corner visible:

Embedded resources

Accessing bitmaps over the Internet is convenient, but sometimes it's not optimum. The process re-quires an Internet connection, an assurance that the bitmaps haven't been moved, and some time for downloading. For fast and guaranteed access to bitmaps, they can be bound right into the application.

If you need access to images that are not platform specific, you can include bitmaps as embedded resources in the shared Portable Class Library project and access them with the `ImageSource.From-Resource` method. The **ResourceBitmapCode** solution demonstrates how to do it.

The **ResourceBitmapCode** PCL project within this solution has a folder named **Images** that con-tains two bitmaps, named ModernUserInterface.jpg (a very large bitmap) and ModernUserInter-face256.jpg (the same picture but with a 256-pixel width).

When adding any type of embedded resource to a PCL project, make sure to set the **Build Action** of the resource to **EmbeddedResource**. This is crucial.

In code, you set the `Source` property of an `Image` element to the `ImageSource` object returned from the static `ImageSource.FromResource` method. This method requires the resource ID. The re-source ID consists of the assembly name followed by a period, then the folder name followed by an-other period, and then the filename, which contains another period for the filename extension. For this example, the resource ID for accessing the smaller of the two bitmaps in the **ResourceBitmapCode** program is:

```
ResourceBitmapCode.Images.ModernUserInterface256.jpg
```

The code in this program references that smaller bitmap and also sets the `HorizontalOptions` and `VerticalOptions` on the `Image` element to `Center`:

```
public class ResourceBitmapCodePage : ContentPage
{
    public ResourceBitmapCodePage()
    {
        Content = new Image
        {
            Source = ImageSource.FromResource(
                        "ResourceBitmapCode.Images.ModernUserInterface256.jpg"),
            VerticalOptions = LayoutOptions.Center,
            HorizontalOptions = LayoutOptions.Center
        };
    }
}
```

As you can see, the bitmap in this instance is *not* stretched to fill the page:

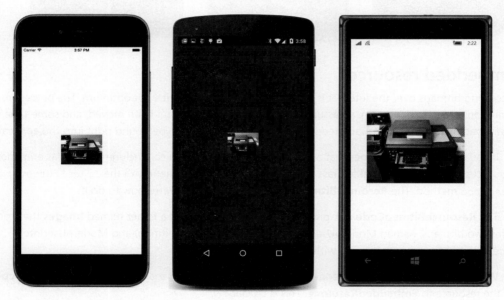

A bitmap is not stretched to fill its container if:

- it is smaller than the container, and

- the `VerticalOptions` and `HorizontalOptions` properties of the `Image` element are not set to `Fill`, or if `Image` is a child of a `StackLayout`.

If you comment out the `VerticalOptions` and `HorizontalOptions` settings, or if you reference the large bitmap (which does not have the "256" at the end of its filename), the image will again stretch to fill the container.

```
        }
}
```

The size of the `Image` element is constrained vertically by the `StackLayout`, so the bitmap is displayed in its pixel size (on iOS and Android) and in device-independent units on Windows Phone. The `Label` displays the size of the `Image` element in device-independent units, which differ on each platform:

The width of the `Image` element displayed by the bottom `Label` includes the aqua background and equals the width of the page in device-independent units. You can use `Aspect` settings of `Fill` or `AspectFill` to make the bitmap fill that entire aqua area.

If you prefer that the size of the `Image` element be the same size as the rendered bitmap in device-independent units, you can set the `HorizontalOptions` property of the `Image` to something other than the default value of `Fill`:

```
<Image Source="{local:ImageResource StackedBitmap.Images.Sculpture_320x240.jpg}"
       HorizontalOptions="Center"
       BackgroundColor="Aqua"
       SizeChanged="OnImageSizeChanged" />
```

Now the bottom `Label` displays only the width of the rendered bitmap. Settings of the `Aspect` property have no effect:

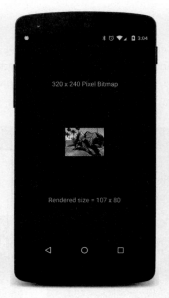

Let's refer to this rendered `Image` size as its *natural size* because it is based on the size of the bitmap being displayed.

The iPhone 6 has a pixel width of 750 pixels, but as you discovered when running the **WhatSize** program in Chapter 5, applications perceive a screen width of 375. There are two pixels to the device-independent unit, so a bitmap with a width of 320 pixels is displayed with a width of 160 units.

The Nexus 5 has a pixel width of 1080, but applications perceive a width of 360, so there are three pixels to the device-independent unit, as the `Image` width of 107 units confirms.

On both iOS and Android devices, when a bitmap is displayed in its natural size, there is a one-to-one mapping between the pixels of the bitmap and the pixels of the display. On Windows Runtime devices, however, that's not the case. The Nokia Lumia 925 used for these screenshots has a pixel width of 768. When running the Windows 10 Mobile operating system, there are 2.25 pixels to the device-independent unit, so applications perceive a screen width of 341. But the 320 × 240 pixel bitmap is displayed in a size of 320 × 240 device-independent units.

This inconsistency between the Windows Runtime and the other two platforms is actually beneficial when you're accessing bitmaps from the individual platform projects. As you'll see, iOS and Android include a feature that lets you supply different sizes of bitmaps for different device resolutions. In effect, this allows you to specify bitmap sizes in device-independent units, which means that Windows devices are consistent with those schemes.

But when using platform-independent bitmaps, you'll probably want to size the bitmaps consistently on all three platforms, and that requires a deeper plunge into the subject.

More on sizing

So far, you've seen two ways to size `Image` elements:

If the `Image` element is not constrained in any way, it will fill its container while maintaining the bitmap's aspect ratio, or fill the area entirely if you set the `Aspect` property to `Fill` or `AspectFill`.

If the bitmap is less than the size of its container and the `Image` is constrained horizontally or vertically by setting `HorizontalOptions` or `VerticalOptions` to something other than `Fill`, or if the `Image` is put in a `StackLayout`, the bitmap is displayed in its natural size. That's the pixel size on iOS and Android devices, but the size in device-independent units on Windows devices.

You can also control size by setting `WidthRequest` or `HeightRequest` to an explicit dimension in device-independent units. However, there are some restrictions.

The following discussion is based on experimentation with the **StackedBitmap** sample. It pertains to `Image` elements that are vertically constrained by being a child of a vertical `StackLayout` or having the `VerticalOptions` property set to something other than `Fill`. The same principles apply to an `Image` element that is horizontally constrained.

If an `Image` element is vertically constrained, you can use `WidthRequest` to reduce the size of the bitmap from its natural size, but you cannot use it to increase the size. For example, try setting `WidthRequest` to 100:

```
<Image Source="{local:ImageResource StackedBitmap.Images.Sculpture_320x240.jpg}"
       WidthRequest="100"
       HorizontalOptions="Center"
       BackgroundColor="Aqua"
       SizeChanged="OnImageSizeChanged" />
```

The resultant height of the bitmap is governed by the specified width and the bitmap's aspect ratio, so now the `Image` is displayed with a size of 100 × 75 device-independent units on all three platforms:

The `HorizontalOptions` setting of `Center` does not affect the size of the rendered bitmap. If you remove that line, the `Image` element will be as wide as the screen (as the aqua background color will demonstrate), but the bitmap will remain the same size.

You cannot use `WidthRequest` to increase the size of the rendered bitmap beyond its natural size. For example, try setting `WidthRequest` to 1000:

```
<Image  Source="{local:ImageResource StackedBitmap.Images.Sculpture_320x240.jpg}"
        WidthRequest="1000"
        HorizontalOptions="Center"
        BackgroundColor="Aqua"
        SizeChanged="OnImageSizeChanged" />
```

Even with `HorizontalOptions` set to `Center`, the resultant `Image` element is now wider than the rendered bitmap, as indicated by the background color:

But the bitmap itself is displayed in its natural size. The vertical `StackLayout` is effectively preventing the height of the rendered bitmap from exceeding its natural height.

To overcome that constraint of the vertical `StackLayout`, you need to set `HeightRequest`. How-ever, you'll also want to leave `HorizontalOptions` at its default value of `Fill`. Otherwise, the `Hori-zontalOptions` setting will prevent the width of the rendered bitmap from exceeding its natural size.

Just as with `WidthRequest`, you can set `HeightRequest` to reduce the size of the rendered bit-map. The following code sets `HeightRequest` to 100 device-independent units:

```
<Image Source="{local:ImageResource StackedBitmap.Images.Sculpture_320x240.jpg}"
       HeightRequest="100"
       BackgroundColor="Aqua"
       SizeChanged="OnImageSizeChanged" />
```

Notice also that the `HorizontalOptions` setting has been removed.

The rendered bitmap is now 100 device-independent units high with a width governed by the as-pect ratio. The `Image` element itself stretches to the sides of the `StackLayout`:

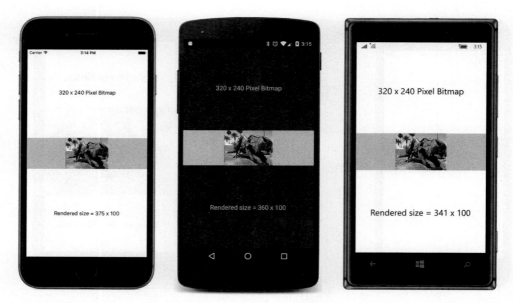

In this particular case, you can set `HorizontalOptions` to `Center` without changing the size of the rendered bitmap. The `Image` element will then be the size of the bitmap (133 × 100), and the aqua background will disappear.

It's important to leave `HorizontalOptions` at its default setting of `Fill` when setting the `HeightRequest` to a value greater than the bitmap's natural height, for example 250:

```
<Image Source="{local:ImageResource StackedBitmap.Images.Sculpture_320x240.jpg}"
       HeightRequest="250"
       BackgroundColor="Aqua"
       SizeChanged="OnImageSizeChanged" />
```

Now the rendered bitmap is larger than its natural size:

However, this technique has a built-in danger, which is revealed when you set the `HeightRequest` to 400:

```
<Image Source="{local:ImageResource StackedBitmap.Images.Sculpture_320x240.jpg}"
       HeightRequest="400"
       BackgroundColor="Aqua"
       SizeChanged="OnImageSizeChanged" />
```

Here's what happens: The `Image` element does indeed get a height of 400 device-independent units. But the width of the rendered bitmap in that `Image` element is limited by the width of the screen, which means that the height of the rendered bitmap is less than the height of the `Image` element:

In a real program you probably wouldn't have the `BackgroundColor` property set, and instead a wasteland of blank screen will occupy the area at the top and bottom of the rendered bitmap.

What this implies is that you should not use `HeightRequest` to control the size of bitmaps in a vertical `StackLayout` unless you write code that ensures that `HeightRequest` is limited to the width of the `StackLayout` times the ratio of the bitmap's height to width.

If you know the pixel size of the bitmap that you'll be displaying, one easy approach is to set `WidthRequest` and `HeightRequest` to that size:

```
<Image Source="{local:ImageResource StackedBitmap.Images.Sculpture_320x240.jpg}"
       WidthRequest="320"
       HeightRequest="240"
       HorizontalOptions="Center"
       BackgroundColor="Aqua"
       SizeChanged="OnImageSizeChanged" />
```

Now the bitmap is displayed in that size in device-independent units on all the platforms:

The problem here is that the bitmap is not being displayed at its optimal resolution. Each pixel of the bitmap occupies at least two pixels of the screen, depending on the device.

If you want to size bitmaps in a vertical `StackLayout` so that they look approximately the same size on a variety of devices, use `WidthRequest` rather than `HeightRequest`. You've seen that `WidthRequest` in a vertical `StackLayout` can only decrease the size of bitmaps. This means that you should use bitmaps that are larger than the size at which they will be rendered. This will give you a more optimal resolution when the image is sized in device-independent units. You can size the bitmap by using a desired metrical size in inches together with the number of device-independent units to the inch for the particular device, which we found to be 160 for these three devices.

Here's a project similar to **StackedBitmap** called **DeviceIndBitmapSize**. It's the same bitmap but now 1200 × 900 pixels, which is wider than the portrait-mode width of even high-resolution 1920 × 1080 displays. The platform-specific requested width of the bitmap corresponds to 1.5 inches:

```
<ContentPage xmlns="http://xamarin.com/schemas/2014/forms"
             xmlns:x="http://schemas.microsoft.com/winfx/2009/xaml"
             xmlns:local="clr-namespace:DeviceIndBitmapSize"
             x:Class="DeviceIndBitmapSize.DeviceIndBitmapSizePage">

    <StackLayout>
        <Label Text="1200 x 900 Pixel Bitmap"
               FontSize="Medium"
               VerticalOptions="CenterAndExpand"
               HorizontalOptions="Center" />

        <!-- 1.5 inch image width -->
        <Image Source="{local:ImageResource DeviceIndBitmapSize.Images.Sculpture_1200x900.jpg}"
               WidthRequest="240"
```

```
                    HorizontalOptions="Center"
                    SizeChanged="OnImageSizeChanged" />
          </Image>

          <Label x:Name="label"
                 FontSize="Medium"
                 VerticalOptions="CenterAndExpand"
                 HorizontalOptions="Center" />
      </StackLayout>
</ContentPage>
```

If the preceding analysis about sizing is correct and all goes well, this bitmap should look approximately the same size on all three platforms relative to the width of the screen, as well as provide higher fidelity resolution than the previous program:

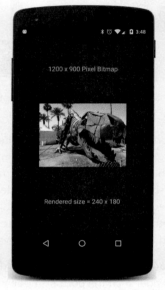

With this knowledge about sizing bitmaps, it is now possible to make a little e-book reader with pictures, because what is the use of a book without pictures?

This e-book reader displays a scrollable `StackLayout` with the complete text of Chapter 7 of Lewis Carroll's *Alice's Adventures in Wonderland,* including three of John Tenniel's original illustrations. The text and illustrations were downloaded from the University of Adelaide's website. The illustrations are included as embedded resources in the **MadTeaParty** project. They have the same names and sizes as those on the website. The names refer to page numbers in the original book:

- image113.jpg — 709 × 553
- image122.jpg — 485 × 545
- image129.jpg — 670 × 596

Recall that the use of `WidthRequest` for `Image` elements in a `StackLayout` can only shrink the size of rendered bitmaps. These bitmaps are not wide enough to ensure that they will all shrink to a proper size on all three platforms, but it's worthwhile examining the results anyway because this is much closer to a real-life example.

The **MadTeaParty** program uses an implicit style for `Image` to set the `WidthRequest` property to a value corresponding to 1.5 inches. Just as in the previous example, this value is 240.

For the three devices used for these screenshots, this width corresponds to:

- 480 pixels on the iPhone 6

- 720 pixels on the Android Nexus 5

- 540 pixels on the Nokia Lumia 925 running Windows 10 Mobile

This means that all three images will shrink in size on the iPhone 6, and they will all have a rendered width of 240 device-independent units.

However, none of the three images will shrink in size on the Nexus 5 because they all have narrower pixel widths than the number of pixels in 1.5 inches. The three images will have a rendered width of (respectively) 236, 162, and 223 device-independent units on the Nexus 5. (That's the pixel width divided by 3.)

On the Windows 10 Mobile device, two will shrink and one will not.

Let's see if the predictions are correct. The XAML file includes a `BackgroundColor` setting on the root element that colors the entire page white, as is appropriate for a book. The `Style` definitions are confined to a `Resources` dictionary in the `StackLayout`. A style for the book title is based on the device `TitleStyle` but with black text and centered, and two implicit styles for `Label` and `Image` serve to style most of the `Label` elements and all three `Image` elements. Only the first and last paragraphs of the chapter's text are shown in this listing of the XAML file:

```
<ContentPage xmlns="http://xamarin.com/schemas/2014/forms"
             xmlns:x="http://schemas.microsoft.com/winfx/2009/xaml"
             xmlns:sys="clr-namespace:System;assembly=mscorlib"
             xmlns:local="clr-namespace:MadTeaParty"
             x:Class="MadTeaParty.MadTeaPartyPage"
             BackgroundColor="White">

    <ContentPage.Padding>
        <OnPlatform x:TypeArguments="Thickness"
                    iOS="5, 20, 5, 0"
                    Android="5, 0"
                    WinPhone="5, 0" />
    </ContentPage.Padding>

    <ScrollView>
        <StackLayout Spacing="10">
            <StackLayout.Resources>
```

```
            <ResourceDictionary>
                <Style x:Key="titleLabel"
                       TargetType="Label"
                       BaseResourceKey="TitleStyle">
                    <Setter Property="TextColor" Value="Black" />
                    <Setter Property="HorizontalTextAlignment" Value="Center" />
                </Style>

                <!-- Implicit styles -->
                <Style TargetType="Label"
                       BaseResourceKey="BodyStyle">
                    <Setter Property="TextColor" Value="Black" />
                </Style>

                <Style TargetType="Image">
                    <Setter Property="WidthRequest" Value="240" />
                </Style>

                <!-- 1/4 inch indent for poetry -->
                <Thickness x:Key="poemIndent">40, 0, 0, 0</Thickness>
            </ResourceDictionary>
        </StackLayout.Resources>

        <!-- Text and images from http://ebooks.adelaide.edu.au/c/carroll/lewis/alice/ -->
        <StackLayout Spacing="0">
            <Label Text="Alice's Adventures in Wonderland"
                   Style="{DynamicResource titleLabel}"
                   FontAttributes="Italic" />

            <Label Text="by Lewis Carroll"
                   Style="{DynamicResource titleLabel}" />
        </StackLayout>

        <Label Style="{DynamicResource SubtitleStyle}"
               TextColor="Black"
               HorizontalTextAlignment="Center">
            <Label.FormattedText>
                <FormattedString>
                    <Span Text="Chapter VII" />
                    <Span Text="{x:Static sys:Environment.NewLine}" />
                    <Span Text="A Mad Tea-Party" />
                </FormattedString>
            </Label.FormattedText>
        </Label>

        <Label Text=
"There was a table set out under a tree in front of the
house, and the March Hare and the Hatter were having tea at
it: a Dormouse was sitting between them, fast asleep, and
the other two were using it as a cushion, resting their
elbows on it, and talking over its head. 'Very uncomfortable
for the Dormouse,' thought Alice; 'only, as it's asleep, I
suppose it doesn't mind.'" />
            ...
```

```
            ...
            ...
            <Label>
                <Label.FormattedText>
                    <FormattedString>
                        <Span Text=
"Once more she found herself in the long hall, and close to
the little glass table. 'Now, I'll manage better this time,'
she said to herself, and began by taking the little golden
key, and unlocking the door that led into the garden. Then
she went to work nibbling at the mushroom (she had kept a
piece of it in her pocket) till she was about a foot high:
then she walked down the little passage: and " />
                        <Span Text="then" FontAttributes="Italic" />
                        <Span Text=
" - she found herself at last in the beautiful garden,
among the bright flower-beds and the cool fountains." />
                    </FormattedString>
                </Label.FormattedText>
            </Label>
        </StackLayout>
    </ScrollView>
</ContentPage>
```

The three `Image` elements simply reference the three embedded resources and are given a setting of the `WidthRequest` property through the implicit style:

```
<Image Source="{local:ImageResource MadTeaParty.Images.image113.jpg}" />
...
<Image Source="{local:ImageResource MadTeaParty.Images.image122.jpg}" />
...
<Image Source="{local:ImageResource MadTeaParty.Images.image129.jpg}" />
```

Here's the first picture:

It's fairly consistent among the three platforms, even though it's displayed in its natural width of 709 pixels on the Nexus 5, but that's very close to the 720 pixels that a width of 240 device-independent units implies.

The difference is much greater with the second image:

This is displayed in its pixel size on the Nexus 5, which corresponds to 162 device-independent units, but is displayed with a width of 240 units on the iPhone 6 and the Nokia Lumia 925.

Although the pictures don't look bad on any of the platforms, getting them all about the same size would require starting out with larger bitmaps.

Browsing and waiting

Another feature of `Image` is demonstrated in the **ImageBrowser** program, which lets you browse the stock photos used for some of the samples in this book. As you can see in the following XAML file, an `Image` element shares the screen with a `Label` and two `Button` views. Notice that a `Property-Changed` handler is set on the `Image`. You learned in Chapter 11, "The bindable infrastructure," that the `PropertyChanged` handler is implemented by `BindableObject` and is fired whenever a bindable property changes value.

```xml
<ContentPage xmlns="http://xamarin.com/schemas/2014/forms"
             xmlns:x="http://schemas.microsoft.com/winfx/2009/xaml"
             x:Class="ImageBrowser.ImageBrowserPage">

    <ContentPage.Padding>
        <OnPlatform x:TypeArguments="Thickness"
                    iOS="0, 20, 0, 0" />
    </ContentPage.Padding>

    <StackLayout>
        <Image x:Name="image"
               VerticalOptions="CenterAndExpand"
               PropertyChanged="OnImagePropertyChanged" />

        <Label x:Name="filenameLabel"
               HorizontalOptions="Center" />

        <ActivityIndicator x:Name="activityIndicator" />

        <StackLayout Orientation="Horizontal">
            <Button x:Name="prevButton"
                    Text="Previous"
                    IsEnabled="false"
                    HorizontalOptions="CenterAndExpand"
                    Clicked="OnPreviousButtonClicked" />

            <Button x:Name="nextButton"
                    Text="Next"
                    IsEnabled="false"
                    HorizontalOptions="CenterAndExpand"
                    Clicked="OnNextButtonClicked" />
        </StackLayout>
    </StackLayout>
</ContentPage>
```

Also on this page is an `ActivityIndicator`. You generally use this element when a program is waiting for a long operation to complete (such as downloading a bitmap) but can't provide any information about the progress of the operation. If your program knows what fraction of the operation has completed, you can use a `ProgressBar` instead. (`ProgressBar` is demonstrated in the next chapter.)

The `ActivityIndicator` has a Boolean property named `IsRunning`. Normally, that property is `false` and the `ActivityIndicator` is invisible. Set the property to `true` to make the `ActivityIndicator` visible. All three platforms implement an animated visual to indicate that the program is working, but it looks a little different on each platform. On iOS it's a spinning wheel, and on Android it's a spinning partial circle. On Windows devices, a series of dots moves across the screen.

To provide browsing access to the stock images, the **ImageBrowser** needs to download a JSON file with a list of all the filenames. Over the years, various versions of .NET have introduced several classes capable of downloading objects over the web. However, not all of these are available in the version of .NET that is available in a Portable Class Library that has the profile compatible with Xamarin.Forms. A class that is available is `WebRequest` and its descendent class `HttpWebRequest`.

The `WebRequest.Create` method returns a `WebRequest` method based on a URI. (The return value is actually an `HttpWebRequest` object.) The `BeginGetResponse` method requires a callback function that is called when the `Stream` referencing the URI is available for access. The `Stream` is accessible from a call to `EndGetResponse` and `GetResponseStream`.

Once the program gets access to the `Stream` object in the following code, it uses the `DataContractJsonSerializer` class together with the embedded `ImageList` class defined near the top of the `ImageBrowserPage` class to convert the JSON file to an `ImageList` object:

```
public partial class ImageBrowserPage : ContentPage
{
    [DataContract]
    class ImageList
    {
        [DataMember(Name = "photos")]
        public List<string> Photos = null;
    }

    WebRequest request;
    ImageList imageList;
    int imageListIndex = 0;

    public ImageBrowserPage()
    {
        InitializeComponent();

        // Get list of stock photos.
        Uri uri = new Uri("https://developer.xamarin.com/demo/stock.json");
        request = WebRequest.Create(uri);
        request.BeginGetResponse(WebRequestCallback, null);
    }

    void WebRequestCallback(IAsyncResult result)
    {
        Device.BeginInvokeOnMainThread(() =>
        {
            try
            {
```

```
                    Stream stream = request.EndGetResponse(result).GetResponseStream();

                    // Deserialize the JSON into imageList;
                    var jsonSerializer = new DataContractJsonSerializer(typeof(ImageList));
                    imageList = (ImageList)jsonSerializer.ReadObject(stream);

                    if (imageList.Photos.Count > 0)
                        FetchPhoto();
                }
                catch (Exception exc)
                {
                    filenameLabel.Text = exc.Message;
                }
            });
    }

    void OnPreviousButtonClicked(object sender, EventArgs args)
    {
        imageListIndex--;
        FetchPhoto();
    }

    void OnNextButtonClicked(object sender, EventArgs args)
    {
        imageListIndex++;
        FetchPhoto();
    }

    void FetchPhoto()
    {
        // Prepare for new image.
        image.Source = null;
        string url = imageList.Photos[imageListIndex];

        // Set the filename.
        filenameLabel.Text = url.Substring(url.LastIndexOf('/') + 1);

        // Create the UriImageSource.
        UriImageSource imageSource = new UriImageSource
        {
            Uri = new Uri(url + "?Width=1080"),
            CacheValidity = TimeSpan.FromDays(30)
        };

        // Set the Image source.
        image.Source = imageSource;

        // Enable or disable buttons.
        prevButton.IsEnabled = imageListIndex > 0;
        nextButton.IsEnabled = imageListIndex < imageList.Photos.Count - 1;
    }

    void OnImagePropertyChanged(object sender, PropertyChangedEventArgs args)
    {
```

```
        if (args.PropertyName == "IsLoading")
        {
            activityIndicator.IsRunning = ((Image)sender).IsLoading;
        }
    }
}
```

The entire body of the `WebRequestCallback` method is enclosed in a lambda function that is the argument to the `Device.BeginInvokeOnMainThread` method. `WebRequest` downloads the file referenced by the URI in a secondary thread of execution. This ensures that the operation doesn't block the program's main thread, which is handling the user interface. The callback method also executes in this secondary thread. However, user-interface objects in a Xamarin.Forms application can be accessed only from the main thread.

The purpose of the `Device.BeginInvokeOnMainThread` method is to get around this problem. The argument to this method is queued to run in the program's main thread and can safely access user-interface objects.

As you click the two buttons, calls to `FetchPhoto` use `UriImageSource` to download a new bitmap. This might take a second or so. The `Image` class defines a Boolean property named `IsLoading` that is `true` when `Image` is in the process of loading (or downloading) a bitmap. `IsLoading` is backed by the bindable property `IsLoadingProperty`. That also means that whenever `IsLoading` changes value, a `PropertyChanged` event is fired. The program uses the `PropertyChanged` event handler—the `OnImagePropertyChanged` method at the very bottom of the class—to set the `IsRunning` property of the `ActivityIndicator` to the same value as the `IsLoading` property of `Image`.

You'll see in Chapter 16, "Data binding," how your applications can link properties like `IsLoading` and `IsRunning` so that they maintain the same value without any explicit event handlers.

Here's **ImageBrowser** in action:

Some of the images have an EXIF orientation flag set, and if the particular platform ignores that flag, the image is displayed sideways.

If you run this program in landscape mode, you'll discover that the buttons disappear. A better layout option for this program is a `Grid`, which is demonstrated in Chapter 17.

Streaming bitmaps

If the `ImageSource` class didn't have `FromUri` or `FromResource` methods, you would still be able to access bitmaps over the web or stored as resources in the PCL. You can do both of these jobs—as well as several others—with `ImageSource.FromStream` or the `StreamImageSource` class.

The `ImageSource.FromStream` method is somewhat easier to use than `StreamImageSource`, but both are a little odd. The argument to `ImageSource.FromStream` is not a `Stream` object but a `Func` object (a method with no arguments) that returns a `Stream` object. The `Stream` property of `Stream-ImageSource` is likewise not a `Stream` object but a `Func` object that has a `CancellationToken` argument and returns a `Task<Stream>` object.

Accessing the streams

The **BitmapStreams** program contains a XAML file with two `Image` elements waiting for bitmaps, each of which is set in the code-behind file by using `ImageSource.FromStream`:

```
<ContentPage xmlns="http://xamarin.com/schemas/2014/forms"
             xmlns:x="http://schemas.microsoft.com/winfx/2009/xaml"
```

```
                     x:Class="BitmapStreams.BitmapStreamsPage">
    <StackLayout>
        <Image x:Name="image1"
               HorizontalOptions="Center"
               VerticalOptions="CenterAndExpand" />

        <Image x:Name="image2"
               HorizontalOptions="Center"
               VerticalOptions="CenterAndExpand" />
    </StackLayout>
</ContentPage>
```

The first `Image` is set from an embedded resource in the PCL; the second is set from a bitmap accessed over the web.

In the **BlackCat** program in Chapter 4, "Scrolling the stack," you saw how to obtain a `Stream` object for any resource stored with a **Build Action** of **EmbeddedResource** in the PCL. You can use this same technique for accessing a bitmap stored as an embedded resource:

```
public partial class BitmapStreamsPage : ContentPage
{
    public BitmapStreamsPage()
    {
        InitializeComponent();

        // Load embedded resource bitmap.
        string resourceID = "BitmapStreams.Images.IMG_0722_512.jpg";
        image1.Source = ImageSource.FromStream(() =>
            {
                Assembly assembly = GetType().GetTypeInfo().Assembly;
                Stream stream = assembly.GetManifestResourceStream(resourceID);
                return stream;
            });
        …
    }
}
```

The argument to `ImageSource.FromStream` is defined as a function that returns a `Stream` object, so that argument is here expressed as a lambda function. The call to the `GetType` method returns the type of the `BitmapStreamsPage` class, and `GetTypeInfo` provides more information about that type, including the `Assembly` object containing the type. That's the **BitmapStream** PCL assembly, which is the assembly with the embedded resource. `GetManifestResourceStream` returns a `Stream` object, which is the return value that `ImageSource.FromStream` wants.

If you ever need a little help with the names of these resources, the `GetManifestResourceNames` returns an array of string objects with all the resource IDs in the PCL. If you can't figure out why your `GetManifestResourceStream` isn't working, first check to make sure your resources have a **Build Action** of **EmbeddedResource**, and then call `GetManifestResourceNames` to get all the resource IDs.

To download a bitmap over the web, you can use the same `WebRequest` method demonstrated earlier in the **ImageBrowser** program. In this program, the `BeginGetResponse` callback is a lambda function:

```
public partial class BitmapStreamsPage : ContentPage
{
    public BitmapStreamsPage()
    {
        ...
        // Load web bitmap.
        Uri uri = new Uri("https://developer.xamarin.com/demo/IMG_0925.JPG?width=512");
        WebRequest request = WebRequest.Create (uri);
        request.BeginGetResponse((IAsyncResult arg) =>
            {
                Stream stream = request.EndGetResponse(arg).GetResponseStream();

                if (Device.OS == TargetPlatform.WinPhone ||
                    Device.OS == TargetPlatform.Windows)
                {
                    MemoryStream memStream = new MemoryStream();
                    stream.CopyTo(memStream);
                    memStream.Seek(0, SeekOrigin.Begin);
                    stream = memStream;
                }
                ImageSource imageSource = ImageSource.FromStream(() => stream);
                Device.BeginInvokeOnMainThread(() => image2.Source = imageSource);
            }, null);
    }
}
```

The `BeginGetResponse` callback also contains two more embedded lambda functions! The first line of the callback obtains the `Stream` object for the bitmap. This `Stream` object is not quite suitable for Windows Runtime so the contents are copied to a `MemoryStream`.

The next statement uses a short lambda function as the argument to `ImageSource.FromStream` to define a function that returns that stream. The last line of the `BeginGetResponse` callback is a call to `Device.BeginInvokeOnMainThread` to set the `ImageSource` object to the `Source` property of the `Image`.

 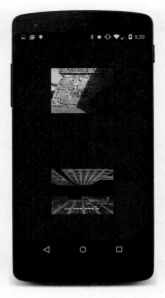 

It might seem as though you have more control over the downloading of images by using `WebRequest` and `ImageSource.FromStream` than with `ImageSource.FromUri`, but the `ImageSource.FromUri` method has a big advantage: it caches the downloaded bitmaps in a storage area private to the application. As you've seen, you can turn off the caching, but if you're using `Image-Source.FromStream` instead of `ImageSource.FromUri`, you might find the need to cache the images, and that would be a much bigger job.

Generating bitmaps at run time

All three platforms support the BMP file format, which dates back to the very beginning of Microsoft Windows. Despite its ancient heritage, the BMP file format is now fairly standardized with more extensive header information.

Although there are some BMP options that allow some rudimentary compression, most BMP files are uncompressed. This lack of compression is usually regarded as a disadvantage of the BMP file format, but in some cases it's not a disadvantage at all. For example, if you want to generate a bitmap algorithmically at run time, it's *much* easier to generate an uncompressed bitmap instead of one of the compressed file formats. (Indeed, even if you had a library function to create a JPEG or PNG file, you'd apply that function to the uncompressed pixel data.)

You can create a bitmap algorithmically at run time by filling a `MemoryStream` with the BMP file headers and pixel data and then passing that `MemoryStream` to the `ImageSource.FromStream` method. The `BmpMaker` class in the **Xamarin.FormsBook.Toolkit** library demonstrates this. It creates a BMP in memory using a 32-bit pixel format—8 bits each for red, green, blue, and alpha (opacity) channels. The `BmpMaker` class was coded with performance in mind, in hopes that it might be used for animation. Maybe someday it will be, but in this chapter the only demonstration is a simple color gradient.

The constructor creates a `byte` array named `buffer` that stores the entire BMP file beginning with the header information and followed by the pixel bits. The constructor then uses a `MemoryStream` for writing the header information to the beginning of this buffer:

```
public class BmpMaker
{
    const int headerSize = 54;
    readonly byte[] buffer;

    public BmpMaker(int width, int height)
    {
        Width = width;
        Height = height;

        int numPixels = Width * Height;
        int numPixelBytes = 4 * numPixels;
        int fileSize = headerSize + numPixelBytes;
        buffer = new byte[fileSize];

        // Write headers in MemoryStream and hence the buffer.
        using (MemoryStream memoryStream = new MemoryStream(buffer))
        {
            using (BinaryWriter writer = new BinaryWriter(memoryStream, Encoding.UTF8))
            {
                // Construct BMP header (14 bytes).
                writer.Write(new char[] { 'B', 'M' });  // Signature
                writer.Write(fileSize);                  // File size
                writer.Write((short)0);                  // Reserved
                writer.Write((short)0);                  // Reserved
                writer.Write(headerSize);                // Offset to pixels

                // Construct BitmapInfoHeader (40 bytes).
                writer.Write(40);                        // Header size
                writer.Write(Width);                     // Pixel width
                writer.Write(Height);                    // Pixel height
                writer.Write((short)1);                  // Planes
                writer.Write((short)32);                 // Bits per pixel
                writer.Write(0);                         // Compression
                writer.Write(numPixelBytes);             // Image size in bytes
                writer.Write(0);                         // X pixels per meter
                writer.Write(0);                         // Y pixels per meter
                writer.Write(0);                         // Number colors in color table
                writer.Write(0);                         // Important color count
            }
        }
    }

    public int Width
    {
```

```
        private set;
        get;
    }

    public int Height
    {
        private set;
        get;
    }

    public void SetPixel(int row, int col, Color color)
    {
        SetPixel(row, col, (int)(255 * color.R),
                           (int)(255 * color.G),
                           (int)(255 * color.B),
                           (int)(255 * color.A));
    }

    public void SetPixel(int row, int col, int r, int g, int b, int a = 255)
    {
        int index = (row * Width + col) * 4 + headerSize;
        buffer[index + 0] = (byte)b;
        buffer[index + 1] = (byte)g;
        buffer[index + 2] = (byte)r;
        buffer[index + 3] = (byte)a;
    }

    public ImageSource Generate()
    {
        // Create MemoryStream from buffer with bitmap.
        MemoryStream memoryStream = new MemoryStream(buffer);

        // Convert to StreamImageSource.
        ImageSource imageSource = ImageSource.FromStream(() =>
        {
            return memoryStream;
        });
        return imageSource;
    }
}
```

After creating a `BmpMaker` object, a program can then call one of the two `SetPixel` methods to set a color at a particular row and column. When making very many calls, the `SetPixel` call that uses a `Color` value is significantly slower than the one that accepts explicit red, green, and blue values.

The last step is to call the `Generate` method. This method instantiates another `MemoryStream` object based on the `buffer` array and uses it to create a `FileImageSource` object. You can call `Generate` multiple times after setting new pixel data. The method creates a new `MemoryStream` each time because `ImageSource.FromStream` closes the `Stream` object when it's finished with it.

The **DiyGradientBitmap** program—"DIY" stands for "Do It Yourself"—demonstrates how to use

`BmpMaker` to make a bitmap with a simple gradient and display it to fill the page. The XAML file includes the `Image` element:

```
<ContentPage xmlns="http://xamarin.com/schemas/2014/forms"
             xmlns:x="http://schemas.microsoft.com/winfx/2009/xaml"
             x:Class="DiyGradientBitmap.DiyGradientBitmapPage">
    <ContentPage.Padding>
        <OnPlatform x:TypeArguments="Thickness"
                    iOS="0, 20, 0, 0" />
    </ContentPage.Padding>

    <Image x:Name="image"
           Aspect="Fill" />

</ContentPage>
```

The code-behind file instantiates a `BmpMaker` and loops through the rows and columns of the bitmap to create a gradient that ranges from red at the top to blue at the bottom:

```
public partial class DiyGradientBitmapPage : ContentPage
{
    public DiyGradientBitmapPage()
    {
        InitializeComponent();

        int rows = 128;
        int cols = 64;
        BmpMaker bmpMaker = new BmpMaker(cols, rows);

        for (int row = 0; row < rows; row++)
            for (int col = 0; col < cols; col++)
            {
                bmpMaker.SetPixel(row, col, 2 * row, 0, 2 * (128 - row));
            }

        ImageSource imageSource = bmpMaker.Generate();
        image.Source = imageSource;
    }
}
```

Here's the result:

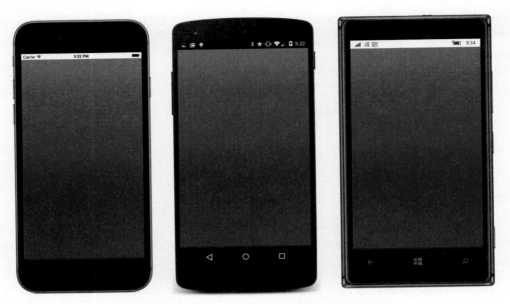

Now use your imagination and see what you can do with `BmpMaker`.

Platform-specific bitmaps

As you've seen, you can load bitmaps over the web or from the shared PCL project. You can also load bitmaps stored as resources in the individual platform projects. The tools for this job are the `Image-Source.FromFile` static method and the corresponding `FileImageSource` class.

You'll probably use this facility mostly for bitmaps connected with user-interface elements. The `Icon` property in `MenuItem` and `ToolBarItem` is of type `FileImageSource`. The `Image` property in `Button` is also of type `FileImageSource`.

Two other uses of `FileImageSource` won't be discussed in this chapter: the `Page` class defines an `Icon` property of type `FileImageSource` and a `BackgroundImage` property of type `string`, but which is assumed to be the name of a bitmap stored in the platform project.

The storage of bitmaps in the individual platform projects allows a high level of platform specificity. You might think you can get the same degree of platform specificity by storing bitmaps for each platform in the PCL project and using the `Device.OnPlatform` method or the `OnPlatform` class to select them. However, as you'll soon discover, all three platforms have provisions for storing bitmaps of different pixel resolutions and then automatically accessing the optimum one. You can take advantage of this valuable feature only if the individual platforms themselves load the bitmaps, and this is the case only when you use `ImageSource.FromFile` and `FileImageSource`.

The platform projects in a newly created Xamarin.Forms solution already contain several bitmaps. In the iOS project, you'll find these in the **Resources** folder. In the Android project, they're in subfolders of the **Resources** folder. In the various Windows projects, they're in the **Assets** folder and subfolders. These bitmaps are application icons and splash screens, and you'll want to replace them when you prepare to bring an application to market.

Let's write a small project called **PlatformBitmaps** that accesses an application icon from each platform project and displays the rendered size of the `Image` element. If you're using `FileImageSource` to load the bitmap (as this program does), you need to set the `File` property to a `string` with the bitmap's filename. Almost always, you'll be using `Device.OnPlatform` in code or `OnPlatform` in XAML to specify the three filenames:

```
public class PlatformBitmapsPage : ContentPage
{
    public PlatformBitmapsPage()
    {
        Image image = new Image
        {
            Source = new FileImageSource
            {
                File = Device.OnPlatform(iOS: "Icon-Small-40.png",
                                         Android: "icon.png",
                                         WinPhone: "Assets/StoreLogo.png")
            },
            HorizontalOptions = LayoutOptions.Center,
            VerticalOptions = LayoutOptions.CenterAndExpand
        };

        Label label = new Label
        {
            FontSize = Device.GetNamedSize(NamedSize.Medium, typeof(Label)),
            HorizontalOptions = LayoutOptions.Center,
            VerticalOptions = LayoutOptions.CenterAndExpand
        };

        image.SizeChanged += (sender, args) =>
            {
                label.Text = String.Format("Rendered size = {0} x {1}",
                                           image.Width, image.Height);
            };

        Content = new StackLayout
        {
            Children =
            {
                image,
                label
            }
        };
    }
}
```

When you access a bitmap stored in the **Resources** folder of the iOS project or the **Resources** folder (or subfolders) of the Android project, do not preface the filename with a folder name. These folders are the standard repositories for bitmaps on these platforms. But bitmaps can be anywhere in the Windows or Windows Phone project (including the project root), so the folder name (if any) is required.

In all three cases, the default icon is the famous hexagonal Xamarin logo (fondly known as the Xamagon), but each platform has different conventions for its icon size, so the rendered sizes are different:

If you begin exploring the icon bitmaps in the iOS and Android projects, you might be a little confused: there seem to be multiple bitmaps with the same names (or similar names) in the iOS and Android projects.

It's time to dive deeper into the subject of bitmap resolution.

Bitmap resolutions

The iOS bitmap filename specified in **PlatformBitmaps** is Icon-Small-40.png, but if you look in the **Resources** folder of the iOS project, you'll see three files with variations of that name. They all have different sizes:

- Icon-Small-40.png — 40 pixels square

- Icon-Small-40@2x.png — 80 pixels square

- Icon-Small-40@3x.png — 120 pixels square

As you discovered earlier in this chapter, when an `Image` is a child of a `StackLayout`, iOS displays the bitmap in its pixel size with a one-to-one mapping between the pixels of the bitmap and the pixels of the screen. This is the optimum display of a bitmap.

However, on the iPhone 6 simulator used in the screenshot, the `Image` has a rendered size of 40 device-independent units. On the iPhone 6 there are two pixels per device-independent unit, which means that the actual bitmap being displayed in that screenshot is not Icon-Small-40.png but Icon-Small-40@2x.png, which is two times 40, or 80 pixels square.

If you instead run the program on the iPhone 6 Plus—which has a device-independent unit equal to three pixels—you'll again see a rendered size of 40 pixels, which means that the Icon-Small-40@3x.png bitmap is displayed. Now try it on the iPad 2 simulator. The iPad 2 has a screen size of just 768 × 1024, and device-independent units are the same as pixels. Now the Icon-Small-40.png bitmap is displayed, and the rendered size is still 40 pixels.

This is what you want. You want to be able to control the rendered size of bitmaps in device-independent units because that's how you can achieve perceptibly similar bitmap sizes on different devices and platforms. When you specify the Icon-Small-40.png bitmap, you want that bitmap to be rendered as 40 device-independent units—or about one-quarter inch—on all iOS devices. But if the program is running on an Apple Retina device, you don't want a 40-pixel-square bitmap stretched to be 40 device-independent units. For maximum visual fidelity, you want a higher resolution bitmap displayed, with a one-to-one mapping of bitmap pixels to screen pixels.

If you look in the Android **Resources** directory, you'll find four different versions of a bitmap named icon.png. These are stored in different subfolders of **Resources**:

- drawable/icon.png — 72 pixels square

- drawable-hdpi/icon.png — 72 pixels square

- drawable-xdpi/icon.png — 96 pixels square

- drawable-xxdpi/icon.png — 144 pixels square

Regardless of the Android device, the icon is rendered with a size of 48 device-independent units. On the Nexus 5 used in the screenshot, there are three pixels to the device-independent unit, which means that the bitmap actually displayed on that screen is the one in the **drawable-xxdpi** folder, which is 144 pixels square.

What's nice about both iOS and Android is that you only need to supply bitmaps of various sizes—and give them the correct names or store them in the correct folders—and the operating system chooses the optimum image for the particular resolution of the device.

The Windows Runtime platform has a similar facility. In the **UWP** project you'll see filenames that include scale-200; for example, Square150x150Logo.scale-200.png. The number after the word *scale* is a percentage, and although the filename seems to indicate that this is a 150×150 bitmap, the image is actually twice as large: 300×300. In the **Windows** project you'll see filenames that include scale-100 and in the **WinPhone** project you'll see scale-240.

However, you've seen that Xamarin.Forms on the Windows Runtime displays bitmaps in their device-independent sizes, and you'll still need to treat the Windows platforms a little differently. But on all three platforms you can control the size of bitmaps in device-independent units.

When creating your own platform-specific images, follow the guidelines in the next three sections.

Device-independent bitmaps for iOS

The iOS naming scheme for bitmaps involves a suffix on the filename. The operating system fetches a particular bitmap with the underlying filename based on the approximate pixel resolution of the device:

- No suffix for 160 DPI devices (1 pixel to the device-independent unit)

- @2x suffix for 320 DPI devices (2 pixels to the DIU)

- @3x suffix: 480 DPI devices (3 pixels to the DIU)

For example, suppose you want a bitmap named MyImage.jpg to show up as about one inch square on the screen. You should supply three versions of this bitmap:

- MyImage.jpg — 160 pixels square

- MyImage@2x.jpg — 320 pixels square

- MyImage@3x.jpg — 480 pixels square

The bitmap will render as 160 device-independent units. For rendered sizes smaller than one inch, decrease the pixels proportionally.

When creating these bitmaps, start with the largest one. Then you can use any bitmap-editing utility to reduce the pixel size. For some images, you might want to fine-tune or completely redraw the smaller versions.

As you might have noticed when examining the various icon files that the Xamarin.Forms template includes with the iOS project, not every bitmap comes in all three resolutions. If iOS can't find a bitmap with the particular suffix it wants, it will fall back and use one of the others, scaling the bitmap up or down in the process.

Device-independent bitmaps for Android

For Android, bitmaps are stored in various subfolders of **Resources** that correspond to a pixel resolution of the screen. Android defines six different directory names for six different levels of device resolution:

- **drawable-ldpi** (low DPI) for 120 DPI devices (0.75 pixels to the DIU)

- **drawable-mdpi** (medium) for 160 DPI devices (1 pixel to the DIU)

- **drawable-hdpi** (high) for 240 DPI devices (1.5 pixels to the DIU))

- **drawable-xhdpi** (extra high) for 320 DPI devices (2 pixels to the DIU)

- **drawable-xxhdpi** (extra extra high) for 480 DPI devices (3 pixels to the DIU)

- **drawable-xxxhdpi** (three extra highs) for 640 DPI devices (4 pixels to the DIU)

If you want a bitmap named MyImage.jpg to render as a one-inch square on the screen, you can supply up to six versions of this bitmap using the same name in all these directories. The size of this one-inch-square bitmap in pixels is equal to the DPI associated with that directory:

- drawable-ldpi/MyImage.jpg — 120 pixels square

- drawable-mdpi/MyImage.jpg — 160 pixels square

- drawable-hdpi/MyImage.jpg — 240 pixels square

- drawable-xhdpi/MyImage.jpg — 320 pixels square

- drawable-xxdpi/MyImage.jpg — 480 pixels square

- drawable-xxxhdpi/MyImage.jpg — 640 pixels square

The bitmap will render as 160 device-independent units.

You are not required to create bitmaps for all six resolutions. The Android project created by the Xamarin.Forms template includes only **drawable-hdpi**, **drawable-xhdpi**, and **drawable-xxdpi**, as well as an unnecessary **drawable** folder with no suffix. These encompass the most common devices. If the Android operating system does not find a bitmap of the desired resolution, it will fall back to a size that is available and scale it.

Device-independent bitmaps for Windows Runtime platforms

The Windows Runtime supports a bitmap naming scheme that lets you embed a scaling factor of pixels per device-independent unit expressed as a percentage. For example, for a one-inch-square bitmap targeted to a device that has two pixels to the unit, use the name:

- MyImage.scale-200.jpg — 320 pixels square

The Windows documentation is unclear about the actual percentages you can use. When building a program, sometimes you'll see error messages in the **Output** window regarding percentages that are not supported on the particular platform.

However, given that Xamarin.Forms displays Windows Runtime bitmaps in their device-independent sizes, this facility is of limited use on these devices.

Let's look at a program that actually does supply custom bitmaps of various sizes for the three platforms. These bitmaps are intended to be rendered about one inch square, which is approximately half the width of the phone's screen in portrait mode.

This **ImageTap** program creates a pair of rudimentary, tappable button-like objects that display not text but a bitmap. The two buttons that **ImageTap** creates might substitute for traditional **OK** and **Cancel** buttons, but perhaps you want to use faces from famous paintings for the buttons. Perhaps you want the **OK** button to display the face of Botticelli's Venus and the **Cancel** button to display the distressed man in Edvard Munch's *The Scream*.

In the sample code for this chapter is a directory named **Images** that contains such images, named Venus_xxx.jpg and Scream_xxx.jpg, where the xxx indicates the pixel size. Each image is in eight different sizes: 60, 80, 120, 160, 240, 320, 480, and 640 pixels square. In addition, some of the files have names of Venus_xxx_id.jpg and Scream_xxx_id.jpg. These versions have the actual pixel size displayed in the lower-right corner of the image so that we can see on the screen exactly what bitmap the operating system has selected.

To avoid confusion, the bitmaps with the original names were added to the **ImageTap** project folders first, and then they were renamed within Visual Studio.

In the **Resources** folder of the iOS project, the following files were renamed:

- Venus_160_id.jpg became Venus.jpg

- Venus_320_id.jpg because Venus@2x.jpg

- Venus_480_id.jpg became Venus@3x.jpg

This was done similarly for the Scream.jpg bitmaps.

In the various subfolders of the Android project **Resources** folder, the following files were renamed:

- Venus_160_id.jpg became drawable-mdpi/Venus.jpg

- Venus_240_id.jpg became drawable-hdpi/Venus.jpg

- Venus_320_id.jpg became drawable-xhdpi/Venus.jpg

- Venus_480_id.jpg became drawable_xxhdpi/Venus.jpg

And similarly for the Scream.jpg bitmaps.

For the Windows Phone 8.1 project, the Venus_160_id.jpg and Scream_160_id.jpg files were copied to an **Images** folder and renamed Venus.jpg and Scream.jpg.

The Windows 8.1 project creates an executable that runs not on phones but on tablets and desktops. These devices have traditionally assumed a resolution of 96 units to the inch, so the Venus_100_id.jpg and Scream_100_id.jpg files were copied to an **Images** folder and renamed Venus.jpg and Scream.jpg.

The UWP project targets all the form factors, so several bitmaps were copied to an **Images** folder and renamed so that the 160-pixel square bitmaps would be used on phones, and the 100-pixel square bitmaps would be used on tablets and desktop screens:

- Venus_160_id.jpg became Venus.scale-200.jpg

- Venus_100_id.jpg became Venus.scale-100.jpg

And similarly for the Scream.jpg bitmaps.

Each of the projects requires a different **Build Action** for these bitmaps. This should be set automatically when you add the files to the projects, but you definitely want to double-check to make sure the **Build Action** is set correctly:

- iOS: **BundleResource**

- Android: **AndroidResource**

- Windows Runtime: **Content**

You don't have to memorize these. When in doubt, just check the **Build Action** for the bitmaps included by the Xamarin.Forms solution template in the platform projects.

The XAML file for the **ImageTap** program puts each of the two `Image` elements on a `ContentView` that is colored white from an implicit style. This white `ContentView` is entirely covered by the `Image`, but (as you'll see) it comes into play when the program flashes the picture to signal that it's been tapped.

```
<ContentPage xmlns="http://xamarin.com/schemas/2014/forms"
             xmlns:x="http://schemas.microsoft.com/winfx/2009/xaml"
             x:Class="ImageTap.ImageTapPage">

    <StackLayout>
        <StackLayout.Resources>
            <ResourceDictionary>
                <Style TargetType="ContentView">
                    <Setter Property="BackgroundColor" Value="White" />
                    <Setter Property="HorizontalOptions" Value="Center" />
                    <Setter Property="VerticalOptions" Value="CenterAndExpand" />
                </Style>
            </ResourceDictionary>
        </StackLayout.Resources>

        <ContentView>
            <Image>
                <Image.Source>
                    <OnPlatform x:TypeArguments="ImageSource"
                                iOS="Venus.jpg"
                                Android="Venus.jpg"
                                WinPhone="Images/Venus.jpg" />
                </Image.Source>
```

```
                            <Image.GestureRecognizers>
                                <TapGestureRecognizer Tapped="OnImageTapped" />
                            </Image.GestureRecognizers>
                        </Image>
                </ContentView>

                <ContentView>
                    <Image>
                        <Image.Source>
                            <OnPlatform x:TypeArguments="ImageSource"
                                        iOS="Scream.jpg"
                                        Android="Scream.jpg"
                                        WinPhone="Images/Scream.jpg" />
                        </Image.Source>

                        <Image.GestureRecognizers>
                            <TapGestureRecognizer Tapped="OnImageTapped" />
                        </Image.GestureRecognizers>
                    </Image>
                </ContentView>

                <Label x:Name="label"
                       FontSize="Medium"
                       HorizontalOptions="Center"
                       VerticalOptions="CenterAndExpand" />

        </StackLayout>
</ContentPage>
```

The XAML file uses `OnPlatform` to select the filenames of the platform resources. Notice that the `x:TypeArguments` attribute of `OnPlatform` is set to `ImageSource` because this type must exactly match the type of the target property, which is the `Source` property of `Image`. `ImageSource` defines an implicit conversion of `string` to itself, so specifying the filenames is sufficient. (The logic for this implicit conversion checks first whether the string has a URI prefix. If not, it assumes that the string is the name of an embedded file in the platform project.)

If you want to avoid using `OnPlatform` entirely in programs that use platform bitmaps, you can put the Windows bitmaps in the root directory of the project rather than in a folder.

Tapping one of these buttons does two things: The `Tapped` handler sets the `Opacity` property of the `Image` to 0.75, which results in partially revealing the white `ContentView` background and simulating a flash. A timer restores the `Opacity` to the default value of one-tenth of a second later. The `Tapped` handler also displays the rendered size of the `Image` element:

```
public partial class ImageTapPage : ContentPage
{
    public ImageTapPage()
    {
        InitializeComponent();
    }

    void OnImageTapped(object sender, EventArgs args)
```

```
    {
        Image image = (Image)sender;
        image.Opacity = 0.75;

        Device.StartTimer(TimeSpan.FromMilliseconds(100), () =>
            {
                image.Opacity = 1;
                return false;
            });

        label.Text = String.Format("Rendered Image is {0} x {1}",
                                    image.Width, image.Height);
    }
}
```

That rendered size compared with the pixel sizes on the bitmaps confirms that the three platforms have indeed selected the optimum bitmap:

These buttons occupy roughly half the width of the screen on all three platforms. This sizing is based entirely on the size of the bitmaps themselves, without any additional sizing information in the code or markup.

Toolbars and their icons

One of the primary uses of bitmaps in the user interface is the Xamarin.Forms toolbar, which appears at the top of the page on iOS and Android devices and at the bottom of the page on Windows Phone devices. Toolbar items are tappable and fire `Clicked` events much like `Button`.

There is no class for toolbar itself. Instead, you add objects of type `ToolbarItem` to the `ToolbarItems` collection property defined by `Page`.

The `ToolbarItem` class does not derive from `View` like `Label` and `Button`. It instead derives from `Element` by way of `MenuItemBase` and `MenuItem`. (`MenuItem` is used only in connection with the `TableView` and won't be discussed until Chapter 19.) To define the characteristics of a toolbar item, use the following properties:

- `Text` — the text that might appear (depending on the platform and `Order`)

- `Icon` — a `FileImageSource` object referencing a bitmap from the platform project

- `Order` — a member of the `ToolbarItemOrder` enumeration: `Default`, `Primary`, or `Secondary`

There is also a `Name` property, but it just duplicates the `Text` property and should be considered obsolete.

The `Order` property governs whether the `ToolbarItem` appears as an image (`Primary`) or text (`Secondary`). The Windows Phone and Windows 10 Mobile platforms are limited to four `Primary` items, and both the iPhone and Android devices start getting crowded with more than that, so that's a reasonable limitation. Additional `Secondary` items are text only. On the iPhone they appear underneath the `Primary` items; on Android and Windows Phone they aren't seen on the screen until the user taps a vertical or horizontal ellipsis.

The `Icon` property is crucial for `Primary` items, and the `Text` property is crucial for `Secondary` items, but the Windows Runtime also uses `Text` to display a short text hint underneath the icons for `Primary` items.

When the `ToolbarItem` is tapped, it fires a `Clicked` event. `ToolbarItem` also has `Command` and `CommandParameter` properties like the `Button`, but these are for data-binding purposes and will be demonstrated in a later chapter.

The `ToolbarItems` collection defined by `Page` is of type `IList<ToolbarItem>`. Once you add a `ToolbarItem` to this collection, the `ToolbarItem` properties cannot be changed. The property settings are instead used internally to construct platform-specific objects.

You can add `ToolbarItem` objects to a `ContentPage` in Windows Phone, but iOS and Android restrict toolbars to a `NavigationPage` or to a page navigated to from a `NavigationPage`. Fortunately, this requirement doesn't mean that the whole topic of page navigation needs to be discussed before you can use the toolbar. Instantiating a `NavigationPage` instead of a `ContentPage` simply involves calling the `NavigationPage` constructor with the newly created `ContentPage` object in the `App` class.

The **ToolbarDemo** program reproduces the toolbar that you saw on the screenshots in Chapter 1. The `ToolbarDemoPage` derives from `ContentPage`, but the `App` class passes the `ToolbarDemoPage` object to a `NavigationPage` constructor:

```
public class App : Application
{
    public App()
    {
        MainPage = new NavigationPage(new ToolbarDemoPage());
    }
    …
}
```

That's all that's necessary to get the toolbar to work on iOS and Android, and it has some other implications as well. A title that you can set with the `Title` property of `Page` is displayed at the top of the iOS and Android screens, and the application icon is also displayed on the Android screen. Another result of using `NavigationPage` is that you no longer need to set some padding at the top of the iOS screen. The status bar is now out of the range of the application's page.

Perhaps the most difficult aspect of using `ToolbarItem` is assembling the bitmap images for the `Icon` property. Each platform has different requirements for the color composition and size of these icons, and each platform has somewhat different conventions for the imagery. The standard icon for **Share**, for example, is different on all three platforms.

For these reasons, it makes sense for each of the platform projects to have its own collection of toolbar icons, and that's why `Icon` is of type `FileImageSource`.

Let's begin with the two platforms that provide collections of icons suitable for `ToolbarItem`.

Icons for Android

The Android website has a downloadable collection of toolbar icons at this URL:

http://developer.android.com/design/downloads

Download the ZIP file identified as **Action Bar Icon Pack**.

The unzipped contents are organized into two main directories: **Core_Icons** (23 images) and **Action Bar Icons** (144 images). These are all PNG files, and the **Action Bar Icons** come in four different sizes, indicated by the directory name:

- **drawable-mdpi** (medium DPI) — 32 pixels square

- **drawable-hdpi** (high DPI) — 48 pixels square

- **drawable-xhdpi** (extra high DPI) — 64 pixels square

- **drawable-xxhdpi** (extra extra high DPI) — 96 pixels square

These directory names are the same as the **Resources** folders in your Android project and imply that the toolbar icons render at 32 device-independent units, or about one-fifth of an inch.

The **Core_Icons** folder also arranges its icons into four directories with the same four sizes, but these directories are named **mdpi**, **hdpi**, **xdpi**, and **unscaled**.

The **Action Bar Icons** folder has an additional directory organization using the names **holo_dark** and **holo_light**:

- **holo_dark**—white foreground image on a transparent background

- **holo_light**—black foreground image on a transparent background

The word "holo" stands for "holographic" and refers to the name Android uses for its color themes. Although the **holo_light** icons are much easier to see in **Finder** and **Windows Explorer**, for most purposes (and especially for toolbar items) you should use the **holo_dark** icons. (Of course, if you know how to change your application theme in the AndroidManifest.xml file, then you probably also know to use the other icon collection.)

The **Core_Icons** folder contains only icons with white foregrounds on a transparent background.

For the **ToolbarDemo** program, three icons were chosen from the **holo_dark** directory in all four resolutions. These were copied to the appropriate subfolders of the **Resources** directory in the Android project:

- From the **01_core_edit** directory, the files named ic_action_edit.png

- From the **01_core_search** directory, the files named ic_action_search.png

- From the **01_core_refresh** directory, the files named ic_action_refresh.png

Check the properties of these PNG files. They must have a **Build Action** of **AndroidResource**.

Icons for Windows Runtime platforms

If you have a version of Visual Studio installed for Windows Phone 8, you can find a collection of PNG files suitable for `ToolbarItem` in the following directory on your hard drive:

C:\Program Files (x86)\Microsoft SDKs\Windows Phone\v8.0\Icons

You can use these for all the Windows Runtime platforms.

There are two subdirectories, **Dark** and **Light**, each containing the same 37 images. As with Android, the icons in the **Dark** directory have white foregrounds on transparent backgrounds, and the icons in the **Light** directory have black foregrounds on transparent backgrounds. You should use the ones in the **Dark** directory for Windows Phone 8.1 and the **Light** directory for Windows 10 Mobile.

The images are a uniform 76 pixels square but have been designed to appear inside a circle. Indeed, one of the files is named basecircle.png, which can serve as a guide if you'd like to design your own, so there are really only 36 usable icons in the collection and a couple of them are the same.

Generally, in a Windows Runtime project, files such as these are stored in the **Assets** folder (which already exists in the project) or a folder named **Images**. The following bitmaps were added to an **Images** folder in all three Windows platforms:

- edit.png

- feature.search.png

- refresh.png

For the Windows 8.1 platform (but not the Windows Phone 8.1 platform), icons are needed for all the toolbar items, so the following bitmaps were added to the **Images** folder of that project:

- Icon1F435.png

- Icon1F440.png

- Icon1F52D.png

These were generated in a Windows program from the Segoe UI Symbol font, which supports emoji characters. The five-digit hexadecimal number in the filename is the Unicode ID for those characters.

When you add icons to a Windows Runtime project, make sure the **Build Action** is **Content**.

Icons for iOS devices

This is the most problematic platform for `ToolbarItem`. If you're programming directly for the native iOS API, a bunch of constants let you select an image for `UIBarButtonItem`, which is the underlying iOS implementation of `ToolbarItem`. But for the Xamarin.Forms `ToolbarItem`, you'll need to obtain icons from another source—perhaps licensing a collection such as the one at glyphish.com—or make your own.

For best results, you should supply two or three image files for each toolbar item in the **Resources** folder. An image with a filename such as image.png should be 20 pixels square, while the same image should also be supplied in a 40-pixel-square dimension with the name image@2x.png and as a 60-pixel-square bitmap named image@3x.png.

Here's a collection of free, unrestricted-use icons used for the program in Chapter 1 and for the **ToolbarDemo** program in this chapter:

http://www.smashingmagazine.com/2010/07/14/gcons-free-all-purpose-icons-for-designers-and-developers-100-icons-psd/

However, they are uniformly 32 pixels square, and some basic ones are missing. Regardless, the following three bitmaps were copied to the **Resources** folder in the iOS project under the assumption that they will be properly scaled:

- edit.png

- search.png

- reload.png

Another option is to use Android icons from the **holo_light** directory and scale the largest image for the various iOS sizes.

For toolbar icons in an iOS project, the **Build Action** must be **BundleResource**.

Here's the **ToolbarDemo** XAML file showing the various `ToolbarItem` objects added to the `ToolbarItems` collection of the page. The `x:TypeArguments` attribute for `OnPlatform` must be `FileImageSource` in this case because that's the type of the `Icon` property of `ToolbarItem`. The three items flagged as `Secondary` have only the `Text` property set and not the `Icon` property.

The root element has a `Title` property set on the page. This is displayed on the iOS and Android screens when the page is instantiated as a `NavigationPage` (or navigated to from a `Navigation-Page`):

```
<ContentPage xmlns="http://xamarin.com/schemas/2014/forms"
             xmlns:x="http://schemas.microsoft.com/winfx/2009/xaml"
             x:Class="ToolbarDemo.ToolbarDemoPage"
             Title="Toolbar Demo">

    <Label x:Name="label"
           FontSize="Medium"
           HorizontalOptions="Center"
           VerticalOptions="Center" />

    <ContentPage.ToolbarItems>
        <ToolbarItem Text="edit"
                     Order="Primary"
                     Clicked="OnToolbarItemClicked">
            <ToolbarItem.Icon>
                <OnPlatform x:TypeArguments="FileImageSource"
                            iOS="edit.png"
                            Android="ic_action_edit.png"
                            WinPhone="Images/edit.png" />
            </ToolbarItem.Icon>
        </ToolbarItem>

        <ToolbarItem Text="search"
                     Order="Primary"
                     Clicked="OnToolbarItemClicked">
            <ToolbarItem.Icon>
                <OnPlatform x:TypeArguments="FileImageSource"
                            iOS="search.png"
                            Android="ic_action_search.png"
                            WinPhone="Images/feature.search.png" />
            </ToolbarItem.Icon>
        </ToolbarItem>

        <ToolbarItem Text="refresh"
                     Order="Primary"
                     Clicked="OnToolbarItemClicked">
            <ToolbarItem.Icon>
                <OnPlatform x:TypeArguments="FileImageSource"
```

```
                                iOS="reload.png"
                                Android="ic_action_refresh.png"
                                WinPhone="Images/refresh.png" />
            </ToolbarItem.Icon>
        </ToolbarItem>

        <ToolbarItem Text="explore"
                     Order="Secondary"
                     Clicked="OnToolbarItemClicked">
            <ToolbarItem.Icon>
                <OnPlatform x:TypeArguments="FileImageSource"
                            WinPhone="Images/Icon1F52D.png" />
            </ToolbarItem.Icon>
        </ToolbarItem>

        <ToolbarItem Text="discover"
                     Order="Secondary"
                     Clicked="OnToolbarItemClicked">
            <ToolbarItem.Icon>
                <OnPlatform x:TypeArguments="FileImageSource"
                            WinPhone="Images/Icon1F440.png" />
            </ToolbarItem.Icon>
        </ToolbarItem>

        <ToolbarItem Text="evolve"
                     Order="Secondary"
                     Clicked="OnToolbarItemClicked">
            <ToolbarItem.Icon>
                <OnPlatform x:TypeArguments="FileImageSource"
                            WinPhone="Images/Icon1F435.png" />
            </ToolbarItem.Icon>
        </ToolbarItem>
    </ContentPage.ToolbarItems>
</ContentPage>
```

Although the OnPlatform element implies that the secondary icons exist for all the Windows Runtime platforms, they do not, but nothing bad happens if the particular icon file is missing from the project.

All the Clicked events have the same handler assigned. You can use unique handlers for the items, of course. This handler just displays the text of the ToolbarItem using the centered Label:

```
public partial class ToolbarDemoPage : ContentPage
{
    public ToolbarDemoPage()
    {
        InitializeComponent();
    }

    void OnToolbarItemClicked(object sender, EventArgs args)
    {
        ToolbarItem toolbarItem = (ToolbarItem)sender;
        label.Text = "ToolbarItem '" + toolbarItem.Text + "' clicked";
    }
}
```

The screenshots show the icon toolbar items (and for iOS, the text items) and the centered `Label` with the most recently clicked item:

If you tap the ellipsis at the top of the Android screen or the ellipsis at the lower-right corner of the Windows 10 Mobile screen, the text items are displayed and, in addition, the text items associated with the icons are also displayed on Windows 10 Mobile:

Regardless of the platform, the toolbar is the standard way to add common commands to a phone application.

Button images

`Button` defines an `Image` property of type `FileImageSource` that you can use to supply a small supplemental image that is displayed to the left of the button text. This feature is *not* intended for an image-only button; if that's what you want, the **ImageTap** program in this chapter is a good starting point.

You want the images to be about one-fifth inch in size. That means you want them to render at 32 device-independent units and to show up against the background of the `Button`. For iOS and the UWP, that means a black image against a white or transparent background. For Android, Windows 8.1, and Windows Phone 8.1, you'll want a white image against a transparent background.

All the bitmaps in the **ButtonImage** project are from the **Action Bar** directory of the **Android Design Icons** collection and the **03_rating_good** and **03_rating_bad** subdirectories. These are "thumbs up" and "thumbs down" images.

The iOS images are from the **holo_light** directory (black images on transparent backgrounds) with the following filename conversions:

- drawable-mdpi/ic_action_good.png not renamed

- drawable-xhdpi/ic_action_good.png renamed to ic_action_good@2x.png

And similarly for ic_action_bad.png.

The Android images are from the **holo_dark** directory (white images on transparent backgrounds) and include all four sizes from the subdirectories **drawable-mdpi** (32 pixels square), **drawable-hdpi** (48 pixels), **drawable-xhdpi** (64 pixels), and **drawable-xxhdpi** (96 pixels square).

The images for the various Windows Runtime projects are all uniformly the 32-pixel bitmaps from the **drawable-mdpi** directories.

Here's the XAML file that sets the `Icon` property for two `Button` elements:

```
<ContentPage xmlns="http://xamarin.com/schemas/2014/forms"
             xmlns:x="http://schemas.microsoft.com/winfx/2009/xaml"
             x:Class="ButtonImage.ButtonImagePage">

    <StackLayout VerticalOptions="Center"
                 Spacing="50">

        <StackLayout.Resources>
            <ResourceDictionary>
                <Style TargetType="Button">
                    <Setter Property="HorizontalOptions" Value="Center" />
                    </Setter.Value>
```

```
                </Setter>
            </Style>
        </ResourceDictionary>
    </StackLayout.Resources>

    <Button Text="Oh Yeah">
        <Button.Image>
            <OnPlatform x:TypeArguments="FileImageSource"
                        iOS="ic_action_good.png"
                        Android="ic_action_good.png"
                        WinPhone="Images/ic_action_good.png" />
        </Button.Image>
    </Button>

    <Button Text="No Way">
        <Button.Image>
            <OnPlatform x:TypeArguments="FileImageSource"
                        iOS="ic_action_bad.png"
                        Android="ic_action_bad.png"
                        WinPhone="Images/ic_action_bad.png" />
        </Button.Image>
    </Button>
    </StackLayout>
</ContentPage>
```

And here they are:

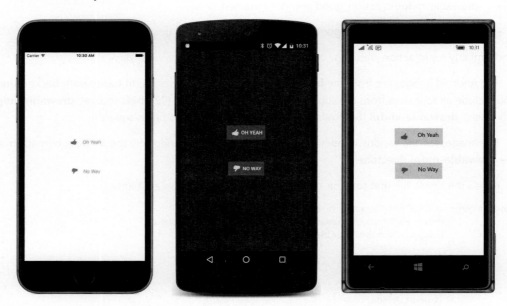

It's not much, but the bitmap adds a little panache to the normally text-only `Button`.

Another significant use for small bitmaps is the context menu available for items in the `TableView`. But a prerequisite for that is a deep exploration of the various views that contribute to the interactive interface of Xamarin.Forms. That's coming up in Chapter 15.

But first let's look at an alternative to `StackLayout` that lets you position child views in a completely flexible manner.

Chapter 14
Absolute layout

In Xamarin.Forms, the concept of layout encompasses all the ways that various views can be assembled on the screen. Here's the class hierarchy showing all the classes that derive from `Layout`:

```
System.Object
    BindableObject
        Element
            VisualElement
                View
                    Layout
                        ContentView
                            Frame
                        ScrollView
                        Layout<T>
                            AbsoluteLayout
                            Grid
                            RelativeLayout
                            StackLayout
```

You've already seen `ContentView`, `Frame`, and `ScrollView` (all of which have a `Content` property that you can set to one child), and you've seen `StackLayout`, which inherits a `Children` property from `Layout<T>` and displays its children in a vertical or horizontal stack. The `Grid` and `Relative-Layout` implement somewhat complex layout models and are explored in future chapters. `Absolute-Layout` is the subject of this chapter.

At first, the `AbsoluteLayout` class seems to implement a rather primitive layout model—one that harks back to the not-so-good old days of graphical user interfaces when programmers were required to individually size and position every element on the screen. Yet, you'll discover that `AbsoluteLay-out` also incorporates a proportional positioning and sizing feature that helps brings this ancient layout model into the modern age.

With `AbsoluteLayout`, many of the rules about layout that you've learned so far no longer apply: the `HorizontalOptions` and `VerticalOptions` properties that are so important when a `View` is the child of a `ContentPage` or `StackLayout` have absolutely no effect when a `View` is a child of an `Ab-soluteLayout`. A program must instead assign to each child of an `AbsoluteLayout` a specific location in device-independent coordinates. The child can also be assigned a specific size or allowed to size itself.

You can use `AbsoluteLayout` either in code or in XAML. Either way, you'll encounter a feature you haven't seen yet that is another part of the support provided by `BindableObject` and `Bindable-Property`. This new feature is the *attached bindable property*. This is a special type of bindable property that is defined by one class (in this case the `AbsoluteLayout`) but which is set on other objects (the children of the `AbsoluteLayout`).

AbsoluteLayout in code

You can add a child view to the `Children` collection of an `AbsoluteLayout` the same way as with `StackLayout`:

```
absoluteLayout.Children.Add(child);
```

However, you also have other options. The `AbsoluteLayout` class redefines its `Children` property to be of type `AbsoluteLayout.IAbsoluteList<View>`, which includes two additional `Add` methods that allow you to specify the position of the child relative to the upper-left corner of the `Absolute-Layout`. You can optionally specify the child's size.

To specify both the position and size, you use a `Rectangle` value. `Rectangle` is a structure, and you can create a `Rectangle` value with a constructor that accepts `Point` and `Size` values:

```
Point point = new Point(x, y);
Size size = new Size(width, height);
Rectangle rect = new Rectangle(point, size);
```

Or you can pass the `x`, `y`, `width`, and `height` arguments directly to a `Rectangle` constructor:

```
Rectangle rect = new Rectangle(x, y, width, height);
```

You can then use an alternative `Add` method to add a view to the `Children` collection of the `Abso-luteLayout`:

```
absoluteLayout.Children.Add(child, rect);
```

The `x` and `y` values indicate the position of the upper-left corner of the child view relative to the upper-left corner of the `AbsoluteLayout` parent in device-independent coordinates. If you prefer the child to size itself, you can use just a `Point` value with no `Size` value:

```
absoluteLayout.Children.Add(child, point);
```

Here's a little demo in a program named **AbsoluteDemo**:

```
public class AbsoluteDemoPage : ContentPage
{
    public AbsoluteDemoPage()
    {
        AbsoluteLayout absoluteLayout = new AbsoluteLayout
        {
            Padding = new Thickness(50)
        };
```

```
absoluteLayout.Children.Add(
    new BoxView
    {
        Color = Color.Accent
    },
    new Rectangle(0, 10, 200, 5));

absoluteLayout.Children.Add(
    new BoxView
    {
        Color = Color.Accent
    },
    new Rectangle(0, 20, 200, 5));

absoluteLayout.Children.Add(
    new BoxView
    {
        Color = Color.Accent
    },
    new Rectangle(10, 0, 5, 65));

absoluteLayout.Children.Add(
    new BoxView
    {
        Color = Color.Accent
    },
    new Rectangle(20, 0, 5, 65));

absoluteLayout.Children.Add(
    new Label
    {
        Text = "Stylish Header",
        FontSize = 24
    },
    new Point(30, 25));

absoluteLayout.Children.Add(
    new Label
    {
        FormattedText = new FormattedString
        {
            Spans =
            {
                new Span
                {
                    Text = "Although the "
                },
                new Span
                {
                    Text = "AbsoluteLayout",
                    FontAttributes = FontAttributes.Italic
                },
                new Span
```

```
            {
                Text = " is usually employed for purposes other " +
                        "than the display of text using "
            },
            new Span
            {
                Text = "Label",
                FontAttributes = FontAttributes.Italic
            },
            new Span
            {
                Text = ", obviously it can be used in that way. " +
                        "The text continues to wrap nicely " +
                        "within the bounds of the container " +
                        "and any padding that might be applied."
            }
        }
    }
},
new Point(0, 80));

this.Content = absoluteLayout;
    }
}
```

Four `BoxView` elements form an overlapping crisscross pattern on the top to set off a header, and then a paragraph of text follows. The program positions and sizes all the `BoxView` elements, while it merely positions the two `Label` views because they size themselves:

A little trial and error was required to get the sizes of the four `BoxView` elements and the header text to be approximately the same size. But notice that the BoxView elements overlap: AbsoluteLayout allows you to overlap views in a very freeform way that's simply impossible with StackLayout (or without using transforms, which are covered in a later chapter).

The big drawback of AbsoluteLayout is that you need to come up with the positioning coordinates yourself or calculate them at run time. Anything not explicitly sized—such as the two Label views—will calculate a size for itself when the page is laid out. But that size is not available until then. If you wanted to add another paragraph after the second Label, what coordinates would you use?

Actually, you can position multiple paragraphs of text by putting a StackLayout (or a StackLayout inside a ScrollView) in the AbsoluteLayout and then putting the Label views in that. Layouts can be nested.

As you can surmise, using AbsoluteLayout is more difficult than using StackLayout. In general it's much easier to let Xamarin.Forms and the other Layout classes handle much of the complexity of layout for you. But for some special uses, AbsoluteLayout is ideal.

Like all visual elements, AbsoluteLayout has its HorizontalOptions and VerticalOptions properties set to Fill by default, which means that AbsoluteLayout fills its container. With other settings of HorizontalOptions and VerticalOptions, an AbsoluteLayout sizes itself to the size of its contents, but there are some exceptions: Try giving the AbsoluteLayout in the **AbsoluteDemo** program a BackgroundColor so that you can see exactly the space it occupies on the screen. It normally fills the whole page, but if you set the HorizontalOptions and VerticalOptions properties of the AbsoluteLayout to Center, you'll see that the size that the AbsoluteLayout computes for itself includes the contents and padding but only one line of the paragraph of text.

Figuring out sizes for visual elements in an AbsoluteLayout can be tricky. One simple approach is demonstrated by the **ChessboardFixed** program below. The program name has the suffix **Fixed** because the position and size of all the squares within the chessboard are set in the constructor. The constructor cannot anticipate the size of the screen, so it arbitrarily sets the size of each square to 35 units, as indicated by the squareSize constant at the top of the class. This value should be sufficiently small for the chessboard to fit on the screen of any device supported by Xamarin.Forms.

Notice that the AbsoluteLayout is centered so it will have a size that accommodates all its children. The board itself is given a color of buff, which is a pale yellow-brown, and then 32 dark-green BoxView elements are displayed in every other square position:

```
public class ChessboardFixedPage : ContentPage
{
    public ChessboardFixedPage()
    {
        const double squareSize = 35;

        AbsoluteLayout absoluteLayout = new AbsoluteLayout
        {
            BackgroundColor = Color.FromRgb(240, 220, 130),
            HorizontalOptions = LayoutOptions.Center,
```

```
            VerticalOptions = LayoutOptions.Center
    };

    for (int row = 0; row < 8; row++)
    {
        for (int col = 0; col < 8; col++)
        {
            // Skip every other square.
            if (((row ^ col) & 1) == 0)
                continue;

            BoxView boxView = new BoxView
                {
                    Color = Color.FromRgb(0, 64, 0)
                };

            Rectangle rect = new Rectangle(col * squareSize,
                                           row * squareSize,
                                           squareSize, squareSize);

            absoluteLayout.Children.Add(boxView, rect);
        }
    }
    this.Content = absoluteLayout;
    }
}
```

The exclusive-or calculation on the row and col variables causes a BoxView to be created only when either the row or col variable is odd but both are not odd. Here's the result:

Attached bindable properties

If we wanted this chessboard to be as large as possible within the confines of the screen, we'd need to add the `BoxView` elements to the `AbsoluteLayout` during the `SizeChanged` handler for the page, or the `SizeChanged` handler would need to find some way to change the position and size of the `BoxView` elements already in the `Children` collection.

Both options are possible, but the second one is preferred because we can fill the `Children` collection of the `AbsoluteLayout` only once in the program's constructor and then adjust the sizes and position later.

At first encounter, the syntax that allows you to set the position and size of a child already in an `AbsoluteLayout` might seem somewhat odd. If `view` is an object of type `View` and `rect` is a `Rectangle` value, here's the statement that gives `view` a location and size of `rect`:

```
AbsoluteLayout.SetLayoutBounds(view, rect);
```

That's not an instance of `AbsoluteLayout` on which you're making a `SetLayoutBounds` call. No. That's a static method of the `AbsoluteLayout` class. You can call `AbsoluteLayout.SetLayoutBounds` either before or after you add the `view` child to the `AbsoluteLayout` children collection. Indeed, because it's a static method, you can call the method before the `AbsoluteLayout` has even been instantiated! A particular instance of `AbsoluteLayout` is not involved at all in this `SetLayoutBounds` method.

Let's look at some code that makes use of this mysterious `AbsoluteLayout.SetLayoutBounds` method and then examine how it works.

The **ChessboardDynamic** program page constructor uses the simple `Add` method without positioning or sizing to add 32 `BoxView` elements to the `AbsoluteLayout` in one `for` loop. To provide a little margin around the chessboard, the `AbsoluteLayout` is a child of a `ContentView` and padding is set on the page. This `ContentView` has a `SizeChanged` handler to position and size the `AbsoluteLayout` children based on the size of the container:

```
public class ChessboardDynamicPage : ContentPage
{
    AbsoluteLayout absoluteLayout;

    public ChessboardDynamicPage()
    {
        absoluteLayout = new AbsoluteLayout
        {
            BackgroundColor = Color.FromRgb(240, 220, 130),
            HorizontalOptions = LayoutOptions.Center,
            VerticalOptions = LayoutOptions.Center
        };

        for (int i = 0; i < 32; i++)
        {
```

```
            BoxView boxView = new BoxView
                {
                    Color = Color.FromRgb(0, 64, 0)
                };
            absoluteLayout.Children.Add(boxView);
        }

        ContentView contentView = new ContentView
        {
            Content = absoluteLayout
        };
        contentView.SizeChanged += OnContentViewSizeChanged;

        this.Padding = new Thickness(5, Device.OnPlatform(25, 5, 5), 5, 5);
        this.Content = contentView;
    }

    void OnContentViewSizeChanged(object sender, EventArgs args)
    {
        ContentView contentView = (ContentView)sender;
        double squareSize = Math.Min(contentView.Width, contentView.Height) / 8;
        int index = 0;

        for (int row = 0; row < 8; row++)
        {
            for (int col = 0; col < 8; col++)
            {
                // Skip every other square.
                if (((row ^ col) & 1) == 0)
                    continue;

                View view = absoluteLayout.Children[index];
                Rectangle rect = new Rectangle(col * squareSize,
                                               row * squareSize,
                                               squareSize, squareSize);

                AbsoluteLayout.SetLayoutBounds(view, rect);
                index++;
            }
        }
    }
}
```

The SizeChanged handler contains much the same logic as the constructor in **ChessboardFixed** except that the BoxView elements are already in the Children collection of the AbsoluteLayout. All that's necessary is to position and size each BoxView when the size of the container changes—for example, during phone orientation changes. The for loop concludes with a call to the static AbsoluteLayout.SetLayoutBounds method for each BoxView with a calculated Rectangle value.

Now the chessboard is sized to fit the screen with a little margin:

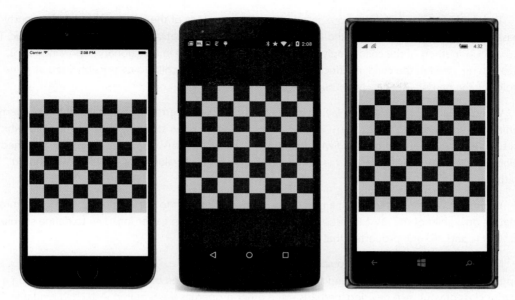

Obviously, the mysterious `AbsoluteLayout.SetLayoutBounds` method works, but how? What does it do? And how does it manage to do what it does without referencing a particular `Absolute-Layout` object?

The `AbsoluteLayout.SetLayoutBounds` call that you've just seen looks like this:

```
AbsoluteLayout.SetLayoutBounds(view, rect);
```

That method call is exactly equivalent to the following call on the child view:

```
view.SetValue(AbsoluteLayout.LayoutBoundsProperty, rect);
```

This is a `SetValue` call on the child view. These two method calls are exactly equivalent because the second one is how `AbsoluteLayout` internally defines the `SetLayoutBounds` static method. `Abso-luteLayout.SetLayoutBounds` is merely a shortcut method, and the similar static `AbsoluteLay-out.GetLayoutBounds` method is a shortcut for a `GetValue` call.

You'll recall that `SetValue` and `GetValue` are defined by `BindableObject` and used to implement bindable properties. Judging solely from the name, `AbsoluteLayout.LayoutBoundsProperty` certainly appears to be a `BindableProperty` object, and that is so. However, it is a very special type of bindable property called an *attached bindable property*.

Normal bindable properties can be set only on instances of the class that defines the property or on instances of a derived class. Attached bindable properties can break that rule: Attached bindable properties are defined by one class—in this case `AbsoluteLayout`—but set on another object, in this case a child of the `AbsoluteLayout`. The property is sometimes said to be *attached* to the child, hence the name.

The child of the `AbsoluteLayout` is ignorant of the purpose of the attached bindable property passed to its `SetValue` method, and the child makes no use of that value in its own internal logic. The `SetValue` method of the child simply saves the `Rectangle` value in a dictionary maintained by `BindableObject` within the child, in effect attaching this value to the child to be possibly used at some point by the parent—the `AbsoluteLayout` object.

When the `AbsoluteLayout` is laying out its children, it can interrogate the value of this property on each child by calling the `AbsoluteLayout.GetLayoutBounds` static method on the child, which in turn calls `GetValue` on the child with the `AbsoluteLayout.LayoutBoundsProperty` attached bindable property. The call to `GetValue` fetches the `Rectangle` value from the dictionary stored within the child.

You might wonder: Why is such a roundabout process required to set positioning and sizing information on a child of the `AbsoluteLayout`? Wouldn't it have been easier for `View` to define simple `X`, `Y`, `Width`, and `Height` properties that an application could set?

Maybe, but those properties would be suitable only for `AbsoluteLayout`. When using the `Grid`, an application needs to specify `Row` and `Column` values on the children of the `Grid`, and when using a layout class of your own devising, perhaps some other properties are required. Attached bindable properties can handle all these cases and more.

Attached bindable properties are a general-purpose mechanism that allows properties defined by one class to be stored in instances of another class. You can define your own attached bindable properties by using static creation methods of `BindableObject` named `CreateAttached` and `CreateAttachedReadOnly`. (You'll see an example in Chapter 27, "Custom renderers.")

Attached properties are mostly used with layout classes. As you'll see, `Grid` defines attached bindable properties to specify the row and column of each child, and `RelativeLayout` also defines attached bindable properties.

Earlier you saw additional `Add` methods defined by the `Children` collection of `AbsoluteLayout`. These are actually implemented using these attached bindable properties. The call

```
absoluteLayout.Children.Add(view, rect);
```

is implemented like this:

```
AbsoluteLayout.SetLayoutBounds(view, rect);
absoluteLayout.Children.Add(view);
```

The `Add` call with only a `Point` argument merely sets the child's position and lets the child size itself:

```
absoluteLayout.Children.Add(view, new Point(x, y));
```

This is implemented with the same static `AbsoluteLayout.SetLayoutBounds` calls but using a special constant for the view's width and height:

```
AbsoluteLayout.SetLayoutBounds(view,
        new Rectangle(x, y, AbsoluteLayout.AutoSize, AbsoluteLayout.AutoSize));
```

```
absoluteLayout.Children.Add(view);
```

You can use that `AbsoluteLayout.AutoSize` constant in your own code.

Proportional sizing and positioning

As you saw, the **ChessboardDynamic** program repositions and resizes the `BoxView` children with calculations based on the size of the `AbsoluteLayout` itself. In other words, the size and position of each child is proportional to the size of the container. Interestingly, this is often the case with an `AbsoluteLayout`, and it might be nice if `AbsoluteLayout` accommodated such situations automatically.

It does!

`AbsoluteLayout` defines a second attached bindable property, named `LayoutFlagsProperty`, and two more static methods, named `SetLayoutFlags` and `GetLayoutFlags`. Setting this attached bindable property allows you to specify child position coordinates or sizes (or both) that are proportional to the size of the `AbsoluteLayout`. When laying out its children, `AbsoluteLayout` scales those coordinates and sizes appropriately.

You select how this feature works with one or more members of the `AbsoluteLayoutFlags` enumeration:

- `None` (equal to 0)

- `XProportional` (1)

- `YProportional` (2)

- `PositionProportional` (3)

- `WidthProportional` (4)

- `HeightProportional` (8)

- `SizeProportional` (12)

- `All` (\xFFFFFFFF)

You can set a proportional position and size on a child of `AbsoluteLayout` using the two static methods:

```
AbsoluteLayout.SetLayoutBounds(view, rect);
AbsoluteLayout.SetLayoutFlags(view, AbsoluteLayoutFlags.All);
```

Or you can use a version of the `Add` method on the `Children` collection that accepts an `AbsoluteLayoutFlags` enumeration member:

```
absoluteLayout.Children.Add(view, rect, AbsoluteLayoutFlags.All);
```

For example, if you use the `SizeProportional` flag and set the width of the child to 0.25 and the height to 0.10, the child will be one-quarter of the width of the `AbsoluteLayout` and one-tenth the height. Easy enough.

The `PositionProportional` flag is similar, but it takes the size of the child into account: a position of (0, 0) puts the child in the upper-left corner, a position of (1, 1) puts the child in the lower-right corner, and a position of (0.5, 0.5) centers the child within the `AbsoluteLayout`. Taking the size of the child into account is great for some tasks—such as centering a child in an `AbsoluteLayout` or displaying it against the right or bottom edge—but a bit awkward for other tasks.

Here's **ChessboardProportional**. The bulk of the job of positioning and sizing has been moved back to the constructor. The `SizeChanged` handler now merely maintains the overall aspect ratio by setting the `WidthRequest` and `HeightRequest` properties of the `AbsoluteLayout` to the minimum of the width and height of the `ContentView`. Remove that `SizeChanged` handling and the chessboard expands to the size of the page less the padding.

```
public class ChessboardProportionalPage : ContentPage
{
    AbsoluteLayout absoluteLayout;

    public ChessboardProportionalPage()
    {
        absoluteLayout = new AbsoluteLayout
        {
            BackgroundColor = Color.FromRgb(240, 220, 130),
            HorizontalOptions = LayoutOptions.Center,
            VerticalOptions = LayoutOptions.Center
        };

        for (int row = 0; row < 8; row++)
        {
            for (int col = 0; col < 8; col++)
            {
                // Skip every other square.
                if (((row ^ col) & 1) == 0)
                    continue;

                BoxView boxView = new BoxView
                {
                    Color = Color.FromRgb(0, 64, 0)
                };

                Rectangle rect = new Rectangle(col / 7.0,    // x
                                               row / 7.0,    // y
                                               1 / 8.0,      // width
                                               1 / 8.0);     // height

                absoluteLayout.Children.Add(boxView, rect, AbsoluteLayoutFlags.All);
            }
        }
    }
}
```

```
        ContentView contentView = new ContentView
        {
            Content = absoluteLayout
        };
        contentView.SizeChanged += OnContentViewSizeChanged;

        this.Padding = new Thickness(5, Device.OnPlatform(25, 5, 5), 5, 5);
        this.Content = contentView;
    }

    void OnContentViewSizeChanged(object sender, EventArgs args)
    {
        ContentView contentView = (ContentView)sender;
        double boardSize = Math.Min(contentView.Width, contentView.Height);
        absoluteLayout.WidthRequest = boardSize;
        absoluteLayout.HeightRequest = boardSize;
    }
}
```

The screen looks the same as the **ChessboardDynamic** program.

Each `BoxView` is added to the `AbsoluteLayout` with the following code. All the denominators are floating-point values, so the results of the divisions are converted to `double`:

```
Rectangle rect = new Rectangle(col / 7.0,      // x
                               row / 7.0,      // y
                               1 / 8.0,        // width
                               1 / 8.0);       // height

absoluteLayout.Children.Add(boxView, rect, AbsoluteLayoutFlags.All);
```

The width and height are always equal to one-eighth the width and height of the `AbsoluteLayout`. That much is clear. But the `row` and `col` variables are divided by 7 (rather than 8) for the relative x and y coordinates. The `row` and `col` variables in the `for` loops range from 0 through 7. The `row` and `col` values of 0 correspond to left or top, but `row` and `col` values of 7 must map to x and y coordinates of 1 to position the child against the right or bottom edge.

If you think you might need some solid rules to derive proportional coordinates, read on.

Working with proportional coordinates

Working with proportional positioning in an `AbsoluteLayout` can be tricky. Sometimes you need to compensate for the internal calculation that takes the size into account. For example, you might prefer to specify coordinates so that an X value of 1 means that the left edge of the child is positioned at the right edge of the `AbsoluteLayout`, and you'll need to convert that to a coordinate that `Absolute-Layout` understands.

In the discussion that follows, a coordinate that does *not* take size into account—a coordinate in which 1 means that the child is positioned just outside the right or bottom edge of the `AbsoluteLay-out`—is referred to as a *fractional* coordinate. The goal of this section is to develop rules for converting a fractional coordinate to a proportional coordinate that you can use with `AbsoluteLayout`. This conversion requires that you know the size of the child view.

Suppose you're putting a view named `child` in an `AbsoluteLayout` named `absoluteLayout`, with a layout bounds rectangle for the child named `layoutBounds`. Let's restrict this analysis to horizontal coordinates and sizes. The process is the same for vertical coordinates and sizes.

This child must first get a width in some way. The child might calculate its own width, or a width in device-independent units might be assigned to it via the `LayoutBounds` attached property. But let's assume that the `AbsoluteLayoutFlags.WidthProportional` flag is set, which means that the width is calculated based on the `Width` field of the layout bounds and the width of the `AbsoluteLayout`:

$$child.Width = layoutBounds.Width * absoluteLayout.Width$$

If the `AbsoluteLayoutFlags.XProportional` flag is also set, then internally the `AbsoluteLayout` calculates a coordinate for the child relative to itself by taking the size of the child into account:

$$relativeChildCoordinate.X = (absoluteLayout.Width - child.Width) * layoutBounds.X$$

For example, if the `AbsoluteLayout` has a width of 400, and the child has a width of 100, and `layoutBounds.X` is 0.5, then `relativeChildCoordinate.X` is calculated as 150. This means that the left edge of the child is 150 pixels from the left edge of the parent. That causes the child to be horizontally centered within the `AbsoluteLayout`.

It's also possible to calculate a fractional child coordinate:

$$fractionalChildCoordinate.X = \frac{relativeChildCoordinate.X}{absoluteLayout.Width}$$

This is not the same as the proportional coordinate because a fractional child coordinate of 1 means that the child's left edge is just outside the right edge of the `AbsoluteLayout`, and hence the child is outside the surface of the `AbsoluteLayout`. To continue the example, the fractional child coordinate is 150 divided by 400 or 0.375. The left of the child view is positioned at (0.375 * 400) or 150 units from the left edge of the `AbsoluteLayout`.

Let's rearrange the terms of the formula that calculates the relative child coordinate to solve for `layoutBounds.X`:

$$layoutBounds.X = \frac{relativeChildCoordinate.X}{(absoluteLayout.Width - child.Width)}$$

And let's divide both the top and bottom of that ratio by the width of the `AbsoluteLayout`:

$$layoutBounds.X = \frac{fractionalChildCoordinate.X}{\left(1 - \frac{child.Width}{absoluteLayout.Width}\right)}$$

If you're also using proportional width, then that ratio in the denominator is `layout-Bounds.Width`:

$$layoutBounds.X = \frac{fractionalChildCoordinate.X}{(1 - \ layoutBounds.Width)}$$

And that is often a very handy formula, for it allows you to convert from a fractional child coordinate to a proportional coordinate for use in the layout bounds rectangle.

In the **ChessboardProportional** example, when `col` equals 7, the `fractionalChildCoordinate.X` is 7 divided by the number of columns (8), or 7/8. The denominator is 1 minus 1/8 (the proportional width of the square), or 7/8 again. The ratio is 1.

Let's look at an example where the formula is applied in code to fractional coordinates. The **ProportionalCoordinateCalc** program attempts to reproduce this simple figure using eight blue `BoxView` elements on a pink `AbsoluteLayout`:

The whole figure has a 2:1 aspect. You can think of the figure as comprising four horizontal rectangles and four vertical rectangles. The pairs of horizontal blue rectangles at the top and bottom have a height of 0.1 fractional units (relative to the height of the `AbsoluteLayout`) and are spaced 0.1 units from the top and bottom and between each other. The vertical blue rectangles appear to be spaced and sized similarly, but because the aspect ratio is 2:1, the vertical rectangles have a width of 0.05 units and are spaced with 0.05 units from the left and right and between each other.

The `AbsoluteLayout` is defined and centered in a XAML file and colored pink:

```
<ContentPage xmlns="http://xamarin.com/schemas/2014/forms"
             xmlns:x="http://schemas.microsoft.com/winfx/2009/xaml"
             x:Class="ProportionalCoordinateCalc.ProportionalCoordinateCalcPage">
    <ContentPage.Padding>
        <OnPlatform x:TypeArguments="Thickness"
                    iOS="5, 25, 5, 5"
                    Android="5"
                    WinPhone="5" />
    </ContentPage.Padding>

    <ContentView SizeChanged="OnContentViewSizeChanged">
        <AbsoluteLayout x:Name="absoluteLayout"
                        BackgroundColor="Pink"
                        HorizontalOptions="Center"
                        VerticalOptions="Center" />
    </ContentView>
```

```
</ContentPage>
```

The code-behind file defines an array of `Rectangle` structures with the fractional coordinates for each of the eight `BoxView` elements. In a `foreach` loop, the program applies a slight variation of the final formula shown above. Rather than a denominator equal to 1 minus the value of `layout-Bounds.Width` (or `layoutBounds.Height`), it uses the `Width` (or `Height`) of the fractional bounds, which is the same value.

```csharp
public partial class ProportionalCoordinateCalcPage : ContentPage
{
    public ProportionalCoordinateCalcPage()
    {
        InitializeComponent();

        Rectangle[] fractionalRects =
        {
            new Rectangle(0.05, 0.1, 0.90, 0.1),     // outer top
            new Rectangle(0.05, 0.8, 0.90, 0.1),     // outer bottom
            new Rectangle(0.05, 0.1, 0.05, 0.8),     // outer left
            new Rectangle(0.90, 0.1, 0.05, 0.8),     // outer right

            new Rectangle(0.15, 0.3, 0.70, 0.1),     // inner top
            new Rectangle(0.15, 0.6, 0.70, 0.1),     // inner bottom
            new Rectangle(0.15, 0.3, 0.05, 0.4),     // inner left
            new Rectangle(0.80, 0.3, 0.05, 0.4),     // inner right
        };

        foreach (Rectangle fractionalRect in fractionalRects)
        {
            Rectangle layoutBounds = new Rectangle
            {
                // Proportional coordinate calculations.
                X = fractionalRect.X / (1 - fractionalRect.Width),
                Y = fractionalRect.Y / (1 - fractionalRect.Height),

                Width = fractionalRect.Width,
                Height = fractionalRect.Height
            };

            absoluteLayout.Children.Add(
                new BoxView
                {
                    Color = Color.Blue
                },
                layoutBounds,
                AbsoluteLayoutFlags.All);
        }
    }

    void OnContentViewSizeChanged(object sender, EventArgs args)
    {
        ContentView contentView = (ContentView)sender;
```

```
        // Figure has an aspect ratio of 2:1.
        double height = Math.Min(contentView.Width / 2, contentView.Height);
        absoluteLayout.WidthRequest = 2 * height;
        absoluteLayout.HeightRequest = height;
    }
}
```

The SizeChanged handler simply fixes the aspect ratio.

Here's the result:

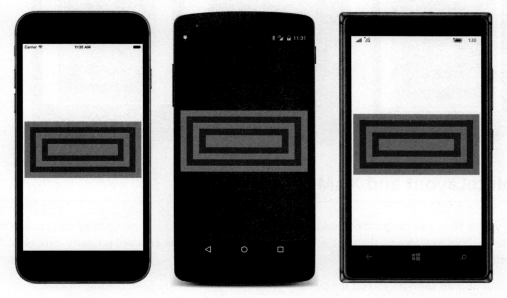

And, of course, you can turn the phone sideways and see a larger figure in landscape mode, which you'll have to view by turning this book sideways:

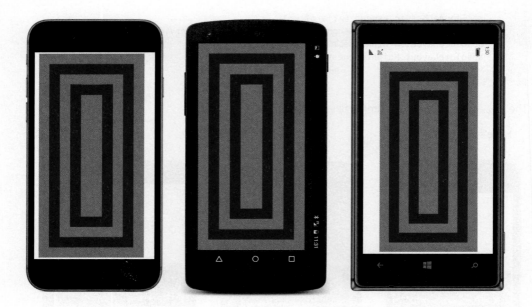

AbsoluteLayout and XAML

As you've seen, you can position and size a child of an `AbsoluteLayout` in code by using one of the `Add` methods available on the `Children` collection or by setting an attached property through a static method call.

But how on earth do you set the position and size of `AbsoluteLayout` children in XAML?

A very special syntax is involved. This syntax is illustrated by this XAML version of the earlier **AbsoluteDemo** program, called **AbsoluteXamlDemo**:

```
<ContentPage xmlns="http://xamarin.com/schemas/2014/forms"
             xmlns:x="http://schemas.microsoft.com/winfx/2009/xaml"
             x:Class="AbsoluteXamlDemo.AbsoluteXamlDemoPage">

    <AbsoluteLayout Padding="50">
        <BoxView Color="Accent"
                 AbsoluteLayout.LayoutBounds="0, 10, 200, 5" />

        <BoxView Color="Accent"
                 AbsoluteLayout.LayoutBounds="0, 20, 200, 5" />

        <BoxView Color="Accent"
                 AbsoluteLayout.LayoutBounds="10, 0, 5, 65" />

        <BoxView Color="Accent"
                 AbsoluteLayout.LayoutBounds="20, 0, 5, 65" />
```

```
                <Label Text="Stylish Header"
                        FontSize="24"
                        AbsoluteLayout.LayoutBounds="30, 25, AutoSize, AutoSize" />

                <Label AbsoluteLayout.LayoutBounds="0, 80, AutoSize, AutoSize">
                    <Label.FormattedText>
                        <FormattedString>
                            <Span Text="Although " />
                            <Span Text="AbsoluteLayout"
                                    FontAttributes="Italic" />
                            <Span Text=
" is usually employed for purposes other
than the display of text using " />
                            <Span Text="Label"
                                    FontAttributes="Italic" />
                            <Span Text=
", obviously it can be used in that way.
The text continues to wrap nicely
within the bounds of the container
and any padding that might be applied." />
                        </FormattedString>
                    </Label.FormattedText>
                </Label>
            </AbsoluteLayout>
</ContentPage>
```

The code-behind file contains only an `InitializeComponent` call.

Here's the first `BoxView`:

```
<BoxView Color="Accent"
         AbsoluteLayout.LayoutBounds="0, 10, 200, 5" />
```

In XAML, an attached bindable property is expressed as an attribute that consists of a class name (`AbsoluteLayout`) and a property name (`LayoutBounds`) separated by a period. Whenever you see such an attribute, it's always an attached bindable property. That's the only application of this attribute syntax.

In summary, combinations of class names and property names only appear in XAML in three specific contexts: If they appear as elements, they are property elements. If they appear as attributes, they are attached bindable properties. And the only other context for a class name and property name is an argument to an `x:Static` markup extension.

The `AbsoluteLayout.LayoutBounds` attribute is commonly set to four numbers separated by commas. You can also express `AbsoluteLayout.LayoutBounds` as a property element:

```
<BoxView Color="Accent">
    <AbsoluteLayout.LayoutBounds>
        0, 10, 200, 5
    </AbsoluteLayout.LayoutBounds>
</BoxView>
```

Those four numbers are parsed by the `BoundsTypeConverter` and not the `RectangleTypeCon-verter` because the `BoundsTypeConverter` allows the use of `AutoSize` for the width and height parts. You can see the `AutoSize` arguments later in the **AbsoluteXamlDemo** XAML file:

```
<Label Text="Stylish Header"
       FontSize="24"
       AbsoluteLayout.LayoutBounds="30, 25, AutoSize, AutoSize" />
```

Or you can leave them out:

```
<Label Text="Stylish Header"
       FontSize="24"
       AbsoluteLayout.LayoutBounds="30, 25" />
```

The odd thing about attached bindable properties that you specify in XAML is that they don't really exist! There is no field, property, or method in `AbsoluteLayout` called `LayoutBounds`. There is certainly a public static read-only field of type `BindableProperty` named `LayoutBoundsProperty`, and there are public static methods named `SetLayoutBounds` and `GetLayoutBounds`, but there is nothing named `LayoutBounds`. The XAML parser recognizes the syntax as referring to an attached bindable property and then looks for `LayoutBoundsProperty` in the `AbsoluteLayout` class. From there it can call `SetValue` on the target view with that `BindableProperty` object together with the value from the `BoundsTypeConverter`.

The **Chessboard** series of programs seems an unlikely candidate for duplicating in XAML because the file would need 32 instances of `BoxView` without the benefit of loops. However, the **ChessboardX-aml** program shows how to specify two properties of `BoxView` in an implicit style, including the `Abso-luteLayout.LayoutFlags` attached bindable property:

```
<ContentPage xmlns="http://xamarin.com/schemas/2014/forms"
             xmlns:x="http://schemas.microsoft.com/winfx/2009/xaml"
             x:Class="ChessboardXaml.ChessboardXamlPage">

    <ContentPage.Padding>
        <OnPlatform x:TypeArguments="Thickness"
                    iOS="5, 25, 5, 5"
                    Android="5"
                    WinPhone="5" />
    </ContentPage.Padding>

    <ContentPage.Resources>
        <ResourceDictionary>
            <Style TargetType="BoxView">
                <Setter Property="Color" Value="#004000" />
                <Setter Property="AbsoluteLayout.LayoutFlags" Value="All" />
            </Style>
        </ResourceDictionary>
    </ContentPage.Resources>

    <ContentView SizeChanged="OnContentViewSizeChanged">
        <AbsoluteLayout x:Name="absoluteLayout"
                        BackgroundColor="#F0DC82"
```

```
                              VerticalOptions="Center"
                              HorizontalOptions="Center">

            <BoxView AbsoluteLayout.LayoutBounds="0.00, 0.00, 0.125, 0.125" />
            <BoxView AbsoluteLayout.LayoutBounds="0.29, 0.00, 0.125, 0.125" />
            <BoxView AbsoluteLayout.LayoutBounds="0.57, 0.00, 0.125, 0.125" />
            <BoxView AbsoluteLayout.LayoutBounds="0.86, 0.00, 0.125, 0.125" />

            <BoxView AbsoluteLayout.LayoutBounds="0.14, 0.14, 0.125, 0.125" />
            <BoxView AbsoluteLayout.LayoutBounds="0.43, 0.14, 0.125, 0.125" />
            <BoxView AbsoluteLayout.LayoutBounds="0.71, 0.14, 0.125, 0.125" />
            <BoxView AbsoluteLayout.LayoutBounds="1.00, 0.14, 0.125, 0.125" />

            <BoxView AbsoluteLayout.LayoutBounds="0.00, 0.29, 0.125, 0.125" />
            <BoxView AbsoluteLayout.LayoutBounds="0.29, 0.29, 0.125, 0.125" />
            <BoxView AbsoluteLayout.LayoutBounds="0.57, 0.29, 0.125, 0.125" />
            <BoxView AbsoluteLayout.LayoutBounds="0.86, 0.29, 0.125, 0.125" />

            <BoxView AbsoluteLayout.LayoutBounds="0.14, 0.43, 0.125, 0.125" />
            <BoxView AbsoluteLayout.LayoutBounds="0.43, 0.43, 0.125, 0.125" />
            <BoxView AbsoluteLayout.LayoutBounds="0.71, 0.43, 0.125, 0.125" />
            <BoxView AbsoluteLayout.LayoutBounds="1.00, 0.43, 0.125, 0.125" />

            <BoxView AbsoluteLayout.LayoutBounds="0.00, 0.57, 0.125, 0.125" />
            <BoxView AbsoluteLayout.LayoutBounds="0.29, 0.57, 0.125, 0.125" />
            <BoxView AbsoluteLayout.LayoutBounds="0.57, 0.57, 0.125, 0.125" />
            <BoxView AbsoluteLayout.LayoutBounds="0.86, 0.57, 0.125, 0.125" />

            <BoxView AbsoluteLayout.LayoutBounds="0.14, 0.71, 0.125, 0.125" />
            <BoxView AbsoluteLayout.LayoutBounds="0.43, 0.71, 0.125, 0.125" />
            <BoxView AbsoluteLayout.LayoutBounds="0.71, 0.71, 0.125, 0.125" />
            <BoxView AbsoluteLayout.LayoutBounds="1.00, 0.71, 0.125, 0.125" />

            <BoxView AbsoluteLayout.LayoutBounds="0.00, 0.86, 0.125, 0.125" />
            <BoxView AbsoluteLayout.LayoutBounds="0.29, 0.86, 0.125, 0.125" />
            <BoxView AbsoluteLayout.LayoutBounds="0.57, 0.86, 0.125, 0.125" />
            <BoxView AbsoluteLayout.LayoutBounds="0.86, 0.86, 0.125, 0.125" />

            <BoxView AbsoluteLayout.LayoutBounds="0.14, 1.00, 0.125, 0.125" />
            <BoxView AbsoluteLayout.LayoutBounds="0.43, 1.00, 0.125, 0.125" />
            <BoxView AbsoluteLayout.LayoutBounds="0.71, 1.00, 0.125, 0.125" />
            <BoxView AbsoluteLayout.LayoutBounds="1.00, 1.00, 0.125, 0.125" />
        </AbsoluteLayout>
    </ContentView>
</ContentPage>
```

Yes, it's a lot of individual `BoxView` elements, but you can't argue with the cleanliness of the file. The code-behind file simply adjusts the aspect ratio:

```
public partial class ChessboardXamlPage : ContentPage
{
    public ChessboardXamlPage()
    {
        InitializeComponent();
```

```
    }

    void OnContentViewSizeChanged(object sender, EventArgs args)
    {
        ContentView contentView = (ContentView)sender;
        double boardSize = Math.Min(contentView.Width, contentView.Height);
        absoluteLayout.WidthRequest = boardSize;
        absoluteLayout.HeightRequest = boardSize;
    }
}
```

Overlays

The ability to overlap children in the `AbsoluteLayout` has some interesting and useful applications, among them being the ability to cover up your entire user interface with something sometimes called an *overlay*. Perhaps your page is carrying out a lengthy job and you don't want the user interacting with the page until the job is completed. You can place a semitransparent overlay over the page and perhaps display an `ActivityIndicator` or a `ProgressBar`.

Here's a program called **SimpleOverlay** that demonstrates this technique. The XAML file begins with an `AbsoluteLayout` filling the entire page. The first child of that `AbsoluteLayout` is a `Stack-Layout`, which you want to fill the page as well. However, the default `HorizontalOptions` and `VerticalOptions` settings of `Fill` on the `StackLayout` don't work for children of an `AbsoluteLayout`. Instead, the `StackLayout` fills the `AbsoluteLayout` through the use of the `AbsoluteLayout.LayoutBounds` and `AbsoluteLayout.LayoutFlags` attached bindable properties:

```xaml
<ContentPage xmlns="http://xamarin.com/schemas/2014/forms"
             xmlns:x="http://schemas.microsoft.com/winfx/2009/xaml"
             x:Class="SimpleOverlay.SimpleOverlayPage">
    <AbsoluteLayout>
        <StackLayout AbsoluteLayout.LayoutBounds="0, 0, 1, 1"
                     AbsoluteLayout.LayoutFlags="All">
            <Label Text=
"This might be a page full of user-interface objects except
that the only functional user-interface object on the page
is a Button."
                   FontSize="Medium"
                   VerticalOptions="CenterAndExpand"
                   HorizontalTextAlignment="Center" />

            <Button Text="Run 5-Second Job"
                    FontSize="Large"
                    VerticalOptions="CenterAndExpand"
                    HorizontalOptions="Center"
                    Clicked="OnButtonClicked" />

            <Button Text="A Do-Nothing Button"
                    FontSize="Large"
                    VerticalOptions="CenterAndExpand"
```

```
                    HorizontalOptions="Center" />

            <Label Text=
"This continues the page full of user-interface objects except
that the only functional user-interface object on the page
is the Button."
                    FontSize="Medium"
                    VerticalOptions="CenterAndExpand"
                    HorizontalTextAlignment="Center" />
        </StackLayout>

        <!-- Overlay -->
        <ContentView x:Name="overlay"
                    AbsoluteLayout.LayoutBounds="0, 0, 1, 1"
                    AbsoluteLayout.LayoutFlags="All"
                    IsVisible="False"
                    BackgroundColor="#C0808080"
                    Padding="10, 0">

            <ProgressBar x:Name="progressBar"
                        VerticalOptions="Center" />

        </ContentView>
    </AbsoluteLayout>
</ContentPage>
```

The second child of the `AbsoluteLayout` is a `ContentView`, which also fills the `AbsoluteLayout` and basically sits on top of the `StackLayout`. However, notice that the `IsVisible` property is set to `False`, which means that this `ContentView` and its children do not participate in the layout. The `ContentView` is still a child of the `AbsoluteLayout`, but it's simply skipped when the layout system is sizing and rendering all the elements of the page.

This `ContentView` is the overlay. When `IsVisible` is set to `True`, it blocks user input to the views below it. The `BackgroundColor` is set to a semitransparent gray, and a `ProgressBar` is vertically centered within it.

A `ProgressBar` resembles a `Slider` without a thumb. A `ProgressBar` is always horizontally oriented. Do not set the `HorizontalOptions` property of a `ProgressBar` to `Start`, `Center`, or `End` unless you also set its `WidthRequest` property.

A program can indicate progress by setting the `Progress` property of the `ProgressBar` to a value between 0 and 1. This is demonstrated in the `Clicked` handler for the only functional `Button` in the program. This handler simulates a lengthy job being performed in code with a timer that determines when five seconds have elapsed:

```
public partial class SimpleOverlayPage : ContentPage
{
    public SimpleOverlayPage()
    {
        InitializeComponent();
    }
```

```
void OnButtonClicked(object sender, EventArgs args)
{
    // Show overlay with ProgressBar.
    overlay.IsVisible = true;

    TimeSpan duration = TimeSpan.FromSeconds(5);
    DateTime startTime = DateTime.Now;

    // Start timer.
    Device.StartTimer(TimeSpan.FromSeconds(0.1), () =>
        {
            double progress = (DateTime.Now - startTime).TotalMilliseconds /
                                duration.TotalMilliseconds;
            progressBar.Progress = progress;
            bool continueTimer = progress < 1;

            if (!continueTimer)
            {
                // Hide overlay.
                overlay.IsVisible = false;
            }
            return continueTimer;
        });
}
}
```

The `Clicked` handler begins by setting the `IsVisible` property of the overlay to `true`, which re-veals the overlay and its child `ProgressBar` and prevents further interaction with the user interface underneath. The timer is set for one-tenth second and calculates a new `Progress` property for the `ProgressBar` based on the elapsed time. When the five seconds are up, the overlay is again hidden and the timer callback returns `false`.

Here's what it looks like with the overlay covering the page and the lengthy job in progress:

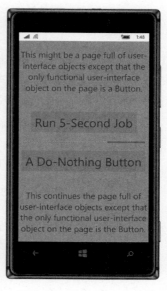

An overlay need not be restricted to a `ProgressBar` or an `ActivityIndicator`. You can include a **Cancel** button or other views.

Some fun

As you can probably see by now, the `AbsoluteLayout` is often used for some special purposes that wouldn't be easy otherwise. Some of these might actually be classified as "fun."

DotMatrixClock displays the digits of the current time using a simulated 5 × 7 dot matrix display. Each dot is a `BoxView`, individually sized and positioned on the screen and colored either red or light-gray depending on whether the dot is on or off. Conceivably, the dots of this clock could be organized in nested `StackLayout` elements or a `Grid`, but each `BoxView` needs to be given a size anyway. The sheer quantity and regularity of these views suggests that the programmer knows better than a layout class how to arrange them on the screen, because `StackLayout` and `Grid` need to perform the location calculations in a more generalized manner. For that reason, this is an ideal job for `AbsoluteLayout`.

A XAML file sets a little padding on the page and prepares an `AbsoluteLayout` for filling by code:

```
<ContentPage xmlns="http://xamarin.com/schemas/2014/forms"
             xmlns:x="http://schemas.microsoft.com/winfx/2009/xaml"
             x:Class="DotMatrixClock.DotMatrixClockPage"
             Padding="10"
             SizeChanged="OnPageSizeChanged">

    <AbsoluteLayout x:Name="absoluteLayout" />
```

```
                                VerticalOptions="Center" />

</ContentPage>
```

The code-behind file contains several fields, including two arrays, named `numberPatterns` and `colonPattern`, that define the dot matrix patterns for the 10 digits and a colon separator:

```
public partial class DotMatrixClockPage : ContentPage
{
    // Total dots horizontally and vertically.
    const int horzDots = 41;
    const int vertDots = 7;

    // 5 x 7 dot matrix patterns for 0 through 9.
    static readonly int[,,] numberPatterns = new int[10,7,5]
    {
        {
            { 0, 1, 1, 1, 0}, { 1, 0, 0, 0, 1}, { 1, 0, 0, 1, 1}, { 1, 0, 1, 0, 1},
            { 1, 1, 0, 0, 1}, { 1, 0, 0, 0, 1}, { 0, 1, 1, 1, 0}
        },
        {
            { 0, 0, 1, 0, 0}, { 0, 1, 1, 0, 0}, { 0, 0, 1, 0, 0}, { 0, 0, 1, 0, 0},
            { 0, 0, 1, 0, 0}, { 0, 0, 1, 0, 0}, { 0, 1, 1, 1, 0}
        },
        {
            { 0, 1, 1, 1, 0}, { 1, 0, 0, 0, 1}, { 0, 0, 0, 0, 1}, { 0, 0, 0, 1, 0},
            { 0, 0, 1, 0, 0}, { 0, 1, 0, 0, 0}, { 1, 1, 1, 1, 1}
        },
        {
            { 1, 1, 1, 1, 1}, { 0, 0, 0, 1, 0}, { 0, 0, 1, 0, 0}, { 0, 0, 0, 1, 0},
            { 0, 0, 0, 0, 1}, { 1, 0, 0, 0, 1}, { 0, 1, 1, 1, 0}
        },
        {
            { 0, 0, 0, 1, 0}, { 0, 0, 1, 1, 0}, { 0, 1, 0, 1, 0}, { 1, 0, 0, 1, 0},
            { 1, 1, 1, 1, 1}, { 0, 0, 0, 1, 0}, { 0, 0, 0, 1, 0}
        },
        {
            { 1, 1, 1, 1, 1}, { 1, 0, 0, 0, 0}, { 1, 1, 1, 1, 0}, { 0, 0, 0, 0, 1},
            { 0, 0, 0, 0, 1}, { 1, 0, 0, 0, 1}, { 0, 1, 1, 1, 0}
        },
        {
            { 0, 0, 1, 1, 0}, { 0, 1, 0, 0, 0}, { 1, 0, 0, 0, 0}, { 1, 1, 1, 1, 0},
            { 1, 0, 0, 0, 1}, { 1, 0, 0, 0, 1}, { 0, 1, 1, 1, 0}
        },
        {
            { 1, 1, 1, 1, 1}, { 0, 0, 0, 0, 1}, { 0, 0, 0, 1, 0}, { 0, 0, 1, 0, 0},
            { 0, 1, 0, 0, 0}, { 0, 1, 0, 0, 0}, { 0, 1, 0, 0, 0}
        },
        {
            { 0, 1, 1, 1, 0}, { 1, 0, 0, 0, 1}, { 1, 0, 0, 0, 1}, { 0, 1, 1, 1, 0},
            { 1, 0, 0, 0, 1}, { 1, 0, 0, 0, 1}, { 0, 1, 1, 1, 0}
        },
        {
            { 0, 1, 1, 1, 0}, { 1, 0, 0, 0, 1}, { 1, 0, 0, 0, 1}, { 0, 1, 1, 1, 1},
```

```
                { 0, 0, 0, 0, 1}, { 0, 0, 0, 1, 0}, { 0, 1, 1, 0, 0}
        },
    };

    // Dot matrix pattern for a colon.
    static readonly int[,] colonPattern = new int[7, 2]
    {
            { 0, 0 }, { 1, 1 }, { 1, 1 }, { 0, 0 }, { 1, 1 }, { 1, 1 }, { 0, 0 }
    };

    // BoxView colors for on and off.
    static readonly Color colorOn = Color.Red;
    static readonly Color colorOff = new Color(0.5, 0.5, 0.5, 0.25);

    // Box views for 6 digits, 7 rows, 5 columns.
    BoxView[,,] digitBoxViews = new BoxView[6, 7, 5];
    ...
}
```

Fields are also defined for an array of BoxView objects for the six digits of the time—two digits each for hour, minutes, and seconds. The total number of dots horizontally (set as horzDots) includes five dots for each of the six digits, four dots for the colon between the hour and minutes, four for the colon between the minutes and seconds, and a one dot width between the digits otherwise.

The program's constructor (shown below) creates a total of 238 BoxView objects and adds them to an AbsoluteLayout, but it also saves the BoxView objects for the digits in the digitBoxViews array. (In theory, the BoxView objects can be referenced later by indexing the Children collection of the AbsoluteLayout. But in that collection, they appear simply as a linear list. Storing them also in a multidimensional array allows them to be more easily identified and referenced.) All the positioning and sizing is proportional based on an AbsoluteLayout that is assumed to have an aspect ratio of 41 to 7, which encompasses the 41 BoxView widths and 7 BoxView heights.

```
public partial class DotMatrixClockPage : ContentPage
{
    ...
    public DotMatrixClockPage()
    {
        InitializeComponent();

        // BoxView dot dimensions.
        double height = 0.85 / vertDots;
        double width = 0.85 / horzDots;

        // Create and assemble the BoxViews.
        double xIncrement = 1.0 / (horzDots - 1);
        double yIncrement = 1.0 / (vertDots - 1);
        double x = 0;

        for (int digit = 0; digit < 6; digit++)
        {
            for (int col = 0; col < 5; col++)
            {
```

```
                double y = 0;

                for (int row = 0; row < 7; row++)
                {
                    // Create the digit BoxView and add to layout.
                    BoxView boxView = new BoxView();
                    digitBoxViews[digit, row, col] = boxView;
                    absoluteLayout.Children.Add(boxView,
                                           new Rectangle(x, y, width, height),
                                           AbsoluteLayoutFlags.All);
                    y += yIncrement;
                }
                x += xIncrement;
            }
            x += xIncrement;

            // Colons between the hour, minutes, and seconds.
            if (digit == 1 || digit == 3)
            {
                int colon = digit / 2;

                for (int col = 0; col < 2; col++)
                {
                    double y = 0;

                    for (int row = 0; row < 7; row++)
                    {
                        // Create the BoxView and set the color.
                        BoxView boxView = new BoxView
                            {
                                Color = colonPattern[row, col] == 1 ?
                                            colorOn : colorOff
                            };
                        absoluteLayout.Children.Add(boxView,
                                               new Rectangle(x, y, width, height),
                                               AbsoluteLayoutFlags.All);
                        y += yIncrement;
                    }
                    x += xIncrement;
                }
                x += xIncrement;
            }
        }

        // Set the timer and initialize with a manual call.
        Device.StartTimer(TimeSpan.FromSeconds(1), OnTimer);
        OnTimer();
    }
    ...
}
```

As you'll recall, the `horzDots` and `vertDots` constants are set to 41 and 7, respectively. To fill up the `AbsoluteLayout`, each `BoxView` needs to occupy a fraction of the width equal to 1 / `horzDots` and a fraction of the height equal to 1 / `vertDots`. The height and width set to each `BoxView` is 85 percent of that value to separate the dots enough so that they don't run into each other:

```
double height = 0.85 / vertDots;
double width = 0.85 / horzDots;
```

To position each `BoxView`, the constructor calculates proportional `xIncrement` and `yIncrement` values like so:

```
double xIncrement = 1.0 / (horzDots - 1);
double yIncrement = 1.0 / (vertDots - 1);
```

The denominators here are 40 and 6 so that the final X and Y positional coordinates are values of 1.

The `BoxView` objects for the time digits are not colored at all in the constructor, but those for the two colons are given a `Color` property based on the `colonPattern` array. The `DotMatrixClockPage` constructor concludes by a one-second timer.

The `SizeChanged` handler for the page is set from the XAML file. The `AbsoluteLayout` is automatically stretched horizontally to fill the width of the page (minus the padding), so the `HeightRequest` really just sets the aspect ratio:

```
public partial class DotMatrixClockPage : ContentPage
{
    …
    void OnPageSizeChanged(object sender, EventArgs args)
    {
        // No chance a display will have an aspect ratio > 41:7
        absoluteLayout.HeightRequest = vertDots * Width / horzDots;
    }
    …
}
```

It seems that the `Device.StartTimer` event handler should be rather complex because it is responsible for setting the `Color` property of each `BoxView` based on the digits of the current time. However, the similarity between the definitions of the `numberPatterns` array and the `digitBoxViews` array makes it surprisingly straightforward:

```
public partial class DotMatrixClockPage : ContentPage
{
    …
    bool OnTimer()
    {
        DateTime dateTime = DateTime.Now;

        // Convert 24-hour clock to 12-hour clock.
        int hour = (dateTime.Hour + 11) % 12 + 1;

        // Set the dot colors for each digit separately.
        SetDotMatrix(0, hour / 10);
        SetDotMatrix(1, hour % 10);
```

```
        SetDotMatrix(2, dateTime.Minute / 10);
        SetDotMatrix(3, dateTime.Minute % 10);
        SetDotMatrix(4, dateTime.Second / 10);
        SetDotMatrix(5, dateTime.Second % 10);
        return true;
    }

    void SetDotMatrix(int index, int digit)
    {
        for (int row = 0; row < 7; row++)
            for (int col = 0; col < 5; col++)
            {
                bool isOn = numberPatterns[digit, row, col] == 1;
                Color color = isOn ? colorOn : colorOff;
                digitBoxViews[index, row, col].Color = color;
            }
    }
}
```

And here's the result:

Of course, bigger is better, so you'll probably want to turn the phone (or the book) sideways for something large enough to read from across the room:

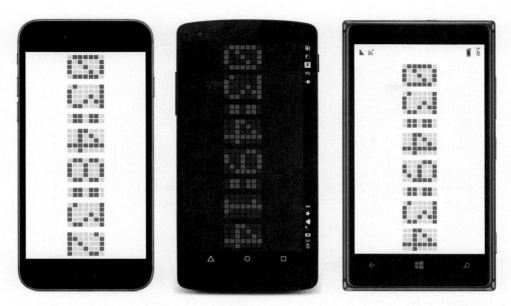

Another special type of application suitable for `AbsoluteLayout` is animation. The **BouncingText** program use its XAML file to instantiate two `Label` elements:

```
<ContentPage xmlns="http://xamarin.com/schemas/2014/forms"
             xmlns:x="http://schemas.microsoft.com/winfx/2009/xaml"
             x:Class="BouncingText.BouncingTextPage">

    <AbsoluteLayout>
        <Label x:Name="label1"
               Text="BOUNCE"
               FontSize="Large"
               AbsoluteLayout.LayoutFlags="PositionProportional" />

        <Label x:Name="label2"
               Text="BOUNCE"
               FontSize="Large"
               AbsoluteLayout.LayoutFlags="PositionProportional" />

    </AbsoluteLayout>
</ContentPage>
```

Notice that the `AbsoluteLayout.LayoutFlags` attributes are set to `PositionProportional`. The `Label` calculates its own size, but the positioning is proportional. Values between 0 and 1 can position the two `Label` elements anywhere within the page.

The code-behind file starts a timer going with a 15-millisecond duration. This is equivalent to approximately 60 ticks per second, which is generally the refresh rate of video displays. A 15-millisecond timer duration is ideal for performing animations:

```
public partial class BouncingTextPage : ContentPage
```

```
{
    const double period = 2000;                         // in milliseconds
    readonly DateTime startTime = DateTime.Now;

    public BouncingTextPage()
    {
        InitializeComponent();
        Device.StartTimer(TimeSpan.FromMilliseconds(15), OnTimerTick);
    }

    bool OnTimerTick()
    {
        TimeSpan elapsed = DateTime.Now - startTime;
        double t = (elapsed.TotalMilliseconds % period) / period;    // 0 to 1
        t = 2 * (t < 0.5 ? t : 1 - t);                               // 0 to 1 to 0

        AbsoluteLayout.SetLayoutBounds(label1,
            new Rectangle(t, 0.5, AbsoluteLayout.AutoSize, AbsoluteLayout.AutoSize));

        AbsoluteLayout.SetLayoutBounds(label2,
            new Rectangle(0.5, 1 - t, AbsoluteLayout.AutoSize, AbsoluteLayout.AutoSize));

        return true;
    }
}
```

The `OnTimerTick` handler computes an elapsed time since the program started and converts that to a value `t` (for time) that goes from 0 to 1 every two seconds. The second calculation of `t` makes it increase from 0 to 1 and then decrease back down to 0 every two seconds. This value is passed directly to the `Rectangle` constructor in the two `AbsoluteLayout.SetLayoutBounds` calls. The result is that the first `Label` moves horizontally across the center of the screen and seems to bounce off the left and right sides. The second `Label` moves vertically up and down the center of the screen and seems to bounce off the top and bottom:

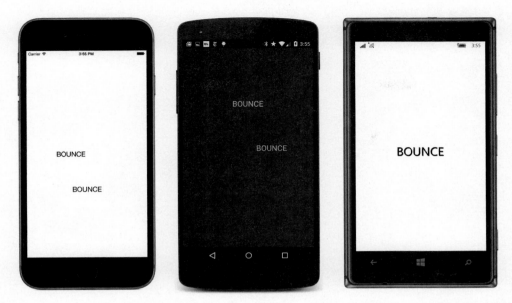

The two `Label` views meet briefly in the center every second, as the Windows 10 Mobile screenshot confirms.

From here on out, the pages of our Xamarin.Forms applications will become more active and animated and dynamic. In the next chapter, you'll see how the interactive views of Xamarin.Forms establish a means of communication between the user and the app.

Chapter 15

The interactive interface

Interactivity is the defining feature of modern computing. The many interactive views that Xamarin.Forms implements respond to touch gestures such as tapping and dragging, and a few even read keystrokes from the phone's virtual keyboard.

These interactive views incorporate paradigms that are familiar to users, and even have names that are familiar to programmers: users can trigger commands with `Button`, specify a number from a range of values with `Slider` and `Stepper`, enter text from the phone's keyboard using `Entry` and `Editor`, and select items from a collection with `Picker`, `ListView`, and `TableView`.

This chapter is devoted to demonstrating many of these interactive views.

View overview

Xamarin.Forms defines 20 instantiable classes that derive from `View` but not from `Layout`. You've already seen six of these classes in previous chapters: `Label`, `BoxView`, `Button`, `Image`, `ActivityIndicator`, and `ProgressBar`.

This chapter focuses on eight views that allow the user to select or interact with basic .NET data types:

Data type	Views
Double	Slider, Stepper
Boolean	Switch
String	Entry, Editor, SearchBar
DateTime	DatePicker, TimePicker

These views are often the visual representations of underlying data items. In the next chapter, you'll begin to explore data binding, which is a feature of Xamarin.Forms that links properties of views with properties of other classes so that these views and underlying data can be structured in correspondences.

Four of the remaining six views are discussed in later chapters. In Chapter 16, "Data binding," you'll see:

- `WebView`, to display webpages or HTML.

Chapter 19, "Collection views" covers these three views:

- `Picker`, selectable strings for program options.

- `ListView`, a scrollable list of data items of the same type.

- `TableView`, a list of items separated into categories, which is flexible enough to be used for data, forms, menus, or settings.

Two views are not covered in this edition of this book:

- `Map`, an interactive map display.

- `OpenGLView`, which allows a program to display 2-D and 3-D graphics by using the Open Graphics Library.

Slider and Stepper

Both `Slider` and `Stepper` let the user select a numeric value from a range. They have nearly identical programming interfaces but incorporate very different visual and interactive paradigms.

Slider basics

The Xamarin.Forms `Slider` is a horizontal bar that represents a range of values between a minimum at the left and a maximum at the right. (The Xamarin.Forms `Slider` does not support a vertical orientation.) The user selects a value on the `Slider` a little differently on the three platforms: On iOS devices, the user drags a round "thumb" along the horizontal bar. The Android and Windows 10 Mobile `Slider` views also have thumbs, but they are too small for a touch target, and the user can simply tap on the horizontal bar, or drag a finger to a specific location.

The `Slider` defines three public properties of type `double`, named `Minimum`, `Maximum`, and `Value`. Whenever the `Value` property changes, the `Slider` fires a `ValueChanged` event indicating the new value.

When displaying a `Slider` you'll want a little padding at the left and right to prevent the `Slider` from extending to the edges of the screen. The XAML file in the **SliderDemo** program applies the `Padding` to the `StackLayout`, which is parent to both a `Slider` and a `Label` that is intended to display the current value of the `Slider`:

```
<ContentPage xmlns="http://xamarin.com/schemas/2014/forms"
             xmlns:x="http://schemas.microsoft.com/winfx/2009/xaml"
             x:Class="SliderDemo.SliderDemoPage">

    <StackLayout Padding="10, 0">
        <Slider VerticalOptions="CenterAndExpand"
                ValueChanged="OnSliderValueChanged" />

        <Label x:Name="label"
               FontSize="Large"
               HorizontalOptions="Center"
               VerticalOptions="CenterAndExpand" />
    </StackLayout>
</ContentPage>
```

When the program starts up, the `Label` displays nothing, and the `Slider` thumb is positioned at the far left:

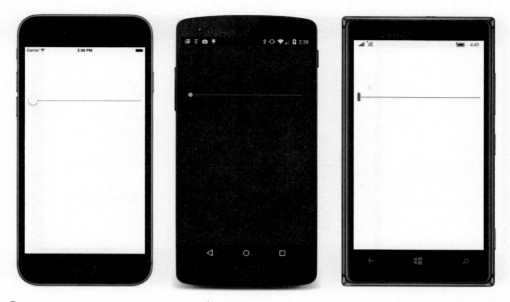

Do not set `HorizontalOptions` on the `Slider` to `Start`, `Center`, or `End` without also setting `WidthRequest` to an explicit value, or the `Slider` will collapse into a very small or even unusable width.

The `Slider` notifies code of changes to the `Value` property by firing the `ValueChanged` event. The event is fired if `Value` is changed programmatically or by user manipulation. Here's the **SliderDemo** code-behind file with the event handler:

```
public partial class SliderDemoPage : ContentPage
{
    public SliderDemoPage()
    {
        InitializeComponent();
    }

    void OnSliderValueChanged(object sender, ValueChangedEventArgs args)
    {
        label.Text = String.Format("Slider = {0}", args.NewValue);
    }
}
```

As usual, the first argument to the event handler is the object firing the event, in this case the `Slider`, and the second argument provides more information about this event. The handler for `ValueChanged` is of type `EventHandler<ValueChangedEventArgs>`, which means that the second argument to the handler is a `ValueChangedEventArgs` object. `ValueChangedEventArgs` defines two properties of type `double` named `OldValue` and `NewValue`. This particular handler simply uses `NewValue` in a string that it sets to the `Text` property of the `Label`:

A little experimentation reveals that the default `Minimum` and `Maximum` settings for `Slider` are 0 and 1. At the time this chapter is being written, the `Slider` on the Windows platforms has a default increment of 0.1. For other settings of `Minimum` and `Maximum`, the `Slider` is restricted to 10 increments or steps of 1, whichever is less. (A more flexible `Slider` is presented in Chapter 27, "Custom renderers.")

If you're not happy with the excessive number of decimal points displayed on the iOS screen, you can reduce the number of decimal places with a formatting specification in `String.Format`:

```
void OnSliderValueChanged(object sender, ValueChangedEventArgs args)
{
    label.Text = String.Format("Slider = {0:F2}", args.NewValue);
}
```

This is not the only way to write the `ValueChanged` handler. An alternative implementation involves casting the first argument to a `Slider` object and then accessing the `Value` property directly:

```
void OnSliderValueChanged(object sender, ValueChangedEventArgs args)
{
    Slider slider = (Slider)sender;
    label.Text = String.Format("Slider = {0}", slider.Value);
}
```

Using the `sender` argument is a good approach if you're sharing the event handler among multiple `Slider` views. By the time the `ValueChanged` event handler is called, the `Value` property already has its new value.

You can set the `Minimum` and `Maximum` properties of the `Slider` to any negative or positive value, with the stipulation that `Maximum` is always greater than `Minimum`. For example, try this:

```
<Slider ValueChanged="OnSliderValueChanged"
        Maximum="100"
        VerticalOptions="CenterAndExpand" />
```

Now the `Slider` value ranges from 0 to 100.

Common pitfalls

Suppose you want the `Slider` value to range from 1 to 100. You can set both `Minimum` and `Maximum` like this:

```
<Slider ValueChanged="OnSliderValueChanged"
        Minimum="1"
        Maximum="100"
        VerticalOptions="CenterAndExpand" />
```

However, when you run the new version of the program, an `ArgumentException` is raised with the text explanation "Value was an invalid value for Minimum." What does that mean?

When the XAML parser encounters the `Slider` tag, a `Slider` is instantiated, and then the properties and events are set in the order in which they appear in the `Slider` tag. But when the `Minimum` property is set to 1, the `Maximum` value now equals the `Minimum` value. That can't be. The `Maximum` property must be *greater* than the `Minimum`. The `Slider` signals this problem by raising an exception.

Internal to the `Slider` class, the `Minimum` and `Maximum` values are compared in a callback method set to the `validateValue` argument to the `BindableProperty.Create` method calls that create the `Minimum` and `Maximum` bindable properties. The `validateValue` callback returns `true` if `Minimum` is less than `Maximum`, indicating that the values are valid. A return value of `false` from this callback triggers the exception. This is the standard way that bindable properties implement validity checks.

This isn't a problem specific to XAML. It also happens if you instantiate and initialize the `Slider` properties in this order in code. The solution is to reverse the order that `Minimum` and `Maximum` are set. First set the `Maximum` property to 100. That's legal because now the range is between 0 and 100. Then set the `Minimum` property to 1:

```
<Slider ValueChanged="OnSliderValueChanged"
        Maximum="100"
        Minimum="1"
        VerticalOptions="CenterAndExpand" />
```

However, this results in another run-time error. Now it's a `NullReferenceException` in the `Value-Changed` handler. Why is that?

The `Value` property of the `Slider` must be within the range of `Minimum` and `Maximum` values, so when the `Minimum` property is set to 1, the `Slider` automatically adjust its `Value` property to 1.

Internally, `Value` is adjusted in a callback method set to the `coerceValue` argument of the `Bindable Property.Create` method calls for the `Minimum`, `Maximum`, and `Value` properties. The callback method returns an adjusted value of the property being set after being subjected to this coercion. In this example, when `Minimum` is set to 1, the `coerceValue` method sets the slider's `Value` property to 1, and the `coerceValue` callback returns the new value of `Minimum`, which remains at the value 1.

However, as a result of the coercion, the `Value` property has changed, and this causes the `Value Changed` event to fire. The `ValueChanged` handler in the code-behind file attempts to set the `Text` property of the `Label`, but the XAML parser has not yet instantiated the `Label` element. The `label` field is `null`.

There are a couple of solutions to this problem. The safest and most general solution is to check for a `null` value for `label` right in the event handler:

```
void OnSliderValueChanged(object sender, ValueChangedEventArgs args)
{
    if (label != null)
    {
        label.Text = String.Format("Slider = {0}", args.NewValue);
    }
}
```

However, you can also fix the problem by moving the assignment of the `ValueChanged` event in the tag to after the `Maximum` and `Minimum` properties have been set:

```
<Slider Maximum="100"
        Minimum="1"
        ValueChanged="OnSliderValueChanged"
        VerticalOptions="CenterAndExpand" />
```

The `Value` property is still coerced to 1 after the `Minimum` property is set, but the `ValueChanged` event handler has not yet been assigned, so no event is fired.

Let's assume that the `Slider` has the default range of 0 to 1. You might want the `Label` to display the initial value of the `Slider` when the program first starts up. You could initialize the `Text` property of the `Label` to "Slider = 0" in the XAML file, but if you ever wanted to change the text to something a little different, you'd need to change it in two places.

You might try giving the `Slider` a name of `slider` in the XAML file and then add some code to the constructor:

```
public SliderDemoPage()
{
    InitializeComponent();

    slider.Value = 0;
}
```

All the elements in the XAML file have been created and initialized when `InitializeComponent` returns, so if this code causes the `Slider` to fire a `ValueChanged` event, that shouldn't be a problem.

But it won't work. The value of the `Slider` is already 0, so setting it to 0 again does nothing. You could try this:

```
public SliderDemoPage()
{
    InitializeComponent();

    slider.Value = 1;
    slider.Value = 0;
}
```

That will work. But you might want to add a comment to the code so that another programmer doesn't later remove the statement that sets `Value` to 1 because it appears to be unnecessary.

Or you could simulate an event by calling the handler directly. The two arguments to the `Value-ChangedEventArgs` constructor are the old value and the new value (in that order), but the `On-SliderValueChanged` handler uses only the `NewValue` property, so it doesn't matter what the other argument is or whether they're equal:

```
public partial class SliderDemoPage : ContentPage
{
    public SliderDemoPage()
    {
        InitializeComponent();

        OnSliderValueChanged(null, new ValueChangedEventArgs(0, 0));
    }

    void OnSliderValueChanged(object sender, ValueChangedEventArgs args)
    {
        label.Text = String.Format("Slider = {0}", args.NewValue);
    }
}
```

That works as well. But remember to set the arguments to the call to `OnSliderValueChanged` so that they agree with what the handler expects. If you replaced the handler body with code that casts the `sender` argument to the `Slider` object, you then need a valid first argument in the `On-SliderValueChanged` call.

The problems involving the event handler disappear when you connect the `Label` with the `Slider` by using data bindings, which you'll learn about in the next chapter. You'll still need to set the properties of the `Slider` in the correct order, but you'll experience none of the problems with the event handler because the event handler will be gone.

Slider color selection

Here's a program named **RgbSliders** that contains three `Slider` elements for selecting red, green, and blue components of a `Color`. An implicit style for `Slider` sets the `Maximum` value to 255:

```
<ContentPage xmlns="http://xamarin.com/schemas/2014/forms"
```

```
                        xmlns:x="http://schemas.microsoft.com/winfx/2009/xaml"
              x:Class="RgbSliders.RgbSlidersPage">
    <ContentPage.Padding>
        <OnPlatform x:TypeArguments="Thickness"
                    iOS="10, 20, 10, 10"
                    Android="10, 0, 10, 10"
                    WinPhone="10, 0, 10, 10" />
    </ContentPage.Padding>

    <StackLayout>
        <StackLayout.Resources>
            <ResourceDictionary>
                <Style TargetType="Slider">
                    <Setter Property="Maximum" Value="255" />
                </Style>

                <Style TargetType="Label">
                    <Setter Property="FontSize" Value="Large" />
                    <Setter Property="HorizontalTextAlignment" Value="Center" />
                </Style>
            </ResourceDictionary>
        </StackLayout.Resources>

        <Slider x:Name="redSlider"
                ValueChanged="OnSliderValueChanged" />

        <Label x:Name="redLabel" />

        <Slider x:Name="greenSlider"
                ValueChanged="OnSliderValueChanged" />

        <Label x:Name="greenLabel" />

        <Slider x:Name="blueSlider"
                ValueChanged="OnSliderValueChanged" />

        <Label x:Name="blueLabel" />

        <BoxView x:Name="boxView"
                 VerticalOptions="FillAndExpand" />
    </StackLayout>
</ContentPage>
```

The Slider elements alternate with three Label elements to display their values, and the StackLayout concludes with a BoxView to show the resultant color.

The constructor of the code-behind file initializes the Slider settings to 128 for a medium gray.
The shared ValueChanged handler checks to see which Slider has changed, and hence which Label
needs to be updated, and then computes a new color for the BoxView:

```
public partial class RgbSlidersPage : ContentPage
{
    public RgbSlidersPage()
```

```
    {
        InitializeComponent();

        redSlider.Value = 128;
        greenSlider.Value = 128;
        blueSlider.Value = 128;
    }

    void OnSliderValueChanged(object sender, ValueChangedEventArgs args)
    {
        if (sender == redSlider)
        {
            redLabel.Text = String.Format("Red = {0:X2}", (int)redSlider.Value);
        }
        else if (sender == greenSlider)
        {
            greenLabel.Text = String.Format("Green = {0:X2}", (int)greenSlider.Value);
        }
        else if (sender == blueSlider)
        {
            blueLabel.Text = String.Format("Blue = {0:X2}", (int)blueSlider.Value);
        }

        boxView.Color = Color.FromRgb((int)redSlider.Value,
                                      (int)greenSlider.Value,
                                      (int)blueSlider.Value);
    }
}
```

Strictly speaking, the if and else statements here are not required. The code can simply set all three labels regardless of which slider is changing. The event handler accesses all three sliders anyway for setting a new color:

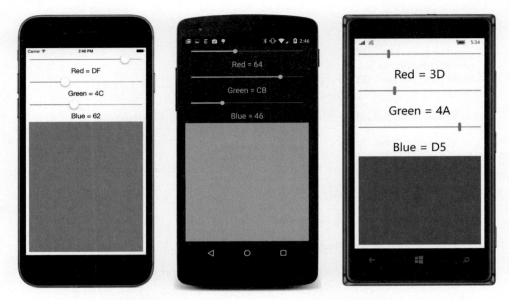

You can turn the phone sideways, but the `BoxView` becomes much shorter, particularly on the Windows 10 Mobile device, where the `Slider` seems to have a vertical height beyond what's required. Once the `Grid` is introduced in Chapter 18, you'll see how it becomes easier for applications to respond to orientation changes.

The following **TextFade** program uses a single `Slider` to control the `Opacity` and horizontal position of two `Label` elements in an `AbsoluteLayout`. In the initial layout, both `Label` elements are positioned at the left center of the `AbsoluteLayout`, but the second one has its `Opacity` set to 0:

```
<ContentPage xmlns="http://xamarin.com/schemas/2014/forms"
             xmlns:x="http://schemas.microsoft.com/winfx/2009/xaml"
             x:Class="TextFade.TextFadePage"
             Padding="10, 0, 10, 20">

    <StackLayout>
        <AbsoluteLayout VerticalOptions="CenterAndExpand">
            <Label x:Name="label1"
                   Text="TEXT"
                   FontSize="Large"
                   AbsoluteLayout.LayoutBounds="0, 0.5"
                   AbsoluteLayout.LayoutFlags="PositionProportional" />

            <Label x:Name="label2"
                   Text="FADE"
                   FontSize="Large"
                   Opacity="0"
                   AbsoluteLayout.LayoutBounds="0, 0.5"
                   AbsoluteLayout.LayoutFlags="PositionProportional" />
        </AbsoluteLayout>
```

```
        <Slider ValueChanged="OnSliderValueChanged" />

    </StackLayout>
</ContentPage>
```

The `Slider` event handler moves both `Label` elements from left to right across the screen. The proportional positioning helps a lot here because the `Slider` values range from 0 to 1, which results in the `Label` elements being positioned progressively from the far left to the far right of the screen:

```
public partial class TextFadePage : ContentPage
{
    public TextFadePage()
    {
        InitializeComponent();
    }

    void OnSliderValueChanged(object sender, ValueChangedEventArgs args)
    {
        AbsoluteLayout.SetLayoutBounds(label1,
            new Rectangle(args.NewValue, 0.5, AbsoluteLayout.AutoSize,
                                             AbsoluteLayout.AutoSize));
        AbsoluteLayout.SetLayoutBounds(label2,
            new Rectangle(args.NewValue, 0.5, AbsoluteLayout.AutoSize,
                                             AbsoluteLayout.AutoSize));

        label1.Opacity = 1 - args.NewValue;
        label2.Opacity = args.NewValue;
    }
}
```

At the same time, the `Opacity` values are set so that one `Label` seems to fade into the other as both labels move across the screen:

The Stepper difference

The `Stepper` view has very nearly the same programming interface as the `Slider`: It has `Minimum`, `Maximum`, and `Value` properties of type `double` and fires a `ValueChanged` event handler.

However, the `Maximum` property of `Stepper` has a default value of 100, and `Stepper` also adds an `Increment` property with a default value of 1. The `Stepper` visuals consist solely of two buttons labeled with minus and plus signs. Presses of those two buttons change the value incrementally between `Minimum` to `Maximum` based on the `Increment` property.

Although `Value` and other properties of `Stepper` are of type `double`, `Stepper` is often used for the selection of integral values. You probably don't want the value of ((`Maximum` – `Minimum`) ÷ `Increment`) to be as high as 100, as the default values suggest. If you press and hold your finger on one of the buttons, you'll trigger a typematic repeat on iOS, but not on Android or Windows 10 Mobile. Unless your program provides another way for the user to change the `Stepper` value (perhaps with a text `Entry` view), you don't want to force the user to press a button 100 times to get from `Minimum` to `Maximum`.

The **StepperDemo** program sets the `Maximum` property of the `Stepper` to 10 and uses the `Stepper` as a rudimentary design aid in determining an optimum border width for a `Button` border. The `Button` at the top of the `StackLayout` is solely for display purposes and has the necessary property settings of `BackgroundColor` and `BorderColor` to enable the border display on Android and Windows 10 Mobile.

The `Stepper` is the last child in the following `StackLayout`. Between the `Button` and `Stepper` are a pair of `Label` elements for displaying the current `Stepper` value:

```
<ContentPage xmlns="http://xamarin.com/schemas/2014/forms"
             xmlns:x="http://schemas.microsoft.com/winfx/2009/xaml"
             x:Class="StepperDemo.StepperDemoPage">

    <StackLayout>
        <Button x:Name="button"
                Text="  Sample Button  "
                FontSize="Large"
                HorizontalOptions="Center"
                VerticalOptions="CenterAndExpand">
            <Button.BackgroundColor>
                <OnPlatform x:TypeArguments="Color"
                            Android="#404040" />
            </Button.BackgroundColor>
            <Button.BorderColor>
                <OnPlatform x:TypeArguments="Color"
                            Android="#C0C0C0"
                            WinPhone="Black" />
            </Button.BorderColor>
        </Button>

        <StackLayout VerticalOptions="CenterAndExpand">

            <StackLayout Orientation="Horizontal"
                         HorizontalOptions="Center">
                <StackLayout.Resources>
                    <ResourceDictionary>
                        <Style TargetType="Label">
                            <Setter Property="FontSize" Value="Medium" />
                        </Style>
                    </ResourceDictionary>
                </StackLayout.Resources>

                <Label Text="Button Border Width =" />
                <Label x:Name="label" />
            </StackLayout>

            <Stepper x:Name="stepper"
                     Maximum="10"
                     ValueChanged="OnStepperValueChanged"
                     HorizontalOptions="Center" />

        </StackLayout>
    </StackLayout>
</ContentPage>
```

The `Label` displaying the `Stepper` value is initialized from the constructor of the code-behind file. With each change in the `Value` property of the `Stepper`, the event handler displays the new value and sets the `Button` border width:

```
public partial class StepperDemoPage : ContentPage
{
    public StepperDemoPage()
    {
```

```
        InitializeComponent();

        // Initialize display.
        OnStepperValueChanged(stepper, null);
    }

    void OnStepperValueChanged(object sender, ValueChangedEventArgs args)
    {
        Stepper stepper = (Stepper)sender;
        button.BorderWidth = stepper.Value;
        label.Text = stepper.Value.ToString("F0");
    }
}
```

Switch and CheckBox

Application programs often need Boolean input from the user, which requires some way for the user to toggle a program option to On or Off, Yes or No, True or False, or however you want to think of it. In Xamarin.Forms, this is a view called the `Switch`.

Switch basics

`Switch` defines just one property on its own, named `IsToggled` of type `bool`, and it fires the `Toggled` event to indicate a change in this property. In code, you might be inclined to give a `Switch` a name of `switch`, but that's a C# keyword, so you'll want to pick something else. In XAML, however, you can set the `x:Name` attribute to `switch`, and the XAML parser will smartly create a field named

@switch, which is how C# allows you to define a variable name using a C# keyword.

The **SwitchDemo** program creates two `Switch` elements with two identifying labels: "Italic" and "Boldface". Each `Switch` has its own event handler, which formats the larger `Label` at the bottom of the `StackLayout`:

```
<ContentPage xmlns="http://xamarin.com/schemas/2014/forms"
             xmlns:x="http://schemas.microsoft.com/winfx/2009/xaml"
             x:Class="SwitchDemo.SwitchDemoPage">

    <StackLayout Padding="10, 0">
        <StackLayout HorizontalOptions="Center"
                     VerticalOptions="CenterAndExpand">
            <StackLayout Orientation="Horizontal"
                         HorizontalOptions="End">
                <Label Text="Italic: "
                       VerticalOptions="Center" />
                <Switch Toggled="OnItalicSwitchToggled"
                        VerticalOptions="Center" />
            </StackLayout>

            <StackLayout Orientation="Horizontal"
                         HorizontalOptions="End">
                <Label Text="Boldface: "
                       VerticalOptions="Center" />
                <Switch Toggled="OnBoldSwitchToggled"
                        VerticalOptions="Center" />
            </StackLayout>
        </StackLayout>

        <Label x:Name="label"
               Text=
"Just a little passage of some sample text that can be formatted
in italic or boldface by toggling the two Switch elements."
               FontSize="Large"
               HorizontalTextAlignment="Center"
               VerticalOptions="CenterAndExpand" />

    </StackLayout>
</ContentPage>
```

The `Toggled` event handler has a second argument of `ToggledEventArgs`, which has a `Value` property of type `bool` that indicates the new state of the `IsToggled` property. The event handlers in **SwitchDemo** use this value to set or clear the particular `FontAttributes` flag in the `FontAttributes` property of the long `Label`:

```
public partial class SwitchDemoPage : ContentPage
{
    public SwitchDemoPage()
    {
        InitializeComponent();
    }
```

```
    void OnItalicSwitchToggled(object sender, ToggledEventArgs args)
    {
        if (args.Value)
        {
            label.FontAttributes |= FontAttributes.Italic;
        }
        else
        {
            label.FontAttributes &= ~FontAttributes.Italic;
        }
    }

    void OnBoldSwitchToggled(object sender, ToggledEventArgs args)
    {
        if (args.Value)
        {
            label.FontAttributes |= FontAttributes.Bold;
        }
        else
        {
            label.FontAttributes &= ~FontAttributes.Bold;
        }
    }
}
```

The `Switch` has a different appearance on the three platforms:

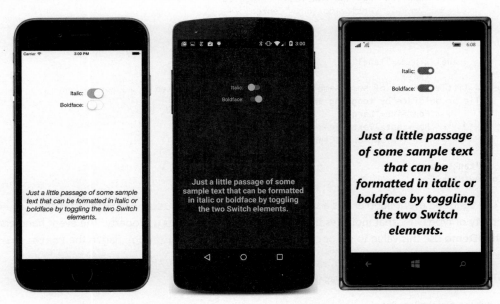

Notice that the program aligns the two `Switch` views, which gives it a more attractive look, but which also means that the text labels are necessarily somewhat misaligned. To accomplish this formatting, the XAML file puts each of the pair of `Label` and `Switch` elements in a horizontal `StackLayout`.

Each horizontal `StackLayout` has its `HorizontalOptions` set to `End`, which aligns each `StackLay-out` at the right, and a parent `StackLayout` centers the collection of labels and switches on the screen with a `HorizontalOptions` setting of `Center`. Within the horizontal `StackLayout`, both views have their `VerticalOptions` properties set to `Center`. If the `Switch` is taller than the `Label`, then the `Label` is vertically centered relative to the `Switch`. But if the `Label` is taller than the `Switch`, the `Switch` is also vertically centered relative to the `Label`.

A traditional CheckBox

In more traditional graphical environments, the user-interface object that allows users to choose a Boolean value is called a `CheckBox`, usually featuring some text with a box that can be empty or filled with an X or a check mark. One advantage of the `CheckBox` over the `Switch` is that the text identifier is part of the visual and doesn't need to be added with a separate `Label`.

One way to create custom views in Xamarin.Forms is by writing special classes called *renderers* that are specific to each platform and that reference views in each platform. That is demonstrated in Chapter 27.

However, it's also possible to create custom views right in Xamarin.Forms by assembling a view from other views. You first derive a class from `ContentView`, set its `Content` property to a `StackLayout` (for example), and then add one or more views on that. (You saw an example of this technique in the `ColorView` class in Chapter 8.) You'll probably also need to define one or more properties, and possibly some events, but you'll want to take advantage of the bindable infrastructure established by the `BindableObject` and `BindableProperty` classes. That allows your properties to be styled and to be targets of data bindings.

A `CheckBox` consists of just two `Label` elements on a `ContentView`: one `Label` displays the text associated with the `CheckBox`, while the other displays a box. A `TapGestureRecognizer` detects when the `CheckBox` is tapped.

A `CheckBox` class has already been added to the **Xamarin.FormsBook.Toolkit** library that is included in the downloadable code for this book. Here's how you would do it on your own:

In Visual Studio, you can select **Forms Xaml Page** from the **Add New Item** dialog box. However, this creates a class that derives from `ContentPage` when you really want a class that derives from `ContentView`. Simply change the root element of the XAML file from `ContentPage` to `ContentView`, and change the base class in the code-behind file from `ContentPage` to `ContentView`.

In Xamarin Studio, however, you can simply choose **Forms ContentView Xaml** from the **New File** dialog.

Here's the CheckBox.xaml file:

```
<ContentView xmlns="http://xamarin.com/schemas/2014/forms"
             xmlns:x="http://schemas.microsoft.com/winfx/2009/xaml"
             x:Class="Xamarin.FormsBook.Toolkit.CheckBox">
```

```
    <StackLayout Orientation="Horizontal">
        <Label x:Name="boxLabel" Text="&#x2610;" />
        <Label x:Name="textLabel" />
    </StackLayout>

    <ContentView.GestureRecognizers>
        <TapGestureRecognizer Tapped="OnCheckBoxTapped" />
    </ContentView.GestureRecognizers>
</ContentView>
```

That Unicode character \u2610 is called the Ballot Box character, and it's just an empty square. Character \u2611 is a Ballot Box with Check, while \u2612 is a Ballot Box with X. To indicate a checked state, this CheckBox code-behind file sets the Text property of boxLabel to \u2611 (as you'll see shortly).

The code-behind file of CheckBox defines three properties:

- Text

- FontSize

- IsChecked

CheckBox also defines an event named IsCheckedChanged.

Should CheckBox also define FontAttributes and FontFamily properties like Label and Button do? Perhaps, but these additional properties are not quite as crucial for views devoted to user interaction.

All three of the properties that CheckBox defines are backed by bindable properties. The code-behind file creates all three BindableProperty objects, and the property-changed handlers are defined as lambda functions within these methods.

Keep in mind that the property-changed handlers are static, so they need to cast the first argument to a CheckBox object to reference the instance properties and events in the class. The property-changed handler for IsChecked is responsible for changing the character representing the checked and unchecked state and firing the IsCheckedChanged event:

```
namespace Xamarin.FormsBook.Toolkit
{
    public partial class CheckBox : ContentView
    {
        public static readonly BindableProperty TextProperty =
            BindableProperty.Create(
                "Text",
                typeof(string),
                typeof(CheckBox),
                null,
                propertyChanged: (bindable, oldValue, newValue) =>
                {
                    ((CheckBox)bindable).textLabel.Text = (string)newValue;
                });
```

```csharp
public static readonly BindableProperty FontSizeProperty =
    BindableProperty.Create(
        "FontSize",
        typeof(double),
        typeof(CheckBox),
        Device.GetNamedSize(NamedSize.Default, typeof(Label)),
        propertyChanged: (bindable, oldValue, newValue) =>
        {
            CheckBox checkbox = (CheckBox)bindable;
            checkbox.boxLabel.FontSize = (double)newValue;
            checkbox.textLabel.FontSize = (double)newValue;
        });

public static readonly BindableProperty IsCheckedProperty =
    BindableProperty.Create(
        "IsChecked",
        typeof(bool),
        typeof(CheckBox),
        false,
        propertyChanged: (bindable, oldValue, newValue) =>
        {
            // Set the graphic.
            CheckBox checkbox = (CheckBox)bindable;
            checkbox.boxLabel.Text = (bool)newValue ? "\u2611" : "\u2610";

            // Fire the event.
            EventHandler<bool> eventHandler = checkbox.CheckedChanged;
            if (eventHandler != null)
            {
                eventHandler(checkbox, (bool)newValue);
            }
        });

public event EventHandler<bool> CheckedChanged;

public CheckBox()
{
    InitializeComponent();
}

public string Text
{
    set { SetValue(TextProperty, value); }
    get { return (string)GetValue(TextProperty); }
}

[TypeConverter(typeof(FontSizeConverter))]
public double FontSize
{
    set { SetValue(FontSizeProperty, value); }
    get { return (double)GetValue(FontSizeProperty); }
}
```

```
        public bool IsChecked
        {
            set { SetValue(IsCheckedProperty, value); }
            get { return (bool)GetValue(IsCheckedProperty); }
        }

        // TapGestureRecognizer handler.
        void OnCheckBoxTapped(object sender, EventArgs args)
        {
            IsChecked = !IsChecked;
        }
    }
}
```

Notice the `TypeConverter` on the `FontSize` property. That allows the property to be set in XAML with attribute values such as "Small" and "Large".

The `Tapped` handler for the `TapGestureRecognizer` is at the bottom of the class and simply toggles the `IsChecked` property by using the C# logical negation operator. An even shorter statement to toggle a Boolean variable uses the exclusive-OR assignment operator:

```
IsChecked ^= true;
```

The **CheckBoxDemo** program is very similar to the **SwitchDemo** program except that the markup is considerably simplified because the `CheckBox` includes its own `Text` property:

```
<ContentPage xmlns="http://xamarin.com/schemas/2014/forms"
             xmlns:x="http://schemas.microsoft.com/winfx/2009/xaml"
             xmlns:toolkit=
                 "clr-namespace:Xamarin.FormsBook.Toolkit;assembly=Xamarin.FormsBook.Toolkit"
             x:Class="CheckBoxDemo.CheckBoxDemoPage">

    <StackLayout Padding="10, 0">
        <StackLayout HorizontalOptions="Center"
                     VerticalOptions="CenterAndExpand">

            <toolkit:CheckBox Text="Italic"
                              FontSize="Large"
                              CheckedChanged="OnItalicCheckBoxChanged" />

            <toolkit:CheckBox Text="Boldface"
                              FontSize="Large"
                              CheckedChanged="OnBoldCheckBoxChanged" />
        </StackLayout>

        <Label x:Name="label"
               Text=
"Just a little passage of some sample text that can be formatted
in italic or boldface by toggling the two custom CheckBox views."
               FontSize="Large"
               HorizontalTextAlignment="Center"
               VerticalOptions="CenterAndExpand" />
    </StackLayout>
```

```
</ContentPage>
```

The code-behind file is also very similar to the earlier program:

```
public partial class CheckBoxDemoPage : ContentPage
{
    public CheckBoxDemoPage()
    {
        InitializeComponent();
    }

    void OnItalicCheckBoxChanged(object sender, bool isChecked)
    {
        if (isChecked)
        {
            label.FontAttributes |= FontAttributes.Italic;
        }
        else
        {
            label.FontAttributes &= ~FontAttributes.Italic;
        }
    }

    void OnBoldCheckBoxChanged(object sender, bool isChecked)
    {
        if (isChecked)
        {
            label.FontAttributes |= FontAttributes.Bold;
        }
        else
        {
            label.FontAttributes &= ~FontAttributes.Bold;
        }
    }
}
```

Interestingly, the character for the checked box shows up in color on the Android and Windows platforms:

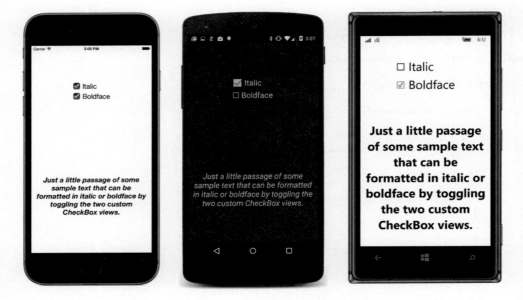

Typing text

Xamarin.Forms defines three views for obtaining text input from the user:

- `Entry` for a single line of text.

- `Editor` for multiple lines of text.

- `SearchBar` for a single line of text specifically for search operations.

Both `Entry` and `Editor` derive from `InputView`, which derives from `View`. `SearchBar` derives directly from `View`.

Both `Entry` and `SearchBar` implement horizontal scrolling if the entered text exceeds the width of the view. The `Editor` implements word wrapping and is capable of vertical scrolling for text that exceeds its height.

Keyboard and focus

`Entry`, `Editor`, and `SearchBar` are different from all the other views in that they make use of the phone's onscreen keyboard, sometimes called the *virtual keyboard*. From the user's perspective, tapping the `Entry`, `Editor`, or `SearchBar` view invokes the onscreen keyboard, which slides in from the bottom. Tapping anywhere else on the screen (except another `Entry`, `Editor`, or `SearchBar` view) often makes the keyboard go away, and sometimes the keyboard can be dismissed in other ways.

From the program's perspective, the presence of the keyboard is closely related to *input focus*, a concept that originated in desktop graphical user interface environments. On both desktop environments and mobile devices, input from the keyboard can be directed to only one user-interface object at a time, and that object must be clearly selectable and identifiable by the user. The object that receives keyboard input is known as the object with *keyboard input focus*, or more simply, just *input focus* or *focus*.

The `VisualElement` class defines several methods, properties, and events related to input focus:

- The `Focus` method attempts to set input focus to a visual element and returns `true` if successful.

- The `Unfocus` method removes input focus from a visual element.

- The `IsFocused` get-only property is `true` if a visual element currently has input focus.

- The `Focused` event is fired when a visual element acquires input focus.

- The `Unfocused` event is fired when a visual element loses input focus.

As you know, mobile environments make far less use of the keyboard than desktop environments do, and most mobile views (such as the `Slider`, `Stepper`, and `Switch` that you've already seen) don't make use of the keyboard at all. Although these five focus-related members of the `VisualElement` class appear to implement a generalized system for passing input focus between visual elements, they really only pertain to `Entry`, `Editor`, and `SearchBar`.

These views signal that they have input focus with a flashing caret showing the text input point, and they trigger the keyboard to slide up. When the view loses input focus, the keyboard slides back down.

A view must have its `IsEnabled` property set to `true` (the default state) to acquire input focus, and of course the `IsVisible` property must also be `true` or the view won't be on the screen at all.

Choosing the keyboard

`Entry` and `Editor` are different from `SearchBar` in that they both derive from `InputView`. Interestingly, although `Entry` and `Editor` define similar properties and events, `InputView` defines just one property: `Keyboard`. This property allows a program to select the type of keyboard that is displayed. For example, a keyboard for typing a URL should be different from a keyboard for entering a phone number. All three platforms have various styles of virtual keyboards appropriate for different types of text input. A program cannot select the keyboard used for `SearchBar`.

This `Keyboard` property is of type `Keyboard`, a class that defines seven static read-only properties of type `Keyboard` appropriate for different keyboard uses:

- `Default`

- `Text`

- `Chat`

- `Url`

- `Email`

- `Telephone`

- `Numeric`

On all three platforms, the `Numeric` keyboard allows typing decimal points but does not allow typing a negative sign, so it's limited to positive numbers.

The following program creates seven `Entry` views that let you see how these keyboards are implemented in the three platforms. The particular keyboard attached to each `Entry` is identified by a property defined by `Entry` named `Placeholder`. This is the text that appears in the `Entry` prior to anything the user types as a hint for the nature of the text the program is expecting. Placeholder text is commonly a short phrase such as "First Name" or "Email Address":

```
<ContentPage xmlns="http://xamarin.com/schemas/2014/forms"
             xmlns:x="http://schemas.microsoft.com/winfx/2009/xaml"
             x:Class="EntryKeyboards.EntryKeyboardsPage">

    <ContentPage.Padding>
        <OnPlatform x:TypeArguments="Thickness"
                    iOS="10, 20, 10, 0"
                    Android="10, 0"
                    WinPhone="10, 0" />
    </ContentPage.Padding>

    <ScrollView>
        <StackLayout>
            <StackLayout.Resources>
                <ResourceDictionary>
                    <Style TargetType="Entry">
                        <Setter Property="VerticalOptions" Value="CenterAndExpand" />
                    </Style>
                </ResourceDictionary>
            </StackLayout.Resources>

            <Entry Placeholder="Default"
                   Keyboard="Default" />

            <Entry Placeholder="Text"
                   Keyboard="Text" />

            <Entry Placeholder="Chat"
                   Keyboard="Chat" />

            <Entry Placeholder="Url"
                   Keyboard="Url" />

            <Entry Placeholder="Email"
```

```
                Keyboard="Email" />

        <Entry Placeholder="Telephone"
               Keyboard="Telephone" />

        <Entry Placeholder="Numeric"
               Keyboard="Numeric" />
    </StackLayout>
  </ScrollView>
</ContentPage>
```

The placeholders appear as gray text. Here's how the display looks when the program first begins to run:

Just as with the `Slider`, you don't want to set `HorizontalOptions` on an `Entry` to `Left`, `Center`, or `Right` unless you also set the `WidthRequest` property. If you do so, the `Entry` collapses to a very small width. It can still be used—the `Entry` automatically provides horizontal scrolling for text longer than the `Entry` can display—but you should really try to provide an adequate size. In this program each `Entry` is as wide as the screen minus a 10-unit padding on the left and right.

You can estimate an adequate `WidthRequest` through experimentation with different text lengths. The next program in this chapter sets the `Entry` width to a value equivalent to one inch.

The **EntryKeyboards** program evenly spaces the seven `Entry` views vertically using a `Vertical-Options` value of `CenterAndExpand` set through an implicit style. Clearly there is enough vertical room for all seven `Entry` views, so you might be puzzled about the use of the `ScrollView` in the XAML file.

The `ScrollView` is specifically for iOS. If you tap an `Entry` close to the bottom of the Android or

Windows 10 Mobile screen, the operating system will automatically move up the contents of the page when the keyboard pops up, so the `Entry` is still visible while you are typing. But iOS doesn't do that unless a `ScrollView` is provided.

Here's how each screen looks when text is being typed in one of the `Entry` views toward the bottom of the screen:

Entry properties and events

Besides inheriting the `Keyboard` property from `InputView`, `Entry` defines four more properties, only one of which you saw in the previous program:

- `Text` — the string that appears in the `Entry`

- `TextColor` — a `Color` value

- `IsPassword` — a Boolean that causes characters to be masked right after they're typed

- `Placeholder` — light-colored text that appears in the `Entry` but disappears as soon as the user begins typing.

Generally, a program obtains what the user typed by accessing the `Text` property, but the program can also initialize the `Text` property. Perhaps the program wishes to suggest some text input.

The `Entry` also defines two events:

- `TextChanged`

- Completed

The `TextChanged` event is fired for every change in the `Text` property, which generally corresponds to every keystroke (except shift and some special keys). A program can monitor this event to perform validity checks. For example, you might check for valid numbers or valid email addresses to enable a **Calculate** or **Send** button.

The `Completed` event is fired when the user presses a particular key on the keyboard to indicate that the text is completed. This key is platform specific:

- iOS: The key is labeled **return**, which is not on the `Telephone` or `Numeric` keyboard.

- Android: The key is a green check mark in the lower-right corner of the keyboard.

- Windows Phone: The key is an enter (or return) symbol (↵) on most keyboards but is a go symbol (→) on the `Url` keyboard. Such a key is not present on the `Telephone` and `Numeric` keyboards.

On iOS and Android, the completed key dismisses the keyboard in addition to generating the `Completed` event. On Windows 10 Mobile it does not.

Android and Windows users can also dismiss the keyboard by using the phone's **Back** button at the bottom left of the portrait screen. This causes the `Entry` to lose input focus but does not cause the `Completed` event to fire.

Let's write a program named **QuadraticEquations** that solves quadratic equations, which are equations of the form:

$$ax^2 + bx + c = 0$$

For any three constants *a*, *b*, and *c*, the program uses the quadratic equation to solve for *x*:

$$x = \frac{-b \pm \sqrt{b^2 - 4ac}}{2a}$$

You enter a, b, and c in three `Entry` views and then press a `Button` labeled **Solve for x**.

Here's the XAML file. Unfortunately, the `Numeric` keyboard is not suitable for this program because on all three platforms it does not allow entering negative numbers. For that reason, no particular keyboard is specified:

```
<ContentPage xmlns="http://xamarin.com/schemas/2014/forms"
             xmlns:x="http://schemas.microsoft.com/winfx/2009/xaml"
             x:Class="QuadaticEquations.QuadraticEquationsPage">

    <ContentPage.Resources>
        <ResourceDictionary>
            <Style TargetType="Label">
                <Setter Property="FontSize" Value="Medium" />
                <Setter Property="VerticalOptions" Value="Center" />
            </Style>
```

```xml
                        <Style TargetType="Entry">
                            <Setter Property="WidthRequest" Value="180" />
                        </Style>
                    </ResourceDictionary>
                </ContentPage.Resources>

                <StackLayout>
                    <!-- Entry section -->
                    <StackLayout Padding="20, 0, 0, 0"
                                 VerticalOptions="CenterAndExpand"
                                 HorizontalOptions="Center">

                        <StackLayout Orientation="Horizontal">
                            <Entry x:Name="entryA"
                                   TextChanged="OnEntryTextChanged"
                                   Completed="OnEntryCompleted" />
                            <Label Text=" x&#178; +" />
                        </StackLayout>

                        <StackLayout Orientation="Horizontal">
                            <Entry x:Name="entryB"
                                   TextChanged="OnEntryTextChanged"
                                   Completed="OnEntryCompleted" />
                            <Label Text=" x +" />
                        </StackLayout>

                        <StackLayout Orientation="Horizontal">
                            <Entry x:Name="entryC"
                                   TextChanged="OnEntryTextChanged"
                                   Completed="OnEntryCompleted" />
                            <Label Text=" = 0" />
                        </StackLayout>
                    </StackLayout>

                    <!-- Button -->
                    <Button x:Name="solveButton"
                            Text="Solve for x"
                            FontSize="Large"
                            IsEnabled="False"
                            VerticalOptions="CenterAndExpand"
                            HorizontalOptions="Center"
                            Clicked="OnSolveButtonClicked" />

                    <!-- Results section -->
                    <StackLayout VerticalOptions="CenterAndExpand"
                                 HorizontalOptions="Center">
                        <Label x:Name="solution1Label"
                               HorizontalTextAlignment="Center" />

                        <Label x:Name="solution2Label"
                               HorizontalTextAlignment="Center" />
                    </StackLayout>
                </StackLayout>
            </ContentPage>
```

The `Label`, `Entry`, and `Button` views are divided into three sections: data input at the top, the `Button` in the middle, and the results at the bottom. Notice the platform-specific `WidthRequest` setting in the implicit `Style` for the `Entry`. This gives each `Entry` a one-inch width.

The program provides two ways to trigger a calculation: by pressing the completion key on the keyboard, or by pressing the `Button` in the middle of the page. Another option in a program such as this would be to perform the calculation for every keystroke (or to be more accurate, every `TextChanged` event). That would work here because the recalculation is very quick. However, in the present design the results are near the bottom of the screen and are covered when the virtual keyboard is active, so the page would have to be reorganized for such a scheme to make sense.

The **QuadraticEquations** program uses the `TextChanged` event but solely to determine the validity of the text typed into each `Entry`. The text is passed to `Double.TryParse`, and if the method returns `false`, the `Entry` text is displayed in red. (On Windows 10 Mobile, the red text coloring shows up only when the `Entry` loses input focus.) Also, the `Button` is enabled only if all three `Entry` views contain valid `double` values. Here's the first half of the code-behind file that shows all the program interaction:

```
public partial class QuadraticEquationsPage : ContentPage
{
    public QuadraticEquationsPage()
    {
        InitializeComponent();

        // Initialize Entry views.
        entryA.Text = "1";
        entryB.Text = "-1";
        entryC.Text = "-1";
    }

    void OnEntryTextChanged(object sender, TextChangedEventArgs args)
    {
        // Clear out solutions.
        solution1Label.Text = " ";
        solution2Label.Text = " ";

        // Color current entry text based on validity.
        Entry entry = (Entry)sender;
        double result;
        entry.TextColor = Double.TryParse(entry.Text, out result) ? Color.Default : Color.Red;

        // Enable the button based on validity.
        solveButton.IsEnabled = Double.TryParse(entryA.Text, out result) &&
                                Double.TryParse(entryB.Text, out result) &&
                                Double.TryParse(entryC.Text, out result);
    }

    void OnEntryCompleted(object sender, EventArgs args)
    {
        if (solveButton.IsEnabled)
        {
            Solve();
```

```
        }
    }

    void OnSolveButtonClicked(object sender, EventArgs args)
    {
        Solve();
    }
    …
}
```

The `Completed` handler for the `Entry` calls the `Solve` method only when the `Button` is enabled, which (as you've seen) indicates that all three `Entry` views contain valid values. Therefore, the `Solve` method can safely assume that all three `Entry` views contain valid numbers that won't cause `Double.Parse` to raise an exception.

The `Solve` method is necessarily complicated because the quadratic equation might have one or two solutions, and each solution might have an imaginary part as well as a real part. The method initializes the real part of the second solution to `Double.NaN` ("not a number") and displays the second result only if that's no longer the case. The imaginary parts are displayed only if they're nonzero, and either a plus sign or an en dash (Unicode \u2013) connects the real and imaginary parts:

```
public partial class QuadraticEquationsPage : ContentPage
{
    …
    void Solve()
    {
        double a = Double.Parse(entryA.Text);
        double b = Double.Parse(entryB.Text);
        double c = Double.Parse(entryC.Text);
        double solution1Real = 0;
        double solution1Imag = 0;
        double solution2Real = Double.NaN;
        double solution2Imag = 0;
        string str1 = " ";
        string str2 = " ";

        if (a == 0 && b == 0 && c == 0)
        {
            str1 = "x = anything";
        }
        else if (a == 0 && b == 0)
        {
            str1 = "x = nothing";
        }
        else
        {
            if (a == 0)
            {
                solution1Real = -c / b;
            }
            else
            {
```

```
                double discriminant = b * b - 4 * a * c;

                if (discriminant == 0)
                {
                    solution1Real = -b / (2 * a);
                }
                else if (discriminant > 0)
                {
                    solution1Real = (-b + Math.Sqrt(discriminant)) / (2 * a);
                    solution2Real = (-b - Math.Sqrt(discriminant)) / (2 * a);
                }
                else
                {
                    solution1Real = -b / (2 * a);
                    solution2Real = solution1Real;

                    solution1Imag = Math.Sqrt(-discriminant) / (2 * a);
                    solution2Imag = -solution1Imag;
                }
            }
            str1 = Format(solution1Real, solution1Imag);
            str2 = Format(solution2Real, solution2Imag);
        }
        solution1Label.Text = str1;
        solution2Label.Text = str2;
    }

    string Format(double real, double imag)
    {
        string str = " ";

        if (!Double.IsNaN(real))
        {
            str = String.Format("x = {0:F5}", real);

            if (imag != 0)
            {
                str += String.Format(" {0} {1:F5} i",
                                     Math.Sign(imag) == 1 ? "+" : "\u2013",
                                     Math.Abs(imag));
            }
        }
        return str;
    }
}
```

Here are a couple of solutions:

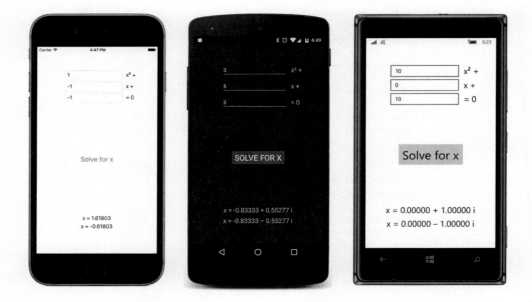

The Editor difference

You might assume that the `Editor` has a more extensive API than the `Entry` because it can handle multiple lines and even paragraphs of text. But in Xamarin.Forms, the API for `Editor` is actually somewhat simpler. Besides inheriting the `Keyboard` property from `InputView`, `Editor` defines just one property on its own: the essential `Text` property. `Editor` also defines the same two events as `Entry`:

- `TextChanged`

- `Completed`

However, the `Completed` event is of necessity a little different. While a return or enter key can signal completion on an `Entry`, these same keys used with the `Editor` instead mark the end of a paragraph.

The `Completed` event for `Editor` works a little differently on the three platforms: For iOS, Xamarin.Forms displays a special **Done** button above the keyboard that dismisses the keyboard and causes a `Completed` event to fire. On Android and Windows 10 Mobile, the system **Back** button—the button at the lower-left corner of the phone in portrait mode—dismisses the keyboard and fires the `Completed` event. This **Back** button does *not* fire the `Completed` event for an `Entry` view, but it does dismiss the keyboard.

It is likely that what users type into an `Editor` is not telephone numbers and URLs but actual words, sentences, and paragraphs. In most cases, you'll want to use the `Text` keyboard for `Editor` because it provides spelling checks, suggestions, and automatic capitalization of the first word of sentences. If you don't want these features, the `Keyboard` class provides an alternative means of specifying a keyboard by using a static `Create` method and the following members of the `KeyboardFlags` enumeration:

- `CapitalizeSentence` (equal to 1)

- `Spellcheck` (2)

- `Suggestions` (4)

- `All` (\xFFFFFFFF)

The `Text` keyboard is equivalent to creating the keyboard with `KeyboardFlags.All`. The `Default` keyboard is equivalent to creating the keyboard with `(KeyboardFlags)0`. You can't create a keyboard in XAML using these flags. It must be done in code.

The **JustNotes** program is intended as a freeform note-taking program that automatically saves and restores the contents of an `Editor` view by using the `Properties` collection of the `Application` class. The page basically consists of a large `Editor`, but to give the user some clue about what the program does, the name of the program is displayed at the top. On iOS and Android, such text can be set by the `Title` property of the page, but to display that property, the `ContentPage` must be wrapped in an `ApplicationPage` (as you discovered with the **ToolbarDemo** program in Chapter 13). That's done in the constructor of the `App` class:

```
public class App : Application
{
    public App()
    {
        MainPage = new NavigationPage(new JustNotesPage());
    }

    protected override void OnStart()
    {
        // Handle when your app starts
    }

    protected override void OnSleep()
    {
        // Handle when your app sleeps
        ((JustNotesPage)(((NavigationPage)MainPage).CurrentPage)).OnSleep();
    }

    protected override void OnResume()
    {
        // Handle when your app resumes
    }
}
```

The `OnSleep` method in `App` calls a method also named `OnSleep` defined in the `JustNotesPage` code-behind file. This is how the contents of the `Editor` are saved in application memory.

The root element of the XAML page sets the `Title` property. The remainder of the page is occupied by an `AbsoluteLayout` filled with the `Editor`:

```
<ContentPage xmlns="http://xamarin.com/schemas/2014/forms"
```

```xml
            xmlns:x="http://schemas.microsoft.com/winfx/2009/xaml"
            x:Class="JustNotes.JustNotesPage"
            Title="Just Notes">

    <StackLayout>
        <AbsoluteLayout VerticalOptions="FillAndExpand">
            <Editor x:Name="editor"
                    Keyboard="Text"
                    AbsoluteLayout.LayoutBounds="0, 0, 1, 1"
                    AbsoluteLayout.LayoutFlags="All"
                    Focused="OnEditorFocused"
                    Unfocused="OnEditorUnfocused" />
        </AbsoluteLayout>
    </StackLayout>
</ContentPage>
```

So why does the program use an `AbsoluteLayout` to host the `Editor`?

The **JustNotes** program is a work in progress. It doesn't quite work right for iOS. As you'll recall, when an `Entry` view is positioned toward the bottom of the screen, you want to put it in a `Scroll-View` so that it scrolls up when the iOS virtual keyboard is displayed. However, because `Editor` implements its own scrolling, you can't put it in a `ScrollView`.

For that reason, the code-behind file sets the height of the `Editor` to one-half the height of the `AbsoluteLayout` when the `Editor` gets input focus so that the keyboard doesn't overlap it, and it restores the `Editor` height when it loses input focus:

```csharp
public partial class JustNotesPage : ContentPage
{
    public JustNotesPage()
    {
        InitializeComponent();

        // Retrieve last saved Editor text.
        IDictionary<string, object> properties = Application.Current.Properties;

        if (properties.ContainsKey("text"))
        {
            editor.Text = (string)properties["text"];
        }
    }

    void OnEditorFocused(object sender, FocusEventArgs args)
    {
        if (Device.OS == TargetPlatform.iOS)
        {
            AbsoluteLayout.SetLayoutBounds(editor, new Rectangle(0, 0, 1, 0.5));
        }
    }

    void OnEditorUnfocused(object sender, FocusEventArgs args)
    {
        if (Device.OS == TargetPlatform.iOS)
```

```
        {
            AbsoluteLayout.SetLayoutBounds(editor, new Rectangle(0, 0, 1, 1));
        }
    }

    public void OnSleep()
    {
        // Save Editor text.
        Application.Current.Properties["text"] = editor.Text;
    }
}
```

That adjustment is only approximate, of course. It varies by device, and it varies by portrait and landscape mode, but sufficient information is not currently available in Xamarin.Forms to do it more accurately. For now, you should probably restrict your use of `Editor` views to the top area of the page.

The code for saving and restoring the `Editor` contents is rather prosaic in comparison with the `Editor` manipulation. The `OnSleep` method (called from the `App` class) saves the text in the `Properties` dictionary with a key of "text" and the constructor restores it.

Here's the program running on all three platforms with the `Text` keyboard in view with word suggestions. On the Windows 10 Mobile screen, a word has been selected and might be copied to the clipboard for a later paste operation:

The SearchBar

The `SearchBar` doesn't derive from `InputView` like `Entry` and `Editor`, and it doesn't have a `Key-`

`board` property. The keyboard that `SearchBar` displays when it acquires input focus is platform specific and appropriate for a search command. The `SearchBar` itself is similar to an `Entry` view, but depending on the platform, it might be adorned with some other graphics and contain a button that erases the typed text.

`SearchBar` defines two events:

- `TextChanged`

- `SearchButtonPressed`

The `TextChanged` event allows your program to access a text entry in progress. Perhaps your program can actually begin a search or offer context-specific suggestions before the user completes typing. The `SearchButtonPressed` event is equivalent to the `Completed` event fired by `Entry`. It is triggered by a particular button on the keyboard in the same location as the completed button for `Entry` but possibly labeled differently.

`SearchBar` defines five properties:

- `Text` — the text entered by the user

- `Placeholder` — hint text displayed before the user begins typing

- `CancelButtonColor` — of type `Color`

- `SearchCommand` — for use with data binding

- `SearchCommandParameter` — for use with data binding

The **SearchBarDemo** program uses only `Text` and `Placeholder`, but the XAML file attaches handlers for both events:

```
<ContentPage xmlns="http://xamarin.com/schemas/2014/forms"
             xmlns:x="http://schemas.microsoft.com/winfx/2009/xaml"
             x:Class="SearchBarDemo.SearchBarDemoPage">
    <ContentPage.Padding>
        <OnPlatform x:TypeArguments="Thickness"
                    iOS="10, 20, 10, 0"
                    Android="10, 0"
                    WinPhone="10, 0" />
    </ContentPage.Padding>

    <StackLayout>
        <SearchBar x:Name="searchBar"
                   Placeholder="Search text"
                   TextChanged="OnSearchBarTextChanged"
                   SearchButtonPressed="OnSearchBarButtonPressed" />

        <ScrollView x:Name="resultsScroll"
                    VerticalOptions="FillAndExpand">
            <StackLayout x:Name="resultsStack" />
        </ScrollView>
```

```
    </StackLayout>
</ContentPage>
```

The program uses the scrollable `StackLayout` named `resultsStack` to display the results of the search.

Here's the `SearchBar` and keyboard for the three platforms. Notice the search icon and a delete button on all three platforms, and the special search keys on the iOS and Android keyboards:

You might guess from the entries in the three `SearchBar` views that the program allows searching through the text of Herman Melville's *Moby-Dick*. That is true! The entire novel is stored as an embedded resource in the **Texts** folder of the Portable Class Library project with the name MobyDick.txt. The file is a plain-text, one-line-per-paragraph format that originated with a file on the Gutenberg.net website.

The constructor of the code-behind file reads that whole file into a string field named `bookText`. The `TextChanged` handler clears the `resultsStack` of any previous search results so that there's no discrepancy between the text being typed into the `SearchBar` and this list. The `SearchButton-Pressed` event initiates the search:

```csharp
public partial class SearchBarDemoPage : ContentPage
{
    const double MaxMatches = 100;
    string bookText;

    public SearchBarDemoPage()
    {
        InitializeComponent();
```

```
        // Load embedded resource bitmap.
        string resourceID = "SearchBarDemo.Texts.MobyDick.txt";
        Assembly assembly = GetType().GetTypeInfo().Assembly;

        using (Stream stream = assembly.GetManifestResourceStream(resourceID))
        {
            using (StreamReader reader = new StreamReader(stream))
            {
                bookText = reader.ReadToEnd();
            }
        }
    }

    void OnSearchBarTextChanged(object sender, TextChangedEventArgs args)
    {
        resultsStack.Children.Clear();
    }

    void OnSearchBarButtonPressed(object sender, EventArgs args)
    {
        // Detach resultsStack from layout.
        resultsScroll.Content = null;

        resultsStack.Children.Clear();
        SearchBookForText(searchBar.Text);

        // Reattach resultsStack to layout.
        resultsScroll.Content = resultsStack;
    }

    void SearchBookForText(string searchText)
    {
        int count = 0;
        bool isTruncated = false;

        using (StringReader reader = new StringReader(bookText))
        {
            int lineNumber = 0;
            string line;

            while (null != (line = reader.ReadLine()))
            {
                lineNumber++;
                int index = 0;

                while (-1 != (index = (line.IndexOf(searchText, index,
                                                StringComparison.OrdinalIgnoreCase))))
                {
                    if (count == MaxMatches)
                    {
                        isTruncated = true;
                        break;
                    }
                    index += 1;
```

```
                    // Add the information to the StackLayout.
                    resultsStack.Children.Add(
                        new Label
                        {
                            Text = String.Format("Found at line {0}, offset {1}",
                                                  lineNumber, index)
                        });

                    count++;
                }

                if (isTruncated)
                {
                    break;
                }
            }
        }

        // Add final count to the StackLayout.
        resultsStack.Children.Add(
            new Label
            {
                Text = String.Format("{0} match{1} found{2}",
                                     count,
                                     count == 1 ? "" : "es",
                                     isTruncated ? " - stopped" : "")
            });
    }
}
```

The `SearchBookForText` method uses the search text with the `IndexOf` method applied to each line of the book for case-insensitive comparison and adds a `Label` to `resultsStack` for each match. However, this process has performance problems because each `Label` that is added to the `StackLayout` potentially triggers a new layout calculation. That's unnecessary. For this reason, before beginning the search, the program detaches the `StackLayout` from the visual tree by setting the `Content` property of its parent (the `ScrollView`) to `null`:

```
resultsScroll.Content = null;
```

After all the `Label` views have been added to the `StackLayout`, the `StackLayout` is added back to the visual tree:

```
resultsScroll.Content = resultsStack;
```

But even that's not a sufficient performance improvement for some searches, and that is why the program limits itself to the first 100 matches. (Notice the `MaxMatches` constant defined at the top of the class.) Here's the program showing the results of the searches you saw entered earlier:

You'll need to reference the actual file to see what those matches are.

Would running the search in a second thread of execution speed things up? No. The actual text search is very fast. The performance issues involve the user interface. If the `SearchBookForText` method were run in a secondary thread, then it would need to use `Device.BeginInvokeOnMain-Thread` to add each `Label` to the `StackLayout`. If that `StackLayout` is attached to the visual tree, this would make the program operate more dynamically—the individual items would appear on the screen following each item added to the list—but the switching back and forth between threads would slow down the overall operation.

Date and time selection

A Xamarin.Forms application that needs a date or time from the user can use the `DatePicker` or `TimePicker` view.

These are very similar: The two views simply display a date or time in a box similar to an `Entry` view. Tapping the view invokes the platform-specific date or time selector. The user then selects (or dials in) a new date or time and signals completion.

The DatePicker

`DatePicker` has three properties of type `DateTime`:

- `MinimumDate`, initialized to January 1, 1900

- `MaximumDate`, initialized to December 31, 2100

- `Date`, initialized to `DateTime.Today`

A program can set these properties to whatever it wants as long as `MinimumDate` is prior to `Maxi-mumDate`. The `Date` property reflects the user's selection.

If you'd like to set those properties in XAML, you can do so using the `x:DateTime` element. Use a format that is acceptable to the `DateTime.Parse` method with a second argument of `Culture-Info.InvariantCulture`. Probably the easiest is the short-date format, which is a two-digit month, a two-digit day, and a four-digit year, separated by slashes:

```
<DatePicker … >
    <DatePicker.MinimumDate>
        03/01/2016
    </DatePicker.MinimumDate>

    <DatePicker.MaximumDate>
        10/31/2016
    </DatePicker.MaximumDate>

    <DatePicker.Date>
        04/24/2016
    </DatePicker.Date>
</DatePicker>
```

The `DatePicker` displays the selected date by using the normal `ToString` method, but you can set the `Format` property of the view to a custom .NET formatting string. The initial value is "d"—the short-date format.

Here's the XAML file from a program called **DaysBetweenDates** that lets you select two dates and then calculates the number of days between them. It contains two `DatePicker` views labeled **To** and **From**:

```
<ContentPage xmlns="http://xamarin.com/schemas/2014/forms"
             xmlns:x="http://schemas.microsoft.com/winfx/2009/xaml"
             x:Class="DaysBetweenDates.DaysBetweenDatesPage">

    <ContentPage.Padding>
        <OnPlatform x:TypeArguments="Thickness"
                    iOS="10, 30, 10, 0"
                    Android="10, 10, 10, 0"
                    WinPhone="10, 10, 10, 0" />
    </ContentPage.Padding>

    <StackLayout>
        <StackLayout.Resources>
            <ResourceDictionary>
                <Style TargetType="DatePicker">
                    <Setter Property="Format" Value="D" />
                    <Setter Property="VerticalOptions" Value="Center" />
                    <Setter Property="HorizontalOptions" Value="FillAndExpand" />
```

```
                </Style>
            </ResourceDictionary>
        </StackLayout.Resources>

        <!-- Underlined text header -->
        <StackLayout Grid.Row="0" Grid.Column="0" Grid.ColumnSpan="2"
                     VerticalOptions="CenterAndExpand"
                     HorizontalOptions="Center">
            <Label Text="Days between Dates"
                   FontSize="Large"
                   FontAttributes="Bold"
                   TextColor="Accent" />
            <BoxView Color="Accent"
                     HeightRequest="3" />
        </StackLayout>

        <StackLayout Orientation="Horizontal"
                     VerticalOptions="CenterAndExpand">
            <Label Text="From:"
                   VerticalOptions="Center" />

            <DatePicker x:Name="fromDatePicker"
                        DateSelected="OnDateSelected" />
        </StackLayout>

        <StackLayout Orientation="Horizontal"
                     VerticalOptions="CenterAndExpand">
            <Label Text="    To:"
                   VerticalOptions="Center" />

            <DatePicker x:Name="toDatePicker"
                        DateSelected="OnDateSelected" />
        </StackLayout>

        <Label x:Name="resultLabel"
               FontSize="Medium"
               HorizontalOptions="Center"
               VerticalOptions="CenterAndExpand" />
    </StackLayout>
</ContentPage>
```

An implicit style sets the `Format` property of the two `DatePicker` views to "D", which is the long-date format, to include the text day of the week and month name. The XAML file uses two horizontal `StackLayout` objects for displaying a `Label` and `DatePicker` side by side.

Watch out: If you use the long-date format, you'll want to avoid setting the `HorizontalOptions` property of the `DatePicker` to `Start`, `Center`, or `End`. If you put the `DatePicker` in a horizontal `StackLayout` (as in this program), set the `HorizontalOptions` to `FillAndExpand`. Otherwise, if the user selects a date with a longer text string than the original date, the result is not formatted well. The **DaysBetweenDates** program uses an implicit style to give the `DatePicker` a `HorizontalOptions` value of `FillAndExpand` so that it occupies the entire width of the horizontal `StackLayout` except for what's occupied by the `Label`.

When you tap one of the `DatePicker` fields, a platform-specific panel comes up. On iOS, it occupies just the bottom part of the screen, but on Android and Windows 10 Mobile, it pretty much takes over the screen:

Notice the **Done** button on iOS, the **OK** button on Android, and the check-mark toolbar button on Windows Phone. All three of these buttons dismiss the date-picking panel and return to the program with a firing of the `DateSelected` event. The event handler in the **DaysBetweenDates** code-behind file accesses both `DatePicker` views and calculates the number of days between the two dates:

```
public partial class DaysBetweenDatesPage : ContentPage
{
    public DaysBetweenDatesPage()
    {
        InitializeComponent();

        // Initialize.
        OnDateSelected(null, null);
    }

    void OnDateSelected(object sender, DateChangedEventArgs args)
    {
        int days = (toDatePicker.Date - fromDatePicker.Date).Days;
        resultLabel.Text = String.Format("{0} day{1} between dates",
                                    days, days == 1 ? "" : "s");
    }
}
```

Here's the result:

The TimePicker (or is it a TimeSpanPicker?)

The `TimePicker` is somewhat simpler than `DatePicker`. It defines only `Time` and `Format` properties, and it doesn't include an event to indicate a new selected `Time` value. If you need to be notified, you can install a handler for the `PropertyChanged` event.

Although `TimePicker` displays the selected time by using the `ToString` method of `DateTime`, the `Time` property is actually of type `TimeSpan`, indicating a duration of time since midnight.

The **SetTimer** program includes a `TimePicker`. The program assumes that the time picked from the `TimePicker` is within the next 24 hours and then notifies you when that time has come. The XAML file puts a `TimePicker`, a `Switch`, and an `Entry` on the page.

```
<ContentPage xmlns="http://xamarin.com/schemas/2014/forms"
             xmlns:x="http://schemas.microsoft.com/winfx/2009/xaml"
             x:Class="SetTimer.SetTimerPage"
             Padding="50">

    <StackLayout Spacing="20"
                 VerticalOptions="Center">
        <TimePicker x:Name="timePicker"
                    PropertyChanged="OnTimePickerPropertyChanged" />

        <Switch x:Name="switch"
                HorizontalOptions="End"
                Toggled="OnSwitchToggled" />

        <Entry x:Name="entry"
               Text="Sample Timer"
```

```
                    Placeholder="label" />
    </StackLayout>
</ContentPage>
```

The `TimePicker` has a `PropertyChanged` event handler attached. The `Entry` lets you remind your-self what the timer is supposed to remind you of.

When you tap the `TimePicker`, a platform-specific panel pops up. As with the `DatePicker`, the Android and Windows 10 Mobile panels obscure much of the screen underneath, but you can see the `SetTimer` user interface in the center of the iPhone screen:

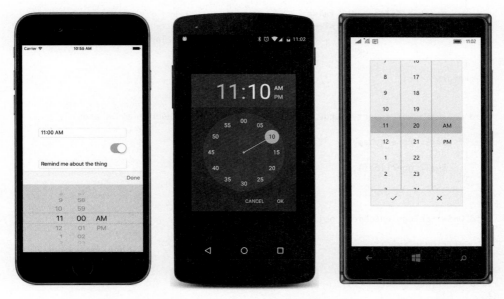

In a real timer program—a timer program that is actually useful and not just a demonstration of the `TimePicker` view—the code-behind file would access the platform-specific notification interfaces so that the user would be notified even if the program were no longer active.

SetTimer doesn't do that. **SetTimer** instead uses a platform-specific alert box that a program can invoke by calling the `DisplayAlert` method that is defined by `Page` and inherited by `ContentPage`.

The `SetTriggerTime` method at the bottom of the code-behind file (shown below) calculates the timer time based on `DateTime.Today`—a property that returns a `DateTime` indicating the current date, but with a time of midnight—and the `TimeSpan` returned from the `TimePicker`. If that time has already passed today, then it's assumed to be tomorrow.

The timer, however, is set for one second. Every second the timer handler checks whether the `Switch` is on and whether the current time is greater than or equal to the timer time:

```
public partial class SetTimerPage : ContentPage
{
    DateTime triggerTime;
```

```
public SetTimerPage()
{
    InitializeComponent();

    Device.StartTimer(TimeSpan.FromSeconds(1), OnTimerTick);
}

bool OnTimerTick()
{
    if (@switch.IsToggled && DateTime.Now >= triggerTime)
    {
        @switch.IsToggled = false;
        DisplayAlert("Timer Alert",
                     "The '" + entry.Text + "' timer has elapsed",
                     "OK");
    }
    return true;
}

void OnTimePickerPropertyChanged(object obj, PropertyChangedEventArgs args)
{
    if (args.PropertyName == "Time")
    {
        SetTriggerTime();
    }
}

void OnSwitchToggled(object obj, ToggledEventArgs args)
{
    SetTriggerTime();
}

void SetTriggerTime()
{
    if (@switch.IsToggled)
    {
        triggerTime = DateTime.Today + timePicker.Time;

        if (triggerTime < DateTime.Now)
        {
            triggerTime += TimeSpan.FromDays(1);
        }
    }
}
}
```

When the timer time has come, the program uses DisplayAlert to signal a reminder to the user. Here's how this alert appears on the three platforms:

Throughout this chapter, you've seen interactive views that define events, and you've seen application programs that implement event handlers. Often these event handlers access a property of the view and set a property of another view.

In the next chapter, you'll see how these event handlers can be eliminated and how properties of different views can be linked, either in code or markup. This is the exciting feature of *data binding*.

Chapter 16
Data binding

Events and event handlers are a vital part of the interactive interface of Xamarin.Forms, but often event handlers perform very rudimentary jobs. They transfer values between properties of different objects and in some cases simply update a `Label` to show the new value of a view.

You can automate such connections between properties of two objects with a powerful feature of Xamarin.Forms called *data binding*. Under the covers, a data binding installs event handlers and handles the transfer of values from one property to another so that you don't have to. In most cases you define these data bindings in the XAML file, so there's no code (or very little code) involved. The use of data bindings helps reduce the number of "moving parts" in the application.

Data bindings also play a crucial role in the Model-View-ViewModel (MVVM) application architecture. As you'll see in Chapter 18, "MVVM," data bindings provide the link between the View (the user interface often implemented in XAML) and the underlying data of the ViewModel and Model. This means that the connections between the user interface and underlying data can be represented in XAML along with the user interface.

Binding basics

Several properties, methods, and classes are involved in data bindings:

- The `Binding` class (which derives from `BindingBase`) defines many characteristics of a data binding.

- The `BindingContext` property is defined by the `BindableObject` class.

- The `SetBinding` method is also defined by the `BindableObject` class.

- The `BindableObjectExtensions` class defines two additional overloads of `SetBinding`.

Two classes support XAML markup extensions for bindings:

- The `BindingExtension` class, which is private to Xamarin.Forms, provides support for the `Binding` markup extension that you use to define a data binding in XAML.

- The `ReferenceExtension` class is also crucial to bindings.

Two interfaces also get involved in data binding. These are:

- `INotifyPropertyChanged` (defined in the `System.ComponentModel` namespace) is the standard interface that classes use when notifying external classes that a property has changed.

This interface plays a major role in MVVM.

- `IValueConverter` (defined in the `Xamarin.Forms` namespace) is used to define small classes that aid data binding by converting values from one type to another.

The most fundamental concept of data bindings is this: Data bindings always have a *source* and a *target*. The source is a property of an object, usually one that changes dynamically at run time. When that property changes, the data binding automatically updates the target, which is a property of another object.

Target ← Source

But as you'll see, sometimes the data flow between the source and target isn't in a constant direction. Even in those cases, however, the distinction between source and target is important because of one basic fact:

The target of a data binding must be backed by a `BindableProperty` *object.*

As you know, the `VisualElement` class derives from `BindableObject` by way of `Element`, and all the visual elements in Xamarin.Forms define most of their properties as bindable properties. For this reason, data-binding targets are almost always visual elements or—as you'll see in Chapter 19, "Collection views"—objects called *cells* that are translated to visual elements.

Although the target of a data binding must be backed by a `BindableProperty` object, there is no such requirement for a data-binding source. The source can be a plain old C# property. However, in all but the most trivial data bindings, a change in the source property causes a corresponding change in the target property. This means that the source object must implement some kind of notification mechanism to signal when the property changes. This notification mechanism is the `INotifyProperty-Changed` interface, which is a standard .NET interface involved in data bindings and used extensively for implementing the MVVM architecture.

The rule for a nontrivial data-binding source—that is, a data-binding source that can dynamically change value—is therefore:

The source of a nontrivial data binding must implement `INotifyPropertyChanged`.

Despite its importance, the `INotifyPropertyChanged` interface has the virtue of being very simple: it consists solely of one event, called `PropertyChanged`, which a class fires when a property has changed.

Very conveniently for our purposes, `BindableObject` implements `INotifyPropertyChanged`. Any property that is backed by a bindable property automatically fires a `PropertyChanged` event when that property changes. This automatic firing of the event extends to bindable properties you might define in your own classes.

This means that you can define data bindings between properties of visual objects. In the grand scheme of things, most data bindings probably link visual objects with underlying data, but for purposes of learning about data bindings and experimenting with them, it's nice to simply link properties of two views without defining data classes.

For the first few examples in this chapter, you'll see data bindings in which the source is the `Value` property of a `Slider` and the target is the `Opacity` property of a `Label`. As you manipulate the `Slider`, the `Label` changes from transparent to opaque. Both properties are of type `double` and range from 0 to 1, so they are a perfect match.

You already know how to do this little job with a simple event handler. Let's see how to do it with a data binding.

Code and XAML

Although most data bindings are defined in XAML, you should know how to do one in code. Here's one way (but not the only way) to set a data binding in code:

- Set the `BindingContext` property on the target object to refer to the source object.

- Call `SetBinding` on the target object to specify both the target and source properties.

The `BindingContext` property is defined by `BindableObject`. (It's the *only* property defined by `BindableObject`.) The `SetBinding` method is also defined by `BindableObject`, but there are two additional overloads of the `SetBinding` method in the `BindableObjectExtensions` class. The target property is specified as a `BindableProperty`; the source property is often specified as a string.

The **OpacityBindingCode** program creates two elements, a `Label` and a `Slider`, and defines a data binding that targets the `Opacity` property of the `Label` from the `Value` property of the `Slider`:

```
public class OpacityBindingCodePage : ContentPage
{
    public OpacityBindingCodePage()
    {
        Label label = new Label
        {
            Text = "Opacity Binding Demo",
            FontSize = Device.GetNamedSize(NamedSize.Large, typeof(Label)),
            VerticalOptions = LayoutOptions.CenterAndExpand,
            HorizontalOptions = LayoutOptions.Center
        };

        Slider slider = new Slider
        {
            VerticalOptions = LayoutOptions.CenterAndExpand
        };

        // Set the binding context: target is Label; source is Slider.
        label.BindingContext = slider;
```

```
        // Bind the properties: target is Opacity; source is Value.
        label.SetBinding(Label.OpacityProperty, "Value");

        // Construct the page.
        Padding = new Thickness(10, 0);
        Content = new StackLayout
        {
            Children = { label, slider }
        };
    }
}
```

Here's the property setting that connects the two objects:

```
label.BindingContext = slider;
```

The `label` object is the target and the `slider` object is the source. Here's the method call that links the two properties:

```
label.SetBinding(Label.OpacityProperty, "Value");
```

The first argument to `SetBinding` is of type `BindableProperty`, and that's the requirement for the target property. But the source property is merely specified as a string. It can be any type of property.

The screenshot demonstrates that you don't need to set an event handler to use the `Slider` for controlling other elements on the page:

Of course, *somebody* is setting an event handler. Under the covers, when the binding initializes it-self, it also performs initialization on the target by setting the `Opacity` property of the `Label` from the

`Value` property of the `Slider`. (As you discovered in the previous chapter, when you set an event handler yourself, this initialization doesn't happen automatically.) Then the internal binding code checks whether the source object (in this case the `Slider`) implements the `INotifyProperty-Changed` interface. If so, a `PropertyChanged` handler is set on the `Slider`. Whenever the `Value` property changes, the binding sets the new value to the `Opacity` property of the `Label`.

Reproducing the binding in XAML involves two markup extensions that you haven't seen yet:

- `x:Reference`, which is part of the XAML 2009 specification.

- `Binding`, which is part of Microsoft's XAML-based user interfaces.

The `x:Reference` binding extension is very simple, but the `Binding` markup extension is the most extensive and complex markup extension in all of Xamarin.Forms. It will be introduced incrementally over the course of this chapter.

Here's how you set the data binding in XAML:

- Set the `BindingContext` property of the target element (the `Label`) to an `x:Reference` markup extension that references the source element (the `Slider`).

- Set the target property (the `Opacity` property of the `Label`) to a `Binding` markup extension that references the source property (the `Value` property of the `Slider`).

The **OpacityBindingXaml** project shows the complete markup:

```
<ContentPage xmlns="http://xamarin.com/schemas/2014/forms"
             xmlns:x="http://schemas.microsoft.com/winfx/2009/xaml"
             x:Class="OpacityBindingXaml.OpacityBindingXamlPage"
             Padding="10, 0">
    <StackLayout>
        <Label Text="Opacity Binding Demo"
               FontSize="Large"
               VerticalOptions="CenterAndExpand"
               HorizontalOptions="Center"
               BindingContext="{x:Reference Name=slider}"
               Opacity="{Binding Path=Value}" />

        <Slider x:Name="slider"
                VerticalOptions="CenterAndExpand" />
    </StackLayout>
</ContentPage>
```

The two markup extensions for the binding are the last two attribute settings in the `Label`. The code-behind file contains nothing except the standard call to `InitializeComponent`.

When setting the `BindingContext` in markup, it is very easy to forget the `x:Reference` markup extension and simply specify the source name, but that doesn't work.

The `Path` argument of the `Binding` markup expression specifies the source property. Why is this argument called `Path` rather than `Property`? You'll see why later in this chapter.

You can make the markup a little shorter. The public class that provides support for `Reference` is `ReferenceExtension`, which defines its content property to be `Name`. The content property of `BindingExtension` (which is not a public class) is `Path`, so you don't need the `Name` and `Path` arguments and equal signs:

```
<Label Text="Opacity Binding Demo"
       FontSize="Large"
       VerticalOptions="CenterAndExpand"
       HorizontalOptions="Center"
       BindingContext="{x:Reference slider}"
       Opacity="{Binding Value}" />
```

Or if you'd like to make the markup longer, you can break out the `BindingContext` and `Opacity` properties as property elements and set them by using regular element syntax for `x:Reference` and `Binding`:

```
<Label Text="Opacity Binding Demo"
       FontSize="Large"
       VerticalOptions="CenterAndExpand"
       HorizontalOptions="Center">

    <Label.BindingContext>
        <x:Reference Name="slider" />
    </Label.BindingContext>

    <Label.Opacity>
        <Binding Path="Value" />
    </Label.Opacity>
</Label>
```

As you'll see, the use of property elements for bindings is sometimes convenient in connection with the data binding.

Source and BindingContext

The `BindingContext` property is actually one of two ways to link the source and target objects. You can alternatively dispense with `BindingContext` and include a reference to the source object within the binding expression itself.

The **BindingSourceCode** project has a page class that is identical to the one in **OpacityBinding-Code** except that the binding is defined in two statements that don't involve the `BindingContext` property:

```
public class BindingSourceCodePage : ContentPage
{
    public BindingSourceCodePage()
    {
        Label label = new Label
        {
```

```
            Text = "Opacity Binding Demo",
            FontSize = Device.GetNamedSize(NamedSize.Large, typeof(Label)),
            VerticalOptions = LayoutOptions.CenterAndExpand,
            HorizontalOptions = LayoutOptions.Center
        };

        Slider slider = new Slider
        {
            VerticalOptions = LayoutOptions.CenterAndExpand
        };

        // Define Binding object with source object and property.
        Binding binding = new Binding
        {
            Source = slider,
            Path = "Value"
        };

        // Bind the Opacity property of the Label to the source.
        label.SetBinding(Label.OpacityProperty, binding);

        // Construct the page.
        Padding = new Thickness(10, 0);
        Content = new StackLayout
        {
            Children = { label, slider }
        };
    }
}
```

The target object and property are still specified in the call to the `SetBinding` method:

```
label.SetBinding(Label.OpacityProperty, binding);
```

However, the second argument references a `Binding` object that specifies the source object and property:

```
Binding binding = new Binding
{
    Source = slider,
    Path = "Value"
};
```

That is not the only way to instantiate and initialize a `Binding` object. An extensive `Binding` constructor allows for specifying many `Binding` properties. Here's how it could be used in the **BindingSourceCode** program:

```
Binding binding = new Binding("Value", BindingMode.Default, null, null, null, slider);
```

Or you can use a named argument to reference the `slider` object:

```
Binding binding = new Binding("Value", source: slider);
```

Binding also has a generic Create method that lets you specify the Path property as a Func object rather than as a string so that it's more immune from misspellings or changes in the property name. However, this Create method doesn't include an argument for the Source property, so you need to set it separately:

```
Binding binding = Binding.Create<Slider>(src => src.Value);
binding.Source = slider;
```

The BindableObjectExtensions class defines two overloads of SetBinding that allow you to avoid explicitly instantiating a Binding object. However, neither of these overloads includes the Source property, so they are restricted to cases where you're using the BindingContext.

The **BindingSourceXaml** program demonstrates how both the source object and source property can be specified in the Binding markup extension:

```
<ContentPage xmlns="http://xamarin.com/schemas/2014/forms"
             xmlns:x="http://schemas.microsoft.com/winfx/2009/xaml"
             x:Class="BindingSourceXaml.BindingSourceXamlPage"
             Padding="10, 0">
    <StackLayout>
        <Label Text="Binding Source Demo"
               FontSize="Large"
               VerticalOptions="CenterAndExpand"
               HorizontalOptions="Center"
               Opacity="{Binding Source={x:Reference Name=slider},
                                 Path=Value}" />

        <Slider x:Name="slider"
                VerticalOptions="CenterAndExpand" />
    </StackLayout>
</ContentPage>
```

The Binding markup extension now has two arguments, one of which is another markup extension for x:Reference, so a pair of curly braces are nested within the main curly braces:

```
Opacity="{Binding Source={x:Reference Name=slider},
                  Path=Value}" />
```

For visual clarity, the two Binding arguments are vertically aligned within the markup extension, but that's not required. Arguments must be separated by a comma (here at the end of the first line), and no quotation marks must appear within the curly braces. You're not dealing with XML attributes within the markup extension. These are markup extension arguments.

You can simplify the nested markup extension by eliminating the Name argument name and equals sign in x:Reference because Name is the content property of the ReferenceExtension class:

```
Opacity="{Binding Source={x:Reference slider},
                  Path=Value}" />
```

However, you *cannot* similarly remove the Path argument name and equals sign. Even though BindingExtension defines Path as its content property, the argument name can be eliminated only when that argument is the first among multiple arguments. You need to switch around the arguments like so:

```
Opacity="{Binding Path=Value,
                 Source={x:Reference slider}}" />
```

And then you can eliminate the `Path` argument name, and perhaps move everything to one line:

```
Opacity="{Binding Value, Source={x:Reference slider}}" />
```

However, because the first argument is missing an argument name and the second argument has an argument name, the whole expression looks a bit peculiar, and it might be difficult to grasp the `Binding` arguments at first sight. Also, it makes sense for the `Source` to be specified *before* the `Path` because the particular property specified by the `Path` makes sense only for a particular type of object, and that's specified by the `Source`.

In this book, whenever the `Binding` markup extension includes a `Source` argument, it will be first, followed by the `Path`. Otherwise, the `Path` will be the first argument, and often the `Path` argument name will be eliminated.

You can avoid the issue entirely by expressing `Binding` in element form:

```
<Label Text="Binding Source Demo"
       FontSize="Large"
       VerticalOptions="CenterAndExpand"
       HorizontalOptions="Center">
    <Label.Opacity>
        <Binding Source="{x:Reference slider}"
                 Path="Value" />
    </Label.Opacity>
</Label>
```

The `x:Reference` markup extension still exists, but you can also express that in element form as well:

```
<Label Text="Binding Source Demo"
       FontSize="Large"
       VerticalOptions="CenterAndExpand"
       HorizontalOptions="Center">
    <Label.Opacity>
        <Binding Path="Value">
            <Binding.Source>
                <x:Reference Name="slider" />
            </Binding.Source>
        </Binding>
    </Label.Opacity>
</Label>
```

You have now seen two ways to specify the link between the source object with the target object:

- Use the `BindingContext` to reference the source object.

- Use the `Source` property of the `Binding` class or the `Binding` markup extension.

If you specify both, the `Source` property takes precedence over the `BindingContext`.

In the examples you've seen so far, these two techniques have been pretty much interchangeable. However, they have some significant differences. For example, suppose you have one object with two properties that are targets of two different data bindings involving two different source objects—for example, a `Label` with the `Opacity` property bound to a `Slider` and the `IsVisible` property bound to a `Switch`. You can't use `BindingContext` for both bindings because `BindingContext` applies to the whole target object and can only specify a single source. You must use the `Source` property of `Binding` for at least one of these bindings.

`BindingContext` is itself backed by a bindable property. This means that `BindingContext` can be set from a `Binding` markup extension. In contrast, you can't set the `Source` property of `Binding` to another `Binding` because `Binding` does not derive from `BindableObject`, which means `Source` is not backed by a bindable property and hence can't be the target of a data binding.

In this variation of the **BindingSourceXaml** markup, the `BindingContext` property of the `Label` is set to a `Binding` markup extension that includes a `Source` and `Path`.

```
<Label Text="Binding Source Demo"
       FontSize="Large"
       VerticalOptions="CenterAndExpand"
       HorizontalOptions="Center"
       BindingContext="{Binding Source={x:Reference Name=slider},
                                Path=Value}"
       Opacity="{Binding}" />
```

This means that the `BindingContext` for this `Label` is not the `slider` object as in previous examples but the `double` that is the `Value` property of the `Slider`. To bind the `Opacity` property to this `double`, all that's required is an empty `Binding` markup extension that basically says "use the `BindingContext` for the entire data-binding source."

Perhaps the most important difference between `BindingContext` and `Source` is a very special characteristic that makes `BindingContext` unlike any other property in all of Xamarin.Forms:

The binding context is propagated through the visual tree.

In other words, if you set `BindingContext` on a `StackLayout`, it applies to all the children of that `StackLayout` and their children as well. The data bindings within that `StackLayout` don't have to specify `BindingContext` or the `Source` argument to `Binding`. They inherit `BindingContext` from the `StackLayout`. Or the children of the `StackLayout` can override that inherited `BindingContext` with `BindingContext` settings of their own or with a `Source` setting in their bindings.

This feature turns out to be exceptionally useful. Suppose a `StackLayout` contains a bunch of visuals with data bindings set to various properties of a particular class. Set the `BindingContext` property of that `StackLayout`. Then, the individual data bindings on the children of the `StackLayout` don't require either a `Source` specification or a `BindingContext` setting. You could then set the `BindingContext` of the `StackLayout` to different instances of that class to display the properties for each instance. You'll see examples of this technique and other data-binding marvels in the chapters ahead, and particularly in Chapter 19.

Meanwhile, let's look at a much simpler example of `BindingContext` propagation through the visual tree.

The `WebView` is intended to embed a web browser inside your application. Alternatively, you can use `WebView` in conjunction with the `HtmlWebViewSource` class to display a chunk of HTML, perhaps saved as an embedded resource in the PCL.

For displaying webpages, you use `WebView` with the `UrlWebViewSource` class to specify an initial URL. However, `UrlWebViewSource` and `HtmlWebViewSource` both derive from the abstract class `WebViewSource`, and that class defines an implicit conversion of `string` and `Uri` to itself, so all you really need to do is set a string with a web address to the `Source` property of `WebView` to direct `WebView` to present that webpage.

`WebView` also defines two methods, named `GoBack` and `GoForward`, that internally implement the **Back** and **Forward** buttons typically found on web browsers. Your program needs to know when it can enable these buttons, so `WebView` also defines two get-only Boolean properties, named `CanGoBack` and `CanGoForward`. These two properties are backed by bindable properties, which means that any changes to these properties result in `PropertyChanged` events being fired, which further means that they can be used as data binding sources to enable and disable two buttons.

Here's the XAML file for **WebViewDemo**. Notice that the nested `StackLayout` containing the two `Button` elements has its `BindingContext` property set to the `WebView`. The two `Button` children in that `StackLayout` inherit the `BindingContext`, so the buttons can have very simple `Binding` expressions on their `IsEnabled` properties that reference only the `CanGoBack` and `CanGoForward` properties:

```
<ContentPage xmlns="http://xamarin.com/schemas/2014/forms"
             xmlns:x="http://schemas.microsoft.com/winfx/2009/xaml"
             x:Class="WebViewDemo.WebViewDemoPage">
    <ContentPage.Padding>
        <OnPlatform x:TypeArguments="Thickness"
                    iOS="10, 20, 10, 0"
                    Android="10, 0"
                    WinPhone="10, 0" />
    </ContentPage.Padding>

    <StackLayout>
        <Entry Keyboard="Url"
               Placeholder="web address"
               Completed="OnEntryCompleted" />

        <StackLayout Orientation="Horizontal"
                     BindingContext="{x:Reference webView}">

            <Button Text="&#x21D0;"
                    FontSize="Large"
```

```
                        HorizontalOptions="FillAndExpand"
                        IsEnabled="{Binding CanGoBack}"
                        Clicked="OnGoBackClicked" />

            <Button Text="&#x21D2;"
                    FontSize="Large"
                    HorizontalOptions="FillAndExpand"
                    IsEnabled="{Binding CanGoForward}"
                    Clicked="OnGoForwardClicked" />
        </StackLayout>

        <WebView x:Name="webView"
                 VerticalOptions="FillAndExpand"
                 Source="https://xamarin.com" />
    </StackLayout>
</ContentPage>
```

The code-behind file needs to handle the `Clicked` events for the **Back** and **Forward** buttons as well as the `Completed` event for the `Entry` that lets you enter a web address of your own:

```
public partial class WebViewDemoPage : ContentPage
{
    public WebViewDemoPage()
    {
        InitializeComponent();
    }

    void OnEntryCompleted(object sender, EventArgs args)
    {
        webView.Source = ((Entry)sender).Text;
    }

    void OnGoBackClicked(object sender, EventArgs args)
    {
        webView.GoBack();
    }

    void OnGoForwardClicked(object sender, EventArgs args)
    {
        webView.GoForward();
    }
}
```

You don't need to enter a web address when the program starts up because the XAML file is hard-coded to go to your favorite website, and you can navigate around from there:

The binding mode

Here is a `Label` whose `FontSize` property is bound to the `Value` property of a `Slider`:

```
<Label FontSize="{Binding Source={x:Reference slider},
                          Path=Value}" />
<Slider x:Name="slider"
        Maximum="100" />
```

That should work, and if you try it, it will work. You'll be able to change the `FontSize` of the `Label` by manipulating the `Slider`.

But here's a `Label` and `Slider` with the binding reversed. Instead of the `FontSize` property of the `Label` being the target, now `FontSize` is the source of the data binding, and the target is the `Value` property of the `Slider`:

```
<Label x:Name="label" />
<Slider Maximum="100"
        Value="{Binding Source={x:Reference label},
                        Path=FontSize}" />
```

That doesn't seem to make any sense. But if you try it, it will work just fine. Once again, the `Slider` will manipulate the `FontSize` property of the `Label`.

The second binding works because of something called the *binding mode*.

You've learned that a data binding sets the value of a target property from the value of a source property, but sometimes the data flow is not so clear cut. The relationship between target and source is defined by members of the `BindingMode` enumeration:

- `Default`

- `OneWay` — changes in the source affect the target (normal).

- `OneWayToSource` — changes in the target affect the source.

- `TwoWay` — changes in the source and target affect each other.

This `BindingMode` enumeration plays a role in two different classes:

When you create a `BindableProperty` object by using one of the static `Create` or `CreateReadOnly` static methods, you can specify a default `BindingMode` value to use when that property is the target of a data binding.

If you don't specify anything, the default binding mode is `OneWay` for bindable properties that are readable and writeable, and `OneWayToSource` for read-only bindable properties. If you specify `BindingMode.Default` when creating a bindable property, the default binding mode for the property is set to `OneWay`. (In other words, the `BindingMode.Default` member is not intended for defining bindable properties.)

You can override that default binding mode for the target property when you define a binding either in code or XAML. You override the default binding mode by setting the `Mode` property of `Binding` to one of the members of the `BindingMode` enumeration. The `Default` member means that you want to use the default binding mode defined for the target property.

When you set the `Mode` property to `OneWayToSource` you are *not* switching the target and the source. The target is still the object on which you've set the `BindingContext` and the property on which you've called `SetBinding` or applied the `Binding` markup extension. But the data flows in a different direction—from target to source.

Most bindable properties have a default binding mode of `OneWay`. However, there are some exceptions. Of the views you've encountered so far in this book, the following properties have a default mode of `TwoWay`:

Class	Property that is TwoWay
`Slider`	`Value`
`Stepper`	`Value`
`Switch`	`IsToggled`
`Entry`	`Text`
`Editor`	`Text`
`SearchBar`	`Text`
`DatePicker`	`Date`
`TimePicker`	`Time`

The properties that have a default binding mode of `TwoWay` are those most likely to be used with underlying data models in an MVVM scenario. With MVVM, the binding targets are visual objects and the binding sources are data objects. In general, you want the data to flow both ways. You want the visual objects to display the underlying data values (from source to target), and you want the interactive visual objects to cause changes in the underlying data (target to source).

The **BindingModes** program connects four `Label` elements and four `Slider` elements with "normal" bindings, meaning that the target is the `FontSize` property of the `Label` and the source is the `Value` property of the `Slider`:

```
<ContentPage xmlns="http://xamarin.com/schemas/2014/forms"
             xmlns:x="http://schemas.microsoft.com/winfx/2009/xaml"
             x:Class="BindingModes.BindingModesPage"
             Padding="10, 0">

    <ContentPage.Resources>
        <ResourceDictionary>
            <Style TargetType="StackLayout">
                <Setter Property="VerticalOptions" Value="CenterAndExpand" />
            </Style>

            <Style TargetType="Label">
                <Setter Property="HorizontalOptions" Value="Center" />
            </Style>
        </ResourceDictionary>
    </ContentPage.Resources>

    <StackLayout VerticalOptions="Fill">
        <StackLayout>
            <Label Text="Default"
                   FontSize="{Binding Source={x:Reference slider1},
                                      Path=Value}" />
            <Slider x:Name="slider1"
                    Maximum="50" />
        </StackLayout>

        <StackLayout>
            <Label Text="OneWay"
                   FontSize="{Binding Source={x:Reference slider2},
                                      Path=Value,
                                      Mode=OneWay}" />
            <Slider x:Name="slider2"
                    Maximum="50" />
        </StackLayout>

        <StackLayout>
            <Label Text="OneWayToSource"
                   FontSize="{Binding Source={x:Reference slider3},
                                      Path=Value,
                                      Mode=OneWayToSource}" />
            <Slider x:Name="slider3"
                    Maximum="50" />
        </StackLayout>

        <StackLayout>
```

```
            <Label Text="TwoWay"
                   FontSize="{Binding Source={x:Reference slider4},
                                      Path=Value,
                                      Mode=TwoWay}" />
            <Slider x:Name="slider4"
                    Maximum="50" />
        </StackLayout>
    </StackLayout>
</ContentPage>
```

The Text of the Label indicates the binding mode. When you first run this program, all the Slider elements are initialized at zero, except for the third one, which is slightly nonzero:

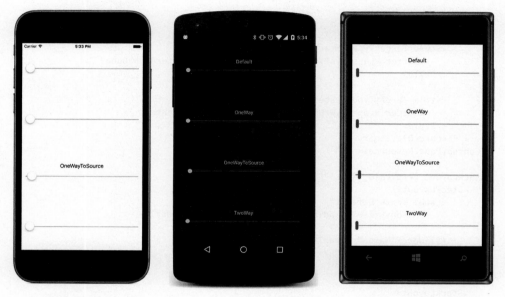

By manipulating each Slider, you can change the FontSize of the Label, but it doesn't work for the third one because the OneWayToSource mode indicates that changes in the target (the FontSize property of the Label) affect the source (the Value property of the Slider):

Although it's not quite evident here, the default binding mode is `OneWay` because the binding is set on the `FontSize` property of the `Label`, and that's the default binding mode for the `FontSize` property.

The **ReverseBinding** program sets the bindings on the `Value` property of the `Slider`:

```xml
<ContentPage xmlns="http://xamarin.com/schemas/2014/forms"
             xmlns:x="http://schemas.microsoft.com/winfx/2009/xaml"
             x:Class="ReverseBinding.ReverseBindingPage"
             Padding="10, 0">

    <ContentPage.Resources>
        <ResourceDictionary>
            <Style TargetType="StackLayout">
                <Setter Property="VerticalOptions" Value="CenterAndExpand" />
            </Style>

            <Style TargetType="Label">
                <Setter Property="HorizontalOptions" Value="Center" />
            </Style>
        </ResourceDictionary>
    </ContentPage.Resources>

    <StackLayout VerticalOptions="Fill">
        <StackLayout>
            <Label x:Name="label1"
                   Text="Default" />
            <Slider Maximum="50"
                    Value="{Binding Source={x:Reference label1},
                                    Path=FontSize}" />
        </StackLayout>
```

```
            <StackLayout>
                <Label x:Name="label2"
                       Text="OneWay" />
                <Slider Maximum="50"
                        Value="{Binding Source={x:Reference label2},
                                        Path=FontSize,
                                        Mode=OneWay}" />
            </StackLayout>

            <StackLayout>
                <Label x:Name="label3"
                       Text="OneWayToSource" />
                <Slider Maximum="50"
                        Value="{Binding Source={x:Reference label3},
                                        Path=FontSize,
                                        Mode=OneWayToSource}" />
            </StackLayout>

            <StackLayout>
                <Label x:Name="label4"
                       Text="TwoWay" />
                <Slider Maximum="50"
                        Value="{Binding Source={x:Reference label4},
                                        Path=FontSize,
                                        Mode=TwoWay}" />
            </StackLayout>
        </StackLayout>
    </StackLayout>
</ContentPage>
```

The default binding mode on these bindings is `TwoWay` because that's the mode set in the `BindableProperty.Create` method for the `Value` property of the `Slider`.

What's interesting about this approach is that for three of the cases here, the `Value` property of the `Slider` is initialized from the `FontSize` property of the `Label`:

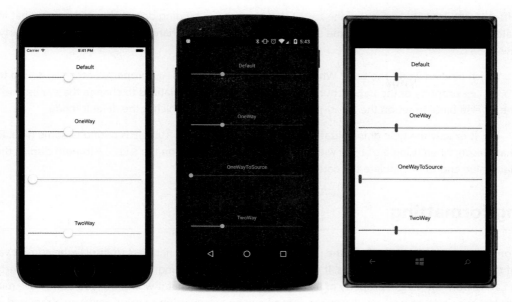

It doesn't happen for OneWayToSource because for that mode, changes to the Value property of the Slider affect the FontSize property of the Label but not the other way around.

Now let's start manipulating these sliders:

Now the OneWayToSource binding works because changes to the Value property of the Slider affect the `FontSize` property of the `Label`, but the `OneWay` binding does not work because that indicates that the `Value` property of the `Slider` is only affected by changes in the `FontSize` property of the `Label`.

Which binding works the best? Which binding initializes the `Value` property of the `Slider` to the `FontSize` property of the `Label`, but also allows `Slider` manipulations to change the `FontSize`? It's the reverse binding set on the `Slider` with a mode of `TwoWay`, which is the default mode.

This is exactly the type of initialization you want to see when a `Slider` is bound to some data. For that reason, when using a `Slider` with MVVM, the binding is set on the `Slider` to both display the data value and to manipulate the data value.

String formatting

Some of the sample programs in the previous chapter used event handlers to display the current values of the `Slider` and `Stepper` views. If you try defining a data binding that targets the `Text` property of a `Label` from the `Value` property of a `Slider`, you'll discover that it works, but you don't have much control over it. In general, you'll want to control any type conversion or value conversion required in data bindings. That's discussed later in this chapter.

String formatting is special, however. The `Binding` class has a `StringFormat` property that allows you to include an entire .NET formatting string. Almost always, the target of such a binding is the `Text` property of a `Label`, but the binding source can be of any type.

The .NET formatting string that you supply to `StringFormat` must be suitable for a call to the `String.Format` static method, which means that it should contain a placeholder of "{0}" with or without a formatting specification suitable for the source data type—for example "{0:F3}" to display a `double` with three decimal places.

In XAML, this placeholder is a bit of a problem because the curly braces can be mistaken for the curly braces used to delimit markup extensions. The easiest solution is to put the entire formatting string in single quotation marks.

The **ShowViewValues** program contains four examples that display the current values of a `Slider`, `Entry`, `Stepper`, and `Switch`. The hexadecimal codes in the formatting string used for displaying the `Entry` contents are Unicode IDs for "smart quotes":

```
<ContentPage xmlns="http://xamarin.com/schemas/2014/forms"
             xmlns:x="http://schemas.microsoft.com/winfx/2009/xaml"
             x:Class="ShowViewValues.ShowViewValuesPage"
             Padding="10, 0">

    <StackLayout>
        <StackLayout VerticalOptions="CenterAndExpand">
            <Label Text="{Binding Source={x:Reference slider},
                        Path=Value,
```

```
                                 StringFormat='The Slider value is {0:F3}'}" />
            <Slider x:Name="slider" />
        </StackLayout>

        <StackLayout VerticalOptions="CenterAndExpand">
            <Label Text="{Binding Source={x:Reference entry},
                                  Path=Text,
                                  StringFormat='The Entry text is &#x201C;{0}&#x201D;'}" />
            <Entry x:Name="entry" />
        </StackLayout>

        <StackLayout VerticalOptions="CenterAndExpand">
            <Label Text="{Binding Source={x:Reference stepper},
                                  Path=Value,
                                  StringFormat='The Stepper value is {0}'}" />
            <Stepper x:Name="stepper" />
        </StackLayout>

        <StackLayout VerticalOptions="CenterAndExpand">
            <Label Text="{Binding Source={x:Reference switch},
                                  Path=IsToggled,
                                  StringFormat='The Switch value is {0}'}" />
            <Switch x:Name="switch" />
        </StackLayout>
    </StackLayout>
</ContentPage>
```

When using `StringFormat` you need to pay particular attention to the placement of commas, single quotation marks, and curly braces.

Here's the result:

You might recall the **WhatSize** program from Chapter 5, "Dealing with sizes." That program used a `SizeChanged` event handler on the page to display the current width and height of the screen in device-independent units.

The **WhatSizeBindings** program does the whole job in XAML. First it adds an `x:Name` attribute to the root tag to give the `WhatSizeBindingsPage` object a name of `page`. Three `Label` views share a horizontal `StackLayout` in the center of the page, and two of them have bindings to the `Width` and `Height` properties. The `Width` and `Height` properties are get-only, but they are backed by bindable properties, so they fire `PropertyChanged` events when they change:

```
<ContentPage xmlns="http://xamarin.com/schemas/2014/forms"
             xmlns:x="http://schemas.microsoft.com/winfx/2009/xaml"
             x:Class="WhatSizeBindings.WhatSizeBindingsPage"
             x:Name="page">

    <StackLayout Orientation="Horizontal"
                 Spacing="0"
                 HorizontalOptions="Center"
                 VerticalOptions="Center">

        <StackLayout.Resources>
            <ResourceDictionary>
                <Style TargetType="Label">
                    <Setter Property="FontSize" Value="Large" />
                </Style>
            </ResourceDictionary>
        </StackLayout.Resources>

        <Label Text="{Binding Source={x:Reference page},
                              Path=Width,
                              StringFormat='{0:F0}'}" />

        <!-- Multiplication sign. -->
        <Label Text=" &#x00D7; " />

        <Label Text="{Binding Source={x:Reference page},
                              Path=Height,
                              StringFormat='{0:F0}'}" />
    </StackLayout>
</ContentPage>
```

Here's the result for the devices used for this book:

The display changes as you turn the phone between portrait and landscape modes.

Alternatively, the `BindingContext` on the `StackLayout` could be set to an `x:Reference` markup extension referencing the `page` object, and the `Source` settings on the bindings wouldn't be necessary.

Why is it called "Path"?

The `Binding` class defines a property named `Path` that you use to set the source property name. But why is it called `Path`? Why isn't it called `Property`?

The `Path` property is called what it's called because it doesn't need to be one property. It can be a stack of properties, subproperties, and even indexers connected with periods.

Using `Path` in this way can be tricky, so here's a program called **BindingPathDemos** that has four `Binding` markup extensions, each of which sets the `Path` argument to a string of property names and indexers:

```
<ContentPage xmlns="http://xamarin.com/schemas/2014/forms"
             xmlns:x="http://schemas.microsoft.com/winfx/2009/xaml"
             xmlns:globe="clr-namespace:System.Globalization;assembly=mscorlib"
             x:Class="BindingPathDemos.BindingPathDemosPage"
             x:Name="page">
    <ContentPage.Padding>
        <OnPlatform x:TypeArguments="Thickness"
                    iOS="10, 20, 10, 0"
                    Android="10, 0"
                    WinPhone="10, 0" />
```

```
            </ContentPage.Padding>

            <ContentPage.Resources>
                <ResourceDictionary>
                    <Style x:Key="baseStyle" TargetType="View">
                        <Setter Property="VerticalOptions" Value="CenterAndExpand" />
                    </Style>

                    <Style TargetType="Label" BasedOn="{StaticResource baseStyle}">
                        <Setter Property="FontSize" Value="Large" />
                        <Setter Property="HorizontalTextAlignment" Value="Center" />
                    </Style>

                    <Style TargetType="Slider" BasedOn="{StaticResource baseStyle}" />
                </ResourceDictionary>
            </ContentPage.Resources>

            <StackLayout BindingContext="{x:Reference page}">
                <Label Text="{Binding Path=Padding.Top,
                                      StringFormat='The top padding is {0}'}" />

                <Label Text="{Binding Path=Content.Children[4].Value,
                                      StringFormat='The Slider value is {0:F2}'}" />

                <Label Text="{Binding Source={x:Static globe:CultureInfo.CurrentCulture},
                                      Path=DateTimeFormat.DayNames[3],
                                      StringFormat='The middle day of the week is {0}'}" />

                <Label Text="{Binding Path=Content.Children[2].Text.Length,
                                      StringFormat='The preceding Label has {0} characters'}" />
                <Slider />
            </StackLayout>
        </ContentPage>
```

Only one element here has an `x:Name`, and that's the page itself. The `BindingContext` of the `StackLayout` is that page, so all the bindings within the `StackLayout` are relative to the page (except for the binding that has an explicit `Source` property set).

The first `Binding` looks like this:

```
<Label Text="{Binding Path=Padding.Top,
                      StringFormat='The top padding is {0}'}" />
```

The `Path` begins with the `Padding` property of the page. That property is of type `Thickness`, so it's possible to access a property of the `Thickness` structure with a property name such as `Top`. Of course, `Thickness` is a structure and therefore does not derive from `BindableObject`, so `Top` can't be a `BindableProperty`. The binding infrastructure can't set a `PropertyChanged` handler on that property, but it will set a `PropertyChanged` handler on the `Padding` property of the page, and if that changes, the binding will update the target.

The second `Binding` references the `Content` property of the page, which is the `StackLayout`. That `StackLayout` has a `Children` property, which is a collection, so it can be indexed:

```
<Label Text="{Binding Path=Content.Children[4].Value,
                    StringFormat='The Slider value is {0:F2}'}" />
```

The view at index 4 of the `Children` collection is a `Slider` (down at the bottom of the markup, with no attributes set), which has a `Value` property, and that's what's displayed here.

The third `Binding` overrides its inherited `BindingContext` by setting the `Source` argument to a static property using `x:Static`. The `globe` prefix is defined in the root tag to refer to the .NET `System.Globalization` namespace, and the `Source` is set to the `CultureInfo` object that encapsulates the culture of the user's phone:

```
<Label Text="{Binding Source={x:Static globe:CultureInfo.CurrentCulture},
                    Path=DateTimeFormat.DayNames[3],
                    StringFormat='The middle day of the week is {0}'}" />
```

One of the properties of `CultureInfo` is `DateTimeFormat`, which is a `DateTimeFormatInfo` object that contains information about date and time formatting, including a property named `DayNames` that is an array of the seven days of the week. The index 3 picks out the middle one.

None of the classes in the `System.Globalization` namespace implement `INotifyPropertyChanged`, but that's okay because the values of these properties don't change at run time.

The final `Binding` references the child of the `StackLayout` with a child index of 2. That's the previous `Label`. It has a `Text` property, which is of type `string`, and `string` has a `Length` property:

```
<Label Text="{Binding Path=Content.Children[2].Text.Length,
                    StringFormat='The preceding Label has {0} characters'}" />
```

The binding system installs a property-changed handler for the `Text` property of the `Label`, so if it changes, the binding will get the new length.

For the following screenshots, the iOS phone was switched to French, and the Android phone was switched to German. This affects the formatting of the `Slider` value—notice the comma rather than a period for the decimal divider—and the name of the middle day of the week:

These `Path` specifications can be hard to configure and debug. Keep in mind that class names do not appear in the `Path` specifications—only property names and indexers. Also keep in mind that you can build up a `Path` specification incrementally, testing each new piece with a placeholder of "{0}" in `StringFormat`. This will often display the fully qualified class name of the type of the value set to the last property in the `Path` specification, and that can be very useful information.

You'll also want to keep an eye on the **Output** window in Visual Studio or Xamarin Studio when running your program under the debugger. You'll see messages there relating to run-time errors encountered by the binding infrastructure.

Binding value converters

You now know how to convert any binding source object to a string by using `StringFormat`. But what about other data conversions? Perhaps you're using a `Slider` for a binding source but the target is expecting an integer rather than a double. Or maybe you want to display the value of a `Switch` as text, but you want "Yes" and "No" rather than "True" and "False".

The tool for this job is a class—often a very tiny class—informally called a *value converter* or (sometimes) a *binding converter*. More formally, such a class implements the `IValueConverter` interface. This interface is defined in the `Xamarin.Forms` namespace, but it is similar to an interface available in Microsoft's XAML-based environments.

An example: Sometimes applications need to enable or disable a `Button` based on the presence of text in an `Entry`. Perhaps the `Button` is labeled **Save** and the `Entry` is a filename. Or the `Button` is labeled **Send** and the `Entry` contains a mail recipient. The `Button` shouldn't be enabled unless the `Entry` contains at least one character of text.

There are a couple of ways to do this job. In a later chapter, you'll see how a data trigger can do it (and can also perform validity checks of the text in the `Entry`). But for this chapter, let's do it with a value converter.

The data-binding target is the `IsEnabled` property of the `Button`. That property is of type `bool`. The binding source is the `Text` property of an `Entry`, or rather the `Length` property of that `Text` property. That `Length` property is of type `int`. The value converter needs to convert an `int` equal to 0 to a `bool` of `false` and a positive `int` to a `bool` of `true`. The code is trivial. We just need to wrap it in a class that implements `IValueConverter`.

Here is that class in the **Xamarin.FormsBook.Toolkit** library, complete with `using` directives. The `IValueConverter` interface consists of two methods, named `Convert` and `ConvertBack`, with identical parameters. You can make the class as generalized or as specialized as you want:

```
using System;
using System.Globalization;
using Xamarin.Forms;

namespace Xamarin.FormsBook.Toolkit
{
    public class IntToBoolConverter : IValueConverter
    {
        public object Convert(object value, Type targetType,
                              object parameter, CultureInfo culture)
        {
            return (int)value != 0;
        }

        public object ConvertBack(object value, Type targetType,
                                  object parameter, CultureInfo culture)
        {
            return (bool)value ? 1 : 0;
        }
    }
}
```

When you include this class in a data binding—and you'll see how to do that shortly—the `Convert` method is called whenever a value passes from the source to the target.

The `value` argument to `Convert` is the value from the data binding source to be converted. You can use `GetType` to determine its type, or you can assume that it's always a particular type. In this example, the `value` argument is assumed to be of type `int`, so casting to an `int` won't raise an exception. More sophisticated value converters can perform more validity checks.

The `targetType` is the type of the data-binding target property. Versatile value converters can use this argument to tailor the conversion for different target types. The `Convert` method should return an object or value that matches this `targetType`. This particular `Convert` method assumes that `target-Type` is `bool`.

The `parameter` argument is an optional conversion parameter that you can specify as a property to the `Binding` class. (You'll see an example in Chapter 18, "MVVM.")

Finally, if you need to perform a culture-specific conversion, the last argument is the `CultureInfo` object that you should use.

The body of this particular `Convert` method assumes that `value` is an `int`, and the method returns a `bool` that is `true` if that integer is nonzero.

The `ConvertBack` method is called only for `TwoWay` or `OneWayToSource` bindings. For the `ConvertBack` method, the `value` argument is the value from the target and the `targetType` argument is actually the type of the source property. If you know that the `ConvertBack` method will never be called, you can simply ignore all the arguments and return `null` or 0 from it. With some value converters, implementing a `ConvertBack` body is virtually impossible, but sometimes it's fairly simple (as in this case).

When you use a value converter in code, you set an instance of the converter to the `Converter` property of `Binding`. You can optionally pass an argument to the value converter by setting the `ConverterParameter` property of `Binding`.

If the binding also has a `StringFormat`, the value that is returned by the value converter is the value that is formatted as a string.

Generally, in a XAML file you'll want to instantiate the value converter in a `Resources` dictionary and then reference it in the `Binding` expression by using `StaticResource`. The value converter shouldn't maintain state and can thus be shared among multiple bindings.

Here's the **ButtonEnabler** program that uses the value converter:

```
<ContentPage xmlns="http://xamarin.com/schemas/2014/forms"
             xmlns:x="http://schemas.microsoft.com/winfx/2009/xaml"
             xmlns:toolkit=
                 "clr-namespace:Xamarin.FormsBook.Toolkit;assembly=Xamarin.FormsBook.Toolkit"
             x:Class="ButtonEnabler.ButtonEnablerPage"
             Padding="10, 50, 10, 0">

    <ContentPage.Resources>
        <ResourceDictionary>
            <toolkit:IntToBoolConverter x:Key="intToBool" />
        </ResourceDictionary>
    </ContentPage.Resources>

    <StackLayout Spacing="20">
        <Entry x:Name="entry"
               Text=""
               Placeholder="text to enable button" />
```

```
            <Button Text="Save or Send (or something)"
                    FontSize="Medium"
                    HorizontalOptions="Center"
                    IsEnabled="{Binding Source={x:Reference entry},
                                        Path=Text.Length,
                                        Converter={StaticResource intToBool}}" />
    </StackLayout>
</ContentPage>
```

The `IntToBoolConverter` is instantiated in the `Resources` dictionary and referenced as a nested markup extension in the `Binding` that is set on the `IsEnabled` property of the `Button`.

Notice that the `Text` property is explicitly initialized in the `Entry` tag to an empty string. By default, the `Text` property is `null`, which means that the binding `Path` setting of `Text.Length` doesn't result in a valid value.

You might remember from previous chapters that a class in the **Xamarin.FormsBook.Toolkit** library that is referenced only in XAML is not sufficient to establish a link from the application to the library. For that reason, the `App` constructor in **ButtonEnabler** calls `Toolkit.Init`:

```
public class App : Application
{
    public App()
    {
        Xamarin.FormsBook.Toolkit.Toolkit.Init();

        MainPage = new ButtonEnablerPage();
    }
    …
}
```

Similar code appears in all the programs in this chapter that use the **Xamarin.FormsBook.Toolkit** library.

The screenshots confirm that the `Button` is not enabled unless the `Entry` contains some text:

If you're using only one instance of a value converter, you don't need to store it in the `Resources` dictionary. You can instantiate it right in the `Binding` tag with the use of property-element tags for the target property and for the `Converter` property of `Binding`:

```
<Button Text="Save or Send (or something)"
        FontSize="Large"
        HorizontalOptions="Center">
    <Button.IsEnabled>
        <Binding Source="{x:Reference entry}"
                 Path="Text.Length">
            <Binding.Converter>
                <toolkit:IntToBoolConverter />
            </Binding.Converter>
        </Binding>
    </Button.IsEnabled>
</Button>
```

Sometimes it's convenient for a value converter to define a couple of simple properties. For example, suppose you want to display some text for the two settings of a `Switch` but you don't want to use "True" and "False", and you don't want to hard-code alternatives into the value converter. Here's a `BoolToStringConverter` with a pair of public properties for two text strings:

```
namespace Xamarin.FormsBook.Toolkit
{
    public class BoolToStringConverter : IValueConverter
    {
        public string TrueText { set; get; }

        public string FalseText { set; get; }
```

```
        public object Convert(object value, Type targetType,
                              object parameter, CultureInfo culture)
        {
            return (bool)value ? TrueText : FalseText;
        }

        public object ConvertBack(object value, Type targetType,
                                  object parameter, CultureInfo culture)
        {
            return false;
        }
    }
}
```

The body of the `Convert` method is trivial: it just selects between the two strings based on the Boolean `value` argument.

A similar value converter converts a Boolean to one of two colors:

```
namespace Xamarin.FormsBook.Toolkit
{
    public class BoolToColorConverter : IValueConverter
    {
        public Color TrueColor { set; get; }

        public Color FalseColor { set; get; }

        public object Convert(object value, Type targetType,
                              object parameter, CultureInfo culture)
        {
            return (bool)value ? TrueColor : FalseColor;
        }

        public object ConvertBack(object value, Type targetType,
                                  object parameter, CultureInfo culture)
        {
            return false;
        }
    }
}
```

The **SwitchText** program instantiates the `BoolToStringConverter` converter twice for two different pairs of strings: once in the `Resources` dictionary, and then within `Binding.Converter` property-element tags. Two properties of the final `Label` are subjected to the `BoolToStringConverter` and the `BoolToColorConverter` based on the same `IsToggled` property from the `Switch`:

```
<ContentPage xmlns="http://xamarin.com/schemas/2014/forms"
             xmlns:x="http://schemas.microsoft.com/winfx/2009/xaml"
             xmlns:toolkit=
                 "clr-namespace:Xamarin.FormsBook.Toolkit;assembly=Xamarin.FormsBook.Toolkit"
             x:Class="SwitchText.SwitchTextPage"
             Padding="10, 0">
```

```
<ContentPage.Resources>
    <ResourceDictionary>
        <toolkit:BoolToStringConverter x:Key="boolToString"
                                       TrueText="Let's do it"
                                       FalseText="Not now" />

        <Style TargetType="Label">
            <Setter Property="FontSize" Value="Medium" />
            <Setter Property="VerticalOptions" Value="Center" />
        </Style>
    </ResourceDictionary>
</ContentPage.Resources>

<StackLayout>
    <!-- First Switch with text. -->
    <StackLayout Orientation="Horizontal"
                 VerticalOptions="CenterAndExpand">
        <Label Text="Learn more?" />

        <Switch x:Name="switch1"
                VerticalOptions="Center" />

        <Label Text="{Binding Source={x:Reference switch1},
                              Path=IsToggled,
                              Converter={StaticResource boolToString}}"
               HorizontalOptions="FillAndExpand" />
    </StackLayout>

    <!-- Second Switch with text. -->
    <StackLayout Orientation="Horizontal"
                 VerticalOptions="CenterAndExpand">
        <Label Text="Subscribe?" />

        <Switch x:Name="switch2"
                VerticalOptions="Center" />

        <Label Text="{Binding Source={x:Reference switch2},
                              Path=IsToggled,
                              Converter={StaticResource boolToString}}"
               HorizontalOptions="FillAndExpand" />
    </StackLayout>

    <!-- Third Switch with text and color. -->
    <StackLayout Orientation="Horizontal"
                 VerticalOptions="CenterAndExpand">
        <Label Text="Leave page?" />

        <Switch x:Name="switch3"
                VerticalOptions="Center" />

        <Label HorizontalOptions="FillAndExpand">
            <Label.Text>
                <Binding Source="{x:Reference switch3}"
                         Path="IsToggled">
```

```
                        <Binding.Converter>
                            <toolkit:BoolToStringConverter TrueText="Yes"
                                                         FalseText="No" />
                        </Binding.Converter>
                    </Binding>
                </Label.Text>

                <Label.TextColor>
                    <Binding Source="{x:Reference switch3}"
                             Path="IsToggled">
                        <Binding.Converter>
                            <toolkit:BoolToColorConverter TrueColor="Green"
                                                        FalseColor="Red" />
                        </Binding.Converter>
                    </Binding>
                </Label.TextColor>
            </Label>
        </StackLayout>
    </StackLayout>
</ContentPage>
```

With the two fairly trivial binding converters, the `Switch` can now display whatever text you want for the two states and can color that text with custom colors:

Now that you've seen a `BoolToStringConverter` and a `BoolToColorConverter`, can you generalize the technique to objects of any type? Here is a generic `BoolToObjectConverter` also in the **Xamarin.FormsBook.Toolkit** library:

```
public class BoolToObjectConverter<T> : IValueConverter
{
    public T TrueObject { set; get; }
```

```
    public T FalseObject { set; get; }

    public object Convert(object value, Type targetType,
                          object parameter, CultureInfo culture)
    {
        return (bool)value ? this.TrueObject : this.FalseObject;
    }

    public object ConvertBack(object value, Type targetType,
                              object parameter, CultureInfo culture)
    {
        return ((T)value).Equals(this.TrueObject);
    }
}
```

The next sample uses this class.

Bindings and custom views

In Chapter 15, "The interactive interface," you saw a custom view named `CheckBox`. This view defines a `Text` property for setting the text of the `CheckBox` as well as a `FontSize` property. It could also have defined all the other text-related properties—`TextColor`, `FontAttributes`, and `FontFamily`—but it did not, mostly because of the work involved. Each property requires a `BindableProperty` definition, a CLR property definition, and a property-changed handler that transfers the new setting of the property to the `Label` views that comprise the visuals of the `CheckBox`.

Data bindings can help simplify this process for some properties by eliminating the property-changed handlers. Here's the code-behind file for a new version of `CheckBox` called `NewCheckBox`. Like the earlier class, it's part of the **Xamarin.FormsBook.Toolkit** library. The file has been reorganized a bit so that each `BindableProperty` definition is paired with its corresponding CLR property definition. You might prefer this type of source-code organization of the properties, or perhaps not.

```
namespace Xamarin.FormsBook.Toolkit
{
    public partial class NewCheckBox : ContentView
    {
        public event EventHandler<bool> CheckedChanged;

        public NewCheckBox()
        {
            InitializeComponent();
        }

        // Text property.
        public static readonly BindableProperty TextProperty =
            BindableProperty.Create(
                "Text",
                typeof(string),
```

```
              typeof(NewCheckBox),
              null);

    public string Text
    {
        set { SetValue(TextProperty, value); }
        get { return (string)GetValue(TextProperty); }
    }

    // TextColor property.
    public static readonly BindableProperty TextColorProperty =
        BindableProperty.Create(
            "TextColor",
            typeof(Color),
            typeof(NewCheckBox),
            Color.Default);

    public Color TextColor
    {
        set { SetValue(TextColorProperty, value); }
        get { return (Color)GetValue(TextColorProperty); }
    }

    // FontSize property.
    public static readonly BindableProperty FontSizeProperty =
        BindableProperty.Create(
            "FontSize",
            typeof(double),
            typeof(NewCheckBox),
            Device.GetNamedSize(NamedSize.Default, typeof(Label)));

    [TypeConverter(typeof(FontSizeConverter))]
    public double FontSize
    {
        set { SetValue(FontSizeProperty, value); }
        get { return (double)GetValue(FontSizeProperty); }
    }

    // FontAttributes property.
    public static readonly BindableProperty FontAttributesProperty =
        BindableProperty.Create(
            "FontAttributes",
            typeof(FontAttributes),
            typeof(NewCheckBox),
            FontAttributes.None);

    public FontAttributes FontAttributes
    {
        set { SetValue(FontAttributesProperty, value); }
        get { return (FontAttributes)GetValue(FontAttributesProperty); }
    }

    // IsChecked property.
    public static readonly BindableProperty IsCheckedProperty =
```

```
            BindableProperty.Create(
                "IsChecked",
                typeof(bool),
                typeof(NewCheckBox),
                false,
                propertyChanged: (bindable, oldValue, newValue) =>
                {
                    // Fire the event.
                    NewCheckBox checkbox = (NewCheckBox)bindable;
                    EventHandler<bool> eventHandler = checkbox.CheckedChanged;
                    if (eventHandler != null)
                    {
                        eventHandler(checkbox, (bool)newValue);
                    }
                });

        public bool IsChecked
        {
            set { SetValue(IsCheckedProperty, value); }
            get { return (bool)GetValue(IsCheckedProperty); }
        }

        // TapGestureRecognizer handler.
        void OnCheckBoxTapped(object sender, EventArgs args)
        {
            IsChecked = !IsChecked;
        }
    }
}
```

Besides the earlier `Text` and `FontSize` properties, this code file now also defines `TextColor` and `FontAttributes` properties. However, the only property-changed handler is for the `IsChecked` handler to fire the `CheckedChanged` event. Everything else is handled by data bindings in the XAML file:

```xml
<ContentView xmlns="http://xamarin.com/schemas/2014/forms"
             xmlns:x="http://schemas.microsoft.com/winfx/2009/xaml"
             xmlns:toolkit="clr-namespace:Xamarin.FormsBook.Toolkit"
             x:Class="Xamarin.FormsBook.Toolkit.NewCheckBox"
             x:Name="checkbox">

    <StackLayout Orientation="Horizontal"
                 BindingContext="{x:Reference checkbox}">

        <Label x:Name="boxLabel" Text="&#x2610;"
                                 TextColor="{Binding TextColor}"
                                 FontSize="{Binding FontSize}">
            <Label.Text>
                <Binding Path="IsChecked">
                    <Binding.Converter>
                        <toolkit:BoolToStringConverter TrueText="&#x2611;"
                                                       FalseText="&#x2610;" />
                    </Binding.Converter>
                </Binding>
            </Label.Text>
```

```
            </Label>

            <Label x:Name="textLabel" Text="{Binding Path=Text}"
                                      TextColor="{Binding TextColor}"
                                      FontSize="{Binding FontSize}"
                                      FontAttributes="{Binding FontAttributes}" />
        </StackLayout>

        <ContentView.GestureRecognizers>
            <TapGestureRecognizer Tapped="OnCheckBoxTapped" />
        </ContentView.GestureRecognizers>
</ContentView>
```

The root element is given a name of `checkbox`, and the `StackLayout` sets that as its `Binding-Context`. All the data bindings within that `StackLayout` can then refer to properties defined by the code-behind file. The first `Label` that displays the box has its `TextColor` and `FontSize` properties bound to the values of the underlying properties, while the `Text` property is targeted by a binding that uses a `BoolToStringConverter` to display an empty box or a checked box based on the `IsChecked` property. The second `Label` is more straightforward: the `Text`, `TextColor`, `FontSize`, and `FontAt-tributes` properties are all bound to the corresponding properties defined in the code-behind file.

If you'll be creating several custom views that include `Text` elements and you need definitions of all the text-related properties, you'll probably want to first create a code-only class (named `CustomView-Base`, for example) that derives from `ContentView` and includes only those text-based property defi-nitions. You can then derive other classes from `CustomViewBase` and have `Text` and all the text-related properties readily available.

Let's write a little program called **NewCheckBoxDemo** that demonstrates the `NewCheckBox` view. Like the earlier **CheckBoxDemo** program, these check boxes control the bold and italic formatting of a paragraph of text. But to demonstrate the new properties, these check boxes are given colors and font attributes, and to demonstrate the `BoolToObjectConverter`, one of the check boxes controls the horizontal alignment of that paragraph:

```
<ContentPage xmlns="http://xamarin.com/schemas/2014/forms"
             xmlns:x="http://schemas.microsoft.com/winfx/2009/xaml"
             xmlns:toolkit=
                 "clr-namespace:Xamarin.FormsBook.Toolkit;assembly=Xamarin.FormsBook.Toolkit"
             x:Class="NewCheckBoxDemo.NewCheckBoxDemoPage">

    <StackLayout Padding="10, 0">
        <StackLayout HorizontalOptions="Center"
                     VerticalOptions="CenterAndExpand">

            <StackLayout.Resources>
                <ResourceDictionary>
                    <Style TargetType="toolkit:NewCheckBox">
                        <Setter Property="FontSize" Value="Large" />
                    </Style>
                </ResourceDictionary>
            </StackLayout.Resources>
```

```
            <toolkit:NewCheckBox Text="Italic"
                                 TextColor="Aqua"
                                 FontSize="Large"
                                 FontAttributes="Italic"
                                 CheckedChanged="OnItalicCheckBoxChanged" />

            <toolkit:NewCheckBox Text="Boldface"
                                 FontSize="Large"
                                 TextColor="Green"
                                 FontAttributes="Bold"
                                 CheckedChanged="OnBoldCheckBoxChanged" />

            <toolkit:NewCheckBox x:Name="centerCheckBox"
                                 Text="Center Text" />
        </StackLayout>

        <Label x:Name="label"
               Text=
"Just a little passage of some sample text that can be formatted
in italic or boldface by toggling the two custom CheckBox views."
               FontSize="Large"
               VerticalOptions="CenterAndExpand">
            <Label.HorizontalTextAlignment>
                <Binding Source="{x:Reference centerCheckBox}"
                         Path="IsChecked">
                    <Binding.Converter>
                        <toolkit:BoolToObjectConverter x:TypeArguments="TextAlignment"
                                                       TrueObject="Center"
                                                       FalseObject="Start" />
                    </Binding.Converter>
                </Binding>
            </Label.HorizontalTextAlignment>
        </Label>
    </StackLayout>
</ContentPage>
```

Notice the `BoolToObjectConverter` between the `Binding.Converter` tags. Because it's a generic class, it requires an `x:TypeArguments` attribute that indicates the type of the `TrueObject` and `FalseObject` properties and the type of the return value of the `Convert` method. Both `TrueObject` and `FalseObject` are set to members of the `TextAlignment` enumeration, and the converter selects one to be set to the `HorizontalTextAlignment` property of the `Label`, as the following screenshots demonstrate:

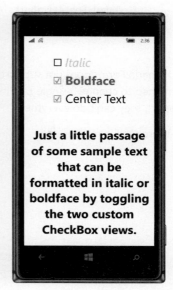

However, this program still needs a code-behind file to manage applying the italic and boldface attributes to the block of text. These methods are identical to those in the early **CheckBoxDemo** program:

```
public partial class NewCheckBoxDemoPage : ContentPage
{
    public NewCheckBoxDemoPage()
    {
        InitializeComponent();
    }

    void OnItalicCheckBoxChanged(object sender, bool isChecked)
    {
        if (isChecked)
        {
            label.FontAttributes |= FontAttributes.Italic;
        }
        else
        {
            label.FontAttributes &= ~FontAttributes.Italic;
        }
    }

    void OnBoldCheckBoxChanged(object sender, bool isChecked)
    {
        if (isChecked)
        {
            label.FontAttributes |= FontAttributes.Bold;
        }
        else
        {
```

```
        label.FontAttributes &= ~FontAttributes.Bold;
    }
  }
}
```

Xamarin.Forms does not support a "multi-binding" that might allow multiple binding sources to be combined to change a single binding target. Bindings can do a lot, but without some additional code support, they can't do everything.

There's still a role for code.

Chapter 17
Mastering the Grid

The `Grid` is a powerful layout mechanism that organizes its children into rows and columns of cells. At first, the `Grid` seems to resemble the HTML `table`, but there is a very important distinction: The HTML `table` is designed for presentation purposes, while the `Grid` is solely for layout. There is no concept of a heading in a `Grid`, for example, and no built-in feature to draw boxes around the cells or to separate rows and columns with divider lines. The strengths of the `Grid` are in specifying cell dimensions with three options of height and width settings.

As you've seen, the `StackLayout` is ideal for one-dimensional collections of children. Although it's possible to nest a `StackLayout` within a `StackLayout` to accommodate a second dimension and mimic a table, often the result can exhibit alignment problems. The `Grid`, however, is designed specifically for two-dimensional arrays of children. As you'll see toward the end of this chapter, the `Grid` can also be very useful for managing layouts that adapt to both portrait and landscape modes.

The basic Grid

A `Grid` can be defined and filled with children in either code or XAML, but the XAML approach is easier and clearer, and hence by far the more common.

The Grid in XAML

When defined in XAML, a `Grid` almost always has a fixed number of rows and columns. The `Grid` definition generally begins with two important properties, named `RowDefinitions` (which is a collection of `RowDefinition` objects) and `ColumnDefinitions` (a collection of `ColumnDefinition` objects). These collections contain one `RowDefinition` for every row in the `Grid` and one `ColumnDefinition` for every column, and they define the row and column characteristics of the `Grid`.

A `Grid` can consist of a single row or single column (in which case it doesn't need one of the two `Definitions` collections), or even just a single cell.

`RowDefinition` has a `Height` property of type `GridLength`, and `ColumnDefinition` has a `Width` property, also of type `GridLength`. The `GridLength` structure specifies a row height or a column width in terms of the `GridUnitType` enumeration, which has three members:

- `Absolute`—the width or height is a value in device-independent units (a number in XAML)

- `Auto`—the width or height is autosized based on the cell contents ("Auto" in XAML)

- `Star`—leftover width or height is allocated proportionally (a number with "*" in XAML)

Here's the first half of the XAML file in the **SimpleGridDemo** project:

```xaml
<ContentPage xmlns="http://xamarin.com/schemas/2014/forms"
             xmlns:x="http://schemas.microsoft.com/winfx/2009/xaml"
             x:Class="SimpleGridDemo.SimpleGridDemoPage">

    <ContentPage.Padding>
        <OnPlatform x:TypeArguments="Thickness"
                    iOS="0, 20, 0, 0" />
    </ContentPage.Padding>

    <Grid>
        <Grid.RowDefinitions>
            <RowDefinition Height="Auto" />
            <RowDefinition Height="100" />
            <RowDefinition Height="2*" />
            <RowDefinition Height="1*" />
        </Grid.RowDefinitions>

        <Grid.ColumnDefinitions>
            <ColumnDefinition Width="*" />
            <ColumnDefinition Width="*" />
        </Grid.ColumnDefinitions>

        ...

    </Grid>
</ContentPage>
```

This `Grid` has four rows and two columns. The height of the first row is "Auto"—meaning that the height is calculated based on the maximum height of all the elements occupying that first row. The second row is 100 device-independent units in height.

The two `Height` settings using "*" (pronounced "star") require some additional explanation: This particular `Grid` has an overall height that is the height of the page minus the `Padding` setting on iOS. Internally, the `Grid` determines the height of the first row based on the contents of that row, and it knows that the height of the second row is 100. It subtracts those two heights from its own height and allocates the remaining height proportionally among the third and fourth rows based on the number in the star setting. The third row is twice the height of the fourth row.

The two `ColumnDefinition` objects both set the `Width` equal to "*," which is the same as "1*," which means that the width of the screen is divided equally between the two columns.

You'll recall from Chapter 14, "Absolute layout," that the `AbsoluteLayout` class defines two attached bindable properties and four static `Set` and `Get` methods that allow a program to specify the position and size of a child of the `AbsoluteLayout` in code or XAML.

The `Grid` is quite similar. The `Grid` class defines four attached bindable properties for specifying the cell or cells that a child of the `Grid` occupies:

- `Grid.RowProperty`—the zero-based row; default value is 0

- Grid.ColumnProperty—the zero-based column; default value is 0

- Grid.RowSpanProperty—the number of rows that the child spans; default value is 1

- Grid.ColumnSpanProperty—the number of columns that the child spans; default value is 1

All four properties are defined to be of type int.

For example, to specify in code that a Grid child named view resides in a particular row and column, you can call:

```
view.SetValue(Grid.RowProperty, 2);
view.SetValue(Grid.ColumnProperty, 1);
```

Those are zero-based row and column numbers, so the child is assigned to the third row and the second column.

The Grid class also defines eight static methods for streamlining the setting and getting of these properties in code:

- Grid.SetRow and Grid.GetRow

- Grid.SetColumn and Grid.GetColumn

- Grid.SetRowSpan and Grid.GetRowSpan

- Grid.SetColumnSpan and Grid.GetColumnSpan

Here's the equivalent of the two SetValue calls you just saw:

```
Grid.SetRow(view, 2);
Grid.SetColumn(view, 1);
```

As you learned in connection with AbsoluteLayout, such static Set and Get methods are implemented with SetValue and GetValue calls on the child of Grid. For example, here's how SetRow is very likely defined within the Grid class:

```
public static void SetRow(BindableObject bindable, int value)
{
    bindable.SetValue(Grid.RowProperty, value);
}
```

You cannot call these methods in XAML, so instead you use the following attributes for setting the attached bindable properties on a child of the Grid:

- Grid.Row

- Grid.Column

- Grid.RowSpan

- Grid.ColumnSpan

These XAML attributes are not actually defined by the `Grid` class, but the XAML parser knows that it must reference the associated attached bindable properties defined by `Grid`.

You don't need to set all these properties on every child of the `Grid`. If the child occupies just one cell, then don't set `Grid.RowSpan` or `Grid.ColumnSpan` because the default value is 1. The `Grid.Row` and `Grid.Column` properties have a default value of 0, so you don't need to set the values if the child occupies the first row or first column. However, for purposes of clarity, the code in this book will usually show the settings of these two properties. To save space, often these attributes will appear on the same line in the XAML listing.

Here's the complete XAML file for **SimpleGridDemo**:

```xml
<ContentPage xmlns="http://xamarin.com/schemas/2014/forms"
             xmlns:x="http://schemas.microsoft.com/winfx/2009/xaml"
             x:Class="SimpleGridDemo.SimpleGridDemoPage">

    <ContentPage.Padding>
        <OnPlatform x:TypeArguments="Thickness"
                    iOS="0, 20, 0, 0" />
    </ContentPage.Padding>

    <Grid>
        <Grid.RowDefinitions>
            <RowDefinition Height="Auto" />
            <RowDefinition Height="100" />
            <RowDefinition Height="2*" />
            <RowDefinition Height="1*" />
        </Grid.RowDefinitions>

        <Grid.ColumnDefinitions>
            <ColumnDefinition Width="*" />
            <ColumnDefinition Width="*" />
        </Grid.ColumnDefinitions>

        <Label Text="Grid Demo"
               Grid.Row="0" Grid.Column="0"
               FontSize="Large"
               HorizontalOptions="End" />

        <Label Text="Demo the Grid"
               Grid.Row="0" Grid.Column="1"
               FontSize="Small"
               HorizontalOptions="End"
               VerticalOptions="End" />

        <Image BackgroundColor="Gray"
               Grid.Row="1" Grid.Column="0" Grid.ColumnSpan="2">
            <Image.Source>
                <OnPlatform x:TypeArguments="ImageSource"
                            iOS="Icon-60.png"
                            Android="icon.png"
                            WinPhone="Assets/StoreLogo.png" />
```

```
            </Image.Source>
        </Image>

        <BoxView Color="Green"
                 Grid.Row="2" Grid.Column="0" />

        <BoxView Color="Red"
                 Grid.Row="2" Grid.Column="1" Grid.RowSpan="2" />

        <BoxView Color="Blue"
                 Opacity="0.5"
                 Grid.Row="3" Grid.Column="0" Grid.ColumnSpan="2" />
    </Grid>
</ContentPage>
```

Two `Label` elements with different `FontSize` settings occupy the two columns of the first row. The height of that row is governed by the tallest element. Settings of `HorizontalOptions` and `VerticalOptions` can position a child within the cell.

The second row has a height of 100 device-independent units. That row is occupied by an `Image` element displaying an application icon with a gray background. The `Image` element spans both columns of that row.

The bottom two rows are occupied by three `BoxView` elements, one that spans two rows, and another that spans two columns, and these overlap in the bottom right cell:

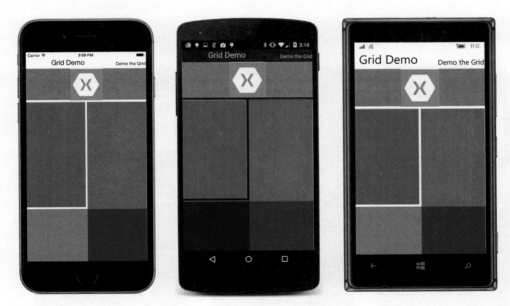

The screenshots confirm that the first row is sized to the height of the large `Label`; the second row is 100 device-independent units tall; and the third and fourth rows occupy all the remaining space. The third row is twice as tall as the fourth. The two columns are equal in width and divide the entire `Grid`

in half. The red and blue `BoxView` elements overlap in the bottom right cell, but the blue `BoxView` is obviously sitting on top of the red one because it has an `Opacity` setting of 0.5 and the result is purple.

The left half of the blue semitransparent `BoxView` is lighter on the iPhone and Windows 10 Mobile device than on the Android phone because of the white background.

As you can see, children of the `Grid` can share cells. The order that the children appear in the XAML file is the order that the children are put into the `Grid`, with later children seemingly sitting on top of (and obscuring) earlier children.

You'll notice that a little gap seems to separate the rows and columns where the background peeks through. This is governed by two `Grid` properties:

- `RowSpacing`—default value of 6

- `ColumnSpacing`—default value of 6

You can set these properties to 0 if you want to close up that space, and you can set the `Background-Color` property of the `Grid` if you want the color peeking through to be something different. You can also add space on the inside of the `Grid` around its perimeter with a `Padding` setting on the `Grid`.

You have now been introduced to all the public properties and methods defined by `Grid`.

Before moving on, let's perform a couple of experiments with **SimpleGridDemo**. First, comment out or delete the entire `RowDefinitions` and `ColumnDefinitions` section near the top of the `Grid`, and then redeploy the program. Here's what you'll see:

When you don't define your own `RowDefinition` and `ColumnDefinition` objects, the `Grid` generates them automatically as views are added to the `Children` collection. However, the default `RowDefinition` and `ColumnDefinition` is "*" (star), meaning that the four rows now equally divide the screen in quarters, and each cell is one-eighth of the total `Grid`.

Here's another experiment. Restore the `RowDefinitions` and `ColumnDefinitions` sections and set the `HorizontalOptions` and `VerticalOptions` properties on the `Grid` itself to `Center`. By default these two properties are `Fill`, which means that the `Grid` fills its container. Here's what happens with `Center`:

The third row is still twice the height of the bottom row, but now the bottom row's height is based on the default `HeightRequest` of `BoxView`, which is 40.

You'll see a similar effect when you put a `Grid` in a `StackLayout`. You can also put a `StackLayout` in a `Grid` cell, or another `Grid` in a `Grid` cell, but don't get carried away with this technique: The deeper you nest `Grid` and other layouts, the more the nested layouts will impact performance.

The Grid in code

It is also possible to define a `Grid` entirely in code, but usually without the clarity or orderliness of the XAML definition. The **GridCodeDemo** program demonstrates the code approach by reproducing the layout of **SimpleGridDemo**.

To specify the height of a `RowDefinition` and the width of the `ColumnDefinition`, you use values of the `GridLength` structure, often in combination with the `GridUnitType` enumeration. The row definitions toward the top of the `GridCodeDemoPage` class demonstrate the variations of

GridLength. The column definitions aren't included because they are the same as those generated by default:

```csharp
public class GridCodeDemoPage : ContentPage
{
    public GridCodeDemoPage()
    {
        Grid grid = new Grid
        {
            RowDefinitions =
            {
                new RowDefinition { Height = GridLength.Auto },
                new RowDefinition { Height = new GridLength(100) },
                new RowDefinition { Height = new GridLength(2, GridUnitType.Star) },
                new RowDefinition { Height = new GridLength(1, GridUnitType.Star) }
            }
        };

        // First Label (row 0 and column 0).
        grid.Children.Add(new Label
        {
            Text = "Grid Demo",
            FontSize = Device.GetNamedSize(NamedSize.Large, typeof(Label)),
            HorizontalOptions = LayoutOptions.End
        });

        // Second Label.
        grid.Children.Add(new Label
            {
                Text = "Demo the Grid",
                FontSize = Device.GetNamedSize(NamedSize.Small, typeof(Label)),
                HorizontalOptions = LayoutOptions.End,
                VerticalOptions = LayoutOptions.End
            },
            1,              // left
            0);             // top

        // Image element.
        grid.Children.Add(new Image
            {
                BackgroundColor = Color.Gray,
                Source = Device.OnPlatform("Icon-60.png",
                                           "icon.png",
                                           "Assets/StoreLogo.png")
            },
            0,              // left
            2,              // right
            1,              // top
            2);             // bottom

        // Three BoxView elements.
        BoxView boxView1 = new BoxView { Color = Color.Green };
        Grid.SetRow(boxView1, 2);
        Grid.SetColumn(boxView1, 0);
```

```
            grid.Children.Add(boxView1);

            BoxView boxView2 = new BoxView { Color = Color.Red };
            Grid.SetRow(boxView2, 2);
            Grid.SetColumn(boxView2, 1);
            Grid.SetRowSpan(boxView2, 2);
            grid.Children.Add(boxView2);

            BoxView boxView3 = new BoxView
            {
                Color = Color.Blue,
                Opacity = 0.5
            };
            Grid.SetRow(boxView3, 3);
            Grid.SetColumn(boxView3, 0);
            Grid.SetColumnSpan(boxView3, 2);
            grid.Children.Add(boxView3);

            Padding = new Thickness(0, Device.OnPlatform(20, 0, 0), 0, 0);
            Content = grid;
        }
}
```

The program shows several different ways to add children to the `Grid` and specify the cells in which they reside. The first `Label` is in row 0 and column 0, so it only needs to be added to the `Children` collection of the `Grid` to get default row and column settings:

```
grid.Children.Add(new Label
{
    …
});
```

The `Grid` redefines its `Children` collection to be of type `IGridList<View>`, which includes several additional `Add` methods. One of these `Add` methods lets you specify the row and column:

```
grid.Children.Add(new Label
    {
        …
    },
    1,              // left
    0);             // top
```

As the comments indicate, the arguments are actually named `left` and `top` rather than `column` and `row`. These names make more sense when you see the syntax for specifying row and column spans:

```
grid.Children.Add(new Image
    {
        …
    },
    0,              // left
    2,              // right
    1,              // top
    2);             // bottom
```

What this means is that the child element goes in the column starting at `left` but ending before `right`—in other words, columns 0 and 1. It occupies the row starting at `top` but ending before `bottom`, which is row 1. The `right` argument must always be greater than `left`, and the `bottom` argument must be greater than `top`. If not, the `Grid` throws an `ArgumentOutOfRangeException`.

The `IGridList<View>` interface also defines `AddHorizontal` and `AddVertical` methods to add children to a single row or single column `Grid`. The `Grid` expands in columns or rows as these calls are made, as well as automatically assigning `Grid.Column` or `Grid.Row` settings on the children. You'll see a use for this facility in the next section.

When adding children to a `Grid` in code, it's also possible to make explicit calls to `Grid.SetRow`, `Grid.SetColumn`, `Grid.SetRowSpan`, and `Grid.SetColumnSpan`. It doesn't matter whether you make these calls before or after you add the child to the `Children` collection of the `Grid`:

```
BoxView boxView1 = new BoxView { … };
Grid.SetRow(boxView1, 2);
Grid.SetColumn(boxView1, 0);
grid.Children.Add(boxView1);

BoxView boxView2 = new BoxView { … };
Grid.SetRow(boxView2, 2);
Grid.SetColumn(boxView2, 1);
Grid.SetRowSpan(boxView2, 2);
grid.Children.Add(boxView2);

BoxView boxView3 = new BoxView
{
    …
};
Grid.SetRow(boxView3, 3);
Grid.SetColumn(boxView3, 0);
Grid.SetColumnSpan(boxView3, 2);
grid.Children.Add(boxView3);
```

The Grid bar chart

The `AddVertical` and `AddHorizontal` methods defined by the `Children` collection of the `Grid` have the capability to add an entire collection of views to the `Grid` in one shot. By default, the new rows or columns get a height or width of "*" (star), so the resultant `Grid` consists of multiple rows or columns, each with the same size.

Let's use the `AddHorizontal` method to make a little bar chart that consists of 50 `BoxView` elements with random heights. The XAML file for the **GridBarChart** program defines an `AbsoluteLayout` that is parent to both a `Grid` and a `Frame`. This `Frame` serves as an overlay to display information about a particular bar in the bar chart. It has its `Opacity` set to 0, so it is initially invisible:

```
<ContentPage xmlns="http://xamarin.com/schemas/2014/forms"
             xmlns:x="http://schemas.microsoft.com/winfx/2009/xaml"
             x:Class="GridBarChart.GridBarChartPage">
```

```
    <AbsoluteLayout>

        <!-- Grid occupying entire page. -->
        <Grid x:Name="grid"
              ColumnSpacing="1"
              AbsoluteLayout.LayoutBounds="0, 0, 1, 1"
              AbsoluteLayout.LayoutFlags="All" />

        <!-- Overlay in center of screen. -->
        <Frame x:Name="overlay"
               OutlineColor="Accent"
               BackgroundColor="#404040"
               Opacity="0"
               AbsoluteLayout.LayoutBounds="0.5, 0.5, AutoSize, AutoSize"
               AbsoluteLayout.LayoutFlags="PositionProportional">

            <Label x:Name="label"
                   TextColor="White"
                   FontSize="Large" />
        </Frame>
    </AbsoluteLayout>
</ContentPage>
```

The code-behind file creates 50 `BoxView` elements with a random `HeightRequest` property be-tween 0 and 300. In addition, the `StyleId` property of each `BoxView` is assigned a string that consists of alternated random consonants and vowels to resemble a name (perhaps of someone from another planet). All these `BoxView` elements are accumulated in a generic `List` collection and then added to the `Grid`. That job is the bulk of the code in the constructor:

```
public partial class GridBarChartPage : ContentPage
{
    const int COUNT = 50;
    Random random = new Random();

    public GridBarChartPage()
    {
        InitializeComponent();

        List<View> views = new List<View>();
        TapGestureRecognizer tapGesture = new TapGestureRecognizer();
        tapGesture.Tapped += OnBoxViewTapped;

        // Create BoxView elements and add to List.
        for (int i = 0; i < COUNT; i++)
        {
            BoxView boxView = new BoxView
            {
                Color = Color.Accent,
                HeightRequest = 300 * random.NextDouble(),
                VerticalOptions = LayoutOptions.End,
                StyleId = RandomNameGenerator()
            };
```

```
            boxView.GestureRecognizers.Add(tapGesture);
            views.Add(boxView);
        }

        // Add whole List of BoxView elements to Grid.
        grid.Children.AddHorizontal(views);

        // Start a timer at the frame rate.
        Device.StartTimer(TimeSpan.FromMilliseconds(15), OnTimerTick);
    }

    // Arrays for Random Name Generator.
    string[] vowels = { "a", "e", "i", "o", "u", "ai", "ei", "ie", "ou", "oo" };
    string[] consonants = { "b", "c", "d", "f", "g", "h", "j", "k", "l", "m",
                            "n", "p", "q", "r", "s", "t", "v", "w", "x", "z" };

    string RandomNameGenerator()
    {
        int numPieces = 1 + 2 * random.Next(1, 4);
        StringBuilder name = new StringBuilder();

        for (int i = 0; i < numPieces; i++)
        {
            name.Append(i % 2 == 0 ?
                consonants[random.Next(consonants.Length)] :
                vowels[random.Next(vowels.Length)]);
        }
        name[0] = Char.ToUpper(name[0]);
        return name.ToString();
    }

    // Set text to overlay Label and make it visible.
    void OnBoxViewTapped(object sender, EventArgs args)
    {
        BoxView boxView = (BoxView)sender;
        label.Text = String.Format("The individual known as {0} " +
                                   "has a height of {1} centimeters.",
                                   boxView.StyleId, (int)boxView.HeightRequest);
        overlay.Opacity = 1;
    }

    // Decrease visibility of overlay.
    bool OnTimerTick()
    {
        overlay.Opacity = Math.Max(0, overlay.Opacity - 0.0025);
        return true;
    }
}
```

The `AddHorizontal` method of the `Children` collection adds the multiple `BoxView` elements to the `Grid` and gives them sequential `Grid.Column` settings. Each column by default has a width of "*" (star), so the width of each `BoxView` is the same while the height is governed by the `HeightRequest` settings. The `Spacing` value of 1 set to the `Grid` in the XAML file provides a little separation between the bars of the bar chart:

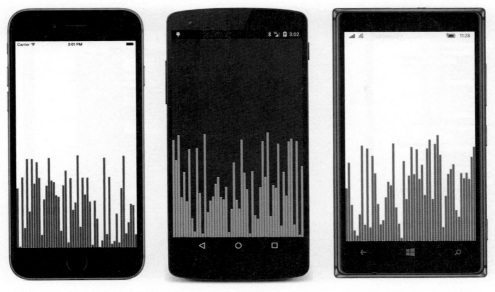

The bars are more distinct when you turn the phone sideways to give them more width:

This program has another feature: When you tap on one of the bars, the overlay is made visible and displays information about that tapped bar—specifically, the interplanetary visitor's name from the

`StyleId` and the height of the bar. But a timer set in the constructor continuously decreases the `Opacity` value on the overlay, so this information gradually fades from view:

Even without a native graphics system, Xamarin.Forms is able to display something that looks quite a lot like graphics.

Alignment in the Grid

A `Grid` row with a `Height` property of `Auto` constrains the height of elements in that row in the same way as a vertical `StackLayout`. Similarly, a column with a `Width` of `Auto` works much like a horizontal `StackLayout`.

As you've seen earlier in this chapter, you can set the `HorizontalOptions` and `VerticalOptions` properties of children of the `Grid` to position them within the cell. Here's a program called **GridAlignment** that creates a `Grid` with nine equal-size cells and then puts six `Label` elements all in the center cell but with different alignment settings:

```
<ContentPage xmlns="http://xamarin.com/schemas/2014/forms"
             xmlns:x="http://schemas.microsoft.com/winfx/2009/xaml"
             x:Class="GridAlignment.GridAlignmentPage">

    <Grid>
        <Grid.RowDefinitions>
            <RowDefinition Height="*" />
            <RowDefinition Height="*" />
            <RowDefinition Height="*" />
        </Grid.RowDefinitions>
```

```
        <Grid.ColumnDefinitions>
            <ColumnDefinition Width="*" />
            <ColumnDefinition Width="*" />
            <ColumnDefinition Width="*" />
        </Grid.ColumnDefinitions>

        <Label Text="Upper Left"
               Grid.Row="1" Grid.Column="1"
               VerticalOptions="Start"
               HorizontalOptions="Start" />

        <Label Text="Upper Right"
               Grid.Row="1" Grid.Column="1"
               VerticalOptions="Start"
               HorizontalOptions="End" />

        <Label Text="Center Left"
               Grid.Row="1" Grid.Column="1"
               VerticalOptions="Center"
               HorizontalOptions="Start" />

        <Label Text="Center Right"
               Grid.Row="1" Grid.Column="1"
               VerticalOptions="Center"
               HorizontalOptions="End" />

        <Label Text="Lower Left"
               Grid.Row="1" Grid.Column="1"
               VerticalOptions="End"
               HorizontalOptions="Start" />

        <Label Text="Lower Right"
               Grid.Row="1" Grid.Column="1"
               VerticalOptions="End"
               HorizontalOptions="End" />
    </Grid>
</ContentPage>
```

As you can see, some of the text overlaps:

But if you turn the phone sideways, the cells resize and the text doesn't overlap:

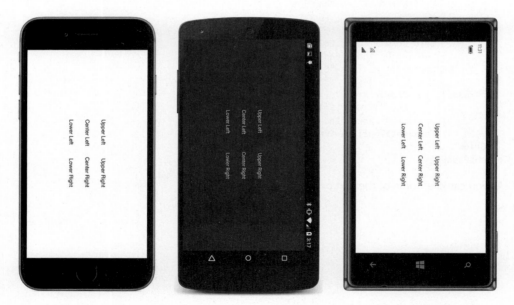

Although you can use `HorizontalOptions` and `VerticalOptions` on children of a `Grid` to set the child's alignment, you cannot use the `Expands` flag. Strictly speaking, you actually *can* use the `Expands` flag, but it has no effect on children of a `Grid`. The `Expands` flag only affects children of a `StackLayout`.

Often you've seen programs that use the `Expands` flag for children of a `StackLayout` to provide extra space to surround elements within the layout. For example, if two `Label` children of a `Stack-Layout` both have their `VerticalOptions` properties set to `CenterAndExpand`, then all the extra space is divided equally between the two slots in the `StackLayout` allocated for these children.

In a `Grid`, you can perform similar layout tricks by using cells sized with the "*" (star) specification together with `HorizontalOptions` and `VerticalOptions` settings on the children. You can even create empty rows or empty columns just for spacing purposes.

The **SpacingButtons** program equally spaces three vertical buttons and three horizontal buttons. The first three buttons occupy a three-row `Grid` that takes up much of the page, and the three horizontal buttons are in a three-column `Grid` down at the bottom of the page. The two grids are in a `StackLayout`:

```
<ContentPage xmlns="http://xamarin.com/schemas/2014/forms"
             xmlns:x="http://schemas.microsoft.com/winfx/2009/xaml"
             x:Class="SpacingButtons.SpacingButtonsPage">
    <StackLayout>
        <Grid VerticalOptions="FillAndExpand">
            <Grid.RowDefinitions>
                <RowDefinition Height="*" />
                <RowDefinition Height="*" />
                <RowDefinition Height="*" />
            </Grid.RowDefinitions>

            <Button Text="Button 1"
                    Grid.Row="0"
                    VerticalOptions="Center"
                    HorizontalOptions="Center" />

            <Button Text="Button 2"
                    Grid.Row="1"
                    VerticalOptions="Center"
                    HorizontalOptions="Center" />

            <Button Text="Button 3"
                    Grid.Row="2"
                    VerticalOptions="Center"
                    HorizontalOptions="Center" />
        </Grid>

        <Grid>
            <Grid.ColumnDefinitions>
                <ColumnDefinition Width="*" />
                <ColumnDefinition Width="*" />
                <ColumnDefinition Width="*" />
            </Grid.ColumnDefinitions>

            <Button Text="Button 4"
                    Grid.Column="0"
                    HorizontalOptions="Center" />

            <Button Text="Button 5"
```

```
                        Grid.Column="1"
                        HorizontalOptions="Center" />

            <Button Text="Button 6"
                        Grid.Column="2"
                        HorizontalOptions="Center" />
        </Grid>
    </StackLayout>
</ContentPage>
```

The second `Grid` has a default `VerticalOptions` value of `Fill`, while the first `Grid` has an explicit setting for `VerticalOptions` to `FillAndExpand`. This means that the first `Grid` will occupy all the area of the screen not occupied by the second `Grid`. The three `RowDefinition` objects of the first `Grid` divide that area into thirds. Within each cell, the `Button` is horizontal and vertically centered:

The second `Grid` divides its area into three equally spaced columns, and each `Button` is horizontally centered within that area.

Although the `Expands` flag of `LayoutOptions` can assist in equally spacing visual objects within a `StackLayout`, the technique breaks down when the visual objects are not a uniform size. The `Expands` option allocates leftover space equally among all the slots in the `StackLayout`, but the total size of each slot depends on the size of the individual visual objects. The `Grid`, however, allocates space equally to the cells, and then the visual objects are aligned within that space.

Cell dividers and borders

The `Grid` doesn't have any built-in cell dividers or borders. But if you'd like some, you can add them yourself. The **GridCellDividers** program defines a `GridLength` value in its `Resources` dictionary named `dividerThickness`. This is used for the height and width of every other row and column in the `Grid`. The idea here is that these rows and columns are for the dividers, while the other rows and columns are for regular content:

```xml
<ContentPage xmlns="http://xamarin.com/schemas/2014/forms"
             xmlns:x="http://schemas.microsoft.com/winfx/2009/xaml"
             x:Class="GridCellDividers.GridCellDividersPage">

    <ContentPage.Padding>
        <OnPlatform x:TypeArguments="Thickness"
                    iOS="0, 20, 0, 0"
                    Android="0"
                    WinPhone="0" />
    </ContentPage.Padding>

    <Grid>
        <Grid.Resources>
            <ResourceDictionary>
                <GridLength x:Key="dividerThickness">2</GridLength>

                <Style TargetType="BoxView">
                    <Setter Property="Color" Value="Accent" />
                </Style>

                <Style TargetType="Label">
                    <Setter Property="HorizontalOptions" Value="Center" />
                    <Setter Property="VerticalOptions" Value="Center" />
                </Style>
            </ResourceDictionary>
        </Grid.Resources>

        <Grid.RowDefinitions>
            <RowDefinition Height="{StaticResource dividerThickness}" />
            <RowDefinition Height="*" />
            <RowDefinition Height="{StaticResource dividerThickness}" />
            <RowDefinition Height="*" />
            <RowDefinition Height="{StaticResource dividerThickness}" />
            <RowDefinition Height="*" />
            <RowDefinition Height="{StaticResource dividerThickness}" />
        </Grid.RowDefinitions>

        <Grid.ColumnDefinitions>
            <ColumnDefinition Width="{StaticResource dividerThickness}" />
            <ColumnDefinition Width="*" />
            <ColumnDefinition Width="{StaticResource dividerThickness}" />
            <ColumnDefinition Width="*" />
            <ColumnDefinition Width="{StaticResource dividerThickness}" />
            <ColumnDefinition Width="*" />
            <ColumnDefinition Width="{StaticResource dividerThickness}" />
        </Grid.ColumnDefinitions>

        <BoxView Grid.Row="0" Grid.Column="0" Grid.ColumnSpan="7" />
        <BoxView Grid.Row="2" Grid.Column="0" Grid.ColumnSpan="7" />
        <BoxView Grid.Row="4" Grid.Column="0" Grid.ColumnSpan="7" />
```

```
            <BoxView Grid.Row="6" Grid.Column="0" Grid.ColumnSpan="7" />

            <BoxView Grid.Row="0" Grid.Column="0" Grid.RowSpan="7" />
            <BoxView Grid.Row="0" Grid.Column="2" Grid.RowSpan="7" />
            <BoxView Grid.Row="0" Grid.Column="4" Grid.RowSpan="7" />
            <BoxView Grid.Row="0" Grid.Column="6" Grid.RowSpan="7" />

            <Label Text="Grid"
                   Grid.Row="1" Grid.Column="1" />

            <Label Text="Cell"
                   Grid.Row="3" Grid.Column="3" />

            <Label Text="Dividers"
                   Grid.Row="5" Grid.Column="5" />
    </Grid>
</ContentPage>
```

Each row and column for the dividers is occupied by a `BoxView` colored with the `Accent` color from an implicit style. For the horizontal dividers, the height is set by the `RowDefinition` and the width is governed by the `Grid.ColumnSpan` attached bindable property; a similar approach is applied for the vertical dividers.

The `Grid` also contains three `Label` elements just to demonstrate how regular content fits in with these dividers:

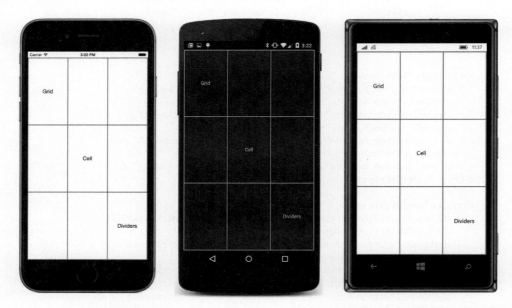

It is not necessary to allocate entire rows and columns to these dividers. Keep in mind that visual objects can share cells, so it's possible to add a `BoxView` (or two or three or four) to a cell and set the horizontal and vertical options so that it hugs the wall of the cell and resembles a border.

Here's a similar program, called **GridCellBorders,** that displays content in the same three cells as **GridCellDividers**, but those three cells are also adorned with borders.

The `Resources` dictionary contains no fewer than seven styles that target `BoxView`! The base style sets the color, two more styles set the `HeightRequest` and `WidthRequest` for the horizontal and vertical borders, and then four more styles set the `VerticalOptions` to `Start` or `End` for the top and bottom borders and `HorizontalOptions` to `Start` and `End` for the left and right borders. The `borderThickness` dictionary entry is a `double` because it's used to set `WidthRequest` and `HeightRequest` properties of the `BoxView` elements:

```
<ContentPage xmlns="http://xamarin.com/schemas/2014/forms"
             xmlns:x="http://schemas.microsoft.com/winfx/2009/xaml"
             x:Class="GridCellBorders.GridCellBordersPage">

    <ContentPage.Padding>
        <OnPlatform x:TypeArguments="Thickness"
                    iOS="10, 20, 10, 10"
                    Android="10"
                    WinPhone="10" />
    </ContentPage.Padding>

    <Grid>
        <Grid.Resources>
            <ResourceDictionary>
                <x:Double x:Key="borderThickness">1</x:Double>

                <Style x:Key="baseBorderStyle" TargetType="BoxView">
                    <Setter Property="Color" Value="Accent" />
                </Style>

                <Style x:Key="horzBorderStyle" TargetType="BoxView"
                       BasedOn="{StaticResource baseBorderStyle}">
                    <Setter Property="HeightRequest" Value="{StaticResource borderThickness}" />
                </Style>

                <Style x:Key="topBorderStyle" TargetType="BoxView"
                       BasedOn="{StaticResource horzBorderStyle}">
                    <Setter Property="VerticalOptions" Value="Start" />
                </Style>

                <Style x:Key="bottomBorderStyle" TargetType="BoxView"
                       BasedOn="{StaticResource horzBorderStyle}">
                    <Setter Property="VerticalOptions" Value="End" />
                </Style>

                <Style x:Key="vertBorderStyle" TargetType="BoxView"
                       BasedOn="{StaticResource baseBorderStyle}">
                    <Setter Property="WidthRequest" Value="{StaticResource borderThickness}" />
                </Style>

                <Style x:Key="leftBorderStyle" TargetType="BoxView"
                       BasedOn="{StaticResource vertBorderStyle}">
```

```xml
                <Setter Property="HorizontalOptions" Value="Start" />
        </Style>

        <Style x:Key="rightBorderStyle" TargetType="BoxView"
                BasedOn="{StaticResource vertBorderStyle}">
            <Setter Property="HorizontalOptions" Value="End" />
        </Style>

        <Style TargetType="Label">
            <Setter Property="HorizontalOptions" Value="Center" />
            <Setter Property="VerticalOptions" Value="Center" />
        </Style>
    </ResourceDictionary>
</Grid.Resources>

<Grid.RowDefinitions>
    <RowDefinition Height="*" />
    <RowDefinition Height="*" />
    <RowDefinition Height="*" />
</Grid.RowDefinitions>

<Grid.ColumnDefinitions>
    <ColumnDefinition Width="*" />
    <ColumnDefinition Width="*" />
    <ColumnDefinition Width="*" />
</Grid.ColumnDefinitions>

<Label Text="Grid"
       Grid.Row="0" Grid.Column="0" />

<BoxView Style="{StaticResource topBorderStyle}"
         Grid.Row="0" Grid.Column="0" />

<BoxView Style="{StaticResource bottomBorderStyle}"
         Grid.Row="0" Grid.Column="0" />

<BoxView Style="{StaticResource leftBorderStyle}"
         Grid.Row="0" Grid.Column="0" />

<BoxView Style="{StaticResource rightBorderStyle}"
         Grid.Row="0" Grid.Column="0" />

<Grid Grid.Row="1" Grid.Column="1">
    <Label Text="Cell" />
    <BoxView Style="{StaticResource topBorderStyle}" />
    <BoxView Style="{StaticResource bottomBorderStyle}" />
    <BoxView Style="{StaticResource leftBorderStyle}" />
    <BoxView Style="{StaticResource rightBorderStyle}" />
</Grid>

<Grid Grid.Row="2" Grid.Column="2">
    <Label Text="Borders" />
    <BoxView Style="{StaticResource topBorderStyle}" />
    <BoxView Style="{StaticResource bottomBorderStyle}" />
```

```
            <BoxView Style="{StaticResource leftBorderStyle}" />
            <BoxView Style="{StaticResource rightBorderStyle}" />
        </Grid>
    </Grid>
</ContentPage>
```

In the cell in the upper-left corner, the `Label` and four `BoxView` elements each gets its `Grid.Row` and `Grid.Column` attributes set to 0. However, for the middle `Grid` and the bottom-right `Grid`, a rather easier approach is taken: Another `Grid` with a single cell occupies the cell, and that single-cell `Grid` contains the `Label` and four `BoxView` elements. The simplicity results from setting `Grid.Row` and `Grid.Column` only on the single-cell `Grid`:

```
<Grid Grid.Row="1" Grid.Column="1">
    <Label Text="Cell" />
    <BoxView Style="{StaticResource topBorderStyle}" />
    <BoxView Style="{StaticResource bottomBorderStyle}" />
    <BoxView Style="{StaticResource leftBorderStyle}" />
    <BoxView Style="{StaticResource rightBorderStyle}" />
</Grid>
```

When nesting a `Grid` inside another `Grid`, the use of the `Grid.Row` and `Grid.Column` attributes can be confusing. This single-cell `Grid` occupies the second row and second column of its parent, which is the `Grid` that occupies the entire page.

Also, keep in mind that when a `Grid` is laying itself out, it looks only at the `Grid.Row` and `Grid.Column` settings of its children, and never its grandchildren or other descendants in the visual tree.

Here's the result:

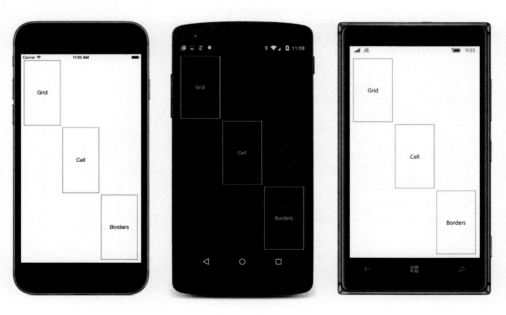

It might be a little disconcerting that the corners of the borders don't meet, but that's due to the default row and column spacing of the `Grid`. Set the `RowSpacing` and `ColumnSpacing` attributes to 0, and the corners will meet although the lines will still seem somewhat discontinuous because the borders are in different cells. If this is unacceptable, use the technique shown in **GridCellDividers**.

If you want all the rows and columns shown with dividers as in **GridCellDividers**, another technique is to set the `BackgroundColor` property of the `Grid` and use the `RowSpacing` and `ColumnSpacing` properties to let that color peek through the spaces between the cells. But all the cells must contain content that has an opaque background for this technique to be visually convincing.

Almost real-life Grid examples

We are now ready to rewrite the **XamlKeypad** program from Chapter 8 to use a `Grid`. The new version is called **KeypadGrid**. The use of a `Grid` not only forces the `Button` elements that make up the keypad to be all the same size, but also allows components of the keypad to span cells.

The `Grid` that makes up the keypad is centered on the page with `HorizontalOptions` and `VerticalOptions` settings. It has five rows and three columns but the `RowDefinitions` and `ColumnDefinitions` collections don't need to be explicitly constructed because every cell has a "*" (star) height and width.

Moreover, the entire `Grid` is given a platform-specific `WidthRequest` and `HeightRequest`, where the width is three-fifths of the height. (The difference for Windows Phone is based on the somewhat larger size of the `Large` font size used for the `Button`.) This causes every cell in the `Grid` to be square:

```
<ContentPage xmlns="http://xamarin.com/schemas/2014/forms"
             xmlns:x="http://schemas.microsoft.com/winfx/2009/xaml"
             x:Class="KeypadGrid.KeypadGridPage">

    <Grid RowSpacing="2"
          ColumnSpacing="2"
          VerticalOptions="Center"
          HorizontalOptions="Center">
        <Grid.WidthRequest>
            <OnPlatform x:TypeArguments="x:Double"
                        iOS="180"
                        Android="180"
                        WinPhone="240" />
        </Grid.WidthRequest>

        <Grid.HeightRequest>
            <OnPlatform x:TypeArguments="x:Double"
                        iOS="300"
                        Android="300"
                        WinPhone="400" />
        </Grid.HeightRequest>

        <Grid.Resources>
```

```
            <ResourceDictionary>
                <Style TargetType="Button">
                    <Setter Property="FontSize" Value="Large" />
                    <Setter Property="BorderWidth" Value="1" />
                </Style>
            </ResourceDictionary>
        </Grid.Resources>

        <Label x:Name="displayLabel"
               Grid.Row="0" Grid.Column="0" Grid.ColumnSpan="2"
               FontSize="Large"
               LineBreakMode="HeadTruncation"
               VerticalOptions="Center"
               HorizontalTextAlignment="End" />

        <Button x:Name="backspaceButton"
                Text="&#x21E6;"
                Grid.Row="0" Grid.Column="2"
                IsEnabled="False"
                Clicked="OnBackspaceButtonClicked" />

        <Button Text="7" StyleId="7"
                Grid.Row="1" Grid.Column="0"
                Clicked="OnDigitButtonClicked" />

        <Button Text="8" StyleId="8"
                Grid.Row="1" Grid.Column="1"
                Clicked="OnDigitButtonClicked" />

        <Button Text="9" StyleId="9"
                Grid.Row="1" Grid.Column="2"
                Clicked="OnDigitButtonClicked" />

        <Button Text="4" StyleId="4"
                Grid.Row="2" Grid.Column="0"
                Clicked="OnDigitButtonClicked" />

        <Button Text="5" StyleId="5"
                Grid.Row="2" Grid.Column="1"
                Clicked="OnDigitButtonClicked" />

        <Button Text="6" StyleId="6"
                Grid.Row="2" Grid.Column="2"
                Clicked="OnDigitButtonClicked" />

        <Button Text="1" StyleId="1"
                Grid.Row="3" Grid.Column="0"
                Clicked="OnDigitButtonClicked" />

        <Button Text="2" StyleId="2"
                Grid.Row="3" Grid.Column="1"
                Clicked="OnDigitButtonClicked" />

        <Button Text="3" StyleId="3"
```

```
                    Grid.Row="3" Grid.Column="2"
                    Clicked="OnDigitButtonClicked" />

        <Button Text="0" StyleId="0"
                    Grid.Row="4" Grid.Column="0" Grid.ColumnSpan="2"
                    Clicked="OnDigitButtonClicked" />

        <Button Text="." StyleId="."
                    Grid.Row="4" Grid.Column="2"
                    Clicked="OnDigitButtonClicked" />

    </Grid>
</ContentPage>
```

The `Label` and the backspace button occupy the top row, but the `Label` spans two columns and the backspace button is in the third column. Similarly, the bottom row of the `Grid` contains the zero button and the decimal-point button, but the zero button spans two columns as is typical on computer keypads.

The code-behind file is the same as the **XamlKeypad** program. In addition, the program saves entries when the program is put to sleep and then restores them when the program starts up again. A border has been added to the `Button` in an implicit style so that it looks more like a real keypad on iOS:

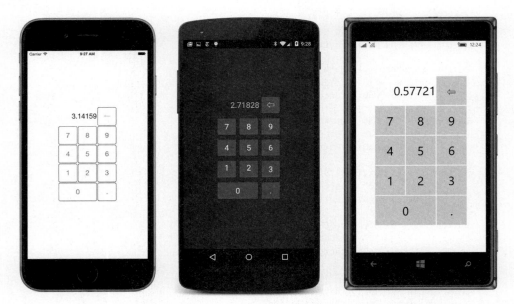

As you might recall, the `OnDigitButtonClicked` handler in the code-behind file uses the `StyleId` property to append a new character to the text string. But as you can see in the XAML file, for each of the buttons with this event handler, the `StyleId` is set to the same character as the `Text` property of the `Button`. Can't the event handler use that instead?

Yes, it can. But suppose you decide that the decimal point in the `Button` doesn't show up very well.

You might prefer to use a heavier and more central dot, such as \u00B7 (called Middle Dot) or \u22C5 (the mathematical Dot Operator) or even \u2022 (the Bullet). Perhaps you'd also like different styles of numbers for these other buttons, such as the set of encircled numbers that begin at \u2460 in the Unicode standard, or the Roman numerals that begin at \u2160. You can replace the `Text` property in the XAML file without touching the code-behind file:

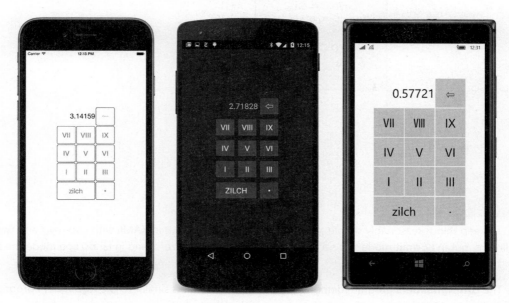

The `StyleId` is one of the tools to keep the visuals and mechanics of the user interface restricted to markup and separated from your code. You'll see more tools to structure your program in the next chapter, which covers the Model-View-ViewModel application architecture. That chapter also presents a variation of the keypad program turned into an adding machine.

Responding to orientation changes

The layout of an application's page is usually tied fairly closely to a particular form factor and aspect ratio. Sometimes, an application will require that it be used only in portrait or landscape mode. But usually an application will attempt to move things around on the screen when the phone changes orientation.

A `Grid` can help an application accommodate itself to orientation changes. The `Grid` can be defined in XAML with certain allowances for both portrait and landscape modes, and then a little code can make the proper adjustments within a `SizeChanged` handler for the page.

This job is easiest if you can divide the entire layout of your application into two large areas that can be arranged vertically when the phone is oriented in portrait mode or horizontally for landscape mode. Put each of these areas in separate cells of a `Grid`. When the phone is in portrait mode, the `Grid` has two rows, and when it's in landscape mode, it has two columns. In the following diagram, the first area is always at the top or the left. The second area can be in either the second row for portrait mode or the second column for landscape mode:

Layout Area 1 Row 0 Column 0	Layout Area 2 (Landscape Mode) Row 0 Column 1
Layout Area 2 (Portrait Mode) Row 1 Column 0	

To keep things reasonably simple, you'll want to define the Grid in XAML with two rows and two columns, but in portrait mode, the second column has a width of zero, and in landscape mode the second row has a zero height.

The **GridRgbSliders** program demonstrates this technique. It is similar to the **RgbSliders** program from Chapter 15, "The interactive interface," except that the layout uses a combination of a Grid and a StackLayout, and the Label elements display the current values of the Slider elements by using data bindings with a value converter and a value converter parameter. (More on this later.) Setting the Color property of the BoxView based on the three Slider elements still requires code because the R, G, and B properties of the Color struct are not backed by bindable properties, and these properties cannot be individually changed anyway because they do not have public set accessors. (However, in the next chapter, on MVVM, you'll see a way to eliminate this logic in the code-behind file.)

As you can see in the following listing, the Grid named mainGrid does indeed have two rows and two columns. However, it is initialized for portrait mode, so the second column has a width of zero. The top row of the Grid contains the BoxView, and that's made as large as possible with a "*" (star) setting, while the bottom row contains a StackLayout with all the interactive controls. This is given a height of Auto:

```
<ContentPage xmlns="http://xamarin.com/schemas/2014/forms"
             xmlns:x="http://schemas.microsoft.com/winfx/2009/xaml"
             xmlns:toolkit=
                 "clr-namespace:Xamarin.FormsBook.Toolkit;assembly=Xamarin.FormsBook.Toolkit"
             x:Class="GridRgbSliders.GridRgbSlidersPage"
             SizeChanged="OnPageSizeChanged">

    <ContentPage.Padding>
```

```
            <OnPlatform x:TypeArguments="Thickness"
                        iOS="0, 20, 0, 0" />
    </ContentPage.Padding>

    <ContentPage.Resources>
        <ResourceDictionary>
            <toolkit:DoubleToIntConverter x:Key="doubleToInt" />

            <Style TargetType="Label">
                <Setter Property="HorizontalTextAlignment" Value="Center" />
            </Style>
        </ResourceDictionary>
    </ContentPage.Resources>

    <Grid x:Name="mainGrid">
        <!-- Initialized for portrait mode. -->
        <Grid.RowDefinitions>
            <RowDefinition Height="*" />
            <RowDefinition Height="Auto" />
        </Grid.RowDefinitions>

        <Grid.ColumnDefinitions>
            <ColumnDefinition Width="*" />
            <ColumnDefinition Width="0" />
        </Grid.ColumnDefinitions>

        <BoxView x:Name="boxView"
                 Grid.Row="0" Grid.Column="0" />

        <StackLayout x:Name="controlPanelStack"
                     Grid.Row="1" Grid.Column="0"
                     Padding="10, 5">

            <StackLayout VerticalOptions="CenterAndExpand">
                <Slider x:Name="redSlider"
                        ValueChanged="OnSliderValueChanged" />

                <Label Text="{Binding Source={x:Reference redSlider},
                                Path=Value,
                                Converter={StaticResource doubleToInt},
                                ConverterParameter=255,
                                StringFormat='Red = {0:X2}'}" />
            </StackLayout>

            <StackLayout VerticalOptions="CenterAndExpand">
                <Slider x:Name="greenSlider"
                        ValueChanged="OnSliderValueChanged" />

                <Label Text="{Binding Source={x:Reference greenSlider},
                                Path=Value,
                                Converter={StaticResource doubleToInt},
                                ConverterParameter=255,
                                StringFormat='Green = {0:X2}'}" />
            </StackLayout>
```

```
<StackLayout VerticalOptions="CenterAndExpand">
    <Slider x:Name="blueSlider"
            ValueChanged="OnSliderValueChanged" />

    <Label Text="{Binding Source={x:Reference blueSlider},
                          Path=Value,
                          Converter={StaticResource doubleToInt},
                          ConverterParameter=255,
                          StringFormat='Blue = {0:X2}'}" />
</StackLayout>
        </StackLayout>
    </Grid>
</ContentPage>
```

And here's the portrait view:

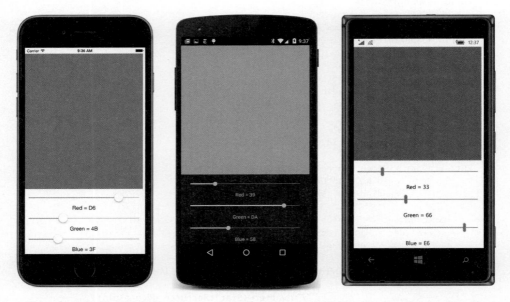

The layout in the XAML file is prepared for landscape mode in a couple of ways. First, the `Grid` already has a second column. This means that to switch to landscape mode, the code-behind file needs to change the height of the second row to zero and the width of the second column to a nonzero value.

Secondly, the `StackLayout` containing all the `Slider` and `Label` elements is accessible from code because it has a name, specifically `controlPanelStack`. The code-behind file can then make `Grid.SetRow` and `Grid.SetColumn` calls on this `StackLayout` to move it from row 1 and column 0 to row 0 and column 1.

In portrait mode, the `BoxView` has a height of "*" (star) and the `StackLayout` has a height of `Auto`. Does this mean that the width of the `StackLayout` should be `Auto` in landscape mode? That wouldn't be wise because it would shrink the widths of the `Slider` elements. A better solution for landscape mode is to give both the `BoxView` and the `StackLayout` a width of "*" (star) to divide the screen in half.

Here's the code-behind file showing the `SizeChanged` handler on the page responsible for switching between portrait and landscape mode, as well as the `ValueChanged` handler for the `Slider` elements that sets the `BoxView` color:

```
public partial class GridRgbSlidersPage : ContentPage
{
    public GridRgbSlidersPage()
    {
        // Ensure link to Toolkit library.
        new Xamarin.FormsBook.Toolkit.DoubleToIntConverter();

        InitializeComponent();
    }

    void OnPageSizeChanged(object sender, EventArgs args)
    {
        // Portrait mode.
        if (Width < Height)
        {
            mainGrid.RowDefinitions[1].Height = GridLength.Auto;
            mainGrid.ColumnDefinitions[1].Width = new GridLength(0, GridUnitType.Absolute);

            Grid.SetRow(controlPanelStack, 1);
            Grid.SetColumn(controlPanelStack, 0);
        }
        // Landscape mode.
        else
        {
            mainGrid.RowDefinitions[1].Height = new GridLength(0, GridUnitType.Absolute);
            mainGrid.ColumnDefinitions[1].Width = new GridLength(1, GridUnitType.Star);

            Grid.SetRow(controlPanelStack, 0);
            Grid.SetColumn(controlPanelStack, 1);
        }
    }

    void OnSliderValueChanged(object sender, ValueChangedEventArgs args)
    {
        boxView.Color = new Color(redSlider.Value, greenSlider.Value, blueSlider.Value);
    }
}
```

And here's the landscape layout, displayed sideways as usual:

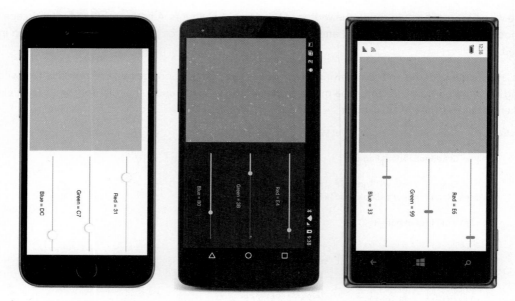

Notice, particularly on the iOS and Android displays, how each pair of `Slider` and `Label` elements is grouped together. This results from a third way that the XAML file is prepared to accommodate landscape mode. Each pair of `Slider` and `Label` elements is grouped in a nested `StackLayout`. This is given a `VerticalOptions` setting of `CenterAndExpand` to perform this spacing.

A little thought was given to arranging the `BoxView` and the control panel: In portrait mode, the fingers manipulating the `Slider` elements won't obscure the result in the `BoxView`, and in landscape mode, the fingers of right-handed users won't obscure the `BoxView` either. (Of course, left-handed users will probably insist on a program option to swap the locations!)

The screenshots show the `Slider` values displayed in hexadecimal. This is done with a data binding, and that would normally be a problem. The `Value` property of the `Slider` is of type `double`, and if you attempt to format a double with "X2" for hexadecimal, an exception will be raised. A type converter (named `DoubleToIntConverter`, for example) must convert the source `double` to an `int` for the string formatting. However, the `Slider` elements are set up for a range of 0 to 1, while integer values formatted as hexadecimal must range from 0 to 255.

A solution is to make use of the `ConverterParameter` property of `Binding`. Whatever is set to this property is passed as the third argument to the `Convert` and `ConvertBack` methods in the value converter. Here's the `DoubleToIntConverter` class in the **Xamarin.FormsBook.Toolkit** library:

```
namespace Xamarin.FormsBook.Toolkit
{
    public class DoubleToIntConverter : IValueConverter
    {
        public object Convert(object value, Type targetType,
                              object parameter, CultureInfo culture)
        {
```

```
        string strParam = parameter as string;
        double multiplier = 1;

        if (!String.IsNullOrEmpty(strParam))
        {
            Double.TryParse(strParam, out multiplier);
        }

        return (int)Math.Round((double)value * multiplier);
    }

    public object ConvertBack(object value, Type targetType,
                              object parameter, CultureInfo culture)
    {
        string strParam = parameter as string;
        double divider = 1;

        if (!String.IsNullOrEmpty(strParam))
        {
            Double.TryParse(strParam, out divider);
        }

        return (int)value / divider;
    }
  }
}
```

The `Convert` and `ConvertBack` methods assume that the `parameter` argument is a string and, if so, attempt to convert it to a `double`. This value is then multiplied by the `double` value being converted, and then the product is cast to an `int`.

The combination of the value converter, the converter parameter, and the string formatting converts values ranging from 0 to 1 coming from the `Slider` to integers in the range of 0 to 255 that are then formatted as two hexadecimal digits:

```
<Label Text="{Binding Source={x:Reference redSlider},
              Path=Value,
              Converter={StaticResource doubleToInt},
              ConverterParameter=255,
              StringFormat='Red = {0:X2}'}" />
```

Of course, if you were defining the `Binding` in code, you would probably set the `ConverterParameter` property to the numeric value of 255 rather than a string of "255", and the logic in the `DoubleToIntConverter` would fail. Simple value converters are usually simpler than they should be for complete bulletproofing.

Can a program like **GridRgbSliders** be entirely realized without the `Slider` event handlers in the code-behind file? Code will certainly still be required, but some of it will be moved away from the user-interface logic. That's the main objective of the Model-View-ViewModel architecture explored in the next chapter.

Chapter 18
MVVM

Can you remember your earliest experiences with programming? It's likely that your main goal was just getting the program working, and then getting it working correctly. You probably didn't think much about the organization or structure of the program. That was something that came later.

The computer industry as a whole has gone through a similar evolution. As developers, we all now realize that once an application begins growing in size, it's usually a good idea to impose some kind of structure or architecture on the code. Experience with this process suggests that it's often best to start thinking about this architecture perhaps before any code is written at all. In most cases, a desirable program structure strives for a "separation of concerns" through which different pieces of the program focus on different sorts of tasks.

In a graphically interactive program, one obvious technique is to separate the user interface from underlying non-user-interface logic, sometimes called *business logic*. The first formal description of such an architecture for graphical user interfaces was called Model-View-Controller (MVC), but this architecture has since given rise to others derived from it.

To some extent, the nature of the programming interface itself influences the application architecture. For example, a programming interface that includes a markup language with data bindings might suggest a particular way to structure an application.

There is indeed an architectural model that was designed specifically with XAML in mind. This is known as Model-View-ViewModel or MVVM. This chapter covers the basics of MVVM (including the command interface), but you'll see more about MVVM in the next chapter, which covers collection views. Also, some other features of Xamarin.Forms are often used in conjunction with MVVM; these features include *triggers* and *behaviors*, and they are the subject of Chapter 23.

MVVM interrelationships

MVVM divides an application into three layers:

- The Model provides underlying data, sometimes involving file or web accesses.

- The ViewModel connects the Model and the View. It helps to manage the data from the Model to make it more amenable to the View, and vice versa.

- The View is the user interface or presentation layer, generally implemented in XAML.

The Model is ignorant of the ViewModel. In other words, the Model knows nothing about the public properties and methods of the ViewModel, and certainly nothing about its internal workings. Similarly, the ViewModel is ignorant of the View. If all the communication between the three layers occurs through method calls and property accesses, then calls in only one direction are allowed. The View only makes calls into the ViewModel or accesses properties of the ViewModel, and the ViewModel similarly only makes calls into the Model or accesses Model properties:

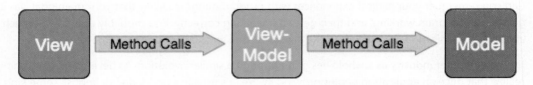

These method calls allow the View to get information from the ViewModel, which in turn gets information from the Model.

In modern environments, however, data is often dynamic. Often the Model will obtain more or newer data that must be communicated to the ViewModel and eventually to the View. For this reason, the View can attach handlers to events that are implemented in the ViewModel, and the ViewModel can attach handlers to events defined by the Model. This allows two-way communication while continuing to hide the View from the ViewModel, and the ViewModel from the Model:

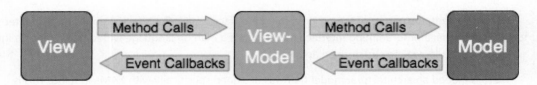

MVVM was designed to take advantage of XAML and particularly XAML-based data bindings. Generally, the View is a page class that uses XAML to construct the user interface. Therefore, the connection between the View and the ViewModel consists largely—and perhaps exclusively—of XAML-based data bindings:

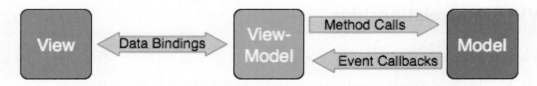

Programmers who are very passionate about MVVM often have an informal goal of expressing all interactions between the View and the ViewModel in a page class with XAML-based data bindings, and in the process reducing the code in the page's code-behind file to a simple `InitializeComponent` call. This goal is difficult to achieve in real-life programming, but it's a pleasure when it happens.

Small programs—such as those in a book like this—often become larger when MVVM is introduced. Do not let this discourage your use of MVVM! Use the examples here to help you determine how

MVVM can be used in a larger program, and you'll eventually see that it helps enormously in architecting your applications.

ViewModels and data binding

In many fairly simple demonstrations of MVVM, the Model is absent or only implied, and the View-Model contains all the business logic. The View and the ViewModel communicate through XAML-based data bindings. The visual elements in the View are data-binding targets, and properties in the ViewModel are data-binding sources.

Ideally, a ViewModel should be independent of any particular platform. This independence allows ViewModels to be shared among other XAML-based environments (such as Windows) in addition to Xamarin.Forms. For this reason, you should try to avoid using the following statement in your View-Models:

```
using Xamarin.Forms;
```

That rule is frequently broken in this chapter! One of the ViewModels is based on the Xamarin.Forms `Color` structure, and another uses `Device.StartTimer`. So let's call the avoidance of anything specific to Xamarin.Forms in the ViewModel a "suggestion" rather than a "rule."

Visual elements in the View qualify as data-binding targets because the properties of these visual elements are backed by bindable properties. To be a data-binding source, a ViewModel must implement a notification protocol to signal when a property in the ViewModel has changed. This notification protocol is the `INotifyPropertyChanged` interface, which is defined in the `System.Component-Model` namespace very simply with just one event:

```
public interface INotifyPropertyChanged
{
    event PropertyChangedEventHandler PropertyChanged;
}
```

The `INotifyPropertyChanged` interface is so central to MVVM that in informal discussions the interface is often abbreviated INPC.

The `PropertyChanged` event in the `INotifyPropertyChanged` interface is of type `Property-Changed-EventHandler`. A handler for this `PropertyChanged` event handler gets an instance of the `PropertyChangedEventArgs` class, which defines a single property named `PropertyName` of type `string` indicating what property in the ViewModel has changed. The event handler can then access that property.

A class that implements `INotifyPropertyChanged` should fire a `PropertyChanged` event whenever a public property changes, but the class should *not* fire the event when the property is merely set but not changed.

Some classes define immutable properties—properties that are initialized in the constructor and then never change. Those properties do not need to fire `PropertyChanged` events because a `PropertyChanged` handler can be attached only after the code in the constructor finishes, and the immutable properties never change after that time.

In theory, a ViewModel class can be derived from `BindableObject` and implement its public properties as `BindableProperty` objects. `BindableObject` implements `INotifyPropertyChanged` and automatically fires a `PropertyChanged` event when any property backed by a `BindableProperty` changes. But deriving from `BindableObject` is overkill for a ViewModel. Because `BindableObject` and `BindableProperty` are specific to Xamarin.Forms, such a ViewModel is no longer platform independent, and the technique provides no real advantages over a simpler implementation of `INotifyPropertyChanged`.

A ViewModel clock

Suppose you are writing a program that needs access to the current date and time, and you'd like to use that information through data bindings. The .NET base class library provides date and time information through the `DateTime` structure. To get the current date and time, just access the `DateTime.Now` property. That's the customary way to write a clock application.

But for data-binding purposes, `DateTime` has a severe flaw: It provides just static information with no notification when the date or time has changed.

In the context of MVVM, the `DateTime` structure perhaps qualifies as a Model in the sense that `DateTime` provides all the data we need but not in a form that's conducive to data bindings. It's necessary to write a ViewModel that makes use of `DateTime` but provides notifications when the date or time has changed.

The **Xamarin.FormsBook.Toolkit** library contains the `DateTimeViewModel` class shown below. The class has only one property, which is named `DateTime` of type `DateTime`, but this property dynamically changes as a result of frequent calls to `DateTime.Now` in a `Device.StartTimer` callback.

Notice that the `DateTimeViewModel` class is based on the `INotifyPropertyChanged` interface and includes a `using` directive for the `System.ComponentModel` namespace that defines this interface. To implement this interface, the class defines a public event named `PropertyChanged`.

Watch out: It is very easy to define a `PropertyChanged` event in your class without explicitly specifying that the class implements `INotifyPropertyChanged`! The notifications will be ignored if you don't explicitly specify that the class is based on the `INotifyPropertyChanged` interface:

```
using System;
using System.ComponentModel;
using Xamarin.Forms;

namespace Xamarin.FormsBook.Toolkit
{
    public class DateTimeViewModel : INotifyPropertyChanged
```

```
    {
        DateTime dateTime = DateTime.Now;

        public event PropertyChangedEventHandler PropertyChanged;

        public DateTimeViewModel()
        {
            Device.StartTimer(TimeSpan.FromMilliseconds(15), OnTimerTick);
        }

        bool OnTimerTick()
        {
            DateTime = DateTime.Now;
            return true;
        }

        public DateTime DateTime
        {
            private set
            {
                if (dateTime != value)
                {
                    dateTime = value;

                    // Fire the event.
                    PropertyChangedEventHandler handler = PropertyChanged;

                    if (handler != null)
                    {
                        handler(this, new PropertyChangedEventArgs("DateTime"));
                    }
                }
            }

            get
            {
                return dateTime;
            }
        }
    }
}
```

The only public property in this class is called `DateTime` of type `DateTime`, and it is associated with a private backing field named `dateTime`. Public properties in ViewModels usually have private backing fields. The `set` accessor of the `DateTime` property is private to the class, and it's updated every 15 milliseconds from the timer callback.

Other than that, the `set` accessor is constructed in a very standard way for ViewModels: It first checks whether the value being set to the property is different from the `dateTime` backing field. If not, it sets that backing field from the incoming value and fires the `PropertyChanged` handler with the name of the property. It is considered very bad practice to fire the `PropertyChanged` handler if the property is merely being set to its existing value, and it might even lead to problems involving infinite cycles of recursive property settings in two-way bindings.

This is the code in the `set` accessor that fires the event:

```
PropertyChangedEventHandler handler = PropertyChanged;

if (handler != null)
{
    handler(this, new PropertyChangedEventArgs("DateTime"));
}
```

That form is preferable to code such as this, which doesn't save the handler in a separate variable:

```
if (PropertyChanged != null)
{
    PropertyChanged(this, new PropertyChangedEventArgs("DateTime"));
}
```

In a multithreaded environment, a `PropertyChanged` handler might be detached between the `if` statement that checks for a `null` value and the actual firing of the event. Saving the handler in a separate variable prevents that from causing a problem, so it's a good habit to adopt even if you're not yet working in a multithreaded environment.

The `get` accessor simply returns the `dateTime` backing field.

The **MvvmClock** program demonstrates how the `DateTimeViewModel` class is capable of providing updated date and time information to the user interface through data bindings:

```
<ContentPage xmlns="http://xamarin.com/schemas/2014/forms"
             xmlns:x="http://schemas.microsoft.com/winfx/2009/xaml"
             xmlns:sys="clr-namespace:System;assembly=mscorlib"
             xmlns:toolkit=
                 "clr-namespace:Xamarin.FormsBook.Toolkit;assembly=Xamarin.FormsBook.Toolkit"
             x:Class="MvvmClock.MvvmClockPage">

    <ContentPage.Resources>
        <ResourceDictionary>
            <toolkit:DateTimeViewModel x:Key="dateTimeViewModel" />

            <Style TargetType="Label">
                <Setter Property="FontSize" Value="Large" />
                <Setter Property="HorizontalTextAlignment" Value="Center" />
            </Style>
        </ResourceDictionary>
    </ContentPage.Resources>

    <StackLayout VerticalOptions="Center">
        <Label Text="{Binding Source={x:Static sys:DateTime.Now},
                        StringFormat='This program started at {0:F}'}" />

        <Label Text="But now..." />
```

```
            <Label Text="{Binding Source={StaticResource dateTimeViewModel},
                                  Path=DateTime.Hour,
                                  StringFormat='The hour is {0}'}" />

            <Label Text="{Binding Source={StaticResource dateTimeViewModel},
                                  Path=DateTime.Minute,
                                  StringFormat='The minute is {0}'}" />

            <Label Text="{Binding Source={StaticResource dateTimeViewModel},
                                  Path=DateTime.Second,
                                  StringFormat='The seconds are {0}'}" />

            <Label Text="{Binding Source={StaticResource dateTimeViewModel},
                                  Path=DateTime.Millisecond,
                                  StringFormat='The milliseconds are {0}'}" />
    </StackLayout>
</ContentPage>
```

The `Resources` section for the page instantiates the `DateTimeViewModel` and also defines an implicit `Style` for the `Label`.

The first of the six `Label` elements sets its `Text` property to a `Binding` object that involves the actual .NET `DateTime` structure. The `Source` property of that binding is an `x:Static` markup extension that references the static `DateTime.Now` property to obtain the date and time when the program first starts running. No `Path` is required in this binding. The "F" formatting specification is for the full date/time pattern, with long versions of the date and time strings. Although this `Label` displays the date and time when the program starts up, it will never get updated.

The final four data bindings *will* be updated. In these data bindings, the `Source` property is set to a `StaticResource` markup extension that references the `DateTimeViewModel` object. The `Path` is set to various subproperties of the `DateTime` property of that ViewModel. Behind the scenes, the binding infrastructure attaches a handler on the `PropertyChanged` event in the `DateTimeViewModel`. This handler checks for a change in the `DateTime` property and updates the `Text` property of the `Label` whenever that property changes.

The code-behind file is empty except for an `InitializeComponent` call. The data bindings of the final four labels display an updated time that changes as fast as the video refresh rate:

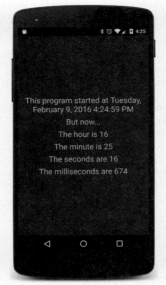
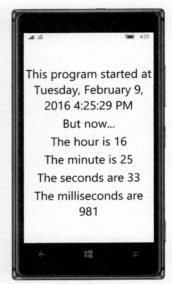

The markup in this XAML file can be simplified by setting the `BindingContext` property of the `StackLayout` to a `StaticResource` markup extension that references the ViewModel. That `BindingContext` is propagated through the visual tree so that you can remove the `Source` settings on the final four `Label` elements:

```
<StackLayout VerticalOptions="Center"
             BindingContext="{StaticResource dateTimeViewModel}">

    <Label Text="{Binding Source={x:Static sys:DateTime.Now},
                     StringFormat='This program started at {0:F}'}" />

    <Label Text="But now..." />

    <Label Text="{Binding Path=DateTime.Hour,
                     StringFormat='The hour is {0}'}" />

    <Label Text="{Binding Path=DateTime.Minute,
                     StringFormat='The minute is {0}'}" />

    <Label Text="{Binding Path=DateTime.Second,
                     StringFormat='The seconds are {0}'}" />

    <Label Text="{Binding Path=DateTime.Millisecond,
                     StringFormat='The milliseconds are {0}'}" />
</StackLayout>
```

The `Binding` on the first `Label` overrides that `BindingContext` with its own `Source` setting.

You can even remove the `DateTimeViewModel` item from the `ResourceDictionary` and instantiate it right in the `StackLayout` between `BindingContext` property-element tags:

```
<StackLayout VerticalOptions="Center">
    <StackLayout.BindingContext>
        <toolkit:DateTimeViewModel />
    </StackLayout.BindingContext>

    <Label Text="{Binding Source={x:Static sys:DateTime.Now},
                        StringFormat='This program started at {0:F}'}" />

    <Label Text="But now..." />

    <Label Text="{Binding Path=DateTime.Hour,
                        StringFormat='The hour is {0}'}" />

    <Label Text="{Binding Path=DateTime.Minute,
                        StringFormat='The minute is {0}'}" />

    <Label Text="{Binding Path=DateTime.Second,
                        StringFormat='The seconds are {0}'}" />

    <Label Text="{Binding Path=DateTime.Millisecond,
                        StringFormat='The milliseconds are {0}'}" />
</StackLayout>
```

Or, you can set the `BindingContext` property of the `StackLayout` to a `Binding` that includes the `DateTime` property. The `BindingContext` then becomes the `DateTime` value, which allows the individual bindings to simply reference properties of the .NET `DateTime` structure:

```
<StackLayout VerticalOptions="Center"
            BindingContext="{Binding Source={StaticResource dateTimeViewModel},
                                Path=DateTime}">

    <Label Text="{Binding Source={x:Static sys:DateTime.Now},
                        StringFormat='This program started at {0:F}'}" />

    <Label Text="But now..." />

    <Label Text="{Binding Path=Hour,
                        StringFormat='The hour is {0}'}" />

    <Label Text="{Binding Path=Minute,
                        StringFormat='The minute is {0}'}" />

    <Label Text="{Binding Path=Second,
                        StringFormat='The seconds are {0}'}" />

    <Label Text="{Binding Path=Millisecond,
                        StringFormat='The milliseconds are {0}'}" />
</StackLayout>
```

You might have doubts that this will work! Behind the scenes, a data binding normally installs a `PropertyChanged` event handler and watches for particular properties being changed, but it can't in this case because the source of the data binding is a `DateTime` value, and `DateTime` doesn't implement `INotifyPropertyChanged`. However, the `BindingContext` of these `Label` elements changes with each change to the `DateTime` property in the ViewModel, so the binding infrastructure accesses new values of these properties at that time.

As the individual bindings on the `Text` properties decrease in length and complexity, you can remove the `Path` attribute name and put everything on one line and nobody will be confused:

```
<StackLayout VerticalOptions="Center">
    <StackLayout.BindingContext>
        <Binding Path="DateTime">
            <Binding.Source>
                <toolkit:DateTimeViewModel />
            </Binding.Source>
        </Binding>
    </StackLayout.BindingContext>

    <Label Text="{Binding Source={x:Static sys:DateTime.Now},
                     StringFormat='This program started at {0:F}'}" />

    <Label Text="But now..." />

    <Label Text="{Binding Hour, StringFormat='The hour is {0}'}" />
    <Label Text="{Binding Minute, StringFormat='The minute is {0}'}" />
    <Label Text="{Binding Second, StringFormat='The seconds are {0}'}" />
    <Label Text="{Binding Millisecond, StringFormat='The milliseconds are {0}'}" />
</StackLayout>
```

In future programs in this book, the individual bindings will mostly be as short and as elegant as possible.

Interactive properties in a ViewModel

The second example of a ViewModel does something so basic that you'd never write a ViewModel for this purpose. The `SimpleMultiplierViewModel` class simply multiplies two numbers together. But it's a good example for demonstrating the overhead and mechanics of a ViewModel that has multiple interactive properties. (And although you'd never write a ViewModel for multiplying two numbers together, you might write a ViewModel for solving quadratic equations or something much more complex.)

The `SimpleMultiplierViewModel` class is part of the **SimpleMultiplier** project:

```
using System;
using System.ComponentModel;

namespace SimpleMultiplier
{
    class SimpleMultiplierViewModel : INotifyPropertyChanged
    {
        double multiplicand, multiplier, product;

        public event PropertyChangedEventHandler PropertyChanged;
```

```
public double Multiplicand
{
    set
    {
        if (multiplicand != value)
        {
            multiplicand = value;
            OnPropertyChanged("Multiplicand");
            UpdateProduct();
        }
    }
    get
    {
        return multiplicand;
    }
}

public double Multiplier
{
    set
    {
        if (multiplier != value)
        {
            multiplier = value;
            OnPropertyChanged("Multiplier");
            UpdateProduct();
        }
    }
    get
    {
        return multiplier;
    }
}

public double Product
{
    protected set
    {
        if (product != value)
        {
            product = value;
            OnPropertyChanged("Product");
        }
    }
    get
    {
        return product;
    }
}

void UpdateProduct()
{
    Product = Multiplicand * Multiplier;
}
```

```
        protected void OnPropertyChanged(string propertyName)
        {
            PropertyChangedEventHandler handler = PropertyChanged;

            if (handler != null)
            {
                PropertyChanged(this, new PropertyChangedEventArgs(propertyName));
            }
        }
    }
}
```

The class defines three public properties of type double, named Multiplicand, Multiplier, and Product. Each property is backed by a private field. The set and get accessors of the first two properties are public, but the set accessor of the Product property is protected to prevent it from being set outside the class while still allowing a descendant class to change it.

The set accessor of each property begins by checking whether the property value is actually changing, and if so, it sets the backing field to that value and calls a method named OnPropertyChanged with that property name.

The INotifyPropertyChanged interface does not require an OnPropertyChanged method, but ViewModel classes often include one to cut down the code repetition. It's usually defined as protected in case you need to derive one ViewModel from another and fire the event in the derived class. Later in this chapter, you'll see techniques to cut down the code repetition in INotifyPropertyChanged classes even more.

The set accessors for both the Multiplicand and Multiplier properties conclude by calling the UpdateProduct method. This is the method that performs the job of multiplying the values of the two properties and setting a new value for the Product property, which then fires its own PropertyChanged event.

Here's the XAML file that makes use of this ViewModel:

```
<ContentPage xmlns="http://xamarin.com/schemas/2014/forms"
             xmlns:x="http://schemas.microsoft.com/winfx/2009/xaml"
             xmlns:local="clr-namespace:SimpleMultiplier"
             x:Class="SimpleMultiplier.SimpleMultiplierPage"
             Padding="10, 0">

    <ContentPage.Resources>
        <ResourceDictionary>
            <local:SimpleMultiplierViewModel x:Key="viewModel" />

            <Style TargetType="Label">
                <Setter Property="FontSize" Value="Large" />
            </Style>
        </ResourceDictionary>
    </ContentPage.Resources>
```

```
<StackLayout BindingContext="{StaticResource viewModel}">

    <StackLayout VerticalOptions="CenterAndExpand">
        <Slider Value="{Binding Multiplicand}" />
        <Slider Value="{Binding Multiplier}" />
    </StackLayout>

    <StackLayout Orientation="Horizontal"
                 Spacing="0"
                 VerticalOptions="CenterAndExpand"
                 HorizontalOptions="Center">
        <Label Text="{Binding Multiplicand, StringFormat='{0:F3}'}" />
        <Label Text="{Binding Multiplier, StringFormat=' x {0:F3}'}" />
        <Label Text="{Binding Product, StringFormat=' = {0:F3}'}" />
    </StackLayout>
</StackLayout>
</ContentPage>
```

The `SimpleMultiplierViewModel` is instantiated in the `Resources` dictionary and set to the `BindingContext` property of the `StackLayout` by using a `StaticResource` markup extension. That `BindingContext` is inherited by all the children and grandchildren of the `StackLayout`, which includes two `Slider` and three `Label` elements. The use of the `BindingContext` allows these bindings to be as simple as possible.

The default binding mode of the `Value` property of the `Slider` is `TwoWay`. Changes in the `Value` property of each `Slider` cause changes to the properties of the ViewModel.

The three `Label` elements display the values of all three properties of the ViewModel with some formatting that inserts times and equals signs with the numbers:

```
<Label Text="{Binding Multiplicand, StringFormat='{0:F3}'}" />
<Label Text="{Binding Multiplier, StringFormat=' x {0:F3}'}" />
<Label Text="{Binding Product, StringFormat=' = {0:F3}'}" />
```

For the first two, you can alternatively bind the `Text` property of the `Label` elements directly to the `Value` property of the corresponding `Slider`, but that would require that you give each `Slider` a name with `x:Name` and reference that name in a `Source` argument by using the `x:Reference` markup extension. The approach used in this program is much cleaner and verifies that data is making a full trip through the ViewModel from each `Slider` to each `Label`.

There is nothing in the code-behind file except a call to `InitializeComponent` in the constructor. All the business logic is in the ViewModel, and the whole user interface is defined in XAML:

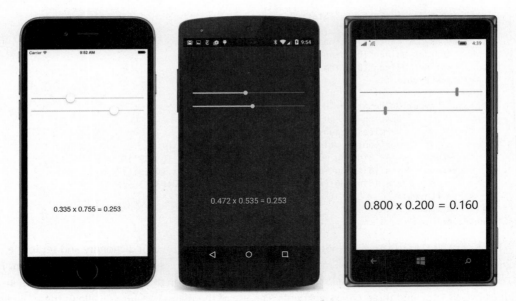

If you'd like to, you can initialize the ViewModel as it is instantiated in the `Resources` dictionary:

```
<local:SimpleMultiplierViewModel x:Key="viewModel"
                                 Multiplicand="0.5"
                                 Multiplier="0.5" />
```

The `Slider` elements will get these initial values as a result of the two-way binding.

The advantage to separating the user interface from the underlying business logic becomes evident when you want to change the user interface somewhat, perhaps by substituting a `Stepper` for the `Slider` for one or both numbers:

```
<StackLayout VerticalOptions="CenterAndExpand">
    <Slider Value="{Binding Multiplicand}" />
    <Stepper Value="{Binding Multiplier}" />
</StackLayout>
```

Aside from the different ranges of the two elements, the functionality is identical:

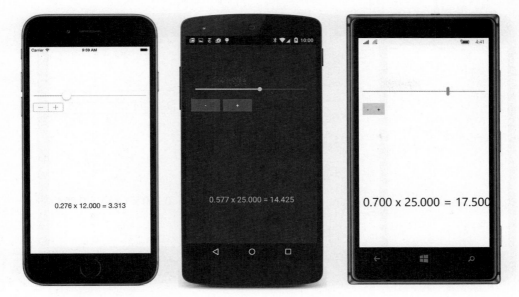

You could also substitute an `Entry`:

```
<StackLayout VerticalOptions="CenterAndExpand">
    <Slider Value="{Binding Multiplicand}" />
    <Entry Text="{Binding Multiplier}" />
</StackLayout>
```

The default binding mode for the `Text` property of the `Entry` is also `TwoWay`, so all you need to worry about is the conversion between the source property `double` and target property `string`. Fortunately, this conversion is automatically handled by the binding infrastructure:

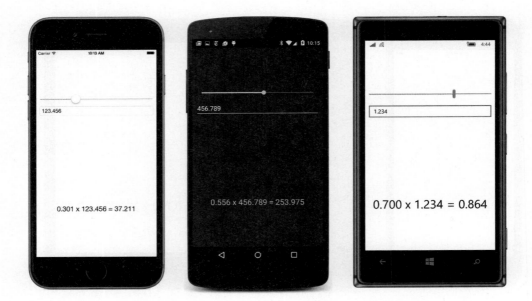

If you type a series of characters that cannot be converted to a `double`, the binding will maintain the last valid value. If you want more sophisticated validation, you'll have to implement your own (such as with a trigger, which will be discussed in Chapter 23).

One interesting experiment is to type **1E-1**, which is scientific notation that is convertible to a `double`. You'll see it immediately change to "0.1" in the `Entry`. This is the effect of the `TwoWay` binding: The `Multiplier` property is set to 1E-1 from the `Entry` but the `ToString` method that the binding infrastructure calls when the value comes back to the `Entry` returns the text "0.1." Because that is different from the existing `Entry` text, the new text is set. To prevent that from happening, you can set the binding mode to `OneWayToSource`:

```
<StackLayout VerticalOptions="CenterAndExpand">
    <Slider Value="{Binding Multiplicand}" />
    <Entry Text="{Binding Multiplier, Mode=OneWayToSource}" />
</StackLayout>
```

Now the `Multiplier` property of the ViewModel is set from the `Text` property of the `Entry`, but not the other way around. If you don't need these two views to be updated from the ViewModel, you can set both of them to `OneWayToSource`. But generally you'll want MVVM bindings to be `TwoWay`.

Should you worry about infinite cycles in two-way bindings? Usually not, because `PropertyChanged` events are fired only when the property actually changes and not when it's merely set to the same value. Generally the source and target will stop updating each other after a bounce or two. However, it is possible to write a "pathological" value converter that doesn't provide for round-trip conversions, and that could indeed cause infinite update cycles in two-way bindings.

A Color ViewModel

Color always provides a good means of exploring the features of a graphical user interface, so you probably won't be surprised to learn that the **Xamarin.FormsBook.Toolkit** library contains a class called `ColorViewModel`.

The `ColorViewModel` class exposes a `Color` property but also `Red`, `Green`, `Blue`, `Alpha`, `Hue`, `Saturation`, and `Luminosity` properties, all of which are individually settable. This is not a feature that the Xamarin.Form `Color` structure provides. Once a `Color` value is created from a `Color` constructor or one of the methods in `Color` beginning with the words `Add`, `From`, `Multiply`, or `With`, it is immutable.

This `ColorViewModel` class is complicated by the interrelationship of its `Color` property and all the component properties. For example, suppose the `Color` property is set. The class should fire a `PropertyChanged` handler not only for `Color` but also for any component (such as `Red` or `Hue`) that also changes. Similarly, if the `Red` property changes, then the class should fire a `PropertyChanged` event for both `Red` and `Color`, and probably `Hue`, `Saturation`, and `Luminosity` as well.

The `ColorViewModel` class solves this problem by storing a backing field for the `Color` property only. All the `set` accessors for the individual components create a new `Color` by using the incoming value with a call to `Color.FromRgba` or `Color.FromHsla`. This new `Color` value is set to the `Color` property rather than the `color` field, which means that the new `Color` value is subjected to processing in the `set` accessor of the `Color` property:

```
public class ColorViewModel : INotifyPropertyChanged
{
    Color color;

    public event PropertyChangedEventHandler PropertyChanged;

    public double Red
    {
        set
        {
            if (Round(color.R) != value)
                Color = Color.FromRgba(value, color.G, color.B, color.A);
        }
        get
        {
            return Round(color.R);
        }
    }

    public double Green
    {
        set
        {
            if (Round(color.G) != value)
                Color = Color.FromRgba(color.R, value, color.B, color.A);
        }
```

```
        get
        {
            return Round(color.G);
        }
    }

    public double Blue
    {
        set
        {
            if (Round(color.B) != value)
                Color = Color.FromRgba(color.R, color.G, value, color.A);
        }
        get
        {
            return Round(color.B);
        }
    }

    public double Alpha
    {
        set
        {
            if (Round(color.A) != value)
                Color = Color.FromRgba(color.R, color.G, color.B, value);
        }
        get
        {
            return Round(color.A);
        }
    }

    public double Hue
    {
        set
        {
            if (Round(color.Hue) != value)
                Color = Color.FromHsla(value, color.Saturation, color.Luminosity, color.A);
        }
        get
        {
            return Round(color.Hue);
        }
    }

    public double Saturation
    {
        set
        {
            if (Round(color.Saturation) != value)
                Color = Color.FromHsla(color.Hue, value, color.Luminosity, color.A);
        }
        get
        {
```

```
                    return Round(color.Saturation);
            }
    }

    public double Luminosity
    {
        set
        {
            if (Round(color.Luminosity) != value)
                Color = Color.FromHsla(color.Hue, color.Saturation, value, color.A);
        }
        get
        {
            return Round(color.Luminosity);
        }
    }

    public Color Color
    {
        set
        {
            Color oldColor = color;

            if (color != value)
            {
                color = value;
                OnPropertyChanged("Color");
            }

            if (color.R != oldColor.R)
                OnPropertyChanged("Red");

            if (color.G != oldColor.G)
                OnPropertyChanged("Green");

            if (color.B != oldColor.B)
                OnPropertyChanged("Blue");

            if (color.A != oldColor.A)
                OnPropertyChanged("Alpha");

            if (color.Hue != oldColor.Hue)
                OnPropertyChanged("Hue");

            if (color.Saturation != oldColor.Saturation)
                OnPropertyChanged("Saturation");

            if (color.Luminosity != oldColor.Luminosity)
                OnPropertyChanged("Luminosity");
        }
        get
        {
            return color;
        }
```

```
    }

    protected void OnPropertyChanged(string propertyName)
    {
        PropertyChangedEventHandler handler = PropertyChanged;

        if (handler != null)
        {
            handler(this, new PropertyChangedEventArgs(propertyName));
        }
    }

    double Round(double value)
    {
        return Device.OnPlatform(value, Math.Round(value, 3), value);
    }
}
```

The set accessor for the Color property is responsible for the firings of all PropertyChanged events based on changes to the properties.

Notice the device-dependent Round method at the bottom of the class and its use in the set and get accessors of the first seven properties. This was added when the **MultiColorSliders** sample in Chapter 23, "Triggers and behaviors," revealed a problem. Android seemed to be internally rounding the color components, causing inconsistencies between the properties being passed to the Color.FromRgba and Color.FromHsla methods and the properties of the resultant Color value, which lead to infinite set and get loops.

The **HslSliders** program instantiates the ColorViewModel between Grid.BindingContext tags so that it becomes the BindingContext for all the Slider and Label elements within the Grid:

```
<ContentPage xmlns="http://xamarin.com/schemas/2014/forms"
             xmlns:x="http://schemas.microsoft.com/winfx/2009/xaml"
             xmlns:toolkit=
                 "clr-namespace:Xamarin.FormsBook.Toolkit;assembly=Xamarin.FormsBook.Toolkit"
             x:Class="HslSliders.HslSlidersPage"
             SizeChanged="OnPageSizeChanged">

    <ContentPage.Padding>
        <OnPlatform x:TypeArguments="Thickness"
                    iOS="0, 20, 0, 0" />
    </ContentPage.Padding>

    <Grid x:Name="mainGrid">
        <Grid.BindingContext>
            <toolkit:ColorViewModel Color="Gray" />
        </Grid.BindingContext>

        <Grid.Resources>
            <ResourceDictionary>
                <Style TargetType="Label">
                    <Setter Property="FontSize" Value="Large" />
```

```
                        <Setter Property="HorizontalTextAlignment" Value="Center" />
                </Style>
            </ResourceDictionary>
        </Grid.Resources>

        <!-- Initialized for portrait mode. -->
        <Grid.RowDefinitions>
            <RowDefinition Height="*" />
            <RowDefinition Height="Auto" />
        </Grid.RowDefinitions>

        <Grid.ColumnDefinitions>
            <ColumnDefinition Width="*" />
            <ColumnDefinition Width="0" />
        </Grid.ColumnDefinitions>

        <BoxView Color="{Binding Color}"
                 Grid.Row="0" Grid.Column="0" />

        <StackLayout x:Name="controlPanelStack"
                     Grid.Row="1" Grid.Column="0"
                     Padding="10, 5">

            <StackLayout VerticalOptions="CenterAndExpand">
                <Slider Value="{Binding Hue}" />
                <Label Text="{Binding Hue, StringFormat='Hue = {0:F2}'}" />
            </StackLayout>

            <StackLayout VerticalOptions="CenterAndExpand">
                <Slider Value="{Binding Saturation}" />
                <Label Text="{Binding Saturation, StringFormat='Saturation = {0:F2}'}" />
            </StackLayout>

            <StackLayout VerticalOptions="CenterAndExpand">
                <Slider Value="{Binding Luminosity}" />
                <Label Text="{Binding Luminosity, StringFormat='Luminosity = {0:F2}'}" />
            </StackLayout>
        </StackLayout>
    </Grid>
</ContentPage>
```

Notice that the `Color` property of `ColorViewModel` is initialized when `ColorViewModel` is instantiated. The two-way bindings of the sliders then pick up the resultant values of the `Hue`, `Saturation`, and `Luminosity` properties.

If you instead want to implement a display of hexadecimal values of `Red`, `Green`, and `Blue`, you can use the `DoubleToIntConverter` class demonstrated in connection with the **GridRgbSliders** program in the previous chapter.

The **HslSliders** program implements the same technique for switching between portrait and landscape modes as that **GridRgbSliders** program. The code-behind file handles the mechanics of this switch:

```
public partial class HslSlidersPage : ContentPage
{
    public HslSlidersPage()
    {
        InitializeComponent();
    }

    void OnPageSizeChanged(object sender, EventArgs args)
    {
        // Portrait mode.
        if (Width < Height)
        {
            mainGrid.RowDefinitions[1].Height = GridLength.Auto;
            mainGrid.ColumnDefinitions[1].Width = new GridLength(0, GridUnitType.Absolute);

            Grid.SetRow(controlPanelStack, 1);
            Grid.SetColumn(controlPanelStack, 0);
        }
        // Landscape mode.
        else
        {
            mainGrid.RowDefinitions[1].Height = new GridLength(0, GridUnitType.Absolute);
            mainGrid.ColumnDefinitions[1].Width = new GridLength(1, GridUnitType.Star);

            Grid.SetRow(controlPanelStack, 0);
            Grid.SetColumn(controlPanelStack, 1);
        }
    }
}
```

This code-behind file isn't quite as pretty as a file that merely calls `InitializeComponent`, but even in the context of MVVM, switching between portrait and landscape modes is a legitimate use of the code-behind file because it is solely devoted to the user interface rather than underlying business logic.

Here's the **HslSliders** program in action:

Streamlining the ViewModel

A typical implementation of `INotifyPropertyChanged` has a private backing field for every public property defined by the class, for example:

```
double number;
```

It also has an `OnPropertyChanged` method responsible for firing the `PropertyChanged` event:

```
protected void OnPropertyChanged(string propertyName)
{
    PropertyChangedEventHandler handler = PropertyChanged;

    if (handler != null)
    {
        PropertyChanged(this, new PropertyChangedEventArgs(propertyName));
    }
}
```

A typical property definition looks like this:

```
public double Number
{
    set
    {
        if (number != value)
        {
            number = value;
            OnPropertyChanged("Number");

            // Do something with the new value.
```

```
        }
    }
    get
    {
        return number;
    }
}
```

A potential problem involves the text string you pass to the `OnPropertyChanged` method. If you misspell it, you won't get any type of error message, and yet bindings involving that property won't work. Also, the backing field appears three times within this single property. If you had several similar properties and defined them through copy-and-paste operations, it's possible to omit the renaming of one of the three appearances of the backing field, and that bug might be very difficult to track down.

You can solve the first problem with a feature introduced in C# 5.0. The `CallerMemberNameAttribute` class allows you to replace an optional method argument with the name of the calling method or property.

You can make use of this feature by redefining the `OnPropertyChanged` method. Make the argument optional by assigning `null` to it and preceding it with the `CallerMemberName` attribute in square brackets. You'll also need a `using` directive for `System.Runtime.CompilerServices`:

```
protected void OnPropertyChanged([CallerMemberName] string propertyName = null)
{
    PropertyChangedEventHandler handler = PropertyChanged;

    if (handler != null)
    {
        PropertyChanged(this, new PropertyChangedEventArgs(propertyName));
    }
}
```

Now the `Number` property can call the `OnPropertyChanged` method without the argument that indicates the property name. That argument will be automatically set to the property name "Number" because that's where the call to `OnPropertyChanged` is originating:

```
public double Number
{
    set
    {
        if (number != value)
        {
            number = value;
            OnPropertyChanged();

            // Do something with the new value.
        }
    }
    get
    {
        return number;
    }
}
```

```
}
```

This approach avoids a misspelled text property name and also allows property names to be changed during program development without worrying about also changing the text strings. Indeed, one of the primary reasons that the `CallerMemberName` attribute was invented was to simplify classes that implement `INotifyPropertyChanged`.

However, this works only when `OnPropertyChanged` is called from the property whose value is changing. In the earlier `ColorViewModel`, explicit property names would still be required in all but one of the calls to `OnPropertyChanged`.

It's possible to go even further to simplify the `set` accessor logic: You'll need to define a generic method, probably named `SetProperty` or something similar. This `SetProperty` method is also defined with the `CallerMemberName` attribute:

```
bool SetProperty<T>(ref T storage, T value, [CallerMemberName] string propertyName = null)
{
    if (Object.Equals(storage, value))
        return false;

    storage = value;
    OnPropertyChanged(propertyName);
    return true;
}

protected void OnPropertyChanged([CallerMemberName] string propertyName = null)
{
    PropertyChangedEventHandler handler = PropertyChanged;
    if (handler != null)
    {
        PropertyChanged(this, new PropertyChangedEventArgs(propertyName));
    }
}
```

The first argument to `SetProperty` is a reference to the backing field, and the second argument is the value being set to the property. `SetProperty` automates the checking and setting of the backing field. Notice that it explicitly includes the `propertyName` argument when calling `OnProperty-Changed`. (Otherwise the `propertyName` argument would become the string "SetProperty"!) The method returns `true` if the property was changed. You can use this return value to perform additional processing with the new value.

Now the `Number` property looks like this:

```
public double Number
{
    set
    {
        if (SetProperty(ref number, value))
        {
            // Do something with the new value.
        }
```

```
        }
    get
    {
        return number;
    }
}
```

Although `SetProperty` is a generic method, the C# compiler can deduce the type from the arguments. If you don't need to do anything with the new value in the property `set` accessor, you can even reduce the two accessors to single lines without obscuring the operations:

```
public double Number
{
    set { SetProperty(ref number, value); }
    get { return number; }
}
```

You might like this streamlining so much that you'll want to put the `SetProperty` and `OnPropertyChanged` methods in their own class and derive from that class when creating your own ViewModels. Such a class, called `ViewModelBase`, is already in the **Xamarin.FormsBook.Toolkit** library:

```
using System;
using System.ComponentModel;
using System.Runtime.CompilerServices;

namespace Xamarin.FormsBook.Toolkit
{
    public class ViewModelBase : INotifyPropertyChanged
    {
        public event PropertyChangedEventHandler PropertyChanged;

        protected bool SetProperty<T>(ref T storage, T value,
                                [CallerMemberName] string propertyName = null)
        {
            if (Object.Equals(storage, value))
                return false;

            storage = value;
            OnPropertyChanged(propertyName);
            return true;
        }

        protected void OnPropertyChanged([CallerMemberName] string propertyName = null)
        {
            PropertyChangedEventHandler handler = PropertyChanged;
            if (handler != null)
            {
                PropertyChanged(this, new PropertyChangedEventArgs(propertyName));
            }
        }
    }
}
```

This class is used in the two remaining examples in this chapter.

The Command interface

Data bindings are very powerful. Data bindings connect properties of visual elements in the View with properties of data in the ViewModel, and allow the direct manipulation of data items through the user interface.

But not everything is a property. Sometimes ViewModels expose public *methods* that must be called from the View based on a user's interaction with a visual element. Without MVVM, you'd probably call such a method from a `Clicked` event handler of a `Button` or a `Tapped` event handler of a `TapGes-tureRecognizer`. When considering these needs, the whole concept of data bindings and MVVM might start to seem hopelessly flawed. How can the code-behind file of a page class be stripped down to an `InitializeComponent` call if it must still make method calls from the View to the ViewModel?

Don't give up on MVVM so quickly! Xamarin.Forms supports a feature that allows data bindings to make method calls in the ViewModel directly from `Button` and `TapGestureRecognizer` and a few other elements. This is a protocol called the *command interface* or the *commanding interface*.

The command interface is supported by eight classes:

- `Button`

- `MenuItem` (covered in Chapter 19, "Collection views"), and hence also `ToolbarItem`

- `SearchBar`

- `TextCell`, and hence also `ImageCell` (also to be covered in Chapter 19)

- `ListView` (also to be covered in Chapter 19)

- `TapGestureRecognizer`

It is also possible to implement commanding in your own custom classes.

The command interface is likely to be a little confusing at first. Let's focus on `Button`.

`Button` defines two ways for code to be notified when the element is clicked. The first is the `Clicked` event. But you can also use the button's command interface as an alternative to (or in addi-tion to) the `Clicked` event. This interface consists of two public properties that `Button` defines:

- `Command` of type `System.Windows.Input.ICommand`.

- `CommandParameter` of type `Object`.

To support commanding, a ViewModel must define a public property of type `ICommand` that is then connected to the `Command` property of the `Button` through a normal data binding.

Like `INotifyPropertyChanged`, the `ICommand` interface is not a part of Xamarin.Forms. It's de-fined in the `System.Windows.Input` namespace and implemented in the **System.ObjectModel** as-sembly, which is one of the .NET assemblies linked to a Xamarin.Forms application. `ICommand` is the *only* type in the `System.Windows.Input` namespace that Xamarin.Forms supports. Indeed it's the only type in *any* `System.Windows` namespace supported by Xamarin.Forms.

Is it a coincidence that `INotifyPropertyChanged` and `ICommand` are both defined in .NET assem-blies rather than Xamarin.Forms? No. These interfaces are often used in ViewModels, and some devel-opers might already have ViewModels developed for one or more of Microsoft's XAML-based environ-ments. It's easiest for developers to incorporate these existing ViewModels into Xamarin.Forms if `INotifyPropertyChanged` and `ICommand` are defined in standard .NET namespaces and assemblies ra-ther than in Xamarin.Forms.

The `ICommand` interface defines two methods and one event:

```
public interface ICommand
{
    void Execute(object arg);

    bool CanExecute(object arg);

    event EventHandler CanExecuteChanged;
}
```

To implement commanding, the ViewModel defines one or more properties of type `ICommand`, meaning that the property is a type that implements these two methods and the event. A property in the ViewModel that implements `ICommand` can then be bound to the `Command` property of a `Button`. When the `Button` is clicked, the `Button` fires its normal `Clicked` event as usual, but it also calls the `Execute` method of the object bound to its `Command` property. The argument to the `Execute` method is the object set to the `CommandParameter` property of the `Button`.

That's the basic technique. However, it could be that certain conditions in the ViewModel prohibit a `Button` click at the current time. In that case, the `Button` should be disabled. This is the purpose of the `CanExecute` method and the `CanExecuteChanged` event in `ICommand`. The `Button` calls `CanEx-ecute` when its `Command` property is first set. If `CanExecute` returns `false`, the `Button` disables itself and doesn't generate `Execute` calls. The `Button` also installs a handler for the `CanExecuteChanged` event. Thereafter, whenever the ViewModel fires the `CanExecuteChanged` event, the button calls `CanExecute` again to determine whether the button should be enabled.

A ViewModel that supports the command interface defines one or more properties of type `ICom-mand` and internally sets this property to a class that implements the `ICommand` interface. What is this class, and how does it work?

If you were implementing the commanding protocol in one of Microsoft's XAML-based environ-ments, you would be writing your own class that implements `ICommand`, or perhaps using one that you found on the web, or one that was included with some MVVM tools. Sometimes such classes are named `CommandDelegate` or something similar.

You can use that same class in the ViewModels of your Xamarin.Forms applications. However, for your convenience, Xamarin.Forms includes two classes that implement `ICommand` that you can use instead. These two classes are named simply `Command` and `Command<T>`, where `T` is the type of the arguments to `Execute` and `CanExecute`.

If you are indeed sharing a ViewModel between Microsoft environments and Xamarin.Forms, you can't use the `Command` classes defined by Xamarin.Forms. However, you'll be using something similar to these `Command` classes, so the following discussion will certainly be applicable regardless.

The `Command` class includes the two methods and event of the `ICommand` interface and also defines a `ChangeCanExecute` method. This method causes the `Command` object to fire the `CanExecute-Changed` event, and that facility turns out to be very handy.

Within the ViewModel, you'll probably create an object of type `Command` or `Command<T>` for every public property in the ViewModel of type `ICommand`. The `Command` or `Command<T>` constructor requires a callback method in the form of an `Action` object that is called when the `Button` calls the `Execute` method of the `ICommand` interface. The `CanExecute` method is optional but takes the form of a `Func` object that returns `bool`.

In many cases, the properties of type `ICommand` are set in the ViewModel's constructor and do not change thereafter. For that reason, these `ICommand` properties do not generally need to fire `PropertyChanged` events.

Simple method executions

Let's look at a simple example. A program called **PowersOfThree** lets you use two buttons to explore various powers of 3. One button increases the exponent and the other button decreases the exponent.

The `PowersViewModel` class derives from the `ViewModelBase` class in the **Xamarin.Forms-Book.Toolkit** library, but the ViewModel itself is in the **PowersOfThree** application project. It is not restricted to powers of 3, but the constructor requires an argument that the class uses as a base value for the power calculation, and which it exposes as the `BaseValue` property. Because this property has a private `set` accessor and doesn't change after the constructor concludes, the property does not fire a `PropertyChanged` event.

Two other properties, named `Exponent` and `Power`, do fire `PropertyChanged` events, but both properties also have private `set` accessors. The `Exponent` property is increased and decreased only from external button clicks.

To implement the response to `Button` taps, the `PowersViewModel` class defines two properties of type `ICommand`, named `IncreaseExponentCommand` and `DecreaseExponentCommand`. Again, both properties have private `set` accessors. As you can see, the constructor sets these two properties by instantiating `Command` objects that reference little private methods immediately following the constructor. These two little methods are called when the `Execute` method of `Command` is called. The View-Model uses the `Command` class rather than `Command<T>` because the program doesn't make use of any argument to the `Execute` methods:

```csharp
class PowersViewModel : ViewModelBase
{
    double exponent, power;

    public PowersViewModel(double baseValue)
    {
        // Initialize properties.
        BaseValue = baseValue;
        Exponent = 0;

        // Initialize ICommand properties.
        IncreaseExponentCommand = new Command(ExecuteIncreaseExponent);
        DecreaseExponentCommand = new Command(ExecuteDecreaseExponent);
    }

    void ExecuteIncreaseExponent()
    {
        Exponent += 1;
    }

    void ExecuteDecreaseExponent()
    {
        Exponent -= 1;
    }

    public double BaseValue { private set; get; }

    public double Exponent
    {
        private set
        {
            if (SetProperty(ref exponent, value))
            {
                Power = Math.Pow(BaseValue, exponent);
            }
        }
        get
        {
            return exponent;
        }
    }

    public double Power
    {
        private set { SetProperty(ref power, value); }
        get { return power; }
    }

    public ICommand IncreaseExponentCommand { private set; get; }

    public ICommand DecreaseExponentCommand { private set; get; }
}
```

The `ExecuteIncreaseExponent` and `ExecuteDecreaseExponent` methods both make a change to the `Exponent` property (which fires a `PropertyChanged` event), and the `Exponent` property recalculates the `Power` property, which also fires a `PropertyChanged` event.

Very often a ViewModel will instantiate its `Command` objects by passing lambda functions to the `Command` constructor. This approach allows these methods to be defined right in the ViewModel constructor, like so:

```
IncreaseExponentCommand = new Command(() =>
    {
        Exponent += 1;
    });

DecreaseExponentCommand = new Command(() =>
    {
        Exponent -= 1;
    });
```

The `PowersOfThreePage` XAML file binds the `Text` properties of three `Label` elements to the `BaseValue`, `Exponent`, and `Power` properties of the `PowersViewModel` class, and binds the `Command` properties of the two `Button` elements to the `IncreaseExponentCommand` and `DecreaseExponentCommand` properties of the ViewModel.

Notice how an argument of 3 is passed to the constructor of `PowersViewModel` as it is instantiated in the `Resources` dictionary. Passing arguments to ViewModel constructors is the primary reason for the existence of the `x:Arguments` tag:

```
<ContentPage xmlns="http://xamarin.com/schemas/2014/forms"
             xmlns:x="http://schemas.microsoft.com/winfx/2009/xaml"
             xmlns:local="clr-namespace:PowersOfThree"
             x:Class="PowersOfThree.PowersOfThreePage">

    <ContentPage.Resources>
        <ResourceDictionary>
            <local:PowersViewModel x:Key="viewModel">
                <x:Arguments>
                    <x:Double>3</x:Double>
                </x:Arguments>
            </local:PowersViewModel>
        </ResourceDictionary>
    </ContentPage.Resources>

    <StackLayout BindingContext="{StaticResource viewModel}">
        <StackLayout Orientation="Horizontal"
                     Spacing="0"
                     HorizontalOptions="Center"
                     VerticalOptions="CenterAndExpand">
            <Label FontSize="Large"
                   Text="{Binding BaseValue, StringFormat='{0}'}" />

            <Label FontSize="Small"
                   Text="{Binding Exponent, StringFormat='{0}'}" />
```

```xml
            <Label FontSize="Large"
                   Text="{Binding Power, StringFormat=' = {0}'}" />
        </StackLayout>

        <StackLayout Orientation="Horizontal"
                     VerticalOptions="CenterAndExpand">

            <Button Text="Increase"
                    Command="{Binding IncreaseExponentCommand}"
                    HorizontalOptions="CenterAndExpand" />

            <Button Text="Decrease"
                    Command="{Binding DecreaseExponentCommand}"
                    HorizontalOptions="CenterAndExpand" />
        </StackLayout>
    </StackLayout>
</ContentPage>
```

Here's what it looks like after several presses of one button or the other:

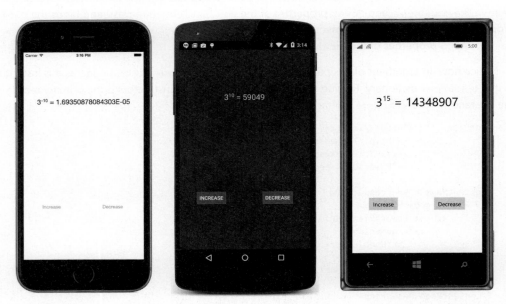

Once again, the wisdom of separating the user interface from the underlying business logic is revealed when the time comes to change the View. For example, suppose you want to replace the buttons with an element with a `TapGestureRecognizer`. Fortunately, `TapGestureRecognizer` has a `Command` property:

```xml
<StackLayout Orientation="Horizontal"
             VerticalOptions="CenterAndExpand">

    <Frame OutlineColor="Accent"
           BackgroundColor="Transparent"
```

```
        Padding="20, 40"
        HorizontalOptions="CenterAndExpand">
    <Frame.GestureRecognizers>
        <TapGestureRecognizer Command="{Binding IncreaseExponentCommand}" />
    </Frame.GestureRecognizers>

    <Label Text="Increase"
           FontSize="Large" />
</Frame>

<Frame OutlineColor="Accent"
       BackgroundColor="Transparent"
       Padding="20, 40"
       HorizontalOptions="CenterAndExpand">
    <Frame.GestureRecognizers>
        <TapGestureRecognizer Command="{Binding DecreaseExponentCommand}" />
    </Frame.GestureRecognizers>

    <Label Text="Decrease"
           FontSize="Large" />
</Frame>
</StackLayout>
```

Without touching the ViewModel or even renaming an event handler so that it applies to a tap rather than a button, the program works the same, but with a different look:

A calculator, almost

Now it's time to make a more sophisticated ViewModel with `ICommand` objects that have both `Execute` and `CanExecute` methods. The next program is almost like a calculator except that it only adds a series of numbers together. The ViewModel is named `AdderViewModel`, and the program is called **AddingMachine**.

Let's look at the screenshots first:

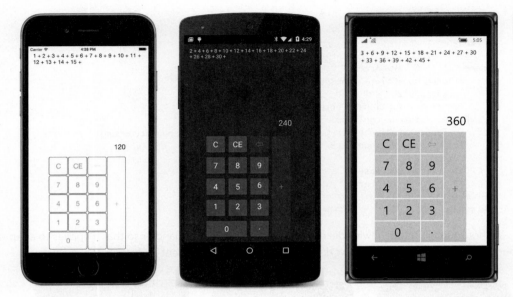

At the top of the page you can see a history of the series of numbers that have already been entered and added. This is a `Label` in a `ScrollView`, so it can get rather long.

The sum of those numbers is displayed in the `Entry` view above the keypad. Normally, that `Entry` view contains the number that you're typing in, but after you hit the big plus sign at the right of the keypad, the `Entry` displays the accumulated sum and the plus sign button becomes disabled. You need to begin typing another number for the accumulated sum to disappear and for the button with the plus sign to be enabled. Similarly, the backspace button is enabled as soon as you begin to type.

These are not the only keys that can be disabled. The decimal point is disabled when the number you're typing already has a decimal point, and all the number keys become disabled when the number contains 16 characters. This is to avoid the number in the `Entry` from becoming too long to display.

The disabling of these buttons is the result of implementing the `CanExecute` method in the `ICommand` interface.

The `AdderViewModel` class is in the **Xamarin.FormsBook.Toolkit** library and derives from `ViewModelBase`. Here is the part of the class with all the public properties and their backing fields:

```
public class AdderViewModel : ViewModelBase
{
    string currentEntry = "0";
    string historyString = "";
```

```
...
public string CurrentEntry
{
    private set { SetProperty(ref currentEntry, value); }
    get { return currentEntry; }
}

public string HistoryString
{
    private set { SetProperty(ref historyString, value); }
    get { return historyString; }
}

public ICommand ClearCommand { private set; get; }

public ICommand ClearEntryCommand { private set; get; }

public ICommand BackspaceCommand { private set; get; }

public ICommand NumericCommand { private set; get; }

public ICommand DecimalPointCommand { private set; get; }

public ICommand AddCommand { private set; get; }
...
}
```

All the properties have private `set` accessors. The two properties of type `string` are only set internally based on the key taps, and the properties of type `ICommand` are set in the `AdderViewModel` constructor (which you'll see shortly).

These eight public properties are the only part of `AdderViewModel` that the XAML file in the **AddingMachine** project needs to know about. Here is that XAML file. It contains a two-row and two-column main `Grid` for switching between portrait and landscape mode, and a `Label`, `Entry`, and 15 `Button` elements, all of which are bound to one of the eight public properties of the `AdderView-Model`. Notice that the `Command` properties of all 10 digit buttons are bound to the `NumericCommand` property and that the buttons are differentiated by the `CommandParameter` property. The setting of this `CommandParameter` property is passed as an argument to the `Execute` and `CanExecute` methods:

```
<ContentPage xmlns="http://xamarin.com/schemas/2014/forms"
             xmlns:x="http://schemas.microsoft.com/winfx/2009/xaml"
             x:Class="AddingMachine.AddingMachinePage"
             SizeChanged="OnPageSizeChanged">

    <ContentPage.Padding>
        <OnPlatform x:TypeArguments="Thickness"
                    iOS="10, 20, 10, 10"
                    Android="10"
                    WinPhone="10" />
    </ContentPage.Padding>
```

```
<Grid x:Name="mainGrid">
    <!-- Initialized for Portrait mode. -->
    <Grid.RowDefinitions>
        <RowDefinition Height="*" />
        <RowDefinition Height="Auto" />
    </Grid.RowDefinitions>

    <Grid.ColumnDefinitions>
        <ColumnDefinition Width="*" />
        <ColumnDefinition Width="0" />
    </Grid.ColumnDefinitions>

    <!-- History display. -->
    <ScrollView Grid.Row="0" Grid.Column="0"
                Padding="5, 0">
        <Label Text="{Binding HistoryString}" />
    </ScrollView>

    <!-- Keypad. -->
    <Grid x:Name="keypadGrid"
          Grid.Row="1" Grid.Column="0"
          RowSpacing="2"
          ColumnSpacing="2"
          WidthRequest="240"
          HeightRequest="360"
          VerticalOptions="Center"
          HorizontalOptions="Center">
        <Grid.Resources>
            <ResourceDictionary>
                <Style TargetType="Button">
                    <Setter Property="FontSize" Value="Large" />
                    <Setter Property="BorderWidth" Value="1" />
                </Style>
            </ResourceDictionary>
        </Grid.Resources>

        <Label Text="{Binding CurrentEntry}"
               Grid.Row="0" Grid.Column="0" Grid.ColumnSpan="4"
               FontSize="Large"
               LineBreakMode="HeadTruncation"
               VerticalOptions="Center"
               HorizontalTextAlignment="End" />

        <Button Text="C"
                Grid.Row="1" Grid.Column="0"
                Command="{Binding ClearCommand}" />

        <Button Text="CE"
                Grid.Row="1" Grid.Column="1"
                Command="{Binding ClearEntryCommand}" />

        <Button Text="&#x21E6;"
                Grid.Row="1" Grid.Column="2"
                Command="{Binding BackspaceCommand}" />
```

```xml
<Button Text="+"
        Grid.Row="1" Grid.Column="3" Grid.RowSpan="5"
        Command="{Binding AddCommand}" />

<Button Text="7"
        Grid.Row="2" Grid.Column="0"
        Command="{Binding NumericCommand}"
        CommandParameter="7" />

<Button Text="8"
        Grid.Row="2" Grid.Column="1"
        Command="{Binding NumericCommand}"
        CommandParameter="8" />

<Button Text="9"
        Grid.Row="2" Grid.Column="2"
        Command="{Binding NumericCommand}"
        CommandParameter="9" />

<Button Text="4"
        Grid.Row="3" Grid.Column="0"
        Command="{Binding NumericCommand}"
        CommandParameter="4" />

<Button Text="5"
        Grid.Row="3" Grid.Column="1"
        Command="{Binding NumericCommand}"
        CommandParameter="5" />

<Button Text="6"
        Grid.Row="3" Grid.Column="2"
        Command="{Binding NumericCommand}"
        CommandParameter="6" />

<Button Text="1"
        Grid.Row="4" Grid.Column="0"
        Command="{Binding NumericCommand}"
        CommandParameter="1" />

<Button Text="2"
        Grid.Row="4" Grid.Column="1"
        Command="{Binding NumericCommand}"
        CommandParameter="2" />

<Button Text="3"
        Grid.Row="4" Grid.Column="2"
        Command="{Binding NumericCommand}"
        CommandParameter="3" />

<Button Text="0"
        Grid.Row="5" Grid.Column="0" Grid.ColumnSpan="2"
        Command="{Binding NumericCommand}"
        CommandParameter="0" />
```

```
        <Button Text="&#x00B7;"
                Grid.Row="5" Grid.Column="2"
                Command="{Binding DecimalPointCommand}" />
    </Grid>
  </Grid>
</ContentPage>
```

What you won't find in the XAML file is a reference to `AdderViewModel`. For reasons you'll see shortly, `AdderViewModel` is instantiated in code.

The core of the adding-machine logic is in the `Execute` and `CanExecute` methods of the six `ICommand` properties. These properties are all initialized in the `AdderViewModel` constructor shown below, and the `Execute` and `CanExecute` methods are all lambda functions.

When only one lambda function appears in the `Command` constructor, that's the `Execute` method (as the parameter name indicates), and the `Button` is always enabled. This is the case for `ClearCommand` and `ClearEntryCommand`.

All the other `Command` constructors have two lambda functions. The first is the `Execute` method, and the second is the `CanExecute` method. The `CanExecute` method returns `true` if the `Button` should be enabled and `false` otherwise.

All the `ICommand` properties are set with the nongeneric form of the `Command` class except for `NumericCommand`, which requires an argument to the `Execute` and `CanExecute` methods to identify which key has been tapped:

```
public class AdderViewModel : ViewModelBase
{
    ...
    bool isSumDisplayed = false;
    double accumulatedSum = 0;

    public AdderViewModel()
    {
        ClearCommand = new Command(
            execute: () =>
            {
                HistoryString = "";
                accumulatedSum = 0;
                CurrentEntry = "0";
                isSumDisplayed = false;
                RefreshCanExecutes();
            });

        ClearEntryCommand = new Command(
            execute: () =>
            {
                CurrentEntry = "0";
                isSumDisplayed = false;
                RefreshCanExecutes();
            });
```

```
BackspaceCommand = new Command(
    execute: () =>
    {
        CurrentEntry = CurrentEntry.Substring(0, CurrentEntry.Length - 1);

        if (CurrentEntry.Length == 0)
        {
            CurrentEntry = "0";
        }

        RefreshCanExecutes();
    },
    canExecute: () =>
    {
        return !isSumDisplayed && (CurrentEntry.Length > 1 || CurrentEntry[0] != '0');
    });

NumericCommand = new Command<string>(
    execute: (string parameter) =>
    {
        if (isSumDisplayed || CurrentEntry == "0")
            CurrentEntry = parameter;
        else
            CurrentEntry += parameter;

        isSumDisplayed = false;
        RefreshCanExecutes();
    },
    canExecute: (string parameter) =>
    {
        return isSumDisplayed || CurrentEntry.Length < 16;
    });

DecimalPointCommand = new Command(
    execute: () =>
    {
        if (isSumDisplayed)
            CurrentEntry = "0.";
        else
            CurrentEntry += ".";

        isSumDisplayed = false;
        RefreshCanExecutes();
    },
    canExecute: () =>
    {
        return isSumDisplayed || !CurrentEntry.Contains(".");
    });

AddCommand = new Command(
    execute: () =>
    {
        double value = Double.Parse(CurrentEntry);
```

```
                HistoryString += value.ToString() + " + ";
                accumulatedSum += value;
                CurrentEntry = accumulatedSum.ToString();
                isSumDisplayed = true;
                RefreshCanExecutes();
            },
            canExecute: () =>
            {
                return !isSumDisplayed;
            });
    }

    void RefreshCanExecutes()
    {
        ((Command)BackspaceCommand).ChangeCanExecute();
        ((Command)NumericCommand).ChangeCanExecute();
        ((Command)DecimalPointCommand).ChangeCanExecute();
        ((Command)AddCommand).ChangeCanExecute();
    }
    ...
}
```

All the `Execute` methods conclude by calling a method named `RefreshCanExecute` following the constructor. This method calls the `ChangeCanExecute` method of each of the four `Command` objects that implement `CanExecute` methods. That method call causes the `Command` object to fire a `ChangeCanExecute` event. Each `Button` responds to that event by making another call to the `CanExecute` method to determine if the `Button` should be enabled or not.

It is not necessary for every `Execute` method to conclude with a call to all four `ChangeCanExecute` methods. For example, the `ChangeCanExecute` method for the `DecimalPointCommand` need not be called when the `Execute` method for `NumericCommand` executes. However, it turned out to be easier—both in terms of logic and code consolidation—to simply call them all after every key tap.

You might be more comfortable implementing these `Execute` and `CanExecute` methods as regular methods rather than lambda functions. Or you might be more comfortable having just one `Command` object that handles all the keys. Each key could have an identifying `CommandParameter` string and you could distinguish between them with a `switch` and `case` statement.

There are lots of ways to implement the commanding logic, but it should be clear that the use of commanding tends to structure the code in a flexible and ideal way.

Once the adding logic is in place, why not add a couple of more buttons for subtraction, multiplication, and division?

Well, it's not quite so easy to enhance the logic to accept multiple operations rather than just one operation. If the program supports multiple operations, then when the user types one of the operation keys, that operation needs to be saved to await the next number. Only after the next number is completed (signaled by the press of another operation key or the equals key) is that saved operation applied.

An easier approach would be to write a Reverse Polish Notation (RPN) calculator, where the operation *follows* the entry of the second number. The simplicity of RPN logic is one big reason why RPN calculators appeal to programmers so much!

ViewModels and the application lifecycle

In a real calculator program on a mobile device, one important feature involves saving the entire state of the calculator when the program is terminated, and restoring it when the program starts up again.

And once again, the concept of the ViewModel seems to break down.

Sure, it's possible to write some application code that accesses the public properties of the View-Model and saves them, but the state of the calculator depends on private fields as well. The `isSum-Displayed` and `accumulatedSum` fields of `AdderViewModel` are essential for restoring the calculator's state.

It's obvious that code external to the `AdderViewModel` can't save and restore the `AdderView-Model` state without the ViewModel exposing more public properties. There's only one class that knows what's necessary to represent the entire internal state of a ViewModel, and that's the ViewModel itself.

The solution is for the ViewModel to define public methods that save and restore its internal state. But because a ViewModel should strive to be platform independent, these methods shouldn't use anything specific to a particular platform. For example, they shouldn't access the Xamarin.Forms `Application` object and then add items to (or retrieve items from) the `Properties` dictionary of that `Application` object. That is much too specific to Xamarin.Forms.

However, working with a generic `IDictionary` object in methods named `SaveState` and `RestoreState` is possible in *any* .NET environment, and that's how `AdderViewModel` implements these methods:

```
public class AdderViewModel : ViewModelBase
{
    ...
    public void SaveState(IDictionary<string, object> dictionary)
    {
        dictionary["CurrentEntry"] = CurrentEntry;
        dictionary["HistoryString"] = HistoryString;
        dictionary["isSumDisplayed"] = isSumDisplayed;
        dictionary["accumulatedSum"] = accumulatedSum;
    }

    public void RestoreState(IDictionary<string, object> dictionary)
    {
        CurrentEntry = GetDictionaryEntry(dictionary, "CurrentEntry", "0");
        HistoryString = GetDictionaryEntry(dictionary, "HistoryString", "");
        isSumDisplayed = GetDictionaryEntry(dictionary, "isSumDisplayed", false);
```

```
            accumulatedSum = GetDictionaryEntry(dictionary, "accumulatedSum", 0.0);

            RefreshCanExecutes();
    }

    public T GetDictionaryEntry<T>(IDictionary<string, object> dictionary,
                                    string key, T defaultValue)
    {
        if (dictionary.ContainsKey(key))
            return (T)dictionary[key];

        return defaultValue;
    }
}
```

The code in **AddingMachine** involved in saving and restoring this state is mostly implemented in the `App` class. The `App` class instantiates the `AdderViewModel` and calls `RestoreState` using the `Properties` dictionary of the current `Application` class. That `AdderViewModel` is then passed as an argument to the `AddingMachinePage` constructor:

```
public class App : Application
{
    AdderViewModel adderViewModel;

    public App()
    {
        // Instantiate and initialize ViewModel for page.
        adderViewModel = new AdderViewModel();
        adderViewModel.RestoreState(Current.Properties);
        MainPage = new AddingMachinePage(adderViewModel);
    }

    protected override void OnStart()
    {
        // Handle when your app starts.
    }

    protected override void OnSleep()
    {
        // Handle when your app sleeps.
        adderViewModel.SaveState(Current.Properties);
    }

    protected override void OnResume()
    {
        // Handle when your app resumes.
    }
}
```

The `App` class is also responsible for calling `SaveState` on `AdderViewModel` during processing of the `OnSleep` method.

The `AddingMachinePage` constructor merely needs to set the instance of `AdderViewModel` to the page's `BindingContext` property. The code-behind file also manages the switch between portrait and landscape layouts:

```
public partial class AddingMachinePage : ContentPage
{
    public AddingMachinePage(AdderViewModel viewModel)
    {
        InitializeComponent();

        // Set ViewModel as BindingContext.
        BindingContext = viewModel;
    }

    void OnPageSizeChanged(object sender, EventArgs args)
    {
        // Portrait mode.
        if (Width < Height)
        {
            mainGrid.RowDefinitions[1].Height = GridLength.Auto;
            mainGrid.ColumnDefinitions[1].Width = new GridLength(0, GridUnitType.Absolute);

            Grid.SetRow(keypadGrid, 1);
            Grid.SetColumn(keypadGrid, 0);
        }
        // Landscape mode.
        else
        {
            mainGrid.RowDefinitions[1].Height = new GridLength(0, GridUnitType.Absolute);
            mainGrid.ColumnDefinitions[1].Width = GridLength.Auto;

            Grid.SetRow(keypadGrid, 0);
            Grid.SetColumn(keypadGrid, 1);
        }
    }
}
```

The **AddingMachine** program demonstrates one way to handle the ViewModel, but it's not the only way. Alternatively, it's possible for `App` to instantiate the `AdderViewModel` but define a property of type `AdderViewModel` that the constructor of `AddingMachinePage` can access.

Or, if you want the page to have full control over the ViewModel, you can do that as well. `Adding-MachinePage` can define its own `OnSleep` method that is called from the `OnSleep` method in the `App` class, and the page class can also handle the instantiation of `AdderViewModel` and the calling of the `RestoreState` and `SaveState` methods. However, this approach might become somewhat clumsy for multipage applications.

In a multipage application, you might have separate ViewModels for each page, perhaps deriving from a ViewModel with properties applicable to the entire application. In such a case, you'll want to avoid properties with the same name using the same dictionary keys for saving each ViewModel's state. You can use more extensive dictionary keys that include the class name, for example, "Adder-ViewModel.CurrentEntry".

Although the power and advantages of data binding and ViewModels should be apparent by now, these features really blossom when used with the Xamarin.Forms `ListView`. That's up in the next chapter.

Chapter 19
Collection views

Many of the views in Xamarin.Forms correspond to basic C# and .NET data types: The `Slider` and `Stepper` are visual representations of a `double`, the `Switch` is a `bool`, and an `Entry` allows the user to edit text exposed as a `string`. But can this correspondence also apply to *collection* types in C# and .NET?

Collections of various sorts have always been essential in digital computing. Even the oldest of high-level programming languages support both arrays and structures. These two archetypal collections complement each other: An array is a collection of values or objects generally of the same type, while a structure is an assemblage of related data items generally of a variety of types.

To supplement these basic collection types, .NET added several useful classes in the `System.Collections` and `System.Collections.Generic` namespaces, most notably `List` and `List<T>`, which are expandable collections of objects of the same type. Underlying these collection classes are three important interfaces that you'll encounter in this chapter:

- `IEnumerable` allows iterating through the items in a collection.

- `ICollection` derives from `IEnumerable` and adds a count of the items in the collection.

- `IList` derives from `ICollection` and supports indexing as well as adding and removing items.

Xamarin.Forms defines three views that maintain collections of various sorts, sometimes also allowing the user to select an item from the collection or interact with the item. The three views discussed in this chapter are:

- `Picker`: A list of text items that lets the user choose one. The `Picker` usually maintains a *short* list of items, generally no more than a dozen or so.

- `ListView`: Very often a long list of data items of the same type rendered in a uniform (or nearly uniform) manner that is specified by a visual tree described by an object called a *cell*.

- `TableView`: A collection of cells, usually of various sorts, to display data or to manage user input. A `TableView` might take the form of a menu, or a fill-out form, or a collection of application settings.

All three of these views provide built-in scrolling.

At first encounter these three views might seem somewhat similar. The purpose of this chapter is to provide enough examples of how these views are used so that you shouldn't have any difficulty choosing the right tool for the job.

Both `Picker` and `ListView` allow selection, but `Picker` is restricted to strings, while `ListView` can display any object rendered in whatever way you want. `Picker` is generally a short list, while `ListView` can maintain must longer lists.

The relationship between `ListView` and `TableView` is potentially confusing because both involve the use of cells, which are derivatives of the `Cell` class. `Cell` derives from `Element` but not `VisualElement`. A cell is not a visual element itself, but instead provides a description of a visual element. These cells are used by `ListView` and `TableView` in two different ways: `ListView` generally displays a list of objects of the same type, the display of which is specified by a single cell. A `TableView` is a collection of multiple cells, each of which displays an individual item in a collection of related items.

If you like to equate Xamarin.Forms views with C# and .NET data types, then:

- `Picker` is a visual representation of an array of `string`.

- `ListView` is a more generalized array of objects, often a `List<T>` collection. The individual items in this collection often implement the `INotifyPropertyChanged` interface.

- `TableView` could be a structure, but it is more likely a class, and possibly a class that implements `INotifyPropertyChanged`, otherwise known as a ViewModel.

Let's begin with the simplest of these three, which is the `Picker`.

Program options with Picker

`Picker` is a good choice when you need a view that allows the user to choose one item among a small collection of several items. `Picker` is implemented in a platform-specific manner and has the limitation that each item is identified solely by a text string.

The Picker and event handling

Here's a program named **PickerDemo** that implements a `Picker` to allow you to choose a specialized keyboard for an `Entry` view. In the XAML file, the `Entry` and the `Picker` are children of a `StackLayout`, and the `Picker` is initialized to contain a list of the various keyboard types supported by the `Keyboard` class:

```
<ContentPage xmlns="http://xamarin.com/schemas/2014/forms"
             xmlns:x="http://schemas.microsoft.com/winfx/2009/xaml"
             x:Class="PickerDemo.PickerDemoPage">
    <ContentPage.Padding>
        <OnPlatform x:TypeArguments="Thickness"
                    iOS="0, 20, 0, 0" />
    </ContentPage.Padding>

    <StackLayout Padding="20"
                 Spacing="50">
```

```
        <Entry x:Name="entry"
               Placeholder="Type something, type anything" />

        <Picker Title="Keyboard Type"
                SelectedIndexChanged="OnPickerSelectedIndexChanged">
            <Picker.Items>
                <x:String>Default</x:String>
                <x:String>Text</x:String>
                <x:String>Chat</x:String>
                <x:String>Url</x:String>
                <x:String>Email</x:String>
                <x:String>Telephone</x:String>
                <x:String>Numeric</x:String>
            </Picker.Items>
        </Picker>
    </StackLayout>
</ContentPage>
```

The program sets two properties of `Picker`: The `Title` property is a string that identifies the function of the `Picker`. The `Items` property is of type `IList<string>`, and generally you initialize it with a list of `x:String` tags in the XAML file. (`Picker` has no content property attribute, so the explicit `Picker.Items` tags are required.) In code, you can use the `Add` or `Insert` method defined by `IList<string>` to put `string` items into the collection.

Here's what you'll see when you first run the program:

The visual representation of the `Picker` is quite similar to the `Entry` but with the `Title` property displayed. Tapping the `Picker` invokes a platform-specific scrollable list of items:

When you press **Done** on the iOS screen, or **OK** on the Android screen, or just tap an item on the Windows list, the `Picker` fires a `SelectedIndexChanged` event. The `SelectedIndex` property of `Picker` is a zero-based number indicating the particular item the user selected. If no item is selected— which is the case when the `Picker` is first created and initialized—`SelectedIndex` equals –1.

The **PickerDemo** program handles the `SelectedIndexChanged` event in the code-behind file. It obtains the `SelectedIndex` from the `Picker`, uses that number to index the `Items` collection of the `Picker`, and then uses reflection to obtain the corresponding `Keyboard` object, which it sets to the `Keyboard` property of the `Entry`:

```
public partial class PickerDemoPage : ContentPage
{
    public PickerDemoPage()
    {
        InitializeComponent();
    }

    void OnPickerSelectedIndexChanged(object sender, EventArgs args)
    {
        if (entry == null)
            return;

        Picker picker = (Picker)sender;
        int selectedIndex = picker.SelectedIndex;

        if (selectedIndex == -1)
            return;

        string selectedItem = picker.Items[selectedIndex];
        PropertyInfo propertyInfo = typeof(Keyboard).GetRuntimeProperty(selectedItem);
```

```
        entry.Keyboard = (Keyboard)propertyInfo.GetValue(null);
    }
}
```

At the same time, the interactive `Picker` display is dismissed, and the `Picker` now displays the selected item:

On iOS and Android, the selection replaces the `Title` property, so in a real-life program you might want to provide a simple `Label` on these two platforms to remind the user of the function of the `Picker`.

You can initialize the `Picker` to display a particular item by setting the `SelectedIndex` property. However, you must set `SelectedIndex` *after* filling the `Items` collection, so you'll probably do it from code or use property-element syntax:

```xml
<Picker Title="Keyboard Type"
        SelectedIndexChanged="OnPickerSelectedIndexChanged">
    <Picker.Items>
        <x:String>Default</x:String>
        <x:String>Text</x:String>
        <x:String>Chat</x:String>
        <x:String>Url</x:String>
        <x:String>Email</x:String>
        <x:String>Telephone</x:String>
        <x:String>Numeric</x:String>
    </Picker.Items>

    <Picker.SelectedIndex>
        6
    </Picker.SelectedIndex>
```

```
</Picker>
```

Data binding the Picker

The `Items` property of `Picker` is not backed by a bindable property; hence, it cannot be the target of a data binding. You cannot bind a collection to a `Picker`. If you need that facility, you'll probably want to use `ListView` instead.

On the other hand, the `SelectedIndex` property of the `Picker` is backed by a `BindableProperty` and has a default binding mode of `TwoWay`. This seems to suggest that you can use `SelectedIndex` in a data binding, and that is true. However, an integer index is usually not what you want in a data binding.

Even if `Picker` had a `SelectedItem` property that provided the actual item rather than the index of the item, that wouldn't be optimum either. This hypothetical `SelectedItem` property would be of type `string`, and usually that's not very useful in data bindings either.

After contemplating this problem—and perhaps being exposed to the `ListView` coming up next—you might try to create a class named `BindablePicker` that derives from `Picker`. Such a class could have an `ObjectItems` property of type `IList<object>` and a `SelectedItem` property of type `object`. However, without any additional information, this `BindablePicker` class would be forced to convert each object in the collection to a string for the underlying `Picker`, and the only generalized way to convert an object to a string is with the object's `ToString` method. Perhaps the string obtained from `ToString` is useful; perhaps not. (You'll see shortly how the `ListView` solves this problem in a very flexible manner.)

Perhaps a better solution for data binding a `Picker` is a value converter that converts between the `SelectedIndex` property of the `Picker` and an object corresponding to each text string in the `Items` collection. To accomplish this conversion, the value converter can maintain its own collection of objects that correspond to the strings displayed by the `Picker`. This means that you'll have two lists associated with the `Picker`—one list of strings displayed by the `Picker` and another list of objects associated with these strings. These two lists must be in exact correspondence, of course, but if the two lists are defined close to each other in the XAML file, there shouldn't be much confusion, and the scheme will have the advantage of being very flexible.

Such a value converter might be called `IndexToObjectConverter`.

Or maybe not. In the general case, you'll want the `SelectedIndex` property of the `Picker` to be the *target* of the data binding. If `SelectedIndex` is the data-binding target, then the `Picker` can be used with a ViewModel as the data-binding source. For that reason, the value converter is better named `ObjectToIndexConverter`. Here's the class in the **Xamarin.FormsBook.Toolkit** library:

```
using System;
using System.Collections.Generic;
using System.Globalization;
using Xamarin.Forms;
```

```
namespace Xamarin.FormsBook.Toolkit
{
    [ContentProperty("Items")]
    public class ObjectToIndexConverter<T> : IValueConverter
    {
        public IList<T> Items { set; get; }

        public ObjectToIndexConverter()
        {
            Items = new List<T>();
        }

        public object Convert(object value, Type targetType,
                              object parameter, CultureInfo culture)
        {
            if (value == null || !(value is T) || Items == null)
                return -1;

            return Items.IndexOf((T)value);
        }

        public object ConvertBack(object value, Type targetType,
                                  object parameter, CultureInfo culture)
        {
            int index = (int)value;

            if (index < 0 || Items == null || index >= Items.Count)
                return null;

            return Items[index];
        }
    }
}
```

This is a generic class, and it defines a public `Items` property of type `IList<T>`, which is also defined as the content property of the converter. The `Convert` method assumes that the `value` parameter is an object of type `T` and returns the index of that object within the collection. The `ConvertBack` method assumes that the `value` parameter is an index into the `Items` collection and returns that object.

The **PickerBinding** program uses the `ObjectToIndexConverter` to define a binding that allows a `Picker` to be used for selecting a font size for a `Label`. The `Picker` is the data-binding target and the `FontSize` property of the `Label` is the source. The `Binding` object is instantiated in element tags to allow the `ObjectToIndexConverter` to be instantiated and initialized locally and provide an easy visual confirmation that the two lists correspond to the same values:

```
<ContentPage xmlns="http://xamarin.com/schemas/2014/forms"
             xmlns:x="http://schemas.microsoft.com/winfx/2009/xaml"
             xmlns:toolkit=
                 "clr-namespace:Xamarin.FormsBook.Toolkit;assembly=Xamarin.FormsBook.Toolkit"
             x:Class="PickerBinding.PickerBindingPage">
```

```
<ContentPage.Padding>
    <OnPlatform x:TypeArguments="Thickness"
                iOS="0, 20, 0, 0" />
</ContentPage.Padding>

<StackLayout Padding="20"
             Spacing="50">

    <Label x:Name="label"
           Text="Sample Text"
           FontSize="16" />

    <Picker Title="Font Size">
        <Picker.Items>
            <x:String>Font Size = 8</x:String>
            <x:String>Font Size = 10</x:String>
            <x:String>Font Size = 12</x:String>
            <x:String>Font Size = 14</x:String>
            <x:String>Font Size = 16</x:String>
            <x:String>Font Size = 20</x:String>
            <x:String>Font Size = 24</x:String>
            <x:String>Font Size = 30</x:String>
        </Picker.Items>

        <Picker.SelectedIndex>
            <Binding Source="{x:Reference label}"
                     Path="FontSize">
                <Binding.Converter>
                    <toolkit:ObjectToIndexConverter x:TypeArguments="x:Double">
                        <x:Double>8</x:Double>
                        <x:Double>10</x:Double>
                        <x:Double>12</x:Double>
                        <x:Double>14</x:Double>
                        <x:Double>16</x:Double>
                        <x:Double>20</x:Double>
                        <x:Double>24</x:Double>
                        <x:Double>30</x:Double>
                    </toolkit:ObjectToIndexConverter>
                </Binding.Converter>
            </Binding>
        </Picker.SelectedIndex>
    </Picker>
</StackLayout>
</ContentPage>
```

By maintaining separate lists of strings and objects, you can make the strings whatever you want. In this case, they include some text to indicate what the number actually means. The Label itself is initialized with a FontSize setting of 16, and the binding picks up that value to display the corresponding string in the Picker when the program first starts up:

The implementations of `Picker` on these three platforms should make it obvious that you don't want to use the `Picker` for more than (say) a dozen items. It's convenient and easy to use, but for lots of items, you want a view made for the job—a view that is designed to display objects not just as simple text strings but with whatever visuals you want.

Rendering data with ListView

Let's move to `ListView`, which is the primary view for displaying collections of items, usually of the same type. The `ListView` always displays the items in a vertical list and implements scrolling if necessary.

`ListView` is the only class that derives from `ItemsView<T>`, but from that class it inherits its most important property: `ItemsSource` of type `IEnumerable`. To this property a program sets an enumerable collection of data, and it can be any type of data. For that reason, `ListView` is one of the backbones of the View part of the Model-View-ViewModel architectural pattern.

`ListView` also supports single-item selection. The `ListView` highlights the selected item and makes it available as the `SelectedItem` property. Notice that this property is named `SelectedItem` rather than `SelectedIndex`. The property is of type `object`. If no item is currently selected in the `ListView`, the property is `null`. `ListView` fires an `ItemSelected` event when the selected item changes, but often you'll be using data binding in connection with the `SelectedItem` property.

ListView defines more properties by far than any other single view in Xamarin.Forms. The discussion in this chapter begins with the most important properties and then progressively covers the more obscure and less common properties.

Collections and selections

The **ListViewList** program defines a ListView that displays 17 Xamarin.Forms Color values. The XAML file instantiates the ListView but leaves the initialization to the code-behind file:

```
<ContentPage xmlns="http://xamarin.com/schemas/2014/forms"
             xmlns:x="http://schemas.microsoft.com/winfx/2009/xaml"
             x:Class="ListViewList.ListViewListPage">
    <ContentPage.Padding>
        <OnPlatform x:TypeArguments="Thickness"
                    iOS="10, 20, 10, 0"
                    Android="10, 0"
                    WinPhone="10, 0" />
    </ContentPage.Padding>

    <ListView x:Name="listView" />

</ContentPage>
```

The bulk of this XAML file is devoted to setting a Padding so that the ListView doesn't extend to the left and right edges of the screen. In some cases, you might want to set an explicit WidthRequest for the ListView based on the width of the widest item that you anticipate.

The ItemsSource property of ListView is of type IEnumerable, an interface implemented by arrays and the List class, but the property is null by default. Unlike the Picker, the ListView does not provide its own collection object. That's your responsibility. The code-behind file of **ListViewList** sets the ItemsSource property to an instance of List<Color> that is initialized with Color values:

```
public partial class ListViewListPage : ContentPage
{
    public ListViewListPage()
    {
        InitializeComponent();

        listView.ItemsSource = new List<Color>
        {
            Color.Aqua, Color.Black, Color.Blue, Color.Fuchsia,
            Color.Gray, Color.Green, Color.Lime, Color.Maroon,
            Color.Navy, Color.Olive, Color.Pink, Color.Purple,
            Color.Red, Color.Silver, Color.Teal, Color.White, Color.Yellow
        };
    }
}
```

When you run this program, you'll discover that you can scroll through the items and select one item by tapping it. These screenshots show how the selected item is highlighted on the three platforms:

Tapping an item also causes the `ListView` to fire both an `ItemTapped` and an `ItemSelected` event. If you tap the same item again, the `ItemTapped` event is fired again but not the `ItemSelected` event. The `ItemSelected` event is fired only if the `SelectedItem` property changes.

Of course, the items themselves aren't very attractive. By default, the `ListView` displays each item by calling the item's `ToString` method, and that's what you see in this `ListView`. But do not fret: Much of the discussion about the `ListView` in this chapter focuses on making the items appear exactly how you'd like!

The row separator

Look closely at the iOS and Android displays and you'll see a thin line separating the rows. You can suppress the display of that row by setting the `SeparatorVisibility` property to the enumeration member `SeparatorVisibility.None`. The default is `SeparatorVisibility.Default`, which means that a separator line is displayed on the iOS and Android screens but not Windows Phone.

For performance reasons, you should set the `SeparatorVisibility` property before adding items to the `ListView`. You can try this in the **ListViewList** program by setting the property in the XAML file:

```
<ListView x:Name="listView"
          SeparatorVisibility="None" />
```

Here's how it looks:

You can also set the separator line to a different color with the `SeparatorColor` property; for example:

```
<ListView x:Name="listView"
          SeparatorColor="Red" />
```

Now it shows up in red:

The line is rendered in a platform-specific manner. On iOS, that means it doesn't extend fully to the left edge of the `ListView`, and on the Windows platforms, that means that there's no separator line at all.

Data binding the selected item

One approach to working with the selected item involves handling the `ItemSelected` event of the `ListView` in the code-behind file and using the `SelectedItem` property to obtain the new selected item. (An example is shown later in this chapter.) But in many cases you'll want to use a data binding with the `SelectedItem` property. The **ListViewArray** program defines a data binding between the `SelectedItem` property of the `ListView` with the `Color` property of a `BoxView`:

```
<ContentPage xmlns="http://xamarin.com/schemas/2014/forms"
             xmlns:x="http://schemas.microsoft.com/winfx/2009/xaml"
             x:Class="ListViewArray.ListViewArrayPage">
    <ContentPage.Padding>
        <OnPlatform x:TypeArguments="Thickness"
                    iOS="10, 20, 10, 0"
                    Android="10, 0"
                    WinPhone="10, 0" />
    </ContentPage.Padding>

    <StackLayout>
        <ListView x:Name="listView"
                  SelectedItem="{Binding Source={x:Reference boxView},
                                         Path=Color,
                                         Mode=TwoWay}">
            <ListView.ItemsSource>
                <x:Array Type="{x:Type Color}">
```

```
                    <x:Static Member="Color.Aqua" />
                    <x:Static Member="Color.Black" />
                    <x:Static Member="Color.Blue" />
                    <x:Static Member="Color.Fuchsia" />
                    <x:Static Member="Color.Gray" />
                    <x:Static Member="Color.Green" />
                    <x:Static Member="Color.Lime" />
                    <x:Static Member="Color.Maroon" />
                    <Color>Navy</Color>
                    <Color>Olive</Color>
                    <Color>Pink</Color>
                    <Color>Purple</Color>
                    <Color>Red</Color>
                    <Color>Silver</Color>
                    <Color>Teal</Color>
                    <Color>White</Color>
                    <Color>Yellow</Color>
                </x:Array>
            </ListView.ItemsSource>
        </ListView>

        <BoxView x:Name="boxView"
                 Color="Lime"
                 HeightRequest="100" />

    </StackLayout>
</ContentPage>
```

This XAML file sets the `ItemsSource` property of the `ListView` directly from an array of items. `ItemsSource` is *not* the content property of `ListView` (in fact, `ListView` has no content property at all), so you'll need explicit `ListView.ItemsSource` tags. The `x:Array` element requires a `Type` attribute indicating the type of the items in the array. For the sake of variety, two different approaches of specifying a `Color` value are shown. You can use anything that results in a value of type `Color`.

The `ItemsSource` property of `ListView` is always populated with objects rather than visual elements. For example, if you want to display strings in the `ListView`, use `string` objects from code or `x:String` elements in the XAML file. Do not fill the `ItemsSource` collection with `Label` elements!

The `ListView` is scrollable, and normally when a scrollable view is a child of a `StackLayout`, a `VerticalOptions` setting of `FillAndExpand` is required. However, the `ListView` itself sets its `HorizontalOptions` and `VerticalOptions` properties to `FillAndExpand`.

The data binding targets the `SelectedItem` property of the `ListView` from the `Color` property of the `BoxView`. You might be more inclined to reverse the source and target property of that binding like this:

```
<BoxView x:Name="boxView"
         Color="{Binding Source={x:Reference listView},
                         Path=SelectedItem}"
         HeightRequest="100" />
```

However, the `SelectedItem` property of the `ListView` is `null` by default, which indicates that nothing is selected, and the binding will fail with a `NullReferenceException`. To make the binding on the `BoxView` work, you would need to initialize the `SelectedItem` property of the `ListView` after the items have been added:

```
<ListView x:Name="listView">
    <ListView.ItemsSource>
        <x:Array Type="{x:Type Color}">
            ...
        </x:Array>
    </ListView.ItemsSource>

    <ListView.SelectedItem>
        <Color>Lime</Color>
    </ListView.SelectedItem>
</ListView>
```

A better approach—and one that you'll be using in conjunction with MVVM—is to set the binding on the `SelectedItem` property of the `ListView`. The default binding mode for `SelectedItem` is `OneWayToSource`, which means that the following binding sets the `Color` of the `BoxView` to whatever item is selected in the `ListView`:

```
<ListView x:Name="listView"
          SelectedItem="{Binding Source={x:Reference boxView},
                                 Path=Color}">
    ...
</ListView>
```

However, if you also want to initialize the `SelectedItem` property from the binding source, use a `TwoWay` binding as shown in the XAML file in the **ListViewArray** program:

```
<StackLayout>
    <ListView x:Name="listView"
              SelectedItem="{Binding Source={x:Reference boxView},
                                     Path=Color,
                                     Mode=TwoWay}">
        ...
    </ListView>

    <BoxView x:Name="boxView"
             Color="Lime"
             HeightRequest="100" />
</StackLayout>
```

You'll see that the "Lime" entry in the `ListView` is selected when the program starts up:

Actually, it's hard to tell whether that really is the "Lime" entry without examining the RGB values. Although the `Color` structure defines a bunch of static fields with color names, `Color` values themselves are not identifiable by name. When the data binding sets a `Lime` color value to the `SelectedItem` property of the `ListView`, the `ListView` probably finds a match among its contents using the `Equals` method of the `Color` structure, which compares the components of the two colors.

The improvement of the `ListView` display is certainly a high priority!

If you examine the **ListViewArray** screen very closely, you'll discover that the `Color` items are not displayed in the same order in which they are defined in the array. The **ListViewArray** program has another purpose: to demonstrate that the `ListView` does not make a copy of the collection set to its `ItemsSource` property. Instead, it uses that collection object directly as a source of the items. In the code-behind file, after the `InitializeComponent` call returns, the constructor of `ListViewArray-Page` performs an in-place array sort to order the items by `Hue`:

```
public partial class ListViewArrayPage : ContentPage
{
    public ListViewArrayPage()
    {
        InitializeComponent();

        Array.Sort<Color>((Color[])listView.ItemsSource,
            (Color color1, Color color2) =>
            {
                if (color1.Hue == color2.Hue)
                    return Math.Sign(color1.Luminosity - color2.Luminosity);

                return Math.Sign(color1.Hue - color2.Hue);
            });
```

```
    }
}
```

This sorting occurs after the `ItemsSource` property is set, which occurs when the XAML is parsed by the `InitializeComponent` call, but before the `ListView` actually displays its contents during the layout process.

This code implies that you can change the collection used by the `ListView` dynamically. However, if you want a `ListView` to change its display when the collection changes, the `ListView` must somehow be notified that changes have occurred in the collection that is referenced by its `ItemsSource` property.

Let's examine this problem in more detail.

The ObservableCollection difference

The `ItemsSource` property of `ListView` is of type `IEnumerable`. Arrays implement the `IEnumerable` interface, and so do the `List` and `List<T>` classes. The `List` and `List<T>` collections are particularly popular for `ListView` because these classes can dynamically reallocate memory to accommodate a collection of almost any size.

You've seen that a collection can be modified after it's been assigned to the `ItemsSource` property of a `ListView`. It should be possible to add items or remove items from the collection referenced by `ItemsSource`, and for the `ListView` to update itself to reflect those changes.

Let's try it. This **ListViewLogger** program instantiates a `ListView` in its XAML file:

```xml
<ContentPage xmlns="http://xamarin.com/schemas/2014/forms"
             xmlns:x="http://schemas.microsoft.com/winfx/2009/xaml"
             x:Class="ListViewLogger.ListViewLoggerPage">
    <ContentPage.Padding>
        <OnPlatform x:TypeArguments="Thickness"
                    iOS="10, 20, 10, 0"
                    Android="10, 0"
                    WinPhone="10, 0" />
    </ContentPage.Padding>

    <ListView x:Name="listView" />
</ContentPage>
```

The code-behind file sets the `ItemsSource` property of the `ListView` to a `List<DateTime>` object and adds a `DateTime` value to this collection every second:

```csharp
public partial class ListViewLoggerPage : ContentPage
{
    public ListViewLoggerPage()
    {
        InitializeComponent();

        List<DateTime> list = new List<DateTime>();
```

```
        listView.ItemsSource = list;

        Device.StartTimer(TimeSpan.FromSeconds(1), () =>
        {
            list.Add(DateTime.Now);
            return true;
        });
    }
}
```

When you first run this program, it will seem as if nothing is happening. But if you turn the phone or emulator sideways, all the items that have been added to the collection since the program started will be displayed. But you won't see any more until you turn the phone's orientation again.

What's happening? When the ListView needs to redraw itself—which is the case when you change the orientation of the phone or emulator—it will use the current IEnumerable collection. (This is how the **ListViewArray** program displayed the sorted array. The array was sorted before the ListView displayed itself for the first time.)

However, if the ListView does not need to redraw itself, there is no way for the ListView to know when an item has been added to or removed from the collection. This is not the fault of ListView. It's really the fault of the List class. The List and List<T> classes don't implement a notification mechanism that signals the ListView when the collection has changed.

To persuade a ListView to keep its display updated with newly added data, we need a class very much like List<T>, but which includes a notification mechanism.

We need a class exactly like ObservableCollection.

ObservableCollection is a .NET class. It is defined in the System.Collections.ObjectModel namespace, and it implements an interface called INotifyCollectionChanged, which is defined in the System.Collections.Specialized namespace. In implementing this interface, an ObservableCollection fires a CollectionChanged event whenever items are added to or removed from the collection, or when items are replaced or reordered.

How does ListView know that an ObservableCollection object is set to its ItemsSource property? When the ItemsSource property is set, the ListView checks whether the object set to the property implements INotifyCollectionChanged. If so, the ListView attaches a CollectionChanged handler to the collection to be notified of changes. Whenever the collection changes, the ListView updates itself.

The **ObservableLogger** program is identical to the **ListViewLogger** program except that it uses an ObservableCollection<DateTime> rather than a List<DateTime> to maintain the collection:

```
public partial class ObservableLoggerPage : ContentPage
{
    public ObservableLoggerPage()
    {
        InitializeComponent();
```

```
            ObservableCollection<DateTime> list = new ObservableCollection<DateTime>();
            listView.ItemsSource = list;

            Device.StartTimer(TimeSpan.FromSeconds(1), () =>
            {
                list.Add(DateTime.Now);
                return true;
            });
        }
    }
```

Now the `ListView` updates itself every second.

Of course, not every application needs this facility, and `ObservableCollection` is overkill for those that don't. But it's an essential part of versatile `ListView` usage.

Sometimes you'll be working with a collection of data items, and the collection itself does not change dynamically—in other words, it always contains the same objects—but properties of the individual items change. Can the `ListView` respond to changes of that sort?

Yes it can, and you'll see an example later in this chapter. Enabling a `ListView` to respond to property changes in the individual items does not require `ObservableCollection` or `INotifyCollectionChanged`. But the data items must implement `INotifyPropertyChanged`, and the `ListView` must display the items using an object called a *cell*.

Templates and cells

The purpose of `ListView` is to display data. In the real world, data is everywhere, and we are compelled to write computer programs to deal with this data. In programming tutorials such as this book, however, data is harder to come by. So let's invent a little bit of data to explore `ListView` in more depth, and if the data turns out to be otherwise useful, so much the better!

As you know, the colors supported by the Xamarin.Forms `Color` structure are based on the 16 colors defined in the HTML 4.01 standard. Another popular collection of colors is defined in the Cascading Style Sheets (CSS) 3.0 standard. That collection contains 147 named colors (seven of which are duplicates for variant spellings) that were originally derived from color names in the X11 windowing system but converted to camel case.

The `NamedColor` class included in the **Xamarin.FormsBook.Toolkit** library lets your Xamarin.Forms program get access to those 147 colors. The bulk of `NamedColor` is the definition of 147 public static read-only fields of type `Color`. Only a few are shown in an abbreviated list toward the end of the class:

```
public class NamedColor
{
    // Instance members.
    private NamedColor()
    {
```

```
        }

    public string Name { private set; get; }

    public string FriendlyName { private set; get; }

    public Color Color { private set; get; }

    public string RgbDisplay { private set; get; }

    // Static members.
    static NamedColor()
    {
        List<NamedColor> all = new List<NamedColor>();
        StringBuilder stringBuilder = new StringBuilder();

        // Loop through the public static fields of type Color.
        foreach (FieldInfo fieldInfo in typeof(NamedColor).GetRuntimeFields ())
        {
            if (fieldInfo.IsPublic &&
                fieldInfo.IsStatic &&
                fieldInfo.FieldType == typeof (Color))
            {
                // Convert the name to a friendly name.
                string name = fieldInfo.Name;
                stringBuilder.Clear();
                int index = 0;

                foreach (char ch in name)
                {
                    if (index != 0 && Char.IsUpper(ch))
                    {
                        stringBuilder.Append(' ');
                    }
                    stringBuilder.Append(ch);
                    index++;
                }

                // Instantiate a NamedColor object.
                Color color = (Color)fieldInfo.GetValue(null);

                NamedColor namedColor = new NamedColor
                {
                    Name = name,
                    FriendlyName = stringBuilder.ToString(),
                    Color = color,
                    RgbDisplay = String.Format("{0:X2}-{1:X2}-{2:X2}",
                                               (int)(255 * color.R),
                                               (int)(255 * color.G),
                                               (int)(255 * color.B))
                };

                // Add it to the collection.
                all.Add(namedColor);
```

```
            }
        }
        all.TrimExcess();
        All = all;
    }

    public static IList<NamedColor> All { private set; get; }

    // Color names and definitions from http://www.w3.org/TR/css3-color/
    // (but with color names converted to camel case).
    public static readonly Color AliceBlue = Color.FromRgb(240, 248, 255);
    public static readonly Color AntiqueWhite = Color.FromRgb(250, 235, 215);
    public static readonly Color Aqua = Color.FromRgb(0, 255, 255);
    ...
    public static readonly Color WhiteSmoke = Color.FromRgb(245, 245, 245);
    public static readonly Color Yellow = Color.FromRgb(255, 255, 0);
    public static readonly Color YellowGreen = Color.FromRgb(154, 205, 50);
}
```

If your application has a reference to **Xamarin.FormsBook.Toolkit** and a `using` directive for the `Xamarin.FormsBook.Toolkit` namespace, you can use these fields just like the static fields in the `Color` structure. For example:

```
BoxView boxView = new BoxView
{
    Color = NamedColor.Chocolate
};
```

You can also use them in XAML without too much more difficulty. If you have an XML namespace declaration for the **Xamarin.FormsBook.Toolkit** assembly, you can reference `NamedColor` in an `x:Static` markup extension:

```
<BoxView Color="{x:Static toolkit:NamedColor.CornflowerBlue}" />
```

But that's not all: In its static constructor, `NamedColor` uses reflection to create 147 instances of the `NamedColor` class that it stores in a list that is publicly available from the static `All` property. Each instance of the `NamedColor` class has a `Name` property, a `Color` property of type `Color`, a `FriendlyName` property that is the same as the `Name` except with some spaces inserted, and an `RgbDisplay` property that formats the hexadecimal color values.

The `NamedColor` class does not derive from `BindableObject` and does not implement `INotifyPropertyChanged`. Regardless, you can use this class as a binding source. That's because these properties remain constant after each `NamedColor` object is instantiated. Only if these properties later changed would the class need to implement `INotifyPropertyChanged` to serve as a successful binding source.

The `NamedColor.All` property is defined to be of type `IList<NamedColor>`, so we can set it to the `ItemsSource` property of a `ListView`. This is demonstrated by the **NaiveNamedColorList** program:

```
<ContentPage xmlns="http://xamarin.com/schemas/2014/forms"
```

```
            xmlns:x="http://schemas.microsoft.com/winfx/2009/xaml"
            xmlns:toolkit=
                "clr-namespace:Xamarin.FormsBook.Toolkit;assembly=Xamarin.FormsBook.Toolkit"
            x:Class="NaiveNamedColorList.NaiveNamedColorListPage">
    <ContentPage.Padding>
        <OnPlatform x:TypeArguments="Thickness"
                    iOS="10, 20, 10, 0"
                    Android="10, 0"
                    WinPhone="10, 0" />
    </ContentPage.Padding>

    <ListView ItemsSource="{x:Static toolkit:NamedColor.All}" />

</ContentPage>
```

Because this program accesses the `NamedColor` class solely from the XAML file, the program calls `Toolkit.Init` from its `App` constructor.

You'll discover that you can scroll this list and select items, but the items themselves might be a little disappointing, for what you'll see is a list of 147 fully qualified class names:

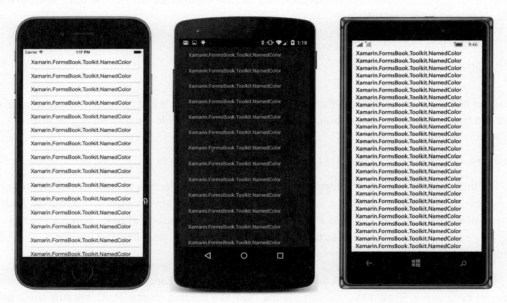

This might seem disappointing, but in your future real-life programming work involving `ListView`, you'll probably cheer when you see something like this display because it means that you've successfully set `ItemsSource` to a valid collection. The objects are there. You just need to display them a little better.

This particular `ListView` displays the fully qualified class name of `NamedColor` because `NamedColor` does not define its own `ToString` method, and the default implementation of `ToString` displays the class name. One simple solution is to add a `ToString` method to `NamedColor`:

```
public override string ToString()
{
    return FriendlyName;
}
```

Now the `ListView` displays the friendly names of all the colors. Simple enough.

However, in real-life programming, you might not have the option to add code to your data classes because you might not have access to the source code. So let's pursue solutions that are independent of the actual implementation of the data.

`ListView` derives from `ItemsView`, and besides defining the `ItemsSource` property, `ItemsView` also defines a property named `ItemTemplate` of type `DataTemplate`. The `DataTemplate` object gives you (the programmer) the power to display the items of your `ListView` in whatever way you want.

When used in connection with `ListView`, the `DataTemplate` references a `Cell` class to render the items. The `Cell` class derives from `Element`, from which it picks up support for parent/child relationships. But unlike `View`, `Cell` does not derive from `VisualElement`. A `Cell` is more like a *description* of a tree of visual elements rather than a visual element itself.

Here's the class hierarchy showing the five classes that derive from `Cell`:

```
Object
    BindableObject
        Element
            Cell

                TextCell — two Label views
                    ImageCell — derives from TextCell and adds an Image view
                EntryCell — an Entry view with a Label
                SwitchCell — a Switch with a Label
                ViewCell — any View (likely with children)
```

The descriptions of `Cell` types are conceptual only: For performance reasons, the actual composition of a `Cell` is defined within each platform.

As you begin exploring these `Cell` classes and contemplating their use in connection with `ListView`, you might question the relevance of a couple of them. But they're not all intended solely for `ListView`. As you'll see later in this chapter, the `Cell` classes also play a major role in the `TableView`, where they are used in somewhat different ways.

The `Cell` derivatives that have the most applicability to `ListView` are probably `TextCell`, `Image-Cell`, and the powerful `ViewCell`, which lets you define your own visuals for the items.

Let's look at `TextCell` first, which defines six properties backed by bindable properties:

- `Text` of type `string`

- TextColor of type Color

- Detail of type string

- DetailColor of type Color

- Command of type ICommand

- CommandParameter of type Object

The TextCell incorporates two Label views that you can set to two different strings and colors. The font characteristics are fixed in a platform-dependent way.

The **TextCellListCode** program contains no XAML. Instead, it demonstrates how to use a TextCell in code to display properties of all the NamedColor objects:

```
public class TextCellListCodePage : ContentPage
{
    public TextCellListCodePage()
    {
        // Define the DataTemplate.
        DataTemplate dataTemplate = new DataTemplate(typeof(TextCell));
        dataTemplate.SetBinding(TextCell.TextProperty, "FriendlyName");
        dataTemplate.SetBinding(TextCell.DetailProperty,
            new Binding(path: "RgbDisplay", stringFormat: "RGB = {0}"));

        // Build the page.
        Padding = new Thickness(10, Device.OnPlatform(20, 0, 0), 10, 0);

        Content = new ListView
        {
            ItemsSource = NamedColor.All,
            ItemTemplate = dataTemplate
        };
    }
}
```

The first step in using a Cell in a ListView is to create an object of type DataTemplate:

```
DataTemplate dataTemplate = new DataTemplate(typeof(TextCell));
```

Notice that the argument to the constructor is not an *instance* of TextCell but the *type* of TextCell.

The second step is to call a SetBinding method on the DataTemplate object, but notice how these SetBinding calls actually target bindable properties of the TextCell:

```
dataTemplate.SetBinding(TextCell.TextProperty, "FriendlyName");
dataTemplate.SetBinding(TextCell.DetailProperty,
    new Binding(path: "RgbDisplay", stringFormat: "RGB = {0}"));
```

These SetBinding calls are identical to bindings that you might set on a TextCell object, but at the time of these calls, there are no instances of TextCell on which to set the bindings!

If you'd like, you can also set some properties of the `TextCell` to constant values by calling the `SetValue` method of the `DataTemplate` class:

```
dataTemplate.SetValue(TextCell.TextColorProperty, Color.Blue);
dataTemplate.SetValue(TextCell.DetailColorProperty, Color.Red);
```

These `SetValue` calls are similar to calls you might make on visual elements instead of setting properties directly.

The `SetBinding` and `SetValue` methods should be very familiar to you because they are defined by `BindableObject` and inherited by very many classes in Xamarin.Forms. However, `DataTemplate` does not derive from `BindableObject` and instead defines its own `SetBinding` and `SetValue` methods. The purpose of these methods is *not* to bind or set properties of the `DataTemplate` instance. Because `DataTemplate` doesn't derive from `BindableObject`, it has no bindable properties of its own. Instead, `DataTemplate` simply saves these settings in two internal dictionaries that are publicly accessible through two properties that `DataTemplate` defines, named `Bindings` and `Values`.

The third step in using a `Cell` with `ListView` is to set the `DataTemplate` object to the `ItemTemplate` property of the `ListView`:

```
Content = new ListView
{
    ItemsSource = NamedColor.All,
    ItemTemplate = dataTemplate
};
```

Here's what happens (conceptually anyway):

When the `ListView` needs to display a particular item (in this case, a `NamedColor` object), it instantiates the type passed to the `DataTemplate` constructor, in this case a `TextCell`. Any bindings or values that have been set on the `DataTemplate` are then transferred to this `TextCell`. The `BindingContext` of each `TextCell` is set to the particular item being displayed, which in this case is a particular `NamedColor` object, and that's how each item in the `ListView` displays properties of a particular `NamedColor` object. Each `TextCell` is a visual tree with identical data bindings, but with a unique `BindingContext` setting. Here's the result:

In general, the `ListView` will not create all the visual trees at once. For performance purposes, it will create them only as necessary as the user scrolls new items into view. You can get some sense of this if you install handlers for the `ItemAppearing` and `ItemDisappearing` events defined by `ListView`. You'll discover that these events don't exactly track the visuals—items are reported as appearing before they scroll into view, and are reported as disappearing after they scroll out of view—but the exercise is instructive nevertheless.

You can also get a sense of what's going on with an alternative constructor for `DataTemplate` that takes a `Func` object:

```
DataTemplate dataTemplate = new DataTemplate(() =>
{
    return new TextCell();
});
```

The `Func` object is called only as the `TextCell` objects are required for the items, although these calls actually are made somewhat in advance of the items scrolling into view.

You might want to include code that actually counts the number of `TextCell` instances being created and displays the result in the **Output** window of Visual Studio or Xamarin Studio:

```
int count = 0;
DataTemplate dataTemplate = new DataTemplate(() =>
    {
        System.Diagnostics.Debug.WriteLine("Text Cell Number " + (++count));
        return new TextCell();
    });
```

As you scroll down to the bottom, you'll discover that a maximum of 147 `TextCell` objects are created for the 147 items in the `ListView`. The `TextCell` objects are cached, but not reused as items scroll in and out of view. However, on a lower level—in particular, involving the platform-specific `TextCellRenderer` objects and the underlying platform-specific visuals created by these renderers—the visuals are reused.

This alternative `DataTemplate` constructor with the `Func` argument might be handy if you need to set some properties on the cell object that you can't set using data bindings. Perhaps you've created a `ViewCell` derivative that requires an argument in its constructor. In general, however, use the constructor with the `Type` argument or define the data template in XAML.

In XAML, the binding syntax somewhat distorts the actual mechanics used to generate visual trees for the `ListView` items, but at the same time the syntax is conceptually clearer and visually more elegant. Here's the XAML file from the **TextCellListXaml** program that is functionally identical to the **TextCellListCode** program:

```
<ContentPage xmlns="http://xamarin.com/schemas/2014/forms"
             xmlns:x="http://schemas.microsoft.com/winfx/2009/xaml"
             xmlns:toolkit=
                 "clr-namespace:Xamarin.FormsBook.Toolkit;assembly=Xamarin.FormsBook.Toolkit"
             x:Class="TextCellListXaml.TextCellListXamlPage">
    <ContentPage.Padding>
        <OnPlatform x:TypeArguments="Thickness"
                    iOS="10, 20, 10, 0"
                    Android="10, 0"
                    WinPhone="10, 0" />
    </ContentPage.Padding>

    <ListView ItemsSource="{x:Static toolkit:NamedColor.All}">
        <ListView.ItemTemplate>
            <DataTemplate>
                <TextCell Text="{Binding FriendlyName}"
                          Detail="{Binding RgbDisplay, StringFormat='RGB = {0}'}" />
            </DataTemplate>
        </ListView.ItemTemplate>
    </ListView>
</ContentPage>
```

In XAML, set a `DataTemplate` to the `ItemTemplate` property of the `ListView` and define `TextCell` as a child of `DataTemplate`. Then simply set the data bindings on the `TextCell` properties as if the `TextCell` were a normal visual element. These bindings don't need `Source` settings because a `BindingContext` has been set on each item by the `ListView`.

You'll appreciate this syntax even more when you define your own custom cells.

Custom cells

One of the classes that derives from `Cell` is named `ViewCell`, which defines a single property named `View` that lets you define a custom visual tree for the display of items in a `ListView`.

There are several ways to define a custom cell, but some are less pleasant than others. Perhaps the greatest amount of work involves mimicking the existing `Cell` classes, which doesn't involve `View-Cell` at all but instead requires that you create platform-specific cell renderers. You can alternatively derive a class from `ViewCell`, define several bindable properties of that class similar to the bindable properties of `TextCell` and the other `Cell` derivatives, and define a visual tree for the cell in either XAML or code, much as you would do for a custom view derived from `ContentView`. You can then use that custom cell in code or XAML just like `TextCell`.

If you want to do the job entirely in code, you can use the `DataTemplate` constructor with the `Func` argument and build the visual tree in code as each item is requested. This approach allows you to define the data bindings as the visual tree is being built instead of setting bindings on the `DataTemplate`.

But certainly the easiest approach is defining the visual tree and bindings of the cell right in XAML within the `ListView` element. The **CustomNamedColorList** program demonstrates this technique. Everything is in the XAML file:

```
<ContentPage xmlns="http://xamarin.com/schemas/2014/forms"
             xmlns:x="http://schemas.microsoft.com/winfx/2009/xaml"
             xmlns:toolkit=
                 "clr-namespace:Xamarin.FormsBook.Toolkit;assembly=Xamarin.FormsBook.Toolkit"
             x:Class="CustomNamedColorList.CustomNamedColorListPage">
    <ContentPage.Padding>
        <OnPlatform x:TypeArguments="Thickness"
                    iOS="10, 20, 10, 0"
                    Android="10, 0"
                    WinPhone="10, 0" />
    </ContentPage.Padding>

    <ListView SeparatorVisibility="None"
              ItemsSource="{x:Static toolkit:NamedColor.All}">
        <ListView.RowHeight>
            <OnPlatform x:TypeArguments="x:Int32"
                        iOS="80"
                        Android="80"
                        WinPhone="90" />
        </ListView.RowHeight>

        <ListView.ItemTemplate>
            <DataTemplate>
                <ViewCell>
                    <ContentView Padding="5">
                        <Frame OutlineColor="Accent"
                               Padding="10">
                            <StackLayout Orientation="Horizontal">
                                <BoxView x:Name="boxView"
                                         Color="{Binding Color}"
                                         WidthRequest="50"
                                         HeightRequest="50" />
                                <StackLayout>
                                    <Label Text="{Binding FriendlyName}"
```

```
                                     FontSize="22"
                                     VerticalOptions="StartAndExpand" />
                      <Label Text="{Binding RgbDisplay, StringFormat='RGB = {0}'}"
                                     FontSize="16"
                                     VerticalOptions="CenterAndExpand" />
                  </StackLayout>
                </StackLayout>
              </Frame>
            </ContentView>
          </ViewCell>
        </DataTemplate>
      </ListView.ItemTemplate>
    </ListView>
</ContentPage>
```

Within the `DataTemplate` property-element tags is a `ViewCell`. The content property of `View‑Cell` is `View`, so you don't need `ViewCell.View` tags. Instead, a visual tree within the `ViewCell` tags is implicitly set to the `View` property. The visual tree begins with a `ContentView` to add a little pad‑ding, then a `Frame` and a pair of nested `StackLayout` elements with a `BoxView` and two `Label` ele‑ments. When the `ListView` renders its items, the `BindingContext` for each displayed item is the item itself, so the `Binding` markup extensions are generally very simple.

Notice that the `RowHeight` property of the `ListView` is set with property element tags for plat‑form-dependent values. These values here were obtained empirically by trial and error, and result in the following displays:

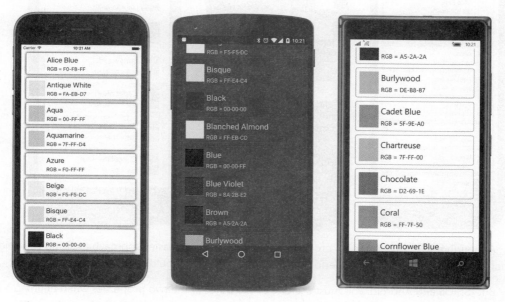

Throughout this book, you have seen several scrollable lists of colors, such as the **ColorBlocks** pro‑gram in Chapter 4, "Scrolling the stack," and the **ColorViewList** program in Chapter 8, "Code and XAML in harmony," but I think you'll agree that this is the most elegant solution to the problem.

Explicitly setting the `RowHeight` property of the `ListView` is one of two ways to set the height of the rows. You can experiment with another approach by removing the `RowHeight` setting and instead setting the `HasUnevenRows` property to `True`. Here's a variation of the **CustomNamedColorList** program:

```
<ListView SeparatorVisibility="None"
          ItemsSource="{x:Static toolkit:NamedColor.All}"
          HasUnevenRows="True">

    <ListView.ItemTemplate>
        …
    </ListView.ItemTemplate>
</ListView>
```

The `HasUnevenRows` property is designed specifically to handle cases when the heights of the cells in the `ListView` are not uniform. However, you can also use it for cases when all the cells are the same height but you don't know precisely what that height is. With this setting, the heights of the individual rows are calculated based on the visual tree, and that height is used to space the rows. In this example, the heights of the cells are governed by the heights of the two `Label` elements. The rows are just a little different than the heights explicitly set from the `RowHeight` property:

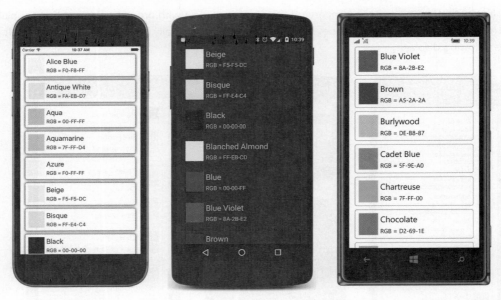

Although the `HasUnevenRows` property seems to provide an easier approach to sizing cell heights than `RowHeight`, it does have a performance penalty and you should avoid it unless you need it.

But for iOS and Android, you must use one or the other of the two properties when defining a custom cell. Here's what happens when neither property is set:

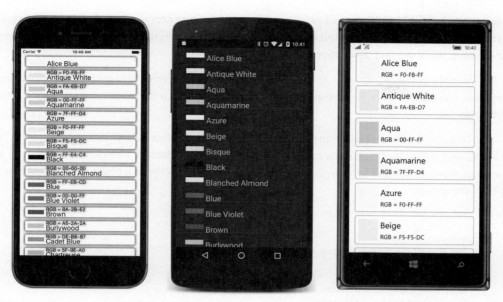

Only the Windows platforms automatically use the rendered size of the visual tree to determine the row height.

In summary, for best `ListView` performance, use one of the predefined `Cell` classes. If you can't, use `ViewCell` and define your own visual tree. Try your best to supply a specific `RowHeight` property setting with `ViewCell`. Use `HasUnevenRows` only when that is not possible.

Grouping the ListView items

It's sometimes convenient for the items in a `ListView` to be grouped in some way. For example, a `ListView` that lists the names of a user's friends or contacts is easily navigable if the items are in alphabetical order, but it's even more navigable if all the A's, B's, C's, and so forth are in separate groups, and a few taps are all that's necessary to navigate to a particular group.

The `ListView` supports such grouping and navigation.

As you've discovered, the object you set to the `ItemsSource` property of `ListView` must implement `IEnumerable`. This `IEnumerable` object is a collection of items.

When using `ListView` with the grouping feature, the `IEnumerable` collection you set to `Items-Source` contains one item for each group, and these items themselves implement `IEnumerable` and contain the objects in that group. In other words, you set the `ItemsSource` property of `ListView` to a collection of collections.

One easy way for the group class to implement `IEnumerable` is to derive from `List` or `Observa-bleCollection`, depending on whether items can be dynamically added to or removed from the collection. However, you'll want to add a couple of other properties to this class: One property (typically called `Title`) should be a text description of the group. Another property is a shorter text description that's used to navigate the list. Based on how this text description is used on Windows 10 Mobile, you should keep this short text description to three letters or fewer.

For example, suppose you want to display a list of colors but divided into groups indicating the dominant hue (or lack of hue). Here are seven such groups: grays, reds, yellows, greens, cyans, blues, and magentas.

The `NamedColorGroup` class in the **Xamarin.FormsBook.Toolkit** library derives from `List<NamedColor>` and hence is a collection of `NamedColor` objects. It also defines text `Title` and `ShortName` properties and a `ColorShade` property intended to serve as a pastel-like representative color of the group:

```
public class NamedColorGroup : List<NamedColor>
{
    // Instance members.
    private NamedColorGroup(string title, string shortName, Color colorShade)
    {
        this.Title = title;
        this.ShortName = shortName;
        this.ColorShade = colorShade;
    }

    public string Title { private set; get; }

    public string ShortName { private set; get; }

    public Color ColorShade { private set; get; }

    // Static members.
    static NamedColorGroup()
    {
        // Create all the groups.
        List<NamedColorGroup> groups = new List<NamedColorGroup>
        {
            new NamedColorGroup("Grays", "Gry", new Color(0.75, 0.75, 0.75)),
            new NamedColorGroup("Reds", "Red", new Color(1, 0.75, 0.75)),
            new NamedColorGroup("Yellows", "Yel", new Color(1, 1, 0.75)),
            new NamedColorGroup("Greens", "Grn", new Color(0.75, 1, 0.75)),
            new NamedColorGroup("Cyans", "Cyn", new Color(0.75, 1, 1)),
            new NamedColorGroup("Blues", "Blu", new Color(0.75, 0.75, 1)),
            new NamedColorGroup("Magentas", "Mag", new Color(1, 0.75, 1))
        };

        foreach (NamedColor namedColor in NamedColor.All)
        {
            Color color = namedColor.Color;
            int index = 0;

            if (color.Saturation != 0)
            {
                index = 1 + (int)((12 * color.Hue + 1) / 2) % 6;
```

```
        }
        groups[index].Add(namedColor);
    }

    foreach (NamedColorGroup group in groups)
    {
        group.TrimExcess();
    }

    All = groups;
}

public static IList<NamedColorGroup> All { private set; get; }
}
```

A static constructor assembles seven `NamedColorGroup` instances and sets the static `All` property to the collection of these seven objects.

The **ColorGroupList** program uses this new class for its `ListView`. Notice that the `ItemsSource` is set to `NamedColorGroup.All` (a collection of seven items) rather than `NamedColor.All` (a collection of 147 items).

```xml
<ContentPage xmlns="http://xamarin.com/schemas/2014/forms"
             xmlns:x="http://schemas.microsoft.com/winfx/2009/xaml"
             xmlns:toolkit=
                 "clr-namespace:Xamarin.FormsBook.Toolkit;assembly=Xamarin.FormsBook.Toolkit"
             x:Class="ColorGroupList.ColorGroupListPage">
    <ContentPage.Padding>
        <OnPlatform x:TypeArguments="Thickness"
                    iOS="10, 20, 10, 0"
                    Android="10, 0"
                    WinPhone="10, 0" />
    </ContentPage.Padding>

    <ListView ItemsSource="{x:Static toolkit:NamedColorGroup.All}"
              IsGroupingEnabled="True"
              GroupDisplayBinding="{Binding Title}"
              GroupShortNameBinding="{Binding ShortName}">
        <ListView.RowHeight>
            <OnPlatform x:TypeArguments="x:Int32"
                        iOS="80"
                        Android="80"
                        WinPhone="90" />
        </ListView.RowHeight>

        <ListView.ItemTemplate>
            <DataTemplate>
                <ViewCell>
                    <ContentView Padding="5">
                        <Frame OutlineColor="Accent"
                               Padding="10">
                            <StackLayout Orientation="Horizontal">
                                <BoxView x:Name="boxView"
```

```
                                        Color="{Binding Color}"
                                        WidthRequest="50"
                                        HeightRequest="50" />
                    <StackLayout>
                        <Label Text="{Binding FriendlyName}"
                               FontSize="22"
                               VerticalOptions="StartAndExpand" />
                        <Label Text="{Binding RgbDisplay, StringFormat='RGB = {0}'}"
                               FontSize="16"
                               VerticalOptions="CenterAndExpand" />
                    </StackLayout>
                </StackLayout>
            </Frame>
        </ContentView>
    </ViewCell>
</DataTemplate>
</ListView.ItemTemplate>
</ListView>
</ContentPage>
```

Setting `IsGroupingEnabled` to `True` is very important. Remove that (as well as the `ItemTemplate` setting), and the `ListView` displays seven items identified by the fully qualified class name "Xamarin.FormsBook.Toolkit.NamedColorGroup".

The `GroupDisplayBinding` property is a `Binding` referencing the name of a property in the group items that contains a heading or title for the group. This is displayed in the `ListView` to identify each group:

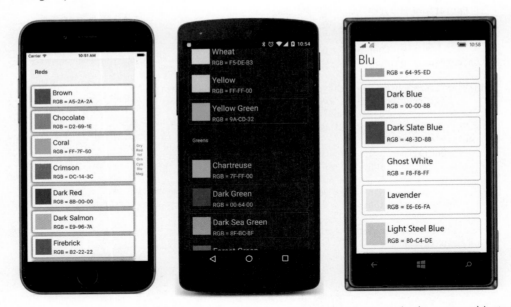

The `GroupShortNameBinding` property is bound to another property in the group objects that displays a condensed version of the header. If the group headings are just the letters A, B, C, and so forth, you can use the same property for the short names.

On the iPhone screen, you can see the short names at the right side of the screen. In iOS terminology, this is called an *index* for the list, and tapping one moves to that part of the list.

On the Windows 10 Mobile screen, the headings incorrectly use the `ShortName` rather than the `Title` property. Tapping a heading goes to a navigation screen (called a *jump list*) where all the short names are arranged in a grid. Tapping one goes back to the `ListView` with the corresponding header at the top of the screen.

Android provides no navigation.

Even though the `ListView` is now really a collection of `NamedColorGroup` objects, `SelectedItem` is still a `NamedColor` object.

In general, if an `ItemSelected` handler needs to determine the group of a selected item, you can do that "manually" by accessing the collection set to the `ItemsSource` property and using one of the `Find` methods defined by `List`. Or you can store a group identifier within each item. The `Tapped` handler provides the group as well as the item.

Custom group headers

If you don't like the particular style of the group headers that Xamarin.Forms supplies, there's something you can do about it. Rather than setting a binding to the `GroupDisplayBinding` property, set a `DataTemplate` to the `GroupHeaderTemplate` property:

```
<ListView ItemsSource="{x:Static toolkit:NamedColorGroup.All}"
          IsGroupingEnabled="True"
          GroupShortNameBinding="{Binding ShortName}">
    ...
    <ListView.GroupHeaderTemplate>
        <DataTemplate>
            <ViewCell>
                <Label Text="{Binding Title}"
                       BackgroundColor="{Binding ColorShade}"
                       TextColor="Black"
                       FontAttributes="Bold,Italic"
                       HorizontalTextAlignment="Center"
                       VerticalTextAlignment="Center">
                    <Label.FontSize>
                        <OnPlatform x:TypeArguments="x:Double"
                                    iOS="30"
                                    Android="30"
                                    WinPhone="45" />
                    </Label.FontSize>
                </Label>
            </ViewCell>
        </DataTemplate>
    </ListView.GroupHeaderTemplate>
</ListView>
```

Notice that the `Label` has a fixed text color of black, so the `BackgroundColor` property should be set to something light that provides a good contrast with the text. Such a color is available from the `NamedColorGroup` class as the `ColorShade` property. This allows the background of the header to reflect the dominant hue associated with the group:

Notice how the header for the topmost item remains fixed at the top on iOS and Windows 10 Mobile and scrolls off the top of the screen only when another header replaces it.

ListView and interactivity

An application can interact with its `ListView` in a variety of ways: If the user taps an item, the `ListView` fires an `ItemTapped` event and, if the item is previously not selected, also an `Item-Selected` event. A program can also define a data binding by using the `SelectedItem` property. The `ListView` has a `ScrollTo` method that lets a program scroll the `ListView` to make a particular item visible. Later in this chapter you'll see a refresh facility implemented by `ListView`.

`Cell` itself defines a `Tapped` event, but you'll probably use that event in connection with `Table-View` rather than `ListView`. `TextCell` defines the same `Command` and `CommandParameter` properties as `Button` and `ToolbarItem`, but you'll probably use those properties in connection with `TableView` as well. You can also define a context menu on a cell; this is demonstrated in the section "Context menus" later in this chapter.

It is also possible for a `Cell` derivative to contain some interactive views. The `EntryCell` and `SwitchCell` allow the user to interact with an `Entry` or a `Switch`. You can also include interactive views in a `ViewCell`.

The **InteractiveListView** program contains in its XAML file a `ListView` named `listView`. The code-behind file sets the `ItemsSource` property of that `ListView` to a collection of type `List<ColorViewModel>`, containing 100 instances of `ColorViewModel`—a class described in Chapter 18, "MVVM," and which can be found in the **Xamarin.FormsBook.Toolkit** library. Each instance of `ColorViewModel` is initialized to a random color:

```
public partial class InteractiveListViewPage : ContentPage
{
    public InteractiveListViewPage()
    {
        InitializeComponent();

        const int count = 100;
        List<ColorViewModel> colorList = new List<ColorViewModel>(count);
        Random random = new Random();

        for (int i = 0; i < count; i++)
        {
            ColorViewModel colorViewModel = new ColorViewModel();
            colorViewModel.Color = new Color(random.NextDouble(),
                                             random.NextDouble(),
                                             random.NextDouble());
            colorList.Add(colorViewModel);
        }
        listView.ItemsSource = colorList;
    }
}
```

The `ListView` in the XAML file contains a data template using a `ViewCell` that contains three `Slider` views, a `BoxView`, and a few `Label` elements to display the hue, saturation, and luminosity values, all of which are bound to properties of the `ColorViewModel` class:

```
<ContentPage xmlns="http://xamarin.com/schemas/2014/forms"
             xmlns:x="http://schemas.microsoft.com/winfx/2009/xaml"
             xmlns:toolkit=
                 "clr-namespace:Xamarin.FormsBook.Toolkit;assembly=Xamarin.FormsBook.Toolkit"
             x:Class="InteractiveListView.InteractiveListViewPage">
    <ContentPage.Padding>
        <OnPlatform x:TypeArguments="Thickness"
                    iOS="10, 20, 10, 0"
                    Android="10, 0"
                    WinPhone="10, 0" />
    </ContentPage.Padding>

    <ContentPage.Resources>
        <ResourceDictionary>
            <toolkit:ColorToContrastColorConverter x:Key="contrastColor" />
        </ResourceDictionary>
    </ContentPage.Resources>

    <ListView x:Name="listView"
              HasUnevenRows="True">
        <ListView.ItemTemplate>
```

```
                <DataTemplate>
                    <ViewCell>
                        <Grid Padding="0, 5">
                            <Grid.RowDefinitions>
                                <RowDefinition Height="Auto" />
                                <RowDefinition Height="Auto" />
                                <RowDefinition Height="Auto" />
                            </Grid.RowDefinitions>

                            <Grid.ColumnDefinitions>
                                <ColumnDefinition Width="*" />
                                <ColumnDefinition Width="Auto" />
                            </Grid.ColumnDefinitions>

                            <Slider Value="{Binding Hue, Mode=TwoWay}"
                                    Grid.Row="0" Grid.Column="0" />

                            <Slider Value="{Binding Saturation, Mode=TwoWay}"
                                    Grid.Row="1" Grid.Column="0" />

                            <Slider Value="{Binding Luminosity, Mode=TwoWay}"
                                    Grid.Row="2" Grid.Column="0" />

                            <ContentView BackgroundColor="{Binding Color}"
                                         Grid.Row="0" Grid.Column="1" Grid.RowSpan="3"
                                         Padding="10">

                                <StackLayout Orientation="Horizontal"
                                             VerticalOptions="Center">
                                    <Label Text="{Binding Hue, StringFormat='{0:F2}, '}"
                                           TextColor="{Binding Color,
                                                Converter={StaticResource contrastColor}" />

                                    <Label Text="{Binding Saturation, StringFormat='{0:F2}, '}"
                                           TextColor="{Binding Color,
                                                Converter={StaticResource contrastColor}" />

                                    <Label Text="{Binding Luminosity, StringFormat='{0:F2}'}"
                                           TextColor="{Binding Color,
                                                Converter={StaticResource contrastColor}" />

                                </StackLayout>
                            </ContentView>
                        </Grid>
                    </ViewCell>
                </DataTemplate>
            </ListView.ItemTemplate>
        </ListView>
</ContentPage>
```

The `Label` elements sit on top of the `BoxView`, so they should be made a color that contrasts with the background. This is accomplished with the `ColorToContrastColorConverter` class (also in **Xamarin.FormsBook.Toolkit**), which calculates the luminance of the color by using a standard formula and then converts to `Color.Black` for a light color and `Color.White` for a dark color:

```
namespace Xamarin.FormsBook.Toolkit
{
    public class ColorToContrastColorConverter : IValueConverter
    {
        public object Convert(object value, Type targetType,
                              object parameter, CultureInfo culture)
        {
            return ColorToContrastColor((Color)value);
        }

        public object ConvertBack(object value, Type targetType,
                                  object parameter, CultureInfo culture)
        {
            return ColorToContrastColor((Color)value);
        }

        Color ColorToContrastColor(Color color)
        {
            // Standard luminance calculation.
            double luminance = 0.30 * color.R +
                               0.59 * color.G +
                               0.11 * color.B;

            return luminance > 0.5 ? Color.Black : Color.White;
        }
    }
}
```

Here's the result:

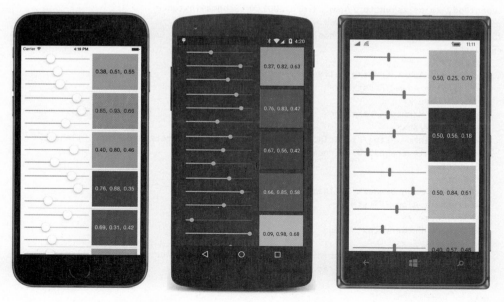

Each of the items independently lets you manipulate the three `Slider` elements to select a new color, and while this example might seem a little artificial, a real-life example involving a collection of identical visual trees is not inconceivable. Even if there are just a few items in the collection, it might make sense to use a `ListView` that displays all the items on the screen and doesn't scroll. `ListView` is one of the most powerful tools that XAML provides to compensate for its lack of programming loops.

ListView and MVVM

`ListView` is one of the major players in the `View` part of the Model-View-ViewModel architecture. Whenever a ViewModel contains a collection, a `ListView` generally displays the items.

A collection of ViewModels

Let's explore the use of `ListView` in MVVM with some data that more closely approximates a real-life example. This is a collection of information about 65 fictitious students of the fictitious School of Fine Art, including images of their overly spherical heads. These images and an XML file containing the student names and references to the bitmaps are in a website at http://xamarin.github.io/xamarin-forms-book-samples/SchoolOfFineArt. This website is hosted from the same GitHub repository as the source code for this book, and the contents of the site can be found in the **gh-pages** branch of that repository.

The Students.xml file at that site contains information about the school and students. Here's the beginning and the end with abbreviated URLs of the photos.

```
<StudentBody xmlns:xsi=http://www.w3.org/2001/XMLSchema-instance
             xmlns:xsd="http://www.w3.org/2001/XMLSchema">
  <School>School of Fine Art</School>
  <Students>
    <Student>
      <FullName>Adam Harmetz</FullName>
      <FirstName>Adam</FirstName>
      <MiddleName />
      <LastName>Harmetz</LastName>
      <Sex>Male</Sex>
      <PhotoFilename>http://xamarin.github.io/.../.../AdamHarmetz.png</PhotoFilename>
      <GradePointAverage>3.01</GradePointAverage>
    </Student>
    <Student>
      <FullName>Alan Brewer</FullName>
      <FirstName>Alan</FirstName>
      <MiddleName />
      <LastName>Brewer</LastName>
      <Sex>Male</Sex>
      <PhotoFilename>http://xamarin.github.io/.../.../AlanBrewer.png</PhotoFilename>
      <GradePointAverage>1.17</GradePointAverage>
    </Student>
    ...
    <Student>
```

```
        <FullName>Tzipi Butnaru</FullName>
        <FirstName>Tzipi</FirstName>
        <MiddleName />
        <LastName>Butnaru</LastName>
        <Sex>Female</Sex>
        <PhotoFilename>http://xamarin.github.io/.../.../TzipiButnaru.png</PhotoFilename>
        <GradePointAverage>3.76</GradePointAverage>
      </Student>
      <Student>
        <FullName>Zrinka Makovac</FullName>
        <FirstName>Zrinka</FirstName>
        <MiddleName />
        <LastName>Makovac</LastName>
        <Sex>Female</Sex>
        <PhotoFilename>http://xamarin.github.io/.../.../ZrinkaMakovac.png</PhotoFilename>
        <GradePointAverage>2.73</GradePointAverage>
      </Student>
    </Students>
</StudentBody>
```

The grade point averages were randomly generated when this file was created.

In the **Libraries** directory among the source code for this book, you'll find a library project named **SchoolOfFineArt** that accesses this XML file and uses XML deserialization to convert it into classes named Student, StudentBody, and SchoolViewModel. Although the Student and StudentBody classes don't have the words ViewModel in their names, they qualify as ViewModels regardless.

The Student class derives from ViewModelBase (a copy of which is included in the **SchoolOfFineArt** library) and defines the seven properties associated with each Student element in the XML file. An eighth property is used in a future chapter. The class also defines four additional properties of type ICommand and a final property named StudentBody. These final five properties are not set from the XML deserialization, as the XmlIgnore attributes indicate:

```
namespace SchoolOfFineArt
{
    public class Student : ViewModelBase
    {
        string fullName, firstName, middleName;
        string lastName, sex, photoFilename;
        double gradePointAverage;
        string notes;

        public Student()
        {
            ResetGpaCommand = new Command(() => GradePointAverage = 2.5m);
            MoveToTopCommand = new Command(() => StudentBody.MoveStudentToTop(this));
            MoveToBottomCommand = new Command(() => StudentBody.MoveStudentToBottom(this));
            RemoveCommand = new Command(() => StudentBody.RemoveStudent(this));
        }

        public string FullName
        {
```

```
        set { SetProperty(ref fullName, value); }
        get { return fullName; }
    }

    public string FirstName
    {
        set { SetProperty(ref firstName, value); }
        get { return firstName; }
    }

    public string MiddleName
    {
        set { SetProperty(ref middleName, value); }
        get { return middleName; }
    }

    public string LastName
    {
        set { SetProperty(ref lastName, value); }
        get { return lastName; }
    }

    public string Sex
    {
        set { SetProperty(ref sex, value); }
        get { return sex; }
    }

    public string PhotoFilename
    {
        set { SetProperty(ref photoFilename, value); }
        get { return photoFilename; }
    }

    public double GradePointAverage
    {
        set { SetProperty(ref gradePointAverage, value); }
        get { return gradePointAverage; }
    }

    // For program in Chapter 25.
    public string Notes
    {
        set { SetProperty(ref notes, value); }
        get { return notes; }
    }

    // Properties for implementing commands.
    [XmlIgnore]
    public ICommand ResetGpaCommand { private set; get; }

    [XmlIgnore]
    public ICommand MoveToTopCommand { private set; get; }
```

```
        [XmlIgnore]
        public ICommand MoveToBottomCommand { private set; get; }

        [XmlIgnore]
        public ICommand RemoveCommand { private set; get; }

        [XmlIgnore]
        public StudentBody StudentBody { set; get; }
    }
}
```

The four properties of type `ICommand` are set in the `Student` constructor and associated with short methods, three of which call methods in the `StudentBody` class. These will be discussed in more detail later.

The `StudentBody` class defines the `School` and `Students` properties. The constructor initializes the `Students` property as an `ObservableCollection<Student>` object. In addition, `StudentBody` defines three methods called from the `Student` class that can remove a student from the list or move a student to the top or bottom of the list:

```
namespace SchoolOfFineArt
{
    public class StudentBody : ViewModelBase
    {
        string school;
        ObservableCollection<Student> students = new ObservableCollection<Student>();

        public string School
        {
            set { SetProperty(ref school, value); }
            get { return school; }
        }

        public ObservableCollection<Student> Students
        {
            set { SetProperty(ref students, value); }
            get { return students; }
        }

        // Methods to implement commands to move and remove students.
        public void MoveStudentToTop(Student student)
        {
            Students.Move(Students.IndexOf(student), 0);
        }

        public void MoveStudentToBottom(Student student)
        {
            Students.Move(Students.IndexOf(student), Students.Count - 1);
        }

        public void RemoveStudent(Student student)
        {
            Students.Remove(student);
```

```
        }
    }
}
```

The `SchoolViewModel` class is responsible for loading the XML file and deserializing it. It contains a single property named `StudentBody`, which corresponds to the root tag of the XAML file. This property is set to the `StudentBody` object obtained from the `Deserialize` method of the `XmlSerializer` class.

```
namespace SchoolOfFineArt
{
    public class SchoolViewModel : ViewModelBase
    {
        StudentBody studentBody;
        Random rand = new Random();

        public SchoolViewModel() : this(null)
        {
        }

        public SchoolViewModel(IDictionary<string, object> properties)
        {
            // Avoid problems with a null or empty collection.
            StudentBody = new StudentBody();
            StudentBody.Students.Add(new Student());

            string uri = "http://xamarin.github.io/xamarin-forms-book-samples" +
                        "/SchoolOfFineArt/students.xml";

            HttpWebRequest request = WebRequest.CreateHttp(uri);

            request.BeginGetResponse((arg) =>
            {
                // Deserialize XML file.
                Stream stream = request.EndGetResponse(arg).GetResponseStream();
                StreamReader reader = new StreamReader(stream);
                XmlSerializer xml = new XmlSerializer(typeof(StudentBody));
                StudentBody = xml.Deserialize(reader) as StudentBody;

                // Enumerate through all the students
                foreach (Student student in StudentBody.Students)
                {
                    // Set StudentBody property in each Student object.
                    student.StudentBody = StudentBody;

                    // Load possible Notes from properties dictionary
                    //      (for program in Chapter 25).
                    if (properties != null && properties.ContainsKey(student.FullName))
                    {
                        student.Notes = (string)properties[student.FullName];
                    }
                }
            }, null);
```

```
            // Adjust GradePointAverage randomly.
            Device.StartTimer(TimeSpan.FromSeconds(0.1),
                () =>
                {
                    if (studentBody != null)
                    {
                        int index = rand.Next(studentBody.Students.Count);
                        Student student = studentBody.Students[index];
                        double factor = 1 + (rand.NextDouble() - 0.5) / 5;
                        student.GradePointAverage = Math.Round(
                            Math.Max(0, Math.Min(5, factor * student.GradePointAverage)), 2);
                    }
                    return true;
                });
        }

        // Save Notes in properties dictionary for program in Chapter 25.
        public void SaveNotes(IDictionary<string, object> properties)
        {
            foreach (Student student in StudentBody.Students)
            {
                properties[student.FullName] = student.Notes;
            }
        }

        public StudentBody StudentBody
        {
            protected set { SetProperty(ref studentBody, value); }
            get { return studentBody; }
        }
    }
}
```

Notice that the data is obtained asynchronously. The properties of the various classes are not set until sometime after the constructor of this class completes. But the implementation of the `INotifyPropertyChanged` interface should allow a user interface to react to data that is acquired sometime after the program starts up.

The callback to `BeginGetResponse` runs in the same secondary thread of execution that is used to download the data in the background. This callback sets some properties that cause `PropertyChanged` events to fire, which result in updates to data bindings and changes to user-interface objects. Doesn't this mean that user-interface objects are being accessed from a second thread of execution? Shouldn't `Device.BeginInvokeOnMainThread` be used to avoid that?

Actually, it's not necessary. Changes in ViewModel properties that are linked to properties of user-interface objects via data bindings don't need to be marshalled to the user-interface thread.

The `SchoolViewModel` class is also responsible for randomly modifying the `GradePointAverage` property of the students, in effect simulating dynamic data. Because `Student` implements `INotify`

`PropertyChanged` (by virtue of deriving from `ViewModelBase`), we should be able to see these values change dynamically when displayed by the `ListView`.

The **SchoolOfFineArt** library also has a static `Library.Init` method that your program should call if it's referring to the library only from XAML to ensure that the assembly is properly bound to the application.

You might want to play around with the `StudentViewModel` class to get a feel for the nested properties and how they are expressed in data bindings. You can create a new Xamarin.Forms project (named **Tryout**, for example), include the **SchoolOfFineArt** project in the solution, and add a reference from **Tryout** to the **SchoolOfFineArt** library. Then create a `ContentPage` that looks something like this:

```
<ContentPage xmlns="http://xamarin.com/schemas/2014/forms"
             xmlns:x="http://schemas.microsoft.com/winfx/2009/xaml"
             xmlns:school="clr-namespace:SchoolOfFineArt;assembly=SchoolOfFineArt"
             x:Class="Tryout.TryoutListPage">
    <ContentPage.Padding>
        <OnPlatform x:TypeArguments="Thickness"
                    iOS="0, 20, 0, 0" />
    </ContentPage.Padding>

    <ContentPage.BindingContext>
        <school:SchoolViewModel />
    </ContentPage.BindingContext>

    <Label />
</ContentPage>
```

The `BindingContext` of the page is set to the `SchoolViewModel` instance, and you can experiment with bindings on the `Text` property of the `Label`. For example, here's an empty binding:

```
<Label Text="{Binding StringFormat='{0}'}" />
```

That displays the fully qualified class name of the inherited `BindingContext`:

SchoolOfFineArt.SchoolViewModel

The `SchoolViewModel` class has one property named `StudentBody`, so set the `Path` of the `Binding` to that:

```
<Label Text="{Binding Path=StudentBody, StringFormat='{0}'}" />
```

Now you'll see the fully-qualified name of the `StudentBody` class:

SchoolOfFineArt.StudentBody

The `StudentBody` class has two properties, named `School` and `Students`. Try the `School` property:

```
<Label Text="{Binding Path=StudentBody.School,
                      StringFormat='{0}'}" />
```

Finally, some actual data is displayed rather than just a class name. It's the string from the XML file set to the `School` property:

School of Fine Art

The `StringFormat` isn't required in the `Binding` expression because the property is of type `string`. Now try the `Students` property:

```
<Label Text="{Binding Path=StudentBody.Students,
                StringFormat='{0}'}" />
```

This displays the fully qualified class name of `ObservableCollection` with a collection of `Student` objects:

System.Collections.ObjectModel.ObservableCollection`1[SchoolOfFineArt.Student]

It should be possible to index this collection, like so:

```
<Label Text="{Binding Path=StudentBody.Students[0],
                StringFormat='{0}'}" />
```

That is an object of type `Student`:

SchoolOfFineArt.Student

If the entire `Students` collection is loaded at the time of this binding, you should be able to specify any index on the `Students` collection, but an index of 0 is always safe.

You can then access a property of that `Student`, for example:

```
<Label Text="{Binding Path=StudentBody.Students[0].FullName,
                StringFormat='{0}'}" />
```

And you'll see that student's name:

Adam Harmetz

Or, try the `GradePointAverage` property:

```
<Label Text="{Binding Path=StudentBody.Students[0].GradePointAverage,
                StringFormat='{0}'}" />
```

Initially you'll see the randomly generated value stored in the XML file:

3.01

But wait a little while and you should see it change.

Would you like to see a picture of Adam Harmetz? Just change the `Label` to an `Image`, and change the target property to `Source` and the source path to `PhotoFilename`:

```
<Image Source="{Binding Path=StudentBody.Students[0].PhotoFilename}" />
```

And there he is, from the class of 2019:

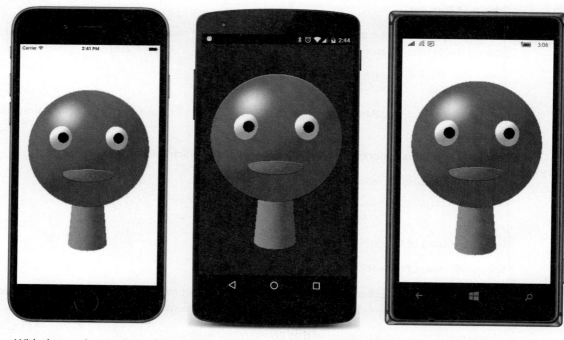

With that understanding of data-binding paths, it should be possible to construct a page that contains both a `Label` that displays the name of the school and a `ListView` that displays all the students with their full names, grade-point averages, and photos. Each item in the `ListView` must display two pieces of text and an image. This is ideal for an `ImageCell`, which derives from `TextCell` and adds an image to the two text items. Here is the **StudentList** program:

```
<ContentPage xmlns="http://xamarin.com/schemas/2014/forms"
             xmlns:x="http://schemas.microsoft.com/winfx/2009/xaml"
             xmlns:school="clr-namespace:SchoolOfFineArt;assembly=SchoolOfFineArt"
             x:Class="StudentList.StudentListPage">
    <ContentPage.Padding>
        <OnPlatform x:TypeArguments="Thickness"
                    iOS="0, 20, 0, 0" />
    </ContentPage.Padding>

    <ContentPage.BindingContext>
        <school:SchoolViewModel />
    </ContentPage.BindingContext>

    <StackLayout BindingContext="{Binding StudentBody}">
        <Label Text="{Binding School}"
               FontSize="Large"
               FontAttributes="Bold"
```

```
                    HorizontalTextAlignment="Center" />

        <ListView ItemsSource="{Binding Students}">
            <ListView.ItemTemplate>
                <DataTemplate>
                    <ImageCell ImageSource="{Binding PhotoFilename}"
                               Text="{Binding FullName}"
                               Detail="{Binding GradePointAverage,
                                             StringFormat='G.P.A. = {0:F2}'}" />
                </DataTemplate>
            </ListView.ItemTemplate>
        </ListView>
    </StackLayout>
</ContentPage>
```

As in the experimental XAML file, the `BindingContext` of the `ContentPage` is the `SchoolView-Model` object. The `StackLayout` inherits that `BindingContext` but sets its own `BindingContext` to the `StudentBody` property, and that's the `BindingContext` inherited by the children of the `Stack-Layout`. The `Text` property of the `Label` is bound to the `School` property of the `StudentBody` class, and the `ItemsSource` property of the `ListView` is bound to the `Students` collection.

This means that the `BindingContext` for each of the items in the `ListView` is a `Student` object, and the `ImageCell` properties can be bound to properties of the `Student` class. The result is scrollable and selectable, although the selection is displayed in a platform-specific manner:

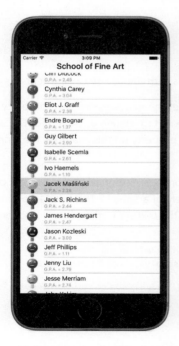  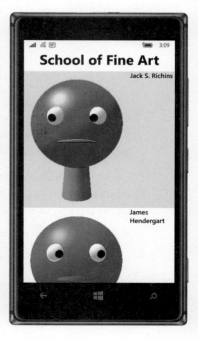

Unfortunately, the Windows Runtime version of the `ImageCell` works a little differently from those on the other two platforms. If you don't like the default size of these rows, you might be tempted to set the `RowHeight` property, but it doesn't work in the same way across the platforms, and the only consistent solution is to switch to a custom `ViewCell` derivative, perhaps one much like the one in **CustomNamedColorList** but with an `Image` rather than a `BoxView`.

The `Label` at the top of the page shares the `StackLayout` with the `ListView` so that the `Label` stays in place as the `ListView` is scrolled. However, you might want such a header to scroll with the contents of the `ListView`, and you might want to add a footer as well. The `ListView` has `Header` and `Footer` properties of type `object` that you can set to a `string` or an object of any type (in which case the header will display the results of that object's `ToString` method) or to a binding.

Here's one approach: The `BindingContext` of the page is set to the `SchoolViewModel` as before, but the `BindingContext` of the `ListView` is set to the `StudentBody` property. This means that the `ItemsSource` property can reference the `Students` collection in a binding, and the `Header` can be bound to the `School` property:

```
<ContentPage … >
    …
    <ContentPage.BindingContext>
        <school:SchoolViewModel />
    </ContentPage.BindingContext>

    <ListView BindingContext="{Binding StudentBody}"
              ItemsSource="{Binding Students}"
              Header="{Binding School}">
        …
    </ListView>
</ContentPage>
```

That displays the text "School of Fine Art" in a header that scrolls with the `ListView` content.

If you'd like to format that header, you can do that as well. Set the `HeaderTemplate` property of the `ListView` to a `DataTemplate`, and within the `DataTemplate` tags define a visual tree. The `BindingContext` for that visual tree is the object set to the `Header` property (in this example, the string with the name of the school).

In the **ListViewHeader** program shown below, the `Header` property is bound to the `School` property. Within the `HeaderTemplate` is a visual tree consisting solely of a `Label`. This `Label` has an empty binding so the `Text` property of that `Label` is bound to the text set to the `Header` property:

```
<ContentPage xmlns="http://xamarin.com/schemas/2014/forms"
             xmlns:x="http://schemas.microsoft.com/winfx/2009/xaml"
             xmlns:school="clr-namespace:SchoolOfFineArt;assembly=SchoolOfFineArt"
             x:Class="ListViewHeader.ListViewHeaderPage">
    <ContentPage.Padding>
        <OnPlatform x:TypeArguments="Thickness"
                    iOS="0, 20, 0, 0" />
    </ContentPage.Padding>

    <ContentPage.BindingContext>
```

```
            <school:SchoolViewModel />
        </ContentPage.BindingContext>

        <ListView BindingContext="{Binding StudentBody}"
                  ItemsSource="{Binding Students}"
                  Header="{Binding School}">

            <ListView.HeaderTemplate>
                <DataTemplate>
                    <Label Text="{Binding}"
                           FontSize="Large"
                           FontAttributes="Bold, Italic"
                           HorizontalTextAlignment="Center" />
                </DataTemplate>
            </ListView.HeaderTemplate>

            <ListView.ItemTemplate>
                <DataTemplate>
                    <ImageCell ImageSource="{Binding PhotoFilename}"
                               Text="{Binding FullName}"
                               Detail="{Binding GradePointAverage,
                                        StringFormat='G.P.A. = {0:F2}'}" />
                </DataTemplate>
            </ListView.ItemTemplate>
        </ListView>
</ContentPage>
```

The header shows up only on the Android platform:

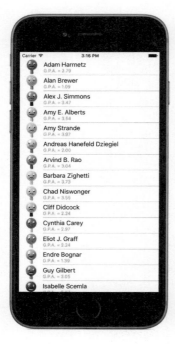

Selection and the binding context

The `StudentBody` class doesn't have a property for the selected student. If it did, you could create a data binding between the `SelectedItem` property of the `ListView` and that selected-student property in `StudentBody`. As usual with MVVM, the property of the view is the data-binding target and the property in the ViewModel is the data-binding source.

However, if you want a detailed view of a student directly, without the intermediary of a View-Model, then the `SelectedItem` property of the `ListView` can be the binding source. The **Select-edStudentDetail** program shows how this might be done. The `ListView` now shares the screen with a `StackLayout` that contains the detail view. To accommodate landscape and portrait orientations, the `ListView` and `StackLayout` are children of a `Grid` that is manipulated in the code-behind file. The code-behind file also sets the `BindingContext` of the page to an instance of the `SchoolViewModel` class.

The `BindingContext` of the `StackLayout` named "detailLayout" is bound to the `SelectedItem` property of the `ListView`. Because the `SelectedItem` property is of type `Student`, bindings within the `StackLayout` can simply refer to properties of the `Student` class:

```
<ContentPage xmlns="http://xamarin.com/schemas/2014/forms"
             xmlns:x="http://schemas.microsoft.com/winfx/2009/xaml"
             x:Class="SelectedStudentDetail.SelectedStudentDetailPage"
             SizeChanged="OnPageSizeChanged">
    <ContentPage.Padding>
```

```xml
                <OnPlatform x:TypeArguments="Thickness"
                            iOS="0, 20, 0, 0" />
        </ContentPage.Padding>

        <Grid x:Name="mainGrid">
            <Grid.RowDefinitions>
                <RowDefinition Height="*" />
                <RowDefinition Height="*" />
            </Grid.RowDefinitions>

            <Grid.ColumnDefinitions>
                <ColumnDefinition Width="*" />
                <ColumnDefinition Width="0" />
            </Grid.ColumnDefinitions>

            <ListView x:Name="listView"
                      Grid.Row="0"
                      Grid.Column="0"
                      ItemsSource="{Binding StudentBody.Students}">
                <ListView.ItemTemplate>
                    <DataTemplate>
                        <ImageCell ImageSource="{Binding PhotoFilename}"
                                   Text="{Binding FullName}"
                                   Detail="{Binding GradePointAverage,
                                                StringFormat='G.P.A. = {0:F2}'}" />
                    </DataTemplate>
                </ListView.ItemTemplate>
            </ListView>

            <StackLayout x:Name="detailLayout"
                         Grid.Row="1"
                         Grid.Column="0"
                         BindingContext="{Binding Source={x:Reference listView},
                                              Path=SelectedItem}">
                <StackLayout Orientation="Horizontal"
                             HorizontalOptions="Center"
                             Spacing="0">
                    <StackLayout.Resources>
                        <ResourceDictionary>
                            <Style TargetType="Label">
                                <Setter Property="FontSize" Value="Large" />
                                <Setter Property="FontAttributes" Value="Bold" />
                            </Style>
                        </ResourceDictionary>
                    </StackLayout.Resources>

                    <Label Text="{Binding LastName}" />
                    <Label Text="{Binding FirstName, StringFormat=', {0}'}" />
                    <Label Text="{Binding MiddleName, StringFormat=' {0}'}" />
                </StackLayout>

                <Image Source="{Binding PhotoFilename}"
                       VerticalOptions="FillAndExpand" />
```

```
                <Label Text="{Binding Sex, StringFormat='Sex = {0}'}"
                       HorizontalOptions="Center" />
                <Label Text="{Binding GradePointAverage, StringFormat='G.P.A. = {0:F2}'}"
                       HorizontalOptions="Center" />
            </StackLayout>
        </Grid>
    </ContentPage>
```

When you first run the program, the `ListView` occupies the top half of the page and the entire bottom half of the page is empty. When you select one of the students, the bottom half displays a different formatting of the name, a larger photo (except on the Windows Phone), and additional information:

Notice that all the `Label` elements in the `StackLayout` named "detailLayout" have their `Text` properties set to bindings of properties of the `Student` class. For example, here are the three `Label` elements that display the full name in a horizontal `StackLayout`:

```
<Label Text="{Binding LastName}" />
<Label Text="{Binding FirstName, StringFormat=', {0}'}" />
<Label Text="{Binding MiddleName, StringFormat=' {0}'}" />
```

An alternative approach is to use separate `Label` elements for the text that separate the last name and first name and the first name and middle name:

```
<Label Text="{Binding LastName}" />
<Label Text=", " />
```

```
<Label Text="{Binding FirstName}" />
<Label Text=" " />
<Label Text="{Binding MiddleName}" />
```

Ostensibly, these two approaches seem visually identical. However, if no student is currently selected, the second approach displays a stray comma that looks like an odd speck on the screen. The advantages of using a binding with `StringFormat` is that the `Label` doesn't appear at all if the `BindingContext` is `null`.

Sometimes it's unavoidable that some spurious text appears in a detail view when the detail view isn't displaying anything otherwise. In such a case you might want to bind the `IsVisible` property of the detail `Layout` object to the `SelectedItem` property of the `ListView` with a binding converter that converts `null` to `false` and non-`null` to `true`.

The code-behind file in the **SelectedStudentDetail** program is responsible for setting the `BindingContext` for the page and also for handling the `SizeChanged` event for the page to adjust the `Grid` and the `detailLayout` object for a landscape orientation:

```
public partial class SelectedStudentDetailPage : ContentPage
{
    public SelectedStudentDetailPage()
    {
        InitializeComponent();

        // Set BindingContext.
        BindingContext = new SchoolViewModel();
    }

    void OnPageSizeChanged(object sender, EventArgs args)
    {
        // Portrait mode.
        if (Width < Height)
        {
            mainGrid.ColumnDefinitions[0].Width = new GridLength(1, GridUnitType.Star);
            mainGrid.ColumnDefinitions[1].Width = new GridLength(0);

            mainGrid.RowDefinitions[0].Height = new GridLength(1, GridUnitType.Star);
            mainGrid.RowDefinitions[1].Height = new GridLength(1, GridUnitType.Star);

            Grid.SetRow(detailLayout, 1);
            Grid.SetColumn(detailLayout, 0);
        }
        // Landscape mode.
        else
        {
            mainGrid.ColumnDefinitions[0].Width = new GridLength(1, GridUnitType.Star);
            mainGrid.ColumnDefinitions[1].Width = new GridLength(1, GridUnitType.Star);

            mainGrid.RowDefinitions[0].Height = new GridLength(1, GridUnitType.Star);
            mainGrid.RowDefinitions[1].Height = new GridLength(0);

            Grid.SetRow(detailLayout, 0);
```

```
        Grid.SetColumn(detailLayout, 1);
    }
}
}
```

Here's a landscape view:

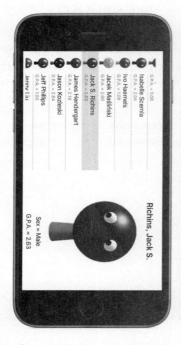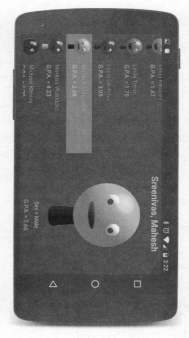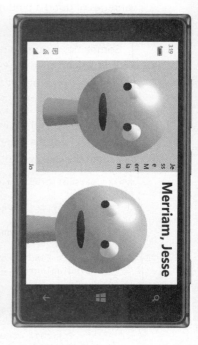

Unfortunately, the large image in the `ListView` on Windows 10 Mobile crowds out the text.

Dividing a page into a `ListView` and detail view is not the only approach. When the user selects an item in the `ListView`, your program could navigate to a separate page to display the detail view. Or you could make use of a `MasterDetailPage` designed specifically for scenarios such as this. You'll see examples with these solutions in the chapters ahead.

Context menus

A cell can define a context menu that is invoked in a platform-specific manner. Such a context menu generally allows a user to perform an operation on a specific item in the `ListView`. When used with a `ListView` displaying students, for example, such a context menu allows the user to perform actions on a specific student.

The **CellContextMenu** program demonstrates this technique. It defines a context menu with four items:

- **Reset GPA** (which sets the grade point average of the student to 2.5)

- **Move to Top** (which moves the student to the top of the list)

- **Move to Bottom** (which similarly moves the student to the bottom)

- **Remove** (which removes the student from the list)

On iOS, the context menu is invoked by sliding the item to the left. On Android and Windows 10 Mobile, you press your finger to the item and hold it until the menu appears. Here's the result:

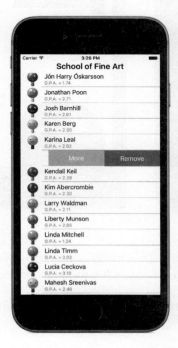

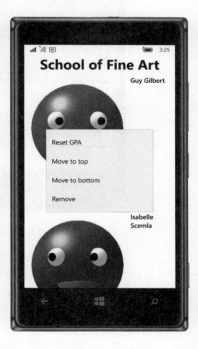

Only one menu item appears on the iOS screen, and that's the item that removes the student from the list. A menu item that removes an entry from the `ListView` must be specially flagged for iOS. The Android screen lists the first two menu items at the top of the screen. Only the Windows Runtime lists them all.

To see the other menu items, you tap the **More** button on iOS and the vertical ellipsis on Android. The other items appear in a list at the bottom of the iOS screen and in a drop-down list at the top right of the Android screen:

Tapping one of the menu items carries out that operation.

To create a context menu for a cell, you add objects of type `MenuItem` to the `ContextActions` collection defined by the `Cell` class. You've already encountered `MenuItem`. It is the base class for the `ToolbarItem` class described in Chapter 13, "Bitmaps."

`MenuItem` defines five properties:

- `Text` of type `string`

- `Icon` of type `FileImageSource` to access a bitmap from a platform project

- `IsDestructive` of type `bool`

- `Command` of type `ICommand`

- `CommandParameter` of type `object`

In addition, `MenuItem` defines a `Clicked` event. You can handle menu actions either in a `Clicked` handler or—if the menu actions are implemented in a ViewModel—an `ICommand` object.

Here's how the `ContextActions` collection is initialized in the **CellContextMenu** program:

```
<ContentPage xmlns="http://xamarin.com/schemas/2014/forms"
             xmlns:x="http://schemas.microsoft.com/winfx/2009/xaml"
             xmlns:school="clr-namespace:SchoolOfFineArt;assembly=SchoolOfFineArt"
             x:Class="CellContextMenu.CellContextMenuPage">
```

```
    <ContentPage.Padding>
        <OnPlatform x:TypeArguments="Thickness"
                    iOS="0, 20, 0, 0" />
    </ContentPage.Padding>

    <ContentPage.BindingContext>
        <school:SchoolViewModel />
    </ContentPage.BindingContext>

    <StackLayout BindingContext="{Binding StudentBody}">
        <Label Text="{Binding School}"
               FontSize="Large"
               FontAttributes="Bold"
               HorizontalTextAlignment="Center" />

        <ListView ItemsSource="{Binding Students}">
            <ListView.ItemTemplate>
                <DataTemplate>
                    <ImageCell ImageSource="{Binding PhotoFilename}"
                               Text="{Binding FullName}"
                               Detail="{Binding GradePointAverage,
                                              StringFormat='G.P.A. = {0:F2}'}">
                        <ImageCell.ContextActions>
                            <MenuItem Text="Reset GPA"
                                      Command="{Binding ResetGpaCommand}" />

                            <MenuItem Text="Move to top"
                                      Command="{Binding MoveToTopCommand}" />

                            <MenuItem Text="Move to bottom"
                                      Command="{Binding MoveToBottomCommand}" />

                            <MenuItem Text="Remove"
                                      IsDestructive="True"
                                      Command="{Binding RemoveCommand}" />
                        </ImageCell.ContextActions>
                    </ImageCell>
                </DataTemplate>
            </ListView.ItemTemplate>
        </ListView>
    </StackLayout>
</ContentPage>
```

Notice that the `IsDestructive` property is set to `True` for the **Remove** item. This is the property that causes the item to be displayed in red on the iOS screen, and which by convention deletes the item from the collection.

`MenuItem` defines an `Icon` property that you can set to a bitmap stored in a platform project (much like the icons used with `ToolbarItem`), but it works only on Android, and the bitmap replaces the `Text` description.

The `Command` properties of all four `MenuItem` objects are bound to properties in the `Student` class.

A `Student` object is the binding context for the cell, so it's also the binding context for these Menu-Item objects. Here's how the properties are defined and initialized in `Student`:

```
public class Student : ViewModelBase
{
    ...
    public Student()
    {
        ResetGpaCommand = new Command(() => GradePointAverage = 2.5);
        MoveToTopCommand = new Command(() => StudentBody.MoveStudentToTop(this));
        MoveToBottomCommand = new Command(() => StudentBody.MoveStudentToBottom(this));
        RemoveCommand = new Command(() => StudentBody.RemoveStudent(this));
    }
    ...
    // Properties for implementing commands.
    [XmlIgnore]
    public ICommand ResetGpaCommand { private set; get; }

    [XmlIgnore]
    public ICommand MoveToTopCommand { private set; get; }

    [XmlIgnore]
    public ICommand MoveToBottomCommand { private set; get; }

    [XmlIgnore]
    public ICommand RemoveCommand { private set; get; }

    [XmlIgnore]
    public StudentBody StudentBody { set; get; }
}
```

Only the `ResetGpaCommand` can be handled entirely within the `Student` class. The other three commands require access to the collection of students in the `StudentBody` class. For that reason, when first loading in the data, the `SchoolViewModel` sets the `StudentBody` property in each `Student` object to the `StudentBody` object with the collection of students. This allows the **Move** and **Remove** commands to be implemented with calls to the following methods in `StudentBody`:

```
public class StudentBody : ViewModelBase
{
    ...
    public void MoveStudentToTop(Student student)
    {
        Students.Move(Students.IndexOf(student), 0);
    }

    public void MoveStudentToBottom(Student student)
    {
        Students.Move(Students.IndexOf(student), Students.Count - 1);
    }

    public void RemoveStudent(Student student)
    {
        Students.Remove(student);
```

```
    }
}
```

Because the `Students` collection is an `ObservableCollection`, the `ListView` redraws itself to reflect the new number or new ordering of the students.

Varying the visuals

Sometimes you don't want every item displayed by the `ListView` to be formatted identically. You might want a little different formatting based on the values of some properties. This is generally a job for *triggers*, which you'll be exploring in Chapter 23. However, you can also vary the visuals of items in a `ListView` by using a value converter.

Here's a view of the **ColorCodedStudents** screen. Every student with a grade-point average less than 2.0 is flagged in red, perhaps to highlight the need for some special attention:

In one sense, this is very simple: The `TextColor` property of the `ImageCell` is bound to the `GradePointAverage` property of `Student`. But that's a property of type `Color` bound to a property of type `double`, so a value converter is required, and one that's capable of performing a test on the `GradePointAverage` property to convert to the proper color.

Here is the `ThresholdToObjectConverter` in the **Xamarin.FormsBook.Toolkit** library:

```
namespace Xamarin.FormsBook.Toolkit
{
```

```
public class ThresholdToObjectConverter<T> : IValueConverter
{
    public T TrueObject { set; get; }

    public T FalseObject { set; get; }

    public object Convert(object value, Type targetType,
                          object parameter, CultureInfo culture)
    {
        // Code assumes that all input is valid!
        double number = (double)value;
        string arg = parameter as string;
        char op = arg[0];
        double criterion = Double.Parse(arg.Substring(1).Trim());

        switch (op)
        {
            case '<': return number < criterion ? TrueObject : FalseObject;
            case '>': return number > criterion ? TrueObject : FalseObject;
            case '=': return number == criterion ? TrueObject : FalseObject;
        }
        return FalseObject;
    }

    public object ConvertBack(object value, Type targetType,
                              object parameter, CultureInfo culture)
    {
        return 0;
    }
}
```

Like the `BoolToObjectConverter` described in Chapter 16, "Data binding," the `ThresholdToOb-jectConverter` is a generic class that defines two properties of type `T`, named `TrueObject` and `FalseObject`. But the choice is based on a comparison of the `value` argument (which is assumed to be of type `double`) and the `parameter` argument, which is specified as the `ConverterParameter` in the binding. This `parameter` argument is assumed to be a string that contains a one-character comparison operator and a number. For purposes of simplicity and clarity, there is no input validation.

Once the value converter is created, the markup is fairly easy:

```
<ContentPage xmlns="http://xamarin.com/schemas/2014/forms"
             xmlns:x="http://schemas.microsoft.com/winfx/2009/xaml"
             xmlns:school="clr-namespace:SchoolOfFineArt;assembly=SchoolOfFineArt"
             xmlns:toolkit=
                 "clr-namespace:Xamarin.FormsBook.Toolkit;assembly=Xamarin.FormsBook.Toolkit"
             x:Class="ColorCodedStudents.ColorCodedStudentsPage">
    <ContentPage.Padding>
        <OnPlatform x:TypeArguments="Thickness"
                    iOS="0, 20, 0, 0" />
    </ContentPage.Padding>

    <ContentPage.Resources>
```

```
        <ResourceDictionary>
            <toolkit:ThresholdToObjectConverter x:Key="thresholdConverter"
                                                x:TypeArguments="Color"
                                                TrueObject="Default"
                                                FalseObject="Red" />
        </ResourceDictionary>
    </ContentPage.Resources>

    <ContentPage.BindingContext>
        <school:SchoolViewModel />
    </ContentPage.BindingContext>

    <ListView ItemsSource="{Binding StudentBody.Students}">
        <ListView.ItemTemplate>
            <DataTemplate>
                <ImageCell ImageSource="{Binding PhotoFilename}"
                           Text="{Binding FullName}"
                           TextColor="{Binding GradePointAverage,
                                       Converter={StaticResource thresholdConverter},
                                       ConverterParameter=>2}"
                           Detail="{Binding GradePointAverage,
                                    StringFormat='G.P.A. = {0:F2}'}" />
            </DataTemplate>
        </ListView.ItemTemplate>
    </ListView>
</ContentPage>
```

When the GPA is greater than or equal to 2, the text is displayed in its default color; otherwise the text is displayed in red.

Refreshing the content

As you've seen, if you use an `ObservableCollection` as a source for `ListView`, any change to the collection causes `ObservableCollection` to fire a `CollectionChanged` event and the `ListView` responds by refreshing the display of items.

Sometimes this type of refreshing must be supplemented with something controlled by the user. For example, consider an email client or RSS reader. Such an application might be configured to look for new email or an update to the RSS file every 15 minutes or so, but the user might be somewhat impatient and might want the program to check right away for new data.

For this purpose a convention has developed that is supported by `ListView`. If the `ListView` has its `IsPullToRefresh` property set to `true`, and if the user swipes down on the `ListView`, the `ListView` will respond by calling the `Execute` method of the `ICommand` object bound to its `RefreshCommand` property. The `ListView` will also set its `IsRefreshing` property to `true` and display some kind of animation indicating that it's busy.

In reality, the `ListView` is not busy. It's just waiting to be notified that new data is available. You've probably written the code invoked by the `Execute` method of the `ICommand` object to perform an asynchronous operation such as a web access. It must notify the `ListView` that it's finished by setting the IsRefreshing property of the ListView back to false. At that time, the ListView displays the new data and the refresh is complete.

This sounds somewhat complicated, but it gets a lot easier if you build this feature into the View-Model that supplies the data. The whole process is demonstrated with a program called **RssFeed** that accesses an RSS feed from NASA.

The RssFeedViewModel class is responsible for downloading the XML with the RSS feed and parsing it. This first happens when the Url property is set and the set accessor calls the LoadRssFeed method:

```
public class RssFeedViewModel : ViewModelBase
{
    string url, title;
    IList<RssItemViewModel> items;
    bool isRefreshing = true;

    public RssFeedViewModel()
    {
        RefreshCommand = new Command(
            execute: () =>
            {
                LoadRssFeed(url);
            },
            canExecute: () =>
            {
                return !IsRefreshing;
            });
    }

    public string Url
    {
        set
        {
            if (SetProperty(ref url, value) && !String.IsNullOrEmpty(url))
            {
                LoadRssFeed(url);
            }
        }
        get
        {
            return url;
        }
    }
    public string Title
    {
        set { SetProperty(ref title, value); }
        get { return title; }
    }

    public IList<RssItemViewModel> Items
    {
        set { SetProperty(ref items, value); }
```

```
                get { return items; }
    }

    public ICommand RefreshCommand { private set; get; }

    public bool IsRefreshing
    {
        set { SetProperty(ref isRefreshing, value); }
        get { return isRefreshing; }
    }

    public void LoadRssFeed(string url)
    {
        WebRequest request = WebRequest.Create(url);
        request.BeginGetResponse((args) =>
        {
            // Download XML.
            Stream stream = request.EndGetResponse(args).GetResponseStream();
            StreamReader reader = new StreamReader(stream);
            string xml = reader.ReadToEnd();

            // Parse XML to extract data from RSS feed.
            XDocument doc = XDocument.Parse(xml);
            XElement rss = doc.Element(XName.Get("rss"));
            XElement channel = rss.Element(XName.Get("channel"));

            // Set Title property.
            Title = channel.Element(XName.Get("title")).Value;

            // Set Items property.
            List<RssItemViewModel> list =
                channel.Elements(XName.Get("item")).Select((XElement element) =>
                {
                    // Instantiate RssItemViewModel for each item.
                    return new RssItemViewModel(element);
                }).ToList();
            Items = list;

            // Set IsRefreshing to false to stop the 'wait' icon.
            IsRefreshing = false;
        }, null);
    }
}
```

The `LoadRssFeed` method uses the LINQ-to-XML interface in the `System.Xml.Linq` namespace to parse the XML file and set both the `Title` property and the `Items` property of the class. The `Items` property is a collection of `RssItemViewModel` objects that define five properties associated with each item in the RSS feed. For each `item` element in the XML file, the `LoadRssFeed` method instantiates an `RssItemViewModel` object:

```
public class RssItemViewModel
{
    public RssItemViewModel(XElement element)
```

```
        {
            // Although this code might appear to be generalized, it is
            //   actually based on desired elements from the particular
            //   RSS feed set in the RssFeedPage.xaml file.
            Title = element.Element(XName.Get("title")).Value;
            Description = element.Element(XName.Get("description")).Value;
            Link = element.Element(XName.Get("link")).Value;
            PubDate = element.Element(XName.Get("pubDate")).Value;

            // Sometimes there's no thumbnail, so check for its presence.
            XElement thumbnailElement = element.Element(
                XName.Get("thumbnail", "http://search.yahoo.com/mrss/"));

            if (thumbnailElement != null)
            {
                Thumbnail = thumbnailElement.Attribute(XName.Get("url")).Value;
            }
        }

    public string Title { protected set; get; }

    public string Description { protected set; get; }

    public string Link { protected set; get; }

    public string PubDate { protected set; get; }

    public string Thumbnail { protected set; get; }
}
```

The constructor of `RssFeedViewModel` also sets its `RefreshCommand` property equal to a `Command` object with an `Execute` method that also calls `LoadRssFeed`, which finishes by setting the `IsRefreshing` property of the class to `false`. To avoid overlapping web accesses, the `CanExecute` method of `RefreshCommand` returns `true` only if `IsRefreshing` is `false`.

Notice that it's not necessary for the `Items` property in `RssFeedViewModel` to be an `ObservableCollection` because once the `Items` collection is created, the items in the collection never change. When the `LoadRssFeed` method gets new data, it creates a whole new `List` object that it sets to the `Items` property, which results in the firing of a `PropertyChanged` event.

The `RssFeedPage` class shown below instantiates the `RssFeedViewModel` and assigns the `Url` property. This object becomes the `BindingContext` for a `StackLayout` that contains a `Label` to display the `Title` property and a `ListView`. The `ItemsSource`, `RefreshCommand`, and `IsRefreshing` properties of the `ListView` are all bound to properties in the `RssFeedViewModel`:

```xml
<ContentPage xmlns="http://xamarin.com/schemas/2014/forms"
             xmlns:x="http://schemas.microsoft.com/winfx/2009/xaml"
             xmlns:local="clr-namespace:RssFeed"
             x:Class="RssFeed.RssFeedPage">
    <ContentPage.Padding>
        <OnPlatform x:TypeArguments="Thickness"
                    iOS="10, 20, 10, 0"
```

```
                        Android="10, 0"
                        WinPhone="10, 0" />
    </ContentPage.Padding>

    <ContentPage.Resources>
        <ResourceDictionary>
            <local:RssFeedViewModel x:Key="rssFeed"
                    Url="http://earthobservatory.nasa.gov/Feeds/rss/eo_iotd.rss" />
        </ResourceDictionary>
    </ContentPage.Resources>

    <Grid>
        <StackLayout x:Name="rssLayout"
                     BindingContext="{StaticResource rssFeed}">

            <Label Text="{Binding Title}"
                   FontAttributes="Bold"
                   HorizontalTextAlignment="Center" />

            <ListView x:Name="listView"
                    ItemsSource="{Binding Items}"
                    ItemSelected="OnListViewItemSelected"
                    IsPullToRefreshEnabled="True"
                    RefreshCommand="{Binding RefreshCommand}"
                    IsRefreshing="{Binding IsRefreshing}">
                <ListView.ItemTemplate>
                    <DataTemplate>
                        <ImageCell Text="{Binding Title}"
                                   Detail="{Binding PubDate}"
                                   ImageSource="{Binding Thumbnail}" />
                    </DataTemplate>
                </ListView.ItemTemplate>
            </ListView>
        </StackLayout>

        <StackLayout x:Name="webLayout"
                     IsVisible="False">

            <WebView x:Name="webView"
                     VerticalOptions="FillAndExpand" />

            <Button Text="&lt; Back to List"
                    HorizontalOptions="Center"
                    Clicked="OnBackButtonClicked" />
        </StackLayout>
    </Grid>
</ContentPage>
```

The items are ideally suited for an `ImageCell`, but perhaps not on the Windows 10 Mobile device:

When you swipe your finger down this list, the `ListView` will go into refresh mode by calling the `Execute` method of the `RefreshCommand` object and displaying an animation indicating that it's busy. When the `IsRefreshing` property is set back to `false` by `RssFeedViewModel`, the `ListView` displays the new data. (This is not implemented on the Windows Runtime platforms.)

In addition, the page contains another `StackLayout` toward the bottom of the XAML file that has its `IsVisible` property set to `false`. The first `StackLayout` with the `ListView` and this second, hidden `StackLayout` share a single-cell `Grid`, so they both essentially occupy the entire page.

When the user selects an item in the `ListView`, the `ItemSelected` event handler in the code-behind file hides the `StackLayout` with the `ListView` and makes the second `StackLayout` visible:

```
public partial class RssFeedPage : ContentPage
{
    public RssFeedPage()
    {
        InitializeComponent();
    }

    void OnListViewItemSelected(object sender, SelectedItemChangedEventArgs args)
    {
        if (args.SelectedItem != null)
        {
            // Deselect item.
            ((ListView)sender).SelectedItem = null;

            // Set WebView source to RSS item
            RssItemViewModel rssItem = (RssItemViewModel)args.SelectedItem;

            // For iOS 9, a NSAppTransportSecurity key was added to
```

```
            // Info.plist to allow accesses to EarthObservatory.nasa.gov sites.
            webView.Source = rssItem.Link;

            // Hide and make visible.
            rssLayout.IsVisible = false;
            webLayout.IsVisible = true;
        }
    }

    void OnBackButtonClicked(object sender, EventArgs args)
    {
        // Hide and make visible.
        webLayout.IsVisible = false;
        rssLayout.IsVisible = true;
    }
}
```

This second `StackLayout` contains a `WebView` for a display of the item referenced by the RSS feed item and a button to go back to the `ListView`:

Notice how the `ItemSelected` event handler sets the `SelectedItem` property of the `ListView` to null, effectively deselecting the item. (However, the selected item is still available in the `SelectedItem` property of the event arguments.) This is a common technique when using the `ListView` for navigational purposes. When the user returns to the `ListView`, you don't want the item to be still selected. Setting the `SelectedItem` property of the `ListView` to null causes another call to the `Item-Selected` event handler, of course, but if the handler begins by ignoring cases when `SelectedItem` is null, the second call shouldn't be a problem.

A more sophisticated program would navigate to a second page or use the detail part of a `MasterDetailPage` for displaying the item. Those techniques will be demonstrated in future chapters.

The TableView and its intents

The third of the three collection views in Xamarin.Forms is `TableView`, and the name might be a little deceptive. When we hear the word "table" in programming contexts, we usually think of a two-dimensional grid, such as an HTML table. The Xamarin.Forms `TableView` is instead a vertical, scrollable list of items that are visually generated from `Cell` classes. This might sound very similar to a `ListView`, but the `ListView` and `TableView` are quite different in use:

The `ListView` generally displays a list of items of the same type, usually instances of a particular data class. These items are in an `IEnumerable` collection. The `ListView` specifies a single `Cell` derivative for rendering these data objects. Items are selectable.

The `TableView` displays a list of items of different types. In real-life programming, often these items are properties of a single class. Each item is associated with its own `Cell` to display the property and often to allow the user to interact with the property. In the general case, the `TableView` displays more than one type of cell.

Properties and hierarchies

`ListView` and `ItemsView` together define 18 properties, while `TableView` has only four:

- `Intent` of type `TableIntent`.
- `Root` of type `TableRoot`. (This is the content property of `TableView`.)
- `RowHeight` of type `int`.
- `HasUnevenRows` of type `bool`.

The `RowHeight` and `HasUnevenRows` properties play the same role in the `TableView` as in the `ListView`.

Perhaps the most revealing property of the `TableView` class is a property that is *not* guaranteed to have any effect on functionality and appearance. This property is named `Intent`, and it indicates how you're using the particular `TableView` in your program. You can set this property (or not) to a member of the `TableIntent` enumeration:

- `Data`
- `Form`
- `Settings`

- `Menu`

These members suggest the various ways that you can use `TableView`. When used for `Data`, the `TableView` usually displays related items, but items of different types. A `Form` is a series of items that the user interacts with to enter information. A `TableView` used for program `Settings` is sometimes known as a *dialog*. This use is similar to `Form`, except that settings usually have default values. You can also use a `TableView` for a `Menu`, in which case the items are generally displayed using text or bitmaps and initiate an action when tapped.

The `Root` property defines the root of the hierarchy of items displayed by the `TableView`. Each item in a `TableView` is associated with a single `Cell` derivative, and the various cells can be organized into sections. To support this hierarchy of items, several classes are defined:

- `TableSectionBase` is an abstract class that derives from `BindableObject` and defines a `Title` property.

- `TableSectionBase<T>` is an abstract class that derives from `TableSectionBase` and implements the `IList<T>` interface, and hence also the `ICollection<T>` and `IEnumerable<T>` interfaces. The class also implements the `INotifyCollectionChanged` interface; internally it maintains an `ObservableCollection<T>` for this collection. This allows items to be dynamically added to or removed from the `TableView`.

- `TableSection` derives from `TableSectionBase<Cell>`.

- `TableRoot` derives from `TableSectionBase<TableSection>`.

In summary, `TableView` has a `Root` property that you set to a `TableRoot` object, which is a collection of `TableSection` objects, each of which is a collection of `Cell` objects.

Notice that both `TableSection` and `TableRoot` inherit a `Title` property from `TableSectionBase`. Depending on the derived class, this is either a title for the section or a title for the entire table. Both `TableSection` and `TableRoot` have constructors that let you set this `Title` property when creating the object.

The `TableSectionBase<T>` class defines two `Add` methods for adding items to the collection. The first `Add` method is required by the `ICollection` interface; the second is not:

- `public void Add(T item)`

- `public void Add(IEnumerable<T> items)`

This second `Add` method seems to allow you to add one `TableSection` to another `TableSection`, and one `TableRoot` to another `TableRoot`, and that process might seem to imply that you can have a nested series of `TableRoot` or `TableSection` instances. But that is not so. This `Add` method just transfers the items from one collection to another. The hierarchy never gets any deeper than a `TableRoot` that is a collection of `TableSection` objects, which are collections of `Cell` objects.

Although the `TableView` makes use of `Cell` objects, it does not use `DataTemplate`. Whether you define a `TableView` in code or in XAML, you always set data bindings directly on the `Cell` objects. Generally these bindings are very simple because you set a `BindingContext` on the `TableView` that is inherited by the individual items.

Visually and functionally, the `TableView` is not very different from a `StackLayout` in a `ScrollView`, where the `StackLayout` contains a collection of short visual trees with bindings. But generally the `TableView` is more convenient in organizing and arranging the information.

A prosaic form

Let's make a data-entry form that lets the program's user enter a person's name and some other information. When you first run the **EntryForm** program, it looks like this:

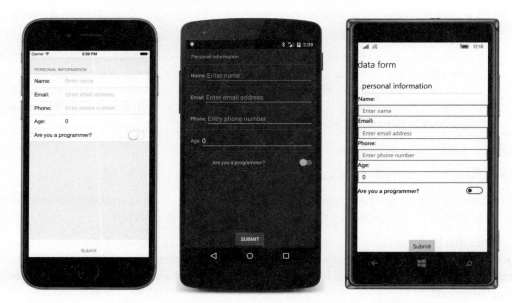

The `TableView` consists of everything on the page except the **Submit** button. This `TableView` has one `TableSection` consisting of five cells—four `EntryCell` elements and one `SwitchCell`. (Those are the only two `Cell` derivatives you haven't seen yet.) The text "Data Form" is the `Title` property of the `TableRoot` object, and it shows up only on the Windows 10 Mobile screen. The text "Personal Information" is the `Title` property for the `TableSection`.

The five cells correspond to five properties of this little class named `PersonalInformation`. Although the class name doesn't explicitly identify this as a ViewModel, the class derives from `View-ModelBase`:

```
class PersonalInformation : ViewModelBase
{
    string name, emailAddress, phoneNumber;
    int age;
```

```
bool isProgrammer;

public string Name
{
    set { SetProperty(ref name, value); }
    get { return name; }
}

public string EmailAddress
{
    set { SetProperty(ref emailAddress, value); }
    get { return emailAddress; }
}

public string PhoneNumber
{
    set { SetProperty(ref phoneNumber, value); }
    get { return phoneNumber; }
}

public int Age
{
    set { SetProperty(ref age, value); }
    get { return age; }
}

public bool IsProgrammer
{
    set { SetProperty(ref isProgrammer, value); }
    get { return isProgrammer; }
}
}
```

When you fill in the information in the form and press the **Submit** button, the program displays the information from the `PersonalInformation` instance in a little paragraph at the bottom of the screen:

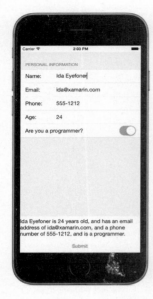

This program maintains just a single instance of `PersonalInformation`. A real application would perhaps create a new instance for each person whose information the user is supplying, and then store each instance in an `ObservableCollection<PersonalInformation>` for display by a `ListView`.

The **EntryForm** XAML file instantiates `PersonalInformation` as the `BindingContext` of the `TableView`. You can see here the `TableRoot`, the `TableSection`, and the five `Cell` objects:

```
<ContentPage xmlns="http://xamarin.com/schemas/2014/forms"
             xmlns:x="http://schemas.microsoft.com/winfx/2009/xaml"
             xmlns:local="clr-namespace:EntryForm"
             x:Class="EntryForm.EntryFormPage">
    <ContentPage.Padding>
        <OnPlatform x:TypeArguments="Thickness"
                    iOS="0, 20, 0, 0" />
    </ContentPage.Padding>

    <StackLayout>
        <TableView x:Name="tableView"
                   Intent="Form">

            <TableView.BindingContext>
                <local:PersonalInformation />
            </TableView.BindingContext>

            <TableRoot Title="Data Form">
                <TableSection Title="Personal Information">
                    <EntryCell Label="Name:"
                               Text="{Binding Name}"
                               Placeholder="Enter name"
                               Keyboard="Text" />
```

```
                        <EntryCell Label="Email:"
                                   Text="{Binding EmailAddress}"
                                   Placeholder="Enter email address"
                                   Keyboard="Email" />

                        <EntryCell Label="Phone:"
                                   Text="{Binding PhoneNumber}"
                                   Placeholder="Enter phone number"
                                   Keyboard="Telephone" />

                        <EntryCell Label="Age:"
                                   Text="{Binding Age}"
                                   Placeholder="Enter age"
                                   Keyboard="Numeric" />

                        <SwitchCell Text="Are you a programmer?"
                                    On="{Binding IsProgrammer}" />
                    </TableSection>
                </TableRoot>
            </TableView>

            <Label x:Name="summaryLabel"
                   VerticalOptions="CenterAndExpand" />

            <Button Text="Submit"
                    HorizontalOptions="Center"
                    Clicked="OnSubmitButtonClicked" />
        </StackLayout>
    </ContentPage>
```

Each of the properties of the `PersonalInformation` class corresponds to a `Cell`. For four of these properties, this is an `EntryCell` that consists (at least conceptually) of an identifying `Label` and an `Entry` view. (In reality, the `EntryCell` consists of platform-specific visual objects, but it's convenient to speak of these objects using Xamarin.Forms names.) The `Label` property specifies the text that appears at the left; the `Placeholder` and `Keyboard` properties of `EntryView` duplicate the same properties in `Entry`. A `Text` property indicates the text in the `Entry` view.

The fifth cell is a `SwitchCell` for the Boolean property `IsProgrammer`. In this case, the `Text` property specifies the text at the left of the cell, and the `On` property indicates the state of the `Switch`.

Because the `BindingContext` of the `TableView` is `PersonalInformation`, the bindings in the `Cell` objects can simply reference the properties of `PersonalInformation`. The binding modes of the `Text` property of the `EntryCell` and the `On` property of the `SwitchCell` are both `TwoWay`. If you only need to transfer data from the view to the data class, this mode can be `OneWayToSource`, but in general you might want to initialize the views from the data class. For example, you can instantiate the `PersonalInformation` instance in the XAML file like this:

```
<TableView.BindingContext>
    <local:PersonalInformation Name="Naomi Name"
                               EmailAddress="naomi@xamarin.com"
                               PhoneNumber="555-1212"
```

```
                                        Age="29"
                                        IsProgrammer="True" />
</TableView.BindingContext>
```

The cells will then be initialized with that information when the program starts up.

Both `EntryCell` and `SwitchCell` fire events if you prefer obtaining information through event handling rather than data binding.

The code-behind file simply processes the `Clicked` event of the **Submit** button by creating a text string with the information from the `PersonalInformation` instance and displaying it with the `Label`:

```
public partial class EntryFormPage : ContentPage
{
    public EntryFormPage()
    {
        InitializeComponent();
    }

    void OnSubmitButtonClicked(object sender, EventArgs args)
    {
        PersonalInformation personalInfo = (PersonalInformation)tableView.BindingContext;

        summaryLabel.Text = String.Format(
            "{0} is {1} years old, and has an email address " +
            "of {2}, and a phone number of {3}, and is {4}" +
            "a programmer.",
            personalInfo.Name, personalInfo.Age,
            personalInfo.EmailAddress, personalInfo.PhoneNumber,
            personalInfo.IsProgrammer ? "" : "not ");
    }
}
```

Custom cells

Of course, few people are entirely happy with the first version of an application, and perhaps that is true for the simple **EntryForm** program. Perhaps the revised design requirements eliminate the integer `Age` property from `PersonalInformation` and substitute a text `AgeRange` property with some fixed ranges. Two more properties are added to the class that pertain only to programmers: These are properties of type `string` that indicate the programmer's preferred computer language and platform, choosable from lists of languages and platforms.

Here's the revised ViewModel class, now called `ProgrammerInformation`:

```
class ProgrammerInformation : ViewModelBase
{
    string name, emailAddress, phoneNumber, ageRange;
    bool isProgrammer;
    string language, platform;
```

```
    public string Name
    {
        set { SetProperty(ref name, value); }
        get { return name; }
    }

    public string EmailAddress
    {
        set { SetProperty(ref emailAddress, value); }
        get { return emailAddress; }
    }

    public string PhoneNumber
    {
        set { SetProperty(ref phoneNumber, value); }
        get { return phoneNumber; }
    }

    public string AgeRange
    {
        set { SetProperty(ref ageRange, value); }
        get { return ageRange; }
    }

    public bool IsProgrammer
    {
        set { SetProperty(ref isProgrammer, value); }
        get { return isProgrammer; }
    }

    public string Language
    {
        set { SetProperty(ref language, value); }
        get { return language; }
    }

    public string Platform
    {
        set { SetProperty(ref platform, value); }
        get { return platform; }
    }
}
```

The AgeRange, Language, and Platform properties seem ideally suited for Picker, but using a Picker inside a TableView requires that the Picker be part of a ViewCell. How do we do this?

When working with a ListView, the simplest way to create a custom cell involves defining a visual tree in a ViewCell within a DataTemplate right in XAML. This approach makes sense because the visual tree that you define is probably tailored specifically to the items in the ListView and is probably not going to be reused somewhere else.

You can use that same technique with a TableView, but with a TableView it's more likely that you'll be reusing particular types of interactive cells. For example, the ProgrammerInformation class has three properties that are suitable for `Picker`. This implies that it makes more sense to create a custom `PickerCell` class that you can use here and elsewhere.

The **Xamarin.FormsBook.Toolkit** library contains a `PickerCell` class that derives from `ViewCell` and is basically a wrapper around a `Picker` view. The class consists of a XAML file and a code-behind file. The code-behind file defines three properties backed by bindable properties: `Label` (which identifies the cell just like the `Label` property in `EntryCell`), `Title` (which corresponds to the `Title` property of `Picker`), and `SelectedValue`, which is the actual string selected in the `Picker`. In addition, a get-only `Items` property exposes the `Items` collection of the `Picker`:

```
namespace Xamarin.FormsBook.Toolkit
{
    [ContentProperty("Items")]
    public partial class PickerCell : ViewCell
    {
        public static readonly BindableProperty LabelProperty =
            BindableProperty.Create(
                "Label", typeof(string), typeof(PickerCell), default(string));

        public static readonly BindableProperty TitleProperty =
            BindableProperty.Create(
                "Title", typeof(string), typeof(PickerCell), default(string));

        public static readonly BindableProperty SelectedValueProperty =
            BindableProperty.Create(
                "SelectedValue", typeof(string), typeof(PickerCell), null,
                BindingMode.TwoWay,
                propertyChanged: (sender, oldValue, newValue) =>
                    {
                        PickerCell pickerCell = (PickerCell)sender;

                        if (String.IsNullOrEmpty(newValue))
                        {
                            pickerCell.picker.SelectedIndex = -1;
                        }
                        else
                        {
                            pickerCell.picker.SelectedIndex =
                                    pickerCell.Items.IndexOf(newValue);
                        }
                    });

        public PickerCell()
        {
            InitializeComponent();
        }

        public string Label
        {
            set { SetValue(LabelProperty, value); }
            get { return (string)GetValue(LabelProperty); }
        }
```

```
        public string Title
        {
            get { return (string)GetValue(TitleProperty); }
            set { SetValue(TitleProperty, value); }
        }

        public string SelectedValue
        {
            get { return (string)GetValue(SelectedValueProperty); }
            set { SetValue(SelectedValueProperty, value); }
        }

        // Items property.
        public IList<string> Items
        {
            get { return picker.Items; }
        }

        void OnPickerSelectedIndexChanged(object sender, EventArgs args)
        {
            if (picker.SelectedIndex == -1)
            {
                SelectedValue = null;
            }
            else
            {
                SelectedValue = Items[picker.SelectedIndex];
            }
        }
    }
}
```

The XAML file defines the visual tree of `PickerCell`, which simply consists of an identifying `Label` and the `Picker` itself. Notice that the root element of the XAML file is `ViewCell`, which is the class that `PickerCell` derives from:

```xml
<ViewCell xmlns="http://xamarin.com/schemas/2014/forms"
          xmlns:x="http://schemas.microsoft.com/winfx/2009/xaml"
          x:Class="Xamarin.FormsBook.Toolkit.PickerCell"
          x:Name="cell">
    <ViewCell.View>
        <StackLayout Orientation="Horizontal"
                     BindingContext="{x:Reference cell}"
                     Padding="16, 0">

            <Label Text="{Binding Label}"
                   VerticalOptions="Center" />

            <Picker x:Name="picker"
                    Title="{Binding Title}"
                    VerticalOptions="Center"
                    HorizontalOptions="FillAndExpand"
                    SelectedIndexChanged="OnPickerSelectedIndexChanged" />
```

```
    </StackLayout>
  </ViewCell.View>
</ViewCell>
```

The `Padding` value set on the `StackLayout` was chosen empirically to be visually consistent with the Xamarin.Forms `EntryCell`.

Normally the `ViewCell.View` property element tags wouldn't be required in this XAML file because `View` is the content property of `ViewCell`. However, the code-behind file defines the content property of `PickerCell` to be the `Items` collection, which means that the content property is no longer `View` and the `ViewCell.View` tags are necessary.

The root element of the XAML file has an `x:Name` attribute that gives the object a name of "cell," and the `StackLayout` sets its `BindingContext` to that object, which means that the `BindingContext` for the children of the `StackLayout` is the `PickerCell` instance itself. This allows the `Label` and `Picker` to contain bindings to the `Label` and `Title` properties defined by `PickerCell` in the code-behind file.

The `Picker` fires a `SelectedIndexChanged` event that is handled in the code-behind file so that the code-behind file can convert the `SelectedIndex` of the `Picker` to a `SelectedValue` of the `PickerCell`.

This is not the only way to create a custom `PickerCell` class. You can also create it by defining individual `PickerCellRenderer` classes for each platform.

The `TableView` in the **ConditionalCells** program uses this `PickerCell` for three of the properties in the `ProgrammerInformation` class and initializes each `PickerCell` with a collection of strings:

```
<ContentPage xmlns="http://xamarin.com/schemas/2014/forms"
             xmlns:x="http://schemas.microsoft.com/winfx/2009/xaml"
             xmlns:local="clr-namespace:ConditionalCells"
             xmlns:toolkit=
                 "clr-namespace:Xamarin.FormsBook.Toolkit;assembly=Xamarin.FormsBook.Toolkit"
             x:Class="ConditionalCells.ConditionalCellsPage">
    <ContentPage.Padding>
        <OnPlatform x:TypeArguments="Thickness"
                    iOS="0, 20, 0, 0" />
    </ContentPage.Padding>

    <StackLayout>
        <TableView Intent="Form">

            <TableView.BindingContext>
                <local:ProgrammerInformation />
            </TableView.BindingContext>

            <TableRoot Title="Data Form">
                <TableSection Title="Personal Information">
                    <EntryCell Label="Name:"
                               Text="{Binding Name}"
```

```
                                     Placeholder="Enter name"
                                     Keyboard="Text" />

                     <EntryCell Label="Email:"
                                Text="{Binding EmailAddress}"
                                Placeholder="Enter email address"
                                Keyboard="Email" />

                     <EntryCell Label="Phone:"
                                Text="{Binding PhoneNumber}"
                                Placeholder="Enter phone number"
                                Keyboard="Telephone" />

                     <toolkit:PickerCell Label="Age Range:"
                                         Title="Age Range"
                                         SelectedValue="{Binding AgeRange}">
                         <x:String>10 - 19</x:String>
                         <x:String>20 - 29</x:String>
                         <x:String>30 - 39</x:String>
                         <x:String>40 - 49</x:String>
                         <x:String>50 - 59</x:String>
                         <x:String>60 - 99</x:String>
                     </toolkit:PickerCell>

                     <SwitchCell Text="Are you a programmer?"
                                 On="{Binding IsProgrammer}" />

                     <toolkit:PickerCell Label="Language:"
                                         Title="Language"
                                         IsEnabled="{Binding IsProgrammer}"
                                         SelectedValue="{Binding Language}">
                         <x:String>C</x:String>
                         <x:String>C++</x:String>
                         <x:String>C#</x:String>
                         <x:String>Objective C</x:String>
                         <x:String>Java</x:String>
                         <x:String>Other</x:String>
                     </toolkit:PickerCell>

                     <toolkit:PickerCell Label="Platform:"
                                         Title="Platform"
                                         IsEnabled="{Binding IsProgrammer}"
                                         SelectedValue="{Binding Platform}">
                         <x:String>iPhone</x:String>
                         <x:String>Android</x:String>
                         <x:String>Windows Phone</x:String>
                         <x:String>Other</x:String>
                     </toolkit:PickerCell>
                 </TableSection>
             </TableRoot>
         </TableView>
     </StackLayout>
</ContentPage>
```

Notice how the `IsEnabled` properties of the `PickerCell` for both the `Platform` and `Language` properties are bound to the `IsProgrammer` property, which means that these cells should be disabled unless the `SwitchCell` is flipped on and the `IsProgrammer` property is `true`. That's why this program is called **ConditionalCells**.

However, it doesn't seem to work, as this screenshot verifies:

Even though the `IsProgrammer` switch is off, and the `IsEnabled` property of each of the last two `PickerCell` elements is set to `false`, those elements still respond and allow selecting a value. Moreover, the `PickerCell` doesn't look or work very well on the Windows 10 Mobile platform.

So let's try another approach.

Conditional sections

A `TableView` can have multiple sections, and you might want a section to be entirely invisible if it doesn't currently apply. In the previous example, a second section, titled "Programmer Information," might contain the two `PickerCell` elements for the `Language` and `Platform` properties. To make the section visible or hidden, the section can be added to or removed from the `TableRoot` based on the setting of the `IsProgrammer` property. (Recall that the internal collections in `TableView` are of type `ObservableCollection`, so the `TableView` should respond to items added or removed dynamically from these collections.) Unfortunately, this can't be handled entirely in XAML, but the code support is fairly easy.

Here is the XAML file in the **ConditionalSection** program. It is the same as the XAML file in the previous program except that the `BindingContext` is no longer set on the `TableView` (that happens in the code-behind file) and the last two `PickerCell` elements have been moved into a second section with the heading "Programmer Information":

```xml
<ContentPage xmlns="http://xamarin.com/schemas/2014/forms"
             xmlns:x="http://schemas.microsoft.com/winfx/2009/xaml"
             xmlns:local="clr-namespace:ConditionalSection"
             xmlns:toolkit=
                 "clr-namespace:Xamarin.FormsBook.Toolkit;assembly=Xamarin.FormsBook.Toolkit"
             x:Class="ConditionalSection.ConditionalSectionPage">
    <ContentPage.Padding>
        <OnPlatform x:TypeArguments="Thickness"
                    iOS="0, 20, 0, 0" />
    </ContentPage.Padding>

    <StackLayout>
        <TableView x:Name="tableView"
                   Intent="Form">
            <TableRoot Title="Data Form">
                <TableSection Title="Personal Information">
                    <EntryCell Label="Name:"
                               Text="{Binding Name}"
                               Placeholder="Enter name"
                               Keyboard="Text" />

                    <EntryCell Label="Email:"
                               Text="{Binding EmailAddress}"
                               Placeholder="Enter email address"
                               Keyboard="Email" />

                    <EntryCell Label="Phone:"
                               Text="{Binding PhoneNumber}"
                               Placeholder="Enter phone number"
                               Keyboard="Telephone" />

                    <toolkit:PickerCell Label="Age Range:"
                                        Title="Age Range"
                                        SelectedValue="{Binding AgeRange}">
                        <x:String>10 - 19</x:String>
                        <x:String>20 - 29</x:String>
                        <x:String>30 - 39</x:String>
                        <x:String>40 - 49</x:String>
                        <x:String>50 - 59</x:String>
                        <x:String>60 - 99</x:String>
                    </toolkit:PickerCell>

                    <SwitchCell x:Name="isProgrammerSwitch"
                                Text="Are you a programmer?"
                                On="{Binding IsProgrammer}" />

                </TableSection>

                <TableSection x:Name="programmerInfoSection"
                              Title="Programmer Information">
                    <toolkit:PickerCell Label="Language:"
```

```
                                    Title="Language"
                                    SelectedValue="{Binding Language}">
                <x:String>C</x:String>
                <x:String>C++</x:String>
                <x:String>C#</x:String>
                <x:String>Objective C</x:String>
                <x:String>Java</x:String>
                <x:String>Other</x:String>
            </toolkit:PickerCell>

            <toolkit:PickerCell Label="Platform:"
                                Title="Platform"
                                SelectedValue="{Binding Platform}">
                <x:String>iPhone</x:String>
                <x:String>Android</x:String>
                <x:String>Windows Phone</x:String>
                <x:String>Other</x:String>
            </toolkit:PickerCell>
          </TableSection>
        </TableRoot>
      </TableView>
    </StackLayout>
</ContentPage>
```

The constructor in the code-behind file handles the rest. It creates the `ProgrammerInformation` object to set to the `BindingContext` of the `TableView` and then removes the second `TableSection` from the `TableRoot`. The page constructor then sets a handler for the `PropertyChanged` event of `ProgrammerInformation` and waits for changes to the `IsProgrammer` property:

```csharp
public partial class ConditionalSectionPage : ContentPage
{
    public ConditionalSectionPage()
    {
        InitializeComponent();

        // Set BindingContext of TableView.
        ProgrammerInformation programmerInfo = new ProgrammerInformation();
        tableView.BindingContext = programmerInfo;

        // Remove programmer-information section!
        tableView.Root.Remove(programmerInfoSection);

        // Watch for changes in IsProgrammer property in ProgrammerInformation.
        programmerInfo.PropertyChanged += (sender, args) =>
        {
            if (args.PropertyName == "IsProgrammer")
            {
                if (programmerInfo.IsProgrammer &&
                    tableView.Root.IndexOf(programmerInfoSection) == -1)
                {
                    tableView.Root.Add(programmerInfoSection);
                }
                if (!programmerInfo.IsProgrammer &&
```

```
                    tableView.Root.IndexOf(programmerInfoSection) != -1)
                {
                    tableView.Root.Remove(programmerInfoSection);
                }
            }
        };
    }
}
```

In theory, the `PropertyChanged` handler doesn't need to check if the `TableSection` is already part of the `TableRoot` collection before adding it, or check if it's not part of the collection before attempting to remove it, but the checks don't hurt.

Here's the program when it first starts up with only one section visible:

Toggling the `SwitchCell` on brings the two additional properties into view:

But not on the Windows 10 Mobile screen.

You don't need to have a single `BindingContext` for the whole `TableView`. Each `TableSection` can have its own `BindingContext`, which means that you can divide your `ViewModels` to coordinate more closely with the `TableView` layout.

A TableView menu

Besides displaying data or serving as a form or settings dialog, a `TableView` can also be a menu. Functionally, a menu is a collection of buttons, although they might not look like traditional buttons. Each menu item is a command that triggers a program operation.

This is why `TextCell` and `ImageCell` have `Command` and `CommandParameter` properties. These cells can trigger commands defined in a ViewModel, or simply some other property of type `ICommand`.

The XAML file in the **MenuCommands** program binds the `Command` properties of four `TextCell` elements with a property named `MoveCommand`, and passes to that `MoveCommand` arguments named "left", "up", "right", and "down":

```
<ContentPage xmlns="http://xamarin.com/schemas/2014/forms"
             xmlns:x="http://schemas.microsoft.com/winfx/2009/xaml"
             x:Class="MenuCommands.MenuCommandsPage"
             x:Name="page">

    <ContentPage.Padding>
        <OnPlatform x:TypeArguments="Thickness"
                    iOS="0, 20, 0, 0" />
    </ContentPage.Padding>
```

```
<StackLayout>
    <TableView Intent="Menu"
               VerticalOptions="Fill"
               BindingContext="{x:Reference page}">
        <TableRoot>
            <TableSection Title="Move the Box">
                <TextCell Text="Left"
                          Command="{Binding MoveCommand}"
                          CommandParameter="left" />

                <TextCell Text="Up"
                          Command="{Binding MoveCommand}"
                          CommandParameter="up" />

                <TextCell Text="Right"
                          Command="{Binding MoveCommand}"
                          CommandParameter="right" />

                <TextCell Text="Down"
                          Command="{Binding MoveCommand}"
                          CommandParameter="down" />
            </TableSection>
        </TableRoot>
    </TableView>

    <AbsoluteLayout BackgroundColor="Maroon"
                    VerticalOptions="FillAndExpand">
        <BoxView x:Name="boxView"
                 Color="Blue"
                 AbsoluteLayout.LayoutFlags="All"
                 AbsoluteLayout.LayoutBounds="0.5, 0.5, 0.2, 0.2" />
    </AbsoluteLayout>
</StackLayout>
</ContentPage>
```

But where is that `MoveCommand` property? If you look at the `BindingContext` of the `TableView`, you'll see that it references the root element of the XAML file, which means that `MoveCommand` property can probably be found as a property in the code-behind file.

And there it is:

```
public partial class MenuCommandsPage : ContentPage
{
    int xOffset = 0;      // ranges from -2 to 2
    int yOffset = 0;      // ranges from -2 to 2

    public MenuCommandsPage()
    {
        // Initialize ICommand property before parsing XAML.
        MoveCommand = new Command<string>(ExecuteMove, CanExecuteMove);

        InitializeComponent();
    }
```

```
public ICommand MoveCommand { private set; get; }

void ExecuteMove(string direction)
{
    switch (direction)
    {
        case "left": xOffset--; break;
        case "right": xOffset++; break;
        case "up": yOffset--; break;
        case "down": yOffset++; break;
    }

    ((Command)MoveCommand).ChangeCanExecute();

    AbsoluteLayout.SetLayoutBounds(boxView,
        new Rectangle((xOffset + 2) / 4.0,
                      (yOffset + 2) / 4.0, 0.2, 0.2));
}

bool CanExecuteMove(string direction)
{
    switch (direction)
    {
        case "left": return xOffset > -2;
        case "right": return xOffset < 2;
        case "up": return yOffset > -2;
        case "down": return yOffset < 2;
    }
    return false;
}
}
```

The `Execute` method manipulates the layout bounds of a `BoxView` in the XAML file so that it moves around the `AbsoluteLayout`. The `CanExecute` method disables an operation if the `BoxView` has been moved to one of the edges.

Only on iOS does the disabled `TextCell` actually appear with a typical gray coloring, but on both the iOS and Android platforms the `TextCell` is no longer functional if the `CanExecute` method returns `false`:

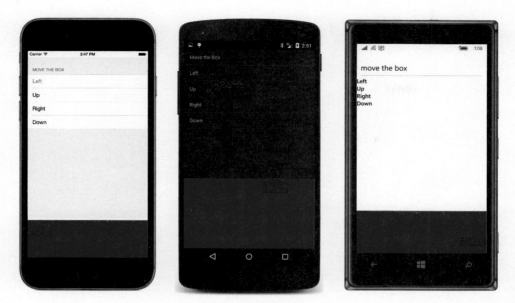

You can also use `TableView` as a menu for page navigation or working with master/detail pages, and for these particular applications you might wonder whether a `ListView` or `TableView` is the right tool for the job. Generally it's `ListView` if you have a collection of items that should all be displayed in the same way, or `TableView` for fewer items that might require individual attention.

What is certain is that you'll definitely see more examples in the chapters ahead.

... are more for page navigation or working with associated pages, and for these particular applications you might wonder whether a ... view ... (is the right tool for the job). Generally a UI... if you will have a collection of items that could all be displayed in the same way ... where navigation in the screen indicates an attempt ...

What is relevant is that you'll probably see more examples in the chapters also.

Chapter 20
Async and file I/O

Graphical user interfaces have a little peculiarity that has far-reaching consequences: User input to an application must be processed sequentially. Regardless of whether user-input events come from a keyboard, a mouse, or touch, each event must be completely processed by an application—either directly or through user-interface objects such as buttons or sliders—before the application obtains the next user-input event from the operating system.

The rationale behind this restriction becomes clear after a little reflection and perhaps an example: Suppose a page contains two buttons, and the user quickly taps one and then the other. Might it be possible for the two buttons to process those two taps concurrently in two separate threads of execution? No, that would not work. It could be that the first button changes the meaning of the second button, perhaps disabling it entirely. For this reason, the first button must be allowed to completely finish processing its tap before the second button begins processing its own tap.

The consequences of this restriction are severe: All user input to a particular application must be processed in a single thread of execution. Moreover, user-interface objects are generally not thread-safe. They cannot be modified from a secondary thread of execution. All code connected with an application's user interface is therefore restricted to a single thread. This thread is known as the *main thread* or the *user-interface thread* or the *UI thread*.

As we users have become more accustomed to graphical user interfaces over the decades, we've become increasingly intolerant of even the slightest lapse in responsiveness. As application programmers, we therefore try our best to keep the user interface responsive to achieve maximum user satisfaction. This means that anything running on the UI thread must perform its processing as quickly as possible and return control back to the operating system. If an event handler running in the UI thread gets bogged down in a long processing job, the entire user interface will seem to freeze and certainly annoy the user.

For this reason, any lengthy jobs that an application must perform should be relegated to secondary threads of execution, often called *worker threads*. These worker threads are said to run "in the background" and do not interfere with the responsiveness of the UI thread.

You've already seen some examples in this book. Several sample programs—the **ImageBrowser** and **BitmapStreams** programs in Chapter 13, "Bitmaps," and the **SchoolOfFineArt** library and **RssFeed** program in Chapter 19, "Collection views"—use the `WebRequest` class to download files over the Internet. A call to the `BeginGetResponse` method of `WebRequest` starts a worker thread that accesses the web resource asynchronously. The `WebRequest` call returns quickly, and the program can handle other user input while the file is being downloaded. An argument to `BeginGetResponse` is a callback method that is invoked when the background process completes. Within this callback method the program calls `EndGetResponse` to get access to the downloaded data.

But the callback method passed to `BeginGetResponse` has a little problem. The callback method runs in the same worker thread that downloads the file, and in the general case, you can't access user-interface objects from anything other than the UI thread. Usually, this means that the callback method must access the UI thread. Each of the three platforms supported by Xamarin.Forms has its own native method for running code from a secondary thread on the UI thread, but in Xamarin.Forms these are all available through the `Device.BeginInvokeOnMainThread` method. (As you'll recall, however, there are some exceptions generally related to ViewModels: Although a secondary thread can't access a user-interface object directly, the secondary thread can set a property that is bound to a user-interface object through a data binding.)

In recent years, asynchronous processing has become more ubiquitous at the same time that it's become easier for programmers. This is an ongoing trend: The future of computing will undoubtedly involve a lot more asynchronous computing and parallel processing, particularly with the increasing use of multicore processor chips. Developers will need good operating-system support and language tools to work with asynchronous operations, and fortunately .NET and C# have been in the forefront of this support.

This chapter will explore some of the basics of working with asynchronous processing in Xamarin.Forms applications, including using the .NET `Task` class to help you define and work with asynchronous methods. The customary hassle of dealing with callback functions has been alleviated greatly with two keywords introduced in C# 5.0: `async` and `await`. The `await` operator has revolutionized asynchronous programming by simplifying the syntax of asynchronous calls, by clarifying program flow surrounding asynchronous calls, by easing the access of user-interface objects, by simplifying the handling of exceptions raised by worker threads, and by unifying the handling of these exceptions and cancellations of background jobs.

This chapter primarily demonstrates how to work with asynchronous processing to perform file input and output, and how to create your own worker threads for performing lengthy jobs.

But Xamarin.Forms itself contains several asynchronous methods.

From callbacks to await

The `Page` class defines three methods that let you display a visual object sometimes called an *alert* or a *message box*. Such a box pops up on the screen with some information or a question for the user. The alert box is modal, meaning that the rest of the application is unavailable while the alert is displayed. The user must dismiss it with the press of a button before returning to interact with the application.

Two of these three methods of the `Page` class are named `DisplayAlert`. The first simply displays some text with a single button to dismiss the box, while the second contains two buttons for yes or no responses. The `DisplayActionSheet` method is similar but displays any number of buttons.

In iOS, Android, and the Windows Runtime, these methods are implemented with platform-specific objects that use events or callback methods to inform the application that the alert box has been dismissed and what button the user pressed to dismiss it. However, Xamarin.Forms has wrapped these objects with an asynchronous interface.

These three methods of the `Page` class are defined like this:

```
Task DisplayAlert (string title, string message, string cancel)

Task<bool> DisplayAlert (string title, string message, string accept, string cancel)

Task<string> DisplayActionSheet (string title, string cancel, string destruction,
                                 params string[] buttons)
```

They all return `Task` objects. The `Task` and `Task<T>` classes are defined in the `System.Threading.Tasks` namespace and they form the core of the Task-based Asynchronous Pattern, known as TAP. TAP is the recommended approach to handling asynchronous operations in .NET. The Task Parallel Library (TPL) builds on TAP.

In contrast, the `BeginGetResponse` and `EndGetResponse` methods of `WebRequest` represent an older approach to asynchronous operations involving `IAsyncResult`. This older approach is called the Asynchronous Programming Model or APM. You might also encounter code that uses the Event-based Asynchronous Model (EAP) to return information from asynchronous jobs through events.

You've already seen the simplest form of `DisplayAlert` in the **SetTimer** program in Chapter 15, "The interactive interface." **SetTimer** used an alert to indicate when a timer elapsed. The program didn't seem to care that `DisplayAlert` returned a `Task` object because the alert box was used strictly for notification purposes. It was not necessary to obtain a response from the user. However, the methods that return `Task<bool>` and `Task<string>` need to convey actual information back to the application indicating which button the user pressed to dismiss the alert.

A return value of `Task<T>` is sometimes referred to as a "promise." The actual value or object isn't available just yet, but it will be available in the future if nothing goes awry.

You can work with a `Task<T>` object in a few different ways. These approaches are fundamentally equivalent, but the C# syntax is quite different.

An alert with callbacks

The intended use of the `DisplayAlert` method that returns a `Task<bool>` is to ask the user a question with a yes or no answer. Obviously the answer isn't available until the user presses a button and the alert is dismissed, at which time a `true` value means Yes and `false` value means No.

One way to work with a `Task<T>` object is with callback methods. The **AlertCallbacks** program demonstrates that approach. It has a XAML file with a `Button` to invoke an alert and a `Label` for the program to display some information:

```
<ContentPage xmlns="http://xamarin.com/schemas/2014/forms"
             xmlns:x="http://schemas.microsoft.com/winfx/2009/xaml"
             x:Class="AlertCallbacks.AlertCallbacksPage">
```

```
        <StackLayout>
            <Button Text="Invoke Alert"
                    FontSize="Large"
                    HorizontalOptions="Center"
                    VerticalOptions="CenterAndExpand"
                    Clicked="OnButtonClicked" />

            <Label x:Name="label"
                   Text="Tap button to invoke alert"
                   FontSize="Large"
                   HorizontalTextAlignment="Center"
                   VerticalOptions="CenterAndExpand" />
        </StackLayout>
</ContentPage>
```

Here's the code-behind file with the `Clicked` event handler and two callback methods:

```
public partial class AlertCallbacksPage : ContentPage
{
    bool result;

    public AlertCallbacksPage()
    {
        InitializeComponent();
    }

    void OnButtonClicked(object sender, EventArgs args)
    {
        Task<bool> task = DisplayAlert("Simple Alert", "Decide on an option",
                                       "yes or ok", "no or cancel");
        task.ContinueWith(AlertDismissedCallback);
        label.Text = "Alert is currently displayed";
    }

    void AlertDismissedCallback(Task<bool> task)
    {
        result = task.Result;
        Device.BeginInvokeOnMainThread(DisplayResultCallback);
    }

    void DisplayResultCallback()
    {
        label.Text = String.Format("Alert {0} button was pressed",
                                   result ? "OK" : "Cancel");
    }
}
```

The `Clicked` handler calls `DisplayAlert` with arguments indicating a title, a question or state-ment, and the text for the two buttons. Generally, these two buttons are labeled "yes" and "no," or "ok" and "cancel," but you can put anything you want in those buttons as this program demonstrates.

If `DisplayAlert` were designed to be a synchronous method, the method would return a `bool` indicating which button the user pressed to dismiss the alert. However, `DisplayAlert` would not be able to return that value until the alert were dismissed, which means that the application would be stuck in the `DisplayAlert` call during the entire time the alert is displayed. Depending on how the operating system handles user-input events, being stuck in the `DisplayAlert` call might not actually block other event handling by the user-interface thread during this time, but it might be a little strange for the UI thread to be seemingly in the `DisplayAlert` call while also handling other events.

Instead of returning a `bool` when the alert is dismissed, `DisplayAlert` returns a `Task<bool>` object that promises a `bool` result sometime in the future. To obtain that value, the `OnButtonClicked` handler in the **AlertCallbacks** program calls the `ContinueWith` method defined by `Task`. This method allows the program to specify a method that is called when the alert is dismissed. The `Clicked` handler concludes by setting some text to the `Label`, and then returns control back to the operating system.

The alert is then displayed:

Of course, the alert essentially disables the user interface of the application, but the application could still be doing some work while the alert is displayed. For example, the program could be using a timer, and that timer would continue to run. You can prove this to yourself by adding the following code to the constructor of the **AlertCallbacks** code-behind file:

```
Device.StartTimer(TimeSpan.FromSeconds(1), () =>
    {
        label.Text = DateTime.Now.ToString();
        return true;
    });
```

When the user dismisses the alert by tapping one of the buttons, the `AlertDismissedCallback` method is called:

```
void AlertDismissedCallback(Task<bool> task)
{
    result = task.Result;
    Device.BeginInvokeOnMainThread(DisplayResultCallback);
}
```

The argument is the same `Task` object originally returned from the `DisplayAlert` method. But now the `Result` property of the `Task` object has been set to `true` or `false` depending on what button the user pressed to dismiss the alert. The program wants to display that value, but unfortunately it cannot because this `AlertDismissedCallback` method is running in a secondary thread that Xamarin.Forms has created. This thread is not allowed to access any user-interface objects of the program. For that reason, the `AlertDismissedCallback` method saves the `bool` result in a field and calls `Device-.BeginInvokeOnMainThread` with a second callback method. That callback method runs in the UI thread:

```
void DisplayResultCallback()
{
    label.Text = String.Format("Alert {0} button was pressed",
                               result ? "OK" : "Cancel");
}
```

The `Label` then displays that text:

The **AlertCallbacks** program demonstrates one traditional way to handle asynchronous methods, but it has a distinct drawback: There are simply too many callbacks, and in one case, data must be passed from one callback to another by using a field.

An alert with lambdas

An obvious approach to simplify callbacks is with lambda functions. This is demonstrated with the **AlertLambdas** program. The XAML file is the same as in the **AlertCallbacks** method, but everything that happens in response to the button click is now inside that `Clicked` handler:

```
public partial class AlertLambdasPage : ContentPage
{
    public AlertLambdasPage()
    {
        InitializeComponent();
    }

    void OnButtonClicked(object sender, EventArgs args)
    {
        Task<bool> task = DisplayAlert("Simple Alert", "Decide on an option",
                                       "yes or ok", "no or cancel");
        task.ContinueWith((Task<bool> taskResult) =>
            {
                Device.BeginInvokeOnMainThread(() =>
                    {
                        label.Text = String.Format("Alert {0} button was pressed",
                                            taskResult.Result ? "OK" : "Cancel");
                    });
            });
        label.Text = "Alert is currently displayed";
    }
}
```

There is really no difference between this program and the previous one except that the callback methods have no name. They are anonymous. But sometimes lambda functions have the tendency to obscure program flow, and that is certainly the case here. The `Text` property of the `Label` is set to the text "Alert is currently displayed" right after the `ContinueWith` method is called and before the callback passed to `ContinueWith` executes, but that statement appears at the bottom of the method.

There should be a better way to denote what you want to happen without distorting program flow. That better way is called `await`.

An alert with await

The **AlertAwait** program has the same XAML file as **AlertCallbacks** and **AlertLambdas**, but the `OnButtonClicked` method is considerably simplified:

```
public partial class AlertAwaitPage : ContentPage
{
    public AlertAwaitPage()
    {
        InitializeComponent();
    }

    async void OnButtonClicked(object sender, EventArgs args)
    {
```

```
            Task<bool> task = DisplayAlert("Simple Alert", "Decide on an option",
                                           "yes or ok", "no or cancel");
            label.Text = "Alert is currently displayed";
            bool result = await task;
            label.Text = String.Format("Alert {0} button was pressed",
                                       result ? "OK" : "Cancel");
        }
    }
```

The key statement is this one:

```
bool result = await task;
```

That `task` variable is the `Task<bool>` object returned from `DisplayAlert`, but the `await` keyword seems to magically extract the Boolean result without any callbacks or lambdas.

The first thing you should know is that `await` doesn't actually wait for the alert to be dismissed! Instead, the C# compiler has performed a lot of surgery on the `OnButtonClicked` method. The method has basically been turned into a state machine. Part of the method is executed when the button is clicked, and part of the method is executed later. When the flow of execution hits the `await` keyword, the remainder of the `OnButtonClicked` method is skipped over for the moment. The `OnButton-Clicked` method exits and returns control back to the operating system. From the perspective of the `Button`, the event handler has completed.

When the user dismisses the alert box, the remainder of the `OnButtonClicked` method resumes execution beginning with the assignment of the Boolean value to the `result` variable. In some circumstances, some optimizations can take place behind the scenes. For example, the flow of execution can just continue normally if the asynchronous operation completes immediately.

The `await` operator has another bonus: Notice that there's no use of `Device.BeginInvokeOn-MainThread`. When the user dismisses the alert, the `OnButtonClicked` method automatically resumes execution in the user-interface thread, which means that it can access the `Label`. (In some cases, you might want to continue running in the background thread for performance reasons. If so, you can use the `ConfigureAwait` method of `Task` to do that. You'll see an example later in this chapter.)

The `await` keyword essentially converts asynchronous code into something that appears to be normal sequential imperative code. Of course, behind the scenes, there is really not much difference between this program and the two previous programs. In all three cases, the `OnButtonClicked` handler returns control back to the operating system when it displays the alert, and resumes execution when the alert is dismissed.

Simply for illustrative purposes, the three programs display some text immediately after the `Dis-playAlert` method is called. If that isn't necessary, then the `DisplayAlert` call can be combined with the `await` operator to get rid of the explicit `Task<bool>` variable entirely:

```
bool result = await DisplayAlert("Simple Alert", "Decide on an option",
                                 "yes or ok", "no or cancel");
```

This is how `await` commonly appears in code. `DisplayAlert` returns `Task<bool>` but the `await` operator effectively extracts the `bool` result after the background task has completed.

Indeed, you can use `await` much like you can any other operator, and it can appear inside a more complex expression. For example, if you don't need the statement that displays the text after the `DisplayAlert` call, you can actually put both the `await` operator and `DisplayAlert` inside the final `String.Format` call:

```
async void OnButtonClicked(object sender, EventArgs args)
{
    label.Text = String.Format("Alert {0} button was pressed",
        await DisplayAlert("Simple Alert", "Decide on an option",
                           "yes or ok", "no or cancel") ? "OK" : "Cancel");
}
```

That might be a little difficult to read, but think of the combination of the `await` operator and the `DisplayAlert` method as a `bool` and the statement makes perfect sense.

You might have noticed that the `OnButtonClicked` method is marked with the `async` keyword. Any method in which you use `await` must be marked as `async`. However, the `async` keyword does not change the signature of the method. `OnButtonClicked` still qualifies as an event handler for the `Clicked` event.

But not every method can be an `async` method.

An alert with nothing

The simpler of the two `DisplayAlert` methods returns a `Task` object. It is intended to display some information to the user that doesn't require a response:

```
Task DisplayAlert (string title, string message, string cancel)
```

Generally, you'll want to use `await` with this simpler `DisplayAlert` method even though it doesn't return any information, and particularly if you need to perform some processing after it has been dismissed. The **NothingAlert** program has the same XAML file as the previous samples but displays this simpler alert box:

```
public partial class NothingAlertPage : ContentPage
{
    public NothingAlertPage()
    {
        InitializeComponent();
    }

    async void OnButtonClicked(object sender, EventArgs args)
    {
        label.Text = "Displaying alert box";
        await DisplayAlert("Simple Alert", "Click 'dismiss' to dismiss", "dismiss");
        label.Text = "Alert has been dismissed";
    }
}
```

Nothing appears to the left of the `await` operator because the return value of `DisplayAlert` is `Task` rather than `Task<T>` and no information is returned.

The first program in this book that used this simpler form of `DisplayAlert` was the **SetTimer** program in Chapter 15. Here's the timer callback method from that program (with the oddly named `@switch` variable so that it doesn't conflict with the `switch` keyword):

```
bool OnTimerTick()
{
    if (@switch.IsToggled && DateTime.Now >= triggerTime)
    {
        @switch.IsToggled = false;
        DisplayAlert("Timer Alert",
                     "The '" + entry.Text + "' timer has elapsed",
                     "OK");
    }
    return true;
}
```

The `DisplayAlert` call returns quickly, and the method continues to execute when the alert box is displayed. The `OnTimerTick` method then returns `true`, and a second later `OnTimerTick` is called again. Fortunately, the `Switch` is no longer toggled, so the program doesn't attempt to call `Display-Alert` a second time. When the alert is dismissed, the user can again interact with the user interface, but no additional code is executed on its return.

What if you wanted to execute a little code after the alert box was dismissed? Try to put an `await` operator in front of `DisplayAlert` and identify the method with the `async` keyword:

```
// Will not compile!
async bool OnTimerTick()
{
    if (@switch.IsToggled && DateTime.Now >= triggerTime)
    {
        @switch.IsToggled = false;
        await DisplayAlert("Timer Alert",
                           "The '" + entry.Text + "' timer has elapsed",
                           "OK");
        // Some code to execute after the alert box is dismissed.
    }
    return true;
}
```

But as the comment says, this code will not compile.

Why not?

When the C# compiler encounters the `await` keyword, it constructs code so that the `OnTimerTick` callback returns to its caller. The remainder of the method then resumes execution when the alert box is dismissed. However, the `Device.StartTimer` method that invokes this callback is expecting the timer callback to return a Boolean value to determine whether it should call the callback again, and the C# compiler cannot construct code that returns a Boolean value because it doesn't know what that

Boolean value should be!

For this reason, methods that contain `await` operators are restricted to return types of `void`, `Task`, or `Task<T>`.

Event handlers usually have `void` return types. This is why the `Clicked` handler of a `Button` can contain `await` operators and be flagged with the `async` keyword. But the timer callback method returns a `bool`, and to use `await` within this method, the return value of the `OnTimerTick` method must be `Task<bool>`:

```
// Method compiles but Device.StartTimer does not!
async Task<bool> OnTimerTick()
{
    if (@switch.IsToggled && DateTime.Now >= triggerTime)
    {
        @switch.IsToggled = false;
        await DisplayAlert("Timer Alert",
                           "The '" + entry.Text + "' timer has elapsed",
                           "OK");
    }
    return true;
}
```

This method now contains entirely legal compilable code. When a method is defined to return `Task<T>`, the body of the method returns an object of type `T` and the compiler does the rest.

However, because the method now returns a `Task<bool>` object, code that calls this method must use `await` with the method (or call `ContinueWith` on the `Task` object) to obtain the Boolean value when the method completes execution. That's a problem for the `Device.StartTimer` call, which is not expecting the callback method to be asynchronous; it's expecting the callback method to return `bool` rather than `Task<bool>`.

If you really did want to execute some code after the alert is dismissed in the **SetTimer** program, you should use `ContinueWith` for that code. The `await` operator is very useful, but it is not a panacea for every asynchronous programming problem.

The `await` operator can only be used in a method, and the method must have a return type of `void`, `Task`, or `Task<T>`. That's it. The `get` accessors of properties cannot use `await`, and they shouldn't be performing asynchronous operations anyway. Constructors cannot use `await` because constructors are not methods and have no return type. You cannot use `await` in the body of a `lock` statement. C# 5 also prohibits using `await` in the `catch` or `finally` blocks of a `try-catch-finally` statement, but C# 6 lifts that restriction.

These restrictions turn out to be most severe for constructors. A constructor should complete promptly because nothing can really be done with an instance of a class until the constructor finishes. Although a constructor can call an asynchronous method that returns `Task`, the constructor can't use `await` with that call. The constructor finishes while the asynchronous method is still processing. (You'll see some examples in this chapter and the next.)

A constructor cannot call an asynchronous method that returns a value required by the constructor to complete. If a constructor needs to obtain an object from an asynchronous operation, it can use `ContinueWith`, in which case the constructor will finish before the object from the asynchronous operation is available. But that's unavoidable.

Saving program settings asynchronously

As you discovered in Chapter 6, "Button clicks," you can save program settings in a dictionary named `Properties` maintained by the `Application` class. Anything you put in the `Properties` dictionary is saved when the program goes into a sleep state and is restored when the program resumes or starts up again. Sometimes it's convenient to save settings in this dictionary as they are changed, and sometimes it's convenient to wait until the `OnSleep` method is called in your `App` class.

There's also another option: The `Application` class has a method named `SavePropertiesAsync` that lets your program take a more proactive role in saving program settings. This allows a program to save program settings whenever it wants to. If the program later crashes or is terminated through the Visual Studio or Xamarin Studio debugger, the settings are saved.

In conformance with recommended practice, the `Async` suffix on the `SavePropertiesAsync` method name identifies this as an asynchronous method. It returns quickly with a `Task` object and saves the settings in a secondary thread of execution.

A program named **SaveProgramSettings** demonstrates this technique. The XAML file contains four `Switch` views and four `Label` views that treat the `Switch` views as digits of a binary number:

```
<ContentPage xmlns="http://xamarin.com/schemas/2014/forms"
             xmlns:x="http://schemas.microsoft.com/winfx/2009/xaml"
             xmlns:toolkit=
                 "clr-namespace:Xamarin.FormsBook.Toolkit;assembly=Xamarin.FormsBook.Toolkit"
             x:Class="SaveProgramSettings.SaveProgramSettingsPage">

    <ContentPage.Resources>
        <ResourceDictionary>
            <toolkit:BoolToStringConverter x:Key="boolToString"
                                           FalseText="Zero"
                                           TrueText="One" />
            <Style TargetType="Label">
                <Setter Property="FontSize" Value="Large" />
                <Setter Property="HorizontalTextAlignment" Value="Center" />
            </Style>

            <Style TargetType="Switch">
                <Setter Property="HorizontalOptions" Value="Center" />
            </Style>
        </ResourceDictionary>
    </ContentPage.Resources>

    <StackLayout>
        <Grid VerticalOptions="CenterAndExpand">
            <Label Text="{Binding Source={x:Reference s3},
```

```
                                    Path=IsToggled,
                                    Converter={StaticResource boolToString}"
                    Grid.Column="0" />

            <Label Text="{Binding Source={x:Reference s2},
                                    Path=IsToggled,
                                    Converter={StaticResource boolToString}"
                    Grid.Column="1" />

            <Label Text="{Binding Source={x:Reference s1},
                                    Path=IsToggled,
                                    Converter={StaticResource boolToString}"
                    Grid.Column="2" />

            <Label Text="{Binding Source={x:Reference s0},
                                    Path=IsToggled,
                                    Converter={StaticResource boolToString}"
                    Grid.Column="3" />
        </Grid>

        <Grid x:Name="switchGrid"
              VerticalOptions="CenterAndExpand">
            <Switch x:Name="s3" Grid.Column="0"
                    Toggled="OnSwitchToggled" />

            <Switch x:Name="s2" Grid.Column="1"
                    Toggled="OnSwitchToggled" />

            <Switch x:Name="s1" Grid.Column="2"
                    Toggled="OnSwitchToggled" />

            <Switch x:Name="s0" Grid.Column="3"
                    Toggled="OnSwitchToggled" />
        </Grid>
    </StackLayout>
</ContentPage>
```

The data bindings on the Label elements allow them to track the values of the Switch views:

The saving and retrieving of program settings is handled in the code-behind file. Notice the handler assigned to the `Toggled` events of the `Switch` elements. The sole purpose of that handler is to store the settings in the `Properties` dictionary—and to save the `Properties` dictionary itself by using `SavePropertiesAsync`—whenever one of the `Switch` elements changes state. The dictionary key is the index of the `Switch` within the `Children` collection of the `Grid`:

```
public partial class SaveProgramSettingsPage : ContentPage
{
    bool isInitialized = false;

    public SaveProgramSettingsPage()
    {
        InitializeComponent();

        // Retrieve settings.
        IDictionary<string, object> properties = Application.Current.Properties;

        for (int index = 0; index < 4; index++)
        {
            Switch switcher = (Switch)(switchGrid.Children[index]);
            string key = index.ToString();

            if (properties.ContainsKey(key))
                switcher.IsToggled = (bool)(properties[key]);
        }
        isInitialized = true;
    }

    async void OnSwitchToggled(object sender, EventArgs args)
    {
        if (!isInitialized)
```

```
            return;

        Switch switcher = (Switch)sender;
        string key = switchGrid.Children.IndexOf(switcher).ToString();
        Application.Current.Properties[key] = switcher.IsToggled;

        // Save settings.
        foreach (View view in switchGrid.Children)
            view.IsEnabled = false;

        await Application.Current.SavePropertiesAsync();

        foreach (View view in switchGrid.Children)
            view.IsEnabled = true;
    }
}
```

One of the purposes of this exercise is to emphasize first, that using `await` doesn't completely solve problems involved with asynchronous operations, but second, that using `await` can help deal with those potential problems.

Here's the problem: The `Toggled` event handler is called every time a `Switch` changes state. It could be that a user toggles a couple of the `Switch` views in succession very quickly. And it could also be the case that the `SavePropertiesAsync` method is slow. Perhaps it saves much more information than four Boolean values. Because this method is asynchronous, there is a danger that it could be called again while it's still working to save the previous collection of settings.

Is `SavePropertiesAsync` reentrant? Can it safely be called again while it's still working? We don't know, and it's better to assume that it's not. For that reason, the handler disables all the `Switch` elements before calling `SavePropertiesAsync` and then reenables them after it's finished. Because `SavePropertiesAsync` returns `Task` rather than `Task<T>`, it's not necessary to use `await` (or `ContinueWith`) to get a value from the method, but it is necessary if you want to execute some code after the method has completed.

In reality, `SavePropertiesAsync` works so fast in this case that it's hard to tell whether this disabling and enabling of the `Switch` views is even working! For testing code such as this, a static method of the `Task` class is very useful. Try inserting this statement right after the `SavePropertiesAsync` call:

```
await Task.Delay(3000);
```

The `Switch` elements are disabled for another 3,000 milliseconds. Of course, if an asynchronous operation really took this long to complete and the user interface is disabled during this time, you'd want to display an `ActivityIndicator` or a `ProgressBar` if possible.

The `Task.Delay` method might seem reminiscent of the `Thread.Sleep` method that you possibly used in some .NET code many years ago. But the two static methods are very different. The `Thread.Sleep` method suspends the current thread, which in this case would be the user-interface thread. That's precisely what you *don't* want. The `Task.Delay` call, however, simulates a do-nothing secondary thread that runs for a specified period of time. The user-interface thread isn't blocked. If you omit the `await` operator, `Task.Delay` would seemingly have no effect on the program at all. When used with the `await` operator, the code in the method that calls `Task.Delay` resumes after the specified period of time.

A platform-independent timer

So far in this book you've seen two ViewModels that have required timers: These are the `DateTime-ViewModel` class used in the `MvvmClock` program in Chapter 18, "MVVM," and the `SchoolViewModel` class in the **SchoolOfFineArt** library, which used the timer to randomly alter the students' grade-point averages for several programs in Chapter 19, "Collection views."

These ViewModels used `Device.StartTimer`, but that's not a good practice. A ViewModel is supposed to be platform independent and usable in any .NET application, but `Device.StartTimer` is specific to Xamarin.Forms.

You can alternatively create your own timer by using `Task.Delay`. Because `Task.Delay` is part of .NET and can be used within Portable Class Libraries, it is much more platform independent than `Device.StartTimer`.

The **TaskDelayClock** demonstrates how to use `Task.Delay` for a timer. The XAML file consists of a `Label` in an `AbsoluteLayout`:

```
<ContentPage xmlns="http://xamarin.com/schemas/2014/forms"
             xmlns:x="http://schemas.microsoft.com/winfx/2009/xaml"
             x:Class="TaskDelayClock.TaskDelayClockPage">
    <ContentPage.Padding>
        <OnPlatform x:TypeArguments="Thickness"
                    iOS="0, 20, 0, 0" />
    </ContentPage.Padding>

    <AbsoluteLayout>
        <Label x:Name="label"
               FontSize="Large"
               AbsoluteLayout.LayoutFlags="PositionProportional" />
    </AbsoluteLayout>
</ContentPage>
```

The code-behind file contains a method called `InfiniteLoop`. Generally, infinite loops are avoided in programming, but this one runs in the user-interface thread for only a very brief period of time four times per second. For the bulk of the time, a `Task.Delay` call allows the user-interface thread to continue to interact with the user:

```
public partial class TaskDelayClockPage : ContentPage
{
    Random random = new Random();

    public TaskDelayClockPage()
    {
        InitializeComponent();
```

```
        InfiniteLoop();
    }

    async void InfiniteLoop()
    {
        while (true)
        {
            label.Text = DateTime.Now.ToString("T");
            label.FontSize = random.Next(12, 49);
            AbsoluteLayout.SetLayoutBounds(label, new Rectangle(random.NextDouble(),
                                                  random.NextDouble(),
                                                  AbsoluteLayout.AutoSize,
                                                  AbsoluteLayout.AutoSize));

            await Task.Delay(250);
        }
    }
}
```

Every 250 milliseconds, the code in the `while` loop runs to give the `Label` the current time, but also to randomly change its font size and its location within the `AbsoluteLayout`:

Yes, it's a rather annoying clock.

This is not truly an "infinite" loop, of course, but it will keep going until the application terminates. If you prefer, you can use a Boolean field as the `while` conditional and exit from the loop by just setting the field to `false`.

Notice how the `InfiniteLoop` method is simply called from the constructor as if it were a normal method. If this method used `Thread.Sleep` rather than `Task.Delay`, it would never return back to the constructor, and the constructor would never finish, and that would not be good at all. This particular `InfiniteLoop` method returns back to the constructor when execution hits the `await` operator for the first time, and the constructor can finish execution. The program can do anything else it wants, but the user-interface thread will be required every 250 milliseconds when `InfiniteLoop` resumes.

Although the `Task.Delay` call simulates a do-nothing secondary thread, it's actually implemented using the `Timer` class from the `System.Threading` namespace. Curiously enough, that `Timer` class is not available in a Xamarin.Forms Portable Class Library, and if it were, it would be a little more difficult to use because the timer callback doesn't run in the user-interface thread.

File input/output

Traditionally, file input/output is one of the most basic programming tasks, but file I/O on mobile devices is a little different from that on the desktop. On the desktop, users and applications generally have access to an entire disk and perhaps additional drives, all of which are organized into directory structures. On mobile devices, several standard folders exist—for pictures or music, for example—but application-specific data is generally restricted to a storage area that is private to each application.

Programmers familiar with .NET know that the `System.IO` namespace contains the bulk of standard file I/O support. This is where you'll find the crucial `Stream` class that provides the basis of reading and writing data organized as a stream of bytes. Building upon this are several `Reader` and `Writer` classes and other classes that allow accessing files and directories. Perhaps the handiest of the file classes is `File` itself, which not only provides a collection of methods to create new files and open existing files but also includes several static methods capable of performing an entire file-read or file-write operation in a single method call.

Particularly if you're working with text files, these static methods of the `File` class can be very convenient. For example, the `File.WriteAllText` method has two arguments of type `string`—a filename and the file contents. The method creates the file (replacing an existing file with the same name if necessary), writes the contents to the file, and then closes it. The `File.ReadAllText` method is similar but returns the contents of the file in one big `string` object. These methods are ideal for writing and reading text files with a minimum of fuss.

At first, file I/O doesn't seem to require asynchronous operations, and in practice, sometimes you have a choice, and sometimes you can avoid asynchronous operations if you want to.

However, other times you do not have a choice. Some platforms require asynchronous functions for file I/O, and even when they're not required, it makes sense to avoid doing file I/O in the user-interface thread.

Good news and bad news

The Xamarin.iOS and Xamarin.Android libraries referenced by your Xamarin.Forms applications include a version of .NET that Xamarin has expressly tailored for these two mobile platforms. The methods in the `File` class in the `System.IO` namespace map to appropriate file I/O functions in the iOS and Android platforms, and the static `Environment.GetFolderPath` method, when used with the `MyDocuments` enumeration member, returns a directory for the application's local storage. This means that you can use simple methods in the `File` class—including the static methods that perform entire file writing or reading operations in a single call—in your iOS and Android applications.

To verify the availability of these classes, let's experiment a little: Go into Visual Studio or Xamarin Studio and load any Xamarin.Forms solution created so far. Bring up one of the code files in the iOS or Android project. In a constructor or method, type the `System.IO` namespace name and then a period. You'll get a list of all the available types in the namespace. If you then type `File` and a period, you'll get all the static methods in the `File` class, including `WriteAllText` and `ReadAllText`.

In the Windows 8.1 and Windows Phone 8.1 projects, however, you're working with a version of .NET created by Microsoft specifically for these platforms. If you type `System.IO` and a period, you won't even see the `File` class at all! It doesn't exist! (However, you'll discover that it does exist in the UWP project.)

Now go into any code file in a Xamarin.Forms Portable Class Library project. As you'll recall, a PCL for Xamarin.Forms targets the following platforms:

- .NET Framework 4.5

- Windows 8

- Windows Phone 8.1

- Xamarin.Android

- Xamarin.iOS

- Xamarin.iOS (Classic)

As you might have already anticipated, the `System.IO` namespace in a PCL is also missing the `File` class. PCLs are configured to support multiple target platforms. Consequently, the APIs implemented within the PCL are necessarily an intersection of the APIs in these target platforms.

Beginning with Windows 8 and the Windows Runtime API, Microsoft completely revamped file I/O and created a whole new set of classes. Your Windows 8.1, Windows Phone 8.1, and UWP applications instead use classes in the `Windows.Storage` namespace for file I/O.

If you are targeting only iOS and Android in your Xamarin.Forms applications, you can share file I/O code between the two platforms. You can use the static `File` methods and everything else in `System.IO`.

If you also want to target one of the Windows or Windows Phone platforms, you'll want to make use of `DependencyService` (discussed in Chapter 9, "Platform-specific API calls") for different file I/O logic for each of the platforms.

A first shot at cross-platform file I/O

In the general case, you'll use `DependencyService` to give your Xamarin.Forms applications access to file I/O functions. As you know from the previous explorations into `DependencyService`, you can define the functions you want in an interface in the Portable Class Library project, while the code to implement these functions resides in separate classes in the individual platforms.

The file I/O functions developed in this chapter will be put to a good use in the **NoteTaker** application in Chapter 24, "Page navigation." For a first shot at file I/O, let's work with a much simpler solution, named **TextFileTryout**, that implements several functions to work with text files. Let's also restrict ourselves to getting this program running on iOS and Android and forget about the Windows platforms for the moment.

The first step in making use of `DependencyService` is creating an interface in the PCL that defines all the methods you'll need. Here is such an interface in the **TextFileTryout** project, named `IFile-Helper`:

```
namespace TextFileTryout
{
    public interface IFileHelper
    {
        bool Exists(string filename);

        void WriteText(string filename, string text);

        string ReadText(string filename);

        IEnumerable<string> GetFiles();

        void Delete(string filename);
    }
}
```

The interface defines functions to determine whether a file exists, to write and read entire text files in one shot, to enumerate all the files created by the application, and to delete a file. In each platform implementation, these functions are restricted to the private file area associated with the application.

You then implement this interface in each of the platforms. Here's the `FileHelper` class in the iOS project, complete with `using` directives and the required `Dependency` attribute:

```
using System;
using System.Collections.Generic;
using System.IO;
using Xamarin.Forms;

[assembly: Dependency(typeof(TextFileTryout.iOS.FileHelper))]

namespace TextFileTryout.iOS
{
    class FileHelper : IFileHelper
    {
```

```
public bool Exists(string filename)
{
    string filepath = GetFilePath(filename);
    return File.Exists(filepath);
}

public void WriteText(string filename, string text)
{
    string filepath = GetFilePath(filename);
    File.WriteAllText(filepath, text);
}

public string ReadText(string filename)
{
    string filepath = GetFilePath(filename);
    return File.ReadAllText(filepath);
}

public IEnumerable<string> GetFiles()
{
    return Directory.GetFiles(GetDocsPath());
}

public void Delete(string filename)
{
    File.Delete(GetFilePath(filename));
}

// Private methods.
string GetFilePath(string filename)
{
    return Path.Combine(GetDocsPath(), filename);
}

string GetDocsPath()
{
    return Environment.GetFolderPath(Environment.SpecialFolder.MyDocuments);
}
    }
}
```

It is essential that this class explicitly implements the `IFileHelper` interface and includes a `Dependency` attribute with the name of the class. These allow the `DependencyService` class in Xamarin.Forms to find this implementation of `IFileHelper` in the platform project. Two private methods at the bottom allow the program to construct a fully qualified filename using the directory of the application's private storage available from the `Environment.GetFolderPath` method.

In both Xamarin.iOS and Xamarin.Android, the implementation of `Environment.GetFolderPath` obtains the platform-specific area of the application's local storage, although the directory names that the method returns for the two platforms are very different.

As a result, the `FileHelper` class in the Android project is exactly the same as the one in the iOS project apart from the different namespace names.

The iOS and Android versions of `FileHelper` make use of the static shortcut methods in the `File` class and a simple static method of `Directory` for obtaining all the files stored with the application. However, the implementation of `IFileHelper` in the Windows 8.1 and Windows Phone 8.1 projects can't use the shortcut methods in the `File` class because they are not available, and the `Environment.GetFolderPath` method isn't available in the UWP project.

Moreover, applications written for these Windows platforms should instead use file I/O functions implemented in the Windows Runtime API. Because the file I/O functions in the Windows Runtime are asynchronous, they do not fit into the interface established by the `IFileHelper` interface. For that reason, the version of `FileHelper` in the three Windows projects is forced to leave the crucial methods unimplemented. Here's the version in the **UWP** project:

```
using System;
using System.Collections.Generic;
using Xamarin.Forms;

[assembly: Dependency(typeof(TextFileTryout.UWP.FileHelper))]

namespace TextFileTryout.UWP
{
    class FileHelper : IFileHelper
    {
        public bool Exists(string filename)
        {
            return false;
        }

        public void WriteText(string filename, string text)
        {
            throw new NotImplementedException("Writing files is not implemented");
        }

        public string ReadText(string filename)
        {
            throw new NotImplementedException("Reading files is not implemented");
        }

        public IEnumerable<string> GetFiles()
        {
            return new string[0];
        }

        public void Delete(string filename)
        {
        }
    }
}
```

The version of `FileHelper` in the Windows 8.1 and Windows Phone 8.1 projects is identical except for the namespace name.

Normally, an application needs to reference the methods in each platform by using the `Dependen-cyService.Get` method. However, the **TextFileTryout** program has made things easy for itself by defining a class named `FileHelper` in the PCL project that also implements `IFileHelper`, but incorporates the call to the `Get` method of `DependencyService` to call the platform versions of these methods:

```
namespace TextFileTryout
{
    class FileHelper : IFileHelper
    {
        IFileHelper fileHelper = DependencyService.Get<IFileHelper>();

        public bool Exists(string filename)
        {
            return fileHelper.Exists(filename);
        }

        public void WriteText(string filename, string text)
        {
            fileHelper.WriteText(filename, text);
        }

        public string ReadText(string filename)
        {
            return fileHelper.ReadText(filename);
        }

        public IEnumerable<string> GetFiles()
        {
            IEnumerable<string> filepaths = fileHelper.GetFiles();
            List<string> filenames = new List<string>();

            foreach (string filepath in filepaths)
            {
                filenames.Add(Path.GetFileName(filepath));
            }
            return filenames;
        }

        public void Delete(string filename)
        {
            fileHelper.Delete(filename);
        }
    }
}
```

Notice that the `GetFiles` method performs a little surgery on the filenames returned from the platform implementation. The filenames that are obtained from the platform implementations of `Get-Files` are fully qualified, and while it might be interesting to see the folder names that iOS and Android use for application local storage, those filenames are going to be displayed in a `ListView` where the folder names will just be a distraction, so this `GetFiles` method strips off the file path.

The `TextFileTryoutPage` class tests these functions. The XAML file includes an `Entry` for a filename, an `Editor` for the file contents, a `Button` labeled "Save", and a `ListView` with all the previously saved filenames:

```xml
<ContentPage xmlns="http://xamarin.com/schemas/2014/forms"
             xmlns:x="http://schemas.microsoft.com/winfx/2009/xaml"
             x:Class="TextFileTryout.TextFileTryoutPage">
    <ContentPage.Padding>
        <OnPlatform x:TypeArguments="Thickness"
                    iOS="0, 20, 0, 0" />
    </ContentPage.Padding>

    <Grid>
        <Grid.RowDefinitions>
            <RowDefinition Height="Auto" />
            <RowDefinition Height="*" />
            <RowDefinition Height="Auto" />
            <RowDefinition Height="*" />
        </Grid.RowDefinitions>

        <Entry x:Name="filenameEntry"
               Grid.Row="0"
               Placeholder="filename" />

        <Editor x:Name="fileEditor"
                Grid.Row="1">
            <Editor.BackgroundColor>
                <OnPlatform x:TypeArguments="Color"
                            WinPhone="#D0D0D0" />
            </Editor.BackgroundColor>
        </Editor>

        <Button x:Name="saveButton"
                Text="Save"
                Grid.Row="2"
                HorizontalOptions="Center"
                Clicked="OnSaveButtonClicked" />

        <ListView x:Name="fileListView"
                  Grid.Row="3"
                  ItemSelected="OnFileListViewItemSelected">
            <ListView.ItemTemplate>
                <DataTemplate>
                    <TextCell Text="{Binding}">
                        <TextCell.ContextActions>
                            <MenuItem Text="Delete"
                                      IsDestructive="True"
                                      Clicked="OnDeleteMenuItemClicked" />
                        </TextCell.ContextActions>
                    </TextCell>
                </DataTemplate>
            </ListView.ItemTemplate>
        </ListView>
    </Grid>
```

```
</ContentPage>
```

Just to keep things simple, all processing is performed in the code-behind file without a ViewModel. The code-behind file implements all the event handlers from the XAML file. The **Save** button checks whether the file exists first and displays an alert box if it does. Selecting one of the files in the ListView loads it in. In addition, the ListView implements a context menu to delete a file. All the file I/O functions are methods of the FileHelper class defined in the PCL and instantiated as a field at the top of the class:

```csharp
public partial class TextFileTryoutPage : ContentPage
{
    FileHelper fileHelper = new FileHelper();

    public TextFileTryoutPage()
    {
        InitializeComponent();

        RefreshListView();
    }

    async void OnSaveButtonClicked(object sender, EventArgs args)
    {
        string filename = filenameEntry.Text;

        if (fileHelper.Exists(filename))
        {
            bool okResponse = await DisplayAlert("TextFileTryout",
                                        "File " + filename +
                                        " already exists. Replace it?",
                                        "Yes", "No");
            if (!okResponse)
                return;
        }

        string errorMessage = null;

        try
        {
            fileHelper.WriteText(filenameEntry.Text, fileEditor.Text);
        }
        catch (Exception exc)
        {
            errorMessage = exc.Message;
        }

        if (errorMessage == null)
        {
            filenameEntry.Text = "";
            fileEditor.Text = "";
            RefreshListView();
        }
        else
        {
```

```
            await DisplayAlert("TextFileTryout", errorMessage, "OK");
        }
    }

    async void OnFileListViewItemSelected(object sender, SelectedItemChangedEventArgs args)
    {
        if (args.SelectedItem == null)
            return;

        string filename = (string)args.SelectedItem;
        string errorMessage = null;

        try
        {
            fileEditor.Text = fileHelper.ReadText((string)args.SelectedItem);
            filenameEntry.Text = filename;
        }
        catch (Exception exc)
        {
            errorMessage = exc.Message;
        }

        if (errorMessage != null)
        {
            await DisplayAlert("TextFileTryout", errorMessage, "OK");
        }
    }

    void OnDeleteMenuItemClicked(object sender, EventArgs args)
    {
        string filename = (string)((MenuItem)sender).BindingContext;
        fileHelper.Delete(filename);
        RefreshListView();
    }

    void RefreshListView()
    {
        fileListView.ItemsSource = fileHelper.GetFiles();
        fileListView.SelectedItem = null;
    }
}
```

The code-behind file calls `DisplayAlert` with the `await` operator on three occasions: The **Save** button uses `DisplayAlert` if the filename you specify already exists. This confirms that your real intention is to replace an existing file. The other two uses are for notification purposes for errors that occur when files are saved or loaded. The file save and file load operations are in `try` and `catch` blocks to catch any errors that might occur. The file save operation will fail for an illegal filename, for example. It is less likely that an error will be encountered on reading a file, but the program checks anyway.

The alerts that notify the user of an error could conceivably be displayed without the `await` operator, but they use `await` anyway to demonstrate a basic principle involved in exception handling: Although C# 6 allows using `await` in a `catch` block, C# 5 does not. To get around this restriction, the catch block simply saves the error message in a variable called errorMessage, and then the code following the catch block uses DisplayAlert to display that text if it exists. This structure allows these event handlers to conclude with different processing depending on successful completion or an error.

Notice also that the constructor concludes with a call to RefreshListView to display all the existing files in the ListView, and the code-behind file also calls that method when a new file has been saved or a file has been deleted.

However, this program does not work on the Windows platforms. Let's fix that.

Accommodating Windows Runtime file I/O

The Windows Runtime API defined a whole new array of file I/O classes. Part of the impetus for this was the recognition of an industry-wide transition away from the relatively unconstrained file access of desktop applications toward a more sandboxed environment.

Much of the new file I/O API can be found in the Windows Runtime namespaces Windows.Storage and Windows.Storage.Streams. To store data that is private to an application, a Windows Runtime program first gets a special StorageFolder object:

```
StorageFolder localFolder = ApplicationData.Current.LocalFolder;
```

ApplicationData defines a static property named Current that returns the ApplicationData object for the application. LocalFolder is an instance property of ApplicationData.

StorageFolder defines methods named CreateFileAsync to create a new file and GetFileAsync to open an existing file. These two methods obtain objects of type StorageFile. With that object, a program can open the file for writing or reading with OpenAsync or OpenReadAsync. These methods obtain an IRandomAccessStream object. From this, DataWriter or DataReader objects are created to perform write or read operations.

This sounds a bit lengthy, and it is. Rather simpler approaches involve static methods of the FileIO class, which are similar to the static methods of the .NET File class. For text files, for example, FileIO.ReadTextAsync and FileIO.WriteTextAsync open a file, perform the read or write access, and close the file in one shot. The first argument to these methods is a StorageFile object.

At any rate, by this time you've undoubtedly noticed the frequent Async suffixes on these method names. Internally, all these methods spin off secondary threads of execution for doing the actual work and return quickly to the caller. The work takes place in the background, and the caller is notified of completion (or error) through callback functions.

Why is this?

When Windows 8 was first being created, the Microsoft developers took a good, hard look at timing and decided that any function call that requires more than 50 milliseconds to execute should be made asynchronous so that it would not interfere with the responsiveness of the user interface. APIs that require more than 50 milliseconds obviously include the file I/O functions, which often need to access potentially slow pieces of hardware like disk drives or a network. Any Windows Runtime file I/O method that could possibly cause a physical storage device to be accessed was made asynchronous and given an `Async` suffix.

However, these asynchronous methods do *not* return `Task` objects. In the Windows Runtime, methods that return data have return types of `IAsyncOperation<TResult>`, while methods that do not return information have return types of `IAsyncAction`. These interfaces can all be found in the `System.Foundations` namespace.

Although these interfaces are not the same as `Task` and `Task<T>`, they are similar, and you can use `await` with them. You can also convert between the two asynchronous protocols. The **System.Runtime.WindowsRuntime** assembly includes a `System` namespace with a `WindowsRuntimeSystemExtensions` class that has extension methods named `AsAsyncAction`, `AsAsyncOpertion`, and `AsTask` that perform these conversions.

Let's rework the **TextFileTryout** program to accommodate asynchronous file I/O. The revised program is called **TextFileAsync and is developed in the next section**. Because asynchronous file I/O functions in the Windows projects will be accessed, all the file functions in the `IFileHelper` interface are defined to return `Task` or `Task<T>` objects.

Platform-specific libraries

Every programmer knows that potentially reusable code should be put in a library, and this is also the case for code used with dependency services. The asynchronous file I/O functions developed here will be reused in the **NoteTaker** program in Chapter 24, and you might want to use these functions in your own applications or perhaps develop your own functions.

However, these file I/O classes can't be put in just one library. Each of the various platform implementations of `FileHelper` must be in a library for that specific platform. This requires separate libraries for each platform.

The **Libraries** directory of the downloadable code for this book contains a solution named **Xamarin.FormsBook.Platform**. The **Platform** part of the name was inspired by the various **Xamarin.Forms.Platform** libraries. Each of the various platforms is a separate library in this solution.

The **Xamarin.FormsBook.Platform** solution contains no fewer than seven library projects, each of which was created somewhat differently:

- **Xamarin.FormsBook.Platform** is a normal Xamarin.Forms Portable Class Library with a profile of 111, which means that it can be accessed by all the platforms. You can create such a library in Visual Studio by selecting **Cross Platform** at the left of the **Add New Project** dialog, and **Class Library (Xamarin.Forms)** in the central area. In the Xamarin Studio **New Project** dialog, select **Multiplatform** and **Library** at the left, and **Xamarin.Forms** and **Class Library** in the central area.

- **Xamarin.FormsBook.Platform.iOS** was created in Visual Studio by selecting **iOS** in the left column of the **Add New Project** dialog, and **Class Library (iOS)** in the central section. In Xamarin Studio select **iOS** and **Library** in the **New Project** dialog, and **Class Library** in the central area.

- **Xamarin.FormsBook.Platform.Android** was created in Visual Studio by selecting **Android** at the left of the **Add New Project** dialog and **Class Library (Android)** in the central section. In Xamarin.Studio, select **Android** and **Library** at the left and **Class Library** in the central section.

- **Xamarin.FormsBook.Platform.UWP** is a library for Windows 10 and Windows 10 Mobile. It was created in Visual Studio by selecting **Windows** and **Universal** at the left, and then **Class Library (Universal Windows)**.

- **Xamarin.FormsBook.Platform.Windows** is a Portable Class Library just for Windows 8.1. It was created in Visual Studio by selecting **Windows**, **Windows 8**, and **Windows** at the left, and then **Class Library (Windows 8.1)**.

- **Xamarin.FormsBook.Platform.WinPhone** is a Portable Class Library just for Windows Phone 8.1. It was created in Visual Studio by selecting **Windows**, **Windows 8**, and **Windows Phone** at the left, and then **Class Library (Windows Phone)**.

- You'll often find that the three Windows platforms can share code because they all use variants of the Windows Runtime API. For this reason, a seventh project was created named **Xamarin.FormsBook.Platform.WinRT**. This is a shared project, and it was created in Visual Studio by searching for "Shared" in the **Add New Project** dialog, and selecting the **Shared Project** for C#.

If you're creating such a solution yourself, you'll also need to use the **Manage Packages for Solution** dialog to install the appropriate Xamarin.Forms NuGet packages for all these libraries.

You'll also need to establish references between the various projects in the solution. All the individual platform projects (with the exception of **Xamarin.FormsBook.Platform.WinRT**) need a reference to **Xamarin.FormsBook.Platform**. You set these references in the **Reference Manager** dialog by selecting **Solution** at the left. In addition, the three Windows projects (**UWP**, **Windows**, and **WinPhone**) all need references to the shared **Xamarin.FormsBook.Platform.WinRT** project. You set these references in the **Reference Manager** dialog by selecting **Shared Projects** at the left.

All the projects have a static `Toolkit.Init` method. Here's the one in the Xamarin.FormsBook.Platform library:

```
namespace Xamarin.FormsBook.Platform
{
    public static class Toolkit
    {
        public static void Init()
        {
        }
    }
}
```

```
}
```

Most of the others are similar except that the version in the Android library actually saves some information that might be useful to classes implemented in this library:

```
namespace Xamarin.FormsBook.Platform.Android
{
    public static class Toolkit
    {
        public static void Init(Activity activity, Bundle bundle)
        {
            Activity = activity;
        }

        public static Activity Activity { private set; get; }
    }
}
```

The `Toolkit.Init` method in each of the Windows platforms calls a do-nothing `Toolkit.Init` method in the shared **Xamarin.FormsBook.Platform.WinRT** project:

```
namespace Xamarin.FormsBook.Platform.UWP
{
    public static class Toolkit
    {
        public static void Init()
        {
            Xamarin.FormsBook.Platform.WinRT.Toolkit.Init();
        }
    }
}
```

The purpose of these methods is to ensure that the libraries are bound to the application even if the application does not directly access anything in the library. It is very often the case when you're working with dependency services and custom renderers that the application does not directly call any library function. However, if you later discover that you really do need to perform some library initialization, the method already exists for you to do so.

You'll discover that the version of the **Xamarin.FormsBook.Platform** libraries included with the downloadable code for this book already includes the `PlatformSoundPlayer` classes from Chapter 9, "Platform-specific API calls." You'll also see some classes beginning with the words `Ellipse` and `StepSlider`. These are discussed in Chapter 27, "Custom renderers."

Let's focus on the new asynchronous `FileHelper` classes. The **Xamarin.FormsBook.Platform** library contains the new `IFileHelper` interface:

```
using System.Collections.Generic;
using System.Threading.Tasks;

namespace Xamarin.FormsBook.Platform
{
    public interface IFileHelper
```

```
    {
        Task<bool> ExistsAsync(string filename);

        Task WriteTextAsync(string filename, string text);

        Task<string> ReadTextAsync(string filename);

        Task<IEnumerable<string>> GetFilesAsync();

        Task DeleteAsync(string filename);
    }
}
```

By convention, methods that return `Task` objects have a suffix of `Async`.

All three Windows platforms can share the same `FileHelper` class, so this shared class is implemented in the shared **Xamarin.FormsBook.Platform.WinRT** project. Each of the five methods in the `FileHelper` class begins with a call to obtain the `StorageFolder` associated with the application's local storage area. Each of them makes asynchronous calls using `await` and is flagged with the `async` keyword:

```
using System;
using System.Collections.Generic;
using System.Linq;
using System.Threading.Tasks;
using Windows.Storage;
using Xamarin.Forms;

[assembly: Dependency(typeof(Xamarin.FormsBook.Platform.WinRT.FileHelper))]

namespace Xamarin.FormsBook.Platform.WinRT
{
    class FileHelper : IFileHelper
    {
        public async Task<bool> ExistsAsync(string filename)
        {
            StorageFolder localFolder = ApplicationData.Current.LocalFolder;

            try
            {
                await localFolder.GetFileAsync(filename);
            }
            catch
            {
                return false;
            }
            return true;
        }

        public async Task WriteTextAsync(string filename, string text)
        {
            StorageFolder localFolder = ApplicationData.Current.LocalFolder;
            IStorageFile storageFile = await localFolder.CreateFileAsync(filename,
```

```
                                          CreationCollisionOption.ReplaceExisting);
        await FileIO.WriteTextAsync(storageFile, text);
    }

    public async Task<string> ReadTextAsync(string filename)
    {
        StorageFolder localFolder = ApplicationData.Current.LocalFolder;
        IStorageFile storageFile = await localFolder.GetFileAsync(filename);
        return await FileIO.ReadTextAsync(storageFile);
    }

    public async Task<IEnumerable<string>> GetFilesAsync()
    {
        StorageFolder localFolder = ApplicationData.Current.LocalFolder;

        IEnumerable<string> filenames =
            from storageFile in await localFolder.GetFilesAsync()
            select storageFile.Name;

        return filenames;
    }

    public async Task DeleteAsync(string filename)
    {
        StorageFolder localFolder = ApplicationData.Current.LocalFolder;
        StorageFile storageFile = await localFolder.GetFileAsync(filename);
        await storageFile.DeleteAsync();
    }
    }
}
```

Although each of the methods is defined as returning a `Task` or a `Task<T>` object, the bodies of the methods don't have any reference to `Task` or `Task<T>`. Instead, the methods that return a `Task` object simply do some work and then end the method with an implicit `return` statement. The `ExistsAsync` method is defined as returning a `Task<bool>` but returns either `true` or `false`. (There is no `Exists` method in the `StorageFolder` class, so a workaround with `try` and `catch` is necessary.)

Similarly, the `ReadTextAsync` method is defined as returning a `Task<string>`, but the body returns a `string`, which is obtained from applying the `await` operator to the `IAsyncOperation<string>` return value of `File.ReadTextAsync`. The C# compiler performs the necessary conversions.

When a program calls this `ReadTextAsync` method, the method executes until the first `await` operator, and then it returns a `Task<string>` object to the caller. The caller can use either `ContinueWith` or `await` to obtain the string when the `FileIO.ReadTextAsync` method has completed.

For iOS and Android, however, we now have a problem. All the methods in `IFileHelper` are now defined as asynchronous methods that return `Task` or `Task<T>` objects, but we've already seen that the methods in the `System.IO` namespace are not asynchronous. What do we do?

The `FileHelper` class in the iOS namespace uses two strategies. In some cases, the `System.IO` classes *do* include asynchronous methods. This is the case for the `WriteAsync` method of `Stream-Writer` and the `ReadAsync` method of `StreamReader`. For the other methods, however, a static `FromResult` method of `Task<T>` is used to convert an object or value to a `Task<T>` object for the method return value. This does not actually convert the method to an asynchronous method, but simply allows the method to have the signature of an asynchronous method:

```
using System;
using System.Collections.Generic;
using System.IO;
using System.Linq;
using System.Threading.Tasks;
using Xamarin.Forms;

[assembly: Dependency(typeof(Xamarin.FormsBook.Platform.iOS.FileHelper))]

namespace Xamarin.FormsBook.Platform.iOS
{
    class FileHelper : IFileHelper
    {
        public Task<bool> ExistsAsync(string filename)
        {
            string filepath = GetFilePath(filename);
            bool exists = File.Exists(filepath);
            return Task<bool>.FromResult(exists);
        }

        public async Task WriteTextAsync(string filename, string text)
        {
            string filepath = GetFilePath(filename);
            using (StreamWriter writer = File.CreateText(filepath))
            {
                await writer.WriteAsync(text);
            }
        }

        public async Task<string> ReadTextAsync(string filename)
        {
            string filepath = GetFilePath(filename);
            using (StreamReader reader = File.OpenText(filepath))
            {
                return await reader.ReadToEndAsync();
            }
        }

        public Task<IEnumerable<string>> GetFilesAsync()
        {
            // Sort the filenames.
            IEnumerable<string> filenames =
                from filepath in Directory.EnumerateFiles(GetDocsFolder())
                select Path.GetFileName(filepath);

            return Task<IEnumerable<string>>.FromResult(filenames);
        }
    }
}
```

```
        public Task DeleteAsync(string filename)
        {
            File.Delete(GetFilePath(filename));
            return Task.FromResult(true);
        }

        string GetDocsFolder()
        {
            return Environment.GetFolderPath(Environment.SpecialFolder.MyDocuments);
        }

        string GetFilePath(string filename)
        {
            return Path.Combine(GetDocsFolder(), filename);
        }
    }
}
```

The Android `FileHelper` class is the same as the iOS class but with a different namespace.

Notice that the only error checking within these platform implementations is for the `ExistsAsync` method in the Windows Runtime platforms, which uses the exception to determine whether the file exists or not. None of the other methods—and particularly the `WriteTextAsync` and `ReadTextAsync` methods—is performing any error checking. One of the nice features of using `await` is that any exception can be caught at a later time when you're actually calling these methods.

You might also have noticed that the individual `GetFilesAsync` methods are now removing the path from the fully qualified filename, so that job doesn't need to be performed by the `FileHelper` class in the **Xamarin.FormsBook.Platform** project:

```
namespace Xamarin.FormsBook.Platform
{
    class FileHelper
    {
        IFileHelper fileHelper = DependencyService.Get<IFileHelper>();

        public Task<bool> ExistsAsync(string filename)
        {
            return fileHelper.ExistsAsync(filename);
        }

        public Task WriteTextAsync(string filename, string text)
        {
            return fileHelper.WriteTextAsync(filename, text);
        }

        public Task<string> ReadTextAsync(string filename)
        {
            return fileHelper.ReadTextAsync(filename);
        }

        public Task<IEnumerable<string>> GetFilesAsync()
```

```
        {
            return fileHelper.GetFilesAsync();
        }

        public Task DeleteAsync(string filename)
        {
            return fileHelper.DeleteAsync(filename);
        }
    }
}
```

Now that we have a library, we need to access this library from an application. The **TextFileAsync** solution was created normally. Then, all seven projects in the **Xamarin.FormsBook.Platform** solution were added to this solution. These projects must be added separately by using the **Add** and **Existing Project** menu item for the solution. There is no **Add All Projects from Solution** menu item, but if you use these libraries in your own projects, you'll wish there were!

At this point, the **TextFileAsync** solution contains 13 projects: Five application projects, a shared PCL with the application code, and seven library projects.

References must be established between these projects by using the **Reference Manager** for the following relationships:

- **TextFileAsync** has a reference to **Xamarin.FormsBook.Platform**.

- **TextFileAsync.iOS** has a reference to **Xamarin.FormsBook.Platform.iOS**.

- **TextFileAsync.Droid** has a reference to **Xamarin.FormsBook.Platform.Android**.

- **TextFileAsync.UWP** has a reference to **Xamarin.FormsBook.Platform.UWP**.

- **TextFileAsync.Windows** has a reference to **Xamarin.FormsBook.Platform.Windows**.

- **TextFileAsync.WinPhone** has a reference to **Xamarin.FormsBook.Platform.WinPhone**.

Of course, all the application projects have normal references to the **TextFileAsync** PCL, and, as you'll recall, the **Xamarin.FormsBook.Platform.UWP**, **Windows**, and **WinPhone** projects all have references to the shared **Xamarin.FormsBook.Platform.WinRT** project.

Also, all the **TextFileAsync** projects should make calls to the various `Toolkit.Init` methods in the libraries. In the `TextFileAsync` project itself, make the call in the constructor of the `App` class:

```
namespace TextFileAsync
{
    public class App : Application
    {
        public App()
        {
            Xamarin.FormsBook.Platform.Toolkit.Init();
            …
        }
        …
```

```
        }
}
```

In the iOS project, make the call after the normal `Forms.Init` call in the `AppDelegate` class:

```
namespace TextFileAsync.iOS
{
    ...
    public partial class AppDelegate :
                            global::Xamarin.Forms.Platform.iOS.FormsApplicationDelegate
    {
        ...
        public override bool FinishedLaunching(UIApplication app, NSDictionary options)
        {
            global::Xamarin.Forms.Forms.Init();
            Xamarin.FormsBook.Platform.iOS.Toolkit.Init();
            LoadApplication(new App());
            ...
        }
    }
}
```

In the Android project, call `Toolkit.Init` with the `MainActivity` and `Bundle` objects in the `MainActivity` class after the normal `Forms.Init` call:

```
namespace TextFileAsync.Droid
{
    ...
    public class MainActivity : global::Xamarin.Forms.Platform.Android.FormsApplicationActivity
    {
        protected override void OnCreate(Bundle bundle)
        {
            ...
            global::Xamarin.Forms.Forms.Init(this, bundle);
            Xamarin.FormsBook.Platform.Android.Toolkit.Init(this, bundle);
            LoadApplication(new App());
        }
    }
}
```

In the three Windows platforms, call `Toolkit.Init` right after `Forms.Init` in the App.xaml.cs file:

```
namespace TextFileAsync.UWP
{
    ...
    sealed partial class App : Application
    {
        ...
                Xamarin.Forms.Forms.Init(e);
                Xamarin.FormsBook.Platform.UWP.Toolkit.Init();
        ...
    }
}
```

With that overhead out of the way, the actual writing of the application can begin. The XAML file for `TextFileAsyncPage` is the same as `TextFileTryoutPage`, but the code-behind file must be fashioned to work with the asynchronous file I/O methods. Any exceptions that might occur in the file I/O functions must be caught here, which means that any method that can throw an exception must be in a `try` block along with the `await` operator:

```
public partial class TextFileAsyncPage : ContentPage
{
    FileHelper fileHelper = new FileHelper();

    public TextFileAsyncPage()
    {
        InitializeComponent();

        RefreshListView();
    }

    async void OnSaveButtonClicked(object sender, EventArgs args)
    {
        saveButton.IsEnabled = false;

        string filename = filenameEntry.Text;

        if (await fileHelper.ExistsAsync(filename))
        {
            bool okResponse = await DisplayAlert("TextFileTryout",
                                        "File " + filename +
                                        " already exists. Replace it?",
                                        "Yes", "No");
            if (!okResponse)
                return;
        }

        string errorMessage = null;

        try
        {
            await fileHelper.WriteTextAsync(filenameEntry.Text, fileEditor.Text);
        }
        catch (Exception exc)
        {
            errorMessage = exc.Message;
        }

        if (errorMessage == null)
        {
            filenameEntry.Text = "";
            fileEditor.Text = "";
            RefreshListView();
        }
        else
        {
            await DisplayAlert("TextFileTryout", errorMessage, "OK");
        }
```

```
            saveButton.IsEnabled = true;
    }

    async void OnFileListViewItemSelected(object sender, SelectedItemChangedEventArgs args)
    {
        if (args.SelectedItem == null)
            return;

        string filename = (string)args.SelectedItem;
        string errorMessage = null;

        try
        {
            fileEditor.Text = await fileHelper.ReadTextAsync((string)args.SelectedItem);
            filenameEntry.Text = filename;
        }
        catch (Exception exc)
        {
            errorMessage = exc.Message;
        }

        if (errorMessage != null)
        {
            await DisplayAlert("TextFileTryout", errorMessage, "OK");
        }
    }

    async void OnDeleteMenuItemClicked(object sender, EventArgs args)
    {
        string filename = (string)((MenuItem)sender).BindingContext;
        await fileHelper.DeleteAsync(filename);
        RefreshListView();
    }

    async void RefreshListView()
    {
        fileListView.ItemsSource = await fileHelper.GetFilesAsync();
        fileListView.SelectedItem = null;
    }
}
```

The result is that this code is structured very much like the previous code that used the synchronous file I/O functions. One difference, however, is that the OnSaveButtonClicked method disables the **Save** button when beginning processing and then reenables it when everything is finished. This is simply to prevent multiple presses of the **Save** button that might cause multiple overlapping calls to FileIO.WriteFileAsync.

Here's the program running on the three platforms:

Keeping it in the background

Some of the `FileHelper` methods in the Windows Runtime implementation have multiple `await` operators to deal with a series of asynchronous calls. This makes sense: Each step in the process must complete before the next step executes. However, one of the characteristics of `await` is that it resumes execution on the same thread that it was invoked on rather than the background thread. This is often convenient when you are obtaining a result to update the user interface. However, within the methods in the `FileHelper` implementations, this isn't necessary. Everything within the body of the `Write-TextAsync` and `ReadTextAsync` methods can occur in a secondary thread.

The `Task` class has a method named `ConfigureAwait` that can control which thread `await` resumes on. If you pass a `false` argument to `ConfigureAwait`, the completed task will resume on the same worker thread used to implement the function. If you'd like to use this in the `FileHelper` code, you'll need to convert the `IAsyncAction` and `IAsyncOperation` objects returned by the Windows Runtime methods to tasks by using `AsTask` and then call `ConfigureAwait` on that `Task` object.

For example, here's how the `WriteTextAsync` and `ReadTextAsync` methods are implemented in the existing **Xamarin.FormsBook.Platform.WinRT** project:

```
namespace Xamarin.FormsBook.Platform.WinRT
{
    class FileHelper : IFileHelper
    {
        ...
        public async Task WriteTextAsync(string filename, string text)
        {
            StorageFolder localFolder = ApplicationData.Current.LocalFolder;
```

```
        IStorageFile storageFile = await localFolder.CreateFileAsync(filename,
                                            CreationCollisionOption.ReplaceExisting);
        await FileIO.WriteTextAsync(storageFile, text);
    }

    public async Task<string> ReadTextAsync(string filename)
    {
        StorageFolder localFolder = ApplicationData.Current.LocalFolder;
        IStorageFile storageFile = await localFolder.GetFileAsync(filename);
        return await FileIO.ReadTextAsync(storageFile);
    }
    …
    }
}
```

These methods have two `await` operators each. To make these methods slightly more efficient, you can use `AsTask` and `ConfigureAwait` to change them to these:

```
namespace Xamarin.FormsBook.Platform.WinRT
{
    class FileHelper : IFileHelper
    {
    …
    public async Task WriteTextAsync(string filename, string text)
    {
        StorageFolder localFolder = ApplicationData.Current.LocalFolder;
        IStorageFile storageFile = await localFolder.CreateFileAsync(filename,
                                        CreationCollisionOption.ReplaceExisting).
                                        AsTask().ConfigureAwait(false);
        await FileIO.WriteTextAsync(storageFile, text).AsTask().ConfigureAwait(false);
    }

    public async Task<string> ReadTextAsync(string filename)
    {
        StorageFolder localFolder = ApplicationData.Current.LocalFolder;
        IStorageFile storageFile = await localFolder.GetFileAsync(filename).
                                        AsTask().ConfigureAwait(false);
        return await FileIO.ReadTextAsync(storageFile).AsTask().ConfigureAwait(false);
    }
    …
    }
}
```

Now the methods following the first `await` operator run in worker threads, and `await` doesn't need to switch back to the user-interface thread just to continue with the method. The switch back to the user-interface thread occurs when `await` is used to call these methods from `TextFileAsyncPage`.

You probably want to restrict this technique to underlying library functions, or for code in your page classes that contain a series of `await` operators that don't access user-interface objects. The technique doesn't make as much sense for functions that contain just one `await` operator that are called from the user-interface thread, because the switch back to the user-interface thread has to occur at some time, and if it doesn't occur in the library function, it will occur in the code that calls the library function.

Don't block the UI thread!

Sometimes, there's a temptation to avoid the hassle of `ContinueWith` or even the lesser hassle of `await` simply by blocking the user-interface thread until a background process completes. Perhaps you know that the background process will complete very quickly and there's nothing much the user can do anyway until it finishes. What's the harm?

Don't do it! Not only is it impolite to the user, but it can introduce subtle bugs into your application.

Let's take an example: In the code-behind file of `TextFileAsyncPage`, the `OnFileListView-ItemSelected` handler has the following code to read the file and set the contents in the `Editor`:

```
fileEditor.Text = await fileHelper.ReadTextAsync((string)args.SelectedItem);
```

You might have discovered, perhaps accidentally or perhaps by experiment, that in a statement like this, you can leave out the `await` operator and just access the `Result` property of the `Task<string>` object returned from `ReadTextAsync`. That `Result` property is the content of the file being read:

```
fileEditor.Text = fileHelper.ReadTextAsync((string)args.SelectedItem).Result;
```

The code seems fine, and it might even work. But the way it works is not good. This statement will block the user-interface thread until the `ReadTextAsync` method has completed and `Result` is available. The user interface will be unresponsive during this time.

Moreover, if you haven't used `ConfigureAwait(false)` in the implementation of `ReadTextAsync` in `FileHelper`, then that `ReadTextAsync` method will require switching to the user-interface thread for resuming execution after each `await` operator. But when it tries to switch back to the user-interface thread, the UI thread will not be available because it's being blocked in the `ReadTextAsync` call in `TextFileAsyncPage`, and a classic deadlock results. The program will simply stop executing entirely.

The rule is simple: Use `ContinueWith` or `await` with every asynchronous method.

Your own awaitable methods

Aside from accessing files over the web or from the local file system, applications sometimes have the need to perform lengthy operations of their own. These operations should be run in the background on secondary threads of execution. While there are now several ways to do this, it's best (and certainly easiest) to use the same Task-based Asynchronous Pattern that is used within Xamarin.Forms and other .NET graphical environments and define your own asynchronous methods just like the others in these environments.

The easiest way to run some code on a worker thread is with the `Task.Run` and `Task.Run<T>`

static methods. The argument is an `Action` object, generally expressed as a lambda function, and the return value is a `Task`. The body of the lambda function is run on a worker thread from the thread pool, which (if you want to use the thread pool yourself) is accessible via the `ThreadPool` class. You can use the `await` operator directly with `Task.Run`:

```
await Task.Run(() =>
{
    // The code that runs in a background thread.
});
```

Although you can use `Task.Run` by itself with other code, generally it's used to construct asynchronous methods. By convention, an asynchronous method has a suffix of `Async`. The method returns either a `Task` object (if the method does not return any value or object) or a `Task<T>` object (if it does return something).

Here's how you can create an asynchronous method that returns `Task`:

```
Task MyMethodAsync(...)
{
    // Perhaps some initialization code.
    return Task.Run(() =>
    {
        // The code that runs in a background thread.
    });
}
```

The `Task.Run` method returns a `Task` object that your method also returns. The `Action` argument to `Task.Run` can use any arguments passed to the `MyMethodAsync`, but you shouldn't define any arguments using `ref` or `out`. Also, watch out for any reference types you pass to `MyMethodAsync`. These can be accessed both from inside the asynchronous code and from outside the method, so you might need to implement synchronization so that the object isn't accessed simultaneously from two threads.

The code within the `Task.Run` call can itself call asynchronous methods using `await`, but in that case you'll need to flag the lambda function passed to `Task.Run` with `async`:

```
return Task.Run(async () =>
{
    // The code that runs in a background thread.
});
```

If the asynchronous method returns something, you'll define the method using the generic form of `Task` and the generic form of `Task.Run`:

```
Task<SomeType> MyMethodAsync(...)
{
    // Perhaps some initialization code.
    return Task.Run<SomeType>(() =>
    {
        // The code that runs in a background thread.
        return anInstanceOfSomeType;
    });
```

}

The value or object returned from the lambda function becomes the `Result` property of the `Task<T>` object returned from `Task.Run` and from your method.

If you need to have more control over the background process, you can use `TaskFactory.Start-New` rather than `Task.Run` to define the asynchronous method.

There are some variations on the basic `Task.Run` patterns, as you'll see in the following several programs. These programs compute and display the famous Mandelbrot set.

The basic Mandelbrot set

The Polish-born French and American mathematician Benoit Mandelbrot (1924–2010) is best known for his work connected with complex self-similar surfaces that he called *fractals*. Among his work involving fractals was an investigation into a recursive formula that generates a fractal image that is now known as the *Mandelbrot set*.

The Mandelbrot set is graphed on the complex plane, where each coordinate is a complex number of the form:

$$c = x + yi$$

The real part x is graphed along the horizontal axis with negative values to the left and positive values to the right. The imaginary part y is graphed along the vertical axis, increasing from negative values on the bottom to positive values going up.

To calculate the Mandelbrot set, begin by taking any point on this plane and call it c, and initialize z to zero:

$$c = x + yi$$

$$z = 0$$

Now perform the following recursive operation:

$$z \leftarrow z^2 + c$$

The result will either diverge to infinity or it will not. If z does *not* diverge to infinity, then c is said to be a member of the Mandelbrot set. Otherwise, it is not a member of the Mandelbrot set.

You need to perform this calculation for every point of interest in the complex plane. Generally, the results are drawn on a bitmap, which means that each pixel in the bitmap corresponds to a particular complex coordinate. In its simplest rendition, points that belong to the Mandelbrot set are colored black and other pixels are colored white.

For some complex numbers, it's easy to determine whether the point belongs to the Mandelbrot set. For example, the complex number (0 + 0i) obviously belongs to the Mandelbrot set, and you can quickly establish that (1 + 0i) does not. But in general, you need to perform the recursive calculation.

And because this is a fractal, you can't take shortcuts. For example, if you know that two values c_1 and c_2 belong to the Mandelbrot set, you can't assume that all points between those two points belong to the Mandelbrot set as well. It is a fundamental characteristic of a fractal to defy interpolation.

How many iterations of the recursive calculation do you need to perform before you can assure yourself that the particular complex number does or does not belong to the Mandelbrot set? It turns out that if the absolute value of z in the recursive calculation ever becomes 2 or greater, then the values will eventually diverge to infinity and the point does not belong to the Mandelbrot set. (The absolute value of a complex number is also referred to as the *magnitude* of the number; it can be calculated as the square root of the sum of the squares of the x and y values, which is the Pythagorean theorem.)

However, if after a certain number of iterations the recursive calculation hasn't yet reached a magnitude of 2, there's no guarantee that it will not diverge with repeated iterations. For this reason, Mandelbrot sets are notoriously computation-intensive, and ideal for secondary threads of execution.

The **MandelbrotSet** program demonstrates how this is done. To render the image, the program makes use of the `BmpMaker` class (introduced in Chapter 13, "Bitmaps") from the **Xamarin.FormsBook.Toolkit** library. That library also contains the following structure to represent a complex number:

```
namespace Xamarin.FormsBook.Toolkit
{
    // Mostly a subset of System.Numerics.Complex.
    public struct Complex : IEquatable<Complex>, IFormattable
    {
        bool gotMagnitude, gotMagnitudeSquared;
        double magnitude, magnitudeSquared;

        public Complex(double real, double imaginary) : this()
        {
            Real = real;
            Imaginary = imaginary;
        }

        public double Real { private set; get; }

        public double Imaginary { private set; get; }

        // MagnitudeSquare and Magnitude calculated on demand and saved.
        public double MagnitudeSquared
        {
            get
            {
                if (gotMagnitudeSquared)
                {
                    return magnitudeSquared;
                }

                magnitudeSquared = Real * Real + Imaginary * Imaginary;
                gotMagnitudeSquared = true;
                return magnitudeSquared;
            }
        }
```

```csharp
        }

        public double Magnitude
        {
            get
            {
                if (gotMagnitude)
                {
                    return magnitude;
                }

                magnitude = Math.Sqrt(magnitudeSquared);
                gotMagnitude = true;
                return magnitude;
            }
        }

        public static Complex operator +(Complex left, Complex right)
        {
            return new Complex(left.Real + right.Real, left.Imaginary + right.Imaginary);
        }

        public static Complex operator -(Complex left, Complex right)
        {
            return new Complex(left.Real - right.Real, left.Imaginary - right.Imaginary);
        }

        public static Complex operator *(Complex left, Complex right)
        {
            return new Complex(left.Real * right.Real - left.Imaginary * right.Imaginary,
                               left.Real * right.Imaginary + left.Imaginary * right.Real);
        }

        public static bool operator ==(Complex left, Complex right)
        {
            return left.Real == right.Real && left.Imaginary == right.Imaginary;
        }

        public static bool operator !=(Complex left, Complex right)
        {
            return !(left == right);
        }

        public static implicit operator Complex(double value)
        {
            return new Complex(value, 0);
        }

        public static implicit operator Complex(int value)
        {
            return new Complex(value, 0);
        }

        public override int GetHashCode()
```

```
        {
            return Real.GetHashCode() + Imaginary.GetHashCode();
        }

        public override bool Equals(Object value)
        {
            return Real.Equals(((Complex)value).Real) &&
                    Imaginary.Equals(((Complex)value).Imaginary);
        }

        public bool Equals(Complex value)
        {
            return Real.Equals(value) && Imaginary.Equals(value);
        }

        public override string ToString()
        {
            return String.Format("{0} {1} {2}i", Real,
                                    RealImaginaryConnector(Imaginary),
                                    Math.Abs(Imaginary));
        }

        public string ToString(string format)
        {
            return String.Format("{0} {1} {2}i", Real.ToString(format),
                                    RealImaginaryConnector(Imaginary),
                                    Math.Abs(Imaginary).ToString(format));
        }

        public string ToString(IFormatProvider formatProvider)
        {
            return String.Format("{0} {1} {2}i", Real.ToString(formatProvider),
                                    RealImaginaryConnector(Imaginary),
                                    Math.Abs(Imaginary).ToString(formatProvider));
        }

        public string ToString(string format, IFormatProvider formatProvider)
        {
            return String.Format("{0} {1} {2}i", Real.ToString(format, formatProvider),
                                    RealImaginaryConnector(Imaginary),
                                 Math.Abs(Imaginary).ToString(format, formatProvider));
        }

        string RealImaginaryConnector(double value)
        {
            return Math.Sign(value) > 0 ? "+" : "\u2013";
        }
    }
}
```

As the comment at the top indicates, this is *mostly* a subset of the Complex structure in the .NET Sys-
tem.Numerics namespace, which unfortunately is not available to a Portable Class Library in a Xama-
rin.Forms project. The ToString methods in this Complex structure work a little differently, however,

and the original `Complex` structure does not have a `MagnitudeSquared` property. A `Magnitude-Squared` property is handy for a Mandelbrot calculation: Checking if the `Magnitude` property is less than 2 is the same as checking if the `MagnitudeSquared` property is less than 4, but without the square root calculation.

The **MandelbrotSet** program has the following XAML file:

```
<ContentPage xmlns="http://xamarin.com/schemas/2014/forms"
             xmlns:x="http://schemas.microsoft.com/winfx/2009/xaml"
             x:Class="MandelbrotSet.MandelbrotSetPage">
    <ContentPage.Padding>
        <OnPlatform x:TypeArguments="Thickness"
                    iOS="0, 20, 0, 0" />
    </ContentPage.Padding>

    <StackLayout>
        <Grid VerticalOptions="FillAndExpand">
            <ContentView Padding="10, 0"
                         VerticalOptions="Center">
                <ActivityIndicator x:Name="activityIndicator" />
            </ContentView>

            <Image x:Name="image" />
        </Grid>

        <Button x:Name="calculateButton"
                Text="Calculate"
                FontSize="Large"
                HorizontalOptions="Center"
                Clicked="OnCalculateButtonClicked" />
    </StackLayout>
</ContentPage>
```

The `ActivityIndicator` informs the user that the program is busy with the background job. The `Image` element and that `ActivityIndicator` share a single-cell `Grid` so that the `ActivityIndicator` can be more toward the vertical center of the screen and then become covered when the bitmap appears. At the bottom is a `Button` to begin the calculation.

The code-behind file below begins by defining several constants. The first four constants relate to the bitmap that the program constructs to display the image of the Mandelbrot set. Throughout this exercise, these bitmaps will always be square, but the code itself is more generalized and should be able to accommodate rectangular dimensions.

The `center` field is the `Complex` point that corresponds to the center of the bitmap, while the `size` field indicates the extent of the real and imaginary coordinates on the bitmaps. These particular `center` and `size` fields imply that the real coordinates range from –2 on the left of the bitmap to 0.5 on the right, and the imaginary coordinates range from –1.25 on the bottom to 1.25 on the top. The `pixelWidth` and `pixelHeight` values indicate the width and height of the bitmap in pixels. The `iterations` field is the maximum number of iterations of the recursive formula before the program assumes that the point belongs to the Mandelbrot set:

```csharp
public partial class MandelbrotSetPage : ContentPage
{
    static readonly Complex center = new Complex(-0.75, 0);
    static readonly Size size = new Size(2.5, 2.5);
    const int pixelWidth = 1000;
    const int pixelHeight = 1000;
    const int iterations = 100;

    public MandelbrotSetPage()
    {
        InitializeComponent();
    }

    async void OnCalculateButtonClicked(object sender, EventArgs args)
    {
        calculateButton.IsEnabled = false;
        activityIndicator.IsRunning = true;

        BmpMaker bmpMaker = new BmpMaker(pixelWidth, pixelHeight);
        await CalculateMandelbrotAsync(bmpMaker);
        image.Source = bmpMaker.Generate();

        activityIndicator.IsRunning = false;
    }

    Task CalculateMandelbrotAsync(BmpMaker bmpMaker)
    {
        return Task.Run(() =>
        {
            for (int row = 0; row < pixelHeight; row++)
            {
                double y = center.Imaginary - size.Height / 2 + row * size.Height / pixelHeight;

                for (int col = 0; col < pixelWidth; col++)
                {
                    double x = center.Real - size.Width / 2 + col * size.Width / pixelWidth;
                    Complex c = new Complex(x, y);
                    Complex z = 0;
                    int iteration = 0;

                    do
                    {
                        z = z * z + c;
                        iteration++;
                    }
                    while (iteration < iterations && z.MagnitudeSquared < 4);

                    bool isMandelbrotSet = iteration == iterations;
                    bmpMaker.SetPixel(row, col, isMandelbrotSet ? Color.Black : Color.White);
                }
            }
        });
    }
}
```

The `OnCalculateButtonClicked` handler is flagged as `async`. It begins by disabling the `Button` to avoid multiple simultaneous calculations and starts the `ActivityIndicator` display. It then creates a `BmpMaker` object with the desired pixel size and passes it to `CalculateMandelbrotAsync`. When that method is finished, the `Clicked` handler continues by setting the bitmap to the `Image` object and turning off the `ActivityIndicator`. The `Button` is not reenabled.

The lambda function passed to the `Task.Run` method loops through the rows and columns of the bitmap created by `BmpMaker`, and for each pixel, it calculates a complex number `c` from the `x` and `y` coordinate values. The little `do-while` loop continues until the maximum number of iterations is reached or the magnitude is 2 or greater. At that point, a pixel can be set to black or white.

After you press the button, your phone might take a minute or so to loop through all the pixels, but then you'll see the classic image:

There's a little danger in the way the `CalculateMandelbrotAsync` method is structured. It is passed a `BmpMaker` object that the background thread fills with pixels, but the main thread also has access to this `BmpMaker` object. If this object were saved as a field, the main thread might contain some code that alters or sets pixels as the background thread is working. That would probably be a bug, of course, but in general you can make your asynchronous methods more bulletproof if arguments are restricted to value types rather than reference types. Don't worry too much if that's not quite possible or convenient, but in the next version of the program, the `CalculateMandelbrotAsync` method will itself create the `BmpMaker` object and return it.

Marking progress

As you've undoubtedly discovered, it's somewhat disconcerting to press the **Calculate** button in **MandelbrotSet** and wait for the bitmap to show up. There's no indication at all how far along the program has gotten in completing the job, or how much longer you need to wait.

If possible, asynchronous methods should report progress. I'm sure you can rig something up yourself to do the job, but there is a standard way of reporting progress for methods that return `Task` objects. This involves the `IProgress<T>` interface and the `Progress<T>` class that implements that interface, both of which are defined in the `System` namespace. `IProgress` is defined like so:

```
public interface IProgress<T>
{
    void Report(T value);
}
```

To make use of this facility, you define an argument to your asynchronous method of type `IProgress`. The asynchronous method then periodically calls `Report` as it's doing the background job. Generally, `T` is either `int`, in which case the values passed to `Report` usually range from 1 to 100, or `double`, for values ranging from 0 to 1. It's your choice. For consistency with the Xamarin.Forms `ProgressBar`, `double` values from 0 to 1 are ideal.

The code that calls the asynchronous method instantiates a `Progress` object and passes to its constructor a lambda function that is called whenever the asynchronous method calls `Report`. (Or you can attach a handler to the `Progress` object's `ProgressChanged` event.) Although `Report` is called on a background thread, the lambda function or event handler is called on the thread that instantiated the `Progress` object, which means that the lambda function or event handler can safely access user-interface objects.

The XAML file for the **MandelbrotProgress** program is the same as the previous XAML file except that a `ProgressBar` has replaced the `ActivityIndicator`:

```
<ContentPage xmlns="http://xamarin.com/schemas/2014/forms"
             xmlns:x="http://schemas.microsoft.com/winfx/2009/xaml"
             x:Class="MandelbrotProgress.MandelbrotProgressPage">
    <ContentPage.Padding>
        <OnPlatform x:TypeArguments="Thickness"
                    iOS="0, 20, 0, 0" />
    </ContentPage.Padding>

    <StackLayout>
        <Grid VerticalOptions="FillAndExpand">
            <ContentView Padding="10, 0"
                         VerticalOptions="Center">
                <ProgressBar x:Name="progressBar" />
            </ContentView>

            <Image x:Name="image" />
        </Grid>
```

```
            <Button x:Name="calculateButton"
                    Text="Calculate"
                    FontSize="Large"
                    HorizontalOptions="Center"
                    Clicked="OnCalculateButtonClicked" />
        </StackLayout>
    </ContentPage>
```

The code-behind file is very similar, except that a `Progress` object named `progressReporter` is defined as a field and the constructor instantiates it with a lambda function that simply sets the argument to the `Progress` property of the `ProgressBar`. This `Progress` object is passed to the `CalculateMandelbrotAsync` method, which in this new version now takes over the responsibility of creating and returning the `BmpMaker` object:

```
public partial class MandelbrotProgressPage : ContentPage
{
    static readonly Complex center = new Complex(-0.75, 0);
    static readonly Size size = new Size(2.5, 2.5);
    const int pixelWidth = 1000;
    const int pixelHeight = 1000;
    const int iterations = 100;

    Progress<double> progressReporter;

    public MandelbrotProgressPage()
    {
        InitializeComponent();

        progressReporter = new Progress<double>((double value) =>
            {
                progressBar.Progress = value;
            });
    }

    async void OnCalculateButtonClicked(object sender, EventArgs args)
    {
        // Configure the UI for a background process.
        calculateButton.IsEnabled = false;

        // Render the Mandelbrot set on a bitmap.
        BmpMaker bmpMaker = await CalculateMandelbrotAsync(progressReporter);
        image.Source = bmpMaker.Generate();
    }

    Task<BmpMaker> CalculateMandelbrotAsync(IProgress<double> progress)
    {
        return Task.Run<BmpMaker>(() =>
        {
            BmpMaker bmpMaker = new BmpMaker(pixelWidth, pixelHeight);

            for (int row = 0; row < pixelHeight; row++)
            {
                double y = center.Imaginary - size.Height / 2 + row * size.Height / pixelHeight;
```

```
            // Report the progress.
            progress.Report((double)row / pixelHeight);

            for (int col = 0; col < pixelWidth; col++)
            {
                double x = center.Real - size.Width / 2 + col * size.Width / pixelWidth;
                Complex c = new Complex(x, y);
                Complex z = 0;
                int iteration = 0;
                bool isMandelbrotSet = false;

                if ((c - new Complex(-1, 0)).MagnitudeSquared < 1.0 / 16)
                {
                    isMandelbrotSet = true;
                }
                else
                {
                    do
                    {
                        z = z * z + c;
                        iteration++;
                    }
                    while (iteration < iterations && z.MagnitudeSquared < 4);

                    isMandelbrotSet = iteration == iterations;
                }
                bmpMaker.SetPixel(row, col, isMandelbrotSet ? Color.Black : Color.White);
            }
        }
        return bmpMaker;
    });
    }
}
```

The asynchronous method reports its progress with every new row:

```
progress.Report((double)row / pixelHeight);
```

Watch out: You don't want to report progress so frequently that you slow down the method! A hundred calls to the `Report` method during the whole operation is plenty, and you can probably reduce that number considerably before the `ProgressBar` begins looking jittery.

If you pay close attention to the `ProgressBar` in **MandelbrotProgress**, you'll see that it moves fast at the start and then slows down. The problem area is the large cardioid—and to a lesser extent, the circle to its left—that makes up the bulk of the Mandelbrot set. For points within these areas, the recursive calculation must run to the maximum iteration count before the point is identified as a member of the set. This new method attempts to reduce the work somewhat by detecting when the point is within the circle. The center of this circle is the complex point –1, and the radius is 1/4:

```
if ((c - new Complex(-1, 0)).MagnitudeSquared < 1.0 / 16)
{
    isMandelbrotSet = true;
```

```
}
```

But the cardioid is a more complex object (although that too can be identified, as the next version of the program demonstrates).

When the asynchronous method creates and returns that `BmpMaker` object, the code to obtain that object and set the bitmap to the `Image` object reduces to just two statements:

```
BmpMaker bmpMaker = await CalculateMandelbrotAsync(progressReporter);
image.Source = bmpMaker.Generate();
```

But if two statements are too many, keep in mind that `await` is pretty much just an ordinary operator and can be part of a more complex statement:

```
image.Source = (await CalculateMandelbrotAsync(progressReporter)).Generate();
```

Cancelling the job

The two Mandelbrot programs shown so far exist for the sole purpose of generating a single image, so it's unlikely that you would want to cancel that job once it's started. However, in the general case, you'll want to provide a facility for the user to bail out of lengthy background jobs.

Although you can probably put together a little cancellation system of your own, the `System.Threading` namespace already has you covered with a class named `CancellationToken-Source` and a structure named `CancellationToken`.

Here's how it works:

A program creates a `CancellationTokenSource` for use with a particular asynchronous method. The `CancellationTokenSource` class defines a property named `Token` that returns a `CancellationToken`. This `CancellationToken` value is passed to the asynchronous method. The asynchronous method periodically calls the `IsCancellationRequested` method of the `CancellationToken`. This method usually returns `false`.

When the program wants to cancel the asynchronous operation (probably in response to some user input), it calls the `Cancel` method of the `CancellationTokenSource`. The next time the asynchronous method calls the `IsCancellationRequested` method of the `CancellationToken`, the method returns `true` because a cancellation has been requested. The asynchronous method can choose how to stop running, perhaps with a simple `return` statement.

Usually, however, a different approach is taken. Rather than calling the `IsCancellationRequested` method of `CancellationToken`, the asynchronous method can instead simply call the `ThrowIfCancellationRequested` method. If a cancellation has been requested, the asynchronous method stops executing by raising an `OperationCanceledException`.

This means that the `await` operator must be part of a `try` block, but as you've seen, this is generally the case when working with files, so it doesn't add much additional code, and the program can process a cancellation as simply another form of exception.

The **MandelbrotCancellation** program demonstrates this technique. The XAML file now has a second button, labeled "Cancel", which is initially disabled:

```
<ContentPage xmlns="http://xamarin.com/schemas/2014/forms"
             xmlns:x="http://schemas.microsoft.com/winfx/2009/xaml"
             x:Class="MandelbrotCancellation.MandelbrotCancellationPage">
    <ContentPage.Padding>
        <OnPlatform x:TypeArguments="Thickness"
                    iOS="0, 20, 0, 0" />
    </ContentPage.Padding>

    <StackLayout>
        <Grid VerticalOptions="FillAndExpand">
            <ContentView Padding="10, 0"
                         VerticalOptions="Center">
                <ProgressBar x:Name="progressBar" />
            </ContentView>

            <Image x:Name="image" />
        </Grid>

        <Grid>
            <Button x:Name="calculateButton"
                    Grid.Column="0"
                    Text="Calculate"
                    FontSize="Large"
                    HorizontalOptions="Center"
                    Clicked="OnCalculateButtonClicked" />

            <Button x:Name="cancelButton"
                    Grid.Column="1"
                    Text="Cancel"
                    FontSize="Large"
                    IsEnabled="False"
                    HorizontalOptions="Center"
                    Clicked="OnCancelButtonClicked" />
        </Grid>
    </StackLayout>
</ContentPage>
```

The code-behind file now has a more extensive `OnCalculateButtonClicked` method. It begins by disabling the **Calculate** button and enabling the **Cancel** button. It creates a new `CancellationTokenSource` object and passes the `Token` property to `CalculateMandelbrotAsync`. The `OnCancelButtonClicked` method is responsible for calling `Cancel` on the `CancellationTokenSource` object. The `CalculateMandelbrotAsync` method calls the `ThrowIfCancellationRequested` method at the same rate that it reports progress. The exception is caught by the `OnCalculateButtonClicked` method, which responds by reenabling the **Calculate** button for another try:

```
public partial class MandelbrotCancellationPage : ContentPage
{
    static readonly Complex center = new Complex(-0.75, 0);
    static readonly Size size = new Size(2.5, 2.5);
    const int pixelWidth = 1000;
```

```
const int pixelHeight = 1000;
const int iterations = 100;

Progress<double> progressReporter;
CancellationTokenSource cancelTokenSource;

public MandelbrotCancellationPage()
{
    InitializeComponent();

    progressReporter = new Progress<double>((double value) =>
        {
            progressBar.Progress = value;
        });
}

async void OnCalculateButtonClicked(object sender, EventArgs args)
{
    // Configure the UI for a background process.
    calculateButton.IsEnabled = false;
    cancelButton.IsEnabled = true;

    cancelTokenSource = new CancellationTokenSource();

    try
    {
        // Render the Mandelbrot set on a bitmap.
        BmpMaker bmpMaker = await CalculateMandelbrotAsync(progressReporter,
                                                  cancelTokenSource.Token);
        image.Source = bmpMaker.Generate();
    }
    catch (OperationCanceledException)
    {
        calculateButton.IsEnabled = true;
        progressBar.Progress = 0;
    }
    catch (Exception)
    {
        // Shouldn't occur in this case.
    }

    cancelButton.IsEnabled = false;
}

void OnCancelButtonClicked(object sender, EventArgs args)
{
    cancelTokenSource.Cancel();
}

Task<BmpMaker> CalculateMandelbrotAsync(IProgress<double> progress,
                                  CancellationToken cancelToken)
{
    return Task.Run<BmpMaker>(() =>
    {
```

```
        BmpMaker bmpMaker = new BmpMaker(pixelWidth, pixelHeight);

        for (int row = 0; row < pixelHeight; row++)
        {
            double y = center.Imaginary - size.Height / 2 + row * size.Height / pixelHeight;

            // Report the progress.
            progress.Report((double)row / pixelHeight);

            // Possibly cancel.
            cancelToken.ThrowIfCancellationRequested();

            for (int col = 0; col < pixelWidth; col++)
            {
                double x = center.Real - size.Width / 2 + col * size.Width / pixelWidth;
                Complex c = new Complex(x, y);
                Complex z = 0;
                int iteration = 0;
                bool isMandelbrotSet = false;

                if ((c - new Complex(-1, 0)).MagnitudeSquared < 1.0 / 16)
                {
                    isMandelbrotSet = true;
                }
                // http://www.reenigne.org/blog/algorithm-for-mandelbrot-cardioid/
                else if (c.MagnitudeSquared * (8 * c.MagnitudeSquared - 3) <
                                                        3.0 / 32 - c.Real)
                {
                    isMandelbrotSet = true;
                }
                else
                {
                    do
                    {
                        z = z * z + c;
                        iteration++;
                    }
                    while (iteration < iterations && z.MagnitudeSquared < 4);

                    isMandelbrotSet = iteration == iterations;
                }
                bmpMaker.SetPixel(row, col, isMandelbrotSet ? Color.Black : Color.White);
            }
        }
        return bmpMaker;
    }, cancelToken);
}
```

The `CancellationToken` is also passed as the second argument to `Task.Run`. This isn't required, but it allows the `Task.Run` method to skip a lot of work if cancellation has already been requested before it even gets started.

Also notice that the code now skips the large cardioid. A comment references a web page that derives the formula in case you want to check the math.

An MVVM Mandelbrot

Although the black-and-white Mandelbrot set is the classic image, most Mandelbrot programs color pixels that are not in the Mandelbrot set based on the number of iterations required for that determination. The penultimate program in this chapter is called **MandelbrotXF**—the XF prefix stands for Xamarin.Forms—and colors the pixels in that way. The program also allows zooming in on specific locations. It is a characteristic of a Mandelbrot set that the image remains interesting no matter how far you zoom. Unfortunately, there is a practical limit to zooming based on the resolution of double-precision floating-point numbers.

The program is architected using MVVM principles, although after seeing the somewhat odd user interface—and how the ViewModel deals with that user interface—you might question the wisdom of that decision.

The odd user interface of **MandelbrotXF** results from a decision to avoid any platform-specific code. At the time this program was originally written, Xamarin.Forms did not support touch operations such as dragging and pinching that might have been helpful in zooming into a particular location. Instead, the program's entire user interface is implemented with two `Slider` elements, two `Stepper` elements, two `Button` elements, a `ProgessBar`, and visuals implemented with `BoxView`.

When you first run the program, here's what you'll see:

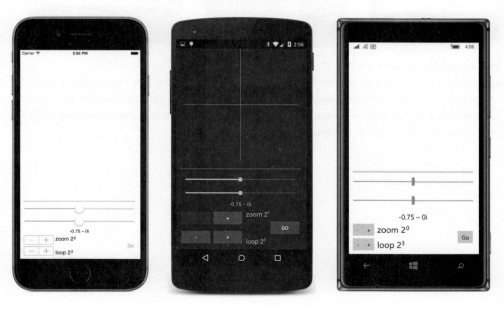

The white crosshairs—which don't show up against the white background of the blank iOS and Windows 10 Mobile screens—fade out over the course of 10 seconds so that they won't obscure the pretty pictures that you'll soon be admiring, but you can bring them back by manipulating either of the sliders or the steppers.

But the first thing you'll want to do is press the **Go** button. The button is replaced with a **Cancel** button and the `ProgressBar` indicates progress. When it's finished, you'll see a colored Mandelbrot set:

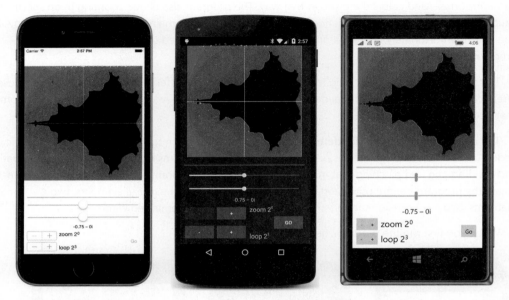

It finishes quickly because the maximum iteration count (indicated by the bottom `Stepper` labeled **loop**) is only 2 to the third power, or 8. As a result, the outline of the black Mandelbrot set is not nearly as sharp as the earlier programs. Many more points are flagged as being a member of the set than would be with a higher maximum iteration count. You can increase that iteration count by powers of 2. Here's a sharper image with a maximum iteration count of 64:

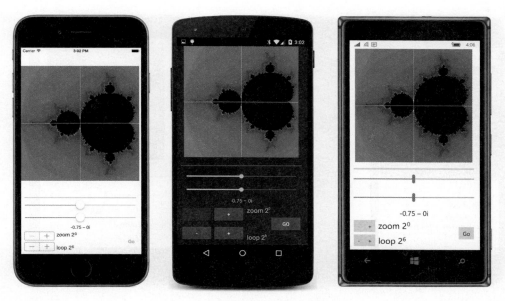

The two `Slider` views allow you to select a new center, which is displayed as a complex number right below the sliders. The first `Stepper` element (labeled **zoom**) allows you to select a magnification factor, also in powers of 2. As you manipulate these three elements, you'll see a box with crosshairs constructed with six thin `BoxView` elements. That box marks the area that will be magnified the next time you press the **Go** button:

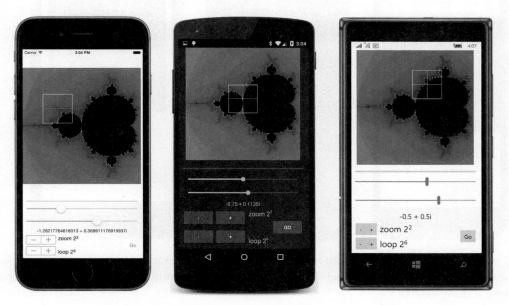

Now press the **Go** button again and wait. Now that previously boxed area fills the bitmap:

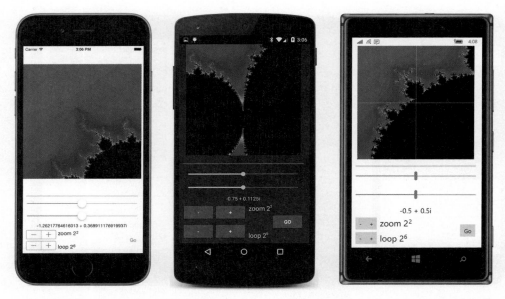

After the new image is calculated, the crosshairs are recentered, and you can reposition the center and zoom in again, and again, and again.

However, generally the more you zoom in, the greater the maximum iterations you'll need to see all the detail. For each device, the image in the previous screenshots acquires visibly more detail with four times as many iterations:

It is a characteristic of the Mandelbrot set that you can just keep zooming in as much as you want and you'll still see just as much detail. However, generally you will need to keep increasing the maximum iteration count as well, and by the time you hit a magnification factor of 2 to the forty-eighth power or so, you've hit a ceiling involving the resolution of double-precision floating-point numbers. Adjacent pixels are no longer associated with distinct complex numbers, and the image begins looking blocky:

That's not an easy obstacle to transcend. There exist implementations of variable-precision floating-point numbers, but because they are not directly handled by the computer's math coprocessor, calculations involving these numbers are necessarily much slower than `float` or `double` types, and it's likely you're not going to want the Mandelbrot calculation to go any slower.

The **MandelbrotXF** program has both a ViewModel and an underlying Model. The Model does the actual number crunching and returns an object of type `BitmapInfo`, which indicates a pixel width and height and an array of integers. The size of the integer array is the product of the pixel width and height, and the elements of the array are iteration counts. A value of −1 indicates a member of the Mandelbrot set:

```
namespace MandelbrotXF
{
    class BitmapInfo
    {
        public BitmapInfo(int pixelWidth, int pixelHeight, int[] iterationCounts)
        {
            PixelWidth = pixelWidth;
            PixelHeight = pixelHeight;
            IterationCounts = iterationCounts;
        }

        public int PixelWidth { private set; get; }

        public int PixelHeight { private set; get; }

        public int[] IterationCounts { private set; get; }
    }
}
```

The `MandelbrotModel` class contains a single asynchronous method. Aside from the `IProgress` object, all the arguments are value types, so there is no danger of any argument changing while the calculation is in progress:

```
namespace MandelbrotXF
{
    class MandelbrotModel
    {
        public Task<BitmapInfo> CalculateAsync(Complex Center,
                                               double width, double height,
                                               int pixelWidth, int pixelHeight,
                                               int iterations,
                                               IProgress<double> progress,
                                               CancellationToken cancelToken)
        {
            return Task.Run(() =>
            {
                int[] iterationCounts = new int[pixelWidth * pixelHeight];
                int index = 0;

                for (int row = 0; row < pixelHeight; row++)
                {
```

```
                    progress.Report((double)row / pixelHeight);
                    cancelToken.ThrowIfCancellationRequested();

                    double y = Center.Imaginary - height / 2 + row * height / pixelHeight;

                    for (int col = 0; col < pixelWidth; col++)
                    {
                        double x = Center.Real - width / 2 + col * width / pixelWidth;
                        Complex c = new Complex(x, y);

                        if ((c - new Complex(-1, 0)).MagnitudeSquared < 1.0 / 16)
                        {
                            iterationCounts[index++] = -1;
                        }
                        // http://www.reenigne.org/blog/algorithm-for-mandelbrot-cardioid/
                        else if (c.MagnitudeSquared * (8 * c.MagnitudeSquared - 3) <
                                                                    3.0 / 32 - c.Real)
                        {
                            iterationCounts[index++] = -1;
                        }
                        else
                        {
                            Complex z = 0;
                            int iteration = 0;

                            do
                            {
                                z = z * z + c;
                                iteration++;
                            }
                            while (iteration < iterations && z.MagnitudeSquared < 4);

                            if (iteration == iterations)
                            {
                                iterationCounts[index++] = -1;
                            }
                            else
                            {
                                iterationCounts[index++] = iteration;
                            }
                        }
                    }
                }
                return new BitmapInfo(pixelWidth, pixelHeight, iterationCounts);
            }, cancelToken);
        }
    }
}
```

This `CalculateAsync` method is called only from the ViewModel. The ViewModel is also intended to provide data-binding sources for the XAML file and to assist the code-behind file in performing those jobs that the XAML data bindings cannot handle. (Drawing the crosshairs and magnification box is a job for that code-behind file.)

For this reason, the `MandelbrotViewModel` class has many properties, but probably not the same properties you'd define if you weren't thinking about the user interface. The `CurrentCenter` property is the complex number for the center of the image currently displayed by the program, and the `CurrentMagnification` also applies to that image. But the `TargetMagnification` is bound to the current setting of the `Stepper`, which will apply to the next calculated image. The `RealOffset` and `ImaginaryOffset` properties are bound to the two `Slider` elements and can range from 0 to 1. From the `CurrentCenter`, `CurrentMagnification`, `RealOffset`, and `ImaginaryOffset` properties, the ViewModel can calculate the `TargetCenter` property. This is the center for the next calculated image. As you'll see, that `TargetCenter` property is used to display the complex number below the two sliders:

```
namespace MandelbrotXF
{
    class MandelbrotViewModel : ViewModelBase
    {
        // Set via constructor arguments.
        readonly double baseWidth;
        readonly double baseHeight;

        // Backing fields for properties.
        Complex currentCenter, targetCenter;
        int pixelWidth, pixelHeight;
        double currentMagnification, targetMagnification;
        int iterations;
        double realOffset, imaginaryOffset;
        bool isBusy;
        double progress;
        BitmapInfo bitmapInfo;

        public MandelbrotViewModel(double baseWidth, double baseHeight)
        {
            this.baseWidth = baseWidth;
            this.baseHeight = baseHeight;

            // Create MandelbrotModel object.
            MandelbrotModel model = new MandelbrotModel();

            // Progress reporter
            Progress<double> progressReporter = new Progress<double>((double progress) =>
            {
                Progress = progress;
            });

            CancellationTokenSource cancelTokenSource = null;

            // Define CalculateCommand and CancelCommand.
            CalculateCommand = new Command(
                execute: async () =>
                    {
                        // Disable this button and enable Cancel button.
                        IsBusy = true;
                        ((Command)CalculateCommand).ChangeCanExecute();
```

```
                ((Command)CancelCommand).ChangeCanExecute();

                // Create CancellationToken.
                cancelTokenSource = new CancellationTokenSource();
                CancellationToken cancelToken = cancelTokenSource.Token;

                try
                {
                    // Perform the calculation.
                    BitmapInfo = await model.CalculateAsync(TargetCenter,
                                                baseWidth / TargetMagnification,
                                                baseHeight / TargetMagnification,
                                                    PixelWidth, PixelHeight,
                                                    Iterations,
                                                    progressReporter,
                                                    cancelToken);

                    // Processing only for a successful completion.
                    CurrentCenter = TargetCenter;
                    CurrentMagnification = TargetMagnification;
                    RealOffset = 0.5;
                    ImaginaryOffset = 0.5;
                }
                catch (OperationCanceledException)
                {
                    // Operation cancelled!
                }
                catch
                {
                    // Another type of exception? This should not occur.
                }

                // Processing regardless of success or cancellation.
                Progress = 0;
                IsBusy = false;

                // Disable Cancel button and enable this button.
                ((Command)CalculateCommand).ChangeCanExecute();
                ((Command)CancelCommand).ChangeCanExecute();
            },
        canExecute: () =>
            {
                return !IsBusy;
            });

    CancelCommand = new Command(
        execute: () =>
            {
                cancelTokenSource.Cancel();
            },
        canExecute: () =>
            {
                return IsBusy;
            });
```

```
    }

    public int PixelWidth
    {
        set { SetProperty(ref pixelWidth, value); }
        get { return pixelWidth; }
    }

    public int PixelHeight
    {
        set { SetProperty(ref pixelHeight, value); }
        get { return pixelHeight; }
    }

    public Complex CurrentCenter
    {
        set
        {
            if (SetProperty(ref currentCenter, value))
                CalculateTargetCenter();
        }
        get { return currentCenter; }
    }

    public Complex TargetCenter
    {
        private set { SetProperty(ref targetCenter, value); }
        get { return targetCenter; }
    }

    public double CurrentMagnification
    {
        set { SetProperty(ref currentMagnification, value); }
        get { return currentMagnification; }
    }

    public double TargetMagnification
    {
        set { SetProperty(ref targetMagnification, value); }
        get { return targetMagnification; }
    }

    public int Iterations
    {
        set { SetProperty(ref iterations, value); }
        get { return iterations; }
    }

    // These two properties range from 0 to 1.
    // They indicate a new center relative to the
    //  current width and height, which is the baseWidth
    //  and baseHeight divided by CurrentMagnification.
    public double RealOffset
    {
```

```
        set
        {
            if (SetProperty(ref realOffset, value))
                CalculateTargetCenter();
        }
        get { return realOffset; }
    }

    public double ImaginaryOffset
    {
        set
        {
            if (SetProperty(ref imaginaryOffset, value))
                CalculateTargetCenter();
        }
        get { return imaginaryOffset; }
    }

    void CalculateTargetCenter()
    {
        double width = baseWidth / CurrentMagnification;
        double height = baseHeight / CurrentMagnification;

        TargetCenter = new Complex(CurrentCenter.Real + (RealOffset - 0.5) * width,
                                   CurrentCenter.Imaginary + (ImaginaryOffset - 0.5) *
                                   height);
    }

    public bool IsBusy
    {
        private set { SetProperty(ref isBusy, value); }
        get { return isBusy; }
    }

    public double Progress
    {
        private set { SetProperty(ref progress, value); }
        get { return progress; }
    }

    public BitmapInfo BitmapInfo
    {
        private set { SetProperty(ref bitmapInfo, value); }
        get { return bitmapInfo; }
    }

    public ICommand CalculateCommand { private set; get; }

    public ICommand CancelCommand { private set; get; }
    }
}
```

MandelbrotViewModel also defines two properties of type ICommand for the **Calculate** and **Cancel** buttons, a Progress property, and an IsBusy property. As you'll see, the IsBusy property is used to display one of those two buttons and hide the other and to disable the rest of the user interface during the calculations. The two `ICommand` properties are implemented with lambda functions in the class's constructor.

The data bindings in the XAML file to the properties in `MandelbrotViewModel` require two new binding converters in the **Xamarin.FormsBook.Toolkit** library. The first simply negates a `bool` value:

```
namespace Xamarin.FormsBook.Toolkit
{
    public class BooleanNegationConverter : IValueConverter
    {
        public object Convert(object value, Type targetType,
                              object parameter, CultureInfo culture)
        {
            return !(bool)value;
        }

        public object ConvertBack(object value, Type targetType,
                                  object parameter, CultureInfo culture)
        {
            return !(bool)value;
        }
    }
}
```

This is used in conjunction with the `IsBusy` property of the ViewModel. When `IsBusy` is `true`, the `IsEnabled` properties of several elements and the `IsVisible` property of the **Go** button need to be set to `false`.

Both `Stepper` elements actually control an exponent of a value in the ViewModel. A `Stepper` value of 8, for example, corresponds to an `Iterations` or `TargetMagnification` value of 256. That conversion requires a base-2 logarithm converter:

```
namespace Xamarin.FormsBook.Toolkit
{
    public class BaseTwoLogConverter : IValueConverter
    {
        public object Convert(object value, Type targetType,
                              object parameter, CultureInfo culture)
        {
            if (value is int)
            {
                return Math.Log((int)value) / Math.Log(2);
            }
            return Math.Log((double)value) / Math.Log(2);
        }

        public object ConvertBack(object value, Type targetType,
                                  object parameter, CultureInfo culture)
        {
            double returnValue = Math.Pow(2, (double)value);

            if (targetType == typeof(int))
```

```
                {
                    return (int) returnValue;
                }
                return returnValue;
            }
        }
    }
```

Here's the XAML file, with bindings to the `Progress`, `RealOffset`, `ImaginaryOffset`, `Tar-getCenter`, `TargetMagnification`, `Iterations`, `IsBusy`, `CalculateCommand`, and `CancelCom-mand` properties of the ViewModel:

```xml
<ContentPage xmlns="http://xamarin.com/schemas/2014/forms"
             xmlns:x="http://schemas.microsoft.com/winfx/2009/xaml"
             xmlns:toolkit=
                 "clr-namespace:Xamarin.FormsBook.Toolkit;assembly=Xamarin.FormsBook.Toolkit"
             x:Class="MandelbrotXF.MandelbrotXFPage"
             SizeChanged="OnPageSizeChanged">
    <ContentPage.Padding>
        <OnPlatform x:TypeArguments="Thickness"
                    iOS="0, 20, 0, 0" />
    </ContentPage.Padding>

    <ContentPage.Resources>
        <ResourceDictionary>
            <toolkit:BooleanNegationConverter x:Key="negate" />
            <toolkit:BaseTwoLogConverter x:Key="base2log" />
        </ResourceDictionary>
    </ContentPage.Resources>

    <Grid x:Name="mainGrid">
        <Grid.RowDefinitions>
            <RowDefinition Height="*" />
            <RowDefinition Height="Auto" />
        </Grid.RowDefinitions>

        <Grid.ColumnDefinitions>
            <ColumnDefinition Width="*" />
            <ColumnDefinition Width="0" />
        </Grid.ColumnDefinitions>

        <!-- Image for determining pixels per unit. -->
        <Image x:Name="testImage"
               Grid.Row="0" Grid.Column="0"
               Opacity="0"
               HorizontalOptions="Center"
               VerticalOptions="Center" />

        <!-- Image for Mandelbrot Set. -->
        <Image x:Name="image"
               Grid.Row="0" Grid.Column="0"
               HorizontalOptions="FillAndExpand"
               VerticalOptions="FillAndExpand"
               SizeChanged="OnImageSizeChanged" />
```

```
            <AbsoluteLayout x:Name="crossHairLayout"
                            Grid.Row="0" Grid.Column="0"
                            HorizontalOptions="Center"
                            VerticalOptions="Center"
                            SizeChanged="OnCrossHairLayoutSizeChanged">

                <AbsoluteLayout.Resources>
                    <ResourceDictionary>
                        <Style TargetType="BoxView">
                            <Setter Property="Color" Value="White" />
                            <Setter Property="AbsoluteLayout.LayoutBounds" Value="0,0,0,0" />
                        </Style>
                    </ResourceDictionary>
                </AbsoluteLayout.Resources>

                <BoxView x:Name="realCrossHair" />
                <BoxView x:Name="imagCrossHair" />
                <BoxView x:Name="topBox" />
                <BoxView x:Name="bottomBox" />
                <BoxView x:Name="leftBox" />
                <BoxView x:Name="rightBox" />
            </AbsoluteLayout>

            <StackLayout x:Name="controlPanelStack"
                         Grid.Row="1" Grid.Column="0"
                         Padding="10">

                <ProgressBar Progress="{Binding Progress}"
                             VerticalOptions="CenterAndExpand" />

                <StackLayout VerticalOptions="CenterAndExpand">
                    <Slider Value="{Binding RealOffset, Mode=TwoWay}"
                            IsEnabled="{Binding IsBusy, Converter={StaticResource negate}}" />

                    <Slider Value="{Binding ImaginaryOffset, Mode=TwoWay}"
                            IsEnabled="{Binding IsBusy, Converter={StaticResource negate}}" />

                    <Label Text="{Binding TargetCenter, StringFormat='{0}'}"
                           FontSize="Small"
                           HorizontalTextAlignment="Center" />
                </StackLayout>

                <Grid VerticalOptions="CenterAndExpand">
                    <Grid.RowDefinitions>
                        <RowDefinition Height="Auto" />
                        <RowDefinition Height="Auto" />
                    </Grid.RowDefinitions>

                    <Grid.ColumnDefinitions>
                        <ColumnDefinition Width="Auto" />
                        <ColumnDefinition Width="*" />
                    </Grid.ColumnDefinitions>
```

```xml
<!-- Magnification factor stepper and display. -->
<Stepper x:Name="magnificationStepper"
         Grid.Row="0" Grid.Column="0"
         Value="{Binding TargetMagnification,
                         Converter={StaticResource base2log}}"
         IsEnabled="{Binding IsBusy, Converter={StaticResource negate}}"
         VerticalOptions="Center" />

<StackLayout Grid.Row="0" Grid.Column="1"
             Orientation="Horizontal"
             Spacing="0"
             VerticalOptions="Start">
    <Label Text="zoom 2"
           FontSize="Medium" />
    <Label Text="{Binding Source={x:Reference magnificationStepper},
                          Path=Value,
                          StringFormat='{0}'}"
           FontSize="Micro" />
</StackLayout>

<!-- Iterations factor stepper and display. -->
<Stepper x:Name="iterationsStepper"
         Grid.Row="1" Grid.Column="0"
         Value="{Binding Iterations, Converter={StaticResource base2log}}"
         IsEnabled="{Binding IsBusy, Converter={StaticResource negate}}"
         VerticalOptions="Center" />

<StackLayout Grid.Row="1" Grid.Column="1"
             Orientation="Horizontal"
             Spacing="0"
             VerticalOptions="End">
    <Label Text="loop 2"
           FontSize="Medium" />
    <Label Text="{Binding Source={x:Reference iterationsStepper},
                          Path=Value,
                          StringFormat='{0}'}"
           FontSize="Micro" />
</StackLayout>

<!-- Go / Cancel buttons. -->
<Grid Grid.Row="0" Grid.Column="1" Grid.RowSpan="2"
      HorizontalOptions="End"
      VerticalOptions="Center">

    <Button Text="Go"
            Command="{Binding CalculateCommand}"
            IsVisible="{Binding IsBusy, Converter={StaticResource negate}}" />

    <Button Text="Cancel"
            Command="{Binding CancelCommand}"
            IsVisible="{Binding IsBusy}" />
    </Grid>
  </Grid>
</StackLayout>
```

```
        </Grid>
</ContentPage>
```

This XAML file only installs three event handlers, and they are all `SizeChanged` handlers.

The first `SizeChanged` handler is on the page itself. This handler is used by the code-behind file to adapt `mainGrid` and its children for portrait or landscape mode using techniques you've seen in previous samples.

The second `SizeChanged` handler is on the `Image` element. The code-behind file uses this to size the `AbsoluteLayout` that displays the crosshairs and magnification box. This `AbsoluteLayout` must be made the same size as the bitmap displayed by the `Image` under the assumption that the `Image` will display a square bitmap.

The third `SizeChanged` handler is on that `AbsoluteLayout`, so the crosshairs and magnification box can be redrawn for a change in size.

The **MandelbrotXF** program also performs a little trick of sorts to ensure that the bitmap contains the optimum number of pixels, which happens when there is a one-to-one mapping between the pixels of the bitmap and the pixels of the display. The XAML file contains a second `Image` element named `testImage`. This `Image` is invisible because the `Opacity` is set to zero, and it is horizontally and vertically centered, which means that it will be displayed with a one-to-one pixel mapping. The code-behind file creates a 120-pixel square bitmap that is set to this `Image`. The resultant size of the `Image` lets the program know how many pixels there are to the device-independent unit, and it can use that to calculate an optimum pixel size for the Mandelbrot bitmap. (Unfortunately it doesn't work for the Windows Runtime platforms.)

Here's roughly the first half of the code-behind file for `MandelbrotXFPage`, showing mostly the instantiation of the `MandelbrotViewModel` class and the interaction of these `SizeChanged` handlers:

```
namespace MandelbrotXF
{
    public partial class MandelbrotXFPage : ContentPage
    {
        MandelbrotViewModel mandelbrotViewModel;
        double pixelsPerUnit = 1;

        public MandelbrotXFPage()
        {
            InitializeComponent();

            // Instantiate ViewModel and get saved values.
            mandelbrotViewModel = new MandelbrotViewModel(2.5, 2.5)
            {
                PixelWidth = 1000,
                PixelHeight = 1000,
                CurrentCenter = new Complex(GetProperty("CenterReal", -0.75),
                                            GetProperty("CenterImaginary", 0.0)),
                CurrentMagnification = GetProperty("Magnification", 1.0),
                TargetMagnification = GetProperty("Magnification", 1.0),
```

```
                Iterations = GetProperty("Iterations", 8),
                RealOffset = 0.5,
                ImaginaryOffset = 0.5
        };

        // Set BindingContext on page.
        BindingContext = mandelbrotViewModel;

        // Set PropertyChanged handler on ViewModel for "manual" processing.
        mandelbrotViewModel.PropertyChanged += OnMandelbrotViewModelPropertyChanged;

        // Create test image to obtain pixels per device-independent unit.
        BmpMaker bmpMaker = new BmpMaker(120, 120);

        testImage.SizeChanged += (sender, args) =>
            {
                pixelsPerUnit = bmpMaker.Width / testImage.Width;
                SetPixelWidthAndHeight();
            };
        testImage.Source = bmpMaker.Generate();

        // Gradually reduce opacity of crosshairs.
        Device.StartTimer(TimeSpan.FromMilliseconds(100), () =>
            {
                realCrossHair.Opacity -= 0.01;
                imagCrossHair.Opacity -= 0.01;
                return true;
            });
    }

    // Method for accessing Properties dictionary if key is not yet present.
    T GetProperty<T>(string key, T defaultValue)
    {
        IDictionary<string, object> properties = Application.Current.Properties;

        if (properties.ContainsKey(key))
        {
            return (T)properties[key];
        }
        return defaultValue;
    }

    // Switch between portrait and landscape mode.
    void OnPageSizeChanged(object sender, EventArgs args)
    {
        if (Width == -1 || Height == -1)
            return;

        // Portrait mode.
        if (Width < Height)
        {
            mainGrid.RowDefinitions[1].Height = GridLength.Auto;
            mainGrid.ColumnDefinitions[1].Width = new GridLength(0, GridUnitType.Absolute);
            Grid.SetRow(controlPanelStack, 1);
```

```
                    Grid.SetColumn(controlPanelStack, 0);
        }
        // Landscape mode.
        else
        {
            mainGrid.RowDefinitions[1].Height = new GridLength(0, GridUnitType.Absolute);
            mainGrid.ColumnDefinitions[1].Width = new GridLength(1, GridUnitType.Star);
            Grid.SetRow(controlPanelStack, 0);
            Grid.SetColumn(controlPanelStack, 1);
        }
    }

    void OnImageSizeChanged(object sender, EventArgs args)
    {
        // Assure that crosshair layout is same size as Image.
        double size = Math.Min(image.Width, image.Height);
        crossHairLayout.WidthRequest = size;
        crossHairLayout.HeightRequest = size;

        // Calculate the pixel size of the Image element.
        SetPixelWidthAndHeight();
    }

    // Sets the Mandelbrot bitmap to optimum pixel width and height.
    void SetPixelWidthAndHeight()
    {
        int pixels = (int)(pixelsPerUnit * Math.Min(image.Width, image.Height));
        mandelbrotViewModel.PixelWidth = pixels;
        mandelbrotViewModel.PixelHeight = pixels;
    }


    // Redraw crosshairs if the crosshair layout changes size.
    void OnCrossHairLayoutSizeChanged(object sender, EventArgs args)
    {
        SetCrossHairs();
    }
    ...

    }
}
```

Rather than attach a bunch of event handlers to user-interface elements in the XAML file, the constructor of the code-behind file instead attaches a `PropertyChanged` handler to the `Mandelbrot-ViewModel` instance. Changes to several properties require that the crosshairs and sizing box be redrawn, and any change to any property brings the crosshairs back into view:

```
namespace MandelbrotXF
{
    {
        ...
        async void OnMandelbrotViewModelPropertyChanged(object sender,
                                        PropertyChangedEventArgs args)
```

```
        {
            // Set opacity back to 1.
            realCrossHair.Opacity = 1;
            imagCrossHair.Opacity = 1;

            switch (args.PropertyName)
            {
                case "RealOffset":
                case "ImaginaryOffset":
                case "CurrentMagnification":
                case "TargetMagnification":
                    // Redraw crosshairs if these properties change
                    SetCrossHairs();
                    break;

                case "BitmapInfo":
                    // Create bitmap based on the iteration counts.
                    DisplayNewBitmap(mandelbrotViewModel.BitmapInfo);

                    // Save properties for the next time program is run.
                    IDictionary<string, object> properties = Application.Current.Properties;
                    properties["CenterReal"] = mandelbrotViewModel.TargetCenter.Real;
                    properties["CenterImaginary"] = mandelbrotViewModel.TargetCenter.Imaginary;
                    properties["Magnification"] = mandelbrotViewModel.TargetMagnification;
                    properties["Iterations"] = mandelbrotViewModel.Iterations;
                    await Application.Current.SavePropertiesAsync();
                    break;
            }
        }

        void SetCrossHairs()
        {
            // Size of the layout for the crosshairs and zoom box.
            Size layoutSize = new Size(crossHairLayout.Width, crossHairLayout.Height);

            // Fractional position of center of crosshair.
            double xCenter = mandelbrotViewModel.RealOffset;
            double yCenter = 1 - mandelbrotViewModel.ImaginaryOffset;

            // Calculate dimension of zoom box.
            double boxSize = mandelbrotViewModel.CurrentMagnification /
                        mandelbrotViewModel.TargetMagnification;

            // Fractional positions of zoom box corners.
            double xLeft = xCenter - boxSize / 2;
            double xRight = xCenter + boxSize / 2;
            double yTop = yCenter - boxSize / 2;
            double yBottom = yCenter + boxSize / 2;

            // Set all the layout bounds.
            SetLayoutBounds(realCrossHair,
                        new Rectangle(xCenter, yTop, 0, boxSize),
                        layoutSize);
            SetLayoutBounds(imagCrossHair,
```

```
                           new Rectangle(xLeft, yCenter, boxSize, 0),
                               layoutSize);
        SetLayoutBounds(topBox, new Rectangle(xLeft, yTop, boxSize, 0), layoutSize);
        SetLayoutBounds(bottomBox, new Rectangle(xLeft, yBottom, boxSize, 0), layoutSize);
        SetLayoutBounds(leftBox, new Rectangle(xLeft, yTop, 0, boxSize), layoutSize);
        SetLayoutBounds(rightBox, new Rectangle(xRight, yTop, 0, boxSize), layoutSize);
    }

    void SetLayoutBounds(View view, Rectangle fractionalRect, Size layoutSize)
    {
        if (layoutSize.Width == -1 || layoutSize.Height == -1)
        {
            AbsoluteLayout.SetLayoutBounds(view, new Rectangle());
            return;
        }

        const double thickness = 1;
        Rectangle absoluteRect = new Rectangle();

        // Horizontal lines.
        if (fractionalRect.Height == 0 && fractionalRect.Y > 0 && fractionalRect.Y < 1)
        {
            double xLeft = Math.Max(0, fractionalRect.Left);
            double xRight = Math.Min(1, fractionalRect.Right);
            absoluteRect = new Rectangle(layoutSize.Width * xLeft,
                                         layoutSize.Height * fractionalRect.Y,
                                         layoutSize.Width * (xRight - xLeft),
                                         thickness);
        }
        // Vertical lines.
        else if (fractionalRect.Width == 0 && fractionalRect.X > 0 && fractionalRect.X < 1)
        {
            double yTop = Math.Max(0, fractionalRect.Top);
            double yBottom = Math.Min(1, fractionalRect.Bottom);
            absoluteRect = new Rectangle(layoutSize.Width * fractionalRect.X,
                                         layoutSize.Height * yTop,
                                         thickness,
                                         layoutSize.Height * (yBottom - yTop));
        }
        AbsoluteLayout.SetLayoutBounds(view, absoluteRect);
    }

    ...

    }
}
```

Early versions of the program attempted to use the proportional sizing and positioning facility of Ab-soluteLayout for the six BoxView elements, but it became too difficult. Fractional values are passed to the SetLayoutBounds method, but those are used to calculate coordinates based on the size of the AbsoluteLayout.

Because Models and ViewModels are supposed to be platform independent, neither `Mandelbrot-Model` nor `MandelbrotViewModel` get involved with creating the actual bitmap. These classes express the image as a `BitmapInfo` value, which is simply a pixel width and height and an array of integers that correspond to iteration counts. Creating and displaying that bitmap mostly involves using `Bmp-Maker` and applying a color scheme based on the iteration count:

```
namespace MandelbrotXF
{
    {
        ...
        void DisplayNewBitmap(BitmapInfo bitmapInfo)
        {
            // Create the bitmap.
            BmpMaker bmpMaker = new BmpMaker(bitmapInfo.PixelWidth, bitmapInfo.PixelHeight);

            // Set the colors.
            int index = 0;
            for (int row = 0; row < bitmapInfo.PixelHeight; row++)
            {
                for (int col = 0; col < bitmapInfo.PixelWidth; col++)
                {
                    int iterationCount = bitmapInfo.IterationCounts[index++];

                    // In the Mandelbrot set: Color black.
                    if (iterationCount == -1)
                    {
                        bmpMaker.SetPixel(row, col, 0, 0, 0);
                    }
                    // Not in the Mandelbrot set: Pick a color based on count.
                    else
                    {
                        double proportion = (iterationCount / 32.0) % 1;

                        if (proportion < 0.5)
                        {
                            bmpMaker.SetPixel(row, col, (int)(255 * (1 - 2 * proportion)),
                                                        0,
                                                        (int)(255 * 2 * proportion));
                        }
                        else
                        {
                            proportion = 2 * (proportion - 0.5);
                            bmpMaker.SetPixel(row, col, 0,
                                                        (int)(255 * proportion),
                                                        (int)(255 * (1 - proportion)));
                        }
                    }
                }
            }
            image.Source = bmpMaker.Generate();
        }
    }
}
```

Feel free to experiment with the color scheme. One easy alternative is to vary the hue of an HSL color with the iteration count:

```
double hue = (iterationCount / 64.0) % 1;
bmpMaker.SetPixel(row, col, Color.FromHsla(hue, 1, 0.5));
```

Back to the web

Prior to this chapter, the only asynchronous code in this book involved web accesses using the only reasonable class available for that purpose in the Portable Class Library, `WebRequest`. The `WebRequest` class uses an older asynchronous protocol called the Asynchronous Programming Model or APM. APM involves two methods, in the case of `WebRequest`, these are called `BeginGetResponse` and `EndGetResponse`.

You can convert this pair of method calls into the Task-based Asynchronous Pattern (TAP) by using the `FromAsync` method of `TaskFactory`, and the **ApmToTap** program demonstrates how. The program uses a web access and `ImageSource.FromStream` to load a bitmap and display it. This technique was shown in Chapter 13 as an alternative to `ImageSource.FromUri`.

The XAML file contains an `Image` element awaiting a bitmap, an `ActivityIndicator` that runs when the bitmap is loading, a `Label` to display a possible error message, and a `Button` to start the download:

```
<ContentPage xmlns="http://xamarin.com/schemas/2014/forms"
             xmlns:x="http://schemas.microsoft.com/winfx/2009/xaml"
             x:Class="ApmToTap.ApmToTapPage">
    <ContentPage.Padding>
        <OnPlatform x:TypeArguments="Thickness"
                    iOS="0, 20, 0, 0" />
    </ContentPage.Padding>

    <StackLayout>
        <Grid VerticalOptions="FillAndExpand">
            <Label x:Name="errorLabel"
                   HorizontalOptions="Center"
                   VerticalOptions="Center" />

            <ActivityIndicator IsRunning="{Binding Source={x:Reference image},
                                                   Path=IsLoading}" />

            <Image x:Name="image" />
        </Grid>

        <Button Text="Load Bitmap"
                HorizontalOptions="Center"
                Clicked="OnLoadButtonClicked" />
    </StackLayout>
</ContentPage>
```

The code-behind file consolidates all the WebRequest code in an asynchronous method named GetStreamAsync. After the TaskFactory and WebRequest objects are instantiated, the method passes the BeginGetResponse and EndGetResponse methods to the FromAsync method of Task-Factory, which then returns a WebResponse object from which a Stream is available:

```
public partial class ApmToTapPage : ContentPage
{
    public ApmToTapPage()
    {
        InitializeComponent();
    }

    async void OnLoadButtonClicked(object sender, EventArgs args)
    {
        try
        {
            Stream stream =
                    await GetStreamAsync("https://developer.xamarin.com/demo/IMG_1996.JPG");
            image.Source = ImageSource.FromStream(() => stream);
        }
        catch (Exception exc)
        {
            errorLabel.Text = exc.Message;
        }
    }

    async Task<Stream> GetStreamAsync(string uri)
    {
        TaskFactory factory = new TaskFactory();
        WebRequest request = WebRequest.Create(uri);
        WebResponse response = await factory.FromAsync<WebResponse>(request.BeginGetResponse,
                                                                    request.EndGetResponse,
                                                                    null);

        return response.GetResponseStream();
    }
}
```

The Clicked handler for the Button can then get that Stream object by calling GetStreamAsync with a URI. As usual, the code with the await operator is in a try block to catch any possible errors. You can experiment a bit by deliberately misspelling the domain or filename to see what kind of errors you get.

Another option for web accesses is a class named HttpClient in the System.Net.Http namespace. This class is not available in the version of .NET included in the Portable Class Library in a Xamarin.Forms solution, but Microsoft has made the class available as a NuGet package:

https://www.nuget.org/packages/Microsoft.Net.Http

From the NuGet manager in Visual Studio or Xamarin Studio, just search for "HttpClient".

HttpClient is based on TAP. The asynchronous methods return Task and Task<T> objects, and some of the methods also have CancellationToken arguments.

None of the methods report progress, however, which suggests that a first-rate modern class for web accesses is still not yet available to Portable Class Libraries.

In the next chapter you'll see many more uses of `await` and explore some other features of the Task-based Asynchronous Pattern in connection with the exciting Xamarin.Forms implementation of animation.

Chapter 21

Transforms

With the help of `StackLayout` and `Grid`, Xamarin.Forms does a good job of sizing and positioning visual elements on the page. Sometimes, however, it's necessary (or convenient) for the application to make some adjustments. You might want to offset the position of elements somewhat, change their size, or even rotate them.

Such changes in location, size, or orientation are possible using a feature of Xamarin.Forms known as *transforms*. The concept of the transform originated in geometry. The transform is a formula that maps points to other points. For example, if you want to shift a geometric object on a Cartesian coordinate system, you can add constant offset factors to all the coordinates that define that object.

These mathematical, geometric transforms play a vital role in computer graphics programming, where they are sometimes known as *matrix transforms* because they are easiest to express mathematically using matrix algebra. Without transforms, there can be no 3D graphics. But over the years, transforms have migrated from graphics programming to user-interface programming. All the platforms supported by Xamarin.Forms support basic transforms that can be applied to user-interface elements such as text, bitmaps, and buttons.

Xamarin.Forms supports three basic types of transforms:

- *Translation*—shifting an element horizontally or vertically or both.

- *Scale*—changing the size of an element.

- *Rotation*—turning an element around a point or axis.

The scaling supported by Xamarin.Forms is uniform in all directions, technically known as *isotropic* scaling. You cannot use scaling to change the aspect ratio of a visual element. Rotation is supported for both the two-dimensional surface of the screen and in 3D space. Xamarin.Forms does not support a skewing transform or a generalized matrix transform.

Xamarin.Forms supports these transforms with eight properties of the `VisualElement` class. These properties are all of type `double`:

- `TranslationX`

- `TranslationY`

- `Scale`

- `Rotation`

- `RotationX`

- RotationY

- AnchorX

- AnchorY

As you'll see in the next chapter, Xamarin.Forms also has an extensive and extensible animation system that can target these properties. But you can also perform transform animations on your own by using `Device.StartTimer` or `Task.Delay`. This chapter demonstrates some animation techniques and perhaps will help get you into an animation frame of mind in preparation for Chapter 22.

The translation transform

An application uses one of the layout classes—`StackLayout`, `Grid`, `AbsoluteLayout`, or `RelativeLayout`—to position a visual element on the screen. Let's call the position established by the layout system the "layout position."

Nonzero values of the `TranslationX` and `TranslationY` properties change the position of a visual element relative to that layout position. Positive values of `TranslationX` shift the element to the right, and positive values of `TranslationY` shift the element down.

The **TranslationDemo** program lets you experiment with these two properties. Everything is in the XAML file:

```
<ContentPage xmlns="http://xamarin.com/schemas/2014/forms"
             xmlns:x="http://schemas.microsoft.com/winfx/2009/xaml"
             x:Class="TranslationDemo.TranslationDemoPage">
    <StackLayout Padding="20, 10">
        <Frame x:Name="frame"
               HorizontalOptions="Center"
               VerticalOptions="CenterAndExpand"
               OutlineColor="Accent">

            <Label Text="TEXT"
                   FontSize="Large" />
        </Frame>

        <Slider x:Name="xSlider"
                Minimum="-200"
                Maximum="200"
                Value="{Binding Source={x:Reference frame},
                            Path=TranslationX}" />

        <Label Text="{Binding Source={x:Reference xSlider},
                          Path=Value,
                          StringFormat='TranslationX = {0:F0}'}"
               HorizontalTextAlignment="Center" />

        <Slider x:Name="ySlider"
```

```
                Minimum="-200"
                Maximum="200"
                Value="{Binding Source={x:Reference frame},
                                Path=TranslationY }" />

        <Label Text="{Binding Source={x:Reference ySlider},
                              Path=Value,
                              StringFormat='TranslationY = {0:F0}'}"
                HorizontalTextAlignment="Center" />
    </StackLayout>
</ContentPage>
```

A `Frame` encloses a `Label` and is centered in the upper part of the `StackLayout`. Two `Slider` elements have bindings to the `TranslationX` and `TranslationY` properties of the `Frame`, and they are initialized for a range of –200 to 200. When you first run the program, the two sliders are set to the default values of `TranslationX` and `TranslationY`, which are zero:

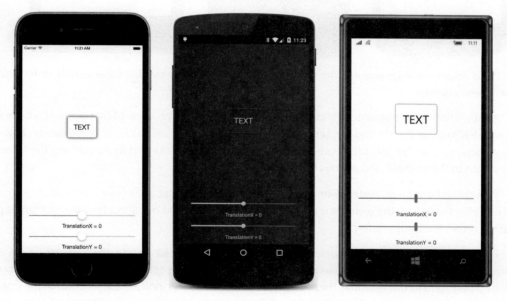

You can manipulate the sliders to move the `Frame` around the screen. The values of `TranslationX` and `TranslationY` specify an offset of the element relative to its original layout position:

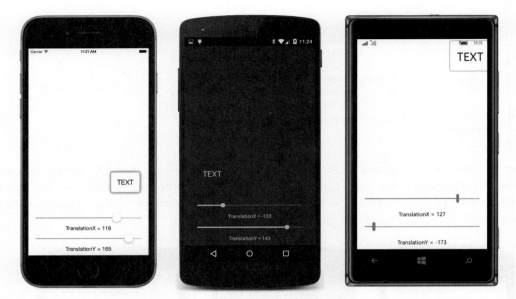

If the values are large enough, the element can be translated to overlap other visuals, or to move off the screen entirely.

A translation of an element such as a `Frame` also affects all the children of that element, which in this case is just the `Label`. You can set the `TranslationX` and `TranslationY` properties on any `VisualElement,` and that includes `StackLayout`, `Grid`, and even `Page` and its derivatives. The transform is applied to the element and all the children of that element.

What might not be so evident without a little investigation is that `TranslationX` and `TranslationY` affect only how the element is *rendered*. These properties do *not* affect how the element is perceived within the layout system.

For example, `VisualElement` defines get-only properties named `X` and `Y` that indicate where an element is located relative to its parent. The `X` and `Y` properties are set when an element is positioned by its parent, and in this example, the `X` and `Y` properties of `Frame` indicate the location of the upper-left corner of the `Frame` relative to the upper-left corner of the `StackLayout`. The `X` and `Y` properties do *not* change when `TranslationX` and `TranslationY` are set. Also, the get-only `Bounds` property—which combines `X` and `Y` along with `Width` and `Height` in a single `Rectangle`—does not change either. The layout system does not get involved when `TranslationX` and `TranslationY` are modified.

What happens if you use `TranslationX` and `TranslationY` to move a `Button` from its original position? Does the `Button` respond to taps at its original layout position or the new rendered position? You'll be happy to know that it's the latter. `TranslationX` and `TranslationY` affect both how the element is rendered and how it responds to taps. You'll see this shortly in a sample program called **ButtonJump**.

If you need to do some extensive movement of elements around the page, you might wonder whether to use `AbsoluteLayout` and specify coordinates explicitly or use `TranslationX` and Trans-lationY to specify offsets. In terms of performance, there's really not much difference. The advantage of `TranslationX` and `TranslationY` is that you can start with a position established by `StackLay-out` or `Grid` and then move the elements relative to that position.

Text effects

One common application of `TranslationX` and `TranslationY` is to apply little offsets to elements that shift them slightly from their layout position. This is sometimes useful if you have multiple overlap-ping elements in a single-cell `Grid` and need to shift one so that it peeks out from under another.

You can even use this technique for common text effects. The XAML-only **TextOffsets** program puts three pairs of `Label` elements in three single-cell `Grid` layouts. The pair of `Label` elements in each `Grid` are the same size and display the same text:

```
<ContentPage xmlns="http://xamarin.com/schemas/2014/forms"
             xmlns:x="http://schemas.microsoft.com/winfx/2009/xaml"
             x:Class="TextOffsets.TextOffsetsPage">
    <ContentPage.Padding>
        <OnPlatform x:TypeArguments="Thickness"
                    iOS="0, 20, 0, 0" />
    </ContentPage.Padding>

    <ContentPage.Resources>
        <ResourceDictionary>
            <Color x:Key="backgroundColor">White</Color>
            <Color x:Key="foregroundColor">Black</Color>

            <Style TargetType="Grid">
                <Setter Property="VerticalOptions" Value="CenterAndExpand" />
            </Style>

            <Style TargetType="Label">
                <Setter Property="FontSize" Value="72" />
                <Setter Property="FontAttributes" Value="Bold" />
                <Setter Property="HorizontalOptions" Value="Center" />
            </Style>
        </ResourceDictionary>
    </ContentPage.Resources>

    <StackLayout BackgroundColor="{StaticResource backgroundColor}">
        <Grid>
            <Label Text="Shadow"
                   TextColor="{StaticResource foregroundColor}"
                   Opacity="0.5"
                   TranslationX="5"
                   TranslationY="5" />

            <Label Text="Shadow"
                   TextColor="{StaticResource foregroundColor}" />
```

```xml
        </Grid>

        <Grid>
            <Label Text="Emboss"
                   TextColor="{StaticResource foregroundColor}"
                   TranslationX="2"
                   TranslationY="2" />

            <Label Text="Emboss"
                   TextColor="{StaticResource backgroundColor}" />
        </Grid>

        <Grid>
            <Label Text="Engrave"
                   TextColor="{StaticResource foregroundColor}"
                   TranslationX="-2"
                   TranslationY="-2" />

            <Label Text="Engrave"
                   TextColor="{StaticResource backgroundColor}" />
        </Grid>
    </StackLayout>
</ContentPage>
```

Normally, the first `Label` in the `Children` collection of the `Grid` would be obscured by the second `Label`, but `TranslationX` and `TranslationY` values applied on the first `Label` allow it to be partially visible. The same basic technique results in three different text effects: a drop shadow, text that appears to be raised up from the surface of the screen, and text that looks like it's chiseled into the screen:

These effects give a somewhat 3D appearance to otherwise flat images. The optical illusion is based on a convention that light illuminates the screen from the upper-left corner. Therefore, shadows are thrown below and to the right of raised objects. The difference between the embossed and engraved effects is entirely due to the relative positions of the obscured black text and the white text on top. If the black text is a little below and to the right, it becomes the shadow of raised white text. If the black text is above and to the left of the white text, it becomes a shadow of text sunk below the surface.

The next example is not something you'll want to use on a regular basis because it requires multiple `Label` elements, but the technique illustrated in the **BlockText** program is useful if you want to supply a little "depth" to your text:

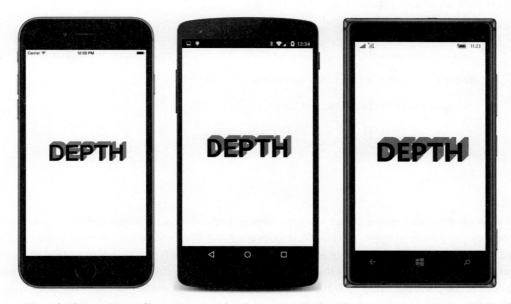

The **BlockText** XAML file uses a single-cell `Grid` to display black text on a white background. The implicit (and extensive) `Style` defined for `Label`, however, specifies a `TextColor` property of `Gray`:

```
<ContentPage xmlns="http://xamarin.com/schemas/2014/forms"
             xmlns:x="http://schemas.microsoft.com/winfx/2009/xaml"
             x:Class="BlockText.BlockTextPage">
    <Grid x:Name="grid"
          BackgroundColor="White">
        <Grid.Resources>
            <ResourceDictionary>
                <Style TargetType="Label">
                    <Setter Property="Text" Value="DEPTH" />
                    <Setter Property="FontSize" Value="72" />
                    <Setter Property="FontAttributes" Value="Bold" />
                    <Setter Property="TextColor" Value="Gray" />
                    <Setter Property="HorizontalOptions" Value="Center" />
                    <Setter Property="VerticalOptions" Value="Center" />
                </Style>
```

```
            </ResourceDictionary>
        </Grid.Resources>

        <Label TextColor="Black" />

    </Grid>
</ContentPage>
```

The constructor in the code-behind file adds several more `Label` elements to the `Grid`. The `Style` ensures that they all get the same properties (including being colored gray), but each of these is offset from the `Label` in the XAML file:

```
public partial class BlockTextPage : ContentPage
{
    public BlockTextPage()
    {
        InitializeComponent();

        for (int i = 0; i < Device.OnPlatform(12, 12, 18); i++)
        {
            grid.Children.Insert(0, new Label
                {
                    TranslationX = i,
                    TranslationY = -i
                });
        }
    }
}
```

Here's another case where `Label` elements overlap each other in the single-cell `Grid`, but now there are many more of them. The black `Label` in the XAML file must be the *last* child in the `Children` collection so that it's on top of all the others. The element with the maximum `TranslationX` and `TranslationY` offset must be the *first* child in the `Children` collection, so it must be on the very bottom of the pile. That's why each successive `Label` is inserted at the beginning of the `Children` collection.

Jumps and animations

The **ButtonJump** program is mostly intended to demonstrate that no matter where you move a `Button` on the screen by using translation, the `Button` still responds to taps in the normal manner. The XAML file centers the `Button` in the middle of the page (less the iOS padding at the top):

```
<ContentPage xmlns="http://xamarin.com/schemas/2014/forms"
             xmlns:x="http://schemas.microsoft.com/winfx/2009/xaml"
             x:Class="ButtonJump.ButtonJumpPage">
    <ContentPage.Padding>
        <OnPlatform x:TypeArguments="Thickness"
                    iOS="0, 20, 0, 0" />
    </ContentPage.Padding>

    <ContentView>
```

```
        <Button Text="Tap me!"
                FontSize="Large"
                HorizontalOptions="Center"
                VerticalOptions="Center"
                Clicked="OnButtonClicked" />
    </ContentView>
</ContentPage>
```

For each call to the `OnButtonClicked` handler, the code-behind file sets the `TranslationX` and `TranslationY` properties to new values. The new values are randomly calculated but restricted so that the `Button` always remains within the edges of the screen:

```
public partial class ButtonJumpPage : ContentPage
{
    Random random = new Random();

    public ButtonJumpPage()
    {
        InitializeComponent();
    }

    void OnButtonClicked(object sender, EventArgs args)
    {
        Button button = (Button)sender;
        View container = (View)button.Parent;

        button.TranslationX = (random.NextDouble() - 0.5) * (container.Width - button.Width);
        button.TranslationY = (random.NextDouble() - 0.5) * (container.Height - button.Height);
    }
}
```

For example, if the `Button` is 80 units wide and the `ContentView` is 320 units wide, the difference is 240 units, which is 120 units on each side of the `Button` when it's in the center of the `ContentView`. The `NextDouble` method of `Random` returns a number between 0 and 1, and subtracting 0.5 yields a number between –0.5 and 0.5, which means that `TranslationX` is set to a random value between –120 and 120. Those values potentially position the `Button` up to the edge of the screen but not beyond.

Keep in mind that `TranslationX` and `TranslationY` are properties rather than methods. They are not cumulative. If you set `TranslationX` to 100 and then to 200, the visual element isn't offset by a total of 300 units from its layout position. The second `TranslationX` value of 200 replaces rather than adds to the initial value of 100.

A few seconds playing with the **ButtonJump** program probably raises a question: Can this be animated? Can the `Button` glide to the new point rather than simply jump there?

Of course. There are several ways to do it, including the Xamarin.Forms animation methods discussed in the next chapter. The XAML file in the **ButtonGlide** program is the same as the one in **ButtonJump,** except that the `Button` now has a name so that the program can easily reference it outside the `Clicked` handler:

```
<ContentPage xmlns="http://xamarin.com/schemas/2014/forms"
             xmlns:x="http://schemas.microsoft.com/winfx/2009/xaml"
             x:Class="ButtonGlide.ButtonGlidePage">
    <ContentPage.Padding>
        <OnPlatform x:TypeArguments="Thickness"
                    iOS="0, 20, 0, 0" />
    </ContentPage.Padding>

    <ContentView>
        <Button x:Name="button"
                Text="Tap me!"
                FontSize="Large"
                HorizontalOptions="Center"
                VerticalOptions="Center"
                Clicked="OnButtonClicked" />
    </ContentView>
</ContentPage>
```

The code-behind file processes the button click by saving several essential pieces of information as fields: a `Point` indicating the starting location obtained from the current values of `TranslationX` and `TranslationY`; a vector (which is also a `Point` value) calculated by subtracting this starting point from a random destination point; and the current `DateTime` when the `Button` is clicked:

```
public partial class ButtonGlidePage : ContentPage
{
    static readonly TimeSpan duration = TimeSpan.FromSeconds(1);
    Random random = new Random();
    Point startPoint;
    Point animationVector;
    DateTime startTime;

    public ButtonGlidePage()
    {
        InitializeComponent();

        Device.StartTimer(TimeSpan.FromMilliseconds(16), OnTimerTick);
    }

    void OnButtonClicked(object sender, EventArgs args)
    {
        Button button = (Button)sender;
        View container = (View)button.Parent;

        // The start of the animation is the current Translation properties.
        startPoint = new Point(button.TranslationX, button.TranslationY);

        // The end of the animation is a random point.
        double endX = (random.NextDouble() - 0.5) * (container.Width - button.Width);
        double endY = (random.NextDouble() - 0.5) * (container.Height - button.Height);

        // Create a vector from start point to end point.
        animationVector = new Point(endX - startPoint.X, endY - startPoint.Y);

        // Save the animation start time.
```

```
            startTime = DateTime.Now;
    }

    bool OnTimerTick()
    {
        // Get the elapsed time from the beginning of the animation.
        TimeSpan elapsedTime = DateTime.Now - startTime;

        // Normalize the elapsed time from 0 to 1.
        double t = Math.Max(0, Math.Min(1, elapsedTime.TotalMilliseconds /
                                        duration.TotalMilliseconds));

        // Calculate the new translation based on the animation vector.
        button.TranslationX = startPoint.X + t * animationVector.X;
        button.TranslationY = startPoint.Y + t * animationVector.Y;
        return true;
    }
}
```

The timer callback is called every 16 milliseconds. That's not an arbitrary number! Video displays commonly have a hardware refresh rate of 60 times per second. Hence, every frame is active for about 16 milliseconds. Pacing the animation at this rate is optimum. Once every 16 milliseconds, the callback calculates an elapsed time from the beginning of the animation and divides it by the duration. That's a value typically called t (for *time*) that ranges from 0 to 1 over the course of the animation. This value is multiplied by the vector, and the result is added to startPoint. That's the new value of Transla-tionX and TranslationY.

Although the timer callback is called continuously while the application is running, the Transla-tionX and TranslationY properties remain constant when the animation has completed. However, you don't have to wait until the Button has stopped moving before you can tap it again. (You need to be quick, or you can change the duration property to something longer.) The new animation starts from the current position of the Button and entirely replaces the previous animation.

One of the advantages of calculating a normalized value of t is that it becomes fairly easy to modify that value so that the animation doesn't have a constant velocity. For example, try adding this state-ment after the initial calculation of t:

```
t = Math.Sin(t * Math.PI / 2);
```

When the original value of t is 0 at the beginning of the animation, the argument to Math.Sin is 0 and the result is 0. When the original value of t is 1, the argument to Math.Sin is $\pi/2$, and the result is 1. However, the values between those two points are not linear. When the initial value of t is 0.5, this statement recalculates t as the sine of 45 degrees, which is 0.707. So by the time the animation is half over, the Button has already moved 70 percent of the distance to its destination. Overall, you'll see an animation that is faster at the beginning and slower toward the end.

You'll see a couple of different approaches to animation in this chapter. Even when you've become familiar with the animation system that Xamarin.Forms provides, sometimes it's useful to do it yourself.

The scale transform

The `VisualElement` class defines a property named `Scale` that you can use to change the rendered size of an element. The `Scale` property does *not* affect layout (as will be demonstrated in the **ButtonScaler** program). It does *not* affect the get-only `Width` and `Height` properties of the element, or the get-only `Bounds` property that incorporates those `Width` and `Height` values. Changes to the `Scale` property do *not* cause a `SizeChanged` event to be triggered.

   `Scale` affects the coordinates of a rendered visual element, but in a very different way from `TranslationX` and `TranslationY`. The two translation properties add values to coordinates, while the `Scale` property is multiplicative. The default value of `Scale` is 1. Values greater than 1 increase the size of the element. For example, a value of 3 makes the element three times its normal size. Values less than 1 decrease the size. A `Scale` value of 0 is legal but causes the element to be invisible. If you're working with `Scale` and your element seems to have disappeared, check whether it's somehow getting a `Scale` value of 0.

   Values less than 0 are also legal and cause the element to be rotated 180 degrees besides being altered in size.

   You can experiment with `Scale` settings using the **SimpleScaleDemo** program. (The program has a **Simple** prefix because it doesn't include the effect of the `AnchorX` and `AnchorY` properties, which will be discussed shortly.) The XAML is similar to the **TranslationDemo** program:

```
<ContentPage xmlns="http://xamarin.com/schemas/2014/forms"
             xmlns:x="http://schemas.microsoft.com/winfx/2009/xaml"
             x:Class="SimpleScaleDemo.SimpleScaleDemoPage">
    <StackLayout Padding="20, 10">
        <Frame x:Name="frame"
               HorizontalOptions="Center"
               VerticalOptions="CenterAndExpand"
               OutlineColor="Accent">

            <Label Text="TEXT"
                   FontSize="Large" />
        </Frame>

        <Slider x:Name="scaleSlider"
                Minimum="-10"
                Maximum="10"
                Value="{Binding Source={x:Reference frame},
                                Path=Scale}" />

        <Label Text="{Binding Source={x:Reference scaleSlider},
                              Path=Value,
                              StringFormat='Scale = {0:F1}'}"
               HorizontalTextAlignment="Center" />
    </StackLayout>
</ContentPage>
```

Here it is in action. Notice the negative `Scale` setting on the Android phone:

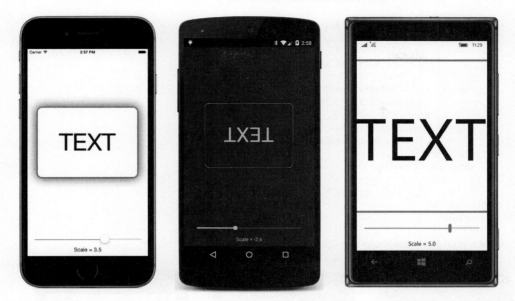

On the Windows 10 Mobile display, the `Frame` has been scaled so large that you can't see its left and right sides.

In real-life programming, you might want to use `Scale` to provide a little feedback to a user when a `Button` is clicked. The `Button` can briefly expand in size and go back down to normal again. However, `Scale` is not the only way to change the size of a `Button`. You can also change the `Button` size by increasing and decreasing the `FontSize` property. These two techniques are very different, however: The `Scale` property doesn't affect layout, but the `FontSize` property does.

This difference is illustrated in the **ButtonScaler** program. The XAML file consists of two `Button` elements sandwiched between two pairs of `BoxView` elements:

```
<ContentPage xmlns="http://xamarin.com/schemas/2014/forms"
             xmlns:x="http://schemas.microsoft.com/winfx/2009/xaml"
             x:Class="ButtonScaler.ButtonScalerPage">
    <StackLayout>
        <!-- "Animate Scale" Button between two BoxViews. -->
        <BoxView Color="Accent"
                 HeightRequest="4"
                 VerticalOptions="EndAndExpand" />

        <Button Text="Animate Scale"
                FontSize="Large"
                BorderWidth="1"
                HorizontalOptions="Center"
                Clicked="OnAnimateScaleClicked" />

        <BoxView Color="Accent"
```

```
                        HeightRequest="4"
                        VerticalOptions="StartAndExpand" />

        <!-- "Animate FontSize" Button between two BoxViews. -->
        <BoxView Color="Accent"
                 HeightRequest="4"
                 VerticalOptions="EndAndExpand" />

        <Button Text="Animate FontSize"
                FontSize="Large"
                BorderWidth="1"
                HorizontalOptions="Center"
                Clicked="OnAnimateFontSizeClicked" />

        <BoxView Color="Accent"
                 HeightRequest="4"
                 VerticalOptions="StartAndExpand" />
    </StackLayout>
</ContentPage>
```

Here's what the page looks like normally:

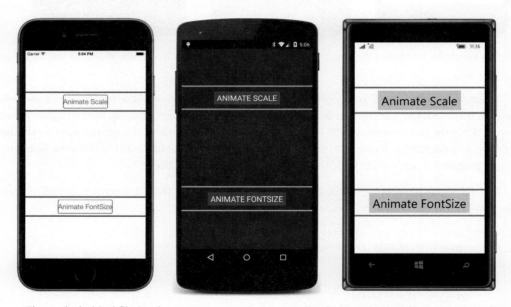

The code-behind file implements a somewhat generalized animation method. It's generalized in the sense that the parameters include two values indicating the starting value and the ending value of the animation. These two values are often called a *from* value and a *to* value. The animation arguments also include the duration of the animation and a callback method. The argument to the callback method is a value between the "from" value and the "to" value, and the calling method can use that value to do whatever it needs to implement the animation.

However, this animation method is not entirely generalized. It actually calculates a value from the *from* value to the *to* value during the first half of the animation, and then calculates a value from the *to* value back to the *from* value during the second half of the animation. This is sometimes called a *reversing* animation.

The method is called `AnimateAndBack`, and it uses a `Task.Delay` call to pace the animation and a .NET `Stopwach` object to determine elapsed time:

```
public partial class ButtonScalerPage : ContentPage
{
    public ButtonScalerPage()
    {
        InitializeComponent();
    }

    void OnAnimateScaleClicked(object sender, EventArgs args)
    {
        Button button = (Button)sender;
        AnimateAndBack(1, 5, TimeSpan.FromSeconds(3), (double value) =>
            {
                button.Scale = value;
            });
    }

    void OnAnimateFontSizeClicked(object sender, EventArgs args)
    {
        Button button = (Button)sender;

        AnimateAndBack(button.FontSize, 5 * button.FontSize,
                        TimeSpan.FromSeconds(3), (double value) =>
            {
                button.FontSize = value;
            });
    }

    async void AnimateAndBack(double fromValue, double toValue,
                        TimeSpan duration, Action<double> callback)
    {
        Stopwatch stopWatch = new Stopwatch();
        double t = 0;
        stopWatch.Start();

        while (t < 1)
        {
            double tReversing = 2 * (t < 0.5 ? t : 1 - t);
            callback(fromValue + (toValue - fromValue) * tReversing);
            await Task.Delay(16);
            t = stopWatch.ElapsedMilliseconds / duration.TotalMilliseconds;
        }

        stopWatch.Stop();
        callback(fromValue);
    }
}
```

The Clicked handler for the text button assigns a various

Another use of the `Scale` property is sizing an element to fit the available space. You might recall the **FitToSizeClock** program toward the end of Chapter 5, "Dealing with sizes." You can do something very similar with the `Scale` property, but you won't need to make estimations or recursive calculations.

The XAML file of the **ScaleToSize** program contains a `Label` missing some text and also missing a `Scale` setting to make the `Label` larger:

```xml
<ContentPage xmlns="http://xamarin.com/schemas/2014/forms"
             xmlns:x="http://schemas.microsoft.com/winfx/2009/xaml"
             x:Class="ScaleToSize.ScaleToSizePage"
             SizeChanged="OnSizeChanged">

    <Label x:Name="label"
           HorizontalOptions="Center"
           VerticalOptions="Center"
           SizeChanged="OnSizeChanged" />

</ContentPage>
```

Both the `ContentPage` and the `Label` have `SizeChanged` handlers installed, and they both use the same handler. This handler simply sets the `Scale` property of the `Label` to the minimum of the width and height of the page divided by the width and height of the `Label`:

```csharp
public partial class ScaleToSizePage : ContentPage
{
    public ScaleToSizePage()
    {
        InitializeComponent();
        UpdateLoop();
    }

    async void UpdateLoop()
    {
        while (true)
        {
            label.Text = DateTime.Now.ToString("T");
            await Task.Delay(1000);
        }
    }

    void OnSizeChanged(object sender, EventArgs args)
    {
        label.Scale = Math.Min(Width / label.Width, Height / label.Height);
    }
}
```

Because setting the `Scale` property doesn't trigger another `SizeChanged` event, there's no danger of triggering an endless recursive loop. But an actual infinite loop using `Task.Delay` keeps the `Label` updated with the current time:

Of course, turning the phone sideways makes the Label larger:

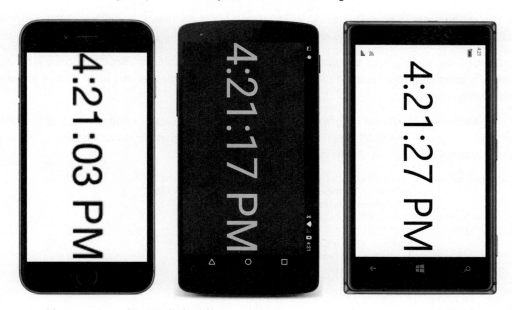

And here you can detect a little difference in the implementation of the Scale property in iOS compared with Android and the Windows Runtime. On Android and Windows, the resultant text looks as though it were drawn with a large font. However, the text on the iOS screen looks a little fuzzy. This fuzziness occurs when the operating system *rasterizes* the prescaled Label, which means that the operating system turns it into a bitmap. The bitmap is then expanded based on the Scale setting.

Anchoring the scale

As you've experimented with the `Scale` property, you've probably noticed that any expansion of the visual element occurs outward from the center of the element, and if you shrink a visual element down to nothing, it contracts toward the center as well.

Here's another way to think about it: The point in the very center of the visual element remains in the same location regardless of the setting of the `Scale` property.

If you're using the `Scale` property to expand a `Button` for visual feedback, or to fit a visual element within a particular space, that's probably precisely what you want. However, for some other applications, you might instead prefer that another point remains in the same location with changes to the `Scale` property. Perhaps you want the upper-left corner of the visual element to remain in the same spot and for expansion of the object to occur toward the right and bottom.

You can control the scaling center with the `AnchorX` and `AnchorY` properties. These properties are of type `double` and are relative to the element being transformed. An `AnchorX` value of 0 indicates the left side of the element, and a value of 1 is the right side of the element. An `AnchorY` value of 0 is the top and 1 is the bottom. The default values are 0.5, which is the center. Setting both properties to 0 allows scaling to be relative to the upper-left corner of the element.

You can also set the properties to values less than 0 or greater than 1, in which case the center of scaling is outside the bounds of the element.

As you'll see, the `AnchorX` and `AnchorY` properties also affect rotation. Rotation occurs around a particular point called the *center of rotation*, and these two properties set that point relative to the element being rotated.

The **AnchoredScaleDemo** program lets you experiment with `AnchorX` and `AnchorY` as they affect the `Scale` property. The XAML files contains two `Stepper` views that let you change the `AnchorX` and `AnchorY` properties from –1 to 2 in increments of 0.25:

```
<ContentPage xmlns="http://xamarin.com/schemas/2014/forms"
             xmlns:x="http://schemas.microsoft.com/winfx/2009/xaml"
             x:Class="AnchoredScaleDemo.AnchoredScaleDemoPage">
    <StackLayout Padding="20, 10">
        <Frame x:Name="frame"
               HorizontalOptions="Center"
               VerticalOptions="CenterAndExpand"
               OutlineColor="Accent">
            <Label Text="TEXT"
                   FontSize="Large" />
        </Frame>

        <Slider x:Name="scaleSlider"
                Minimum="-10"
                Maximum="10"
                Value="{Binding Source={x:Reference frame},
                        Path=Scale}" />
```

```
        <Label Text="{Binding Source={x:Reference scaleSlider},
                               Path=Value,
                               StringFormat='Scale = {0:F1}'}"
               HorizontalTextAlignment="Center" />

    <StackLayout Orientation="Horizontal"
                 HorizontalOptions="Center">
        <Stepper x:Name="anchorXStepper"
                 Minimum="-1"
                 Maximum="2"
                 Increment="0.25"
                 Value="{Binding Source={x:Reference frame},
                                 Path=AnchorX}" />

        <Label Text="{Binding Source={x:Reference anchorXStepper},
                              Path=Value,
                              StringFormat='AnchorX = {0:F2}'}"
               VerticalOptions="Center"/>
    </StackLayout>

    <StackLayout Orientation="Horizontal"
                 HorizontalOptions="Center">
        <Stepper x:Name="anchorYStepper"
                 Minimum="-1"
                 Maximum="2"
                 Increment="0.25"
                 Value="{Binding Source={x:Reference frame},
                                 Path=AnchorY}" />

        <Label Text="{Binding Source={x:Reference anchorYStepper},
                              Path=Value,
                              StringFormat='AnchorY = {0:F2}'}"
               VerticalOptions="Center"/>
    </StackLayout>
    </StackLayout>
</ContentPage>
```

Here are some screenshots showing (from left to right) scaling that is relative to the upper-left corner, relative to the lower-right corner, and relative to the center bottom:

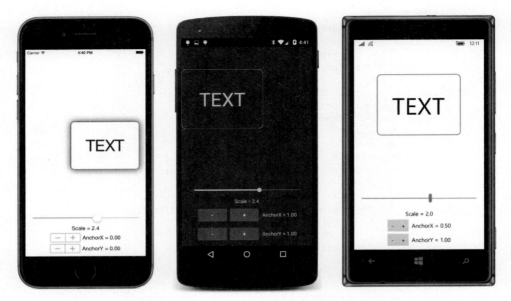

If you are familiar with iOS programming, you know about the similar anchorPoint property. In iOS, this property affects both positioning and the transform center. In Xamarin.Forms, the AnchorX and AnchorY properties specify only the transform center.

This means that the iOS implementation of Xamarin.Forms must compensate for the difference between anchorPoint and the AnchorX and AnchorY properties, and in the latest version of Xamarin.Forms available as this edition was going to print, that compensation is not working quite right.

To see the problem, deploy the **AnchoredScaleDemo** program to an iPhone or iPhone simulator. Leave Scale set at its default value of 1, but set both AnchorX and AnchorY to 1. The Frame with the Label should not move from the center of its slot in the StackLayout because the AnchorX and AnchorY properties should only affect the center of scaling and rotation.

Now change the orientation of the phone or simulator from portrait to landscape. The Frame is no longer centered. Now change it back to portrait. It doesn't return to its original centered position.

This problem affects every program in this chapter (and the next chapter) that use nondefault values of AnchorX and AnchorY. Sometimes the sample programs in these chapters set AnchorX and AnchorY after an element has been resized to try to avoid the problem, but as long as the phone can change orientation from portrait to landscape, the problem cannot be circumvented, and there's nothing an application can do to compensate for the problem.

The rotation transform

The `Rotation` property rotates a visual element on the surface of the screen. Set the `Rotation` property to an angle in degrees (not radians). Positive angles rotate the element clockwise. You can set `Rotation` to angles less than 0 or greater than 360. The actual rotation angle is the value of the `Rotation` property modulo 360. The element is rotated around a point relative to itself specified with the `AnchorX` and `AnchorY` properties.

The **PlaneRotationDemo** program lets you experiment with these three properties. The XAML file is very similar to the **AnchoredScaleDemo** program:

```
<ContentPage xmlns="http://xamarin.com/schemas/2014/forms"
             xmlns:x="http://schemas.microsoft.com/winfx/2009/xaml"
             x:Class="PlaneRotationDemo.PlaneRotationDemoPage">
    <StackLayout Padding="20, 10">
        <Frame x:Name="frame"
               HorizontalOptions="Center"
               VerticalOptions="CenterAndExpand"
               OutlineColor="Accent">
            <Label Text="TEXT"
                   FontSize="Large" />
        </Frame>

        <Slider x:Name="rotationSlider"
                Maximum="360"
                Value="{Binding Source={x:Reference frame},
                                Path=Rotation}" />

        <Label Text="{Binding Source={x:Reference rotationSlider},
                              Path=Value,
                              StringFormat='Rotation = {0:F0}'}"
               HorizontalTextAlignment="Center" />

        <StackLayout Orientation="Horizontal"
                     HorizontalOptions="Center">
            <Stepper x:Name="anchorXStepper"
                     Minimum="-1"
                     Maximum="2"
                     Increment="0.25"
                     Value="{Binding Source={x:Reference frame},
                                     Path=AnchorX}" />

            <Label Text="{Binding Source={x:Reference anchorXStepper},
                                  Path=Value,
                                  StringFormat='AnchorX = {0:F2}'}"
                   VerticalOptions="Center"/>
        </StackLayout>

        <StackLayout Orientation="Horizontal"
                     HorizontalOptions="Center">
            <Stepper x:Name="anchorYStepper"
```

```
                            Minimum="-1"
                            Maximum="2"
                            Increment="0.25"
                            Value="{Binding Source={x:Reference frame},
                                            Path=AnchorY}" />

            <Label Text="{Binding Source={x:Reference anchorYStepper},
                                  Path=Value,
                                  StringFormat='AnchorY = {0:F2}'}"
                   VerticalOptions="Center"/>
        </StackLayout>
    </StackLayout>
</ContentPage>
```

Here are several combinations of `Rotation` angles and rotation centers:

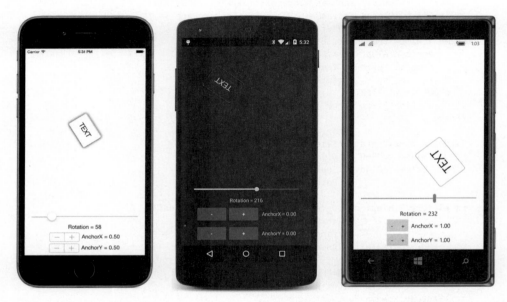

The iOS screen shows rotation around the center of the element (which is always safe on iOS despite the `AnchorX` and `AnchorY` bug), while the rotation on the Android screen is around the upper-left corner, and the rotation on the Windows 10 Mobile screen is centered on the bottom-right corner.

Rotated text effects

Rotation is fun. It's more fun when rotation is animated (as you'll see in the next chapter), but it's fun even with static images.

Several of the rotation examples in this chapter and the next involve arranging visual elements in a circle, so let's begin by attempting to display a simple circle. Of course, without an actual graphics system in Xamarin.Forms, we'll need to be inventive and construct this circle with `BoxView`. If you use many small `BoxView` elements and arrange them properly, it should be possible to create something that looks like a smooth round circle, like this:

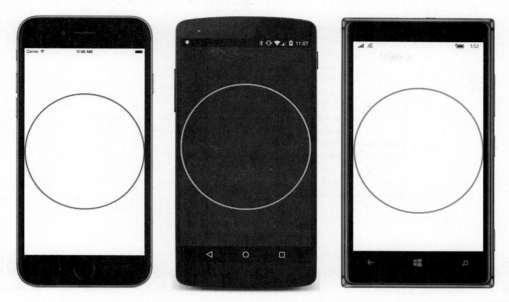

Each circle is composed of 64 `BoxView` elements, each of which is 4 units in thickness. These two values are defined as constants in the code-only **BoxViewCircle** program:

```
public class BoxViewClockPage : ContentPage
{
    const int COUNT = 64;
    const double THICKNESS = 4;

    public BoxViewClockPage()
    {
        AbsoluteLayout absoluteLayout = new AbsoluteLayout();
        Content = absoluteLayout;

        for (int index = 0; index < COUNT; index++)
        {
            absoluteLayout.Children.Add(new BoxView
                {
                    Color = Color.Accent,
                });
        }

        absoluteLayout.SizeChanged += (sender, args) =>
            {
                Point center = new Point(absoluteLayout.Width / 2, absoluteLayout.Height / 2);
                double radius = Math.Min(absoluteLayout.Width, absoluteLayout.Height) / 2;
                double circumference = 2 * Math.PI * radius;
                double length = circumference / COUNT;

                for (int index = 0; index < absoluteLayout.Children.Count; index++)
```

```
            {
                BoxView boxView = (BoxView)absoluteLayout.Children[index];

                // Position every BoxView at the top.
                AbsoluteLayout.SetLayoutBounds(boxView,
                    new Rectangle(center.X - length / 2,
                                  center.Y - radius,
                                  length,
                                  THICKNESS));

                // Set the AnchorX and AnchorY properties so rotation is
                //      around the center of the AbsoluteLayout.
                boxView.AnchorX = 0.5;
                boxView.AnchorY = radius / THICKNESS;

                // Set a unique Rotation for each BoxView.
                boxView.Rotation = index * 360.0 / COUNT;
            }
        };
    }
}
```

All the calculations occur in the `SizeChanged` handler of the `AbsoluteLayout`. The minimum of the width and height of the `AbsoluteLayout` is the radius of a circle. Knowing that radius allows calculating a circumference, and hence a length for each individual `BoxView`.

The `for` loop positions each `BoxView` in the same location: at the center top of the circle. Each `BoxView` must then be rotated around the center of the circle. This requires setting an `AnchorY` property that corresponds to the distance from the top of the `BoxView` to the center of the circle. That distance is the `radius` value, but it must be in units of the `BoxView` height, which means that `radius` must be divided by `THICKNESS`.

There's an alternative way to position and rotate each `BoxView` that doesn't require setting the `AnchorX` and `AnchorY` properties. This approach is better for iOS. The `for` loop begins by calculating `x` and `y` values corresponding to the center of each `BoxView` around the perimeter of the circle. These calculations require using sine and cosine functions with a `radius` value that compensates for the thickness of the `BoxView`:

```
for (int index = 0; index < absoluteLayout.Children.Count; index++)
{
    BoxView boxView = (BoxView)absoluteLayout.Children[index];

    // Find point in center of each positioned BoxView.
    double radians = index * 2 * Math.PI / COUNT;
    double x = center.X + (radius - THICKNESS / 2) * Math.Sin(radians);
    double y = center.Y - (radius - THICKNESS / 2) * Math.Cos(radians);

    // Position each BoxView at that point.
    AbsoluteLayout.SetLayoutBounds(boxView,
        new Rectangle(x - length / 2,
                      y - THICKNESS / 2,
                      length,
```

```
                              THICKNESS));

    // Set a unique Rotation for each BoxView.
    boxView.Rotation = index * 360.0 / COUNT;
}
```

The x and y values indicate the position desired for the center of each BoxView, while AbsoluteLay-
out.SetLayoutBounds requires the location of the top-left corner of each BoxView, so these x and y
values are adjusted for that difference when used with SetLayoutBounds. Each BoxView is then rotated around its own center.

Now let's rotate some text. The **RotatedText** program is implemented entirely in XAML:

```xml
<ContentPage xmlns="http://xamarin.com/schemas/2014/forms"
             xmlns:x="http://schemas.microsoft.com/winfx/2009/xaml"
             x:Class="RotatedText.RotatedTextPage">
    <Grid>
        <Grid.Resources>
            <ResourceDictionary>
                <Style TargetType="Label">
                    <Setter Property="Text" Value="      ROTATE" />
                    <Setter Property="FontSize" Value="32" />
                    <Setter Property="Grid.Column" Value="1" />
                    <Setter Property="VerticalOptions" Value="Center" />
                    <Setter Property="HorizontalOptions" Value="Start" />
                    <Setter Property="AnchorX" Value="0" />
                </Style>
            </ResourceDictionary>
        </Grid.Resources>

        <Label Rotation="0" />
        <Label Rotation="22.5" />
        <Label Rotation="45" />
        <Label Rotation="67.5" />
        <Label Rotation="90" />
        <Label Rotation="112.5" />
        <Label Rotation="135" />
        <Label Rotation="157.5" />
        <Label Rotation="180" />
        <Label Rotation="202.5" />
        <Label Rotation="225" />
        <Label Rotation="246.5" />
        <Label Rotation="270" />
        <Label Rotation="292.5" />
        <Label Rotation="315" />
        <Label Rotation="337.5" />
    </Grid>
</ContentPage>
```

The program consists of 16 Label elements in a Grid with an implicit Style setting six properties,
including the Text and FontSize. Although this Grid might seem to be only a single cell, it's actually
a two-column Grid because the Style sets the Grid.Column property of each Label to 1, which is
the second column. The Style centers each Label vertically within the second column and starts it at

the left of that column, which is the center of the page. However, the text begins with several blank spaces, so it seems to start a bit to the right of the center of the page.

The `Style` concludes by setting the `AnchorX` value to 0, which sets the center of rotation to the vertical center of the left edge of each `Label`. Each `Label` then gets a unique `Rotation` setting:

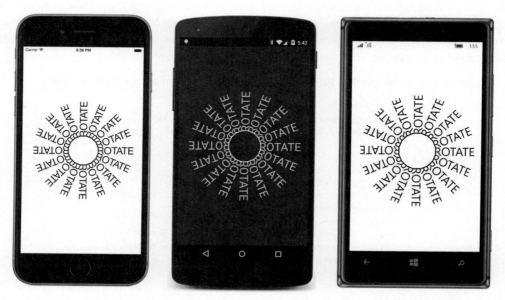

Obviously, the spaces preceding the "ROTATE" string were chosen so that the vertical bars of the R combine to form a 16-sided polygon that seems almost like a circle.

You can also rotate individual letters in a text string if each letter is a separate `Label` element. You begin by positioning these `Label` elements in an `AbsoluteLayout` and then apply a `Rotation` property to make it appear as if the letters follow a particular nonlinear path. The **CircularText** program arranges these letters in a circle.

CircularText is a code-only program and is similar to the alternate **BoxViewCircle** algorithm. The constructor is responsible for creating all the individual `Label` elements and adding them to the `Children` collection of the `AbsoluteLayout`. No positioning or rotating is performed during the constructor because the program doesn't yet know how large these individual `Label` elements are, or how large the `AbsoluteLayout` is:

```
public class CircularTextPage : ContentPage
{
    AbsoluteLayout absoluteLayout;
    Label[] labels;

    public CircularTextPage()
    {
        // Create the AbsoluteLayout.
        absoluteLayout = new AbsoluteLayout();
```

```
        absoluteLayout.SizeChanged += (sender, args) =>
            {
                LayOutLabels();
            };
        Content = absoluteLayout;

        // Create the Labels.
        string text = "Xamarin.Forms makes me want to code more with ";
        labels = new Label[text.Length];
        double fontSize = 32;
        int countSized = 0;

        for (int index = 0; index < text.Length; index++)
        {
            char ch = text[index];

            Label label = new Label
            {
                Text = ch == ' ' ? "-" : ch.ToString(),
                Opacity = ch == ' ' ? 0 : 1,
                FontSize = fontSize,
            };
            label.SizeChanged += (sender, args) =>
                {
                    if (++countSized >= labels.Length)
                        LayOutLabels();
                };

            labels[index] = label;
            absoluteLayout.Children.Add(label);
        }
    }

    void LayOutLabels()
    {
        // Calculate the total width of the Labels.
        double totalWidth = 0;

        foreach (Label label in labels)
        {
            totalWidth += label.Width;
        }

        // From that, get a radius of the circle to center of Labels.
        double radius = totalWidth / 2 / Math.PI + labels[0].Height / 2;
        Point center = new Point(absoluteLayout.Width / 2, absoluteLayout.Height / 2);
        double angle = 0;

        for (int index = 0; index < labels.Length; index++)
        {
            Label label = labels[index];

            // Set the position of the Label.
            double x = center.X + radius * Math.Sin(angle) - label.Width / 2;
```

```
            double y = center.Y - radius * Math.Cos(angle) - label.Height / 2;

            AbsoluteLayout.SetLayoutBounds(label, new Rectangle(x, y, AbsoluteLayout.AutoSize,
                                                               AbsoluteLayout.AutoSize));
            // Set the rotation of the Label.
            label.Rotation = 360 * angle / 2 / Math.PI;

            // Increment the rotation angle.
            if (index < labels.Length - 1)
            {
                angle += 2 * Math.PI * (label.Width + labels[index + 1].Width) / 2 / totalWidth;
            }
        }
    }
}
```

Notice the code that creates each `Label` element: If the character in the original text string is a space, the `Text` property of the `Label` is assigned a dash, but the `Opacity` property is set to 0 so that the dash is invisible. This is a little trick to fix a problem that showed up on the Windows Runtime platforms: If the `Label` contains only a space, then the width of the `Label` is calculated as zero and all the words run together.

All the action happens in the `LayOutLabels` method. This method is called from two `Size-Changed` handlers expressed as lambda functions in the constructor. The `SizeChanged` handler for the `AbsoluteLayout` is called soon after the program starts up or when the phone changes orientation. The `SizeChanged` handler for the `Label` elements keeps track of how many have been sized so far, and only calls `LayOutLabels` when they are all ready.

The `LayOutLabels` method calculates the total width of all the `Label` elements. If that's assumed to be the circumference of a circle, then the method can easily compute a radius of that circle. But that radius is actually extended by half the height of each `Label`. The endpoint of that radius thus coincides with the center of each `Label`. The `Label` is positioned within the `AbsoluteLayout` by subtracting half the `Label` width and height from that point.

An accumulated angle is used both for finding the endpoint of the radius for the next `Label` and for rotating the `Label`. Because the endpoint of each radius coincides with the center of each `Label`, the angle is incremented based on half the width of the current `Label` and half the width of the next `Label`.

Although the math is a bit tricky, the result is worth it:

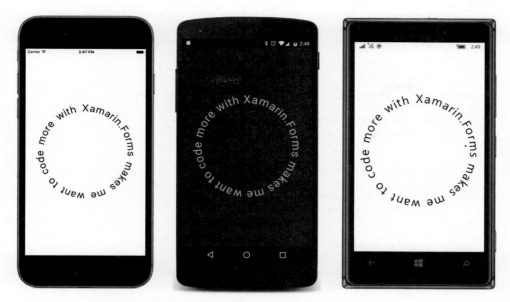

This program does not set nondefault values of `AnchorX` and `AnchorY`, so there is no problem changing the phone orientation on iOS.

An analog clock

One of the classic sample programs for a graphical user interface is an analog clock. Once again, `Box-View` comes to the rescue for the hands of the clock. These `BoxView` elements must be rotated based on the hours, minutes, and seconds of the current time.

Let's first take care of the rotation mathematics with a class named `AnalogClockViewModel`, which is included in the **Xamarin.FormsBook.Toolkit** library:

```
namespace Xamarin.FormsBook.Toolkit
{
    public class AnalogClockViewModel : ViewModelBase
    {
        double hourAngle, minuteAngle, secondAngle;

        public AnalogClockViewModel()
        {
            UpdateLoop();
        }

        async void UpdateLoop()
        {
            while (true)
            {
                DateTime dateTime = DateTime.Now;
                HourAngle = 30 * (dateTime.Hour % 12) + 0.5 * dateTime.Minute;
                MinuteAngle = 6 * dateTime.Minute + 0.1 * dateTime.Second;
```

```
                SecondAngle = 6 * dateTime.Second + 0.006 * dateTime.Millisecond;

                await Task.Delay(16);
            }
        }

        public double HourAngle
        {
            private set { SetProperty(ref hourAngle, value); }
            get { return hourAngle; }
        }

        public double MinuteAngle
        {
            private set { SetProperty(ref minuteAngle, value); }
            get { return minuteAngle; }
        }

        public double SecondAngle
        {
            private set { SetProperty(ref secondAngle, value); }
            get { return secondAngle; }
        }
    }
}
```

Each of the three properties is updated 60 times per second in a loop paced by a `Task.Delay` call. Of course, the hour hand rotation angle is based not only on the hour, but on a fractional part of that hour available from the `Minute` part of the `DateTime` value. Similarly, the angle of the minute hand is based on the `Minute` and `Second` properties, and the second hand is based on the `Second` and `Millisecond` properties.

These three properties of the ViewModel can be bound to the `Rotation` properties of the three hands of the analog clock.

As you know, some clocks have a smoothly gliding second hand, while the second hand of other clocks moves in discrete ticks. The `AnalogClockViewModel` class seems to impose a smooth second hand, but if you want discrete ticks, you can supply a value converter for that purpose:

```
namespace Xamarin.FormsBook.Toolkit
{
    public class SecondTickConverter : IValueConverter
    {
        public object Convert(object value, Type targetType,
                              object parameter, CultureInfo culture)
        {
            return 6.0 * (int)((double)value / 6);
        }

        public object ConvertBack(object value, Type targetType,
                                  object parameter, CultureInfo culture)
        {
            return (double)value;
```

```
        }
    }
}
```

The name of this class and even the tiny code might be obscure if you didn't know what it was supposed to do: The `Convert` method converts an angle of type `double` ranging from 0 to 360 degrees with fractional parts into discrete angle values of 0, 6, 12, 18, 24, and so forth. These angles correspond to the discrete positions of the second hand.

The **MinimalBoxViewClock** program instantiates three `BoxView` elements in its XAML file and binds the `Rotation` properties to the three properties of `AnalogClockViewModel`:

```xml
<ContentPage xmlns="http://xamarin.com/schemas/2014/forms"
             xmlns:x="http://schemas.microsoft.com/winfx/2009/xaml"
             xmlns:toolkit=
                 "clr-namespace:Xamarin.FormsBook.Toolkit;assembly=Xamarin.FormsBook.Toolkit"
             x:Class="MinimalBoxViewClock.MinimalBoxViewClockPage">
    <ContentPage.Padding>
        <OnPlatform x:TypeArguments="Thickness"
                    iOS="0, 20, 0, 0" />
    </ContentPage.Padding>

    <ContentPage.Resources>
        <ResourceDictionary>
            <toolkit:SecondTickConverter x:Key="secondTick" />
        </ResourceDictionary>
    </ContentPage.Resources>

    <AbsoluteLayout BackgroundColor="White"
                    SizeChanged="OnAbsoluteLayoutSizeChanged">

        <AbsoluteLayout.BindingContext>
            <toolkit:AnalogClockViewModel  />
        </AbsoluteLayout.BindingContext>

        <BoxView x:Name="hourHand"
                 Color="Black"
                 Rotation="{Binding HourAngle}" />

        <BoxView x:Name="minuteHand"
                 Color="Black"
                 Rotation="{Binding MinuteAngle}" />

        <BoxView x:Name="secondHand"
                 Color="Black"
                 Rotation="{Binding SecondAngle, Converter={StaticResource secondTick}}" />
    </AbsoluteLayout>
</ContentPage>
```

The code-behind file sets the sizes of these `BoxView` clock hands based on the size of the `AbsoluteLayout`, and it sets the locations so that all hands point up from the center of the clock in the 12:00 position:

```
public partial class MinimalBoxViewClockPage : ContentPage
{
    public MinimalBoxViewClockPage()
    {
        InitializeComponent();
    }

    void OnAbsoluteLayoutSizeChanged(object sender, EventArgs args)
    {
        AbsoluteLayout absoluteLayout = (AbsoluteLayout)sender;

        // Calculate a center and radius for the clock.
        Point center = new Point(absoluteLayout.Width / 2, absoluteLayout.Height / 2);
        double radius = Math.Min(absoluteLayout.Width, absoluteLayout.Height) / 2;

        // Position all hands pointing up from center.
        AbsoluteLayout.SetLayoutBounds(hourHand,
            new Rectangle(center.X - radius * 0.05,
                          center.Y - radius * 0.6,
                          radius * 0.10, radius * 0.6));

        AbsoluteLayout.SetLayoutBounds(minuteHand,
            new Rectangle(center.X - radius * 0.025,
                          center.Y - radius * 0.7,
                          radius * 0.05, radius * 0.7));

        AbsoluteLayout.SetLayoutBounds(secondHand,
            new Rectangle(center.X - radius * 0.01,
                          center.Y - radius * 0.9,
                          radius * 0.02, radius * 0.9));

        // Set the anchor to bottom center of BoxView.
        hourHand.AnchorY = 1;
        minuteHand.AnchorY = 1;
        secondHand.AnchorY = 1;
    }
}
```

For example, the hour hand is given a length of 0.60 of the clock's radius and a width of 0.10 of the clock's radius. This means that the horizontal position of the hour hand's top-left corner must be set to half its width (0.05 times the radius) to the left of the clock's center. The vertical position of the hour hand is the hand's height above the clock's center. The settings of AnchorY ensure that all rotations are relative to the center bottom of each clock hand:

Of course, this program is called **MinimalBoxViewClock** for a reason. It doesn't have convenient tick marks around the circumference, so it's a little hard to discern the actual time. Also, the clock hands should more properly overlap the center of the clock face so that they at least seem to be attached to a rotating pin or tube.

Both these problems are addressed in the nonminimal **BoxViewClock**. The XAML file is very similar to **MinimalBoxViewClock**, but the code-behind file is more extensive. It begins with a small structure named `HandParams`, which defines the size of each hand relative to the radius but also includes an `Offset` value. This is a fraction of the total length of the hand, indicating where it aligns with the center of the clock face. It also becomes the `AnchorY` value for rotations:

```
public partial class BoxViewClockPage : ContentPage
{
    // Structure for storing information about the three hands.
    struct HandParams
    {
        public HandParams(double width, double height, double offset) : this()
        {
            Width = width;
            Height = height;
            Offset = offset;
        }

        public double Width { private set; get; }   // fraction of radius
        public double Height { private set; get; }  // ditto
        public double Offset { private set; get; }  // relative to center pivot
    }

    static readonly HandParams secondParams = new HandParams(0.02, 1.1, 0.85);
    static readonly HandParams minuteParams = new HandParams(0.05, 0.8, 0.9);
```

```
    static readonly HandParams hourParams = new HandParams(0.125, 0.65, 0.9);

    BoxView[] tickMarks = new BoxView[60];

    public BoxViewClockPage()
    {
        InitializeComponent();

        // Create the tick marks (to be sized and positioned later).
        for (int i = 0; i < tickMarks.Length; i++)
        {
            tickMarks[i] = new BoxView { Color = Color.Black };
            absoluteLayout.Children.Add(tickMarks[i]);
        }
    }

    void OnAbsoluteLayoutSizeChanged(object sender, EventArgs args)
    {
        // Get the center and radius of the AbsoluteLayout.
        Point center = new Point(absoluteLayout.Width / 2, absoluteLayout.Height / 2);
        double radius = 0.45 * Math.Min(absoluteLayout.Width, absoluteLayout.Height);

        // Position, size, and rotate the 60 tick marks.
        for (int index = 0; index < tickMarks.Length; index++)
        {
            double size = radius / (index % 5 == 0 ? 15 : 30);
            double radians = index * 2 * Math.PI / tickMarks.Length;
            double x = center.X + radius * Math.Sin(radians) - size / 2;
            double y = center.Y - radius * Math.Cos(radians) - size / 2;
            AbsoluteLayout.SetLayoutBounds(tickMarks[index], new Rectangle(x, y, size, size));
            tickMarks[index].Rotation = 180 * radians / Math.PI;
        }

        // Position and size the three hands.
        LayoutHand(secondHand, secondParams, center, radius);
        LayoutHand(minuteHand, minuteParams, center, radius);
        LayoutHand(hourHand, hourParams, center, radius);
    }

    void LayoutHand(BoxView boxView, HandParams handParams, Point center, double radius)
    {
        double width = handParams.Width * radius;
        double height = handParams.Height * radius;
        double offset = handParams.Offset;

        AbsoluteLayout.SetLayoutBounds(boxView,
            new Rectangle(center.X - 0.5 * width,
                          center.Y - offset * height,
                          width, height));

        // Set the AnchorY property for rotations.
        boxView.AnchorY = handParams.Offset;
    }
}
```

The tick marks around the circumference of the clock face are also `BoxView` elements, but there are 60 of them with two different sizes, and they are positioned using techniques you've already seen. The visuals are surprisingly good considering the absence of a Xamarin.Forms graphics system:

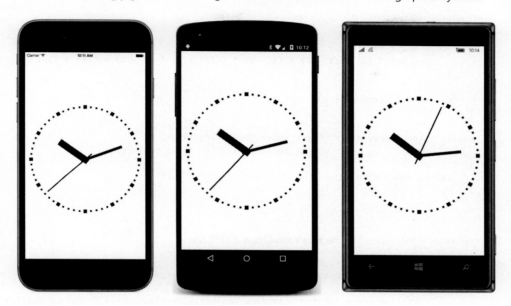

Best of all, you can actually tell the time.

This clock has another interesting feature that makes the movement of the hands quite mesmerizing. The second hand neither glides from second to second or makes discrete jumps; instead it has a more complex movement. It pulls back slightly, then jumps ahead but slightly overshooting its mark, and then backs up and comes to rest. How is this done?

In the next chapter, you'll see that Xamarin.Forms implements several *easing functions* that can add realism to an animation by changing the animation's velocity—by speeding it up and slowing it down—over the course of the animation. Such easing functions have become fairly standard throughout the computer industry, and **Xamarin.FormsBook.Toolkit** contains a value converter that implements an easing function called the *back ease*:

```
namespace Xamarin.FormsBook.Toolkit
{
    public class SecondBackEaseConverter : IValueConverter
    {
        public object Convert(object value, Type targetType,
                              object parameter, CultureInfo culture)
        {
            int seconds = (int)((double)value / 6);    // 0, 1, 2, ... 60
            double t = (double)value / 6 % 1;          // 0 --> 1
            double v = 0;                              // 0 --> 1

            // Back-ease in and out functions from http://robertpenner.com/easing/
```

```
            if (t < 0.5)
            {
                t *= 2;
                v = 0.5 * t * t * ((1.7 + 1) * t - 1.7);
            }
            else
            {
                t = 2 * (t - 0.5);
                v = 0.5 * (1 + ((t - 1) * (t - 1) * ((1.7 + 1) * (t - 1) + 1.7) + 1));
            }

            return 6 * (seconds + v);
        }

        public object ConvertBack(object value, Type targetType,
                                  object parameter, CultureInfo culture)
        {
            return (double)value;
        }
    }
}
```

This converter is referenced in the **BoxViewClock** XAML file:

```xml
<ContentPage xmlns="http://xamarin.com/schemas/2014/forms"
             xmlns:x="http://schemas.microsoft.com/winfx/2009/xaml"
             xmlns:toolkit=
                 "clr-namespace:Xamarin.FormsBook.Toolkit;assembly=Xamarin.FormsBook.Toolkit"
             x:Class="BoxViewClock.BoxViewClockPage">
    <ContentPage.Padding>
        <OnPlatform x:TypeArguments="Thickness"
                    iOS="0, 20, 0, 0" />
    </ContentPage.Padding>

    <ContentPage.Resources>
        <ResourceDictionary>
            <toolkit:SecondBackEaseConverter x:Key="secondBackEase" />
        </ResourceDictionary>
    </ContentPage.Resources>

    <AbsoluteLayout x:Name="absoluteLayout"
                    BackgroundColor="White"
                    SizeChanged="OnAbsoluteLayoutSizeChanged">

        <AbsoluteLayout.BindingContext>
            <toolkit:AnalogClockViewModel />
        </AbsoluteLayout.BindingContext>

        <BoxView x:Name="hourHand"
                 Color="Black"
                 Rotation="{Binding HourAngle}" />

        <BoxView x:Name="minuteHand"
                 Color="Black"
                 Rotation="{Binding MinuteAngle}" />
```

```
                   <BoxView x:Name="secondHand"
                            Color="Black"
                            Rotation="{Binding SecondAngle, Converter={StaticResource secondBackEase}}" />
        </AbsoluteLayout>
</ContentPage>
```

You'll see more easing functions in the next chapter.

Vertical sliders?

Can certain views be rotated and still work as they should? More specifically, can the normal horizontal `Slider` elements of Xamarin.Forms be rotated to become vertical sliders?

Let's try it. The **VerticalSliders** program contains three sliders in a `StackLayout`, and the `Stack-Layout` itself is rotated 90 degrees counterclockwise:

```
<ContentPage xmlns="http://xamarin.com/schemas/2014/forms"
             xmlns:x="http://schemas.microsoft.com/winfx/2009/xaml"
             x:Class="VerticalSliders.VerticalSlidersPage">

    <StackLayout VerticalOptions="Center"
                 Spacing="50"
                 Rotation="-90">

        <Slider Value="0.25" />

        <Slider Value="0.5" />

        <Slider Value="0.75" />
    </StackLayout>
</ContentPage>
```

Sure enough, all three sliders are now oriented vertically:

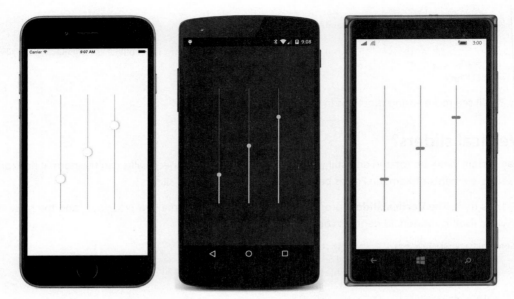

And they work! You can manipulate these vertical sliders just as though they had been designed for that purpose. The `Minimum` value corresponds to a thumb position at the bottom, and the `Maximum` value corresponds to the top.

However, the Xamarin.Forms layout system is completely unaware of the new locations of these sliders. For example, if you turn the phone to landscape mode, the sliders are resized for the width of the portrait screen and are much too large to be rotated into a vertical position. You'll need to spend some extra effort in getting rotated sliders positioned and sized intelligently.

But it does work.

3D-ish rotations

Even though computer screens are flat and two-dimensional, it's possible to draw visual objects on these screens that give the appearance of a third dimension. Earlier in this chapter you saw some text effects that give the hint of a third dimension, and Xamarin.Forms supports two additional rotations, named `RotationX` and `RotationY`, that also seem to break through the inherent two-dimensional flatness of the screen.

When dealing with 3D graphics, it's convenient to think of the screen as part of a 3D coordinate system. The X axis is horizontal and the Y axis is vertical, as usual. But there is also an implicit Z axis that is orthogonal to the screen. This Z axis sticks out from the screen and extends through the back of the screen.

In 2D space, rotation occurs around a point. In 3D space, rotation occurs around an axis. The `Rotation X` property is rotation around the X axis. The top and bottom of a visual object seem to move toward the viewer or away from the viewer. Similarly, `RotationY` is rotation around the Y axis. The left and right sides of a visual object seem to move toward the viewer or away from the viewer. By extension, the basic `Rotation` property is rotation around the Z axis. For consistency, the `Rotation` property should probably be named `RotationZ`, but that might confuse people who are thinking only in two dimensions.

The **ThreeDeeRotationDemo** program allows you to experiment with combinations of `RotationX`, `RotationY`, and `Rotation`, as well as explore how the `AnchorX` and `AnchorY` affect these two additional rotation properties:

```
<ContentPage xmlns="http://xamarin.com/schemas/2014/forms"
             xmlns:x="http://schemas.microsoft.com/winfx/2009/xaml"
             x:Class="ThreeDeeRotationDemo.ThreeDeeRotationDemoPage">
    <StackLayout Padding="20, 10">
        <Frame x:Name="frame"
               HorizontalOptions="Center"
               VerticalOptions="CenterAndExpand"
               OutlineColor="Accent">

            <Label Text="TEXT"
                   FontSize="72" />
        </Frame>

        <Slider x:Name="rotationXSlider"
                Maximum="360"
                Value="{Binding Source={x:Reference frame},
                        Path=RotationX}" />

        <Label Text="{Binding Source={x:Reference rotationXSlider},
                      Path=Value,
                      StringFormat='RotationX = {0:F0}'}"
               HorizontalTextAlignment="Center" />

        <Slider x:Name="rotationYSlider"
                Maximum="360"
                Value="{Binding Source={x:Reference frame},
                        Path=RotationY}" />

        <Label Text="{Binding Source={x:Reference rotationYSlider},
                      Path=Value,
                      StringFormat='RotationY = {0:F0}'}"
               HorizontalTextAlignment="Center" />

        <Slider x:Name="rotationZSlider"
                Maximum="360"
                Value="{Binding Source={x:Reference frame},
                        Path=Rotation}" />

        <Label Text="{Binding Source={x:Reference rotationZSlider},
                      Path=Value,
```

```
                                    StringFormat='Rotation(Z) = {0:F0}'}"
                    HorizontalTextAlignment="Center" />

        <StackLayout Orientation="Horizontal"
                     HorizontalOptions="Center">
            <Stepper x:Name="anchorXStepper"
                     Minimum="-1"
                     Maximum="2"
                     Increment="0.25"
                     Value="{Binding Source={x:Reference frame},
                                     Path=AnchorX}" />

            <Label Text="{Binding Source={x:Reference anchorXStepper},
                                  Path=Value,
                                  StringFormat='AnchorX = {0:F2}'}"
                   VerticalOptions="Center"/>
        </StackLayout>

        <StackLayout Orientation="Horizontal"
                     HorizontalOptions="Center">
            <Stepper x:Name="anchorYStepper"
                     Minimum="-1"
                     Maximum="2"
                     Increment="0.25"
                     Value="{Binding Source={x:Reference frame},
                                     Path=AnchorY}" />

            <Label Text="{Binding Source={x:Reference anchorYStepper},
                                  Path=Value,
                                  StringFormat='AnchorY = {0:F2}'}"
                   VerticalOptions="Center"/>
        </StackLayout>
    </StackLayout>
</ContentPage>
```

Here's a sample screen showing combinations of all three rotations:

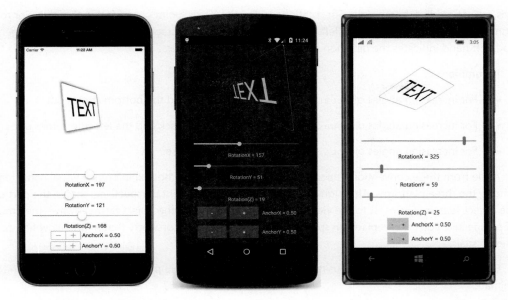

You'll discover that the AnchorY property affects RotationX but not RotationY. For the default AnchorY value of 0.5, RotationX causes rotation to occur around the horizontal center of the visual object. When you set AnchorY to 0, rotation is around the top of the object, and for a value of 1, rotation is around the bottom.

Similarly, the AnchorX property affects RotationY but not RotationX. An AnchorX value of 0 causes RotationY to rotate the visual object around its left edge, while a value of 1 causes rotation around the right edge.

The directions of rotation are consistent among the three platforms, but they are best described in connection with conventions of 3D coordinate systems:

You might think there are many ways to arrange orthogonal X, Y, and Z axes. For example, increasing values of X might increase corresponding to leftward or rightward movement on the X axis, and increasing values of Y might correspond with up or down movement on the Y axis. However, many of these variations become equivalent when the axes are viewed from different directions. In reality, there are only two different ways to arrange X, Y, and Z axes. These two ways are known as *right-hand* and *left-hand* coordinate systems.

The 3D coordinate system implied by the three Rotation properties in Xamarin.Forms is left-handed: If you point the forefinger of your left hand in the direction of increasing X coordinates (which is to the right), and your middle finger in the direction of increasing Y coordinates (which is down), then your thumb points in the direction of increasing Z coordinates, which are coming out of the screen.

Your left hand can also be used to predict the direction of rotation: For rotation around a particular axis, first point your thumb in the direction of increasing values on that axis. For rotation around the X axis, point your left thumb right. For rotation around the Y axis, point your left thumb down. For rotation around the Z axis, point your left thumb coming out of the screen. The curl of the other fingers of your left hand indicates the direction of rotation for positive angles.

In summary:

- For increasing angles of `RotationX`, the top goes back and the bottom comes out.

- For increasing angles of `RotationY`, the right side goes back and the left side comes out.

- For increasing angles of `Rotation`, the rotation is clockwise.

Aside from these conventions, `RotationX` and `RotationY` do not exhibit much visual consistency among the three platforms. Although all three platforms implement perspective—that is, the part of the object seemingly closest to the view is larger than the part of the object farther away—the amount of perspective you'll see is platform specific. There is no `AnchorZ` property that might allow fine-tuning these visuals.

But what's perhaps most obvious is that these various `Rotation` properties would be very fun to animate.

Chapter 22
Animation

Animation is life, action, vitality, and on computers we try to imitate those qualities despite being restricted to manipulating tiny pixels on a flat screen.

Computer animation usually refers to any type of dynamic visual change. A `Button` that simply appears on a page is not animation. But a `Button` that fades into view, or moves into place, or grows in size from a dot—that's animation. Very often, visual elements respond to user input with a change in appearance, such as a `Button` flash, a `Stepper` increment, or a `ListView` scroll. That, too, is animation.

It's sometimes desirable for an application to go beyond those automatic and conventional animations and add its own. That's what this chapter is all about.

You started seeing some of this in the previous chapter. You saw how to set transforms on visual elements and then use the timer or `Task.Delay` to animate them. Xamarin.Forms also includes its own animation infrastructure that exists in three levels of programming interfaces corresponding to the classes `ViewExtensions`, `Animation`, and `AnimationExtensions`. This animation system is versatile enough for complex jobs but exceptionally easy for simple jobs. This chapter begins with the easy high-level class (`ViewExtensions`) and then drills down to the more versatile lower levels.

The Xamarin.Forms animation classes are generally used to target properties of visual elements. A typical animation progressively changes a property from one value to another value over a period of time. The properties that are targeted by animations should be backed by bindable properties. This is not a requirement, but bindable properties are generally designed to respond to dynamic changes through the implementation of a property-changed handler. It does no good to animate a property of an object if the object doesn't even realize that the property is being changed!

There is no XAML interface for the Xamarin.Forms animation system. Consequently, all the animations in this chapter are realized in code. However, as you'll see in the next chapter, you can encapsulate animations in classes called *trigger actions* and *behaviors*, and then reference them from XAML files. Triggers and behaviors are generally the easiest way (and the recommended way) to incorporate animations within MVVM applications.

Exploring basic animations

Let's dive in with a tiny program called **AnimationTryout**. The XAML file contains nothing but a centered `Button`:

```
<ContentPage xmlns="http://xamarin.com/schemas/2014/forms"
             xmlns:x="http://schemas.microsoft.com/winfx/2009/xaml"
             x:Class="AnimationTryout.AnimationTryoutPage">

    <Button x:Name="button"
            Text="Tap Me!"
            FontSize="Large"
            HorizontalOptions="Center"
            VerticalOptions="Center"
            Clicked="OnButtonClicked" />

</ContentPage>
```

For this exercise, let's ignore the actual essential function that the Button presumably performs within the application. In addition to wanting the button to carry out that function, suppose you'd like to spin it around in a circle when the user taps it. The Clicked handler in the code-behind file can do that by calling a method named RotateTo with an argument of 360 for the number of degrees to rotate:

```
public partial class AnimationTryoutPage : ContentPage
{
    public AnimationTryoutPage()
    {
        InitializeComponent();
    }

    void OnButtonClicked(object sender, EventArgs args)
    {
        button.RotateTo(360);
    }
}
```

The RotateTo method is an animation that targets the Rotation property of Button. However, the RotateTo method is not defined in the VisualElement class like the Rotation property. It is, instead, an extension method defined in the ViewExtensions class.

When you run this program and tap the button, the RotateTo method animates the button to spin around in a full 360 degree circle. Here it is in progress:

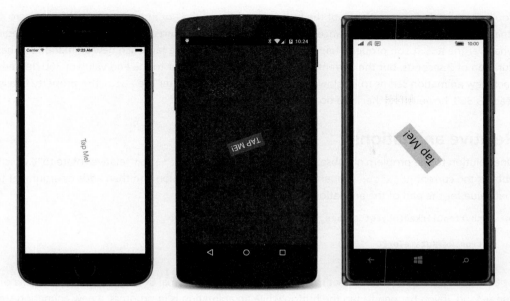

The complete trip takes 250 milliseconds (one quarter of a second), which is the default duration of this RotateTo animation.

However, this program has a flaw. After you've watched the button spin around, try tapping it again. It does not rotate.

That program flaw reveals a little bit about what's going on internally: On the first call to OnButtonClicked, the RotateTo method obtains the current Rotation property, which is 0, and then defines an animation of the Rotation property from that value to the argument of RotateTo, which is 360. When the animation concludes after a quarter second, the Rotation property is left at 360.

The next time the button is pressed, the current value is 360 and the argument to RotateTo is also 360. Internally, the animation still occurs, but the Rotation property doesn't budge. It's stuck at 360.

Setting the animation duration

Here's a little variation of the Clicked handler in **AnimationTryout**. It doesn't fix the problem with multiple taps of the Button, but it does extend the animation to two seconds so you can enjoy the animation longer. The duration is specified in milliseconds as the second argument to RotateTo. That second argument is optional and has a default value of 250:

```
void OnButtonClicked(object sender, EventArgs args)
{
    button.RotateTo(360, 2000);
}
```

With this variation, try tapping the Button and then tapping it again several times as it's rotating.

You'll discover that repeated taps of the button do not send the Rotation property back to zero. Instead, the previous animation is cancelled and a new animation starts. But this new animation begins at whatever the Rotation property happens to be at the time of the tap. Each new animation still has a duration of 2 seconds, but the current Rotation property is closer to the end value of 360 degrees, so each new animation seems to be slower than the one before it. After the Rotation property finally reaches 360, however, further taps do nothing.

Relative animations

One solution to the problem of subsequent taps is to use RelRotateTo ("relative rotate to"), which obtains the current Rotation property for the start of the animation and then adds its argument to that value for the end of the animation. Here's an example:

```
void OnButtonClicked(object sender, EventArgs args)
{
    button.RelRotateTo(90, 1000);
}
```

Each tap starts an animation that rotates the button an additional 90 degrees over the course of one second. If you happen to tap the button while an animation is in progress, a new animation starts from that position, so it might end at a position that is not an increment of 90 degrees. There is no change in velocity with multiple taps because the animation is always going at the rate of 90 degrees per second.

Both RotateTo and RelRotateTo have a common underlying structure. During the course of the animation, a value is calculated—often called *t* (for time) or, sometimes, *progress*. This value is based on elapsed time and the animation's duration:

$$t = \frac{elapsedTime}{duration}$$

Values of *t* range from 0 at the beginning of the animation to 1 at the end of the animation. The animation is also defined by two values (often the values of a property), one for the start of the animation and one for the end. These are often called *start* and *end* values, or *from* and *to* values. The animation calculates a value between *from* and *to* based on a simple interpolation formula:

$$value = fromValue + t \cdot (toValue - fromValue)$$

When *t* equals 0, *value* equals *fromValue* and when *t* equals 1, *value* equals *toValue*.

Both RotateTo and RelRotateTo obtain *fromValue* from the current value of the Rotation property at the time the method is called. RotateTo sets *toValue* equal to its argument, while RelRotateTo sets *toValue* equal to *fromValue* plus its argument.

Awaiting animations

Another way to fix the problem with subsequent taps is to initialize the Rotation property prior to the call to RotateTo:

```
void OnButtonClicked(object sender, EventArgs args)
{
    button.Rotation = 0;
    button.RotateTo(360, 2000);
}
```

Now you can tap the Button again after it's stopped and it will begin the animation from the beginning. Repeated taps while the Button is rotating also behave differently: They start over from 0 degrees.

Interestingly, this slight variation in the code does *not* allow subsequent taps:

```
void OnButtonClicked(object sender, EventArgs args)
{
    button.RotateTo(360, 2000);
    button.Rotation = 0;
}
```

This version behaves just like the version with only the RotateTo method. It seems as if setting the Rotation property to 0 after that call does nothing.

Why doesn't it work? It doesn't work because the RotateTo method is asynchronous. The method returns quickly after initiating the animation, but the animation itself occurs in the background. Setting the Rotation property to 0 at the time the RotateTo method returns has no apparent effect because the setting is very quickly superseded by the background RotateTo animation.

Because the method is asynchronous, RotateTo returns a Task object—more specifically, a Task<bool> object—and that means that you can call ContinueWith to specify a callback function that is invoked when the animation terminates. The callback can then set the Rotation property back to 0 after the animation has completed:

```
void OnButtonClicked(object sender, EventArgs args)
{
    button.RotateTo(360, 2000).ContinueWith((task) =>
        {
            button.Rotation = 0;
        });
}
```

The task object passed to ContinueWith is of type Task<bool>, and the ContinueWith callback can use the Result property to obtain that Boolean value. The value is true if the animation was cancelled and false if it ran to completion. You can easily confirm this by displaying the return value using a Debug.WriteLine call and looking at the results in the **Output** window of Visual Studio or Xamarin Studio:

```
void OnButtonClicked(object sender, EventArgs args)
{
    button.RotateTo(360, 2000).ContinueWith((task) =>
        {
            System.Diagnostics.Debug.WriteLine("Cancelled? " + task.Result);
            button.Rotation = 0;
```

```
        });
}
```

If you tap the `Button` while it's being animated, you'll see `true` values returned. Every new call to `RotateTo` cancels the previous animation. If you let the animation run to completion, you'll see a `false` value returned.

It's more likely that you'll use `await` with the `RotateTo` method than `ContinueWith`:

```
async void OnButtonClicked(object sender, EventArgs args)
{
    bool wasCancelled = await button.RotateTo(360, 2000);
    button.Rotation = 0;
}
```

Or, if you don't care about the return value:

```
async void OnButtonClicked(object sender, EventArgs args)
{
    await button.RotateTo(360, 2000);
    button.Rotation = 0;
}
```

Notice the `async` modifier on the handler, which is required for any method that contains `await` operators.

If you've used other animation systems, it's very likely that you were required to define a callback method if you wanted the application to be notified when an animation is completed. With `await`, determining when an animation is completed—perhaps to execute some other code—becomes trivial. In this particular example the code that is executed is fairly simple, but of course it could be more complex.

Sometimes you'll want to let your animations just run to completion in the background—in which case it's not necessary to use `await` with them—and sometimes you'll want to do something when the animation has completed. But watch out: If the `Button` is also triggering some actual application function, you might not want to wait until the animation finishes before carrying that out.

`RotateTo` and `RelRotateTo` are two of several similar methods defined in the `ViewExtensions` class. Others that you'll see in this chapter include `ScaleTo`, `TranslateTo`, `FadeTo`, and `LayoutTo`. They all return `Task<bool>` objects—`false` if the animation completed without interruption and `true` if it was cancelled.

Your application can cancel one or more of these animations with a call to the static method `ViewExtensions.CancelAnimations`. Unlike all the other methods in `ViewExtensions`, this is not an extension method. You need to call it like so:

```
ViewExtensions.CancelAnimations(button);
```

That will immediately cancel all animations initiated by the extension methods in the `ViewExtensions` class that are currently running on the `button` object.

Using `await` is particularly useful for stacking sequential animations:

```
async void OnButtonClicked(object sender, EventArgs args)
{
    await button.RotateTo(90, 250);
    await button.RotateTo(-90, 500);
    await button.RotateTo(0, 250);
}
```

The total animation defined here requires one second. The `Button` swings 90 degrees clockwise in the first quarter second, then 180 degrees counterclockwise in the next half second, and then 90 degrees clockwise to end up at 0 degrees again. You need `await` on the first two so that they're sequential, but you don't need it on the third if there's nothing else to execute in the `Clicked` handler after the third animation has completed.

A composite animation like this is often known as a *key-frame animation*. You are specifying a series of rotation angles and times, and the overall animation is interpolating between those. In most animation systems, key-frame animations are often more difficult to use than simple animations. But with `await`, key-frame animations become trivial.

The return value of `Task<bool>` does not necessarily indicate that the animation is running in a secondary thread. In fact, at least part of the animation—the part that actually sets the `Rotation` property—must run in the user-interface thread. It is theoretically possible for the entire animation to run in the user-interface thread. As you saw in the previous chapter, animations that you create with `Device.StartTimer` or `Task.Delay` run entirely in the user-interface thread, although the underlying timer mechanism might involve a secondary thread.

You'll see later in this chapter how an animation method can still return a `Task` object but run entirely in the user-interface thread. This technique allows code to use timers for pacing animations but still provide a structured `Task`-based notification when the code has completed.

Composite animations

You can mix awaited and nonawaited calls to create composite animations. For example, suppose you want the button to spin around 360 degrees at the same time it expands in size and then contracts.

The `ViewExtensions` class defines a method name `ScaleTo` that animates the `Scale` property just as `RotateTo` animates the `Rotate` property. The expansion and contraction of the `Button` size requires two sequential animations, but these should occur at the same time as the rotation, which only requires one call. For that reason, the `RotateTo` call can execute without an `await`, and while that animation is running in the background, the method can make two sequential calls to `ScaleTo`. Try this in **AnimationTryout**:

```
async void OnButtonClicked(object sender, EventArgs args)
{
    button.Rotation = 0;
    button.RotateTo(360, 2000);
    await button.ScaleTo(5, 1000);
```

```
    await button.ScaleTo(1, 1000);
}
```

The durations are made somewhat longer than they would be normally so that you can see what's happening. The RotateTo method returns immediately, and the first ScaleTo animation begins at that time. But that await operator on the first ScaleTo delays the call of the second ScaleTo until the first ScaleTo has completed. At that time, the RotateTo animation is only half finished and the Button has rotated 180 degrees. During the next 1,000 milliseconds, that RotateTo completes at about the same time the second ScaleTo animation completes.

Here's the Button as it's making its way through the animation:

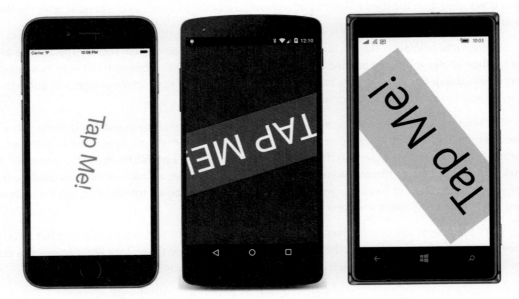

Because the OnButtonClicked method is flagged with the async keyword and the first RotateTo does not have an await operator, you'll get a warning message from the compiler that states: "Because this call is not awaited, execution of the current method continues before the call is completed. Consider applying the 'await' operator to the result of the call."

If you prefer not to see that warning message, you can turn it off with a #pragma statement that disables that particular warning:

```
#pragma warning disable 4014
```

You could place that statement at the top of your source code file to disable warnings throughout the file. Or you can place it before the offending call and reenable those warnings after the call by using:

```
#pragma warning restore 4014
```

Task.WhenAll and Task.WhenAny

Another powerful option is available that lets you combine animations in a very structured way without worrying about compiler warnings. The static `Task.WhenAll` and `Task.WhenAny` methods of the `Task` class are intended to run multiple asynchronous methods concurrently. Each of these methods can accept an array or other collection of multiple arguments, each of which is a method that returns a `Task` object. The `Task.WhenAll` and `Task.WhenAny` methods also return `Task` objects. The `WhenAll` method completes when all the methods in its collection have completed. The `WhenAny` method completes when any method in its collection completes execution while the other methods in the `WhenAny` collection continue to run.

Watch out: The `Task` class also includes static methods named `WaitAll` and `WaitAny`. You don't want to use those methods. They block the user-interface thread until the task or tasks have completed.

Because the `Task.WhenAll` and `Task.WhenAny` methods themselves return `Task` objects, you can use `await` with them. Here's one way to implement the composite animation shown above without any compiler warnings: The `Task.WhenAny` call contains two tasks, the first of which runs for two seconds and the second runs for one second. When that second task completes, the `Task.WhenAny` call also completes. The `RotateTo` method is still running, but now the second `ScaleTo` method can start:

```
async void OnButtonClicked(object sender, EventArgs args)
{
    button.Rotation = 0;

    await Task.WhenAny<bool>
        (
            button.RotateTo(360, 2000),
            button.ScaleTo(5, 1000)
        );
    await button.ScaleTo(1, 1000);
}
```

You can also use `Task.Delay` with these methods to introduce little delays into the composite animation.

Rotation and anchors

The `AnchorX` and `AnchorY` properties set the center of scaling or rotation for the `Scale` and `Rotation` properties, so they also affect the `ScaleTo` and `RotateTo` animations.

The **CircleButton** program rotates a `Button` in a circle, but not like the code you've seen previously. This program rotates a `Button` around the center of the screen, and for that it requires `AnchorX` and `AnchorY`.

The XAML file puts the `Button` in an `AbsoluteLayout`:

```
<ContentPage xmlns="http://xamarin.com/schemas/2014/forms"
             xmlns:x="http://schemas.microsoft.com/winfx/2009/xaml"
```

```
                    x:Class="CircleButton.CircleButtonPage">
    <ContentPage.Padding>
        <OnPlatform x:TypeArguments="Thickness"
                    iOS="0, 20, 0, 0" />
    </ContentPage.Padding>

    <AbsoluteLayout x:Name="absoluteLayout"
                    SizeChanged="OnSizeChanged">
        <Button x:Name="button"
                Text="Tap Me!"
                FontSize="Large"
                SizeChanged="OnSizeChanged"
                Clicked="OnButtonClicked" />
    </AbsoluteLayout>
</ContentPage>
```

The only reason this program uses an `AbsoluteLayout` for the `Button` is to place the `Button` precisely at a particular location on the screen. The XAML file sets the same `SizeChanged` handler on both the `AbsoluteLayout` and the `Button`. That event handler saves the center of the `Absolute-Layout` as the `Point` field named `center` and also saves the distance from that center to the nearest edge as the `radius` field:

```
public partial class CircleButtonPage : ContentPage
{
    Point center;
    double radius;

    public CircleButtonPage()
    {
        InitializeComponent();
    }

    void OnSizeChanged(object sender, EventArgs args)
    {
        center = new Point(absoluteLayout.Width / 2, absoluteLayout.Height / 2);
        radius = Math.Min(absoluteLayout.Width, absoluteLayout.Height) / 2;
        AbsoluteLayout.SetLayoutBounds(button,
            new Rectangle(center.X - button.Width / 2, center.Y - radius,
                          AbsoluteLayout.AutoSize,
                          AbsoluteLayout.AutoSize));
    }
    ...
}
```

The `OnSizeChanged` handler concludes by positioning the `Button` in the horizontal center of the page, but with its top edge a distance of `radius` above the center of the `AbsoluteLayout`:

Recall that the `AnchorX` and `AnchorY` properties must be set to numbers that are relative to the width and height of the `Button`. An `AnchorX` value of 0 refers to the left edge of the `Button` and a value of 1 refers to the right edge. Similarly, an `AnchorY` value of 0 refers to the top of the `Button` and a value of 1 refers to the bottom.

To rotate this `Button` around the point saved as `center`, `AnchorX` and `AnchorY` must be set to values based on the `center` point. The center of the `Button` is directly above the center of the page, so the default 0.5 value of `AnchorX` is fine. `AnchorY`, however, needs a value from the top of the `Button` to the center point, but in units of the button's height:

```
public partial class CircleButtonPage : ContentPage
{
    …
    async void OnButtonClicked(object sender, EventArgs args)
    {
        button.Rotation = 0;
        button.AnchorY = radius / button.Height;
        await button.RotateTo(360, 1000);
    }
}
```

The `Button` then makes a full rotation of 360 degrees around the center of the page. Here it is in progress:

Easing functions

You've already seen the following key-frame animation that swings the Button one way and then the other:

```
async void OnButtonClicked(object sender, EventArgs args)
{
    await button.RotateTo(90, 250);
    await button.RotateTo(-90, 500);
    await button.RotateTo(0, 250);
}
```

But the animation doesn't quite look right. The movement seems very mechanical and robotic because the rotations have a constant angular velocity. Shouldn't the Button at least slow down as it reverses direction and then speed up again?

You can control velocity changes in animations with the use of easing functions. You already saw a couple of homemade easing functions in Chapter 21, "Transforms." Xamarin.Forms includes an Easing class that allows you to specify a simple transfer function that controls how animations speed up or slow down as they're running.

You'll recall that animations generally involve a variable named *t* or *progress* that increases from 0 to 1 over the course of the animation. This *t* variable is then used in an interpolation between *from* and *to* values:

$$value = fromValue + t \cdot (toValue - fromValue)$$

The easing function introduces a little transfer function into this calculation:

$$value = fromValue + EasingFunc(t) \cdot (toValue - fromValue)$$

The `Easing` class defines a method named `Ease` that performs this job. For an input of 0, the `Ease` method returns 0, and for an input of 1, `Ease` returns 1. Between those two values, some mathematics—often a rather *tiny* chunk of mathematics—gives the animation a nonconstant velocity. (As you'll see later, it's not entirely necessary that the `Ease` method maps 0 to 0 and 1 to 1, but that's certainly the normal case.)

You can define your own easing functions, but the `Easing` class defines 11 static read-only fields of type `Easing` for your convenience:

- `Linear` (the default)

- `SinIn`, `SinOut`, and `SinInOut`

- `CubicIn`, `CubicOut`, and `CubicInOut`

- `BounceIn` and `BounceOut`

- `SpringIn` and `SpringOut`

The `In` and `Out` suffixes indicate whether the effect is prominent at the beginning of the animation, at the end, or both.

The `SinIn`, `SinOut`, and `SinInOut` easing functions are based on sine and cosine functions:

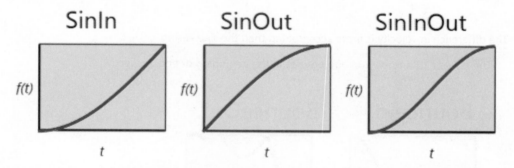

In each of these graphs, the horizontal axis is linear time, left to right from 0 to 1. The vertical axis shows the output of the `Ease` method, 0 to 1 from bottom to top. A steeper, more vertical slope is faster, while a more horizontal slope is slower.

The `SinIn` is the first quadrant of a cosine curve but subtracted from 1 so it goes from 0 to 1; it starts off slow but gets faster. The `SinOut` is the first quadrant of a sine curve, starting off somewhat faster than a linear animation but slowing down toward the end. The `SinInOut` is the first half of a cosine curve (again adjusted to go from 0 to 1); it's slow at the beginning and the end.

Because harmonic motion is best described by sine curves, these easing functions are ideal for a

Button swinging to and fro. You can specify an object of type `Easing` as the last argument to the RotateTo methods:

```
async void OnButtonClicked(object sender, EventArgs args)
{
    await button.RotateTo(90, 250, Easing.SinOut);
    await button.RotateTo(-90, 500, Easing.SinInOut);
    await button.RotateTo(0, 250, Easing.SinIn);
}
```

And now the movement is much more natural. The `Button` slows down as it approaches the point
when it reverses movement and then speeds up again.

The `CubicIn` easing function is simply the input raised to the third power. The `CubicOut` is the reverse of that, and `CubicInOut` combines the two effects:

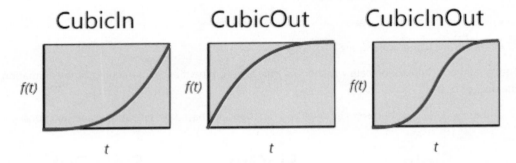

The difference in velocity is more accentuated than the sine easing.

The `BounceIn` and `BounceOut` bounce at the beginning or end, respectively:

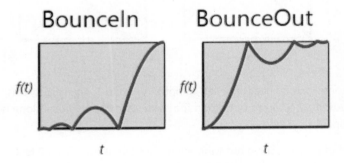

As you might imagine, the `BounceOut` is great for animating transforms that seem to come up against
an obstacle.

The output of the `SpringIn` and `SpringOut` functions actually go beyond the range of 0 to 1. The
`SpringIn` has an output that drops below 0 initially, and the `SpringOut` output goes beyond the

value of 1:

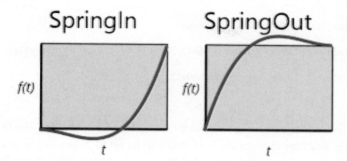

In other animation systems, these SpringIn and SpringOut patterns are usually known as *back-ease* functions, and you saw the underlying mathematics in the **BoxViewClock** sample in the previous chapter. In fact, you can rewrite the Convert method in SecondBackEaseConverter like this and it will work the same:

```
public object Convert(object value, Type targetType,
                      object parameter, CultureInfo culture)
{
    int seconds = (int)((double)value / 6);    // 0, 1, 2, ... 60
    double t = (double)value / 6 % 1;          // 0 --> 1
    double v = 0;                              // 0 --> 1

    if (t < 0.5)
    {
        v = 0.5 * Easing.SpringIn.Ease(2 * t);
    }
    else
    {
        v = 0.5 * (1 + Easing.SpringOut.Ease(2 * (t - 0.5)));
    }

    return 6 * (seconds + v);
}
```

There is no SpringInOut object, so the Convert method must break each second into two halves. When t is less than 0.5, the SpringIn object is applied. However, the input to the Ease method needs to be doubled to range from 0 to 1, and the output needs to be halved to range from 0 to 0.5. The SpringOut call must be adjusted likewise: When t ranges from 0.5 to 1, the input to the Ease method needs to range from 0 to 1, and the output needs to be adjusted to range from 0.5 to 1.

Let's try some more easing functions. The **BounceButton** program has a XAML file that is the same as **AnimationTryout**, and the Clicked handler for the Button has just three statements:

```
public partial class BounceButtonPage : ContentPage
{
    public BounceButtonPage()
```

```
    {
        InitializeComponent();
    }

    async void OnButtonClicked(object sender, EventArgs args)
    {
        await button.TranslateTo(0, (Height - button.Height) / 2, 1000, Easing.BounceOut);
        await Task.Delay(2000);
        await button.TranslateTo(0, 0, 1000, Easing.SpringOut);
    }
}
```

The `TranslateTo` method animates the `TranslationX` and `TranslationY` properties. The first two arguments are named `x` and `y`, and they indicate the final values to be set to `TranslationX` and `TranslationY`. The first `TranslateTo` call here does not move the `Button` horizontally, so the first argument is 0. The second argument is the distance between the bottom of the `Button` and the bottom of the page. The `Button` is vertically centered on the page, so that distance is half the height of the page minus half the height of the `Button`.

That first animation is performed in 1,000 milliseconds. Then there's a two-second delay, and the `Button` is translated back to its original position with `x` and `y` arguments of 0. The second `TranslateTo` animation uses the `Easing.SpringOut` function, so you probably expect the `Button` to overshoot its mark and then settle back into its final position.

However, the `TranslateTo` method clamps the output of any easing function that goes outside the range of 0 to 1. Later on in this chapter you'll see a fix for that flaw in the `TranslateTo` method.

Your own easing functions

It's easy to make your own easing functions. All that's required is a method of type `Func<double, double>`, which is a function with a `double` argument and a `double` return value. This is a transfer function: It should return 0 for an argument of 0, and 1 for an argument of 1. But between those two values, anything goes.

Generally you'll define a custom easing function as the argument to the `Easing` constructor. That's the only constructor `Easing` defines, but the `Easing` class also defines an implicit conversion from a `Func<double, double>` to `Easing`.

The Xamarin.Forms animation functions call the `Ease` method of the `Easing` object. That `Ease` method also has a `double` argument and a `double` return value, and it basically provides public access to the easing function you specify in the `Easing` constructor. (The graphs earlier in this chapter that showed the various predefined easing functions were generated by a program that accessed the `Ease` methods of the various predefined `Easing` objects.)

Here's a program that incorporates two custom easing functions to control the scaling of a `Button`. These functions somewhat contradict the meaning of the word "ease," which is why the program is called **UneasyScale**. The first of these two easing functions truncates the incoming value to the discrete values 0, 0.2, 0.4, 0.6, 0.8, and 1, so the Button increases in size in jumps. The Button is then decreased in size with another easing function that applies a little random variation to the incoming value.

The first of these easing functions is specified as a lambda function argument to the Easing constructor. The second is a method cast to an Easing object:

```
public partial class UneasyScalePage : ContentPage
{
    Random random = new Random();

    public UneasyScalePage()
    {
        InitializeComponent();
    }

    async void OnButtonClicked(object sender, EventArgs args)
    {
        double scale = Math.Min(Width / button.Width, Height / button.Height);
        await button.ScaleTo(scale, 1000, new Easing(t => (int)(5 * t) / 5.0));
        await button.ScaleTo(1, 1000, (Easing)RandomEase);
    }

    double RandomEase(double t)
    {
        return t == 0 || t == 1 ? t : t + 0.25 * (random.NextDouble() - 0.5);
    }
}
```

Unfortunately, it's easier to make disjointed functions like these rather than smoother and more interesting transfer functions. Those tend to be necessarily a bit more complex.

For example, suppose you want an easing function that looks like this:

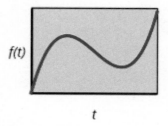

It starts off fast, then slows down and reverses course, but then reverses course again to rise quickly into the final stretch.

You might guess that this is a polynomial equation, or at least that it can be approximated by a polynomial equation. It has two points where the slope is zero, which further suggests that this is a cubic and can be represented like this:

$$f(t) = a \cdot t^3 + b \cdot t^2 + c \cdot t + d$$

Now all we need to find are values of *a, b, c,* and *d* that will cause the transfer function to behave as we want.

For the endpoints, we know that:

$$f(0) = 0$$
$$f(1) = 1$$

This means that:

$$d = 0$$

and:

$$1 = a + b + c$$

If we say further that the two dips in the curve are at *t* equal to 1/3 and 2/3, and the values of *f(t)* at those points are 2/3 and 1/3, respectively, then:

$$\frac{2}{3} = a \cdot \frac{1}{27} + b \cdot \frac{1}{9} + c \cdot \frac{1}{3}$$

$$\frac{1}{3} = a \cdot \frac{8}{27} + b \cdot \frac{4}{9} + c \cdot \frac{2}{3}$$

Those two equations are somewhat more readable and manipulable if they are converted to integer coefficients, so what we have are three equations with three unknowns:

$$1 = a + b + c$$

$$18 = a + 3 \cdot b + 9 \cdot c$$

$$9 = 8 \cdot a + 12 \cdot b + 18 \cdot c$$

And with a little manipulation and combination and work, you can find *a, b,* and *c*:

$$a = 9$$

$$b = -\frac{27}{2}$$

$$c = \frac{11}{2}$$

Let's see if it does what we think it will do. The **CustomCubicEase** program has a XAML file that is the same as the previous projects. The easing function is here expressed directly as a `Func<double, double>` object so that it can be conveniently used in two `ScaleTo` calls. The `Button` is first scaled up in size, and then after a one-second pause, the `Button` is scaled back to normal:

```
public partial class CustomCubicEasePage : ContentPage
```

```
{
    public CustomCubicEasePage()
    {
        InitializeComponent();
    }

    async void OnButtonClicked(object sender, EventArgs args)
    {
        Func<double, double> customEase = t => 9 * t * t * t - 13.5 * t * t + 5.5 * t;

        double scale = Math.Min(Width / button.Width, Height / button.Height);
        await button.ScaleTo(scale, 1000, customEase);
        await Task.Delay(1000);
        await button.ScaleTo(1, 1000, customEase);
    }
}
```

If you don't consider the job of making your own easing functions to be "fun and relaxing," one good source for many standard easing functions is the website http://robertpenner.com/easing/.

It's also possible to construct easing functions from `Math.Sin` and `Math.Cos` if you need simple harmonic motion and to combine those with `Math.Exp` for exponential increases or decay.

Let's take an example: Suppose you want a `Button` that, when clicked, swings down from its lower-left corner, almost as if the `Button` were a picture attached to a wall with a couple of nails, and one of the nails falls out, so the picture slips down and hangs by a single nail in its lower-left corner.

You can follow along with this exercise in the **AnimationTryout** program. In the `Clicked` handler for the `Button`, let's begin by setting the `AnchorX` and `AnchorY` properties and then call `RotateTo` for a 90-degree swing:

```
button.AnchorX = 0;
button.AnchorY = 1;
await button.RotateTo(90, 3000);
```

Here's the result when that animation has completed:

But this really cries out for an easing function so that the `Button` swings back and forth a bit from that corner before settling. To begin, let's first add a do-nothing linear easing function to the `Rotate-To` call:

```
await button.RotateTo(90, 3000, new Easing(t => t));
```

Let's now add some sinusoidal behavior. That's either a sine or a cosine. We want the swing to be slow at the beginning, so that would imply a cosine rather than a sine. Let's set the argument to the `Math.Cos` method so that as `t` goes from 0 to 1, the angle is 0 through 10π. That's five complete cycles of the cosine curve, which means that the `Button` swings five times back and forth:

```
await button.RotateTo(90, 3000, new Easing(t => Math.Cos(10 * Math.PI * t)));
```

Of course, this is not right at all. When `t` is zero, the `Math.Cos` method returns 1, so the animation starts off by jumping to a value of 90 degrees. For subsequent values of `t`, the `Math.Cos` function returns values ranging from 1 through –1, so the `Button` swings five times from 90 degrees to –90 degrees and back to 90 degrees, finally coming to a rest at 90 degrees. That is indeed where we want the animation to end, but we want the animation to start at 0 degrees

Nevertheless, let's ignore that problem for a moment. Let's instead tackle what initially seems to be the more complex problem. We don't want the `Button` to swing a full 180 degrees five times. We want the swings of the `Button` to decay over time before it comes to rest.

There's an easy way to do that. We can multiply the `Math.Cos` method by a `Math.Exp` call with a negative argument based on `t`:

```
Math.Exp(-5 * t)
```

The `Math.Exp` method raises the mathematical constant *e* (approximately 2.7) to the specified power.

When t is 0 at the beginning of the animation, *e* to the 0 power is 1. And when t is 1, *e* to the negative fifth power is less than .01, which is very close to zero. (You don't need to use –5 in this call; you can experiment to find a value that seems best.)

Let's multiply the `Math.Cos` result by the `Math.Exp` result:

```
await button.RotateTo(90, 3000, new Easing(t => Math.Cos(10 * Math.PI * t) * Math.Exp(-5 * t)));
```

We are very very close. The `Math.Exp` does indeed damp the `Math.Cos` call, but the product is backward The product is 1 when t is 0 and nearly 0 when t is 1. Can we fix this by simply subtracting the whole expression from 1? Let's try it:

```
await button.RotateTo(90, 3000,
    new Easing(t => 1 - Math.Cos(10 * Math.PI * t) * Math.Exp(-5 * t)));
```

Now the easing function properly returns 0 when t is 0, and close enough to 1 when t is 1.

And, what's more important, the easing function is now visually satisfactory as well. It really looks as if the `Button` drops from its mooring and swings several times before coming to rest.

Let's now call `TranslateTo` to make the `Button` drop off and fall to the bottom of the page. How far does the `Button` need to drop?

The `Button` was originally positioned in the center of the page. That means that the distance between the bottom of the `Button` and the page was half the height of the page minus the height of the `Button`:

```
(Height - button.Height) / 2
```

But now the `Button` has swung 90 degrees from its lower-left corner, so the `Button` is closer to the bottom of the page by its width. Here's the full call to `TranslateTo` to drop the `Button` to the bottom of the page and make it bounce a little:

```
await button.TranslateTo(0, (Height - button.Height) / 2 - button.Width,
                    1000, Easing.BounceOut);
```

The `Button` comes to rest like this:

Now let's make the `Button` keel over and land upside down, which means that we want to rotate the `Button` around the upper-right corner. This requires a change in the `AnchorX` and `AnchorY` properties:

```
button.AnchorX = 1;
button.AnchorY = 0;
```

But that's a problem—a *big* problem—because a change in the `AnchorX` and `AnchorY` properties actually changes the location of the `Button`. Try it! The `Button` suddenly leaps up and to the right. Where the `Button` jumps to is exactly the position it would be if the first `RotateTo` had been based on these new `AnchorX` and `AnchorY` values—a rotation around its upper-right corner rather than its lower-left corner.

Can you visualize that? Here's a little mockup that shows the original position of the `Button`, the `Button` rotated 90 degrees clockwise from its lower-left corner, and the `Button` rotated 90 degrees clockwise from its upper-right corner:

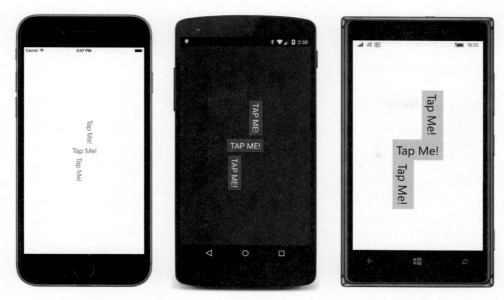

When we set new values of AnchorX and AnchorY, we need to adjust the TranslationX and TranslationY properties so that the Button essentially moves from the rotated position in the upper-right to the rotated position in the lower-left. TranslationX needs to be decreased by the width of the Button and then increased by its height. TranslationY needs to be increased by both the height of the Button and the width of the Button. Let's try that:

```
button.TranslationX -= button.Width - button.Height;
button.TranslationY += button.Width + button.Height;
```

And that preserves the position of the Button when the AnchorX and AnchorY properties are changed to the button's upper-right corner.

Now the Button can be rotated around its upper-right corner as it falls over, with another little bounce, of course:

```
await button.RotateTo(180, 1000, Easing.BounceOut);
```

And now the Button can ascend up the screen and simultaneously fade out:

```
await Task.WhenAll
    (
        button.FadeTo(0, 4000),
        button.TranslateTo(0, -Height, 5000, Easing.CubicIn)
    );
```

The FadeTo method animates the Opacity property, in this case from its default value of 1 to the value 0 specified as the first argument.

Here's the complete program, called **SwingButton** (referring to the first animation) and concluding with a restoration of the Button to its original position so that you can try it again:

```
public partial class SwingButtonPage : ContentPage
{
    public SwingButtonPage()
    {
        InitializeComponent();
    }

    async void OnButtonClicked(object sender, EventArgs args)
    {
        // Swing down from lower-left corner.
        button.AnchorX = 0;
        button.AnchorY = 1;

        await button.RotateTo(90, 3000,
            new Easing(t => 1 - Math.Cos(10 * Math.PI * t) * Math.Exp(-5 * t)));

        // Drop to the bottom of the screen.
        await button.TranslateTo(0, (Height - button.Height) / 2 - button.Width,
                                 1000, Easing.BounceOut);

        // Prepare AnchorX and AnchorY for next rotation.
        button.AnchorX = 1;
        button.AnchorY = 0;

        // Compensate for the change in AnchorX and AnchorY.
        button.TranslationX -= button.Width - button.Height;
        button.TranslationY += button.Width + button.Height;

        // Fall over.
        await button.RotateTo(180, 1000, Easing.BounceOut);

        // Fade out while ascending to the top of the screen.
        await Task.WhenAll
            (
                button.FadeTo(0, 4000),
                button.TranslateTo(0, -Height, 5000, Easing.CubicIn)
            );

        // After three seconds, return the Button to normal.
        await Task.Delay(3000);
        button.TranslationX = 0;
        button.TranslationY = 0;
        button.Rotation = 0;
        button.Opacity = 1;
    }
}
```

An easing function is supposed to return 0 when the input is 0 and 1 when the input is 1, but it's possible to break these rules, and sometimes that makes sense. For example, suppose you want an animation that moves an element a little—perhaps it vibrates it in some way—but the animation should return the element to its original position at the end. For something like this it makes sense for the easing function to return 0 when the input is both 0 and 1, but something other than 0 between those values.

This is the idea behind `JiggleButton`, which is in the **Xamarin.FormsBook.Toolkit** library. `JiggleButton` derives from `Button` and installs a `Clicked` handler for the sole purpose of jiggling the button when you click it:

```
namespace Xamarin.FormsBook.Toolkit
{
    public class JiggleButton : Button
    {
        bool isJiggling;

        public JiggleButton()
        {
            Clicked += async (sender, args) =>
                {
                    if (isJiggling)
                        return;

                    isJiggling = true;

                    await this.RotateTo(15, 1000, new Easing(t =>
                                            Math.Sin(Math.PI * t) *
                                            Math.Sin(Math.PI * 20 * t)));
                    isJiggling = false;
                };
        }
    }
}
```

The `RotateTo` method seems to rotate the button by 15 degrees over the course of one second. However, the custom `Easing` object has a different idea. It consists solely of the product of two sine functions. As `t` goes from 0 to 1, the first `Math.Sin` function sweeps the first half of a sine curve, so it goes from 0 when `t` is 0, to 1 when `t` is 0.5, and back to 0 when `t` is 1.

The second `Math.Sin` call is the jiggle part. As `t` goes from 0 to 1, this call goes through 10 cycles of a sine curve. Without the first `Math.Sin` call, this would rotate the button from 0 to 15 degrees, then to –15 degrees, and back to 0 ten times. But the first `Math.Sin` call dampens that rotation at the beginning and end of the animation, allowing only a full 15 and –15 degree rotation in the middle.

A little code involving the `isJiggling` field protects the `Clicked` handler from starting a new animation when one is already in progress. This is an advantage of using `await` with the animation methods: You know exactly when the animation is completed.

The **JiggleButtonDemo** XAML file creates three `JiggleButton` objects so that you can play with them:

```
<ContentPage xmlns="http://xamarin.com/schemas/2014/forms"
             xmlns:x="http://schemas.microsoft.com/winfx/2009/xaml"
             xmlns:toolkit=
                 "clr-namespace:Xamarin.FormsBook.Toolkit;assembly=Xamarin.FormsBook.Toolkit"
             x:Class="JiggleButtonDemo.JiggleButtonDemoPage">
```

```
    <StackLayout>
        <toolkit:JiggleButton Text="Tap Me!"
                              FontSize="Large"
                              HorizontalOptions="Center"
                              VerticalOptions="CenterAndExpand" />

        <toolkit:JiggleButton Text="Tap Me!"
                              FontSize="Large"
                              HorizontalOptions="Center"
                              VerticalOptions="CenterAndExpand" />

        <toolkit:JiggleButton Text="Tap Me!"
                              FontSize="Large"
                              HorizontalOptions="Center"
                              VerticalOptions="CenterAndExpand" />

    </StackLayout>
</ContentPage>
```

Entrance animations

One common type of animation in real-life programming occurs when a page is first made visible. The various elements on the page can be animated briefly before settling into their final states. This is often called an *entrance animation* and can involve:

- Translation, to move elements into their final positions.

- Scale, to enlarge or shrink elements to their final sizes.

- Changes in Opacity to fade elements into view.

- 3D rotation to make it seem as if a whole page swings into view.

Generally you'll want the elements on the page to come to rest with default values of these properties: TranslationX and TranslationY values of 0, Scale and Opacity values of 1, and all Rotation properties set to 0.

In other words, the entrance animations should *end* at each property's default value, which means that they begin at nondefault values. This approach also allows the program to apply other transforms to these elements at a later time without taking the entrance animations into account.

When designing the layout in XAML you'll want to simply ignore these animations. As an example, here is a page with several elements solely for demonstration purposes. The program is called **FadingEntrance**:

```
<ContentPage xmlns="http://xamarin.com/schemas/2014/forms"
             xmlns:x="http://schemas.microsoft.com/winfx/2009/xaml"
             x:Class="FadingEntrance.FadingEntrancePage">
    <ContentPage.Padding>
        <OnPlatform x:TypeArguments="Thickness"
                    iOS="10, 20, 10, 10"
                    Android="10"
                    WinPhone="10" />
```

```
        </ContentPage.Padding>

        <StackLayout x:Name="stackLayout">
            <Label Text="The App"
                   Style="{DynamicResource TitleStyle}"
                   FontAttributes="Italic"
                   HorizontalOptions="Center" />

            <Button Text="Countdown"
                    FontSize="Large"
                    HorizontalOptions="Center" />

            <Label Text="Primary Slider"
                   HorizontalOptions="Center" />

            <Slider Value="0.5" />

            <ListView HorizontalOptions="Center"
                      WidthRequest="200">
                <ListView.ItemsSource>
                    <x:Array Type="{x:Type Color}">
                        <Color>Red</Color>
                        <Color>Green</Color>
                        <Color>Blue</Color>
                        <Color>Aqua</Color>
                        <Color>Purple</Color>
                        <Color>Yellow</Color>
                    </x:Array>
                </ListView.ItemsSource>

                <ListView.ItemTemplate>
                    <DataTemplate>
                        <ViewCell>
                            <BoxView Color="{Binding}" />
                        </ViewCell>
                    </DataTemplate>
                </ListView.ItemTemplate>
            </ListView>

            <Label Text="Secondary Slider"
                   HorizontalOptions="Center" />

            <Slider Value="0.5" />

            <Button Text="Launch"
                    FontSize="Large"
                    HorizontalOptions="Center" />
        </StackLayout>
</ContentPage>
```

The code-behind file overrides the `OnAppearing` method. The `OnAppearing` method is called after the page is laid out but before the page becomes visible. All the elements on the page have been sized and positioned, so if you need to obtain that information you can do so during this method. In the

FadingEntrance program, the `OnAppearing` override sets the `Opacity` property of the `StackLayout` to `0` (thus making everything within the `StackLayout` invisible) and then animates it to 1:

```
public partial class FadingEntrancePage : ContentPage
{
    public FadingEntrancePage()
    {
        InitializeComponent();
    }

    protected override void OnAppearing()
    {
        base.OnAppearing();

        stackLayout.Opacity = 0;
        stackLayout.FadeTo(1, 3000);
    }
}
```

Here's the page in the process of fading into view:

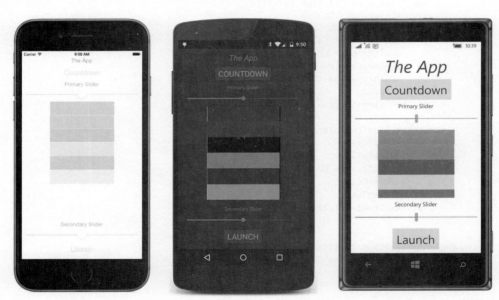

Let's try another. The XAML file in the **SlidingEntrance** program is the same as **FadingEntrance**, but the `OnAppearing` override begins by setting all the `TranslationX` properties of the children of the `StackLayout` to alternating values of 1000 and –1000:

```
public partial class SlidingEntrancePage : ContentPage
{
    public SlidingEntrancePage()
    {
        InitializeComponent();
    }
```

```
async protected override void OnAppearing()
{
    base.OnAppearing();

    double offset = 1000;

    foreach (View view in stackLayout.Children)
    {
        view.TranslationX = offset;
        offset *= -1;
    }

    foreach (View view in stackLayout.Children)
    {
        await Task.WhenAny(view.TranslateTo(0, 0, 1000, Easing.SpringOut),
                           Task.Delay(100));
    }
}
```

The second `foreach` loop then animates these children back to the default settings of `TranslationX` and `TranslationY`. However, the animations are staggered and overlapped. Here's how: The first call to `Task.WhenAny` starts the first `TranslateTo` animation, which completes after one second. However, the second argument to `Task.WhenAny` is `Task.Delay`, which completes in one-tenth of a second, and that's when `Task.WhenAny` also completes. The `foreach` loop fetches the next child, which then begins its own one-second animation. Every animation begins one-tenth of a second after the previous one.

Here's the result in process:

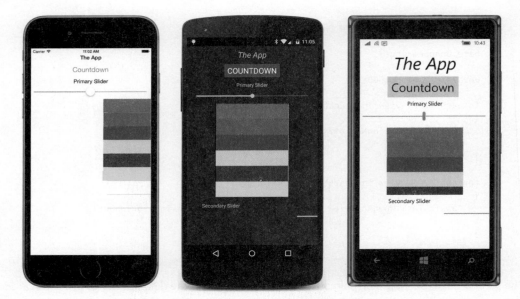

The `TranslateTo` call uses the `Easing.SpringOut` function, which means that each animated element should overshoot its destination and then move backward to come at rest in the center of the page. However, you won't see this happen. As you've already discovered, the `TranslateTo` method stops working when an easing function has an output that exceeds 1.

You'll see a solution for this—and a version of this program with elements that do overshoot their destinations—later in this chapter.

Finally, here's a **SwingingEntrance** animation:

```
public partial class SwingingEntrancePage : ContentPage
{
    public SwingingEntrancePage()
    {
        InitializeComponent();
    }

    async protected override void OnAppearing()
    {
        base.OnAppearing();

        stackLayout.AnchorX = 0;
        stackLayout.RotationY = 180;
        await stackLayout.RotateYTo(0, 1000, Easing.CubicOut);
        stackLayout.AnchorX = 0.5;
    }
}
```

The `RotateYTo` method rotates the entire `StackLayout` and its children around the Y axis from 180 degrees to 0 degrees. With an `AnchorX` setting of 0, the rotation is actually around the left edge of the `StackLayout`. The `StackLayout` won't be visible until the `RotationY` value is less than 90 degrees, but the result looks a little better if the rotation starts before the page actually becomes visible. The `CubicOut` easing function causes the animation to slow down as it nears completion. Here it is in progress:

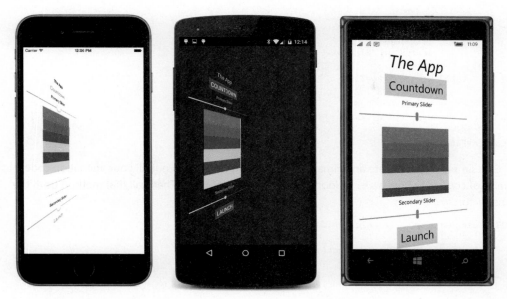

After the animation has completed, the `OnAppearing` method returns `AnchorX` to its original value so that everything has default values for any future animations that the program might want to implement.

Forever animations

At the opposite extreme from entrance animations are *forever animations*. An application can implement an animation that goes on "forever," or at least until the program ends. Often the sole purpose of such animations is to demonstrate the capabilities of an animation system, but preferably in a delightful or amusing manner.

The first example is called **FadingTextAnimation** and uses `FadeTo` to fade two `Label` elements in and out. The XAML file puts both `Label` elements in a single-cell `Grid` so that they overlap. The second one has its `Opacity` property set to 0:

```
<ContentPage xmlns="http://xamarin.com/schemas/2014/forms"
             xmlns:x="http://schemas.microsoft.com/winfx/2009/xaml"
             x:Class="FadingTextAnimation.FadingTextAnimationPage"
             BackgroundColor="White"
             SizeChanged="OnPageSizeChanged">
    <ContentPage.Resources>
        <ResourceDictionary>
            <Style TargetType="Label">
```

```
                <Setter Property="HorizontalTextAlignment" Value="Center" />
                <Setter Property="VerticalTextAlignment" Value="Center" />
            </Style>
        </ResourceDictionary>
    </ContentPage.Resources>

    <Grid>
        <Label x:Name="label1"
               Text="MORE"
               TextColor="Blue" />

        <Label x:Name="label2"
               Text="CODE"
               TextColor="Red"
               Opacity="0" />
    </Grid>
</ContentPage>
```

One simple way to create an animation that runs "forever" is to put all your animation code—using `await` of course—within a `while` loop with a condition of `true`. Then call that method from the constructor:

```
public partial class FadingTextAnimationPage : ContentPage
{
    public FadingTextAnimationPage()
    {
        InitializeComponent();

        // Start the animation going.
        AnimationLoop();
    }

    void OnPageSizeChanged(object sender, EventArgs args)
    {
        if (Width > 0)
        {
            double fontSize = 0.3 * Width;
            label1.FontSize = fontSize;
            label2.FontSize = fontSize;
        }
    }

    async void AnimationLoop()
    {
        while (true)
        {
            await Task.WhenAll(label1.FadeTo(0, 1000),
                               label2.FadeTo(1, 1000));

            await Task.WhenAll(label1.FadeTo(1, 1000),
                               label2.FadeTo(0, 1000));
        }
    }
}
```

Infinite loops are usually dangerous, but this one executes very briefly once every second when the `Task.WhenAll` method signals a completion of the two animations—the first fading out one `Label` and the second fading in the other `Label`. The `SizeChanged` handler for the page sets the `FontSize` of the text, so the text approaches the width of the page:

Does it mean "More code" or "Code more"? Perhaps both.

Here's another animation that targets text. The **PalindromeAnimation** program spins individual characters 180 degress to turn them upside down. Fortunately, the characters comprise a palindrome that reads the same forward and backward:

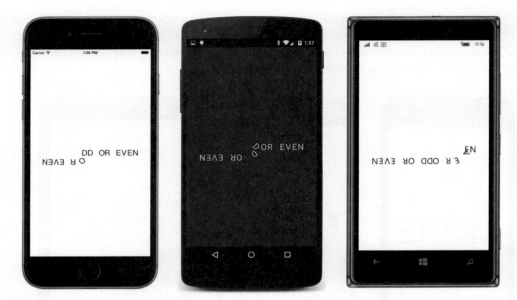

When all the characters are flipped upside down, the whole collection of characters is flipped, and the animation starts again.

The XAML file simply contains a horizontal `StackLayout`, without any children just yet:

```
<ContentPage xmlns="http://xamarin.com/schemas/2014/forms"
             xmlns:x="http://schemas.microsoft.com/winfx/2009/xaml"
             x:Class="PalindromeAnimation.PalindromeAnimationPage"
             SizeChanged="OnPageSizeChanged">

    <StackLayout x:Name="stackLayout"
                 Orientation="Horizontal"
                 HorizontalOptions="Center"
                 VerticalOptions="Center"
                 Spacing="0" />
</ContentPage>
```

The constructor of the code-behind file fills this `StackLayout` with 17 `Label` elements to spell out the palindromic phrase "NEVER ODD OR EVEN." As in the previous program, the `SizeChanged` handler for the page adjusts the size of these labels. Each `Label` is given a uniform `WidthRequest` and a `FontSize` based on that width. Each character in the text string must occupy the same width so that they are still spaced the same when they flip upside down:

```
public partial class PalindromeAnimationPage : ContentPage
{
    string text = "NEVER ODD OR EVEN";
    double[] anchorX = { 0.5, 0.5, 0.5, 0.5, 1, 0,
                         0.5, 1, 1, -1,
                         0.5, 1, 0,
                         0.5, 0.5, 0.5, 0.5 };
```

```
public PalindromeAnimationPage()
{
    InitializeComponent();

    // Add a Label to the StackLayout for each character.
    for (int i = 0; i < text.Length; i++)
    {
        Label label = new Label
        {
            Text = text[i].ToString(),
            HorizontalTextAlignment = TextAlignment.Center
        };
        stackLayout.Children.Add(label);
    }

    // Start the animation.
    AnimationLoop();
}

void OnPageSizeChanged(object sender, EventArgs args)
{
    // Adjust the size and font based on the display width.
    double width = 0.8 * this.Width / stackLayout.Children.Count;

    foreach (Label label in stackLayout.Children.OfType<Label>())
    {
        label.FontSize = 1.4 * width;
        label.WidthRequest = width;
    }
}

async void AnimationLoop()
{
    bool backwards = false;

    while (true)
    {
        // Let's just sit here a second.
        await Task.Delay(1000);

        // Prepare for overlapping rotations.
        Label previousLabel = null;

        // Loop through all the labels.
        IEnumerable<Label> labels = stackLayout.Children.OfType<Label>();

        foreach (Label label in backwards ? labels.Reverse() : labels)
        {
            uint flipTime = 250;

            // Set the AnchorX and AnchorY properties.
            int index = stackLayout.Children.IndexOf(label);
            label.AnchorX = anchorX[index];
            label.AnchorY = 1;
```

```
                    if (previousLabel == null)
                    {
                        // For the first Label in the sequence, rotate it 90 degrees.
                        await label.RelRotateTo(90, flipTime / 2);
                    }
                    else
                    {
                        // For the second and subsequent, also finish the previous flip.
                        await Task.WhenAll(label.RelRotateTo(90, flipTime / 2),
                                           previousLabel.RelRotateTo(90, flipTime / 2));
                    }

                    // If it's the last one, finish the flip.
                    if (label == (backwards ? labels.First() : labels.Last()))
                    {
                        await label.RelRotateTo(90, flipTime / 2);
                    }

                    previousLabel = label;
                }

                // Rotate the entire stack.
                stackLayout.AnchorY = 1;
                await stackLayout.RelRotateTo(180, 1000);

                // Flip the backwards flag.
                backwards ^= true;
            }
        }
}
```

Much of the complexity of the `AnimationLoop` method results from overlapping animations. Each letter needs to rotate by 180 degrees. However, the final 90 degrees of each letter rotation overlaps with the first 90 degrees of the next letter. This requires that the first letter and the last letter be handled differently.

The letter rotations are further complicated by the settings of the `AnchorX` and `AnchorY` properties. For each rotation, `AnchorY` is set to 1 and the rotation occurs around the bottom of the `Label`. But the setting of the `AnchorX` property depends on where the letter occurs in the phrase. The first four letters of "NEVER" can spin around the bottom center of the letter because they form the word "EVEN" when inverted. But the "R" needs to spin around its lower-right corner so that it becomes the end of the word "OR". The space after "NEVER" needs to spin around its lower-left corner so that it becomes the space between "OR" and "EVEN". Essentially, the "R" of "NEVER" and the space swap places. The rest of the phrase continues similarly. The various `AnchorX` values for each letter are stored in the `anchorX` array at the top of the class.

When all the letters have been individually rotated, then the whole `StackLayout` is rotated by 180 degrees. Although that rotated `StackLayout` looks the same as the `StackLayout` when the program started running, it is not the same. The last letter of the phrase is now the first child in the `StackLay-out` and the first letter is now the last child in the `StackLayout`. That's the reason for the `backwards` variable. The `foreach` statement uses that to enumerate through the `StackLayout` children in a forward or backward direction.

You'll notice that all the `AnchorX` and `AnchorY` properties are set in the `AnimationLoop` right before the animation is started, even though they never change over the course of the program. This is to accommodate the problem with iOS. The properties must be set after the element has been sized, and setting those properties within this loop is simply convenient.

If that problem with iOS did not exist, all the `AnchorX` and `AnchorY` properties could be set in the program's constructor or even in the XAML file. It's not unreasonable to define all 17 `Label` elements in the XAML file with unique `AnchorX` settings on each `Label` and the common `AnchorY` setting in a `Style`.

As it is, on iOS devices, the **PalindromeAnimation** program cannot survive a change in orientation from portrait to landscape and back. After the `Label` elements are resized, there is nothing the application can do to fix the internal use of the `AnchorX` and `AnchorY` properties.

The **CopterAnimation** program simulates a little helicopter flying in a circle around the page. The simulation, however, is very simple: The helicopter is simply two `BoxView` elements sized and arranged to look like wings:

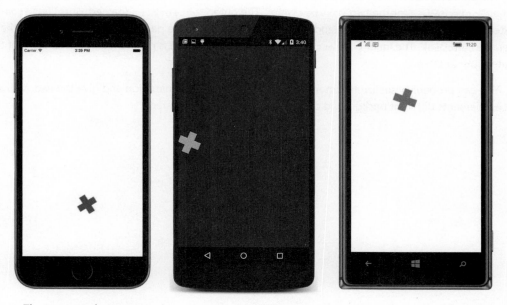

The program has two continuous rotations. The fast one spins the helicopter's blades around its center. A slower rotation moves the wing assemblage in a circle around the center of the page. Both rotations use the default `AnchorX` and `AnchorY` settings of 0.5, so there's no problem on iOS.

However, the program implicitly uses the width of the phone for the circumference of the circle that the copter wings fly around. If you turn the phone sideways to landscape mode, the copter will actually fly outside the bounds of the phone.

The secret to the simplicity of **CopterAnimation** is the XAML file:

```xml
<ContentPage xmlns="http://xamarin.com/schemas/2014/forms"
             xmlns:x="http://schemas.microsoft.com/winfx/2009/xaml"
             x:Class="CopterAnimation.CopterAnimationPage">
    <ContentView x:Name="revolveTarget"
                 HorizontalOptions="Fill"
                 VerticalOptions="Center">
        <ContentView x:Name="copterView"
                     HorizontalOptions="End">
            <AbsoluteLayout>
                <BoxView AbsoluteLayout.LayoutBounds="20, 0, 20, 60"
                         Color="Accent" />

                <BoxView AbsoluteLayout.LayoutBounds="0, 20, 60, 20"
                         Color="Accent" />
            </AbsoluteLayout>
        </ContentView>
    </ContentView>
</ContentPage>
```

The entire layout consists of two nested `ContentView` elements, with an `AbsoluteLayout` in the inner `ContentView` for the two `BoxView` wings. The outer `ContentView` (named `revolveTarget`) extends to the width of the phone and is vertically centered on the page, but it is only as tall as the inner `ContentView`. The inner `ContentView` (named `copterView`) is positioned at the far right of the outer `ContentView`.

You can probably visualize this more easily if you turn off the animation and give the two `Content-View` elements different background colors, for example, blue and red:

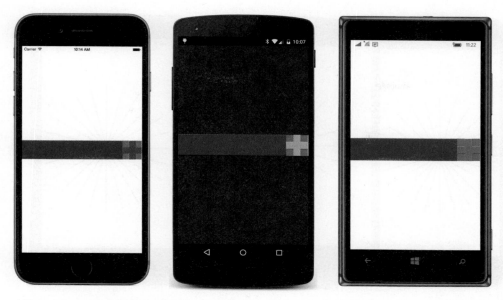

Now you can see fairly easily that both these `ContentView` elements can be rotated around their centers to achieve the effect of rotating wings flying in a circle:

```
public partial class CopterAnimationPage : ContentPage
{
    public CopterAnimationPage()
    {
        InitializeComponent();

        AnimationLoop();
    }

    async void AnimationLoop()
    {
        while (true)
        {
            revolveTarget.Rotation = 0;
            copterView.Rotation = 0;

            await Task.WhenAll(revolveTarget.RotateTo(360, 5000),
                               copterView.RotateTo(360 * 5, 5000));
        }
    }
}
```

Both animations have a duration of five seconds, but during that time, the outer `ContentView` rotates only once around its center while the copter wing assembly rotates five times around its center.

The **RotatingSpokes** program draws 24 spokes emanating from the center of the page with a length based on the lesser of the height and width of the page. Of course, each of the spokes is a thin `BoxView` element:

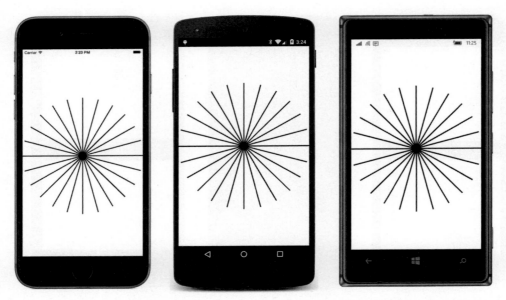

After three seconds, the assemblage of spokes begins to rotate around the center. That goes on for a little while, and then each individual spoke begins rotating around *its* center, making an interesting changing pattern:

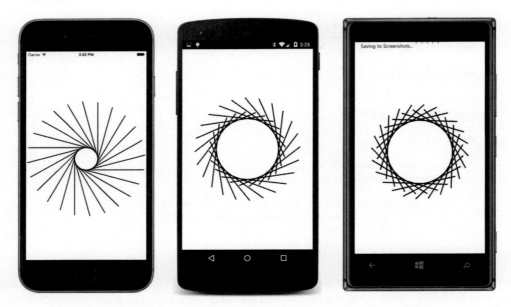

As with **CopterAnimation**, the **RotatingSpokes** program uses default values of AnchorX and An-chorY for all the rotations, so there's no problem changing the phone orientation on iOS devices.

But the XAML file in **RotatingSpokes** consists solely of an AbsoluteLayout and suggests nothing about how the program works:

```
<ContentPage xmlns="http://xamarin.com/schemas/2014/forms"
             xmlns:x="http://schemas.microsoft.com/winfx/2009/xaml"
             x:Class="RotatingSpokes.RotatingSpokesPage"
             BackgroundColor="White"
             SizeChanged="OnPageSizeChanged">
    <AbsoluteLayout x:Name="absoluteLayout"
                    HorizontalOptions="Center"
                    VerticalOptions="Center" />
</ContentPage>
```

Everything else is done in code. The constructor adds 24 black BoxView elements to the AbsoluteLayout, and the SizeChanged handler for the page positions them in the spoke pattern:

```
public partial class RotatingSpokesPage : ContentPage
{
    const int numSpokes = 24;
    BoxView[] boxViews = new BoxView[numSpokes];

    public RotatingSpokesPage()
    {
        InitializeComponent();

        // Create all the BoxView elements.
        for (int i = 0; i < numSpokes; i++)
        {
            BoxView boxView = new BoxView
            {
                Color = Color.Black
            };
            boxViews[i] = boxView;
            absoluteLayout.Children.Add(boxView);
        }

        AnimationLoop();
    }

    void OnPageSizeChanged(object sender, EventArgs args)
    {
        // Set AbsoluteLayout to a square dimension.
        double dimension = Math.Min(this.Width, this.Height);
        absoluteLayout.WidthRequest = dimension;
        absoluteLayout.HeightRequest = dimension;

        // Find the center and a size for the BoxView.
        Point center = new Point(dimension / 2, dimension / 2);
        Size boxViewSize = new Size(dimension / 2, 3);

        for (int i = 0; i < numSpokes; i++)
        {
            // Find an angle for each spoke.
            double degrees = i * 360 / numSpokes;
            double radians = Math.PI * degrees / 180;
```

```
        // Find the point of the center of each BoxView spoke.
        Point boxViewCenter =
            new Point(center.X + boxViewSize.Width / 2 * Math.Cos(radians),
                      center.Y + boxViewSize.Width / 2 * Math.Sin(radians));

        // Find the upper-left corner of the BoxView and position it.
        Point boxViewOrigin = boxViewCenter - boxViewSize * 0.5;
        AbsoluteLayout.SetLayoutBounds(boxViews[i],
                          new Rectangle(boxViewOrigin, boxViewSize));

        // Rotate the BoxView around its center.
        boxViews[i].Rotation = degrees;
    }
}
...
}
```

Certainly the easiest way to render these spokes would be to position all 24 thin `BoxView` elements extending straight up from the center of the `AbsoluteLayout`—much like the initial 12:00 position of the hands of the `BoxViewClock` in the previous chapter—and then to rotate each of them around its bottom edge by an increment of 15 degrees. However, that requires that the `AnchorY` properties of these `BoxView` elements be set to 1 for that bottom edge rotation. That wouldn't work for this program because each of the `BoxView` elements must later be animated to rotate around its center.

The solution is to first calculate a position within the `AbsoluteLayout` for the *center* of each `Box-View`. This is the `Point` value in the `SizeChanged` handler called `boxViewCenter`. The `box-ViewOrigin` is then the upper-left corner of the `BoxView` if the center of the `BoxView` is positioned at `boxViewCenter`. If you comment out the last statement in the `for` loop that sets the `Rotation` property of each `BoxView`, you'll see the spokes positioned like this:

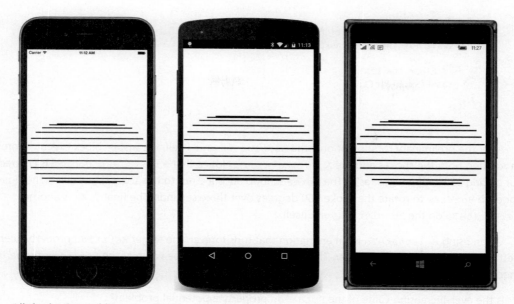

All the horizontal lines (except for the top and bottom ones) are actually two aligned spokes. The center of each spoke is half the length of the spoke from the center of the page. Rotating each of the spokes around its center then creates the initial pattern you saw earlier.

Here's the `AnimationLoop` method:

```
public partial class RotatingSpokesPage : ContentPage
{
    ...
    async void AnimationLoop()
    {
        // Keep still for 3 seconds.
        await Task.Delay(3000);

        // Rotate the configuration of spokes 3 times.
        uint count = 3;
        await absoluteLayout.RotateTo(360 * count, 3000 * count);

        // Prepare for creating Task objects.
        List<Task<bool>> taskList = new List<Task<bool>>(numSpokes + 1);

        while (true)
        {
            foreach (BoxView boxView in boxViews)
            {
                // Task to rotate each spoke.
                taskList.Add(boxView.RelRotateTo(360, 3000));
            }

            // Task to rotate the whole configuration.
            taskList.Add(absoluteLayout.RelRotateTo(360, 3000));
```

```
        // Run all the animations; continue in 3 seconds.
        await Task.WhenAll(taskList);

        // Clear the List.
        taskList.Clear();
    }
  }
}
```

After the preliminary rotation of only the `AbsoluteLayout` itself, the `while` block executes forever in rotating both the spokes and the `AbsoluteLayout`. Notice that a `List<Task<bool>>` is created for storing 25 simultaneous tasks. The `foreach` loop adds a `Task` to this `List` that calls `RelRotateTo` for each `BoxView` to rotate the spoke 360 degrees over three seconds. The final `Task` is another `RelRotateTo` on the `AbsoluteLayout` itself.

When using `RelRotateTo` in an animation that runs forever, the target `Rotation` property keeps getting larger and larger and larger. The actual rotation angle is the value of the `Rotation` property modulo 360.

Is the ever-increasing value of the `Rotation` property a potential problem?

In theory, no. Even if the underlying platform used a single-precision floating-point number to represent `Rotation` values, a problem wouldn't arise until the value exceeds 3.4×10^{38}. Even if you're increasing the `Rotation` property by 360 degrees every second, and you started the animation at the time of the Big Bang (13.8 billion years ago), the `Rotation` value would be only 4.4×10^{17}.

However, in reality, a problem can creep up, and much sooner than you might think. A `Rotation` angle of 36,000,000—just 100,000 rotations of 360 degrees—causes an object to be rendered a little differently than a `Rotation` angle of 0, and the deviation gets larger for higher `Rotation` angles.

If you'd like to explore this, you'll find a program named **RotationBreakdown** among the source code for this chapter. The program spins two `BoxView` elements at the same pace, one with `RotateTo` from 0 to 360 degrees, and the other with `RelRotateTo` with an argument of 36000. The `BoxView` rotated with `RotateTo` normally obscures the `BoxView` rotated with `RelRotateTo`, but that underlying `BoxView` is colored red, and within a minute you'll start seeing the red `BoxView` peek through. The deviation becomes greater the longer the program runs.

Often when you're combining animations, you want them all to start and end at the same time. But other times—and particularly with animations that run forever—you want several animations to run independently of each other, or at least seeming to run independently.

This is the case with the **SpinningImage** program. The program displays a bitmap using the `Image` element:

```
<ContentPage xmlns="http://xamarin.com/schemas/2014/forms"
             xmlns:x="http://schemas.microsoft.com/winfx/2009/xaml"
             x:Class="SpinningImage.SpinningImagePage">
```

```
<Image x:Name="image"
       Source="https://developer.xamarin.com/demo/IMG_0563.JPG"
       Scale="0.5" />

</ContentPage>
```

Normally, the `Image` would render the bitmap to fit within the screen while maintaining the bitmap's aspect ratio. In portrait mode, the width of the rendered bitmap would be the same as the width of the phone. However, with a `Scale` setting of 0.5, the `Image` is half that size.

The code-behind file then animates it by using `RotateTo`, `RotateXTo`, and `RotateYTo` to make it twist and turn almost randomly in space:

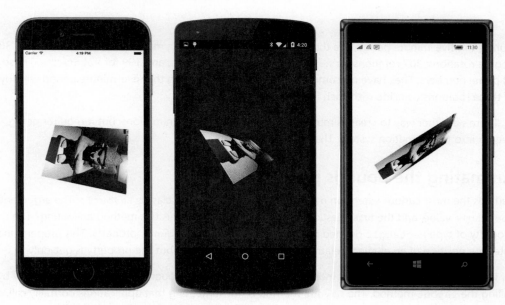

However, you probably don't want the `RotateTo`, `RotateXTo`, and `RotateYTo` to be synchronized in any way because that would result in repetitive patterns.

The solution here actually does create a repetitive pattern, but one that is five minutes in length. This is the duration for the three animations in the `Task.WhenAll` method:

```
public partial class SpinningImagePage : ContentPage
{
    public SpinningImagePage()
    {
        InitializeComponent();

        AnimationLoop();
    }

    async void AnimationLoop()
    {
```

```
        uint duration = 5 * 60 * 1000;   // 5 minutes

        while (true)
        {
            await Task.WhenAll(
                image.RotateTo(307 * 360, duration),
                image.RotateXTo(251 * 360, duration),
                image.RotateYTo(199 * 360, duration));

            image.Rotation = 0;
            image.RotationX = 0;
            image.RotationY = 0;
        }
    }
}
```

During this five-minute period, the three separate animations each makes a different number of 360 degree rotations: 307 rotations for `RotateTo`, 251 for `RotateXTo`, and 199 for `RotateYTo`. Those are all prime numbers. They have no common factors. So never during that five-minute period will any two of these rotations coincide with each other in the same way.

There's another way to create simultaneous but autonomous animations, but it requires going deeper into the animation system. That will be coming up soon.

Animating the Bounds property

Perhaps the most curious extension method in `ViewExtensions` class is `LayoutTo`. The argument is a `Rectangle` value, and the first question might be: What property is this method animating? The only property of type `Rectangle` defined by `VisualElement` is the `Bounds` property. This property indicates the position of an element relative to its parent and its size, but the property is get-only.

The `LayoutTo` animation does indeed animate the `Bounds` property, but it does so indirectly by calling the `Layout` method. The `Layout` method is not something that applications normally call. As the name suggests, it's commonly used within the layout system to position and size children relative to their parents. The only time you'll probably have an occasion to call `Layout` is when you write a custom layout class that derives from `Layout<View>`, as you'll see in Chapter 26, "Custom layouts."

You probably don't want to use the `LayoutTo` animation for children of a `StackLayout` or `Grid` because the animation overrides the position and size set by the parent. As soon as you turn the phone sideways, the page undergoes another layout pass that causes the `StackLayout` or `Grid` to move and size the child based on the normal layout process, and that will override your animation.

You'll have the same problem with a child of an `AbsoluteLayout`. After the `LayoutTo` animation completes, if you turn the phone sideways, the `AbsoluteLayout` then moves and sizes the child based on the child's `LayoutBounds` attached bindable property. But with `AbsoluteLayout` you also have a solution to this problem: After the `LayoutTo` animation concludes, the program can set the child's `LayoutBounds` attached bindable property to the same rectangle specified in the animation, perhaps using the final setting of the `Bounds` property set by the animation.

Keep in mind, however, that the `Layout` method and the `LayoutTo` animation have no knowledge of the proportional positioning and sizing feature in `AbsoluteLayout`. If you use proportional positioning and sizing, you might need to translate between proportional and absolute coordinates and sizes. The `Bounds` property always reports position and size in absolute coordinates.

The **BouncingBox** program uses `LayoutTo` to methodically bounce a `BoxView` around the interior of a square `Frame`. The `BoxView` starts at the center of the top edge, then moves in an arc to the center of the right edge, and then to the center of the bottom edge, the center of the left edge, and back up to the top, from where the journey continues. As the `BoxView` hits each edge, it realistically compresses and then expands like a rubber ball:

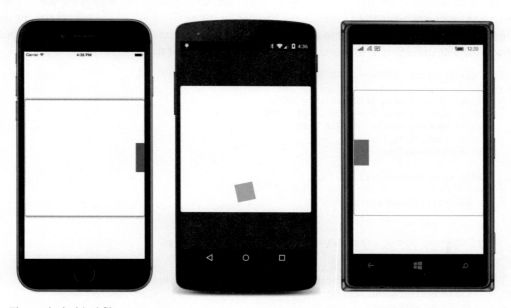

The code-behind file uses `AbsoluteLayout.SetLayoutBounds` to position the `BoxView` against each of the four edges, `LayoutTo` for the compression and decompression against the edge, and `RotateTo` to move the `BoxView` in an arc to the next edge.

The XAML file creates the `Frame`, the `AbsoluteLayout`, and the `BoxView`:

```
<ContentPage xmlns="http://xamarin.com/schemas/2014/forms"
             xmlns:x="http://schemas.microsoft.com/winfx/2009/xaml"
             x:Class="BouncingBox.BouncingBoxPage">
    <ContentPage.Padding>
        <OnPlatform x:TypeArguments="Thickness"
                    iOS="0, 20, 0, 0" />
    </ContentPage.Padding>

    <ContentView SizeChanged="OnContentViewSizeChanged">
        <Frame x:Name="frame"
               OutlineColor="Accent"
               BackgroundColor="White"
```

```
                    Padding="0"
                    HorizontalOptions="Center"
                    VerticalOptions="Center">
                <AbsoluteLayout SizeChanged="OnAbsoluteLayoutSizeChanged">
                    <BoxView x:Name="boxView"
                             Color="Accent"
                             IsVisible="False" />
                </AbsoluteLayout>
            </Frame>
        </ContentView>
    </ContentPage>
```

In the code-behind file, the `SizeChanged` handler for the `ContentView` adjusts the size of the `Frame` to be square, while the `SizeChanged` handler for the `AbsoluteLayout` saves its size for the animation calculations and starts the animation going if the size appears to be legitimate. (Without this check, the animation begins too early, and it uses an invalid size of the `AbsoluteLayout`.)

```
public partial class BouncingBoxPage : ContentPage
{
    static readonly uint arcDuration = 1000;
    static readonly uint bounceDuration = 250;
    static readonly double boxSize = 50;
    double layoutSize;
    bool animationGoing;

    public BouncingBoxPage()
    {
        InitializeComponent();
    }

    void OnContentViewSizeChanged(object sender, EventArgs args)
    {
        ContentView contentView = (ContentView)sender;
        double size = Math.Min(contentView.Width, contentView.Height);
        frame.WidthRequest = size;
        frame.HeightRequest = size;
    }

    void OnAbsoluteLayoutSizeChanged(object sender, EventArgs args)
    {
        AbsoluteLayout absoluteLayout = (AbsoluteLayout)sender;
        layoutSize = Math.Min(absoluteLayout.Width, absoluteLayout.Height);

        // Only start the animation with a valid size.
        if (!animationGoing && layoutSize > 100)
        {
            animationGoing = true;
            AnimationLoop();
        }
    }
    ...
}
```

The `AnimationLoop` method is lengthy, but that's only because it uses separate logic for each of

the four sides and the transitions between those sides. For each side, the first step is to position the
BoxView by using AbsoluteLayout.SetLayoutBounds. Then the BoxView is rotated in an arc to
the next side. This requires setting the AnchorX and AnchorY properties so that the center of animation is close to the corner of the Frame but expressed in units of the BoxView size.

Then come the two calls to LayoutTo to animate the compression of the BoxView as it hits the inside of the Frame, and the subsequent expansion of BoxView as it bounces off:

```
public partial class BoxingBoxPage : ContentPage
{
    ...
    async void AnimationLoop()
    {
        while (true)
        {
            // Initial position at top.
            AbsoluteLayout.SetLayoutBounds(boxView,
                new Rectangle((layoutSize - boxSize) / 2, 0, boxSize, boxSize));

            // Arc from top to right.
            boxView.AnchorX = layoutSize / 2 / boxSize;
            boxView.AnchorY = 0.5;
            await boxView.RotateTo(-90, arcDuration);

            // Bounce on right.
            Rectangle rectNormal = new Rectangle(layoutSize - boxSize,
                                                 (layoutSize - boxSize) / 2,
                                                 boxSize, boxSize);

            Rectangle rectSquashed = new Rectangle(rectNormal.X + boxSize / 2,
                                                   rectNormal.Y - boxSize / 2,
                                                   boxSize / 2, 2 * boxSize);

            boxView.BatchBegin();
            boxView.Rotation = 0;
            boxView.AnchorX = 0.5;
            boxView.AnchorY = 0.5;
            AbsoluteLayout.SetLayoutBounds(boxView, rectNormal);
            boxView.BatchCommit();

            await boxView.LayoutTo(rectSquashed, bounceDuration, Easing.SinOut);
            await boxView.LayoutTo(rectNormal, bounceDuration, Easing.SinIn);

            // Arc from right to bottom.
            boxView.AnchorX = 0.5;
            boxView.AnchorY = layoutSize / 2 / boxSize;
            await boxView.RotateTo(-90, arcDuration);

            // Bounce at bottom.
            rectNormal = new Rectangle((layoutSize - boxSize) / 2,
                                       layoutSize - boxSize,
                                       boxSize, boxSize);
```

```
rectSquashed = new Rectangle(rectNormal.X - boxSize / 2,
                             rectNormal.Y + boxSize / 2,
                             2 * boxSize, boxSize / 2);

boxView.BatchBegin();
boxView.Rotation = 0;
boxView.AnchorX = 0.5;
boxView.AnchorY = 0.5;
AbsoluteLayout.SetLayoutBounds(boxView, rectNormal);
boxView.BatchCommit();

await boxView.LayoutTo(rectSquashed, bounceDuration, Easing.SinOut);
await boxView.LayoutTo(rectNormal, bounceDuration, Easing.SinIn);

// Arc from bottom to left.
boxView.AnchorX = 1 - layoutSize / 2 / boxSize;
boxView.AnchorY = 0.5;
await boxView.RotateTo(-90, arcDuration);

// Bounce at left.
rectNormal = new Rectangle(0, (layoutSize - boxSize) / 2,
                           boxSize, boxSize);

rectSquashed = new Rectangle(rectNormal.X,
                             rectNormal.Y - boxSize / 2,
                             boxSize / 2, 2 * boxSize);

boxView.BatchBegin();
boxView.Rotation = 0;
boxView.AnchorX = 0.5;
boxView.AnchorY = 0.5;
AbsoluteLayout.SetLayoutBounds(boxView, rectNormal);
boxView.BatchCommit();

await boxView.LayoutTo(rectSquashed, bounceDuration, Easing.SinOut);
await boxView.LayoutTo(rectNormal, bounceDuration, Easing.SinIn);

// Arc from left to top.
boxView.AnchorX = 0.5;
boxView.AnchorY = 1 - layoutSize / 2 / boxSize;
await boxView.RotateTo(-90, arcDuration);

// Bounce on top.
rectNormal = new Rectangle((layoutSize - boxSize) / 2, 0,
                           boxSize, boxSize);

rectSquashed = new Rectangle(rectNormal.X - boxSize / 2, 0,
                             2 * boxSize, boxSize / 2);

boxView.BatchBegin();
boxView.Rotation = 0;
boxView.AnchorX = 0.5;
boxView.AnchorY = 0.5;
AbsoluteLayout.SetLayoutBounds(boxView, rectNormal);
```

```
        boxView.BatchCommit();

        await boxView.LayoutTo(rectSquashed, bounceDuration, Easing.SinOut);
        await boxView.LayoutTo(rectNormal, bounceDuration, Easing.SinIn);
    }
  }
}
```

The `SinOut` and `SinIn` easing functions provide a little realism for the compression to slow down as it's ending, and for the expansion to speed up after it's started.

Notice the calls to `BatchBegin` and `BatchCommit` that surround a number of property settings that accompany the positioning of the `BoxView` at one of the edges. These were added because there seemed to be a little flickering on the iPhone simulator, as if the properties were not being set simultaneously. However, the flickering remained even with these calls.

The `LayoutTo` animation is also used in one of the first games that was written for Xamarin.Forms. It's a version of the famous 15-Puzzle that consists of 15 tiles and one empty square in a four-by-four grid. The tiles can be shifted around but only by moving a tile into the empty spot.

On the early Apple Macintosh, this puzzle was named Puzzle. In the first Windows Software Development Kit, it was the only sample program using Microsoft Pascal, and it had the name Muzzle (for "Microsoft puzzle"). The version for Xamarin.Forms is thus called **Xuzzle**.

The original version of **Xuzzle** is here:

https://developer.xamarin.com/samples/xamarin-forms/Xuzzle/

The somewhat simplified version presented in this chapter doesn't include the animation that awards you for successfully completing the puzzle. However, rather than displaying letters or numbers, the tiles in this new version display 15/16 of the beloved Xamarin logo, called the Xamagon, and hence this new version is called **XamagonXuzzle**. Here's the startup screen:

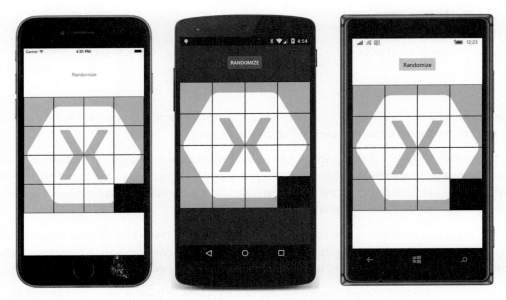

When you press the **Randomize** button, the tiles are shifted around:

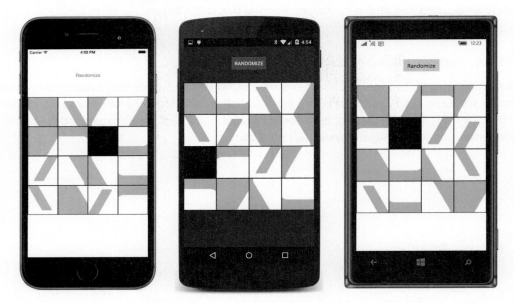

Your job is to shift the tiles back into their original configuration. You do this by tapping any tile adjacent to the empty square. The program applies an animation to shift the tapped tile into that empty square, and the empty square now replaces the tile you tapped.

You can also move multiple tiles with one tap. For example, suppose you tap the rightmost tile in the third row of the Android screen. The second tile in that row moves left, followed by the third and fourth tiles also moving left, again leaving the empty square replacing the tile you tapped.

The bitmaps for the 15 tiles were created especially for this program, and the **XamagonXuzzle** project contains them in the **Images** folder of the Portable Class Library, all with a **Build Action** of **Embedded Resource**.

Each tile is a `ContentView` that simply contains an `Image` with a little `Padding` applied for the gaps between the tiles that you see in the screenshots:

```
class XamagonXuzzleTile : ContentView
{
    public XamagonXuzzleTile (int row, int col, ImageSource imageSource)
    {
        Row = row;
        Col = col;

        Padding = new Thickness(1);
        Content = new Image
        {
            Source = imageSource
        };
    }

    public int Row { set; get; }

    public int Col { set; get; }
}
```

Each tile has an initial row and column, but the `Row` and `Col` properties are public, so the program can change them as the tiles are moved around. Also supplied to the constructor of the `XamagonXuzzleTile` class is an `ImageSource` object that references one of the bitmap resources.

The XAML file instantiates the `Button` and an `AbsoluteLayout` for the tiles:

```
<ContentPage xmlns="http://xamarin.com/schemas/2014/forms"
             xmlns:x="http://schemas.microsoft.com/winfx/2009/xaml"
             x:Class="XamagonXuzzle.XamagonXuzzlePage">
    <ContentPage.Padding>
        <OnPlatform x:TypeArguments="Thickness"
                    iOS="0, 20, 0, 0" />
    </ContentPage.Padding>

    <ContentView SizeChanged="OnContentViewSizeChanged">
        <StackLayout x:Name="stackLayout">
            <Button Text="Randomize"
                    Clicked="OnRandomizeButtonClicked"
                    HorizontalOptions="CenterAndExpand"
                    VerticalOptions="CenterAndExpand" />

            <AbsoluteLayout x:Name="absoluteLayout"
                            BackgroundColor="Black" />

            <!-- Balance out layout with invisible button. -->
```

```
            <Button Text="Randomize"
                    Opacity="0"
                    HorizontalOptions="CenterAndExpand"
                    VerticalOptions="CenterAndExpand" />
        </StackLayout>
    </ContentView>
</ContentPage>
```

As you'll see, the `SizeChanged` handler for the `ContentView` changes the orientation of the `Stack-Layout` to accommodate portrait and landscape modes.

The constructor of the code-behind file instantiates all 15 tiles and gives each one an `ImageSource` based on one of the 15 bitmaps.

```
public partial class XamagonXuzzlePage : ContentPage
{
    // Number of tiles horizontally and vertically,
    //  but if you change it, some code will break.
    static readonly int NUM = 4;

    // Array of tiles, and empty row & column.
    XamagonXuzzleTile[,] tiles = new XamagonXuzzleTile[NUM, NUM];
    int emptyRow = NUM - 1;
    int emptyCol = NUM - 1;

    double tileSize;
    bool isBusy;

    public XamagonXuzzlePage()
    {
        InitializeComponent();

        // Loop through the rows and columns.
        for (int row = 0; row < NUM; row++)
        {
            for (int col = 0; col < NUM; col++)
            {
                // But skip the last one!
                if (row == NUM - 1 && col == NUM - 1)
                    break;

                // Get the bitmap for each tile and instantiate it.
                ImageSource imageSource =
                    ImageSource.FromResource("XamagonXuzzle.Images.Bitmap" +
                                                row + col + ".png");

                XamagonXuzzleTile tile = new XamagonXuzzleTile(row, col, imageSource);

                // Add tap recognition.
                TapGestureRecognizer tapGestureRecognizer = new TapGestureRecognizer
                {
                    Command = new Command(OnTileTapped),
                    CommandParameter = tile
                };
```

```
            tile.GestureRecognizers.Add(tapGestureRecognizer);

            // Add it to the array and the AbsoluteLayout.
            tiles[row, col] = tile;
            absoluteLayout.Children.Add(tile);
        }
    }
}
    ...
}
```

The `SizeChanged` handler for the `ContentView` has the responsibility of setting the `Orientation` property of the `StackLayout`, sizing the `AbsoluteLayout`, and sizing and positioning all the tiles within the `AbsoluteLayout`. Notice that each tile's position is calculated based on the `Row` and `Col` properties of that tile:

```
public partial class XamagonXuzzlePage : ContentPage
{
    ...
    void OnContentViewSizeChanged(object sender, EventArgs args)
    {
        ContentView contentView = (ContentView)sender;
        double width = contentView.Width;
        double height = contentView.Height;

        if (width <= 0 || height <= 0)
            return;

        // Orient StackLayout based on portrait/landscape mode.
        stackLayout.Orientation = (width < height) ? StackOrientation.Vertical :
                                                     StackOrientation.Horizontal;

        // Calculate tile size and position based on ContentView size.
        tileSize = Math.Min(width, height) / NUM;
        absoluteLayout.WidthRequest = NUM * tileSize;
        absoluteLayout.HeightRequest = NUM * tileSize;

        foreach (View view in absoluteLayout.Children)
        {
            XamagonXuzzleTile tile = (XamagonXuzzleTile)view;

            // Set tile bounds.
            AbsoluteLayout.SetLayoutBounds(tile, new Rectangle(tile.Col * tileSize,
                                                               tile.Row * tileSize,
                                                               tileSize,
                                                               tileSize));
        }
    }
    ...
}
```

The constructor has set a `TapGestureRecognizer` on each tile, and that's handled by the `OnTile-`

`Tapped` method. It's possible for a single tap to result in up to three tiles being shifted. That job is handled by the `ShiftIntoEmpty` method, which loops through all the shifted tiles and calls `Animate-Tile` for each one. That method defines the `Rectangle` value for the call to `LayoutTo`—which is the one and only animation method in this entire program—and then other variables are adjusted for the new configuration:

```
public partial class XamagonXuzzlePage : ContentPage
{
    ...
    async void OnTileTapped(object parameter)
    {
        if (isBusy)
            return;

        isBusy = true;
        XamagonXuzzleTile tappedTile = (XamagonXuzzleTile)parameter;
        await ShiftIntoEmpty(tappedTile.Row, tappedTile.Col);
        isBusy = false;
    }

    async Task ShiftIntoEmpty(int tappedRow, int tappedCol, uint length = 100)
    {
        // Shift columns.
        if (tappedRow == emptyRow && tappedCol != emptyCol)
        {
            int inc = Math.Sign(tappedCol - emptyCol);
            int begCol = emptyCol + inc;
            int endCol = tappedCol + inc;

            for (int col = begCol; col != endCol; col += inc)
            {
                await AnimateTile(emptyRow, col, emptyRow, emptyCol, length);
            }
        }
        // Shift rows.
        else if (tappedCol == emptyCol && tappedRow != emptyRow)
        {
            int inc = Math.Sign(tappedRow - emptyRow);
            int begRow = emptyRow + inc;
            int endRow = tappedRow + inc;

            for (int row = begRow; row != endRow; row += inc)
            {
                await AnimateTile(row, emptyCol, emptyRow, emptyCol, length);
            }
        }
    }

    async Task AnimateTile(int row, int col, int newRow, int newCol, uint length)
    {
        // The tile to be animated.
        XamagonXuzzleTile animaTile = tiles[row, col];
```

```
            // The destination rectangle.
            Rectangle rect = new Rectangle(emptyCol * tileSize,
                                           emptyRow * tileSize,
                                           tileSize,
                                           tileSize);

            // Animate it!
            await animaTile.LayoutTo(rect, length);

            // Set layout bounds to same Rectangle.
            AbsoluteLayout.SetLayoutBounds(animaTile, rect);

            // Set several variables and properties for new layout.
            tiles[newRow, newCol] = animaTile;
            animaTile.Row = newRow;
            animaTile.Col = newCol;
            tiles[row, col] = null;
            emptyRow = row;
            emptyCol = col;
        }
        ...
}
```

The `AnimateTile` method uses `await` for the `LayoutTo` call. If it did not use `await`—if it let the `LayoutTo` animation run in the background while it proceeded with its other work—then the program would not know when the `LayoutTo` animation concluded. That means that if `ShiftIntoEmpty` were shifting two or three tiles, those animations would occur simultaneously instead of sequentially.

Because `AnimateTile` uses `await`, the method must have the `async` modifier. However, if the method returned `void`, then the `AnimateTile` method would return when the `LayoutTo` animation begins, and again the `ShiftIntoEmpty` method would not know when the animation completes. For this reason, `AnimateTile` returns a `Task` object. The `AnimateTile` method still returns when the `LayoutTo` animation begins, but it returns a `Task` object that can signal when the `AnimateTile` method completes. This means that `ShiftIntoEmpty` can call `AnimateTile` using `await` and move the tiles sequentially.

`ShiftIntoEmpty` uses `await`, so it must also be defined with the `async` modifier, but it could return `void`. If so, then `ShiftIntoEmpty` would return at the time it makes its first call to `AnimateTile`, which means that the `OnTileTapped` method would not know when the entire animation has completed. But `OnTileTapped` needs to prevent tiles from being tapped and animated if they are already in the process of being animated, which requires that `ShiftIntoEmpty` return `Task`. This means that `OnTileTapped` can use `await` with `ShiftIntoEmpty`, which means that `OnTileTapped` must also include the `async` modifier.

The `OnTileTapped` handler is called from the `Button` itself, so it cannot return `Task`. It must return `void`, just as the method is defined. But you can see how the use of `await` and `async` seems to ripple up the chain of method calls.

Once the code exists for handling taps, implementing the **Randomize** button becomes fairly trivial.

It simply makes multiple calls to `ShiftIntoEmpty` with a faster animation speed:

```
public partial class XamagonXuzzlePage : ContentPage
{
    …
    async void OnRandomizeButtonClicked(object sender, EventArgs args)
    {
        Button button = (Button)sender;
        button.IsEnabled = false;
        Random rand = new Random();
        isBusy = true;

        // Simulate some fast crazy taps.
        for (int i = 0; i < 100; i++)
        {
            await ShiftIntoEmpty(rand.Next(NUM), emptyCol, 25);
            await ShiftIntoEmpty(emptyRow, rand.Next(NUM), 25);
        }
        button.IsEnabled = true;
        isBusy = false;
    }
}
```

Again, using `await` with the `ShiftIntoEmpty` calls allows the calls to be executed sequentially (which is exciting to watch) and allows the `OnRandomizeButtonClicked` handler to know when everything is completed so it can reenable the `Button` and allow taps on the tiles.

Your own awaitable animations

In the next section of this chapter, you'll see the underlying animation infrastructure that Xamarin.Forms implements. These underlying methods allow you to define your own animation functions that return `Task` objects and which can be used with `await`.

In Chapter 20, "Async and file I/O," you saw how to use the static `Task.Run` method to create a secondary thread of execution for carrying out an intensive background job like a Mandelbrot computation. The `Task.Run` method returns a `Task` object that can signal when the background job has completed.

But animation is not quite like that. An animation doesn't need to spend a lot of time crunching numbers. It merely needs to do something very brief and simple—such as setting a `Rotation` property—once every 16 milliseconds. That job can run in the user-interface thread—in fact, the actual property access *must* run in the user-interface thread—and the timing can be handled by using `Device.StartTimer` or `Task.Delay`.

You shouldn't use `Task.Run` for implementing animations, because a secondary thread of execution is unnecessary and wasteful. However, when you actually sit down to write an animation method similar to the Xamarin.Forms animation methods such as `RotateTo`, you might encounter an obstacle. The method must return a `Task` object and perhaps use `Device.StartTimer` for the timing, but that doesn't seem possible.

Here's a first stab at writing such a method. The parameters include the target VisualElement, *from* and *to* values, and a duration. It uses Device.StartTimer and a Stopwatch to calculate the current setting of the Rotation property, and it exits the Device.StartTimer callback when the animation has completed:

```
Task MyRotate(VisualElement visual, double fromValue, double toValue, uint duration)
{
    Stopwatch stopwatch = new Stopwatch();
    stopwatch.Start();

    Device.StartTimer(TimeSpan.FromMilliseconds(16), () =>
        {
            double t = Math.Min(1, stopwatch.ElapsedMilliseconds / (double)duration);
            double value = fromValue + t * (toValue - fromValue);
            visual.Rotation = value;
            bool completed = t == 1;

            if (completed)
            {
                // Need to signal that the Task has completed. But how?
            }
            return !completed;
        });

    // Need to return a Task object here but where does it come from?
}
```

At two crucial points the method doesn't know what to do. After the method calls Device.StartTimer, it needs to exit and return a Task object to the caller. But where does this Task object come from? The Task class has a constructor, but like Task.Run, that constructor creates a second thread of execution, and there's no reason to create that thread. Moreover, when the animation has finished, the method somehow needs to signal that the Task has completed.

Fortunately, there exists a class that does exactly what you want. It's called TaskCreationSource. It's a generic class in which the type parameter is the same as the type parameter of the Task object that you want to create. The Task property of the TaskCreationSource object provides the Task object you need. This is what your asynchronous method returns. When your method has completed processing the background job, it can call SetResult on the TaskCreationSource object, signaling that the job is finished.

The following **TryAwaitableAnimation** program shows how to use TaskCreationSource in a MyRotateTo method that is called from the Clicked handler of a Button:

```
public partial class TryAwaitableAnimationPage : ContentPage
{
    public TryAwaitableAnimationPage()
    {
        InitializeComponent();
    }

    async void OnButtonClicked(object sender, EventArgs args)
```

```
    {
        Button button = (Button)sender;
        uint milliseconds = UInt32.Parse((string)button.StyleId);
        await MyRotate(button, 0, 360, milliseconds);
    }

    Task MyRotate(VisualElement visual, double fromValue, double toValue, uint duration)
    {
        TaskCompletionSource<object> taskCompletionSource = new TaskCompletionSource<object>();

        Stopwatch stopwatch = new Stopwatch();
        stopwatch.Start();

        Device.StartTimer(TimeSpan.FromMilliseconds(16), () =>
            {
                double t = Math.Min(1, stopwatch.ElapsedMilliseconds / (double)duration);
                double value = fromValue + t * (toValue - fromValue);
                visual.Rotation = value;
                bool completed = t == 1;

                if (completed)
                {
                    taskCompletionSource.SetResult(null);
                }
                return !completed;
            });

        return taskCompletionSource.Task;
    }
}
```

Notice the instantiation of `TaskCreationSource`, the return value of the `Task` property of that object, and the call to `SetResult` within the `Device.StartTimer` callback when the animation has finished.

There is no nongeneric form of `TaskCreationSource`, so if your method just returns a `Task` object rather than a `Task<T>` object, you'll need to specify a type when defining the `TaskCreationSource` instance. By convention, you can use `object` for this purpose, in which case your method calls `SetResult` with a `null` argument.

The **TryAwaitableAnimation** XAML file instantiates three `Button` elements that share this `Clicked` handler. Each of them defines its own animation duration as the `StyleId` property. (As you'll recall, `StyleId` is not used within Xamarin.Forms and exists solely to be used by an application programmer as a convenient way to attach arbitrary data to an element.)

```
<ContentPage xmlns="http://xamarin.com/schemas/2014/forms"
             xmlns:x="http://schemas.microsoft.com/winfx/2009/xaml"
             x:Class="TryAwaitableAnimation.TryAwaitableAnimationPage">
    <StackLayout>
        <StackLayout.Resources>
            <ResourceDictionary>
                <Style TargetType="Button">
```

```
                    <Setter Property="Text" Value="Tap Me!" />
                    <Setter Property="FontSize" Value="Large" />
                    <Setter Property="HorizontalOptions" Value="Center" />
                    <Setter Property="VerticalOptions" Value="CenterAndExpand" />
                </Style>
            </ResourceDictionary>
        </StackLayout.Resources>

        <Button Clicked="OnButtonClicked" StyleId="5000" />

        <Button Clicked="OnButtonClicked" StyleId="2500" />

        <Button Clicked="OnButtonClicked" StyleId="1000" />
    </StackLayout>
</ContentPage>
```

Even though each of these `Button` elements is animating itself by a call to `MyRotate`, you can have all buttons spinning at the same time. Each call to `MyRotate` gets its own set of local variables, and these local variables are used in each `Device.StartTimer` callback.

However, if you tap a `Button` while it's still spinning, then a second animation is applied to that `Button` and the two animations battle each other. What the code requires is a way to cancel the previous animation when a new animation is applied.

One approach is for the `MyRotate` method to maintain a dictionary of type `Dictionary<VisualElement, bool>` defined as a field. Whenever it begins an animation, `MyRotate` adds the target `VisualElement` as a key to this dictionary with a value of `false`. When the animation ends, it removes this entry from the dictionary. A separate method (named `CancelMyRotate`, perhaps) can set the value in the dictionary to `true`, meaning to cancel the animation. The `Device.StartTimer` callback can begin by checking the value of the dictionary for the particular `VisualElement` and return `false` from the callback if the animation has been cancelled. But you'll discover in the discussion that follows how to do it with less code.

Now that you've seen the high-level animation functions implemented in the `ViewExtensions` class, let's explore how the rest of the Xamarin.Forms animation system implements these functions and allows you to start, control, and cancel animations.

Deeper into animation

On first encounter, the complete Xamarin.Forms animation system can be a little confusing. Let's begin with a global view of the three public classes that you can use to define animations.

Sorting out the classes

In addition to the `Easing` class, the Xamarin.Forms animation system comprises three public classes. Here they are in hierarchical order from high level to low level:

ViewExtensions class

This is the class you've already seen. `ViewExtensions` is a static class that contains several extension methods for `VisualElement`, which is the parent class to `View` and `Page`:

- `TranslateTo` animates the `TranslationX` and `TranslationY` properties

- `ScaleTo` animates the `Scale` property

- `RelScaleTo` applies an animated incremental increase or decrease to the `Scale` property

- `RotateTo` animates the `Rotation` property

- `RelRotateTo` applies an animated incremental increase or decrease to the `Rotation` property

- `RotateXTo` animates the `RotationX` property

- `RotateYTo` animates the `RotationY` property

- `FadeTo` animates the `Opacity` property

- `LayoutTo` animates the get-only `Bounds` property by calling the `Layout` method

As you can see, the first seven methods target transform properties. These properties do not cause any change to how the element is perceived in layout. Although the animated view can move, change size, and rotate, none of the other views on the page are affected, except possibly being obscured by the new location or size.

The `FadeTo` animation changes only the `Opacity` property, so that doesn't cause layout changes either.

As you've seen, the `LayoutTo` animation is a little different. The argument is a `Rectangle` value, and the method essentially overrides the location and size assigned to the view by the element's parent `Layout` or `Layout<T>` object. `LayoutTo` is most useful for animating children of an `Absolute-Layout` because you can call `AbsoluteLayout.SetLayoutBounds` with the same `Rectangle` object after the animation has completed. In Chapter 26, you'll learn how to use `LayoutTo` in a class that derives from `Layout<View>`.

These are all asynchronous methods that return `Task<bool>`. The Boolean return value is `true` if the animation was cancelled and `false` if it ran to completion.

In addition, `ViewExtensions` also contains a static `ViewExtensions.CancelAnimations` method (not an extension method) that has a single argument of type `VisualElement`. This method cancels any and all animations started with this class on that `VisualElement` object.

All the extension methods in `ViewExtensions` work by creating one or more `Animation` objects and then calling the `Commit` method defined by that `Animation` class.

The Animation class

The `Animation` class has two constructors: a parameterless constructor and another with five parameters, although only one of the arguments is required:

```
public Animation (Action<double> callback,
                  double start = 0.0f,
                  double end = 1.0f,
                  Easing easing = null,
                  Action finished = null)
```

This defines an animation of a `double` value that begins at `start` and ends at `end`. Often, these two arguments will have their default values of 0 and 1, respectively. The animated value is passed to the callback method as an argument, where it is generally named `t` or `progress`. The callback can do whatever it wants with this value, but generally it's used to change a value of a property. If the target property is of type `double`, then `start` and `end` values can define the start and end values of the animated property directly.

`Animation` implements the `IEnumerable` interface. It can maintain a collection of child animations that can then be uniformly started and remain synchronized. To allow a program to add items to this collection, `Animation` defines four methods:

- `Add`

- `Insert`

- `WithConcurrent` (two versions)

These are all fundamentally the same in that they all add a child `Animation` object to an internal collection maintained by `Animation`. You'll see examples shortly.

Starting the animation (which might or might not include child animations) requires a call to the `Commit` method. The `Commit` method specifies the duration of the animation and also includes two more callbacks:

```
animation.Commit(IAnimatable owner,
                 string name,
                 uint rate = 16,
                 uint length = 250,
                 Easing easing = null,
                 Action<double, bool> finished = null,
                 Func<bool> repeat = null);
```

Notice the first argument is `IAnimatable`. The `IAnimatable` interface defines just two methods, named `BatchBegin` and `BatchCommit`. The only class that implements `IAnimatable` is `VisualElement`, which is the class associated with the `ViewExtensions` methods.

The `name` argument identifies the animation. You can use methods in the `AnimationExtensions` class (coming up) to determine if an animation of that name is running or to cancel it. You don't need to use unique names for every animation that you're running, but if you're making multiple overlapping `Commit` calls on the same visual object, then those names should be unique.

In theory, the `rate` argument indicates the number of milliseconds between each call to the callback method defined in the `Animation` constructor. It is set at 16 for an animation speed of 60 frames per second, but changing it has no effect.

The `repeat` callback allows the animation to be repeated. It's called at the end of the animation, and if the callback returns `true`, that signals that the animation should be repeated. As you'll see, it works in some configurations but not others.

The `Commit` method in the `Animation` class works by calling an `Animate` method in the `AnimationExtensions` class.

AnimationExtensions class

Like `ViewExtensions`, `AnimationExtentions` is a static class containing mostly extension methods. But while the first parameter in the `ViewExtensions` methods is a `VisualElement`, the first parameter in the `AnimationExtensions` methods is an `IAnimatable` to be consistent with the `Commit` method in the `Animation` class.

`AnimationExtensions` defines several overloads of the `Animate` method with callbacks and other information. The most extensive version of `Animate` is this generic method:

```
public static void Animate<T>(this IAnimatable self,
                    string name,
                    Func<double, T> transform,
                    Action<T> callback,
                    uint rate = 16,
                    uint length = 250,
                    Easing easing = null,
                    Action<T, bool> finished = null,
                    Func<bool> repeat = null);
```

In one sense, this is the only animation method you need. By now many of these parameters should be recognizable. But notice the `transform` method that can help structure the logic of animations that target properties that are not of type `double`.

For example, suppose you want to animate a property of type `Color`. You first write a little `transform` method that accepts a `double` argument ranging from 0 to 1 (and often named `t` or `progress`) and returns a `Color` value corresponding to that value. The `callback` method obtains that `Color` value and can then set it to a particular property of a particular object. You'll see this precise application at the end of this chapter.

Other public methods in the `AnimationExtensions` class are `AnimationIsRunning` to determine if a particular animation on a particular `VisualElement` instance is running, and `AbortAnimation` to cancel an animation. Both are extension methods for `IAnimatable` and require a name consistent with the name passed to the `Animate` method or the `Commit` method of `Animation`.

Working with the Animation class

Let's experiment a bit with the `Animation` class. This involves instantiating objects of type `Animation` and then calling `Commit`, which actually starts the animation going. The `Commit` method does not return a `Task` object; instead, the `Animation` class provides notifications entirely through callbacks.

There are several different ways to configure an `Animation` object, and some of these might involve child animations, which is why the project that demonstrates the `Animation` class is called **ConcurrentAnimations**. But not all the demonstrations in this program involve child animations.

The XAML file defines mostly a bunch of buttons that serve both to trigger animations and to be the targets of these animations:

```
<ContentPage xmlns="http://xamarin.com/schemas/2014/forms"
             xmlns:x="http://schemas.microsoft.com/winfx/2009/xaml"
             x:Class="ConcurrentAnimations.ConcurrentAnimationsPage">
    <StackLayout>
        <StackLayout.Resources>
            <ResourceDictionary>
                <Style TargetType="Button">
                    <Setter Property="HorizontalOptions" Value="Center" />
                    <Setter Property="VerticalOptions" Value="CenterAndExpand" />
                </Style>
            </ResourceDictionary>
        </StackLayout.Resources>

        <Button Text="Animation 1 (Scale)"
                Clicked="OnButton1Clicked" />

        <Button Text="Animation 2 (Repeated)"
                Clicked="OnButton2Clicked" />

        <Button Text="Stop Animation 2"
                Clicked="OnStop2Clicked" />

        <Button Text="Animation 3 (Scale up &amp; down)"
                Clicked="OnButton3Clicked" />

        <Button Text="Animation 4 (Scale &amp; Rotate)"
                Clicked="OnButton4Clicked" />

        <Button Text="Animation 5 (Dots)"
                Clicked="OnButton5Clicked" />

        <Label x:Name="waitLabel"
               FontSize="Large"
               WidthRequest="100" />

        <Button Text="Turn off dots"
                Clicked="OnTurnOffButtonClicked" />

        <Button Text="Animation 6 (Color)"
                Clicked="OnButton6Clicked" />
```

```
    </StackLayout>
</ContentPage>
```

The code-behind file contains the event handlers for each of these buttons.

The code in the `Clicked` handler for the first `Button` uses comments to identify all the arguments for the `Animation` constructor and the `Commit` call. There are a total of four callback methods, each of which are expressed here as a lambda function but not with the most concise syntax:

```
public partial class ConcurrentAnimationsPage : ContentPage
{
    ...
    public ConcurrentAnimationsPage()
    {
        InitializeComponent();
    }

    void OnButton1Clicked(object sender, EventArgs args)
    {
        Button button = (Button)sender;

        Animation animation = new Animation(
            (double value) =>
                {
                    button.Scale = value;
                },              // callback
            1,                  // start
            5,                  // end
            Easing.Linear,      // easing
            () =>
                {
                    Debug.WriteLine("finished");
                }               // finished (but doesn't fire in this configuration)
        );

        animation.Commit(
            this,               // owner
            "Animation1",       // name
            16,                 // rate (but has no effect here)
            1000,               // length (in milliseconds)
            Easing.Linear,
            (double finalValue, bool wasCancelled) =>
                {
                    Debug.WriteLine("finished: {0} {1}", finalValue, wasCancelled);
                    button.Scale = 1;
                },              // finished
            () =>
                {
                    Debug.WriteLine("repeat");
                    return false;
                }               // repeat
        );
    }
```

```
    ...
}
```

The callback in the `Animation` constructor sets the `Scale` property of the `Button` to the value passed to that callback. This value ranges from 1 to 5 as the next two arguments indicate.

The `Commit` method assigns an owner to the animation. This can be the visual element on which the animation is applied or another visual element, such as the page. The `name` is combined with the owner to uniquely identify the animation if it must be cancelled. The same owner should be used for calls to `AnimationIsRunning` or `AbortAnimation` in the `AnimationExtensions` class. (You'll see how to cancel an animation shortly.)

The last argument to the `Animation` constructor is named `finished`, and it's a callback that is supposed to be invoked when the animation completes, but in this configuration it is not called. Fortunately, the `Commit` method also has a `finished` callback with two arguments. The first should indicate a final value (but in this configuration that value is always 1), and the second argument is a `bool` that is set to `true` if the animation was cancelled.

In this example, both `finished` callbacks make calls to `Debug.WriteLine` so that you can confirm that one is called but not the other. The `finished` callback included with the `Commit` call sets the `Scale` property back to 1, so the `Button` snaps back to its original size.

If you want to apply an easing function, you can specify it either in the constructor or in the `Commit` method call.

The `Clicked` handler for the second `Button` is very similar to the first except that the syntax is considerably more concise. Many of the parameters to the constructor and the `Commit` method have default values, and the constructor has taken advantage of those. The syntax for the lambda functions has also been simplified:

```
public partial class ConcurrentAnimationsPage : ContentPage
{
    ...
    void OnButton2Clicked(object sender, EventArgs args)
    {
        Button button = (Button)sender;

        Animation animation = new Animation(v => button.Scale = v, 1, 5);
        animation.Commit(this, "Animation2", 16, 1000, Easing.Linear,
                    (v, c) => button.Scale = 1,
                    () => true);
    }

    void OnStop2Clicked(object sender, EventArgs args)
    {
        this.AbortAnimation("Animation2");
    }
    ...
}
```

The only functional difference between the code for this `Button` and the previous `Button` involves the `repeat` callback. When the animation completes—that is, after a value of 5 is passed to the `callback` method—both the `repeat` and `finished` callbacks passed to the `Commit` method are called. If `repeat` returns `true`, then the animation starts over from the beginning, and at the end of that, `repeat` and `finished` are called again.

Fortunately, the XAML file includes another `Button` that calls `AbortAnimation` to terminate the animation. `AbortAnimation` is an extension method, so it must be called on the same element passed as the first argument to the `Commit` method, which in this case is the page object.

If you want several concurrent forever animations that run independently of each other, you can create an `Animation` object for each of them and then call `Commit` on each one with a `repeat` callback that returns `true`.

Child animations

Those first two examples in **ConcurrentAnimations** are single animations. The `Animation` class also supports child animations, and that's what the handler for the `Button` labeled "Animation 3" demonstrates. It first creates a parent `Animation` object with the parameterless constructor. It then creates two additional `Animation` objects and adds them to the parent `Animation` object with the `Add` and `Insert` methods:

```
public partial class ConcurrentAnimationsPage : ContentPage
{
    ...
    void OnButton3Clicked(object sender, EventArgs args)
    {
        Button button = (Button)sender;

        // Create parent animation object.
        Animation parentAnimation = new Animation();

        // Create "up" animation and add to parent.
        Animation upAnimation = new Animation(
            v => button.Scale = v,
            1, 5, Easing.SpringIn,
            () => Debug.WriteLine("up finished"));

        parentAnimation.Add(0, 0.5, upAnimation);

        // Create "down" animation and add to parent.
        Animation downAnimation = new Animation(
            v => button.Scale = v,
            5, 1, Easing.SpringOut,
            () => Debug.WriteLine("down finished"));

        parentAnimation.Insert(0.5, 1, downAnimation);

        // Commit parent animation.
        parentAnimation.Commit(
```

```
            this, "Animation3", 16, 5000, null,
            (v, c) => Debug.WriteLine("parent finished: {0} {1}", v, c));
    }
    …
}
```

These `Add` and `Insert` methods are basically the same, and in practical use are interchangeable. The only difference is that `Insert` returns the parent `Animation` object while `Add` does not.

Both methods require two arguments of type `double` with the names `beginAt` and `finishAt`. These two arguments must be between 0 and 1, and `finishAt` must be greater than `beginAt`. These two arguments indicate the relative period within the total animation that these particular child animations are active.

The total animation is five seconds long. That's the argument of 5000 in the `Commit` method. The first child animation animates the `Scale` property from 1 to 5. The `beginAt` and `finishAt` arguments are 0 and 0.5, respectively, which means that this child animation is active during the first half of the overall animation—that is, during the first 2.5 seconds. The second child animation takes the `Scale` property from 5 back down to 1. The `beginAt` and `finishAt` arguments are 0.5 and 1, respectively, which means that this animation occurs in the second half of the overall five-second animation.

The result is that the `Button` is scaled to five times its size over 2.5 seconds and then scaled back down to 1 over the final 2.5 seconds. But notice the two `Easing` functions set on the two child animations. The `Easing.SpringIn` object causes the `Button` to initially shrink in size before getting larger, and the `Easing.SpringOut` function also causes the `Button` to become smaller than its actual size toward the end of the complete animation.

As you'll see when you click the button to run this code, all the `finished` callbacks are now called. That is one difference between using the `Animation` class for a single animation and using it with child animations. The `finished` callback on the child animations indicates when that particular child has completed, and the `finished` callback passed to the `Commit` method indicates when the entire animation has finished.

There are two more differences when using child animations:

- When using child animations, returning `true` from the `repeat` callback on the `Commit` method doesn't cause the animation to repeat, but the animation will nevertheless continue to run with no new values.

- If you include an `Easing` function in the `Commit` method, and the `Easing` function returns a value greater than 1, the animation will be terminated at that point. If the `Easing` function returns a value less than 0, the value is clamped to equal 0.

If you want to use an `Easing` function that returns a value less than 0 or greater than 1 (for example, the `Easing.SpringIn` or `Easing.SpringOut` function), specify it in one or more of the child animations, as the example demonstrates, rather than the `Commit` method.

The C# compiler recognizes the `Add` method of a class that implements `IEnumerable` as a collection initializer. To keep the animation syntax to a minimum, you can follow the `new` operator on the parent `Animation` object with a pair of curly braces to initialize the contents with children. Each pair of curly braces within those outer curly braces encloses the arguments to the `Add` method. Here is an animation with three children:

```
public partial class ConcurrentAnimationsPage : ContentPage
{
    ...
    void OnButton4Clicked(object sender, EventArgs args)
    {
        Button button = (Button)sender;

        new Animation
        {
            { 0, 0.5, new Animation(v => button.Scale = v, 1, 5) },
            { 0.25, 0.75, new Animation(v => button.Rotation = v, 0, 360) },
            { 0.5, 1, new Animation(v => button.Scale = v, 5, 1) }
        }.Commit(this, "Animation4", 16, 5000);
    }
    ...
}
```

Notice also that `Commit` is called directly on the `Animation` constructor. This is as concise as you can make this code.

The first two arguments to these implicit `Add` methods indicate where within the entire parent animation the child is active. The first child animates the `Scale` property and is active during the first half of the parent animation, and the last child also animates the `Scale` property and is active for the last half of the parent animation. That's the same as the previous example. But now there's also an animation of the `Rotation` property with start and end values of 0.25 and 0.75. This `Rotation` animation begins halfway through the first `Scale` animation and ends halfway through the second `Scale` animation. This is how child animations can be overlapped.

The `Animation` class also includes two methods named `WithConcurrent` to add child animations to a parent `Animation` object. These are similar to the `Add` and `Insert` methods, except that the `beginAt` and `finishAt` arguments (or `start` and `end` as they're called in one of the `WithConcurrent` methods) are not restricted to the range of 0 through 1. However, only that part of the child animation that corresponds to a range of 0 through 1 will be active.

For example, suppose you call `WithConcurrent` to define a child animation that targets a `Scale` property from 1 to 4, but with a `beginAt` argument of −1 and a `finishAt` argument of 2. The `beginAt` value of −1 corresponds to a `Scale` value of 1, and the `finishAt` value of 2 corresponds to a `Scale` value of 4, but values outside the range of 0 and 1 don't play a role in the animation, so the `Scale` property will only be animated from 2 to 3.

Beyond the high-level animation methods

The examples in **ConcurrentAnimations** that you've seen so far have restricted themselves to animations of the `Scale` and `Rotate` properties, so they haven't shown anything you can't do with the
methods in the `ViewExtensions` class. But because you have access to the actual callback method,
you can do anything you want during that callback.

Here's an animation that you might use to indicate that your application is performing an operation
that might take some time to complete. Rather than displaying an `ActivityIndicator`, you've chosen to display a string of periods that repetitively increases in length from 0 to 10. Those two values are
specified as arguments to the `Animation` constructor. The callback method casts the current value to
an integer for use with one of the lesser-known `string` constructors to construct a string with that
number of dots:

```
public partial class ConcurrentAnimationsPage : ContentPage
{
    bool keepAnimation5Running = false;
    ...
    void OnButton5Clicked(object sender, EventArgs args)
    {
        Animation animation =
                new Animation(v => dotLabel.Text = new string('.', (int)v), 0, 10);
        animation.Commit(this, "Animation5", 16, 3000, null,
                    (v, cancelled) => dotLabel.Text = "",
                    () => keepAnimation5Running);
        keepAnimation5Running = true;
    }

    void OnTurnOffButtonClicked(object sender, EventArgs args)
    {
        keepAnimation5Running = false;
    }
    ...
}
```

The `OnButton5Clicked` method concludes by setting the `keepAnimation5Running` field to
`true`, and the `repeat` callback in the `Commit` method returns that value. The animation will keep running until `keepAnimation5Running` is set to `false`, which is what the next `Button` does.

The difference between this technique and cancelling the animation is that this technique does not
immediately end the animation. The `repeat` callback is only called after the animation reaches its end
value (which is 10 in this case), so the animation could continue to run for almost another three seconds after `keepAnimation5Running` is set to `false`.

The final example in the **ConcurrentAnimations** program animates the `BackgroundColor` property of the page by setting it to `Color` values created by the `Color.FromHsla` method with hue values ranging from 0 through 1. This animation gives the effect of sweeping through the colors of the
rainbow:

```
public partial class ConcurrentAnimationsPage : ContentPage
```

```
{
    …
    void OnButton6Clicked(object sender, EventArgs args)
    {
        new Animation(callback: v => BackgroundColor = Color.FromHsla(v, 1, 0.5),
                        start: 0,
                        end: 1).Commit(owner: this,
                                name: "Animation6",
                                length: 5000,
                                finished: (v, c) => BackgroundColor = Color.Default);
    }
}
```

This code uses named arguments and hence illustrates yet another syntax variation for instantiating an Animation object and calling Commit on it.

More of your own awaitable methods

Earlier, you saw how to use TaskCompletionSource together with Device.StartTimer to write your own asynchronous animation methods. You can also combine TaskCompletionSource with the Animation class to write you own asynchronous animation methods similar to those in the ViewExtensions class.

Suppose you like the idea of the **SlidingEntrance** program, but you are dissatisfied that the Easing.SpringOut function doesn't work with the TranslateTo method. You can write your own translation animation method. If you only need to animate the TranslationX property, you can call it TranslateXTo:

```
public static Task<bool> TranslateXTo(this VisualElement view, double x,
                                        uint length = 250, Easing easing = null)
{
    easing = easing ?? Easing.Linear;
    TaskCompletionSource<bool> taskCompletionSource = new TaskCompletionSource<bool>();

    Animation animation = new Animation(
        (value) => view.TranslationX = value, // callback
        view.TranslationX,      // start
        x,                      // end
        easing);                // easing

    animation.Commit(
        view,                   // owner
        "TranslateXTo",         // name
        16,                     // rate
        length,                 // length
        null,                   // easing
        (finalValue, cancelled) => taskCompletionSource.SetResult(cancelled)); // finished

    return taskCompletionSource.Task;
}
```

Notice that the current value of the TranslationX property is passed to the Animation constructor for the `start` argument, and the `x` parameter to `TranslateXTo` is passed as the `end` argument. The `TaskCompletionSource` has a type argument of `bool` so that the method can indicate if it's been cancelled or not. The method returns the `Task` property of the `TaskCompletionSource` object and calls `SetResult` in the `finished` callback of the `Commit` method.

However, there is a subtle flaw in this `TranslateXTo` method. What happens if the visual element being animated is removed from the visual tree during the course of the animation? In theory, if there are no other references to that object, it should become eligible for garbage collection. However, there *will* be a reference to that object in the animation method. The element will continue to be animated— and prevented from being garbage collected—even though there are no other references to that element!

You can avoid this peculiar situation if the animation method creates a `WeakReference` object to the animated element. The `WeakReference` allows the animation method to refer to the element but does not increase the reference count for purposes of garbage collection. While this is something you don't need to bother with for animation methods in your own application—because you're probably aware when elements are removed from visual trees—it's something you should probably do in any animation method that appears in a library.

The `TranslateXTo` method is in the **Xamarin.FormsBook.Toolkit** library, so it includes the use of `WeakReference`. Because the element could be gone when the callback method is called, the method must get a reference to the element with the `TryGetTarget` method. That method returns `false` if the object is no longer available:

```
namespace Xamarin.FormsBook.Toolkit
{
    public static class MoreViewExtensions
    {
        public static Task<bool> TranslateXTo(this VisualElement view, double x,
                                        uint length = 250, Easing easing = null)
        {
            easing = easing ?? Easing.Linear;
            TaskCompletionSource<bool> taskCompletionSource = new TaskCompletionSource<bool>();
            WeakReference<VisualElement> weakViewRef = new WeakReference<VisualElement>(view);

            Animation animation = new Animation(
                (value) =>
                    {
                        VisualElement viewRef;
                        if (weakViewRef.TryGetTarget(out viewRef))
                        {
                            viewRef.TranslationX = value;
                        }
                    },              // callback
                view.TranslationX,  // start
                x,                  // end
                easing);            // easing

            animation.Commit(
                view,               // owner
```

```
                    "TranslateXTo",        // name
                    16,                    // rate
                    length,                // length
                    null,                  // easing
                    (finalValue, cancelled) =>
                            taskCompletionSource.SetResult(cancelled)); // finished

          return taskCompletionSource.Task;
      }

      public static void CancelTranslateXTo(VisualElement view)
      {
          view.AbortAnimation("TranslateXTo");
      }
      …
}
```

Notice that a method to cancel the animation named "TranslateX" is also included.

This `TranslateXTo` method is demonstrated in the **SpringSlidingEntrance** program, which is the same as **SlidingEntrance** except that it has a reference to the **Xamarin.FormsBook.Toolkit** library and the `OnAppearing` override calls `TranslateXTo`:

```
public partial class SpringSlidingEntrancePage : ContentPage
{
    public SpringSlidingEntrancePage()
    {
        InitializeComponent();
    }

    async protected override void OnAppearing()
    {
        base.OnAppearing();

        double offset = 1000;

        foreach (View view in stackLayout.Children)
        {
            view.TranslationX = offset;
            offset *= -1;
        }

        foreach (View view in stackLayout.Children)
        {
            await Task.WhenAny(view.TranslateXTo(0, 1000, Easing.SpringOut),
                               Task.Delay(100));
        }
    }
}
```

The difference is, I'm sure you'll agree, well worth the effort. The elements on the page slide in and overshoot their destinations before settling into a well-ordered page.

The **Xamarin.FormsBook.Toolkit** library also has a `TranslateYTo` method that is basically the same as `TranslateXTo`, but with more concise syntax:

```
namespace Xamarin.FormsBook.Toolkit
{
    public static class MoreViewExtensions
    {
        ...
        public static Task<bool> TranslateYTo(this VisualElement view, double y,
                                              uint length = 250, Easing easing = null)
        {
            easing = easing ?? Easing.Linear;
            TaskCompletionSource<bool> taskCompletionSource = new TaskCompletionSource<bool>();
            WeakReference<VisualElement> weakViewRef = new WeakReference<VisualElement>(view);

            Animation animation = new Animation((value) =>
                {
                    VisualElement viewRef;
                    if (weakViewRef.TryGetTarget(out viewRef))
                    {
                        viewRef.TranslationY = value;
                    }
                }, view.TranslationY, y, easing);

            animation.Commit(view, "TranslateYTo", 16, length, null,
                             (v, c) => taskCompletionSource.SetResult(c));

            return taskCompletionSource.Task;
        }

        public static void CancelTranslateYTo(VisualElement view)
        {
            view.AbortAnimation("TranslateYTo");
        }
        ...
    }
}
```

As a replacement for `TranslateTo`, you can use `TranslateXYTo`. As you learned earlier in this chapter, an `Easing` function that returns values less than 0 or greater than 1 shouldn't be passed to the `Commit` method for an animation with children. Instead, the `Easing` function should be passed to the `Animation` constructors of the children. This is what `TranslateXYTo` does:

```
namespace Xamarin.FormsBook.Toolkit
{
    public static class MoreViewExtensions
    {
        ...
        public static Task<bool> TranslateXYTo(this VisualElement view, double x, double y,
                                               uint length = 250, Easing easing = null)
        {
            easing = easing ?? Easing.Linear;
            TaskCompletionSource<bool> taskCompletionSource = new TaskCompletionSource<bool>();
            WeakReference<VisualElement> weakViewRef = new WeakReference<VisualElement>(view);

            Action<double> callbackX = value =>
```

```
        {
            VisualElement viewRef;
            if (weakViewRef.TryGetTarget(out viewRef))
            {
                viewRef.TranslationX = value;
            }
        };

    Action<double> callbackY = value =>
        {
            VisualElement viewRef;
            if (weakViewRef.TryGetTarget(out viewRef))
            {
                viewRef.TranslationY = value;
            }
        };

    Animation animation = new Animation
    {
        { 0, 1, new Animation(callbackX, view.TranslationX, x, easing) },
        { 0, 1, new Animation(callbackY, view.TranslationY, y, easing) }
    };

    animation.Commit(view, "TranslateXYTo", 16, length, null,
                    (v, c) => taskCompletionSource.SetResult(c));

    return taskCompletionSource.Task;
}

public static void CancelTranslateXYTo(VisualElement view)
{
    view.AbortAnimation("TranslateXYTo");
}
    ...
    }
}
```

Implementing a Bezier animation

Some graphics systems implement an animation that moves a visual object along a Bezier curve and even (optionally) rotates the visual object so it remains tangent to the curve.

The Bezier curve is named after Pierre Bézier, a French engineer and mathematician who developed the use of the curve in interactive computer-aided designs of automobile bodies while working at Renault. The curve is a type of spline defined by a start point and an end point and two control points. The curve passes through the start and end points but usually not the two control points. Instead, the control points function like "magnets" to pull the curve toward them.

In its two-dimensional form, the Bezier curve is represented mathematically as a pair of parametric cubic equations. Here is a `BezierSpline` structure in the **Xamarin.FormsBook.Toolkit** library:

```
namespace Xamarin.FormsBook.Toolkit
{
```

```
public struct BezierSpline
{
    public BezierSpline(Point point0, Point point1, Point point2, Point point3)
        : this()
    {
        Point0 = point0;
        Point1 = point1;
        Point2 = point2;
        Point3 = point3;
    }

    public Point Point0 { private set; get; }

    public Point Point1 { private set; get; }

    public Point Point2 { private set; get; }

    public Point Point3 { private set; get; }

    public Point GetPointAtFractionLength(double t, out Point tangent)
    {
        // Calculate point on curve.
        double x = (1 - t) * (1 - t) * (1 - t) * Point0.X +
                   3 * t * (1 - t) * (1 - t) * Point1.X +
                   3 * t * t * (1 - t) * Point2.X +
                   t * t * t * Point3.X;

        double y = (1 - t) * (1 - t) * (1 - t) * Point0.Y +
                   3 * t * (1 - t) * (1 - t) * Point1.Y +
                   3 * t * t * (1 - t) * Point2.Y +
                   t * t * t * Point3.Y;

        Point point = new Point(x, y);

        // Calculate tangent to curve.
        x = 3 * (1 - t) * (1 - t) * (Point1.X - Point0.X) +
            6 * t * (1 - t) * (Point2.X - Point1.X) +
            3 * t * t * (Point3.X - Point2.X);

        y = 3 * (1 - t) * (1 - t) * (Point1.Y - Point0.Y) +
            6 * t * (1 - t) * (Point2.Y - Point1.Y) +
            3 * t * t * (Point3.Y - Point2.Y);

        tangent = new Point(x, y);
        return point;
    }
}
```

The Point0 and Point3 points are the start and end points, while Point1 and Point2 are the two control points.

The GetPointAtFractionLength method returns the point on the curve corresponding to values

of t ranging from 0 to 1. The first calculations of x and y in this method involve the standard parametric equations of the Bezier curve. When t is 0, the point on the curve is Point0, and when t is 1, the
point on the curve is Point3.

GetPointAtFractionLength also has a second calculation of x and y based on the first derivative
of the curve, so these values indicate the tangent of the curve at that point. Generally, we think of the
tangent as a straight line that touches the curve but does not intersect it, so it might seem peculiar to
express the tangent as another point. But this is not really a point. It's a vector in the direction from the
point (0, 0) to the point (x, y). That vector can be turned into a rotation angle by using the inverse tangent function, also known as the arctangent, and available most conveniently to the .NET programmers
as Math.Atan2, which has two arguments, y and x in that order, and returns an angle in radians. You'll
need to convert to degrees for setting the Rotation property.

The BezierPathTo method in the **Xamarin.FormsBook.Toolkit** library moves the target visual
element by calling the Layout method, which means that BezierPathTo is similar to LayoutTo. The
method also optionally rotates the element by setting its Rotation property. Rather than splitting the
job into two child animations, BezierPathTo does everything in the callback method of a single animation.

The start point of the Bezier curve is assumed to be the center of the visual element that the animation targets. The BezierPathTo method requires two control points and an end point. All points generated from the Bezier curve are also assumed to refer to the center of the visual element, so the points
must be adjusted by half the element's width and height:

```
namespace Xamarin.FormsBook.Toolkit
{
    public static class MoreViewExtensions
    {
        ...
        public static Task<bool> BezierPathTo(this VisualElement view,
                                  Point pt1, Point pt2, Point pt3,
                                  uint length = 250,
                                  BezierTangent bezierTangent = BezierTangent.None,
                                  Easing easing = null)
        {
            easing = easing ?? Easing.Linear;
            TaskCompletionSource<bool> taskCompletionSource = new TaskCompletionSource<bool>();
            WeakReference<VisualElement> weakViewRef = new WeakReference<VisualElement>(view);

            Rectangle bounds = view.Bounds;
            BezierSpline bezierSpline = new BezierSpline(bounds.Center, pt1, pt2, pt3);

            Action<double> callback = t =>
                {
                    VisualElement viewRef;
                    if (weakViewRef.TryGetTarget(out viewRef))
                    {
                        Point tangent;
                        Point point = bezierSpline.GetPointAtFractionLength(t, out tangent);
                        double x = point.X - bounds.Width / 2;
```

```
                        double y = point.Y - bounds.Height / 2;
                        viewRef.Layout(new Rectangle(new Point(x, y), bounds.Size));

                        if (bezierTangent != BezierTangent.None)
                        {
                            viewRef.Rotation = 180 * Math.Atan2(tangent.Y, tangent.X) / Math.PI;

                            if (bezierTangent == BezierTangent.Reversed)
                            {
                                viewRef.Rotation += 180;
                            }
                        }
                    }
                };

            Animation animation = new Animation(callback, 0, 1, easing);
            animation.Commit(view, "BezierPathTo", 16, length,
                finished: (value, cancelled) => taskCompletionSource.SetResult(cancelled));

            return taskCompletionSource.Task;
        }

        public static void CancelBezierPathTo(VisualElement view)
        {
            view.AbortAnimation("BezierPathTo");
        }
        ...
    }
}
```

Applying the `Rotation` angle is still a bit tricky, however. If the points of a Bezier curve are defined so that the curve goes roughly from left to right across the screen, then the tangent is a vector that also goes from left to right, and the rotation of the animated element should preserve its orientation. But if the points of the Bezier curve go from right to left, then the tangent is also from right to left, and the mathematics dictate that the element should be flipped 180 degrees.

To control the orientation of the target element, a tiny enumeration is defined:

```
namespace Xamarin.FormsBook.Toolkit
{
    public enum BezierTangent
    {
        None,
        Normal,
        Reversed
    }
}
```

The `BezierPathTo` animation uses this to control how the tangent angle is applied to the `Rotation` property.

The **BezierLoop** program demonstrates the use of `BezierPathTo`. A `Button` sits in the upper-left corner of an `AbsoluteLayout`:

```
<ContentPage xmlns="http://xamarin.com/schemas/2014/forms"
             xmlns:x="http://schemas.microsoft.com/winfx/2009/xaml"
             x:Class="BezierLoop.BezierLoopPage">
    <ContentPage.Padding>
        <OnPlatform x:TypeArguments="Thickness"
                    iOS="0, 20, 0, 0" />
    </ContentPage.Padding>

    <AbsoluteLayout>
        <Button Text="Click for Loop"
                Clicked="OnButtonClicked" />
    </AbsoluteLayout>
</ContentPage>
```

The `Clicked` handler for the `Button` begins by calculating the start and end points of the Bezier curve and the two control points. The start point is the upper-left corner where the `Button` initially sits. The end point is the upper-right corner. The two control points are the lower-right corner and the lower-left corner, respectively. This type of configuration actually creates a loop in the Bezier curve:

```
public partial class BezierLoopPage : ContentPage
{
    public BezierLoopPage()
    {
        InitializeComponent();
    }

    async void OnButtonClicked(object sender, EventArgs args)
    {
        Button button = (Button)sender;
        Layout parent = (Layout)button.Parent;

        // Center of Button in upper-left corner.
        Point point0 = new Point(button.Width / 2, button.Height / 2);

        // Lower-right corner of page.
        Point point1 = new Point(parent.Width, parent.Height);

        // Lower-left corner of page.
        Point point2 = new Point(0, parent.Height);

        // Center of Button in upper-right corner.
        Point point3 = new Point(parent.Width - button.Width / 2, button.Height / 2);

        // Initial angle of Bezier curve (vector from Point0 to Point1).
        double angle = 180 / Math.PI * Math.Atan2(point1.Y - point0.Y,
                                                  point1.X - point0.X);

        await button.RotateTo(angle, 1000, Easing.SinIn);

        await button.BezierPathTo(point1, point2, point3, 5000,
                                  BezierTangent.Normal, Easing.SinOut);

        await button.BezierPathTo(point2, point1, point0, 5000,
                                  BezierTangent.Reversed, Easing.SinIn);
```

```
        await button.RotateTo(0, 1000, Easing.SinOut);
    }
}
```

The tangent to the Bezier curve at its very beginning is the line from `point0` to `point1`. This is the `angle` variable that the method calculates so it can first use `RotateTo` to rotate the `Button` to avoid a jump when the `BezierPathTo` animation begins. The first `BezierPathTo` moves the `Button` from the upper-left corner to the upper-right corner with a loop near the bottom of the screen:

A second `BezierPathTo` then reverses the trip back to the upper-left corner. (This is where the `BezierTangent` enumeration comes into play. Without it, the `Button` suddenly flips upside down as the second `BezierPathTo` begins.) A final `RotateTo` restores it to its original orientation.

Working with AnimationExtensions

Why does `ViewExtensions` not include a `ColorTo` animation? There are three plausible reasons why such a method isn't as obvious as you might initially assume:

Firstly, the only `Color` property defined by `VisualElement` is `BackgroundColor`, but that's usually not the `Color` property you want to animate. It's more likely you want to animate the `TextColor` property of `Label` or the `Color` property of `BoxView`.

Secondly, all the methods in `ViewExtensions` animate a property from its current value to a specified value. But often the current value of a property of type `Color` is `Color.Default`, which is not a real color and which cannot be used in an interpolation calculation.

Thirdly, the interpolation between two `Color` values can be calculated in a variety of different ways, but two stand out as the most likely: You might want to interpolate the red-green-blue values or the hue-saturation-luminosity values. The intermediate values will be different in these two cases.

Let's take care of these three problems with three different solutions:

Firstly, let's not have the color-animation method target a particular property. Let's write the method with a callback method that passes the interpolated `Color` value back to the caller.

Secondly, let's require that both a start `Color` value and an end `Color` value be supplied to the animation method.

Thirdly, let's write two different methods, `RgbColorAnimation` and `HslColorAnimation`.

You could certainly use the `Animation` class and `Commit` for this job, but let's instead dive deeper into the Xamarin.Forms animation system and use a method in the `AnimationExtensions` class.

`AnimationExtensions` has four different methods named `Animate`, as well as an `AnimateKinetic` method. The `AnimateKinetic` method is intended to apply a "drag" value to an animation so that it slows down as if by friction. However, it's not yet working in a way that allows the results to be easily predicted, and it is not demonstrated in this chapter.

Of the four `Animate` methods, the generic form is the most versatile:

```
public static void Animate<T>(this IAnimatable self,
                              string name,
                              Func<double, T> transform,
                              Action<T> callback,
                              uint rate = 16,
                              uint length = 250,
                              Easing easing = null,
                              Action<T, bool> finished = null,
                              Func<bool> repeat = null);
```

The generic type is the type of the property you want to animate—for example, `Color`. By this time you should recognize all these parameters except for the callback method named `transform`. The input to that callback is always a `t` or `progress` value ranging from 0 to 1. The output is a value of the generic type—for example, `Color`. That value is then passed to the `callback` method for application to a particular property.

Here are `RgbColorAnimation` and `HslColorAnimation` in the `MoreViewExtensions` class of the **Xamarin.FormsBook.Toolkit** library:

```
namespace Xamarin.FormsBook.Toolkit
{
    public static class MoreViewExtensions
    {
        ...
        public static Task<bool> RgbColorAnimation(this VisualElement view,
                                                   Color fromColor, Color toColor,
                                                   Action<Color> callback,
                                                   uint length = 250,
```

```
                                                    Easing easing = null)
    {
        Func<double, Color> transform = (t) =>
            {
                return Color.FromRgba(fromColor.R + t * (toColor.R - fromColor.R),
                                      fromColor.G + t * (toColor.G - fromColor.G),
                                      fromColor.B + t * (toColor.B - fromColor.B),
                                      fromColor.A + t * (toColor.A - fromColor.A));
            };

        return ColorAnimation(view, "RgbColorAnimation", transform,
                              callback, length, easing);
    }

    public static void CancelRgbColorAnimation(VisualElement view)
    {
        view.AbortAnimation("RgbColorAnimation");
    }

    public static Task<bool> HslColorAnimation(this VisualElement view,
                                               Color fromColor, Color toColor,
                                               Action<Color> callback,
                                               uint length = 250,
                                               Easing easing = null)
    {
        Func<double, Color> transform = (t) =>
        {
            return Color.FromHsla(
                fromColor.Hue + t * (toColor.Hue - fromColor.Hue),
                fromColor.Saturation + t * (toColor.Saturation - fromColor.Saturation),
                fromColor.Luminosity + t * (toColor.Luminosity - fromColor.Luminosity),
                fromColor.A + t * (toColor.A - fromColor.A));
        };

        return ColorAnimation(view, "HslColorAnimation", transform,
                              callback, length, easing);
    }

    public static void CancelHslColorAnimation(VisualElement view)
    {
        view.AbortAnimation("HslColorAnimation");
    }

    static Task<bool> ColorAnimation(VisualElement view,
                                     string name,
                                     Func<double, Color> transform,
                                     Action<Color> callback,
                                     uint length,
                                     Easing easing)
    {
        easing = easing ?? Easing.Linear;
        TaskCompletionSource<bool> taskCompletionSource = new TaskCompletionSource<bool>();

        view.Animate<Color>(name, transform, callback, 16,
```

```
                                 length, easing, (value, canceled) =>
            {
                taskCompletionSource.SetResult(canceled);
            });

            return taskCompletionSource.Task;
        }
    }
}
```

The two methods define their own `transform` functions and then make use of the private `ColorAnimation` method to actually make the call to the `Animate` method in `AnimationExtensions`. Because these methods don't explicitly target a particular visual element, there is no need for the `WeakReference` class.

The **ColorAnimations** program demonstrates these methods for animating various color properties in various ways. The XAML file as a `Label`, two `Button` elements, and two `BoxView` elements:

```xml
<ContentPage xmlns="http://xamarin.com/schemas/2014/forms"
             xmlns:x="http://schemas.microsoft.com/winfx/2009/xaml"
             x:Class="ColorAnimations.ColorAnimationsPage">
    <StackLayout>
        <Label x:Name="label"
               Text="TEXT"
               FontSize="48"
               FontAttributes="Bold"
               HorizontalOptions="Center"
               VerticalOptions="CenterAndExpand" />

        <Button Text="Rainbow Background"
                Clicked="OnRainbowBackgroundButtonClicked"
                HorizontalOptions="Center"
                VerticalOptions="CenterAndExpand" />

        <Button Text="BoxView Color"
                Clicked="OnBoxViewColorButtonClicked"
                HorizontalOptions="Center"
                VerticalOptions="CenterAndExpand" />

        <StackLayout Orientation="Horizontal">
            <BoxView x:Name="boxView1"
                     Color="Blue"
                     HeightRequest="100"
                     HorizontalOptions="FillAndExpand" />

            <BoxView x:Name="boxView2"
                     Color="Blue"
                     HeightRequest="100"
                     HorizontalOptions="FillAndExpand" />
        </StackLayout>
    </StackLayout>
</ContentPage>
```

The code-behind file uses a mix of `RgbColorAnimation` and `HslColorAnimation` to animate the colors of the `Label` text and its background, the background of the page, and the two `BoxView` elements.

The `Label` text and its background are continuously animated oppositely between black and white. Only midway through the animations—when both the text and the background are medium gray—is the text invisible:

```
public partial class ColorAnimationsPage : ContentPage
{
    public ColorAnimationsPage()
    {
        InitializeComponent();

        AnimationLoop();
    }

    async void AnimationLoop()
    {
        while (true)
        {
            Action<Color> textCallback = color => label.TextColor = color;
            Action<Color> backCallback = color => label.BackgroundColor = color;

            await Task.WhenAll(
                    label.RgbColorAnimation(Color.White, Color.Black, textCallback, 1000),
                    label.HslColorAnimation(Color.Black, Color.White, backCallback, 1000));

            await Task.WhenAll(
                    label.RgbColorAnimation(Color.Black, Color.White, textCallback, 1000),
                    label.HslColorAnimation(Color.White, Color.Black, backCallback, 1000));
        }
    }
    ...
}
```

When animating between `Color.Black` and `Color.White`, it doesn't matter whether you use `Rgb-ColorAnimation` or `HslColorAnimation`. The result is the same. Black is represented in RGB as (0, 0, 0) and in HSL as (0, 0, 0). White is (1, 1, 1) in RGB and (0, 0, 1) in HSL. At the midway point, the RGB color (0.5, 0.5, 0.5) is the same as the HSL color (0, 0, 0.5).

The `HslColorAnimation` is great for animating through all the hues, which roughly correspond to the colors of the rainbow, traditionally red, orange, yellow, green, blue, indigo, and violet. In color animations, a final animation back to red usually occurs at the end. Animating RGB colors through this sequence requires first animating from `Color.Red` to `Color.Yellow`, then `Color.Yellow` to `Color.Green`, then `Color.Green` to `Color.Aqua`, then `Color.Aqua` to `Color.Blue`, then `Color.Blue` to `Color.Fuchsia`, and finally `Color.Fuchsia` to `Color.Red`.

With `HslColorAnimation`, all that's necessary is to animate between two representations of red, one with the `Hue` set to 0 and the other with the `Hue` set to 1:

```
public partial class ColorAnimationsPage : ContentPage
{
    ...
    async void OnRainbowBackgroundButtonClicked(object sender, EventArgs args)
    {
        // Animate from Red to Red.
        await this.HslColorAnimation(Color.FromHsla(0, 1, 0.5),
                                     Color.FromHsla(1, 1, 0.5),
                                     color => BackgroundColor = color,
                                     10000);

        BackgroundColor = Color.Default;
    }
    ...
}
```

Even with simple animations between two primary colors, RgbColorAnimation and HslColorAnimation can produce different results. Consider an animation from blue to red. The **ColorAnimations** program demonstrates the difference by animating the colors of two BoxView elements with the two animation methods:

```
public partial class ColorAnimationsPage : ContentPage
{
    ...
    async void OnBoxViewColorButtonClicked(object sender, EventArgs args)
    {
        Action<Color> callback1 = color => boxView1.Color = color;
        Action<Color> callback2 = color => boxView2.Color = color;

        await Task.WhenAll(boxView1.RgbColorAnimation(Color.Blue, Color.Red, callback1, 2000),
                           boxView2.HslColorAnimation(Color.Blue, Color.Red, callback2, 2000));

        await Task.WhenAll(boxView1.RgbColorAnimation(Color.Red, Color.Blue, callback1, 2000),
                           boxView2.HslColorAnimation(Color.Red, Color.Blue, callback2, 2000));

    }
}
```

Blue has an RGB representation of (0, 0, 1) and an HSL representation of (0.67, 1, 0.5). Red has an RGB representation of (1, 0, 0) and in HSL is (1, 0, 0.5). Halfway through the RGB animation, the interpolated color is (0.5, 0, 0.5), which is known in Xamarin.Forms as Color.Magenta. However, midway through the HslColorAnimation, the interpolated color is (0.83, 1, 0.5), which is the lighter Color.Fuchsia, which has an RGB representation of (1, 0, 1).

This screenshot shows the progress (from left to right) of the animation of the two BoxView elements from blue to red:

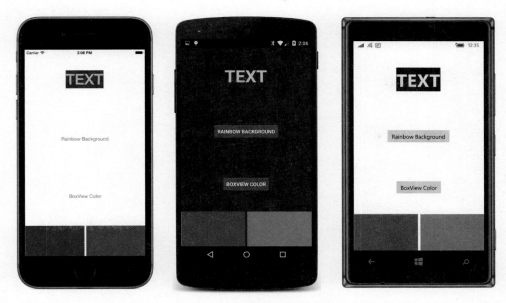

Neither is "right" or "wrong." It's just two different ways of interpolating between two colors, and the reason why a simple `ColorAnimation` method is inadequate.

Structuring your animations

There is no XAML representation of animations, so much of the focus of this chapter has necessarily been on code rather than markup.

However, when you're using animations in conjunction with styles, and with MVVM and data binding, you'll probably want a way to refer to animations in XAML. This is possible, and you'll see in the next chapter how you can encapsulate animations within classes called *trigger actions* and *behaviors*, and then make them part of the styling and data binding of your application's visuals.

Chapter 23
Triggers and behaviors

The introduction of a markup language such as XAML into a graphical programming environment might seem at first to be merely an alternative way to construct an assemblage of user-interface elements. But we've seen that the markup language tends to have much more profound consequences. The markup language induces us to divide the program more decisively between the interactive visuals and the underlying business logic. This further suggests that we might benefit from formalizing such a separation in an application architecture such as MVVM, and that turns out to be quite valuable.

At the same time, markup languages like XAML tend to have some intrinsic deficiencies in comparison with code. While code generally defines a dynamic process, markup languages are usually restricted to describing a fixed state. Several features have been added to Xamarin.Forms to help compensate for these deficiencies. These features include markup extensions, the resource dictionary, styles, and data binding.

In this chapter, you'll see two more of these features, called *triggers* and *behaviors*. Triggers cause changes to the user interface in response to events or property changes, while behaviors are more open-ended, allowing entire chunks of functionality to be added to existing visual elements. Both triggers and behaviors can be part of a `Style` definition. Often triggers and behaviors are supported by code that can contain animations.

It is unlikely that triggers and behaviors would have even been conceived or invented in a code-only programming environment. However, like the resource dictionary, styles, and data binding, these features help developers structure their applications more productively by suggesting additional ways to conceptualize the various pieces and components of these programs—and additional ways to reuse and share code.

Triggers and behaviors are implemented with several classes that will be introduced in the course of this chapter. You'll make use of these triggers and behaviors with two collection properties that are defined by both `VisualElement` and `Style`:

- `Triggers` property of type `IList<TriggerBase>`
- `Behaviors` property of type `IList<Behavior>`

Let's begin with triggers.

Triggers

In the most general (and vaguest) sense, a trigger is a condition that results in a response. More specifically, a trigger responds to a property change or the firing of an event by setting another property or running some code. Almost always, the properties that are set, or the code that is run, involve the user interface and are represented in XAML.

Both `VisualElement` and `Style` define a `Triggers` property of type `IList<TriggerBase>`. The abstract `TriggerBase` class derives from `BindableObject`. Four sealed classes derive from `Trigger-Base`:

- `Trigger` for setting properties (or running code) in response to a property change.

- `EventTrigger` for running code in response to an event.

- `DataTrigger` for setting properties (or running code) in response to a property change referenced in a data binding.

- `MultiTrigger` for setting properties (or running code) when multiple triggers occur.

The differences between these will become much clearer in practice.

The simplest trigger

In its usual form, the `Trigger` class checks for a property change of an element and responds by setting another property of the same element.

For example, suppose you've designed a page that contains several `Entry` views. You've decided that when a particular `Entry` gets the input focus, you want the `Entry` to become larger. You want to make the `Entry` stand out, including the text that the user types.

Much more specifically, when the `IsFocused` property of the `Entry` becomes `True`, you want the `Scale` property of the `Entry` to be set to 1.5. When the `IsFocused` property reverts back to `False`, you want the `Scale` property to also revert to its previous value.

To accommodate this concept, `Trigger` defines three properties:

- `Property` of type `BindableProperty`.

- `Value` of type `Object`.

- `Setters` of type `IList<Setter>`. This is the content property of `Trigger`.

All these properties must be set for the `Trigger` to work. From `TriggerBase`, `Trigger` inherits another essential property:

- `TargetType` of type `Type`.

This is the type of the element on which the `Trigger` is attached.

The `Property` and `Value` properties of `Trigger` are sometimes said to constitute a *condition*. When the value of the property referenced by `Property` equals `Value`, the condition is true, and the collection of `Setter` objects are applied to the element.

As you'll recall from Chapter 12, "Styles," `Setter` defines two properties that happen to be the same as the first two `Trigger` properties:

- `Property` of type `BindableProperty`.

- `Value` of type `Object`.

With triggers we're only dealing with bindable properties. The `Trigger` condition property must be backed by a `BindableProperty` as well as the property set by the `Setter`.

When the condition becomes false, the `Setter` objects are "un-applied," meaning that the property referenced by the `Setter` reverts to what its value would be without the `Setter`, which might be the default value of the property, a value set directly on the element, or a value applied through a `Style`.

Here's the XAML file for the **EntryPop** program. Each of the three `Entry` views on the page has a single `Trigger` object added to its `Triggers` collection using the `Entry.Triggers` property-element tag. Each of the `Trigger` objects has a single `Setter` added to its `Setters` collection. Because `Setters` is the content property of `Trigger`, the `Trigger.Setters` property-element tags are not required:

```
<ContentPage xmlns="http://xamarin.com/schemas/2014/forms"
             xmlns:x="http://schemas.microsoft.com/winfx/2009/xaml"
             x:Class="EntryPop.EntryPopPage"
             Padding="20, 50, 120, 0">

    <StackLayout Spacing="20">
        <Entry Placeholder="enter name"
               AnchorX="0">
            <Entry.Triggers>
                <Trigger TargetType="Entry" Property="IsFocused" Value="True">
                    <Setter Property="Scale" Value="1.5" />
                </Trigger>
            </Entry.Triggers>
        </Entry>

        <Entry Placeholder="enter address"
               AnchorX="0">
            <Entry.Triggers>
                <Trigger TargetType="Entry" Property="IsFocused" Value="True">
                    <Setter Property="Scale" Value="1.5" />
                </Trigger>
            </Entry.Triggers>
        </Entry>

        <Entry Placeholder="enter city and state"
```

```
            AnchorX="0">
        <Entry.Triggers>
            <Trigger TargetType="Entry" Property="IsFocused" Value="True">
                <Setter Property="Scale" Value="1.5" />
            </Trigger>
        </Entry.Triggers>
    </Entry>
  </StackLayout>
</ContentPage>
```

Each `Trigger` object must have its `TargetType` set, and in this case that's an `Entry`. Internally, the `Trigger` uses a `PropertyChanged` handler to monitor the value of the `IsFocused` property. When that property equals `True`, then the single `Setter` object sets the `Scale` property to 1.5. The `AnchorX` setting of zero directs the scaling to occur from the left side of the `Entry`. (The nondefault value of `AnchorX` means that the `Entry` views won't be positioned correctly if you change the orientation of the iOS screen.)

When the `Entry` loses input focus and the `IsFocused` property becomes `False` again, the `Trigger` automatically removes the application of the `Setter`, in which case the `Scale` property reverts to its pre-`Trigger` value, which isn't necessarily its default value.

Here are the enlarged `Entry` views with input focus:

Each `Entry` view in this example has only one `Trigger`, and each `Trigger` has only one `Setter`, but in the general case, a visual element can have multiple `Trigger` objects in its `Triggers` collection, and each `Trigger` can have multiple `Setter` objects in its `Setters` collection.

If you were to do something like this in code, you'd attach a `PropertyChanged` event handler to each `Entry` and respond to changes in the `IsFocused` property by setting the `Scale` property. The advantage of the `Trigger` is that you can do the entire job in markup right where the element is de-fined, leaving code for jobs presumably more important than increasing the size of an `Entry` element!

For this reason, it's unlikely that you will have the need to create `Trigger` objects in code. Never-theless, the **EntryPopCode** program demonstrates how you'd do it. The code has been fashioned to resemble the XAML as much as possible:

```
public class EntryPopCodePage : ContentPage
{
    public EntryPopCodePage()
    {
        Padding = new Thickness(20, 50, 120, 0);
        Content = new StackLayout
        {
            Spacing = 20,
            Children =
            {
                new Entry
                {
                    Placeholder = "enter name",
                    AnchorX = 0,
                    Triggers =
                    {
                        new Trigger(typeof(Entry))
                        {
                            Property = Entry.IsFocusedProperty,
                            Value = true,
                            Setters =
                            {
                                new Setter
                                {
                                    Property = Entry.ScaleProperty,
                                    Value = 1.5
                                }
                            }
                        }
                    }
                },
                new Entry
                {
                    Placeholder = "enter addresss",
                    AnchorX = 0,
                    Triggers =
                    {
                        new Trigger(typeof(Entry))
                        {
                            Property = Entry.IsFocusedProperty,
                            Value = true,
                            Setters =
                            {
                                new Setter
                                {
                                    Property = Entry.ScaleProperty,
                                    Value = 1.5
```

```
                                   }
                                 }
                              }
                           }
                        },
                        new Entry
                        {
                            Placeholder = "enter city and state",
                            AnchorX = 0,
                            Triggers =
                            {
                                new Trigger(typeof(Entry))
                                {
                                    Property = Entry.IsFocusedProperty,
                                    Value = true,
                                    Setters =
                                    {
                                        new Setter
                                        {
                                            Property = Entry.ScaleProperty,
                                            Value = 1.5
                                        }
                                    }
                                }
                            }
                        }
                    }
                };
            }
        }
```

The only real difference between the XAML and the code is the treatment of the `TargetType` property. In XAML, the `TargetType` property is set to "Entry" in each of the three `Trigger` definitions. In code, however, `typeof(Entry)` must be passed as an argument to the `Trigger` constructor. If you check the documentation of the `Trigger` class, you'll find that the `TargetType` property is get-only. The XAML parser uses the `TargetType` attribute setting to instantiate the `Trigger` object.

The `Style` class also defines a `Triggers` property of type `IList<TriggerBase>`, which means that you can use a `Style` to share `Trigger` objects among multiple elements. The **StyledTriggers** program shows how. Notice that both the `Style` and the `Trigger` tags contain a `TargetType` property setting. The `Style` contains one `Setter` object and uses `Style.Triggers` property-element tags for the single `Trigger` object, which also contains a `Setter` object:

```
<ContentPage xmlns="http://xamarin.com/schemas/2014/forms"
             xmlns:x="http://schemas.microsoft.com/winfx/2009/xaml"
             x:Class="StyledTriggers.StyledTriggersPage"
             Padding="20, 50, 120, 0">

    <ContentPage.Resources>
        <ResourceDictionary>
            <Style TargetType="Entry">
                <Setter Property="AnchorX" Value="0" />
```

```
                <Style.Triggers>
                    <Trigger TargetType="Entry" Property="IsFocused" Value="True">
                        <Setter Property="Scale" Value="1.5" />
                    </Trigger>
                </Style.Triggers>
            </Style>
        </ResourceDictionary>
    </ContentPage.Resources>

    <StackLayout Spacing="20">

        <Entry Placeholder="enter name" />

        <Entry Placeholder="enter address" />

        <Entry Placeholder="enter city and state" />

    </StackLayout>
</ContentPage>
```

Because the `Style` has no dictionary key, it is an implicit style that is automatically applied to all the elements of type `Entry`. The individual `Entry` elements need only contain what is unique to each element.

Perhaps after experimenting with the **EntryPop** program (or the two variations), you decide that you don't want the `Scale` property to simply "pop" to a value of 1.5. You want an animation. You want it to "swell" in size when it gains input focus, and to be animated back down to normal when it loses input focus.

That, too, is possible.

Trigger actions and animations

Although some triggers can be realized entirely in XAML, others require a little support from code. As you know, Xamarin.Forms has no direct support for implementing animations in XAML, so if you want to use a trigger to animate an element, you'll need some code.

There are a couple of ways to invoke an animation from XAML. The most obvious way is to use `EventTrigger`, which defines two properties:

- `Event` of type `string`.

- `Actions` of type `IList<TriggerAction>`.

When the element on which you've attached the trigger fires that particular event, the `EventTrigger` invokes all the `TriggerAction` objects in the `Actions` collection.

For example, `VisualElement` defines two events related to input focus: `Focused` and `Unfocused`. You can set those event names to the `Event` property of two different `EventTrigger` objects. When the element fires the event, the objects of type `TriggerAction` are invoked. Your job is to supply a class that derives from `TriggerAction`. This derived class overrides a method named `Invoke` to respond to the event.

Xamarin.Forms defines both a `TriggerAction` class and a `TriggerAction<T>` class, but both classes are abstract. Generally you'll derive from `TriggerAction<T>` and set the type parameter to the most generalized class the trigger action can support.

For example, suppose you want to derive from `TriggerAction<T>` for a class that calls `ScaleTo` to animate the `Scale` property. Set the type parameter to `VisualElement` because that's the class that is referenced by the `ScaleTo` extension method. An object of that type is also passed to `Invoke`.

By convention, a class that derives from `TriggerAction` has an `Action` suffix in its name. Such a class can be as simple as this:

```
public class ScaleAction : TriggerAction<VisualElement>
{
    protected override void Invoke(VisualElement visual)
    {
        visual.ScaleTo(1.5);
    }
}
```

When you include this class in an `EventTrigger` that is attached to an `Entry` view, the particular `Entry` object is passed as an argument to the `Invoke` method, which animates that `Entry` object using `ScaleTo`. The `Entry` expands to 150 percent of its original size in a default duration of a quarter second.

Of course, you probably don't want to make the class that specific. That simple `ScaleAction` class would work fine for the `Focused` event, but you would need a different one for the `Unfocused` event to animate the `Scale` property back down to 1.

Your `Action<T>` derivative can include properties to make the class very generalized. You can even make the `ScaleAction` class so generalized that it essentially becomes a wrapper for the `ScaleTo` method. Here's the version of `ScaleAction` in the **Xamarin.FormsBook.Toolkit** library:

```
namespace Xamarin.FormsBook.Toolkit
{
    public class ScaleAction : TriggerAction<VisualElement>
    {
        public ScaleAction()
        {
            // Set defaults.
            Anchor = new Point (0.5, 0.5);
            Scale = 1;
            Length = 250;
            Easing = Easing.Linear;
        }

        public Point Anchor { set; get; }
```

```
        public double Scale { set; get; }

        public int Length { set; get; }

        [TypeConverter(typeof(EasingConverter))]
        public Easing Easing { set; get; }

        protected override void Invoke(VisualElement visual)
        {
            visual.AnchorX = Anchor.X;
            visual.AnchorY = Anchor.Y;
            visual.ScaleTo(Scale, (uint)Length, Easing);
        }
    }
}
```

You might wonder whether you should back these properties with bindable properties so that they can be targets of data bindings. You can't do that, however, because `TriggerAction` derives from `Object` rather than `BindableObject`. Keep the properties simple.

Notice the `TypeConverter` attribute on the `Easing` property. This `Easing` property will probably be set in XAML, but the XAML parser doesn't know how to convert text strings like "SpringIn" and "SinOut" to objects of type `Easing`. The following custom type converter (also in **Xamarin.Forms-Book.Toolkit**) assists the XAML parser in converting text strings into `Easing` objects:

```
namespace Xamarin.FormsBook.Toolkit
{
    public class EasingConverter : TypeConverter
    {
        public override bool CanConvertFrom(Type sourceType)
        {
            if (sourceType == null)
                throw new ArgumentNullException("EasingConverter.CanConvertFrom: sourceType");

            return (sourceType == typeof(string));
        }

        public override object ConvertFrom(CultureInfo culture, object value)
        {
            if (value == null || !(value is string))
                return null;

            string name = ((string)value).Trim();

            if (name.StartsWith("Easing"))
            {
                name = name.Substring(7);
            }

            FieldInfo field = typeof(Easing).GetRuntimeField(name);

            if (field != null && field.IsStatic)
```

```
            {
                return (Easing)field.GetValue(null);
            }

            throw new InvalidOperationException(
                String.Format("Cannot convert \"{0}\" into Xamarin.Forms.Easing", value));
        }
    }
}
```

The **EntrySwell** program defines an implicit `Style` for `Entry` in its `Resources` dictionary. That `Style` has two `EventTrigger` objects in its `Triggers` collection, one for `Focused` and the other for `Unfocused`. Both invoke a `ScaleAction` but with different property settings:

```xml
<ContentPage xmlns="http://xamarin.com/schemas/2014/forms"
             xmlns:x="http://schemas.microsoft.com/winfx/2009/xaml"
             xmlns:toolkit=
                 "clr-namespace:Xamarin.FormsBook.Toolkit;assembly=Xamarin.FormsBook.Toolkit"
             x:Class="EntrySwell.EntrySwellPage"
             Padding="20, 50, 120, 0">

    <ContentPage.Resources>
        <ResourceDictionary>
            <Style TargetType="Entry">
                <Style.Triggers>
                    <EventTrigger Event="Focused">
                        <toolkit:ScaleAction Anchor="0, 0.5"
                                             Scale="1.5"
                                             Easing="SpringOut" />
                    </EventTrigger>

                    <EventTrigger Event="Unfocused">
                        <toolkit:ScaleAction Anchor="0, 0.5"
                                             Scale="1" />
                    </EventTrigger>
                </Style.Triggers>
            </Style>
        </ResourceDictionary>
    </ContentPage.Resources>

    <StackLayout Spacing="20">
        <Entry Placeholder="enter name" />

        <Entry Placeholder="enter address" />

        <Entry Placeholder="enter city and state" />
    </StackLayout>
</ContentPage>
```

Notice that `EventTrigger` does not require the `TargetType` property. The only constructor that `EventTrigger` defines has no parameters.

As each `Entry` gets input focus, you'll see it grow larger and then briefly overshoot the 1.5 `Scale` value. That's the effect of the `SpringOut` easing function.

What if you wanted to use a custom easing function? You would need to define such an easing function in code, of course, and you can do that in the code-behind file. But how would you reference that easing function in XAML? Here's how:

First, remove the `ResourceDictionary` tags from the XAML file. Those tags instantiate the `ResourceDictionary` and set it to the `Resources` property.

Second, in the constructor of the code-behind file, instantiate the `ResourceDictionary` and set it to the `Resources` property. Do this before `InitializeComponent` so that it exists when the XAML file is parsed:

```
Resources = new ResourceDictionary();
InitializeComponent();
```

Third, between those two statements, add an `Easing` object with a custom easing function to the `Resources` dictionary:

```
Resources = new ResourceDictionary();
Resources.Add("customEase", new Easing(t => -6 * t * t + 7 * t));
InitializeComponent();
```

This quadratic formula maps 0 to 0 and 1 to 1, but 0.5 to 2, so it will be obvious if this easing function is correctly used by the animation.

Finally, reference that dictionary entry using `StaticResource` in the `EventTrigger` definition:

```
<EventTrigger Event="Focused">
    <toolkit:ScaleAction Anchor="0, 0.5"
                         Scale="1.5"
                         Easing="{StaticResource customEase}" />
</EventTrigger>
```

Because the object in the `Resources` dictionary is of type `Easing`, the XAML parser will assign it directly to the `Easing` property of `ScaleAction` and bypass the `TypeConverter`.

Among the code samples for this chapter is a solution named **CustomEasingSwell** that demonstrates this technique.

Do not use `DynamicResource` to set the custom `Easing` object to the `Easing` property, perhaps in hopes of defining the easing function in code at a later time. `DynamicResource` requires the target property to be backed by a bindable property; `StaticResource` does not.

You've seen how you can use `Trigger` to set a property in response to a property change, and `EventTrigger` to invoke a `TriggerAction` object in response to an event firing.

But what if you wanted to invoke a `TriggerAction` in response to a property change? Perhaps you want to invoke an animation from XAML but there is no appropriate event for an `EventTrigger`.

There is a second way to invoke a `TriggerAction` derivative that involves the regular `Trigger` class rather than `EventTrigger`. If you look at the documentation of `TriggerBase` (the class from which all the other trigger classes derive), you'll see the following two properties:

- `EnterActions` of type `IList<TriggerAction>`

- `ExitActions` of type `IList<TriggerAction>`

When used with `Trigger`, all the `TriggerAction` objects in the `EnterActions` collection are invoked when the `Trigger` condition becomes true, and all the objects in the `ExitActions` collection are invoked when the condition becomes false again.

The **EnterExitSwell** program demonstrates this technique. It uses `Trigger` to monitor the `IsFocused` property and invokes two instances of `ScaleAction` to increase the size of the `Entry` when `IsFocused` becomes `True` and to decrease the size of the `Entry` when `IsFocused` stops being `True`:

```xml
<ContentPage xmlns="http://xamarin.com/schemas/2014/forms"
             xmlns:x="http://schemas.microsoft.com/winfx/2009/xaml"
             xmlns:toolkit=
                 "clr-namespace:Xamarin.FormsBook.Toolkit;assembly=Xamarin.FormsBook.Toolkit"
             x:Class="EnterExitSwell.EnterExitSwellPage"
             Padding="20, 50, 120, 0">

    <ContentPage.Resources>
        <ResourceDictionary>
            <Style TargetType="Entry">
                <Style.Triggers>
                    <Trigger TargetType="Entry" Property="IsFocused" Value="True">
                        <Trigger.EnterActions>
                            <toolkit:ScaleAction Anchor="0, 0.5"
                                                 Scale="1.5"
                                                 Easing="SpringOut" />
                        </Trigger.EnterActions>

                        <Trigger.ExitActions>
                            <toolkit:ScaleAction Anchor="0, 0.5"
                                                 Scale="1" />
                        </Trigger.ExitActions>
                    </Trigger>
                </Style.Triggers>
            </Style>
        </ResourceDictionary>
    </ContentPage.Resources>

    <StackLayout Spacing="20">
        <Entry Placeholder="enter name" />

        <Entry Placeholder="enter address" />

        <Entry Placeholder="enter city and state" />
    </StackLayout>
</ContentPage>
```

In summary, you can invoke a class derived from `TriggerAction<T>` either with a change in a property by using `Trigger` or with an event firing by using `EventTrigger`.

But don't use `EnterActions` and `ExitActions` with `EventTrigger`. `EventTrigger` invokes only the `TriggerAction` objects in its `Actions` collection.

More event triggers

The previous chapter on animation showed several examples of a `Button` that rotated or scaled itself when it was clicked. While most of those animation examples were taken to extremes for purposes of making amusing demonstrations, it's not unreasonable for a `Button` to respond to a click with a little animation. This is a perfect job for `EventTrigger`.

Here's another `TriggerAction` derivative. It's similar to `ScaleAction` but includes two calls to `ScaleTo` rather than just one and hence is named `ScaleUpAndDownAction`:

```
namespace Xamarin.FormsBook.Toolkit
{
    public class ScaleUpAndDownAction : TriggerAction<VisualElement>
    {
        public ScaleUpAndDownAction()
        {
            Anchor = new Point(0.5, 0.5);
            Scale = 2;
            Length = 500;
        }

        public Point Anchor { set; get; }

        public double Scale { set; get; }

        public int Length { set; get; }

        protected override async void Invoke(VisualElement visual)
        {
            visual.AnchorX = Anchor.X;
            visual.AnchorY = Anchor.Y;
            await visual.ScaleTo(Scale, (uint)Length / 2, Easing.SinOut);
            await visual.ScaleTo(1, (uint)Length / 2, Easing.SinIn);
        }
    }
}
```

This class hard-codes the `Easing` functions to keep the code simple.

The **ButtonGrowth** program defines an intrinsic `Style` that sets three `Button` properties and includes an `EventTrigger` that invokes `ScaleUpAndDownAction` with default parameters in response to the `Clicked` event:

```
<ContentPage xmlns="http://xamarin.com/schemas/2014/forms"
             xmlns:x="http://schemas.microsoft.com/winfx/2009/xaml"
```

```
        xmlns:toolkit=
            "clr-namespace:Xamarin.FormsBook.Toolkit;assembly=Xamarin.FormsBook.Toolkit"
        x:Class="ButtonGrowth.ButtonGrowthPage">

    <ContentPage.Resources>
        <ResourceDictionary>
            <Style TargetType="Button">
                <Setter Property="HorizontalOptions" Value="Center" />
                <Setter Property="VerticalOptions"   Value="CenterAndExpand" />
                <Setter Property="FontSize"          Value="Large" />

                <Style.Triggers>
                    <EventTrigger Event="Clicked">
                        <toolkit:ScaleUpAndDownAction />
                    </EventTrigger>
                </Style.Triggers>
            </Style>
        </ResourceDictionary>
    </ContentPage.Resources>

    <StackLayout>
        <Button Text="Button #1" />
        <Button Text="Button #2" />
        <Button Text="Button #3" />
    </StackLayout>
</ContentPage>
```

Here are three buttons as they've grown in size in response to clicks:

Would it have been possible to use two instances of `ScaleAction` here instead of `ScaleUpAnd-DownAction`—one instance that scaled the `Button` up in size and the other that scaled it down? No.

We're only dealing with one event—the `Clicked` event—and everything has to be invoked when that event is fired. An `EventTrigger` can certainly invoke multiple actions, but these actions occur simultaneously. Two `ScaleAction` instances running simultaneously would battle each other.

However, there is a solution. Here's a `DelayedScaleAction` class that derives from `ScaleAction` but includes a `Task.Delay` call prior to the `ScaleTo` call:

```
namespace Xamarin.FormsBook.Toolkit
{
    public class DelayedScaleAction : ScaleAction
    {
        public DelayedScaleAction() : base()
        {
            // Set defaults.
            Delay = 0;
        }

        public int Delay { set; get; }

        async protected override void Invoke(VisualElement visual)
        {
            visual.AnchorX = Anchor.X;
            visual.AnchorY = Anchor.Y;
            await Task.Delay(Delay);
            await visual.ScaleTo(Scale, (uint)Length, Easing);
        }
    }
}
```

You can now modify the **ButtonGrowth** XAML file to include two `DelayedScaleAction` objects triggered by the `Clicked` event. These are both invoked simultaneously, but the second has its `Delay` property set to the same value as the `Length` property of the first, so the first `ScaleTo` ends as the second `ScaleTo` begins:

```
<Style TargetType="Button">

    ...
    <Style.Triggers>
        <EventTrigger Event="Clicked">
            <toolkit:DelayedScaleAction Scale="2"
                                        Length="250"
                                        Easing="SinOut" />

            <toolkit:DelayedScaleAction Delay="250"
                                        Scale="1"
                                        Length="250"
                                        Easing="SinIn" />
        </EventTrigger>
    </Style.Triggers>
</Style>
```

`DelayedScaleAction` is a little more difficult to use than `ScaleUpAndDownAction`, but it's more flexible, and you can also define classes named `DelayedTranslateAction` and `DelayedRotate-Action` to add to the mix.

In the previous chapter you saw a `Button` derivative named `JiggleButton` that runs a brief animation when the `Button` is clicked. This is a type of animation that you can alternatively implement using a `TriggerAction`. The advantage is that you can use it with the normal `Button` class, and potentially separate the effect from a particular type of view and a particular event so it could be used with other views and other events.

Here's a `TriggerAction` derivative that implements the same type of animation as `JiggleButton` but with three properties to make it more flexible. To more clearly distinguish it from the earlier code, the name of this class is `ShiverAction`:

```
namespace Xamarin.FormsBook.Toolkit
{
    public class ShiverAction : TriggerAction<VisualElement>
    {
        public ShiverAction()
        {
            Length = 1000;
            Angle = 15;
            Vibrations = 10;
        }

        public int Length { set; get; }

        public double Angle { set; get; }

        public int Vibrations { set; get; }

        protected override void Invoke(VisualElement visual)
        {
            visual.Rotation = 0;
            visual.AnchorX = 0.5;
            visual.AnchorY = 0.5;
            visual.RotateTo(Angle, (uint)Length,
                new Easing(t => Math.Sin(Math.PI * t) *
                            Math.Sin(Math.PI * 2 * Vibrations * t)));
        }
    }
}
```

Notice that `Invoke` initializes the `Rotation` property of the target visual element to zero. This is to avoid problems when the `Button` is pressed twice in succession and `Invoke` is called while the previous animation is still running.

The XAML file of the **ShiverButtonDemo** program defines an implicit `Style` that includes the `ShiverAction` with rather extreme values set to its three properties:

```
<ContentPage xmlns="http://xamarin.com/schemas/2014/forms"
             xmlns:x="http://schemas.microsoft.com/winfx/2009/xaml"
             xmlns:toolkit=
```

```
                "clr-namespace:Xamarin.FormsBook.Toolkit;assembly=Xamarin.FormsBook.Toolkit"
             x:Class="ShiverButtonDemo.ShiverButtonDemoPage">

    <ContentPage.Resources>
        <ResourceDictionary>
            <Style TargetType="Button">
                <Setter Property="HorizontalOptions" Value="Center" />
                <Setter Property="VerticalOptions"   Value="CenterAndExpand" />
                <Setter Property="FontSize"          Value="Large" />

                <Style.Triggers>
                    <EventTrigger Event="Clicked">
                        <toolkit:ShiverAction Length="3000"
                                              Angle="45"
                                              Vibrations="25" />

                    </EventTrigger>
                </Style.Triggers>
            </Style>
        </ResourceDictionary>
    </ContentPage.Resources>

    <StackLayout>
        <Button Text="Button #1" />
        <Button Text="Button #2" />
        <Button Text="Button #3" />
    </StackLayout>
</ContentPage>
```

The three `Button` elements share the same instance of `ShiverAction`, but each call to the `Invoke` method is for a specific `Button` object. Each button's shivering is independent of the others.

But what if you want to use `ShiverAction` to respond to `Tapped` events on an element rather than `Clicked` events on a `Button`—for example, to vibrate a `Frame` with some content, or an `Image`? The `Tapped` event is only defined by `TapGestureRecognizer`, but you can't attach an `EventTrigger` to a `TapGestureRecognizer` because `TapGestureRecognizer` does not have a `Triggers` collection. Nor can you attach an `EventTrigger` to a `View` object and specify the `Tapped` event. That `Tapped` event won't be found on the `View` object.

The solution is to use a behavior, as will be demonstrated later in this chapter.

It's also possible to use `EventTrigger` objects for entry validation. Here's a `TriggerAction` derivative named `NumericValidationAction` with a generic argument of `Entry`, so it applies only to `Entry` views. When `Invoke` is called, the argument is an `Entry` object, so it can access properties specific to `Entry`, in this case `Text` and `TextColor`. The method checks whether the `Text` property of the `Entry` can be parsed into a valid `double`. If not, the text is colored red to alert the user:

```
namespace Xamarin.FormsBook.Toolkit
{
    public class NumericValidationAction : TriggerAction<Entry>
    {
        protected override void Invoke(Entry entry)
        {
```

```
            double result;
            bool isValid = Double.TryParse(entry.Text, out result);
            entry.TextColor = isValid ? Color.Default : Color.Red;
        }
    }
}
```

You can attach this code to an `Entry` with an `EventTrigger` for the `TextChanged` event, as demonstrated in the **TriggerEntryValidation** program:

```
<ContentPage xmlns="http://xamarin.com/schemas/2014/forms"
             xmlns:x="http://schemas.microsoft.com/winfx/2009/xaml"
             xmlns:toolkit=
                 "clr-namespace:Xamarin.FormsBook.Toolkit;assembly=Xamarin.FormsBook.Toolkit"
             x:Class="TriggerEntryValidation.TriggerEntryValidationPage"
             Padding="50">

    <StackLayout>
        <Entry Placeholder="Enter a System.Double">
            <Entry.Triggers>
                <EventTrigger Event="TextChanged">
                    <toolkit:NumericValidationAction />
                </EventTrigger>
            </Entry.Triggers>
        </Entry>
    </StackLayout>
</ContentPage>
```

Whenever the text changes, the `Invoke` method of `NumericValidationAction` is called.

The screenshot shows valid numeric entries for the iOS and Windows 10 Mobile devices, but an invalid number in the Android device:

Unfortunately, this doesn't work quite right on the Universal Windows Platform. If an invalid number is typed in the `Entry`, the text turns red only when the `Entry` loses input focus. However, it works fine on the other Windows Runtime platforms (Windows 8.1 and Windows Phone 8.1).

Data triggers

So far, you've only seen triggers that operate within the context of a particular object. A `Trigger` responds to a change in a property of an object by changing another property of that same object, or by invoking an `Action` that affects that object. The `EventTrigger` similarly responds to an event fired by an object to invoke an `Action` on that same object.

The `DataTrigger` is different. Like the other `TriggerBase` derivatives, the `DataTrigger` is attached to a visual element or defined in a `Style`. However, the `DataTrigger` can detect a property change in *another* object through a data binding, and either change a property in the object that it's attached to or (by using the `EnterActions` and `ExitActions` collection inherited from `Trigger-Base`) invoke a `TriggerAction` on that object.

`DataTrigger` defines the following three properties.

- `Binding` of type `BindingBase`.

- `Value` of type `Object`.

- `Setters` of type `IList<Setter>`. This is the content property of `DataTrigger`.

From the perspective of an application program, the `DataTrigger` is very similar to `Trigger` except that the property of `Trigger` named `Property` is replaced with the `Binding` property. Both `Trigger` and `DataTrigger` require the `TargetType` property to be set.

What is the other object that the `Binding` property of `DataTrigger` references? It can be part of a ViewModel in an MVVM scenario or another element on the page.

You might recall the **SchoolOfFineArt** library from Chapter 19, "Collection views." The `Student` class in that library defines a property named `Sex` of type `string` that is set to either "Male" or "Female". The **GenderColors** program presented below uses that property in conjunction with a `DataTrigger` to set a blue or pink color for the student (regardless how hopelessly old-fashioned that color scheme might seem).

A `ListView` displays all the students of the high school, and a `ViewCell` formats each student to display the student's photo, full name, and the current grade-point average:

```
<ContentPage xmlns="http://xamarin.com/schemas/2014/forms"
             xmlns:x="http://schemas.microsoft.com/winfx/2009/xaml"
             xmlns:school="clr-namespace:SchoolOfFineArt;assembly=SchoolOfFineArt"
             x:Class="GenderColors.GenderColorsPage">
    <ContentPage.Padding>
        <OnPlatform x:TypeArguments="Thickness"
                    iOS="0, 20, 0, 0" />
    </ContentPage.Padding>

    <ContentPage.BindingContext>
        <school:SchoolViewModel />
    </ContentPage.BindingContext>

    <StackLayout BindingContext="{Binding StudentBody}">
        <Label Text="{Binding School}"
               FontSize="Large"
               FontAttributes="Bold"
               HorizontalTextAlignment="Center" />

        <ListView ItemsSource="{Binding Students}"
                  VerticalOptions="FillAndExpand">
            <ListView.RowHeight>
                <OnPlatform x:TypeArguments="x:Int32"
                            iOS="70"
                            Android="70"
                            WinPhone="100" />
            </ListView.RowHeight>

            <ListView.ItemTemplate>
                <DataTemplate>
                    <ViewCell>
                        <Grid Padding="0, 5">
                            <Grid.ColumnDefinitions>
                                <ColumnDefinition Width="80" />
                                <ColumnDefinition Width="*" />
                            </Grid.ColumnDefinitions>

                            <Image Grid.Column="0"
                                   Source="{Binding PhotoFilename}"
```

```
                                      VerticalOptions="Center" />

                        <StackLayout Grid.Column="1"
                                     VerticalOptions="Center">
                            <Label Text="{Binding FullName}"
                                   FontSize="22"
                                   TextColor="Pink">
                                <Label.Triggers>
                                    <DataTrigger TargetType="Label"
                                                 Binding="{Binding Sex}"
                                                 Value="Male">
                                        <Setter Property="TextColor" Value="#8080FF" />
                                    </DataTrigger>
                                </Label.Triggers>
                            </Label>

                            <Label Text="{Binding GradePointAverage,
                                            StringFormat='G.P.A. = {0:F2}'}"
                                   FontSize="16" />
                        </StackLayout>
                    </Grid>
                </ViewCell>
            </DataTemplate>
        </ListView.ItemTemplate>
    </ListView>
</StackLayout>
</ContentPage>
```

The program uses `ViewCell` rather than `ImageCell`, so it has access to a `Label` onto which it can attach a `DataTrigger`. A trigger cannot be attached directly to a `Cell` or `Cell` derivative because there's no `Triggers` collection defined for these classes.

The `Label` displays the `FullName` property of the `Student` object and the `TextColor` is set to `Pink`. But a `DataTrigger` checks whether the `Sex` property of the `Student` object equals "Male", and if so it uses a `Setter` to set the `TextColor` to a light blue. Here is that `Label` isolated from the rest of the cell:

```
<Label Text="{Binding FullName}"
       FontSize="Large"
       TextColor="Pink">
    <Label.Triggers>
        <DataTrigger TargetType="Label"
                     Binding="{Binding Sex}"
                     Value="Male">
            <Setter Property="TextColor" Value="#8080FF" />
        </DataTrigger>
    </Label.Triggers>
</Label>
```

The `BindingContext` of the `DataTrigger` is the same as the `BindingContext` of the `Label` to which it is attached. That `BindingContext` is a particular `Student` object, so the `Binding` on the `DataTrigger` only needs to specify the `Sex` property.

Here it is in action:

Something quite similar can be done with a data binding directly from the `Sex` property of the `Student` object to the `TextColor` property of the `Label` (or the `ImageCell`), but it would require a binding converter. The `DataTrigger` does the job without any additional code.

However, by itself the `DataTrigger` cannot mimic the **ColorCodedStudents** program in Chapter 19. That program displays a student in red if that student's grade-point average falls dangerously below a 2.0 criterion. The less-than numeric comparison requires some code. This too is a job for a behavior, and once you learn about behaviors later in this chapter, you should be able to code something like this yourself.

It's also possible for `DataTrigger` to reference another element on the page to monitor a property of that element.

For example, one of the classic tasks in graphical environments is to disable a button if nothing has been typed into a text-entry field. Perhaps the text-entry field is a filename, and the button executes some code to load or save that file. It doesn't make any sense for the button to be enabled if the filename is blank.

You can do that job entirely in XAML with a `DataTrigger`. Here's the markup in the **ButtonEnabler** project:

```
<ContentPage xmlns="http://xamarin.com/schemas/2014/forms"
             xmlns:x="http://schemas.microsoft.com/winfx/2009/xaml"
             x:Class="ButtonEnabler.ButtonEnablerPage"
             Padding="20, 50">
```

```
<StackLayout Spacing="20">
    <Entry x:Name="entry"
           Text=""
           Keyboard="Url"
           Placeholder="enter filename" />

    <Button Text="Save"
            FontSize="Large"
            HorizontalOptions="Center">
        <Button.Triggers>
            <DataTrigger TargetType="Button"
                         Binding="{Binding Source={x:Reference entry},
                                           Path=Text.Length}"
                         Value="0">
                <Setter Property="IsEnabled" Value="False" />
            </DataTrigger>
        </Button.Triggers>
    </Button>
</StackLayout>
</ContentPage>
```

The `DataTrigger` on the `Button` sets its `Binding` property with a `Source` referencing the `Entry` element. The `Path` is set to `Text.Length`. The `Text` property of the `Entry` element is of type `string`, and `Length` is a property of `string`, so this binding refers to the number of characters entered in the `Entry` element. The `Value` property of `DataTrigger` is set to zero, so when there are zero characters entered into the `Entry`, the `Setter` property is invoked, which sets the `IsEnabled` property of the `Button` to `False`.

Based on the input in the `Entry` element, the `Button` is disabled on the iPhone and Windows 10 Mobile screens shown here but enabled on the Android screen:

Although this represents a tiny enhancement to the user interface, if you didn't have a `DataTrigger` you'd need to implement this enhancement in code in a `TextChanged` handler of the `Entry`, or you'd need to write a binding converter for a `Binding` between the `IsEnabled` property of the `Button` and the `Text.Length` property of the `Entry`.

The XAML file in **ButtonEnabler** contains a crucial property setting that you might not have noticed:

```
<Entry … Text="" … />
```

When an `Entry` is first created, the `Text` property is not an empty string but `null`, which means that the data binding in the `DataTrigger` is trying to reference the `Length` property of a `null` string object, and it will fail. Because the binding fails, the `Button` will be enabled when the program first starts up. It only becomes disabled after the user types a character and backspaces.

Initializing the `Text` property to an empty string has no other effect but to allow the `DataTrigger` to work when the program starts up.

Combining conditions in the MultiTrigger

Both the `Trigger` and the `DataTrigger` effectively monitor a property to determine if it's equal to a particular value. That's called the trigger's *condition*, and if the condition is true, then a collection of `Setter` objects are invoked.

As a programmer, you might begin wondering whether you can have multiple conditions in a trigger. But once you start talking about multiple conditions, you need to determine whether you want to combine conditions with a logical OR operation or an AND operation—whether the trigger is invoked if *any* of the conditions are true, or if it requires that *all* the conditions be true.

If you want a trigger invoked when multiple conditions are all true—the logical AND case—that's the last of the four classes that derive from `TriggerBase`. The `MultiTrigger` defines two collection properties:

- `Conditions` of type `IList<Condition>`

- `Setters` of type `IList<Setter>`

`Condition` is an abstract class and has two descendent classes:

- `PropertyCondition`, which has `Property` and `Value` properties like `Trigger`

- `BindingCondition`, which has `Binding` and `Value` properties like `DataTrigger`

You can mix multiple `PropertyCondition` and `BindingCondition` objects in the same `Conditions` collection of the `MultiTrigger`. When all the conditions are true, all the `Setter` objects in the `Setters` collection are applied.

Let's look at a simple example: In the **AndConditions** program, four `Switch` elements share the page with a blue `BoxView`. When all the `Switch` elements are turned on, the `BoxView` turns red:

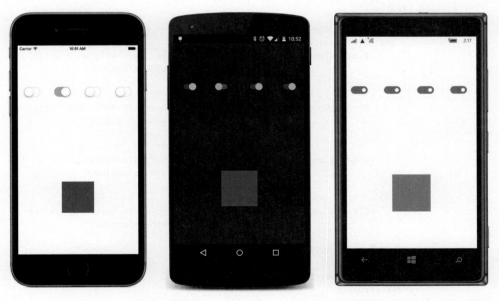

The XAML file shows how this is done. The `Triggers` collection of the `BoxView` contains a `Multi-`

Trigger. The TargetType property is required. The Conditions collection contains four Binding-Condition objects, each of which references the IsToggled property of one of the four Switch elements and checks for a True value. If all the conditions are true, the MultiTrigger sets the Color property of the BoxView to Red:

```xaml
<ContentPage xmlns="http://xamarin.com/schemas/2014/forms"
             xmlns:x="http://schemas.microsoft.com/winfx/2009/xaml"
             x:Class="AndConditions.AndConditionsPage">
    <StackLayout>
        <Grid VerticalOptions="CenterAndExpand">
            <Switch x:Name="switch1" Grid.Column="0"
                    HorizontalOptions="Center" />

            <Switch x:Name="switch2" Grid.Column="1"
                    HorizontalOptions="Center" />

            <Switch x:Name="switch3" Grid.Column="2"
                    HorizontalOptions="Center" />

            <Switch x:Name="switch4" Grid.Column="3"
                    HorizontalOptions="Center" />
        </Grid>

        <BoxView WidthRequest="100"
                 HeightRequest="100"
                 VerticalOptions="CenterAndExpand"
                 HorizontalOptions="Center"
                 Color="Blue">
            <BoxView.Triggers>
                <MultiTrigger TargetType="BoxView">
                    <MultiTrigger.Conditions>
                        <BindingCondition Binding="{Binding Source={x:Reference switch1},
                                                            Path=IsToggled}"
                                          Value="True" />

                        <BindingCondition Binding="{Binding Source={x:Reference switch2},
                                                            Path=IsToggled}"
                                          Value="True" />

                        <BindingCondition Binding="{Binding Source={x:Reference switch3},
                                                            Path=IsToggled}"
                                          Value="True" />

                        <BindingCondition Binding="{Binding Source={x:Reference switch4},
                                                            Path=IsToggled}"
                                          Value="True" />
                    </MultiTrigger.Conditions>

                    <Setter Property="Color" Value="Red" />
                </MultiTrigger>
            </BoxView.Triggers>
        </BoxView>
    </StackLayout>
</ContentPage>
```

That's the AND combination. What about an OR combination?

Because the `Triggers` collection can accommodate multiple `DataTrigger` objects, you might think that this would work:

```
<BoxView WidthRequest="100"
         HeightRequest="100"
         VerticalOptions="CenterAndExpand"
         HorizontalOptions="Center"
         Color="Blue">
    <BoxView.Triggers>
        <DataTrigger TargetType="BoxView"
                     Binding="{Binding Source={x:Reference switch1}, Path=IsToggled}"
                     Value="True">
            <Setter Property="Color" Value="Red" />
        </DataTrigger>

        <DataTrigger TargetType="BoxView"
                     Binding="{Binding Source={x:Reference switch2}, Path=IsToggled}"
                     Value="True">
            <Setter Property="Color" Value="Red" />
        </DataTrigger>

        <DataTrigger TargetType="BoxView"
                     Binding="{Binding Source={x:Reference switch3}, Path=IsToggled}"
                     Value="True">
            <Setter Property="Color" Value="Red" />
        </DataTrigger>

        <DataTrigger TargetType="BoxView"
                     Binding="{Binding Source={x:Reference switch4}, Path=IsToggled}"
                     Value="True">
            <Setter Property="Color" Value="Red" />
        </DataTrigger>
    </BoxView.Triggers>
</BoxView>
```

And if you try it, you might find that it does seem to work at first. But as you further experiment with turning various `Switch` elements on and off, you'll find that it really does *not* work.

Whether it should work or shouldn't work is open to debate. The four `DataTrigger` objects all target the same `Color` property, and if each `DataTrigger` works independently to determine whether that `Setter` should be applied or not, then this really shouldn't work as a logical OR.

However, keep in mind Victorian mathematician Augustus De Morgan's laws of logic, which state (using C# syntax for AND, OR, logical negation, and equivalence):

$$A \mid B \ == \ !(!A \ \& \ !B)$$

$$A \ \& \ B \ == \ !(!A \mid !B)$$

This means you can use `MultiTrigger` to perform a logical OR as the **OrConditions** program demonstrates:

```xml
<ContentPage xmlns="http://xamarin.com/schemas/2014/forms"
             xmlns:x="http://schemas.microsoft.com/winfx/2009/xaml"
             x:Class="OrConditions.OrConditionsPage">
    <StackLayout>
        <Grid VerticalOptions="CenterAndExpand">
            <Switch x:Name="switch1" Grid.Column="0"
                    HorizontalOptions="Center" />

            <Switch x:Name="switch2" Grid.Column="1"
                    HorizontalOptions="Center" />

            <Switch x:Name="switch3" Grid.Column="2"
                    HorizontalOptions="Center" />

            <Switch x:Name="switch4" Grid.Column="3"
                    HorizontalOptions="Center" />
        </Grid>

        <BoxView WidthRequest="100"
                 HeightRequest="100"
                 VerticalOptions="CenterAndExpand"
                 HorizontalOptions="Center"
                 Color="Red">
            <BoxView.Triggers>
                <MultiTrigger TargetType="BoxView">
                    <MultiTrigger.Conditions>
                        <BindingCondition Binding="{Binding Source={x:Reference switch1},
                                                            Path=IsToggled}"
                                          Value="False" />

                        <BindingCondition Binding="{Binding Source={x:Reference switch2},
                                                            Path=IsToggled}"
                                          Value="False" />

                        <BindingCondition Binding="{Binding Source={x:Reference switch3},
                                                            Path=IsToggled}"
                                          Value="False" />

                        <BindingCondition Binding="{Binding Source={x:Reference switch4},
                                                            Path=IsToggled}"
                                          Value="False" />
                    </MultiTrigger.Conditions>

                    <Setter Property="Color" Value="Blue" />
                </MultiTrigger>
            </BoxView.Triggers>
        </BoxView>
    </StackLayout>
</ContentPage>
```

It's the same as **AndConditions** except all the logic is flipped around. All the BindingCondition objects check for a False value of the IsToggled property, and if all the conditions are satisfied, the normally red BoxView is colored blue:

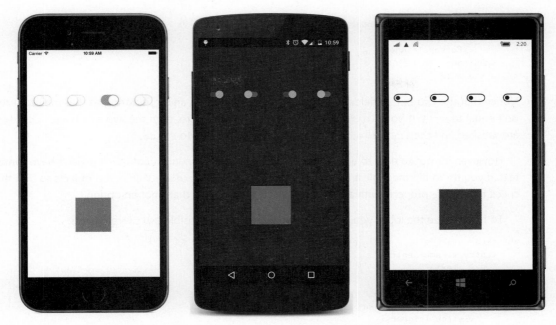

Here's another way you can think of these two programs: In **AndConditions**, the `BoxView` is always
blue unless all the `Switch` elements are toggled on. In **OrConditions**, the `BoxView` is always red unless all the `Switch` elements are off.

Suppose you have a scenario involving two `Entry` fields and a `Button`. You want to enable the
`Button` if either `Entry` field contains some text.

Flip the logic upside down: You really want to disable the `Button` if both `Entry` fields contain no
text. That's fairly easy:

```
<StackLayout>
    <Entry x:Name="entry1"
           Text="" />

    <Entry x:Name="entry2"
           Text="" />

    <Button Text="Send">
        <Button.Triggers>
            <MultiTrigger TargetType="Button">
                <MultiTrigger.Conditions>
                    <BindingCondition Binding="{Binding Source={x:Reference entry1},
                                                        Path=Text.Length}"
                                      Value="0" />
                    <BindingCondition Binding="{Binding Source={x:Reference entry2},
                                                        Path=Text.Length}"
                                      Value="0" />
                </MultiTrigger.Conditions>
```

```
                    <Setter Property="IsEnabled" Value="False" />
                </MultiTrigger>
            </Button.Triggers>
        </Button>
    </StackLayout>
```

Notice that the two `Entry` fields initialize the `Text` property to an empty string so that the property isn't equal to `null`. If both `Text` properties have a length of zero, then the two `BindingConditions` are satisfied and the `IsEnabled` property of the `Button` is set to `False`.

However, it's not so easy to adapt this to enable the `Button` only if *both* `Entry` views have some text. If you try to flip the logic around, you must change the `BindingCondition` objects so that they check for a `Text` property with a length *not* equal to zero, and that's not an option.

To help realize the logic, you can use some intermediary invisible `Switch` elements:

```
<StackLayout>
    <Entry x:Name="entry1"
           Text="" />

    <Switch x:Name="switch1"
            IsVisible="False">
        <Switch.Triggers>
            <DataTrigger TargetType="Switch"
                         Binding="{Binding Source={x:Reference entry1},
                                           Path=Text.Length}"
                         Value="0">
                <Setter Property="IsToggled" Value="True" />
            </DataTrigger>
        </Switch.Triggers>
    </Switch>

    <Entry x:Name="entry2"
           Text="" />

    <Switch x:Name="switch2"
            IsVisible="False">
        <Switch.Triggers>
            <DataTrigger TargetType="Switch"
                         Binding="{Binding Source={x:Reference entry2},
                                           Path=Text.Length}"
                         Value="0">
                <Setter Property="IsToggled" Value="True" />
            </DataTrigger>
        </Switch.Triggers>
    </Switch>

    <Button Text="Send"
            IsEnabled="False">
        <Button.Triggers>
            <MultiTrigger TargetType="Button">
                <MultiTrigger.Conditions>
```

```
                    <BindingCondition Binding="{Binding Source={x:Reference switch1},
                                                        Path=IsToggled}"
                                      Value="False" />
                    <BindingCondition Binding="{Binding Source={x:Reference switch2},
                                                        Path=IsToggled}"
                                      Value="False" />
                </MultiTrigger.Conditions>

                <Setter Property="IsEnabled" Value="True" />
            </MultiTrigger>
        </Button.Triggers>
    </Button>
</StackLayout>
```

Each `Entry` now has a companion `Switch` that uses a `DataTrigger` to set its `IsToggled` property to `True` if the length of the `Text` property of the `Entry` is zero. The two `Switch` elements can then be used in the `MultiTrigger`. If both `Switch` elements have their `IsToggled` properties set to `True`, then both `Entry` fields contain some text, and the `IsEnabled` property of the `Button` can be set to `True`.

If you want to actually combine AND and OR operations, you'll need to engage in some deeper levels of logic.

For example, suppose you have a scenario with two `Entry` views and a `Button`, and the `Button` should be enabled only if either of the two `Entry` views contains some text, but not if both `Entry` views contain some text:

Perhaps (as this screenshot suggests) one of the `Entry` views is for a filename and the other is for a URL, and the program needs one and only one of these two text strings.

What you need is an exclusive-OR (XOR) operation, and it's a combination of AND, OR, and negation operators:

$$A \text{ ^ } B \text{ == } (A \text{ | } B) \text{ \& } !(A \text{ \& } B)$$

This can be done with three `MultiTrigger` objects, two of which are on intermediary invisible `Switch` elements and the final one is on the `Button` itself. Here's the **XorConditions** XAML file with comments describing the various pieces of the logic:

```xml
<ContentPage xmlns="http://xamarin.com/schemas/2014/forms"
             xmlns:x="http://schemas.microsoft.com/winfx/2009/xaml"
             x:Class="XorConditions.XorConditionsPage"
             Padding="50, 20">

    <StackLayout>
        <Label Text="Enter:" />

        <Entry x:Name="entry1"
               Text=""
               Placeholder="filename" />

        <!-- IsToggled is true if entry1 has no text -->
        <Switch x:Name="switch1"
                IsVisible="False">
            <Switch.Triggers>
                <DataTrigger TargetType="Switch"
                             Binding="{Binding Source={x:Reference entry1},
                                               Path=Text.Length}"
                             Value="0">
                    <Setter Property="IsToggled" Value="True" />
                </DataTrigger>
            </Switch.Triggers>
        </Switch>

        <Label Text="Or:" />

        <Entry x:Name="entry2"
               Text=""
               Placeholder="url" />

        <!-- IsToggled is true if entry2 has no text -->
        <Switch x:Name="switch2"
                IsVisible="False">
            <Switch.Triggers>
                <DataTrigger TargetType="Switch"
                             Binding="{Binding Source={x:Reference entry2},
                                               Path=Text.Length}"
                             Value="0">
                    <Setter Property="IsToggled" Value="True" />
                </DataTrigger>
            </Switch.Triggers>
        </Switch>

        <!-- IsToggled is true if either Entry has some text (OR operation) -->
```

```xml
            <Switch x:Name="switch3"
                    IsToggled="True"
                    IsVisible="False">
                <Switch.Triggers>
                    <MultiTrigger TargetType="Switch">
                        <MultiTrigger.Conditions>
                            <BindingCondition Binding="{Binding Source={x:Reference switch1},
                                                                Path=IsToggled}"
                                              Value="True" />
                            <BindingCondition Binding="{Binding Source={x:Reference switch2},
                                                                Path=IsToggled}"
                                              Value="True" />
                        </MultiTrigger.Conditions>

                        <Setter Property="IsToggled" Value="False" />
                    </MultiTrigger>
                </Switch.Triggers>
            </Switch>

            <!-- IsToggled is true if both Entry's have some text (AND operation) -->
            <Switch x:Name="switch4"
                    IsVisible="False">
                <Switch.Triggers>
                    <MultiTrigger TargetType="Switch">
                        <MultiTrigger.Conditions>
                            <BindingCondition Binding="{Binding Source={x:Reference switch1},
                                                                Path=IsToggled}"
                                              Value="False" />
                            <BindingCondition Binding="{Binding Source={x:Reference switch2},
                                                                Path=IsToggled}"
                                              Value="False" />
                        </MultiTrigger.Conditions>

                        <Setter Property="IsToggled" Value="True" />
                    </MultiTrigger>
                </Switch.Triggers>
            </Switch>

            <!-- Button is enabled if either Entry has some text but not both (XOR operation) -->
            <Button Text="Load"
                    IsEnabled="False"
                    FontSize="Large">
                <Button.Triggers>
                    <MultiTrigger TargetType="Button">
                        <MultiTrigger.Conditions>
                            <BindingCondition Binding="{Binding Source={x:Reference switch3},
                                                                Path=IsToggled}"
                                              Value="True" />
                            <BindingCondition Binding="{Binding Source={x:Reference switch4},
                                                                Path=IsToggled}"
                                              Value="False" />
                        </MultiTrigger.Conditions>

                        <Setter Property="IsEnabled" Value="True" />
```

```
                    </MultiTrigger>
                </Button.Triggers>
            </Button>
        </StackLayout>
</ContentPage>
```

Of course, once the XAML gets this extravagant, nobody will fault you if you simply decide to enable or disable the `Button` in code!

Behaviors

Triggers and behaviors are generally discussed in tandem because they have some applicational overlap. Sometimes you'll be puzzled whether to use a trigger or behavior because either seems to do the job.

Anything you can do with a trigger you can also do with a behavior. However, a behavior always involves some code, which is a class that derives from `Behavior<T>`. Triggers only involve code if you're writing an `Action<T>` derivative for an `EventTrigger` or for `EnterActions` or `ExitActions` collections of the other triggers.

Obviously, if you can do what you need using one of the triggers without writing any code, then don't use a behavior. But sometimes it's not so clear.

Let's compare a trigger and behavior that do the same job.

The **TriggerEntryValidation** program shown earlier in this chapter uses a class named `NumericEntryAction` that checks whether a number typed into an `Entry` view qualifies as a valid `double` value and colors the text red if it doesn't:

```
namespace Xamarin.FormsBook.Toolkit
{
    public class NumericValidationAction : TriggerAction<Entry>
    {
        protected override void Invoke(Entry entry)
        {
            double result;
            bool isValid = Double.TryParse(entry.Text, out result);
            entry.TextColor = isValid ? Color.Default : Color.Red;
        }
    }
}
```

This is referenced in an `EventTrigger` attached to an `Entry`:

```
<Entry Placeholder="Enter a System.Double">
    <Entry.Triggers>
        <EventTrigger Event="TextChanged">
            <toolkit:NumericValidationAction />
        </EventTrigger>
    </Entry.Triggers>
```

```
</Entry>
```

You can use a behavior for this same job. The first step is to derive a class from `Behavior<T>`. The generic argument is the most generalized base class that the behavior can handle. In this example, that's an `Entry` view. Then, override two virtual methods, named `OnAttachedTo` and `OnDetaching-From`. The `OnAttachedTo` method is called when the behavior is attached to a particular visual object, and it gives your behavior a chance to initialize itself. Often this involves attaching some event handlers to the object. The `OnDetachingFrom` method is called when the behavior is removed from the visual object. Even if this occurs only when the program is terminating, you should undo anything the `OnAt-tachedTo` method does.

Here's the `NumericValidationBehavior` class:

```
namespace Xamarin.FormsBook.Toolkit
{
    public class NumericValidationBehavior : Behavior<Entry>
    {
        protected override void OnAttachedTo(Entry entry)
        {
            base.OnAttachedTo(entry);
            entry.TextChanged += OnEntryTextChanged;
        }

        protected override void OnDetachingFrom(Entry entry)
        {
            base.OnDetachingFrom(entry);
            entry.TextChanged -= OnEntryTextChanged;
        }

        void OnEntryTextChanged(object sender, TextChangedEventArgs args)
        {
            double result;
            bool isValid = Double.TryParse(args.NewTextValue, out result);
            ((Entry)sender).TextColor = isValid ? Color.Default : Color.Red;
        }
    }
}
```

The `OnAttachedTo` method attaches a handler for the `TextChanged` event of the `Entry`, and the `OnDetachingFrom` method detaches that handler. The handler itself does the same job as the `Invoke` method in `NumericValidationAction`.

Because the `NumericValidationBehavior` class installs the handler for the `TextChanged` event, the behavior can be used without specifying anything beyond the class name. Here's the XAML file for the **BehaviorEntryValidation** program, which differs from the earlier program that used an `EventTrigger` by specifying the behavior in an implicit style that is applied to four `Entry` views:

```
<ContentPage xmlns="http://xamarin.com/schemas/2014/forms"
             xmlns:x="http://schemas.microsoft.com/winfx/2009/xaml"
             xmlns:toolkit=
                 "clr-namespace:Xamarin.FormsBook.Toolkit;assembly=Xamarin.FormsBook.Toolkit"
```

```
                x:Class="BehaviorEntryValidation.BehaviorEntryValidationPage"
                Padding="50">

    <ContentPage.Resources>
        <ResourceDictionary>
            <Style TargetType="Entry">
                <Style.Behaviors>
                    <toolkit:NumericValidationBehavior />
                </Style.Behaviors>
            </Style>
        </ResourceDictionary>
    </ContentPage.Resources>

    <StackLayout>
        <Entry Placeholder="Enter a System.Double" />

        <Entry Placeholder="Enter a System.Double" />

        <Entry Placeholder="Enter a System.Double" />

        <Entry Placeholder="Enter a System.Double" />
    </StackLayout>
</ContentPage>
```

This `Style` object is shared among the four `Entry` views, so only a single `NumericValidationBe-`
`havior` object is instantiated. As this single object is attached to each of the four `Entry` views, it attaches a `TextChanged` handler on each one so that the single `NumericValidationBehavior` object
operates independently on the four views:

In this particular example, the `TriggerAction` would be preferred over the `Behavior` because it's less code and the code doesn't refer to a particular event, so it's more generalized.

But a behavior can be as generalized or as specific as you want; and behaviors also have the ability to participate more fully within the XAML file through data bindings.

Behaviors with properties

The `Behavior<T>` class derives from the `Behavior` class, which derives from `BindableObject`. This suggests that your `Behavior<T>` derivative can define its own bindable properties.

Earlier you saw some `Action<T>` derivatives such as `ScaleAction` and `ShiverAction` that defined some properties to give them more flexibility. But a `Behavior<T>` derivative can define bindable properties that can serve as source properties for data bindings. This means that you don't have to hard-code the behavior to modify a particular property, such as setting the `TextColor` property of an `Entry` to `Red`. You can instead decide later how you want the behavior to affect the user interface, and implement that right in the XAML file. This gives the behavior a greater amount of flexibility and allows the XAML to play a greater role in the aspect of the behavior that pertains to the user interface.

Here is a class in the **Xamarin.FormsBook.Toolkit** library called `ValidEmailBehavior`, which is similar to `NumericValidationBehavior` except that it uses a regular expression to determine whether the `Text` property of an `Entry` is a valid email address:

```
namespace Xamarin.FormsBook.Toolkit
{
    public class ValidEmailBehavior : Behavior<Entry>
    {
        static readonly BindablePropertyKey IsValidPropertyKey =
            BindableProperty.CreateReadOnly("IsValid",
                                            typeof(bool),
                                            typeof(ValidEmailBehavior),
                                            false);

        public static readonly BindableProperty IsValidProperty =
            IsValidPropertyKey.BindableProperty;

        public bool IsValid
        {
            private set { SetValue(IsValidPropertyKey, value); }
            get { return (bool)GetValue(IsValidProperty); }
        }

        protected override void OnAttachedTo(Entry entry)
        {
            entry.TextChanged += OnEntryTextChanged;
            base.OnAttachedTo(entry);
        }

        protected override void OnDetachingFrom(Entry entry)
        {
            entry.TextChanged -= OnEntryTextChanged;
            base.OnDetachingFrom(entry);
```

```
        }

        void OnEntryTextChanged(object sender, TextChangedEventArgs args)
        {
            Entry entry = (Entry)sender;
            IsValid = IsValidEmail(entry.Text);
        }

        bool IsValidEmail(string strIn)
        {
            if (String.IsNullOrEmpty(strIn))
                return false;

            try
            {
                // from https://msdn.microsoft.com/en-us/library/01escwtf(v=vs.110).aspx
                return Regex.IsMatch(strIn,
                    @"^(?("")("".+?(?<!\\)"")@)|(([0-9a-z]((\.(?!\.))|" +
                    @"[-!#\$%&'\*\+/=\?\^`\{\}\|~\w])*)" +
                    @"(?<=[0-9a-z])@))(?(\[)(\[(\d{1,3}\.){3}\d{1,3}\])|" +
                    @"(([0-9a-z][-\w]*[0-9a-z]*\.)+[a-z0-9][\-a-z0-9]{0,22}[a-z0-9]))$",
                    RegexOptions.IgnoreCase, TimeSpan.FromMilliseconds(250));
            }
            catch (RegexMatchTimeoutException)
            {
                return false;
            }
        }
    }
}
```

Instead of setting the `Text` property of the `Entry` to `Red`, `ValidEmailBehavior` defines an `IsValid`
property that is backed by a bindable property. Because it makes no sense for code external to this
class to set the `IsValid` property, it is a read-only bindable property. The `Bindable.CreateRead-
Only` call creates a private bindable-property key that is used by the `SetValue` call in the private `set`
accessor of `IsValid`. The public `IsValidProperty` bindable property is referenced by the `GetValue`
call as usual.

How you use that `IsValid` property is entirely up to you.

For example, the **EmailValidationDemo** program binds that `IsValid` property to the `IsVisible`
property of an `Image` displaying a "thumb up" picture. That "thumb up" bitmap sits on top of another
`Image` element with a "thumb down" to indicate when a valid email address has been typed. That `Is-
Valid` property is also bound to the `IsEnabled` property of a **Send** button. Notice that the `Source` of
both data bindings is the `ValidEmailBehavior` object:

```
<ContentPage xmlns="http://xamarin.com/schemas/2014/forms"
             xmlns:x="http://schemas.microsoft.com/winfx/2009/xaml"
             xmlns:local="clr-namespace:EmailValidationDemo"
             xmlns:toolkit=
                "clr-namespace:Xamarin.FormsBook.Toolkit;assembly=Xamarin.FormsBook.Toolkit"
             x:Class="EmailValidationDemo.EmailValidationDemoPage"
```

```
                Padding="20, 50">

    <StackLayout>
        <StackLayout Orientation="Horizontal">
            <Entry Placeholder="Enter email address"
                   Keyboard="Email"
                   HorizontalOptions="FillAndExpand">
                <Entry.Behaviors>
                    <toolkit:ValidEmailBehavior x:Name="validEmail" />
                </Entry.Behaviors>
            </Entry>

            <Grid HeightRequest="40">
                <Image Source=
                       "{local:ImageResource EmailValidationDemo.Images.ThumbsDown.png}" />

                <Image Source="{local:ImageResource EmailValidationDemo.Images.ThumbsUp.png}"
                       IsVisible="{Binding Source={x:Reference validEmail},
                                           Path=IsValid}"/>

            </Grid>
        </StackLayout>

        <Button Text="Send!"
                FontSize="Large"
                HorizontalOptions="Center"
                IsEnabled="{Binding Source={x:Reference validEmail},
                                    Path=IsValid}" />
    </StackLayout>
</ContentPage>
```

As you're typing an email address, it's not considered valid until it has at least a two-character top-level domain:

The two bitmaps are part of the common **EmailValidationDemo** project. The `ImageResource` markup extension class used to reference the bitmaps was discussed in Chapter 13, "Bitmaps," and it must be part of the same assembly that contains the bitmaps:

```
namespace EmailValidationDemo
{
    [ContentProperty ("Source")]
    public class ImageResourceExtension : IMarkupExtension
    {
        public string Source { get; set; }

        public object ProvideValue (IServiceProvider serviceProvider)
        {
            if (Source == null)
                return null;

            return ImageSource.FromResource(Source);
        }
    }
}
```

What if you have multiple `Entry` views on the same page that need to check for valid email addresses. Could you include the `ValidEmailBehavior` class in a `Behaviors` collection of a `Style`?

No you cannot. The `ValidEmailBehavior` class defines a property named `IsValid`. This means that a particular instance of `ValidEmailBehavior` always has a particular state, which is the value of this property. This has a significant implication:

A behavior that maintains state—such as a field or a property—cannot be shared, which means it shouldn't be included in a `Style`.

If you need to use `ValidEmailBehavior` for multiple `Entry` views on the same page, don't put it in a `Style`. Add a separate instance to the `Behaviors` collections of each of the `Entry` views.

The advantage of this `IsValid` property outweighs the disadvantages, however, because you can use the property in a variety of ways. Here's a program called **EmailValidationConverter** that uses the `IsValid` property with a binding converter already in the **Xamarin.FormsBook.Toolkit** library to choose between two text strings:

```
<ContentPage xmlns="http://xamarin.com/schemas/2014/forms"
             xmlns:x="http://schemas.microsoft.com/winfx/2009/xaml"
             xmlns:toolkit=
                 "clr-namespace:Xamarin.FormsBook.Toolkit;assembly=Xamarin.FormsBook.Toolkit"
             x:Class="EmailValidationConverter.EmailValidationConverterPage"
             Padding="50">

    <StackLayout>
        <StackLayout Orientation="Horizontal">
            <Entry Placeholder="Enter email address"
                   HorizontalOptions="FillAndExpand">
                <Entry.Behaviors>
                    <toolkit:ValidEmailBehavior x:Name="validEmail" />
                </Entry.Behaviors>
            </Entry>

            <Label HorizontalTextAlignment="Center"
                   VerticalTextAlignment="Center">
                <Label.Text>
                    <Binding Source="{x:Reference validEmail}"
                             Path="IsValid">
                        <Binding.Converter>
                            <toolkit:BoolToObjectConverter x:TypeArguments="x:String"
                                                           FalseObject="Not yet!"
                                                           TrueObject="OK!" />
                        </Binding.Converter>
                    </Binding>
                </Label.Text>
            </Label>
        </StackLayout>

        <Button Text="Send!"
                FontSize="Large"
                HorizontalOptions="Center"
                IsEnabled="{Binding Source={x:Reference validEmail},
                                    Path=IsValid}" />
    </StackLayout>
</ContentPage>
```

The `BoolToObjectConverter` chooses between the two text strings "Not yet!" and "OK!".

However, you can do this same thing with a little more straightforward logic and no binding converter by using a `DataTrigger`, as the **EmailValidationTrigger** program demonstrates. The "Not yet!" text is assigned to the `Text` property of the `Label`, while a `DataTrigger` on the `Label` contains a binding to the `IsValid` property to set the "OK!" text:

```xml
<ContentPage xmlns="http://xamarin.com/schemas/2014/forms"
             xmlns:x="http://schemas.microsoft.com/winfx/2009/xaml"
             xmlns:toolkit=
                 "clr-namespace:Xamarin.FormsBook.Toolkit;assembly=Xamarin.FormsBook.Toolkit"
             x:Class="EmailValidationTrigger.EmailValidationTriggerPage"
             Padding="50">

    <StackLayout>
        <StackLayout Orientation="Horizontal">
            <Entry Placeholder="Enter email address"
                   HorizontalOptions="FillAndExpand">
                <Entry.Behaviors>
                    <toolkit:ValidEmailBehavior x:Name="validEmail" />
                </Entry.Behaviors>
            </Entry>

            <Label Text="Not yet!"
                   HorizontalTextAlignment="Center"
                   VerticalTextAlignment="Center">
                <Label.Triggers>
                    <DataTrigger TargetType="Label"
                                 Binding="{Binding Source={x:Reference validEmail},
                                                   Path=IsValid}"
                                 Value="True">
                        <Setter Property="Text" Value="OK!" />
                    </DataTrigger>
                </Label.Triggers>
            </Label>
        </StackLayout>

        <Button Text="Send!"
                FontSize="Large"
                HorizontalOptions="Center"
                IsEnabled="{Binding Source={x:Reference validEmail},
                                    Path=IsValid}" />
    </StackLayout>
</ContentPage>
```

Referencing a behavior from a data binding in a `DataTrigger` is a powerful technique.

Toggles and check boxes

In Chapter 15, "The interactive interface," and Chapter 16, "Data binding," you saw how to construct traditional `CheckBox` views. However, another approach to custom views is to incorporate the interactive logic of the view in a behavior and then realize the visuals entirely in XAML. This approach gives you the flexibility of customizing the visuals with markup rather than code. Because the visual appearance is not part of the underlying logic, you can create ad hoc visuals whenever you use the behavior.

Here is a class in the **Xamarin.FormsBook.Toolkit** library named `ToggleBehavior`. Like the Xamarin.Forms `Switch` element, it defines a property named `IsToggled` that is backed by a bindable property. `ToggleBehavior` simply installs a `TapGestureRecognizer` to the visual that it's attached to and toggles the state of the `IsToggled` property whenever a tap is detected:

```
namespace Xamarin.FormsBook.Toolkit
{
    public class ToggleBehavior : Behavior<View>
    {
        TapGestureRecognizer tapRecognizer;

        public static readonly BindableProperty IsToggledProperty =
            BindableProperty.Create<ToggleBehavior, bool>(tb => tb.IsToggled, false);

        public bool IsToggled
        {
            set { SetValue(IsToggledProperty, value); }
            get { return (bool)GetValue(IsToggledProperty); }
        }

        protected override void OnAttachedTo(View view)
        {
            base.OnAttachedTo(view);

            tapRecognizer = new TapGestureRecognizer ();
            tapRecognizer.Tapped += OnTapped;
            view.GestureRecognizers.Add(tapRecognizer);
        }

        protected override void OnDetachingFrom(View view)
        {
            base.OnDetachingFrom(view);

            view.GestureRecognizers.Remove(tapRecognizer);
            tapRecognizer.Tapped -= OnTapped;
        }

        void OnTapped(object sender, EventArgs args)
        {
            IsToggled = !IsToggled;
        }
    }
}
```

The `ToggleBehavior` class defines a property, which means that you cannot share a `ToggleBehav-ior` in a `Style`.

Here's a simple application. The **ToggleLabel** program attaches `ToggleBehavior` to a `Label` and uses the `IsToggled` property with a `DataTrigger` to switch the text of the `Label` between "Paused" and "Playing," perhaps for a music application:

```
<ContentPage xmlns="http://xamarin.com/schemas/2014/forms"
             xmlns:x="http://schemas.microsoft.com/winfx/2009/xaml"
             xmlns:toolkit=
                 "clr-namespace:Xamarin.FormsBook.Toolkit;assembly=Xamarin.FormsBook.Toolkit"
```

```
                   x:Class="ToggleLabel.ToggleLabelPage">

        <Label Text="Paused"
               FontSize="Large"
               HorizontalOptions="Center"
               VerticalOptions="Center">
            <Label.Behaviors>
                <toolkit:ToggleBehavior x:Name="toggleBehavior" />
            </Label.Behaviors>

            <Label.Triggers>
                <DataTrigger TargetType="Label"
                             Binding="{Binding Source={x:Reference toggleBehavior},
                                               Path=IsToggled}"
                             Value="True">
                    <Setter Property="Text" Value="Playing" />
                </DataTrigger>
            </Label.Triggers>
        </Label>
</ContentPage>
```

Of course, such a program would probably need to run some code when the `Label` is toggled. Keep in mind that `Behavior` derives from `BindableObject`, which means that any `BindableProperty` that you define in a behavior automatically generates a `PropertyChanged` event when the property changes.

This means that you can attach a handler to the `PropertyChanged` event of `ToggleBehavior` and check for changes in the `IsToggled` property. This is demonstrated in the **FormattedTextToggle** program, which expands the **ToggleLabel** program to include a `Frame` and some formatted text that more clearly indicates the two options that the tap switches between:

```
<ContentPage xmlns="http://xamarin.com/schemas/2014/forms"
             xmlns:x="http://schemas.microsoft.com/winfx/2009/xaml"
             xmlns:toolkit=
                 "clr-namespace:Xamarin.FormsBook.Toolkit;assembly=Xamarin.FormsBook.Toolkit"
             x:Class="FormattedTextToggle.FormattedTextTogglePage">

    <StackLayout>
        <Frame HorizontalOptions="Center"
               VerticalOptions="CenterAndExpand"
               OutlineColor="Accent"
               BackgroundColor="Transparent">

            <Frame.Behaviors>
                <toolkit:ToggleBehavior x:Name="toggleBehavior"
                                        PropertyChanged="OnBehaviorPropertyChanged" />
            </Frame.Behaviors>

            <Label>
                <Label.FormattedText>
                    <FormattedString>
                        <FormattedString.Spans>
                            <Span Text="Paused / "
```

```
                                        FontSize="Large"
                                        FontAttributes="Bold" />

                            <Span Text="Playing"
                                  FontSize="Small" />
                        </FormattedString.Spans>
                    </FormattedString>
                </Label.FormattedText>

                <Label.Triggers>
                    <DataTrigger TargetType="Label"
                                 Binding="{Binding Source={x:Reference toggleBehavior},
                                                   Path=IsToggled}"
                                 Value="True">
                        <Setter Property="FormattedText">
                            <Setter.Value>
                                <FormattedString>
                                    <FormattedString.Spans>
                                        <Span Text="Paused"
                                              FontSize="Small" />

                                        <Span Text=" / Playing"
                                              FontSize="Large"
                                              FontAttributes="Bold" />
                                    </FormattedString.Spans>
                                </FormattedString>
                            </Setter.Value>
                        </Setter>
                    </DataTrigger>
                </Label.Triggers>
            </Label>
        </Frame>

        <Label x:Name="eventLabel"
               Text=""
               FontSize="Large"
               Opacity="0"
               HorizontalOptions="Center"
               VerticalOptions="CenterAndExpand" />
    </StackLayout>
</ContentPage>
```

The `ToggleBehavior` is attached to the `Frame`, and the `Frame` contains a `Label`. (Notice that the `BackgroundColor` of the `Frame` is set to `Transparent` rather than the default value of `null`. This is necessary to trap the tap events on the Windows Runtime platforms.)

This program demonstrates one way to solve a common problem with toggle buttons: Does the text (or icon) refer to a state or an action? The `Label` here makes it clear by displaying the text "Paused / Playing" but with the word "Paused" larger than the word "Playing". When the `IsToggled` property is `True`, the `DataTrigger` changes that display so that the word "Playing" is larger than the word "Paused".

The `PropertyChanged` event on the `ToggleBehavior` is handled in the code-behind file:

```
public partial class FormattedTextTogglePage : ContentPage
{
    public FormattedTextTogglePage()
    {
        InitializeComponent();
    }

    void OnBehaviorPropertyChanged(object sender, PropertyChangedEventArgs args)
    {
        if (args.PropertyName == "IsToggled")
        {
            eventLabel.Text = "IsToggled = " + ((ToggleBehavior)sender).IsToggled;
            eventLabel.Opacity = 1;
            eventLabel.FadeTo(0, 1000);
        }
    }
}
```

The `OnBehaviorPropertyChanged` handler checks for a change in the property named "IsToggled". Keep in mind that the `sender` argument to the event handler is not the visual element whose taps are being detected (which is the `Frame`) but the `ToggleBehavior` itself. The code sets the `Text` property of the `Label` at the bottom of the page and sets the `Opacity` to 1, but then fades it out over the course of a second to give a sense of an event firing:

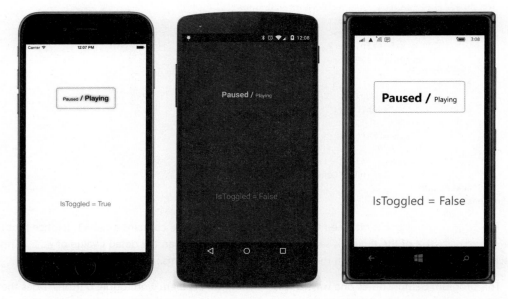

If you like the idea of defining the visuals of a toggle view in XAML but prefer a little more structure, the **Xamarin.FormsBook.Toolkit** library has a class named `ToggleBase` that derives from `Content-View` and incorporates `ToggleBehavior`. The constructor adds the `ToggleBehavior` to the `Behaviors` collection of the class and then attaches an event handler to it. The class also defines a `Toggled` event and its own `IsToggled` property that fires that event:

```
namespace Xamarin.FormsBook.Toolkit
{
    public class ToggleBase : ContentView
    {
        public event EventHandler<ToggledEventArgs> Toggled;

        public static readonly BindableProperty IsToggledProperty =
            BindableProperty.Create("IsToggled", typeof(bool), typeof(ToggleBase), false,
                            BindingMode.TwoWay,
                propertyChanged: (bindable, oldValue, newValue) =>
                {
                    EventHandler<ToggledEventArgs> handler = ((ToggleBase)bindable).Toggled;
                    if (handler != null)
                        handler(bindable, new ToggledEventArgs((bool)newValue));
                });

        public ToggleBase()
        {
            ToggleBehavior toggleBehavior = new ToggleBehavior();
            toggleBehavior.PropertyChanged += OnToggleBehaviorPropertyChanged;
            Behaviors.Add(toggleBehavior);
        }

        public bool IsToggled
        {
            set { SetValue(IsToggledProperty, value); }
            get { return (bool)GetValue(IsToggledProperty); }
        }

        protected void OnToggleBehaviorPropertyChanged(object sender,
                                                PropertyChangedEventArgs args)
        {
            if (args.PropertyName == "IsToggled")
            {
                IsToggled = ((ToggleBehavior)sender).IsToggled;
            }
        }
    }
}
```

The `ToggleBase` class defines all the logic of a toggle view without the visuals. In truth, it doesn't require the `ToggleBehaviors` class. It could install its own `TapGestureRecognizer`, but the result would be basically the same.

You can instantiate the `ToggleBase` class in a XAML file and supply the visuals as content of the `ToggleBase`. Here's a program called **TraditionalCheckBox** that uses two Unicode characters for an unchecked box and a checked box, similar to the `CheckBox` views in Chapters 15 and 16:

```
<ContentPage xmlns="http://xamarin.com/schemas/2014/forms"
             xmlns:x="http://schemas.microsoft.com/winfx/2009/xaml"
             xmlns:toolkit=
                 "clr-namespace:Xamarin.FormsBook.Toolkit;assembly=Xamarin.FormsBook.Toolkit"
             x:Class="TraditionalCheckBox.TraditionalCheckBoxPage">
```

```
        <StackLayout>
            <toolkit:ToggleBase x:Name="checkbox"
                                HorizontalOptions="Center"
                                VerticalOptions="CenterAndExpand"
                                Toggled="OnToggleBaseToggled">
                <StackLayout Orientation="Horizontal">
                    <Label Text="&#x2610;"
                           FontSize="Large">
                        <Label.Triggers>
                            <DataTrigger TargetType="Label"
                                         Binding="{Binding Source={x:Reference checkbox},
                                                           Path=IsToggled}"
                                         Value="True">
                                <Setter Property="Text" Value="&#x2611;" />
                            </DataTrigger>
                        </Label.Triggers>
                    </Label>

                    <Label Text="Italicize Text"
                           FontSize="Large" />
                </StackLayout>
            </toolkit:ToggleBase>

            <Label Text="Sample text to italicize"
                   FontSize="Large"
                   HorizontalOptions="Center"
                   VerticalOptions="CenterAndExpand">
                <Label.Triggers>
                    <DataTrigger TargetType="Label"
                                 Binding="{Binding Source={x:Reference checkbox},
                                                   Path=IsToggled}"
                                 Value="True">
                        <Setter Property="FontAttributes" Value="Italic" />
                    </DataTrigger>
                </Label.Triggers>
            </Label>

            <Label x:Name="eventLabel"
                   Text=""
                   FontSize="Large"
                   Opacity="0"
                   HorizontalOptions="Center"
                   VerticalOptions="CenterAndExpand" />

        </StackLayout>
</ContentPage>
```

The XAML file uses the `IsToggled` property as the source of two very similar data bindings, each within a `DataTrigger`. In both cases the `Source` property is set to the `ToggleBase` instance, and the `Path` property is set to the `IsToggled` property of `ToggleBase`. The first `DataTrigger` switches between the empty box and the checked box to indicate the state of the toggle, and the second `DataTrigger` italicizes some text when the `CheckBox` is toggled on.

In addition, the `Toggled` event of `ToggleBase` is handled in the code-behind file with a fade-out `Label`:

```
public partial class TraditionalCheckBoxPage : ContentPage
{
    public TraditionalCheckBoxPage()
    {
        InitializeComponent();
    }

    void OnToggleBaseToggled(object sender, ToggledEventArgs args)
    {
        eventLabel.Text = "IsToggled = " + args.Value;
        eventLabel.Opacity = 1;
        eventLabel.FadeTo(0, 1000);
    }
}
```

Here's the result:

If you need multiple instances of a particular type of toggle view, you can encapsulate the visuals in a class that derives from `ToggleBase`.

The next example derives from `ToggleBase` to make a view that is very much like the Xamarin.Forms `Switch`, except with visuals created entirely in XAML. This "switch clone" is realized with a little `BoxView` that moves back and forth in a `Frame`. For implementing the animation, the **Xamarin.FormsBook.Toolkit** library includes a `TranslateAction` class with properties that provide arguments for a call to `TranslateTo`:

```
namespace Xamarin.FormsBook.Toolkit
```

```
{
    public class TranslateAction : TriggerAction<VisualElement>
    {
        public TranslateAction()
        {
            // Set defaults.
            Length = 250;
            Easing = Easing.Linear;
        }

        public double X { set; get; }

        public double Y { set; get; }

        public int Length { set; get; }

        [TypeConverter(typeof(EasingConverter))]
        public Easing Easing { set; get; }

        protected override void Invoke(VisualElement visual)
        {
            visual.TranslateXYTo(X, Y, (uint)Length, Easing);
        }
    }
}
```

The `SwitchClone` class that mimics the `Switch` is part of the **SwitchCloneDemo** project. It's entirely done in XAML. The root element is the base class of `ToggleBase`, and the `x:Class` attribute indicates the derived class of `SwitchClone`. The `Resources` dictionary defines several constants that allow for visuals that are not too large, but still big enough to be a proper touch target:

```
<toolkit:ToggleBase
        xmlns="http://xamarin.com/schemas/2014/forms"
        xmlns:x="http://schemas.microsoft.com/winfx/2009/xaml"
        xmlns:toolkit=
            "clr-namespace:Xamarin.FormsBook.Toolkit;assembly=Xamarin.FormsBook.Toolkit"
        x:Class="SwitchCloneDemo.SwitchClone"
        x:Name="toggle">

    <toolkit:ToggleBase.Resources>
        <ResourceDictionary>
            <x:Double x:Key="height">20</x:Double>
            <x:Double x:Key="width">50</x:Double>
            <x:Double x:Key="halfWidth">25</x:Double>
        </ResourceDictionary>
    </toolkit:ToggleBase.Resources>

    <Frame Padding="2"
            OutlineColor="Accent"
            BackgroundColor="Transparent">
        <AbsoluteLayout WidthRequest="{StaticResource width}">
            <BoxView Color="Accent"
                    WidthRequest="{StaticResource halfWidth}"
                    HeightRequest="{StaticResource height}">
```

```
                    <BoxView.Triggers>
                        <DataTrigger TargetType="BoxView"
                                     Binding="{Binding Source={x:Reference toggle},
                                                       Path=IsToggled}"
                                     Value="True">
                            <DataTrigger.EnterActions>
                                <toolkit:TranslateAction X="{StaticResource halfWidth}"
                                                         Length="100" />
                            </DataTrigger.EnterActions>

                            <DataTrigger.ExitActions>
                                <toolkit:TranslateAction Length="100" />
                            </DataTrigger.ExitActions>
                        </DataTrigger>
                    </BoxView.Triggers>
                </BoxView>
            </AbsoluteLayout>
        </Frame>
</toolkit:ToggleBase>
```

Notice that the root element has a name of "toggle." This allows the data binding in the `DataTrigger` on the `BoxView` to reference the `IsToggled` property defined by the `ToggleBase` class. The `DataTrigger` does not include a `Setter` but instead uses `EnterActions` and `ExitActions` to invoke the `TranslateAction` for shifting the `BoxView` back and forth.

The code-behind file for `SwitchClone` has nothing but an `InitializeComponent` call, but if you need other properties (for example, for color or some accompanying text) you can define them there.

At least that's the way it was originally coded. Later on, the program refused to build on the Windows Runtime platforms. Perhaps the problem had something to do with the root element in the XAML file referencing a class in a library. Regardless, a code-only version of the class did work, and this is the one included with the sample code for this chapter:

```
class SwitchClone : ToggleBase
{
    const double height = 20;
    const double width = 50;
    const double halfWidth = 25;

    public SwitchClone()
    {
        BoxView boxView = new BoxView
        {
            Color = Color.Accent,
            WidthRequest = halfWidth,
            HeightRequest = height
        };

        DataTrigger dataTrigger = new DataTrigger(typeof(BoxView))
        {
            Binding = new Binding("IsToggled", source: this),
            Value = true,
        };
```

```
dataTrigger.EnterActions.Add(new TranslateAction
{
    X = halfWidth,
    Length = 100
});

dataTrigger.ExitActions.Add(new TranslateAction
{
    Length = 100
});

boxView.Triggers.Add(dataTrigger);

Content = new Frame
{
    Padding = 2,
    OutlineColor = Color.Accent,
    BackgroundColor = Color.Transparent,
    Content = new AbsoluteLayout
    {
        WidthRequest = width,
        Children =
        {
            boxView
        }
    }
};
    }
}
```

The `SwitchCloneDemoPage` class displays four of these switch clones in a row:

```
<ContentPage xmlns="http://xamarin.com/schemas/2014/forms"
             xmlns:x="http://schemas.microsoft.com/winfx/2009/xaml"
             xmlns:local="clr-namespace:SwitchCloneDemo"
             x:Class="SwitchCloneDemo.SwitchCloneDemoPage">

    <Grid VerticalOptions="Center">
        <local:SwitchClone Grid.Column="0"
                           HorizontalOptions="Center" />

        <local:SwitchClone Grid.Column="1"
                           HorizontalOptions="Center" />

        <local:SwitchClone Grid.Column="2"
                           HorizontalOptions="Center" />

        <local:SwitchClone Grid.Column="3"
                           HorizontalOptions="Center" />
    </Grid>
</ContentPage>
```

And here they are:

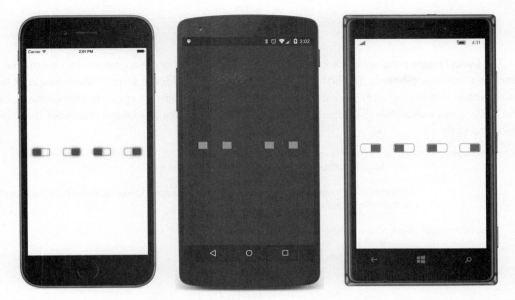

Of course, once you start thinking about using animations, you might start getting some interesting (or perhaps downright odd) ideas of what a toggle view might look like. To give you a few more options, here's a `RotateAction` class:

```
namespace Xamarin.FormsBook.Toolkit
{
    public class RotateAction : TriggerAction<VisualElement>
    {
        public RotateAction()
        {
            // Set defaults.
            Anchor = new Point (0.5, 0.5);
            Rotation = 0;
            Length = 250;
            Easing = Easing.Linear;
        }

        public Point Anchor { set; get; }

        public double Rotation { set; get; }

        public int Length { set; get; }

        [TypeConverter(typeof(EasingConverter))]
        public Easing Easing { set; get; }

        protected override void Invoke(VisualElement visual)
        {
            visual.AnchorX = Anchor.X;
            visual.AnchorY = Anchor.Y;
            visual.RotateTo(Rotation, (uint)Length, Easing);
```

```
        }
    }
}
```

The **LeverToggle** program has a XAML file that is devoted to a single toggle switch constructed from two `BoxView` elements. The first `BoxView` resembles a base for the second, which functions like a lever. Notice that the `DataTrigger` on the second `BoxView` contains a `Setter` to change the color of the `BoxView` as well as `EnterActions` and `ExitActions` to invoke animations that move the lever back and forth:

```xml
<ContentPage xmlns="http://xamarin.com/schemas/2014/forms"
             xmlns:x="http://schemas.microsoft.com/winfx/2009/xaml"
             xmlns:toolkit=
                "clr-namespace:Xamarin.FormsBook.Toolkit;assembly=Xamarin.FormsBook.Toolkit"
             x:Class="LeverToggle.LeverTogglePage">

    <toolkit:ToggleBase x:Name="toggle"
                        HorizontalOptions="Center"
                        VerticalOptions="Center">
        <AbsoluteLayout>
            <BoxView Color="Gray"
                     AbsoluteLayout.LayoutBounds="0, 75, 100, 25">
                <BoxView.Triggers>
                    <DataTrigger TargetType="BoxView"
                                 Binding="{Binding Source={x:Reference toggle},
                                                   Path=IsToggled}"
                                 Value="True">
                        <Setter Property="Color" Value="Lime" />
                    </DataTrigger>
                </BoxView.Triggers>
            </BoxView>

            <BoxView Color="Gray"
                     AbsoluteLayout.LayoutBounds="45, 0, 10, 100"
                     AnchorX="0.5"
                     AnchorY="1"
                     Rotation="-30">
                <BoxView.Triggers>
                    <DataTrigger TargetType="BoxView"
                                 Binding="{Binding Source={x:Reference toggle},
                                                   Path=IsToggled}"
                                 Value="True">

                        <Setter Property="Color" Value="Lime" />

                        <DataTrigger.EnterActions>
                            <toolkit:RotateAction Anchor="0.5, 1" Rotation="30" />
                        </DataTrigger.EnterActions>

                        <DataTrigger.ExitActions>
                            <toolkit:RotateAction Anchor="0.5, 1" Rotation="-30" />
                        </DataTrigger.ExitActions>
                    </DataTrigger>
```

```
                    </BoxView.Triggers>
                  </BoxView>
                </AbsoluteLayout>
              </toolkit:ToggleBase>
</ContentPage>
```

The untoggled state is shown on the Android screen, while the iOS and Windows 10 Mobile screens show the toggled state:

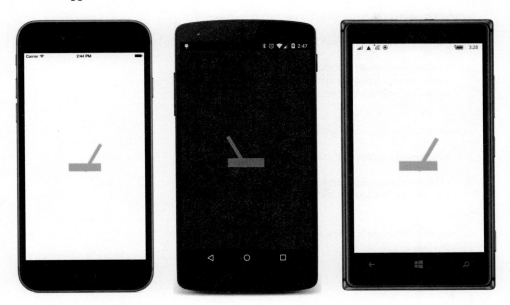

Responding to taps

The various manifestations of toggle views demonstrate one way to respond to taps within a XAML file. If tap events were integrated into the `VisualElement` class, you could get at them more directly and with greater ease using `EventTrigger`. But you can't attach an `EventTrigger` to a `TapGestureRecognizer`.

Getting around that little restriction is the purpose of a behavior devoted solely to a tap. This is called `TapBehavior`:

```
namespace Xamarin.FormsBook.Toolkit
{
    public class TapBehavior : Behavior<View>
    {
        TapGestureRecognizer tapGesture;

        static readonly BindablePropertyKey IsTriggeredKey =
            BindableProperty.CreateReadOnly("IsTriggered", typeof(bool),
                                typeof(TapBehavior), false);
```

```
        public static readonly BindableProperty IsTriggeredProperty =
                                    IsTriggeredKey.BindableProperty;

        public bool IsTriggered
        {
            private set { SetValue(IsTriggeredKey, value); }
            get { return (bool)GetValue(IsTriggeredProperty); }
        }

        protected override void OnAttachedTo(View view)
        {
            base.OnAttachedTo(view);

            tapGesture = new TapGestureRecognizer();
            tapGesture.Tapped += OnTapped;
            view.GestureRecognizers.Add(tapGesture);
        }

        protected override void OnDetachingFrom(View view)
        {
            base.OnDetachingFrom(view);

            view.GestureRecognizers.Remove(tapGesture);
            tapGesture.Tapped -= OnTapped;
        }

        async void OnTapped(object sender, EventArgs args)
        {
            IsTriggered = true;
            await Task.Delay(100);
            IsTriggered = false;
        }
    }
}
```

The `TapBehavior` class defines a Boolean property named `IsTriggered`, but it doesn't function exactly like a normal property. For one thing, it's backed by a read-only bindable property. This means that the `IsTriggered` property can be set only within the `TapBehavior` class, and the only time the class sets `IsTriggered` is in the event handler for the `TapGestureRecognizer`, when the `IsTriggered` property becomes `true` for a mere one-tenth of a second.

In other words, the `Tapped` event is converted into a very brief spike of a property value—somewhat reminiscent of how events are triggered in digital hardware. But the `IsTriggered` property can then be referenced in a `DataTrigger`.

Suppose you like the idea of the `ShiverButton`, but you'd like to apply the concept to something other than a `Button`, which means you need to respond to `Tapped` events. You can't use an `EventTrigger`, but the `TapBehavior` lets you use a `DataTrigger` instead.

To demonstrate, here's **BoxViewTapShiver**, which attaches `TapBehavior` objects to three `BoxView` elements, each of which also includes a `DataTrigger` that references the behavior and invokes a

`ShiverAction` in its `EnterActions` collection:

```xml
<ContentPage xmlns="http://xamarin.com/schemas/2014/forms"
             xmlns:x="http://schemas.microsoft.com/winfx/2009/xaml"
             xmlns:toolkit=
                 "clr-namespace:Xamarin.FormsBook.Toolkit;assembly=Xamarin.FormsBook.Toolkit"
             x:Class="BoxViewTapShiver.BoxViewTapShiverPage">

    <ContentPage.Resources>
        <ResourceDictionary>
            <Style TargetType="BoxView">
                <Setter Property="WidthRequest" Value="200" />
                <Setter Property="HeightRequest" Value="50" />
                <Setter Property="HorizontalOptions" Value="Center" />
                <Setter Property="VerticalOptions"   Value="CenterAndExpand" />
            </Style>
        </ResourceDictionary>
    </ContentPage.Resources>

    <StackLayout>
        <BoxView Color="Red">
            <BoxView.Behaviors>
                <toolkit:TapBehavior x:Name="tapBehavior1" />
            </BoxView.Behaviors>

            <BoxView.Triggers>
                <DataTrigger TargetType="BoxView"
                             Binding="{Binding Source={x:Reference tapBehavior1},
                                               Path=IsTriggered}"
                             Value="True">
                    <DataTrigger.EnterActions>
                        <toolkit:ShiverAction />
                    </DataTrigger.EnterActions>
                </DataTrigger>
            </BoxView.Triggers>
        </BoxView>

        <BoxView Color="Green">
            <BoxView.Behaviors>
                <toolkit:TapBehavior x:Name="tapBehavior2" />
            </BoxView.Behaviors>

            <BoxView.Triggers>
                <DataTrigger TargetType="BoxView"
                             Binding="{Binding Source={x:Reference tapBehavior2},
                                               Path=IsTriggered}"
                             Value="True">
                    <DataTrigger.EnterActions>
                        <toolkit:ShiverAction />
                    </DataTrigger.EnterActions>
                </DataTrigger>
            </BoxView.Triggers>
        </BoxView>
```

```
        <BoxView Color="Blue">
            <BoxView.Behaviors>
                <toolkit:TapBehavior x:Name="tapBehavior3" />
            </BoxView.Behaviors>

            <BoxView.Triggers>
                <DataTrigger TargetType="BoxView"
                             Binding="{Binding Source={x:Reference tapBehavior3},
                                               Path=IsTriggered}"
                             Value="True">
                    <DataTrigger.EnterActions>
                        <toolkit:ShiverAction />
                    </DataTrigger.EnterActions>
                </DataTrigger>
            </BoxView.Triggers>
        </BoxView>
    </StackLayout>
</ContentPage>
```

Each of the three `TapBehavior` objects has a unique name, which is referenced by the corresponding `DataTrigger`. When you tap a `BoxView`, it shivers, and they all work independently.

It is very tempting to put the `TapBehavior` and `DataTrigger` objects in a `Style` to cut down on the repetitive markup, but that won't work. That would cause a single `TapBehavior` to be shared among the three `BoxView` elements. Moreover, each `DataTrigger` refers to a corresponding `Tap-Behavior` by name.

If you want to cut down on the markup in this case, you'll once again need to define a new class. The **ShiverViews** program demonstrates this. It first defines a class named `ShiverView` that derives from `BoxView` and adds the `TapBehavior` and `DataTrigger`:

```
<BoxView xmlns="http://xamarin.com/schemas/2014/forms"
         xmlns:x="http://schemas.microsoft.com/winfx/2009/xaml"
         xmlns:toolkit=
             "clr-namespace:Xamarin.FormsBook.Toolkit;assembly=Xamarin.FormsBook.Toolkit"
         x:Class="ShiverViews.ShiverView">

    <BoxView.Behaviors>
        <toolkit:TapBehavior x:Name="tapBehavior" />
    </BoxView.Behaviors>

    <BoxView.Triggers>
        <DataTrigger TargetType="BoxView"
                     Binding="{Binding Source={x:Reference tapBehavior},
                                       Path=IsTriggered}"
                     Value="True">
            <DataTrigger.EnterActions>
                <toolkit:ShiverAction />
            </DataTrigger.EnterActions>
        </DataTrigger>
    </BoxView.Triggers>
</BoxView>
```

As with the `SwitchClone` class, you could also add some properties in the code-behind file and reference them in the XAML file.

The `ShiverViewsPage` XAML file can then just instantiate three independent `ShiverView` objects with an implicit style:

```
<ContentPage xmlns="http://xamarin.com/schemas/2014/forms"
             xmlns:x="http://schemas.microsoft.com/winfx/2009/xaml"
             xmlns:local="clr-namespace:ShiverViews"
             x:Class="ShiverViews.ShiverViewsPage">

    <StackLayout>
        <StackLayout.Resources>
            <ResourceDictionary>
                <Style TargetType="local:ShiverView">
                    <Setter Property="WidthRequest" Value="200" />
                    <Setter Property="HeightRequest" Value="50" />
                    <Setter Property="HorizontalOptions" Value="Center" />
                    <Setter Property="VerticalOptions"   Value="CenterAndExpand" />
                </Style>
            </ResourceDictionary>
        </StackLayout.Resources>

        <local:ShiverView Color="Red" />
        <local:ShiverView Color="Green" />
        <local:ShiverView Color="Blue" />
    </StackLayout>
</ContentPage>
```

Radio buttons

The radios built into the dashboards of old automobiles often featured a row of half a dozen (or so) buttons that could be "programmed" for various radio stations. Pushing in one of these buttons caused the radio to jump to that preselected station, and also caused the button for the previous selection to pop out.

Those old car radios are now antiques, but mutually exclusive options on our computer screens are still represented by visual objects we call *radio buttons*.

Radio buttons are somewhat similar to toggles or check boxes. But radio buttons are always found in a group of two or more. Selecting or checking any button in that group causes the others to become unchecked.

The logic behind radio buttons is complicated because an application might feature several groups of radio buttons on the same page, and these groups should function independently. Pressing a button in one group should only affect the other buttons within that group, and not the buttons in any other group.

Traditionally, radio buttons were grouped with a common parent. In Xamarin.Forms terminology, radio buttons that are children of one `StackLayout` are considered to be in the same group, while radio buttons that are children of another `StackLayout` are in another independent group.

However, there is a more generalized way to distinguish groups of radio buttons, and that is by giving each group a unique name, which really means that each radio button within that group references the same name.

The problem with these names is that they add some extra overhead, particularly when you need only one group of radio buttons. For that reason, there should be an allowance for a group of radio buttons that is *not* identified by a name. This is called the *default* group.

Here is a `RadioBehavior` class in the **Xamarin.FormsBook.Toolkit** library that is based on those principles. You attach this behavior to every view that you want to convert into a radio button. Like the `ToggleBehavior` class, `RadioBehavior` sets a `TapGestureRecognizer` on the visual element to which it's attached. It doesn't define an `IsToggled` property like `ToggleBehavior`, but it does define an `IsChecked` property that is quite similar and indicates whether the radio button is checked or unchecked. The `RadioBehavior` class also defines a `GroupName` property of type `string` to identify the group; a `null` value or an empty string indicates the default group.

The `RadioBehavior` class needs to store all the instantiated radio buttons by group, so it defines two static collections, one of which is a simple `List<RadioBehavior>` for all the objects in the default group, and the other is a `Dictionary` with a key corresponding to the group name that references a `List<RadioBehavior>` collection for all the objects in that named group:

```
namespace Xamarin.FormsBook.Toolkit
{
    public class RadioBehavior : Behavior<View>
    {
        TapGestureRecognizer tapRecognizer;
        static List<RadioBehavior> defaultGroup = new List<RadioBehavior>();
        static Dictionary<string, List<RadioBehavior>> radioGroups =
                            new Dictionary<string, List<RadioBehavior>>();

        public RadioBehavior()
        {
            defaultGroup.Add(this);
        }

        public static readonly BindableProperty IsCheckedProperty =
            BindableProperty.Create("IsChecked",
                                typeof(bool),
                                typeof(RadioBehavior),
                                false,
                                propertyChanged: OnIsCheckedChanged);

        public bool IsChecked
        {
            set { SetValue(IsCheckedProperty, value); }
            get { return (bool)GetValue(IsCheckedProperty); }
        }

        static void OnIsCheckedChanged(BindableObject bindable, object oldValue,
```

```
                                      object newValue)
{
    RadioBehavior behavior = (RadioBehavior)bindable;

    if ((bool)newValue)
    {
        string groupName = behavior.GroupName;
        List<RadioBehavior> behaviors = null;

        if (String.IsNullOrEmpty(groupName))
        {
            behaviors = defaultGroup;
        }
        else
        {
            behaviors = radioGroups[groupName];
        }

        foreach (RadioBehavior otherBehavior in behaviors)
        {
            if (otherBehavior != behavior)
            {
                otherBehavior.IsChecked = false;
            }
        }
    }
}

public static readonly BindableProperty GroupNameProperty =
    BindableProperty.Create("GroupName",
                            typeof(string),
                            typeof(RadioBehavior),
                            null,
                            propertyChanged: OnGroupNameChanged);

public string GroupName
{
    set { SetValue(GroupNameProperty, value); }
    get { return (string)GetValue(GroupNameProperty); }
}

static void OnGroupNameChanged(BindableObject bindable, object oldValue,
                               object newValue)
{
    RadioBehavior behavior = (RadioBehavior)bindable;
    string oldGroupName = (string)oldValue;
    string newGroupName = (string)newValue;

    if (String.IsNullOrEmpty(oldGroupName))
    {
        // Remove the Behavior from the default group.
        defaultGroup.Remove(behavior);
    }
    else
```

```
        {
            // Remove the RadioBehavior from the radioGroups collection.
            List<RadioBehavior> behaviors = radioGroups[oldGroupName];
            behaviors.Remove(behavior);

            // Get rid of the collection if it's empty.
            if (behaviors.Count == 0)
            {
                radioGroups.Remove(oldGroupName);
            }
        }

        if (String.IsNullOrEmpty(newGroupName))
        {
            // Add the new Behavior to the default group.
            defaultGroup.Add(behavior);
        }
        else
        {
            List<RadioBehavior> behaviors = null;

            if (radioGroups.ContainsKey(newGroupName))
            {
                // Get the named group.
                behaviors = radioGroups[newGroupName];
            }
            else
            {
                // If that group doesn't exist, create it.
                behaviors = new List<RadioBehavior>();
                radioGroups.Add(newGroupName, behaviors);
            }

            // Add the Behavior to the group.
            behaviors.Add(behavior);
        }
    }

    protected override void OnAttachedTo(View view)
    {
        base.OnAttachedTo(view);

        tapRecognizer = new TapGestureRecognizer ();
        tapRecognizer.Tapped += OnTapRecognizerTapped;
        view.GestureRecognizers.Add(tapRecognizer);
    }

    protected override void OnDetachingFrom(View view)
    {
        base.OnDetachingFrom(view);

        view.GestureRecognizers.Remove(tapRecognizer);
        tapRecognizer.Tapped -= OnTapRecognizerTapped;
    }
```

```
        void OnTapRecognizerTapped(object sender, EventArgs args)
        {
            IsChecked = true;
        }
    }
}
```

The `TapGestureRecognizer` handler at the bottom of the listing is very simple: When the visual object is tapped, the `RadioBehavior` object attached to that visual object sets its `IsChecked` property to `true`. If the `IsChecked` property was previously `false`, that change causes a call to the `OnIsCheckedChanged` method, which sets the `IsChecked` property of all the `RadioBehavior` objects in the same group to `false`.

Here's a simple demonstration of some interactive logic for selecting the size of a T-shirt. The three radio buttons are simple `Label` elements with text properties of "Small", "Medium", and "Large", and that's why the program is called **RadioLabels**. Each `Label` has a `RadioBehavior` in its `Behaviors` collection. Each `RadioBehavior` is given an `x:Name` for data bindings, but all the `RadioBehavior` objects have a default `GroupName` property setting of `null`. Each `Label` also has a `DataTrigger` in its `Triggers` collection that is bound to the corresponding `RadioBehavior` to turn the `TextColor` of the `Label` to green when the `IsChecked` property is `true`.

Notice that the `IsChecked` property for the middle `RadioBehavior` property is initialized to `true` to select that object when the program starts up:

```
<ContentPage xmlns="http://xamarin.com/schemas/2014/forms"
             xmlns:x="http://schemas.microsoft.com/winfx/2009/xaml"
             xmlns:toolkit=
                 "clr-namespace:Xamarin.FormsBook.Toolkit;assembly=Xamarin.FormsBook.Toolkit"
             xmlns:local="clr-namespace:RadioLabels"
             x:Class="RadioLabels.RadioLabelsPage"
             Padding="0, 50, 0, 0">

    <StackLayout>
        <Grid>
            <Grid.Resources>
                <ResourceDictionary>
                    <Style TargetType="Label">
                        <Setter Property="FontSize" Value="Medium" />
                        <Setter Property="HorizontalTextAlignment" Value="Center" />
                    </Style>
                </ResourceDictionary>
            </Grid.Resources>

            <Label Text="Small"
                   TextColor="Gray"
                   Grid.Column="0">
                <Label.Behaviors>
                    <toolkit:RadioBehavior x:Name="smallRadio" />
                </Label.Behaviors>
```

```
                    <Label.Triggers>
                        <DataTrigger TargetType="Label"
                                     Binding="{Binding Source={x:Reference smallRadio},
                                                       Path=IsChecked}"
                                     Value="True">
                            <Setter Property="TextColor" Value="Green" />
                        </DataTrigger>
                    </Label.Triggers>
                </Label>

                <Label Text="Medium"
                       TextColor="Gray"
                       Grid.Column="1">
                    <Label.Behaviors>
                        <toolkit:RadioBehavior x:Name="mediumRadio"
                                               IsChecked="True" />
                    </Label.Behaviors>

                    <Label.Triggers>
                        <DataTrigger TargetType="Label"
                                     Binding="{Binding Source={x:Reference mediumRadio},
                                                       Path=IsChecked}"
                                     Value="True">
                            <Setter Property="TextColor" Value="Green" />
                        </DataTrigger>
                    </Label.Triggers>
                </Label>

                <Label Text="Large"
                       TextColor="Gray"
                       Grid.Column="2">
                    <Label.Behaviors>
                        <toolkit:RadioBehavior x:Name="largeRadio" />
                    </Label.Behaviors>

                    <Label.Triggers>
                        <DataTrigger TargetType="Label"
                                     Binding="{Binding Source={x:Reference largeRadio},
                                                       Path=IsChecked}"
                                     Value="True">
                            <Setter Property="TextColor" Value="Green" />
                        </DataTrigger>
                    </Label.Triggers>
                </Label>
            </Grid>

            <Grid VerticalOptions="CenterAndExpand"
                  HorizontalOptions="Center">

                <Image Source="{local:ImageResource RadioLabels.Images.tee200.png}"
                       IsVisible="{Binding Source={x:Reference smallRadio},
                                           Path=IsChecked}" />

                <Image Source="{local:ImageResource RadioLabels.Images.tee250.png}"
```

```
                    IsVisible="{Binding Source={x:Reference mediumRadio},
                                        Path=IsChecked}" />

        <Image Source="{local:ImageResource RadioLabels.Images.tee300.png}"
               IsVisible="{Binding Source={x:Reference largeRadio},
                                   Path=IsChecked}" />
      </Grid>
    </StackLayout>
</ContentPage>
```

Another complication intrinsic to radio buttons involves making use of the selected item. In some cases you want each radio button within a group to be represented by a particular enumeration member. (In this example, such an enumeration might have three members, named Small, Medium, and Large.) Consolidating a group of radio buttons into an enumeration value obviously involves more code.

The **RadioLabels** program avoids those issues and simply binds the IsChecked properties of the three RadioBehavior objects to the IsVisible properties of three Image elements sharing a single-cell Grid at the bottom of the XAML file. These display a different size bitmap depending on the selection.

The relative sizes of these bitmaps is not so obvious in these screenshots because each platform displays the bitmaps in somewhat different sizes:

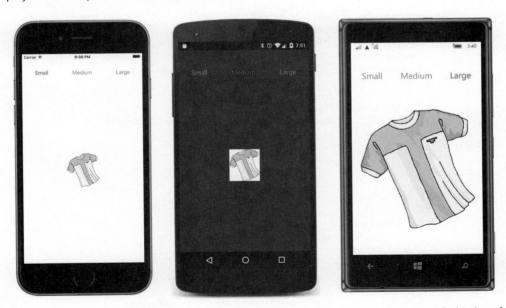

The DataTrigger attached to each Label changes the TextColor from its styled color of Gray to Green when that item is selected.

If you want to change multiple properties of each Label when that item is selected, you can add more Setter objects to the DataTrigger. But a better approach is to consolidate the Setter objects in a `Style`, and then to reference the `Style` in the `DataTrigger`.

This is demonstrated in the **RadioStyle** program. The `Resources` dictionary for the page defines a `Style` with the key of "baseStyle" that defines the appearance of an unchecked `Label`, and a `Style` with the key of "selectedStyle" that is based on "baseStyle" but defines the appearance of a checked `Label`. The `Resources` collection concludes with an implicit style for `Label` that is the same as "baseStyle":

```xml
<ContentPage xmlns="http://xamarin.com/schemas/2014/forms"
             xmlns:x="http://schemas.microsoft.com/winfx/2009/xaml"
             xmlns:local="clr-namespace:RadioStyle"
             xmlns:toolkit=
                "clr-namespace:Xamarin.FormsBook.Toolkit;assembly=Xamarin.FormsBook.Toolkit"
             x:Class="RadioStyle.RadioStylePage"
             Padding="0, 50, 0, 0">

    <ContentPage.Resources>
        <ResourceDictionary>
            <Style x:Key="baseStyle" TargetType="Label">
                <Setter Property="TextColor" Value="Gray" />
                <Setter Property="FontSize" Value="Small" />
                <Setter Property="HorizontalTextAlignment" Value="Center" />
                <Setter Property="VerticalTextAlignment" Value="Center" />
            </Style>

            <Style x:Key="selectedStyle" TargetType="Label"
                   BasedOn="{StaticResource baseStyle}">
                <Setter Property="TextColor" Value="Green" />
                <Setter Property="FontSize" Value="Medium" />
                <Setter Property="FontAttributes" Value="Bold,Italic" />
            </Style>

            <!-- Implicit style -->
            <Style TargetType="Label" BasedOn="{StaticResource baseStyle}" />
        </ResourceDictionary>
    </ContentPage.Resources>

    <StackLayout>
        <Grid>
            <Label Text="Small"
                   Grid.Column="0">
                <Label.Behaviors>
                    <toolkit:RadioBehavior x:Name="smallRadio" />
                </Label.Behaviors>

                <Label.Triggers>
                    <DataTrigger TargetType="Label"
                                 Binding="{Binding Source={x:Reference smallRadio},
                                                   Path=IsChecked}"
                                 Value="True">
                        <Setter Property="Style" Value="{StaticResource selectedStyle}" />
                    </DataTrigger>
                </Label.Triggers>
```

```
            </Label>

            <Label Text="Medium"
                   Grid.Column="1">
                <Label.Behaviors>
                    <toolkit:RadioBehavior x:Name="mediumRadio"
                                           IsChecked="True" />
                </Label.Behaviors>

                <Label.Triggers>
                    <DataTrigger TargetType="Label"
                                 Binding="{Binding Source={x:Reference mediumRadio},
                                                   Path=IsChecked}"
                                 Value="True">
                        <Setter Property="Style" Value="{StaticResource selectedStyle}" />
                    </DataTrigger>
                </Label.Triggers>
            </Label>

            <Label Text="Large"
                   Grid.Column="2">
                <Label.Behaviors>
                    <toolkit:RadioBehavior x:Name="largeRadio" />
                </Label.Behaviors>

                <Label.Triggers>
                    <DataTrigger TargetType="Label"
                                 Binding="{Binding Source={x:Reference largeRadio},
                                                   Path=IsChecked}"
                                 Value="True">
                        <Setter Property="Style" Value="{StaticResource selectedStyle}" />
                    </DataTrigger>
                </Label.Triggers>
            </Label>
        </Grid>

        <Grid VerticalOptions="CenterAndExpand"
              HorizontalOptions="Center">

            <Image Source="{local:ImageResource RadioStyle.Images.tee200.png}"
                   IsVisible="{Binding Source={x:Reference smallRadio},
                                       Path=IsChecked}" />

            <Image Source="{local:ImageResource RadioStyle.Images.tee250.png}"
                   IsVisible="{Binding Source={x:Reference mediumRadio},
                                       Path=IsChecked}" />

            <Image Source="{local:ImageResource RadioStyle.Images.tee300.png}"
                   IsVisible="{Binding Source={x:Reference largeRadio},
                                       Path=IsChecked}" />
        </Grid>
    </StackLayout>
</ContentPage>
```

Prior to this chapter, `Setter` objects were only found in `Style` definitions, so it might seem a little odd to see a `Setter` object in the `DataTrigger` that sets the `Style` property for the `Label`. But the screenshots demonstrate that it works fine. Now the selected item is in a larger font with bold and italic in addition to a different color:

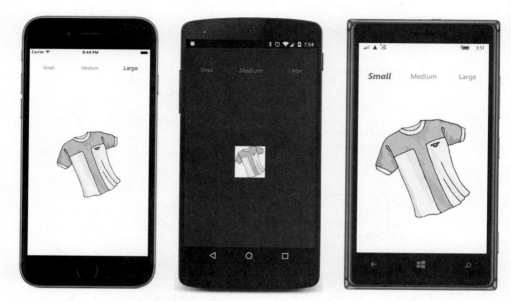

You might also have fun creating new types of visuals to identify the selected item in a group of radio buttons. The **RadioImages** program contains four bitmaps indicating different modes of transportation. The `Image` elements that reference these bitmaps are each a child of a `ContentView` to which is attached the `RadioBehavior` and a `DataTrigger` that changes the color of the `ContentView`:

```
<ContentPage xmlns="http://xamarin.com/schemas/2014/forms"
             xmlns:x="http://schemas.microsoft.com/winfx/2009/xaml"
             xmlns:local="clr-namespace:RadioImages"
             xmlns:toolkit=
                 "clr-namespace:Xamarin.FormsBook.Toolkit;assembly=Xamarin.FormsBook.Toolkit"
             x:Class="RadioImages.RadioImagesPage">

    <ContentPage.Resources>
        <ResourceDictionary>
            <Style TargetType="ContentView">
                <Setter Property="WidthRequest"    Value="75" />
                <Setter Property="HeightRequest"   Value="75" />
                <Setter Property="Padding"         Value="10" />
            </Style>

            <Color x:Key="selectedColor">#80C0FF</Color>
        </ResourceDictionary>
    </ContentPage.Resources>

    <StackLayout HorizontalOptions="Start"
```

```
                            VerticalOptions="Center"
                            Padding="20, 0"
                            Spacing="0">
        <ContentView>
            <ContentView.Behaviors>
                <toolkit:RadioBehavior x:Name="pedestrianRadio" />
            </ContentView.Behaviors>

            <ContentView.Triggers>
                <DataTrigger TargetType="ContentView"
                             Binding="{Binding Source={x:Reference pedestrianRadio},
                                               Path=IsChecked}"
                             Value="True">
                    <Setter Property="BackgroundColor" Value="{StaticResource selectedColor}" />
                </DataTrigger>
            </ContentView.Triggers>

            <Image Source="{local:ImageResource RadioImages.Images.pedestrian.png}" />
        </ContentView>

        <ContentView>
            <ContentView.Behaviors>
                <toolkit:RadioBehavior x:Name="carRadio" />
            </ContentView.Behaviors>

            <ContentView.Triggers>
                <DataTrigger TargetType="ContentView"
                             Binding="{Binding Source={x:Reference carRadio},
                                               Path=IsChecked}"
                             Value="True">
                    <Setter Property="BackgroundColor" Value="{StaticResource selectedColor}" />
                </DataTrigger>
            </ContentView.Triggers>

            <Image Source="{local:ImageResource RadioImages.Images.car.png}" />
        </ContentView>

        <ContentView>
            <ContentView.Behaviors>
                <toolkit:RadioBehavior x:Name="trainRadio" />
            </ContentView.Behaviors>

            <ContentView.Triggers>
                <DataTrigger TargetType="ContentView"
                             Binding="{Binding Source={x:Reference trainRadio},
                                               Path=IsChecked}"
                             Value="True">
                    <Setter Property="BackgroundColor" Value="{StaticResource selectedColor}" />
                </DataTrigger>
            </ContentView.Triggers>

            <Image Source="{local:ImageResource RadioImages.Images.train.png}" />
        </ContentView>
```

```
<ContentView>
    <ContentView.Behaviors>
        <toolkit:RadioBehavior x:Name="busRadio" />
    </ContentView.Behaviors>

    <ContentView.Triggers>
        <DataTrigger TargetType="ContentView"
                     Binding="{Binding Source={x:Reference busRadio},
                                       Path=IsChecked}"
                     Value="True">
            <Setter Property="BackgroundColor" Value="{StaticResource selectedColor}" />
        </DataTrigger>
    </ContentView.Triggers>

    <Image Source="{local:ImageResource RadioImages.Images.bus.png}" />
</ContentView>
    </StackLayout>
</ContentPage>
```

Sometimes, you'll want to set an initial selected item by setting the `IsChecked` property on one of the `RadioBehavior` objects to `true`, and sometimes not. This program leaves them all unchecked at program startup, but once the user selects one of the items, there is no way to unselect them all.

The crucial factor in this scheme is that the `ContentView` is given a significant `Padding` value so it seems to surround the `Image` element when that item is selected:

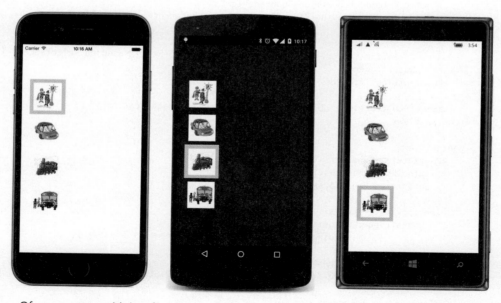

Of course, even with just four items, the repetitive markup looks a bit ominous. You could derive a class from `ContentView` to consolidate the `RadioBehavior` and `DataTrigger` interaction, but you'd need to define a property on this derived class to specify the particular bitmap associated with the button, and very likely another property or an event to indicate when that item has been selected. Generally, it's easier to keep the markup for each radio button to a minimum by defining common properties using a `Style` or other resources.

If you want to create more traditional radio button visuals, that's possible as well. The Unicode characters \u25CB and \u25C9 resemble the traditional unchecked and checked radio button circles and dots.

The **TraditionalRadios** program has six radio buttons, but they are divided into two groups of three buttons each, so the `GroupName` properties need to be set for at least one of the two groups. The program chooses to set the `GroupName` for *all* the radio buttons to either "platformGroup" or "languageGroup". Each `RadioBehavior` is attached to a horizontal `StackLayout` that contains one `Label` with a `DataTrigger` that switches between the "○" and "◉" strings, and a second `Label` that displays the text to the right of that symbol:

```
<ContentPage xmlns="http://xamarin.com/schemas/2014/forms"
             xmlns:x="http://schemas.microsoft.com/winfx/2009/xaml"
             xmlns:toolkit=
                 "clr-namespace:Xamarin.FormsBook.Toolkit;assembly=Xamarin.FormsBook.Toolkit"
             x:Class="TraditionalRadios.TraditionalRadiosPage">

    <ContentPage.Resources>
        <ResourceDictionary>
            <x:String x:Key="uncheckedRadio">&#x25CB;</x:String>
            <x:String x:Key="checkedRadio">&#x25C9;</x:String>
        </ResourceDictionary>
    </ContentPage.Resources>

    <Grid VerticalOptions="Center" Padding="5, 0">
        <!-- Left column -->
        <StackLayout Grid.Column="0" Spacing="24">

            <!-- Header -->
            <StackLayout HorizontalOptions="Start" Spacing="0">
                <Label Text="Choose Platform" />
                <BoxView Color="Accent" HeightRequest="1" />
            </StackLayout>

            <!-- Stack of radio buttons -->
            <StackLayout Spacing="12">

                <StackLayout Orientation="Horizontal">
                    <StackLayout.Behaviors>
                        <toolkit:RadioBehavior x:Name="iosRadio"
                                               GroupName="platformGroup" />
                    </StackLayout.Behaviors>

                    <Label Text="{StaticResource uncheckedRadio}">
                        <Label.Triggers>
                            <DataTrigger TargetType="Label"
                                         Binding="{Binding Source={x:Reference iosRadio},
                                                           Path=IsChecked}"
```

```
                                        Value="True">
                        <Setter Property="Text" Value="{StaticResource checkedRadio}" />
                    </DataTrigger>
                </Label.Triggers>
            </Label>
            <Label Text="iOS" />
        </StackLayout>

        <StackLayout Orientation="Horizontal">
            <StackLayout.Behaviors>
                <toolkit:RadioBehavior x:Name="androidRadio"
                                       GroupName="platformGroup" />
            </StackLayout.Behaviors>

            <Label Text="{StaticResource uncheckedRadio}">
                <Label.Triggers>
                    <DataTrigger TargetType="Label"
                                 Binding="{Binding Source={x:Reference androidRadio},
                                                   Path=IsChecked}"
                                 Value="True">
                        <Setter Property="Text" Value="{StaticResource checkedRadio}" />
                    </DataTrigger>
                </Label.Triggers>
            </Label>
            <Label Text="Android" />
        </StackLayout>

        <StackLayout Orientation="Horizontal">
            <StackLayout.Behaviors>
                <toolkit:RadioBehavior x:Name="winPhoneRadio"
                                       GroupName="platformGroup" />
            </StackLayout.Behaviors>

            <Label Text="{StaticResource uncheckedRadio}">
                <Label.Triggers>
                    <DataTrigger TargetType="Label"
                                 Binding="{Binding Source={x:Reference winPhoneRadio},
                                                   Path=IsChecked}"
                                 Value="True">
                        <Setter Property="Text" Value="{StaticResource checkedRadio}" />
                    </DataTrigger>
                </Label.Triggers>
            </Label>
            <Label Text="Windows Phone" />
        </StackLayout>
    </StackLayout>
</StackLayout>
<!-- Left column -->
<StackLayout Grid.Column="1" Spacing="24">

    <!-- Header -->
    <StackLayout HorizontalOptions="Start" Spacing="0">
        <Label Text="Choose Language" />
        <BoxView Color="Accent" HeightRequest="1" />
```

```xml
        </StackLayout>

        <!-- Stack of radio buttons -->
        <StackLayout Spacing="12">

            <StackLayout Orientation="Horizontal">
                <StackLayout.Behaviors>
                    <toolkit:RadioBehavior x:Name="objectiveCRadio"
                                           GroupName="languageGroup" />
                </StackLayout.Behaviors>

                <Label Text="{StaticResource uncheckedRadio}">
                    <Label.Triggers>
                        <DataTrigger TargetType="Label"
                                     Binding="{Binding Source={x:Reference objectiveCRadio},
                                                       Path=IsChecked}"
                                     Value="True">
                            <Setter Property="Text" Value="{StaticResource checkedRadio}" />
                        </DataTrigger>
                    </Label.Triggers>
                </Label>
                <Label Text="Objective-C" />
            </StackLayout>

            <StackLayout Orientation="Horizontal">
                <StackLayout.Behaviors>
                    <toolkit:RadioBehavior x:Name="javaRadio"
                                           GroupName="languageGroup" />
                </StackLayout.Behaviors>

                <Label Text="{StaticResource uncheckedRadio}">
                    <Label.Triggers>
                        <DataTrigger TargetType="Label"
                                     Binding="{Binding Source={x:Reference javaRadio},
                                                       Path=IsChecked}"
                                     Value="True">
                            <Setter Property="Text" Value="{StaticResource checkedRadio}" />
                        </DataTrigger>
                    </Label.Triggers>
                </Label>
                <Label Text="Java" />
            </StackLayout>

            <StackLayout Orientation="Horizontal">
                <StackLayout.Behaviors>
                    <toolkit:RadioBehavior x:Name="cSharpRadio"
                                           GroupName="languageGroup" />
                </StackLayout.Behaviors>

                <Label Text="{StaticResource uncheckedRadio}">
                    <Label.Triggers>
                        <DataTrigger TargetType="Label"
                                     Binding="{Binding Source={x:Reference cSharpRadio},
                                                       Path=IsChecked}"
```

```
                                        Value="True">
                        <Setter Property="Text" Value="{StaticResource checkedRadio}" />
                    </DataTrigger>
                </Label.Triggers>
            </Label>
            <Label Text="C&#x266F;" />
        </StackLayout>
    </StackLayout>
</StackLayout>
    </Grid>
</ContentPage>
```

In the context of modern user interfaces, these radio buttons look very quaint and old-fashioned, but at the same time quite authentic:

Fades and orientation

Already in this book, you've seen a couple of color-selection programs that let you interactively form a color by using three `Slider` elements. The final sample in this chapter is yet another color-selection program, but this one gives you options: It contains three radio buttons (actually, simple `Label` elements) labeled "RGB Hex", "RGB Float", and "HSL". These allow you to select a color in three different ways:

- As red, green, and blue hexadecimal values ranging from 00 to FF.

- As red, green, and blue floating-point values ranging from 0 to 1.

- As hue, saturation, and luminosity floating-point values ranging from 0 to 1.

It might at first seem complex to switch between these three options. You might imagine that code is required to redefine the range of the `Slider` elements and to reformat the text that is displayed to show the values. However, you can actually define the entire user interface in XAML.

The first trick is that the XAML file actually contains nine `Slider` elements with accompanying `Label` elements to display the values. Each set of three `Slider` and `Label` elements occupies a `StackLayout` with its `IsVisible` property bound to one of the `RadioBehavior` objects attached to the three radio buttons. The three `StackLayout` elements occupy a single-cell `Grid`, much like the pictures of the T-shirts in the **RadioLabels** and **RadioStyle** programs.

But let's make it more challenging: When you select one of the radio buttons, you probably expect one set of three `Slider` and `Label` elements to be replaced by another. Let's instead have the former set fade out and the new set fade in.

How can this be done?

Let's build the markup. If you just wanted to replace one `StackLayout` with another, you would bind the `IsVisible` property of the `StackLayout` to the `IsChecked` property of the corresponding `RadioBehavior`:

```
<StackLayout IsVisible="{Binding Source={x:Reference hexRadio},
                                 Path=IsChecked}">

    <!-- Trio of Slider and Label elements -->

</StackLayout>
```

To instead fade out the old and fade in the new, you would first need to initialize the `IsVisible` property of the `StackLayout` to `False` and attach a `DataTrigger` that references the `IsChecked` property of the `RadioBehavior`:

```
<StackLayout IsVisible="False">
    <StackLayout.Triggers>
        <DataTrigger TargetType="StackLayout"
                     Binding="{Binding Source={x:Reference hexRadio},
                                       Path=IsChecked}"
                     Value="True">

            ...

        </DataTrigger>
    </StackLayout.Triggers>

    <!-- Trio of Slider and Label elements -->

</StackLayout>
```

Then, instead of adding a `Setter` or two to the `DataTrigger`, you need to add an `Action` derivative to the `EnterActions` and `ExitActions` collections:

```
<StackLayout IsVisible="False">
```

```
        <StackLayout.Triggers>
            <DataTrigger TargetType="StackLayout"
                         Binding="{Binding Source={x:Reference hexRadio},
                                           Path=IsChecked}"
                         Value="True">
                <DataTrigger.EnterActions>
                    <toolkit:FadeEnableAction Enable="True" />
                </DataTrigger.EnterActions>

                <DataTrigger.ExitActions>
                    <toolkit:FadeEnableAction Enable="False" />
                </DataTrigger.ExitActions>
            </DataTrigger>
        </StackLayout.Triggers>

        <!-- Trio of Slider and Label elements -->

    </StackLayout>
```

As you'll recall, the `EnterActions` are invoked when the condition becomes true (which in this case is when the `IsChecked` property of the corresponding `RadioBehavior` is `True`), and the `ExitActions` are invoked when the condition becomes false.

This hypothetical `FadeEnableAction` class has a Boolean property named `Enable`. When the `Enable` property is `True`, we want `FadeEnableAction` to use the `FadeTo` extension method to animate the `Opacity` property from 0 (invisible) to 1 (fully visible). When `Enable` is `False`, we want `FadeTo` to animate the `Opacity` from 1 to 0. Keep in mind that as one `StackLayout` (and its children) fades out, another one simultaneously fades in.

However, the `StackLayout` won't be visible at all unless `FadeEnableAction` begins by setting `IsVisible` to `true` when `Enable` is set to `True`. Similarly, when `Enable` is set to `False`, `FadeEnableAction` must conclude by setting `IsVisible` back to `false`.

During the transition between two sets of `Slider` and `Label` elements, you probably don't want both sets responding to user input. For this reason, `FadeEnableAction` must also manipulate the `IsEnabled` property of the `StackLayout`, which enables or disables all its children. Since two animations will be going on simultaneously—as one `StackLayout` fades out and the other fades in—it makes sense to change the `IsEnabled` property halfway through the animation.

Here is a `FadeEnableAction` class in **Xamarin.FormsBook.Toolkit** that satisfies all these criteria:

```
namespace Xamarin.FormsBook.Toolkit
{
    public class FadeEnableAction : TriggerAction<VisualElement>
    {
        public FadeEnableAction()
        {
            Length = 500;
        }

        public bool Enable { set; get; }
```

```
public int Length { set; get; }

async protected override void Invoke(VisualElement view)
{
    if (Enable)
    {
        // Transition to visible and enabled.
        view.IsVisible = true;
        view.Opacity = 0;
        await view.FadeTo(0.5, (uint)Length / 2);
        view.IsEnabled = true;
        await view.FadeTo(1, (uint)Length / 2);
    }
    else
    {
        // Transition to invisible and disabled.
        view.Opacity = 1;
        await view.FadeTo(0.5, (uint)Length / 2);
        view.IsEnabled = false;
        await view.FadeTo(0, (uint)Length / 2);
        view.IsVisible = false;
    }
}
}
}
```

Let's give ourselves yet another challenge. In Chapter 17, "Mastering the Grid," in the section "Responding to orientation changes," you saw how to use the Grid to change your layout between portrait and landscape modes. Basically, all the layout on the page is divided roughly in half, and becomes two children of a Grid. In portrait mode, those two children go in two rows of the Grid, and in landscape mode, they go into two columns.

Can something like this be handled by a behavior? Accommodating a generalized response to orientation would be hard, but a simple approach might be to assume that in portrait mode, the second row should be autosized while the first row uses the rest of the available space. In landscape mode, the screen is simply divided equally in half. This is how the **GridRgbSliders** program in Chapter 17 worked, and also the **MandelbrotXF** program in Chapter 20.

The following GridOrientationBehavior can be attached only to a Grid. The Grid must *not* have any row definitions or column definitions defined—the behavior takes care of that—and it must contain only two children. The behavior monitors the SizeChanged event of the Grid. When that size changes, the Behavior sets the row and column definitions of the Grid and the row and column settings of the two children of the Grid:

```
namespace Xamarin.FormsBook.Toolkit
{
    // Assumes Grid with two children without any
    //      row or column definitions set.
    public class GridOrientationBehavior : Behavior<Grid>
    {
```

```csharp
protected override void OnAttachedTo(Grid grid)
{
    base.OnAttachedTo(grid);

    // Add row and column definitions.
    grid.RowDefinitions.Add(new RowDefinition());
    grid.RowDefinitions.Add(new RowDefinition());
    grid.ColumnDefinitions.Add(new ColumnDefinition());
    grid.ColumnDefinitions.Add(new ColumnDefinition());

    grid.SizeChanged += OnGridSizeChanged;
}
protected override void OnDetachingFrom(Grid grid)
{
    base.OnDetachingFrom(grid);
    grid.SizeChanged -= OnGridSizeChanged;
}

private void OnGridSizeChanged(object sender, EventArgs args)
{
    Grid grid = (Grid)sender;

    if (grid.Width <= 0 || grid.Height <= 0)
        return;

    // Portrait mode
    if (grid.Height > grid.Width)
    {
        // Set row definitions.
        grid.RowDefinitions[0].Height = new GridLength(1, GridUnitType.Star);
        grid.RowDefinitions[1].Height = GridLength.Auto;

        // Set column definitions.
        grid.ColumnDefinitions[0].Width = new GridLength(1, GridUnitType.Star);
        grid.ColumnDefinitions[1].Width = new GridLength(0);

        //Position first child.
        Grid.SetRow(grid.Children[0], 0);
        Grid.SetColumn(grid.Children[0], 0);

        // Position second child.
        Grid.SetRow(grid.Children[1], 1);
        Grid.SetColumn(grid.Children[1], 0);
    }
    // Landscape mode
    else
    {
        // Set row definitions.
        grid.RowDefinitions[0].Height = new GridLength(1, GridUnitType.Star);
        grid.RowDefinitions[1].Height = new GridLength(0);

        // Set column definitions.
        grid.ColumnDefinitions[0].Width = new GridLength(1, GridUnitType.Star);
        grid.ColumnDefinitions[1].Width = new GridLength(1, GridUnitType.Star);
```

```
            //Position first child.
            Grid.SetRow(grid.Children[0], 0);
            Grid.SetColumn(grid.Children[0], 0);

            // Position second child.
            Grid.SetRow(grid.Children[1], 0);
            Grid.SetColumn(grid.Children[1], 1);
        }
    }
}
}
```

Now let's put it all together in a program call **MultiColorSliders**. The backbone of the program is the `ColorViewModel` introduced in Chapter 18, "MVVM," and can be found in the **Xamarin.Forms-Book.Toolkit** library. An instance of `ColorViewModel` is set as the `BindingContext` of the `Grid` that contains all the content of the page. The three sets of `Slider` and `Label` elements all contain bindings to the `Red`, `Green`, `Blue`, `Hue`, `Saturation`, and `Luminosity` properties of that ViewModel. For the hexadecimal option, the `DoubleToIntConverter` introduced in Chapter 17 converts from the `double` values of the `Red`, `Green`, and `Blue` properties to integers with a multiplication by 255 for display by each `Label`.

Here is the XAML file. It's rather long because it contains three sets of three `Slider` and `Label` elements, but several comments help to guide you through the various sections:

```
<ContentPage xmlns="http://xamarin.com/schemas/2014/forms"
             xmlns:x="http://schemas.microsoft.com/winfx/2009/xaml"
             xmlns:toolkit=
                 "clr-namespace:Xamarin.FormsBook.Toolkit;assembly=Xamarin.FormsBook.Toolkit"
             x:Class="MultiColorSliders.MultiColorSlidersPage">
    <ContentPage.Padding>
        <OnPlatform x:TypeArguments="Thickness"
                    iOS="0, 20, 0, 0"  />
    </ContentPage.Padding>

    <ContentPage.Resources>
        <ResourceDictionary>
            <toolkit:ColorViewModel x:Key="colorViewModel" />

            <toolkit:DoubleToIntConverter x:Key="doubleToInt" />

            <Style x:Key="baseStyle" TargetType="Label">
                <Setter Property="HorizontalTextAlignment" Value="Center" />
            </Style>

            <Style x:Key="unselectedStyle" TargetType="Label"
                   BasedOn="{StaticResource baseStyle}">
                <Setter Property="TextColor" Value="Gray" />
            </Style>

            <Style x:Key="selectedStyle" TargetType="Label"
                   BasedOn="{StaticResource baseStyle}">
```

```xml
                    <Setter Property="TextColor" Value="Accent" />
                    <Setter Property="Scale" Value="1.5" />
                </Style>

                <!-- Implicit style for labels underneath sliders -->
                <Style TargetType="Label" BasedOn="{StaticResource baseStyle}" />
            </ResourceDictionary>
        </ContentPage.Resources>

        <Grid>
            <Grid.BindingContext>
                <toolkit:ColorViewModel Alpha="1" />
            </Grid.BindingContext>

            <!-- The GridOrientationBehavior takes care of the row and
                    column definitions, and the row and column settings
                    of the two Grid children. -->
            <Grid.Behaviors>
                <toolkit:GridOrientationBehavior />
            </Grid.Behaviors>

            <!-- First child of Grid is on top or at left. -->
            <BoxView Color="{Binding Color}" />

            <!-- Second child of Grid is on bottom or at right. -->
            <StackLayout Padding="10">

                <!-- Three-column Grid for radio labels -->
                <Grid>
                    <Label Text="RGB Hex" Grid.Column="0"
                           Style="{StaticResource unselectedStyle}">
                        <Label.Behaviors>
                            <toolkit:RadioBehavior x:Name="hexRadio"
                                                   IsChecked="true" />
                        </Label.Behaviors>

                        <Label.Triggers>
                            <DataTrigger TargetType="Label"
                                         Binding="{Binding Source={x:Reference hexRadio},
                                                           Path=IsChecked}"
                                         Value="True">
                                <Setter Property="Style" Value="{StaticResource selectedStyle}" />
                            </DataTrigger>
                        </Label.Triggers>
                    </Label>

                    <Label Text="RGB Float" Grid.Column="1"
                           Style="{StaticResource unselectedStyle}">
                        <Label.Behaviors>
                            <toolkit:RadioBehavior x:Name="floatRadio" />
                        </Label.Behaviors>

                        <Label.Triggers>
                            <DataTrigger TargetType="Label"
```

```
                                 Binding="{Binding Source={x:Reference floatRadio},
                                                   Path=IsChecked}"
                          Value="True">
                    <Setter Property="Style" Value="{StaticResource selectedStyle}" />
                </DataTrigger>
            </Label.Triggers>
        </Label>

        <Label Text="HSL" Grid.Column="2"
               Style="{StaticResource unselectedStyle}">
            <Label.Behaviors>
                <toolkit:RadioBehavior x:Name="hslRadio" />
            </Label.Behaviors>

            <Label.Triggers>
                <DataTrigger TargetType="Label"
                             Binding="{Binding Source={x:Reference hslRadio},
                                               Path=IsChecked}"
                             Value="True">
                    <Setter Property="Style" Value="{StaticResource selectedStyle}" />
                </DataTrigger>
            </Label.Triggers>
        </Label>
    </Grid>

    <!-- Single-cell Grid for three sets of sliders and labels -->
    <Grid>

        <!-- StackLayout for RGB Hex sliders and labels -->
        <StackLayout>
            <StackLayout.Triggers>
                <DataTrigger TargetType="StackLayout"
                             Binding="{Binding Source={x:Reference hexRadio},
                                               Path=IsChecked}"
                             Value="True">
                    <DataTrigger.EnterActions>
                        <toolkit:FadeEnableAction Enable="True" />
                    </DataTrigger.EnterActions>

                    <DataTrigger.ExitActions>
                        <toolkit:FadeEnableAction Enable="False" />
                    </DataTrigger.ExitActions>
                </DataTrigger>
            </StackLayout.Triggers>

            <Slider Value="{Binding Red, Mode=TwoWay}" />

            <Label Text="{Binding Red, StringFormat='Red = {0:X2}',
                                  Converter={StaticResource doubleToInt},
                                  ConverterParameter=255}" />

            <Slider Value="{Binding Green, Mode=TwoWay}" />

            <Label Text="{Binding Green, StringFormat='Green = {0:X2}',
```

```
                                        Converter={StaticResource doubleToInt},
                                        ConverterParameter=255}" />

        <Slider Value="{Binding Blue, Mode=TwoWay}" />

        <Label Text="{Binding Blue, StringFormat='Blue = {0:X2}',
                            Converter={StaticResource doubleToInt},
                            ConverterParameter=255}" />
    </StackLayout>

    <!-- StackLayout for RGB float sliders and labels -->
    <StackLayout IsVisible="False">
        <StackLayout.Triggers>
            <DataTrigger TargetType="StackLayout"
                         Binding="{Binding Source={x:Reference floatRadio},
                                           Path=IsChecked}"
                         Value="True">
                <DataTrigger.EnterActions>
                    <toolkit:FadeEnableAction Enable="True" />
                </DataTrigger.EnterActions>

                <DataTrigger.ExitActions>
                    <toolkit:FadeEnableAction Enable="False" />
                </DataTrigger.ExitActions>
            </DataTrigger>
        </StackLayout.Triggers>

        <Slider Value="{Binding Red, Mode=TwoWay}" />
        <Label Text="{Binding Red, StringFormat='Red = {0:F2}'}" />
        <Slider Value="{Binding Green, Mode=TwoWay}" />
        <Label Text="{Binding Green, StringFormat='Green = {0:F2}'}" />
        <Slider Value="{Binding Blue, Mode=TwoWay}" />
        <Label Text="{Binding Blue, StringFormat='Blue = {0:F2}'}" />
    </StackLayout>

    <!-- StackLayout for HSL sliders and labels -->
    <StackLayout IsVisible="False">
        <StackLayout.Triggers>
            <DataTrigger TargetType="StackLayout"
                         Binding="{Binding Source={x:Reference hslRadio},
                                           Path=IsChecked}"
                         Value="True">
                <DataTrigger.EnterActions>
                    <toolkit:FadeEnableAction Enable="True" />
                </DataTrigger.EnterActions>

                <DataTrigger.ExitActions>
                    <toolkit:FadeEnableAction Enable="False" />
                </DataTrigger.ExitActions>
            </DataTrigger>
        </StackLayout.Triggers>

        <!-- Trio of Slider and Label elements -->
```

```
                    <Slider Value="{Binding Hue, Mode=TwoWay}" />
                    <Label Text="{Binding Hue, StringFormat='Hue = {0:F2}'}" />
                    <Slider Value="{Binding Saturation, Mode=TwoWay}" />
                    <Label Text="{Binding Saturation, StringFormat='Saturation = {0:F2}'}" />
                    <Slider Value="{Binding Luminosity, Mode=TwoWay}" />
                    <Label Text="{Binding Luminosity, StringFormat='Luminosity = {0:F2}'}" />
                </StackLayout>
            </Grid>
        </StackLayout>
    </Grid>
</ContentPage>
```

You might recall that the `ColorViewModel` class introduced in Chapter 18 rounded the color components, both coming into and going out of the ViewModel. **MultiColorSliders** happens to be the program that revealed a problem with the unrounded values. Here's the problem:

For Android, Xamarin.Forms implements the `Slider` using a `SeekBar`, and the Android `SeekBar` only has integer `Progress` values ranging from 0 to the integer `Max` property. To convert to the floating-point `Value` property of the `Slider`, Xamarin.Forms sets the `Max` property of the `SeekBar` to 1000 and then performs a calculation based on the `Minimum` and `Maximum` properties of the `Slider`. This means that when `Minimum` and `Maximum` have their default values of 0 and 1, respectively, the `Value` property only increases in increments of 0.001, and is always representable with three decimal places.

However, the `ColorViewModel` uses the `Color` structure to convert between RGB and HSL representations, and in this particular program all the properties representing RGB and HSL values are bound to `Slider` elements. Even if the values of the `Red`, `Green`, and `Blue` properties set by the `Slider` elements are rounded to the nearest 0.001, the resultant `Hue`, `Saturation`, and `Luminosity` values will have more than three decimal places. If these values are not rounded by the ViewModel, that's an issue. When the `Value` properties of the `Slider` elements are set from these values, the `Slider` effectively rounds them to three decimal places and then triggers a `PropertyChanged` event that the `ColorViewModel` responds to by creating a new `Color`, which results in new `Red`, `Green`, and `Blue` properties, and an infinite loop ensues.

The solution—as you saw in Chapter 18—was to add rounding to the `ColorViewModel`. That avoids the infinite loop.

Here's the program running in portrait mode. Each platform shows a different option selected, but you'll have to run the program yourself to see the fading animation:

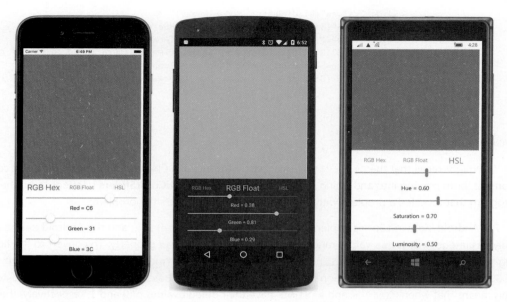

Turn this book (or your computer screen or perhaps your head) sideways, and you'll see how the program responds to landscape mode:

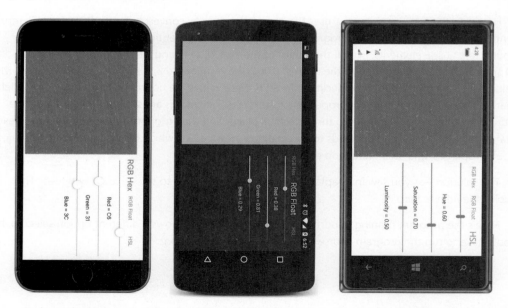

Perhaps the best part of the **MultiColorSliders** program is the code-behind file, which contains merely a call to `InitializeComponent`:

```
namespace MultiColorSliders
{
```

```
public partial class MultiColorSlidersPage : ContentPage
{
    public MultiColorSlidersPage()
    {
        InitializeComponent();
    }
}
}
```

There is, of course, a considerable amount of code support in **MultiColorSliders**, consisting of two `Behavior<T>` derivatives, an `Action<T>` derivative, an `IValueConverter` implementation, and an `INotifyPropertyChanged` implementation that functions as a ViewModel.

However, all this code is isolated in reusable components, which makes this program a model of MVVM design philosophy.

Chapter 24
Page navigation

Different types of computing environments tend to develop different metaphors for presenting information to the user. Sometimes a metaphor developed within one environment is so good that it influences other environments.

Such is the case with the page and navigation metaphor that evolved on the World Wide Web. Prior to that, desktop computer applications simply were not organized around the concept of navigable pages. But the web demonstrated the power and convenience of the page metaphor, and now mobile and desktop operating systems generally support a page-based architecture, and many applications have taken advantage of that.

A page architecture is particularly popular in mobile applications, and for that reason such an architecture is supported by Xamarin.Forms. A Xamarin.Forms application can contain multiple classes that derive from `ContentPage`, and the user can navigate between these pages. (In the next chapter, you'll see several alternatives to `ContentPage`. Those other page types can also participate in navigation.)

Generally, a page will include a `Button` (or perhaps a `Label` or an `Image` with a `TapGestureRecognizer`) that the user taps to navigate to another page. Sometimes, that second page will allow further navigation to other pages.

But there also must be a way for the user to return to the previous page, and here's where platform differences begin manifesting themselves: Android and Windows Phone devices incorporate a standard **Back** button (symbolized as a left-pointing arrow or triangle) at the bottom of the screen; iOS devices do not, and neither does Windows running on the desktop or a tablet.

Also, as you'll see, standard software **Back** buttons are provided at the top of some (but not all) navigable pages as part of the standard user interface by iOS and Android, and also by the Windows Runtime when running on desktop computers or tablets.

From the programmer's perspective, page navigation is implemented with the familiar concept of a stack. When one page navigates to another, the new page is pushed on the stack and becomes the active page. When the second page returns back to the first page, a page is popped from the stack, and the new topmost page then becomes active. The application has access to the navigation stack that Xamarin.Forms maintains for the application and supports methods to manipulate the stack by inserting pages or removing them.

An application that is structured around multiple pages always has one page that is special because it's the starting point of the application. This is often called the *main* page, or the *home* page, or the *start* page.

All the other pages in the application are intrinsically different from that start page, however, because they fall into two different categories: modal pages and modeless pages.

Modal pages and modeless pages

In user interface design, "modal" refers to something that requires user interaction before the application can continue. Computer applications on the desktop sometimes display modal windows or modal dialogs. When one of these modal objects is displayed, the user can't simply use the mouse to switch to the application's main window. The modal object demands more attention from the user before it goes away.

A window or dialog that is not modal is often called *modeless* when it's necessary to distinguish between the two types.

The Xamarin.Forms page-navigation system likewise implements modal and modeless pages by defining two different methods that a page can call to navigate to another page:

```
Task PushAsync(Page page)

Task PushModalAsync(Page page)
```

The page to navigate to is passed as the argument. As the name of the second method implies, it navigates to a modal page. The simple `PushAsync` method navigates to a modeless page, which in real-life programming is the more common page type.

Two other methods are defined to go back to the previous page:

```
Task<Page> PopAsync()

Task<Page> PopModalAsync()
```

In many cases an application does not need to call `PopAsync` directly if it relies on the back navigation provided by the phone or operating system.

The `Task` return value and the `Async` suffix on these `Push` and `Pop` method names indicate that they are asynchronous, but this does not mean that a navigated page runs in a different thread of execution! What the completion of the task indicates is discussed later in this chapter.

These four methods—as well as other navigation methods and properties—are defined in the `INavigation` interface. The object that implements this interface is internal to Xamarin.Forms, but `VisualElement` defines a read-only property named `Navigation` of type `INavigation`, and this gives you access to the navigation methods and properties.

This means that you can use these navigation methods from an instance of any class that derives from `VisualElement`. Generally, however, you'll use the `Navigation` property of the page object, so the code to navigate to a new page often looks like this:

```
await Navigation.PushAsync(new MyNewPage());
```

or this:

```
await Navigation.PushModalAsync(new MyNewModalPage());
```

The difference between modal and modeless pages mostly involves the user interface that the operating system provides on the page to return back to the previous page. This difference varies by platform. A greater difference in the user interface between modeless and modal pages exists on iOS and the Windows desktop or tablets; somewhat less difference is found on Android and the Windows phone platforms.

Generally, you'll use modal pages when your application needs some information from the user and you don't want the user to return to the previous page until that information is provided. To work across all platforms, a modal page must provide its own user-interface for navigating back to the previous page.

Let's begin by exploring the difference between modeless and modal pages in more detail. The **ModelessAndModal** program contains three pages with the class names `MainPage`, `ModalPage`, and `ModelessPage`. The pages themselves are rather simple, so to keep the file bulk to a minimum, these are code-only pages. In a real application, pages can be implemented with XAML or—at the other extreme—generated dynamically by code. (You'll see examples of both options later in this chapter.)

`MainPage` creates two `Button` elements, one that navigates to a modeless page and the other that navigates to a modal page. Notice the `Title` property set at the top of the constructor. This `Title` property has no effect in a single-page application but plays an important role in multipage applications:

```
public class MainPage : ContentPage
{
    public MainPage()
    {
        Title = "Main Page";

        Button gotoModelessButton = new Button
        {
            Text = "Go to Modeless Page",
            HorizontalOptions = LayoutOptions.Center,
            VerticalOptions = LayoutOptions.CenterAndExpand
        };
        gotoModelessButton.Clicked += async (sender, args) =>
        {
            await Navigation.PushAsync(new ModelessPage());
        };

        Button gotoModalButton = new Button
        {
            Text = "Go to Modal Page",
            HorizontalOptions = LayoutOptions.Center,
            VerticalOptions = LayoutOptions.CenterAndExpand
```

```
        };
        gotoModalButton.Clicked += async (sender, args) =>
        {
            await Navigation.PushModalAsync(new ModalPage());
        };

        Content = new StackLayout
        {
            Children =
            {
                gotoModelessButton,
                gotoModalButton
            }
        };
    }
}
```

The `Clicked` handler for the first `Button` calls `PushAsync` with a new instance of `ModelessPage`, and the second calls `PushModalAsync` with a new instance of `ModalPage`. The `Clicked` handlers are flagged with the `async` keyword and call the `Push` methods with `await`.

A program that makes calls to `PushAsync` or `PushModalAsync` must have slightly different startup code in the constructor of the `App` class. Rather than setting the `MainPage` property of `App` to an instance of the application's sole page, an instance of the application's startup page is generally passed to the `NavigationPage` constructor, and this is set to the `MainPage` property.

Here's how the constructor of your `App` class usually looks when the application incorporates page navigation:

```
public class App : Application
{
    public App()
    {
        MainPage = new NavigationPage(new MainPage());
    }
    ...
}
```

Most of the `App` classes in all the programs in this chapter contain similar code. As an alternative you can instantiate `NavigationPage` by using its parameterless constructor and then call the `PushAsync` method of the `NavigationPage` to go to the home page.

The use of `NavigationPage` results in a visible difference in the page. The `Title` property is displayed at the top of `MainPage`, and it is accompanied by the application icon on the Android screen:

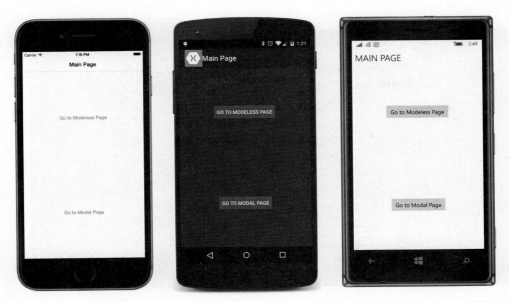

Another big difference is that you no longer need to set `Padding` on the iOS page to avoid overwriting the status bar at the top of the screen.

The title is also displayed at the top of the Windows 10 program running in tablet mode:

A rather larger title is displayed on the Windows 8.1 and Windows Phone 8.1 platforms:

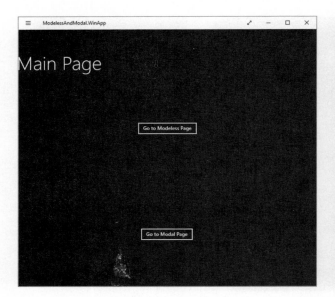

Clicking the **Go to Modeless Page** button causes the following code to execute:

```
await Navigation.PushAsync(new ModelessPage());
```

This code instantiates a new `ModelessPage` and navigates to that page.

The `ModelessPage` class defines a `Title` property with the text "Modeless Page" and a `Button` element labeled **Back to Main** with a `Clicked` handler that calls `PopAsync`:

```
public class ModelessPage : ContentPage
{
    public ModelessPage()
    {
        Title = "Modeless Page";

        Button goBackButton = new Button
        {
            Text = "Back to Main",
            HorizontalOptions = LayoutOptions.Center,
            VerticalOptions = LayoutOptions.Center
        };
        goBackButton.Clicked += async (sender, args) =>
        {
            await Navigation.PopAsync();
        };

        Content = goBackButton;
    }
}
```

You don't actually need the **Back to Main** button on the iOS and Android pages because a left-pointing arrow at the top of the page performs that same function. The Windows Phone doesn't need that `Button` either because it has a **Back** button at the bottom of the screen, as does the Android device:

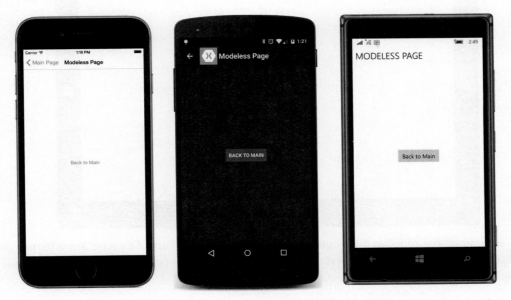

That top area on the iOS and Android pages is called the *navigation bar*. In that navigation bar, both the iOS and Android pages show the `Title` property of the current page, and the iOS page also displays the `Title` property of the previous page in another color.

A program running in tablet mode under Windows 10 contains a **Back** button in the lower-left corner, directly to the right of the Windows logo:

In contrast, the Windows 8.1 program displays a button in the form of a circled arrow to navigate back to the previous page. The Windows Phone 8.1 screen doesn't need that button because it has a **Back** button on the bottom of the screen:

In summary, you don't need to include your own **Back to Main** button (or its equivalent) on a modeless page. Either the navigation interface or the device itself provides a **Back** button.

Let's go back to `MainPage`. When you click the **Go to Modal Page** button on the main page, the

`Clicked` handler executes the following code:

```
await Navigation.PushModalAsync(new ModalPage(), true);
```

The `ModalPage` class is nearly identical to the `ModelessPage` except for the different `Title` setting and the call to `PopModalAsync` in the `Clicked` handler:

```
public class ModalPage : ContentPage
{
    public ModalPage()
    {
        Title = "Modal Page";

        Button goBackButton = new Button
        {
            Text = "Back to Main",
            HorizontalOptions = LayoutOptions.Center,
            VerticalOptions = LayoutOptions.Center
        };
        goBackButton.Clicked += async (sender, args) =>
        {
            await Navigation.PopModalAsync();
        };

        Content = goBackButton;
    }
}
```

Despite the `Title` property setting in the class, none of the three platforms displays the `Title` or any other page-navigation interface:

These screens now look like typical single-page applications. Although it's not quite obvious, you'll once again need to be careful to avoid overwriting the status bar on the iOS page.

You don't need the **Back to Main** button on the Android and Windows Phone pages because you can use the **Back** button on the bottom of the phone, but you definitely need it on the iOS page: That **Back to Main** button on the iPhone is the only path back to `MainPage`.

The UWP application running under Windows 10 in tablet mode doesn't display a title, but the **Back** button in the lower-left corner still works to navigate back to `MainPage`.

However, the Windows 8.1 page needs the **Back to Main** button, while the Windows Phone 8.1 page does not because it has a **Back** button on the bottom of the phone:

Nothing internal to the page definition distinguishes a modeless page and a modal page. It depends on how the page is invoked—whether through `PushAsync` or `PushModalAsync`. However, a particular page must know how it was invoked so that it can call either `PopAsync` or `PopModalAsync` to navigate back.

Throughout the time this program is running, there is only one instance of `MainPage`. It continues to remain in existence when `ModelessPage` and `ModalPage` are active. This is always the case in a multipage application. A page that calls `PushAsync` or `PushModalAsync` does not cease to exist when the next page is active.

However, in this program, each time you navigate to `ModelessPage` or `ModalPage`, a new instance of that page is created. When that page returns back to `MainPage`, there are no further references to that instance of `ModelessPage` or `ModalPage`, and that object becomes eligible for garbage collection. This is *not* the only way to manage navigable pages, and you'll see alternatives later in this chapter, but in general it is best to instantiate a page right before navigating to it.

A page always occupies the full screen. Sometimes it's desirable for a modal page to occupy only part of the screen, and for the previous page to be visible (but disabled) underneath that popup. You can't do this with Xamarin.Forms pages. If you want something like that, look at the **SimpleOverlay** program in Chapter 14, "Absolute layout."

Animated page transitions

All four of the methods you've seen are also available with an overload that has an additional argument of type `bool`:

```
Task PushAsync(Page page, bool animated)

Task PushModalAsync(Page page, bool animated)

Task<Page> PopAsync(bool animated)

Task<Page> PopModalAsync(bool animated)
```

Setting this argument to `true` enables a page-transition animation if such an animation is supported by the underlying platform. However, the simpler `Push` and `Pop` methods enable this animation by default, so you'll only need these four overloads if you want to *suppress* the animation, in which case you set the Boolean argument to `false`.

Toward the end of this chapter, you'll see some code that saves and restores the entire page navigation stack when a multipage application is terminated. To restore the navigation stack, these pages must be created and navigated to during program startup. In this case, the animations should be suppressed, and these overloads are handy for that.

You'll also want to suppress the animation if you provide one of your own page-entrance animations, such as demonstrated in Chapter 22, "Animation."

In general, however, you'll want to use the simpler forms of the `Push` and `Pop` methods.

Visual and functional variations

`NavigationPage` defines several properties—and several attached bindable properties—that have the power to change the appearance of the navigation bar and even to eliminate it altogether.

You can set the `BarBackgroundColor` and `BarTextColor` properties when you instantiate the `NavigationPage` in the `App` class. Try this in the **ModalAndModeless** program:

```
public class App : Application
{
    public App()
    {
        MainPage = new NavigationPage(new MainPage())
        {
            BarBackgroundColor = Color.Blue,
            BarTextColor = Color.Pink
        };
    }
}
```

The various platforms use these colors in different ways. The iOS navigation bar is affected by both colors, but on the Android screen, only the background color appears. All these screenshots show `ModelessPage`, but the top area of `MainPage` is colored in the same way:

The Windows 10 application in tablet mode looks quite similar to the Windows 10 Mobile screen:

The other two Windows Runtime platforms also make use of the `BarTextColor`, and the Windows 8.1 page uses `BarBackgroundColor` as well:

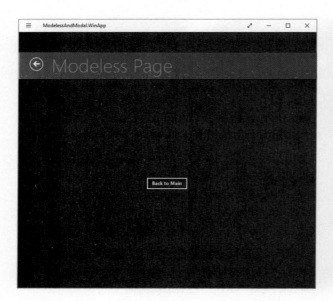 

The `NavigationPage` class also defines a `Tint` property, but that property is deprecated and should be considered obsolete.

`NavigationPage` also defines four attached bindable properties that affect the particular `Page` class on which they are set. For example, suppose you don't want the **Back** button to appear on a modeless page. Here's how you set the `NavigationPage.HasBackButton` attached bindable property in code in the `ModelessPage` constructor:

```
public class ModelessPage : ContentPage
{
    public ModelessPage()
    {
        Title = "Modeless Page";

        NavigationPage.SetHasBackButton(this, false);
        …
    }
}
```

In XAML, you would do it like so:

```
<ContentPage xmlns="http://xamarin.com/schemas/2014/forms"
             xmlns:x="http://schemas.microsoft.com/winfx/2009/xaml"
             x:Class="ModelessAndModal.ModelessPage"
             Title="Modeless Page"
             NavigationPage.HasBackButton="False">
    …
</ContentPage>
```

And sure enough, when you navigate to `ModelessPage`, the **Back** button in the navigation bar is gone:

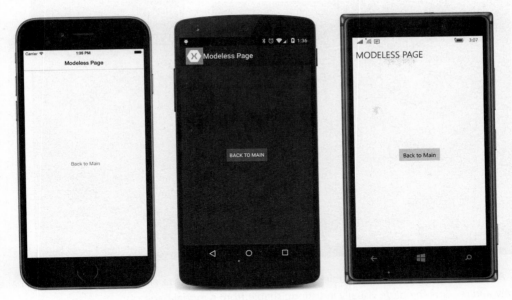

However, a functional **Back** button continues to exist on Windows 10:

The **Back** button is also gone from the Windows 8.1 screen:

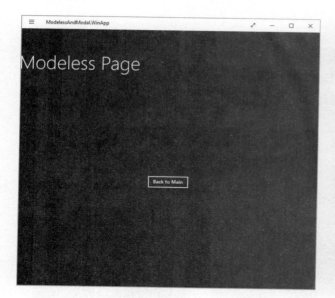

A more extreme attached bindable property of `NavigationPage` eliminates the navigation bar entirely and renders the page visually indistinguishable from a modal page:

```
public class ModelessPage : ContentPage
{
    public ModelessPage()
    {
        Title = "Modeless Page";

        NavigationPage.SetHasNavigationBar(this, false);
        ...
    }
}
```

Two more attached bindable properties affect the text and the icon in the navigation bar. As you've seen, all the platforms display the `Title` property at the top of the main page and a modeless page. However, on a modeless page, the iOS screen also displays the `Title` property of the *previous* page—the page from which you navigated to the modeless page. The `NavigationPage.BackButtonTitle` attached bindable property can change that text on the iOS page. You need to set it on the page from which you navigate to the modeless page. In the **ModelessAndModal** program, you can set the property on `MainPage` like so:

```
public class MainPage : ContentPage
{
    public MainPage()
    {
        Title = "Main Page";

        NavigationPage.SetBackButtonTitle(this, "go back");
        ...
```

```
        }
    }
```

This does not affect the title on `MainPage` itself, but only the text that accompanies the **Back** button on the navigation bar on `ModelessPage`, and then only on iOS. You'll see a screenshot shortly.

The second attached bindable property is `NavigationPage.TitleIcon`, which replaces the application icon on the Android navigation bar and replaces the title with an icon on the iOS page. The property is of type `FileImageSource`, which refers to a bitmap file in the platform project. In use, it's similar to the `Icon` property of `MenuItem` and `ToolbarItem`.

To let you experiment with this, some appropriate icons have been added to the iOS and Android projects in the **ModelessAndModal** solution. These icons come from the Android **Action Bar Icon Pack** discussed in Chapter 13, "Bitmaps." (In Chapter 13, look for the section "Platform-specific bitmaps," and then "Toolbars and their icons," and finally "Icons for Android.")

For iOS, the icons are from the **ActionBarIcons/holo_light/08_camera_flash_on** directory. These icons display a lightning bolt. The images in the **mdpi**, **xdpi**, and **xxdpi** directories are 32, 64, and 96 pixels square, respectively. Within the **Resources** folder of the iOS project, the 32-pixel square bitmap has the original name of ic_action_flash_on.png, and the two larger files were renamed with @2 and @3 suffixes, respectively.

For Android, the icons are from the **ActionBarIcons/holo_dark/08_camera_flash_on** directory; these are white foregrounds on transparent backgrounds. The files in the **mdpi**, **hdpi**, **xdpi**, and **xxdpi** directories were added to the Android project.

You can display these icons on the modeless page by adding the following code to the `Modeless-Page` constructor:

```
public class ModelessPage : ContentPage
{
    public ModelessPage()
    {
        Title = "Modeless Page";

        if (Device.OS == TargetPlatform.iOS || Device.OS == TargetPlatform.Android)
            NavigationPage.SetTitleIcon(this, "ic_action_flash_on.png");

        ...
    }
}
```

Here is `ModelessPage` with both the alternate **Back** button text of "go back" set on `MainPage` and the icons set on `ModelessPage`:

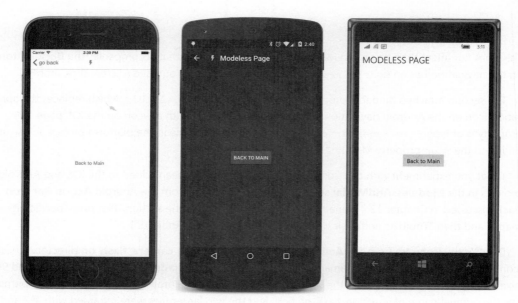

As you can see, the icon replaces the normal `Title` text on the iOS page.

Neither the `NavigationPage.BackButtonTitle` nor the `NavigationPage.TitleIcon` attached bindable property affect any of the Windows or Windows Phone platforms.

Programmers familiar with Android architecture are sometimes curious how Xamarin.Forms page navigation integrates with the aspect of Android application architecture known as the *activity*. A Xamarin.Forms application running on an Android device comprises only one activity, and the page navigation is built on top of that. A `ContentPage` is a Xamarin.Forms object; it is not an Android activity, or a fragment of an activity.

Exploring the mechanics

As you've seen, the `Push` and `Pop` methods return `Task` objects. Generally you'll use `await` when calling those methods. Here's the call to `PushAsync` in the `MainPage` class of **ModelessAndModal**:

```
await Navigation.PushAsync(new ModelessPage());
```

Suppose you have some code following this statement. When does that code get executed? We know it executes when the `PushAsync` task completes, but when is that? Is it after the user has tapped a **Back** button on `ModelessPage` to return back to `MainPage`?

No, that is not the case. The `PushAsync` task completes rather quickly. The completion of this task doesn't indicate that the process of page navigation has completed, but it *does* indicate when it is safe to obtain the current status of the page-navigation stack.

Following a `PushAsync` or `PushModalAsync` call, the following events occur. However, the precise order in which these events occur is platform dependent:

- The page calling `PushAsync` or `PushModalAsync` generally gets a call to its `OnDisappearing` override.

- The page being navigated to gets a call to its `OnAppearing` override.

- The `PushAsync` or `PushModalAsync` task completes.

To repeat: The order in which these events occur is dependent on the platform and also on whether navigation is to a modeless page or a modal page.

Following a `PopAsync` or `PopModalAsync` call, the following events occur, again in an order that is platform dependent:

- The page calling `PopAsync` or `PopModalAsync` gets a call to its `OnDisappearing` override.

- The page being returned to generally gets a call to its `OnAppearing` override.

- The `PopAsync` or `PopModalAsync` task returns.

You'll notice two uses of the word "generally" in those descriptions. This word refers to an exception to these rules when an Android device navigates to a modal page. The page that calls `PushModalAsync` does not get a call to its `OnDisappearing` override, and that same page does not get a call to its `OnAppearing` override when the modal page calls `PopModalAsync`.

Also, calls to the `OnDisappearing` and `OnAppearing` overrides do not necessarily indicate page navigation. On iOS, the `OnDisappearing` override is called on the active page when the program terminates. On the Windows Phone Silverlight platform (which is no longer supported by Xamarin.Forms), a page received `OnDisappearing` calls when the user invokes a `Picker`, `DatePicker`, or `TimePicker` on the page. For these reasons, the `OnDisappearing` and `OnAppearing` overrides cannot be treated as guaranteed indications of page navigation, although there are times when they must be used for that purpose.

The `INavigation` interface that defines these `Push` and `Pop` calls also defines two properties that provide access to the actual navigation stack:

- `NavigationStack`, which contains the modeless pages

- `ModalStack`, which contains the modal pages

The `set` accessors of these two properties are not public, and the properties themselves are of type `IReadOnlyList<Page>`, so you cannot directly modify them. (As you'll see, methods are available to modify the page stack in a more structured manner.) Although these properties are not implemented with `Stack<T>` classes, they function like a stack anyway. The item in the `IReadOnlyList` with an index of zero is the oldest page, and the last item is the most recent page.

The existence of these two collections for modeless and modal pages suggests that modeless and modal page navigation cannot be intermixed, and this is true: A modeless page can navigate to a modal page, but a modal page *cannot* navigate to a modeless page.

Some experimentation reveals that the `Navigation` property of different page instances retains different collections of the navigation stack. (In particular, after navigation to a modal page, the `NavigationStack` associated with that modal page is empty.) The most foolproof approach is to work with the instances of these collections maintained by the `Navigation` property of the `NavigationPage` instance set to the `MainPage` property of the `App` class.

With each call to `PushAsync` or `PopAsync`, the contents of the `NavigationStack` change—either a new page is added to the collection or a page is removed from the collection. Similarly, with each call to `PushModalAsync` or `PopModalAsync`, the contents of the `ModalStack` change.

Experimentation reveals that it is not safe to use the contents of the `NavigationStack` or `ModalStack` during calls to the `OnAppearing` or `OnDisappearing` overrides while the page navigation is in progress. The only approach that works for all the platforms is to wait until the `PushAsync`, `PushModalAsync`, `PopAsync`, or `PopModalAsync` task completes. That's your indication that these stack collections are stable and accurate.

The `NavigationPage` class also defines a get-only property named `CurrentPage`. This page instance is the same as the last item in the `NavigationStack` collections available from `NavigationPage`. However, when a modal page is active, `CurrentPage` continues to indicate the last *modeless* page that was active before navigation to a modal page.

Let's explore the details and mechanics of page navigation with a program called **SinglePageNavigation**, so called because the program contains only one page class, named `SinglePageNavigationPage`. The program navigates between various instances of this one class.

One of the purposes of the **SinglePageNavigation** program is to prepare you for writing an application that saves the navigation stack when the application is suspended or terminated, and to restore the stack when the application is restarted. Doing this depends on your application's ability to extract trustworthy information from the `NavigationStack` and `ModalStack` properties.

Here's the XAML file for the `SinglePageNavigationPage` class:

```
<ContentPage xmlns="http://xamarin.com/schemas/2014/forms"
             xmlns:x="http://schemas.microsoft.com/winfx/2009/xaml"
             x:Class="SinglePageNavigation.SinglePageNavigationPage"
             x:Name="page">

    <StackLayout>
        <StackLayout.Resources>
            <ResourceDictionary>
                <Style x:Key="baseStyle" TargetType="View">
                    <Setter Property="VerticalOptions" Value="CenterAndExpand" />
                </Style>

                <Style TargetType="Button" BasedOn="{StaticResource baseStyle}">
```

```
                <Setter Property="HorizontalOptions" Value="Center" />
            </Style>

            <Style TargetType="Label" BasedOn="{StaticResource baseStyle}">
                <Setter Property="HorizontalTextAlignment" Value="Center" />
            </Style>
        </ResourceDictionary>
    </StackLayout.Resources>

    <Label Text="{Binding Source={x:Reference page}, Path=Title}" />

    <Button x:Name="modelessGoToButton"
            Text="Go to Modeless Page"
            Clicked="OnGoToModelessClicked" />

    <Button x:Name="modelessBackButton"
            Text="Back from Modeless Page"
            Clicked="OnGoBackModelessClicked" />

    <Button x:Name="modalGoToButton"
            Text="Go to Modal Page"
            Clicked="OnGoToModalClicked" />

    <Button x:Name="modalBackButton"
            Text="Back from Modal Page"
            Clicked="OnGoBackModalClicked" />

    <Label x:Name="currentPageLabel"
           Text=" " />

    <Label x:Name="modelessStackLabel"
           Text=" " />

    <Label x:Name="modalStackLabel"
           Text=" " />
    </StackLayout>
</ContentPage>
```

The XAML file instantiates four `Button` and four `Label` elements. The first `Label` has a data binding to display the page's `Title` property so that the title is visible regardless of the platform and whether the page is modal or modeless. The four buttons are for navigating to and from modeless or modal pages. The remaining three labels display other information set from code.

Here's roughly the first half of the code-behind file. Notice the constructor code that sets the `Title` property to the text "Page #," where the hash sign indicates a number starting at zero for the first instantiated page. Each time this class is instantiated, that number is increased:

```
public partial class SinglePageNavigationPage : ContentPage
{
    static int count = 0;
    static bool firstPageAppeared = false;
    static readonly string separator = new string('-', 20);
```

```csharp
public SinglePageNavigationPage()
{
    InitializeComponent();

    // Set Title to zero-based instance of this class.
    Title = "Page " + count++;
}

async void OnGoToModelessClicked(object sender, EventArgs args)
{
    SinglePageNavigationPage newPage = new SinglePageNavigationPage();
    Debug.WriteLine(separator);
    Debug.WriteLine("Calling PushAsync from {0} to {1}", this, newPage);
    await Navigation.PushAsync(newPage);
    Debug.WriteLine("PushAsync completed");

    // Display the page stack information on this page.
    newPage.DisplayInfo();
}

async void OnGoToModalClicked(object sender, EventArgs args)
{
    SinglePageNavigationPage newPage = new SinglePageNavigationPage();
    Debug.WriteLine(separator);
    Debug.WriteLine("Calling PushModalAsync from {0} to {1}", this, newPage);
    await Navigation.PushModalAsync(newPage);
    Debug.WriteLine("PushModalAsync completed");

    // Display the page stack information on this page.
    newPage.DisplayInfo();
}

async void OnGoBackModelessClicked(object sender, EventArgs args)
{
    Debug.WriteLine(separator);
    Debug.WriteLine("Calling PopAsync from {0}", this);
    Page page = await Navigation.PopAsync();
    Debug.WriteLine("PopAsync completed and returned {0}", page);

    // Display the page stack information on the page being returned to.
    NavigationPage navPage = (NavigationPage)App.Current.MainPage;
    ((SinglePageNavigationPage)navPage.CurrentPage).DisplayInfo();
}

async void OnGoBackModalClicked(object sender, EventArgs args)
{
    Debug.WriteLine(separator);
    Debug.WriteLine("Calling PopModalAsync from {0}", this);
    Page page = await Navigation.PopModalAsync();
    Debug.WriteLine("PopModalAsync completed and returned {0}", page);

    // Display the page stack information on the page being returned to.
    NavigationPage navPage = (NavigationPage)App.Current.MainPage;
    ((SinglePageNavigationPage)navPage.CurrentPage).DisplayInfo();
```

```
    }

    protected override void OnAppearing()
    {
        base.OnAppearing();
        Debug.WriteLine("{0} OnAppearing", Title);

        if (!firstPageAppeared)
        {
            DisplayInfo();
            firstPageAppeared = true;
        }
    }

    protected override void OnDisappearing()
    {
        base.OnDisappearing();
        Debug.WriteLine("{0} OnDisappearing", Title);
    }

    // Identify each instance by its Title.
    public override string ToString()
    {
        return Title;
    }
    …
}
```

Each of the `Clicked` handlers for the four buttons displays some information using `Debug.Write-Line`. When you run the program under the debugger in Visual Studio or Xamarin Studio, this text appears in the **Output** window.

The code-behind file also overrides the `OnAppearing` and `OnDisappearing` methods. These are important, for they generally tell you when the page is being navigated to (`OnAppearing`) or navigated from (`OnDisappearing`).

But, as mentioned earlier, Android is a little different: An Android page that calls `PushModalAsync` does not get a call to its `OnDisappearing` method, and when the modal page returns to that page, the original page does not get a corresponding call to its `OnAppearing` method. It's as if the page stays in the background while the modal page is displayed, and that's very much the case: If you go back to **ModelessAndModal** and set the `BackgroundColor` of the modal page to `Color.From-Rgba(0, 0, 0, 0.5)`, you can see the previous page behind the modal page. But this is only the case for Android.

All the `Clicked` handlers in `SinglePageNavigationPage` make a call to a method named `Dis-playInfo`. This method is shown below and displays information about the `NavigationStack` and `ModalStack`—including the pages in the stacks—and the `CurrentPage` property maintained by the `NavigationPage` object.

However, these `Clicked` handlers do *not* call the `DisplayInfo` method in the current instance of the page because the Clicked handlers are effecting a transition to another page. The Clicked handlers must call the DisplayInfo method in the page instance to which they are navigating.

The calls to DisplayInfo in the Clicked handlers that call PushAsync and PushModalAsync are easy because each Clicked handler already has the new page instance being navigated to. The calls to DisplayInfo in the Clicked handlers that call PopAsync and PopModalAsync are a little more difficult because they need to obtain the page being returned to. This is not the Page instance returned from the PopAsync and PopModalAsync tasks. That Page instance turns out to be the same page that calls these methods.

Instead, the Clicked handlers that call PopAsync and PopModalAsync obtain the page being returned to from the CurrentPage property of NavigationPage:

```
NavigationPage navPage = (NavigationPage)App.Current.MainPage;
((SinglePageNavigationPage)navPage.CurrentPage).DisplayInfo();
```

What's crucial is that the code to obtain this new CurrentPage property and the calls to DisplayInfo all occur *after* the asynchronous Push or Pop task has completed. That's when this information becomes valid.

However, the DisplayInfo method must also be called when the program first starts up. As you'll see, DisplayInfo makes use of the MainPage property of the App class to obtain the NavigationPage instantiated in the App constructor. However, that MainPage property has not yet been set in the App constructor when the SinglePageNavigationPage constructor executes, so the page constructor cannot call DisplayInfo. Instead, the OnAppearing override makes that call, but only for the first page instance:

```
if (!firstPageAppeared)
{
    DisplayInfo();
    firstPageAppeared = true;
}
```

Besides displaying the value of CurrentPage and the NavigationStack and ModalStack collections, the DisplayInfo method also enables and disables the four Button elements on the page so that it's always legal to press an enabled Button.

Here's DisplayInfo and the two methods it uses to display the stack collections:

```
public partial class SinglePageNavigationPage : ContentPage
{
    ...
    public void DisplayInfo()
    {
        // Get the NavigationPage and display its CurrentPage property.
        NavigationPage navPage = (NavigationPage)App.Current.MainPage;

        currentPageLabel.Text = String.Format("NavigationPage.CurrentPage = {0}",
                                              navPage.CurrentPage);
```

```
        // Get the navigation stacks from the NavigationPage.
        IReadOnlyList<Page> navStack = navPage.Navigation.NavigationStack;
        IReadOnlyList<Page> modStack = navPage.Navigation.ModalStack;

        // Display the counts and contents of these stacks.
        int modelessCount = navStack.Count;
        int modalCount = modStack.Count;

        modelessStackLabel.Text = String.Format("NavigationStack has {0} page{1}{2}",
                                            modelessCount,
                                            modelessCount == 1 ? "" : "s",
                                            ShowStack(navStack));

        modalStackLabel.Text = String.Format("ModalStack has {0} page{1}{2}",
                                            modalCount,
                                            modalCount == 1 ? "" : "s",
                                            ShowStack(modStack));

        // Enable and disable buttons based on the counts.
        bool noModals = modalCount == 0 || (modalCount == 1 && modStack[0] is NavigationPage);

        modelessGoToButton.IsEnabled = noModals;
        modelessBackButton.IsEnabled = modelessCount > 1 && noModals;
        modalBackButton.IsEnabled = !noModals;
    }

    string ShowStack(IReadOnlyList<Page> pageStack)
    {
        if (pageStack.Count == 0)
            return "";

        StringBuilder builder = new StringBuilder();

        foreach (Page page in pageStack)
        {
            builder.Append(builder.Length == 0 ? " (" : ", ");
            builder.Append(StripNamespace(page));
        }

        builder.Append(")");
        return builder.ToString();
    }

    string StripNamespace(Page page)
    {
        string pageString = page.ToString();

        if (pageString.Contains("."))
            pageString = pageString.Substring(pageString.LastIndexOf('.') + 1);

        return pageString;
    }
}
```

Some of the logic involving the enabling and disabling of the `Button` elements will become apparent when you see some of the screens that the program displays. You can always comment out that enabling and disabling code to explore what happens when you press an invalid `Button`.

The general rules are these:

- A modeless page can navigate to another modeless page or a modal page.

- A modal page can navigate only to another modal page.

When you first run the program, you'll see the following. The XAML includes a display of the `Title` property at the top, so it's visible on all the pages:

The three `Label` elements on the bottom of the page display the `CurrentPage` property of the `NavigationPage` object and the `NavigationStack` and `ModalStack`, both obtained from the `Navigation` property of the `NavigationPage`.

On all three platforms, the `NavigationStack` contains one item, which is the home page. The contents of the `ModalStack`, however, vary by platform. On the Android and Windows Runtime platforms, the modal stack contains one item (the `NavigationPage` object), but the modal stack is empty on iOS.

This is why the `DisplayInfo` method sets the `noModals` Boolean variable to `true` if either the modal stack has a count of zero or if it contains one item but that item is `NavigationPage`:

```
bool noModals = modalCount == 0 || (modalCount == 1 && modStack[0] is NavigationPage);
```

Notice that the `CurrentPage` property and the item in `NavigationStack` are not instances of `NavigationPage`, but instead are instances of `SinglePageNavigationPage`, which derives from

`ContentPage`. It is `SinglePageNavigationPage` that defines its `ToString` method to display the page title.

Now press the **Go to Modeless Page** button five times and here's what you'll see. The screens are consistent aside from the modal stack on the iOS screen:

As soon as you press the **Go to Modeless Page** button once, the **Back from Modeless Page** button is enabled. The logic is this:

```
modelessBackButton.IsEnabled = modelessCount > 1 && noModals;
```

In plain English, the **Back from Modeless Page** button should be enabled if there are at least two items in the modeless stack (the original page and the current page) and if the current page is not a modal page.

If you press that **Back from ModelessPage** button at this point, you'll see the `NavigationStack` shrink in size until you get back to **Page 0**. Throughout, the `CurrentPage` property continues to indicate the last item in `NavigationStack`.

If you then press **Go to Modeless Page** again, you will see more items added to the `Navigation-Stack` with ever-increasing page numbers because new `SinglePageNavigationPage` objects are being instantiated.

Instead, try pressing the **Go to Modal Page** button:

Now `ModalStack` contains that new page, but `CurrentPage` still refers to the last modeless page. The iOS modal stack is still missing that initial `NavigationPage` object present in the other platforms.

If you then press **Back from Modal Page**, the modal stack is properly restored to its initial state.

Multipage applications usually try to save the navigation stack when they are suspended or terminated, and then restore that stack when they start up again. Toward the end of this chapter, you'll see code that uses `NavigationStack` and `ModalStack` to do that job.

Enforcing modality

In general, your applications will probably use modeless pages except for special circumstances when the application needs to obtain crucial information from the user. The application can then display a modal page that the user cannot dismiss until this crucial information has been entered.

One little problem, however, is that an Android or Windows Phone user can always return to the previous page by pressing the standard **Back** button on the device. To enforce modality—to make sure that the user enters the desired information before leaving the page—the application must disable that button.

This technique is demonstrated in the **ModalEnforcement** program. The home page consists solely of a `Button`:

```
<ContentPage xmlns="http://xamarin.com/schemas/2014/forms"
             xmlns:x="http://schemas.microsoft.com/winfx/2009/xaml"
             x:Class="ModalEnforcement.ModalEnforcementHomePage"
             Title="Main Page">
```

```
<Button Text="Go to Modal Page"
        HorizontalOptions="Center"
        VerticalOptions="Center"
        Clicked="OnGoToButtonClicked" />
```

```
</ContentPage>
```

The code-behind file handles the `Clicked` event of the button by navigating to a modal page:

```
public partial class ModalEnforcementHomePage : ContentPage
{
    public ModalEnforcementHomePage()
    {
        InitializeComponent();
    }

    async void OnGoToButtonClicked(object sender, EventArgs args)
    {
        await Navigation.PushModalAsync(new ModalEnforcementModalPage());
    }
}
```

The XAML file for the `ModalEnforcementModalPage` contains two `Entry` elements, a `Picker` element, and a `Button` labeled **Done**. The markup is more extensive than you might anticipate because it contains a `MultiTrigger` to set the `IsEnabled` property of the button to `True` only if something has been typed into the two `Entry` elements and something has also been entered into the `Picker`. This `MultiTrigger` requires three hidden `Switch` elements, using a technique discussed in Chapter 23, "Triggers and behaviors":

```
<ContentPage xmlns="http://xamarin.com/schemas/2014/forms"
             xmlns:x="http://schemas.microsoft.com/winfx/2009/xaml"
             x:Class="ModalEnforcement.ModalEnforcementModalPage"
             Title="Modal Page">

    <StackLayout Padding="20, 0">
        <Entry x:Name="entry1"
               Text=""
               Placeholder="Enter Name"
               VerticalOptions="CenterAndExpand" />

        <!-- Invisible Switch to help with MultiTrigger logic -->
        <Switch x:Name="switch1" IsVisible="False">
            <Switch.Triggers>
                <DataTrigger TargetType="Switch"
                             Binding="{Binding Source={x:Reference entry1}, Path=Text.Length}"
                             Value="0">
                    <Setter Property="IsToggled" Value="True" />
                </DataTrigger>
            </Switch.Triggers>
        </Switch>

        <Entry x:Name="entry2"
               Text=""
```

```
            Placeholder="Enter Email Address"
            VerticalOptions="CenterAndExpand" />

<!-- Invisible Switch to help with MultiTrigger logic -->
<Switch x:Name="switch2" IsVisible="False">
    <Switch.Triggers>
        <DataTrigger TargetType="Switch"
                     Binding="{Binding Source={x:Reference entry2}, Path=Text.Length}"
                     Value="0">
            <Setter Property="IsToggled" Value="True" />
        </DataTrigger>
    </Switch.Triggers>
</Switch>


<Picker x:Name="picker"
        Title="Favorite Programming Language"
        VerticalOptions="CenterAndExpand">
    <Picker.Items>
        <x:String>C#</x:String>
        <x:String>F#</x:String>
        <x:String>Objective C</x:String>
        <x:String>Swift</x:String>
        <x:String>Java</x:String>
    </Picker.Items>
</Picker>

<!-- Invisible Switch to help with MultiTrigger logic -->
<Switch x:Name="switch3" IsVisible="False">
    <Switch.Triggers>
        <DataTrigger TargetType="Switch"
                     Binding="{Binding Source={x:Reference picker}, Path=SelectedIndex}"
                     Value="-1">
            <Setter Property="IsToggled" Value="True" />
        </DataTrigger>
    </Switch.Triggers>
</Switch>


<Button x:Name="doneButton"
        Text="Done"
        IsEnabled="False"
        HorizontalOptions="Center"
        VerticalOptions="CenterAndExpand"
        Clicked="OnDoneButtonClicked">
    <Button.Triggers>
        <MultiTrigger TargetType="Button">
            <MultiTrigger.Conditions>
                <BindingCondition Binding="{Binding Source={x:Reference switch1},
                                                    Path=IsToggled}"
                                  Value="False" />

                <BindingCondition Binding="{Binding Source={x:Reference switch2},
                                                    Path=IsToggled}"
                                  Value="False" />
```

```
                    <BindingCondition Binding="{Binding Source={x:Reference switch3},
                                                        Path=IsToggled}"
                                      Value="False" />
                </MultiTrigger.Conditions>

                <Setter Property="IsEnabled" Value="True" />
            </MultiTrigger>
        </Button.Triggers>
    </Button>
    </StackLayout>
</ContentPage>
```

In a real-life program, there would probably also be a check that the email address is valid. The simple logic in the XAML file simply checks for the presence of at least one character.

Here's the modal page as it first appears, when nothing has yet been entered. Notice that the **Done** button is disabled:

Normally the user can still press the standard **Back** button at the bottom left of the Android and Windows Phone screens to return back to the main page. To inhibit the normal behavior of the **Back** button, the modal page must override the virtual `OnBackButtonPressed` method. You can supply your own **Back** button processing in this override and return `true`. To entirely disable the **Back** button, simply return `true` without doing anything else. To allow the default **Back** button processing to occur, call the base class implementation. Here's how the code-behind file of `ModalEnforcementModalPage` does it:

```
public partial class ModalEnforcementModalPage : ContentPage
{
    public ModalEnforcementModalPage()
```

```
    {
        InitializeComponent();
    }

    protected override bool OnBackButtonPressed()
    {
        if (doneButton.IsEnabled)
        {
            return base.OnBackButtonPressed();
        }
        return true;
    }

    async void OnDoneButtonClicked(object sender, EventArgs args)
    {
        await Navigation.PopModalAsync();
    }
}
```

Only if the **Done** button in the XAML file is enabled will the `OnBackButtonPressed` override call the base class implementation of the method and return the value that is returned from that implementation. This causes the modal page to return to the page that invoked it. If the **Done** button is disabled, then the override returns `true` indicating that it is finished performing all the handling that it desires for the **Back** button.

The `Clicked` handler for the **Done** button simply calls `PopModalAsync`, as usual.

The `Page` class also defines a `SendBackButtonPressed` that causes the `OnBackButtonPressed` method to be called. It should be possible to implement the `Clicked` handler for the **Done** button by calling this method:

```
void OnDoneButtonClicked(object sender, EventArgs args)
{
    SendBackButtonPressed();
}
```

Although this works on iOS and Android, it currently does not work on the Windows Runtime platforms.

In real-world programming, it's more likely that you'll be using a ViewModel to accumulate the information that the user enters into the modal page. In that case, the ViewModel itself can contain a property that indicates whether all the information entered is valid.

The **MvvmEnforcement** program uses this technique, and includes a little ViewModel—appropriately named `LittleViewModel`:

```
namespace MvvmEnforcement
{
    public class LittleViewModel : INotifyPropertyChanged
    {
        string name, email;
        string[] languages = {  "C#", "F#", "Objective C", "Swift", "Java" };
```

```
int languageIndex = -1;
bool isValid;

public event PropertyChangedEventHandler PropertyChanged;

public string Name
{
    set
    {
        if (name != value)
        {
            name = value;
            OnPropertyChanged("Name");
            TestIfValid();
        }
    }
    get { return name; }
}

public string Email
{
    set
    {
        if (email != value)
        {
            email = value;
            OnPropertyChanged("Email");
            TestIfValid();
        }
    }
    get { return email; }
}

public IEnumerable<string> Languages
{
    get { return languages; }
}

public int LanguageIndex
{
    set
    {
        if (languageIndex != value)
        {
            languageIndex = value;
            OnPropertyChanged("LanguageIndex");

            if (languageIndex >= 0 && languageIndex < languages.Length)
            {
                Language = languages[languageIndex];
                OnPropertyChanged("Language");
            }
            TestIfValid();
        }
```

```
        }
        get { return languageIndex; }
    }

    public string Language { private set; get; }

    public bool IsValid
    {
        private set
        {
            if (isValid != value)
            {
                isValid = value;
                OnPropertyChanged("IsValid");
            }
        }
        get { return isValid; }
    }

    void TestIfValid()
    {
        IsValid = !String.IsNullOrWhiteSpace(Name) &&
                  !String.IsNullOrWhiteSpace(Email) &&
                  !String.IsNullOrWhiteSpace(Language);
    }

    void OnPropertyChanged(string propertyName)
    {
        PropertyChangedEventHandler handler = PropertyChanged;

        if (handler != null)
            handler(this, new PropertyChangedEventArgs(propertyName));
    }
  }
}
```

The `Name` and `Email` properties are of type `string` for the purpose of binding with the `Text` properties of an `Entry` element. The `LanguageIndex` property is intended to be bound to the `SelectedIndex` property of the `Picker`. But the `set` accessor for `LanguageIndex` uses that value to set the `Language` property of type `string` from an array of strings in the `Languages` collection.

Whenever the `Name`, `Email`, or `LanguageIndex` property changes, the `TestIfValid` method is called to set the `IsValid` property. This property can be bound to the `IsEnabled` property of the `Button`.

The home page in **MvvmEnforcement** is the same as the one in **ModalEnforcement,** but of course the XAML file for the modal page is quite a bit simpler and implements all the data bindings:

```
<ContentPage xmlns="http://xamarin.com/schemas/2014/forms"
             xmlns:x="http://schemas.microsoft.com/winfx/2009/xaml"
             x:Class="MvvmEnforcement.MvvmEnforcementModalPage"
             Title="Modal Page">
```

```
    <StackLayout Padding="20, 0">
        <Entry Text="{Binding Name}"
               Placeholder="Enter Name"
               VerticalOptions="CenterAndExpand" />

        <Entry Text="{Binding Email}"
               Placeholder="Enter Email Address"
               VerticalOptions="CenterAndExpand" />

        <Picker x:Name="picker"
                Title="Favorite Programming Language"
                SelectedIndex="{Binding LanguageIndex}"
                VerticalOptions="CenterAndExpand" />

        <Button Text="Done"
                IsEnabled="{Binding IsValid}"
                HorizontalOptions="Center"
                VerticalOptions="CenterAndExpand"
                Clicked="OnDoneButtonClicked" />
    </StackLayout>
</ContentPage>
```

The markup contains four bindings to properties in the ViewModel.

The modal page's code-behind file is responsible for instantiating `LittleViewModel` and setting the object to the `BindingContext` property of the page, which it does in the constructor. The constructor also accesses the `Languages` collection of the ViewModel to set the `Items` property of the `Picker`. (Unfortunately the `Items` property is not backed by a bindable property and hence is not bindable.)

The remainder of the file is fairly similar to the modal page in **ModalEnforcement** except that the `OnBackButtonPressed` override accesses the `IsValid` property of `LittleViewModel` to determine whether to call the base class implementation or return `true`:

```
public partial class MvvmEnforcementModalPage : ContentPage
{
    public MvvmEnforcementModalPage()
    {
        InitializeComponent();

        LittleViewModel viewModel = new LittleViewModel();
        BindingContext = viewModel;

        // Populate Picker Items list.
        foreach (string language in viewModel.Languages)
        {
            picker.Items.Add(language);
        }
    }

    protected override bool OnBackButtonPressed()
    {
        LittleViewModel viewModel = (LittleViewModel)BindingContext;
```

```
            return viewModel.IsValid ? base.OnBackButtonPressed() : true;
    }

    async void OnDoneButtonClicked(object sender, EventArgs args)
    {
        await Navigation.PopModalAsync();
    }
}
```

Navigation variations

As you've experimented with the **ModalEnforcement** and **MvvmEnforcement** programs, you might have felt disconcerted by the failure of the modal pages to retain any information. We've all encountered programs and websites that navigate to a page used to enter information, but when you leave that page and then later return, all the information you entered is gone! Such pages can be very annoying.

Even in simple demonstration samples like **ModalEnforcement** and **MvvmEnforcement**, it's possible to fix that problem very easily by creating only a single instance of the modal page—perhaps when the program starts up—and then using that single instance throughout.

Despite the apparent ease of this solution, it is not a good generalized approach to the problem of retaining page information. This technique should probably be avoided except for the simplest of cases. Keeping a lot of pages active could result in memory issues, and you must be careful to avoid having the same page instance in the navigation stack more than once.

Nevertheless, here's how you can modify the ModalEnforcementHomePage code-behind file for this technique:

```
public partial class ModalEnforcementHomePage : ContentPage
{
    ModalEnforcementModalPage modalPage = new ModalEnforcementModalPage();

    public ModalEnforcementHomePage()
    {
        InitializeComponent();
    }

    async void OnGoToButtonClicked(object sender, EventArgs args)
    {
        await Navigation.PushModalAsync(modalPage);
    }
}
```

The ModalEnforcementHomePage saves an instance of ModalEnforcementModalPage as a field and then always passes that single instance to PushModalAsync.

In less-simple applications, this technique can easily go wrong: Sometimes a particular type of page in an application can be navigated to from several different pages, and that might result in two sepa-rate, inconsistent instances of `ModalPage`.

This technique collapses entirely if you need to save the state of the program when it terminates and restore it when it executes again. You can't save and restore the page instances themselves. It's generally the data associated with the page that must be saved.

In real-life programming, ViewModels often form the backbone of page types in a multipage appli-cation, and the best way that an application can retain page data is through the ViewModel rather than the page.

A much better way to maintain page state when a modal page is invoked several times in succes-sion can be demonstrated using **MvvmEnforcement**. First, add a property to the `App` page for `LittleViewModel` and instantiate that class in the `App` constructor:

```
namespace MvvmEnforcement
{
    public class App : Application
    {
        public App()
        {
            ModalPageViewModel = new LittleViewModel();

            MainPage = new NavigationPage(new MvvmEnforcementHomePage());
        }

        public LittleViewModel ModalPageViewModel { private set; get; }
        ...

    }
}
```

Because the `LittleViewModel` is instantiated just once, it maintains the information for the dura-tion of the application. Each new instance of `MvvmEnforcementModalPage` can then simply access this property and set the `ViewModel` object to its `BindingContext`:

```
public partial class MvvmEnforcementModalPage : ContentPage
{
    public MvvmEnforcementModalPage()
    {
        InitializeComponent();

        LittleViewModel viewModel = ((App)Application.Current).ModalPageViewModel;
        BindingContext = viewModel;

        // Populate Picker Items list.
        foreach (string language in viewModel.Languages)
        {
            picker.Items.Add(language);
        }
    }
    ...
}
```

Of course, once the program terminates, the information is lost, but the `App` class can also save that information in the `Properties` property of `Application`—a technique first demonstrated in the **PersistentKeypad** program toward the end of Chapter 6, "Button clicks"—and then retrieve it when the application starts up again.

The problems of retaining data—and passing data between pages—will occupy much of the focus of the later sections of this chapter.

Making a navigation menu

If your application consists of a variety of different but architecturally identical pages, all of which are navigable from the home page, you might be interested in constructing what is sometimes called a *navigation menu*. This is a menu in which each entry is a particular page type.

The **ViewGalleryType** program is intended to demonstrate all the `View` classes in Xamarin.Forms. It contains a home page and one page for every instantiable class in Xamarin.Forms that derives from `View`—but not `Layout`—with the exception of `Map` and `OpenGLView`. That's 18 classes and 18 `ContentPage` derivatives, plus the home page. (The reason for the **Type** suffix on the project name will become apparent shortly.)

These 18 page classes are all stored in a folder named **ViewPages** in the Portable Class Library. Here is one example: SliderPage.xaml. It's just a `Slider` with a `Label` bound to the `Value` property:

```
<ContentPage xmlns="http://xamarin.com/schemas/2014/forms"
             xmlns:x="http://schemas.microsoft.com/winfx/2009/xaml"
             x:Class="ViewGalleryType.SliderPage"
             Title="Slider">

    <StackLayout Padding="10, 0">
        <Slider x:Name="slider"
                VerticalOptions="CenterAndExpand" />

        <Label Text="{Binding Source={x:Reference slider},
                              Path=Value,
                              StringFormat='The Slider value is {0}'}"
               VerticalOptions="CenterAndExpand"
               HorizontalAlignment="Center" />
    </StackLayout>
</ContentPage>
```

The other 17 are similar. Some of the pages have a little code in the code-behind file, but most of them simply have a call to `InitializeComponent`.

In addition, the **ViewGalleryType** project has a folder named **Images** that contains 18 bitmaps with the name of each `View` derivative stretched out to nearly fill the bitmap's surface. These bitmaps were generated by a Windows Presentation Foundation program and are flagged as **EmbeddedResource** in the project. The project also contains an `ImageResourceExtension` class described in Chapter 13, in the section "Embedded resources," to reference the bitmaps from the XAML file.

The home page is named `ViewGalleryTypePage`. It assembles 18 `ImageCell` elements in six different sections of a `Table`:

```xml
<ContentPage xmlns="http://xamarin.com/schemas/2014/forms"
             xmlns:x="http://schemas.microsoft.com/winfx/2009/xaml"
             xmlns:local="clr-namespace:ViewGalleryType;assembly=ViewGalleryType"
             x:Class="ViewGalleryType.ViewGalleryTypePage"
             Title="View Gallery">
    <TableView Intent="Menu">
        <TableRoot>
            <TableSection Title="Presentation Views">
                <ImageCell ImageSource="{local:ImageResource ViewGalleryType.Images.Label.png}"
                           Text="Display text"
                           Command="{Binding NavigateCommand}"
                           CommandParameter="{x:Type local:LabelPage}" />

                <ImageCell ImageSource="{local:ImageResource ViewGalleryType.Images.Image.png}"
                           Text="Display a bitmap"
                           Command="{Binding NavigateCommand}"
                           CommandParameter="{x:Type local:ImagePage}" />

                <ImageCell ImageSource=
                               "{local:ImageResource ViewGalleryType.Images.BoxView.png}"
                           Text="Display a block"
                           Command="{Binding NavigateCommand}"
                           CommandParameter="{x:Type local:BoxViewPage}" />

                <ImageCell ImageSource=
                               "{local:ImageResource ViewGalleryType.Images.WebView.png}"
                           Text="Display a web site"
                           Command="{Binding NavigateCommand}"
                           CommandParameter="{x:Type local:WebViewPage}" />
            </TableSection>

            <TableSection Title="Command Views">
                <ImageCell ImageSource="{local:ImageResource ViewGalleryType.Images.Button.png}"
                           Text="Initiate a command"
                           Command="{Binding NavigateCommand}"
                           CommandParameter="{x:Type local:ButtonPage}" />

                <ImageCell ImageSource=
                               "{local:ImageResource ViewGalleryType.Images.SearchBar.png}"
                           Text="Initiate a text search"
                           Command="{Binding NavigateCommand}"
                           CommandParameter="{x:Type local:SearchBarPage}" />
            </TableSection>

            <TableSection Title="Data-Type Views">
                <ImageCell ImageSource="{local:ImageResource ViewGalleryType.Images.Slider.png}"
                           Text="Range of doubles"
                           Command="{Binding NavigateCommand}"
                           CommandParameter="{x:Type local:SliderPage}" />

                <ImageCell ImageSource=
```

```
                                "{local:ImageResource ViewGalleryType.Images.Stepper.png}"
                                Text="Discrete doubles"
                                Command="{Binding NavigateCommand}"
                                CommandParameter="{x:Type local:StepperPage}" />

        <ImageCell ImageSource="{local:ImageResource ViewGalleryType.Images.Switch.png}"
                                Text="Select true or false"
                                Command="{Binding NavigateCommand}"
                                CommandParameter="{x:Type local:SwitchPage}" />

        <ImageCell ImageSource=
                                "{local:ImageResource ViewGalleryType.Images.DatePicker.png}"
                                Text="Select a date"
                                Command="{Binding NavigateCommand}"
                                CommandParameter="{x:Type local:DatePickerPage}" />

        <ImageCell ImageSource=
                                "{local:ImageResource ViewGalleryType.Images.TimePicker.png}"
                                Text="Select a time"
                                Command="{Binding NavigateCommand}"
                                CommandParameter="{x:Type local:TimePickerPage}" />
    </TableSection>

    <TableSection Title="Text-Editing Views">
        <ImageCell ImageSource="{local:ImageResource ViewGalleryType.Images.Entry.png}"
                                Text="Edit a single line"
                                Command="{Binding NavigateCommand}"
                                CommandParameter="{x:Type local:EntryPage}" />

        <ImageCell ImageSource="{local:ImageResource ViewGalleryType.Images.Editor.png}"
                                Text="Edit a paragraph"
                                Command="{Binding NavigateCommand}"
                                CommandParameter="{x:Type local:EditorPage}" />
    </TableSection>

    <TableSection Title="Activity Indicator Views">
        <ImageCell ImageSource=
                                "{local:ImageResource ViewGalleryType.Images.ActivityIndicator.png}"
                                Text="Show activity"
                                Command="{Binding NavigateCommand}"
                                CommandParameter="{x:Type local:ActivityIndicatorPage}" />

        <ImageCell ImageSource=
                                "{local:ImageResource ViewGalleryType.Images.ProgressBar.png}"
                                Text="Show progress"
                                Command="{Binding NavigateCommand}"
                                CommandParameter="{x:Type local:ProgressBarPage}" />
    </TableSection>

    <TableSection Title="Collection Views">
        <ImageCell ImageSource="{local:ImageResource ViewGalleryType.Images.Picker.png}"
                                Text="Pick item from list"
                                Command="{Binding NavigateCommand}"
                                CommandParameter="{x:Type local:PickerPage}" />
```

```
        <ImageCell ImageSource=
                   "{local:ImageResource ViewGalleryType.Images.ListView.png}"
                   Text="Show a collection"
                   Command="{Binding NavigateCommand}"
                   CommandParameter="{x:Type local:ListViewPage}" />

        <ImageCell ImageSource=
                   "{local:ImageResource ViewGalleryType.Images.TableView.png}"
                   Text="Show form or menu"
                   Command="{Binding NavigateCommand}"
                   CommandParameter="{x:Type local:TableViewPage}" />
      </TableSection>
    </TableRoot>
  </TableView>
</ContentPage>
```

Each `ImageCell` has a reference to a bitmap indicating the view's name and a `Text` property that briefly describes the view. The `Command` property of `ImageCell` is bound to an `ICommand` object that is implemented in the code-behind file, and the `CommandParameter` is an `x:Type` markup extension that references one of the page classes. As you'll recall, the `x:Type` markup extension is the XAML equivalent of the C# `typeof` operator and results in each `CommandParameter` being of type `Type`.

Here's what the home page looks like on the three platforms:

The code-behind file defines the `NavigateCommand` property that each `ImageCell` references in a binding. The `Execute` method is implemented as a lambda function: It passes the `Type` argument (set from the `CommandParameter` in the XAML file) to `Activator.CreateInstance` to instantiate the page and then navigates to that page:

```
public partial class ViewGalleryTypePage : ContentPage
{
    public ViewGalleryTypePage()
    {
        InitializeComponent();

        NavigateCommand = new Command<Type>(async (Type pageType) =>
        {
            Page page = (Page)Activator.CreateInstance(pageType);
            await Navigation.PushAsync(page);
        });

        BindingContext = this;
    }

    public ICommand NavigateCommand { private set; get; }
}
```

The constructor concludes by setting its `BindingContext` property to itself, so each `ImageCell` in the XAML file can reference the `NavigateCommand` property with a simple `Binding`.

Taping the `Slider` entry (for example) navigates to `SliderPage`:

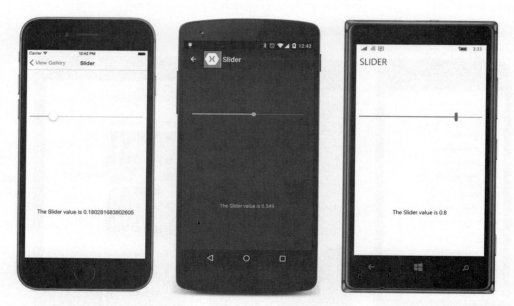

Returning to the home page requires using the navigation bar on the iOS and Android screens or the **Back** button on the Android and Windows 10 Mobile screens.

A new instance of each page is created each time you navigate to that page, so of course these different instances of `SliderPage` won't retain the value of the `Slider` you might have previously set.

Is it possible to create just a single instance of each of these 18 pages? Yes, and that is demonstrated in **ViewGalleryInst**. The **Inst** suffix stands for "instance" to distinguish the program from the use of a page type in **ViewGalleryType**.

The 18 page classes for each view are the same, as are the bitmaps. The home page, however, now expresses the CommandParameter property of each ImageCell as a property element to instantiate each page class. Here is an excerpt:

```
<ContentPage xmlns="http://xamarin.com/schemas/2014/forms"
             xmlns:x="http://schemas.microsoft.com/winfx/2009/xaml"
             xmlns:local="clr-namespace:ViewGalleryInst;assembly=ViewGalleryInst"
             x:Class="ViewGalleryInst.ViewGalleryInstPage"
             Title="View Gallery">
    <TableView Intent="Menu">
        <TableRoot>
            <TableSection Title="Presentation Views">
                <ImageCell ImageSource="{local:ImageResource ViewGalleryInst.Images.Label.png}"
                           Text="Display text"
                           Command="{Binding NavigateCommand}">
                    <ImageCell.CommandParameter>
                        <local:LabelPage />
                    </ImageCell.CommandParameter>
                </ImageCell>

                ...

                <ImageCell ImageSource=
                           "{local:ImageResource ViewGalleryInst.Images.TableView.png}"
                           Text="Show form or menu"
                           Command="{Binding NavigateCommand}">
                    <ImageCell.CommandParameter>
                        <local:TableViewPage />
                    </ImageCell.CommandParameter>
                </ImageCell>
            </TableSection>
        </TableRoot>
    </TableView>
</ContentPage>
```

Now when you manipulate the Slider on the SliderPage, and then return back to home and navigate to the SliderPage again, the Slider will be the same because it's the same page instance.

Keep in mind that with this configuration, a total of 19 page classes are instantiated when your program starts up, and that means 19 XAML files are being parsed, and that might affect the startup performance, and occupy a lot of memory as well.

Moreover, any errors in the XAML files that are found during this run-time parsing will also manifest themselves at program startup. It might be difficult to discover exactly which XAML file has the problem! When building a program that instantiates many page classes in one shot, you'll want to add new classes incrementally to make sure everything works well before proceeding.

Better yet, avoid this technique entirely. Instantiate each page as you need it, and retain data associated with the page by using a ViewModel.

Manipulating the navigation stack

Sometimes it's necessary to alter the normal stack-oriented flow of navigation. For example, suppose a page needs some information from the user, but first it navigates to a page that provides some instructions or a disclaimer, and then from there navigates to the page that actually obtains the information. When the user is finished and goes back, you'll want to skip that page with the instructions or disclaimer. That page should be removed from the navigation stack.

Here's a similar example: Suppose the user is interacting with a page that obtains some information and then wants to go back to the previous page. However, the program detects that something is wrong with this information that requires an extended discussion on a separate page. The program could insert a new page into the navigation stack to provide that discussion.

Or a certain sequence of pages might end with a `Button` labeled **Go to Home**, and all the pages in between can simply be skipped when navigating back to the home page.

The `INavigation` interface defines methods for all three of these cases. They are named `Remove-Page`, `InsertPageBefore`, and `PopToRootAsync`.

The **StackManipulation** program demonstrates these three methods, but in a very abstract manner. The program consists of five code-only pages, named `PageA`, `PageB`, `PageBAlternative`, `PageC`, and `PageD`. Each page sets its `Title` property to identify itself.

`PageA` has a `Button` to navigate to `PageB`:

```
public class PageA : ContentPage
{
    public PageA()
    {
        Button button = new Button
        {
            Text = "Go to Page B",
            FontSize = Device.GetNamedSize(NamedSize.Large, typeof(Button)),
            HorizontalOptions = LayoutOptions.Center,
            VerticalOptions = LayoutOptions.Center
        };
        button.Clicked += async (sender, args) =>
        {
            await Navigation.PushAsync(new PageB());
        };

        Title = "Page A";
        Content = new button;
    }
}
```

`PageB` is similar, except that it navigates to `PageC`. `PageBAlternative` is the same as `PageB` except that it identifies itself as "Page B Alt". `PageC` has a `Button` to navigate to `PageD`, and `PageD` has two buttons:

```csharp
public class PageD : ContentPage
{
    public PageD()
    {
        // Create Button to go directly to PageA.
        Button homeButton = new Button
        {
            Text = "Go Directly to Home",
            FontSize = Device.GetNamedSize(NamedSize.Large, typeof(Button)),
            HorizontalOptions = LayoutOptions.Center,
            VerticalOptions = LayoutOptions.CenterAndExpand
        };

        homeButton.Clicked += async (sender, args) =>
        {
            await Navigation.PopToRootAsync();
        };

        // Create Button to swap pages.
        Button swapButton = new Button
        {
            Text = "Swap B and Alt B",
            FontSize = Device.GetNamedSize(NamedSize.Large, typeof(Button)),
            HorizontalOptions = LayoutOptions.Center,
            VerticalOptions = LayoutOptions.CenterAndExpand
        };

        swapButton.Clicked += (sender, args) =>
        {
            IReadOnlyList<Page> navStack = Navigation.NavigationStack;
            Page pageC = navStack[navStack.Count - 2];
            Page existingPageB = navStack[navStack.Count - 3];
            bool isOriginal = existingPageB is PageB;
            Page newPageB = isOriginal ? (Page)new PageBAlternative() : new PageB();

            // Swap the pages.
            Navigation.RemovePage(existingPageB);
            Navigation.InsertPageBefore(newPageB, pageC);

            // Finished: Disable the Button.
            swapButton.IsEnabled = false;
        };

        Title = "Page D";
        Content = new StackLayout
        {
            Children =
            {
                homeButton,
                swapButton
            }
        };
    }
}
```

The button labeled **Go Directly to Home** has a `Clicked` handler that calls `PopToRootAsync`. This causes the program to jump back to `PageA` and effectively clears the navigation stack of all intermediary pages.

The button labeled **Swap B and Alt B** is a little more complex. The `Clicked` handler for this button replaces `PageB` with `PageBAlternative` in the navigation stack (or vice versa), so when you go back through the pages, you'll encounter a different page B. Here's how the `Clicked` handler does it:

At the time the `Button` is clicked, the `NavigationStack` has four items with indices 0, 1, 2, and 3. These four indices correspond to objects in the stack of type `PageA`, `PageB` (or `PageBAlternative`), `PageC`, and `PageD`. The handler accesses the `NavigationStack` to obtain these actual instances:

```
IReadOnlyList<Page> navStack = Navigation.NavigationStack;
Page pageC = navStack[navStack.Count - 2];
Page existingPageB = navStack[navStack.Count - 3];
```

That `existingPageB` object might be of type `PageB` or `PageBAlternative`, so a `newPageB` object is created of the other type:

```
bool isOriginal = existingPageB is PageB;
Page newPageB = isOriginal ? (Page)new PageBAlternative() : new PageB();
```

The next two statements remove the `existingPageB` object from the navigation stack and then insert the `newPageB` object in the slot before `pageC`, effectively swapping the pages:

```
// Swap the pages.
Navigation.RemovePage(existingPageB);
Navigation.InsertPageBefore(newPageB, pageC);
```

Obviously, the first time you click this button, `existingPageB` will be a `PageB` object and `newPageB` will be a `PageBAlternative` object, but you can then go back to `PageC` or `PageBAlternative`, and navigate forward again to `PageD`. Clicking the button again will replace the `PageBAlternative` object with a `PageB` object.

Dynamic page generation

The **BuildAPage** program is a multipage application, but the **BuildAPage** project contains only a single page class named `BuildAPageHomePage`. As the name suggests, the program constructs a new page from code and then navigates to it.

The XAML file lets you specify what you want on this constructed page:

```
<ContentPage xmlns="http://xamarin.com/schemas/2014/forms"
             xmlns:x="http://schemas.microsoft.com/winfx/2009/xaml"
             x:Class="BuildAPage.BuildAPageHomePage"
             Title="Build-a-Page"
             Padding="10, 5">

    <StackLayout>
        <Label Text="Enter page title:" />
```

```xml
<Entry x:Name="titleEntry"
       Placeholder="page title" />

<Grid VerticalOptions="FillAndExpand">
    <ContentView Grid.Row="0">
        <StackLayout>
        <Label Text="Tap to add to generated page:" />
            <ListView x:Name="viewList"
                        ItemSelected="OnViewListItemSelected">
                <ListView.ItemsSource>
                    <x:Array Type="{x:Type x:String}">
                        <x:String>BoxView</x:String>
                        <x:String>Button</x:String>
                        <x:String>DatePicker</x:String>
                        <x:String>Entry</x:String>
                        <x:String>Slider</x:String>
                        <x:String>Stepper</x:String>
                        <x:String>Switch</x:String>
                        <x:String>TimePicker</x:String>
                    </x:Array>
                </ListView.ItemsSource>
            </ListView>
        </StackLayout>
    </ContentView>

    <ContentView Grid.Row="1">
        <StackLayout>
            <Label Text="Tap to remove from generated page:" />
            <ListView x:Name="pageList"
                        ItemSelected="OnPageListItemSelected" />
        </StackLayout>
    </ContentView>
</Grid>

<Button x:Name="generateButton"
        Text="Generate the Page!"
        IsEnabled="False"
        HorizontalOptions="Center"
        VerticalOptions="Center"
        Clicked="OnGenerateButtonClicked" />
    </StackLayout>
</ContentPage>
```

Use the `Entry` at the top of the page to specify a `Title` property for the constructed page. A `ListView` then lists eight common views that you might want on your page. As you select these views, they are transferred to the second `ListView`. If you want to delete one of them from the page, just tap it in this second `ListView`.

Here's how it might look after you've selected a few elements for the page. Notice that you can select multiple elements of the same type and each is given a unique number:

When you're all finished "designing" your page, simply tap the **Generate the Page!** button on the bottom, and the program builds that page and navigates to it:

The code-behind file has `ItemSelected` handlers for the two `ListView` elements to add items and remove items from the second `ListView`, but the more interesting processing occurs in the `Clicked` handler for the `Button`:

```
public partial class BuildAPageHomePage : ContentPage
```

```
{
    ObservableCollection<string> viewCollection = new ObservableCollection<string>();
    Assembly xamarinForms = typeof(Label).GetTypeInfo().Assembly;

    public BuildAPageHomePage()
    {
        InitializeComponent();

        pageList.ItemsSource = viewCollection;
    }

    void OnViewListItemSelected(object sender, SelectedItemChangedEventArgs args)
    {
        if (args.SelectedItem != null)
        {
            viewList.SelectedItem = null;
            int number = 1;
            string item = null;

            while (-1 != viewCollection.IndexOf(
                item = ((string)args.SelectedItem) + ' ' + number))
            {
                number++;
            }

            viewCollection.Add(item);
            generateButton.IsEnabled = true;
        }
    }

    void OnPageListItemSelected(object sender, SelectedItemChangedEventArgs args)
    {
        if (args.SelectedItem != null)
        {
            pageList.SelectedItem = null;
            viewCollection.Remove((string)args.SelectedItem);
            generateButton.IsEnabled = viewCollection.Count > 0;
        }
    }

    async void OnGenerateButtonClicked(object sender, EventArgs args)
    {
        ContentPage contentPage = new ContentPage
        {
            Title = titleEntry.Text,
            Padding = new Thickness(10, 0)
        };
        StackLayout stackLayout = new StackLayout();
        contentPage.Content = stackLayout;

        foreach (string item in viewCollection)
        {
            string viewString = item.Substring(0, item.IndexOf(' '));
            Type viewType = xamarinForms.GetType("Xamarin.Forms." + viewString);
```

```
            View view = (View)Activator.CreateInstance(viewType);
            view.VerticalOptions = LayoutOptions.CenterAndExpand;

            switch (viewString)
            {
                case "BoxView":
                    ((BoxView)view).Color = Color.Accent;
                    goto case "Stepper";

                case "Button":
                    ((Button)view).Text = item;
                    goto case "Stepper";

                case "Stepper":
                case "Switch":
                    view.HorizontalOptions = LayoutOptions.Center;
                    break;
            }
            stackLayout.Children.Add(view);
        }
        await Navigation.PushAsync(contentPage);
    }
}
```

This `Clicked` handler creates a `ContentPage` and a `StackLayout` and then simply loops through the strings in the second `ListView`, finding a corresponding `Type` object by using the `GetType` method defined by the `Assembly` class. (Notice the `Assembly` object named `xamarinForms` defined as a field.) A call to `Activator.CreateInstance` creates the actual element, which can then be tailored slightly for the final layout.

Creating a `ContentPage` object in code and adding elements to it isn't new. In fact, the standard Xamarin.Forms project template includes an `App` class with a constructor that instantiates `ContentPage` and adds a `Label` to it, so you were introduced to this technique way back in Chapter 2. But that approach was quickly abandoned in favor of the more flexible technique of deriving a class from `ContentPage`. Deriving a class is more powerful because the derived class has access to protected methods such as `OnAppearing` and `OnDisappearing`.

Sometimes, however, it's helpful to go back to basics.

Patterns of data transfer

It's often necessary for pages within a multipage application to share data, and particularly for one page to pass information to another page. Sometimes this process resembles a function call: When `HomePage` displays a list of items and navigates to `DetailPage` to display a detailed view of one of these items, `HomePage` must pass that particular item to `DetailPage`. Or when the user enters information into `FillOutFormPage`, that information must be returned back to the page that invoked `FillOutFormPage`.

Several techniques are available to transfer data between pages. Which one you use depends on the particular application. Keep in mind throughout this discussion that you'll probably also need to save the contents of the page when the application terminates, and restore the contents when the program starts up again. Some of the data-sharing techniques are more conducive to saving and restoring page state than others. This issue is explored in more detail later in this chapter.

Constructor arguments

When one page navigates to another page and needs to pass data to that page, one obvious way to pass that data is through the second page's constructor.

The **SchoolAndStudents** program illustrates this technique. The program makes use of the **SchoolOfFineArt** library introduced in Chapter 19, "Collection views." The program consists of two pages named `SchoolPage` and `StudentPage`. The `SchoolPage` class uses a `ListView` to display a scrollable list of all the students in the school. When the user selects one, the program navigates to a `StudentPage` that displays details about the individual student. The program is similar to the **SelectedStudentDetail** program in Chapter 19, except that the list and detail have been separated into two pages.

Here's `SchoolPage`. To keep things as simple as possible, the `ListView` uses an `ImageCell` to display each student in the school:

```
<ContentPage xmlns="http://xamarin.com/schemas/2014/forms"
             xmlns:x="http://schemas.microsoft.com/winfx/2009/xaml"
             x:Class="SchoolAndStudents.SchoolPage"
             Title="School">

    <StackLayout BindingContext="{Binding StudentBody}">
        <Label Text="{Binding School}"
               FontSize="Large"
               FontAttributes="Bold"
               HorizontalTextAlignment="Center" />

        <ListView x:Name="listView"
                  ItemsSource="{Binding Students}"
                  ItemSelected="OnListViewItemSelected">
            <ListView.ItemTemplate>
                <DataTemplate>
                    <ImageCell ImageSource="{Binding PhotoFilename}"
                               Text="{Binding FullName}"
                               Detail="{Binding GradePointAverage,
                                        StringFormat='G.P.A. = {0:F2}'}" />
                </DataTemplate>
            </ListView.ItemTemplate>
        </ListView>
    </StackLayout>
</ContentPage>
```

The data bindings in this XAML file assume that the `BindingContext` for the page is set to an object of type `SchoolViewModel` defined in the **SchoolOfFineArt** Library. The `SchoolViewModel` has a property of type `StudentBody`, which is set to the `BindingContext` of the `StackLayout`. The `Label` is bound to the `School` property of `StudentBody`, and the `ItemsSource` of the `ListView` is bound to the `Students` collection property of `StudentBody`. This means that each item in the `ListView` has a `BindingContext` of type `Student`. The `ImageCell` references the `PhotoFilename`, `FullName`, and `GradePointAverage` properties of that `Student` object.

Here's that `ListView` running on iOS, Android, and Windows 10 Mobile:

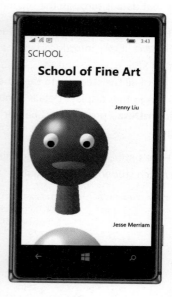

The constructor in the code-behind file is responsible for setting the `BindingContext` of the page from an instance of `SchoolViewModel`. The code-behind file also contains a handler for the `Item-Selected` event of the `ListView`. This event is fired when the user taps one of the students:

```
public partial class SchoolPage : ContentPage
{
    public SchoolPage()
    {
        InitializeComponent();

        // Set BindingContext.
        BindingContext = new SchoolViewModel();
    }

    async void OnListViewItemSelected(object sender, SelectedItemChangedEventArgs args)
    {
        // The selected item is null or of type Student.
        Student student = args.SelectedItem as Student;
```

```
        // Make sure that an item is actually selected.
        if (student != null)
        {
            // Deselect the item.
            listView.SelectedItem = null;

            // Navigate to StudentPage with Student argument.
            await Navigation.PushAsync(new StudentPage(student));
        }
    }
}
```

The `SelectedItem` property of the event arguments is the `Student` object that is tapped, and the handler uses that as an argument to the `StudentPage` class in the `PushAsync` call.

Notice also that the handler sets the `SelectedItem` property of the `ListView` to `null`. This deselects the item so that it won't still be selected when the user returns to the `SchoolPage`, and the user can tap it again. But setting that `SelectedItem` property to `null` also causes another call to the `ItemSelected` event handler. Fortunately, the handler ignores the event if the `SelectedItem` is `null`.

The code-behind file for `StudentPage` simply uses that constructor argument to set the `BindingContext` of the page:

```
public partial class StudentPage : ContentPage
{
    public StudentPage(Student student)
    {
        InitializeComponent();
        BindingContext = student;
    }
}
```

The XAML file for the `StudentPage` class contains bindings to various properties of the `Student` class:

```
<ContentPage xmlns="http://xamarin.com/schemas/2014/forms"
             xmlns:x="http://schemas.microsoft.com/winfx/2009/xaml"
             x:Class="SchoolAndStudents.StudentPage"
             Title="Student">

    <StackLayout>
        <!-- Name -->
        <StackLayout Orientation="Horizontal"
                     HorizontalOptions="Center"
                     Spacing="0">
            <StackLayout.Resources>
                <ResourceDictionary>
                    <Style TargetType="Label">
                        <Setter Property="FontSize" Value="Large" />
                        <Setter Property="FontAttributes" Value="Bold" />
                    </Style>
```

```
                </ResourceDictionary>
            </StackLayout.Resources>

            <Label Text="{Binding LastName}" />
            <Label Text="{Binding FirstName, StringFormat=', {0}'}" />
            <Label Text="{Binding MiddleName, StringFormat=' {0}'}" />
        </StackLayout>

        <!-- Photo -->
        <Image Source="{Binding PhotoFilename}"
               VerticalOptions="FillAndExpand" />

        <!-- Sex -->
        <Label Text="{Binding Sex, StringFormat='Sex = {0}'}"
               HorizontalOptions="Center" />

        <!-- GPA -->
        <Label Text="{Binding GradePointAverage, StringFormat='G.P.A. = {0:F2}'}"
               HorizontalOptions="Center" />
    </StackLayout>
</ContentPage>
```

The XAML file doesn't require a button or any other user-interface object to return back to `SchoolPage` because that's provided automatically, either as part of the standard navigation user interface for the platform or as part of the phone itself:

Passing information to the navigated page through the constructor is versatile, but for this particular example, it's unnecessary. `StudentPage` could have a parameterless constructor, and the `School-Page` could set the `BindingContext` of the newly created `StudentPage` right in the `PushAsync` call:

```
await Navigation.PushAsync(new StudentPage { BindingContext = student });
```

One of the problems with either approach is preserving the application state when the program is suspended. If you want `StudentPage` to save the current student when the program terminates, it needs to save all the properties of the `Student` object. But when that `Student` object is re-created when the program starts up again, it's a different object from the particular `Student` object for the same student in the `Students` collection even though all the properties are the same.

If the `Students` collection is known to be constant, it makes more sense for `StudentPage` to save only an index into the `Students` collection that references this particular `Student` object. But in this example, `StudentPage` does not have access to that index or to the `Students` collection.

Properties and method calls

A page calling `PushAsync` or `PushModalAsync` obviously has direct access to the class that it's navigating to, so it can set properties or call methods in that page object to pass information to it. A page calling `PopAsync` or `PopModalAsync`, however, has some more work to do to determine the page that it's returning to. In the general case, a page can't always be expected to be familiar with the page type of the page that navigated to it.

You'll need to exercise caution when setting properties or calling methods from one page to another. You can't make any assumptions about the sequence of calls to the `OnAppearing` and `OnDisappearing` overrides and the completion of the `PushAsync`, `PopAsync`, `PushModalAsync`, and `PopModalAsync` tasks.

Let's assume you have pages named `HomePage` and `InfoPage`. As the names suggest, `HomePage` uses `PushAsync` to navigate to `InfoPage` to obtain some information from the user, and somehow `InfoPage` must transfer that information to `HomePage`.

Here are some ways that `HomePage` and `InfoPage` can interact (or not interact):

`HomePage` can access a property in `InfoPage` or call a method in `InfoPage` after instantiating `InfoPage` or after the `PushAsync` task completes. This is straightforward, and you already saw an example in the **SinglePageNavigation** program.

`InfoPage` can access a property in `HomePage` or call a method in `HomePage` at any time during its existence. Most conveniently, `InfoPage` can perform these operations during its `OnAppearing` override (for initialization) or the `OnDisappearing` override (to prepare final values). For the duration of its existence, `InfoPage` can obtain the `HomePage` instance from the `NavigationStack` collection. However, depending on the order of the `OnAppearing` and `OnDisappearing` calls relative to the completion of the `PushAsync` or `PopAsync` tasks, `HomePage` might be the last item in the `NavigationStack`, or `InfoPage` might be the last item in the `NavigationStack`, in which case `HomePage` is the next to last item.

HomePage can be informed that InfoPage has returned control back to HomePage by overriding its OnAppearing method. (But keep in mind that this method is not called on Android devices when a modal page has returned back to the page that invoked it.) However, during the OnAppearing override of HomePage, HomePage cannot be entirely certain that the instance of InfoPage is still in the NavigationStack collection, or even that it exists at all. HomePage can save the instance of InfoPage when it navigates to InfoPage, but that creates problems if the application needs to save the page state when it terminates.

Let's examine a program named **DataTransfer1** that uses a second page to obtain information from the user and then adds that information as an item to a ListView. The user can add multiple items to the ListView or edit an existing item by tapping it. To focus entirely on the mechanism of interpage communication, the program uses no data bindings, and the class that stores the information does not implement INotifyPropertyChanged:

```
public class Information
{
    public string Name { set; get; }

    public string Email { set; get; }

    public string Language { set; get; }

    public DateTime Date { set; get; }

    public override string ToString()
    {
        return String.Format("{0} / {1} / {2} / {3:d}",
                             String.IsNullOrWhiteSpace(Name) ? "???" : Name,
                             String.IsNullOrWhiteSpace(Email) ? "???" : Email,
                             String.IsNullOrWhiteSpace(Language) ? "???" : Language,
                             Date);
    }
}
```

The ToString method allows the ListView to display the items with minimum fuss.

The **DataTransfer1** program has two pages, named DataTransfer1HomePage and DataTransfer1InfoPage, that communicate to each other by calling public methods. The DataTransfer1HomePage has a XAML file with a Button for invoking a page to obtain information and a ListView for displaying each item and allowing an item to be edited:

```
<ContentPage xmlns="http://xamarin.com/schemas/2014/forms"
             xmlns:x="http://schemas.microsoft.com/winfx/2009/xaml"
             x:Class="DataTransfer1.DataTransfer1HomePage"
             Title="Home Page">
    <Grid>
        <Button Text="Add New Item"
                Grid.Row="0"
```

```
                    FontSize="Large"
                    HorizontalOptions="Center"
                    VerticalOptions="Center"
                    Clicked="OnGetInfoButtonClicked" />

        <ListView x:Name="listView"
                  Grid.Row="1"
                  ItemSelected="OnListViewItemSelected" />
    </Grid>
</ContentPage>
```

Let's bounce back and forth between the two classes to examine the transfer of data. Here's the portion of the code-behind file showing the initialization of the ListView with an ObservableCollection so that the ListView updates its display whenever the collection changes:

```
public partial class DataTransfer1HomePage : ContentPage
{
    ObservableCollection<Information> list = new ObservableCollection<Information>();

    public DataTransfer1HomePage()
    {
        InitializeComponent();

        // Set collection to ListView.
        listView.ItemsSource = list;
    }

    // Button Clicked handler.
    async void OnGetInfoButtonClicked(object sender, EventArgs args)
    {
        await Navigation.PushAsync(new DataTransfer1InfoPage());
    }
    ...
}
```

This code also implements the Clicked handler for the Button simply by instantiating the Data-Transfer1InfoPage and navigating to it.

The XAML file of DataTransfer1InfoPage has two Entry elements, a Picker, and a Date-Picker corresponding to the properties of Information. This page relies on each platform's standard user interface for returning to the home page:

```
<ContentPage xmlns="http://xamarin.com/schemas/2014/forms"
             xmlns:x="http://schemas.microsoft.com/winfx/2009/xaml"
             x:Class="DataTransfer1.DataTransfer1InfoPage"
             Title="Info Page">

    <StackLayout Padding="20, 0"
                 Spacing="20">
        <Entry x:Name="nameEntry"
               Placeholder="Enter Name" />

        <Entry x:Name="emailEntry"
```

```
                    Placeholder="Enter Email Address" />

        <Picker x:Name="languagePicker"
                Title="Favorite Programming Language">
            <Picker.Items>
                <x:String>C#</x:String>
                <x:String>F#</x:String>
                <x:String>Objective C</x:String>
                <x:String>Swift</x:String>
                <x:String>Java</x:String>
            </Picker.Items>
        </Picker>

        <DatePicker x:Name="datePicker" />
    </StackLayout>
</ContentPage>
```

The code-behind file of the info page instantiates an `Information` object that is associated with this page instance:

```
public partial class DataTransfer1InfoPage : ContentPage
{
    // Instantiate an Information object for this page instance.
    Information info = new Information();

    public DataTransfer1InfoPage()
    {
        InitializeComponent();
    }
    ...
}
```

The user interacts with the elements on the page by entering some information:

Nothing else happens in the class until `DataTransfer1InfoPage` gets a call to its `OnDisappearing` override. This usually indicates that the user has pressed the **Back** button that is either part of the navigation bar (on iOS and Android) or below the screen (on Android and Windows Phone).

However, you might be aware that in a platform no longer supported by Xamarin.Forms (Windows Phone Silverlight), `OnDisappearing` was called when the user invoked the `Picker` or `DatePicker`, and you might be nervous about it being called in other circumstances on the current platforms. This implies that nothing should be done in the `OnDisappearing` override that can't be undone when `OnDisappearing` is called as part of the normal navigation back to the home page. This is why `DataTransfer1InfoPage` instantiates its `Information` object when the page is first created and not during the `OnDisappearing` override.

The `OnDisappearing` override sets the properties of the `Information` object from the four views and then obtains the instance of `DataTransfer1HomePage` that invoked it from the `Navigation-Stack` collection. It then calls a method named `InformationReady` in that home page:

```
public partial class DataTransfer1InfoPage : ContentPage
{
    …
    protected override void OnDisappearing()
    {
        base.OnDisappearing();

        // Set properties of Information object.
        info.Name = nameEntry.Text;
        info.Email = emailEntry.Text;

        int index = languagePicker.SelectedIndex;
        info.Language = index == -1 ? null : languagePicker.Items[index];
```

```
        info.Date = datePicker.Date;

        // Get the DataTransfer1HomePage that invoked this page.
        NavigationPage navPage = (NavigationPage)Application.Current.MainPage;
        IReadOnlyList<Page> navStack = navPage.Navigation.NavigationStack;
        int lastIndex = navStack.Count - 1;
        DataTransfer1HomePage homePage = navStack[lastIndex] as DataTransfer1HomePage;

        if (homePage == null)
        {
            homePage = navStack[lastIndex - 1] as DataTransfer1HomePage;
        }
        // Transfer Information object to DataTransfer1HomePage.
        homePage.InformationReady(info);
    }
}
```

The `InformationReady` method in `DataTransfer1HomePage` checks whether the `Information` object is already in the `ObservableCollection` set to the `ListView`, and if so, it replaces it. Otherwise, it adds the object to that collection:

```
public partial class DataTransfer1HomePage : ContentPage
{
    ...
    // Called from InfoPage.
    public void InformationReady(Information info)
    {
        // If the object has already been added, replace it.
        int index = list.IndexOf(info);

        if (index != -1)
        {
            list[index] = info;
        }
        // Otherwise, add it.
        else
        {
            list.Add(info);
        }
    }
}
```

There are two reasons for checking whether the `Information` object is already in the `ListView` collection. It might be there already if the info page received an earlier call to its `OnDisappearing` override, which then results in a call to `InformationReady` in the home page. Also—as you'll see— existing items in the `ListView` can be edited.

The code that replaces the `Information` object with itself in the `ObservableCollection` might seem superfluous. However, the act of replacing the item causes the `ObservableCollection` to fire a `CollectionChanged` event, and the `ListView` redraws itself. Another solution would be for `Infor-`

`mation` to implement `INotifyPropertyChanged`, in which case the change in the values of a property would cause the `ListView` to update the display of that item.

At this point, we're back on the home page, and the `ListView` displays the newly added item:

You can now tap the `Button` again to create a new item, or you can tap an existing item in the `ListView`. The `ItemSelected` handler for the `ListView` also navigates to `DataTransfer1Info-Page`:

```
public partial class DataTransfer1HomePage : ContentPage
{
    ...
    // ListView ItemSelected handler.
    async void OnListViewItemSelected(object sender, SelectedItemChangedEventArgs args)
    {
        if (args.SelectedItem != null)
        {
            // Deselect the item.
            listView.SelectedItem = null;

            DataTransfer1InfoPage infoPage = new DataTransfer1InfoPage();
            await Navigation.PushAsync(infoPage);
            infoPage.InitializeInfo((Information)args.SelectedItem);
        }
    }
    ...
}
```

However, after the `PushAsync` task completes, the handler calls a method in `DataTransfer1Info-Page` named `InitializeInfo` with the selected item.

The `InitializeInfo` method in `DataTransfer1InfoPage` replaces the `Information` object it originally created as a field with this existing instance and initializes the views on the page with the properties of the object:

```
public partial class DataTransfer1InfoPage : ContentPage
{
    …
    public void InitializeInfo(Information info)
    {
        // Replace the instance.
        this.info = info;

        // Initialize the views.
        nameEntry.Text = info.Name ?? "";
        emailEntry.Text = info.Email ?? "";

        if (!String.IsNullOrWhiteSpace(info.Language))
        {
            languagePicker.SelectedIndex = languagePicker.Items.IndexOf(info.Language);
        }
        datePicker.Date = info.Date;
    }
    …
}
```

Now the user is editing an existing item instead of a new instance.

Generally, a program that allows editing of existing items will also give the user an opportunity to abandon any changes already made to the item. To allow that, the `DataTransfer1InfoPage` would need to differentiate between returning back to the home page with changes and cancelling the edit operation. At least one `Button` or `ToolbarItem` is required, and that should probably be a **Cancel** button so that the standard **Back** button saves the changes.

Such a program should also have a facility to delete items. Later on in this chapter, you'll see such a program.

The messaging center

You might not like the idea of the two page classes making method calls directly to each other. It seems to work well for a small sample, but for a larger program with lots of interclass communication, you might prefer something a little more flexible that doesn't require actual page instances.

Such a facility is the Xamarin.Forms `MessagingCenter` class. This is a static class with three methods, named `Subscribe`, `Unsubscribe`, and `Send`. Messages are identified with a text string and can be accompanied by any object. The `Send` method broadcasts a message that is received by any subscriber to that message.

The **DataTransfer2** program has the same `Information` class and the same XAML files as **Data-Transfer1,** but it uses the `MessagingCenter` class rather than direct method calls.

The constructor of the home page subscribes to a message identified by the text string "InformationReady." The generic arguments to `Subscribe` indicate what object type sends this message—an object of type `DataTransfer2InfoPage`—and the type of the data, which is `Information`. The `Subscribe` method arguments indicate the object receiving the message (`this`), the message name, and a lambda function. The body of this lambda function is the same as the body of the `InformationReady` method in the previous program:

```
public partial class DataTransfer2HomePage : ContentPage
{
    ObservableCollection<Information> list = new ObservableCollection<Information>();

    public DataTransfer2HomePage()
    {
        InitializeComponent();

        // Set collection to ListView.
        listView.ItemsSource = list;

        // Subscribe to "InformationReady" message.
        MessagingCenter.Subscribe<DataTransfer2InfoPage, Information>
            (this, "InformationReady", (sender, info) =>
            {
                // If the object has already been added, replace it.
                int index = list.IndexOf(info);

                if (index != -1)
                {
                    list[index] = info;
                }
                // Otherwise, add it.
                else
                {
                    list.Add(info);
                }
            });
    }

    // Button Clicked handler.
    async void OnGetInfoButtonClicked(object sender, EventArgs args)
    {
        await Navigation.PushAsync(new DataTransfer2InfoPage());
    }

    // ListView ItemSelected handler.
    async void OnListViewItemSelected(object sender, SelectedItemChangedEventArgs args)
    {
        if (args.SelectedItem != null)
        {
            // Deselect the item.
            listView.SelectedItem = null;

            DataTransfer2InfoPage infoPage = new DataTransfer2InfoPage();
            await Navigation.PushAsync(infoPage);
```

```
            // Send "InitializeInfo" message to info page.
            MessagingCenter.Send<DataTransfer2HomePage, Information>
                (this, "InitializeInfo", (Information)args.SelectedItem);
        }
    }
}
```

The `ItemSelected` handler of the `ListView` contains a call to `MessagingCenter.Send`. The generic arguments indicate the type of the message sender and the type of the data. The arguments to the method indicate the object sending the message, the message name, and the data, which is the `SelectedItem` of the `ListView`.

The `DataTransfer2InfoPage` code-behind file contains complementary calls to `Messaging-Center.Subscribe` and `MessageCenter.Send`. The info page constructor subscribes to the "Initial-izeInfo" message; the body of the lambda function is the same as the `InitializeInfo` method in the previous program except that it ends with a call to unsubscribe from the message. Unsubscribing ensures that there is no longer a reference to the info page object and allows the info page object to be garbage collected. Strictly speaking, however, unsubscribing shouldn't be necessary because the `Mes-sagingCenter` maintains `WeakReference` objects for subscribers:

```
public partial class DataTransfer2InfoPage : ContentPage
{
    // Instantiate an Information object for this page instance.
    Information info = new Information();

    public DataTransfer2InfoPage()
    {
        InitializeComponent();

        // Subscribe to "InitializeInfo" message.
        MessagingCenter.Subscribe<DataTransfer2HomePage, Information>
            (this, "InitializeInfo", (sender, info) =>
            {
                // Replace the instance.
                this.info = info;

                // Initialize the views.
                nameEntry.Text = info.Name ?? "";
                emailEntry.Text = info.Email ?? "";

                if (!String.IsNullOrWhiteSpace(info.Language))
                {
                    languagePicker.SelectedIndex = languagePicker.Items.IndexOf(info.Language);
                }
                datePicker.Date = info.Date;

                // Don't need "InitializeInfo" any more so unsubscribe.
                MessagingCenter.Unsubscribe<DataTransfer2HomePage, Information>
                    (this, "InitializeInfo");
            });
    }
```

```
    protected override void OnDisappearing()
    {
        base.OnDisappearing();

        // Set properties of Information object.
        info.Name = nameEntry.Text;
        info.Email = emailEntry.Text;

        int index = languagePicker.SelectedIndex;
        info.Language = index == -1 ? null : languagePicker.Items[index];

        info.Date = datePicker.Date;

        // Send "InformationReady" message back to home page.
        MessagingCenter.Send<DataTransfer2InfoPage, Information>
            (this, "InformationReady", info);
    }
}
```

The OnDisappearing override is considerably shorter than the version in the previous program. To call a method in the home page, the previous program had to go into the NavigationStack collection. In this version, all that's necessary is to use MessagingCenter.Send to send an "Information-Ready" message to whoever has subscribed to it, and that happens to be the home page.

Events

In both the method-call approach and the messaging-center approach to interclass communication, the info page needs to know the type of the home page. This is sometimes undesirable if the same info page can be called from different types of pages.

One solution to this problem is for the info class to implement an event, and that's the approach taken in **DataTransfer3**. The Information class and XAML files are the same as the previous programs, but DataTransfer3InfoPage now implements a public event named InformationReady:

```
public partial class DataTransfer3InfoPage : ContentPage
{
    // Define a public event for transferring data.
    public EventHandler<Information> InformationReady;

    // Instantiate an Information object for this page instance.
    Information info = new Information();

    public DataTransfer3InfoPage()
    {
        InitializeComponent();
    }

    public void InitializeInfo(Information info)
    {
        // Replace the instance.
```

```
        this.info = info;

        // Initialize the views.
        nameEntry.Text = info.Name ?? "";
        emailEntry.Text = info.Email ?? "";

        if (!String.IsNullOrWhiteSpace(info.Language))
        {
            languagePicker.SelectedIndex = languagePicker.Items.IndexOf(info.Language);
        }
        datePicker.Date = info.Date;
    }

    protected override void OnDisappearing()
    {
        base.OnDisappearing();

        // Set properties of Information object.
        info.Name = nameEntry.Text;
        info.Email = emailEntry.Text;

        int index = languagePicker.SelectedIndex;
        info.Language = index == -1 ? null : languagePicker.Items[index];

        info.Date = datePicker.Date;

        // Raise the InformationReady event.
        EventHandler<Information> handler = InformationReady;

        if (handler != null)
            handler(this, info);
    }
}
```

During the OnDisappearing override, the class sets the Information properties from the elements and raises an InformationReady event with the Information object.

The home page can set a handler for the InformationReady event either after it instantiates the info page or after it navigates to the page. The event handler adds the Information object to the ListView or replaces an existing item:

```
public partial class DataTransfer3HomePage : ContentPage
{
    ObservableCollection<Information> list = new ObservableCollection<Information>();

    public DataTransfer3HomePage()
    {
        InitializeComponent();

        // Set collection to ListView.
        listView.ItemsSource = list;
    }
```

```
// Button Clicked handler.
async void OnGetInfoButtonClicked(object sender, EventArgs args)
{
    DataTransfer3InfoPage infoPage = new DataTransfer3InfoPage();
    await Navigation.PushAsync(infoPage);

    // Set event handler for obtaining information.
    infoPage.InformationReady += OnInfoPageInformationReady;
}

// ListView ItemSelected handler.
async void OnListViewItemSelected(object sender, SelectedItemChangedEventArgs args)
{
    if (args.SelectedItem != null)
    {
        // Deselect the item.
        listView.SelectedItem = null;

        DataTransfer3InfoPage infoPage = new DataTransfer3InfoPage();
        await Navigation.PushAsync(infoPage);
        infoPage.InitializeInfo((Information)args.SelectedItem);

        // Set event handler for obtaining information.
        infoPage.InformationReady += OnInfoPageInformationReady;
    }
}

void OnInfoPageInformationReady(object sender, Information info)
{
    // If the object has already been added, replace it.
    int index = list.IndexOf(info);

    if (index != -1)
    {
        list[index] = info;
    }
    // Otherwise, add it.
    else
    {
        list.Add(info);
    }
}
}
```

There are a couple of problems with this approach. The first problem is that there is no convenient place to detach the event handler. The info page raises the event in its OnDisappearing override. If you are not confident that OnDisappearing is called only when navigation is occurring, then the home page can't detach the event hander in the handler itself.

Nor can the home page detach the event handler in its OnAppearing override because when the info page returns back to the home page, the order in which the OnAppearing and OnDisappearing overrides are called is platform dependent.

If the home page can't detach the handler from the info page, then each instance of info page will continue to maintain a reference to the home page and can't be garbage collected.

The event-handler approach is also not good when an application needs to save and restore page state. The info page cannot save the state of the event to restore it when the program executes again.

The App class intermediary

In a Xamarin.Forms application, the first code that executes in the common code project is the constructor of a class customarily named `App` that derives from `Application`. This `App` object remains constant until the program terminates, and it is always available to any code in the program through the static `Application.Current` property. The return value of that property is of type `Application`, but it's simple to cast it to `App`.

This implies that the `App` class is a great place to store data that must be accessed throughout the application, including data that is transferred from one page to another.

The `Information` class in the **DataTransfer4** version of the program is just a little different from the version you've seen previously:

```
public class Information
{
    public Information()
    {
        Date = DateTime.Today;
    }

    public string Name { set; get; }

    public string Email { set; get; }

    public string Language { set; get; }

    public DateTime Date { set; get; }

    public override string ToString()
    {
        return String.Format("{0} / {1} / {2} / {3:d}",
                        String.IsNullOrWhiteSpace(Name) ? "???" : Name,
                        String.IsNullOrWhiteSpace(Email) ? "???" : Email,
                        String.IsNullOrWhiteSpace(Language) ? "???" : Language,
                        Date);
    }
}
```

The constructor of this version sets the `Date` property to today's date. In previous versions of the program, the properties of an `Information` instance are set from the various elements on the info page. In that case, the `Date` property is set from the `DatePicker`, which by default sets its `Date` property to the current date. In **DataTransfer4**, as you'll see, the elements on the info page are initialized from the properties in the `Information` object, so setting the `Date` property in the `Information` class merely keeps the functionality of the programs consistent.

Here's the `App` class in **DataTransfer4**. Notice the public properties named `InfoCollection` and `CurrentInfoItem`. The constructor initializes `InfoCollection` to an `ObservableCollection<Information>` object before creating `DataTransfer4HomePage`:

```
public class App : Application
{
    public App()
    {
        // Create the ObservableCollection for the Information items.
        InfoCollection = new ObservableCollection<Information>();

        MainPage = new NavigationPage(new DataTransfer4HomePage());
    }

    public IList<Information> InfoCollection { private set; get; }

    public Information CurrentInfoItem { set; get; }
    ...
}
```

The availability of the `InfoCollection` property in `App` allows `DataTransfer4HomePage` to set it directly to the `ItemsSource` property of the `ListView`:

```
public partial class DataTransfer4HomePage : ContentPage
{
    App app = (App)Application.Current;

    public DataTransfer4HomePage()
    {
        InitializeComponent();

        // Set collection to ListView.
        listView.ItemsSource = app.InfoCollection;
    }

    // Button Clicked handler.
    async void OnGetInfoButtonClicked(object sender, EventArgs args)
    {
        // Create new Information item.
        app.CurrentInfoItem = new Information();

        // Navigate to info page.
        await Navigation.PushAsync(new DataTransfer4InfoPage());
    }

    // ListView ItemSelected handler.
    async void OnListViewItemSelected(object sender, SelectedItemChangedEventArgs args)
    {
        if (args.SelectedItem != null)
        {
            // Deselect the item.
```

```
            listView.SelectedItem = null;

            // Get existing Information item.
            app.CurrentInfoItem = (Information)args.SelectedItem;

            // Navigate to info page.
            await Navigation.PushAsync(new DataTransfer4InfoPage());
        }
    }
}
```

Notice the two different but similar ways that the `Clicked` handler for the `Button` and the `Item-Selected` handler for the `ListView` are implemented. Before navigating to `DataTransfer4Info-Page`, both handlers set the `CurrentInfoItem` property of the `App` class to an instance of `Information`. But the `Clicked` handler sets the `CurrentInfoItem` property to a new instance, whereas the `ItemSelected` handler sets it to the selected item in the `ListView`.

Everything else is handled by `DataTransfer4InfoPage`. The info page can initialize the elements on the page from the `Information` object stored in the `CurrentInfoItem` property of the `App` class:

```
public partial class DataTransfer4InfoPage : ContentPage
{
    App app = (App)Application.Current;

    public DataTransfer4InfoPage()
    {
        InitializeComponent();

        // Initialize the views.
        Information info = app.CurrentInfoItem;

        nameEntry.Text = info.Name ?? "";
        emailEntry.Text = info.Email ?? "";

        if (!String.IsNullOrWhiteSpace(info.Language))
        {
            languagePicker.SelectedIndex = languagePicker.Items.IndexOf(info.Language);
        }
        datePicker.Date = info.Date;
    }

    protected override void OnDisappearing()
    {
        base.OnDisappearing();

        // Set properties of Information object.
        Information info = app.CurrentInfoItem;

        info.Name = nameEntry.Text;
        info.Email = emailEntry.Text;

        int index = languagePicker.SelectedIndex;
        info.Language = index == -1 ? null : languagePicker.Items[index];
```

```
            info.Date = datePicker.Date;

            // If the object has already been added to the collection, replace it.
            IList<Information> list = app.InfoCollection;

            index = list.IndexOf(info);

            if (index != -1)
            {
                list[index] = info;
            }
            // Otherwise, add it.
            else
            {
                list.Add(info);
            }
        }
    }
}
```

The info page still needs to override its `OnDisappearing` method to set the properties of the `Information` object and possibly add it to the `ListView` collection or replace the same object to trigger a redraw. But the info page doesn't need to directly access the `ListView` because it can obtain the `ObservableCollection` from the `InfoCollection` property of the `App` class.

Moreover, if you need to save and restore page state, everything is available right in the `App` class.

Let's see how that might work.

Switching to a ViewModel

At this point it should be obvious that the `Information` class should really implement `INotifyPropertyChanged`. In **DataTransfer5**, the `Information` class has become an `InformationViewModel` class. It derives from `ViewModelBase` in the **Xamarin.FormsBook.Toolkit** library to reduce the overhead:

```
public class InformationViewModel : ViewModelBase
{
    string name, email, language;
    DateTime date = DateTime.Today;

    public string Name
    {
        set { SetProperty(ref name, value); }
        get { return name; }
    }

    public string Email
    {
        set { SetProperty(ref email, value); }
        get { return email; }
    }
```

```
    public string Language
    {
        set { SetProperty(ref language, value); }
        get { return language; }
    }

    public DateTime Date
    {
        set { SetProperty(ref date, value); }
        get { return date; }
    }
}
```

A new class has been added to **DataTransfer5** called AppData. This class includes an Observable-Collection of Information objects for the ListView as well as a separate Information instance for the info page:

```
public class AppData
{
    public AppData()
    {
        InfoCollection = new ObservableCollection<InformationViewModel>();
    }

    public IList<InformationViewModel> InfoCollection { private set; get; }

    public InformationViewModel CurrentInfo { set; get; }
}
```

The App class instantiates AppData before instantiating the home page and makes it available as a public property:

```
public class App : Application
{
    public App()
    {
        // Ensure link to Toolkit library.
        new Xamarin.FormsBook.Toolkit.ObjectToIndexConverter<object>();

        // Instantiate AppData and set property.
        AppData = new AppData();

        // Go to the home page.
        MainPage = new NavigationPage(new DataTransfer5HomePage());
    }

    public AppData AppData { private set; get; }
    ...
}
```

The XAML file of DataTransfer5HomePage sets the BindingContext for the page with a binding that incorporates the static Application.Current property (which returns the App object) and the

AppData instance. This means that the `ListView` can bind its `ItemsSource` property to the `Info-Collection` property of `AppData`:

```xml
<ContentPage xmlns="http://xamarin.com/schemas/2014/forms"
             xmlns:x="http://schemas.microsoft.com/winfx/2009/xaml"
             x:Class="DataTransfer5.DataTransfer5HomePage"
             Title="Home Page"
             BindingContext="{Binding Source={x:Static Application.Current},
                                      Path=AppData}">
    <Grid>
        <Button Text="Add New Item"
                Grid.Row="0"
                FontSize="Large"
                HorizontalOptions="Center"
                VerticalOptions="Center"
                Clicked="OnGetInfoButtonClicked" />

        <ListView x:Name="listView"
                  Grid.Row="1"
                  ItemsSource="{Binding InfoCollection}"
                  ItemSelected="OnListViewItemSelected">
            <ListView.ItemTemplate>
                <DataTemplate>
                    <ViewCell>
                        <StackLayout Orientation="Horizontal">
                            <Label Text="{Binding Name}" />
                            <Label Text=" / " />
                            <Label Text="{Binding Email}" />
                            <Label Text=" / " />
                            <Label Text="{Binding Language}" />
                            <Label Text=" / " />
                            <Label Text="{Binding Date, StringFormat='{0:d}'}" />
                        </StackLayout>
                    </ViewCell>
                </DataTemplate>
            </ListView.ItemTemplate>
        </ListView>
    </Grid>
</ContentPage>
```

Previous versions of the program relied upon the `ToString` override in `Information` to display the items. Now that `Information` has been replaced with `InformationViewModel`, the `ToString` method isn't adequate because there's no notification that the `ToString` method might return something different. Instead, the `ListView` uses a `ViewCell` containing elements with bindings to properties of `InformationViewModel`.

The code-behind file continues to implement the `Clicked` handler for the `Button` and the `Item-Selected` handler for the `ListView`, but they are now so similar they can make use of a common method named `GoToInfoPage`:

```csharp
public partial class DataTransfer5HomePage : ContentPage
{
```

```
public DataTransfer5HomePage()
{
    InitializeComponent();
}

// Button Clicked handler.
void OnGetInfoButtonClicked(object sender, EventArgs args)
{
    // Navigate to the info page.
    GoToInfoPage(new InformationViewModel(), true);
}

// ListView ItemSelected handler.
void OnListViewItemSelected(object sender, SelectedItemChangedEventArgs args)
{
    if (args.SelectedItem != null)
    {
        // Deselect the item.
        listView.SelectedItem = null;

        // Navigate to the info page.
        GoToInfoPage((InformationViewModel)args.SelectedItem, false);
    }
}

async void GoToInfoPage(InformationViewModel info, bool isNewItem)
{
    // Get AppData object (set to BindingContext in XAML file).
    AppData appData = (AppData)BindingContext;

    // Set info item to CurrentInfo property of AppData.
    appData.CurrentInfo = info;

    // Navigate to the info page.
    await Navigation.PushAsync(new DataTransfer5InfoPage());

    // Add new info item to the collection.
    if (isNewItem)
    {
        appData.InfoCollection.Add(info);
    }
}
}
```

For both cases, the GoToInfoPage method sets the CurrentInfo property of AppData. For a Clicked event, it's set to a new InformationViewModel object. For the ItemSelected event, it's set to an existing InformationViewModel from the ListView collection. The isNewItem parameter of the GoToInfoPage method indicates whether this InformationViewModel object should also be added to the InfoCollection of AppData.

Notice that the new item is added to the InfoCollection after the PushAsync task completes. If the item is added prior to the PushAsync call, then—depending on the platform—you might notice this new item suddenly appearing in the `ListView` immediately before the page transition. That could be a bit disturbing!

The XAML file for the `DataTransfer5InfoPage` sets the `BindingContext` for the page to the `CurrentInfo` property of `AppData`. (The home page sets the `CurrentInfo` property of `AppData` prior to instantiating the info page, so it's not necessary for `AppData` to implement `INotifyProperty-tyChanged`.) The setting of the `BindingContext` allows all the visual elements on the page to be bound to properties in the `InformationViewModel` class:

```xml
<ContentPage xmlns="http://xamarin.com/schemas/2014/forms"
             xmlns:x="http://schemas.microsoft.com/winfx/2009/xaml"
             xmlns:toolkit=
                 "clr-namespace:Xamarin.FormsBook.Toolkit;assembly=Xamarin.FormsBook.Toolkit"
             x:Class="DataTransfer5.DataTransfer5InfoPage"
             Title="Info Page"
             BindingContext="{Binding Source={x:Static Application.Current},
                             Path=AppData.CurrentInfo}">

    <StackLayout Padding="20, 0"
                 Spacing="20">
        <Entry Text="{Binding Name}"
               Placeholder="Enter Name" />

        <Entry Text="{Binding Email}"
               Placeholder="Enter Email Address" />

        <Picker x:Name="languagePicker"
                Title="Favorite Programming Language">
            <Picker.Items>
                <x:String>C#</x:String>
                <x:String>F#</x:String>
                <x:String>Objective C</x:String>
                <x:String>Swift</x:String>
                <x:String>Java</x:String>
            </Picker.Items>

            <Picker.SelectedIndex>
                <Binding Path="Language">
                    <Binding.Converter>
                        <toolkit:ObjectToIndexConverter x:TypeArguments="x:String">
                            <x:String>C#</x:String>
                            <x:String>F#</x:String>
                            <x:String>Objective C</x:String>
                            <x:String>Swift</x:String>
                            <x:String>Java</x:String>
                        </toolkit:ObjectToIndexConverter>
                    </Binding.Converter>
                </Binding>
            </Picker.SelectedIndex>
        </Picker>

        <DatePicker Date="{Binding Date}" />
    </StackLayout>
```

```
</ContentPage>
```

Notice the use of the `ObjectToIndexConverter` in the binding between the `SelectedIndex` property of the `Picker` and the string `Language` property of `InformationViewModel`. This binding converter was introduced in Chapter 19, "Collection views," in the section "Data binding the Picker."

The code-behind file of `DataTransfer5InfoPage` achieves the MVVM goal of being nothing but a call to `InitializeComponent`:

```
public partial class DataTransfer5InfoPage : ContentPage
{
    public DataTransfer5InfoPage()
    {
        InitializeComponent();
    }
}
```

The other convenient aspect of **DataTransfer5** is that there is no longer a need to override the `OnAppearing` and `OnDisappearing` methods, and no need to wonder about the order of these method calls during page navigation.

But what's really nice is that it's easy to migrate **DataTransfer5** to a version that saves application data when the program is terminated and restores it the next time the program is run.

Saving and restoring page state

Particularly as you begin working more with multipage applications, it's very beneficial to treat the pages of your application *not* as the primary repositories of data, but merely as temporary visual and interactive views of underlying data. The key word here is *temporary*. If you keep the underlying data up to date as the user interacts with it, then pages can appear and disappear without worry.

The final program in this series is **DataTransfer6**, which saves the contents of `AppData` (and some other information) in application local storage when the program is suspended—and hence when the program is terminated—and then retrieves that data the next time the program starts up.

Besides saving data that the user has painstakingly entered, you'll probably also want to save the state of the page navigation stack. This means that if the user is entering data on the info page and the program terminates, then the next time the program runs, it navigates to that info page with the partially entered data restored.

As you'll recall, the `Application` class defines a property named `Properties` that is a dictionary with `string` keys and `object` values. You can set items in the `Properties` dictionary either before or during the `OnSleep` override in your `App` class. The items will then be available the next time the `App` constructor executes.

The underlying platform serializes objects in the `Properties` dictionary by converting the objects to a form in which they can be saved to a file. It doesn't matter to the application programmer whether this is a binary form or a string form, perhaps XML or JSON.

For integer or floating-point numbers, for `DateTime` values, or for strings, the serialization is straightforward. On some platforms, it might be possible to save an instance of a more complex class, such as `InformationViewModel`, directly to the `Properties` collection. However, this doesn't work on all the platforms. It's much safer to serialize classes yourself to XML or JSON strings and then save the resultant strings in the `Properties` collection. With the version of .NET available to Xamarin.Forms Portable Class Libraries, XML serialization is a bit easier than JSON serialization, and that's what **Data-Transfer6** uses.

When performing serialization and deserialization, you need to watch out for object references. Serialization does not preserve object equality. Let's see how this can be an issue:

The version of `AppData` introduced in **DataTransfer5** has two properties: `InfoCollection`, which is a collection of `InformationViewModel` objects, and `CurrentInfo`, which is an `Information-ViewModel` object that is currently being edited.

The program relies on the fact that the `CurrentInfo` object is also an item in the `InfoCollection`. The `CurrentInfo` becomes the `BindingContext` for the info page, and the properties of that `InformationViewModel` instance are interactively altered by the user. But only because that same object is part of `InfoCollection` will the new values show up in the `ListView`.

What happens when you serialize the `InfoCollection` and `CurrentInfo` properties of `AppData` and then deserialize to create a new `AppData`?

In the deserialized version, the `CurrentInfo` object will have the exact same properties as one of the items in the `InfoCollection`, but it won't be the same instance. If the program is restored to allow the user to continue editing an item on the info page, none of those edits will be reflected in the object in the `ListView` collection.

With that mental preparation, it is now time to look at the version of `AppData` in **DataTransfer6**.

```csharp
public class AppData
{
    public AppData()
    {
        InfoCollection = new ObservableCollection<InformationViewModel>();
        CurrentInfoIndex = -1;
    }

    public ObservableCollection<InformationViewModel> InfoCollection { private set; get; }

    [XmlIgnore]
    public InformationViewModel CurrentInfo { set; get; }

    public int CurrentInfoIndex { set; get; }

    public string Serialize()
    {
        // If the CurrentInfo is valid, set the CurrentInfoIndex.
        if (CurrentInfo != null)
```

```
        {
            CurrentInfoIndex = InfoCollection.IndexOf(CurrentInfo);
        }
        XmlSerializer serializer = new XmlSerializer(typeof(AppData));
        using (StringWriter stringWriter = new StringWriter())
        {
            serializer.Serialize(stringWriter, this);
            return stringWriter.GetStringBuilder().ToString();
        }
    }

    public static AppData Deserialize(string strAppData)
    {
        XmlSerializer serializer = new XmlSerializer(typeof(AppData));
        using (StringReader stringReader = new StringReader(strAppData))
        {
            AppData appData = (AppData)serializer.Deserialize(stringReader);

            // If the CurrentInfoIndex is valid, set the CurrentInfo.
            if (appData.CurrentInfoIndex != -1)
            {
                appData.CurrentInfo = appData.InfoCollection[appData.CurrentInfoIndex];
            }
            return appData;
        }
    }
}
```

This version has an `InfoCollection` property and a `CurrentInfo` property like the previous version, but it also includes a `CurrentInfoIndex` property of type `int`, and the `CurrentInfo` property is flagged with the `XmlIgnore` attribute, which means that it won't be serialized.

The class also has two methods, named `Serialize` and `Deserialize`. `Serialize` begins by setting the `CurrentInfoIndex` property to the index of `CurrentInfo` within the `InfoCollection`. It then converts the instance of the class to an XML string and returns that string.

`Deserialize` does the opposite. It is a static method with a `string` argument. The string is assumed to be the XML representation of an `AppData` object. After it's converted into an `AppData` instance, the method sets the `CurrentInfo` property based on the `CurrentInfoIndex` property. Now `CurrentInfo` is once again the identical object to one of the members of the `InfoCollection`. The method returns that `AppData` instance.

The only other change from **DataTransfer5** to **DataTransfer6** is the `App` class. The `OnSleep` override serializes the `AppData` object and saves it in the `Properties` dictionary with a key of "appData". But it also saves a Boolean value with the key "isInfoPageActive" if the user has navigated to `Data-Transfer6InfoPage` and is possibly in the process of entering or editing information.

The `App` constructor deserializes the string available from the "appData" `Properties` entry or sets the `AppData` property to a new instance if that dictionary entry doesn't exist. If the "isInfoPageActive" entry is true, it must not only instantiate `DataTransfer6MainPage` as the argument to the `NavigationPage` constructor (as usual), but must also navigate to `DataTransfer6InfoPage`:

```csharp
public class App : Application
{
    public App()
    {
        // Ensure link to Toolkit library.
        Xamarin.FormsBook.Toolkit.Toolkit.Init;

        // Load previous AppData if it exists.
        if (Properties.ContainsKey("appData"))
        {
            AppData = AppData.Deserialize((string)Properties["appData"]);
        }
        else
        {
            AppData = new AppData();
        }

        // Launch home page.
        Page homePage = new DataTransfer6HomePage();
        MainPage = new NavigationPage(homePage);

        // Possibly navigate to info page.
        if (Properties.ContainsKey("isInfoPageActive") &&
            (bool)Properties["isInfoPageActive"])
        {
            homePage.Navigation.PushAsync(new DataTransfer6InfoPage(), false);
        }
    }

    public AppData AppData { private set; get; }

    protected override void OnStart()
    {
        // Handle when your app starts
    }

    protected override void OnSleep()
    {
        // Save AppData serialized into string.
        Properties["appData"] = AppData.Serialize();

        // Save Boolean for info page active.
        Properties["isInfoPageActive"] =
            MainPage.Navigation.NavigationStack.Last() is DataTransfer6InfoPage;
    }

    protected override void OnResume()
    {
        // Handle when your app resumes
    }
}
```

To test this program, it is necessary to terminate the program in such a way that the App class gets a call to its OnSleep method. If you're running the program under the Visual Studio or Xamarin Studio debugger, do *not* terminate the program from the debugger. Instead, terminate the application on the phone.

Perhaps the best way of terminating a program on phones and phone emulators is to first display all the currently running programs:

- On iOS, double tap the **Home** button.

- On Android, tap the (rightmost) **MultiTask** button.

- On Windows Phone, hold down the (leftmost) **Back** button.

This action causes the OnSleep method to be called. You can then terminate the program:

- On iOS, swipe the application up.

- On Android, swipe it to the side.

- On Windows Phone, swipe it down.

When running the Windows program in a window, you can terminate the program simply by clicking the **Close** button. In tablet mode, swipe the program down from the top.

You can then use Visual Studio or Xamarin Studio to stop debugging the application (if necessary). Then run the program again to see whether it "remembers" where it left off.

Saving and restoring the navigation stack

Many multipage applications have a page architecture that is more complex than **DataTransfer6**, and you'll want a generalized way to save and restore the entire navigation stack. Moreover, you'll probably want to integrate the preservation of the navigation stack with a systematic way to save and restore the state of each page, particularly if you're not using MVVM.

In an MVVM application, generally a ViewModel is responsible for saving the data that underlies the various pages of an application. But in the absence of a ViewModel, that job is left up to each individual page, generally involving the Properties dictionary implemented by the Application class. However, you need to be careful not to have duplicate dictionary keys in two or more pages. Duplicate keys are particularly likely if a particular page type might have multiple instances in the navigation stack.

The problem of duplicate dictionary keys can be avoided if each page in the navigation stack uses a unique prefix for its dictionary keys. For example, the home page might use a prefix of "0" for all its dictionary keys, the next page in the navigation stack might use a prefix of "1" and so forth.

The **Xamarin.FormsBook.Toolkit** library has an interface and a class that work together to help you with saving and restoring the navigation stack, and saving and restoring page state using unique dictionary key prefixes. This interface and class do not preclude the use of MVVM with your application.

The interface is called `IPersistentPage`, and it has methods named `Save` and `Restore` that include the dictionary-key prefix as an argument:

```
namespace Xamarin.FormsBook.Toolkit
{
    public interface IPersistentPage
    {
        void Save(string prefix);

        void Restore(string prefix);
    }
}
```

Any page in your application can implement `IPersistentPage`. The `Save` and `Restore` methods are responsible for using the `prefix` parameter when adding items to the `Properties` dictionary or accessing those items. You'll see examples shortly.

These `Save` and `Restore` methods are called from a class named `MultiPageRestorableApp`, which derives from `Application` and is intended to be a base class for the `App` class. When you derive `App` from `MultiPageRestorableApp`, you have two responsibilities:

- From the `App` class's constructor, call the `Startup` method of `MultiPageRestorableApp` with the type of the application's home page.

- Call the base class's `OnSleep` method from the `OnSleep` override of the `App` class.

There are also two requirements when using `MultiPageRestoreableApp`:

- Each page in the application must have a parameterless constructor.

- When you derive `App` from `MultiPageRestorableApp`, this base class becomes a public type exposed from the application's Portable Class Library. This means that all the individual platform projects also require a reference to the **Xamarin.FormsBook.Toolkit** library.

`MultiPageRestorableApp` implements its `OnSleep` method by looping through the contents of `NavigationStack` and `ModalStack`. Each page is given a unique index starting at 0, and each page is reduced to a short string that includes the page type, the page's index, and a Boolean indicating whether the page is modal:

```
namespace Xamarin.FormsBook.Toolkit
{
    // Derived classes must call Startup(typeof(YourStartPage));
    // Derived classes must call base.OnSleep() in override
    public class MultiPageRestorableApp : Application
    {
```

```
...
protected override void OnSleep()
{
    StringBuilder pageStack = new StringBuilder();
    int index = 0;

    // Accumulate the modeless pages in pageStack.
    IReadOnlyList<Page> stack = (MainPage as NavigationPage).Navigation.NavigationStack;
    LoopThroughStack(pageStack, stack, ref index, false);

    // Accumulate the modal pages in pageStack.
    stack = (MainPage as NavigationPage).Navigation.ModalStack;
    LoopThroughStack(pageStack, stack, ref index, true);

    // Save the list of pages.
    Properties["pageStack"] = pageStack.ToString();
}

void LoopThroughStack(StringBuilder pageStack, IReadOnlyList<Page> stack,
                      ref int index, bool isModal)
{
    foreach (Page page in stack)
    {
        // Skip the NavigationPage that's often at the bottom of the modal stack.
        if (page is NavigationPage)
            continue;

        pageStack.AppendFormat("{0} {1} {2}", page.GetType().ToString(),
                                              index, isModal);
        pageStack.AppendLine();

        if (page is IPersistentPage)
        {
            string prefix = index.ToString() + ' ';
            ((IPersistentPage)page).Save(prefix);
        }
        index++;
    }
}
```

In addition, each page that implements `IPersistentPage` gets a call to its `Save` method with the integer prefix converted to a string.

The `OnSleep` method concludes by saving the composite string containing one line per page to the `Properties` dictionary with the key "pageStack".

An `App` class that derives from `MultiPageRestorableApp` must call the `Startup` method from its constructor. The `Startup` method accesses the "pageStack" entry in the `Properties` dictionary. For each line, it instantiates a page of that type. If the page implements `IPersistentPage`, then the Restore method is called. Each page is added to the navigation stack with a call to PushAsync or Push-ModalAsync. Notice the second argument to PushAsync and PushModalAsync is set to false to suppress any page-transition animation the platform might implement:

```
namespace Xamarin.FormsBook.Toolkit
{
    // Derived classes must call Startup(typeof(YourStartPage));
    // Derived classes must call base.OnSleep() in override
    public class MultiPageRestorableApp : Application
    {
        protected void Startup(Type startPageType)
        {
            object value;

            if (Properties.TryGetValue("pageStack", out value))
            {
                MainPage = new NavigationPage();
                RestorePageStack((string)value);
            }
            else
            {
                // First time the program is run.
                Assembly assembly = this.GetType().GetTypeInfo().Assembly;
                Page page = (Page)Activator.CreateInstance(startPageType);
                MainPage = new NavigationPage(page);
            }
        }

        async void RestorePageStack(string pageStack)
        {
            Assembly assembly = GetType().GetTypeInfo().Assembly;
            StringReader reader = new StringReader(pageStack);
            string line = null;

            // Each line is a page in the navigation stack.
            while (null != (line = reader.ReadLine()))
            {
                string[] split = line.Split(' ');
                string pageTypeName = split[0];
                string prefix = split[1] + ' ';
                bool isModal = Boolean.Parse(split[2]);

                // Instantiate the page.
                Type pageType = assembly.GetType(pageTypeName);
                Page page = (Page)Activator.CreateInstance(pageType);

                // Call Restore on the page if it's available.
                if (page is IPersistentPage)
                {
                    ((IPersistentPage)page).Restore(prefix);
                }

                if (!isModal)
                {
```

```
                            // Navigate to the next modeless page.
                            await MainPage.Navigation.PushAsync(page, false);

                            // HACK: to allow page navigation to complete!
                            if (Device.OS == TargetPlatform.Windows &&
                                    Device.Idiom != TargetIdiom.Phone)
                                await Task.Delay(250);
                        }
                        else
                        {
                            // Navigate to the next modal page.
                            await MainPage.Navigation.PushModalAsync(page, false);

                            // HACK: to allow page navigation to complete!
                            if (Device.OS == TargetPlatform.iOS)
                                await Task.Delay(100);
                        }
                    }
                }
            }
            ...
        }
}
```

This code contains two comments that begin with the word "HACK". These indicate statements that are intended to fix two problems encountered in Xamarin.Forms:

- On iOS, nested modal pages don't properly restore unless a little time separates the PushModalAsync calls.

- On Windows 8.1, modeless pages do not contain left arrow **Back** buttons unless a little time separates the calls to PushAsync.

Let's try it out!

The **StackRestoreDemo** program has three pages, named DemoMainPage, DemoModelessPage, and DemoModalPage, each of which contains a Stepper and implements IPersistentPage to save and restore the Value property associated with that Stepper. You can set different Stepper values on each page and then check whether they're restored correctly.

The App class derives from MultiPageRestorableApp. It calls Startup from its constructor and calls the base class OnSleep method from its OnSleep override:

```
public class App : Xamarin.FormsBook.Toolkit.MultiPageRestorableApp
{
    public App()
    {
        // Must call Startup with type of start page!
        Startup(typeof(DemoMainPage));
    }

    protected override void OnSleep()
    {
```

```
            // Must call base implementation!
            base.OnSleep();
        }
    }
}
```

The XAML for `DemoMainPage` instantiates a `Stepper`, a `Label` showing the value of that `Stepper`, and two `Button` elements:

```xaml
<ContentPage xmlns="http://xamarin.com/schemas/2014/forms"
             xmlns:x="http://schemas.microsoft.com/winfx/2009/xaml"
             x:Class="StackRestoreDemo.DemoMainPage"
             Title="Main Page">

    <StackLayout>
        <Label Text="Main Page"
               FontSize="Large"
               VerticalOptions="CenterAndExpand"
               HorizontalOptions="Center" />

        <Grid VerticalOptions="CenterAndExpand">
            <Stepper x:Name="stepper"
                     Grid.Column="0"
                     VerticalOptions="Center"
                     HorizontalOptions="Center" />

            <Label Grid.Column="1"
                   Text="{Binding Source={x:Reference stepper},
                                  Path=Value,
                                  StringFormat='{0:F0}'}"
                   FontSize="Large"
                   VerticalOptions="Center"
                   HorizontalOptions="Center" />
        </Grid>

        <Button Text="Go to Modeless Page"
                FontSize="Large"
                VerticalOptions="CenterAndExpand"
                HorizontalOptions="Center"
                Clicked="OnGoToModelessPageClicked" />

        <Button Text="Go to Modal Page"
                FontSize="Large"
                VerticalOptions="CenterAndExpand"
                HorizontalOptions="Center"
                Clicked="OnGoToModalPageClicked" />

    </StackLayout>
</ContentPage>
```

The event handlers for the two `Button` elements navigate to `DemoModelessPage` and `DemoModal-Page`. The implementation of `IPersistentPage` saves and restores the `Value` property of the `Step-per` element by using the `Properties` dictionary. Notice the use of the `prefix` parameter in defining the dictionary key:

```
public partial class DemoMainPage : ContentPage, IPersistentPage
{
    public DemoMainPage()
    {
        InitializeComponent();
    }

    async void OnGoToModelessPageClicked(object sender, EventArgs args)
    {
        await Navigation.PushAsync(new DemoModelessPage());
    }

    async void OnGoToModalPageClicked(object sender, EventArgs args)
    {
        await Navigation.PushModalAsync(new DemoModalPage());
    }

    public void Save(string prefix)
    {
        App.Current.Properties[prefix + "stepperValue"] = stepper.Value;
    }

    public void Restore(string prefix)
    {
        object value;
        if (App.Current.Properties.TryGetValue(prefix + "stepperValue", out value))
            stepper.Value = (double)value;
    }
}
```

The DemoModelessPage class is essentially the same as DemoMainPage except for the Title property and the Label that displays the same text as the Title.

The DemoModalPage is somewhat different. It also has a Stepper and a Label that displays the value of the Stepper, but one Button returns to the previous page and the other Button navigates to another modal page:

```
<ContentPage xmlns="http://xamarin.com/schemas/2014/forms"
             xmlns:x="http://schemas.microsoft.com/winfx/2009/xaml"
             x:Class="StackRestoreDemo.DemoModalPage"
             Title="Modal Page">

    <StackLayout>
        <Label Text="Modal Page"
               FontSize="Large"
               VerticalOptions="CenterAndExpand"
               HorizontalOptions="Center" />

        <Grid VerticalOptions="CenterAndExpand">
            <Stepper x:Name="stepper"
                     Grid.Column="0"
                     VerticalOptions="Center"
                     HorizontalOptions="Center" />
```

```xml
            <Label Grid.Column="1"
                   Text="{Binding Source={x:Reference stepper},
                                  Path=Value,
                                  StringFormat='{0:F0}'}"
                   FontSize="Large"
                   VerticalOptions="Center"
                   HorizontalOptions="Center" />
        </Grid>

        <Button Text="Go Back"
                FontSize="Large"
                VerticalOptions="CenterAndExpand"
                HorizontalOptions="Center"
                Clicked="OnGoBackClicked" />

        <Button x:Name="gotoModalButton"
                Text="Go to Modal Page"
                FontSize="Large"
                VerticalOptions="CenterAndExpand"
                HorizontalOptions="Center"
                Clicked="OnGoToModalPageClicked" />

    </StackLayout>
</ContentPage>
```

The code-behind file contains handlers for those two buttons and also implements IPersis-tantPage:

```csharp
public partial class DemoModalPage : ContentPage, IPersistentPage
{
    public DemoModalPage()
    {
        InitializeComponent();
    }

    async void OnGoBackClicked(object sender, EventArgs args)
    {
        await Navigation.PopModalAsync();
    }

    async void OnGoToModalPageClicked(object sender, EventArgs args)
    {
        await Navigation.PushModalAsync(new DemoModalPage());
    }

    public void Save(string prefix)
    {
        App.Current.Properties[prefix + "stepperValue"] = stepper.Value;
    }

    public void Restore(string prefix)
    {
        object value;
```

```
        if (App.Current.Properties.TryGetValue(prefix + "stepperValue", out value))
            stepper.Value = (double)value;
    }
}
```

One easy way to test the program is to progressively navigate to several modeless and then modal pages, setting a different value on the `Stepper` on each page. Then terminate the application from the phone or emulator (as described earlier) and start it up again. You should be on the same page as the page you left and see the same `Stepper` values as you go back through the pages.

Something like a real-life app

Ideally, users should not be aware when an application is terminated and restarted. The application experience should be continuous and seamless. A half-entered `Entry` that was never completed should still be in the same state a week later even if the program hasn't been running all that time.

The **NoteTaker** program allows a user to take notes consisting of a title and some text. Because there may be quite a few of these notes, and they have the potential of becoming quite long, they are not stored in the `Properties` dictionary. Instead, the program makes use of the `IFileHelper` interface and `FileHelper` classes demonstrated in the **TextFileAsync** program in Chapter 20, "Async and file I/O." Each note is a separate file. Like **TextFileAsync**, the **NoteTaker** solution also contains all the projects in the **Xamarin.FormsBook.Platform** solution and references to those library projects.

NoteTaker is structured much like the `DataTransfer` programs earlier in this chapter, with pages named `NoteTakerHomePage` and `NoteTakerNotePage`.

The home page consists of an `ItemsView` that dominates the page and an **Add** button. This **Add** button is a `ToolbarItem` that takes the form of a plus sign in the upper-right corner of the iOS, Android, and Windows Phone screens:

Pressing that button causes the program to navigate to the `NoteTakerNotePage`. At the top is an `Entry` for a title, but most of the page is occupied by an `Editor` for the text of the note itself. You can now type in a title and note:

It is not necessary to enter a title. If there is none, an identifier is constructed that consists of the beginning of the text. Nor is it necessary to enter the note text. A note can consist solely of a title. (At the time this chapter was written, the Windows Runtime `Editor` didn't properly wrap text.)

If either the title or note isn't blank, the note is considered to be a valid note. When you go back to the home page by using the standard **Back** button either in the navigation bar or at the bottom of the screen, the new note is added to the `ListView`:

You can now add more new notes or edit an existing note by tapping the entry in the `ListView`. The `ListView` tap navigates to the same page as the **Add** button, but notice that the `Title` property on the second page is now "Edit Note" rather than "New Note":

You can now make changes to the note and return back to the home page. Two toolbar items are also available on this page: The first is a **Cancel** button that allows you to abandon any edits you've made. An alert asks whether you're sure. You can also tap the **Delete** item to delete the note, also with an alert for confirmation.

One of the tricky aspects of this program involves the **Cancel** button. Suppose you're in the middle of editing a note and you get distracted, and eventually the program is terminated. The next time you start up the program, you should return to the edit screen and see your edits. If you then invoke the **Cancel** command, your edits should be abandoned.

This means that when the application is suspended while a note is being edited, the note must essentially be saved in two different forms: The pre-edit note and the note with the edits. The program handles this by saving each note to a file only when NoteTakerNotePage gets a call to its OnDisappearing override. (However, some special consideration needs to accommodate the case in iOS when the page gets a call to OnDisappearing when the program terminates.) The file version of the Note object is the one without the edits. The edited version is reflected by the current contents of the Entry and Editor; NoteTakerNotePage saves those two text strings in the Save method of its IPersistantPage implementation.

The Note class implements INotifyPropertyChanged by virtue of deriving from ViewModelBase in the **Xamarin.FormsBook.Toolkit** library. The class defines four public properties: Filename, Title, Text, and Identifier, which is either the same as Title or the first 30 characters of Text, truncated to display complete words only. The Filename property is set from the constructor and never changes:

```
public class Note : ViewModelBase, IEquatable<Note>
{
    string title, text, identifier;
    FileHelper fileHelper = new FileHelper();

    public Note(string filename)
    {
        Filename = filename;
    }

    public string Filename { private set; get; }

    public string Title
    {
        set
        {
            if (SetProperty(ref title, value))
            {
                Identifier = MakeIdentifier();
            }
        }
        get { return title; }
    }

    public string Text
```

```csharp
    {
        set
        {
            if (SetProperty(ref text, value) && String.IsNullOrWhiteSpace(Title))
            {
                Identifier = MakeIdentifier();
            }
        }
        get { return text; }
    }

    public string Identifier
    {
        private set { SetProperty(ref identifier, value); }
        get { return identifier; }
    }

    string MakeIdentifier()
    {
        if (!String.IsNullOrWhiteSpace(this.Title))
            return Title;

        int truncationLength = 30;

        if (Text == null || Text.Length <= truncationLength)
        {
            return Text;
        }

        string truncated = Text.Substring(0, truncationLength);

        int index = truncated.LastIndexOf(' ');

        if (index != -1)
            truncated = truncated.Substring(0, index);

        return truncated;
    }

    public Task SaveAsync()
    {
        string text = Title + Environment.NewLine + Text;
        return fileHelper.WriteTextAsync(Filename, text);
    }

    public async Task LoadAsync()
    {
        string text = await fileHelper.ReadTextAsync(Filename);

        // Break string into Title and Text.

        int index = text.IndexOf(Environment.NewLine);
        Title = text.Substring(0, index);
        Text = text.Substring(index + Environment.NewLine.Length);
```

```
    }

    public async Task DeleteAsync()
    {
        await fileHelper.DeleteAsync(Filename);
    }

    public bool Equals(Note other)
    {
        return other == null ? false : Filename == other.Filename;
    }
}
```

The `Note` class also defines methods to save, load, or delete the file associated with the particular instance of the class. The first line of the file is the `Title` property, and the remainder of the file is the `Text` property.

In most cases, there is a one-to-one correspondence between `Note` files and instances of the `Note` class. However, if the `DeleteAsync` method is called, then the `Note` object still exists, but the file does not. (However, as you'll see, all references to a `Note` object whose `DeleteAsync` method is called are quickly detached and the object become eligible for garbage collection.)

The program does not maintain a list of these files when the program isn't running. Instead, the `NoteFolder` class obtains all the files in the application's local storage with a filename extension of ".note" and creates a collection of `Note` objects from these files:

```
public class NoteFolder
{
    public NoteFolder()
    {
        this.Notes = new ObservableCollection<Note>();
        GetFilesAsync();
    }

    public ObservableCollection<Note> Notes { private set; get; }

    async void GetFilesAsync()
    {
        FileHelper fileHelper = new FileHelper();

        // Sort the filenames.
        IEnumerable<string> filenames =
            from filename in await fileHelper.GetFilesAsync()
            where filename.EndsWith(".note")
            orderby (filename)
            select filename;

        // Store them in the Notes collection.
        foreach (string filename in filenames)
        {
            Note note = new Note(filename);
            await note.LoadAsync();
```

```
            Notes.Add(note);
        }
    }
}
```

As you'll see, the filename is constructed from a `DateTime` object at the time the note is first created, consisting of the year followed by the month, day, and time, which means that when these `Note` files are sorted by filename, they appear in the collection in the same order in which they are created.

The `App` class instantiates `NoteFolder` and makes it available as a public property. `App` derives from `MultiPageRestorableApp`, so it calls `Startup` with the `NoteTakerHomePage` type, and also implements the `OnSleep` override by calling the base class implementation:

```
public class App : MultiPageRestorableApp
{
    public App()
    {
        // This loads all the existing .note files.
        NoteFolder = new NoteFolder();

        // Make call to method in MultiPageRestorableApp.
        Startup(typeof(NoteTakerHomePage));
    }

    public NoteFolder NoteFolder { private set; get; }

    protected override void OnSleep()
    {
        // Required call when deriving from MultiPageRestorableApp.
        base.OnSleep();
    }

    // Special processing for iOS.
    protected override void OnResume()
    {
        NoteTakerNotePage notePage =
            ((NavigationPage)MainPage).CurrentPage as NoteTakerNotePage;

        if (notePage != null)
            notePage.OnResume();
    }
}
```

The `App` class also overrides the `OnResume` method. If `NoteTakerNotePage` is currently active, the method calls an `OnResume` method in the note page. This is some special processing for iOS. As you'll see, `NoteTakerNotePage` saves a `Note` object to a file during its `OnDisappearing` override, but it shouldn't do that if the `OnDisappearing` override indicates that the application is terminating.

The XAML file for the `NoteTakerHomePage` instantiates the `ListView` for displaying all the `Note` objects. The `ItemsSource` is bound to the `Notes` collection of the `NoteFolder` that is stored in the `App` class. Each `Note` object is displayed in the `ListView` with its `Identifier` property:

```
<ContentPage xmlns="http://xamarin.com/schemas/2014/forms"
             xmlns:x="http://schemas.microsoft.com/winfx/2009/xaml"
             x:Class="NoteTaker.NoteTakerHomePage"
             Title="Note Taker">

    <ListView ItemsSource="{Binding Source={x:Static Application.Current},
                                    Path=NoteFolder.Notes}"
              ItemSelected="OnListViewItemSelected"
              VerticalOptions="FillAndExpand">
        <ListView.ItemTemplate>
            <DataTemplate>
                <TextCell Text="{Binding Identifier}" />
            </DataTemplate>
        </ListView.ItemTemplate>
    </ListView>

    <ContentPage.ToolbarItems>
        <ToolbarItem Name="Add Note"
                     Order="Primary"
                     Activated="OnAddNoteActivated">
            <ToolbarItem.Icon>
                <OnPlatform x:TypeArguments="FileImageSource"
                            iOS="new.png"
                            Android="ic_action_new.png"
                            WinPhone="Images/add.png" />
            </ToolbarItem.Icon>
        </ToolbarItem>
    </ContentPage.ToolbarItems>
</ContentPage>
```

The code-behind file is dedicated to handling just two events: The `ItemSelected` event of the `ListView` for editing an existing `Note`, and the `Activated` event of the `ToolbarItem` for creating a new `Note`:

```
partial class NoteTakerHomePage : ContentPage
{
    public NoteTakerHomePage()
    {
        InitializeComponent();
    }

    async void OnListViewItemSelected(object sender, SelectedItemChangedEventArgs args)
    {
        if (args.SelectedItem != null)
        {
            // Deselect the item.
            ListView listView = (ListView)sender;
            listView.SelectedItem = null;

            // Navigate to NotePage.
            await Navigation.PushAsync(new NoteTakerNotePage
                {
                    Note = (Note)args.SelectedItem,
                    IsNoteEdit = true
```

```
                });
        }
    }

    async void OnAddNoteActivated(object sender, EventArgs args)
    {
        // Create unique filename.
        DateTime dateTime = DateTime.UtcNow;
        string filename = dateTime.ToString("yyyyMMddHHmmssfff") + ".note";

        // Navigate to NotePage.
        await Navigation.PushAsync(new NoteTakerNotePage
            {
                Note = new Note(filename),
                IsNoteEdit = false
            });
    }
}
```

In both cases, the event handler instantiates NoteTakerNotePage, sets two properties, and navigates to that page. For a new note, a filename is constructed and a Note object is instantiated. For an existing note, the Note object is simply the selected item from the ListView. Notice that the new note has a filename but is not yet saved to a file or made part of the Notes collection in NoteFolder.

The XAML file for NoteTakerNotePage has an Entry and Editor for entering a note's title and text. The data bindings on the Text properties of these elements imply that the BindingContext for the page is a Note object:

```xml
<ContentPage xmlns="http://xamarin.com/schemas/2014/forms"
             xmlns:x="http://schemas.microsoft.com/winfx/2009/xaml"
             x:Class="NoteTaker.NoteTakerNotePage"
             Title="New Note">

    <StackLayout>
        <Label Text="Title:" />

        <Entry Text="{Binding Title}"
               Placeholder="Title (optional)" />

        <Label Text="Note:" />

        <Editor Text="{Binding Text}"
                Keyboard="Text"
                VerticalOptions="FillAndExpand" />
    </StackLayout>

    <ContentPage.ToolbarItems>
        <ToolbarItem Name="Cancel"
                     Order="Primary"
                     Activated="OnCancelActivated">
            <ToolbarItem.Icon>
                <OnPlatform x:TypeArguments="FileImageSource"
                            iOS="cancel.png"
```

```
                                   Android="ic_action_cancel.png"
                                   WinPhone="Images/cancel.png" />
                </ToolbarItem.Icon>
            </ToolbarItem>

            <ToolbarItem Name="Delete"
                         Order="Primary"
                         Activated="OnDeleteActivated">
                <ToolbarItem.Icon>
                    <OnPlatform x:TypeArguments="FileImageSource"
                                iOS="discard.png"
                                Android="ic_action_discard.png"
                                WinPhone="Images/delete.png" />
                </ToolbarItem.Icon>
            </ToolbarItem>
        </ContentPage.ToolbarItems>
</ContentPage>
```

The two ToolbarItem elements toward the bottom should be visible only when an existing note is being edited. The removal of these toolbar items occurs in the code-behind file when the IsNoteEdit property is set from the home page. That code also changes the Title property for the page. The set accessor for the Note property is responsible for setting the page's BindingContext:

```
public partial class NoteTakerNotePage : ContentPage, IPersistentPage
{
    Note note;
    bool isNoteEdit;
    …
    public NoteTakerNotePage()
    {
        InitializeComponent();
    }

    public Note Note
    {
        set
        {
            note = value;
            BindingContext = note;
        }
        get { return note; }
    }

    public bool IsNoteEdit
    {
        set
        {
            isNoteEdit = value;
            Title = IsNoteEdit ? "Edit Note" : "New Note";

            // No toolbar items if it's a new Note!
            if (!IsNoteEdit)
            {
```

```
                ToolbarItems.Clear();
            }
        }
        get { return isNoteEdit; }
    }
    ...
}
```

The `NoteTakerNotePage` class implements the `IPersistentPage` interface, which means that it has methods named `Save` and `Restore` for saving and restoring the page state. These methods use the `Properties` dictionary to save and restore the three properties of `Note` that define a `Note` object—the `Filename`, `Title`, and `Text` properties—and the `IsNoteEdit` property of `NoteTaker-NotePage`. This is the `Note` object in its current edited state:

```csharp
public partial class NoteTakerNotePage : ContentPage, IPersistentPage
{
    ...
    // Special field for iOS.
    bool isInSleepState;
    ...
    // IPersistent implementation
    public void Save(string prefix)
    {
        // Special code for iOS.
        isInSleepState = true;

        Application app = Application.Current;
        app.Properties["fileName"] = Note.Filename;
        app.Properties["title"] = Note.Title;
        app.Properties["text"] = Note.Text;
        app.Properties["isNoteEdit"] = IsNoteEdit;
    }

    public void Restore(string prefix)
    {
        Application app = Application.Current;

        // Create a new Note object.
        Note note = new Note((string)app.Properties["fileName"])
        {
            Title = (string)app.Properties["title"],
            Text = (string)app.Properties["text"]
        };

        // Set the properties of this class.
        Note = note;
        IsNoteEdit = (bool)app.Properties["isNoteEdit"];
    }

    // Special code for iOS.
    public void OnResume()
    {
        isInSleepState = false;
```

```
        }
        ...
}
```

The class also defines a method named `OnResume` that is called from the `App` class. Thus, the `isInSleepState` field is `true` when the application has been suspended.

The purpose of the `isInSleepState` field is to avoid saving the `Note` to a file when the `OnDisappearing` override is called as the application is being terminated under iOS. Saving this `Note` object to a file would not allow the user to later abandon edits of the `Note` by pressing the **Cancel** button on this page.

If the `OnDisappearing` override indicates that the user is returning back to the home page—as it otherwise does in this application—then the `Note` object can be saved to a file, and possibly added to the `Notes` collection in `NoteFolder`:

```
public partial class NoteTakerNotePage : ContentPage, IPersistentPage
{
    ...
    async protected override void OnDisappearing()
    {
        base.OnDisappearing();

        // Special code for iOS:
        //      Do not save note when program is terminating.
        if (isInSleepState)
            return;

        // Only save the note if there's some text somewhere.
        if (!String.IsNullOrWhiteSpace(Note.Title) ||
            !String.IsNullOrWhiteSpace(Note.Text))
        {
            // Save the note to a file.
            await Note.SaveAsync();

            // Add it to the collection if it's a new note.
            NoteFolder noteFolder = ((App)App.Current).NoteFolder;

            // IndexOf method finds match based on Filename property
            //      based on implementation of IEquatable in Note.
            int index = noteFolder.Notes.IndexOf(note);
            if (index == -1)
            {
                // No match -- add it.
                noteFolder.Notes.Add(note);
            }
            else
            {
                // Match -- replace it.
                noteFolder.Notes[index] = note;
            }
        }
    }
}
```

```
    ...
}
```

The Note class implements the IEquatable interface and defines two Note objects to be equal if their Filename properties are the same. The OnDisappearing override relies on that definition of equality to avoid adding a Note object to the collection if another one already exists with the same Filename property.

Finally, the NoteTakerNotePage code-behind file has handlers for the two ToolbarItem elements. In both cases, the processing begins with a call to DisplayAlert to get user confirmation, and either reloads the Note object from the file (effectively overwriting any edits), or deletes the file and removes it from the Notes collection:

```
public partial class NoteTakerNotePage : ContentPage, IPersistentPage
{
    ...
    async void OnCancelActivated(object sender, EventArgs args)
    {
        if (await DisplayAlert("Note Taker", "Cancel note edit?",
                                            "Yes", "No"))
        {
            // Reload note.
            await Note.LoadAsync();

            // Return to home page.
            await Navigation.PopAsync();
        }
    }

    async void OnDeleteActivated(object sender, EventArgs args)
    {
        if (await DisplayAlert("Note Taker", "Delete this note?",
                                            "Yes", "No"))
        {
            // Delete Note file and remove from collection.
            await Note.DeleteAsync();
            ((App)App.Current).NoteFolder.Notes.Remove(Note);

            // Wipe out Entry and Editor so the Note
            //   won't be saved during OnDisappearing.
            Note.Title = "";
            Note.Text = "";

            // Return to home page.
            await Navigation.PopAsync();
        }
    }
}
```

Of course, this is not the only way to write a program like this. It's possible to move a lot of the logic for creating, editing, and deleting notes into AppData and make it a proper ViewModel. AppData would probably need a new property of type Note called CurrentNote, and several properties of type

`ICommand` for binding to the `Command` property of each of the `ToolbarItem` elements.

Some programmers even try to move page-navigation logic into ViewModels, but not everyone agrees that this is a proper approach to MVVM. Is a page part of the user interface and hence part of the View? Or are pages really more like a collection of related data items?

Philosophical questions such as those might become even more vexing as the varieties of page types in Xamarin.Forms are explored in the next chapter.

Chapter 25
Page varieties

If you think of a Xamarin.Forms application as a building, then you construct this building from bricks that take the form of views and elements. You arrange them into walls using layout classes, and then form them into rooms with `ContentPage`, with passages from room to room made possible with navigational functions structured around `NavigationPage`.

This visual architecture can be enhanced a bit more with other instantiable classes that derive from `Page`. Here's the complete hierarchy:

```
Page
     TemplatedPage
           ContentPage
     NavigationPage
     MasterDetailPage
     MultiPage<T>
           TabbedPage
           CarouselPage
```

This chapter is devoted to these additional `Page` derivatives, which are similar in that they serve as parents to manage the visual presentation of two or more other pages:

- `MasterDetailPage` manages two pages: The *master* is generally a collection of data or a list of items, and the *detail* generally displays a particular item from the collection.

- `TabbedPage` consists of multiple child pages identified by tabs. You can populate `TabbedPage` with a collection of discrete pages or automatically generate tabs and pages based on a collection of data in much the same way that a `ListView` generates items based on a data collection. With this second option, each tab is associated with a member of the collection, formatted with a template, but this option is not suitable for iOS platforms.

The `CarouselPage` is slated for deprecation in favor of a forthcoming `CarouselView`, so it will not be discussed in this chapter. `MultiPage<T>` is abstract and cannot be instantiated itself, but it defines most of the properties and events for `TabbedPage`.

Master and Detail

The `MasterDetailPage` defines two properties, named `Master` and `Detail` of type `Page`. Generally, you'll set these two properties to objects of type `ContentPage`, but currently, to get `MasterDetail-Page` to work on the Universal Windows Platform, the detail page must be a `NavigationPage`.

How the `MasterDetailPage` displays and switches between these two pages depends on several factors: the underlying operating system, whether you're running the program on a phone or tablet, the portrait or landscape orientation of the device, and the setting of a property of `MasterDetail-Page` named `MasterBehavior`. Several behaviors are possible:

- *split*: The master and detail pages are displayed side by side, the master on the left and the detail on the right.

- *popover*: The detail page is animated to cover, or partially cover, the master page. There are three possibilities:

    o *slide*: The detail and master page slide back and forth.

    o *overlap*: The detail page partially covers the master page.

    o *swap*: The detail page entirely obscures the master page.

In theory, the `MasterBehavior` property of `MasterDetailPage` allows you to choose between the *split* and *popover* behaviors. You set this property to one of the five members of the `MasterBehavior` enumeration:

- `Default`

- `Split`

- `SplitOnLandscape`

- `SplitOnPortrait`

- `Popover`

As you'll see, however, the setting of the `MasterBehavior` property has *no effect* for applications running on phones. It only affects applications running on a tablet or the desktop. Phones always exhibit a *popover* behavior. Whether this behavior results in a *slide*, *overlap*, or *swap* depends on the platform.

Exploring the behaviors

Let's explore these behaviors with a program named **MasterDetailBehaviors**. The program defines three pages, named `DemoPage` (which derives from `MasterDetailPage`), and two `ContentPage` derivatives that are children of the `MasterDetailPage`. These are named `MasterPage` and `Detail-Page`.

`MasterPage` and `DetailPage` are very similar. Here's `MasterPage`:

```
<ContentPage xmlns="http://xamarin.com/schemas/2014/forms"
             xmlns:x="http://schemas.microsoft.com/winfx/2009/xaml"
             x:Class="MasterDetailBehaviors.MasterPage"
             Title="Master Page"
             Padding="10"
             x:Name="masterPage">
```

```
<ContentPage.Padding>
    <OnPlatform x:TypeArguments="Thickness"
                iOS="0, 20, 0, 0" />
</ContentPage.Padding>

<Frame OutlineColor="Accent">
    <StackLayout Orientation="Horizontal"
                 Spacing="0"
                 HorizontalOptions="Center"
                 VerticalOptions="Center">

        <Label Text="{Binding Source={x:Reference masterPage},
                              Path=Width,
                              StringFormat='Master: {0:F0}'}"
               FontSize="Large" />

        <Label Text="{Binding Source={x:Reference masterPage},
                              Path=Height,
                              StringFormat=' &#x00D7; {0:F0}'}"
               FontSize="Large" />
    </StackLayout>
</Frame>
</ContentPage>
```

It contains a `Frame` with a pair of `Label` elements to display the width and height of the page. Notice that a `Title` property is set and the page contains the standard `Padding` to avoid overlapping the status bar on the iPhone.

The `DetailPage` does not contain that `Padding`. You'll see that it's unnecessary. But like `Master-Page`, this page also sets the `Title` property and contains a `Frame` with a pair of `Label` elements to display the width and height:

```
<ContentPage xmlns="http://xamarin.com/schemas/2014/forms"
             xmlns:x="http://schemas.microsoft.com/winfx/2009/xaml"
             x:Class="MasterDetailBehaviors.DetailPage"
             Title="Detail Page"
             Padding="10"
             x:Name="detailPage">

    <Frame OutlineColor="Accent">
        <StackLayout Orientation="Horizontal"
                     Spacing="0"
                     VerticalOptions="CenterAndExpand"
                     HorizontalOptions="Center">
            <Label Text="{Binding Source={x:Reference detailPage},
                                  Path=Width,
                                  StringFormat='Detail: {0:F0}'}"
                   FontSize="Large"/>

            <Label Text="{Binding Source={x:Reference detailPage},
                                  Path=Height,
                                  StringFormat=' &#x00D7; {0:F0}'}"
                   FontSize="Large" />
```

```
            </StackLayout>
        </Frame>
</ContentPage>
```

You'll also need a page that derives from `MasterDetailPage`. To add such a page in Visual Studio, add a new item to the project by using the **Forms Xaml Page** template; in Xamarin Studio, add a new file to the project by using the **Forms ContentPage Xaml** template. This creates a page that derives from `ContentPage`, but you can then simply change `ContentPage` to `MasterDetailPage` in both the XAML file and C# code-behind file.

Here's the XAML file for `DemoPage` with `MasterDetailPage` as the root element:

```
<MasterDetailPage xmlns="http://xamarin.com/schemas/2014/forms"
                  xmlns:x="http://schemas.microsoft.com/winfx/2009/xaml"
                  xmlns:local="clr-namespace:MasterDetailBehaviors"
                  x:Class="MasterDetailBehaviors.DemoPage"
                  Title="Demo Page"
                  MasterBehavior="Default">

    <MasterDetailPage.Master>
        <local:MasterPage />
    </MasterDetailPage.Master>

    <MasterDetailPage.Detail>
        <NavigationPage>
            <x:Arguments>
                <local:DetailPage />
            </x:Arguments>
        </NavigationPage>
    </MasterDetailPage.Detail>
</MasterDetailPage>
```

The `MasterDetailPage.Master` and `MasterDetailPage.Detail` property elements are set to instances of `MasterPage` and `DetailPage`, respectively, but with a little difference: The `Detail` property is set to a `NavigationPage`, and the `x:Arguments` tags specify the `DetailPage` as the constructor argument. This is necessary to enable the user interface that lets the user switch between the master and detail pages on the Universal Windows Platform.

Also notice that the `MasterBehavior` property is set to `Default` in the root tag. You can experiment with different settings.

The `App` constructor sets the `MainPage` property to `DemoPage`. A Xamarin.Forms program should not navigate to a `MasterDetailPage`:

```
namespace MasterDetailBehaviors
{
    public class App : Application
    {
        public App()
        {
            MainPage = new DemoPage();
        }
```

```
        ...
    }
}
```

When you first run the program, by default the detail page is initially displayed:

On all three platforms, the heading identifies this as the detail page by displaying the `Title` property of `DetailPage`. The iPhone also displays the `Title` of the `MasterPage`.

The operation to switch from the detail page to the master is different on the three platforms:

- On iOS, swipe the detail page to the right, or tap the Master Page text in the heading.

- On Android, swipe right from the left edge of the phone, or tap the arrow in the upper-left corner.

- On Windows 10 Mobile, tap the menu icon in the upper-left corner.

Here's the result after the switch:

The master page is now visible. In terms of the `MasterBehavior` enumeration, the master page becomes visible with a `Popover` behavior, but the three screenshots illustrate differences between the platforms:

- The behavior on iOS is a *slide*. The detail page slides to the right as the master page slides in from the left; you can still see the left part of the detail page.

- The Android is an *overlay*. It's hard to tell because the detail page is faded out, but look closely, and you can see the `Frame` in the `DetailPage` at the far right of the screen.

- Windows 10 Mobile is also a *slide*. You can see the detail page behind the master page.

On both iOS and Android, the width of the master page is somewhat less than the width of the screen.

To return to the detail page on iOS, swipe to the left. On Android, swipe the master page to the left, tap the visible part of the detail page at the far right of the screen, or tap the **Back** triangle at the bottom of the screen. On Windows Phone, tap the menu icon again or the **Back** arrow.

You'll see similar behavior for these three platforms in landscape mode, except that master page has a similar width as the master page in portrait mode, which results in much more of the detail page being visible:

If you experiment with different settings of the `MasterBehavior` property of `MasterDetailPage`, you'll discover that this property has no effect on phones. Phones always have a *popover* behavior. Only on the iPad and on Windows tablets and the desktop will you see a *split* behavior.

On the iPad in landscape mode, the `MasterBehavior.Default` setting results in a *split* behavior:

However, you can control the behavior. If you set the `MasterBehavior` property to `Popover`, you'll get a master page that overlays the detail page much like on the iPhone.

For an iPad in portrait mode, the default setting is the same as `Popover`, and you'll need to select `Split` or `SplitOnPortrait` to get a split screen in portrait mode.

The `SplitOnLandscape` and `SplitOnPortrait` options allow you to have a different behavior for portrait and landscape modes. The `SplitOnLandscape` setting makes the most sense, and that is why it's the same as `Default` for tablets and the desktop: The master and detail views share the screen in landscape mode, but when the tablet is turned to portrait mode, the detail view occupies the full screen and the master page overlays it.

Here's the program running on the Surface Pro 3 in tablet mode:

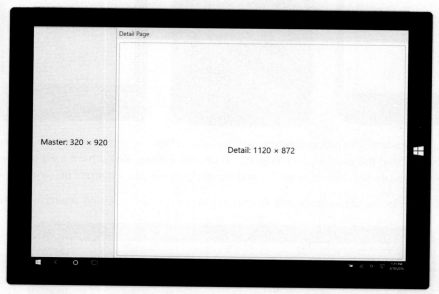

This is a split behavior. You'll see a popover behavior if you start the program with the tablet in portrait mode, and you can control the behavior with different settings of the `MasterBehavior` property.

The user interface to switch between master and detail is a bit different on Windows 8.1 and Windows Phone 8.1. A toolbar item is automatically provided to switch between master and detail:

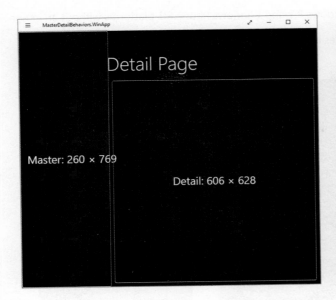

The Windows 8.1 screen shows the split behavior, but if you set it for popover, you'll need to right-click the screen to display the toolbar. The Windows Phone 8.1 screen displays the toolbar normally. You are responsible for setting the toolbar button image and the associated text. The image and text are the same regardless of whether the master or detail view is visible. The text is set from the `Title` property of the master page., which in this case is "Master Page".

The bitmap for the button is set from the `Icon` property of the master page. (This `Icon` property is actually defined by `Page` and inherited by all the other page derivatives.) The Windows 8.1 and Windows Phone 8.1 projects were both given a folder named **Images**. The content of this folder is a PNG file. The constructor in the code-behind file for `MasterPage` sets that bitmap to the `Icon` property:

```
public partial class MasterPage : ContentPage
{
    public MasterPage()
    {
        InitializeComponent();

        if (Device.OS == TargetPlatform.WinPhone ||
            Device.OS == TargetPlatform.Windows)
        {
            Icon = new FileImageSource
            {
                File = "Images/ApplicationBar.Select.png"
            };
        }
    }
}
```

If you do not set that `Icon` property—either in the code-behind file or in the XAML file—the toolbar button will be displayed on the Windows 8.1 and Windows Phone 8.1 platforms without an image.

Tapping that toolbar icon switches between detail and master:

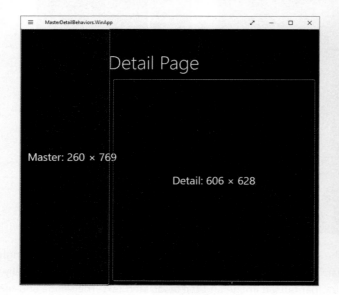

Back to school

So far in this book you've seen a couple of programs that use a `ListView` to display the students of the School of Fine Art. These programs all have different approaches for displaying a detailed look at one of the students. The **SelectedStudentDetail** program in Chapter 19, "Collection views," displayed the `ListView` in the top half of the screen and the detail in the bottom half. The **SchoolAndStudents** program in Chapter 24, "Page navigation," used page navigation to display the student from the `ListView`. Now let's use a `MasterDetailPage` for this job and call it **SchoolAndDetail**.

One major difference between the **SchoolAndDetail** program and **MasterDetailBehaviors** involves how the program is constructed. Rather than having separate classes for the master and detail page, everything is consolidated in one class that derives from `MasterDetailPage`.

This single class (shown below) is named `SchoolAndDetailPage`. The layout of the master and detail pages are defined within the `MasterDetailPage.Master` and `MasterDetailPage.Detail` property-element tags.

The root tag sets a property of `MasterDetailPage` named `IsPresented`. This property allows a program to switch between master and detail views programmatically or declaratively in XAML. The default value is `false`, which means to display the detail page, but the root element of this XAML file sets it to `True` to display the master page at startup:

```
<MasterDetailPage xmlns="http://xamarin.com/schemas/2014/forms"
```

```
                    xmlns:x="http://schemas.microsoft.com/winfx/2009/xaml"
                    xmlns:school="clr-namespace:SchoolOfFineArt;assembly=SchoolOfFineArt"
                    x:Class="SchoolAndDetail.SchoolAndDetailPage"
                    IsPresented="True">

    <MasterDetailPage.Master>
        <ContentPage Title="School">
            <ContentPage.Padding>
                <OnPlatform x:TypeArguments="Thickness"
                            iOS="0, 20, 0, 0" />
            </ContentPage.Padding>

            <ContentPage.Icon>
                <OnPlatform x:TypeArguments="FileImageSource"
                            WinPhone="Images/refresh.png" />
            </ContentPage.Icon>

            <ContentPage.BindingContext>
                <school:SchoolViewModel />
            </ContentPage.BindingContext>

            <StackLayout BindingContext="{Binding StudentBody}">
                <Label Text="{Binding School}"
                       FontSize="Large"
                       FontAttributes="Bold"
                       HorizontalTextAlignment="Center" />

                <ListView x:Name="listView"
                          ItemsSource="{Binding Students}"
                          ItemTapped="OnListViewItemTapped">
                    <ListView.ItemTemplate>
                        <DataTemplate>
                            <ImageCell ImageSource="{Binding PhotoFilename}"
                                       Text="{Binding FullName}"
                                       Detail="{Binding GradePointAverage,
                                                StringFormat='G.P.A. = {0:F2}'}" />
                        </DataTemplate>
                    </ListView.ItemTemplate>
                </ListView>
            </StackLayout>
        </ContentPage>
    </MasterDetailPage.Master>

    <!-- Detail Page -->
    <MasterDetailPage.Detail>
        <NavigationPage>
            <x:Arguments>
                <ContentPage Title="{Binding FirstName}"
                             BindingContext="{Binding Source={x:Reference listView},
                                              Path=SelectedItem}">
                    <StackLayout>
                        <!-- Name -->
                        <StackLayout Orientation="Horizontal"
                                     HorizontalOptions="Center"
```

```
                        Spacing="0">
                <StackLayout.Resources>
                    <ResourceDictionary>
                        <Style TargetType="Label">
                            <Setter Property="FontSize" Value="Large" />
                            <Setter Property="FontAttributes" Value="Bold" />
                        </Style>
                    </ResourceDictionary>
                </StackLayout.Resources>

                <Label Text="{Binding LastName}" />
                <Label Text="{Binding FirstName, StringFormat=', {0}'}" />
                <Label Text="{Binding MiddleName, StringFormat=' {0}'}" />
            </StackLayout>

            <!-- Photo -->
            <Image Source="{Binding PhotoFilename}"
                   VerticalOptions="FillAndExpand" />

            <!-- Sex -->
            <Label Text="{Binding Sex, StringFormat='Sex = {0}'}"
                   HorizontalOptions="Center" />

            <!-- GPA -->
            <Label Text="{Binding GradePointAverage, StringFormat='G.P.A. =
                          {0:F2}'}"
                   HorizontalOptions="Center" />

        </StackLayout>
    </ContentPage>
</x:Arguments>
</NavigationPage>
</MasterDetailPage.Detail>
</MasterDetailPage>
```

Notice also that the `Title` and `Icon` properties are set on the master page. The Windows 8.1 and Windows Phone 8.1 projects contain an **Images** directory with a **Refresh** icon that might also suggest a toggle operation. The master page also instantiates `SchoolViewModel` as an object in the `Master-PageBase.BindingContext` property-element tags.

One advantage of putting everything within a single XAML file is that you can establish a data binding between the master and detail pages. The `BindingContext` of the `ContentPage` that serves as the detail page is bound to the `SelectedItem` property of the `ListView`.

Other than those differences, the page definitions themselves are quite similar to the **SchoolAnd-Students** program in the previous chapter.

The program starts up displaying the master page, which includes the `ListView` with the students:

This program has another way to switch from the master page to the detail page. The code-behind file contains a simple handler for the `ItemTapped` event of the `ListView`:

```
public partial class SchoolAndDetailPage : MasterDetailPage
{
    public SchoolAndDetailPage()
    {
        InitializeComponent();
    }

    void OnListViewItemTapped(object sender, ItemTappedEventArgs args)
    {
        // Show the detail page.
        IsPresented = false;
    }
}
```

The difference between `ItemTapped` and `ItemSelected` is that `ItemTapped` works even if the item is already selected. The `ItemTapped` handler doesn't deselect the item. This maintains a consistency between the selected item in the `ListView` and the contents of the detail page.

Here's the detail page that you'll see after a tap:

To return to the master page on iOS, swipe right. On Android, swipe right from the left edge or tap the arrow at the top. On Windows 10 Mobile, tap the menu icon in the upper-left corner.

On both Android and Windows Phone, tapping the **Back** arrow at the bottom of the screen will exit the program. That **Back** arrow will switch from master to detail, but not from detail to master.

Here's the program running on the iPad Air 2 simulator showing the side-by-side display of the master and detail:

Your own user interface

If you'd like to supply your own user interface for switching between the master and detail views, you'll probably also want to disable the interface automatically provided by the MasterDetailPage. You can do this in two ways:

- Set the IsGestureEnabled property to false to disable the swipe gesture support on iOS and Android.

- Override the protected ShouldShowToolbarButton method and return false to hide the toolbar buttons on Windows 8.1 and Windows Phone 8.1.

However, you won't be able to disable the interface entirely. Setting the IsGestureEnabled property to false means you can no longer use swipes to switch between master and detail on iOS and Android. The property does not affect taps, however. For both iOS and Android, when the display has a *popover* behavior and the master page is overlaying the detail page, you can dismiss the master page with a tap on the detail page at the right. IsGestureEnabled does not disable those taps.

If you set the IsGestureEnabled property to false, you'll need to supply your own user interface for displaying the master view from the detail page on iOS and Android.

The toolbar button that accompanies the MasterDetailPage on Windows 8.1 and Windows Phone 8.1 platforms is attached to the underlying native page. It cannot be accessed from the ToolbarItems collections of the MasterDetailPage or of the two pages set to the Master and Detail properties. Overriding the ShouldShowToolbarButton and returning false suppresses that toolbar button. Again, if you do that, you must supply you own user interface for switching between master and detail views.

Another problem is that you don't need an interface at all to switch between the views when the MasterDetailPage is using a *split* mode. You know that you only get a split mode on iPad and Windows Runtime tablets, but if you specify a MasterBehavior as Default or SplitOnLandscape, how can you tell when the screen is in a *split* mode or *overlay* mode?

On the Windows Runtime tablets, a call to the base implementation of ShouldShowToolbarButton will tell you. This method returns true for phones and for tablets in an *overlay* mode, but it returns false for tablets in a *split* mode. However, this method is only implemented on Windows 8.1 and Windows Phone 8.1.

For iOS, you can determine whether the iPad is in an *overlay* or *split* mode by checking the dimensions of the page. If the page is in portrait mode, it's overlay; for landscape mode, it's split.

Let's put all this knowledge to use. The **ColorsDetails** program displays all the colors in the NamedColor collection in a ListView in the master page and provides detailed information about the selected color in its detail page. Here's the master page definition first:

```
<MasterDetailPage xmlns="http://xamarin.com/schemas/2014/forms"
                  xmlns:x="http://schemas.microsoft.com/winfx/2009/xaml"
```

```
                        xmlns:toolkit=
                        "clr-namespace:Xamarin.FormsBook.Toolkit;assembly=Xamarin.FormsBook.Toolkit"
                        x:Class="ColorsDetails.ColorDetailsPage"
                        IsPresented="True"
                        x:Name="page">

        <MasterDetailPage.Master>
            <ContentPage Title="Colors">
                <ContentPage.Padding>
                    <OnPlatform x:TypeArguments="Thickness"
                                iOS="0, 20, 0, 0" />
                </ContentPage.Padding>

                <ListView x:Name="listView"
                          SeparatorVisibility="None"
                          ItemsSource="{x:Static toolkit:NamedColor.All}"
                          ItemTapped="OnListViewItemTapped">
                    <ListView.RowHeight>
                        <OnPlatform x:TypeArguments="x:Int32"
                                    iOS="80"
                                    Android="80"
                                    WinPhone="90" />
                    </ListView.RowHeight>

                    <ListView.ItemTemplate>
                        <DataTemplate>
                            <ViewCell>
                                <ContentView Padding="5">
                                    <Frame OutlineColor="Accent"
                                           Padding="10">
                                        <StackLayout Orientation="Horizontal">
                                            <BoxView x:Name="boxView"
                                                     Color="{Binding Color}"
                                                     WidthRequest="50"
                                                     HeightRequest="50" />
                                            <StackLayout>
                                                <Label Text="{Binding Name}"
                                                       FontSize="Medium"
                                                       VerticalOptions="StartAndExpand" />
                                                <Label Text="{Binding RgbDisplay,
                                                                StringFormat='RGB = {0}'}"
                                                       FontSize="Small"
                                                       VerticalOptions="CenterAndExpand" />
                                            </StackLayout>
                                        </StackLayout>
                                    </Frame>
                                </ContentView>
                            </ViewCell>
                        </DataTemplate>
                    </ListView.ItemTemplate>
                </ListView>
            </ContentPage>
        </MasterDetailPage.Master>
        …
```

```
</MasterDetailPage>
```

The markup for this `ListView` is quite similar to that in the **CustomNamedColorList** program in Chapter 19. In this new version, however, the `ItemTapped` event of the `ListView` is handled in the code-behind file. (You'll see that code shortly.)

Here's the list of colors on the three platforms:

The `ContentPage` that serves as the detail view has its `BindingContext` set to the `SelectedItem` property of the `ListView`. Most of the contents—which include a `BoxView` of the color; the red, green, and blue values; and the hue, saturation, and luminosity values—are in a `ScrollView`. This is for the benefit of phones in landscape mode. The only elements not in this `ScrollView` are a `Label` with the color name at the top of the page and a `Button` on the bottom:

```
<MasterDetailPage … >

    …
    <MasterDetailPage.Detail>
        <NavigationPage>
            <x:Arguments>
                <ContentPage Title="Color"
                             BindingContext="{Binding Source={x:Reference listView},
                                                       Path=SelectedItem}">
                    <ContentPage.Padding>
                        <OnPlatform x:TypeArguments="Thickness"
                                    iOS="0, 20, 0, 0" />
                    </ContentPage.Padding>

                    <StackLayout>
                        <Label Text="{Binding FriendlyName}"
                               Style="{DynamicResource TitleStyle}"
```

```
                              HorizontalTextAlignment="Center" />

            <ScrollView VerticalOptions="FillAndExpand">
                <StackLayout>
                    <BoxView Color="{Binding Color}"
                             WidthRequest="144"
                             HeightRequest="144"
                             VerticalOptions="CenterAndExpand"
                             HorizontalOptions="Center" />

                    <StackLayout VerticalOptions="CenterAndExpand"
                                 HorizontalOptions="Center">
                        <StackLayout.Resources>
                            <ResourceDictionary>
                                <Style TargetType="Label">
                                    <Setter Property="HorizontalTextAlignment"
                                            Value="End" />
                                </Style>
                            </ResourceDictionary>
                        </StackLayout.Resources>

                        <Label Text="{Binding Color.R,
                                      StringFormat='Red = {0:F2}'}" />
                        <Label Text="{Binding Color.G,
                                      StringFormat='Green = {0:F2}'}" />
                        <Label Text="{Binding Color.B,
                                      StringFormat='Blue = {0:F2}'}" />
                        <Label Text="{Binding Color.A,
                                      StringFormat='Alpha = {0:F2}'}" />
                        <Label Text=" " />
                        <Label Text="{Binding Color.Hue,
                                      StringFormat='Hue = {0:F2}'}" />
                        <Label Text="{Binding Color.Saturation,
                                      StringFormat='Saturation = {0:F2}'}"
/>

                        <Label Text="{Binding Color.Luminosity,
                                      StringFormat='Luminosity = {0:F2}'}"
/>
                    </StackLayout>
                </StackLayout>
            </ScrollView>

            <Button x:Name="returnButton"
                    Text="Return to list"
                    HorizontalOptions="Center"
                    Clicked="OnReturnButtonClicked">
                <Button.IsEnabled>
                    <Binding Source="{x:Reference page}"
                             Path="IsPresented">
                        <Binding.Converter>
                            <toolkit:BooleanNegationConverter />
                        </Binding.Converter>
                    </Binding>
                </Button.IsEnabled>
            </Button.IsEnabled>
```

```
                        </Button>
                    </StackLayout>
                </ContentPage>
            </x:Arguments>
        </NavigationPage>
    </MasterDetailPage.Detail>
</MasterDetailPage>
```

The `Button` on the bottom has a `Clicked` event handler in the code-behind file, of course, but also notice the data binding to its `IsEnabled` property. The source of the data binding is the `IsPresented` property of the `MasterDetailPage`. If `IsPresented` is `true`—which means that master view is displayed—then the `Button` is disabled. (If you'd like to do something similar in code, `MasterDetailPage` defines an `IsPresentedChanged` event.)

You can see the `Button` at the bottom of the detail view for returning to the master view:

The code-behind file handles the event handlers for the `ListView` and `Button` (toward the bottom of the file). These merely set the `IsPresented` property to `false` and `true`, respectively, and have no effect when the `MasterDetailPage` is in *split* mode:

```
public partial class ColorDetailsPage : MasterDetailPage
{
    public ColorDetailsPage()
    {
        InitializeComponent();

        IsGestureEnabled = false;

        // Special processing for iPads.
        if (Device.OS == TargetPlatform.iOS &&
```

```
                    Device.Idiom == TargetIdiom.Tablet)
        {
            SizeChanged += (sender, args) =>
            {
                // Enable button for portrait mode.
                returnButton.IsVisible = Height > Width;
            };
        }
    }

    public override bool ShouldShowToolbarButton()
    {
        // Only works for Windows and Windows Phone platforms.
        returnButton.IsVisible = base.ShouldShowToolbarButton();

        return false;
    }

    void OnListViewItemTapped(object sender, ItemTappedEventArgs args)
    {
        IsPresented = false;
    }

    void OnReturnButtonClicked(object sender, EventArgs args)
    {
        IsPresented = true;
    }
}
```

The more interesting parts of the code-behind file are in the constructor and the override of the `ShouldShowToolbarButton`. These sections of code attempt two jobs:

First, they disable the existing user interface for switching between master and detail views by setting `IsGestureEnabled` to `false` and returning `false` from `ShouldShowToolbarButton`. This means that no toolbar item is displayed on the Windows 8.1 and Windows Phone 8.1 platforms. The `MasterDetailPage` still requires that a `Title` be set on the `ContentPage` that serves as the master view, but that `Title` is not used anywhere on these platforms.

The second job is to hide that `Button` entirely when the `MasterDetailPage` is in split view. The `SizeChanged` handler for the page is set in the constructor when the program is running on an iPad, and it sets the `IsVisible` property to `true` only if the page dimensions indicate portrait mode. The `ShouldShowToolbarButton` override handles Windows tablets by showing the `Button` if the base implementation of `ShouldShowToolbarButton` returns `true`.

That's one way to implement your own user interface for switching between master and detail views. The **MasterDetailTaps** program shows another approach. This program is similar to the **MasterDetailBehavior** program that began this chapter, but with the definitions of the master and detail views consolidated in one XAML file. This new program disables the existing UI for transitioning between master and detail views and replaces it with simple taps.

`MasterDetailTapsPage` derives from `MasterDetailPage` and includes similar `Frame` and `Label` elements as the earlier program:

```
<MasterDetailPage xmlns="http://xamarin.com/schemas/2014/forms"
                  xmlns:x="http://schemas.microsoft.com/winfx/2009/xaml"
                  x:Class="MasterDetailTaps.MasterDetailTapsPage"
                  Title="Demo Page">

    <MasterDetailPage.Master>
        <ContentPage Title="Master"
                     Padding="10"
                     x:Name="masterPage">

            <Frame OutlineColor="Accent"
                   BackgroundColor="Transparent">
                <Frame.GestureRecognizers>
                    <TapGestureRecognizer Tapped="OnMasterTapped" />
                </Frame.GestureRecognizers>

                <StackLayout Orientation="Horizontal"
                             Spacing="0"
                             HorizontalOptions="Center"
                             VerticalOptions="Center">

                    <Label Text="{Binding Source={x:Reference masterPage},
                                          Path=Width,
                                          StringFormat='Master: {0:F0}'}"
                           FontSize="Large" />

                    <Label Text="{Binding Source={x:Reference masterPage},
                                          Path=Height,
                                          StringFormat=' &#x00D7; {0:F0}'}"
                           FontSize="Large" />
                </StackLayout>
            </Frame>
        </ContentPage>
    </MasterDetailPage.Master>

    <MasterDetailPage.Detail>
        <NavigationPage>
            <x:Arguments>
                <ContentPage Title="Detail"
                             Padding="10"
                             x:Name="detailPage">
                    <ContentPage.Padding>
                        <OnPlatform x:TypeArguments="Thickness"
                                    iOS="0, 20, 0, 0" />
                    </ContentPage.Padding>

                    <Frame OutlineColor="Accent"
                           BackgroundColor="Transparent">
                        <Frame.GestureRecognizers>
                            <TapGestureRecognizer Tapped="OnDetailTapped" />
                        </Frame.GestureRecognizers>
```

```
            <StackLayout Orientation="Horizontal"
                         Spacing="0"
                         VerticalOptions="CenterAndExpand"
                         HorizontalOptions="Center">
              <Label Text="{Binding Source={x:Reference detailPage},
                                     Path=Width,
                                     StringFormat='Detail: {0:F0}'}"
                     FontSize="Large"/>

              <Label Text="{Binding Source={x:Reference detailPage},
                                     Path=Height,
                                     StringFormat=' &#x00D7; {0:F0}'}"
                     FontSize="Large" />
            </StackLayout>
          </Frame>
        </ContentPage>
      </x:Arguments>
    </NavigationPage>
  </MasterDetailPage.Detail>
</MasterDetailPage>
```

Notice the `TapGestureRecognizer` attached to the `Frame` element on both the master and detail pages.

Notice also that the `BackgroundColor` of each `Frame` is set to `Transparent`. This is for the benefit of the Windows platforms. The default background of a `Frame` in these platforms is `null`, which lets taps fall through to the underlying element. Setting the background to `Transparent` doesn't change the appearance but captures the taps.

The `Tapped` handlers simply set `IsPresented`:

```
public partial class MasterDetailTapsPage : MasterDetailPage
{
    public MasterDetailTapsPage()
    {
        InitializeComponent();

        // Disable swipe interface.
        IsGestureEnabled = false;
    }

    public override bool ShouldShowToolbarButton()
    {
        // Hide toolbar button on Windows platforms.
        return false;
    }

    void OnMasterTapped(object sender, EventArgs args)
    {
        // Catch exceptions when setting IsPresented in split mode.
        try
        {
```

```
            IsPresented = false;
        }
        catch
        {
        }
    }

    void OnDetailTapped(object sender, EventArgs args)
    {
        IsPresented = true;
    }
}
```

The normal user interface is disabled as in the previous program but no logic is required to hide the new user interface in *split* mode.

The `try` and `catch` block in the `OnMasterTapped` method is used to avoid an `InvalidOpera-tionException` that occurs on both Windows and iPads in split mode. The error message that accompanies the exception states "Can't change IsPresented when setting Split."

TabbedPage

`TabbedPage` derives from the abstract class `MultiPage<Page>`. It maintains a collection of children of type `Page`, only one of which is fully visible at a time. `TabbedPage` identifies each child by a series of tabs across the top or bottom of the page. An iOS application that uses a `TabbedPage` must include an icon for each tab; otherwise, Apple will not accept the program for the App Store. This icon is set via each page's `Icon` property.

`MultiPage<T>` defines all the important properties and events for `TabbedPage`, the most important of which is:

- `Children` property of type `IList<T>`.

Normally, you fill this `Children` collection with page objects.

However, you can use `TabbedPage` in a somewhat different way by observing that `MultiPage<T>` is quite similar to `ItemsView<T>`, the base class of `ListView`, in that it defines:

- the `ItemsSource` property of type `IEnumerable`, and

- the `ItemTemplate` property of type `DataTemplate`.

If you supply an `IEnumerable` collection of objects with public properties suitable for data bindings, and a template with a page type as the root element, then the children are generated dynamically. The `BindingContext` of each generated page is set equal to the particular object from `ItemsSource`.

`MultiPage<T>` defines two properties that can help your application keep track of which page in the `Children` collection the user is currently viewing:

- CurrentPage of type T (Page for TabbedPage).

- SelectedItem of type object, referring to an object in the ItemsSource collection.

Both properties are gettable and settable.

MultiPage<T> also defines two events:

- PagesChanged is fired when the ItemsSource collection changes

- CurrentPageChanged is fired when the viewed page changes.

Most commonly, you'll add ContentPage derivatives directly to the Children collection. If you want to use TabbedPage for displaying a collection of similar pages based on a collection of data, you can alternatively set the ItemsSource property to that collection and define a page by using ItemTemplate, but this approach should be avoided on iOS.

Discrete tab pages

The most common use of TabbedPage is to navigate between different functions within an app, which typically means each tab presents a different type of page. It is common for these pages to be related in some way—perhaps multiple pages for application settings—even if they don't look the same.

The **DiscreteTabbedColors** program has three tabs: the first displaying a list of the built-in Xamarin.Forms colors, the second displaying a list of colors from the NamedColor class in the **Xamarin.FormsBook.Toolkit** (introduced in earlier chapters), and the third containing a color-tester (with which you can select arbitrary RGB values to preview).

The **DiscreteTabbedColors** program begins with three ContentPage derivatives. The first is code-only and consists of a simple list of the standard Xamarin.Forms colors.

```
class BuiltInColorsPage : ContentPage
{
    public BuiltInColorsPage()
    {
        Title = "Built-in";
        Icon = Device.OnPlatform("ic_action_computer.png", null, null);
        Padding = new Thickness(5, Device.OnPlatform(20, 5, 5), 5, 5);
        double fontSize = Device.GetNamedSize(NamedSize.Large, typeof(Label));
        Content = new ScrollView
        {
            Content = new StackLayout
            {
                Spacing = 0,
                Children =
                {
                    new Label
                    {
                        Text = "White",
                        TextColor = Color.White,
                        FontSize = fontSize
```

```
                },

                ...

                new Label
                {
                    Text = "Purple",
                    TextColor = Color.Purple,
                    FontSize = fontSize
                }
            }
        }
    };
}
}
```

Notice that the `Title` property is set. This is essential for the tab text on all the platforms. The code also sets the `Icon` property for iOS. The particular icon is part of the Android set of icons described in Chapter 13, "Bitmaps," and is 32-pixels square.

The `NamedColorsPage` consists of a `ListView` of all the `NamedColor` objects. Notice again the `Title` property and `Icon` property for iOS:

```xml
<ContentPage xmlns="http://xamarin.com/schemas/2014/forms"
             xmlns:x="http://schemas.microsoft.com/winfx/2009/xaml"
             xmlns:toolkit=
                "clr-namespace:Xamarin.FormsBook.Toolkit;assembly=Xamarin.FormsBook.Toolkit"
             x:Class="DiscreteTabbedColors.NamedColorsPage"
             Title="Toolkit">
    <ContentPage.Icon>
        <OnPlatform x:TypeArguments="FileImageSource"
                    iOS="ic_action_storage.png" />
    </ContentPage.Icon>

    <ListView ItemsSource="{x:Static toolkit:NamedColor.All}">
        <ListView.RowHeight>
            <OnPlatform x:TypeArguments="x:Int32"
                        iOS="80"
                        Android="80"
                        WinPhone="90" />
        </ListView.RowHeight>

        <ListView.ItemTemplate>
            <DataTemplate>
                <ViewCell>
                    <ContentView Padding="5">
                        <StackLayout Orientation="Horizontal">
                            <BoxView x:Name="boxView"
                                     Color="{Binding Color}"
                                     WidthRequest="50"
                                     HeightRequest="50" />
                            <StackLayout>
                                <Label Text="{Binding Name}"
                                       FontSize="Medium"
```

```
                                                VerticalOptions="StartAndExpand" />
                            <Label Text="{Binding RgbDisplay, StringFormat='RGB = {0}'}"
                                   FontSize="Small"
                                   VerticalOptions="CenterAndExpand" />
                        </StackLayout>
                    </StackLayout>
                </ContentView>
            </ViewCell>
        </DataTemplate>
    </ListView.ItemTemplate>
</ListView>
</ContentPage>
```

The third page contains a trio of `Slider` elements to select a color, such as you've seen before:

```
<ContentPage xmlns="http://xamarin.com/schemas/2014/forms"
             xmlns:x="http://schemas.microsoft.com/winfx/2009/xaml"
             xmlns:toolkit=
                 "clr-namespace:Xamarin.FormsBook.Toolkit;assembly=Xamarin.FormsBook.Toolkit"
             x:Class="DiscreteTabbedColors.ColorTestPage"
             Title="Test">
    <ContentPage.Icon>
        <OnPlatform x:TypeArguments="FileImageSource"
                    iOS="ic_action_gamepad.png" />
    </ContentPage.Icon>

    <StackLayout Padding="20, 40">
        <StackLayout.BindingContext>
            <toolkit:ColorViewModel Color="Gray" />
        </StackLayout.BindingContext>

        <Label Text="{Binding Red, StringFormat='Red = {0:F2}'}"
               HorizontalOptions="Center" />

        <Slider Value="{Binding Red}" />

        <Label Text="{Binding Green, StringFormat='Green = {0:F2}'}"
               HorizontalOptions="Center" />

        <Slider Value="{Binding Green}" />

        <Label Text="{Binding Blue, StringFormat='Blue = {0:F2}'}"
               HorizontalOptions="Center" />

        <Slider Value="{Binding Blue}" />

        <BoxView Color="{Binding Color}"
                 VerticalOptions="FillAndExpand" />
    </StackLayout>
</ContentPage>
```

Here's the `DiscreteTabbedColorsPage`. Notice the root element of `TabbedPage`. This XAML file simply adds instances of these three page types to the `Children` collection of the `TabbedPage`:

```
<TabbedPage xmlns="http://xamarin.com/schemas/2014/forms"
```

```
      xmlns:x="http://schemas.microsoft.com/winfx/2009/xaml"
      xmlns:local="clr-namespace:DiscreteTabbedColors"
      x:Class="DiscreteTabbedColors.DiscreteTabbedColorsPage">

  <local:BuiltInColorsPage />
  <local:NamedColorsPage />
  <local:ColorTestPage />

</TabbedPage>
```

Here are the three tabs on the three platforms:

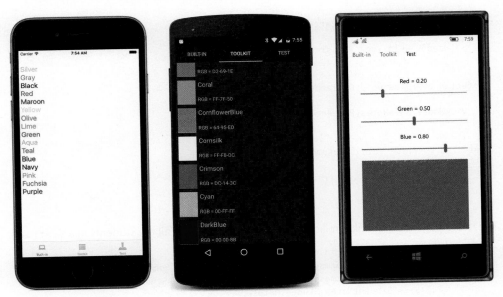

On iOS, the tabs are at the bottom, identified with text and icons, and the selected tab is highlighted. Both Android and Windows 10 Mobile display the tabs at the top of the screen but highlight the selected tab in different ways.

The **StudentNotes** program has a home page that lists all the students in a `ListView`, but selecting a student from this list causes the program to navigate to a `TabbedPage`. The page has three tabs: the first displays textual information about the student, the second displays the photograph of the student, and the third displays an `Editor` that allows a teacher or other school administrator to enter some notes about the student. (This feature makes use of the `Notes` property in the `Student` class in the **SchoolOfFineArt** library.)

The `App` class in the **StudentNotes** program passes the `Properties` dictionary defined by `Application` to the `SchoolViewModel` constructor, and also passes the `Properties` dictionary to the `SaveNotes` method of the ViewModel when the program goes to sleep, possibly in preparation for being terminated:

```
public class App : Application
```

```
{
    public App()
    {
        ViewModel = new SchoolViewModel(Properties);

        MainPage = new NavigationPage(new StudentNotesHomePage());
    }

    public SchoolViewModel ViewModel
    {
        private set; get;
    }

    protected override void OnStart()
    {
        // Handle when your app starts
    }

    protected override void OnSleep()
    {
        ViewModel.SaveNotes(Properties);
    }

    protected override void OnResume()
    {
        // Handle when your app resumes
    }
}
```

The home page should look familiar by now. It simply displays all the students in a `ListView`:

```xml
<ContentPage xmlns="http://xamarin.com/schemas/2014/forms"
             xmlns:x="http://schemas.microsoft.com/winfx/2009/xaml"
             xmlns:local="clr-namespace:StudentNotes;assembly=StudentNotes"
             x:Class="StudentNotes.StudentNotesHomePage"
             Title="Students"
             BindingContext="{Binding Source={x:Static Application.Current},
                                     Path=ViewModel}">

    <StackLayout BindingContext="{Binding StudentBody}">
        <Label Text="{Binding School}"
               FontSize="Large"
               FontAttributes="Bold"
               HorizontalTextAlignment="Center" />

        <ListView x:Name="listView"
                  ItemsSource="{Binding Students}"
                  ItemSelected="OnListViewItemSelected">
            <ListView.ItemTemplate>
                <DataTemplate>
                    <ImageCell ImageSource="{Binding PhotoFilename}"
                               Text="{Binding FullName}"
                               Detail="{Binding GradePointAverage,
                                        StringFormat='G.P.A. = {0:F2}'}" />
                </DataTemplate>
```

```
            </ListView.ItemTemplate>
        </ListView>
    </StackLayout>
</ContentPage>
```

The code-behind file contains the `ItemSelected` handler for the `ListView` to navigate to `StudentNotesDataPage`, setting the page's `BindingContext` to the selected `Student` object:

```
public partial class StudentNotesHomePage : ContentPage
{
    public StudentNotesHomePage()
    {
        InitializeComponent();
    }

    async void OnListViewItemSelected(object sender, SelectedItemChangedEventArgs args)
    {
        if (args.SelectedItem != null)
        {
            listView.SelectedItem = null;

            await Navigation.PushAsync(new StudentNotesDataPage
            {
                BindingContext = args.SelectedItem
            });
        }
    }
}
```

The `StudentNotesDataPage` derives from `TabbedPage`. Within the start and end tags of the `TabbedPage`, three `ContentPage` definitions are added to the `Children` property of `TabbedPage`. Each has its `Title` property set to the text to use in the tab, and `Icon` definitions are included for iOS:

```
<TabbedPage xmlns="http://xamarin.com/schemas/2014/forms"
            xmlns:x="http://schemas.microsoft.com/winfx/2009/xaml"
            x:Class="StudentNotes.StudentNotesDataPage"
            Title="Student Data">

    <ContentPage Title="Info">
        <ContentPage.Icon>
            <OnPlatform x:TypeArguments="FileImageSource"
                        iOS="ic_action_about.png" />
        </ContentPage.Icon>

        <StackLayout>
            <Label Text="{Binding FullName}"
                   FontSize="Large"
                   HorizontalOptions="Center" />

            <StackLayout Spacing="12"
                         VerticalOptions="CenterAndExpand"
                         HorizontalOptions="Center">
                <StackLayout.Resources>
                    <ResourceDictionary>
```

```
                    <Style TargetType="Label">
                        <Setter Property="FontSize" Value="Large" />
                    </Style>
                </ResourceDictionary>
            </StackLayout.Resources>

            <Label Text="{Binding LastName,
                                 StringFormat='Last name: {0}'}" />

            <Label Text="{Binding FirstName,
                                 StringFormat='First name: {0}'}" />

            <Label Text="{Binding MiddleName,
                                 StringFormat='Middle name: {0}'}" />

            <Label Text="{Binding Sex,
                                 StringFormat='Sex: {0}'}" />

            <Label Text="{Binding GradePointAverage,
                                 StringFormat='G.P.A. = {0:F2}'}" />
        </StackLayout>
    </StackLayout>
</ContentPage>


<ContentPage Title="Photo">
    <ContentPage.Icon>
        <OnPlatform x:TypeArguments="FileImageSource"
                    iOS="ic_action_person.png" />
    </ContentPage.Icon>

    <StackLayout>
        <Label Text="{Binding FullName}"
               FontSize="Large"
               HorizontalOptions="Center" />

        <Image Source="{Binding PhotoFilename}"
               VerticalOptions="FillAndExpand" />
    </StackLayout>
</ContentPage>


<ContentPage Title="Notes">
    <ContentPage.Icon>
        <OnPlatform x:TypeArguments="FileImageSource"
                    iOS="ic_action_edit.png" />
    </ContentPage.Icon>

    <StackLayout>
        <Label Text="{Binding FullName}"
               FontSize="Large"
               HorizontalOptions="Center" />

        <Editor Text="{Binding Notes}"
                Keyboard="Text"
                VerticalOptions="FillAndExpand" />
```

```
            </StackLayout>
        </ContentPage>
    </TabbedPage>
```

This is perhaps not enough information to spread over three pages, but you can easily imagine situations where this approach would be ideal.

Here's how the three tabs look on the three platforms:

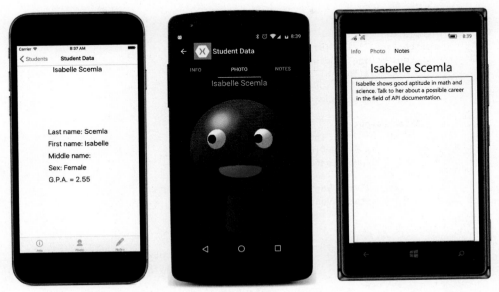

You can navigate back to the list of students in the normal way: By tapping the left arrow at the top of the screen on iOS and Android, or by pressing the **Back** arrow at the bottom of the screen on Android and Windows 10 Mobile.

Using an ItemTemplate

The TabbedPage can also be used to present a small data set, each item of which is a separate page identified by a tab. You do this by setting the ItemsSource property of TabbedPage and specifying an ItemTemplate for rendering each page.

The **MultiTabbedColors** project contains a single page class that was added to the project as a ContentPage, but which was then modified to be a TabbedPage. The project also has a reference to the **Xamarin.FormsBook.Toolkit** library.

Notice that the root element of the XAML file sets the ItemsSource property of TabbedPage to the collection available from the NamedColor.All static property. The remainder of the file defines the ItemTemplate property. The TabbedPage.ItemTemplate property-element tags enclose a pair of DataTemplate tags, in which a page definition appears, beginning with ContentPage. The data

bindings reference properties of the objects in the `ItemsSource` collection, in this case properties of
`NamedColor`:

```xml
<TabbedPage xmlns="http://xamarin.com/schemas/2014/forms"
            xmlns:x="http://schemas.microsoft.com/winfx/2009/xaml"
            xmlns:toolkit=
                "clr-namespace:Xamarin.FormsBook.Toolkit;assembly=Xamarin.FormsBook.Toolkit"
            x:Class="MultiTabbedColors.MultiTabbedColorsPage"
            ItemsSource="{x:Static toolkit:NamedColor.All}">

    <TabbedPage.ItemTemplate>
        <DataTemplate>
            <ContentPage Title="{Binding Name}">
                <ContentPage.Padding>
                    <OnPlatform x:TypeArguments="Thickness"
                                iOS="0, 20, 0, 0" />
                </ContentPage.Padding>

                <StackLayout>
                    <Label Text="{Binding FriendlyName}"
                           Style="{DynamicResource TitleStyle}"
                           HorizontalTextAlignment="Center" />

                    <ScrollView VerticalOptions="FillAndExpand">
                        <StackLayout>
                            <BoxView Color="{Binding Color}"
                                     WidthRequest="144"
                                     HeightRequest="144"
                                     VerticalOptions="CenterAndExpand"
                                     HorizontalOptions="Center" />

                            <StackLayout VerticalOptions="CenterAndExpand"
                                         HorizontalOptions="Center">
                                <StackLayout.Resources>
                                    <ResourceDictionary>
                                        <Style TargetType="Label">
                                            <Setter Property="HorizontalTextAlignment"
                                                    Value="End" />
                                        </Style>
                                    </ResourceDictionary>
                                </StackLayout.Resources>

                                <Label Text="{Binding Color.R,
                                              StringFormat='Red = {0:F2}'}" />
                                <Label Text="{Binding Color.G,
                                              StringFormat='Green = {0:F2}'}" />
                                <Label Text="{Binding Color.B,
                                              StringFormat='Blue = {0:F2}'}" />
                                <Label Text="{Binding Color.A,
                                              StringFormat='Alpha = {0:F2}'}" />
                                <Label Text=" " />
                                <Label Text="{Binding Color.Hue,
                                              StringFormat='Hue = {0:F2}'}" />
                                <Label Text="{Binding Color.Saturation,
```

```
                                                  StringFormat='Saturation = {0:F2}'}" />
                         <Label Text="{Binding Color.Luminosity,
                                                  StringFormat='Luminosity = {0:F2}'}" />

                      </StackLayout>
                   </StackLayout>
                </ScrollView>
             </StackLayout>
          </ContentPage>
       </DataTemplate>
    </TabbedPage.ItemTemplate>
</TabbedPage>
```

To avoid overwriting the status bar at the top of the iOS screen, set `Padding` on the `ContentPage` template rather than on the `TabbedPage` itself.

Set the `Title` property of this `ContentPage` template to the text you want to appear in the tabs to identify each page. Notice that the `Title` is bound to the `Name` property of `NamedColor`, but the contents of the page also include a `Label` with a `TitleStyle` to display the `FriendlyName` property, which is similar to the `Name` property but includes spaces if the color name consists of multiple words.

Here is **TabbedColors** running on the three standard platforms:

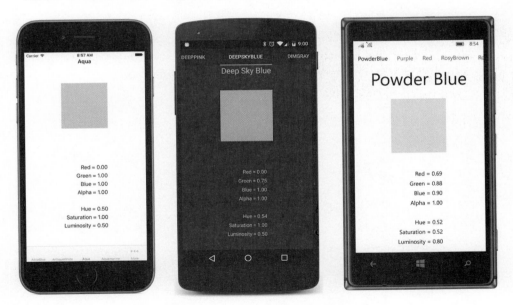

The tabs function like a menu that allow you to select a particular page.

The good news is that this works great on Android and Windows 10 Mobile. You can scroll quickly through the headers on the top of the Android screen, and swipe the actual pages on Windows 10 Mobile. On iOS, however, only four items are displayed, and the **more** button and the ellipsis do not work. Moreover, there are no icons, and you need icons on a `TabbedPage` for Apple to approve the app for the App Store. While this facility of `TabbedPage` appears to be quite an interesting way to generate pages, it's not suitable for a cross-platform application. More suitable would be the `Carou-selView`, which unfortunately was not quite ready by the time this book went to print.

Chapter 26

Custom layouts

Customization is a crucial aspect of any graphical programming environment. Has the system been designed for flexibility? Can you create new types of user-interface elements? How well do these new elements integrate into the system?

Xamarin.Forms has several features that facilitate customization. You've already seen the dependency service (first discussed in Chapter 9, "Platform-specific API calls"), which allows your application to execute platform-specific code from the common Portable Class Library.

In the next chapter, you'll see how to create specialized user-interface elements in the form of new `View` derivatives. You create these new elements by coding custom *renderers* that implement the element in the individual platforms.

This chapter focuses instead on those powerful classes that typically inhabit the visual tree *between* the page and the individual user-interface objects. These classes are known as *layouts* because they derive from `Layout<View>`. Xamarin.Forms defines four such classes—`StackLayout`, `AbsoluteLayout`, `RelativeLayout`, and `Grid`—each of which arranges its children in a different way. As you've seen throughout this book, these `Layout<View>` derivatives are vital for defining the visual organization of your page.

The classes that derive from `Layout<View>` are somewhat unusual in Xamarin.Forms in that they make use of no platform-specific code. They are instead implemented entirely within Xamarin.Forms.

This chapter describes how to derive a class from `Layout<View>` to write your own custom layouts. This is a very useful skill that comes to the rescue whenever you need to organize your page in a manner that's not handled by the standard layout classes. For example, suppose you want to present data by using a card-file metaphor with overlapping cards, or as items that wrap in both columns and scrollable rows, or that pan from side to side with finger swipes. This chapter will show you how to write such classes.

Writing custom layouts also provides you with the best insights into how the layout system in Xamarin.Forms works. This knowledge will help you design your own pages even if you restrict yourself to the standard layout classes.

An overview of layout

In Xamarin.Forms, there is no centralized system that handles layout. Instead, the process is very decentralized. Layout is handled by the elements themselves, or within the classes they derive from. For example, every visual element is responsible for determining its own preferred size. This is known as a *requested* size because there might not be enough room to fit the whole element, or there might be more than enough room for the element.

The elements that get most involved in layout have a single child or multiple children. These are the `Page` derivatives, `Layout` derivatives (`ContentView`, `Frame`, and `ScrollView`), and `Layout<View>` derivatives. These elements are responsible for determining the location and size of their child or children relative to themselves. The child location and size is usually based on the child's requested size, so layout often involves a give-and-take relationship between parents and children. Children have requests, but parents lay down the law.

Let's look at a few simple examples.

Parents and children

Consider the following markup:

```
<ContentPage … >
    <Frame OutlineColor="Accent" >
        <Label Text="Sample text" />
    </Frame>
</ContentPage>
```

It's a `Label` in a `Frame` in a `ContentPage`. Like most `View` derivatives, the `Frame` has default `HorizontalOptions` and `VerticalOptions` property settings of `LayoutOptions.Fill`, which means that the `Frame` fills the page except for a possible `Padding` setting on the page. The size of the `Frame` is based on the size of the page and not on the size of the text displayed by the `Label`.

Now set the `HorizontalOptions` and `VerticalOptions` properties on the `Frame`:

```
<ContentPage … >
    <Frame OutlineColor="Accent"
           VerticalOptions="Center"
           HorizontalOptions="Center">
        <Label Text="Sample text" />
    </Frame>
</ContentPage>
```

The `Frame` now hugs the rendered text of the `Label`, which means that the size of the `Frame` is based on the size of the `Label` rather than on the size of the page.

But not entirely! If you add more and more text to the `Label`, the `Frame` will grow, but it won't ever get larger than the page. Instead, the text will be truncated. With more text than can fit on the page, the `Label` becomes limited by the maximum size of the `Frame`, which is limited by the size of the `ContentPage`.

But now put the `Frame` in a `ScrollView`:

```
<ContentPage … >
    <ScrollView>
        <Frame OutlineColor="Accent">
```

```
            <Label Text="Very long text ... " />
        </Frame>
    </ScrollView>
</ContentPage>
```

Now the `ScrollView` is the size of the page, but the `Frame` can grow larger than the `ScrollView`. The `ScrollView` allows the user to scroll the bottom of the `Frame` into view.

The `Frame` can also extend past the bottom of the page if it's in a `StackLayout`:

```
<ContentPage … >
    <StackLayout>
        <Frame OutlineColor="Accent">
            <Label Text="Very long text ... " />
        </Frame>
    </StackLayout>
</ContentPage>
```

Ultimately, it is the parent that determines what the size of its children should be, and imposes that size on its children, but often the parent will base that size on the requested size of the child.

Sizing and positioning

The process of layout begins at the top of the visual tree with the page, and it then proceeds through all the branches of the visual tree to encompass every visual element on the page. Elements that are parents to other elements are responsible for sizing and positioning their children relative to themselves. This requires that parent elements call certain public methods in the child elements. These public methods often result in calls to other methods within each element, for properties to be set, and for events to be fired.

Perhaps the most important public method involved in layout is named (quite appropriately) `Layout`. This method is defined by `VisualElement` and inherited by every class that derives from `VisualElement`:

```
public void Layout(Rectangle bounds)
```

The `Layout` method specifies two characteristics of the element:

- the rectangular area in which the element is rendered (indicated by the `Width` and `Height` properties of the `Rectangle` value); and

- the position of the element's upper-left corner relative to its parent's upper-left corner (the `X` and `Y` properties).

When an application starts up and the first page needs to be displayed, the first `Layout` call is to a `Page` object, and the `Width` and `Height` properties indicate the size of the screen, or the area of the screen that the page occupies. Beginning with that first `Layout` call, the `Layout` calls are effectively propagated through the visual tree: Every element that is a parent to other elements—`Page`, `Layout`, and `Layout<View>` derivatives—is responsible for calling the `Layout` method on its children, resulting in every visual element on the page getting a call to its `Layout` method. (You'll see how this works shortly.)

This whole process is known as a *layout cycle*, and if you turn the phone sideways, the layout cycle starts again from the beginning at the top of the visual tree with the `Page` object. Layout cycles can also occur on a subset of the visual tree if something changes to affect the layout. These changes include items being added or removed from a collection such as that in a `ListView` or a `StackLayout` or another `Layout` class, a change in the `IsVisible` property of an element, or a change in the size of an element (for one reason or another).

Internal to `VisualElement`, the `Layout` method causes five properties of the element to be set. These properties are all defined by `VisualElement`:

- `Bounds` of type `Rectangle`

- `X` of type `double`

- `Y` of type `double`

- `Width` of type `double`

- `Height` of type `double`

These properties are all synchronized. The `X`, `Y`, `Width`, and `Height` properties of `VisualElement` are always the same values as the `X`, `Y`, `Width`, and `Height` properties of the `Bounds` rectangle. These properties indicate the element's actual rendered size and its position relative to the upper-left corner of its parent.

None of these five properties have public `set` accessors. To external code, these properties are `get`-only.

Prior to an element's first `Layout` call, the `X` and `Y` properties have values of 0, but the `Width` and `Height` properties have "mock" values of –1, which indicates that the properties have not yet been set. Valid values of these properties are available only after a layout cycle has occurred. Valid values are *not* available during execution of the constructors of the elements that make up the visual tree.

The `X`, `Y`, `Width`, and `Height` properties are all backed by bindable properties, so they can be sources of data bindings. The `Bounds` property is *not* backed by a bindable property and does not fire a `PropertyChanged` event. Do not use `Bounds` as a data-binding source.

A call to `Layout` also triggers a call to the `SizeAllocated` method, which is defined by `Visual-Element` like so:

```
protected void SizeAllocated(double width, double height)
```

The two arguments are the same as the `Width` and `Height` properties of the `Bounds` rectangle. The `SizeAllocated` method calls a protected virtual method name `OnSizeAllocated`:

```
protected virtual void OnSizeAllocated(double width, double height)
```

After the `OnSizeAllocated` method returns, and the size has changed from its previous value, `Visu-alElement` fires a `SizeChanged` event, defined like so:

```
public event EventHandler SizeChanged;
```

This indicates that the element's size has been set or has subsequently changed. As you've seen in previous chapters, when you need to implement some size-specific handling, the `SizeChanged` event is an excellent opportunity to access the `Bounds` property or the `Width` and `Height` properties to obtain a valid size of the page or any element on the page. The call to the `Layout` method is completed with the firing of the `SizeChanged` event.

As an alternative to the `SizeChanged` event, it is possible for an application to override `OnSizeAl-located` in a `ContentPage` derivative to obtain the new size of the page. (If you do so, be sure to call the base class implementation of `OnSizeAllocated`.) You'll find that `OnSizeAllocated` is sometimes called when the element's size doesn't actually change. The `SizeChanged` event is fired only when the size changes, and it's better for size-specific handling on the application level.

The `OnSizeAllocated` method is not defined as virtual so that applications can override it, but to allow classes within Xamarin.Forms to override it. Only two classes override `OnSizeAllocated` to perform their own specialized processing, but they are exceptionally important classes:

- `Page`

- `Layout`

These are the base classes for all the Xamarin.Forms elements that serve as parents to other elements within a Xamarin.Forms visual tree. (Although `ListView` and `TableView` seem to have children as well, the layout of those children are handled within the platform implementations of these views.)

Some of the classes that derive from `Page` and `Layout` have a `Content` property of type `View`. These classes are `ContentPage`, `ContentView`, `Frame`, and `ScrollView`. The `Content` property is a single child. The other classes that derive from `Page` (`MasterDetailPage`, `TabbedPage`, and `Carou-selPage`) have multiple children. The classes that derive from `Layout<View>` have a `Children` property of type `IList<View>`; these classes are `StackLayout`, `AbsoluteLayout`, `RelativeLayout`, and `Grid`.

The `Page` and `Layout` classes have a parallel structure beginning with an override of the `On-SizeAllocated` method. Both classes define the following method that is called from the `OnSize-Allocated` override:

```
protected void UpdateChildrenLayout()
```

Both versions of `UpdateChildrenLayout` call a method named `LayoutChildren`. This method is defined just a little differently in `Page` and `Layout`. In `Page`, the `LayoutChildren` method is defined as virtual:

```
protected virtual void LayoutChildren(double x, double y, double width, double height)
```

In `Layout` it's defined as abstract:

```
protected abstract void LayoutChildren(double x, double y, double width, double height);
```

Every Xamarin.Forms class that has a `Content` or a `Children` property also has an overridable `LayoutChildren` method. When you write your own class that derives from `Layout<View>` (which is the primary objective of this chapter), you'll override `LayoutChildren` to provide a custom organization of the layout's children.

The responsibility of a `LayoutChildren` override is to call the `Layout` method on all the element's children, which is usually the `View` object set to the element's `Content` property or the `View` objects in the element's `Children` collection. This is the most important part of layout.

As you'll recall, a call to the `Layout` method results in the `Bounds`, `X`, `Y`, `Width`, and `Height` properties being set and in calls to `SizeAllocated` and `OnSizeAllocated`. If the element is a `Layout` derivative, then `OnSizeAllocated` calls `UpdateChildrenLayout` and `LayoutChildren`. `LayoutChildren` then calls `Layout` on its children. This is how the `Layout` calls propagate from the top of the visual tree through all the branches and every element on the page.

Both `Page` and `Layout` also define a `LayoutChanged` event:

```
public event EventHandler LayoutChanged;
```

The `UpdateChildrenLayout` method concludes by firing this event, but only if at least one child has a new `Bounds` property.

You've seen that the `Page` and `Layout` classes both override the `OnSizeAllocated` method, and both define `UpdateChildrenLayout` and `LayoutChildren` methods and a `LayoutChanged` event. The `Page` and `Layout` classes have yet another similarity: They both define a `Padding` property. This padding is automatically reflected in the arguments to `LayoutChildren`.

For example, consider the following page definition:

```
<ContentPage … Padding="20">
    <ContentView Padding="15">
        <Label Text="Sample text" />
    </ContentView>
</ContentPage>
```

Suppose the screen in portrait mode measures 360 by 640. The `ContentPage` gets a call to its `Layout` method with a bounds rectangle equal to (0, 0, 360, 640). This kicks off the layout cycle.

Although the `Layout` method in `ContentPage` has an argument of (0, 0, 360, 640), the `LayoutChildren` call in that page is adjusted for the `Padding` property of 20. Both the `width` and `height` are decreased by 40 (20 on each side) and the `x` and `y` arguments are increased by 20, so the `LayoutChildren` arguments are (20, 20, 320, 600). This is the rectangle relative to the page in which `ContentPage` can position its child.

The `LayoutChildren` method in `ContentPage` calls the `Layout` method in its child (the `ContentView`) to give the `ContentView` the entire space available to the page minus the padding on the page. The bounds rectangle argument to this `Layout` call is (20, 20, 320, 600), which positions the upper-left corner of the `ContentView` 20 units to the right and below the upper-left corner of the `ContentPage`.

The call to the `LayoutChildren` override in `ContentView` reflects that layout area, but decreased by the `Padding` setting of 15, so the arguments to the `LayoutChildren` override in `ContentView` are (15, 15, 290, 570). This `LayoutChildren` method calls the `Layout` method in `Label` with that value.

Now let's make a little change:

```
<ContentPage … Padding="20">
    <ContentView Padding="15"
                 VerticalOptions="Center">
        <Label Text="Sample text" />
    </ContentView>
</ContentPage>
```

The `LayoutChildren` override in `ContentPage` now needs to do things a little differently. It can't simply call `Layout` on the `ContentView` with its own size minus the padding. It must call the `Layout` method in `ContentView` to vertically center the `ContentView` within the space it has available.

But how? To vertically center the `ContentView` relative to itself, the `ContentPage` must know the height of the `ContentView`. But the height of the `ContentView` depends on the height of the `Label`, and that height depends on the text and perhaps on various font properties that might be set on the `Label`. Moreover, the `Label` is capable of wrapping text to multiple rows, and the `Label` can't figure how many rows it requires without also knowing the horizontal space that's available to it.

This problem implies that more steps are involved.

Constraints and size requests

You just saw how, in some cases, a `LayoutChildren` override can call `Layout` on its child or children based solely on the `LayoutChildren` arguments. But in the more general case, `LayoutChildren` needs to know the size of its children before calling those children's `Layout` methods. For this reason, a `LayoutChildren` override generally calls *two* public methods in this order on each of its children:

- `GetSizeRequest`

- `Layout`

Why does a parent need to call `GetSizeRequest` on its child? Why can't the parent simply obtain the child's size by accessing the child's `Bounds` property or its `Width` and `Height` properties?

Because, in the general case, those properties have not been set yet! Recall that these properties are set by a call to `Layout`, and the `Layout` call hasn't yet occurred. In the general case, the `Layout` call can't occur until the parent knows the child's requested size. In the general case, the `GetSizeRequest` call is a prerequisite for the `Layout` call.

The information that `GetSizeRequest` returns is entirely independent of any information that might be set by `Layout`. Instead, the argument to `Layout` usually depends on the information returned from `GetSizeRequest`.

The `GetSizeRequest` call obtains what is sometimes called a *desired* size of an element. This is often related to the element's *native size*, and that generally depends on the particular platform. In contrast, the `Layout` call imposes a particular size on the element. Sometimes these two sizes are the same and sometimes not. These two sizes are usually *not* the same if the element's `HorizontalOptions` and `VerticalOptions` settings are `LayoutOptions.Fill`. In that case, the size that the element occupies is usually based on the area available to the element's parent rather than the size that the element needs.

The native size of some elements is fixed and inflexible. For example, in any particular platform, a `Switch` is always a fixed size determined by its implementation in that platform. But that's not always the case for other types of elements. Sometimes one dimension of the size is fixed but the other dimension is more flexible. The height of a horizontal `Slider` is fixed by the platform implementation, but the width of the `Slider` can be as wide as its parent.

Sometimes the size of an element depends on its property settings. The size of a `Button` or `Label` is dependent on the text displayed by the element and font size. Because the text displayed by a `Label` can wrap to multiple lines, the height of a `Label` depends on how many rows are displayed, and that's governed by the width available for the `Label`. Sometimes the height or width of an element depends on the height or width of its children. Such is the case with `StackLayout`.

These complications require that an element determine its size based on *constraints*, which generally indicate how much space is available within the element's parent for that element.

Like `Layout`, the `GetSizeRequest` method is defined by `VisualElement`. This is a public method that a parent element calls to obtain the size of each of its children:

```
public virtual SizeRequest GetSizeRequest(double widthConstraint, double heightConstraint)
```

The `widthConstraint` and `heightConstraint` arguments generally indicate the size that the parent has available for the child; the child is responsible for implementing this method to determine an appropriate size for itself based on those constraints. For example, a `Label` determines how many lines it needs for its text based on a particular width.

`VisualElement` also defines a very similar protected method named `OnSizeRequest`:

```
protected virtual SizeRequest OnSizeRequest(double widthConstraint, double heightConstraint)
```

Obviously these two methods are related and easily confused. Both methods are defined as `virtual`, but throughout all of Xamarin.Forms, only one class overrides the `GetSizeRequest` method, and that's the `Layout` class, which marks the method as `sealed`.

On the other hand, every class that derives from `Layout` or `Layout<View>` overrides `OnSize-Request`. This is where a layout class determines the size that it needs to be by making calls to the `GetSizeRequest` methods of its children.

For `View` derivatives (but not `Layout` derivatives), the public `GetSizeRequest` method calls the protected `OnSizeRequest` method which is responsible for obtaining the native size of the element from the platform-specific implementation.

The `SizeRequest` structure returned from `GetSizeRequest` and `OnSizeRequest` has two properties:

- `Request` of type `Size`

- `Minimum` of type `Size`

It's tempting to try to call `GetSizeRequest` on newly created objects, such as `Label` and `BoxView` and `Slider`, and examine what sizes are returned. However, the `GetSizeRequest` call will not work unless the element is part of an actual visual tree because only then is the Xamarin.Forms element implemented with an underlying platform object.

Most elements return `SizeRequest` values with identical `Request` and `Minimum` sizes. The only elements for which they're uniformly different is `ListView` and `TableView`, where the `Minimum` size is (40, 40), perhaps to allow some portion of the `ListView` or `TableView` to be displayed even if there isn't enough room for the whole thing.

In general, however, the `Minimum` size does not seem to play much of a role in the Xamarin.Forms layout system, and you don't need to go to extraordinary lengths to accommodate it. The `Size-Request` structure has a constructor that lets you set both properties to the same `Size` value.

You might recall that `VisualElement` defines four properties that have the word `Request` as part of their names:

- `WidthRequest` of type `double`

- `HeightRequest` of type `double`

- `MinimumWidthRequest` of type `double`

- `MinimumHeightRequest` of type `double`

Unlike the `Width` and `Height` properties, these four properties have public `set` accessors. Your application can set the `WidthRequest` and `HeightRequest` properties of an element to override its customary size. This is particularly useful for a `BoxView`, which initializes its `WidthRequest` and `Height-Request` values to 40. You can set these properties to different values to make a `BoxView` whatever size you want.

By default, these four properties have "mock" values of –1. If they are set to actual values, here's how `GetSizeRequest` and `OnSizeRequest` interact with them:

First, `GetSizeRequest` finds the minimum of its `widthConstraint` argument and the element's `WidthRequest` property and the minimum of `heightConstraint` and `HeightRequest`. These are the values passed to `OnSizeRequest`. In essence, the element is being offered only as much size as the `WidthRequest` and `HeightRequest` properties indicate.

Based on those constraints, `OnSizeRequest` returns a `SizeRequest` value back to `GetSize-Request`. That `SizeRequest` value has `Request` and `Minimum` properties. `GetSizeRequest` then finds the minimum of the `Width` and `Height` properties of the `Request` property and the `WidthRequest` and `HeightRequest` properties set on the element. It also finds the minimum of the `Width` and `Height` properties of the `Minimum` property, and the `MinimumWidthRequest` and `MinimumHeightRequest` properties set on the element. `GetSizeRequest` then returns a new `SizeRequest` value based on these minimums.

Here's some simple markup:

```
<ContentPage … Padding="20">
    <Label Text="Sample text"
           HorizontalOptions="Center"
           VerticalOptions="Center" />
</ContentPage>
```

Suppose the screen in portrait mode is 360 by 640. The layout cycle begins with a call to the `Lay-out` method of `ContentPage` with a bounds rectangle of (0, 0, 360, 640). The arguments to the `Lay-outChildren` override in `ContentPage` are adjusted for the padding, so the arguments are (20, 20, 320, 600).

Because `Label` has its `HorizontalOptions` and `VerticalOptions` properties not set to `Lay-outOptions.Fill`, the page must determine the size of the `Label` by calling `GetSizeRequest` with constraints of (320, 600). The information that `Label` returns depends on the platform, but let's assume the `Label` returns a size of (100, 24). The `ContentPage` must then position that `Label` in the center of the (320, 600) area available for its child. From the width of 320, it subtracts the `Label` width of 100 and divides by 2. That's 110, but that's relative to the area available for the child, and not relative to the upper-left corner of the page, which includes the margin of 20. So the horizontal offset of the `Label` from the `ContentPage` is actually 130.

The `ContentPage` performs a similar calculation for the height: 600 minus 24, divided by 2, plus 20, or 308. The `ContentPage` then calls the `Layout` method of the `Label` with the bounds rectangle (130, 308, 100, 24) to position and size the `Label` relative to itself.

How do `WidthRequest` and `HeightRequest` settings on the `Label` affect this? Here's a `WidthRe-quest` that is more than what the `Label` needs but a `HeightRequest` that is less:

```
<Label Text="Sample text"
       WidthRequest="200"
       HeightRequest="12"
       HorizontalOptions="Center"
       VerticalOptions="Center" />
```

The `ContentPage` still calls the `GetSizeRequest` method of the `Label` with constraints of (320, 600), but the `GetSizeRequest` modifies those constraints to be (200, 12), and that's what is passed to the `OnSizeRequest` override. The `Label` still returns a requested size of (100, 24), but `GetSizeRequest` again adjusts those for the `Width` and `Height` request and returns (200, 12) back to the `ContentPage`.

The `ContentPage` then calls the `Layout` method of `Label` based on `Label` dimensions of (200, 12) rather than (100, 24). The `Layout` call on the `Label` now has a bounds rectangle of (80, 314, 200, 12). The `Label` is displayed with twice as much width as is necessary for the text, but with half as much height. The text is cropped off at the bottom.

If instead the `WidthRequest` setting on the `Label` is set to be less than 100—for example, 50— then the `OnSizeRequest` method is called with a `widthConstraint` argument of 50, and the `Label` calculates a height for the text that results in wrapping the text into multiple lines.

Infinite constraints

Now here's some markup that at first seems very similar to the earlier example but with quite a profound difference:

```
<ContentPage … Padding="20">
    <StackLayout>
        <Label Text="Sample text" />
        …
    </StackLayout>
</ContentPage>
```

The `ContentPage` still gets an initial `Layout` call with the arguments (0, 0, 360, 640), and the arguments to the `LayoutChildren` override are (20, 20, 320, 600). It has one child, the `StackLayout`. The `StackLayout` has default settings of `HorizontalOptions` and `VerticalOptions` of `LayoutOptions.Fill`, which means that the `StackLayout` can be positioned relative to `ContentPage` with a `Layout` call of (20, 20, 320, 600).

This results in `StackLayout` getting a `LayoutChildren` call with arguments of (0, 0, 320, 600). How does `StackLayout` size and position its children?

As we know from working with `StackLayout` since Chapter 4, a vertical `StackLayout` gives its children the same horizontal size as itself, but a vertical size based on what the child needs. This means that `StackLayout` must call `GetSizeRequest` on all its children prior to calling `Layout`. But what constraints should it specify with those `GetSizeRequest` calls?

The initial impulse might be that `StackLayout` calls `GetSizeRequest` on its children with constraints that reflect its own size of (320, 600). But that's not right. The `StackLayout` doesn't limit its children to its own height. It allows its children to be any height they need to be. This implies that the height constraint should actually be infinite.

And this is true. `StackLayout` calls `GetSizeRequest` on its children with a height of (320, ∞), or, in terms of .NET, (320, `Double.PositiveInfinity`).

This is important: Constraints passed to `GetSizeRequest` and `OnSizeRequest` can range from 0 through `Double.PositiveInfinity`. However, `GetSizeRequest` and `OnSizeRequest` can never themselves request an infinite dimension by returning a `SizeRequest` value with a property set to `Double.PositiveInfinity`.

Let's try another common layout pattern:

```
<ContentPage … Padding="20">
    <ScrollView>
        <StackLayout>
            <Label Text="Sample text" />
            …
        </StackLayout>
    </ScrollView>
</ContentPage>
```

As usual, `ContentPage` gets a call to `Layout` with a bounds rectangle of (0, 0, 360, 640) and a call to its `LayoutChildren` method with arguments of (20, 20, 320, 600). The `ScrollView` has default `HorizontalOptions` and `VerticalOptions` settings of `LayoutOptions.Fill`, so the page doesn't need to know what size the `ScrollView` is. The page simply calls the `Layout` method of `ScrollView` with a bounds rectangle of (20, 20, 320, 600).

`ScrollView` then gets a call to its `LayoutChildren` method with arguments of (0, 0, 320, 600). It needs to determine the size of its child (the `StackLayout`), so it calls the `GetSizeRequest` method of `StackLayout`. What should the constraints be?

In the general case, the `StackLayout` will have a height greater than the height of `ScrollView`. That's why you're including a `ScrollView` in the visual tree! `ScrollView` needs to know that height if it is to successfully scroll its child. Therefore, `ScrollView` calls the `GetSizeRequest` method of `StackLayout` with constraints of (320, `Double.PositiveInfinity`). This translates into a call to `On-SizeRequest` with the same constraint arguments, which `StackLayout` overrides and handles.

You can also think of an infinite constraint as an autosize indication. A vertical `StackLayout` requests a child size with an infinite height constraint to obtain the child's requested height. Similarly, a child of a `Grid` cell whose row height or column width is `GridLength.Auto` will see an infinite `heightConstraint` or `widthConstraint`, or both. A child of an `AbsoluteLayout` with a `Layout-Bounds` height or width of `Auto` will also see an infinite `heightConstraint` or `widthConstraint`.

Sometimes the words *constrained* and *unconstrained* are used to refer to these differences. An element is *constrained* when it receives a call to its `GetSizeRequest` method with noninfinite arguments. The element is constrained to a particular size. An element is *unconstrained* when it gets a call to `Get-SizeRequest` with one or both arguments equal to `Double.PositiveInfinity`. Sometimes the term *partially constrained* is used to refer to a `GetSizeRequest` call with one `Double.PositiveIn-finity` argument, and the term *fully constrained* makes it clear that neither argument is infinite.

When you write your own custom layout classes by deriving from `Layout<View>`, you must override both the `OnSizeRequest` and `LayoutChildren` methods, and you must be aware that under certain circumstances, one or both of the constraints arguments to `OnSizeRequest` will be `Double.PositiveInfinity`. However, `OnSizeRequest` must never request an infinite size.

Peeking inside the process

Much of the information presented so far in this chapter has been assembled from test programs that contain classes that derive from various elements (such as `StackLayout`, `ScrollView`, and `Label`), override virtual methods (such as `GetSizeRequest`, `OnSizeRequest`, `OnSizeAllocated`, and `LayoutChildren`), and simply display information in the **Output** window of Visual Studio or Xamarin Studio by using the `Debug.WriteLine` method from the `System.Diagnostics` namespace.

A little bit of that exploratory process—but using the phone itself to display this information—is shown in the **ExploreChildSizes** sample.

ExploreChildSizes uses a `MasterDetailPage` to display a bunch of radio buttons on the `Master` page and a visual tree on the `Detail` part. The radio buttons make use of the `RadioButtonManager` and `RadioButtonItem` classes presented in Chapter 25, "Page varieties." Here's the `Master` page with radio buttons to select `HorizontalOptions` and `VerticalOptions` properties for the child views on the `Detail` page:

```
<MasterDetailPage xmlns="http://xamarin.com/schemas/2014/forms"
                  xmlns:x="http://schemas.microsoft.com/winfx/2009/xaml"
                  xmlns:local="clr-namespace:ExploreChildSizes;assembly=ExploreChildSizes"
                  xmlns:toolkit=
                  "clr-namespace:Xamarin.FormsBook.Toolkit;assembly=Xamarin.FormsBook.Toolkit"
                  x:Class="ExploreChildSizes.ExploreChildSizesPage">

    <MasterDetailPage.Master>
        <ContentPage Title="swap">
            <ContentPage.Icon>
                <OnPlatform x:TypeArguments="FileImageSource"
                            WinPhone="Images/refresh.png" />
            </ContentPage.Icon>

            <ContentPage.Padding>
                <OnPlatform x:TypeArguments="Thickness"
                            iOS="0, 20, 0, 0" />
            </ContentPage.Padding>

            <ScrollView>
                <StackLayout Padding="20"
                             Spacing="20">

                    <StackLayout>
                        <StackLayout.BindingContext>
                            <toolkit:RadioButtonManager x:Name="vertRadios"
                                                        x:TypeArguments="LayoutOptions" />
                        </StackLayout.BindingContext>

                        <StackLayout HorizontalOptions="Start">
                            <Label Text="Child VerticalOptions"
```

```
                                        FontSize="Medium" />
                        <BoxView Color="Accent"
                                 HeightRequest="3" />
                    </StackLayout>

                    <local:RadioButton BindingContext="{Binding Items[0]}" />
                    <local:RadioButton BindingContext="{Binding Items[1]}" />
                    <local:RadioButton BindingContext="{Binding Items[2]}" />
                    <local:RadioButton BindingContext="{Binding Items[3]}" />
                    <local:RadioButton BindingContext="{Binding Items[4]}" />
                    <local:RadioButton BindingContext="{Binding Items[5]}" />
                    <local:RadioButton BindingContext="{Binding Items[6]}" />
                    <local:RadioButton BindingContext="{Binding Items[7]}" />
                </StackLayout>

                <StackLayout>
                    <StackLayout.BindingContext>
                        <toolkit:RadioButtonManager x:Name="horzRadios"
                                                    x:TypeArguments="LayoutOptions" />
                    </StackLayout.BindingContext>

                    <StackLayout HorizontalOptions="Start">
                        <Label Text="Child HorizontalOptions"
                               FontSize="Medium" />
                        <BoxView Color="Accent"
                                 HeightRequest="3" />
                    </StackLayout>

                    <local:RadioButton BindingContext="{Binding Items[0]}" />
                    <local:RadioButton BindingContext="{Binding Items[1]}" />
                    <local:RadioButton BindingContext="{Binding Items[2]}" />
                    <local:RadioButton BindingContext="{Binding Items[3]}" />
                    <local:RadioButton BindingContext="{Binding Items[4]}" />
                    <local:RadioButton BindingContext="{Binding Items[5]}" />
                    <local:RadioButton BindingContext="{Binding Items[6]}" />
                    <local:RadioButton BindingContext="{Binding Items[7]}" />
                </StackLayout>
            </StackLayout>
        </ScrollView>
    </ContentPage>
</MasterDetailPage.Master>
    ...
</MasterDetailPage>
```

This page uses a class named `RadioButtonManager` in the **Xamarin.FormsBook.Toolkit** library, which you can peruse at your leisure. It allows for being a binding source for an item associated with the selected button. The `RadioButton` class uses the `Accent` color and the `Bold` attribute to indicate the selected item:

```
<ContentView xmlns="http://xamarin.com/schemas/2014/forms"
             xmlns:x="http://schemas.microsoft.com/winfx/2009/xaml"
             x:Class="ExploreChildSizes.RadioButton">
    <Label Text="{Binding Name}"
           FontSize="Medium">
```

```
            <Label.GestureRecognizers>
                <TapGestureRecognizer Command="{Binding Command}"
                                      CommandParameter="{Binding Value}"/>
            </Label.GestureRecognizers>

            <Label.Triggers>
                <DataTrigger TargetType="Label"
                             Binding="{Binding IsSelected}"
                             Value="True">
                    <Setter Property="TextColor" Value="Accent" />
                    <Setter Property="FontAttributes" Value="Bold" />
                </DataTrigger>
            </Label.Triggers>
        </Label>
</ContentView>
```

Here's the `Master` page on the three platforms. On the right side of all three screens, you can see a slice of the `Detail` page with a yellow background of a `StackLayout`:

The `Detail` page (shown below) is divided by a grid into two rows of equal height. The top row is a simple visual tree consisting of a `StackLayout` with a `Label` and `BoxView`. However, the classes in this visual tree are actually *derived* from `StackLayout`, `Label`, and `BoxView` and are called `Open-StackLayout`, `OpenLabel`, and `OpenBoxView`. Notice that the `VerticalOptions` and `Horizontal-Options` properties of `OpenLabel` and `OpenBoxView` are bound to the two `RadioButtonManager` objects on the `Master` page:

```
<MasterDetailPage … >
    …
    <MasterDetailPage.Detail>
        <ContentPage>
```

```
                    <ContentPage.Padding>
                        <OnPlatform x:TypeArguments="Thickness"
                                    iOS="0, 20, 0, 0" />
                    </ContentPage.Padding>

                    <Grid>
                        <local:OpenStackLayout x:Name="openStackLayout"
                                               Grid.Row="0"
                                               BackgroundColor="Yellow"
                                               Padding="15">
                            <local:OpenLabel
                                    x:Name="openLabel"
                                    Text="This is a label with text sufficiently long enough to wrap"
                                    FontSize="Large"
                                    BackgroundColor="Gray"
                                    VerticalOptions="{Binding Source={x:Reference vertRadios},
                                                              Path=SelectedValue}"
                                    HorizontalOptions="{Binding Source={x:Reference horzRadios},
                                                                Path=SelectedValue}" />

                            <local:OpenBoxView
                                    x:Name="openBoxView"
                                    Color="Pink"
                                    VerticalOptions="{Binding Source={x:Reference vertRadios},
                                                              Path=SelectedValue}"
                                    HorizontalOptions="{Binding Source={x:Reference horzRadios},
                                                                Path=SelectedValue}" />
                        </local:OpenStackLayout>
                        ...
                    </Grid>
                </ContentPage>
            </MasterDetailPage.Detail>
        </MasterDetailPage>
```

The `Open` prefix in this context means that these classes define public properties that reveal the arguments and return values of the `GetSizeRequest` calls and (in the case of `OpenStackLayout`) the arguments to `LayoutChildren`. All these properties are backed by read-only bindable properties so that they can serve as sources for data bindings. In addition, the `Bounds` property is mirrored in a property named `ElementBounds`, also backed by a read-only bindable property:

Here's the `OpenLabel` class. The other two are similar:

```
class OpenLabel : Label
{
    static readonly BindablePropertyKey ConstraintKey =
        BindableProperty.CreateReadOnly(
            "Constraint",
            typeof(Size),
            typeof(OpenLabel),
            new Size());

    public static readonly BindableProperty ConstraintProperty =
        ConstraintKey.BindableProperty;
```

```
static readonly BindablePropertyKey SizeRequestKey =
    BindableProperty.CreateReadOnly(
        "SizeRequest",
        typeof(SizeRequest),
        typeof(OpenLabel),
        new SizeRequest());

public static readonly BindableProperty SizeRequestProperty =
    SizeRequestKey.BindableProperty;

static readonly BindablePropertyKey ElementBoundsKey =
    BindableProperty.CreateReadOnly(
        "ElementBounds",
        typeof(Rectangle),
        typeof(OpenLabel),
        new Rectangle());

public static readonly BindableProperty ElementBoundsProperty =
    ElementBoundsKey.BindableProperty;

public OpenLabel()
{
    SizeChanged += (sender, args) =>
    {
        ElementBounds = Bounds;
    };
}

public Size Constraint
{
    private set { SetValue(ConstraintKey, value); }
    get { return (Size)GetValue(ConstraintProperty); }
}

public SizeRequest SizeRequest
{
    private set { SetValue(SizeRequestKey, value); }
    get { return (SizeRequest)GetValue(SizeRequestProperty); }
}
public Rectangle ElementBounds
{
    private set { SetValue(ElementBoundsKey, value); }
    get { return (Rectangle)GetValue(ElementBoundsProperty); }
}

public override SizeRequest GetSizeRequest(double widthConstraint, double heightConstraint)
{
    Constraint = new Size(widthConstraint, heightConstraint);
    SizeRequest sizeRequest = base.GetSizeRequest(widthConstraint, heightConstraint);
    SizeRequest = sizeRequest;
    return sizeRequest;
}
}
```

The bottom half of the `Grid` on the `Detail` page contains a scrollable `StackLayout` with data bindings to display these properties:

```xml
<MasterDetailPage … >
    …
    <MasterDetailPage.Detail>
        <ContentPage>
            <ContentPage.Padding>
                <OnPlatform x:TypeArguments="Thickness"
                            iOS="0, 20, 0, 0" />
            </ContentPage.Padding>

            <Grid>
                …
                <ScrollView Grid.Row="1"
                            Padding="10, 0">
                    <StackLayout>
                        <StackLayout.Resources>
                            <ResourceDictionary>
                                <Style TargetType="Label">
                                    <Setter Property="FontSize" Value="Small" />
                                </Style>
                            </ResourceDictionary>
                        </StackLayout.Resources>

                        <StackLayout
                            BindingContext="{Binding Source={x:Reference openStackLayout}}">
                            <Label Text="StackLayout:"
                                   FontAttributes="Bold" />

                            <Label Text="{Binding Path=Constraint,
                                         StringFormat='Constraint = {0}'}" />

                            <Label Text="{Binding Path=SizeRequest.Request,
                                         StringFormat='Request = {0}'}" />

                            <Label Text="{Binding Path=SizeRequest.Minimum,
                                         StringFormat='Minimum = {0}'}" />

                            <Label Text="{Binding Path=ElementBounds,
                                         StringFormat='Bounds = {0}'}" />

                            <Label Text="{Binding Path=LayoutBounds,
                                         StringFormat='Layout = {0}'}" />
                        </StackLayout>

                        <StackLayout BindingContext="{Binding Source={x:Reference openLabel}}">
                            <Label Text="Label:"
                                   FontAttributes="Bold" />

                            <Label Text="{Binding Path=Constraint,
                                         StringFormat='Constraint = {0}'}" />

                            <Label Text="{Binding Path=SizeRequest.Request,
```

```
                                              StringFormat='Request = {0}'}" />

                        <Label Text="{Binding Path=SizeRequest.Minimum,
                                      StringFormat='Minimum = {0}'}" />

                        <Label Text="{Binding Path=ElementBounds,
                                      StringFormat='Bounds = {0}'}" />
                </StackLayout>

                <StackLayout BindingContext="{Binding Source={x:Reference openBoxView}">
                        <Label Text="BoxView:"
                               FontAttributes="Bold" />

                        <Label Text="{Binding Path=Constraint,
                                      StringFormat='Constraint = {0}'}" />

                        <Label Text="{Binding Path=SizeRequest.Request,
                                      StringFormat='Request = {0}'}" />

                        <Label Text="{Binding Path=SizeRequest.Minimum,
                                      StringFormat='Minimum = {0}'}" />

                        <Label Text="{Binding Path=ElementBounds,
                                      StringFormat='Bounds = {0}'}" />
                </StackLayout>
            </StackLayout>
          </ScrollView>
        </Grid>
      </ContentPage>
    </MasterDetailPage.Detail>
</MasterDetailPage>
```

You can then set various combinations of VerticalOptions and HorizontalOptions on the Label and BoxView and see how these affect the arguments and return values from the GetSizeRequest method and the arguments to the Layout method (which are reflected in the Bounds property):

The `VerticalOptions` settings on the `Label` and `BoxView` have no effect except when the `Expands` flag is `true`. The `HorizontalOptions` settings position the items at the left, center, or right.

You might notice a couple of oddities: First, the `OpenStackLayout` does not get a call to its `GetSizeRequest` method. This is why the top three items in the bottom half of the screen are all zero. This `GetSizeRequest` call would normally come from the `Grid`, which is its parent. However, the `Grid` has a size based on the size of the screen, and the `Grid` contains two rows of equal size. The `OpenStackLayout` has its `VerticalOptions` and `HorizontalOptions` properties set to `LayoutOptions.Fill`, so it will have a size that is based on the `Grid` and not its contents.

If you'd like to investigate this behavior further, you'll need to change the `VerticalOptions` or `HorizontalOptions` properties of the `OpenStackLayout` in the markup on the `Detail` page. In that case, the `Grid` will call the `GetSizeRequest` method of `OpenStackLayout`—and `OpenStackLayout` then makes `GetSizeRequest` calls to `Label` and `BoxView`—because it needs to know the `OpenStackLayout` size to position it.

Both `OpenLabel` and `OpenBoxView` get calls to their `GetSizeRequest` methods with height constraints of `Double.PositiveInfinity`, but the `Label` shows some inconsistencies among the platforms.

On the various Windows platforms, it appears from the displayed values that the constraint width of the `Label` does not equal the layout width of the `StackLayout`. But further exploration reveals that the `GetSizeRequest` method is called more than once—the first time with the layout width, and then with the requested width of the `Label`.

The Android `Label` returns the width constraint as its requested width, which means that the `HorizontalOptions` setting on the `Label` has no effect on its horizontal position. This difference in the

Android implementation disappears when the text occupies just one line.

Deriving from Layout<View>

We are now armed with sufficient knowledge to create our own layout classes.

Most of the public and protected methods involved in layout are defined by the nongeneric `Layout` class. The `Layout<T>` class derives from `Layout` and constrains the generic type to `View` and its derivatives. `Layout<T>` defines a single public property named `Children` of type `IList<T>` and a couple of protected methods described shortly.

A custom layout class almost always derives from `Layout<View>`. If you want to restrict the children to certain types, you can derive from `Layout<Label>` or `Layout<BoxView>`, but that is not common. (You'll see an example toward the end of this chapter.)

A custom layout class has just two responsibilities:

- Override `OnSizeRequest` to call `GetSizeRequest` on all the layout's children. Return a requested size for the layout itself.

- Override `LayoutChildren` to call `Layout` on all the layout's children.

Both methods typically use `foreach` or `for` to enumerate through all the children in the custom layout's `Children` collection.

It is particularly important for your layout class to call `Layout` on each child. Otherwise, the child never gets a proper size or position and will not be visible.

However, the enumeration of children in the `OnSizeRequest` and `LayoutChildren` overrides should skip any child whose `IsVisible` property is set to `false`. Such children will not be visible anyway, but if you don't deliberately skip those children, it's likely that your layout class will leave room for these invisible children, and that's not correct behavior.

As you've seen, it is not guaranteed that the `OnSizeRequest` override will be called. The method doesn't need to be called if the size of the layout is governed by its parent rather than its children. The method definitely *will* be called if one or both of the constraints are infinite, or if the layout class has nondefault settings of `VerticalOptions` or `HorizontalOptions`. Otherwise, a call to `OnSizeRequest` is not guaranteed and you shouldn't rely on it.

You've also seen that the `OnSizeRequest` call might have constraint arguments set to `Double.PositiveInfinity`. However, `OnSizeRequest` cannot return a requested size with infinite dimensions. There is sometimes a temptation to implement `OnSizeRequest` in a very simple manner like this:

```
// This is very bad code!
protected override SizeRequest OnSizeRequest(double widthConstraint, double heightConstraint)
```

```
{
    return new SizeRequest(new Size(widthConstraint, heightConstraint));
}
```

Don't do it! If your `Layout<View>` derivative can't deal with infinite constraints for some reason—and you'll see an example later in this chapter—then raise an exception indicating that.

Very often, the `LayoutChildren` override will also require knowing the size of the children. The `LayoutChildren` method can also call `GetSizeRequest` on all the children before calling `Layout`. It is possible to cache the size of the children obtained in the `OnSizeRequest` override to avoid later `GetSizeRequest` calls in the `LayoutChildren` override, but the layout class will need to know when the sizes need to be obtained again. You'll see some guidelines shortly.

An easy example

A good technique for learning how to write custom layouts is to duplicate the functionality of an existing layout but simplify it somewhat.

The `VerticalStack` class described below is intended to mimic a `StackLayout` with an `Orientation` setting of `Vertical`. The `VerticalStack` class therefore does not have an `Orientation` property, and to keep things simple, `VerticalStack` doesn't have a `Spacing` property either. Moreover, `VerticalStack` does not recognize the `Expands` flag on the `HorizontalOptions` and `VerticalOptions` settings of its children. Ignoring the `Expands` flag simplifies the stacking logic *enormously*.

`VerticalStack` therefore defines just two members: overrides of the `OnSizeRequest` and `LayoutChildren` methods. Typically, both methods enumerate through the `Children` property defined by `Layout<T>`, and generally both methods make calls to the `GetSizeRequest` of the children. Any child with an `IsVisible` property set to `false` should be skipped.

The `OnSizeRequest` override in `VerticalStack` calls `GetSizeRequest` on each child with a constraint width equal to the `widthConstraint` argument to the override and a constraint height equal to `Double.PositiveInfinity`. This constrains the width of the child to the width of the `VerticalStack`, but allows each child to be as tall as it wants. That's the fundamental characteristic of a vertical stack:

```
public class VerticalStack : Layout<View>
{
    protected override SizeRequest OnSizeRequest(double widthConstraint,
                                                 double heightConstraint)
    {
        Size reqSize = new Size();
        Size minSize = new Size();

        // Enumerate through all the children.
        foreach (View child in Children)
        {
            // Skip the invisible children.
            if (!child.IsVisible)
                continue;
```

```
            // Get the child's requested size.
            SizeRequest childSizeRequest = child.GetSizeRequest(widthConstraint,
                                                   Double.PositiveInfinity);

            // Find the maximum width and accumulate the height.
            reqSize.Width = Math.Max(reqSize.Width, childSizeRequest.Request.Width);
            reqSize.Height += childSizeRequest.Request.Height;

            // Do the same for the minimum size request.
            minSize.Width = Math.Max(minSize.Width, childSizeRequest.Minimum.Width);
            minSize.Height += childSizeRequest.Minimum.Height;
        }
        return new SizeRequest(reqSize, minSize);
    }
    ...
}
```

The `foreach` loop over the `Children` collection accumulates the size of the children separately for the `Request` and `Minimum` properties of the `SizeRequest` object returned from the child. These accumulations involve two `Size` values, named `reqSize` and `minSize`. Because this is a *vertical* stack, the `reqSize.Width` and `minSize.Width` values are set to the *maximum* of the child widths, while the `reqSize.Height` and `minSize.Height` values are set to the *sum* of the child heights.

It is possible that the `widthConstraint` argument to `OnSizeRequest` is `Double.PositiveInfinity`, in which case the arguments to the `GetSizeRequest` call of the child are both infinite. (For example, the `VerticalStack` could be a child of a `StackLayout` with a horizontal orientation.) Generally, the body of the `OnSizeRequest` doesn't need to worry about situations like that because the `SizeRequest` value returned from `GetSizeRequest` never contains infinite values.

The second method in a custom layout—an override of `LayoutChildren`—is shown below. This is generally called as a consequence of a call to the parent's `Layout` method.

The `width` and `height` arguments to `LayoutChildren` indicate the size of the layout's area available for its children. Both values are finite. If an argument to `OnSizeRequest` was infinite, the corresponding argument to `LayoutChildren` will be the width or height returned from the `OnSizeRequest` override. Otherwise, it depends on the `HorizontalOptions` and `VerticalOptions` settings. For `Fill`, the argument to `LayoutChildren` is the same as the corresponding argument to `OnSizeRequest`. Otherwise, it's the requested width or height returned from the `OnSizeRequest`.

`LayoutChildren` also has x and y arguments that reflect the `Padding` property set on the layout. For example, if the left padding is 20 and the top padding is 50, then x is 20 and y is 50. These generally indicate a starting position for the children of the layout:

```
public class VerticalStack : Layout<View>
{
    ...
    protected override void LayoutChildren(double x, double y, double width, double height)
    {
        // Enumerate through all the children.
```

```
        foreach (View child in Children)
        {
            // Skip the invisible children.
            if (!child.IsVisible)
                continue;

            // Get the child's requested size.
            SizeRequest childSizeRequest = child.GetSizeRequest(width, Double.PositiveInfinity);

            // Initialize child position and size.
            double xChild = x;
            double yChild = y;
            double childWidth = childSizeRequest.Request.Width;
            double childHeight = childSizeRequest.Request.Height;

            // Adjust position and size based on HorizontalOptions.
            switch (child.HorizontalOptions.Alignment)
            {
                case LayoutAlignment.Start:
                    break;

                case LayoutAlignment.Center:
                    xChild += (width - childWidth) / 2;
                    break;

                case LayoutAlignment.End:
                    xChild += (width - childWidth);
                    break;

                case LayoutAlignment.Fill:
                    childWidth = width;
                    break;
            }

            // Layout the child.
            child.Layout(new Rectangle(xChild, yChild, childWidth, childHeight));

            // Get the next child's vertical position.
            y += childHeight;
        }
    }
}
```

This is a vertical stack, so LayoutChildren needs to vertically position each child based on the child's requested height. If the child has a HorizontalOptions setting of Fill, then the width of each child is the same as the width of the VerticalStack (minus the padding). Otherwise, the child's width is its requested width, and the stack must position that child within its own width.

To perform these calculations, LayoutChildren calls GetSizeRequest on its children again, but this time with the actual width and height arguments to LayoutChildren rather than the constraint arguments used in OnSizeRequest. Then it calls Layout on each child. The height argument to the Rectangle constructor is always the height of the child. The width argument could be either the width of the child or the width of the `VerticalStack` passed to the `LayoutChildren` override, depending on the `HorizontalOptions` setting on the child. Notice that each child is positioned x units from the left of the `VerticalStack`, and the first child is positioned y units from the top of the `VerticalStack`. That y variable is then increased at the bottom of the loop based on the child's height. That creates the stack.

The `VerticalStack` class is part of the **VerticalStackDemo** program, which contains a home page that navigates to two pages to test it out. Of course, you can add more test pages (which is something you should do for any `Layout<View>` classes that you develop).

The two test pages are instantiated in the home page:

```
<ContentPage xmlns="http://xamarin.com/schemas/2014/forms"
             xmlns:x="http://schemas.microsoft.com/winfx/2009/xaml"
             xmlns:sys="clr-namespace:System;assembly=mscorlib"
             xmlns:local="clr-namespace:VerticalStackDemo;assembly=VerticalStackDemo"
             x:Class="VerticalStackDemo.VerticalStackDemoHomePage"
             Title="VerticalStack Demo">

    <ListView ItemSelected="OnListViewItemSelected">
        <ListView.ItemsSource>
            <x:Array Type="{x:Type Page}">
                <local:LayoutOptionsTestPage />
                <local:ScrollTestPage />
            </x:Array>
        </ListView.ItemsSource>

        <ListView.ItemTemplate>
            <DataTemplate>
                <TextCell Text="{Binding Title}" />
            </DataTemplate>
        </ListView.ItemTemplate>
    </ListView>
</ContentPage>
```

The code-behind file navigates to the selected page:

```
public partial class VerticalStackDemoHomePage : ContentPage
{
    public VerticalStackDemoHomePage()
    {
        InitializeComponent();
    }

    async void OnListViewItemSelected(object sender, SelectedItemChangedEventArgs args)
    {
        ((ListView)sender).SelectedItem = null;

        if (args.SelectedItem != null)
        {
            Page page = (Page)args.SelectedItem;
            await Navigation.PushAsync(page);
        }
    }
```

```
        }
    }
```

The first of the test pages uses `VerticalStack` to display five `Button` elements with different `HorizontalOptions` settings. The `VerticalStack` itself is given a `VerticalOptions` setting that should position it in the middle of the page:

```xml
<ContentPage xmlns="http://xamarin.com/schemas/2014/forms"
             xmlns:x="http://schemas.microsoft.com/winfx/2009/xaml"
             xmlns:local="clr-namespace:VerticalStackDemo;assembly=VerticalStackDemo"
             x:Class="VerticalStackDemo.LayoutOptionsTestPage"
             Title="Test Layout Options">

    <local:VerticalStack Padding="50, 0"
                         VerticalOptions="Center">
        <Button Text="Default" />

        <Button Text="Start"
                HorizontalOptions="Start" />

        <Button Text="Center"
                HorizontalOptions="Center" />

        <Button Text="End"
                HorizontalOptions="End" />

        <Button Text="Fill"
                HorizontalOptions="Fill" />
    </local:VerticalStack>
</ContentPage>
```

Sure enough, the logic for the various `HorizontalOptions` settings on the children of `VerticalStack` seems to work:

Obviously, the Windows 10 Mobile platform would benefit from some spacing between the buttons!

If you remove the `VerticalOptions` setting on the `VerticalStack`, the `VerticalStack` will *not* get a call at all to its `OnSizeRequest` override. There is no need for it. The arguments to `Layout-Children` will reflect the whole size of the page less the `Padding`, and the page does not need to know how much space the `VerticalStack` requires.

The second test program puts the `VerticalStack` in a `ScrollView`:

```
<ContentPage xmlns="http://xamarin.com/schemas/2014/forms"
             xmlns:x="http://schemas.microsoft.com/winfx/2009/xaml"
             xmlns:local="clr-namespace:VerticalStackDemo;assembly=VerticalStackDemo"
             x:Class="VerticalStackDemo.ScrollTestPage"
             Title="Test Scrolling">
    <ScrollView>
        <local:VerticalStack x:Name="stack" />
    </ScrollView>
</ContentPage>
```

The code-behind file fills the `VerticalStack` with 125 instances of a regular `StackLayout`, each one containing a `BoxView`, and another `VerticalStack` with three `Label` elements:

```
public partial class ScrollTestPage : ContentPage
{
    public ScrollTestPage()
    {
        InitializeComponent();

        for (double r = 0; r <= 1.0; r += 0.25)
            for (double g = 0; g <= 1.0; g += 0.25)
                for (double b = 0; b <= 1.0; b += 0.25)
```

```
            {
                    stack.Children.Add(new StackLayout
                    {
                        Orientation = StackOrientation.Horizontal,
                        Padding = 6,
                        Children =
                        {
                            new BoxView
                            {
                                Color = Color.FromRgb(r, g, b),
                                WidthRequest = 100,
                                HeightRequest = 100
                            },

                            new VerticalStack
                            {
                                VerticalOptions = LayoutOptions.Center,
                                Children =
                                {
                                    new Label { Text = "Red = " + r.ToString("F2") },
                                    new Label { Text = "Green = " + g.ToString("F2") },
                                    new Label { Text = "Blue = " + b.ToString("F2") }
                                }
                            }
                        }
                    });
            }
        }
}
```

The VerticalStack is a child of a ScrollView with a vertical scrolling orientation, so it receives an OnSizeRequest call with a height of Double.PositiveInfinity. The VerticalStack responds with a height that encompasses all its children. The ScrollView uses that height together with its own height (which is based on the size of the screen) to scroll its contents:

Vertical and horizontal positioning simplified

Toward the end of the `LayoutChildren` override in `VerticalStack` is a `switch` statement that assists in positioning each child horizontally based on the child's `HorizontalOptions` property setting. Here's that whole method again:

```
public class VerticalStack : Layout<View>
{
    ...
    protected override void LayoutChildren(double x, double y, double width, double height)
    {
        // Enumerate through all the children.
        foreach (View child in Children)
        {
            // Skip the invisible children.
            if (!child.IsVisible)
                continue;

            // Get the child's requested size.
            SizeRequest childSizeRequest = child.GetSizeRequest(width, Double.PositiveInfinity);

            // Initialize child position and size.
            double xChild = x;
            double yChild = y;
            double childWidth = childSizeRequest.Request.Width;
            double childHeight = childSizeRequest.Request.Height;

            // Adjust position and size based on HorizontalOptions.
            switch (child.HorizontalOptions.Alignment)
            {
```

```
                    case LayoutAlignment.Start:
                        break;

                    case LayoutAlignment.Center:
                        xChild += (width - childWidth) / 2;
                        break;

                    case LayoutAlignment.End:
                        xChild += (width - childWidth);
                        break;

                    case LayoutAlignment.Fill:
                        childWidth = width;
                        break;
                }

                // Layout the child.
                child.Layout(new Rectangle(xChild, yChild, childWidth, childHeight));

                // Get the next child's vertical position.
                y += childHeight;
            }
        }
    }
}
```

Positioning a child within a rectangle based on its HorizontalOptions and VerticalOptions settings is something that comes up fairly frequently when writing layouts. For that reason, the Layout<T> class includes a public static method that does it for you:

```
public static void LayoutChildIntoBoundingRegion(VisualElement child, Rectangle region)
```

You can rewrite the LayoutChildren method to use this helper method like so:

```
protected override void LayoutChildren(double x, double y, double width, double height)
{
    // Enumerate through all the children.
    foreach (View child in Children)
    {
        // Skip the invisible children.
        if (!child.IsVisible)
            continue;

        // Get the child's requested size.
        SizeRequest childSizeRequest = child.GetSizeRequest(width, Double.PositiveInfinity);
        double childHeight = childSizeRequest.Request.Height;

        // Layout the child.
        LayoutChildIntoBoundingRegion(child, new Rectangle(x, y, width, childHeight));

        // Calculate the next child vertical position.
        y += childHeight;
    }
}
```

That's a considerable simplification! But as this call is used in other layout classes in this chapter, keep in mind that it is equivalent to making a call to the child's `Layout` method.

Notice that the rectangle you pass to `LayoutChildIntoBoundingRegion` encompasses the whole area in which the child can reside. In this case, the `width` argument to the `Rectangle` constructor is the `width` argument passed to `LayoutChildren`, which is the width of the `VerticalLayout` itself. But the `height` argument to the `Rectangle` constructor is the height the specific child requires, which is available from `GetSizeRequest`.

Unless the child has default `HorizontalOptions` and `VerticalOptions` settings of `Fill`, the `LayoutChildIntoBoundingRegion` method itself needs to call `GetSizeRequest` on the child using the `Width` and `Height` properties of that `Rectangle` value. That's the only way it knows how to position the child within the area provided in that `Rectangle` passed to the method call.

That means that when using the `LayoutChildIntoBoundingRegion` method, the `VerticalLayout` class could very well call `GetSizeRequest` three times on every child in each layout cycle.

Moreover, just as `VerticalLayout` calls `GetSizeRequest` on its children multiple times, and sometimes with different arguments, the parent of `VerticalLayout` might call `GetSizeRequest` on the `VerticalLayout` more than once with different arguments, which then results in more `OnSizeRequest` calls.

Calls to `GetSizeRequest` should not have any side effects. The calls don't result in any other properties being set, and should merely retrieve information based on particular width and height constraints. `GetSizeRequest` may therefore be called more freely than `Layout`, which actually affects how the element is sized and positioned.

But don't call `GetSizeRequest` if you don't need to. A call to `GetSizeRequest` is not required for an element to be displayed on the screen. Only `Layout` is required.

In your own layout classes, it's best to handle `OnSizeRequest` calls "blindly" without trying to figure out where the call is coming from, or why the arguments are what they are, or what it means to get several calls with different arguments.

However, it is possible for your layout class to cache the result of the `OnSizeRequest` call so that you can streamline subsequent calls. But doing this properly requires knowing about the process of *invalidation*.

Invalidation

Suppose you've assembled some layouts and views on a page, and for some reason the code-behind file (or perhaps a trigger or behavior) changes the text of a `Button`, or maybe just a font size or attribute. That change might affect the size of the button, which might potentially have a ripple effect of changes in layout through the rest of the page.

The process by which a change in an element on the page triggers a new layout is referred to as *invalidation*. When something on the page is invalid, it's means that it no longer has a correct size or position. A new layout cycle is required.

The process of invalidation begins with a protected virtual method defined by `VisualElement`:

```
protected virtual void InvalidateMeasure()
```

This method is protected. You can't invalidate an element from external code. Elements must invalidate themselves, generally when a property of the element changes. This commonly happens in the implementations of bindable properties. Whenever there's a change in one of the element's bindable properties that might result in a new size of the element, the property-changed handler usually calls `InvalidateMeasure`.

The `InvalidateMeasure` method fires an event so that any object external to the element might be informed when the element no longer has a correct size:

```
public event EventHandler MeasureInvalidated;
```

The element's parent generally handles this `MeasureInvalidated` event. However, the element doesn't do anything beyond firing this event. It doesn't change its own layout size. That's the responsibility of the element's parent. But any future call to `GetSizeRequest` will reflect the new size.

`VisualElement` itself defines 28 public properties, but only a few of them trigger calls to `InvalidateMeasure` and a subsequent firing of the `MeasureInvalidated` event. These properties are:

- `IsVisible`

- `WidthRequest` and `MinimumWidthRequest`

- `HeightRequest` and `MinimumHeightRequest`

These are the only properties that `VisualElement` defines that cause a change to the layout size of the element.

`VisualElement` defines some properties that might cause a change in the *appearance* of the element but not a change to the layout size. These are `BackgroundColor`, `IsEnabled`, `IsFocused`, and `Opacity`. Changes to these properties do not cause calls to `InvalidateMeasure`.

In addition, `VisualElement` defines eight transform properties that change the size of a rendered element but do not change the size of the element as perceived in layout. These are `AnchorX`, `AnchorY`, `Rotation`, `RotationX`, `RotationY`, `Scale`, `TranslationX`, and `TranslationY`.

The `Behaviors`, `Style`, and `Triggers` properties might *indirectly* affect layout size, but changes to these properties (or the collections that these properties maintain) do not themselves cause `InvalidateMeasure` to be called. In addition, changes to the `InputTransparent`, `Navigation`, and `Resources` properties do not affect layout size.

And then there are the five properties that are set by a call to `Layout`. These are `Bounds`, `X`, `Y`,

`Width`, and `Height`. These properties definitely should not—and do not—cause a call to `InvalidateMeasure`.

The `View` class adds three more properties to those defined by `VisualElement`. The `GestureRecognizers` property doesn't affect layout size, but changes to the following two properties cause a call to `InvalidateMeasure`:

- `HorizontalOptions`

- `VerticalOptions`

The classes that derive from `View` also make calls to `InvalidateMeasure` whenever a property changes that might cause a change in the element's size. For example, `Label` calls `InvalidateMeasure` whenever any of the following properties change:

- `Text` and `FormattedText`

- `FontFamily`, `FontSize`, and `FontAttributes`

- `LineBreakMode`

`Label` does *not* call `InvalidateMeasure` when the `TextColor` property changes. That affects the appearance of the text but not its size. `Label` also does *not* call `InvalidateMeasure` when the `HorizontalTextAlignment` and `VerticalTextAlignment` properties change. These properties govern the alignment of the text within the total size of the `Label`, but they do not affect the size of the `Label` itself.

The `Layout` class builds on the invalidation infrastructure in several crucial ways. First, `Layout` defines a method similar to `InvalidateMeasure` called `InvalidateLayout`:

```
protected virtual void InvalidateLayout()
```

A `Layout` derivative class should call `InvalidateLayout` whenever a change is made that affects how the layout class positions and sizes its children.

The `Layout` class itself calls `InvalidateLayout` whenever a child is added or removed from its `Content` property (in the case of `ContentView`, `Frame`, and `ScrollView`) or its `Children` collection (in the case of `Layout<View>` derivatives).

If you do *not* want your layout class to call `InvalidateLayout` when a child is added or removed, you can override the `ShouldInvalidateOnChildAdded` and `ShouldInvalidateOnChildRemoved` methods and simply return `false` instead of `true`. Your class can then implement a custom process when children are added or removed. The `Layout<T>` class overrides the virtual methods named `OnChildAdded` and `OnChildRemoved` defined by the `Element` class, but your class should instead override the `OnAdded` and `OnRemoved` methods for custom processing.

In addition, the `Layout` class sets a handler for the `MeasureInvalidated` event on every child added to its `Content` property or `Children` collection, and detaches the handler when the child is re-moved. The `Page` class does something similar. Both the `Page` and `Layout` classes expose overridable `OnChildMeasureInvalidated` methods if you want to be notified when these events are fired.

These `MeasureInvalidated` event handlers are really the crucial part of the process because every element in the visual tree that has children is alerted whenever one of its children changes size. This is how a change in the size of an element very deep in the visual tree can cause changes that ripple up the tree.

The `Layout` class, however, attempts to restrict the impact of a change in a child's size on the total layout of the page. If the particular layout is constrained in size, then a change in the size of a child need not affect anything higher than this layout in the visual tree.

In most cases, a change in the size of a layout affects how the layout arranges its children. For this reason, any change in a layout's size will precipitate a layout cycle for the layout. The layout will get calls to its `OnSizeRequested` and `LayoutChildren` methods.

However, the opposite is not always true. The way in which a layout arranges its children might af-fect the layout's size, or it might not. Most obviously, the layout's size will *not* be affected by how the layout arranges its children if the layout's size is fully constrained.

This difference becomes important when the layout defines its own properties such as the `Spacing` and `Orientation` properties defined by `StackLayout`. When such a property changes value, the lay-out must invalidate itself to cause a new layout cycle to occur. Should the layout call `Invalidate-Measure` or `InvalidateLayout`?

In most cases, the layout should call `InvalidateLayout`. This guarantees that the layout gets a call to its `LayoutChildren` method even if the layout is fully constrained in size. If the layout calls `Inval-idateMeasure`, then a new layout pass will be generated only if the layout is not fully constrained in size. If the layout is constrained in size, then a call to `InvalidateMeasure` will do nothing.

Some rules for coding layouts

From the discussion above, you can formulate several rules for your own `Layout<View>` derivatives:

Rule 1: If your layout class defines properties such as `Spacing` or `Orientation`, these properties should be backed by bindable properties. In most cases, the property-changed handlers of these bind-able properties should call `InvalidateLayout`. Calling `InvalidateMeasure` should be restricted to cases where a property change affects the size of the layout only and not how it arranges its children, but a real-life example is hard to imagine.

Rule 2: Your layout class might define attached bindable properties for its children similar to the `Row`, `Column`, `RowSpan`, and `ColumnSpan` properties defined by `Grid`. As you know, these properties are defined by the layout class, but they are intended to be set on the children of the layout. In this case, your layout class should override the `OnAdded` method to add a `PropertyChanged` handler to each child of the layout, and override `OnRemoved` to remove that handler. The `PropertyChanged` handler should check whether the property being changed on the child is one of the attached bindable properties that your class has defined, and if so, your layout should usually respond by calling `InvalidateLayout`.

Rule 3: If you want to implement a cache (or retain other information) to minimize repetitive processing of calls to the `GetSizeRequest` methods of the layout's children, then you should also override the `InvalidateLayout` method to be notified when children are added to or removed from the layout, and the `OnChildMeasureInvalidated` method to be notified when one of the layout's children changes size. In both cases, your layout class should respond by clearing that cache or discarding the retained information.

It's possible for the layout to also clear the cache or discard retained information when the layout gets a call to its `InvalidateMeasure` method. However, generally the cache is a dictionary based on sizes passed to the `OnSizeRequest` and `LayoutChildren` override, so those sizes will be different anyway.

All these techniques will be demonstrated in the pages ahead.

A layout with properties

The `StackLayout` is certainly handy, but it's only a single row or column of children. If you want multiple rows and columns, you can use the `Grid`, but the application must explicitly set the number of rows and columns, and that requires having a good idea of the size of the children.

A more useful layout to accommodate an indefinite number of children would begin positioning children in a row much like a horizontal `StackLayout`, but then go to a second row if necessary, and to a third, continuing for however many rows are necessary. If the number of rows is expected to exceed the height of the screen, then the layout could be made a child of a `ScrollView`.

This is the idea behind `WrapLayout`. It arranges its children in columns horizontally across the screen until it gets to the edge, at which point it wraps the display of subsequent children to the next row, and so forth.

But let's make it a little more versatile: Let's give it an `Orientation` property like `StackLayout`. This allows a program using `WrapLayout` to specify that it begin by arranging its children in rows down the screen, and should then go to a second column if necessary. With this alternative orientation, the `WrapLayout` could be horizontally scrolled.

Let's also give `WrapLayout` two properties, named `ColumnSpacing` and `RowSpacing`, just like `Grid`.

The `WrapLayout` has the potential of being algorithmically rather complex if it really allows for children of a variety of different sizes. The first row might have four children, then three children in the second row, and so forth.

Let's instead make a simple assumption that all the children have the same size—or more precisely, that the same amount of space is allocated for each child based on the maximum size of the children. This is sometimes called a *cell size*, and WrapLayout will calculate a cell size that is large enough for every child. Children smaller than the cell size can be positioned within that cell based on their HorizontalOptions and VerticalOptions settings.

WrapLayout is useful enough to justify its inclusion in the **Xamarin.FormsBook.Toolkit** library. The following enumeration contains the two orientation options with wordy but unambiguous descriptions:

```
namespace Xamarin.FormsBook.Toolkit
{
    public enum WrapOrientation
    {
        HorizontalThenVertical,
        VerticalThenHorizontal
    }
}
```

WrapLayout defines three properties backed by bindable properties. The property-changed handler of each bindable property simply calls InvalidateLayout to trigger a new layout pass on the layout:

```
namespace Xamarin.FormsBook.Toolkit
{
    public class WrapLayout : Layout<View>
    {
        ...
        public static readonly BindableProperty OrientationProperty =
            BindableProperty.Create(
                "Orientation",
                typeof(WrapOrientation),
                typeof(WrapLayout),
                WrapOrientation.HorizontalThenVertical,
                propertyChanged: (bindable, oldValue, newValue) =>
                {
                    ((WrapLayout)bindable).InvalidateLayout();
                });

        public static readonly BindableProperty ColumnSpacingProperty =
            BindableProperty.Create(
                "ColumnSpacing",
                typeof(double),
                typeof(WrapLayout),
                6.0,
                propertyChanged: (bindable, oldvalue, newvalue) =>
                {
                    ((WrapLayout)bindable).InvalidateLayout();
                });

        public static readonly BindableProperty RowSpacingProperty =
            BindableProperty.Create(
                "RowSpacing",
                typeof(double),
```

```
                    typeof(WrapLayout),
                    6.0,
                    propertyChanged: (bindable, oldvalue, newvalue) =>
                    {
                        ((WrapLayout)bindable).InvalidateLayout();
                    });

        public WrapOrientation Orientation
        {
            set { SetValue(OrientationProperty, value); }
            get { return (WrapOrientation)GetValue(OrientationProperty); }
        }

        public double ColumnSpacing
        {
            set { SetValue(ColumnSpacingProperty, value); }
            get { return (double)GetValue(ColumnSpacingProperty); }
        }

        public double RowSpacing
        {
            set { SetValue(RowSpacingProperty, value); }
            get { return (double)GetValue(RowSpacingProperty); }
        }
        …
    }
}
```

WrapLayout also defines a private structure for storing information about a particular collection of children. The CellSize property is the maximum size of all the children but adjusted to the size of the layout. The Rows and Cols properties are the number of rows and columns.

```
namespace Xamarin.FormsBook.Toolkit
{
    public class WrapLayout : Layout<View>
    {
        struct LayoutInfo
        {
            public LayoutInfo(int visibleChildCount, Size cellSize, int rows, int cols) : this()
            {
                VisibleChildCount = visibleChildCount;
                CellSize = cellSize;
                Rows = rows;
                Cols = cols;
            }

            public int VisibleChildCount { private set; get; }

            public Size CellSize { private set; get; }

            public int Rows { private set; get; }

            public int Cols { private set; get; }
        }
```

```
        Dictionary<Size, LayoutInfo> layoutInfoCache = new Dictionary<Size, LayoutInfo>();
        …
    }
}
```

Notice also the definition of a `Dictionary` to store multiple `LayoutInfo` values. The `Size` key is either the constraint arguments to the `OnSizeRequest` override, or the `width` and `height` arguments to the `LayoutChildren` override.

If the `WrapLayout` is in a constrained `ScrollView` (which will normally be the case), then one of the constraint arguments will be infinite, but that will not be the case for the `width` and `height` arguments to `LayoutChildren`. In that case, there will be two dictionary entries.

If you then turn the phone sideways, `WrapLayout` will get another `OnSizeRequest` call with an infinite constraint, and another `LayoutChildren` call. That's two more dictionary entries. But then if you turn the phone back to portrait mode, no further calculations need occur because the cache already has that case.

Here is the `GetLayoutInfo` method in `WrapLayout` that calculates the properties of the `LayoutInfo` structure based on a particular size. Notice that the method begins by checking if a calculated `LayoutInfo` value is already available in the cache. At the end of the `GetLayoutInfo` method, the new `LayoutInfo` value is stored in the cache:

```
namespace Xamarin.FormsBook.Toolkit
{
    public class WrapLayout : Layout<View>
    {
        …
        LayoutInfo GetLayoutInfo(double width, double height)
        {
            Size size = new Size(width, height);

            // Check if cached information is available.
            if (layoutInfoCache.ContainsKey(size))
            {
                return layoutInfoCache[size];
            }

            int visibleChildCount = 0;
            Size maxChildSize = new Size();
            int rows = 0;
            int cols = 0;
            LayoutInfo layoutInfo = new LayoutInfo();

            // Enumerate through all the children.
            foreach (View child in Children)
            {
                // Skip invisible children.
                if (!child.IsVisible)
                    continue;
```

```
            // Count the visible children.
            visibleChildCount++;

            // Get the child's requested size.
            SizeRequest childSizeRequest = child.GetSizeRequest(Double.PositiveInfinity,
                                                                Double.PositiveInfinity);

            // Accumulate the maximum child size.
            maxChildSize.Width =
                Math.Max(maxChildSize.Width, childSizeRequest.Request.Width);

            maxChildSize.Height =
                Math.Max(maxChildSize.Height, childSizeRequest.Request.Height);
        }

        if (visibleChildCount != 0)
        {
            // Calculate the number of rows and columns.
            if (Orientation == WrapOrientation.HorizontalThenVertical)
            {
                if (Double.IsPositiveInfinity(width))
                {
                    cols = visibleChildCount;
                    rows = 1;
                }
                else
                {
                    cols = (int)((width + ColumnSpacing) /
                                (maxChildSize.Width + ColumnSpacing));
                    cols = Math.Max(1, cols);
                    rows = (visibleChildCount + cols - 1) / cols;
                }
            }
            else // WrapOrientation.VerticalThenHorizontal
            {
                if (Double.IsPositiveInfinity(height))
                {
                    rows = visibleChildCount;
                    cols = 1;
                }
                else
                {
                    rows = (int)((height + RowSpacing) /
                                (maxChildSize.Height + RowSpacing));
                    rows = Math.Max(1, rows);
                    cols = (visibleChildCount + rows - 1) / rows;
                }
            }

            // Now maximize the cell size based on the layout size.
            Size cellSize = new Size();

            if (Double.IsPositiveInfinity(width))
            {
```

```
                    cellSize.Width = maxChildSize.Width;
                }
                else
                {
                    cellSize.Width = (width - ColumnSpacing * (cols - 1)) / cols;
                }

                if (Double.IsPositiveInfinity(height))
                {
                    cellSize.Height = maxChildSize.Height;
                }
                else
                {
                    cellSize.Height = (height - RowSpacing * (rows - 1)) / rows;
                }

                layoutInfo = new LayoutInfo(visibleChildCount, cellSize, rows, cols);
            }

            layoutInfoCache.Add(size, layoutInfo);
            return layoutInfo;
        }
        …
    }
}
```

The logic of `GetLayoutInfo` is divided into three major sections:

The first section is a `foreach` loop that enumerates through all the children, calls `GetSizeRequest` with an infinite width and height, and determines the maximum child size.

The second and third sections are executed only if there is at least one visible child. The second section has different processing based on the `Orientation` property and calculates the number of rows and columns. It will usually be the case that a `WrapPanel` with the default `Orientation` setting (`HorizontalThenVertical`) will be a child of a vertical `ScrollView`, in which case the `heightConstraint` argument to the `OnSizeRequest` override will be infinite. It might also be the case that the `widthConstraint` argument to `OnSizeRequest` (and `GetLayoutInfo`) is also infinite, which results in all the children being displayed in a single row. But that would be unusual.

The third section then calculates a cell size for the children based on the dimensions of the `WrapLayout`. For an `Orientation` of `HorizontalThenVertical`, this cell size is usually a bit wider than the maximum child size, but it might be smaller if the `WrapLayout` is not wide enough for the widest child or tall enough for the tallest child.

The cache must be entirely destroyed when the layout receives calls to `InvalidateLayout` (which could result when children are added to or removed from the collection, or when one of the properties of `WrapLayout` changes value) or to `OnChildMeasureInvalidated`. This is simply a matter of clearing the dictionary:

```
namespace Xamarin.FormsBook.Toolkit
{
```

```
public class WrapLayout : Layout<View>
{
    ...

    protected override void InvalidateLayout()
    {
        base.InvalidateLayout();

        // Discard all layout information for children added or removed.
        layoutInfoCache.Clear();
    }

    protected override void OnChildMeasureInvalidated()
    {
        base.OnChildMeasureInvalidated();

        // Discard all layout information for child size changed.
        layoutInfoCache.Clear();
    }
}
}
```

Finally, we're ready to look at the two required methods. The `OnSizeRequest` override simply calls `GetLayoutInfo` and constructs a `SizeRequest` value from the returned information together with the `RowSpacing` and `ColumnSpacing` properties:

```
namespace Xamarin.FormsBook.Toolkit
{
    public class WrapLayout : Layout<View>
    {
        ...

        protected override SizeRequest OnSizeRequest(double widthConstraint,
                                                     double heightConstraint)
        {
            LayoutInfo layoutInfo = GetLayoutInfo(widthConstraint, heightConstraint);

            if (layoutInfo.VisibleChildCount == 0)
            {
                return new SizeRequest();
            }

            Size totalSize = new Size(layoutInfo.CellSize.Width * layoutInfo.Cols +
                                          ColumnSpacing * (layoutInfo.Cols - 1),
                                      layoutInfo.CellSize.Height * layoutInfo.Rows +
                                          RowSpacing * (layoutInfo.Rows - 1));

            return new SizeRequest(totalSize);
        }
        ...
    }
}
```

The `LayoutChildren` override begins with a call to `GetLayoutInfo` and then enumerates all the children to size and position them within each child's cell. This logic also requires separate processing based on the `Orientation` property:

```
namespace Xamarin.FormsBook.Toolkit
{
    public class WrapLayout : Layout<View>
    {
        ...
        protected override void LayoutChildren(double x, double y, double width, double height)
        {
            LayoutInfo layoutInfo = GetLayoutInfo(width, height);

            if (layoutInfo.VisibleChildCount == 0)
                return;

            double xChild = x;
            double yChild = y;
            int row = 0;
            int col = 0;

            foreach (View child in Children)
            {
                if (!child.IsVisible)
                    continue;

                LayoutChildIntoBoundingRegion(child,
                        new Rectangle(new Point(xChild, yChild), layoutInfo.CellSize));

                if (Orientation == WrapOrientation.HorizontalThenVertical)
                {
                    if (++col == layoutInfo.Cols)
                    {
                        col = 0;
                        row++;
                        xChild = x;
                        yChild += RowSpacing + layoutInfo.CellSize.Height;
                    }
                    else
                    {
                        xChild += ColumnSpacing + layoutInfo.CellSize.Width;
                    }
                }
                else // Orientation == WrapOrientation.VerticalThenHorizontal
                {
                    if (++row == layoutInfo.Rows)
                    {
                        col++;
                        row = 0;
                        xChild += ColumnSpacing + layoutInfo.CellSize.Width;
                        yChild = y;
                    }
                    else
                    {
                        yChild += RowSpacing + layoutInfo.CellSize.Height;
                    }
                }
```

```
                  }
              }
          }
        ...
    }
}
```

Let's try it out! The XAML file of the **PhotoWrap** program simply contains a `WrapPanel` with default property settings in a `ScrollView`:

```xml
<ContentPage xmlns="http://xamarin.com/schemas/2014/forms"
             xmlns:x="http://schemas.microsoft.com/winfx/2009/xaml"
             xmlns:toolkit=
                 "clr-namespace:Xamarin.FormsBook.Toolkit;assembly=Xamarin.FormsBook.Toolkit"
             x:Class="PhotoWrap.PhotoWrapPage">
    <ContentPage.Padding>
        <OnPlatform x:TypeArguments="Thickness"
                    iOS="0, 20, 0, 0" />
    </ContentPage.Padding>

    <ScrollView>
        <toolkit:WrapLayout x:Name="wrapLayout" />
    </ScrollView>
</ContentPage>
```

The code-behind file accesses the JSON file containing the list of stock photos previously used in several sample programs in this book. The constructor creates an `Image` element for each bitmap in the list and adds it to the `WrapLayout`:

```csharp
public partial class PhotoWrapPage : ContentPage
{
    [DataContract]
    class ImageList
    {
        [DataMember(Name = "photos")]
        public List<string> Photos = null;
    }

    WebRequest request;
    static readonly int imageDimension = Device.OnPlatform(240, 240, 120);
    static readonly string urlSuffix =
        String.Format("?width={0}&height={0}&mode=max", imageDimension);

    public PhotoWrapPage()
    {
        InitializeComponent();

        // Get list of stock photos.
        Uri uri = new Uri("http://docs.xamarin.com/demo/stock.json");
        request = WebRequest.Create(uri);
        request.BeginGetResponse(WebRequestCallback, null);
    }

    void WebRequestCallback(IAsyncResult result)
```

```
    {
        try
        {
            Stream stream = request.EndGetResponse(result).GetResponseStream();

            // Deserialize the JSON into imageList.
            var jsonSerializer = new DataContractJsonSerializer(typeof(ImageList));
            ImageList imageList = (ImageList)jsonSerializer.ReadObject(stream);

            Device.BeginInvokeOnMainThread(() =>
            {
                foreach (string filepath in imageList.Photos)
                {
                    Image image = new Image
                    {
                        Source = ImageSource.FromUri(new Uri(filepath + urlSuffix))
                    };
                    wrapLayout.Children.Add(image);
                }
            });
        }
        catch (Exception)
        {
        }
    }
}
```

The number of columns in each row depends on the size of the bitmaps, the screen width, and the number of pixels per device-independent unit:

Turn the phones sideways, and you'll see something a bit different:

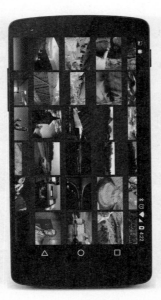

The `ScrollView` allows the layout to be vertically scrolled. If you want to check the different orientation of the `WrapPanel`, you'll need to change the orientation of the `ScrollView` as well:

```
<ScrollView Orientation="Horizontal">
    <toolkit:WrapLayout x:Name="wrapLayout"
                        Orientation="VerticalThenHorizontal" />
</ScrollView>
```

Now the screen scrolls horizontally:

The `Image` elements load the bitmaps in the background, so the `WrapLayout` class will get numerous calls to its `Layout` method as each `Image` element gets a new size based on the loaded bitmap. Consequently, you might see some shifting of the rows and columns as the bitmaps are being loaded.

No unconstrained dimensions allowed!

There are times when you want to see *everything* on the screen, perhaps in an array of uniformly sized rows and columns. You can do something like this with a `Grid` with all the row and column definitions defined with the asterisk to make them all the same size. The only problem is that you probably also want the number of rows and columns to be based on the number of children, and optimized for the best use of the screen real estate.

Let's write a custom layout called `UniformGridLayout`. Like `WrapLayout`, `UniformGridLayout` requires `Orientation`, `RowSpacing`, and `ColumnSpacing` properties, so let's eliminate some of the work involved in redefining properties by deriving `UniformGridLayout` from `WrapLayout`.

Because `UniformGridLayout` makes no sense with an unconstrained dimension, the `OnSize-Request` override checks for infinite constraints and raises an exception if it encounters such a thing.

To assist in the ability of `UniformGridLayout` to optimize the use of the screen real estate, let's give it a property named `AspectRatio` of type `AspectRatio`. This property indicates the expected aspect ratio of the children as a `double` value. The value 1.33, for example, indicates an aspect ratio of 4:3, which is a width that is 33 percent longer than the height. By default, however, `UniformGridLayout` will calculate an average aspect ratio of its children.

This `AspectRatio` structure is similar to the `GridLength` structure defined for the `Grid` class in that it allows a `double` value as well as an "Auto" option to force `UniformGridLayout` to calculate that average aspect ratio:

```
namespace Xamarin.FormsBook.Toolkit
{
    [TypeConverter(typeof(AspectRatioTypeConverter))]
    public struct AspectRatio
    {
        public AspectRatio(double value)
        {
            if (value < 0)
                throw new FormatException("AspectRatio value must be greater than 0, " +
                                          "or set to 0 to indicate Auto");

            Value = value;
        }

        public static AspectRatio Auto
        {
            get
            {
                return new AspectRatio();
            }
        }

        public double Value { private set; get; }

        public bool IsAuto { get { return Value == 0; } }

        public override string ToString()
        {
            return Value == 0 ? "Auto" : Value.ToString();
        }
    }
}
```

The "Auto" option is indicated by a `Value` property of 0. An application using `UniformGridLayout` can create such an `AspectRatio` value with the parameterless constructor, or by passing a 0 to the defined constructor, or by using the static `Auto` property.

I'm sure you'd like to be able to set an `AspectRatio` property in XAML, so the structure is flagged with a `TypeConverter` attribute. The `AspectRatioTypeConverter` class can handle a string with the word "Auto" or a `double`:

```
namespace Xamarin.FormsBook.Toolkit
{
    public class AspectRatioTypeConverter : TypeConverter
    {
        public override bool CanConvertFrom(Type sourceType)
        {
            return sourceType == typeof(string);
        }

        public override object ConvertFrom(CultureInfo culture, object value)
        {
```

```
                    string str = value as string;

                    if (String.IsNullOrWhiteSpace(str))
                        return null;

                    str = str.Trim();
                    double aspectValue;

                    if (String.Compare(str, "auto", StringComparison.OrdinalIgnoreCase) == 0)
                        return AspectRatio.Auto;

                    if (Double.TryParse(str, NumberStyles.Number,
                                        CultureInfo.InvariantCulture, out aspectValue))
                        return new AspectRatio(aspectValue);

                    throw new FormatException("AspectRatio must be Auto or numeric");
                }
            }
        }
```

The `UniformGridLayout` class derives from `WrapLayout` solely for inheriting the three bindable properties that `WrapLayout` defines. To those properties, `UniformGridLayout` adds the `AspectRatio` property:

```
namespace Xamarin.FormsBook.Toolkit
{
    public class UniformGridLayout : WrapLayout
    {
        public static readonly BindableProperty AspectRatioProperty =
            BindableProperty.Create(
                "AspectRatio",
                typeof(AspectRatio),
                typeof(UniformGridLayout),
                AspectRatio.Auto,
                propertyChanged: (bindable, oldvalue, newvalue) =>
                {
                    ((UniformGridLayout)bindable).InvalidateLayout();
                });

        public AspectRatio AspectRatio
        {
            set { SetValue(AspectRatioProperty, value); }
            get { return (AspectRatio)GetValue(AspectRatioProperty); }
        }
        ...
    }
}
```

The `OnSizeRequest` override begins by checking if the constraints are infinite and raising an exception if that is the case. Otherwise, it requests the entire area unless it has no visible children:

```
namespace Xamarin.FormsBook.Toolkit
{
    public class UniformGridLayout : WrapLayout
```

```
    {
        ...
        protected override SizeRequest OnSizeRequest(double widthConstraint,
                                                     double heightConstraint)
        {
            if (Double.IsInfinity(widthConstraint) || Double.IsInfinity(heightConstraint))
                throw new InvalidOperationException(
                    "UniformGridLayout cannot be used with unconstrained dimensions.");

            // Just check to see if there aren't any visible children.
            int childCount = 0;

            foreach (View view in Children)
                childCount += view.IsVisible ? 1 : 0;

            if (childCount == 0)
                return new SizeRequest();

            // Then request the entire (noninfinite) size.
            return new SizeRequest(new Size(widthConstraint, heightConstraint));
        }
        ...
    }
}
```

The hard part is the `LayoutChildren` override, and it has three main sections:

```
namespace Xamarin.FormsBook.Toolkit
{
    public class UniformGridLayout : WrapLayout
    {
        ...
        protected override void LayoutChildren(double x, double y, double width, double height)
        {
            int childCount = 0;

            foreach (View view in Children)
                childCount += view.IsVisible ? 1 : 0;

            if (childCount == 0)
                return;

            double childAspect = AspectRatio.Value;

            // If AspectRatio is Auto, calculate an average aspect ratio
            if (AspectRatio.IsAuto)
            {
                int nonZeroChildCount = 0;
                double accumAspectRatio = 0;

                foreach (View view in Children)
                {
                    if (view.IsVisible)
                    {
                        SizeRequest sizeRequest = view.GetSizeRequest(Double.PositiveInfinity,
```

```
                                                        Double.PositiveInfinity);

            if (sizeRequest.Request.Width > 0 && sizeRequest.Request.Height > 0)
            {
                nonZeroChildCount++;
                accumAspectRatio += sizeRequest.Request.Width /
                                        sizeRequest.Request.Height;
            }
        }
    }

    if (nonZeroChildCount > 0)
    {
        childAspect = accumAspectRatio / nonZeroChildCount;
    }
    else
    {
        childAspect = 1;
    }
}

int bestRowsCount = 0;
int bestColsCount = 0;
double bestUsage = 0;
double bestChildWidth = 0;
double bestChildHeight = 0;

// Test various possibilities of the number of columns.
for (int colsCount = 1; colsCount <= childCount; colsCount++)
{
    // Find the number of rows for that many columns.
    int rowsCount = (int)Math.Ceiling((double)childCount / colsCount);

    // Determine if we have more rows or columns than we need.
    if ((rowsCount - 1) * colsCount >= childCount ||
        rowsCount * (colsCount - 1) >= childCount)
    {
        continue;
    }

    // Get the aspect ratio of the resultant cells.
    double cellWidth = (width - ColumnSpacing * (colsCount - 1)) / colsCount;
    double cellHeight = (height - RowSpacing * (rowsCount - 1)) / rowsCount;
    double cellAspect = cellWidth / cellHeight;
    double usage = 0;

    // Compare with the average aspect ratio of the child.
    if (cellAspect > childAspect)
    {
        usage = childAspect / cellAspect;
    }
    else
    {
        usage = cellAspect / childAspect;
```

```
        }

        // If we're using more space, save the numbers.
        if (usage > bestUsage)
        {
            bestRowsCount = rowsCount;
            bestColsCount = colsCount;
            bestUsage = usage;
            bestChildWidth = cellWidth;
            bestChildHeight = cellHeight;
        }
    }

    int colIndex = 0;
    int rowIndex = 0;
    double xChild = x;
    double yChild = y;

    foreach (View view in Children)
    {
        // Position and size the child.
        LayoutChildIntoBoundingRegion(view,
            new Rectangle(xChild, yChild, bestChildWidth, bestChildHeight));

        // Increment the coordinates and indices.
        if (Orientation == WrapOrientation.HorizontalThenVertical)
        {
            xChild += bestChildWidth + ColumnSpacing;

            if (++colIndex == bestColsCount)
            {
                colIndex = 0;
                xChild = x;
                yChild += bestChildHeight + RowSpacing;
            }
        }
        else // Orientation == WrapOrientation.VerticalThenHorizontal
        {
            yChild += bestChildHeight + RowSpacing;

            if (++rowIndex == bestRowsCount)
            {
                rowIndex = 0;
                xChild += bestChildWidth + ColumnSpacing;
                yChild = y;
            }
        }
    }
  }
 }
}
```

The first section calculates an average aspect ratio of the children if the "Auto" option has been specified.

The second section loops through different combinations of rows and columns and determines which combination results in the best use of the available space. The crucial calculation is this:

```
if (cellAspect > childAspect)
{
    usage = childAspect / cellAspect;
}
else
{
    usage = cellAspect / childAspect;
}
```

For example, suppose that the `childAspect` that is calculated based on the average of all the children is 1.5, and for a particular combination of rows and columns the `cellAspect` value is 2. A child with an aspect ratio of 1.5 will occupy only 75 percent of a cell with an aspect ratio of 2. If the `cellAspect` is instead 0.75, then the child will occupy only 50 percent of that cell.

The third section then gives each child a size and position within the grid. This requires different processing based on the `Orientation` property.

Let's try it out. The **PhotoGrid** XAML file fills the page (except for the top padding on the iPhone) with a `UniformGridLayout` with two properties set:

```
<ContentPage xmlns="http://xamarin.com/schemas/2014/forms"
             xmlns:x="http://schemas.microsoft.com/winfx/2009/xaml"
             xmlns:toolkit=
                "clr-namespace:Xamarin.FormsBook.Toolkit;assembly=Xamarin.FormsBook.Toolkit"
             x:Class="PhotoGrid.PhotoGridPage">
    <ContentPage.Padding>
        <OnPlatform x:TypeArguments="Thickness"
                    iOS="0, 20, 0, 0" />
    </ContentPage.Padding>

    <toolkit:UniformGridLayout x:Name="uniformGridLayout"
                               Orientation="VerticalThenHorizontal"
                               AspectRatio="Auto" />

</ContentPage>
```

The code-behind file is virtually identical to the one in **PhotoWrap**, and here's the result:

Again, as the `Image` elements load the bitmaps, you might see some shifting of the rows and columns.

It's fun to run this on the Windows desktop and change the size and aspect ratio of the window to see how the bitmaps are reordered into rows and columns. This is a good way also to check for some bugs in your code.

Overlapping children

Can a `Layout<View>` class call the `Layout` method on its children so that the children overlap? Yes, but that probably raises another question in your mind: What determines the order that the children are rendered? Which children seemingly sit in the foreground and might partially or totally obscure other children displayed in the background?

In some graphical environments, programmers have access to a value called *Z-index*. The name comes from visualizing a three-dimensional coordinate system on a two-dimensional computer screen. The X and Y axes define the horizontal surface of the screen, while the Z axis is perpendicular to the screen. Visual elements with a higher Z-index appear to be closer to the viewer in the foreground, and hence might possibly obscure elements with a lower Z-index in the background.

There is no explicit Z-index in Xamarin.Forms. You might guess that a Z-index is implied by the order in which the layout class calls the `Layout` method on its children, but this is not the case. A layout class can call the `Layout` methods on its children in whatever order you want without any change in the display. These calls give each child a size and position relative to its parent, but the children are *not* rendered in that order.

Instead, the children are rendered in their order in the `Children` collection. The children earlier in the collection are rendered first, so they appear in the background, which means that children later in the collection appear to be in the foreground and can obscure those earlier children.

The `Layout` class defines two methods that allow you to move a child to the beginning or end of the `Children` collection. These methods are:

- `LowerChild` — moves a child to the beginning of the `Children` collection, and visually to the background.

- `RaiseChild` — moves a child to the end of the `Children` collection, and visually to the foreground.

The child must already be a part of the `Children` collection for these methods to work. These calls result in a call to the protected `OnChildrenReordered` method defined by `VisualElement` and a firing of the `ChildrenReordered` event.

At the time this chapter was written, the `LowerChild` and `RaiseChild` methods do not work on the various Windows platforms. However, the `Children` property defined by `Layout<T>` is of type `IList<T>`, so you can also move children in and out of the collection with calls to `Add`, `Insert`, `Remove`, and `RemoveAt`. Regardless of how you do it, any change to the contents of the `Children` collection results in a call to `LayoutInvalidated` and a new layout cycle.

These issues arise when you want to write a layout class that overlaps its children, but you also want the option to bring a partially obscured child out of hiding, perhaps with a tap. To move a child to the visual foreground, you'll need to manipulate the `Children` collection, but you'll also need to make sure that these manipulations don't interfere with the rendering of the children.

You'll see one possible solution in the `OverlapLayout` class. This layout class displays its children in a vertical or horizontal stack but overlapped. Each child is positioned slightly lower (or to the right of) the previous child, specified by a property that `OverlapLayout` defines called `Offset`.

Here is program called **StudentCardFile** that uses `OverlapLayout` in a `ScrollView` to display the students of the School of Fine Art by using a card-file metaphor:

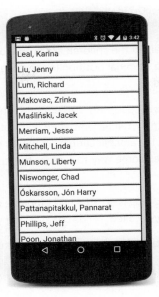

The students are ordered by last name. The iOS screen shows the very top of the list. The Android screen is scrolled to somewhere in the middle, and the Windows 10 Mobile screen is scrolled to the end. The only entirely visible student is the one at the end of the `Children` collection, with a last name very late in the alphabet.

To view a student, you can tap the top of the student's card:

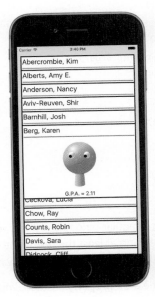
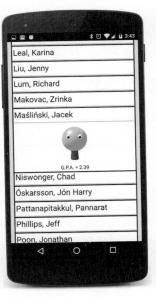

The child is brought to the foreground with calls to two methods that simulate a `RaiseChild` call:

```
overlapLayout.Children.Remove(tappedChild);
overlapLayout.Children.Add(tappedChild);
```

You can now scroll the list like normal. All the children are in the same order from top to bottom. You can cause that child to be restored to its initial position in the `Children` collection with another tap on that child or by tapping another child.

If you think about the logic of `VerticalStack` earlier in this chapter, you can imagine that there might be a bit of a problem if you simply call `RaiseChild` without doing anything else. `RaiseChild` sends the child to the end of the `Children` collection, so it would normally be rendered last and appear at the bottom of the list. We need some way to reorder the `Children` collection while keeping the rendering order constant.

The solution that `OverlapLayout` uses is an attached bindable property that can be set on each child by the application. This property is called `RenderOrder`, and you'll see how it works shortly.

Here's how to define an attached bindable property in a layout class. It's a little different from a regular bindable property:

```
namespace Xamarin.FormsBook.Toolkit
{
    public class OverlapLayout : Layout<View>
    {
        ...
        // Attached bindable property.
        public static readonly BindableProperty RenderOrderProperty =
            BindableProperty.CreateAttached("RenderOrder",
                                            typeof(int),
                                            typeof(OverlapLayout),
                                            0);

        // Helper methods for attached bindable property.
        public static void SetRenderOrder(BindableObject bindable, int order)
        {
            bindable.SetValue(RenderOrderProperty, order);
        }

        public static int GetRenderOrder(BindableObject bindable)
        {
            return (int)bindable.GetValue(RenderOrderProperty);
        }
        ...
    }
}
```

The definition of the public static read-only field is similar to defining a regular bindable property except that you use the static `Bindable.CreateAttached` method, defining at least the text name of the property, the type of the property, the type of the class defining the property, and a default value.

However, unlike with a regular bindable property, you do *not* define a C# property. Instead, you define two static methods for setting and getting the property. These two static helper methods—called

SetRenderOrder and GetRenderOrder—are not strictly required. Any code that uses the attached bindable property can simply call SetValue and GetValue instead, as the bodies of the methods demonstrate. But they are customary.

As you'll see, code or markup using OverlapLayout sets this RenderOrder property on each of the layout's children. The **StudentCardFile** sample you'll see shortly sets the property when the children are first created and never changes it. However, in the general case, the attached bindable properties set on children can change, in which case another layout pass is required.

For this reason, layouts that implement attached bindable properties should override the OnAdded and OnRemoved methods to attach (and detach) a handler for the PropertyChanged event on each child in the Children collection of the layout. This handler then checks for changes in the attached bindable property and invalidates the layout if the property value has changed:

```
namespace Xamarin.FormsBook.Toolkit
{
    public class OverlapLayout : Layout<View>
    {
        ...
        // Monitor PropertyChanged events for items in the Children collection.
        protected override void OnAdded(View view)
        {
            base.OnAdded(view);
            view.PropertyChanged += OnChildPropertyChanged;
        }

        protected override void OnRemoved(View view)
        {
            base.OnRemoved(view);
            view.PropertyChanged -= OnChildPropertyChanged;
        }

        void OnChildPropertyChanged(object sender, PropertyChangedEventArgs args)
        {
            if (args.PropertyName == "RenderOrder")
            {
                InvalidateLayout();
            }
        }
        ...
    }
}
```

Rather than explicitly referencing the text name of the property in the PropertyChanged handler (and possibly misspelling it), you can alternatively reference the PropertyName property of the RenderOrderProperty bindable property object.

OverlapLayout also defines two regular bindable properties. The Orientation property is based on the existing StackOrientation enumeration (because the layout is very similar to a stack) and Offset indicates the difference between each successive child:

```
namespace Xamarin.FormsBook.Toolkit
{
    public class OverlapLayout : Layout<View>
    {
        public static readonly BindableProperty OrientationProperty =
            BindableProperty.Create(
                "Orientation",
                typeof(StackOrientation),
                typeof(OverlapLayout),
                StackOrientation.Vertical,
                propertyChanged: (bindable, oldValue, newValue) =>
                {
                    ((OverlapLayout)bindable).InvalidateLayout();
                });

        public static readonly BindableProperty OffsetProperty =
            BindableProperty.Create(
                "Offset",
                typeof(double),
                typeof(OverlapLayout),
                20.0,
                propertyChanged: (bindable, oldvalue, newvalue) =>
                {
                    ((OverlapLayout)bindable).InvalidateLayout();
                });
        ...
        public StackOrientation Orientation
        {
            set { SetValue(OrientationProperty, value); }
            get { return (StackOrientation)GetValue(OrientationProperty); }
        }

        public double Offset
        {
            set { SetValue(OffsetProperty, value); }
            get { return (double)GetValue(OffsetProperty); }
        }
        ...
    }
}
```

The two required method overrides are quite simple compared with some of the other layout classes in this chapter. OnSizeRequest simply determines the maximum size of the children and calculates a requested size based on the size of one child—because initially only one child is fully visible—plus the product of the Offset value and the number of children minus one:

```
namespace Xamarin.FormsBook.Toolkit
{
    public class OverlapLayout : Layout<View>
    {
        ...
        protected override SizeRequest OnSizeRequest(double widthConstraint,
                                                     double heightConstraint)
        {
```

```
        int visibleChildCount = 0;
        Size maxChildSize = new Size();

        foreach (View child in Children)
        {
            if (!child.IsVisible)
                continue;

            visibleChildCount++;

            // Get the child's desired size.
            SizeRequest childSizeRequest = new SizeRequest();

            if (Orientation == StackOrientation.Vertical)
            {
                childSizeRequest = child.GetSizeRequest(widthConstraint,
                                            Double.PositiveInfinity);
            }
            else // Orientation == StackOrientation.Horizontal
            {
                childSizeRequest = child.GetSizeRequest(Double.PositiveInfinity,
                                            heightConstraint);
            }

            // Find the maximum child width and height.
            maxChildSize.Width = Math.Max(maxChildSize.Width,
                                    childSizeRequest.Request.Width);
            maxChildSize.Height = Math.Max(maxChildSize.Height,
                                    childSizeRequest.Request.Height);
        }

        if (visibleChildCount == 0)
        {
            return new SizeRequest();
        }
        else if (Orientation == StackOrientation.Vertical)
        {
            return new SizeRequest(
                new Size(maxChildSize.Width,
                    maxChildSize.Height + Offset * (visibleChildCount - 1)));
        }
        else // Orientation == StackOrientation.Horizontal
        {
            return new SizeRequest(
                new Size(maxChildSize.Width + Offset * (visibleChildCount - 1),
                    maxChildSize.Height));
        }
    }
    ...
}
```

If we didn't need to worry about bringing hidden children to the foreground, the `LayoutChildren` method would position each successive child by incrementing `x` or `y` (depending on the orientation) by

Offset units. Instead, the method calculates a `childOffset` value for each child by multiplying the `Offset` property by the `RenderOrder` property:

```
namespace Xamarin.FormsBook.Toolkit
{
    public class OverlapLayout : Layout<View>
    {
        ...
        protected override void LayoutChildren(double x, double y, double width, double height)
        {
            foreach (View child in Children)
            {
                if (!child.IsVisible)
                    continue;

                SizeRequest childSizeRequest = child.GetSizeRequest(width, height);
                double childOffset = Offset * GetRenderOrder(child);

                if (Orientation == StackOrientation.Vertical)
                {
                    LayoutChildIntoBoundingRegion(child,
                        new Rectangle(x, y + childOffset,
                                      width, childSizeRequest.Request.Height));
                }
                else // Orientation == StackOrientation.Horizontal
                {
                    LayoutChildIntoBoundingRegion(child,
                        new Rectangle(x + childOffset, y,
                                      childSizeRequest.Request.Width, height));
                }
            }
        }
    }
}
```

The statement that performs the multiplication of the `Offset` and the `RenderOrder` property is

```
double childOffset = Offset * GetRenderOrder(child);
```

You can do the same thing without the static `GetRenderOrder` property by using `GetValue`:

```
double childOffset = Offset * (int)child.GetValue(RenderOrderProperty);
```

But the `GetRenderOrder` method is definitely easier.

The **StudentCardFile** program defines a page with an `OverlapLayout` in a `ScrollView`:

```
<ContentPage xmlns="http://xamarin.com/schemas/2014/forms"
             xmlns:x="http://schemas.microsoft.com/winfx/2009/xaml"
             xmlns:toolkit=
                "clr-namespace:Xamarin.FormsBook.Toolkit;assembly=Xamarin.FormsBook.Toolkit"
             x:Class="StudentCardFile.StudentCardFilePage"
             BackgroundColor="Yellow">
    <ContentPage.Padding>
        <OnPlatform x:TypeArguments="Thickness"
```

```
                        iOS="0, 20, 0, 0" />
    </ContentPage.Padding>

    <ScrollView>
        <toolkit:OverlapLayout x:Name="overlapLayout"
                               Padding="10" />
    </ScrollView>
</ContentPage>
```

The code-behind file instantiates the `SchoolViewModel` and uses the `PropertyChanged` event to determine when the `StudentBody` property is valid. The students are first sorted by last name. Then, for each `Student` object, the code creates a `StudentView` (which you'll see shortly) and assigns the `Student` object to the view's `BindingContext`:

```csharp
public partial class StudentCardFilePage : ContentPage
{
    ...
    public StudentCardFilePage()
    {
        InitializeComponent();

        // Set a platform-specific Offset on the OverlapLayout.
        overlapLayout.Offset = 2 * Device.GetNamedSize(NamedSize.Large, typeof(Label));

        SchoolViewModel viewModel = new SchoolViewModel();

        viewModel.PropertyChanged += (sender, args) =>
        {
            if (args.PropertyName == "StudentBody")
            {
                // Sort the students by last name.
                var students =
                    viewModel.StudentBody.Students.OrderBy(student => student.LastName);

                Device.BeginInvokeOnMainThread(() =>
                {
                    int index = 0;

                    // Loop through the students.
                    foreach (Student student in students)
                    {
                        // Create a StudentView for each.
                        StudentView studentView = new StudentView
                        {
                            BindingContext = student
                        };

                        // Set the Order attached bindable property.
                        OverlapLayout.SetRenderOrder(studentView, index++);

                        // Attach a Tap gesture handler.
                        TapGestureRecognizer tapGesture = new TapGestureRecognizer();
                        tapGesture.Tapped += OnStudentViewTapped;
                        studentView.GestureRecognizers.Add(tapGesture);
```

```
                                        // Add it to the OverlapLayout.
                                        overlapLayout.Children.Add(studentView);
                                }
                        });
                }
            };
        }
        ...
    }
```

The `RenderOrder` property is simply set to sequential values:

```
OverlapLayout.SetRenderOrder(studentView, index++);
```

It doesn't seem like much, but it's crucial for maintaining the rendering order of the students when the `Children` collection is altered.

The `Children` collection is altered in the `Tapped` handler. Keep in mind that the code needs to handle three different (but related) cases: A tap on a student card requires that the card be moved to the foreground with manipulation of the `Children` collection, equivalent to a call to `RaiseChild`— except if the student card is already in the foreground, in which case the card needs to be put back where it was. If one card is already in the foreground when another card is tapped, then the first card must be moved back and the second card moved to the foreground:

```
public partial class StudentCardFilePage : ContentPage
{
    View exposedChild = null;
    ...
    void OnStudentViewTapped(object sender, EventArgs args)
    {
        View tappedChild = (View)sender;
        bool retractOnly = tappedChild == exposedChild;

        // Retract the exposed child.
        if (exposedChild != null)
        {
            overlapLayout.Children.Remove(exposedChild);
            overlapLayout.Children.Insert(
                OverlapLayout.GetRenderOrder(exposedChild), exposedChild);
            exposedChild = null;
        }
        // Expose a new child.
        if (!retractOnly)
        {
            // Raise child.
            overlapLayout.Children.Remove(tappedChild);
            overlapLayout.Children.Add(tappedChild);

            exposedChild = tappedChild;
        }
    }
}
```

The `StudentView` class derives from `ContentView` and is meant to resemble an index card. The borders are thin `BoxView` elements, and another `BoxView` draws a horizontal line under the name at the top of the card:

```xml
<ContentView xmlns="http://xamarin.com/schemas/2014/forms"
             xmlns:x="http://schemas.microsoft.com/winfx/2009/xaml"
             x:Class="StudentCardFile.StudentView"
             BackgroundColor="White">
    <ContentView.Resources>
        <ResourceDictionary>
            <x:Double x:Key="thickness">3</x:Double>

            <Style TargetType="Label">
                <Setter Property="TextColor" Value="Black" />
            </Style>

            <Style TargetType="BoxView">
                <Setter Property="Color" Value="Black" />
            </Style>
        </ResourceDictionary>
    </ContentView.Resources>

    <Grid>
        <BoxView VerticalOptions="Start"
                 HeightRequest="{StaticResource thickness}" />

        <BoxView VerticalOptions="End"
                 HeightRequest="{StaticResource thickness}" />

        <BoxView HorizontalOptions="Start"
                 WidthRequest="{StaticResource thickness}" />

        <BoxView HorizontalOptions="End"
                 WidthRequest="{StaticResource thickness}" />

        <StackLayout Padding="5">
            <StackLayout Orientation="Horizontal">
                <Label Text="{Binding LastName, StringFormat='{0},'}"
                       FontSize="Large" />

                <Label Text="{Binding FirstName}"
                       FontSize="Large" />

                <Label Text="{Binding MiddleName}"
                       FontSize="Large" />
            </StackLayout>

            <BoxView Color="Accent"
                     HeightRequest="2" />

            <Image Source="{Binding PhotoFilename}" />

            <Label Text="{Binding GradePointAverage, StringFormat='G.P.A. = {0:F2}'}"
                   HorizontalTextAlignment="Center" />
```

```
        </StackLayout>
    </Grid>
</ContentView>
```

You've already seen the screenshots.

More attached bindable properties

Attached bindable properties can also be set in XAML and set with a `Style`. To see how this works, let's examine a class named `CartesianLayout` that mimics a two-dimensional, four-quadrant Cartesian coordinate system. This layout lets you use `BoxView` to draw lines by specifying relative X and Y coordinates ranging from −1 to 1 with a particular line thickness in device units.

`CartesianLayout` derives from `Layout<BoxView>`, so it is restricted to children of that type. This layout doesn't make much sense with other types of elements. The class begins by defining three attached bindable properties and static `Set` and `Get` methods:

```
namespace Xamarin.FormsBook.Toolkit
{
    public class CartesianLayout : Layout<BoxView>
    {
        public static readonly BindableProperty Point1Property =
            BindableProperty.CreateAttached("Point1",
                                    typeof(Point),
                                    typeof(CartesianLayout),
                                    new Point());

        public static readonly BindableProperty Point2Property =
            BindableProperty.CreateAttached("Point2",
                                    typeof(Point),
                                    typeof(CartesianLayout),
                                    new Point());

        public static readonly BindableProperty ThicknessProperty =
            BindableProperty.CreateAttached("Thickness",
                                    typeof(Double),
                                    typeof(CartesianLayout),
                                    1.0);        // must be explicitly Double!

        public static void SetPoint1(BindableObject bindable, Point point)
        {
            bindable.SetValue(Point1Property, point);
        }

        public static Point GetPoint1(BindableObject bindable)
        {
            return (Point)bindable.GetValue(Point1Property);
        }

        public static void SetPoint2(BindableObject bindable, Point point)
        {
            bindable.SetValue(Point2Property, point);
```

```
        }

        public static Point GetPoint2(BindableObject bindable)
        {
            return (Point)bindable.GetValue(Point2Property);
        }

        public static void SetThickness(BindableObject bindable, double thickness)
        {
            bindable.SetValue(ThicknessProperty, thickness);
        }

        public static double GetThickness(BindableObject bindable)
        {
            return (double)bindable.GetValue(ThicknessProperty);
        }
        …
    }
}
```

As with any attached properties defined in a layout, you should invalidate the layout whenever an attached property changes that might affect the layout. This `PropertyChanged` handler uses the `PropertyName` property of the bindable property to avoid misspellings:

```
namespace Xamarin.FormsBook.Toolkit
{
    public class CartesianLayout : Layout<BoxView>
    {
        …
        // Monitor PropertyChanged events for items in the Children collection.
        protected override void OnAdded(BoxView boxView)
        {
            base.OnAdded(boxView);
            boxView.PropertyChanged += OnChildPropertyChanged;
        }

        protected override void OnRemoved(BoxView boxView)
        {
            base.OnRemoved(boxView);
            boxView.PropertyChanged -= OnChildPropertyChanged;
        }

        void OnChildPropertyChanged(object sender, PropertyChangedEventArgs args)
        {
            if (args.PropertyName == Point1Property.PropertyName ||
                args.PropertyName == Point2Property.PropertyName ||
                args.PropertyName == ThicknessProperty.PropertyName)
            {
                InvalidateLayout();
            }
        }
    }
    …
}
```

The `OnSizeRequest` override requires that at least one of the dimensions be constrained and requests a size that is square:

```
namespace Xamarin.FormsBook.Toolkit
{
    public class CartesianLayout : Layout<BoxView>
    {
        ...
        protected override SizeRequest OnSizeRequest(double widthConstraint,
                                                     double heightConstraint)
        {
            if (Double.IsInfinity(widthConstraint) && Double.IsInfinity(heightConstraint))
                throw new InvalidOperationException(
                    "CartesianLayout requires at least one dimension to be constrained.");

            // Make it square!
            double minimum = Math.Min(widthConstraint, heightConstraint);
            return new SizeRequest(new Size(minimum, minimum));
        }
        ...
    }
}
```

However, the resultant layout will *not* be square if it has default `HorizontalOptions` and `VerticalOptions` settings of `Fill`.

The `LayoutChildren` override calls a method that contains the mathematics to translate the `Point1`, `Point2`, and `Thickness` properties into a `Rectangle` suitable for a `Layout` call. The `Layout` call always renders the `BoxView` as a horizontal line positioned midway between `Point1` and `Point2`. The `Rotation` property then rotates the `BoxView` to coincide with the points. The math is a little more complex than the alternative (positioning the `BoxView` so that it begins at one point, and then rotating the `BoxView` so that it meets the other point), but this approach doesn't require setting the `AnchorX` and `AnchorY` properties:

```
namespace Xamarin.FormsBook.Toolkit
{
    public class CartesianLayout : Layout<BoxView>
    {
        ...
        protected override void LayoutChildren(double x, double y, double width, double height)
        {
            foreach (View child in Children)
            {
                if (!child.IsVisible)
                    continue;

                double angle;
                Rectangle bounds = GetChildBounds(child, x, y, width, height, out angle);

                // Lay out the child.
                child.Layout(bounds);
```

```
            // Rotate the child.
            child.Rotation = angle;
        }
    }

    protected Rectangle GetChildBounds(View child,
                                       double x, double y, double width, double height,
                                       out double angle)
    {
        // Get coordinate system information.
        Point coordCenter = new Point(x + width / 2, y + height / 2);
        double unitLength = Math.Min(width, height) / 2;

        // Get child information.
        Point point1 = GetPoint1(child);
        Point point2 = GetPoint2(child);
        double thickness = GetThickness(child);
        double length = unitLength * Math.Sqrt(Math.Pow(point2.X - point1.X, 2) +
                                               Math.Pow(point2.Y - point1.Y, 2));

        // Calculate child bounds.
        Point centerChild = new Point((point1.X + point2.X) / 2,
                                      (point1.Y + point2.Y) / 2);

        double xChild = coordCenter.X + unitLength * centerChild.X - length / 2;
        double yChild = coordCenter.Y - unitLength * centerChild.Y - thickness / 2;
        Rectangle bounds = new Rectangle(xChild, yChild, length, thickness);
        angle = 180 / Math.PI * Math.Atan2(point1.Y - point2.Y,
                                           point2.X - point1.X);

        return bounds;
    }
  }
}
```

You can set the attached bindable properties in XAML and even in a `Style`, but because the class name is required when referencing attached bindable properties, the properties also require the XML namespace declaration. The **UnitCube** program draws the outline of a 3D cube:

```xml
<ContentPage xmlns="http://xamarin.com/schemas/2014/forms"
             xmlns:x="http://schemas.microsoft.com/winfx/2009/xaml"
             xmlns:toolkit=
                 "clr-namespace:Xamarin.FormsBook.Toolkit;assembly=Xamarin.FormsBook.Toolkit"
             x:Class="UnitCube.UnitCubePage">

    <toolkit:CartesianLayout BackgroundColor="Yellow"
                             HorizontalOptions="Center"
                             VerticalOptions="Center">
        <toolkit:CartesianLayout.Resources>
            <ResourceDictionary>
                <Style x:Key="baseStyle" TargetType="BoxView">
                    <Setter Property="Color" Value="Blue" />
                    <Setter Property="toolkit:CartesianLayout.Thickness" Value="3" />
                </Style>
```

```xml
                    <Style x:Key="hiddenStyle" TargetType="BoxView"
                            BasedOn="{StaticResource baseStyle}">
                        <Setter Property="Opacity" Value="0.25" />
                    </Style>

                    <!-- Implicit style. -->
                    <Style TargetType="BoxView"
                            BasedOn="{StaticResource baseStyle}" />

                </ResourceDictionary>
            </toolkit:CartesianLayout.Resources>

            <!-- Three "hidden" edges first in the background -->
            <!-- Rear edges -->
            <BoxView toolkit:CartesianLayout.Point1="0.25, 0.75"
                     toolkit:CartesianLayout.Point2="0.25, -0.25"
                     Style="{StaticResource hiddenStyle}" />

            <BoxView toolkit:CartesianLayout.Point1="0.25, -0.25"
                     toolkit:CartesianLayout.Point2="-0.75, -0.25"
                     Style="{StaticResource hiddenStyle}" />

            <!-- Front to rear edge -->
            <BoxView toolkit:CartesianLayout.Point1="0.5, -0.5"
                     toolkit:CartesianLayout.Point2="0.25, -0.25"
                     Style="{StaticResource hiddenStyle}" />

            <!-- Front edges -->
            <BoxView toolkit:CartesianLayout.Point1="-0.5, 0.5"
                     toolkit:CartesianLayout.Point2="0.5, 0.5" />

            <BoxView toolkit:CartesianLayout.Point1="0.5, 0.5"
                     toolkit:CartesianLayout.Point2="0.5, -0.5" />

            <BoxView toolkit:CartesianLayout.Point1="0.5, -0.5"
                     toolkit:CartesianLayout.Point2="-0.5, -0.5" />

            <BoxView toolkit:CartesianLayout.Point1="-0.5, -0.5"
                     toolkit:CartesianLayout.Point2="-0.5, 0.5" />

            <!-- Rear edges -->
            <BoxView toolkit:CartesianLayout.Point1="-0.75, 0.75"
                     toolkit:CartesianLayout.Point2="0.25, 0.75" />

            <BoxView toolkit:CartesianLayout.Point1="-0.75, -0.25"
                     toolkit:CartesianLayout.Point2="-0.75, 0.75" />

            <!-- Front to rear edges -->
            <BoxView toolkit:CartesianLayout.Point1="-0.5, 0.5"
                     toolkit:CartesianLayout.Point2="-0.75, 0.75" />

            <BoxView toolkit:CartesianLayout.Point1="0.5, 0.5"
                     toolkit:CartesianLayout.Point2="0.25, 0.75" />
```

```
        <BoxView toolkit:CartesianLayout.Point1="-0.5, -0.5"
                 toolkit:CartesianLayout.Point2="-0.75, -0.25" />
    </toolkit:CartesianLayout>
</ContentPage>
```

The background "lines" are drawn with an `Opacity` value that makes them seem as if they're viewed through a translucent side:

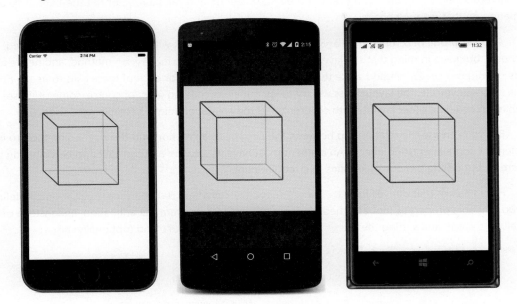

Layout and LayoutTo

`VisualElement` defines a collection of transform properties. These are `AnchorX`, `AnchorY`, `Rotation`, `RotationX`, `RotationY`, `Scale`, `TranslationX`, and `TranslationY`, and they don't affect layout at all. In other words, setting these properties does not generate calls to `InvalidateMeasure` or `InvalidateLayout`. Element sizes returned from `GetSizeRequest` are not affected by these properties. The `Layout` call sizes and positions elements as if these properties do not exist.

This means that you can animate these properties without generating a bunch of layout cycles. The `TranslateTo`, `ScaleTo`, `RotateTo`, `RotateXTo`, and `RotateYTo` animation methods defined as extension methods in `ViewExtensions` are entirely independent of layout.

However, `ViewExtensions` also defines a method named `LayoutTo` that makes animated calls to the `Layout` method. This results in changing the layout size or position of the element relative to its parent and setting new values of the element's `Bounds`, `X`, `Y`, `Width`, and `Height` properties.

Using `LayoutTo` therefore requires exercising some precautions.

For example, suppose an element is a child of a `StackLayout`. When `StackLayout` gets a `LayoutChildren` call, it will call `Layout` on that element to size and position it at a particular location relative to itself. Suppose your program then calls `LayoutTo` on that element to give it a new size and position. The `StackLayout` doesn't know about that, so if the `StackLayout` undergoes another layout cycle, it will move the element back to where it thinks it should be. If you still need the element to be somewhere other than where the `StackLayout` thinks it should be, you might want to attach a handler to the `LayoutChanged` event of the `StackLayout` and call `Layout` or run the `LayoutTo` animation on that element again.

Another problem is running a `LayoutTo` animation on a layout with many children. It's allowed, of course, but keep in mind that the layout will get numerous calls to its `Layout` method, and hence also its `LayoutChildren` method while the animation is in progress. For each of these calls to its `LayoutChildren` override, the layout class will try to lay out all its children (and, of course, some of those children could be other layouts with children), and the animation might become quite choppy.

But you can use the relationship between the `LayoutTo` animation and the `Layout` method to implement some interesting effects. An element must have its `Layout` method called to be visible on the screen, but calling `LayoutTo` satisfies that requirement.

Here's a class that derives from `CartesianLayout`, called `AnimatedCartesianLayout`. It defines two bindable properties (not attached bindable properties) to govern the animation, and instead of calling `Layout` and setting the `Rotation` property, it calls `LayoutTo` and (optionally) `RotateTo`:

```
namespace Xamarin.FormsBook.Toolkit
{
    public class AnimatedCartesianLayout : CartesianLayout
    {
        public static readonly BindableProperty AnimationDurationProperty =
            BindableProperty.Create(
                "AnimatedDuration",
                typeof(int),
                typeof(AnimatedCartesianLayout),
                1000);

        public int AnimationDuration
        {
            set { SetValue(AnimationDurationProperty, value); }
            get { return (int)GetValue(AnimationDurationProperty); }
        }

        public static readonly BindableProperty AnimateRotationProperty =
            BindableProperty.Create(
                "AnimateRotation",
                typeof(bool),
                typeof(AnimatedCartesianLayout),
                true);

        public bool AnimateRotation
        {
            set { SetValue(AnimateRotationProperty, value); }
```

```
            get { return (bool)GetValue(AnimateRotationProperty); }
        }

        protected override void LayoutChildren(double x, double y, double width, double height)
        {
            foreach (View child in Children)
            {
                if (!child.IsVisible)
                    continue;

                double angle;
                Rectangle bounds = GetChildBounds(child, x, y, width, height, out angle);

                // Lay out the child.
                if (child.Bounds.Equals(new Rectangle(0, 0, -1, -1)))
                {
                    child.Layout(new Rectangle(x + width / 2, y + height / 2, 0, 0));
                }
                child.LayoutTo(bounds, (uint)AnimationDuration);

                // Rotate the child.
                if (AnimateRotation)
                {
                    child.RotateTo(angle, (uint)AnimationDuration);
                }
                else
                {
                    child.Rotation = angle;
                }
            }
        }
    }
}
```

The only tricky part involves a child that hasn't yet received its first `Layout` call. The `Bounds` property of such a child is the rectangle (0, 0, −1, −1), and the `LayoutTo` animation will use that value as the starting point for the animation. In that case, the `LayoutChildren` method first calls `Layout` to position the child in the center and to give it a size of (0, 0).

The **AnimatedUnitCube** program has a XAML file nearly identical to the **UnitCube** program but with an `AnimatedCartesianLayout` with an animation duration of 3 seconds:

```xml
<ContentPage xmlns="http://xamarin.com/schemas/2014/forms"
             xmlns:x="http://schemas.microsoft.com/winfx/2009/xaml"
             xmlns:toolkit=
                 "clr-namespace:Xamarin.FormsBook.Toolkit;assembly=Xamarin.FormsBook.Toolkit"
             x:Class="AnimatedUnitCube.AnimatedUnitCubePage">

    <toolkit:AnimatedCartesianLayout BackgroundColor="Yellow"
                                     AnimationDuration="3000"
                                     HorizontalOptions="Center"
                                     VerticalOptions="Center">
        <toolkit:AnimatedCartesianLayout.Resources>
```

```
            <ResourceDictionary>
                <Style  x:Key="baseStyle" TargetType="BoxView">
                    <Setter Property="Color" Value="Blue" />
                    <Setter Property="toolkit:CartesianLayout.Thickness" Value="3" />
                </Style>

                <Style x:Key="hiddenStyle" TargetType="BoxView"
                        BasedOn="{StaticResource baseStyle}">
                    <Setter Property="Opacity" Value="0.25" />
                </Style>

                <!-- Implicit style. -->
                <Style TargetType="BoxView"
                        BasedOn="{StaticResource baseStyle}" />

            </ResourceDictionary>
        </toolkit:AnimatedCartesianLayout.Resources>
        ...

    </toolkit:AnimatedCartesianLayout>
</ContentPage>
```

The following screenshots show the progression from left to right almost to the point where the cube is complete:

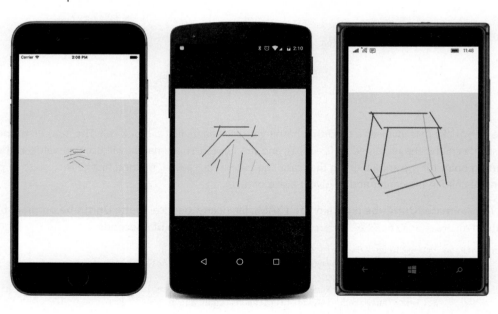

Depending on how they're defined, some of the horizontal lines aren't rotated at all, while others (the ones on the bottom, for example) must be rotated 180 degrees.

As you know, user interfaces have become more animated and dynamic in recent years, so exploring various techniques that are possible by using `LayoutTo` rather than `Layout` can become a whole new area for adventurous programmers to pursue.

Chapter 27
Custom renderers

At the core of Xamarin.Forms is something that might seem like magic: the ability of a single element such as `Button` to appear as a native button under the iOS, Android, and Windows operating systems. In this chapter, you'll see how on all three platforms each element in Xamarin.Forms is supported by a special class known as a *renderer*. For example, the `Button` class in Xamarin.Forms is supported by several classes in the various platforms, each named `ButtonRenderer`.

The good news is that you can also write your own renderers, and this chapter will show you how. However, keep in mind that writing custom renderers is a big topic, and this chapter can only get you started.

Writing custom renderers is not quite as easy as writing a Xamarin.Forms application. You'll need to be familiar with the individual iOS, Android, and Windows Runtime platforms. But obviously it's a powerful technique. Indeed, some developers think of the ultimate value of Xamarin.Forms as providing a structured framework in which to write custom renderers.

The complete class hierarchy

In Chapter 11, "The bindable infrastructure," you saw a program called **ClassHierarchy** that displays the Xamarin.Forms class hierarchy. However, that program only displays the types in the **Xamarin.Forms.Core** and **Xamarin.Forms.Xaml** assemblies, which are the types that a Xamarin.Forms application generally uses.

Xamarin.Forms also contains additional assemblies associated with each platform. These assemblies play a crucial role by providing the platform support for Xamarin.Forms, including all the renderers.

You're probably already familiar with the names of these assemblies from seeing them in the **Reference** sections of the various projects in your Xamarin.Forms solution:

- **Xamarin.Forms.Platform** (very small)

- **Xamarin.Forms.Platform.iOS**

- **Xamarin.Forms.Platform.Android**

- **Xamarin.Forms.Platform.UAP**

- **Xamarin.Forms.Platform.WinRT** (larger than the next two on this list)

- **Xamarin.Forms.Platform.WinRT.Tablet**

- **Xamarin.Forms.Platform.WinRT.Phone**

In this discussion, these will be referred to collectively as the *platform assemblies*.

Is it possible to write a Xamarin.Forms application that displays a class hierarchy of the types in these platform assemblies?

Yes! However, if you restrict yourself to examining only the assemblies normally loaded with an application—and this is certainly the simplest approach—then an application can only display the types in the assemblies that are part of that application. For example, you can only display the types in the **Xamarin.Forms.Platform.iOS** assembly with a Xamarin.Forms program running under iOS, and similarly for the other assemblies.

But there's still a problem: As you might recall, the original **ClassHierarchy** program began by obtaining .NET `Assembly` objects for the **Xamarin.Forms.Core** and **Xamarin.Forms.Xaml** assemblies based on two classes (`View` and `Extensions`) that it knew to be in those two assemblies:

```
typeof(View).GetTypeInfo().Assembly
typeof(Extensions).GetTypeInfo().Assembly
```

However, a Xamarin.Forms application's Portable Class Library doesn't have direct access to the platform assemblies. The platform assemblies are referenced only by the application projects. This means that a Xamarin.Forms Portable Class Library can't use similar code to get a reference to the platform assembly. This won't work:

```
typeof(ButtonRenderer).GetTypeInfo().Assembly
```

However, these platform assemblies are loaded when the application runs, so the PCL can instead obtain `Assembly` objects for the platform assemblies based on the assembly name. The **PlatformClassHierarchy** program begins like this:

```
public partial class PlatformClassHierarchyPage : ContentPage
{
    public PlatformClassHierarchyPage()
    {
        InitializeComponent();

        List<TypeInformation> classList = new List<TypeInformation>();

        string[] assemblyNames = Device.OnPlatform(
            iOS: new string[] { "Xamarin.Forms.Platform.iOS" },
            Android: new string[] { "Xamarin.Forms.Platform.Android" },
            WinPhone: new string[] { "Xamarin.Forms.Platform.UAP",
                                     "Xamarin.Forms.Platform.WinRT",
                                     "Xamarin.Forms.Platform.WinRT.Tablet",
                                     "Xamarin.Forms.Platform.WinRT.Phone" }
        );

        foreach (string assemblyName in assemblyNames)
        {
            try
```

```
        {
            Assembly assembly = Assembly.Load(new AssemblyName(assemblyName));
            GetPublicTypes(assembly, classList);
        }
        catch
        {
        }
    }
    ...
}
```

And from there the **PlatformClassHierarchy** program is the same as the original **ClassHierarchy** program.

As you can see, the `foreach` loop obtains the `Assembly` object from the static `Assembly.Load` method. However, there's not a straightforward way for the program to determine whether it's running under the Universal Windows Platform or one of the other Windows Runtime platforms, so if `Device.OnPlatform` indicates that it's the `WinPhone` device, the program tries all four assemblies and uses `try` and `catch` to just ignore the ones that don't work.

Some of the class names—and particularly the fully qualified class names for classes outside the assembly—are a little too long for the portrait display and wrap awkwardly, but here's part of the display on the three platforms. Each has been scrolled to the part of the class hierarchy that begins with the generic `ViewRenderer` class. This is generally the class you'll derive from to create your own custom renderers:

Notice the generic parameters for the `ViewRenderer` class named either `TView` and `TNativeView`, or `TElement` and `TNativeElement`: As you'll see, `TView` or `TElement` is the Xamarin.Forms element, such as `Button`, while `TNativeView` or `TNativeElement` is the native control for that `Button`.

Although the **PlatformClassHierarchy** program doesn't indicate this, the constraints for the `ViewRenderer` generic parameters are platform dependent:

- On iOS:
  - ○   `TView` is constrained to `Xamarin.Forms.View`
  - ○   `TNativeView` is constrained to `UIKit.UIView`
- On Android:
  - ○   `TView` is constrained to `Xamarin.Forms.View`
  - ○   `TNativeView` is constrained to `Android.Views.View`
- On the Windows platforms:
  - ○   `TElement` is constrained to `Xamarin.Forms.View`
  - ○   `TNativeElement` is constrained to `Windows.UI.Xaml.FrameworkElement`

To write a custom renderer, you derive a class from `ViewRenderer`. To accommodate all the platforms, you must implement the iOS renderer by using a class that derives from `UIView`, implement the Android renderer with a class that derives from `View`, and implement a renderer for the Windows platforms with a class that derives from `FrameworkElement`.

Let's try it!

Hello, custom renderers!

The **HelloRenderers** program mostly demonstrates the overhead required to write simple renderers. The program defines a new `View` derivative named `HelloView` that is intended to display a simple fixed string of text. Here's the complete HelloView.cs file in the **HelloRenderers** Portable Class Library project:

```
using Xamarin.Forms;

namespace HelloRenderers
{
    public class HelloView : View
    {
    }
}
```

That's it! However, note that the class is defined as `public`. Even though you might think that this class is only referenced within the PCL, that's not the case. It must be visible to the platform assemblies.

The **HelloRenderers** PCL is so simple that it doesn't even bother with a page class. Instead, it instantiates and displays a `HelloView` object centered on the page right in the App.cs file:

```
namespace HelloRenderers
{
    public class App : Application
    {
        public App()
        {
            MainPage = new ContentPage
            {
                Content = new HelloView
                {
                    VerticalOptions = LayoutOptions.Center,
                    HorizontalOptions = LayoutOptions.Center
                }
            };
        }
        ...
    }
}
```

Without any other code, this program runs fine, but you won't actually see the `HelloView` object on the screen because it's just a blank transparent view. What we need are some platform renderers for `HelloView`.

When a Xamarin.Forms application starts up, Xamarin.Forms uses .NET reflection to search through the various assemblies that comprise the application, looking for assembly attributes named `Export-Renderer`. An `ExportRenderer` attribute indicates the presence of a custom renderer that can supply support for a Xamarin.Forms element.

The **HelloRenderers.iOS** project contains the following HelloViewRenderer.cs file, shown in its entirety. Notice the `ExportRenderer` attribute right under the `using` directives. Because this is an assembly attribute, it must be outside a `namespace` declaration. This particular `ExportRenderer` attribute basically says "The `HelloView` class is supported by a renderer of type `HelloViewRenderer`":

```
using Xamarin.Forms;
using Xamarin.Forms.Platform.iOS;

using UIKit;

using HelloRenderers;
using HelloRenderers.iOS;

[assembly: ExportRenderer(typeof(HelloView), typeof(HelloViewRenderer))]

namespace HelloRenderers.iOS
{
    public class HelloViewRenderer : ViewRenderer<HelloView, UILabel>
    {
        protected override void OnElementChanged(ElementChangedEventArgs<HelloView> args)
        {
```

```
            base.OnElementChanged(args);

            if (Control == null)
            {
                UILabel label = new UILabel
                {
                    Text = "Hello from iOS!",
                    Font = UIFont.SystemFontOfSize(24)
                };

                SetNativeControl(label);
            }
        }
    }
}
```

The definition of the `HelloViewRenderer` class follows the `ExportRenderer` attribute. The class must be public. It derives from the generic `ViewRenderer` class. The two generic parameters are named `TView`, which is the Xamarin.Forms class, and `TNativeView`, which is the class in this particular case that is native to iOS.

In iOS, a class that displays text is `UILabel` in the `UIKit` namespace, and that's what's used here. The two generic arguments to `ViewRenderer` basically say "A `HelloView` object is actually rendered as an iOS `UILabel` object."

The one essential job for a `ViewRenderer` derivative is to override the `OnElementChanged` method. This method is called when a `HelloView` object is created, and its job is to create a native control for rendering the `HelloView` object.

The `OnElementChanged` override begins by checking the `Control` property that the class inherits from `ViewRenderer`. This `Control` property is defined by `ViewRenderer` to be of type `TNativeView`, so in `HelloViewRenderer` it is of type `UILabel`. The first time that `OnElementChanged` is called, this `Control` property will be null. The `UILabel` object must be created. This is what the method does, assigning to it some text and a font size. That `UILabel` method is then passed to the `SetNativeControl` method. Thereafter, the `Control` property will be this `UILabel` object.

The `using` directives at the top of the file are divided into three groups:

- The `using` directive for the `Xamarin.Forms` namespace is required for the `ExportRenderer` attribute, while `Xamarin.Forms.Platform.iOS` is required for the `ViewRenderer` class.

- The iOS `UIKit` namespace is required for `UILabel`.

- The `using` directives for `HelloRenderers` and `HelloRenderers.iOS` are required only for the `HelloView` and `HelloViewRenderer` references in the `ExportRenderer` attribute because the attribute must be outside the `HelloRenderer.iOS` namespace block.

Those last two `using` directives are particularly annoying because they're only required for a single purpose. If you'd like, you can get rid of those two `using` directives by fully qualifying the class names within the `ExportRenderer` attribute.

This is done in the following renderer. Here's the complete HelloViewRenderer.cs file in the **Hello-Renderers.Droid** project. The Android widget for displaying text is `TextView` in the `Android.Widget` namespace:

```
using Xamarin.Forms;
using Xamarin.Forms.Platform.Android;

using Android.Util;
using Android.Widget;

[assembly: ExportRenderer(typeof(HelloRenderers.HelloView),
                          typeof(HelloRenderers.Droid.HelloViewRenderer))]

namespace HelloRenderers.Droid
{
    public class HelloViewRenderer : ViewRenderer<HelloView, TextView>
    {
        protected override void OnElementChanged(ElementChangedEventArgs<HelloView> args)
        {
            base.OnElementChanged(args);

            if (Control == null)
            {
                SetNativeControl(new TextView(Context)
                {
                    Text = "Hello from Android!"
                });

                Control.SetTextSize(ComplexUnitType.Sp, 24);
            }
        }
    }
}
```

This `HelloViewRenderer` class derives from the Android version of `ViewRenderer`. The generic arguments for `ViewRenderer` indicate that the `HelloView` class is supported by the Android `TextView` widget.

Once again, on the first call to `OnElementChanged`, the `Control` property will be `null`. The method must create a native Android `TextView` widget and call `SetNativeControl`. To save a little space, the newly instantiated `TextView` object is passed directly to the `SetNativeControl` method. Notice that the `TextView` constructor requires the Android `Context` object. This is available as a property of `OnElementChanged`.

After the call to `SetNativeControl`, the `Control` property defined by `ViewRenderer` is the native Android widget, in this case the `TextView` object. The method uses this `Control` property to call `SetTextSize` on the `TextView` object. In Android, text sizes can be scaled in a variety of ways. The `ComplexUnitType.Sp` enumeration member indicates "scaled pixels," which is compatible with how

Xamarin.Forms handles font sizes for `Label` in Android.

Here's the UWP version of `HelloViewRenderer` in the **HelloRenderers.UWP** project:

```
using Xamarin.Forms.Platform.UWP;

using Windows.UI.Xaml.Controls;

[assembly: ExportRenderer (typeof(HelloRenderers.HelloView),
                           typeof(HelloRenderers.UWP.HelloViewRenderer))]

namespace HelloRenderers.UWP
{
    public class HelloViewRenderer : ViewRenderer<HelloView, TextBlock>
    {
        protected override void OnElementChanged(ElementChangedEventArgs<HelloView> args)
        {
            base.OnElementChanged(args);

            if (Control == null)
            {
                SetNativeControl(new TextBlock
                {
                    Text = "Hello from the UWP!",
                    FontSize = 24,
                });
            }
        }
    }
}
```

In all the Windows platforms, the `HelloView` object is rendered by a Windows Runtime `TextBlock` in the `Windows.UI.Xaml.Controls` namespace.

The `HelloViewRenderer` classes in the **HelloRenderers.Windows** and **HelloRenderers.Win-Phone** projects are mostly the same except for namespaces and the text used to set the `Text` property of `TextBlock`.

Here's the program running on the three standard platforms:

Notice how the text is properly centered through the use of the normal `HorizontalOptions` and `VerticalOptions` properties set on the `HelloView` object. However, you can't set the `Horizontal-TextAlignment` and `VerticalTextAlignment` properties on `HelloView`. Those properties are defined by `Label` and not by `HelloView`.

To turn `HelloView` into a full-fledged view for displaying text, you'd need to start adding properties to the `HelloView` class. Let's examine how properties are added to renderers with a different example.

Renderers and properties

Xamarin.Forms includes a `BoxView` element for displaying rectangular blocks of color. Have you ever wished you had something similar for drawing a circle, or to make it more generalized, an ellipse?

That's the purpose of `EllipseView`. However, because you might want to use `EllipseView` in multiple applications, it is implemented in the **Xamarin.FormsBook.Platform** libraries, introduced in Chapter 20, "Async and file I/O."

`BoxView` defines one property on its own—a `Color` property of type `Color`—and `EllipseView` can do the same. It doesn't need properties to set the width and height of the ellipse because it inherits `WidthRequest` and `HeightRequest` from `VisualElement`.

So here's `EllipseView` as defined in the **Xamarin.FormsBook.Platform** library project:

```
namespace Xamarin.FormsBook.Platform
{
```

```
public class EllipseView : View
{
    public static readonly BindableProperty ColorProperty =
        BindableProperty.Create(
            "Color",
            typeof(Color),
            typeof(EllipseView),
            Color.Default);

    public Color Color
    {
        set { SetValue(ColorProperty, value); }
        get { return (Color)GetValue(ColorProperty); }
    }

    protected override SizeRequest OnSizeRequest(double widthConstraint,
                                                 double heightConstraint)
    {
        return new SizeRequest(new Size(40, 40));
    }
}
}
```

The `Color` property simply involves a basic definition of a bindable property with no property-changed handler. The property is defined, but it doesn't seem to be doing anything. Somehow, the `Color` property defined in `EllipseView` has to be linked up with a property on the object that the renderer is rendering.

The only other code in `EllipseView` is an override of `OnSizeRequest` to set a default size of the ellipse, the same as `BoxView`.

Let's begin with the Windows platform. It turns out that a Windows renderer for `EllipseView` is simpler than the iOS and Android renderers.

As you'll recall, the **Xamarin.FormsBook.Platform** solution created in Chapter 20 has a facility to allow sharing code among the various Windows platforms: The **Xamarin.FormsBook.Platform.UWP** library, the **Xamarin.FormsBook.Platform.Windows** library, and the **Xamarin.FormsBook.Platform.WinPhone** library all have references to the **Xamarin.FormsBook.Platform.WinRT** library, which is not a library at all but actually a shared project. This shared project is where the `Ellipse-ViewRenderer` class for all the Windows platforms can reside.

On the Windows platforms, an `EllipseView` can be rendered by a native Windows element called `Ellipse` in the `Windows.UI.Xaml.Shapes` namespace, because `Ellipse` satisfies the criteria of deriving from `Windows.UI.Xaml.FrameworkElement`.

The `Ellipse` is specified as the second generic argument to the `ViewRenderer` class. Because this file is shared by all the Windows platforms, it needs some preprocessing directives to include the correct namespace for the `ExportRendererAttribute` and `ViewRenderer` classes:

```
using System.ComponentModel;
```

```
using Windows.UI.Xaml.Media;
using Windows.UI.Xaml.Shapes;

#if WINDOWS_UWP
using Xamarin.Forms.Platform.UWP;
#else
using Xamarin.Forms.Platform.WinRT;
#endif

[assembly: ExportRenderer(typeof(Xamarin.FormsBook.Platform.EllipseView),
                          typeof(Xamarin.FormsBook.Platform.WinRT.EllipseViewRenderer))]

namespace Xamarin.FormsBook.Platform.WinRT
{
    public class EllipseViewRenderer : ViewRenderer<EllipseView, Ellipse>
    {
        protected override void OnElementChanged(ElementChangedEventArgs<EllipseView> args)
        {
            base.OnElementChanged(args);

            if (Control == null)
            {
                SetNativeControl(new Ellipse());
            }

            if (args.NewElement != null)
            {
                SetColor();
            }
        }
        ...
    }
}
```

As you might expect by now, the `OnElementChanged` override first checks whether the `Control` property is `null`, and if so, it creates the native object, in this case an `Ellipse`, and passes it to `SetNativeControl`. Thereafter, the `Control` property is set to this `Ellipse` object.

This `OnElementChanged` override also contains some additional code involving the `Element-ChangedEventArgs` argument. This requires a little explanation:

Each renderer instance—in this example, an instance of this `EllipseViewRenderer` class—maintains a single instance of a native object, in this example an `Ellipse`.

However, the rendering infrastructure has a facility both to attach a renderer instance to a Xamarin.Forms element and to detach it and attach another Xamarin.Forms element to the same renderer. Perhaps Xamarin.Forms needs to re-create the element or substitute another element for the one already associated with the renderer.

Changes of this sort are communicated to the renderer with calls to `OnElementChanged`. The `Ele-mentChangedEventArgs` argument includes two properties, `OldElement` and `NewElement`, both of the type indicated in the generic argument to `ElementChangedEventArgs`, in this case `El-lipseView`. In many cases, you don't have to worry about different Xamarin.Forms elements being attached and detached from a single renderer instance. But in some cases you might want to use the opportunity to clean up or free some resources that your renderer uses.

In the simplest and most common case, each renderer instance will get one call to `OnElement-Changed` for the Xamarin.Forms view that uses that renderer. You'll use the call to `OnElementChanged` to create the native element and pass it to `SetNativeControl`, as you've already seen. After that call to `SetNativeControl`, the `Control` property defined by `ViewRenderer` is the native object, in this case the `Ellipse`.

At the time you get that call to `OnElementChanged`, the Xamarin.Forms object (in this case an `El-lipseView`) has probably already been created and it might also have some properties set. (In other words, the element might be initialized with a few property settings by the time the renderer is required to display the element.) But the system is designed so that this is not necessarily the case. It's possible that a subsequent call to `OnElementChanged` indicates that an `EllipseView` has been created.

What's important is the `NewElement` property of the event arguments. If that property is not `null` (which is the normal case), that property is the Xamarin.Forms element, and you should transfer property settings from that Xamarin.Forms element to the native object. That's the purpose of the call to the `SetColor` method shown above. You'll see the body of that method shortly.

The `ViewRenderer` defines a property named `Element` that it sets to the Xamarin.Forms element, in this case an `EllipseView`. If the most recent call to `OnElementChanged` contained a non-`null` `NewElement` property, then `Element` is that same object.

In summary, these are the two essential properties that you can use throughout your renderer class:

- `Element`—the Xamarin.Forms element, valid if the most recent `OnElementChanged` call had a non-`null` `NewElement` property.

- `Control`—the native view, or widget, or control object, valid after a call to `SetNativeView`.

As you know, properties of Xamarin.Forms elements can change. For example, the `Color` property of `EllipseView` might be animated. If a property such as `Color` is backed by a bindable property, any change to that property causes a `PropertyChanged` event to be fired.

The renderer is also notified of that property change. Any change to a bindable property in a Xamarin.Forms element attached to a renderer also causes a call to the protected virtual `OnElementProp-ertyChanged` method in the `ViewRenderer` class. In this particular example, any change to *any* bindable property in `EllipseView` (including the `Color` property) generates a call to `OnElementProper-tyChanged`. Your renderer should override that method and check for which property has changed:

```
namespace Xamarin.FormsBook.Platform.WinRT
{
    public class EllipseViewRenderer : ViewRenderer<EllipseView, Ellipse>
```

```
    {
        ...
        protected override void OnElementPropertyChanged(object sender,
                                                PropertyChangedEventArgs args)
        {
            base.OnElementPropertyChanged(sender, args);

            if (args.PropertyName == EllipseView.ColorProperty.PropertyName)
            {
                SetColor();
            }
        }
        ...
    }
}
```

If the `Color` property has changed, the `PropertyName` property of the event argument is "Color," the text name specified when the `EllipseView.ColorProperty` bindable property was created. But to avoid misspelling the name, the `OnElementPropertyChanged` method checks the actual string value in the bindable property. The renderer must respond by transferring that new setting of the `Color` property to the native object, in this case the Windows `Ellipse` object.

This `SetColor` method is called from only two places—the `OnElementChanged` override and the `OnElementPropertyChanged` override. Don't think you can skip the call in `OnElementChanged` under the assumption that the property hasn't changed prior to the call to `OnElementChanged`. It is very often the case that `OnElementChanged` is called *after* an element has been initialized with property settings.

However, `SetColor` can make some valid assumptions about the existence of the Xamarin.Forms element and the native control: When `SetColor` is called from `OnElementChanged`, the native control has been created and `NewElement` is non-null. This means that both the `Control` and `Element` properties are valid. The `Element` property is also valid when `OnElementPropertyChanged` is called because that's the object whose property has just changed.

This means that the `SetColor` method can simply transfer a color from `Element` (the Xamarin.Forms element) to `Control`, the native object. To avoid namespace clashes, this `SetColor` method fully qualifies all references to any structure named `Color`:

```
namespace Xamarin.FormsBook.Platform.WinRT
{
    public class EllipseViewRenderer : ViewRenderer<EllipseView, Ellipse>
    {
        ...
        void SetColor()
        {
            if (Element.Color == Xamarin.Forms.Color.Default)
            {
                Control.Fill = null;
            }
            else
```

```
            {
                Xamarin.Forms.Color color = Element.Color;

                global::Windows.UI.Color winColor =
                    global::Windows.UI.Color.FromArgb((byte)(color.A * 255),
                                                      (byte)(color.R * 255),
                                                      (byte)(color.G * 255),
                                                      (byte)(color.B * 255));

                Control.Fill = new SolidColorBrush(winColor);
            }
        }
    }
}
```

The Windows `Ellipse` object has a property named `Fill` of type `Brush`. By default, this property is `null`, and that's what the `SetColor` method sets it to if the `Color` property of `EllipseView` is `Color.Default`. Otherwise, the Xamarin.Forms `Color` must be converted to a Windows `Color`, which is then passed to the `SolidColorBrush` constructor. The `SolidColorBrush` objects is set to the `Fill` property of `Ellipse`.

That's the Windows version, but when it comes time to create iOS and Android renderers for `EllipseView`, you might feel a little stymied. Here again are the constraints for the second generic parameter to `ViewRenderer`:

- iOS: `TNativeView` is constrained to `UIKit.UIView`

- Android: `TNativeView` is constrained to `Android.View.Views`

- Windows: `TNativeElement` is constrained to `Windows.UI.Xaml.FrameworkElement`

This means that to make an `EllipseView` renderer for iOS, you need a `UIView` derivative that displays an ellipse. Does something like that exist? No, it does not. Therefore, you must make one yourself. This is the first step to making the iOS renderer.

For that reason, the **Xamarin.FormsBook.Platform.iOS** library contains a class named `EllipseUIView` that derives from `UIView` for the sole purpose of drawing an ellipse:

```
using CoreGraphics;
using UIKit;

namespace Xamarin.FormsBook.Platform.iOS
{
    public class EllipseUIView : UIView
    {
        UIColor color = UIColor.Clear;

        public EllipseUIView()
        {
            BackgroundColor = UIColor.Clear;
        }
```

```
        public override void Draw(CGRect rect)
        {
            base.Draw(rect);

            using (CGContext graphics = UIGraphics.GetCurrentContext())
            {
                //Create ellipse geometry based on rect field.
                CGPath path = new CGPath();
                path.AddEllipseInRect(rect);
                path.CloseSubpath();

                //Add geometry to graphics context and draw it.
                color.SetFill();
                graphics.AddPath(path);
                graphics.DrawPath(CGPathDrawingMode.Fill);
            }
        }

        public void SetColor(UIColor color)
        {
            this.color = color;
            SetNeedsDisplay();
        }
    }
}
```

The class overrides the OnDraw method to create a graphics path of an ellipse and then to draw it on the graphics context. The color it uses is stored as a field and is initially set to UIColor.Clear, which is transparent. However, you'll notice a SetColor method at the bottom. This delivers new color to the class and then calls SetNeedsDisplay, which invalidates the drawing surface and generates another call to OnDraw.

Notice also that the BackgroundColor of the UIView is set in the constructor to UIColor.Clear. Without that setting, the view has a black background in the area not covered by the ellipse.

Now that the EllipseUIView class exists for iOS, the EllipseViewRenderer can be written using EllipseUIView as the native control. Structurally, this class is virtually identical to the Windows renderer:

```
using System.ComponentModel;

using UIKit;

using Xamarin.Forms;
using Xamarin.Forms.Platform.iOS;

[assembly: ExportRenderer(typeof(Xamarin.FormsBook.Platform.EllipseView),
                          typeof(Xamarin.FormsBook.Platform.iOS.EllipseViewRenderer))]

namespace Xamarin.FormsBook.Platform.iOS
{
    public class EllipseViewRenderer : ViewRenderer<EllipseView, EllipseUIView>
```

```
{
    protected override void OnElementChanged(ElementChangedEventArgs<EllipseView> args)
    {
        base.OnElementChanged(args);

        if (Control == null)
        {
            SetNativeControl(new EllipseUIView());
        }

        if (args.NewElement != null)
        {
            SetColor();
        }
    }

    protected override void OnElementPropertyChanged(object sender,
                                                     PropertyChangedEventArgs args)
    {
        base.OnElementPropertyChanged(sender, args);

        if (args.PropertyName == EllipseView.ColorProperty.PropertyName)
        {
            SetColor();
        }
    }

    void SetColor()
    {
        if (Element.Color != Color.Default)
        {
            Control.SetColor(Element.Color.ToUIColor());
        }
        else
        {
            Control.SetColor(UIColor.Clear);
        }
    }
}
}
```

The only real differences between this renderer and the Windows version is that the `Control` property is set to an instance of `ColorUIView`, and the body of the `SetColor` method at the bottom is different. It now calls the `SetColor` method in `ColorUIView`. This `SetColor` method is also able to make use of a public extension method in the **Xamarin.Forms.Platform.iOS** library called `ToUIColor` to convert a Xamarin.Forms color to an iOS color.

You might have noticed that neither the Windows renderer nor the iOS renderer had to worry about sizing. As you'll see shortly, an `EllipseView` can be set to a variety of sizes, and the size calculated in the Xamarin.Forms layout system becomes the size of the native control.

This unfortunately turned out *not* to be the case with the Android renderer. The Android renderer needs some sizing logic. Like iOS, Android is also missing a native control that renders an ellipse. Therefore, the **Xamarin.FormsBook.Platform.Android** library contains a class named `EllipseDraw-ableView` that derives from `View` and draws an ellipse:

```
using Android.Content;
using Android.Views;
using Android.Graphics.Drawables;
using Android.Graphics.Drawables.Shapes;
using Android.Graphics;

namespace Xamarin.FormsBook.Platform.Android
{
    public class EllipseDrawableView : View
    {
        ShapeDrawable drawable;

        public EllipseDrawableView(Context context) : base(context)
        {
            drawable = new ShapeDrawable(new OvalShape());
        }

        protected override void OnDraw(Canvas canvas)
        {
            base.OnDraw(canvas);
            drawable.Draw(canvas);
        }

        public void SetColor(Xamarin.Forms.Color color)
        {
            drawable.Paint.SetARGB((int)(255 * color.A),
                                   (int)(255 * color.R),
                                   (int)(255 * color.G),
                                   (int)(255 * color.B));
            Invalidate();
        }

        public void SetSize(double width, double height)
        {
            float pixelsPerDip = Resources.DisplayMetrics.Density;
            drawable.SetBounds(0, 0, (int)(width * pixelsPerDip),
                                     (int)(height * pixelsPerDip));
            Invalidate();
        }
    }
}
```

Structurally, this is similar to the `EllipseUIView` class defined for iOS, except that the constructor creates a `ShapeDrawable` object for an ellipse, and the `OnDraw` override renders it.

This class has two methods to set properties of this ellipse. The `SetColor` method converts a Xamarin.Forms color to set the `Paint` property of the `ShapeDrawable` object, and the `SetSize` method converts a size in device-independent units to pixels for setting the bounds of the `ShapeDrawable` object. Both `SetColor` and `SetSize` conclude with a call to `Invalidate` to invalidate the drawing surface and generate another call to `OnDraw`.

The Android renderer makes use of the `EllipseDrawableView` class as its native object:

```csharp
using System.ComponentModel;

using Xamarin.Forms;
using Xamarin.Forms.Platform.Android;

[assembly: ExportRenderer(typeof(Xamarin.FormsBook.Platform.EllipseView),
                          typeof(Xamarin.FormsBook.Platform.Android.EllipseViewRenderer))]

namespace Xamarin.FormsBook.Platform.Android
{
    public class EllipseViewRenderer : ViewRenderer<EllipseView, EllipseDrawableView>
    {
        double width, height;

        protected override void OnElementChanged(ElementChangedEventArgs<EllipseView> args)
        {
            base.OnElementChanged(args);

            if (Control == null)
            {
                SetNativeControl(new EllipseDrawableView(Context));
            }

            if (args.NewElement != null)
            {
                SetColor();
                SetSize();
            }
        }

        protected override void OnElementPropertyChanged(object sender,
                                                         PropertyChangedEventArgs args)
        {
            base.OnElementPropertyChanged(sender, args);

            if (args.PropertyName == VisualElement.WidthProperty.PropertyName)
            {
                width = Element.Width;
                SetSize();
            }
            else if (args.PropertyName == VisualElement.HeightProperty.PropertyName)
            {
                height = Element.Height;
                SetSize();
            }
            else if (args.PropertyName == EllipseView.ColorProperty.PropertyName)
            {
                SetColor();
            }
```

```
        }

        void SetColor()
        {
            Control.SetColor(Element.Color);
        }

        void SetSize()
        {
            Control.SetSize(width, height);
        }
    }
}
```

Notice that the `OnElementPropertyChanged` method needs to check for changes to both the `Width` and `Height` properties and save them in fields so they can be combined into a single `Bounds` setting for the `SetSize` call to `EllipseDrawableView`.

With all the renderers in place, it's time to see whether it works. The **EllipseDemo** solution also contains links to the various projects of the **Xamarin.FormsBook.Platform** solution, and each of the projects in **EllipseDemo** contains a reference to the corresponding library project in **Xamarin.Forms-Book.Platform**.

Each of the projects in **EllipseDemo** also contains a call to the `Toolkit.Init` method in the corresponding library project. This is not always necessary. But keep in mind that the various renderers are not directly referenced by any code in any of the projects, and some optimizations can cause the code not to be available at run time. The call to `Toolkit.Init` avoids that.

The XAML file in **EllipseDemo** creates several `EllipseView` objects with different colors and sizes, some constrained in size while others are allowed to fill their container:

```
<?xml version="1.0" encoding="utf-8" ?>
<ContentPage xmlns="http://xamarin.com/schemas/2014/forms"
             xmlns:x="http://schemas.microsoft.com/winfx/2009/xaml"
             xmlns:platform=
                 "clr-namespace:Xamarin.FormsBook.Platform;assembly=Xamarin.FormsBook.Platform"
             x:Class="EllipseDemo.EllipseDemoPage">
    <Grid>
        <platform:EllipseView Color="Aqua" />

        <StackLayout>
            <StackLayout.Padding>
                <OnPlatform x:TypeArguments="Thickness"
                            iOS="0, 20, 0, 0" />
            </StackLayout.Padding>

            <platform:EllipseView Color="Red"
                                  WidthRequest="40"
                                  HeightRequest="80"
                                  HorizontalOptions="Center" />

            <platform:EllipseView Color="Green"
```

```
                                          WidthRequest="160"
                                          HeightRequest="80"
                                          HorizontalOptions="Start" />

            <platform:EllipseView Color="Blue"
                                          WidthRequest="160"
                                          HeightRequest="80"
                                          HorizontalOptions="End" />

            <platform:EllipseView Color="#80FF0000"
                                          HorizontalOptions="Center" />

            <ContentView Padding="50"
                         VerticalOptions="FillAndExpand">

                <platform:EllipseView Color="Red"
                                          BackgroundColor="#80FF0000" />

            </ContentView>
        </StackLayout>
    </Grid>
</ContentPage>
```

Take note in particular of the penultimate `EllipseView` that gives itself a half-opaque red color. Against the `Aqua` of the large ellipse filling the page, this should render as medium gray.

The last `EllipseView` gives itself a `BackgroundColor` setting of half-opaque red. Again, this should render as gray against the large `Aqua` ellipse, but as a light red against a white background and dark red against a black background. Here they are:

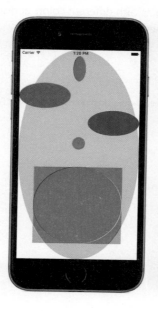
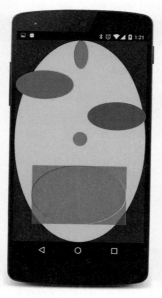

Once you have an `EllipseView`, of course you'll want to write a bouncing-ball program. The **BouncingBall** solution also includes links to all the projects in the **Xamarin.FormsBook.Platform** solution, and all the application projects have references to the corresponding library projects. The **BouncingBall** PCL also has a reference to the **Xamarin.FormsBook.Toolkit** library for a structure called `Vector2`, a two-dimensional vector.

The XAML file positions an `EllipseView` in the center of the page:

```
<ContentPage xmlns="http://xamarin.com/schemas/2014/forms"
             xmlns:x="http://schemas.microsoft.com/winfx/2009/xaml"
             xmlns:platform=
                 "clr-namespace:Xamarin.FormsBook.Platform;assembly=Xamarin.FormsBook.Platform"
             x:Class="BouncingBall.BouncingBallPage">

    <platform:EllipseView x:Name="ball"
                          WidthRequest="100"
                          HeightRequest="100"
                          HorizontalOptions="Center"
                          VerticalOptions="Center" />

</ContentPage>
```

The code-behind file starts up two animations that run "forever." The first animation is defined in the constructor and animates the `Color` property of the bouncing ball to take it through the colors of the rainbow every 10 seconds.

The second animation bounces the ball on the four "walls" of the screen. For each cycle through the `while` loop, the code first determines which wall it will hit first and the distance to that wall in device-independent units. The new calculation of `center` toward the end of the `while` loop is the position of the ball as it strikes a wall. The new calculation of `vector` determines a deflection vector based on an existing vector and a vector that is perpendicular to the surface that it's hitting (called a *normal* vector):

```
public partial class BouncingBallPage : ContentPage
{
    public BouncingBallPage()
    {
        InitializeComponent();

        // Color animation: cycle through rainbow every 10 seconds.
        new Animation(callback: v => ball.Color = Color.FromHsla(v, 1, 0.5),
                      start: 0,
                      end: 1
                      ).Commit(owner: this,
                               name: "ColorAnimation",
                               length: 10000,
                               repeat: () => true);

        BounceAnimationLoop();
    }

    async void BounceAnimationLoop()
```

```
    {
        // Wait until the dimensions are good.
        while (Width == -1 && Height == -1)
        {
            await Task.Delay(100);
        }

        // Initialize points and vectors.
        Point center = new Point();
        Random rand = new Random();
        Vector2 vector = new Vector2(rand.NextDouble(), rand.NextDouble());
        vector = vector.Normalized;
        Vector2[] walls = { new Vector2(1, 0), new Vector2(0, 1),        // left, top
                            new Vector2(-1, 0), new Vector2(0, -1) };   // right, bottom

        while (true)
        {
            // The locations of the four "walls" (taking ball size into account).
            double right = Width / 2 - ball.Width / 2;
            double left = -right;
            double bottom = Height / 2 - ball.Height / 2;
            double top = -bottom;

            // Find the number of steps till a wall is hit.
            double nX = Math.Abs(((vector.X > 0 ? right : left) - center.X) / vector.X);
            double nY = Math.Abs(((vector.Y > 0 ? bottom : top) - center.Y) / vector.Y);
            double n = Math.Min(nX, nY);

            // Find the wall that's being hit.
            Vector2 wall = walls[nX < nY ? (vector.X > 0 ? 2 : 0) : (vector.Y > 0 ? 3 : 1)];

            // New center and vector after animation.
            center += n * vector;
            vector -= 2 * Vector2.DotProduct(vector, wall) * wall;

            // Animate at 3 msec per unit.
            await ball.TranslateTo(center.X, center.Y, (uint)(3 * n));
        }
    }
}
```

Of course, a still photograph can't possibly capture the exciting action of the animation:

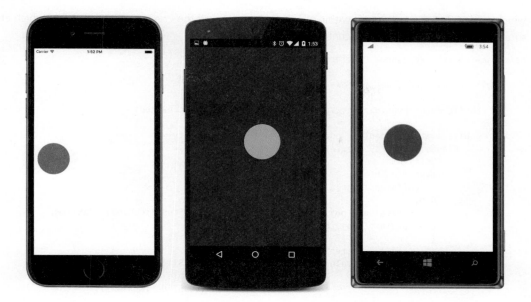

Renderers and events

Most Xamarin.Forms elements are interactive. They respond to user input by firing events. If you implement an event in your Xamarin.Forms custom element, you probably also need to define an event handler in the renderers for the corresponding event that the native control fires. This section will show you how.

The `StepSlider` element was inspired by a problem with the Xamarin.Forms implementation of the Windows `Slider` element. By default, the Xamarin.Forms `Slider` when running on the Windows platforms has only 10 steps from 0 through 1, so it is only capable of `Value` values of 0, 0.1, 0.2, and so forth up to 1.0.

Like the regular Xamarin.Forms `Slider`, the `StepSlider` element has `Minimum`, `Maximum`, and `Value` properties, but it also defines a `Step` property to specify the number of steps between `Minimum` and `Maximum`. For example, if `Minimum` is set to 5, `Maximum` is set to 10, and `Step` is set to 20, then the possible values of the `Value` property are 5.00, 5.25, 5.50, 5.75, 6.00, and so forth up to 10. The number of possible `Value` values is equal to the `Step` value plus 1.

Interestingly, implementing this `Step` property turned out to require a different approach on all three platforms, but the primary purpose of this exercise is to demonstrate how to implement events.

Here is the `StepSlider` class in the **Xamarin.FormsBook.Platform** library. Notice the definition of the `ValueChanged` event at the top and the firing of that event by changes in the `Value` property. Much of the bulk of the bindable property definitions are devoted to the `validateValue` methods, which ensure that the property is within allowable bounds, and the `coerceValue` methods, which ensure that the properties are consistent among themselves:

```
namespace Xamarin.FormsBook.Platform
{
    public class StepSlider : View
    {
        public event EventHandler<ValueChangedEventArgs> ValueChanged;

        public static readonly BindableProperty MinimumProperty =
            BindableProperty.Create(
                "Minimum",
                typeof(double),
                typeof(StepSlider),
                0.0,
                validateValue: (obj, min) => (double)min < ((StepSlider)obj).Maximum,
                coerceValue: (obj, min) =>
                {
                    StepSlider stepSlider = (StepSlider)obj;
                    stepSlider.Value = stepSlider.Coerce(stepSlider.Value,
                                                         (double)min,
                                                         stepSlider.Maximum);

                    return min;
                });

        public static readonly BindableProperty MaximumProperty =
            BindableProperty.Create(
                "Maximum",
                typeof(double),
                typeof(StepSlider),
                100.0,
                validateValue: (obj, max) => (double)max > ((StepSlider)obj).Minimum,
                coerceValue: (obj, max) =>
                {
                    StepSlider stepSlider = (StepSlider)obj;
                    stepSlider.Value = stepSlider.Coerce(stepSlider.Value,
                                                         stepSlider.Minimum,
                                                         (double)max);

                    return max;
                });

        public static readonly BindableProperty StepsProperty =
            BindableProperty.Create(
                "Steps",
                typeof(int),
                typeof(StepSlider),
                100,
                validateValue: (obj, steps) => (int)steps > 1);

        public static readonly BindableProperty ValueProperty =
            BindableProperty.Create(
                "Value",
                typeof(double),
                typeof(StepSlider),
```

```
                              0.0,
                              BindingMode.TwoWay,
                              coerceValue: (obj, value) =>
                              {
                                  StepSlider stepSlider = (StepSlider)obj;
                                  return stepSlider.Coerce((double)value,
                                                           stepSlider.Minimum,
                                                           stepSlider.Maximum);
                              },
                              propertyChanged: (obj, oldValue, newValue) =>
                              {
                                  StepSlider stepSlider = (StepSlider)obj;
                                  EventHandler<ValueChangedEventArgs> handler = stepSlider.ValueChanged;
                                  if (handler != null)
                                      handler(obj, new ValueChangedEventArgs((double)oldValue,
                                                                             (double)newValue));
                              });

        public double Minimum
        {
            set { SetValue(MinimumProperty, value); }
            get { return (double)GetValue(MinimumProperty); }
        }

        public double Maximum
        {
            set { SetValue(MaximumProperty, value); }
            get { return (double)GetValue(MaximumProperty); }
        }

        public int Steps
        {
            set { SetValue(StepsProperty, value); }
            get { return (int)GetValue(StepsProperty); }
        }

        public double Value
        {
            set { SetValue(ValueProperty, value); }
            get { return (double)GetValue(ValueProperty); }
        }

        double Coerce(double value, double min, double max)
        {
            return Math.Max(min, Math.Min(value, max));
        }
    }
}
```

The `StepSlider` class fires the `ValueChanged` property when the `Value` property changes, but there's nothing in this class that changes the `Value` property when the user manipulates the platform renderer for `StepSlider`. That's left to the renderer class.

Once again, let's first look at the Windows implementation of `StepSliderRenderer` in the **Xamarin.FormsBook.Platform.WinRT** shared project because it's a little more straightforward. The renderer uses the `Windows.UI.Xaml.Controls.Slider` for the native control. To avoid a namespace clash between the Windows `Slider` and the Xamarin.Forms `Slider`, a `using` directive defines the `win` prefix to refer to the Windows namespace and uses that to reference the Windows `Slider`:

```
using System.ComponentModel;

using Xamarin.Forms;

using Win = Windows.UI.Xaml.Controls;
using Windows.UI.Xaml.Controls.Primitives;

#if WINDOWS_UWP
using Xamarin.Forms.Platform.UWP;
#else
using Xamarin.Forms.Platform.WinRT;
#endif

[assembly: ExportRenderer(typeof(Xamarin.FormsBook.Platform.StepSlider),
                          typeof(Xamarin.FormsBook.Platform.WinRT.StepSliderRenderer))]

namespace Xamarin.FormsBook.Platform.WinRT
{
    public class StepSliderRenderer : ViewRenderer<StepSlider, Win.Slider>
    {
        protected override void OnElementChanged(ElementChangedEventArgs<StepSlider> args)
        {
            base.OnElementChanged(args);

            if (Control == null)
            {
                SetNativeControl(new Win.Slider());
            }

            if (args.NewElement != null)
            {
                SetMinimum();
                SetMaximum();
                SetSteps();
                SetValue();

                Control.ValueChanged += OnWinSliderValueChanged;
            }
            else
            {
                Control.ValueChanged -= OnWinSliderValueChanged;
            }
        }
        ...
    }
}
```

The big difference between this renderer and the one you've seen earlier is that this one sets an event handler on the `ValueChanged` event of the native Windows `Slider`. (You'll see the event handler shortly.) If `args.NewElement` becomes `null`, however, that means that there is no longer a Xamarin.Forms element attached to the renderer and that the event handler is no longer needed. Moreover, you'll see soon that the event handler refers to the `Element` property inherited from the `ViewRenderer` class, and that property will also be `null` if `args.NewElement` is `null`.

For that reason, `OnElementChanged` detaches the event handler when `args.NewElement` becomes `null`. Likewise, any resources you've allocated for the renderer should be freed whenever `args.NewElement` becomes `null`.

The override of the `OnElementPropertyChanged` method checks for changes in the four properties that `StepSlider` defines:

```
namespace Xamarin.FormsBook.Platform.WinRT
{
    public class StepSliderRenderer : ViewRenderer<StepSlider, Win.Slider>
    {
        …
        protected override void OnElementPropertyChanged(object sender,
                                                  PropertyChangedEventArgs args)
        {
            base.OnElementPropertyChanged(sender, args);

            if (args.PropertyName == StepSlider.MinimumProperty.PropertyName)
            {
                SetMinimum();
            }
            else if (args.PropertyName == StepSlider.MaximumProperty.PropertyName)
            {
                SetMaximum();
            }
            else if (args.PropertyName == StepSlider.StepsProperty.PropertyName)
            {
                SetSteps();
            }
            else if (args.PropertyName == StepSlider.ValueProperty.PropertyName)
            {
                SetValue();
            }
        }
        …
    }
}
```

The Windows `Slider` defines `Minimum`, `Maximum`, and `Value` properties just like the Xamarin.Forms `Slider` and the new `StepSlider`. But it doesn't define a `Steps` property. Instead, it defines a `StepFrequency` property, which is the opposite of a `Steps` property. To reproduce the earlier example (`Minimum` set to 5, `Maximum` set to 10, and `Steps` set to 20), you'd set `StepFrequency` to 0.25. The conversion is fairly simple:

```
namespace Xamarin.FormsBook.Platform.WinRT
{
    public class StepSliderRenderer : ViewRenderer<StepSlider, Win.Slider>
    {
        ...
        void SetMinimum()
        {
            Control.Minimum = Element.Minimum;
        }

        void SetMaximum()
        {
            Control.Maximum = Element.Maximum;
        }

        void SetSteps()
        {
            Control.StepFrequency = (Element.Maximum - Element.Minimum) / Element.Steps;
        }

        void SetValue()
        {
            Control.Value = Element.Value;
        }
        ...
    }
}
```

Finally, here's the `ValueChanged` handler for the Windows `Slider`. This has the responsibility of setting the `Value` property in the `StepSlider`, which then fires its own `ValueChanged` event. However, a special method exists for setting a value from a renderer. This method, called `SetValueFromRenderer`, is defined by the `IElementController` interface and implemented by the Xamarin.Forms `Element` class:

```
namespace Xamarin.FormsBook.Platform.WinRT
{
    public class StepSliderRenderer : ViewRenderer<StepSlider, Win.Slider>
    {
        ...
        void OnControlValueChanged(object sender, RangeBaseValueChangedEventArgs args)
        {
            ((IElementController)Element).SetValueFromRenderer(StepSlider.ValueProperty,
                                                              args.NewValue);
        }
    }
}
```

The iOS `UISlider` has `MinValue`, `MaxValue`, and `Value` properties and defines a `ValueChanged` event, but it doesn't have anything like a `Steps` or `StepFrequency` property. Instead, the iOS `StepSliderRenderer` class in **Xamarin.FormsBook.Platform.iOS** makes a manual adjustment to the `Value` property before calling `SetValueFromRenderer` from the `ValueChanged` event handler:

```
using System;
using System.ComponentModel;

using UIKit;

using Xamarin.Forms;
using Xamarin.Forms.Platform.iOS;

[assembly: ExportRenderer(typeof(Xamarin.FormsBook.Platform.StepSlider),
                          typeof(Xamarin.FormsBook.Platform.iOS.StepSliderRenderer))]

namespace Xamarin.FormsBook.Platform.iOS
{
    public class StepSliderRenderer : ViewRenderer<StepSlider, UISlider>
    {
        int steps;

        protected override void OnElementChanged(ElementChangedEventArgs<StepSlider> args)
        {
            base.OnElementChanged(args);

            if (Control == null)
            {
                SetNativeControl(new UISlider());
            }

            if (args.NewElement != null)
            {
                SetMinimum();
                SetMaximum();
                SetSteps();
                SetValue();

                Control.ValueChanged += OnUISliderValueChanged;
            }
            else
            {
                Control.ValueChanged -= OnUISliderValueChanged;
            }
        }

        protected override void OnElementPropertyChanged(object sender,
                                                  PropertyChangedEventArgs args)
        {
            base.OnElementPropertyChanged(sender, args);

            if (args.PropertyName == StepSlider.MinimumProperty.PropertyName)
            {
                SetMinimum();
            }
            else if (args.PropertyName == StepSlider.MaximumProperty.PropertyName)
            {
                SetMaximum();
            }
```

```
            else if (args.PropertyName == StepSlider.StepsProperty.PropertyName)
            {
                SetSteps();
            }
            else if (args.PropertyName == StepSlider.ValueProperty.PropertyName)
            {
                SetValue();
            }
        }

        void SetMinimum()
        {
            Control.MinValue = (float)Element.Minimum;
        }

        void SetMaximum()
        {
            Control.MaxValue = (float)Element.Maximum;
        }

        void SetSteps()
        {
            steps = Element.Steps;
        }

        void SetValue()
        {
            Control.Value = (float)Element.Value;
        }

        void OnUISliderValueChanged(object sender, EventArgs args)
        {
            double increment = (Element.Maximum - Element.Minimum) / Element.Steps;
            double value = increment * Math.Round(Control.Value / increment);
            ((IElementController)Element).SetValueFromRenderer(StepSlider.ValueProperty, value);
        }
    }
}
```

Interestingly enough, the Android `SeekBar` widget has an equivalent to the `Steps` property but no equivalents to the `Minimum` and `Maximum` properties! How is this possible? The `SeekBar` actually defines an integer property named `Max`, and the `Progress` property of the `SeekBar` is always an integer that ranges from 0 to `Max`. So the `Max` property really indicates the number of steps the `SeekBar` can make, and a conversion is necessary between the `Progress` property of the `SeekBar` and the `Value` property of the `StepSlider`.

This conversion occurs in two places: The `SetValue` method converts from the `Value` property of the `StepSlider` to the `Progress` property of the `SeekBar`, and the `OnProgressChanged` method converts from the `Progress` property of the `SeekBar` to the `Value` property of the `StepSlider`.

In addition, the event handler is a little different. The `SetOnSeekBarChangeListener` method accepts an argument of type `IOnSeekBarChangeListener`, which defines three methods that report changes to the `Seekbar`, including the method `OnProgressChanged`. The renderer itself implements that interface.

Here's the complete `StepSliderRenderer` class in the **Xamarin.FormsBook.Platform.Android** library:

```
using System.ComponentModel;

using Android.Widget;

using Xamarin.Forms;
using Xamarin.Forms.Platform.Android;

[assembly: ExportRenderer(typeof(Xamarin.FormsBook.Platform.StepSlider),
                          typeof(Xamarin.FormsBook.Platform.Android.StepSliderRenderer))]

namespace Xamarin.FormsBook.Platform.Android
{
    public class StepSliderRenderer : ViewRenderer<StepSlider, SeekBar>,
                                      SeekBar.IOnSeekBarChangeListener
    {
        double minimum, maximum;

        protected override void OnElementChanged(ElementChangedEventArgs<StepSlider> args)
        {
            base.OnElementChanged(args);

            if (Control == null)
            {
                SetNativeControl(new SeekBar(Context));
            }
            if (args.NewElement != null)
            {
                SetMinimum();
                SetMaximum();
                SetSteps();
                SetValue();

                Control.SetOnSeekBarChangeListener(this);
            }
            else
            {
                Control.SetOnSeekBarChangeListener(null);
            }
        }

        protected override void OnElementPropertyChanged(object sender,
                                                         PropertyChangedEventArgs args)
        {
            base.OnElementPropertyChanged(sender, args);

            if (args.PropertyName == StepSlider.MinimumProperty.PropertyName)
            {
                SetMinimum();
```

```
            }
            else if (args.PropertyName == StepSlider.MaximumProperty.PropertyName)
            {
                SetMaximum();
            }
            else if (args.PropertyName == StepSlider.StepsProperty.PropertyName)
            {
                SetSteps();
            }
            else if (args.PropertyName == StepSlider.ValueProperty.PropertyName)
            {
                SetValue();
            }
        }

        void SetMinimum()
        {
            minimum = Element.Minimum;
        }

        void SetMaximum()
        {
            maximum = Element.Maximum;
        }

        void SetSteps()
        {
            Control.Max = Element.Steps;
        }

        void SetValue()
        {
            double value = Element.Value;
            Control.Progress = (int)((value - minimum) / (maximum - minimum) * Element.Steps);
        }

        // Implementation of SeekBar.IOnSeekBarChangeListener
        public void OnProgressChanged(SeekBar seekBar, int progress, bool fromUser)
        {
            double value = minimum + (maximum - minimum) * Control.Progress / Control.Max;
            ((IElementController)Element).SetValueFromRenderer(StepSlider.ValueProperty, value);
        }

        public void OnStartTrackingTouch(SeekBar seekBar)
        {
        }

        public void OnStopTrackingTouch(SeekBar seekBar)
        {
        }
    }
}
```

The **StepSliderDemo** solution contains links to the **Xamarin.FormsBook.Platform** libraries and